P9-CKX-871

FOR REFERENCE

Do Not Take From This Room

THE WEATHER HANDBOOK

A summary of climatic conditions and weather
phenomena for selected cities in the United States and
around the world.

Edited by McKinley Conway and Linda L. Liston

Revised edition 1990

Copyright © 1963, 1974 and 1990 by Conway Data, Inc.
40 Technology Park/Atlanta
Norcross, Georgia 30092 USA

Riverside Community College
Library
4800 Magnolia Avenue
Riverside, California 92506

Cataloging in Publication

Conway, McKinley
The Weather Handbook
Includes Index
1. Weather statistics 2. Climatic conditions 3. Natural
phenomena
I. Liston, Linda L., Co-author
II. Title

Copyright © 1990 by Conway Data, Inc. All rights reserved. No
part of this publication may be reproduced, stored in a retrieval
system or transmitted, in any form or by any means, electronic,
mechanical, photocopying, recording, or otherwise, without prior
written permission of the publisher.

International Standard Book Number: 0-910436-29-0

Printed in the United States of America

Acknowledgements

The weather summaries in this book are based on data from the National Climatic Data Center of the U.S. Dept. of Commerce, Asheville, N.C.; the National Center for Atmospheric Research (operated by the University Corporation for Atmospheric Research under the sponsorship of the National Science Foundation), Boulder, Colo.; the National Hurricane Center, Coral Gables, Fla.; and the Royal Meteorological Society of Great Britain. Other information came from such sources as the U.S. Army Engineer Topographic Laboratories, Ft. Belvoir, Va.; and the World Meteorological Organization.

We are pleased to acknowledge the efforts of Timothy A. Meers for computer analysis and programming of the weather tapes, Susan Dunwody Andes for compiling and verifying the data, and staff geographer Dr. Michael O'Connor for assistance in selection of the cities to be included.

Staff artist Martin Bozone and Production Manager Claire Fleisig contributed their talents to design, maps and production of the book.

Lastly, we'd like to say a word of thanks to the hundreds of meteorologists and weather briefers with whom we have consulted over the years. Almost always they were polite, thoughtful and accommodating. Thank you!

Preface

This is the third, revised edition of the book originally issued in 1963. This edition contains new data for the reporting stations and has been broadened to include many more stations.

Altogether, this compilation covers some 250 U.S. cities and more than 600 cities in other nations.

Users should find this work to be an excellent basis for comparing climatic conditions and for estimating the probability of various weather phenomena in different areas. Care has been taken to insure accuracy. However, meteorology is not an exact science and discrepancies undoubtedly exist. Also, it should be kept in mind that new weather records are set somewhere almost every day.

A casual glance at the contents will reveal the tremendous complexity of world weather patterns. It is evident that terrain, elevation, ocean currents, bodies of water and other factors combine to produce a wide range of conditions. Stations located only 100 miles apart may have distinctly different climates.

Contents

Index of Figures

Introduction

"There are no atheists in thunderstorms."

For outdoor people the weather defines recreational opportunities. For farmers it determines good or bad times. And for those of us who fly small airplanes it is even more — it is truly a matter of life and death.

Pilots who survive to a ripe old age have learned to have a very healthy respect for a variety of weather phenomena. Probably the biggest concern is thunderstorms because they are so common and so lethal if ignored.

In many parts of the world thunderstorms can occur any day. In much of the United States they are a threat during about six warm months of the year. Usually the storms come on summer afternoons, and they are scattered over wide areas.

Whether one flies a heavy jet or a light plane, the pilot's strategy is to avoid thunderstorm cells by zig-zagging around them. Life only gets grim when a line of heavy storms is encountered and the gaps between cells are narrow.

Sometimes a pilot gets boxed in and finds himself plowing through a cell. That is the source of the old saw that among pilots there are no atheists in thunderstorms.

At the least, going through an active cell is a nerve-wracking experience and a test of the ability of the pilot and the strength of the airframe. As thunderstorms grow in intensity they spawn violent vertical gusts and hail. For the pilot, this means the possibility of loss of control, structural failure and a fatal accident.

Tornados are believed to develop from severe thunderstorms. Flying into such a cell is suicidal.

When the weather cools off and the thunderstorms wane, a new problem emerges — ice. While icing can be encountered at very high altitudes any time, anywhere, the biggest exposure for most pilots comes during the winter at lower altitudes.

The veteran pilot knows that there are different kinds of ice to be found in different weather systems and that there is a temperature range in which icing is most likely. He also knows that it can get too cold for icing to be a problem.

Another range of problems is associated with low ceilings and visibilities. Fog, which occurs when the temperature and dewpoint converge, is a major culprit.

There are many localities which have microclimates conducive to fog, smog, haze and other contributors to low ceilings and visibilities. The Los Angeles basin is a well-known example.

Around the world there are airports located many miles from the cities they serve because sites near the city are too often fog-bound. A good example is Halifax, Nova Scotia.

Elevations are also of critical importance to the pilot. Without consulting any reference book, an experienced pilot can tell you that

Denver and Colorado Springs are more than 5,000 feet above sea level and Bogotá and Quito are much higher.

Altitude also tells a lot about wind patterns. Below 12,000 feet in the Caribbean the trade winds blow steadily out of the east. Airports in the region have east/west runways wherever terrain permits.

At altitudes above 30,000 to 40,000 feet the winds always come from the west — because of the rotation of the earth. And, in the northern hemisphere the winds circulate counter-clockwise around a low pressure center, while they go clockwise south of the equator.

Similarly, in the Caribbean the hurricanes track from southeast toward the northwest, while in the South Pacific the typhoons may follow different routes.

Veteran pilots can also make easy estimates of latitude and longitude of key cities and suggest which ones may enjoy very long summer days or very short winter days.

With all of these and other variations, it is no wonder that weather is a universal topic of interest and conversation among those who fly.

The idea for this handbook emerged sometime in the years after WWII as the author was planning flights to remote parts of the U.S., Canada and Latin America. In those days it was difficult to get weather data quickly and conveniently for many locations.

Over a period of years we managed to compile a considerable amount of data from various sources. In Central America, for example, we discovered military records of observations made at bases built by U.S. units during WWII and later abandoned. Also, we got access to records kept by other governments.

For some routes we collected enough data that other pilots began asking to borrow our files. Someone then suggested we put the data into a book. While that idea was germinating, better official sources at home and abroad became available, and so we launched the project.

We hasten to say that this new edition relies on data from current official records and not on our own spotty observations. Today, coverage is more complete and more reliable than ever.

We should say also that we practice what we preach. We have used the kind of data contained in this book as background for planning flights around the Caribbean and throughout Mexico and Central America, all in small aircraft.

We made one memorable flight across the Amazon basin from the Pacific coast to the Atlantic. That's about 3,000 miles, most of it over trackless rain forest.

We have made numerous flights to Alaska and to points throughout Canada. Several years ago we flew a small single- engined Mooney from Atlanta up across Quebec to Baffin Island, then to Greenland, Iceland and Scotland. After stops at Prestwick, Gatwick, Amsterdam, Brussels and Shannon, we returned across the North Atlantic.

It was a magnificent experience which could not have been enjoyed as much without reliable weather reporting services.

This volume, however, was not compiled solely for the benefit of those who fly. We learned with earlier editions that the kind of data it contains is very useful for world travelers. Will a raincoat be needed in Bombay in February? How cold will it be in Rome in April?

Also, the previous editions found wide use among those involved in the planning of outdoor activities and those engaged in the design of facilities. Using the weather profiles for reporting stations, one can quickly get an idea of requirements for heating, air conditioning and energy needs.

And now, we have a new and even wider audience — those who are interested in global weather patterns and threats to our environment. The news media give much space to alarmist predictions of global warming via the greenhouse effect. There are concerns regarding ozone depletion.

Just now, with satellite observations and other extensions of our observation capabilities, we are learning much about the intricate systems which affect the weather of the world. We now know, for example, that "El Nino" is a global phenomenon. Events which occur in one part of the world may be related to events in another hemisphere.

There are many rumors, myths and misconceptions in circulation. Extremists press the panic button, while apathetic segments of society ignore significant warnings.

We have reached the point, we believe, where every thoughtful citizen needs to have facts at hand. We hope this book will be helpful to many who want to deal with the realities of global weather.

—McKinley Conway

II. Weather Phenomena

A. Cold Waves and Blizzards

In northern latitudes, cold waves are common occurrences taken in stride by winter-wise residents. Low temperatures, snow, sleet and frigid winds are not strangers. Yet, when these factors combine in an area, blizzards occur and major disasters are possible.

Areas most vulnerable include the states of the upper Midwest, the Midwest and the Northeast.

But the Southern states are not immune to damage. Big Arctic air masses sometimes push sub-freezing air all the way to Florida and through the Rio Grande Valley, causing large losses in the citrus and truck farming industries.

The Southern states are also victimized some winters by ice storms — freezing rain which clings to trees, wires and all exposed structures. A severe ice storm can cut off electric power and telephone service, halt transportation and otherwise convert an area into something akin to an attack zone, with everyone huddled under shelter unable to move.

Fig. 11 indicates generally how great the snow risk is in various parts of the nation. Those who live in areas which have much snow have long since learned to prepare their homes each fall for blizzards which might pin them down for several days. Also, they know when they travel to carry warm clothing and emergency supplies in the vehicle, whether it be an automobile, snowmobile or airplane.

B. Droughts and Heat Waves

Droughts cause great damage, and heat waves take a surprising toll of human life. We refer not to annual dry seasons or periodic summer heat, but to severe, atypical situations, such as the disastrous drought which struck Europe in 1976 and parts of the United States in the late 1980s. Water was rationed in many areas, and agricultural losses were devastating.

A drought hit the U.S. Pacific Northwest in 1978, draining reservoirs to the point that electric utility systems depending on hydro power experienced "brown-outs," and large industrial plants were shut down.

In some parts of the world, repeated droughts in successive years have accelerated the conversion of arable land into desert. Noteworthy is the Sahel region of Africa, south of the Sahara, where droughts of the 1970s have displaced a substantial portion of the 20 million residents.

C. Floods

In the earliest days of man, camp sites were located near streams which provided drinking water. As man developed, his first mode of transportation was a dugout canoe, and for a long while there after, boat transportation was dominant. Thus, early communities sprouted where rivers met or where natural harbors occurred.

A great many of these communities, which later became cities, were built on lowlands that we now know to be flood plains. They are particularly prevalent in the United States where new areas were opened for commerce and development first by riverboats plying the Ohio, Mississippi and other rivers.

Despite great investment in flood control measures, many parts of many cities and towns still are exposed to the hazards of a flood. But these are not the only exposed areas. Today we know that virtually everyone lives in or close to an area which is vulnerable to some type of flood risk.

Most widespread is the risk of flash flooding which may result from a deluge in a particular local area. Records reveal that such a phenomenon can occur almost anywhere, and the possibility of serious flooding depends on the features of the area.

Flash flooding is common even in arid lands. High risks occur where there is little vegetation to slow run-off. The same is true in urban areas where unplanned development has brought large paved areas without attention to drainage requirements. Terrain features are also highly significant. A dry canyon can become a raging torrent when heavy rains fall along the slopes above.

Another common type of flood is the riverine flood which occurs in the spring along streams fed by melting snow in the upstream hinterland. If this comes concurrently with heavy rains, disaster can occur.

Altogether, floods are the most common natural disaster, and they are very expensive. One of the most devastating floods in U.S. history struck Johnstown, Pennsylvania, in 1889, killing 2,200 people. Yet many are unaware that as recently as 1977 another flood at Johnstown killed 68!

Indicative of the lethal surprises inherent in flash floods was the downpour which caught campers and fishermen in the Big Thompson Canyon in Colorado in 1976, killing 130.

Fig. 48 shows on a state-by-state basis the percentage of population living in flood-prone areas. The range is from 4.4 percent in Tennessee to 14.8 percent in Massachusetts. These percentages may seem small, but when applied to the total population, the data reveal an enormous risk.

Monetary damage is likely to be highest in California, Texas, Missouri, Illinois, Indiana, Michigan, Ohio, Pennsylvania and New York. States likely to have lowest dollar losses generally are found in the area from Montana and the Dakotas down to Arizona and New Mexico.

Still another kind of flood is caused by tidal waves or tsunamis. These waves result from earth tremors and may travel for thousands of miles across the ocean before striking a shore with devastating effect.

Of course, the tidal wave risk follows an entirely different pattern, being confined to coastal areas, particularly those on the Pacific Rim. Fig. 52 shows the location of seismographic monitoring stations and identifies wave-prone areas such as Alaska and Hawaii.

Tidal waves may be more prevalent in the Pacific, but they can and do occur elsewhere. A freak tidal wave has even been reported in the Mediterranean. Triggered by an underwater mud slide, the wave in 1979 killed 13 people and did $10 million damage on the Riviera east of Nice.

While most flood hazards are old and plainly identifiable, some observers see in the future even greater perils. They do not think the anticipated melting of the polar ice cap is millions of years in the future. Instead, they see this as a possible early consequence of alteration of the earth's atmosphere via ozone depletion, greenhouse effect or other event.

D. Wind Storms: Hurricanes, Typhoons and Cyclones

Hurricanes and, as they are known in the Western Pacific, typhoons, clearly are important risks in many parts of the world wherever tropical cyclones (masses of warm, moist air rotating around a low pressure area) develop. Cyclonic activity grows seasonally over the oceans and, under conditions not fully understood, develops strength until the circulating air mass reaches hurricane velocity of at least 74 miles per hour.

Three regions of the globe spawn most of the hurricane activity: the Atlantic and Caribbean, the Eastern Pacific off Mexico and the Western Pacific. Substantial cyclonic activity is also found in the Indian Ocean, but few typhoons are reported.

The area of greatest risk is the Western Pacific where huge typhoons develop over great expanses of open water and spend themselves against the coast lines of Southeast Asia, China, Japan, the Philippines, Okinawa and lesser islands. The fury of these storms was confirmed during World War II when large "unsinkable" warships were capsized by monster waves.

In the Central and Western Pacific, it is estimated that, on the average, there are 20 typhoons each year. In addition, there are about 10 significant typhoon systems per year in this region and in the coastal zones of Australia. Peak activity occurs in the months from July through October.

Cyclonic activity in the Indian Ocean is heaviest in the Bay of Bengal. That a storm does not need to reach hurricane strength to be deadly has been proven many times in this area when cyclones have pushed water onto the lowlands of the Ganges Delta. One such storm a few years ago killed 300,000 people, making it one of the greatest disasters in recorded history.

Another area of hurricane risk is the Eastern Pacific. Storms which build in the waters off the Mexican coast sometimes travel northeast across the Baja Peninsula and Gulf of Cortez, bringing high winds and flood-producing downpours to southwestern states. The hurricane season falls generally in the period June through October.

This area produces about eight significant cyclones in a typical year, with three of them reaching hurricane strength. While most

of the storms move west toward open water, a few wreak havoc in
Mexico.

But the area of greatest interest is the Atlantic, Caribbean and Gulf
of Mexico, where hurricanes annually threaten millions of people.
From the spawning zone off the northeast coast of South America and
along the Windward and Leeward chain, cyclones build and move
toward Puerto Rico, Central America, the Yucatan, the Gulf Coast
Florida and the Atlantic seaboard. This region produces about eight
major tropical cyclones and five hurricanes per year.

Much has been learned about hurricanes in this area, and this
knowledge is being extended steadily by the National Hurricane Center
of NOAA in Miami. Looking, for example, at data on direct hurricane
hits on the U.S. mainland for the period 1900-1977, we find this state
tally:

Florida 50
Texas 31
Louisiana 20
North Carolina .. 19
South Carolina .. 10
Alabama 7
New York 7
Connecticut 6
Massachusetts 5
Mississippi............ 5
Georgia................. 4
Rhode Island 4
Maine.................... 4
Virginia................. 3
New Jersey 1
New Hampshire... 1

This does not mean, of course, that these are the only states suffering
hurricane risk. In fact, a major storm may strike land first in Mississippi
but cause catastrophic flooding several days later in West Virginia.

Of the direct hits recorded, more than half occurred in September,
and most of the remainder were in August or October.

Much has been learned, also, about the relative strength and
damage potential of hurricanes. First, it is well established by now that
nearly one-half of the deaths and destruction caused by hurricanes
results not from the wind but from the surge of water driven ashore
ahead of the storm, causing extreme tides. Second, it is impossible to
predict the level of the surge at a specific location simply from
knowledge of the velocity of the winds. The slope of the continental
shelf and the shape of the shoreline must be considered.

Additional analysis of hurricane data reveals that most of those
residents of coastal areas who have "experienced" hurricanes have not
actually experienced the full fury of an intense storm (scale 4 or 5).
This produces a false sense of security in many areas.

Public officials in several hurricane-prone areas have asked, "Why
continue to rebuild facilities on coastal barrier islands and exposed

dunes?" Of course, environmentalists have long argued that these areas should have little development. The occasional sweep of a hurricane across such areas is, in fact, beneficial to the environment, they say.

The confrontation can only increase in intensity. Population growth in hurricane-prone areas is increasing at twice the national average. Continued high-density construction on some barrier islands may well be creating death traps for the future.

Many such resort and retirement communities rest on sand three to eight feet above sea level. In an emergency evacuation, thousands of residents would rely on one two-lane road connected to the mainland by bridge or causeway which would be subject to blockage by a single mishap.

Perhaps the greatest area of risk to lives and property is in the Florida Keys. Throughout the string of islands connected by bridge and causeway for nearly 100 miles, the only lifeline is the Overseas Highway which ranges in elevation from three to 10 feet above sea level. Given 24 hours warning of a direct hit, it is doubtful that the populace could be evacuated.

Another highly vulnerable area is found in Florida's lower West Coast where a cluster of islands, including Sanibel and Captiva, sit a few feet above sea level. A major hurricane could produce a surge here of 15 to 20 feet, sweeping over the island. Again, the only lifeline is a two-lane road connected to the mainland by causeway and bridge. Should a major storm in the Gulf change course abruptly and aim directly at this area, it is unlikely the islands could be evacuated, particularly during a season of heavy tourist population.

Vulnerable areas can be found along the entire coastline. For example, the Cape May, New Jersey, resort area is cited as particularly exposed to disaster risk. The normal population is about 50,000 but on a late summer weekend may be several times that. Access is primarily via one road which can handle fewer than 5,000 cars per hour if all goes well. A major hurricane veering in from the Atlantic, pushing a surge ahead, could trap a great many people.

Because predicting the speed and path of hurricanes is still very much an inexact science, the National Hurricane Center builds a margin of safety into its forecasts whenever possible. A typical hurricane warning may be issued, for example, for a 300-mile stretch of the Gulf Coast, with the expectation that the damaging winds and water will impact from 100 miles of the center, leaving another 100-mile swath on either side which is relatively safe. These two areas are thus "overwarned" if the hurricane stays on course.

NHC is very conscious of the "overwarning" situation. First, the alerting of large areas unnecessarily promotes complacency when the next hurricane comes. Second, there is a huge cost involved in an alert area. Businesses close, schools are suspended, homes are shuttered, and countless activities are interrupted.

Clearly, those who wish to survive must be aware of the hurricane risk, pay attention to warnings, know how to evaluate them and, most important, have a plan for responding.

E. Thunderstorms, Tornados and Related Phenomena

Thunderstorms are fascinating. Lie on the beach at Daytona almost any summer day and watch them grow. At mid-morning, the sky is clear. An hour later, wispy scattered clouds appear. By noon they are puffy cumulus, the cotton-ball variety. Some, but not all, now begin to grow vertically. By mid-afternoon, there are great towering columns of heavy cumulus, dark at the bottom.

Then comes the first crack of lightning, the rumble of thunder and spatters of big drops of rain. A few of the cumulus giants grow fat and black and dump deluges below. At the center of these cells is a fury of turbulence, including powerful down drafts which bring cool air from high altitude. The area beneath the cell is cooled, soaked and blasted by gusts.

An hour later, the cell is dissipating, and by late in the day, most are gone. The show is over until the next day.

The same performance can be witnessed around the world, wherever warm, moist air and conditions for convection development occur.

Thunderstorms can be beautiful, majestic and inspiring, and they can be ominous, intimidating and awesome. The same storm can be safe and brilliantly white on top and black and deadly underneath.

The storms found in the U.S. include not only those which start from tropical conditions but also those of other origins.

Thunderstorms develop along mountain ranges where prevailing winds drive warm, moist surface air up the slopes to a point that condensation occurs. Downwind, the storms build regularly. Find a lounge chair and sit on a Colorado Springs patio on just about any late-summer afternoon and you can see them grow along the east front of the Rockies.

Still other thunderstorms result from air mass movements, typically the collision of a fast-moving cold front with warm, moist air. While this can occur almost anywhere, certain parts of the country offer prime conditions more frequently.

As indicated in Fig. 16, areas of greatest thunderstorm activity include Florida, the Gulf Coast and the east slopes of the Rockies. Some areas are almost immune. Those living in the San Francisco Bay area seldom see anything resembling a thunderstorm.

Having made it clear, we hope, that a thunderstorm can occur almost anywhere, we should now stress that the intensity of thunderstorms and their potential for doing damage varies greatly. While none may be taken lightly, some are more deadly than others.

To a degree, the intensity of a thunderstorm is related to its height. U-2 pilots have confirmed tops above 100,000 feet. The number and frequency of lightning strikes may also reveal strength.

Thunderstorms present many mysteries. Specifically, we do not yet know how or why some thunderstorm cells develop into severe storms with large hail, or even into tornados, the deadliest of storms.

The conditions most likely to yield hail are found in the Great Plains from the Texas Panhandle north to Nebraska and Iowa. Other states are also vulnerable, however.

Another major risk related to thunderstorms is fire. Many deadly fires are started by lightning. When forests are relatively dry, such fires are numerous.

Lightning itself is a killer. Each year there are scores of deaths recorded on playgrounds, golf courses, farms and wherever people may be caught out in the open in a thunderstorm.

Thunderstorms also pose hazards, of course, to those who travel, especially to aircraft and boats. Veteran pilots avoid thunderstorms no matter how big or sophisticated the airplane they are flying. Somewhere, they say, there lurks a great granddaddy of a cell capable of breaking up any aircraft ever built.

At one time, the U.S. was committed to building a fleet of great dirigibles to serve as aircraft carriers in the sky. But the flagship of that fleet, the Akron, in 1933 ran into a thunderstorm off the New Jersey coast, broke up and crashed, killing 73 Navy crewmen. The loss, coupled with another accident with the sister ship, the Macon, doomed the program. Those who travel in boats are also wary of thunderstorms. The gusts which come with active cells can whip up hazardous waves on a shallow body of water within a few minutes. And, most boats are too slow to dodge.

Despite all of these threats, by far the worst aspect of thunderstorms is that they are involved somehow in the birth of tornados.

Whatever the process, tornados emerge in areas where there are line squalls or clusters of severe thunderstorms. Tornados occur in most parts of the world, favoring the locations and seasons where warm air and moisture occur.

When thunderstorm-tornado conditions are ripe, many storms can occur on the same day in the same region. It is not uncommon for one or more tornados to travel along a line or arc, striking the ground, then lifting over a segment and striking again several miles away.

Such was the case in the Spring of 1974 when one of the worst tornado days in U.S. history occurred. One body of storms struck a line extending from Central Kentucky to Central Ohio; another moved across North Alabama into Georgia; while a third skipped from Indiana into Michigan. More than 100 tornados were reported, producing a death toll of 329, injuries to 6,000 and property damage of $1 billion. Hardest hit was Xenia, Ohio, where 34 were killed.

In an average year, more than 700 tornados are recorded in the U.S. To provide some indication of areas of greatest risk, NOAA has tallied, by state, the number of thunderstorms per 10,000 square miles. For such an area, measuring 100 miles wide by 100 miles long, this is the number of tornados which might be expected in a typical year in the more tornado-prone states:

    Oklahoma........ 7.97
    Florida 6.55
    Indiana............. 6.38
    Massachusetts. 5.63
    Kansas.............. 5.55

Illinois 5.45
Iowa 4.88
Mississippi 4.77
Missouri 4.54
Nebraska 4.53
Texas 4.46
Louisiana 4.22
Delaware 4.13

To estimate potential property damage, it is necessary to weigh the tornado probability in each state against the density of population and development. One analysis suggested that loss risk is highest in Texas and Illinois.

Looking at the total risk due to windstorms, it is important to recognize that hurricanes and tornados are not the only offenders. High winds are also generated by weather systems which do not spawn tropical cyclones, thunderstorms or tornados.

F. Other Weather-Related Phenomena

Certain other natural phenomena can influence the weather, or can result from the weather. In the former category are volcanos; in the latter are mudslides.

1. Volcanos

Best known volcanic eruption in history occurred when Vesuvius destroyed Pompeii in 79 A.D. Perhaps the deadliest eruption was that of Mont Pelee on Martinique in the Caribbean. In 1902 the volcano exploded and destroyed the city of St. Pierre, killing 30,000 inhabitants. The destruction was wreaked by lava gushing down the slopes, by earthquakes and by hot toxic gases.

Volcanos can have an impact far from their sites. The famous Pacific island volcano, Krakatoa, blew up in 1883 with such a blast that the island disappeared and smoke and ash drifted around the world. Yet it was not the greatest eruption on record.

That dubious honor goes to Mount Tambora on the island of Sumbawa in Indonesia, which in 1816 exploded and produced the largest quantity of atmospheric dust ever recorded.

This blanket of insulation shielded the earth from the sun for more than a year and caused areas in the north to report they had missed a summer. New England had several inches of snow in June and frost in July and August. Most summer crops were lost.

In recent times destructive volcanos have erupted in Chile, the Philippines, in Java, Costa Rica, Iceland and the U.S.

Five volcanos on the U.S. mainland are classified as active. These include Mt. Shasta and Mt. Lassen in California and Mt. Baker, Mt. Rainer and Mt. St. Helens in Washington. (See Fig. 49.) The eruption of Mt. St. Helens in 1980 was one of the most devastating geological events of the century in the U.S.

2. Mudslides

There is nothing glamorous about a mudslide. Yet, in some years they are the main topic of conversation in California. Heavy rains and the mudslides that result can inflict heavy property damage and have been credited with the loss of dozens of lives.

The risk of land, rock and mudslides is related first to the soil and earth structure of the area: where certain geologic conditions exist, slides are more prevalent. This tendency to slip may also be triggered or accentuated by earth tremors, rain or man-made changes. Slides may occur slowly and deliberately or may strike swiftly without warning.

The risk of slides is encountered around the world. In 1979 major slide disasters occurred in such diverse locations as Korea and Sumatra. Closer to home, a disaster of recent years wiped out the Quebec village of Saint-Jean-Vianney.

High-risk areas for land-slides in the U.S. include the states of California, Illinois, Ohio, Pennsylvania, New Jersey and New York. Slightly less slide-prone are Texas, Missouri, Minnesota and Michigan.

Not included in these forecasts are other phenomena, such as land subsidence, sink holes and expansive soil. In areas of general land subsidence — the Houston ship channel area, California's San Joaquin Valley, metropolitan Las Vegas — the problem is serious and expensive, but the situation moves slowly enough to avoid being classified as a disaster.

At specific points in the Southeast, however, there is a possibility of small local disasters due to land sinks which can occur without warning overnight.

This is an area resting on a limestone strata in which cavities develop and, from time to time, surface areas collapse. While the area involved in these collapses is usually small — typically only one or two houses might be swallowed — the record shows thousands of different collapses.

From the viewpoint of damage, the problem of expansive soils is much more serious. This type of disaster, almost unknown to the general public, creates more than $2 billion in damage per year. The risk extends to every state.

The obscure expansive soil hazard results from the characteristics of certain clays in the soil. These clays, when wet, can expand more than 10 times and generate enough force to break up concrete structures.

The problem is most prevalent in areas which have distinct wet and dry seasons. States most vulnerable to this damage include California, Texas and Missouri. Other states where major damage is forecast include Louisiana, Kansas, Illinois, Michigan, Ohio, Pennsylvania and New York.

3. Acid Rain

Acid rain occurs when such gases as sulfur dioxide and nitrogen oxide are discharged into the atmosphere by coal-burning generators, plants and automobiles, and — encountering clouds and moisture — fall back to earth in the form of rain or snow. Prevailing winds may carry the acid rain hundreds of miles from the source of the pollutants.

There is growing evidence that acid rain occurrence is increasing and has already reduced fish population, especially trout and salmon, in areas far from urban and industrial centers.

Again, we are reminded that we live in a very complex environment, and as man seeks to manage the ecosystem, he discovers that he has a lot to learn. Responsible researchers argue that it is pollution control programs that have caused the acid rain problem. They point out that ash from coal burning neutralizes nitrogen and sulfur dioxide acidity and in the past controlled acid rain. However, in recent years EPA regulations have required installation of expensive scrubbers to eliminate ash, permitting the acid rain to develop.

This is small comfort to the trout fishing industry of the Adirondacks where fish depletion has been so catastrophic that heroic and costly counter measures have been necessary. Lakes and streams have been restored only by treating with lime and restocking.

An even greater risk is projected by the depletion of the ozone layer which protects the earth from cancer-producing ultraviolet radiation.

In this same family of large-scale potential ecodoom situations is the threat of increasing carbon dioxide in the atmosphere. This so-called "greenhouse effect" is caused by cutting forests, burning fossil fuels and otherwise upsetting the carbon dioxide balance. The predicted long-term result is a gradual warming of the earth, leading to melting of the polar ice cap sufficiently to flood coastal areas.

To protect the ozone layer, the EPA is limiting production and use of fluorocarbon gas. The use of fluorocarbon gas as a propellant in aerosol sprays has already been banned. The limits affect fluorocarbons used in refrigeration, plastic foams and solvents.

Even among those most concerned about this possibility, the opinion is that serious problems lie in the 21st century. Also, one must balance against the possible warming trend the forecast of a cooling trend being made by other scientists who expect new volcanic eruptions to spout more dust particles into the upper atmosphere, reducing the heat received from the sun.

In any event, high levels of exhaust fumes in local areas cannot be disregarded. There is growing evidence that areas immediately adjacent to heavily-travelled freeways may accumulate toxic risks under certain combinations of wind direction, terrain and foliage pattern.

G. Combinations of Risks

Among pilots there is an axiom which says that single malfunctions don't hurt, but combinations will kill you. Certainly, weather disasters which occur in combination can be far more deadly.

In Indonesia recently, a landslide of little consequence plunged into the ocean and propelled a tidal wave onto a nearby island. Five hundred people drowned. This is not a rare occurrence: earthquakes often trigger landslides which cause damaging floods or wave action.

Fig. 53 provides some indication of the types of weather hazards which may be encountered around the world. A more detailed indication is given in Chapter VII, which contains excerpts from the records of the Agency for International Development. Since our chart is based on reported loss of life, Asia shows badly on all counts as a result of its great population density and exposure.

Looking at the U.S., we have considerably more data for our evaluation. The state weather risk profiles in Chapter V provide quick comparisons.

Unless placed in proper context, these state comparisons can be very misleading. A large state with several different climate zones, such as California, may indicate a high risk for blizzard conditions, and this might be a real factor at a high elevation in the Sierras. However, the risk does not exist for San Diego, which has one of the mildest climates in the nation.

III. Maps and Special Observations

In this section, the reader will find a variety of maps which provide a graphic view of weather patterns. Such a presentation is useful in making comparisons of large areas, as well as in finding specific data for locations not listed in the Weather Summaries.

Fig. 1. Average Annual Temperature (°F)

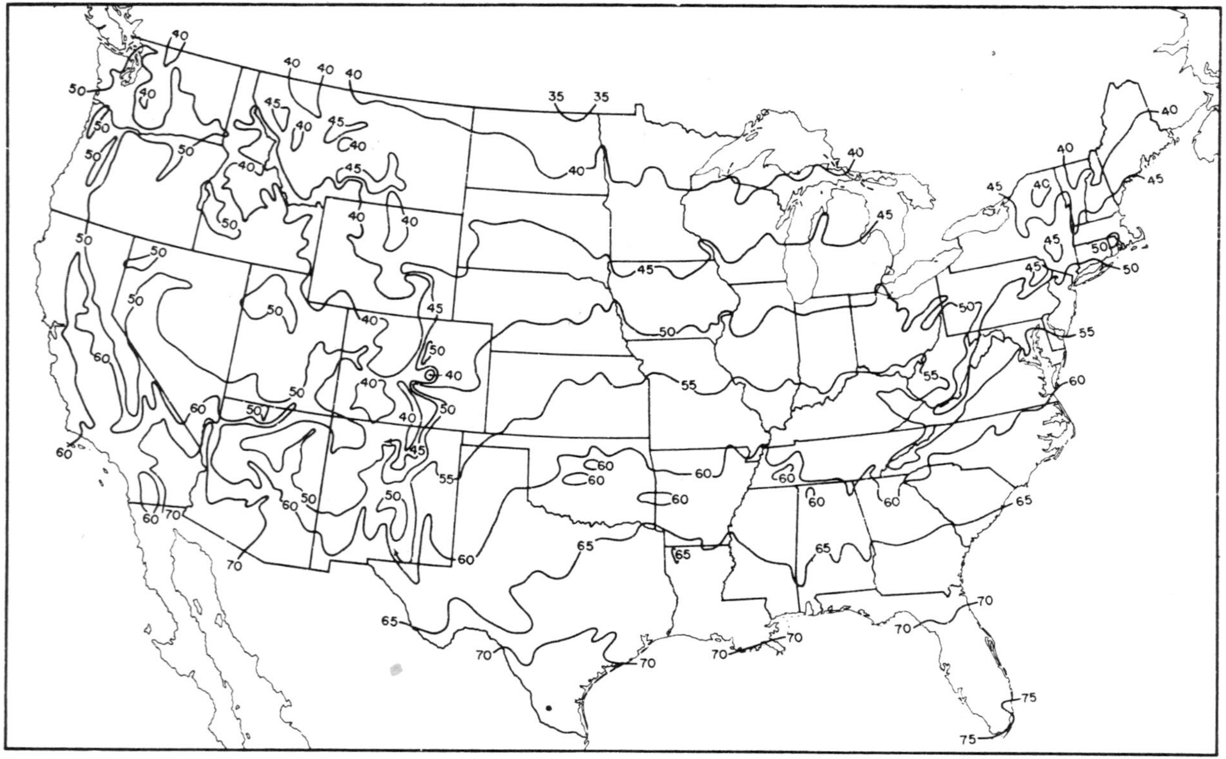

Fig. 2. Normal Daily Minimum Temperature (°F), January

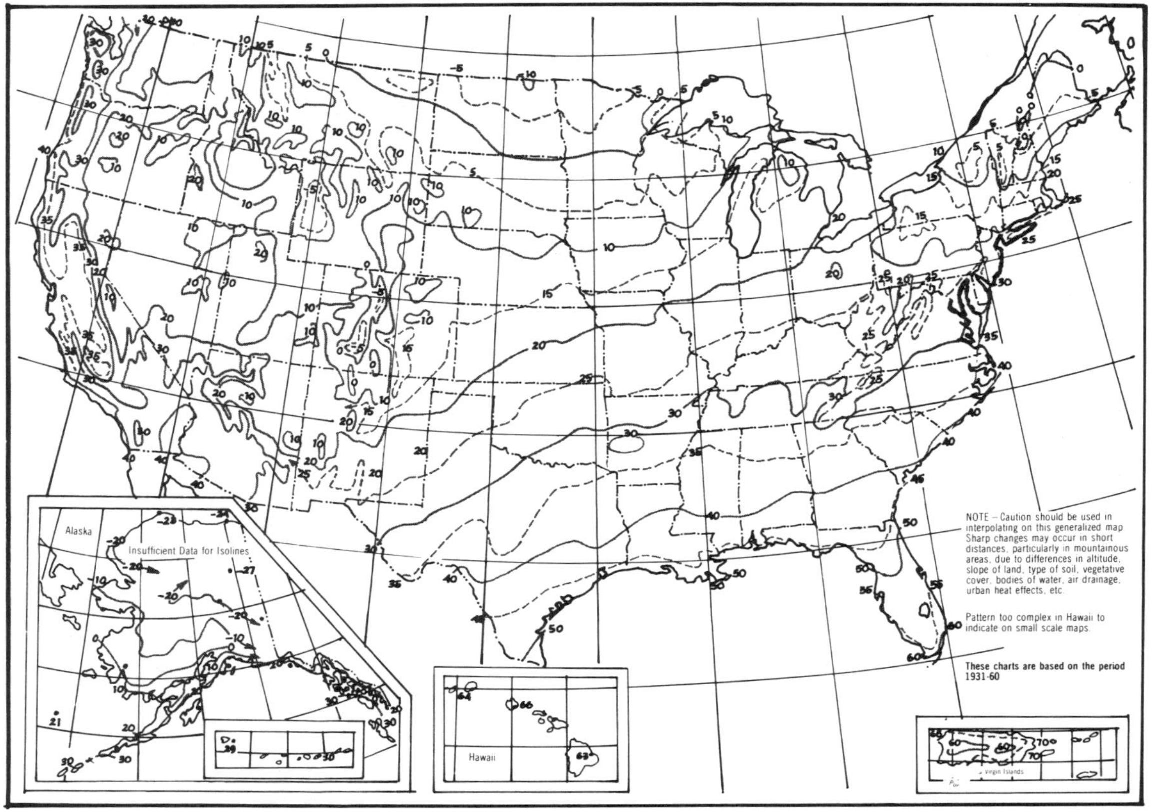

NOTE: Caution should be used in interpolating on this generalized map. Sharp changes may occur in short distances, particularly in mountainous areas, due to differences in altitude, slope of land, type of soil, vegetative cover, bodies of water, air drainage, urban heat effects, etc.

Pattern too complex in Hawaii to indicate on small scale maps.

These charts are based on the period 1931-60

Virgin Islands

Hawaii

Insufficient Data for Isolines

Alaska

Fig. 3. Normal Daily Maximum Temperature (°F), January

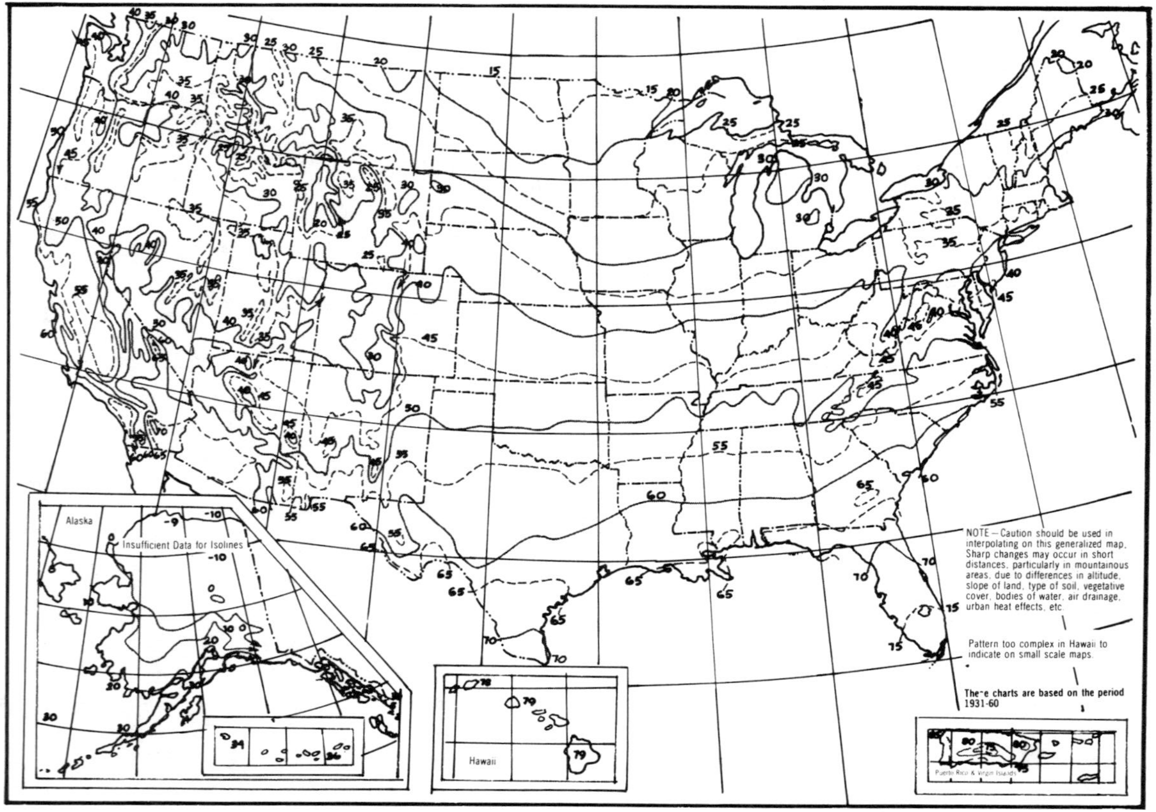

NOTE—Caution should be used in interpolating on this generalized map. Sharp changes may occur in short distances, particularly in mountainous areas, due to differences in altitude, slope of land, type of soil, vegetative cover, bodies of water, air drainage, urban heat effects, etc.

Pattern too complex in Hawaii to indicate on small scale maps.

These charts are based on the period 1931-60

Hawaii

Alaska

Insufficient Data for Isolines

Fig. 4. Normal Daily Minimum Temperature (° F), July

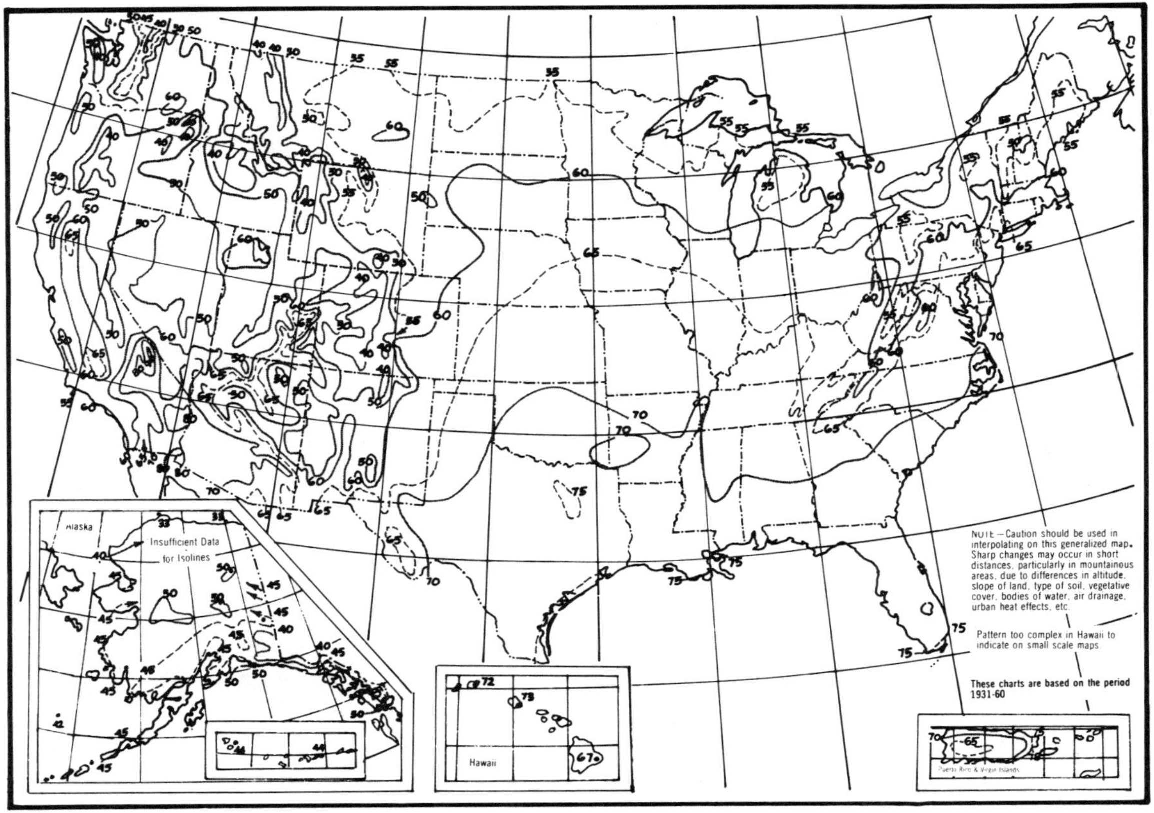

Alaska
Insufficient Data for Isolines
Hawaii
Puerto Rico & Virgin Islands
NOTE—Caution should be used in interpolating on this generalized map. Sharp changes may occur in short distances, particularly in mountainous areas, due to differences in altitude, slope of land, type of soil, vegetative cover, bodies of water, air drainage, urban heat effects, etc.
Pattern too complex in Hawaii to indicate on small scale maps.
These charts are based on the period 1931-60

Fig. 5. Normal Daily Maximum Temperature (°F), July

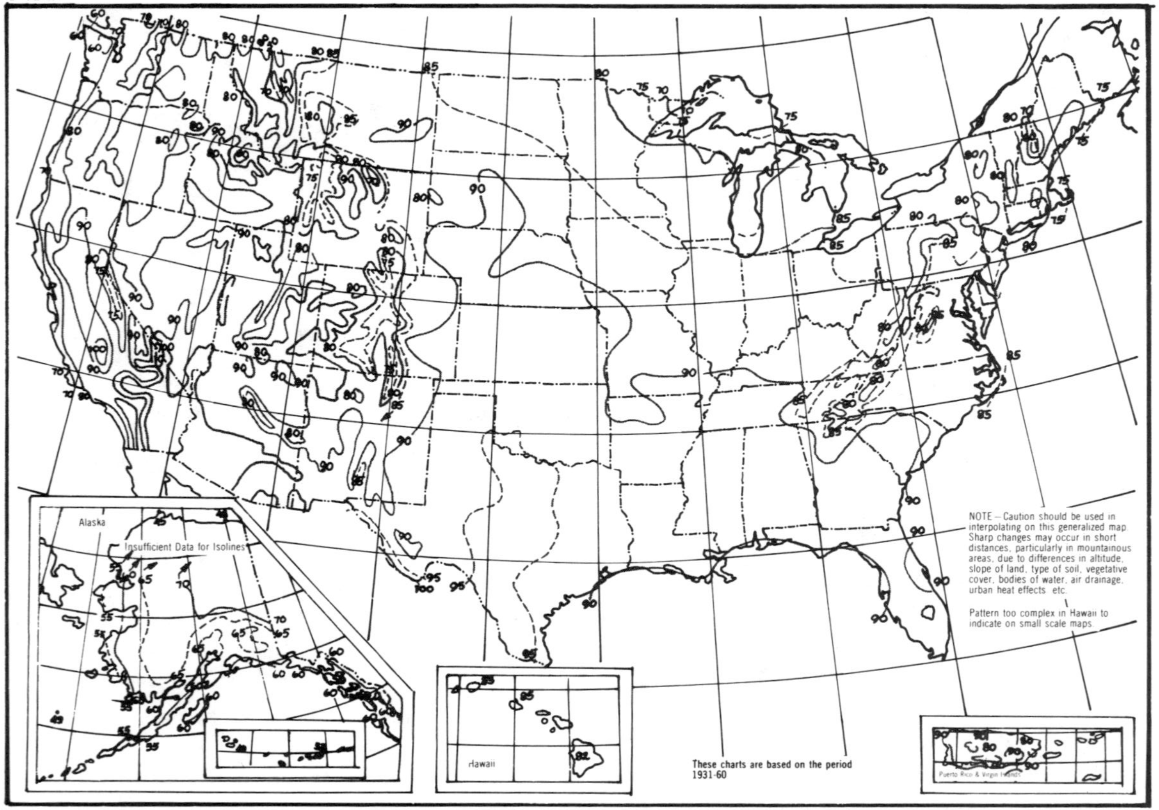
Alaska
Insufficient Data for Isolines
Hawaii
Puerto Rico & Virgin Islands
These charts are based on the period 1931-60
NOTE—Caution should be used in interpolating on this generalized map. Sharp changes may occur in short distances, particularly in mountainous areas, due to differences in altitude, slope of land, type of soil, vegetative cover, bodies of water, air drainage, urban heat effects, etc.
Pattern too complex in Hawaii to indicate on small scale maps

Fig. 6. Mean Annual Number of Days with Maximum Temperature 90° F and Above (Except 70° F and Above in Alaska)

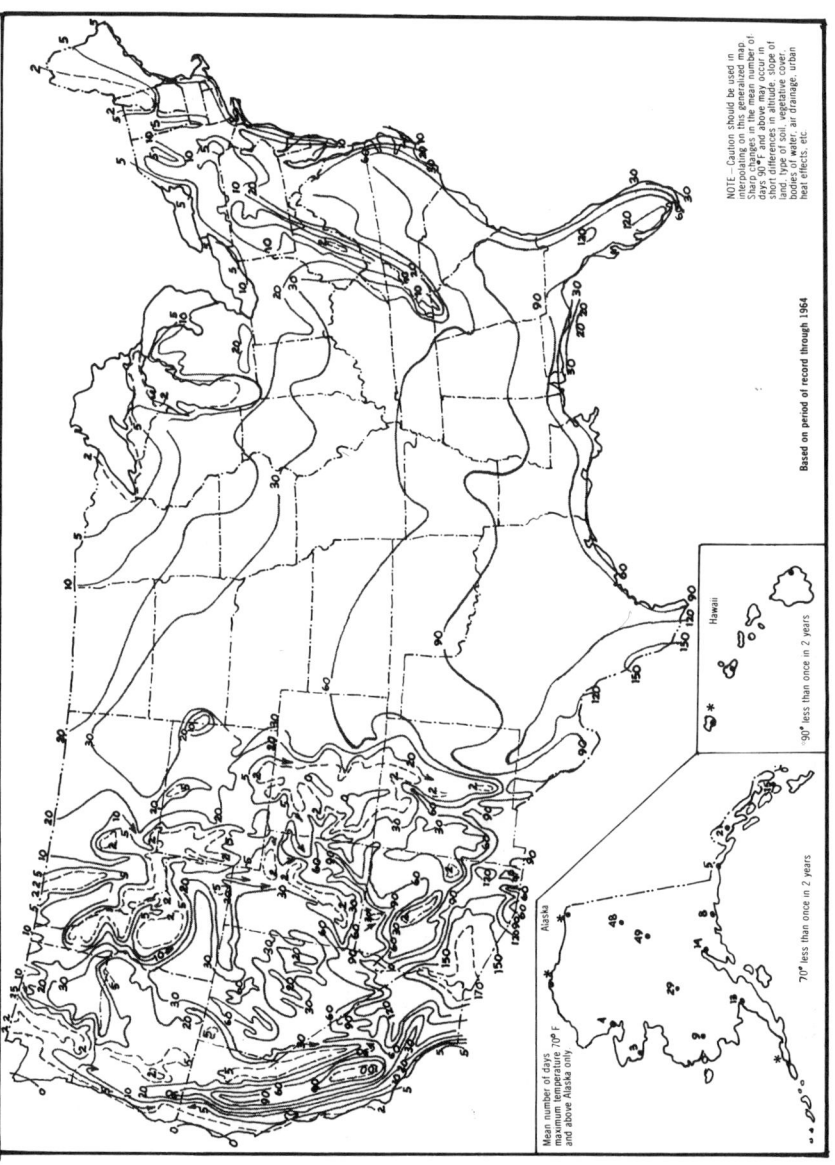

Mean number of days
maximum temperature 70° F
and above Alaska only

Alaska

70° less than once in 2 years

90° less than once in 2 years

Hawaii

Based on period of record through 1964

NOTE — Caution should be used in interpolating on this generalized map. Sharp changes in the mean number of days 90° F and above may occur in short differences in altitude, slope of land, type of soil, vegetative cover, bodies of water, air drainage, urban heat effects, etc.

Fig. 7. Mean Annual Number of Days with Minimum Temperature of 32° F and Below

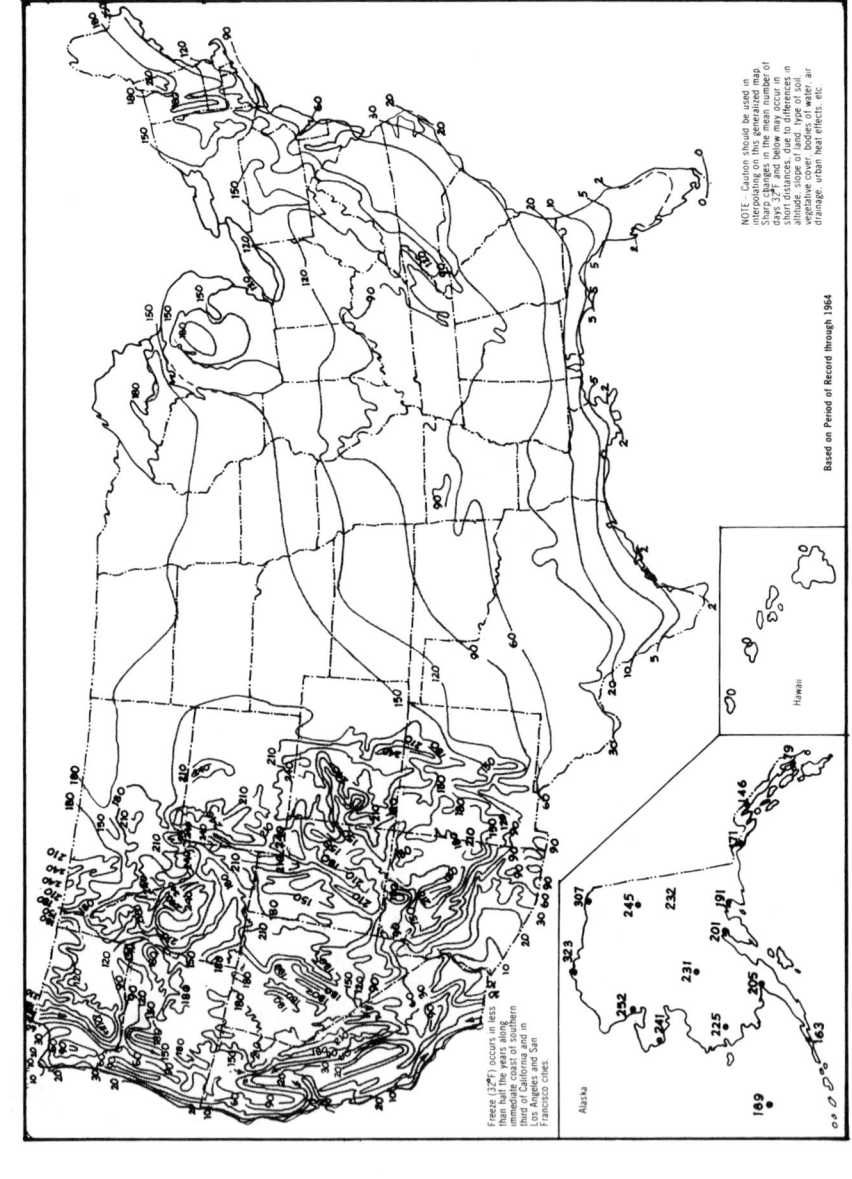

Freeze (32°F) occurs in less than half the years along immediate coast of southern third of California and in Los Angeles and San Francisco cities.

NOTE: Caution should be used in interpolating on this generalized map. Sharp changes in the mean number of days 32°F and below may occur in short distances, due to differences in altitude, slope of land, type of soil, vegetative cover, bodies of water, air drainage, urban heat effects, etc.

Based on Period of Record through 1964

Fig. 8. Mean Date of Last 32° F Temperature in Spring

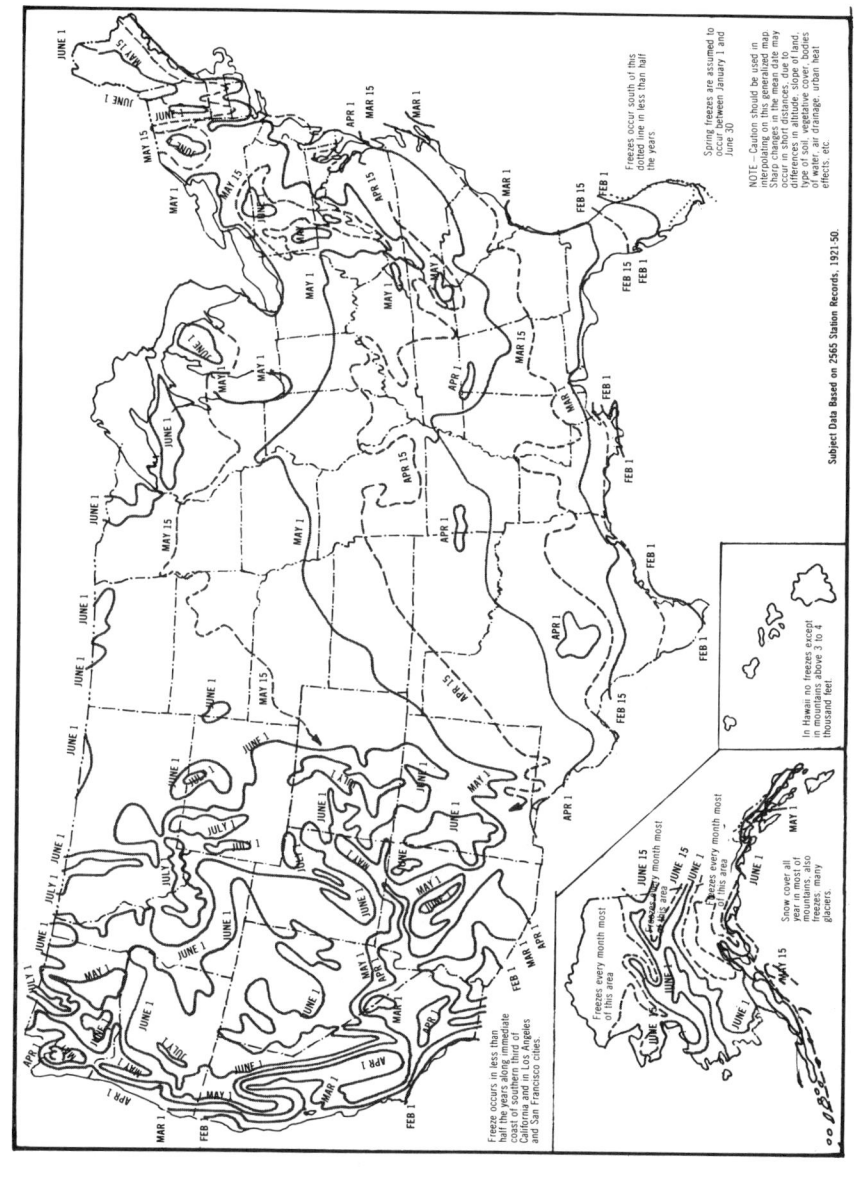

Freeze occurs in less than half the years along immediate coast of southern third of California and in Los Angeles and San Francisco cities.

Freezes occur south of this dotted line in less than half the years.

Spring freezes are assumed to occur between January 1 and June 30

NOTE.—Caution should be used in interpolating on this generalized map. Sharp changes in the mean date may occur in short distances, due to differences in altitude, slope of land, type of soil, vegetative cover, bodies of water, air drainage, urban heat effects, etc.

Subject Data Based on 2565 Station Records, 1921-50.

In Hawaii no freezes except in mountains above 3 to 4 thousand feet.

Snow cover all year in most of mountains, also freezes, many glaciers.

Freezes every month most of this area.

Freezes every month most of this area.

25

Fig. 9. Mean Date of First 32° F Temperature in Autumn

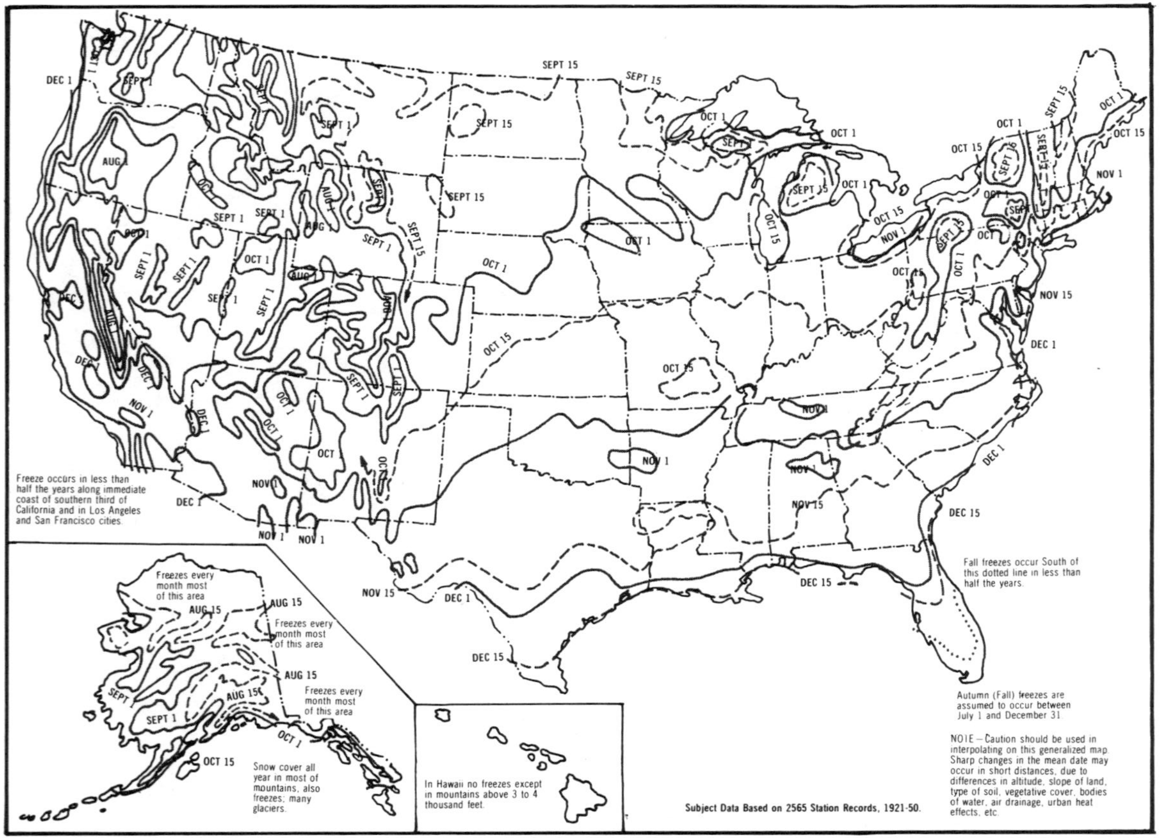
Freeze occurs in less than half the years along immediate coast of southern third of California and in Los Angeles and San Francisco cities.
Fall freezes occur South of this dotted line in less than half the years.
Autumn (Fall) freezes are assumed to occur between July 1 and December 31.
NOTE—Caution should be used in interpolating on this generalized map. Sharp changes in the mean date may occur in short distances, due to differences in altitude, slope of land, type of soil, vegetative cover, bodies of water, air drainage, urban heat effects, etc.
Subject Data Based on 2565 Station Records, 1921-50.
Freezes every month most of this area
Freezes every month most of this area
Freezes every month most of this area
Snow cover all year in most of mountains, also freezes; many glaciers.
In Hawaii no freezes except in mountains above 3 to 4 thousand feet.
SEPT 15
OCT 1
OCT 15
NOV 1
NOV 15
DEC 1
DEC 15
AUG 15
SEPT 1
AUG 1

Fig. 10. Normal Annual Total Precipitation (Inches)

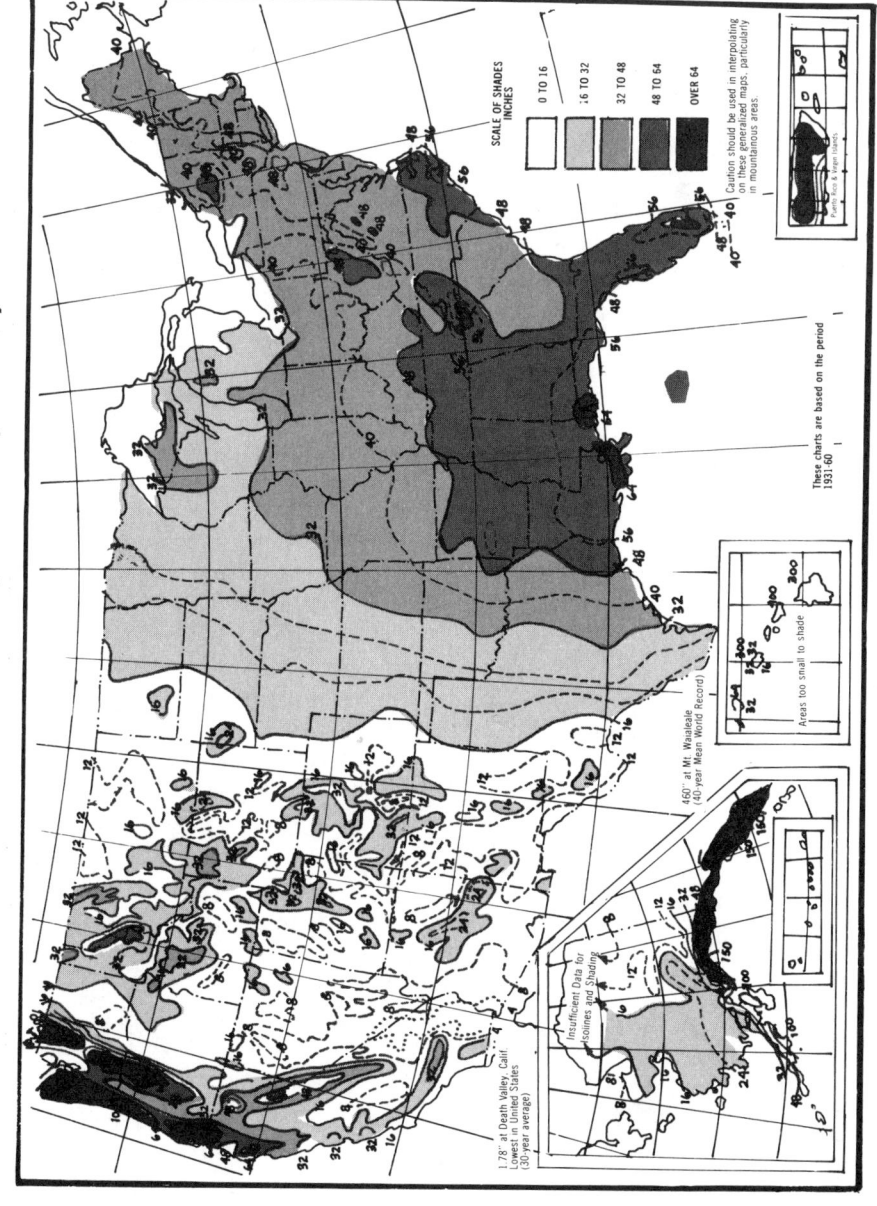

SCALE OF SHADES
INCHES

0 TO 16

16 TO 32

32 TO 48

48 TO 64

OVER 64

Caution should be used in interpolating on these generalized maps, particularly in mountainous areas.

These charts are based on the period 1931-60

460" at Mt. Waialeale (40-year Mean World Record)

Areas too small to shade

1.78" at Death Valley, Calif. Lowest in United States (30-year average)

Insufficient Data for Isolines and Shading

Fig. 11. Mean Annual Total Snowfall (Inches)

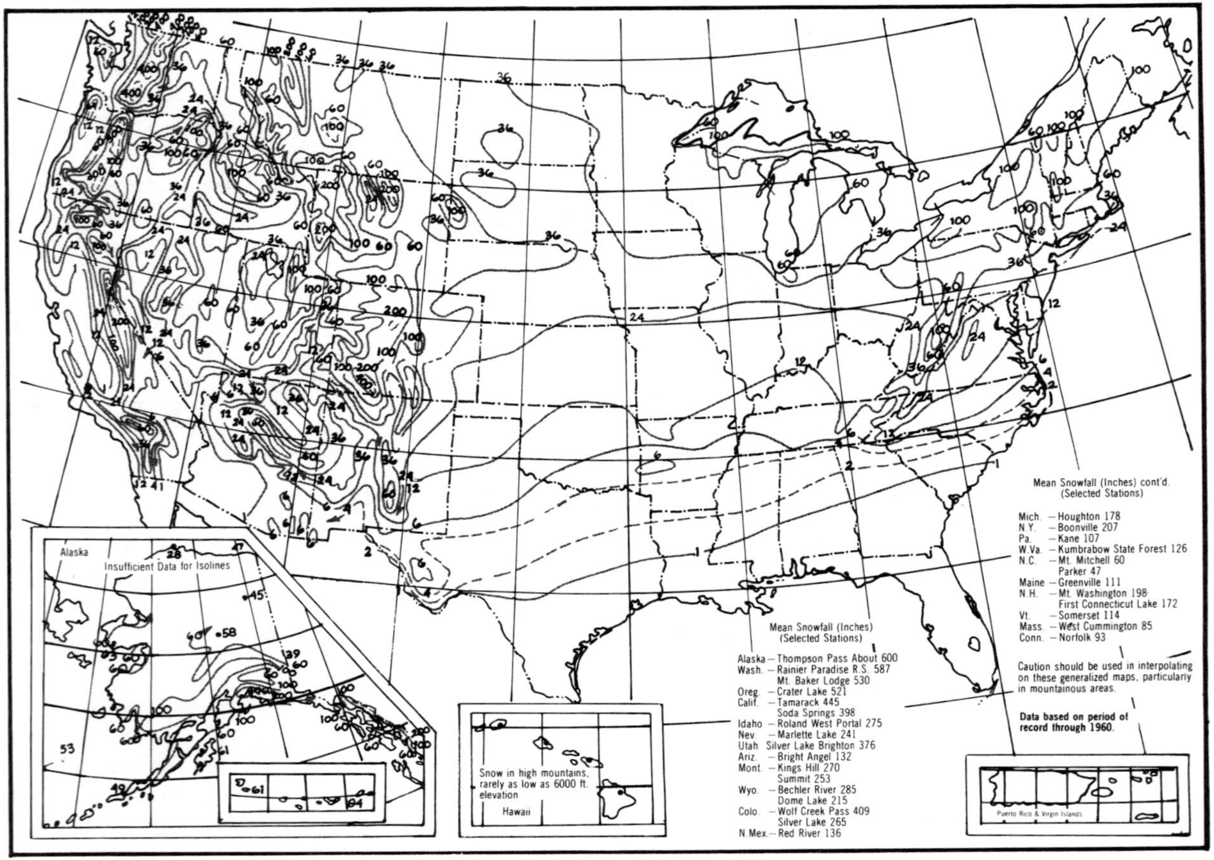
Alaska
Insufficient Data for Isolines
Snow in high mountains, rarely as low as 6000 ft. elevation
Hawaii
Puerto Rico & Virgin Islands
Mean Snowfall (Inches)
(Selected Stations)
Alaska — Thompson Pass About 600
Wash. — Rainier Paradise R.S. 587
Mt. Baker Lodge 530
Oreg. — Crater Lake 521
Calif. — Tamarack 445
Soda Springs 398
Idaho — Roland West Portal 275
Nev. — Marlette Lake 241
Utah Silver Lake Brighton 376
Ariz. — Bright Angel 132
Mont. — Kings Hill 270
Summit 253
Wyo. — Bechler River 285
Dome Lake 215
Colo. — Wolf Creek Pass 409
Silver Lake 265
N.Mex. — Red River 136
Mean Snowfall (Inches) cont'd.
(Selected Stations)
Mich. — Houghton 178
N.Y. — Boonville 207
Pa. — Kane 107
W.Va. — Kumbrabow State Forest 126
N.C. — Mt. Mitchell 60
Parker 47
Maine — Greenville 111
N.H. — Mt. Washington 198
First Connecticut Lake 172
Vt. — Somerset 114
Mass. — West Cummington 85
Conn. — Norfolk 93
Caution should be used in interpolating on these generalized maps, particularly in mountainous areas.
Data based on period of record through 1960.

Fig. 12. Mean Relative Humidity (%), January

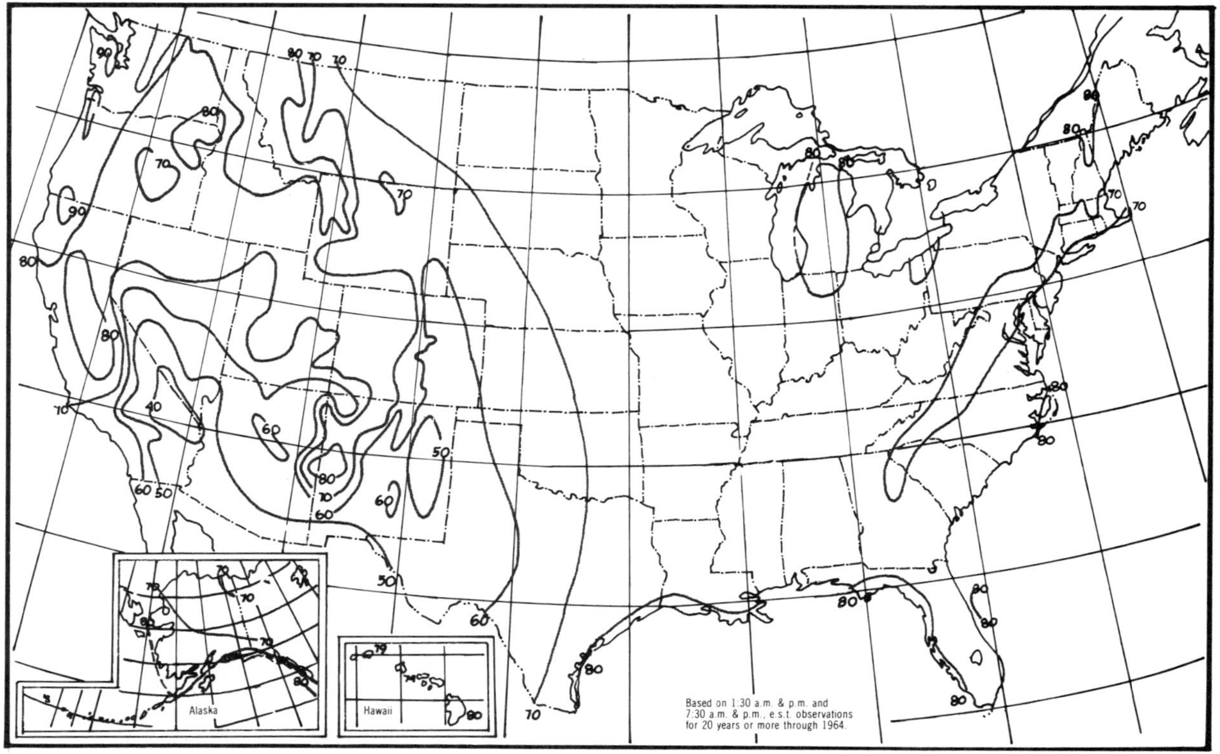

Based on 1:30 a.m. & p.m. and
7:30 a.m. & p.m. e.s.t. observations
for 20 years or more through 1964

Fig. 13. Mean Relative Humidity (%), July

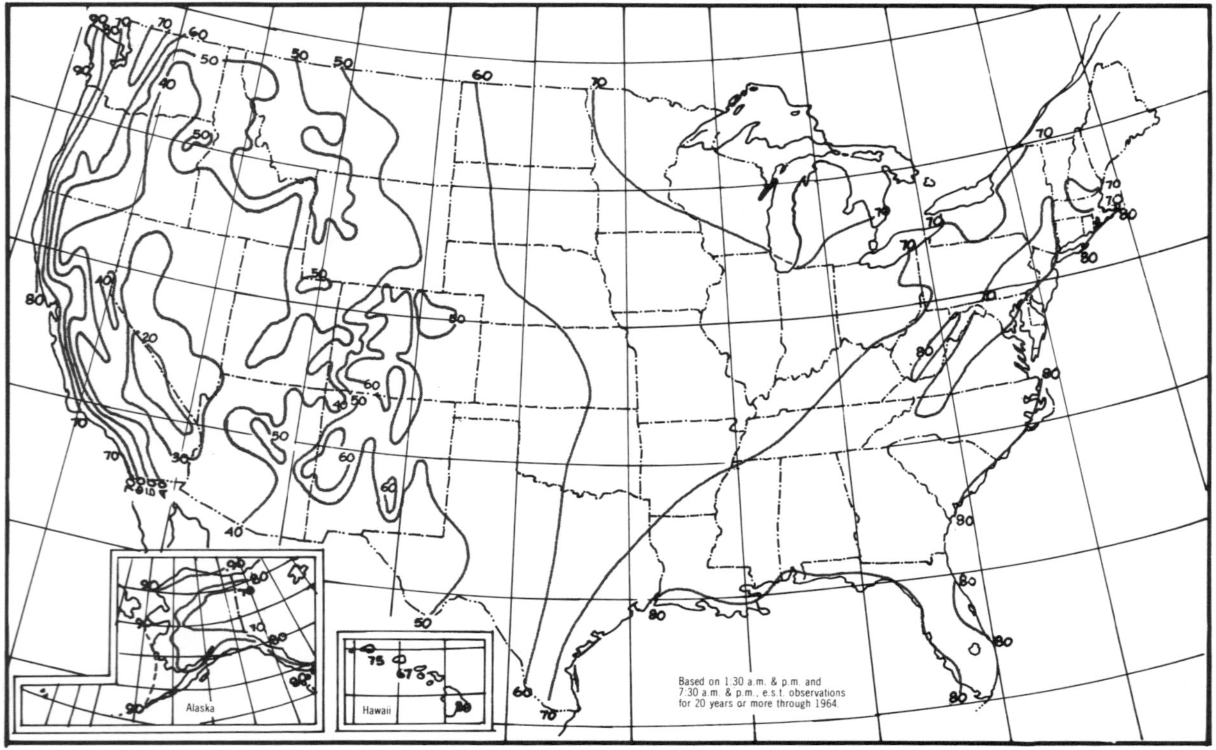

Based on 1:30 a.m. & p.m. and
7:30 a.m. & p.m. e.s.t. observations
for 20 years or more through 1964

Hawaii

Alaska

Fig. 14. Mean Annual Total Heating Degree Days (Base 65° F)

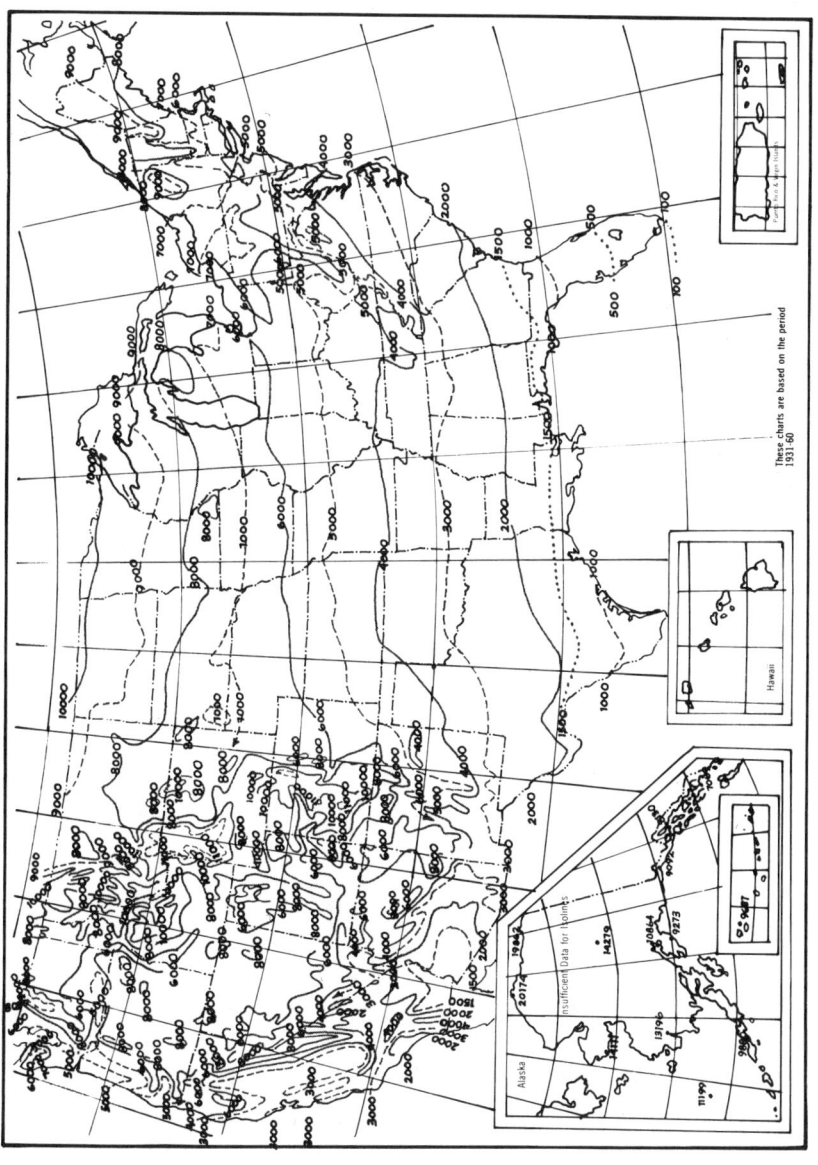

Fig. 15. Mean Annual Total Cooling Degree Days (Base 65° F)

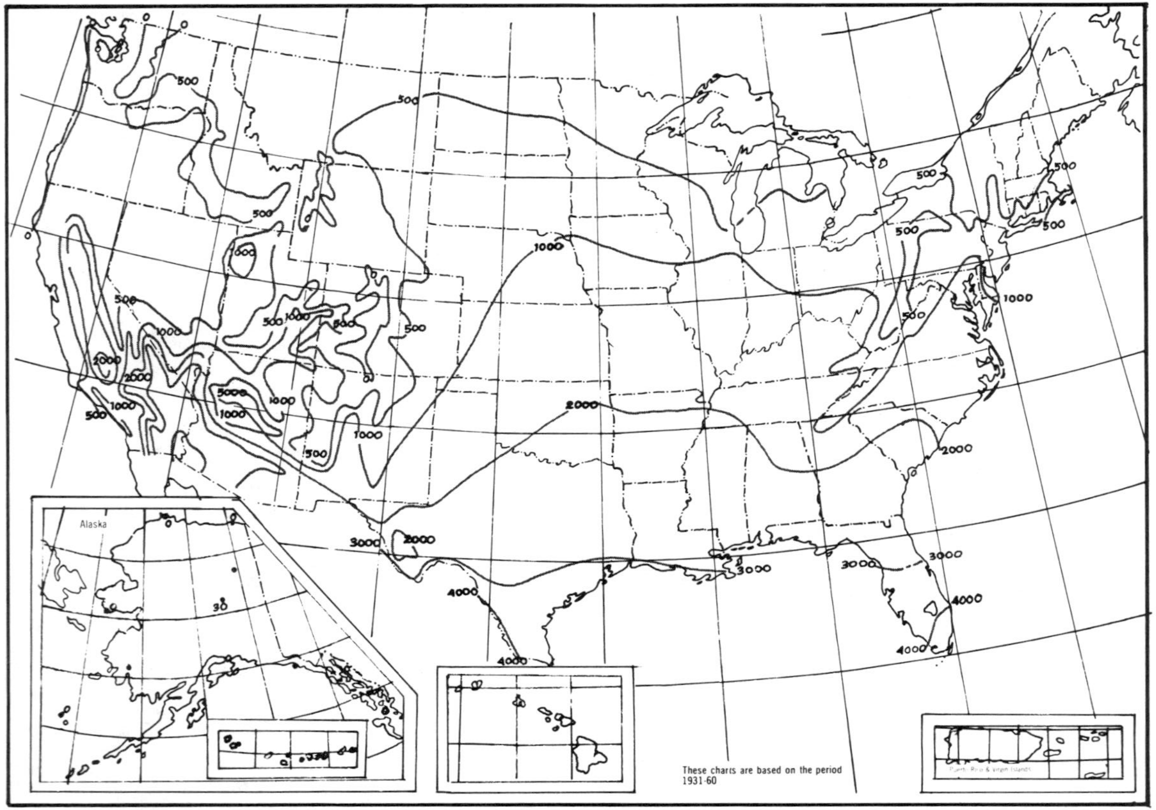

These charts are based on the period 1931-60

Alaska

Fig. 16. Mean Annual Number of Days with Thunderstorms

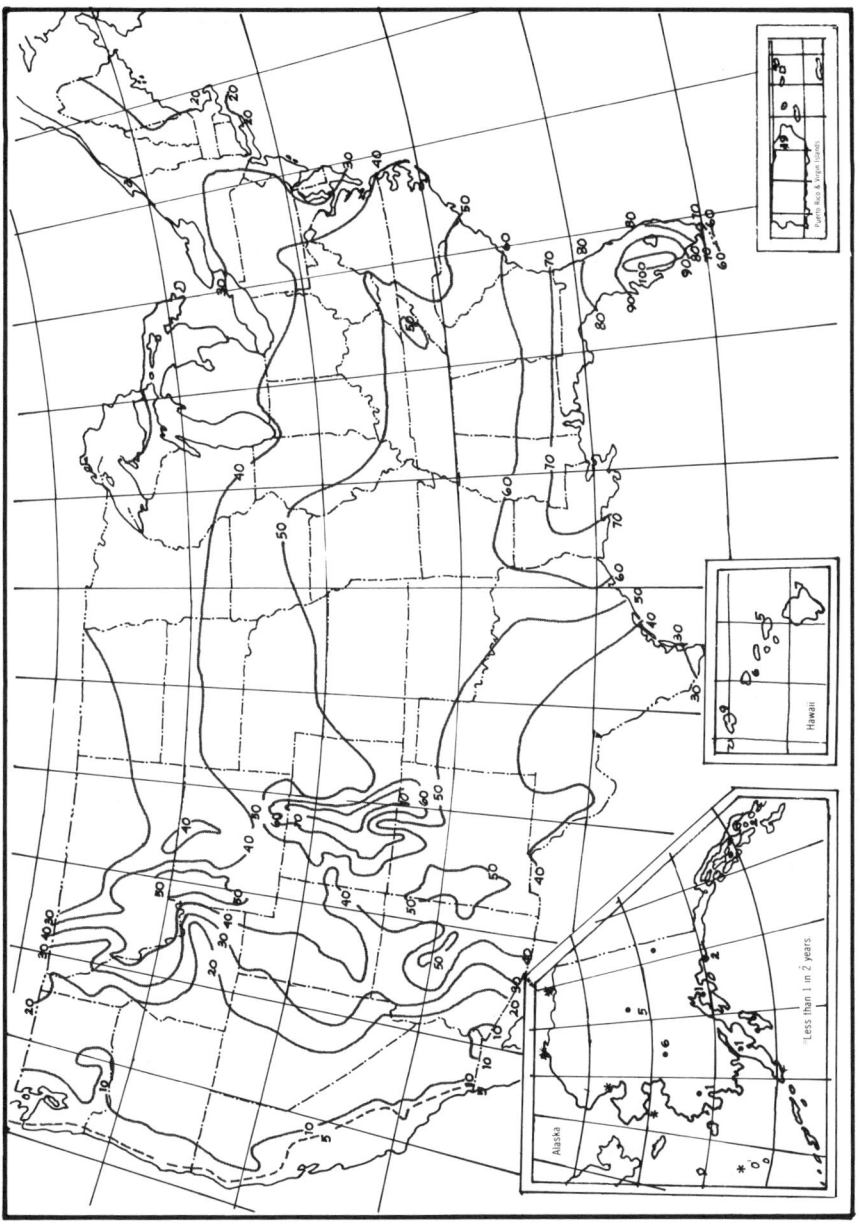

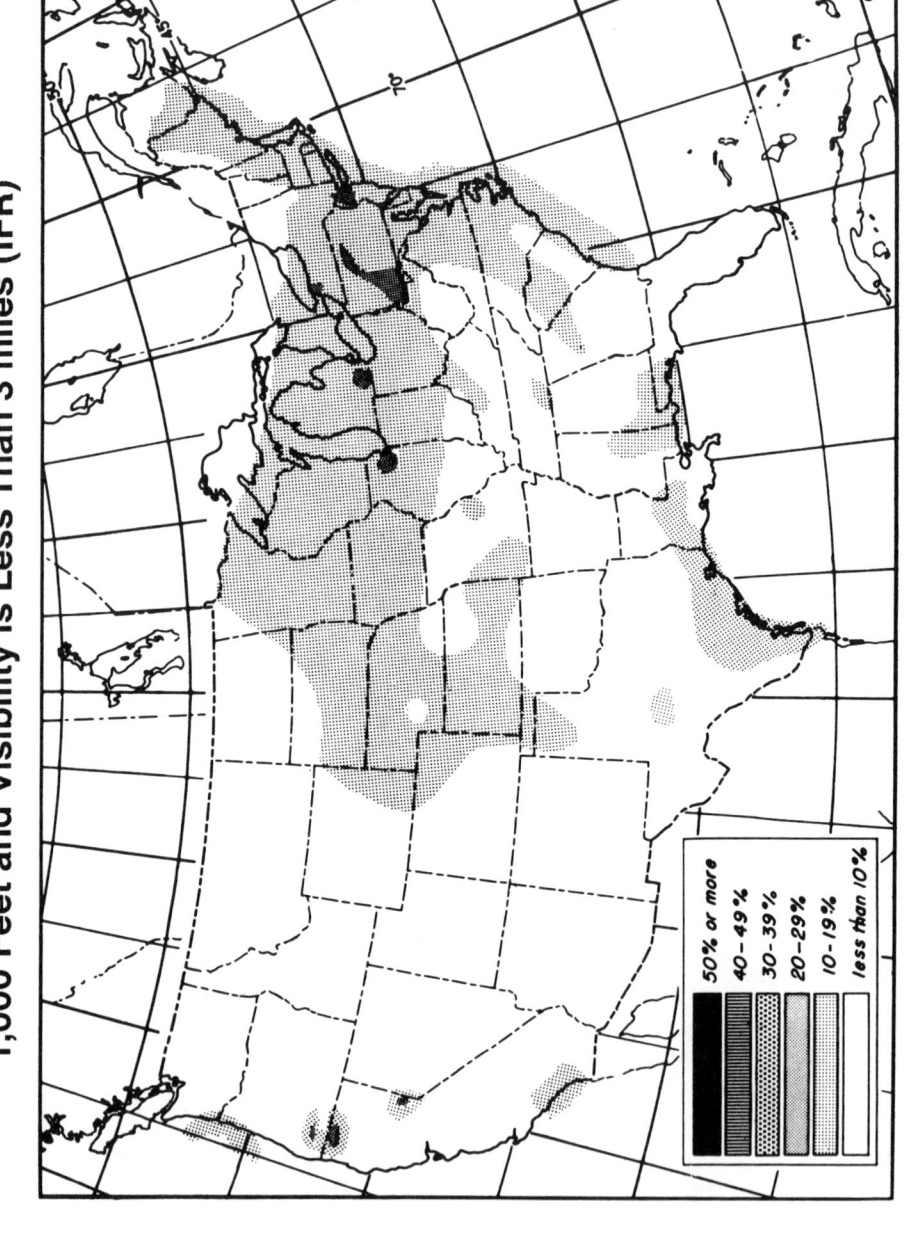

Fig. 17. Percentage of Hours in the Spring When the Ceiling is Below 1,000 Feet and Visibility Is Less Than 3 miles (IFR)

50% or more
40-49%
30-39%
20-29%
10-19%
less than 10%

Fig. 18. Percentage of Hours in the Summer When the Ceiling Is Below 1,000 Feet and Visibility Is Less Than 3 Miles (IFR)

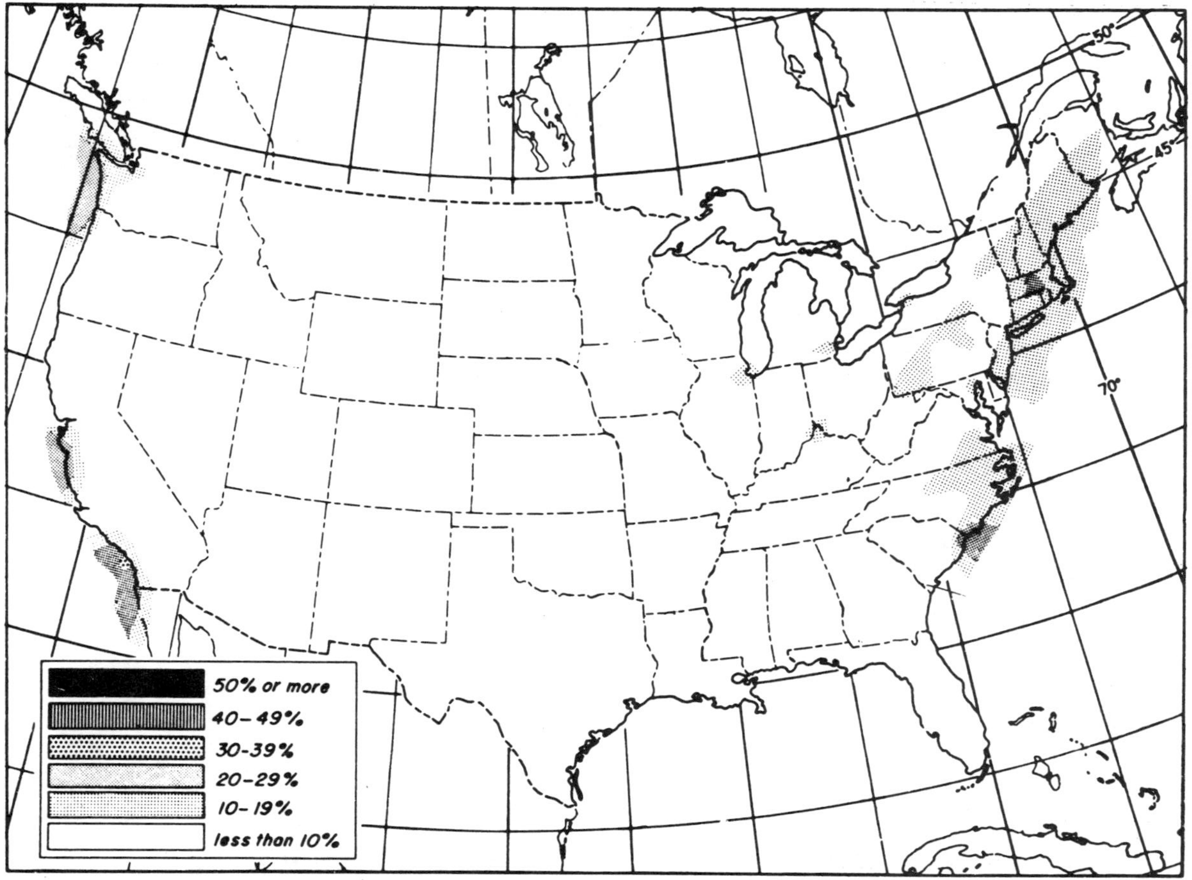

Legend:
- 50% or more
- 40–49%
- 30–39%
- 20–29%
- 10–19%
- less than 10%

Fig. 19. Percentage of Hours in the Fall When the Ceiling is Below 1,000 Feet and Visibility Is Less Than 3 miles (IFR)

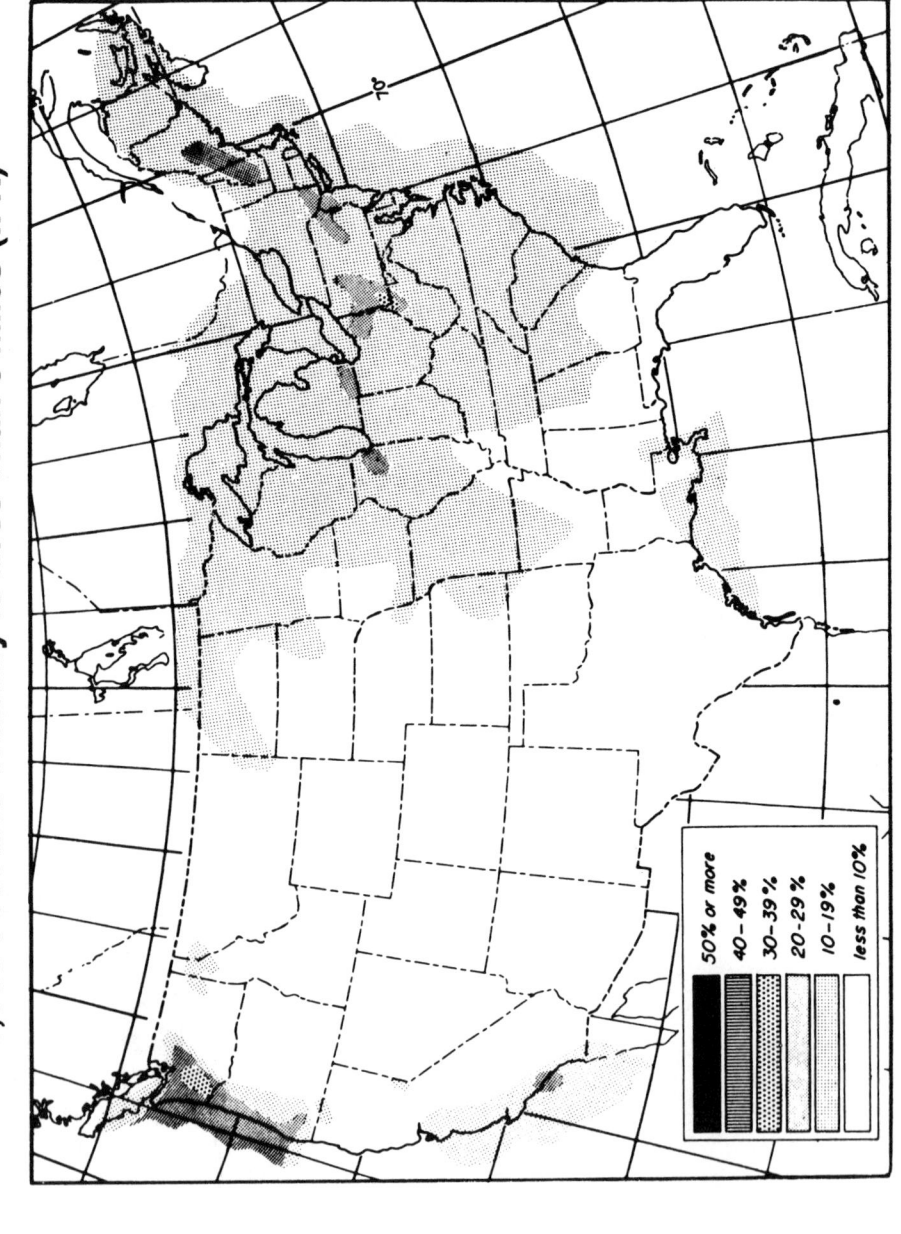

Legend:
- 50% or more
- 40 – 49 %
- 30 – 39 %
- 20 – 29 %
- 10 – 19%
- less than 10%

Fig. 20. Percentage of Hours in the Winter When the Ceiling Is Below 1,000 Feet and Visibility Is Less Than 3 Miles (IFR)

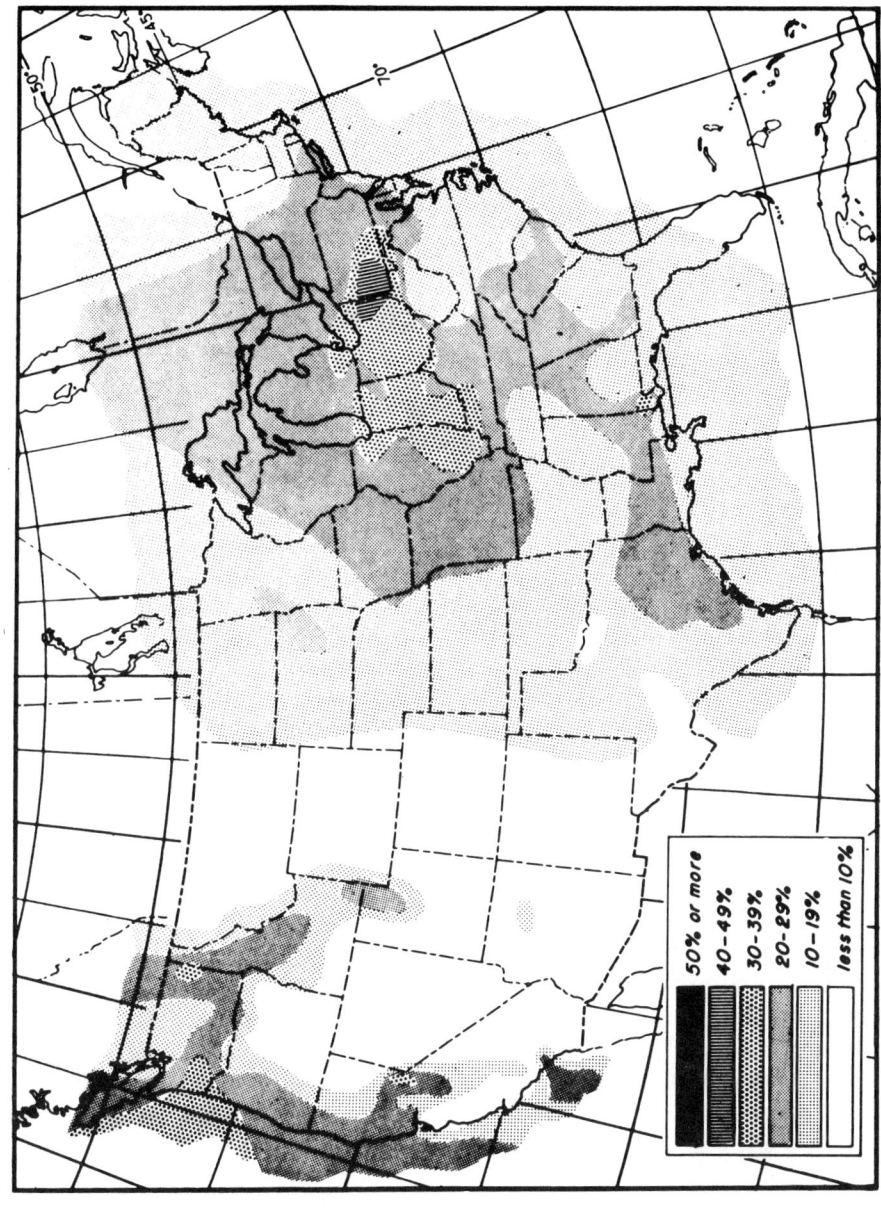

50% or more
40–49%
30–39%
20–29%
10–19%
less than 10%

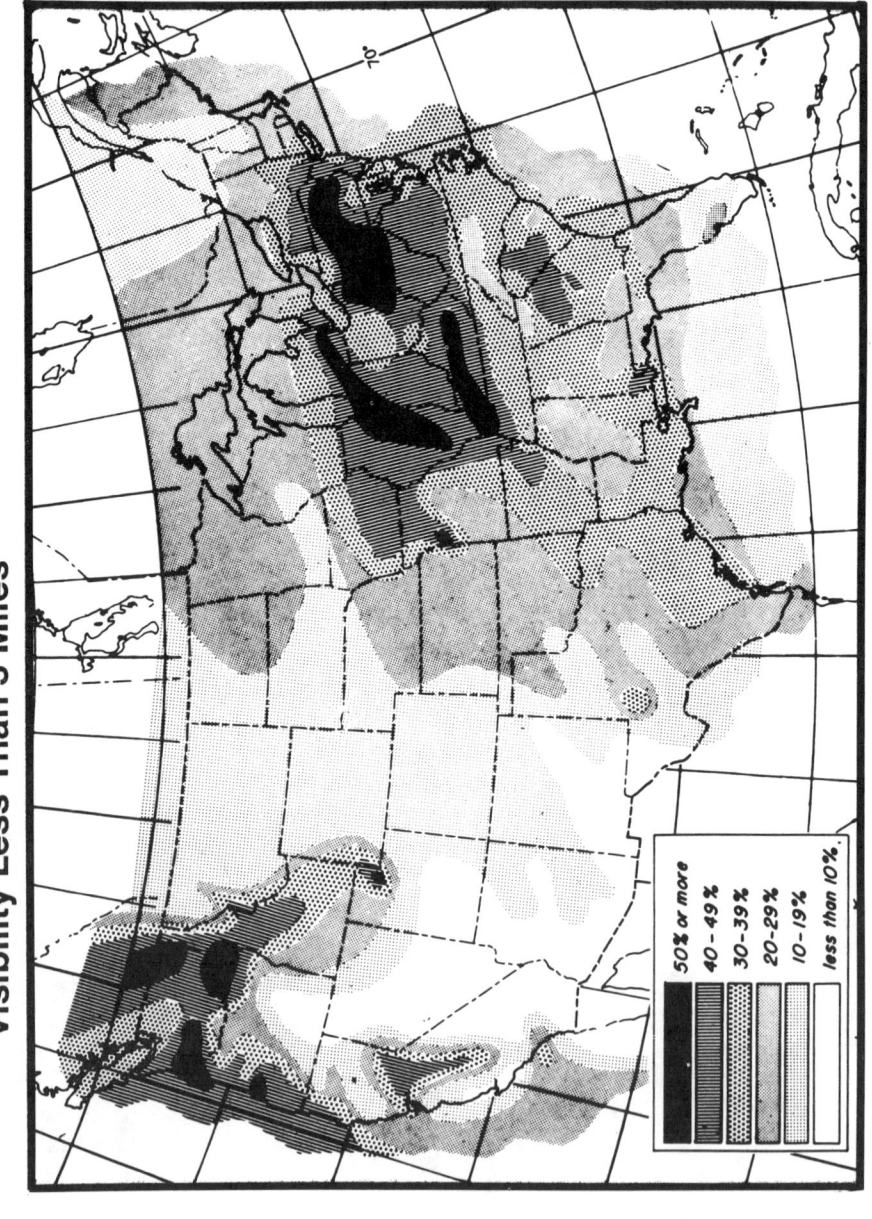

Fig. 21. Percentage of Hours Observed During Any One Month in the Winter Season, with the Ceiling 1,000 Feet or Less and Visibility Less Than 3 Miles

50% or more
40 – 49%
30 – 39%
20 – 29%
10 – 19%
less than 10%

Fig. 22. Mean Monthly Percentage of Possible Sunshine, January

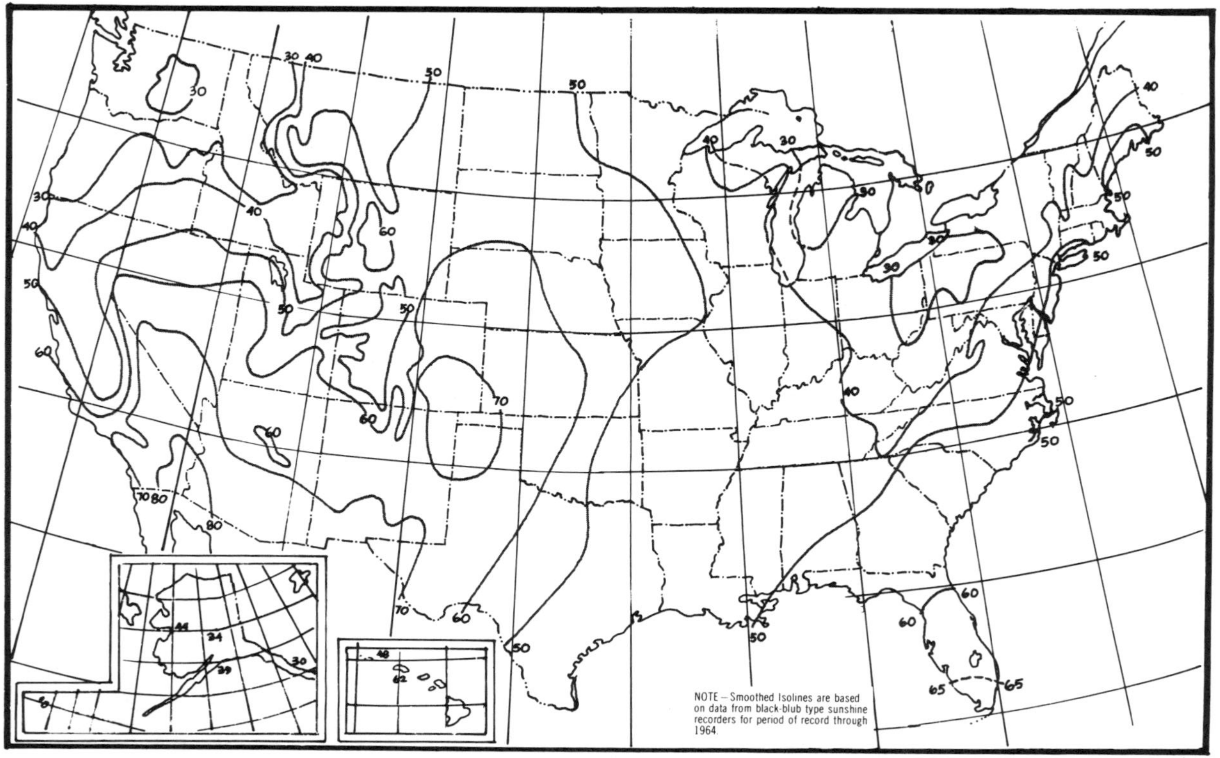

NOTE—Smoothed isolines are based on data from black-blub type sunshine recorders for period of record through 1964

Fig. 23. Mean Monthly Percentage of Possible Sunshine, July

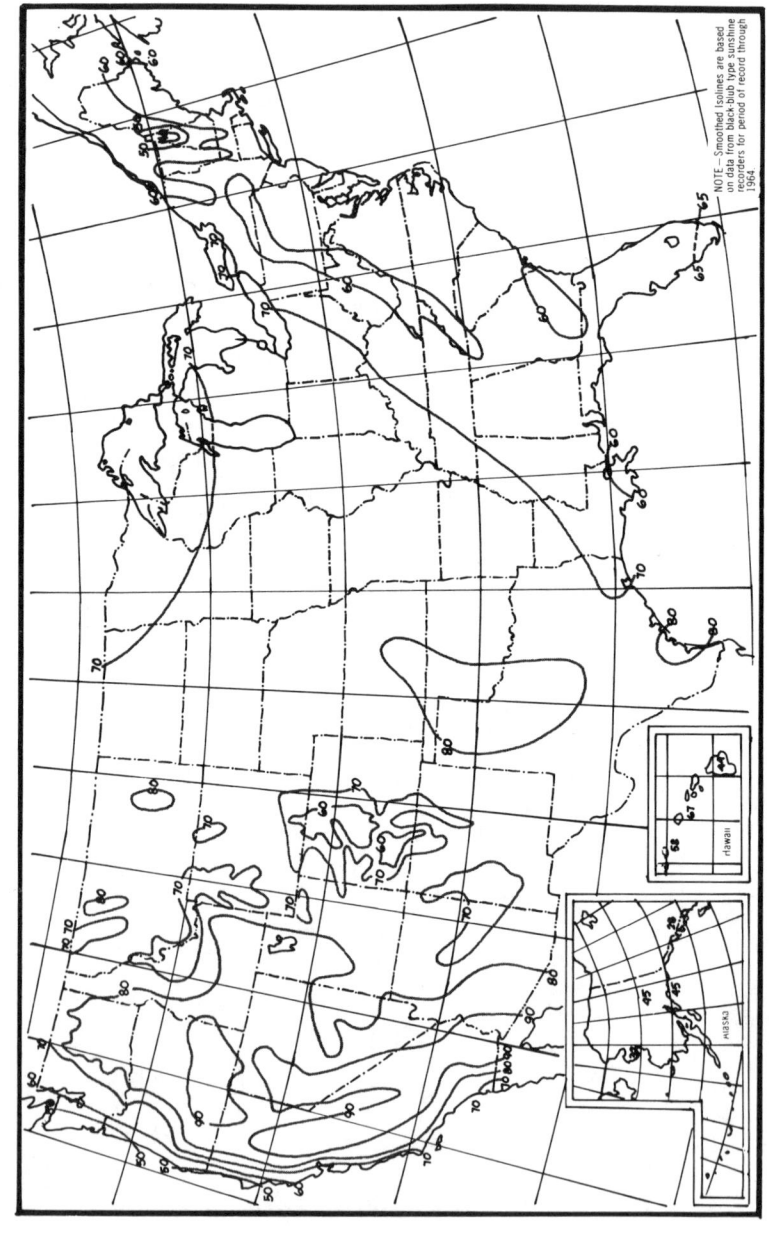

NOTE — Smoothed isolines are based on data from black-bulb type sunshine recorders for period of record through 1964

Fig. 24. Gross Total Energy Requirements, Heating and Cooling

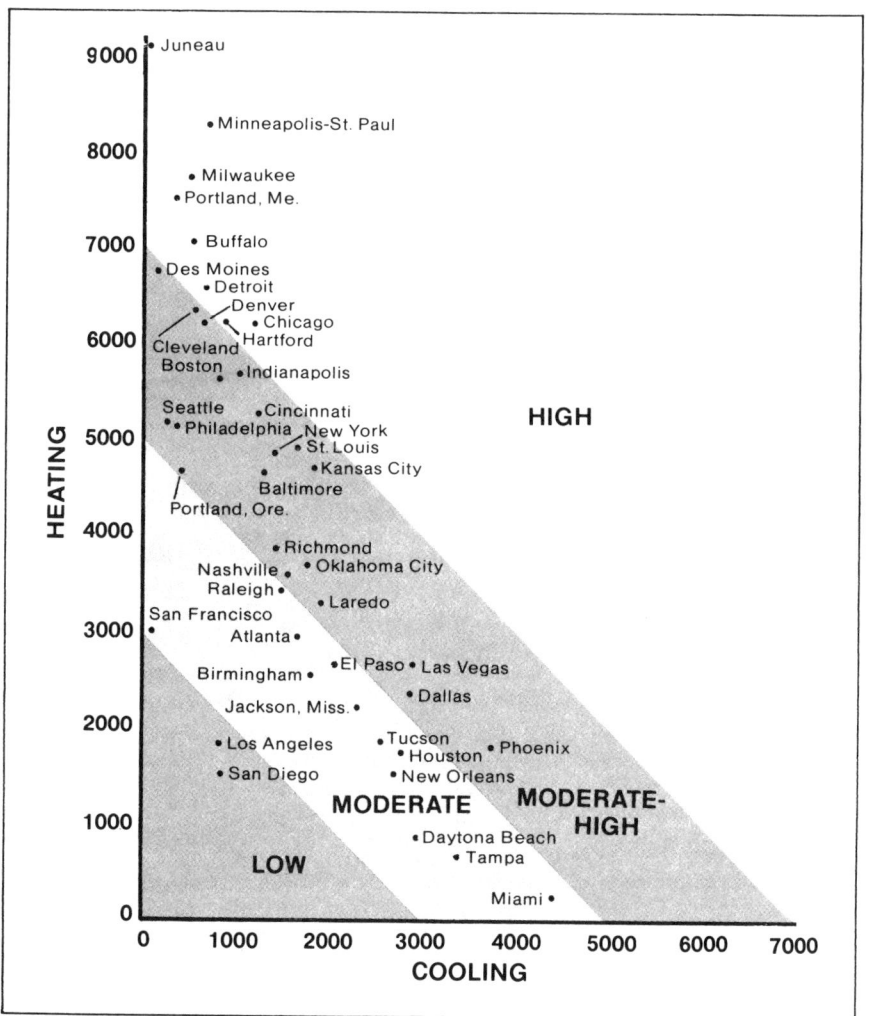

Fig. 25. Hurricane Tracks, 1961-62

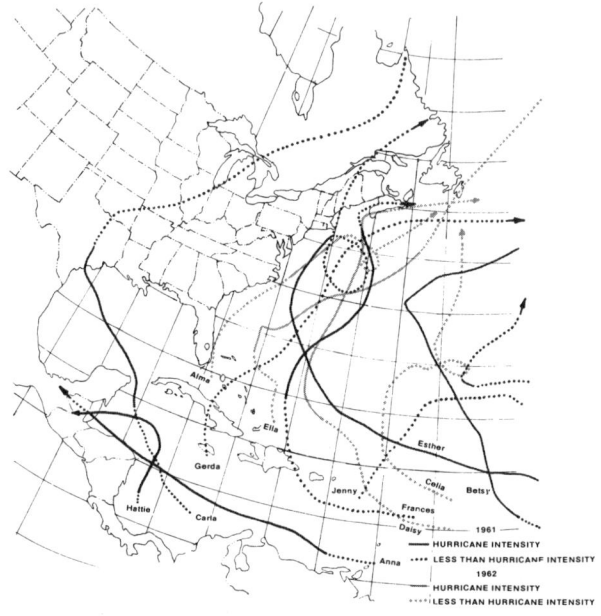

Fig. 26. Hurricane Tracks, 1963-64

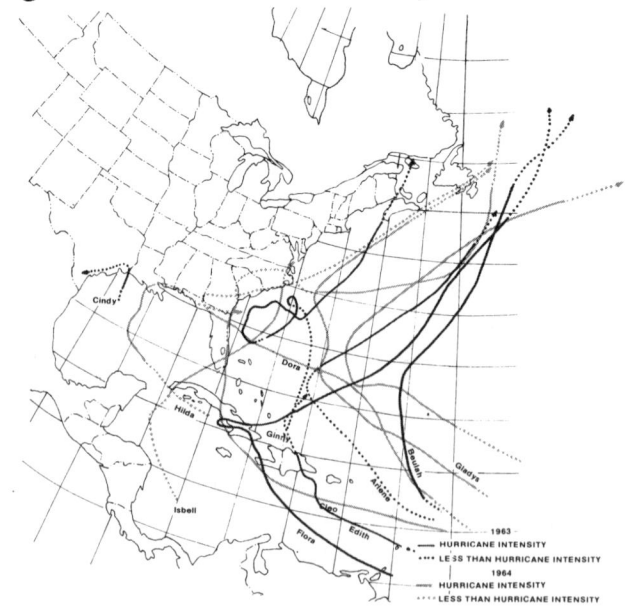

Fig. 27. Hurricane Tracks, 1965-66

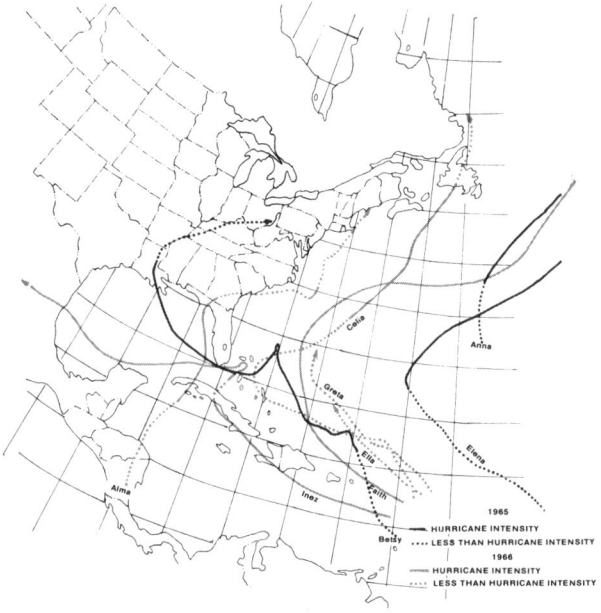

Fig. 28. Hurricane Tracks, 1967-68

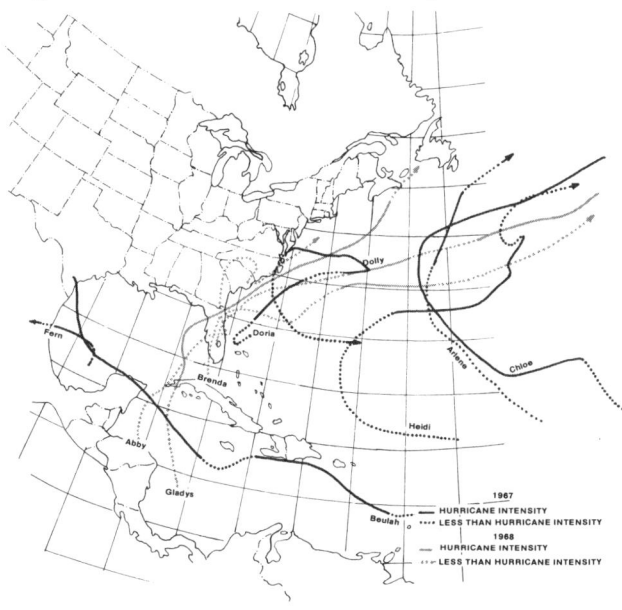

Fig. 29. Hurricane Tracks, 1969-70

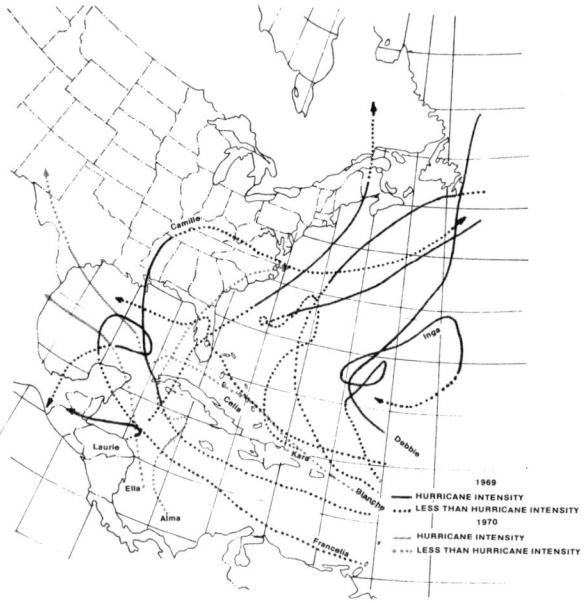

Fig. 30. Hurricane Tracks, 1971

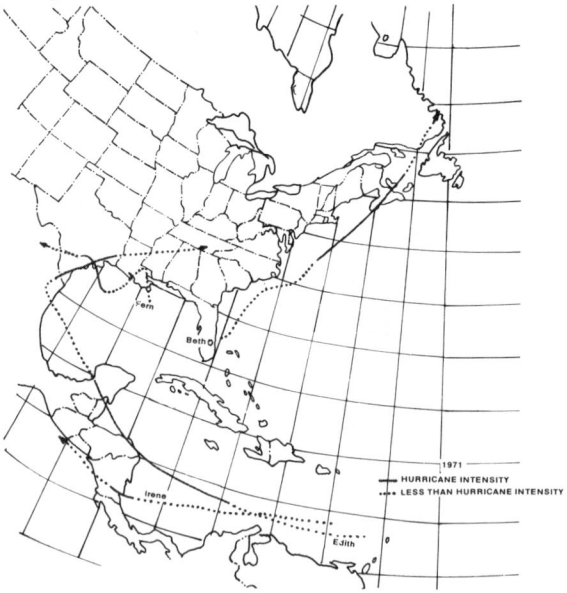

Fig. 31. Hurricane Tracks, 1972

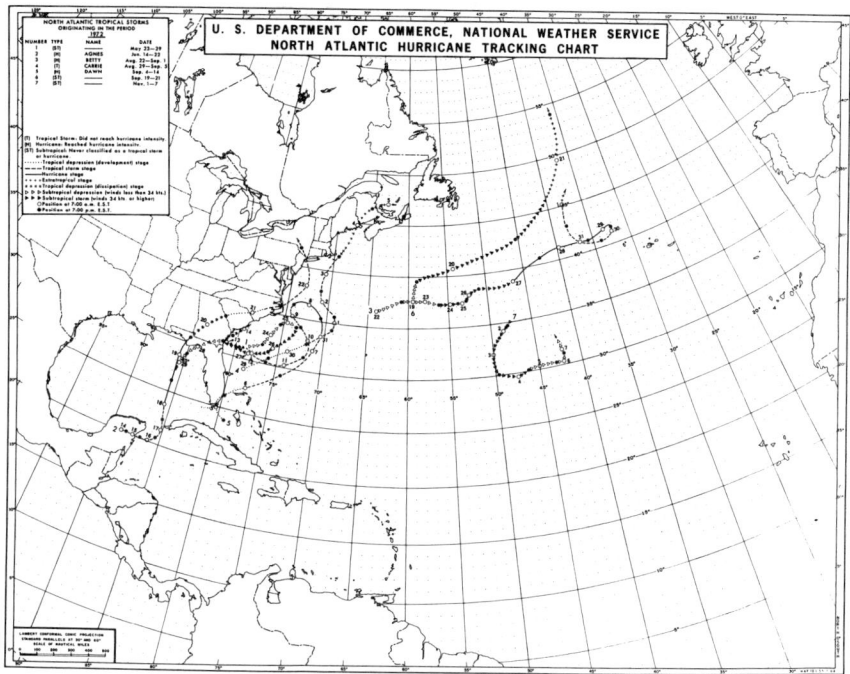

Fig. 32. Hurricane Tracks, 1973

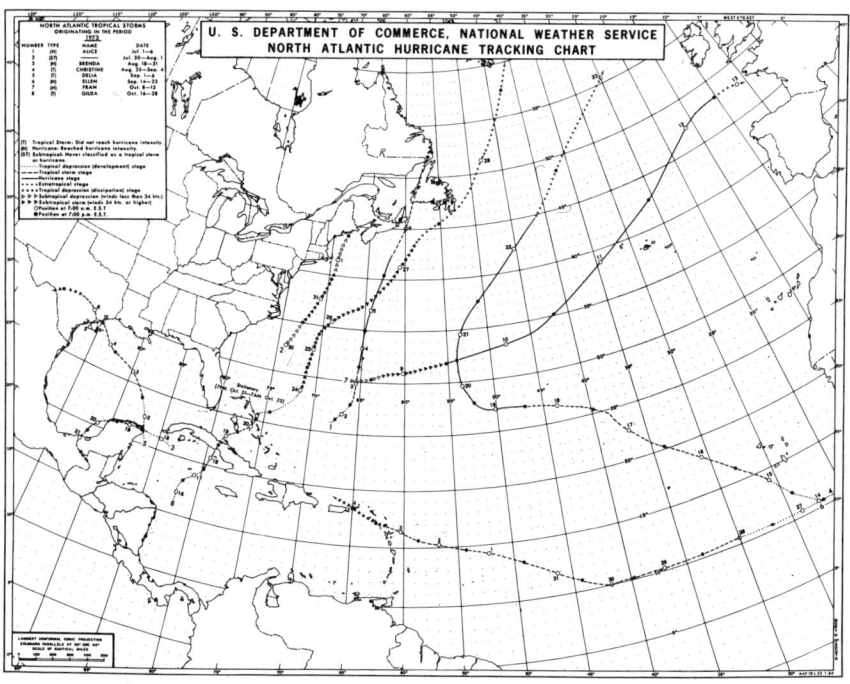

Fig. 33. Hurricane Tracks, 1974

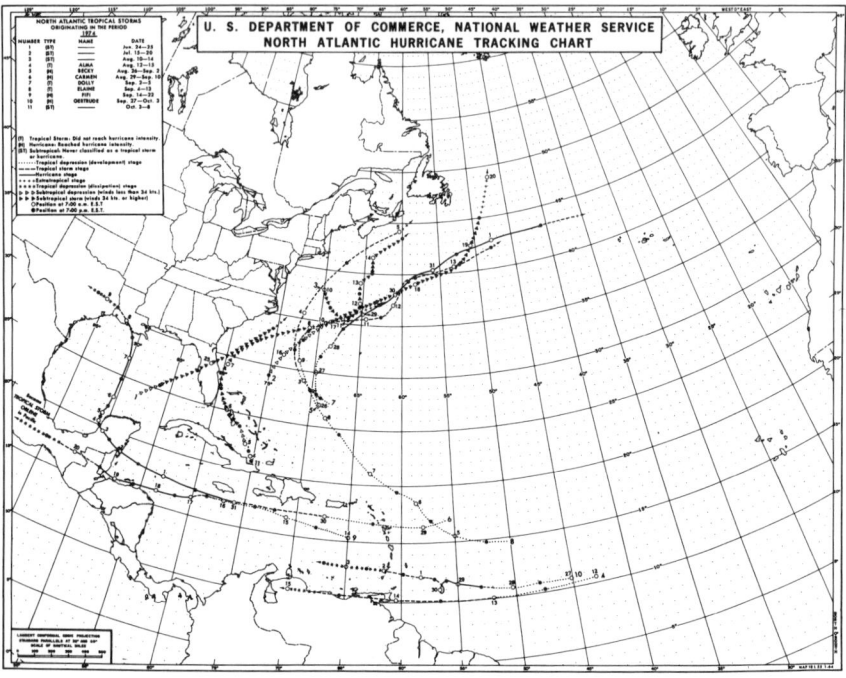

Fig. 34. Hurricane Tracks, 1975

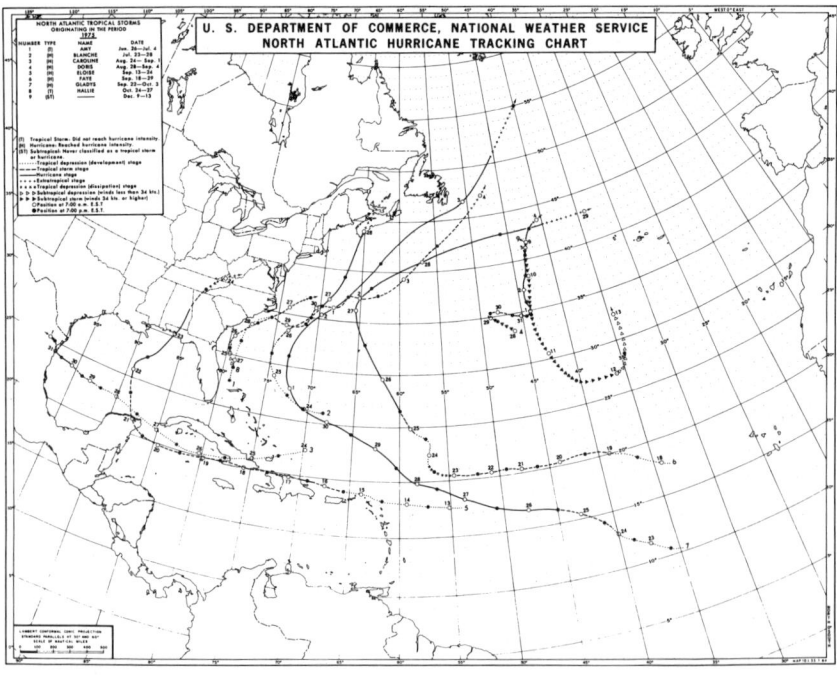

Fig. 35. Hurricane Tracks, 1976

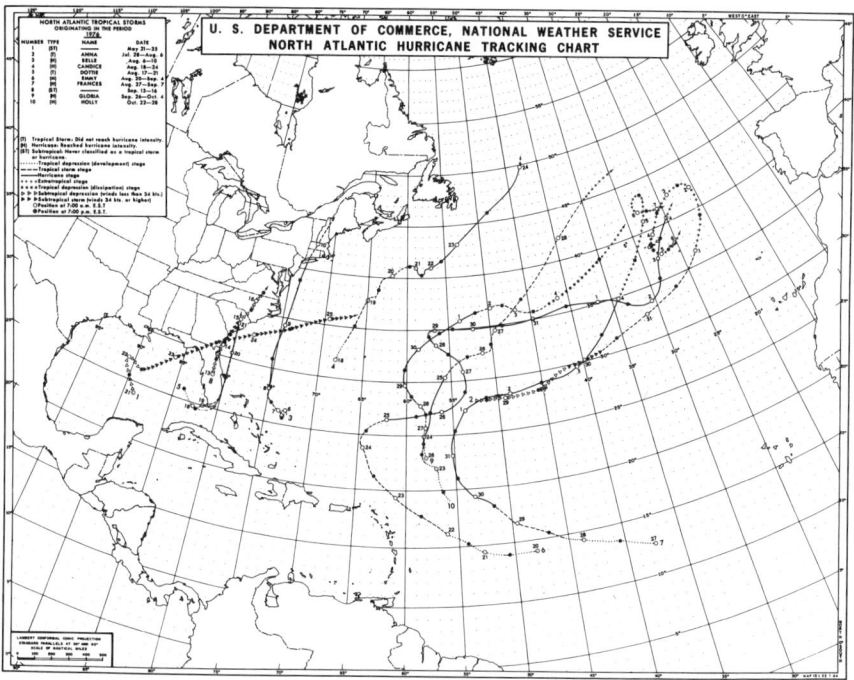

Fig. 36. Hurricane Tracks, 1977

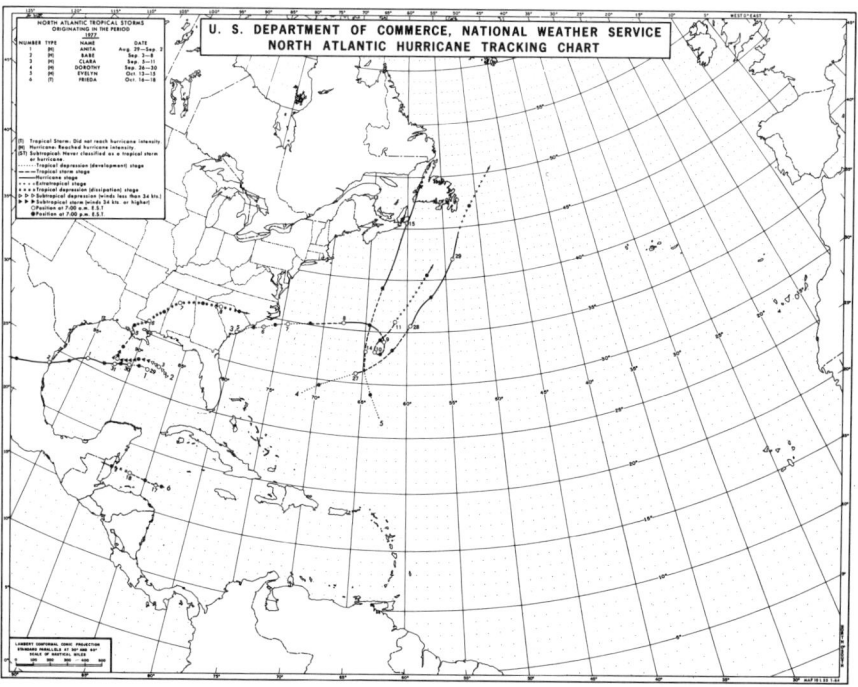

Fig. 37. Hurricane Tracks, 1978

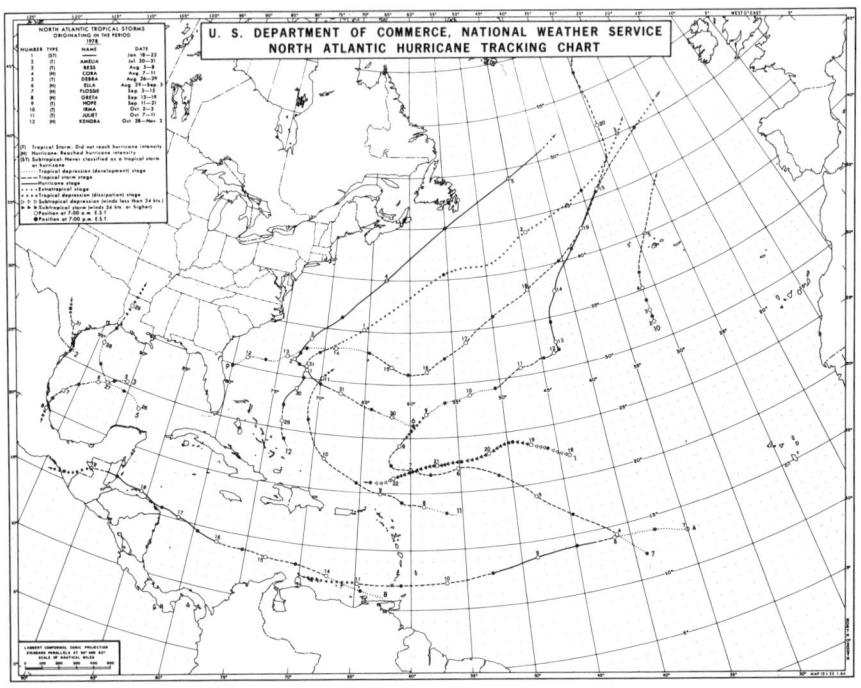

Fig. 38. Hurricane Tracks, 1979

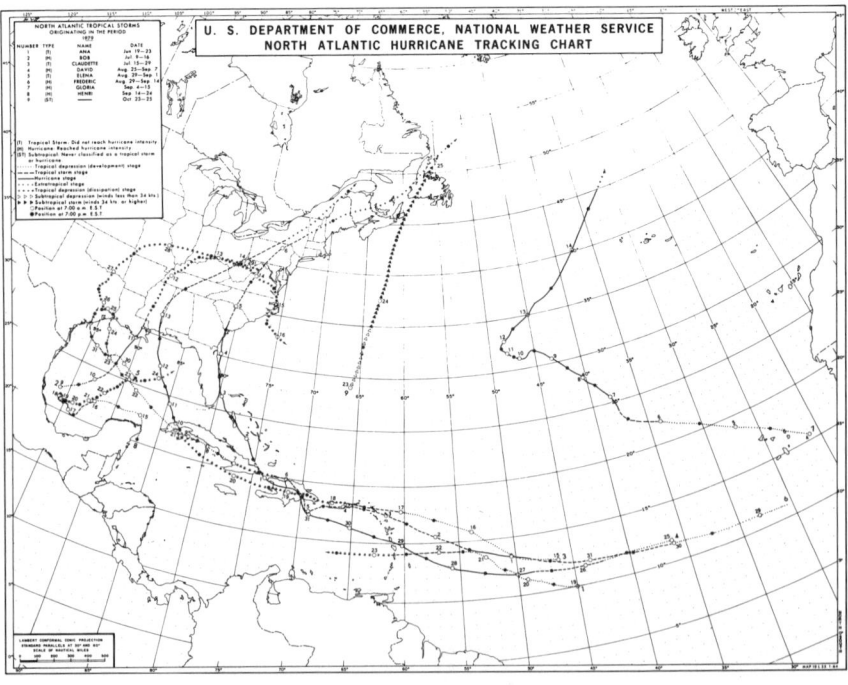

Fig. 39. Hurricane Tracks, 1980

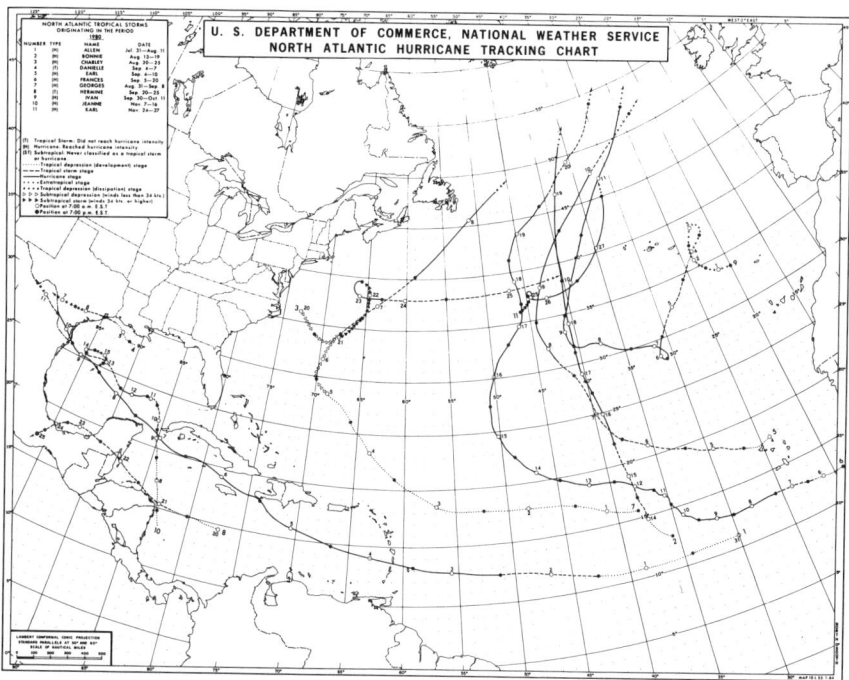

Fig. 40. Hurricane Tracks, 1981

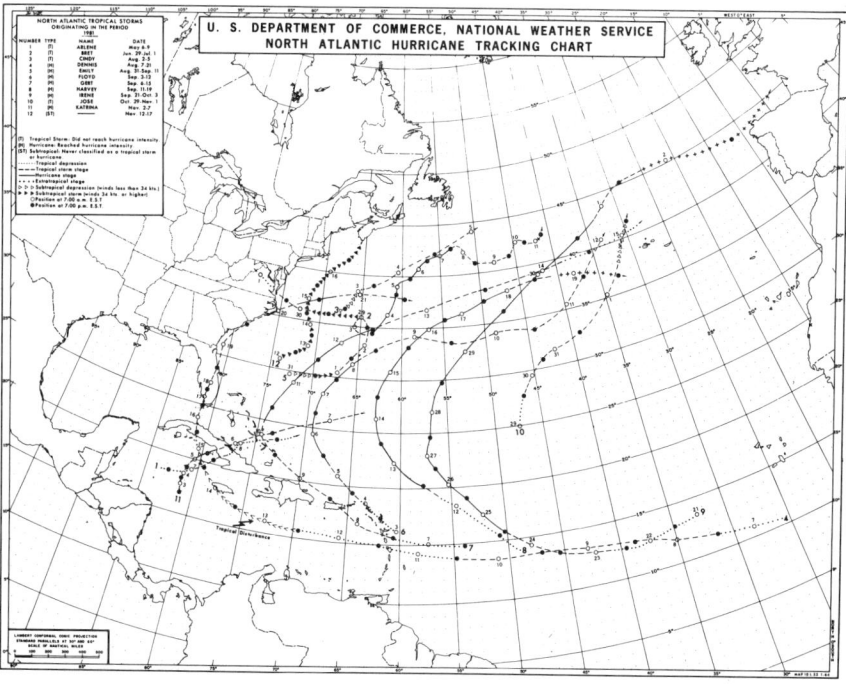

Fig. 41. Hurricane Tracks, 1982

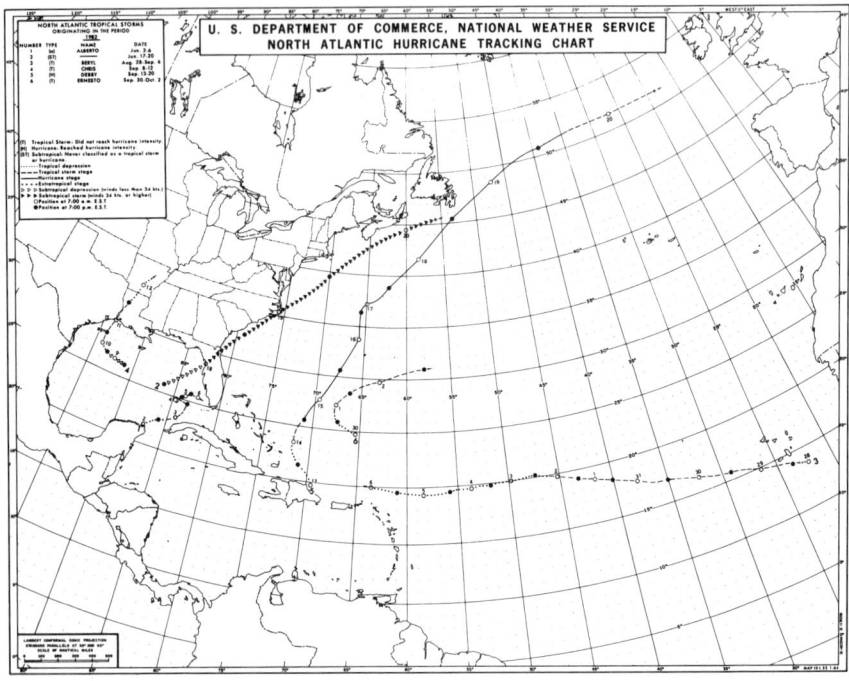

Fig. 42. Hurricane Tracks, 1983

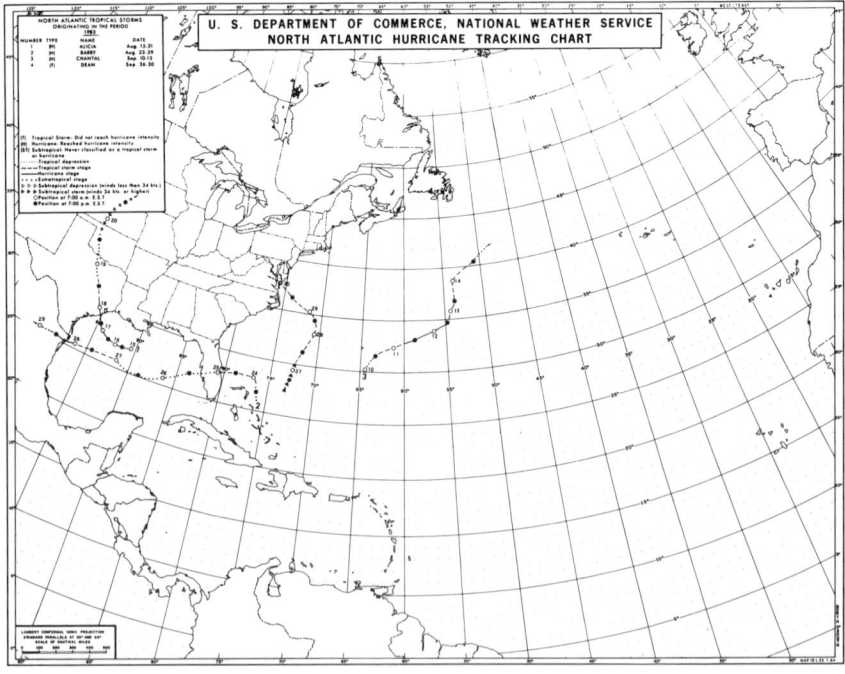

Fig. 43. Hurricane Tracks, 1984

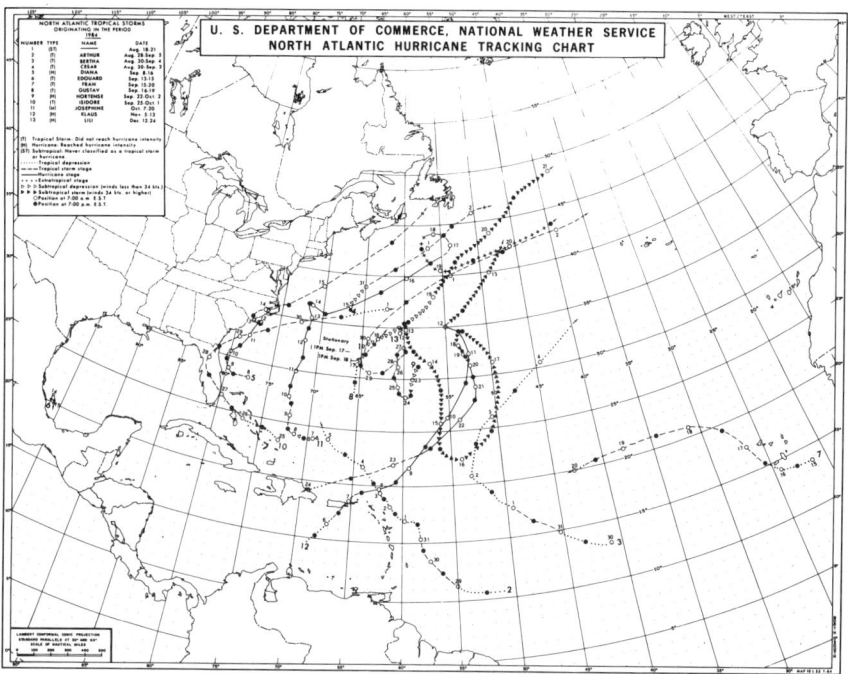

Fig. 44. Hurricane Tracks, 1985

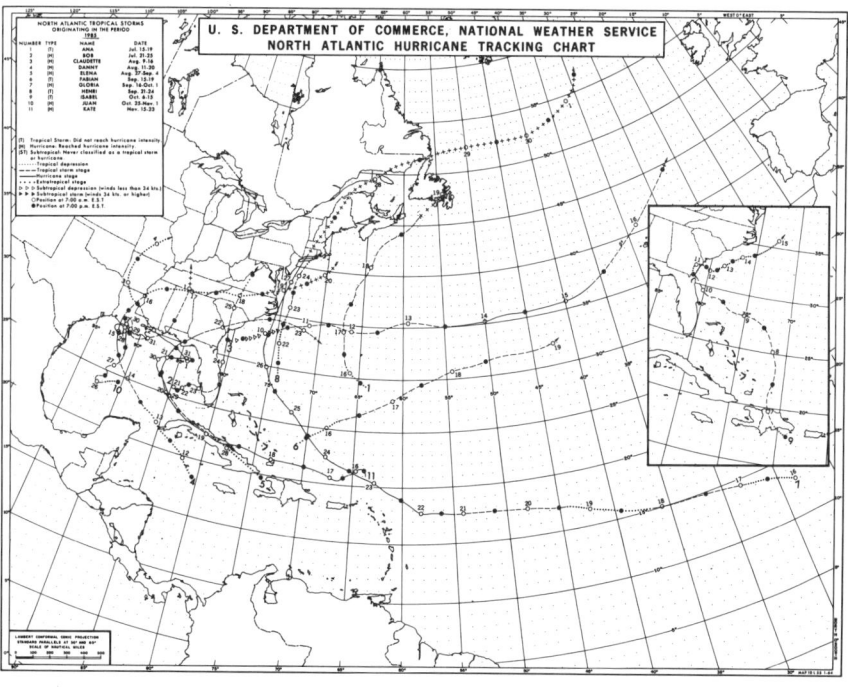

Fig. 45. Hurricane Tracks, 1986

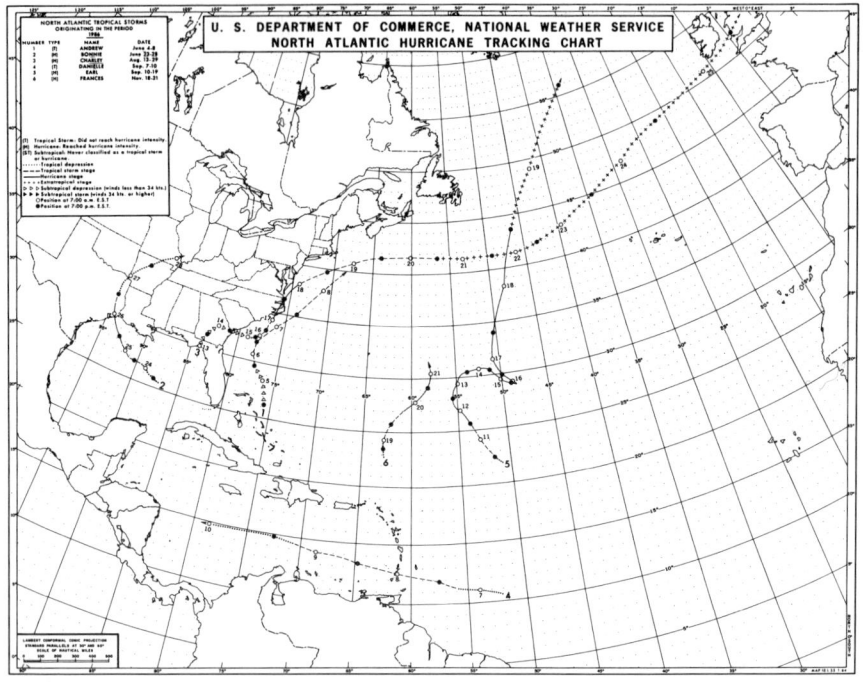

Fig. 46. Hurricane Tracks, 1987

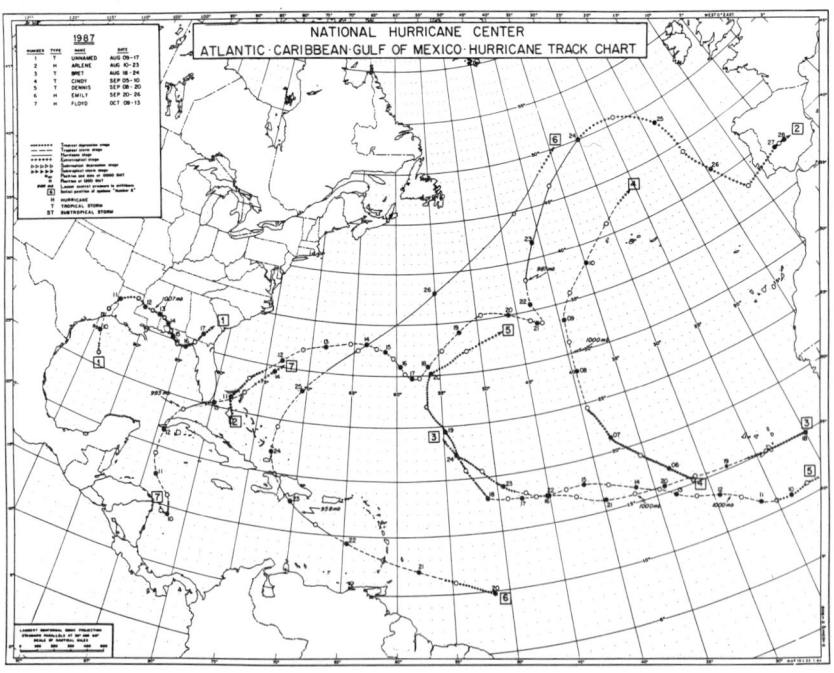

Fig. 47. Wind Chill Table

Equivalent Temperature (°F)

Calm	35	30	25	20	15	10	5	0	-5	-10	-15	-20
5	33	27	21	16	12	7	1	-6	-11	-15	-20	-26
10	21	16	9	2	-2	-9	-15	-22	-27	-31	-38	-45
15	16	11	1	-6	-11	-18	-25	-33	-40	-45	-51	-60
20	12	3	-4	-9	-17	-24	-32	-40	-46	-52	-60	-68
25	7	0	-7	-15	-22	-29	-37	-45	-52	-58	-67	-75
30	5	-2	-11	-18	-26	-33	-41	-49	-56	-63	-70	-78
35	3	-4	-13	-20	-27	-35	-43	-52	-60	-67	-72	-83
40	1	-4	-15	-22	-29	-36	-45	-54	-62	-69	-76	-87

Windspeed (Miles per hour)

Fig. 48. Percentage of Population Residing in Flood-Prone Areas

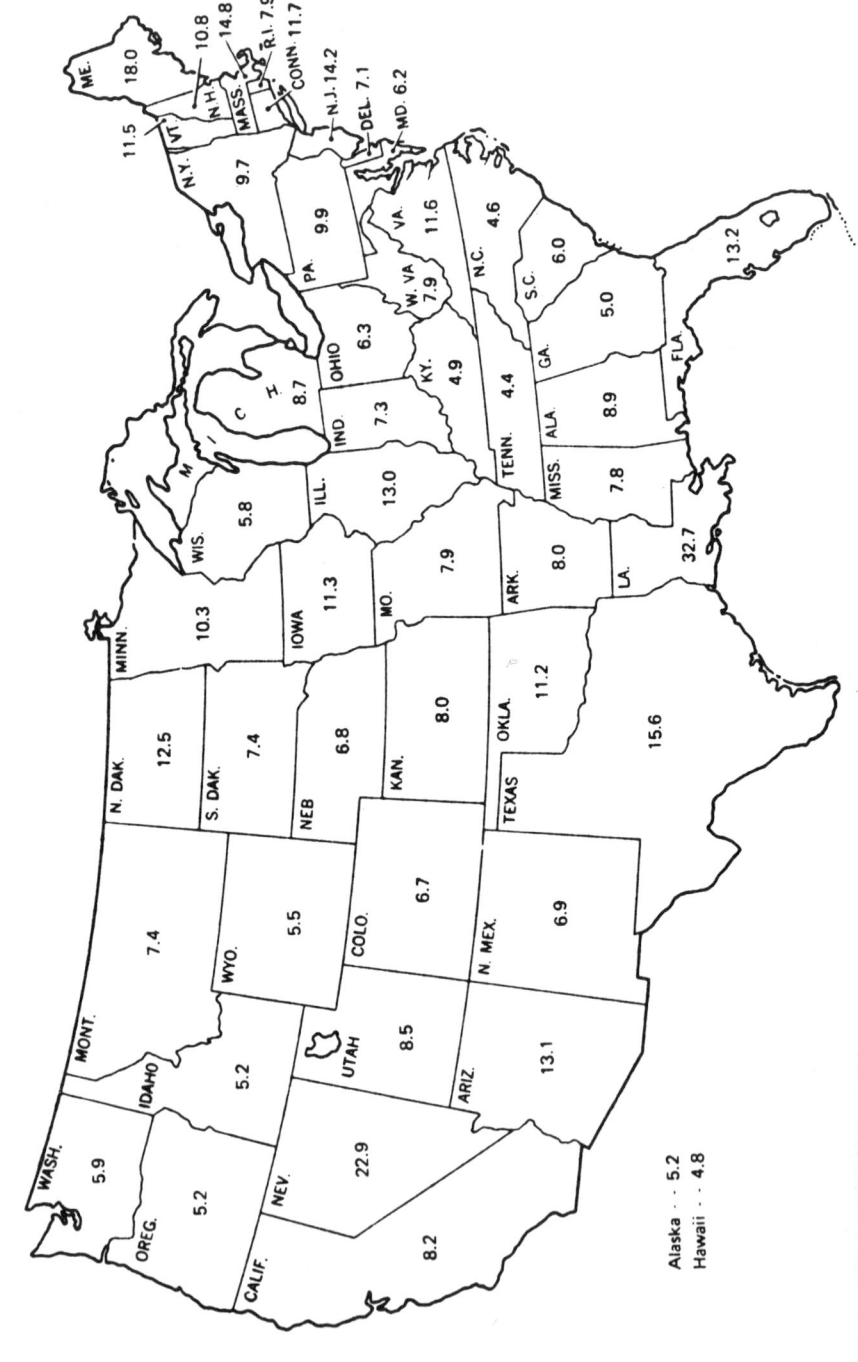

ME. 18.0
N.H. 10.8
MASS. 14.8
R.I. 7.9
CONN. 11.7
N.J. 14.2
DEL. 7.1
MD. 6.2
VT. 11.5
N.Y. 9.7
PA. 9.9
VA. 11.6
W. VA. 7.9
N.C. 4.6
S.C. 6.0
OHIO 6.3
KY. 4.9
GA. 8.9
FLA. 13.2
MICH. 8.7
IND. 7.3
TENN. 4.4
ALA. 7.8
MISS. 8.0
ILL. 13.0
WIS. 5.8
MINN. 10.3
IOWA 11.3
MO. 7.9
ARK. 8.0
LA. 32.7
N. DAK. 12.5
S. DAK. 7.4
NEB. 6.8
KAN. 8.0
OKLA. 11.2
TEXAS 15.6
MONT. 7.4
WYO. 5.5
COLO. 6.7
N. MEX. 6.9
WASH. 5.9
IDAHO 5.2
UTAH 8.5
ARIZ. 13.1
OREG. 5.2
NEV. 22.9
CALIF. 8.2

Alaska -- 5.2
Hawaii -- 4.8

54

Fig. 49. Volcanic Activity in the United States

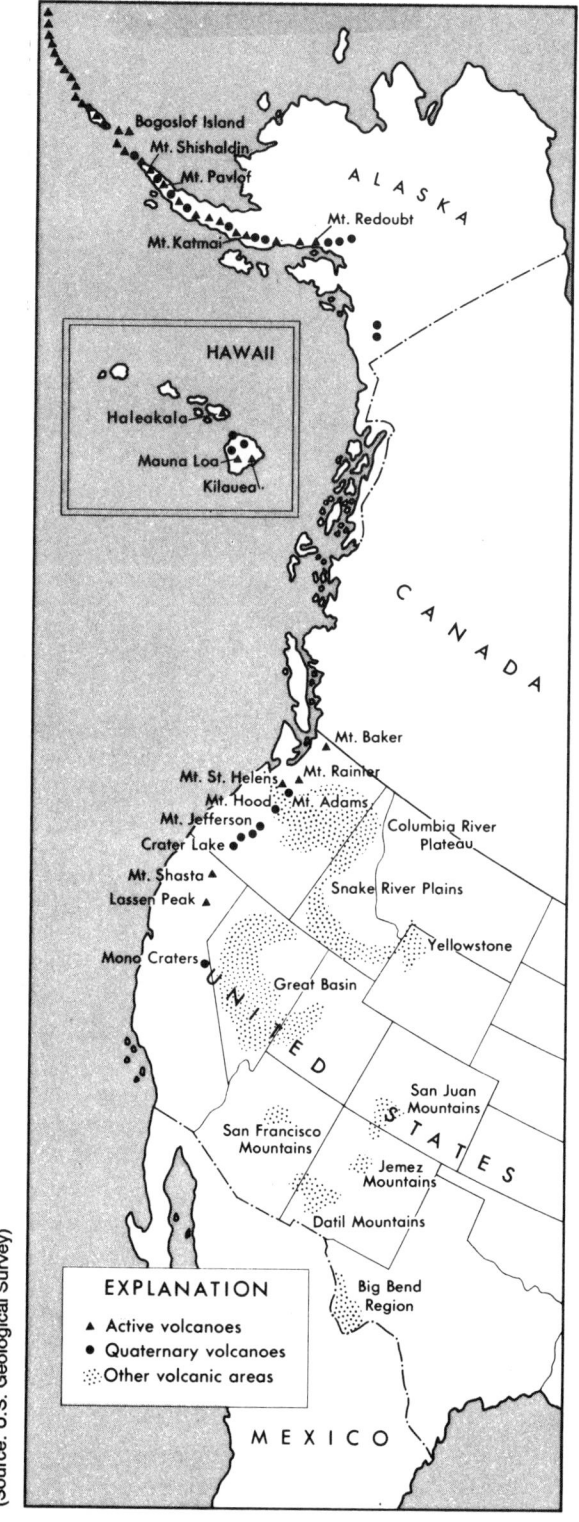

Bogoslof Island
Mt. Shishaldin
Mt. Pavlof
Mt. Redoubt
Mt. Katmai

A L A S K A

HAWAII
Haleakala
Mauna Loa
Kilauea

C A N A D A

Mt. Baker
Mt. St. Helens
Mt. Rainier
Mt. Hood
Mt. Adams
Mt. Jefferson
Crater Lake
Columbia River Plateau
Mt. Shasta
Lassen Peak
Snake River Plains
Mono Craters
Yellowstone
Great Basin
U N I T E D
San Juan Mountains
S T A T E S
San Francisco Mountains
Jemez Mountains
Datil Mountains
Big Bend Region

EXPLANATION
▲ Active volcanoes
● Quaternary volcanoes
∴ Other volcanic areas

M E X I C O

(Source: U.S. Geological Survey)

55

Fig. 50. Global Precipitation

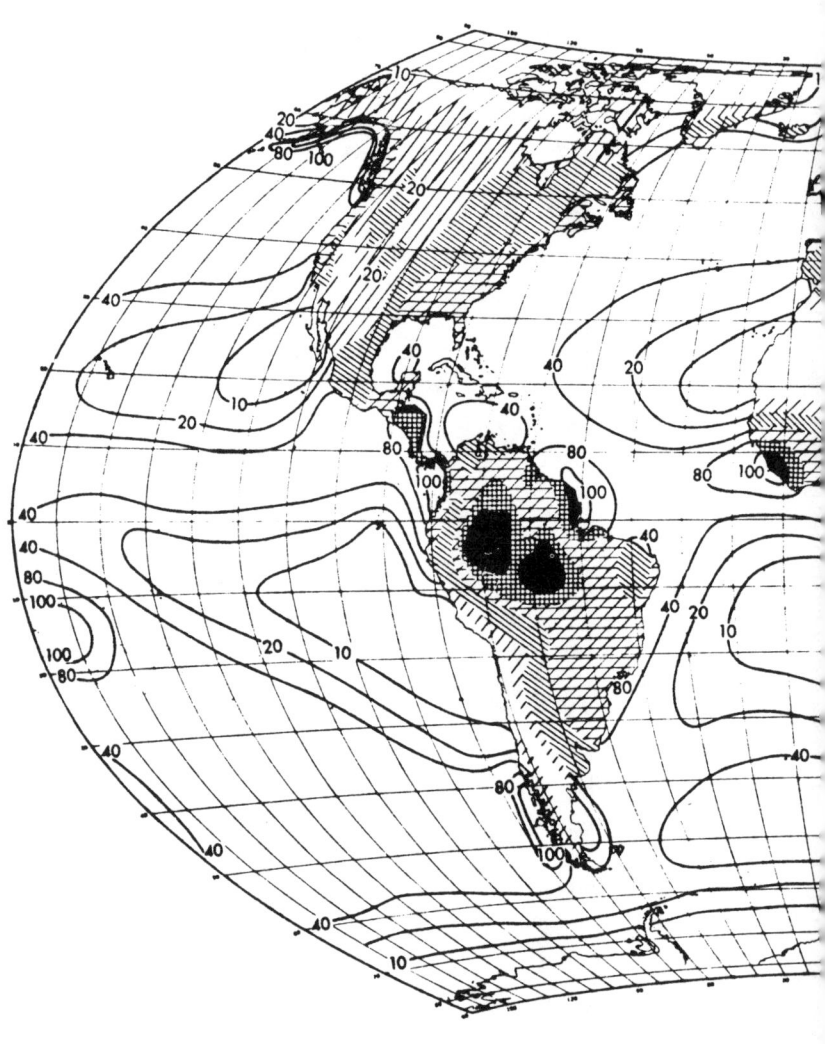

(Source: *Climates of the World,* U.S. Dept. of Commerce, 1972)

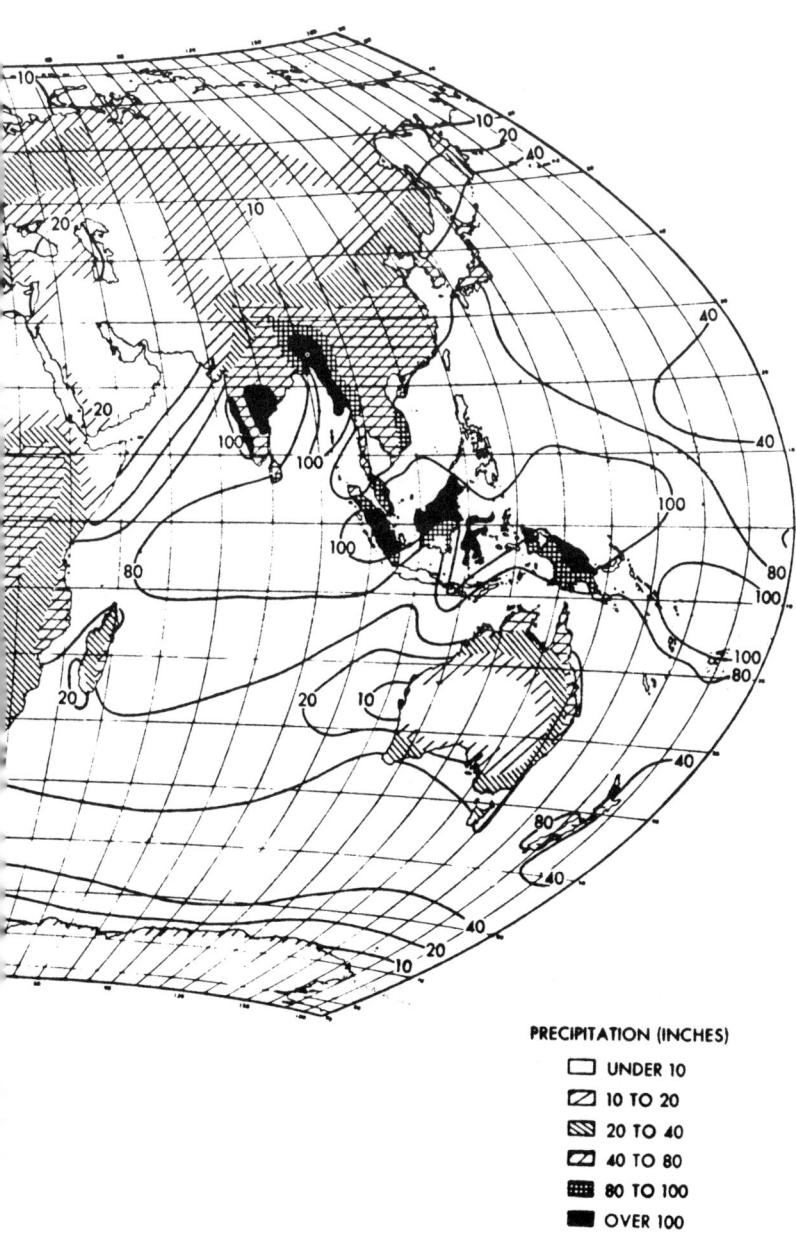

PRECIPITATION (INCHES)

☐ UNDER 10
▧ 10 TO 20
▨ 20 TO 40
▨ 40 TO 80
▦ 80 TO 100
■ OVER 100

Fig. 51. Arid Desert Regions

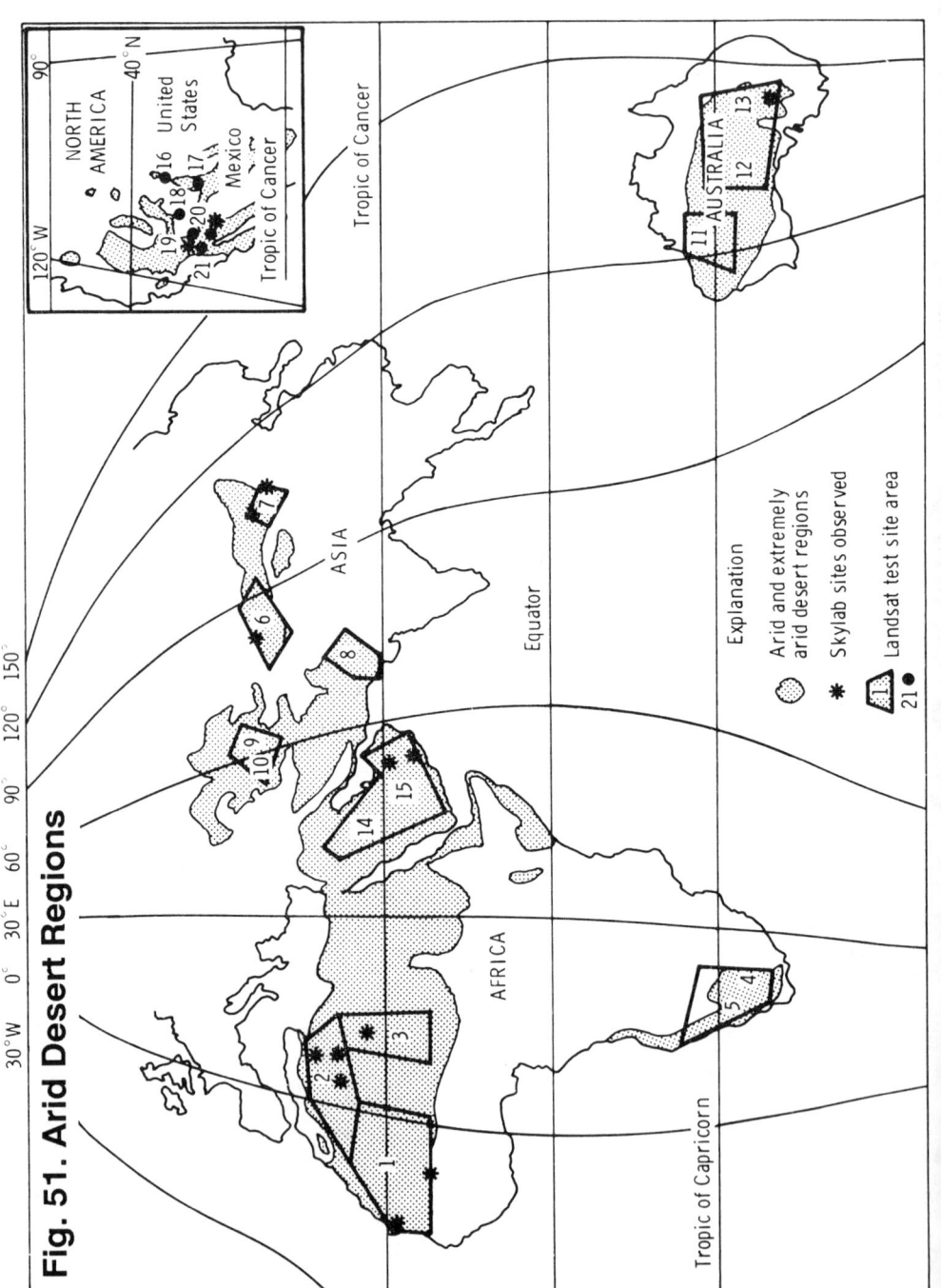

Explanation

⬭ Arid and extremely arid desert regions

✳ Skylab sites observed

▱ 11 Landsat test site area

21 ●

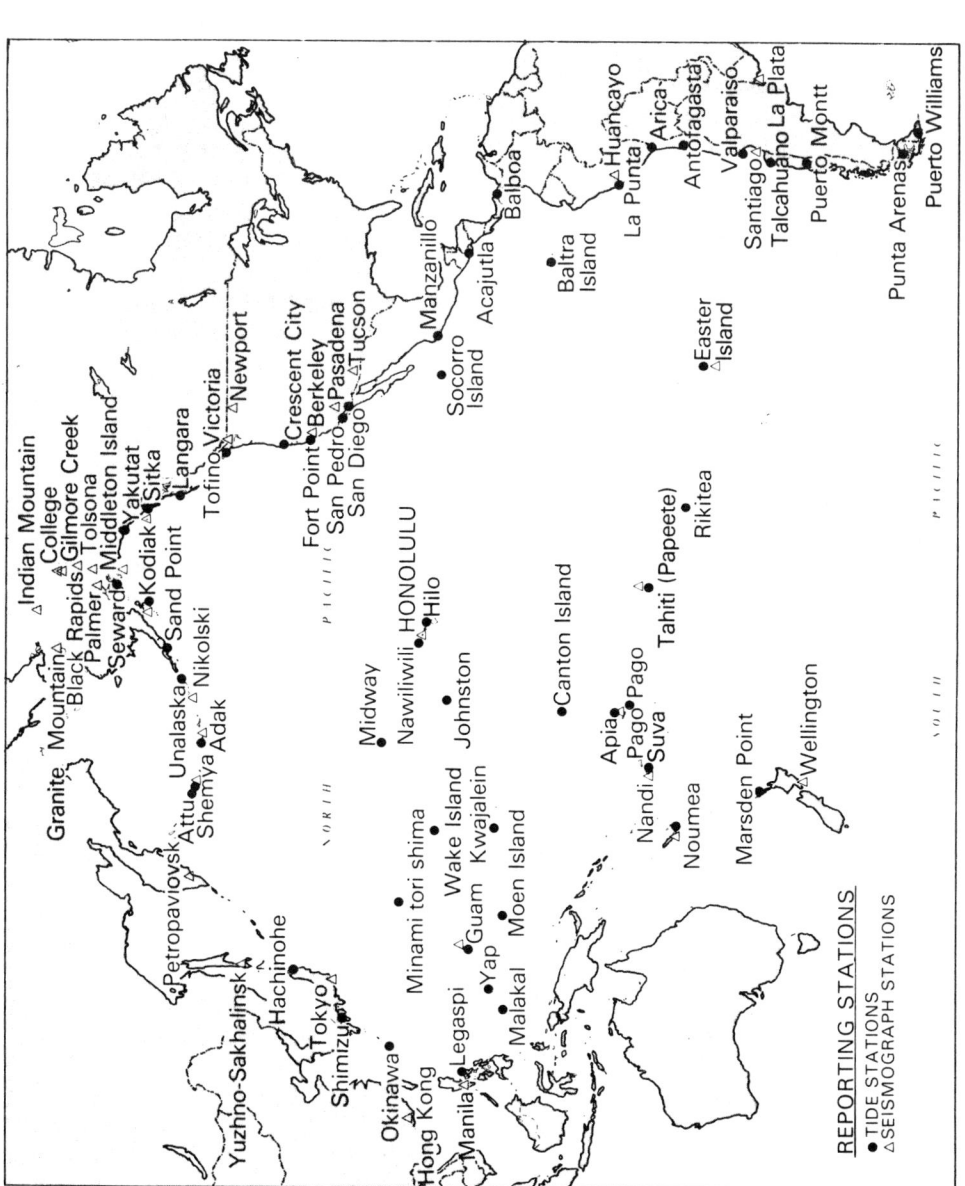

(Source: *Tsunami*, U.S. Dept. of Commerce, 1975)

59

Fig. 53. Weather Extremes Around the World

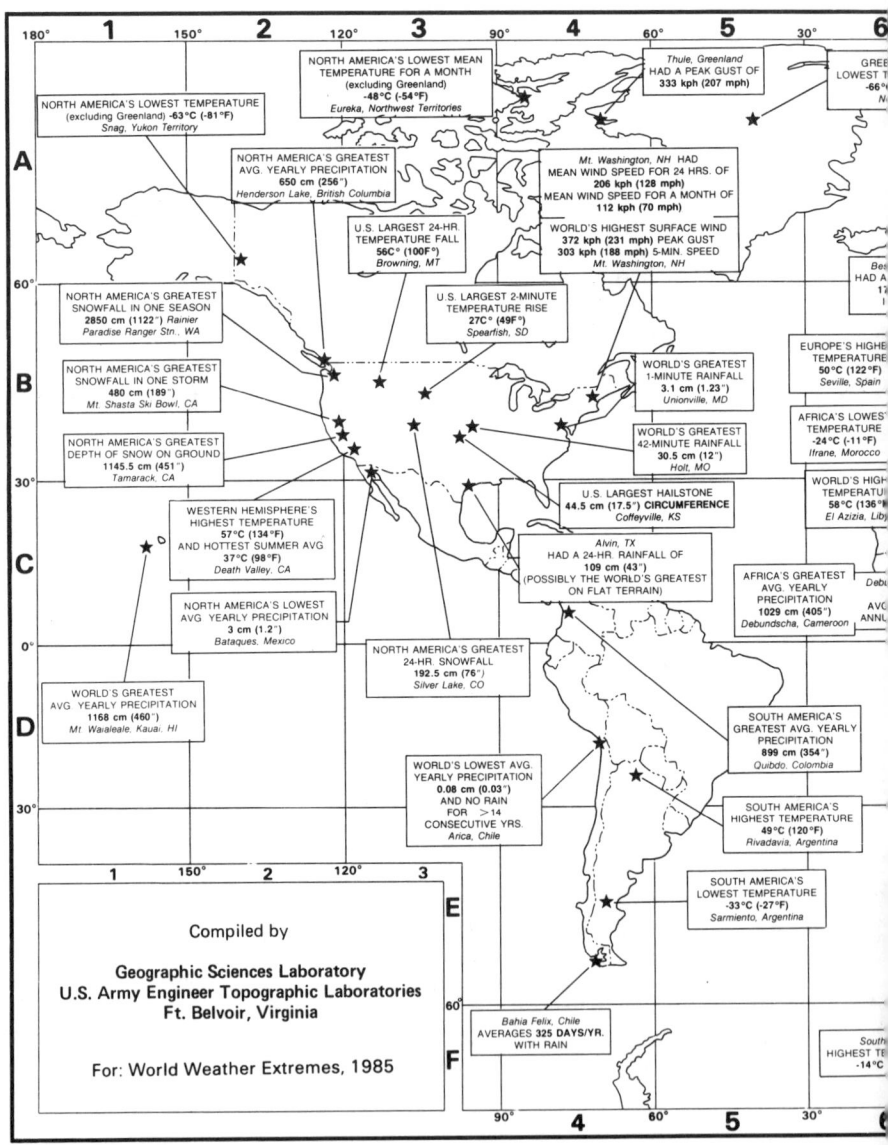

NORTH AMERICA'S LOWEST TEMPERATURE
(excluding Greenland) -63°C (-81°F)
Snag, Yukon Territory

NORTH AMERICA'S LOWEST MEAN
TEMPERATURE FOR A MONTH
(excluding Greenland)
-48°C (-54°F)
Eureka, Northwest Territories

Thule, Greenland
HAD A PEAK GUST OF
333 kph (207 mph)

GREE
LOWEST T
-66°
N

NORTH AMERICA'S GREATEST
AVG. YEARLY PRECIPITATION
650 cm (256")
Henderson Lake, British Columbia

Mt. Washington, NH HAD
MEAN WIND SPEED FOR 24 HRS. OF
206 kph (128 mph)
MEAN WIND SPEED FOR A MONTH OF
112 kph (70 mph)

U.S. LARGEST 24-HR.
TEMPERATURE FALL
56C° (100F°)
Browning, MT

WORLD'S HIGHEST SURFACE WIND
372 kph (231 mph) PEAK GUST
303 kph (188 mph) 5-MIN. SPEED
Mt. Washington, NH

Bes
HAD A
1:
I

NORTH AMERICA'S GREATEST
SNOWFALL IN ONE SEASON
2850 cm (1122") Rainier
Paradise Ranger Stn., WA

U.S. LARGEST 2-MINUTE
TEMPERATURE RISE
27C° (49F°)
Spearfish, SD

EUROPE'S HIGHE
TEMPERATURE
50°C (122°F)
Seville, Spain

NORTH AMERICA'S GREATEST
SNOWFALL IN ONE STORM
480 cm (189")
Mt. Shasta Ski Bowl, CA

WORLD'S GREATEST
1-MINUTE RAINFALL
3.1 cm (1.23")
Unionville, MD

AFRICA'S LOWEST
TEMPERATURE
-24°C (-11°F)
Ifrane, Morocco

NORTH AMERICA'S GREATEST
DEPTH OF SNOW ON GROUND
1145.5 cm (451")
Tamarack, CA

WORLD'S GREATEST
42-MINUTE RAINFALL
30.5 cm (12")
Holt, MO

WORLD'S HIGH
TEMPERATU
58°C (136°
El Azizia, Liby

WESTERN HEMISPHERE'S
HIGHEST TEMPERATURE
57°C (134°F)
AND HOTTEST SUMMER AVG
37°C (98°F)
Death Valley, CA

U.S. LARGEST HAILSTONE
44.5 cm (17.5") CIRCUMFERENCE
Coffeyville, KS

Alvin, TX
HAD A 24-HR. RAINFALL OF
109 cm (43")
(POSSIBLY THE WORLD'S GREATEST
ON FLAT TERRAIN)

AFRICA'S GREATEST
AVG. YEARLY
PRECIPITATION
1029 cm (405")
Debundscha, Cameroon

Deb
AVG
ANNU

NORTH AMERICA'S LOWEST
AVG. YEARLY PRECIPITATION
3 cm (1.2")
Bataques, Mexico

NORTH AMERICA'S GREATEST
24-HR. SNOWFALL
192.5 cm (76")
Silver Lake, CO

WORLD'S GREATEST
AVG. YEARLY PRECIPITATION
1168 cm (460")
Mt. Waaleale, Kauai, HI

SOUTH AMERICA'S
GREATEST AVG. YEARLY
PRECIPITATION
899 cm (354")
Quibdo, Colombia

WORLD'S LOWEST AVG.
YEARLY PRECIPITATION
0.08 cm (0.03")
AND NO RAIN
FOR   >14
CONSECUTIVE YRS.
Arica, Chile

SOUTH AMERICA'S
HIGHEST TEMPERATURE
49°C (120°F)
Rivadavia, Argentina

SOUTH AMERICA'S
LOWEST TEMPERATURE
-33°C (-27°F)
Sarmiento, Argentina

Compiled by

**Geographic Sciences Laboratory
U.S. Army Engineer Topographic Laboratories
Ft. Belvoir, Virginia**

For: World Weather Extremes, 1985

Bahia Felix, Chile
AVERAGES 325 DAYS/YR.
WITH RAIN

South
HIGHEST TE
-14°C

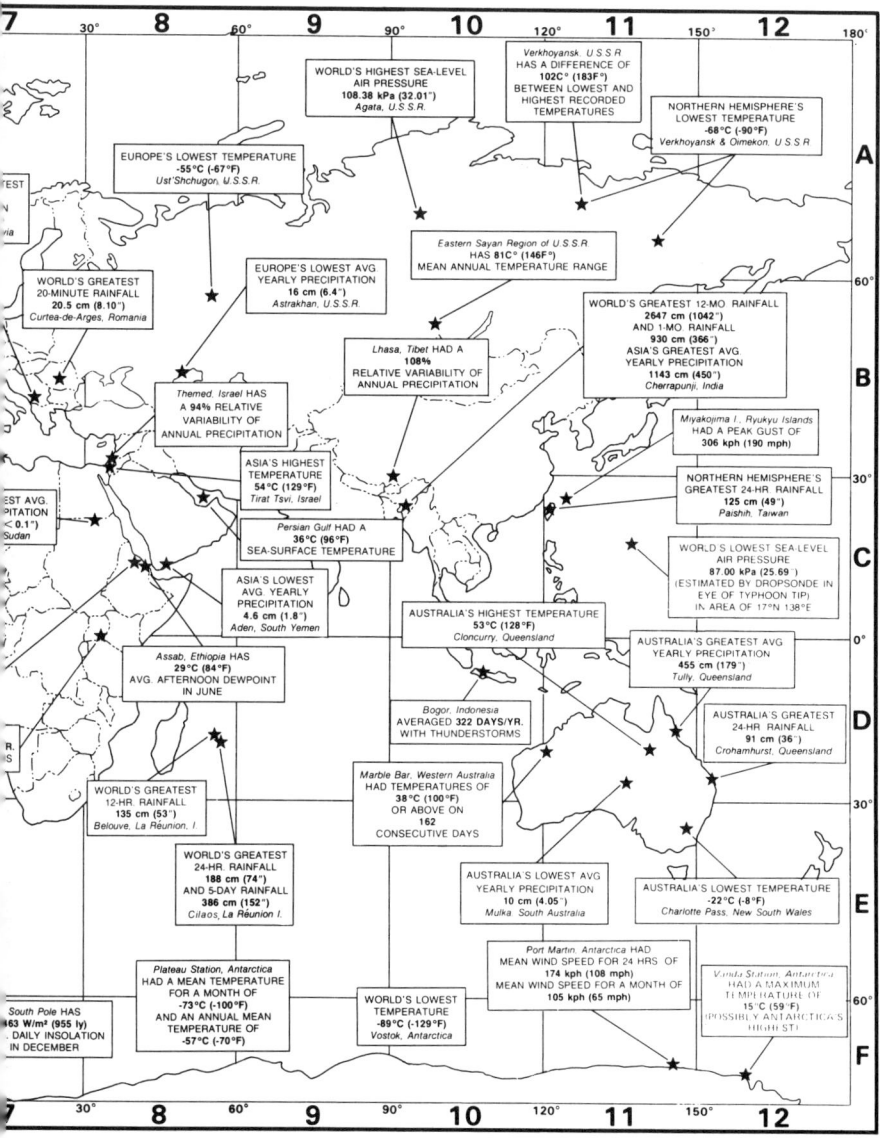

WORLD'S HIGHEST SEA-LEVEL
AIR PRESSURE
108.38 kPa (32.01")
Agata, U.S.S.R.

Verkhoyansk, U.S.S.R.
HAS A DIFFERENCE OF
102C° (183F°)
BETWEEN LOWEST AND
HIGHEST RECORDED
TEMPERATURES

NORTHERN HEMISPHERE'S
LOWEST TEMPERATURE
-68°C (-90°F)
Verkhoyansk & Oimekon, U.S.S.R.

EUROPE'S LOWEST TEMPERATURE
-55°C (-67°F)
Ust'Shchugor, U.S.S.R.

Eastern Sayan Region of U.S.S.R.
HAS **81C° (146F°)**
MEAN ANNUAL TEMPERATURE RANGE

WORLD'S GREATEST
20-MINUTE RAINFALL
20.5 cm (8.10")
Curtea-de-Arges, Romania

EUROPE'S LOWEST AVG.
YEARLY PRECIPITATION
16 cm (6.4")
Astrakhan, U.S.S.R.

WORLD'S GREATEST 12-MO. RAINFALL
2647 cm (1042")
AND 1-MO. RAINFALL
930 cm (366")
ASIA'S GREATEST AVG.
YEARLY PRECIPITATION
1143 cm (450")
Cherrapunji, India

Lhasa, Tibet HAD A
108%
RELATIVE VARIABILITY OF
ANNUAL PRECIPITATION

Themed, Israel HAS
A **94%** RELATIVE
VARIABILITY OF
ANNUAL PRECIPITATION

Miyakojima I., Ryukyu Islands
HAD A PEAK GUST OF
306 kph (190 mph)

ASIA'S HIGHEST
TEMPERATURE
54°C (129°F)
Tirat Tsvi, Israel

NORTHERN HEMISPHERE'S
GREATEST 24-HR. RAINFALL
125 cm (49")
Paishih, Taiwan

Persian Gulf HAD A
36°C (96°F)
SEA-SURFACE TEMPERATURE

WORLD'S LOWEST SEA-LEVEL
AIR PRESSURE
87.00 kPa (25.69")
(ESTIMATED BY DROPSONDE IN
EYE OF TYPHOON TIP)
IN AREA OF 17°N 138°E

ASIA'S LOWEST
AVG. YEARLY
PRECIPITATION
4.6 cm (1.8")
Aden, South Yemen

AUSTRALIA'S HIGHEST TEMPERATURE
53°C (128°F)
Cloncurry, Queensland

AUSTRALIA'S GREATEST AVG.
YEARLY PRECIPITATION
455 cm (179")
Tully, Queensland

Assab, Ethiopia HAS
29°C (84°F)
AVG. AFTERNOON DEWPOINT
IN JUNE

Bogor, Indonesia
AVERAGED **322 DAYS/YR.**
WITH THUNDERSTORMS

AUSTRALIA'S GREATEST
24-HR. RAINFALL
91 cm (36")
Crohamhurst, Queensland

WORLD'S GREATEST
12-HR. RAINFALL
135 cm (53")
Belouve, La Réunion, I.

Marble Bar, Western Australia
HAD TEMPERATURES OF
38°C (100°F)
OR ABOVE ON
162
CONSECUTIVE DAYS

WORLD'S GREATEST
24-HR. RAINFALL
188 cm (74")
AND 5-DAY RAINFALL
386 cm (152")
Cilaos, La Réunion I.

AUSTRALIA'S LOWEST AVG
YEARLY PRECIPITATION
10 cm (4.05")
Mulka, South Australia

AUSTRALIA'S LOWEST TEMPERATURE
-22°C (-8°F)
Charlotte Pass, New South Wales

Plateau Station, Antarctica
HAD A MEAN TEMPERATURE
FOR A MONTH OF
-73°C (-100°F)
AND AN ANNUAL MEAN
TEMPERATURE OF
-57°C (-70°F)

Port Martin, Antarctica HAD
MEAN WIND SPEED FOR 24 HRS. OF
174 kph (108 mph)
MEAN WIND SPEED FOR A MONTH OF
105 kph (65 mph)

Vanda Station, Antarctica
HAD A MAXIMUM
TEMPERATURE OF
15°C (59°F)
(POSSIBLY ANTARCTICA'S
HIGHEST)

South Pole HAS
463 W/m² (955 ly)
DAILY INSOLATION
IN DECEMBER

WORLD'S LOWEST
TEMPERATURE
-89°C (-129°F)
Vostok, Antarctica

IV. Weather Summaries for Key U.S. Cities

The following weather profiles of major U.S. cities depict for each month and for the year:
- Normal daily minimum and maximum temperatures;
- Normal monthly temperature;
- Extreme temperatures and years of occurrence;
- Degree days (a factor used to estimate amounts of energy required to maintain comfortable indoor temperature levels. Daily values are computed from each day's mean temperature. Each degree that a day's mean temperature is below or above 65 degrees Fahrenheit is counted as one heating or cooling degree day.)
- Percent of possible sunshine (the total time that sunshine reaches the surface of the earth expressed as the percentage of the maximum amount possible from sunrise to sunset with clear sky conditions);
- Average sky cover;
- Number of clear (0 to 0.3 sky cover), cloudy (0.4 to 0.7 sky cover) and cloudy (0.8 to complete sky cover) days;
- Number of days with precipitation of .01 inch or more (including the liquid water equivalent of frozen precipitation); snow or ice pellets (including sleet) of one inch or more; thunderstorms, fog, and temperatures above 90 degrees or below 32 degrees;
- Relative humidity in the morning and afternoon (expressed as a percentage measure of the amount of moisture in the air compared to the maximum amount of moisture the air can hold at the same temperature and pressure. Maximum relative humidity values usually occur during the morning hours);
- Normal and maximum precipitation (the normal precipitation includes the liquid water equivalent of snowfall);
- Maximum amounts of snow and ice pellets;
- Mean wind speed.

The elevation and latitude and longitude given are for the weather observation station — usually at the airport.

The presence of an asterisk (*) indicates an average frequency of occurrence greater than zero but smaller than .5. T denotes trace, or less than 0.05 inch of precipitation or snow.

Data for cities in the United States are presented in Fahrenheit readings for temperature and in the U.S. Customary system (inches) for precipitation. Conversions to Celsius and the metric system may be accomplished as follows:

Fahrenheit from Celsius: $1.8 \times °C + 32 = °F$
Celsius from Fahrenheit: Subtract 32 from $°F$ and divide by 1.8
1 inch = 24.4 millimeters (mm)

Most of the summaries reflect averages for a period of 30 years. Normals data are for the period 1951 through 1980. Observed data are from the 1860s through 1985.

BIRMINGHAM

Elev. 620'   33° 34'N — 86° 45'W   **Alabama**

NORMALS, MEANS, EXTREMES

	JAN	FEB	MAR	APR	MAY	JUN	JUL	AUG	SEP	OCT	NOV	DEC	YEAR
TEMPERATURE													
Normal daily maximum	52.7	57.3	65.2	75.2	81.6	87.9	90.3	89.7	84.6	74.8	63.7	55.9	73.2
Normal daily minimum	33.0	35.2	42.1	50.4	58.3	65.9	69.8	69.1	63.6	50.4	40.5	35.2	51.1
Normal monthly	42.9	46.3	53.7	62.8	70.0	76.9	80.1	79.4	74.1	62.6	52.1	45.6	62.2
Extreme highest	81	83	89	90	99	102	106	103	100	94	84	80	106
Extreme highest date	1949	1962	1982	1955	1962	1954	1980	1947	1980	1954	1961	1951	1980
Extreme lowest	-6	3	11	26	35	42	51	51	37	27	5	1	-6
Extreme lowest date	1985	1958	1980	1973	1944	1966	1967	1946	1967	1956	1950	1962	1985
DEGREE DAYS BASE 65° F													
Heating	685	532	368	110	36	0	0	0	7	137	387	601	2863
Cooling	0	8	18	44	191	360	468	450	280	62	0	0	1881
% OF POSSIBLE SUNSHINE	42	50	55	63	66	65	59	63	61	66	55	46	58
AVERAGE SKY COVER													
Sunrise - Sunset	6.9	6.5	6.5	5.8	5.9	5.9	6.4	5.8	5.6	4.6	5.7	6.5	6.0
NUMBER OF DAYS (Sunrise-Sunset)													
Clear	6.9	7.1	7.3	8.9	8.0	7.0	4.7	6.7	9.7	13.8	10.1	8.3	98.5
Partly cloudy	6.2	6.6	8.0	7.9	10.9	12.6	14.5	14.6	9.3	7.8	6.8	6.7	112.0
Cloudy	17.9	14.6	15.7	13.3	12.1	10.4	11.7	9.7	11.0	9.4	13.1	16.0	154.8
Precipitation .01" or more	11.2	10.2	11.3	9.3	9.5	9.5	12.6	9.9	7.8	6.2	9.0	10.5	117.1
Snow, Ice pellets 1.0" or more	0.3	0.1	0.1	0.0	0.0	0.0	0.0	0.0	0.0	0.0	*	0.1	0.5
Thunderstorms	1.7	2.3	4.6	5.3	7.0	8.2	11.5	9.2	4.0	1.3	1.7	1.2	58.0
Fog, Visibility 1/4 mile or less	1.4	0.7	0.7	0.2	0.4	0.7	0.5	0.5	0.5	0.8	1.1	1.1	8.6
Temperature Maximum:													
90° and above	0.0	0.0	0.0	0.0	1.8	10.2	15.8	13.1	5.8	0.1	0.0	0.0	46.7
32° and below	1.8	0.5	*	0.0	0.0	0.0	0.0	0.0	0.0	0.0	*	0.5	2.9
Temperature Minimum:													
32° and below	17.9	14.4	6.2	0.9	0.0	0.0	0.0	0.0	0.0	0.4	7.0	14.2	60.9
0° and below	0.2	0.0	0.0	0.0	0.0	0.0	0.0	0.0	0.0	0.0	0.0	0.0	0.2
RELATIVE HUMIDITY (%)													
Morning	76	72	72	77	84	84	85	86	85	83	80	77	80
Afternoon	62	55	53	52	56	57	61	61	59	55	57	60	57
PRECIPITATION (inches)													
Water Equivalent													
Normal	5.2	4.7	6.6	5.0	4.5	3.6	5.3	3.8	4.3	2.6	3.6	4.9	54.5
Maximum monthly	11.0	17.6	15.8	13.7	11.1	8.4	13.7	10.8	10.4	7.5	15.2	13.9	17.6
Date	1949	1961	1980	1979	1969	1963	1950	1967	1977	1977	1948	1961	1961
Minimum monthly	1.0	1.2	1.7	1.3	1.1	0.6	0.3	0.8	T	0.1	0.4	0.8	T
Date	1981	1968	1985	1967	1951	1968	1983	1955	1955	1963	1949	1980	1955
Maximum in 24 hrs	5.8	6.5	7.0	5.0	4.6	3.8	5.4	5.1	5.0	3.7	4.8	5.2	7.0
Date	1949	1961	1970	1966	1969	1957	1985	1952	1977	1977	1948	1961	1970
SNOW, ICE PELLETS													
Maximum monthly	6.6	2.3	2.0	T	0.0	0.0	0.0	0.0	0.0	T	1.4	8.0	8.0
Date	1982	1960	1984	1971	—	—	—	—	—	1955	1950	1963	1963
Maximum in 24 hrs	4.5	2.3	2.0	T	0.0	0.0	0.0	0.0	0.0	T	1.4	8.4	8.4
Date	1948	1960	1984	1971	—	—	—	—	—	1955	1950	1963	1963
WIND (Resultant)													
Mean speed (mph)	8.4	8.8	9.3	8.4	6.8	6.1	5.7	5.4	6.4	6.2	7.3	8.0	7.2

HUNTSVILLE
Elev. 624' 34° 39'N — 86° 46'W **Alabama**

NORMALS, MEANS, EXTREMES

	JAN	FEB	MAR	APR	MAY	JUN	JUL	AUG	SEP	OCT	NOV	DEC	YEAR
TEMPERATURE													
Normal daily maximum	49.4	53.9	61.9	73.0	79.9	86.8	89.4	89.2	83.5	73.4	61.6	53.0	71.2
Normal daily minimum	31.0	33.2	40.6	50.0	57.6	65.3	69.1	67.9	62.0	49.1	39.4	33.6	49.9
Normal monthly	40.2	43.6	51.3	61.5	68.8	76.1	79.3	78.6	72.8	61.3	50.5	43.3	60.6
Extreme highest	76	77	84	90	92	101	102	102	96	89	83	77	102
Extreme highest date	1972	1982	1982	1971	1970	1969	1980	1983	1978	1982	1982	1978	1983
Extreme lowest	-11	6	6	28	36	45	54	55	40	29	15	-1	-11
Extreme lowest date	1985	1981	1980	1983	1971	1972	1972	1976	1981	1982	1976	1983	1985
DEGREE DAYS BASE 65° F													
Heating	769	606	441	136	41	0	0	0	12	166	435	673	3279
Cooling	0	7	16	31	159	333	443	422	246	51	0	0	1708
% OF POSSIBLE SUNSHINE	na	na	na	na	na	na	na	na	na	na	na	na	na
AVERAGE SKY COVER													
Sunrise - Sunset	6.9	6.6	6.7	6.0	6.1	5.6	5.9	5.5	5.7	5.3	6.1	6.6	6.1
NUMBER OF DAYS (Sunrise-Sunset)													
Clear	7.1	6.9	6.8	9.4	8.4	8.6	7.1	9.0	8.9	12.1	9.1	8.1	101.6
Partly cloudy	6.1	6.1	7.7	6.7	9.6	11.3	13.4	12.7	9.6	6.9	6.5	5.8	102.4
Cloudy	17.8	15.3	16.5	13.9	13.0	10.1	10.5	9.3	11.5	12.0	14.4	17.1	161.3
Precipitation .01" or more	11.5	9.3	12.0	9.9	10.9	9.2	10.6	9.0	8.4	7.0	9.7	10.7	118.2
Snow, Ice pellets 1.0" or more	0.5	0.6	0.1	0.0	0.0	0.0	0.0	0.0	0.0	0.0	0.0	0.1	1.3
Thunderstorms	1.3	2.2	4.7	5.0	7.4	8.2	10.3	9.1	4.6	2.2	2.3	1.1	58.2
Fog, Visibility 1/4 mile or less	3.0	1.7	1.1	0.7	1.3	1.3	1.9	2.0	2.3	2.6	2.0	1.2	20.9
Temperature Maximum:													
90° and above	0.0	0.0	0.0	0.1	0.7	8.6	15.7	12.7	4.9	0.0	0.0	0.0	42.6
32° and below	3.8	1.0	0.1	0.0	0.0	0.0	0.0	0.0	0.0	0.0	0.1	1.3	6.3
Temperature Minimum:													
32° and below	20.2	15.9	7.1	0.7	0.0	0.0	0.0	0.0	0.0	0.5	7.8	15.9	68.1
0° and below	0.3	0.0	0.0	0.0	0.0	0.0	0.0	0.0	0.0	0.0	0.0	0.1	0.4
RELATIVE HUMIDITY (%)													
Morning	78	74	74	75	82	84	86	86	86	83	79	77	80
Afternoon	66	58	57	52	57	55	60	59	60	56	58	62	58
PRECIPITATION (inches)													
Water Equivalent													
Normal	5.1	4.7	6.7	4.9	4.6	3.7	5.0	3.1	3.9	2.9	4.2	5.4	54.7
Maximum monthly	10.9	9.5	17.0	10.0	11.8	7.3	9.4	7.1	9.7	12.0	11.5	11.7	17.0
Date	1982	1971	1980	1982	1983	1976	1973	1985	1980	1975	1977	1983	1980
Minimum monthly	1.7	0.5	2.7	1.8	3.0	0.7	0.7	0.9	0.5	0.7	1.8	0.9	0.5
Date	1970	1978	1982	1976	1970	1968	1983	1973	1982	1971	1971	1980	1982
Maximum in 24 hrs	4.9	3.8	7.7	3.8	5.9	4.4	4.4	3.7	3.9	6.0	3.3	5.8	7.7
Date	1982	1971	1973	1983	1983	1969	1975	1985	1980	1975	1973	1973	1973
SNOW, ICE PELLETS													
Maximum monthly	4.3	4.2	2.1	T	0.0	0.0	0.0	0.0	0.0	0.0	0.8	1.0	4.3
Date	1982	1985	1968	1973	—	—	—	—	—	—	1974	1974	1982
Maximum in 24 hrs	4.0	3.6	2.1	T	0.0	0.0	0.0	0.0	0.0	0.0	0.8	1.0	4.0
Date	1985	1985	1968	1973	—	—	—	—	—	—	1974	1974	1985
WIND (Resultant)													
Mean speed (mph)	9.5	9.6	10.2	9.2	8.0	7.0	6.3	5.9	6.8	7.6	8.5	9.5	8.2

MOBILE

NORMALS, MEANS, EXTREMES

	JAN	FEB	MAR	APR	MAY	JUN	JUL	AUG	SEP	OCT	NOV	DEC	YEAR
TEMPERATURE													
Normal daily maximum	60.6	63.9	70.3	78.3	84.9	90.2	91.2	90.7	87.0	79.4	69.3	63.1	77.4
Normal daily minimum	40.9	43.2	49.8	57.7	64.8	70.8	73.2	72.9	69.3	57.5	47.9	42.9	57.6
Normal monthly	50.8	53.6	60.1	68.0	74.9	80.5	82.2	81.8	78.2	68.5	58.6	53.0	67.5
Extreme highest	84	82	90	92	100	102	104	102	99	93	87	81	104
Extreme highest date	1949	1981	1946	1943	1953	1952	1952	1968	1980	1963	1971	1974	1952
Extreme lowest	3	11	21	36	43	49	60	59	42	32	22	8	3
Extreme lowest date	1985	1951	1943	1973	1960	1984	1947	1956	1967	1957	1950	1983	1985
DEGREE DAYS BASE 65° F													
Heating	469	342	191	43	0	0	0	0	0	50	218	382	1695
Cooling	29	23	39	133	307	465	533	521	396	158	26	13	2643
% OF POSSIBLE SUNSHINE	na	na	na	na	na	na	na	na	na	na	na	na	na
AVERAGE SKY COVER													
Sunrise - Sunset	6.6	6.2	6.2	5.8	5.7	5.8	6.6	6.0	5.7	4.5	5.3	6.2	5.9
NUMBER OF DAYS (Sunrise-Sunset)													
Clear	7.7	7.9	8.4	8.9	8.5	7.2	3.5	5.9	8.8	14.3	11.1	9.2	101.4
Partly cloudy	6.3	6.7	8.1	8.7	11.7	14.0	15.2	14.9	10.2	7.9	7.2	6.5	117.3
Cloudy	17.0	13.6	14.5	12.4	10.8	8.8	12.2	10.3	11.0	8.8	11.7	15.4	146.6
Precipitation .01" or more	10.7	9.6	10.7	7.5	8.3	11.2	16.4	14.1	10.3	5.8	7.7	10.4	122.5
Snow, Ice pellets 1.0" or more	*	0.1	*	0.0	0.0	0.0	0.0	0.0	0.0	0.0	0.0	*	0.2
Thunderstorms	1.9	2.2	5.0	4.9	7.0	11.7	18.2	14.3	7.4	2.2	2.0	2.4	79.1
Fog, Visibility 1/4 mile or less	6.0	4.5	5.3	4.5	2.6	0.9	1.0	1.4	2.0	2.5	4.4	4.9	40.0
Temperature Maximum:													
90° and above	0.0	0.0	0.0	0.3	4.2	17.9	22.3	20.5	10.3	1.0	0.0	0.0	76.6
32° and below	0.3	0.0	0.0	0.0	0.0	0.0	0.0	0.0	0.0	0.0	0.0	0.1	0.4
Temperature Minimum:													
32° and below	9.0	6.0	1.2	0.0	0.0	0.0	0.0	0.0	0.0	0.0	1.2	5.7	23.1
0° and below	0.0	0.0	0.0	0.0	0.0	0.0	0.0	0.0	0.0	0.0	0.0	0.0	0.0
RELATIVE HUMIDITY (%)													
Morning	77	76	80	82	83	84	85	87	84	82	82	79	82
Afternoon	61	55	55	53	54	54	60	61	59	53	57	61	57
PRECIPITATION (inches)													
Water Equivalent													
Normal	4.5	4.9	6.4	5.3	5.4	5.0	7.7	6.7	6.5	2.6	3.6	5.4	64.6
Maximum monthly	10.4	11.8	15.5	17.6	15.0	13.0	19.2	15.1	13.6	13.2	13.6	11.3	19.2
Date	1978	1983	1946	1955	1980	1961	1949	1984	1957	1985	1948	1953	1949
Minimum monthly	0.9	1.3	0.5	0.4	0.4	1.1	1.7	2.3	0.5	T	0.2	1.2	T
Date	1968	1948	1967	1962	1962	1966	1983	1972	1963	1978	1960	1980	1978
Maximum in 24 hrs	8.3	5.3	6.5	13.3	8.0	7.3	5.3	6.6	8.5	5.6	7.0	5.5	13.3
Date	1965	1981	1951	1955	1981	1961	1975	1969	1979	1985	1975	1968	1955
SNOW, ICE PELLETS													
Maximum monthly	3.5	3.6	1.6	0.0	0.0	0.0	0.0	0.0	0.0	0.0	T	3.0	3.6
Date	1955	1973	1954	—	—	—	—	—	—	—	1966	1963	1973
Maximum in 24 hrs	3.5	3.6	1.6	0.0	0.0	0.0	0.0	0.0	0.0	0.0	T	3.0	3.6
Date	1955	1973	1954	—	—	—	—	—	—	—	1966	1963	1973
WIND (Resultant)													
Mean speed (mph)	10.5	10.7	11.0	10.4	8.9	7.7	7.0	6.8	8.0	8.2	9.3	10.1	9.0

MONTGOMERY

Elev. 192'   32° 18N — 86° 24W   **Alabama**

NORMALS, MEANS, EXTREMES

	JAN	FEB	MAR	APR	MAY	JUN	JUL	AUG	SEP	OCT	NOV	DEC	YEAR
TEMPERATURE													
Normal daily maximum	57.0	60.9	68.1	77.0	83.6	89.8	91.5	91.2	86.9	77.5	67.0	59.8	75.9
Normal daily minimum	36.4	38.8	45.5	53.3	61.1	68.4	71.8	71.1	66.4	53.1	43.0	37.9	53.9
Normal monthly	46.7	49.9	56.8	65.2	72.4	79.1	81.7	81.2	76.7	65.3	55.0	48.9	64.9
Extreme highest	83	85	89	91	98	105	105	104	101	100	87	85	105
Extreme highest date	1949	1962	1954	1972	1953	1954	1952	1983	1980	1954	1975	1982	1954
Extreme lowest	0	10	19	31	40	49	59	57	39	26	13	5	0
Extreme lowest date	1985	1951	1980	1950	1971	1984	1947	1968	1967	1952	1950	1983	1985
DEGREE DAYS BASE 65° F													
Heating	580	439	284	72	10	0	0	0	0	86	307	499	2277
Cooling	13	17	30	78	240	423	518	502	351	95	7	0	2274
% OF POSSIBLE SUNSHINE	48	54	59	65	65	65	62	65	63	65	56	51	60
AVERAGE SKY COVER													
Sunrise - Sunset	6.6	6.2	6.2	5.6	5.7	5.6	6.2	5.6	5.5	4.7	5.4	6.1	5.8
NUMBER OF DAYS													
(Sunrise-Sunset)													
Clear	7.4	8.0	8.0	9.6	9.2	8.6	5.4	8.1	10.0	13.8	11.0	9.5	108.7
Partly cloudy	6.5	6.4	7.9	8.1	10.2	11.5	14.1	13.8	9.1	7.5	6.3	6.0	107.5
Cloudy	17.1	13.8	15.1	12.3	11.6	9.9	11.5	9.1	11.0	9.7	12.6	15.5	149.1
Precipitation .01" or more	10.7	9.3	10.3	8.2	8.5	9.0	11.9	9.1	7.5	5.7	7.7	10.1	108.0
Snow, Ice pellets 1.0" or more	0.1	*	0.0	0.0	0.0	0.0	0.0	0.0	0.0	0.0	0.0	*	0.2
Thunderstorms	1.7	2.2	4.9	5.5	6.7	8.9	11.8	8.9	4.0	1.4	1.8	1.8	59.6
Fog, Visibility 1/4 mile or less	3.5	1.9	1.7	1.2	1.2	0.7	1.0	1.0	1.7	2.0	3.1	3.3	22.2
Temperature Maximum:													
90° and above	0.0	0.0	0.0	*	3.0	16.0	20.7	19.0	11.5	1.0	0.0	0.0	71.3
32° and below	0.5	0.0	0.0	0.0	0.0	0.0	0.0	0.0	0.0	0.0	0.0	0.2	0.7
Temperature Minimum:													
32° and below	14.0	9.6	2.6	0.0	0.0	0.0	0.0	0.0	0.0	0.2	4.1	10.1	40.6
0° and below	*	0.0	0.0	0.0	0.0	0.0	0.0	0.0	0.0	0.0	0.0	0.0	*
RELATIVE HUMIDITY (%)													
Morning	76	72	74	77	82	83	86	87	85	84	81	78	80
Afternoon	60	55	53	52	55	55	60	61	57	54	55	59	56
PRECIPITATION (inches)													
Water Equivalent													
Normal	4.2	4.5	5.9	4.4	4.0	3.5	4.8	3.2	4.7	2.3	3.0	4.8	49.2
Maximum monthly	7.6	13.4	10.8	15.6	12.0	9.9	8.9	10.4	10.6	9.1	21.3	11.4	21.3
Date	1947	1961	1958	1964	1978	1946	1956	1984	1953	1959	1948	1961	1948
Minimum monthly	0.7	1.5	1.9	0.9	1.1	0.3	1.6	0.8	0.4	0.0	0.3	1.4	0.0
Date	1954	1947	1985	1965	1962	1979	1952	1958	1954	1978	1949	1955	1978
Maximum in 24 hrs	4.7	5.6	7.1	4.6	6.4	7.0	4.5	5.7	8.8	4.3	8.2	4.3	8.8
Date	1965	1982	1958	1957	1978	1946	1970	1984	1953	1964	1948	1953	1953
SNOW, ICE PELLETS													
Maximum monthly	6.0	3.1	T	0.0	0.0	0.0	0.0	0.0	0.0	0.0	T	1.0	6.0
Date	1977	1973	1983	**	**	**	**	**	**	**	1971	1963	1977
Maximum in 24 hrs	3.0	3.1	T	0.0	0.0	0.0	0.0	0.0	0.0	0.0	T	1.0	3.1
Date	1977	1973	1983	—	—	—	—	—	—	—	1971	1963	1973
WIND (Resultant)													
Mean speed (mph)	7.8	8.3	8.4	7.4	6.2	5.9	5.7	5.2	6.0	5.7	6.6	7.2	6.7

ANCHORAGE　　Elev. 114'　　61° 13'N — 149° 53'W　　Alaska

NORMALS, MEANS, EXTREMES

	JAN	FEB	MAR	APR	MAY	JUN	JUL	AUG	SEP	OCT	NOV	DEC	YEAR
TEMPERATURE													
Normal daily maximum	20.0	25.5	31.7	42.6	54.2	61.8	65.1	63.2	55.2	40.8	27.9	20.4	42.4
Normal daily minimum	6.0	10.3	15.7	28.2	38.3	47.0	51.1	49.2	41.1	28.4	15.4	7.1	28.2
Normal monthly	13.0	17.9	23.7	35.4	46.3	54.4	58.1	56.2	48.2	34.6	21.7	13.8	35.3
Extreme highest	50	48	51	65	77	85	81	82	73	61	53	47	85
Extreme highest date	1961	1977	1984	1976	1969	1969	1977	1978	1957	1969	1979	1985	1969
Extreme lowest	-34	-26	-24	-4	17	33	38	31	20	-5	-21	-30	-34
Extreme lowest date	1975	1956	1971	1985	1964	1961	1964	1984	1956	1956	1956	1964	1975
DEGREE DAYS BASE 65° F													
Heating	1612	1319	1280	888	580	318	214	273	504	942	1299	1587	10816
Cooling	0	0	0	0	0	0	0	0	0	0	0	0	0
% OF POSSIBLE SUNSHINE	39	44	53	52	51	47	43	41	42	38	36	32	43
AVERAGE SKY COVER													
Sunrise - Sunset	6.7	7.0	6.8	7.2	7.6	8.0	7.9	7.9	7.8	7.6	7.3	7.2	7.4
NUMBER OF DAYS (Sunrise-Sunset)													
Clear	8.0	6.6	7.3	5.2	3.9	2.5	3.3	3.5	3.9	5.1	5.7	6.6	61.7
Partly cloudy	4.7	3.8	5.5	6.5	6.7	6.9	5.6	6.1	5.4	4.9	5.0	4.2	65.3
Cloudy	18.3	17.8	18.1	18.3	20.3	20.7	22.0	21.4	20.7	21.0	19.4	20.2	238.1
Precipitation .01" or more	7.3	8.3	7.8	6.9	6.8	8.4	11.6	13.0	13.7	12.0	9.2	10.4	115.4
Snow, Ice pellets 1.0" or more	2.6	3.1	2.6	0.0	0.0	0.0	0.0	0.0	0.3	2.4	2.9	4.3	20.2
Thunderstorms	0.0	0.0	0.0	0.0	0.1	0.2	0.4	0.3	0.1	0.0	0.0	0.0	1.0
Fog, Visibility 1/4 mile or less	6.5	4.0	1.3	0.7	0.3	0.1	0.2	1.0	1.4	2.1	4.0	5.3	26.8
Temperature Maximum:													
90° and above	0.0	0.0	0.0	0.0	0.5	2.8	6.4	3.3	0.2	0.0	0.0	0.0	13.1
32° and below	24.9	19.9	11.8	2.3	0.0	0.0	0.0	0.0	0.0	4.7	20.8	25.4	109.9
Temperature Minimum:													
32° and below	30.5	26.8	27.9	21.4	2.9	0.0	0.0	0.1	3.2	19.7	28.1	30.3	190.9
0° and below	10.9	7.4	2.4	*	0.0	0.0	0.0	0.0	0.0	0.1	3.2	8.6	32.7
RELATIVE HUMIDITY (%)													
Morning	71	72	70	72	72	74	79	82	81	76	77	75	75
Afternoon	71	66	56	54	49	55	61	64	63	65	73	74	63
PRECIPITATION (inches)													
Water Equivalent													
Normal	0.8	0.9	0.6	0.6	0.5	1.0	1.9	2.1	2.4	1.7	1.1	1.1	15.2
Maximum monthly	2.0	3.0	2.7	1.9	1.6	3.4	4.4	4.9	5.4	3.4	2.8	2.6	5.4
Date	1963	1955	1979	1977	1980	1962	1958	1981	1961	1981	1976	1955	1961
Minimum monthly	0.0	0.0	T	T	0.0	0.1	0.4	0.3	0.7	0.3	0.0	0.1	T
Date	1982	1958	1983	1969	1957	1969	1972	1969	1973	1960	1985	1982	1983
Maximum in 24 hrs	1.1	1.1	0.7	0.6	1.1	1.8	2.0	1.6	1.9	1.1	1.6	1.6	2.0
Date	1961	1956	1979	1975	1980	1962	1956	1955	1961	1980	1964	1955	1956
SNOW, ICE PELLETS													
Maximum monthly	21.1	48.5	31.0	27.6	3.9	0.0	0.0	0.0	4.6	27.1	32.4	41.6	48.5
Date	1955	1955	1979	1963	1963	—	—	—	1965	1982	1956	1955	1955
Maximum in 24 hrs	10.5	12.4	14.5	9.1	3.9	0.0	0.0	0.0	3.5	9.6	16.4	17.7	17.7
Date	1955	1956	1959	1955	1963	—	—	—	1965	1955	1964	1955	1955
WIND (Resultant)													
Mean speed (mph)	6.2	6.7	6.7	7.2	8.4	8.2	7.2	6.7	6.3	6.5	6.1	5.9	6.8

BARROW

Elev. 31' 71° 18'N — 156° 47'W **Alaska**

NORMALS, MEANS, EXTREMES

	JAN	FEB	MAR	APR	MAY	JUN	JUL	AUG	SEP	OCT	NOV	DEC	YEAR
TEMPERATURE													
Normal daily maximum	-8.0	-13.8	-9.7	5.4	23.6	37.4	44.6	42.4	33.8	18.9	4.6	-7.0	14.4
Normal daily minimum	-20.8	-25.5	-22.1	-8.8	13.9	29.3	33.2	33.5	27.3	9.5	-6.6	-18.8	3.7
Normal monthly	-14.4	-19.7	-15.9	-1.7	18.8	33.4	38.9	38.0	30.6	14.2	-1.0	-12.9	9.0
Extreme highest	36	36	33	42	45	70	78	76	62	43	39	34	78
Extreme highest date	1974	1982	1967	1936	1927	1942	1927	1968	1957	1954	1937	1932	1927
Extreme lowest	-53	-56	-52	-42	-19	4	22	20	1	-32	-40	-55	-56
Extreme lowest date	1975	1924	1971	1924	1984	1969	1936	1925	1975	1970	1948	1924	1924
DEGREE DAYS BASE 65° F													
Heating	2461	2369	2508	2001	1432	951	809	837	1032	1575	1980	2415	20370
Cooling	0	0	0	0	0	0	0	0	0	0	0	0	0
% OF POSSIBLE SUNSHINE	na	na	na	na	na	na	na	na	na	na	na	na	na
AVERAGE SKY COVER													
Sunrise - Sunset	0.0	5.1	4.7	5.5	8.3	8.0	7.8	8.9	9.2	8.6	0.0	0.0	0.0
NUMBER OF DAYS (Sunrise-Sunset)													
Clear	3.3	12.1	14.0	11.0	3.3	3.8	3.5	1.4	1.4	2.2	4.1	0.0	60.2
Partly cloudy	1.6	5.7	7.1	7.1	5.0	5.6	7.0	3.8	2.7	4.1	2.7	0.0	52.3
Cloudy	2.5	10.4	9.9	11.9	22.8	20.5	20.5	25.8	25.9	24.7	10.7	0.0	185.5
Precipitation .01" or more	4.5	4.3	3.6	4.2	4.3	4.7	8.7	10.5	10.3	11.3	6.3	4.8	77.5
Snow, Ice pellets 1.0" or more	0.5	0.4	0.3	0.8	0.3	0.2	0.1	0.2	0.9	1.7	0.8	0.5	6.7
Thunderstorms	0.0	0.0	0.0	0.0	0.0	*	*	*	0.0	0.0	0.0	0.0	0.1
Fog, Visibility 1/4 mile or less	2.2	1.5	1.3	2.6	7.4	10.6	12.0	11.7	5.2	3.1	2.3	1.3	61.3
Temperature Maximum:													
90° and above	0.0	0.0	0.0	0.0	0.0	0.1	0.9	0.6	0.0	0.0	0.0	0.0	1.6
32° and below	30.9	28.2	31.0	29.4	26.6	5.0	0.4	1.8	13.2	28.6	29.8	31.0	255.9
Temperature Minimum:													
32° and below	31.0	28.2	31.0	30.0	30.8	24.2	14.6	15.6	25.9	30.8	30.0	31.0	323.2
0° and below	29.0	27.4	30.3	23.1	3.4	0.0	0.0	0.0	0.0	6.7	21.5	28.9	170.3
RELATIVE HUMIDITY (%)													
Morning	68	65	66	74	88	93	94	95	92	85	77	69	81
Afternoon	68	65	67	73	83	86	84	87	88	84	77	70	78
PRECIPITATION (inches)													
Water Equivalent													
Normal	0.2	0.1	0.1	0.2	0.1	0.3	0.8	0.9	0.5	0.5	0.3	0.1	4.7
Maximum monthly	1.0	0.8	1.4	1.3	0.8	1.1	2.4	2.8	1.5	1.6	1.1	0.7	2.8
Date	1962	1959	1963	1963	1933	1955	1922	1963	1958	1925	1965	1967	1963
Minimum monthly	0.0	0.0	0.0	0.0	T	T	T	T	0.0	0.1	T	0.0	0.0
Date	1939	1936	1928	1938	1939	1937	1937	1934	1969	1936	1936	1936	1939
Maximum in 24 hrs	0.7	0.3	0.7	0.4	0.3	0.8	0.8	0.8	0.5	1.0	0.4	0.2	1.0
Date	1937	1959	1963	1963	1969	1955	1954	1960	1959	1926	1925	1930	1926
SNOW, ICE PELLETS													
Maximum monthly	11.9	9.4	15.8	15.4	12.9	6.6	9.0	4.0	12.9	21.2	19.0	9.7	21.2
Date	1962	1944	1963	1963	1933	1933	1922	1969	1972	1925	1925	1925	1925
Maximum in 24 hrs	5.4	3.6	7.1	4.2	4.5	3.2	6.0	2.5	5.0	15.0	6.0	5.0	15.0
Date	1962	1959	1963	1963	1923	1981	1922	1936	1950	1926	1925	1922	1926
WIND (Resultant)													
Mean speed (mph)	11.4	10.9	11.1	11.3	11.6	11.4	11.6	12.3	13.0	13.3	12.4	11.2	11.8

FAIRBANKS

Elev. 436' 64° 49'N — 147° 52'W **Alaska**

NORMALS, MEANS, EXTREMES

	JAN	FEB	MAR	APR	MAY	JUN	JUL	AUG	SEP	OCT	NOV	DEC	YEAR
TEMPERATURE													
Normal daily maximum	-3.9	7.3	21.7	40.8	59.2	70.1	71.8	66.5	54.4	32.6	12.4	-1.7	35.9
Normal daily minimum	-21.6	-15.4	-4.8	19.5	37.2	48.5	51.2	46.5	35.4	17.5	-4.6	-18.4	15.9
Normal monthly	-12.8	-4.1	8.5	30.2	48.2	59.3	61.5	56.5	44.9	25.1	3.9	-10.1	25.9
Extreme highest	50	45	51	74	89	96	94	90	84	65	46	44	96
Extreme highest date	1981	1980	1970	1960	1960	1969	1975	1976	1957	1969	1970	1985	1969
Extreme lowest	-61	-56	-49	-21	-1	31	35	30	10	-27	-43	-62	-62
Extreme lowest date	1969	1968	1956	1964	1964	1963	1959	1981	1983	1975	1964	1961	1961
DEGREE DAYS BASE 65° F													
Heating	2412	1932	1752	1044	521	198	141	270	603	1240	1833	2328	14274
Cooling	0	0	0	0	0	27	33	10	0	0	0	0	70
% OF POSSIBLE SUNSHINE	na	na	na	na	na	na	na	na	na	na	na	na	na
AVERAGE SKY COVER													
Sunrise - Sunset	6.1	6.2	6.0	6.7	6.9	7.4	7.5	7.8	7.5	8.0	6.9	6.8	7.0
NUMBER OF DAYS (Sunrise-Sunset)													
Clear	9.6	8.2	9.5	6.4	4.4	2.6	3.4	3.0	4.5	3.5	6.8	7.4	69.4
Partly cloudy	5.7	5.7	6.9	7.3	10.8	9.9	8.5	6.7	6.1	5.4	5.3	5.8	84.2
Cloudy	15.6	14.3	14.5	16.3	15.8	17.5	19.1	21.3	19.4	22.1	17.9	17.8	211.7
Precipitation .01" or more	7.1	6.5	6.2	5.4	6.8	10.4	12.7	12.6	9.5	10.9	9.6	8.6	106.3
Snow, Ice pellets 1.0" or more	3.1	2.4	2.4	1.2	0.2	0.0	0.0	0.0	0.3	4.1	4.0	4.0	21.8
Thunderstorms	0.0	0.0	0.0	*	0.4	2.3	2.0	0.7	0.1	0.0	0.0	0.0	5.5
Fog, Visibility 1/4 mile or less	5.0	2.4	0.6	0.2	0.2	0.3	0.8	1.9	1.5	1.8	1.2	3.7	19.6
Temperature Maximum:													
90° and above	0.0	0.0	0.0	*	3.0	16.0	20.0	10.6	1.3	0.0	0.0	0.0	51.0
32° and below	29.7	26.0	21.0	6.2	0.2	0.0	0.0	0.0	0.2	16.1	27.7	29.6	156.8
Temperature Minimum:													
32° and below	31.0	28.3	30.9	27.0	6.5	0.0	0.0	0.5	8.3	28.3	30.0	31.0	221.7
0° and below	25.8	22.5	16.2	2.1	*	0.0	0.0	0.0	0.0	3.9	18.2	25.0	113.7
RELATIVE HUMIDITY (%)													
Morning	67	65	66	67	67	75	82	85	81	78	72	69	73
Afternoon	67	62	54	47	38	43	51	55	55	67	72	69	57
PRECIPITATION (inches)													
Water Equivalent													
Normal	0.5	0.4	0.4	0.2	0.5	1.3	1.7	1.8	1.0	0.7	0.6	0.7	10.3
Maximum monthly	1.9	1.7	2.1	0.9	1.6	3.5	4.3	6.2	3.0	2.1	3.3	3.2	6.2
Date	1957	1966	1963	1982	1955	1955	1962	1967	1960	1983	1970	1984	1967
Minimum monthly	0.0	0.0	T	T	0.0	0.1	0.4	0.4	0.1	0.0	T	T	T
Date	1966	1976	1968	1969	1957	1966	1957	1957	1968	1954	1953	1969	1969
Maximum in 24 hrs	0.5	0.9	0.9	0.4	0.8	1.5	1.6	3.4	1.2	2.2	0.8	1.2	3.4
Date	1968	1966	1963	1979	1955	1955	1962	1967	1954	1976	1970	1968	1967
SNOW, ICE PELLETS													
Maximum monthly	26.3	43.1	29.6	11.4	4.7	T	0.0	T	7.8	25.9	54.0	50.7	54.0
Date	1957	1966	1963	1982	1964	1974	—	1969	1972	1982	1970	1984	1970
Maximum in 24 hrs	9.4	20.1	12.6	5.8	4.5	T	0.0	T	7.0	10.4	14.6	14.7	20.1
Date	1968	1966	1963	1982	1964	1985	—	1969	1972	1974	1970	1968	1966
WIND (Resultant)													
Mean speed (mph)	3.1	4.0	5.3	6.6	7.8	7.2	6.6	6.2	6.2	5.4	3.8	3.1	5.4

HOMER

Elev. 67' **59° 38'N — 151° 30'W** **Alaska**

NORMALS, MEANS, EXTREMES

	JAN	FEB	MAR	APR	MAY	JUN	JUL	AUG	SEP	OCT	NOV	DEC	YEAR
TEMPERATURE													
Normal daily maximum	27.0	31.2	34.4	42.1	49.8	56.3	60.5	60.3	54.8	44.0	34.9	27.7	43.6
Normal daily minimum	14.4	17.4	19.3	28.1	34.6	41.2	45.1	45.2	39.7	30.6	22.8	15.8	29.5
Normal monthly	20.7	24.3	26.9	35.1	42.2	48.8	52.8	52.8	47.3	37.3	28.9	21.8	36.6
Extreme highest	51	51	53	63	69	80	78	78	68	64	52	50	80
Extreme highest date	1961	1954	1974	1965	1964	1953	1967	1944	1965	1954	1962	1969	1953
Extreme lowest	-18	-18	-21	-9	6	29	34	31	20	2	-7	-16	-21
Extreme lowest date	1972	1947	1971	1944	1949	1950	1959	1955	1956	1975	1963	1964	1971
DEGREE DAYS BASE 65° F													
Heating	1370	1140	1181	897	707	486	378	378	531	859	1083	1339	10349
Cooling	0	0	0	0	0	0	0	0	0	0	0	0	0
% OF POSSIBLE SUNSHINE	na	na	na	na	na	na	na	na	na	na	na	na	na
AVERAGE SKY COVER													
Sunrise - Sunset	6.8	6.9	7.0	7.2	7.7	7.3	7.6	7.1	7.3	7.4	7.1	6.8	7.2
NUMBER OF DAYS (Sunrise-Sunset)													
Clear	7.7	6.8	6.1	5.4	3.7	3.9	3.3	5.3	4.8	5.2	5.9	7.4	65.4
Partly cloudy	4.2	4.4	6.3	6.3	6.8	8.1	8.6	7.7	7.0	5.2	5.3	5.3	75.1
Cloudy	19.1	17.1	18.7	18.3	20.5	17.9	19.1	18.1	18.1	20.6	18.9	18.3	224.7
Precipitation .01" or more	12.8	11.3	11.7	9.2	9.5	8.9	11.1	12.4	15.2	15.4	12.1	14.0	143.8
Snow, Ice pellets 1.0" or more	3.1	4.2	3.4	2.1	0.2	0.0	0.0	0.0	0.0	1.1	2.5	4.2	20.9
Thunderstorms	0.0	0.0	0.0	0.0	0.1	0.0	0.3	0.1	0.0	0.1	0.0	0.0	0.5
Fog, Visibility 1/4 mile or less	0.6	1.1	0.8	0.5	0.4	0.3	1.2	2.1	0.9	0.4	0.7	0.9	9.9
Temperature Maximum:													
90° and above	0.0	0.0	0.0	0.0	0.0	0.3	0.7	0.8	0.0	0.0	0.0	0.0	1.8
32° and below	17.4	12.6	8.7	1.7	0.1	0.0	0.0	0.0	0.0	1.6	10.5	17.4	69.9
Temperature Minimum:													
32° and below	28.8	24.8	27.4	22.5	9.9	0.6	0.0	*	3.7	17.7	25.2	27.7	188.4
0° and below	4.2	2.4	1.4	*	0.0	0.0	0.0	0.0	0.0	0.0	0.2	3.4	11.6
RELATIVE HUMIDITY (%)													
Morning	78	78	77	81	84	88	91	90	88	82	79	78	83
Afternoon	76	72	67	66	65	67	71	72	70	69	74	77	71
PRECIPITATION (inches)													
Water Equivalent													
Normal	1.6	1.9	1.2	1.3	1.0	1.0	1.4	2.3	2.8	3.2	2.9	2.5	23.7
Maximum monthly	6.6	5.6	6.0	3.4	2.2	3.3	3.7	5.5	5.3	8.5	8.7	8.0	8.7
Date	1981	1978	1981	1959	1980	1941	1948	1939	1961	1969	1983	1939	1983
Minimum monthly	0.3	0.1	0.2	0.0	0.0	0.0	0.1	0.4	0.8	0.9	0.1	0.0	0.0
Date	1969	1979	1953	1954	1974	1957	1953	1978	1969	1933	1955	1933	1933
Maximum in 24 hrs	2.3	1.6	1.3	1.4	1.0	1.2	1.3	1.8	1.5	2.2	3.2	2.1	3.2
Date	1984	1941	1981	1980	1977	1978	1980	1936	1982	1946	1983	1979	1983
SNOW, ICE PELLETS													
Maximum monthly	33.8	46.0	38.1	17.4	6.6	T	0.0	0.0	0.5	21.9	37.4	54.7	54.7
Date	1962	1974	1976	1972	1971	1963	—	—	1962	1976	1945	1979	1979
Maximum in 24 hrs	24.0	19.2	15.2	7.4	6.0	T	0.0	0.0	0.4	6.0	24.5	20.2	24.5
Date	1939	1945	1954	1972	1971	1963	—	—	1968	1940	1945	1979	1945
WIND (Resultant)													
Mean speed (mph)	8.0	8.0	7.6	7.6	7.9	7.3	6.8	5.9	6.3	6.9	7.6	7.4	7.3

JUNEAU

Elev. 12'   58° 22'N — 134° 35'W   **Alaska**

NORMALS, MEANS, EXTREMES

	JAN	FEB	MAR	APR	MAY	JUN	JUL	AUG	SEP	OCT	NOV	DEC	YEAR
TEMPERATURE													
Normal daily maximum	27.4	33.7	37.4	46.8	54.7	61.1	64.0	62.6	55.9	47.0	37.5	31.5	46.6
Normal daily minimum	16.1	21.9	25.0	31.3	38.1	44.2	47.4	46.6	42.3	36.5	28.0	22.1	33.3
Normal monthly	21.8	27.8	31.2	39.1	46.4	52.7	55.7	54.6	49.1	41.8	32.8	26.8	40.0
Extreme highest	57	55	59	71	82	86	90	83	72	61	56	54	90
Extreme highest date	1958	1977	1981	1958	1947	1969	1975	1977	1949	1954	1949	1944	1975
Extreme lowest	-22	-22	-15	6	25	31	36	27	23	11	-5	-21	-22
Extreme lowest date	1972	1968	1972	1963	1972	1971	1950	1948	1972	1984	1966	1949	1972
DEGREE DAYS BASE 65° F													
Heating	1339	1042	1048	777	574	369	288	322	474	719	969	1184	9105
Cooling	0	0	0	0	0	0	0	0	0	0	0	0	0
% OF POSSIBLE SUNSHINE	32	32	37	39	39	34	31	32	26	19	23	20	30
AVERAGE SKY COVER													
Sunrise - Sunset	7.6	8.1	8.2	8.2	8.0	8.1	8.3	8.0	8.5	8.9	8.4	8.5	8.2
NUMBER OF DAYS (Sunrise-Sunset)													
Clear	6.0	3.9	4.0	3.3	3.8	3.4	3.0	3.9	2.8	2.1	3.6	3.7	43.4
Partly cloudy	2.7	2.9	2.9	3.9	3.9	4.1	4.6	4.7	3.2	2.1	2.3	1.8	39.1
Cloudy	22.3	21.4	24.1	22.8	23.3	22.5	23.3	22.5	24.1	26.7	24.1	25.6	282.7
Precipitation .01" or more	17.8	16.9	17.8	16.9	17.1	15.7	16.8	17.6	20.0	23.5	19.2	20.5	219.9
Snow, Ice pellets 1.0" or more	7.0	5.4	4.4	1.0	0.0	0.0	0.0	0.0	0.0	0.3	3.3	6.3	27.8
Thunderstorms	*	0.0	0.0	0.0	0.0	*	0.1	*	0.1	0.0	0.1	0.0	0.3
Fog, Visibility 1/4 mile or less	2.1	2.5	1.8	0.8	0.7	0.2	0.2	1.1	3.0	3.1	3.3	2.3	21.1
Temperature Maximum:													
90° and above	0.0	0.0	0.0	*	1.3	5.0	7.1	5.6	0.1	0.0	0.0	0.0	19.2
32° and below	16.9	9.8	4.0	0.3	0.0	0.0	0.0	0.0	0.0	0.2	6.7	13.2	51.2
Temperature Minimum:													
32° and below	26.0	22.8	23.8	15.7	4.2	0.1	0.0	0.1	1.7	7.9	18.8	24.2	145.3
0° and below	4.9	1.9	0.6	0.0	0.0	0.0	0.0	0.0	0.0	0.0	0.2	2.2	9.8
RELATIVE HUMIDITY (%)													
Morning	79	83	83	85	86	86	86	90	92	88	85	83	86
Afternoon	75	75	67	63	62	65	70	74	77	78	80	81	72
PRECIPITATION (inches)													
Water Equivalent													
Normal	3.6	3.7	3.3	2.9	3.4	2.9	4.1	5.0	6.4	7.7	5.1	4.6	53.1
Maximum monthly	8.1	8.4	6.3	5.3	6.3	5.3	7.8	12.3	11.6	15.2	11.2	9.8	15.2
Date	1976	1964	1966	1980	1966	1949	1969	1961	1981	1974	1956	1956	1974
Minimum monthly	0.9	0.6	0.5	0.2	1.2	1.0	1.1	0.5	2.3	2.7	1.1	0.4	0.2
Date	1969	1969	1983	1948	1946	1950	1972	1979	1965	1950	1983	1983	1948
Maximum in 24 hrs	2.7	2.3	1.8	1.5	1.6	1.9	1.9	2.6	3.1	4.6	3.3	3.5	4.6
Date	1948	1949	1948	1952	1981	1953	1984	1974	1952	1946	1949	1956	1946
SNOW, ICE PELLETS													
Maximum monthly	69.2	86.3	52.6	46.3	1.2	T	0.0	0.0	T	15.6	32.5	54.7	86.3
Date	1982	1965	1948	1963	1964	1970	—	—	1974	1956	1975	1964	1965
Maximum in 24 hrs	20.1	23.7	31.0	24.2	0.7	T	0.0	0.0	T	8.8	16.5	25.6	31.0
Date	1975	1949	1948	1963	1945	1970	—	—	1974	1956	1963	1962	1948
WIND (Resultant)													
Mean speed (mph)	8.3	8.7	8.6	8.7	8.3	7.8	7.5	7.4	7.9	9.6	8.5	9.0	8.4

NORMALS, MEANS, EXTREMES

	JAN	FEB	MAR	APR	MAY	JUN	JUL	AUG	SEP	OCT	NOV	DEC	YEAR
TEMPERATURE													
Normal daily maximum	36.6	34.8	38.3	43.3	48.4	56.1	59.3	61.0	55.9	47.1	39.9	35.2	46.3
Normal daily minimum	27.2	24.0	27.0	32.7	38.0	43.3	48.1	48.5	43.9	35.2	29.4	24.0	35.1
Normal monthly	31.9	29.4	32.7	38.0	43.2	49.7	53.7	54.8	49.9	41.2	34.7	29.6	40.7
Extreme highest	54	56	57	64	80	86	82	83	73	62	54	56	86
Extreme highest date	1963	1957	1963	1965	1968	1953	1967	1968	1985	1983	1970	1984	1953
Extreme lowest	-8	-12	-6	7	20	30	37	36	26	10	0	-1	-12
Extreme lowest date	1975	1971	1971	1977	1949	1968	1966	1973	1968	1975	1971	1970	1971
DEGREE DAYS BASE 65° F													
Heating	1026	997	1001	810	676	459	355	316	453	738	909	1097	8837
Cooling	0	0	0	0	0	0	0	0	0	0	0	0	0
% OF POSSIBLE SUNSHINE	na	na	na	na	na	na	na	na	na	na	na	na	na
AVERAGE SKY COVER													
Sunrise - Sunset	7.2	7.2	7.3	7.3	8.1	7.7	8.0	7.5	7.5	6.9	6.9	7.2	7.4
NUMBER OF DAYS (Sunrise-Sunset)													
Clear	5.3	6.1	5.7	4.9	2.9	3.9	3.3	4.6	4.3	6.6	7.4	6.5	61.5
Partly cloudy	5.5	4.9	6.5	7.2	5.6	6.3	5.7	7.3	7.4	7.3	5.7	5.8	75.1
Cloudy	20.2	17.2	18.8	17.9	22.5	19.8	22.0	19.1	18.3	17.1	16.9	18.7	228.5
Precipitation .01" or more	17.0	16.0	16.5	15.2	17.8	14.8	14.8	14.3	15.5	16.0	17.0	16.8	191.7
Snow, Ice pellets 1.0" or more	3.9	5.4	4.5	2.5	0.2	0.0	0.0	0.0	0.0	0.9	1.7	3.6	22.8
Thunderstorms	0.0	0.0	0.0	0.0	0.0	0.1	0.0	0.1	0.0	0.0	0.0	0.1	0.3
Fog, Visibility 1/4 mile or less	1.2	1.2	1.1	0.3	1.1	1.3	2.7	2.7	0.9	0.3	0.1	0.8	13.6
Temperature Maximum:													
90° and above	0.0	0.0	0.0	0.0	0.3	1.0	2.3	3.2	0.4	0.0	0.0	0.0	7.3
32° and below	8.7	7.6	4.3	1.0	*	0.0	0.0	0.0	0.0	1.1	3.4	8.0	34.2
Temperature Minimum:													
32° and below	20.9	20.9	20.5	14.5	3.7	0.1	0.0	0.0	0.5	12.3	18.0	22.1	133.5
0° and below	0.5	0.7	0.4	0.0	0.0	0.0	0.0	0.0	0.0	0.0	*	0.2	1.8
RELATIVE HUMIDITY (%)													
Morning	79	78	78	77	83	85	87	86	85	79	78	76	81
Afternoon	75	73	70	68	72	75	76	74	73	69	73	73	73
PRECIPITATION (inches)													
Water Equivalent													
Normal	8.2	6.2	4.0	4.8	7.7	3.3	3.9	5.2	7.6	9.9	6.6	6.2	74.2
Maximum monthly	15.7	12.4	9.9	6.4	12.6	11.7	10.2	11.1	12.6	14.5	15.3	19.8	19.8
Date	1977	1977	1984	1978	1983	1965	1985	1977	1957	1977	1983	1985	1985
Minimum monthly	0.2	1.4	1.3	1.1	1.0	0.7	0.8	0.7	1.2	1.5	0.1	1.2	0.1
Date	1969	1956	1977	1954	1964	1978	1980	1983	1977	1956	1950	1977	1950
Maximum in 24 hrs	3.2	4.0	1.9	1.7	3.6	2.3	3.1	3.3	2.6	4.4	2.9	4.4	4.4
Date	1960	1977	1984	1985	1979	1971	1985	1976	1965	1974	1983	1985	1974
SNOW, ICE PELLETS													
Maximum monthly	40.1	38.8	74.5	34.8	6.0	T	0.0	0.0	0.4	14.9	24.3	33.1	74.5
Date	1971	1984	1956	1985	1971	1965	—	—	1977	1961	1965	1975	1956
Maximum in 24 hrs	12.0	13.6	17.8	11.3	4.0	T	0.0	0.0	0.4	10.0	14.0	11.9	17.8
Date	1976	1973	1956	1985	1968	1965	—	—	1977	1970	1965	1975	1956
WIND (Resultant)													
Mean speed (mph)	12.7	12.3	12.0	11.2	10.4	8.8	7.3	7.8	9.3	11.1	12.1	12.4	10.6

Elev. 13' 64° 30'N — 165° 26'W **Alaska**

NORMALS, MEANS, EXTREMES

	JAN	FEB	MAR	APR	MAY	JUN	JUL	AUG	SEP	OCT	NOV	DEC	YEAR
TEMPERATURE													
Normal daily maximum	13.4	11.8	15.7	25.8	42.1	52.0	56.6	55.7	48.5	33.8	22.7	12.0	32.5
Normal daily minimum	-1.9	-5.1	-2.6	9.9	29.3	38.6	44.4	44.0	36.1	22.2	9.7	-3.3	18.4
Normal monthly	5.8	3.4	6.6	17.9	35.7	45.3	50.5	49.9	42.3	28.0	16.2	4.4	25.5
Extreme highest	43	47	43	51	78	81	86	81	71	59	45	43	86
Extreme highest date	1977	1970	1984	1953	1981	1957	1977	1977	1979	1954	1983	1969	1977
Extreme lowest	-40	-42	-46	-30	-11	23	31	27	15	-10	-39	-41	-46
Extreme lowest date	1971	1978	1971	1968	1949	1974	1976	1984	1970	1966	1948	1961	1971
DEGREE DAYS BASE 65° F													
Heating	1835	1728	1810	1413	908	588	450	468	681	1147	1464	1879	14371
Cooling	0	0	0	0	0	0	0	0	0	0	0	0	0
% OF POSSIBLE SUNSHINE	39	53	53	53	49	41	36	30	33	35	30	35	41
AVERAGE SKY COVER													
Sunrise - Sunset	6.3	5.3	5.8	6.1	6.5	6.9	7.7	8.1	7.5	6.9	7.2	6.1	6.7
NUMBER OF DAYS (Sunrise-Sunset)													
Clear	9.7	11.9	11.0	9.3	7.4	5.6	3.8	3.0	4.8	7.3	6.4	10.5	90.7
Partly cloudy	4.4	3.4	5.0	6.1	7.5	8.5	6.8	5.7	5.8	5.4	4.3	3.8	66.7
Cloudy	16.9	13.0	15.0	14.6	16.0	15.9	20.3	22.3	19.4	18.4	19.3	16.7	207.8
Precipitation .01" or more	10.8	8.0	9.6	9.1	8.1	9.2	12.7	15.2	13.2	10.4	12.3	9.7	128.2
Snow, Ice pellets 1.0" or more	3.1	1.7	2.5	2.2	0.7	*	0.0	0.0	0.2	1.5	3.5	2.9	18.2
Thunderstorms	0.0	0.0	0.0	0.0	0.0	0.1	0.2	0.1	0.0	0.0	0.0	0.0	0.4
Fog, Visibility 1/4 mile or less	2.1	1.5	1.6	1.3	3.0	4.1	3.2	1.5	0.5	0.5	1.1	1.7	22.2
Temperature Maximum:													
90° and above	0.0	0.0	0.0	0.0	0.3	1.7	3.6	1.4	0.1	0.0	0.0	0.0	7.1
32° and below	27.6	25.8	27.6	21.8	4.4	0.0	0.0	0.0	0.1	12.3	24.4	26.8	170.8
Temperature Minimum:													
32° and below	31.0	28.2	30.9	29.4	19.6	3.7	0.4	1.7	9.8	25.6	29.3	30.8	240.3
0° and below	14.8	17.6	14.7	9.3	0.5	0.0	0.0	0.0	0.0	0.7	6.8	15.9	80.5
RELATIVE HUMIDITY (%)													
Morning	74	72	73	78	81	85	89	89	84	80	77	74	80
Afternoon	74	70	70	74	73	75	79	79	74	72	76	74	74
PRECIPITATION (inches)													
Water Equivalent													
Normal	0.8	0.5	0.5	0.6	0.5	1.1	2.2	3.1	2.3	1.2	0.9	0.6	14.7
Maximum monthly	2.1	1.6	1.9	2.1	1.2	4.1	4.2	7.8	5.7	3.8	4.3	2.1	7.8
Date	1957	1975	1954	1961	1952	1978	1954	1951	1964	1972	1979	1951	1951
Minimum monthly	T	T	T	0.0	0.1	0.0	0.2	0.4	0.3	T	0.0	0.0	T
Date	1970	1979	1971	1969	1974	1964	1964	1971	1968	1974	1962	1956	1979
Maximum in 24 hrs	1.2	0.7	0.6	0.6	0.7	2.0	1.7	2.9	1.4	2.2	0.8	1.0	2.9
Date	1963	1975	1954	1978	1948	1953	1954	1976	1978	1957	1979	1951	1976
SNOW, ICE PELLETS													
Maximum monthly	23.7	21.3	19.7	23.3	10.0	2.5	0.0	0.1	3.1	13.6	25.9	23.4	25.9
Date	1950	1975	1954	1961	1977	1982	—	1965	1958	1958	1970	1977	1970
Maximum in 24 hrs	7.8	9.0	5.0	6.3	5.3	1.7	0.0	0.1	2.6	6.6	8.7	8.4	9.0
Date	1947	1975	1948	1961	1952	1982	—	1965	1948	1948	1979	1951	1975
WIND (Resultant)													
Mean speed (mph)	11.7	10.8	10.4	10.5	10.2	10.0	10.0	10.5	11.1	11.0	12.0	10.4	10.7

VALDEZ

Elev. 37'   61° 08'N — 146° 21'W   **Alaska**

NORMALS, MEANS, EXTREMES

	JAN	FEB	MAR	APR	MAY	JUN	JUL	AUG	SEP	OCT	NOV	DEC	YEAR
TEMPERATURE													
Normal daily maximum	29.3	30.0	36.2	43.9	51.1	57.5	62.1	61.5	54.1	43.2	33.8	25.1	44.0
Normal daily minimum	20.9	19.4	24.1	31.4	38.2	44.5	47.8	46.6	41.3	34.5	25.5	16.8	32.6
Normal monthly	25.1	24.7	30.2	37.7	44.7	51.0	55.0	54.1	47.7	38.9	29.7	21.0	38.3
Extreme highest	46	51	51	61	73	73	85	81	73	56	50	52	85
Extreme highest date	1980	1982	1974	1983	1982	1985	1979	1977	1979	1984	1977	1983	1979
Extreme lowest	-20	-3	-6	5	21	31	33	32	25	8	5	-6	-20
Extreme lowest date	1972	1972	1972	1972	1972	1972	1972	1984	1983	1975	1982	1980	1972
DEGREE DAYS BASE 65° F													
Heating	1237	1128	1079	819	629	420	310	338	519	809	1059	1364	9711
Cooling	0	0	0	0	0	0	0	0	0	0	0	0	0
% OF POSSIBLE SUNSHINE	na	na	na	na	na	na	na	na	na	na	na	na	na
AVERAGE SKY COVER													
Sunrise - Sunset	7.3	7.4	7.2	7.8	8.1	8.2	8.4	7.4	7.7	8.1	7.0	7.5	7.7
NUMBER OF DAYS (Sunrise-Sunset)													
Clear	6.5	6.2	7.3	5.0	3.7	2.2	2.7	5.7	4.8	4.7	6.8	6.8	62.3
Partly cloudy	3.3	2.7	3.5	3.8	4.5	6.0	4.7	6.0	5.2	2.7	3.8	1.7	47.8
Cloudy	21.2	19.5	20.2	21.2	22.8	21.8	23.7	19.3	20.0	23.7	19.3	22.5	255.2
Precipitation .01" or more	15.7	13.8	15.7	13.5	15.3	14.7	16.9	16.8	19.2	19.5	14.5	15.9	191.5
Snow, Ice pellets 1.0" or more	9.0	8.5	9.9	5.1	0.3	0.0	0.0	0.0	0.0	3.2	7.8	10.8	54.5
Thunderstorms	0.0	0.0	0.0	0.0	0.0	0.1	0.1	0.0	0.1	0.3	0.0	0.0	0.6
Fog, Visibility 1/4 mile or less	1.1	2.0	0.9	0.3	0.0	0.1	4.5	5.6	2.3	1.4	2.4	0.4	20.9
Temperature Maximum:													
90° and above	0.0	0.0	0.0	0.0	0.4	0.8	3.1	3.2	0.2	0.0	0.0	0.0	7.5
32° and below	18.9	14.2	6.0	0.8	0.0	0.0	0.0	0.0	0.0	1.7	13.5	20.3	75.3
Temperature Minimum:													
32° and below	29.2	27.7	29.7	19.9	1.3	0.2	0.0	0.1	1.7	12.4	27.5	30.4	180.0
0° and below	1.6	0.1	0.2	0.0	0.0	0.0	0.0	0.0	0.0	0.0	0.0	1.1	2.9
RELATIVE HUMIDITY (%)													
Morning	80	77	81	83	87	90	93	93	90	83	79	76	84
Afternoon	76	70	68	65	63	66	72	71	73	73	72	75	70
PRECIPITATION (Inches)													
Water Equivalent													
Normal	5.0	4.1	3.4	3.1	2.4	2.1	3.9	3.7	8.2	9.1	6.0	5.3	56.7
Maximum monthly	12.5	9.6	9.9	8.1	4.7	4.5	8.9	18.2	16.6	15.4	20.5	16.8	20.5
Date	1981	1980	1979	1977	1985	1981	1981	1981	1982	1979	1976	1985	1976
Minimum monthly	0.0	1.0	0.8	0.5	0.7	0.9	1.4	2.1	2.7	3.7	0.4	1.3	0.0
Date	1974	1979	1983	1981	1984	1983	1972	1978	1973	1985	1975	1983	1974
Maximum in 24 hrs	3.7	2.3	2.2	1.4	0.9	1.5	1.9	3.4	3.2	3.9	2.0	3.0	3.9
Date	1981	1985	1981	1983	1985	1981	1981	1981	1982	1983	1979	1985	1983
SNOW, ICE PELLETS													
Maximum monthly	96.1	100.8	113.9	71.4	5.8	0.0	0.0	0.0	T	39.0	75.6	105.5	113.9
Date	1976	1984	1985	1977	1985	—	—	—	1981	1983	1981	1979	1985
Maximum in 24 hrs	19.9	27.5	32.3	15.7	5.8	0.0	0.0	0.0	T	15.3	19.9	29.2	32.3
Date	1984	1978	1982	1983	1985	—	—	—	1981	1982	1981	1981	1982
WIND (Resultant)													
Mean speed (mph)	7.8	8.2	4.9	5.5	5.8	5.7	4.5	4.2	4.3	6.8	6.8	7.0	6.0

YAKUTAT

Elev. 28'　　　**59° 31'N — 139° 40'W**　　　# Alaska

NORMALS, MEANS, EXTREMES

	JAN	FEB	MAR	APR	MAY	JUN	JUL	AUG	SEP	OCT	NOV	DEC	YEAR
TEMPERATURE													
Normal daily maximum	30.1	34.8	37.2	43.2	49.7	55.6	59.5	59.7	55.3	47.2	38.4	32.7	45.3
Normal daily minimum	16.3	20.6	22.1	28.7	35.8	43.2	47.5	46.3	41.1	34.4	26.5	20.6	31.9
Normal monthly	23.2	27.7	29.7	36.0	42.8	49.4	53.5	53.0	48.2	40.8	32.5	26.7	38.6
Extreme highest	55	54	59	68	79	81	84	86	77	63	55	52	86
Extreme highest date	1981	1963	1981	1976	1963	1961	1955	1957	1957	1967	1976	1960	1957
Extreme lowest	-22	-20	-20	3	21	29	35	29	21	6	-6	-24	-24
Extreme lowest date	1952	1969	1972	1948	1972	1971	1968	1974	1971	1966	1966	1964	1964
DEGREE DAYS BASE 65° F													
Heating	1296	1044	1094	870	688	468	357	369	504	750	975	1190	9605
Cooling	0	0	0	0	0	0	0	0	0	0	0	0	0
% OF POSSIBLE SUNSHINE	na	na	na	na	na	na	na	na	na	na	na	na	na
AVERAGE SKY COVER													
Sunrise - Sunset	7.6	8.0	7.9	8.0	8.4	8.6	8.6	8.3	8.5	8.6	8.1	8.2	8.2
NUMBER OF DAYS (Sunrise-Sunset)													
Clear	5.5	4.1	4.2	3.9	2.4	1.6	2.0	3.3	2.5	3.0	4.1	4.3	40.9
Partly cloudy	3.6	3.1	4.2	4.6	4.6	4.6	4.5	4.1	3.6	2.6	2.8	2.9	45.2
Cloudy	21.9	21.0	22.6	21.5	24.1	23.8	24.5	23.6	23.9	25.4	23.1	23.8	279.1
Precipitation .01" or more	18.6	18.2	19.3	17.9	19.1	16.7	18.0	18.3	20.6	24.2	20.7	21.6	233.1
Snow, Ice pellets 1.0" or more	8.5	9.2	9.0	5.1	0.6	0.0	0.0	0.0	0.0	1.6	5.3	9.5	48.9
Thunderstorms	*	*	*	*	0.1	0.0	0.1	0.2	0.3	0.7	0.4	0.2	2.0
Fog, Visibility 1/4 mile or less	2.2	2.8	2.5	2.1	2.2	3.0	3.8	5.6	3.5	0.8	0.9	2.0	31.4
Temperature Maximum:													
90° and above	0.0	0.0	0.0	0.0	0.3	0.6	1.4	1.0	0.1	0.0	0.0	0.0	3.4
32° and below	17.0	9.8	3.3	0.1	0.0	0.0	0.0	0.0	0.0	0.4	6.8	13.5	51.0
Temperature Minimum:													
32° and below	24.9	23.2	24.0	21.4	7.7	0.5	0.0	0.2	4.5	11.0	22.0	25.4	164.9
0° and below	5.6	3.0	1.1	0.0	0.0	0.0	0.0	0.0	0.0	0.0	0.6	2.7	13.0
RELATIVE HUMIDITY (%)													
Morning	81	84	86	90	92	94	96	95	95	91	87	83	90
Afternoon	79	77	73	70	72	74	78	79	78	80	81	82	77
PRECIPITATION (inches)													
Water Equivalent													
Normal	9.3	10.0	9.5	8.6	9.1	5.5	8.2	10.0	15.7	20.1	15.5	12.9	134.
Maximum monthly	31.8	32.1	27.3	19.1	18.9	16.2	21.4	26.9	29.2	36.8	43.8	29.8	43.8
Date	1985	1964	1979	1977	1965	1965	1959	1981	1975	1965	1956	1985	1956
Minimum monthly	1.5	1.6	2.0	0.7	2.7	0.5	1.7	2.8	9.0	6.6	3.2	3.7	0.5
Date	1950	1979	1958	1948	1960	1946	1957	1954	1946	1950	1985	1983	1946
Maximum in 24 hrs	5.1	4.9	7.8	3.9	4.9	6.0	5.3	5.5	7.8	6.9	7.1	6.1	7.8
Date	1962	1964	1979	1966	1965	1979	1959	1965	1974	1963	1956	1963	1974
SNOW, ICE PELLETS													
Maximum monthly	75.5	87.3	111.0	55.6	15.0	T	0.0	0.0	T	36.0	77.1	91.6	111.0
Date	1975	1965	1959	1985	1965	1984	—	—	1983	1966	1975	1957	1959
Maximum in 24 hrs	23.5	20.7	32.4	18.6	10.0	T	0.0	0.0	T	14.7	17.3	23.1	32.4
Date	1971	1959	1960	1982	1965	1984	—	—	1983	1956	1961	1961	1960
WIND (Resultant)													
Mean speed (mph)	7.6	7.8	7.3	7.3	7.7	7.2	6.7	6.5	7.0	8.2	7.6	8.0	7.4

FLAGSTAFF

Elev. 7006' 35° 08'N — 111° 40'W **Arizona**

NORMALS, MEANS, EXTREMES

	JAN	FEB	MAR	APR	MAY	JUN	JUL	AUG	SEP	OCT	NOV	DEC	YEAR
TEMPERATURE													
Normal daily maximum	41.7	44.5	48.6	57.1	66.7	77.6	81.9	78.9	74.1	63.7	51.0	43.6	60.8
Normal daily minimum	14.7	16.9	20.4	25.9	32.9	40.9	50.3	48.7	40.9	30.6	21.5	15.9	30.0
Normal monthly	28.2	30.7	34.5	41.5	49.8	59.3	66.1	63.8	57.5	47.2	36.3	29.8	45.4
Extreme highest	66	70	73	78	87	96	97	92	90	85	74	68	97
Extreme highest date	1971	1977	1966	1981	1974	1970	1973	1978	1950	1980	1977	1950	1973
Extreme lowest	-22	-23	-16	-2	14	22	32	24	23	-2	-13	-23	-23
Extreme lowest date	1971	1985	1966	1975	1975	1955	1955	1968	1971	1971	1958	1978	1985
DEGREE DAYS BASE 65° F													
Heating	1141	960	946	702	468	194	34	76	229	552	861	1091	7254
Cooling	0	0	0	0	0	20	68	39	0	0	0	0	127
% OF POSSIBLE SUNSHINE	75	71	71	80	88	87	70	77	80	76	73	71	77
AVERAGE SKY COVER													
Sunrise - Sunset	5.3	5.1	5.2	4.6	3.9	2.9	5.4	5.0	3.6	3.6	4.2	4.8	4.5
NUMBER OF DAYS (Sunrise-Sunset)													
Clear	12.4	11.4	11.8	13.0	15.8	19.1	8.8	10.3	16.0	17.2	15.5	13.9	165.1
Partly cloudy	6.0	6.0	7.7	8.4	8.9	7.4	13.1	12.9	9.6	6.9	6.3	6.4	99.4
Cloudy	12.7	10.9	11.5	8.6	6.3	3.6	9.1	7.8	4.5	6.8	8.2	10.7	100.8
Precipitation .01" or more	7.5	6.5	8.4	5.8	4.1	2.5	11.8	11.0	6.4	4.7	5.4	6.2	80.2
Snow, Ice pellets 1.0" or more	4.2	3.8	5.1	2.5	0.7	0.0	0.0	0.0	*	0.6	2.0	3.4	22.3
Thunderstorms	*	0.3	0.6	1.3	2.6	3.7	16.6	15.7	6.7	2.2	0.7	0.2	50.5
Fog, Visibility 1/4 mile or less	1.8	1.8	1.6	1.2	0.2	*	0.1	0.3	0.5	0.9	1.1	1.8	11.4
Temperature Maximum:													
90° and above	0.0	0.0	0.0	0.0	0.0	1.2	1.5	0.3	*	0.0	0.0	0.0	3.1
32° and below	4.7	2.6	1.9	0.2	0.0	0.0	0.0	0.0	0.0	0.1	1.2	4.5	15.2
Temperature Minimum:													
32° and below	30.3	27.7	29.9	25.6	14.4	3.2	0.1	0.1	2.8	18.7	28.0	30.2	210.8
0° and below	3.5	1.5	0.7	0.1	0.0	0.0	0.0	0.0	0.0	*	0.5	2.1	8.4
RELATIVE HUMIDITY (%)													
Morning	74	73	71	66	63	54	69	76	74	71	71	72	70
Afternoon	51	44	41	32	26	20	39	43	37	36	43	52	39
PRECIPITATION (inches)													
Water Equivalent													
Normal	2.1	1.9	2.1	1.3	0.7	0.5	2.4	2.6	1.4	1.5	1.6	2.2	20.8
Maximum monthly	6.5	7.8	6.7	5.6	2.1	2.9	5.2	5.5	6.7	9.8	6.6	7.3	9.8
Date	1980	1980	1970	1965	1979	1955	1964	1951	1983	1972	1985	1967	1972
Minimum monthly	0.0	T	T	0.0	T	0.0	0.3	0.2	T	T	T	T	0.0
Date	1972	1967	1972	1962	1974	1971	1963	1962	1973	1952	1980	1958	1972
Maximum in 24 hrs	2.1	2.5	2.9	1.7	1.1	2.7	2.5	2.6	3.4	2.7	3.6	3.1	3.6
Date	1979	1980	1970	1985	1965	1956	1964	1951	1965	1972	1978	1951	1978
SNOW, ICE PELLETS													
Maximum monthly	63.4	42.1	77.4	58.3	8.2	T	0.0	0.0	2.0	24.7	40.7	86.0	86.0
Date	1980	1969	1973	1965	1975	1955	—	—	1965	1971	1985	1967	1967
Maximum in 24 hrs	23.1	19.9	26.3	17.2	6.6	T	0.0	0.0	2.0	13.5	18.4	27.3	27.3
Date	1980	1976	1970	1977	1965	1955	—	—	1965	1974	1985	1967	1967
WIND (Resultant)													
Mean speed (mph)	7.5	7.3	8.1	8.5	7.9	7.6	5.9	5.7	6.3	6.4	7.4	7.3	7.2

PHOENIX
Elev. 1110' 33° 26'N — 112° 01'W ## Arizona

NORMALS, MEANS, EXTREMES

	JAN	FEB	MAR	APR	MAY	JUN	JUL	AUG	SEP	OCT	NOV	DEC	YEAR
TEMPERATURE													
Normal daily maximum	65.2	69.7	74.5	83.1	92.4	102.3	105.0	102.3	98.2	87.7	74.3	66.4	85.1
Normal daily minimum	39.4	42.5	46.7	53.0	61.5	70.6	79.5	77.5	70.9	59.1	46.9	40.2	57.3
Normal monthly	52.3	56.1	60.6	68.1	77.0	86.5	92.3	89.9	84.6	73.4	60.6	53.3	71.2
Extreme highest	88	89	95	104	113	117	118	116	118	107	93	88	118
Extreme highest date	1971	1963	1972	1949	1984	1979	1958	1975	1950	1980	1980	1950	1958
Extreme lowest	17	22	25	32	40	50	61	60	47	34	25	22	17
Extreme lowest date	1950	1948	1966	1945	1967	1944	1944	1942	1965	1971	1938	1948	1950
DEGREE DAYS BASE 65° F													
Heating	394	269	187	52	0	0	0	0	0	13	159	368	1442
Cooling	0	20	51	142	376	645	846	772	588	273	27	6	3746
% OF POSSIBLE SUNSHINE	78	80	83	88	93	94	85	85	89	88	83	77	85
AVERAGE SKY COVER													
Sunrise - Sunset	4.7	4.5	4.4	3.3	2.6	1.9	3.7	3.2	2.2	2.7	3.5	4.1	3.4
NUMBER OF DAYS (Sunrise-Sunset)													
Clear	13.8	12.7	14.5	17.4	21.1	23.4	16.4	17.6	21.9	20.4	17.4	15.2	211.6
Partly cloudy	6.9	6.7	7.9	7.1	6.3	4.5	10.3	9.6	5.1	6.1	6.3	6.2	83.1
Cloudy	10.3	8.8	8.6	5.5	3.6	2.2	4.4	3.8	3.0	4.5	6.4	9.6	70.6
Precipitation .01" or more	3.9	3.9	3.5	1.8	0.9	0.7	4.3	4.7	3.0	2.7	2.5	3.8	35.6
Snow, Ice pellets 1.0" or more	0.0	0.0	0.0	0.0	0.0	0.0	0.0	0.0	0.0	0.0	0.0	0.0	0.0
Thunderstorms	0.3	0.5	0.8	0.7	0.9	1.0	6.3	7.2	3.7	1.2	0.5	0.7	23.8
Fog, Visibility 1/4 mile or less	0.6	0.2	0.1	0.0	0.0	0.0	0.0	0.0	0.0	*	0.2	0.5	1.6
Temperature Maximum:													
90° and above	0.0	0.0	1.4	8.6	22.6	29.1	31.0	30.8	27.4	13.8	0.4	0.0	164.9
32° and below	0.0	0.0	0.0	0.0	0.0	0.0	0.0	0.0	0.0	0.0	0.0	0.0	0.0
Temperature Minimum:													
32° and below	4.3	1.6	0.5	0.0	0.0	0.0	0.0	0.0	0.0	0.0	0.2	2.1	8.7
0° and below	0.0	0.0	0.0	0.0	0.0	0.0	0.0	0.0	0.0	0.0	0.0	0.0	0.0
RELATIVE HUMIDITY (%)													
Morning	68	61	58	44	36	32	45	51	51	52	59	68	52
Afternoon	32	27	24	16	13	12	20	23	23	23	28	34	23
PRECIPITATION (inches)													
Water Equivalent													
Normal	0.7	0.5	0.8	0.2	0.1	0.1	0.7	1.0	0.6	0.6	0.5	0.8	7.1
Maximum monthly	2.4	2.2	4.1	2.1	1.0	1.7	5.1	5.5	4.2	4.4	3.0	3.9	5.5
Date	1955	1944	1941	1941	1976	1972	1984	1951	1939	1972	1952	1967	1951
Minimum monthly	0.0	0.0	0.0	0.0	0.0	0.0	T	T	0.0	0.0	0.0	0.0	0.0
Date	1972	1967	1959	1962	1983	1983	1947	1975	1973	1973	1980	1981	1983
Maximum in 24 hrs	1.3	1.2	2.0	1.3	0.9	1.6	2.7	3.0	2.4	2.2	1.1	1.8	3.0
Date	1951	1978	1983	1941	1976	1972	1984	1943	1970	1972	1978	1967	1943
SNOW, ICE PELLETS													
Maximum monthly	T	0.6	T	T	0.0	0.0	0.0	0.0	0.0	0.0	0.0	0.1	0.6
Date	1962	1939	1976	1949	—	—	—	—	—	—	—	1985	1939
Maximum in 24 hrs	T	0.6	T	T	0.0	0.0	0.0	0.0	0.0	0.0	0.0	0.1	0.6
Date	1962	1939	1976	1949	—	—	—	—	—	—	—	1985	1939
WIND (Resultant)													
Mean speed (mph)	5.3	5.9	6.7	7.0	7.1	6.9	7.2	6.7	6.4	5.9	5.4	5.2	6.3

TUCSON

Elev. 2584'   32° 07'N — 110° 56'W   Arizona

NORMALS, MEANS, EXTREMES

	JAN	FEB	MAR	APR	MAY	JUN	JUL	AUG	SEP	OCT	NOV	DEC	YEAR
TEMPERATURE													
Normal daily maximum	64.1	67.4	71.8	80.1	88.8	98.5	98.5	95.9	93.5	84.1	72.2	65.0	81.7
Normal daily minimum	38.1	40.0	43.8	49.7	57.5	67.4	73.8	72.0	67.3	56.7	45.2	39.0	54.2
Normal monthly	51.1	53.7	57.8	64.9	73.2	83.0	86.2	84.0	80.4	70.4	58.7	52.0	67.9
Extreme highest	87	92	92	102	107	111	111	109	107	101	90	84	111
Extreme highest date	1953	1957	1950	1943	1958	1985	1983	1944	1983	1980	1947	1954	1985
Extreme lowest	16	20	20	27	38	47	62	61	44	26	24	16	16
Extreme lowest date	1949	1955	1965	1945	1950	1955	1982	1956	1965	1971	1979	1974	1974
DEGREE DAYS BASE 65° F													
Heating	431	326	246	86	8	0	0	0	0	30	204	403	1734
Cooling	0	12	22	86	262	537	657	589	462	198	15	0	2840
% OF POSSIBLE SUNSHINE	80	84	86	92	94	93	78	82	87	88	85	80	86
AVERAGE SKY COVER													
Sunrise - Sunset	4.7	4.4	4.5	3.3	2.7	2.2	5.2	4.4	2.9	2.9	3.5	4.4	3.8
NUMBER OF DAYS (Sunrise-Sunset)													
Clear	13.7	13.0	14.7	17.4	20.6	21.8	10.0	12.8	19.6	20.0	17.6	15.0	196.3
Partly cloudy	7.0	6.7	6.8	7.2	6.5	5.9	12.4	11.9	6.7	6.3	6.0	6.0	89.5
Cloudy	10.3	8.6	9.5	5.3	4.0	2.3	8.5	6.3	3.7	4.6	6.3	10.0	79.5
Precipitation .01" or more	4.5	3.6	4.2	2.0	1.3	1.6	10.6	9.2	4.8	3.3	2.9	4.3	52.5
Snow, Ice pellets 1.0" or more	0.1	0.2	0.1	*	0.0	0.0	0.0	0.0	0.0	0.0	*	0.1	0.5
Thunderstorms	0.4	0.2	0.4	0.6	1.2	2.5	14.1	13.3	5.7	1.9	0.4	0.3	41.2
Fog, Visibility 1/4 mile or less	0.2	0.2	*	0.0	0.0	0.0	0.0	0.0	*	0.0	0.2	0.4	1.0
Temperature Maximum:													
90° and above	0.0	*	0.2	3.8	16.8	28.0	29.3	28.5	23.4	8.2	*	0.0	138.3
32° and below	0.0	0.0	0.0	0.0	0.0	0.0	0.0	0.0	0.0	0.0	0.0	0.0	0.0
Temperature Minimum:													
32° and below	6.4	4.4	1.2	*	0.0	0.0	0.0	0.0	0.0	*	1.4	5.1	18.6
0° and below	0.0	0.0	0.0	0.0	0.0	0.0	0.0	0.0	0.0	0.0	0.0	0.0	0.0
RELATIVE HUMIDITY (%)													
Morning	63	58	53	42	34	32	57	65	55	52	54	61	52
Afternoon	33	27	23	16	13	13	28	33	27	25	28	34	25
PRECIPITATION (inches)													
Water Equivalent													
Normal	0.8	0.6	0.6	0.3	0.1	0.2	2.4	2.1	1.3	0.8	0.6	0.9	11.1
Maximum monthly	2.9	2.9	2.2	1.6	0.8	1.4	6.1	7.9	5.1	4.9	1.9	5.0	7.9
Date	1979	1980	1952	1951	1943	1954	1981	1955	1964	1983	1952	1965	1955
Minimum monthly	T	0.0	0.0	0.0	0.0	0.0	0.2	0.2	0.0	0.0	0.0	0.0	0.0
Date	1970	1972	1956	1972	1974	1983	1947	1976	1953	1982	1980	1981	1983
Maximum in 24 hrs	1.4	1.4	1.1	0.7	0.8	1.2	3.9	2.4	3.0	3.5	1.8	1.5	3.9
Date	1946	1942	1952	1952	1943	1954	1958	1961	1964	1983	1968	1967	1958
SNOW, ICE PELLETS													
Maximum monthly	4.7	3.9	5.7	2.0	0.0	0.0	0.0	0.0	0.0	T	6.4	6.8	6.8
Date	1949	1965	1964	1976	—	—	—	—	—	1959	1958	1971	1971
Maximum in 24 hrs	3.5	3.9	5.7	2.0	0.0	0.0	0.0	0.0	0.0	T	6.4	6.8	6.8
Date	1949	1965	1964	1976	—	—	—	—	—	1959	1958	1971	1971
WIND (Resultant)													
Mean speed (mph)	7.8	8.1	8.5	8.9	8.6	8.6	8.3	7.7	8.2	8.1	8.1	7.8	8.2

WINSLOW

Elev. 4895'   35° 01'N — 110° 44'W   # Arizona

NORMALS, MEANS, EXTREMES

	JAN	FEB	MAR	APR	MAY	JUN	JUL	AUG	SEP	OCT	NOV	DEC	YEAR
TEMPERATURE													
Normal daily maximum	45.0	53.2	60.7	70.0	79.9	91.0	94.5	91.1	85.2	73.1	57.9	46.0	70.6
Normal daily minimum	19.0	23.6	29.1	36.0	44.4	53.6	63.0	61.1	52.7	40.1	27.8	19.3	39.1
Normal monthly	32.0	38.4	44.9	53.0	62.2	72.3	78.8	76.1	69.0	56.6	42.9	32.7	54.9
Extreme highest	75	78	85	92	101	106	109	103	99	93	79	74	109
Extreme highest date	1971	1957	1971	1943	1951	1970	1971	1979	1950	1972	1980	1958	1971
Extreme lowest	-18	-7	6	16	23	35	46	41	31	13	-1	-12	-18
Extreme lowest date	1937	1939	1948	1975	1964	1979	1935	1968	1978	1970	1952	1967	1937
DEGREE DAYS BASE 65° F													
Heating	1023	745	623	360	132	10	0	0	12	270	663	1001	4839
Cooling	0	0	0	0	45	229	428	344	132	9	0	0	1187
% OF POSSIBLE SUNSHINE	na	na	na	na	na	na	na	na	na	na	na	na	na
AVERAGE SKY COVER													
Sunrise - Sunset	5.3	4.9	4.7	3.9	3.5	2.9	5.0	4.5	3.1	3.1	3.9	4.7	4.1
NUMBER OF DAYS (Sunrise-Sunset)													
Clear	12.2	11.5	12.8	14.8	17.2	19.8	10.7	12.1	18.0	18.6	15.9	13.7	177.4
Partly cloudy	7.1	6.9	8.8	8.6	8.5	6.6	12.2	12.6	7.9	6.7	6.4	6.8	99.3
Cloudy	11.7	9.8	9.5	6.5	5.3	3.5	8.1	6.3	4.0	5.7	7.6	10.5	88.6
Precipitation .01" or more	4.0	4.4	4.6	3.3	2.9	2.1	7.4	8.9	5.3	3.9	3.0	4.4	54.1
Snow, Ice pellets 1.0" or more	1.0	0.6	0.9	0.1	0.0	0.0	0.0	0.0	0.0	0.1	0.3	1.0	4.0
Thunderstorms	0.1	0.4	0.5	1.0	2.0	3.1	11.4	10.7	5.4	1.4	0.2	0.1	36.3
Fog, Visibility 1/4 mile or less	1.1	0.5	0.3	0.1	0.0	0.0	0.0	0.0	0.1	0.4	0.6	1.4	4.3
Temperature Maximum:													
90° and above	0.0	0.0	0.0	*	3.2	17.5	25.1	20.7	6.0	0.1	0.0	0.0	72.6
32° and below	5.3	0.5	0.0	0.0	0.0	0.0	0.0	0.0	0.0	0.0	0.2	3.5	9.6
Temperature Minimum:													
32° and below	28.5	24.2	19.2	9.6	1.5	0.0	0.0	0.0	0.1	5.3	20.0	28.2	136.6
0° and below	2.5	0.0	0.0	0.0	0.0	0.0	0.0	0.0	0.0	0.0	*	1.2	3.8
RELATIVE HUMIDITY (%)													
Morning	79	70	62	52	44	38	58	64	64	61	69	77	62
Afternoon	50	35	26	19	16	14	27	30	28	28	35	50	30
PRECIPITATION (inches)													
Water Equivalent													
Normal	0.4	0.4	0.5	0.3	0.3	0.3	1.1	1.4	0.8	0.9	0.4	0.5	7.6
Maximum monthly	1.6	2.0	2.0	1.5	1.3	3.2	2.8	4.8	2.5	5.6	1.6	3.7	5.6
Date	1935	1973	1973	1934	1979	1972	1946	1963	1975	1972	1952	1967	1972
Minimum monthly	T	T	T	T	T	0.0	0.0	0.1	0.0	0.0	0.0	T	0.0
Date	1984	1972	1971	1962	1977	1971	1962	1968	1957	1952	1932	1981	1971
Maximum in 24 hrs	0.7	0.7	1.0	0.4	0.9	2.1	1.6	2.0	1.2	2.2	0.8	1.5	2.2
Date	1980	1956	1984	1953	1969	1955	1982	1964	1983	1974	1973	1967	1974
SNOW, ICE PELLETS													
Maximum monthly	10.6	10.7	11.0	4.8	0.6	0.0	0.0	0.0	T	8.2	7.4	39.6	39.6
Date	1949	1973	1973	1977	1978	—	—	—	1945	1961	1952	1967	1967
Maximum in 24 hrs	6.4	8.0	4.7	2.9	0.6	0.0	0.0	0.0	T	6.6	4.8	17.0	17.0
Date	1980	1977	1970	1977	1978	—	—	—	1945	1961	1966	1967	1967
WIND (Resultant)													
Mean speed (mph)	7.1	8.5	10.6	11.3	10.9	10.6	9.1	8.4	8.2	7.7	7.3	6.7	8.9

YUMA
Elev. 194' 32° 39'N — 114° 36'W **Arizona**

NORMALS, MEANS, EXTREMES

	JAN	FEB	MAR	APR	MAY	JUN	JUL	AUG	SEP	OCT	NOV	DEC	YEAR
TEMPERATURE													
Normal daily maximum	68.6	73.9	78.5	85.7	93.6	102.9	106.8	105.3	101.4	90.9	77.4	69.1	87.8
Normal daily minimum	43.2	46.1	49.9	55.6	63.0	71.4	80.4	79.5	73.1	61.8	50.2	43.8	59.8
Normal monthly	55.9	60.0	64.2	70.7	78.3	87.2	93.6	92.4	87.3	76.4	63.8	56.5	73.8
Extreme highest	88	92	98	106	116	116	119	120	115	112	98	86	120
Extreme highest date	1971	1981	1966	1980	1983	1985	1958	1981	1982	1980	1962	1958	1981
Extreme lowest	24	28	32	41	46	54	63	63	53	35	30	27	24
Extreme lowest date	1971	1956	1951	1977	1967	1955	1956	1968	1965	1971	1958	1968	1971
DEGREE DAYS BASE 65° F													
Heating	290	176	104	37	0	0	0	0	0	8	92	276	983
Cooling	8	36	80	208	412	666	887	849	669	361	56	12	4244
% OF POSSIBLE SUNSHINE	83	87	90	94	96	97	90	91	93	92	86	82	90
AVERAGE SKY COVER													
Sunrise - Sunset	4.3	3.8	3.6	2.5	1.9	1.3	2.8	2.5	1.7	2.2	3.1	3.8	2.8
NUMBER OF DAYS (Sunrise-Sunset)													
Clear	15.2	15.1	17.2	20.6	23.5	25.4	20.1	21.6	24.4	22.8	19.0	16.7	241.6
Partly cloudy	7.0	6.7	7.4	5.9	5.3	3.6	7.7	6.4	3.8	5.3	5.8	6.5	71.4
Cloudy	8.8	6.5	6.4	3.6	2.2	1.0	3.3	3.0	1.8	2.8	5.2	7.8	52.3
Precipitation .01" or more	2.5	1.7	1.9	0.8	0.3	0.2	1.1	2.3	1.2	1.2	1.5	2.5	17.1
Snow, Ice pellets 1.0" or more	0.0	0.0	0.0	0.0	0.0	0.0	0.0	0.0	0.0	0.0	0.0	0.0	0.0
Thunderstorms	0.1	0.2	0.2	0.2	0.1	0.3	1.6	2.2	1.3	0.7	0.1	0.2	7.2
Fog, Visibility 1/4 mile or less	0.5	0.2	0.0	0.0	0.0	0.0	0.0	*	0.0	0.0	0.2	0.6	1.5
Temperature Maximum:													
90° and above	0.0	0.1	2.3	9.8	22.2	28.6	30.9	30.8	27.9	16.6	1.1	0.0	170.3
32° and below	0.0	0.0	0.0	0.0	0.0	0.0	0.0	0.0	0.0	0.0	0.0	0.0	0.0
Temperature Minimum:													
32° and below	0.8	*	0.0	0.0	0.0	0.0	0.0	0.0	0.0	0.0	0.0	0.7	1.5
0° and below	0.0	0.0	0.0	0.0	0.0	0.0	0.0	0.0	0.0	0.0	0.0	0.0	0.0
RELATIVE HUMIDITY (%)													
Morning	57	56	53	48	45	42	50	56	57	54	56	59	53
Afternoon	28	24	21	17	15	13	22	24	24	23	27	32	23
PRECIPITATION (inches)													
Water Equivalent													
Normal	0.3	0.2	0.1	0.1	0.0	0.0	0.1	0.4	0.2	0.2	0.2	0.3	2.6
Maximum monthly	2.1	1.8	1.1	1.2	0.3	0.2	2.1	2.9	2.4	2.6	1.6	2.0	2.9
Date	1979	1958	1982	1965	1965	1972	1984	1977	1963	1957	1969	1982	1977
Minimum monthly	T	0.0	0.0	0.0	0.0	0.0	0.0	0.0	0.0	0.0	0.0	0.0	0.0
Date	1975	1974	1972	1982	1983	1983	1983	1976	1980	1981	1980	1981	1983
Maximum in 24 hrs	1.2	1.3	0.6	1.0	0.3	0.2	1.4	2.7	2.4	2.2	1.4	1.8	2.7
Date	1979	1958	1973	1965	1965	1972	1984	1977	1963	1972	1969	1982	1977
SNOW, ICE PELLETS													
Maximum monthly	0.0	0.0	0.0	0.0	0.0	0.0	0.0	0.0	0.0	0.0	0.0	T	T
Date	—	—	—	—	—	—	—	—	—	—	—	1967	1967
Maximum in 24 hrs	0.0	0.0	0.0	0.0	0.0	0.0	0.0	0.0	0.0	0.0	0.0	T	T
Date	—	—	—	—	—	—	—	—	—	—	—	1967	1967
WIND (Resultant)													
Mean speed (mph)	7.4	7.4	7.9	8.3	8.3	8.5	9.5	8.9	7.3	6.6	6.9	7.2	7.8

FORT SMITH

Elev. 447'   35° 20'N — 94° 22'W   **Arkansas**

NORMALS, MEANS, EXTREMES

	JAN	FEB	MAR	APR	MAY	JUN	JUL	AUG	SEP	OCT	NOV	DEC	YEAR
TEMPERATURE													
Normal daily maximum	48.4	53.8	62.5	73.7	81.0	88.5	93.6	92.9	85.7	75.9	61.9	52.1	72.5
Normal daily minimum	26.6	30.9	38.5	49.1	58.2	66.3	70.5	68.9	62.1	49.0	37.7	30.2	49.0
Normal monthly	37.5	42.4	50.5	61.4	69.6	77.4	82.1	80.9	73.9	62.5	49.8	41.2	60.8
Extreme highest	81	86	94	93	98	105	111	110	106	96	86	82	111
Extreme highest date	1952	1962	1974	1962	1951	1953	1954	1964	1947	1963	1955	1951	1954
Extreme lowest	-10	-9	7	22	35	47	50	51	33	22	8	-1	-10
Extreme lowest date	1977	1951	1948	1975	1954	1972	1972	1967	1967	1952	1976	1983	1977
DEGREE DAYS BASE 65° F													
Heating	853	633	461	147	33	0	0	0	13	143	456	738	3477
Cooling	0	0	11	39	175	375	530	493	280	66	0	0	1969
% OF POSSIBLE SUNSHINE	50	55	56	59	63	69	73	72	66	65	55	51	61
AVERAGE SKY COVER													
Sunrise - Sunset	6.4	6.1	6.3	6.0	6.0	5.4	5.0	4.8	5.0	4.9	5.5	6.0	5.6
NUMBER OF DAYS (Sunrise-Sunset)													
Clear	8.8	8.8	8.5	9.0	8.2	9.8	11.8	12.3	11.9	13.4	11.0	9.7	123.1
Partly cloudy	6.3	6.0	7.3	6.9	9.7	10.3	10.8	10.7	8.5	6.8	6.0	6.7	95.8
Cloudy	15.9	13.5	15.3	14.1	13.1	9.9	8.5	8.1	9.6	10.8	12.9	14.6	146.3
Precipitation .01" or more	7.6	7.7	9.3	10.0	10.5	8.2	7.7	7.1	7.5	6.7	6.9	7.1	96.0
Snow, Ice pellets 1.0" or more	1.0	0.8	0.3	0.0	0.0	0.0	0.0	0.0	0.0	0.0	0.3	0.4	2.8
Thunderstorms	1.2	1.6	4.7	6.8	8.4	7.6	7.4	6.6	4.4	3.2	2.6	1.5	56.0
Fog, Visibility 1/4 mile or less	2.4	1.6	1.2	0.5	1.0	0.6	0.8	0.7	1.4	2.0	1.4	1.7	14.9
Temperature Maximum:													
90° and above	0.0	0.0	0.2	0.3	0.9	11.3	22.8	21.4	10.0	1.7	0.0	0.0	68.6
32° and below	4.3	1.5	0.1	0.0	0.0	0.0	0.0	0.0	0.0	0.0	*	1.6	7.5
Temperature Minimum:													
32° and below	24.2	18.0	7.7	0.9	0.0	0.0	0.0	0.0	0.0	0.8	8.7	19.9	80.1
0° and below	0.3	*	0.0	0.0	0.0	0.0	0.0	0.0	0.0	0.0	0.0	0.1	0.4
RELATIVE HUMIDITY (%)													
Morning	76	74	72	74	82	82	80	80	83	81	79	78	78
Afternoon	60	57	53	52	57	57	54	53	55	51	56	60	55
PRECIPITATION (inches)													
Water Equivalent													
Normal	1.8	2.5	3.8	4.2	4.7	3.6	3.1	3.0	3.2	3.2	3.5	2.8	39.9
Maximum monthly	11.3	7.9	8.5	10.3	12.0	10.4	10.4	6.5	8.9	12.0	14.0	10.0	14.0
Date	1949	1951	1953	1957	1957	1958	1960	1971	1974	1951	1946	1971	1946
Minimum monthly	0.3	0.1	0.8	0.9	0.7	0.3	0.1	0.4	0.0	T	0.5	0.2	T
Date	1976	1947	1971	1955	1970	1954	1947	1973	1956	1964	1954	1981	1964
Maximum in 24 hrs	5.4	4.4	3.6	5.1	5.5	3.4	7.1	5.0	3.9	5.9	6.9	5.7	7.1
Date	1949	1985	1953	1964	1982	1977	1960	1971	1974	1951	1973	1971	1960
SNOW, ICE PELLETS													
Maximum monthly	13.0	11.5	5.3	T	0.0	0.0	0.0	0.0	0.0	0.0	4.7	7.2	13.0
Date	1977	1960	1968	1973	—	—	—	—	—	—	1976	1975	1977
Maximum in 24 hrs	7.4	5.8	5.3	T	0.0	0.0	0.0	0.0	0.0	0.0	4.7	7.1	7.4
Date	1977	1978	1968	1973	—	—	—	—	—	—	1976	1975	1977
WIND (Resultant)													
Mean speed (mph)	8.1	8.5	9.4	8.9	7.7	6.6	6.2	6.3	6.6	6.7	7.7	8.1	7.6

LITTLE ROCK

Elev. 257'   34° 44'N — 92° 14'W   **Arkansas**

NORMALS, MEANS, EXTREMES

	JAN	FEB	MAR	APR	MAY	JUN	JUL	AUG	SEP	OCT	NOV	DEC	YEAR
TEMPERATURE													
Normal daily maximum	49.8	54.5	63.2	73.8	81.7	89.5	92.7	92.3	85.6	75.8	62.4	53.2	72.9
Normal daily minimum	29.9	33.6	41.2	50.9	59.2	67.5	71.4	69.6	63.0	50.4	40.0	33.2	50.8
Normal monthly	39.9	44.1	52.2	62.4	70.5	78.5	82.1	81.0	74.3	63.1	51.2	43.2	61.9
Extreme highest	83	84	91	92	98	104	109	108	106	97	86	80	109
Extreme highest date	1950	1980	1974	1955	1964	1954	1980	1980	1947	1963	1955	1956	1980
Extreme lowest	-4	-5	11	28	40	46	54	52	37	30	17	-1	-5
Extreme lowest date	1962	1951	1951	1971	1971	1969	1972	1967	1942	1981	1976	1963	1951
DEGREE DAYS BASE 65° F													
Heating	778	585	417	124	18	0	0	0	8	132	414	676	3152
Cooling	0	0	20	46	188	405	530	496	287	73	0	0	2045
% OF POSSIBLE SUNSHINE	46	54	57	62	68	73	71	73	68	69	56	48	62
AVERAGE SKY COVER													
Sunrise - Sunset	6.5	6.0	6.2	6.1	6.0	5.4	5.5	5.0	5.2	4.5	5.5	6.2	5.7
NUMBER OF DAYS (Sunrise-Sunset)													
Clear	8.6	9.1	8.6	8.7	8.0	9.5	8.8	11.6	11.2	14.4	11.0	9.2	118.7
Partly cloudy	6.1	5.7	7.0	7.5	10.8	11.6	12.9	10.9	8.6	7.1	5.9	5.9	99.9
Cloudy	16.3	13.5	15.4	13.8	12.3	8.9	9.3	8.5	10.1	9.5	13.1	16.0	146.6
Precipitation .01" or more	9.7	8.9	10.4	10.3	10.0	8.1	8.3	7.1	7.2	6.7	8.0	9.0	103.6
Snow, Ice pellets 1.0" or more	1.0	0.5	0.2	0.0	0.0	0.0	0.0	0.0	0.0	0.0	0.1	0.3	2.0
Thunderstorms	1.8	2.4	4.8	6.5	7.2	7.5	8.7	6.3	3.8	2.4	3.0	1.8	56.4
Fog, Visibility 1/4 mile or less	2.8	1.8	1.1	0.8	0.8	0.3	0.5	0.7	1.0	1.8	1.8	2.5	16.0
Temperature Maximum:													
90° and above	0.0	0.0	*	0.1	3.7	16.0	22.1	19.3	8.5	1.4	0.0	0.0	71.2
32° and below	4.0	1.0	0.1	0.0	0.0	0.0	0.0	0.0	0.0	0.0	0.0	1.5	6.7
Temperature Minimum:													
32° and below	21.4	14.8	4.4	0.4	0.0	0.0	0.0	0.0	0.0	0.2	5.4	15.6	62.2
0° and below	0.1	0.0	0.0	0.0	0.0	0.0	0.0	0.0	0.0	0.0	0.0	0.1	0.2
RELATIVE HUMIDITY (%)													
Morning	76	74	71	74	82	82	83	83	84	81	78	76	79
Afternoon	61	59	57	57	58	55	57	56	58	53	58	62	58
PRECIPITATION (inches)													
Water Equivalent													
Normal	3.9	3.8	4.6	5.4	5.2	3.6	3.6	3.0	4.2	2.8	4.3	4.2	49.2
Maximum monthly	12.5	11.0	9.4	14.2	12.7	7.8	7.6	14.4	10.1	15.3	9.7	11.5	15.3
Date	1950	1956	1953	1973	1968	1974	1951	1966	1978	1984	1982	1978	1984
Minimum monthly	0.7	0.5	0.7	1.0	0.6	T	0.8	0.1	0.2	0.0	0.2	1.2	T
Date	1961	1947	1966	1960	1970	1952	1942	1980	1956	1944	1949	1958	1952
Maximum in 24 hrs	5.1	5.1	3.4	7.9	7.7	4.6	3.4	7.3	4.0	5.1	5.0	3.6	7.9
Date	1969	1950	1944	1974	1955	1960	1959	1966	1967	1984	1957	1971	1974
SNOW, ICE PELLETS													
Maximum monthly	12.0	9.8	7.0	T	0.0	0.0	0.0	0.0	0.0	0.0	4.8	9.8	12.0
Date	1966	1979	1971	1983	—	—	—	—	—	—	1971	1963	1966
Maximum in 24 hrs	11.3	9.6	6.7	T	0.0	0.0	0.0	0.0	0.0	0.0	4.8	9.8	11.3
Date	1960	1966	1971	1973	—	—	—	—	—	—	1971	1963	1960
WIND (Resultant)													
Mean speed (mph)	8.7	9.1	9.8	9.2	7.8	7.4	6.8	6.5	6.8	6.9	8.1	8.4	7.9

BAKERSFIELD

Elev. 496' **35° 25'N — 119° 03'W** **California**

NORMALS, MEANS, EXTREMES

	JAN	FEB	MAR	APR	MAY	JUN	JUL	AUG	SEP	OCT	NOV	DEC	YEAR
TEMPERATURE													
Normal daily maximum	57.4	63.7	68.6	75.1	83.9	92.2	98.8	96.4	90.8	81.0	67.4	57.6	77.7
Normal daily minimum	38.9	42.6	45.5	50.1	57.2	64.3	70.1	68.5	63.8	54.9	44.9	38.7	53.3
Normal monthly	48.2	53.2	57.1	62.6	70.6	78.3	84.5	82.5	77.3	68.0	56.2	48.2	65.5
Extreme highest	82	85	92	101	107	114	115	112	112	103	91	83	115
Extreme highest date	1984	1977	1969	1981	1982	1976	1950	1981	1955	1980	1949	1979	1950
Extreme lowest	20	26	31	34	40	45	53	52	45	29	28	21	20
Extreme lowest date	1963	1949	1966	1984	1950	1953	1948	1942	1948	1971	1941	1962	1963
DEGREE DAYS BASE 65° F													
Heating	521	335	255	137	35	6	0	0	0	50	268	521	2128
Cooling	0	0	10	68	208	405	605	539	369	143	0	0	2347
% OF POSSIBLE SUNSHINE	na	na	na	na	na	na	na	na	na	na	na	na	na
AVERAGE SKY COVER													
Sunrise - Sunset	6.6	5.9	5.4	4.3	3.0	1.6	1.3	1.3	1.7	3.0	5.0	6.5	3.8
NUMBER OF DAYS (Sunrise-Sunset)													
Clear	7.1	7.7	10.2	13.1	18.5	23.5	26.6	26.1	23.9	19.5	11.8	7.3	195.3
Partly cloudy	8.1	8.5	9.5	9.1	8.4	4.6	3.0	3.6	4.2	6.7	8.1	7.5	81.3
Cloudy	15.8	12.1	11.3	7.8	4.2	1.9	1.3	1.4	1.9	4.8	10.0	16.2	88.6
Precipitation .01" or more	5.9	6.2	6.6	4.2	1.6	0.5	0.1	0.4	0.9	1.7	3.6	5.3	36.9
Snow, Ice pellets 1.0" or more	0.0	0.0	*	0.0	0.0	0.0	0.0	0.0	0.0	0.0	0.0	0.0	*
Thunderstorms	0.1	0.2	0.4	0.5	0.2	0.2	0.1	0.2	0.5	0.4	0.1	0.1	2.9
Fog, Visibility 1/4 mile or less	8.5	2.8	0.4	0.1	*	0.0	*	*	*	0.1	2.7	8.0	22.7
Temperature Maximum:													
90° and above	0.0	0.0	0.1	1.6	10.6	19.6	28.5	26.3	17.1	5.4	*	0.0	109.4
32° and below	0.0	0.0	0.0	0.0	0.0	0.0	0.0	0.0	0.0	0.0	0.0	0.0	0.0
Temperature Minimum:													
32° and below	4.2	0.9	0.2	0.0	0.0	0.0	0.0	0.0	0.0	0.1	0.2	3.9	9.5
0° and below	0.0	0.0	0.0	0.0	0.0	0.0	0.0	0.0	0.0	0.0	0.0	0.0	0.0
RELATIVE HUMIDITY (%)													
Morning	83	78	72	65	55	50	48	53	57	63	75	83	65
Afternoon	62	51	43	33	25	22	21	24	28	34	50	62	38
PRECIPITATION (inches)													
Water Equivalent													
Normal	0.9	1.0	0.8	0.7	0.2	0.0	0.0	0.0	0.1	0.3	0.6	0.6	5.7
Maximum monthly	2.8	4.6	4.6	2.6	2.3	1.1	0.3	1.1	1.0	1.8	3.0	1.8	4.6
Date	1943	1978	1938	1967	1971	1972	1965	1983	1976	1974	1960	1977	1978
Minimum monthly	T	0.0	T	0.0	0.0	0.0	0.0	0.0	0.0	0.0	0.0	T	0.0
Date	1972	1967	1972	1966	1982	1983	1983	1981	1981	1978	1959	1962	1983
Maximum in 24 hrs	1.0	3.0	1.6	1.0	1.4	1.1	0.3	1.0	0.6	1.5	1.5	1.1	3.0
Date	1954	1978	1938	1943	1971	1972	1965	1983	1978	1940	1960	1974	1978
SNOW, ICE PELLETS													
Maximum monthly	T	T	1.5	0.0	0.0	0.0	0.0	0.0	0.0	0.0	0.0	T	1.5
Date	1979	1953	1974	—	—	—	—	—	—	—	—	1968	1974
Maximum in 24 hrs	T	T	1.5	0.0	0.0	0.0	0.0	0.0	0.0	0.0	0.0	T	1.5
Date	1979	1953	1974	—	—	—	—	—	—	—	—	1968	1974
WIND (Resultant)													
Mean speed (mph)	5.2	5.8	6.5	7.1	7.9	7.9	7.2	6.8	6.2	5.5	5.1	5.0	6.4

BISHOP

Elev. 4110' 37° 22'N — 118° 22'W ## California

NORMALS, MEANS, EXTREMES

	JAN	FEB	MAR	APR	MAY	JUN	JUL	AUG	SEP	OCT	NOV	DEC	YEAR
TEMPERATURE													
Normal daily maximum	52.9	58.2	63.4	70.9	80.2	90.4	97.5	95.2	88.2	77.1	63.5	55.1	74.4
Normal daily minimum	21.4	25.9	29.5	35.8	43.5	50.8	56.3	53.8	46.8	37.4	27.7	22.1	37.6
Normal monthly	37.2	42.1	46.5	53.4	61.9	70.6	76.9	74.5	67.5	57.3	45.6	38.6	56.0
Extreme highest	77	78	87	93	101	109	109	107	106	97	84	78	109
Extreme highest date	1948	1951	1966	1981	1951	1954	1972	1981	1950	1980	1960	1958	1972
Extreme lowest	-7	-2	9	15	25	29	40	37	26	16	5	-4	-7
Extreme lowest date	1982	1969	1971	1953	1964	1967	1983	1959	1948	1970	1958	1967	1982
DEGREE DAYS BASE 65° F													
Heating	862	641	574	357	156	20	0	0	31	250	582	815	4288
Cooling	0	0	0	9	60	191	372	295	106	12	0	0	1045
% OF POSSIBLE SUNSHINE	na	na	na	na	na	na	na	na	na	na	na	na	na
AVERAGE SKY COVER													
Sunrise - Sunset	5.3	5.0	4.7	4.3	4.1	2.6	2.4	2.2	1.9	2.9	4.1	4.5	3.7
NUMBER OF DAYS (Sunrise-Sunset)													
Clear	11.5	11.0	13.0	13.7	14.8	20.2	21.9	22.9	23.2	19.7	14.9	14.3	201.0
Partly cloudy	8.0	7.5	8.9	9.0	9.8	6.8	6.7	6.0	4.7	6.7	7.9	7.4	89.3
Cloudy	11.6	9.8	9.0	7.3	6.4	3.0	2.4	2.2	2.1	4.7	7.2	9.3	75.0
Precipitation .01" or more	3.9	3.2	3.1	2.4	2.7	1.5	2.3	1.8	1.9	1.7	2.7	3.1	30.3
Snow, Ice pellets 1.0" or more	1.0	0.3	0.3	0.2	*	0.0	0.0	0.0	0.0	*	0.2	0.5	2.5
Thunderstorms	0.0	0.0	0.0	0.2	1.4	1.6	5.4	3.1	1.1	0.5	0.1	0.0	13.4
Fog, Visibility 1/4 mile or less	0.1	0.0	0.0	0.1	0.0	0.0	0.0	0.0	0.0	0.0	0.1	0.1	0.3
Temperature Maximum:													
90° and above	0.0	0.0	0.0	0.3	5.1	18.3	29.2	26.4	14.1	1.3	0.0	0.0	94.7
32° and below	0.7	0.1	0.0	0.0	0.0	0.0	0.0	0.0	0.0	0.0	0.0	0.2	0.9
Temperature Minimum:													
32° and below	29.2	24.2	20.9	8.6	1.0	0.1	0.0	0.0	0.2	6.4	23.5	29.3	143.4
0° and below	0.3	0.1	0.0	0.0	0.0	0.0	0.0	0.0	0.0	0.0	0.0	0.1	0.4
Afternoon	35	27	21	16	16	13	14	13	14	18	26	34	21
PRECIPITATION (inches)													
Water Equivalent													
Normal	1.3	0.9	0.4	0.3	0.3	0.1	0.1	0.1	0.1	0.1	0.4	1.0	5.6
Maximum monthly	8.9	6.0	2.0	2.2	1.3	1.2	1.4	0.6	1.1	1.5	2.5	5.7	8.9
Date	1969	1969	1952	1956	1962	1982	1976	1983	1975	1957	1960	1966	1969
Minimum monthly	0.0	T	0.0	0.0	0.0	0.0	0.0	0.0	0.0	0.0	0.0	0.0	0.0
Date	1976	1967	1972	1973	1983	1981	1982	1980	1974	1973	1976	1975	1983
Maximum in 24 hrs	3.3	3.6	1.4	1.5	0.9	0.7	0.8	0.4	0.7	1.0	1.7	3.3	3.6
Date	1952	1969	1974	1982	1953	1982	1976	1977	1982	1957	1950	1966	1969
SNOW, ICE PELLETS													
Maximum monthly	23.2	31.9	14.5	8.8	2.3	0.0	0.0	0.0	T	1.8	3.9	13.2	31.9
Date	1969	1969	1952	1956	1964	—	—	—	1955	1978	1964	1967	1969
Maximum in 24 hrs	18.0	14.2	7.5	8.8	2.3	0.0	0.0	0.0	T	1.8	3.9	6.7	18.0
Date	1969	1976	1952	1956	1964	—	—	—	1955	1978	1964	1967	1969

BLUE CANYON

Elev. 5280'   39° 17'N — 120° 42'W   **California**

NORMALS, MEANS, EXTREMES

	JAN	FEB	MAR	APR	MAY	JUN	JUL	AUG	SEP	OCT	NOV	DEC	YEAR
TEMPERATURE													
Normal daily maximum	43.5	44.9	45.3	51.3	60.3	69.2	77.7	76.5	72.4	62.8	51.4	46.3	58.5
Normal daily minimum	30.7	31.3	31.0	35.2	42.8	51.0	58.9	57.3	53.3	45.5	37.1	32.7	42.2
Normal monthly	37.1	38.1	38.2	43.3	51.6	60.1	68.3	66.9	62.9	54.2	44.3	39.5	50.4
Extreme highest	71	73	72	82	88	92	95	97	93	88	78	75	97
Extreme highest date	1962	1954	1966	1985	1984	1950	1972	1981	1955	1980	1976	1958	1981
Extreme lowest	5	6	9	17	21	28	37	35	27	17	13	3	3
Extreme lowest date	1950	1949	1956	1972	1950	1952	1983	1968	1971	1971	1945	1972	1972
DEGREE DAYS BASE 65° F													
Heating	865	753	831	658	432	200	35	76	132	356	621	791	5750
Cooling	0	0	0	7	14	53	137	135	66	21	0	0	433
% OF POSSIBLE SUNSHINE	na	na	na	na	na	na	na	na	na	na	na	na	na
AVERAGE SKY COVER													
Sunrise - Sunset	6.7	6.4	6.4	5.8	4.9	3.3	1.4	1.8	2.2	3.9	5.9	6.4	4.6
NUMBER OF DAYS (Sunrise-Sunset)													
Clear	8.7	8.1	8.7	9.6	12.0	18.5	26.1	24.7	22.4	16.5	10.2	8.8	174.4
Partly cloudy	5.5	5.1	5.6	7.0	8.0	5.4	3.5	4.1	4.2	5.7	5.2	5.1	64.3
Cloudy	16.7	15.1	16.7	13.4	10.8	6.1	1.4	2.2	3.4	8.7	14.7	17.1	126.4
Precipitation .01" or more	12.3	11.6	13.1	9.8	7.2	3.5	0.8	1.3	2.7	6.0	10.5	11.9	90.6
Snow, Ice pellets 1.0" or more	6.9	7.0	8.3	5.1	1.6	0.1	0.0	0.0	0.1	0.8	4.4	6.3	40.5
Thunderstorms	0.1	0.4	0.6	1.3	2.6	1.9	1.4	1.0	1.1	1.0	0.3	0.0	11.6
Fog, Visibility 1/4 mile or less	9.6	9.1	10.8	7.3	5.6	2.1	0.0	0.3	0.8	4.5	7.0	9.9	67.1
Temperature Maximum:													
90° and above	0.0	0.0	0.0	0.0	0.0	0.1	0.3	0.5	0.2	0.0	0.0	0.0	1.1
32° and below	4.4	2.9	3.2	1.5	0.1	0.0	0.0	0.0	0.0	*	1.1	3.4	16.8
Temperature Minimum:													
32° and below	18.0	16.5	19.1	11.4	4.3	0.4	0.0	0.0	0.2	2.6	10.6	15.3	98.4
0° and below	0.0	0.0	0.0	0.0	0.0	0.0	0.0	0.0	0.0	0.0	0.0	0.0	0.0
RELATIVE HUMIDITY (%)													
Morning	56	64	69	63	55	47	41	44	49	52	58	55	54
Afternoon	57	63	64	54	46	38	33	35	42	50	61	58	50
PRECIPITATION (inches)													
Water Equivalent													
Normal	14.1	9.9	8.9	5.4	2.7	0.8	0.3	0.5	0.9	3.9	8.4	11.7	67.8
Maximum monthly	33.8	23.2	22.2	16.5	10.8	3.0	5.8	3.6	5.7	22.3	28.3	45.1	45.1
Date	1970	1962	1983	1948	1957	1947	1974	1976	1978	1962	1973	1955	1955
Minimum monthly	0.7	0.8	1.8	0.3	0.0	0.0	0.0	0.0	0.0	0.0	T	0.3	0.0
Date	1984	1964	1956	1946	1985	1973	1981	1981	1980	1966	1959	1976	1981
Maximum in 24 hrs	9.1	8.3	5.2	5.3	5.1	1.9	4.7	2.7	3.1	7.9	8.6	9.3	9.3
Date	1963	1960	1983	1982	1957	1971	1974	1968	1978	1962	1950	1964	1964
SNOW, ICE PELLETS													
Maximum monthly	176.3	128.6	146.8	119.4	26.1	8.0	0.0	0.0	7.4	22.0	69.9	154.1	176.3
Date	1952	1969	1952	1948	1964	1954	—	—	1971	1956	1984	1952	1952
Maximum in 24 hrs	38.5	33.1	34.0	33.7	19.6	5.5	0.0	0.0	7.4	14.6	30.2	29.0	38.5
Date	1952	1959	1952	1955	1980	1954	—	—	1971	1984	1982	1952	1952
WIND (Resultant)													
Mean speed (mph)	8.7	8.6	8.4	7.2	7.2	7.0	6.2	6.4	6.8	7.4	7.6	7.2	7.4

EUREKA

Elev. 43' 40° 47'N — 124° 09'W **California**

NORMALS, MEANS, EXTREMES

	JAN	FEB	MAR	APR	MAY	JUN	JUL	AUG	SEP	OCT	NOV	DEC	YEAR
TEMPERATURE													
Normal daily maximum	53.4	54.6	54.0	54.7	57.0	59.1	60.3	61.3	62.2	60.3	57.5	54.5	57.4
Normal daily minimum	41.3	42.6	42.5	44.0	47.3	50.2	51.9	52.6	51.5	48.3	45.2	42.2	46.6
Normal monthly	47.4	48.6	48.3	49.4	52.2	54.7	56.1	57.0	56.9	54.3	51.4	48.4	52.0
Extreme highest	75	85	78	79	84	85	76	82	86	82	77	77	86
Extreme highest date	1981	1930	1914	1982	1939	1945	1985	1968	1983	1917	1950	1963	1983
Extreme lowest	25	27	29	32	36	41	45	44	41	32	29	21	21
Extreme lowest date	1937	1962	1917	1929	1954	1966	1924	1935	1946	1971	1935	1972	1972
DEGREE DAYS BASE 65° F							—						
Heating	549	456	518	468	397	309	276	248	246	332	408	518	4725
Cooling	0	0	0	0	0	0	0	0	0	0	0	0	0
% OF POSSIBLE SUNSHINE	42	45	51	56	57	58	54	49	54	49	42	40	50
AVERAGE SKY COVER													
Sunrise - Sunset	7.2	7.5	7.3	6.9	6.8	6.5	6.6	6.9	5.9	6.5	7.2	7.3	6.9
NUMBER OF DAYS (Sunrise-Sunset)													
Clear	6.0	5.2	5.8	6.4	6.6	7.3	6.4	5.5	8.8	8.1	6.1	6.1	78.4
Partly cloudy	6.1	5.8	7.6	8.3	9.8	9.7	10.9	10.9	8.7	8.4	6.5	6.4	98.9
Cloudy	18.9	17.2	17.7	15.3	14.7	13.0	13.7	14.7	12.6	14.5	17.4	18.5	187.9
Precipitation .01" or more	16.0	14.3	15.5	11.7	8.3	5.2	2.1	2.6	4.6	8.7	13.3	15.6	118.0
Snow, Ice pellets 1.0" or more	0.1	0.0	0.0	0.0	0.0	0.0	0.0	0.0	0.0	0.0	0.0	*	0.1
Thunderstorms	0.7	0.7	0.4	0.2	0.2	0.2	0.2	0.1	0.4	0.4	0.7	0.6	4.7
Fog, Visibility 1/4 mile or less	4.0	2.8	1.8	1.7	1.2	2.2	3.4	5.2	7.4	9.3	6.3	4.4	49.7
Temperature Maximum:													
90° and above	0.0	0.0	0.0	0.0	0.0	0.0	0.0	0.0	0.0	0.0	0.0	0.0	0.0
32° and below	0.0	0.0	0.0	0.0	0.0	0.0	0.0	0.0	0.0	0.0	0.0	0.0	0.0
Temperature Minimum:													
32° and below	2.1	0.8	0.3	*	0.0	0.0	0.0	0.0	0.0	*	0.2	1.3	4.7
0° and below	0.0	0.0	0.0	0.0	0.0	0.0	0.0	0.0	0.0	0.0	0.0	0.0	0.0
PRECIPITATION (inches)													
Water Equivalent													
Normal	6.9	5.2	5.0	2.9	1.6	0.5	0.1	0.3	0.9	2.7	5.9	6.2	38.5
Maximum monthly	13.9	13.9	13.9	10.6	6.0	2.5	1.3	3.4	3.5	13.0	16.5	14.1	16.5
Date	1969	1938	1938	1963	1960	1954	1916	1983	1925	1950	1973	1983	1973
Minimum monthly	0.6	0.5	0.0	0.3	0.0	0.0	0.0	0.0	0.0	0.0	T	0.5	0.0
Date	1985	1923	1926	1956	1955	1917	1967	1940	1929	1917	1929	1976	1967
Maximum in 24 hrs	4.4	4.8	4.0	2.5	2.2	1.7	1.1	2.2	1.5	5.8	4.5	4.1	5.8
Date	1912	1959	1975	1983	1943	1943	1916	1983	1977	1950	1926	1939	1950
SNOW, ICE PELLETS													
Maximum monthly	3.0	0.8	1.0	T	0.0	0.0	0.0	0.0	0.0	0.0	0.1	1.9	3.0
Date	1935	1955	1966	1982	—	—	—	—	—	—	1977	1972	1935
Maximum in 24 hrs	3.0	0.8	1.0	T	0.0	0.0	0.0	0.0	0.0	0.0	0.1	1.9	3.0
Date	1935	1955	1966	1982	—	—	—	—	—	—	1977	1972	1935
WIND (Resultant)													
Mean speed (mph)	6.9	7.2	7.6	8.0	7.9	7.4	6.8	5.8	5.5	5.6	6.0	6.4	6.8

FRESNO
Elev. 328' 36° 46'N — 119° 43'W **California**

NORMALS, MEANS, EXTREMES

	JAN	FEB	MAR	APR	MAY	JUN	JUL	AUG	SEP	OCT	NOV	DEC	YEAR
TEMPERATURE													
Normal daily maximum	54.2	61.2	66.5	73.7	82.7	91.1	97.9	95.5	90.3	79.9	65.2	54.4	76.1
Normal daily minimum	36.8	39.7	42.0	46.5	52.7	58.9	64.1	62.2	57.8	49.7	41.1	36.3	49.0
Normal monthly	45.5	50.5	54.3	60.1	67.7	75.0	81.0	78.9	74.1	64.8	53.2	45.4	62.5
Extreme highest	75	79	90	100	107	110	111	111	111	102	89	76	111
Extreme highest date	1984	1981	1972	1981	1984	1964	1984	1981	1955	1980	1949	1958	1984
Extreme lowest	19	25	26	32	36	44	50	49	37	27	26	21	19
Extreme lowest date	1963	1971	1966	1982	1975	1955	1955	1966	1950	1972	1975	1967	1963
DEGREE DAYS BASE 65° F													
Heating	605	406	336	187	52	8	0	0	0	88	354	611	2647
Cooling	0	0	0	40	135	308	496	431	277	82	0	0	1769
% OF POSSIBLE SUNSHINE	48	65	78	85	90	94	96	96	93	88	65	46	79
AVERAGE SKY COVER													
Sunrise - Sunset	7.3	6.2	5.3	4.2	3.1	1.9	1.2	1.4	1.7	2.9	5.4	7.0	4.0
NUMBER OF DAYS (Sunrise-Sunset)													
Clear	5.2	7.5	11.2	14.5	19.4	23.3	26.7	26.0	23.8	20.0	10.8	6.6	194.9
Partly cloudy	7.1	8.0	8.3	7.8	7.0	4.3	3.0	3.6	3.9	6.2	7.4	6.0	72.5
Cloudy	18.6	12.8	11.5	7.7	4.6	2.5	1.3	1.5	2.4	4.8	11.8	18.4	97.8
Precipitation .01" or more	7.8	7.0	7.0	4.5	1.9	0.7	0.3	0.4	0.9	2.1	5.8	7.0	45.3
Snow, Ice pellets 1.0" or more	*	0.0	0.0	0.0	0.0	0.0	0.0	0.0	0.0	0.0	0.0	*	0.1
Thunderstorms	0.3	0.3	0.8	0.6	0.5	0.4	0.3	0.3	0.7	0.6	0.3	0.3	5.4
Fog, Visibility 1/4 mile or less	11.5	6.6	1.8	0.4	0.1	0.0	0.0	*	0.1	0.9	6.2	12.2	39.8
Temperature Maximum:													
90° and above	0.0	0.0	*	1.7	10.5	19.5	28.5	26.5	17.1	4.0	0.0	0.0	107.7
32° and below	0.0	0.0	0.0	0.0	0.0	0.0	0.0	0.0	0.0	0.0	0.0	0.1	0.1
Temperature Minimum:													
32° and below	7.0	3.2	0.9	0.1	0.0	0.0	0.0	0.0	0.0	0.2	2.0	8.4	21.7
0° and below	0.0	0.0	0.0	0.0	0.0	0.0	0.0	0.0	0.0	0.0	0.0	0.0	0.0
RELATIVE HUMIDITY (%)													
Morning	91	90	86	80	71	65	61	68	72	78	87	92	78
Afternoon	68	56	47	35	25	23	22	25	28	35	56	70	41
PRECIPITATION (inches)													
Water Equivalent													
Normal	2.0	1.8	1.6	1.1	0.3	0.0	0.0	0.0	0.1	0.4	1.2	1.6	10.5
Maximum monthly	8.5	5.9	5.7	4.4	1.5	0.6	0.0	0.2	1.1	1.5	3.5	6.7	8.5
Date	1969	1962	1958	1967	1957	1972	1979	1964	1976	1982	1972	1955	1969
Minimum monthly	0.0	T	0.0	0.0	0.0	0.0	0.0	0.0	0.0	0.0	0.0	0.0	0.0
Date	1976	1964	1972	1962	1982	1983	1983	1981	1981	1978	1959	1960	1983
Maximum in 24 hrs	2.5	1.9	1.6	1.3	0.9	0.6	0.0	0.2	0.9	1.5	1.3	1.7	2.5
Date	1969	1969	1958	1983	1957	1972	1979	1964	1978	1976	1953	1955	1969
SNOW, ICE PELLETS													
Maximum monthly	2.2	T	T	0.0	0.0	0.0	0.0	0.0	0.0	T	0.0	1.2	2.2
Date	1962	1979	1979	—	—	—	—	—	—	1974	—	1968	1962
Maximum in 24 hrs	1.5	T	T	0.0	0.0	0.0	0.0	0.0	0.0	T	0.0	1.2	1.5
Date	1962	1979	1985	—	—	—	—	—	—	1974	—	1968	1962
WIND (Resultant)													
Mean speed (mph)	5.3	5.7	6.8	7.3	8.1	8.3	7.3	6.8	6.1	5.2	4.8	5.0	6.4

LOS ANGELES

Elev. 97'   33° 56'N — 118° 24'W   **California**

NORMALS, MEANS, EXTREMES

	JAN	FEB	MAR	APR	MAY	JUN	JUL	AUG	SEP	OCT	NOV	DEC	YEAR
TEMPERATURE													
Normal daily maximum	64.6	65.5	65.1	66.7	69.1	72.0	75.3	76.5	76.4	74.0	70.3	66.1	70.1
Normal daily minimum	47.3	48.6	49.7	52.2	55.7	59.1	62.6	64.0	62.5	58.5	52.1	47.8	55.0
Normal monthly	56.0	57.1	57.4	59.5	62.4	65.6	69.0	70.3	69.5	66.3	61.2	57.0	62.6
Extreme highest	88	92	93	95	97	104	97	98	110	106	101	94	110
Extreme highest date	1976	1963	1978	1966	1979	1981	1985	1955	1963	1961	1966	1958	1963
Extreme lowest	23	32	34	39	43	48	49	51	47	41	34	32	23
Extreme lowest date	1937	1942	1939	1942	1938	1950	1942	1948	1948	1942	1939	1968	1937
DEGREE DAYS BASE 65° F													
Heating	286	233	240	180	106	54	17	12	18	55	139	255	1595
Cooling	7	12	0	15	25	72	141	176	153	95	25	7	728
% OF POSSIBLE SUNSHINE	na	na	na	na	na	na	na	na	na	na	na	na	na
AVERAGE SKY COVER													
Sunrise - Sunset	5.2	5.1	5.1	4.7	5.2	5.0	3.9	3.8	4.3	4.4	4.6	4.7	4.7
NUMBER OF DAYS (Sunrise-Sunset)													
Clear	12.1	11.3	11.7	11.5	10.0	9.3	12.7	13.4	12.9	13.1	14.0	12.7	144.7
Partly cloudy	8.1	6.4	8.6	9.0	10.8	11.3	13.0	12.1	10.5	10.1	8.0	8.5	116.3
Cloudy	10.8	10.6	10.7	9.5	10.1	9.4	5.3	5.4	6.6	7.9	8.0	9.8	104.2
Precipitation .01" or more	6.0	6.0	5.8	3.5	1.2	0.5	0.5	0.4	1.1	2.0	3.6	5.3	35.9
Snow, Ice pellets 1.0" or more	0.0	0.0	0.0	0.0	0.0	0.0	0.0	0.0	0.0	0.0	0.0	0.0	0.0
Thunderstorms	0.3	0.4	0.7	0.4	0.1	*	0.2	0.3	0.3	0.3	0.3	0.4	3.9
Fog, Visibility 1/4 mile or less	4.6	3.5	3.2	2.5	1.5	1.5	1.6	2.3	3.6	4.8	5.3	5.6	40.0
Temperature Maximum:													
90° and above	0.0	*	0.1	0.2	0.3	0.5	0.2	0.3	1.9	1.6	0.3	*	5.5
32° and below	0.0	0.0	0.0	0.0	0.0	0.0	0.0	0.0	0.0	0.0	0.0	0.0	0.0
Temperature Minimum:													
32° and below	*	0.0	0.0	0.0	0.0	0.0	0.0	0.0	0.0	0.0	0.0	*	0.1
0° and below	0.0	0.0	0.0	0.0	0.0	0.0	0.0	0.0	0.0	0.0	0.0	0.0	0.0
RELATIVE HUMIDITY (%)													
Morning	70	74	78	79	82	85	86	85	82	78	73	70	79
Afternoon	59	62	65	63	65	67	67	68	66	64	62	61	64
PRECIPITATION (inches)													
Water Equivalent													
Normal	3.0	2.4	1.7	0.9	0.1	0.0	0.0	0.1	0.1	0.2	1.5	1.6	12.0
Maximum monthly	9.6	11.0	6.3	4.5	2.5	0.2	0.1	2.4	4.3	2.3	7.9	6.5	11.0
Date	1969	1962	1983	1965	1977	1964	1969	1977	1939	1936	1946	1936	1962
Minimum monthly	0.0	T	0.0	0.0	0.0	0.0	0.0	0.0	0.0	0.0	0.0	T	0.0
Date	1976	1964	1959	1979	1943	1978	1983	1981	1968	1969	1980	1963	1983
Maximum in 24 hrs	6.1	4.1	3.5	1.8	1.7	0.2	0.1	2.4	4.2	1.7	5.6	3.0	6.1
Date	1956	1962	1968	1960	1977	1964	1969	1977	1939	1972	1967	1951	1956
SNOW, ICE PELLETS													
Maximum monthly	T	T	0.0	0.0	0.0	0.0	0.0	0.0	0.0	0.0	0.0	T	T
Date	1982	1951	—	—	—	—	—	—	—	—	—	1971	1982
Maximum in 24 hrs	T	T	0.0	0.0	0.0	0.0	0.0	0.0	0,0	0.0	0.0	T	T
Date	1982	1951	—	—	—	—	—	—	—	—	—	1971	1982
WIND (Resultant)													
Mean speed (mph)	6.7	7.4	8.1	8.5	8.3	7.9	7.7	7.6	7.3	6.9	6.7	6.5	7.5

MOUNT SHASTA   Elev. 3535'   41° 19'N — 122° 19'W   California

NORMALS, MEANS, EXTREMES

	JAN	FEB	MAR	APR	MAY	JUN	JUL	AUG	SEP	OCT	NOV	DEC	YEAR
TEMPERATURE													
Normal daily maximum	42.1	47.3	50.9	57.9	67.0	75.4	85.1	83.3	77.5	65.4	50.9	43.9	62.2
Normal daily minimum	25.5	28.6	29.6	33.2	39.6	46.2	50.7	49.0	44.3	37.4	30.8	26.7	36.8
Normal monthly	33.8	38.0	40.3	45.6	53.3	60.8	67.9	66.2	60.9	51.4	40.9	35.3	49.5
Extreme highest	65	71	80	86	94	98	100	105	103	93	80	72	105
Extreme highest date	1961	1953	1966	1981	1984	1985	1979	1981	1955	1980	1949	1958	1981
Extreme lowest	-2	1	11	14	21	25	31	34	25	19	9	-5	-5
Extreme lowest date	1962	1950	1945	1955	1954	1952	1947	1968	1965	1946	1977	1972	1972
DEGREE DAYS BASE 65° F													
Heating	964	756	769	582	369	165	30	67	163	422	723	921	5931
Cooling	0	0	0	0	7	42	123	105	40	0	0	0	317
% OF POSSIBLE SUNSHINE	na	na	na	na	na	na	na	na	na	na	na	na	na
AVERAGE SKY COVER													
Sunrise - Sunset	6.9	6.4	6.6	5.6	5.1	3.6	1.5	2.1	2.5	4.3	6.0	6.7	4.8
NUMBER OF DAYS (Sunrise-Sunset)													
Clear	8.6	8.0	8.1	9.9	12.4	16.0	24.5	24.1	21.4	14.4	9.3	7.4	164.1
Partly cloudy	6.4	7.1	7.5	9.8	8.5	7.3	4.7	4.4	4.8	7.4	7.3	7.9	83.1
Cloudy	16.0	13.1	15.4	10.3	10.1	6.6	1.8	2.5	3.9	9.3	13.4	15.7	118.0
Precipitation .01" or more	12.0	11.4	12.1	8.9	7.2	4.9	1.8	2.4	3.3	6.5	10.3	12.0	92.8
Snow, Ice pellets 1.0" or more	5.1	3.4	3.8	1.7	0.3	0.0	0.0	0.0	0.0	0.2	1.8	4.0	20.3
Thunderstorms	*	0.3	0.2	0.9	2.4	2.6	3.1	1.9	1.0	0.3	0.2	0.1	13.1
Fog, Visibility 1/4 mile or less	1.4	0.8	0.4	0.4	0.0	0.1	0.0	0.0	0.1	0.1	1.0	2.4	6.7
Temperature Maximum:													
90° and above	0.0	0.0	0.0	0.0	0.2	2.0	9.0	6.9	3.0	0.1	0.0	0.0	21.1
32° and below	3.4	0.7	0.2	0.0	0.0	0.0	0.0	0.0	0.0	0.0	0.2	1.9	6.4
Temperature Minimum:													
32° and below	25.7	21.3	21.7	13.7	3.7	0.3	*	0.0	0.8	6.3	17.9	25.0	136.5
0° and below	0.1	0.0	0.0	0.0	0.0	0.0	0.0	0.0	0.0	0.0	0.0	0.1	0.2
RELATIVE HUMIDITY (%)													
Morning	76	76	75	72	69	67	64	65	67	72	78	78	72
Afternoon	66	60	52	43	39	36	28	29	33	46	62	67	47
PRECIPITATION (inches)													
Water Equivalent													
Normal	7.2	5.6	4.2	2.7	1.5	0.8	0.2	0.4	0.8	2.0	5.1	6.0	37.0
Maximum monthly	21.1	17.6	14.7	9.6	5.2	3.5	1.7	2.5	6.8	13.8	17.2	17.4	21.1
Date	1978	1958	1983	1948	1957	1982	1958	1976	1957	1950	1973	1955	1978
Minimum monthly	0.1	0.2	0.2	0.0	0.0	0.0	0.0	0.0	T	T	T	0.4	0.0
Date	1984	1971	1956	1985	1954	1973	1970	1981	1975	1966	1959	1956	1981
Maximum in 24 hrs	6.9	4.4	3.8	3.0	2.0	1.6	1.5	1.8	5.9	4.7	4.3	4.9	6.9
Date	1974	1958	1983	1958	1957	1968	1985	1954	1957	1950	1981	1960	1974
SNOW, ICE PELLETS													
Maximum monthly	119.8	83.7	67.0	50.2	16.4	T	0.0	0.0	0.0	7.1	41.9	137.7	137.7
Date	1952	1969	1952	1967	1960	1975	—	—	—	1971	1970	1952	1952
Maximum in 24 hrs	34.9	29.1	26.5	29.5	14.2	T	0.0	0.0	0.0	5.5	29.0	37.4	37.4
Date	1966	1956	1952	1958	1960	1975	—	—	—	1971	1961	1952	1952
WIND (Resultant)													
Mean speed (mph)	5.0	5.2	5.8	6.2	5.4	5.4	4.4	4.2	4.6	4.2	5.2	5.5	5.1

RED BLUFF

Elev. 342' 40° 09'N — 122° 15'W **California**

NORMALS, MEANS, EXTREMES

	JAN	FEB	MAR	APR	MAY	JUN	JUL	AUG	SEP	OCT	NOV	DEC	YEAR
TEMPERATURE													
Normal daily maximum	53.9	60.0	64.0	71.2	81.2	90.3	98.2	95.7	90.4	78.8	63.6	55.2	75.2
Normal daily minimum	37.1	40.7	42.5	46.6	53.9	61.8	66.3	64.4	60.0	51.5	43.0	37.8	50.5
Normal monthly	45.5	50.4	53.3	58.9	67.6	76.1	82.3	80.1	75.2	65.2	53.3	46.5	62.8
Extreme highest	79	85	92	98	108	114	119	121	114	107	93	83	121
Extreme highest date	1948	1977	1960	1947	1984	1950	1972	1981	1950	1980	1949	1980	1981
Extreme lowest	20	23	26	29	35	42	52	52	42	32	24	20	20
Extreme lowest date	1975	1949	1966	1982	1970	1952	1964	1959	1971	1946	1985	1972	1975
DEGREE DAYS BASE 65° F													
Heating	605	409	363	226	59	8	0	0	0	90	348	574	2682
Cooling	0	0	0	43	137	341	536	468	310	96	0	0	1931
% OF POSSIBLE SUNSHINE	54	64	70	81	86	89	96	94	92	81	61	53	77
AVERAGE SKY COVER													
Sunrise - Sunset	6.7	6.6	6.2	5.4	4.3	3.2	1.4	1.9	2.2	4.1	6.1	6.7	4.6
NUMBER OF DAYS (Sunrise-Sunset)													
Clear	7.9	7.1	8.6	10.8	14.8	18.5	26.2	24.1	22.1	15.7	9.5	7.6	172.9
Partly cloudy	5.8	5.7	7.0	7.7	7.8	6.4	3.4	4.5	4.7	6.9	5.1	5.9	70.8
Cloudy	17.3	15.5	15.4	11.6	8.4	5.0	1.5	2.4	3.2	8.5	15.3	17.5	121.6
Precipitation .01" or more	11.0	9.2	9.7	6.6	4.0	2.6	0.6	1.2	1.9	4.9	9.0	10.5	71.3
Snow, Ice pellets 1.0" or more	0.4	0.1	*	0.0	0.0	0.0	0.0	0.0	0.0	0.0	0.1	0.1	0.7
Thunderstorms	0.2	0.7	1.4	1.3	1.4	1.6	0.8	0.9	0.8	0.6	0.3	0.1	10.2
Fog, Visibility 1/4 mile or less	6.5	1.8	0.6	0.1	*	0.0	0.0	0.0	*	0.2	2.2	6.2	17.7
Temperature Maximum:													
90° and above	0.0	0.0	*	0.8	7.4	16.1	27.4	24.9	16.9	4.4	0.1	0.0	97.9
32° and below	*	0.0	0.0	0.0	0.0	0.0	0.0	0.0	0.0	0.0	0.0	*	0.1
Temperature Minimum:													
32° and below	9.1	2.6	0.9	0.1	0.0	0.0	0.0	0.0	0.0	*	1.4	6.5	20.6
0° and below	0.0	0.0	0.0	0.0	0.0	0.0	0.0	0.0	0.0	0.0	0.0	0.0	0.0
RELATIVE HUMIDITY (%)													
Morning	81	79	75	69	63	55	52	54	54	64	76	82	67
Afternoon	59	51	45	36	28	23	19	20	23	33	51	61	37
PRECIPITATION (inches)													
Water Equivalent													
Normal	4.5	3.3	2.3	1.5	0.7	0.4	0.0	0.2	0.4	1.1	3.1	3.5	21.4
Maximum monthly	10.1	11.3	9.2	5.7	4.0	1.6	0.6	1.5	2.4	4.3	8.4	10.2	11.3
Date	1978	1958	1983	1948	1956	1982	1974	1965	1957	1957	1970	1983	1958
Minimum monthly	0.2	0.0	0.0	0.0	0.0	0.0	0.0	0.0	0.0	0.0	T	T	0.0
Date	1976	1964	1956	1985	1969	1979	1976	1982	1974	1978	1959	1956	1982
Maximum in 24 hrs	3.1	2.6	2.6	2.2	1.7	1.5	0.4	1.0	1.5	2.5	4.0	3.6	4.0
Date	1978	1959	1978	1953	1956	1982	1958	1968	1964	1962	1954	1960	1954
SNOW, ICE PELLETS													
Maximum monthly	13.6	2.5	8.0	T	0.0	0.0	0.0	0.0	0.0	T	2.0	10.7	13.6
Date	1950	1949	1976	1975	—	—	—	—	—	1971	1977	1972	1950
Maximum in 24 hrs	9.9	1.5	8.0	T	0.0	0.0	0.0	0.0	0.0	T	2.0	9.2	9.9
Date	1950	1962	1976	1975	—	—	—	—	—	1971	1977	1972	1950
WIND (Resultant)													
Mean speed (mph)	8.7	9.1	9.7	9.5	9.2	9.2	8.0	7.5	7.9	8.1	8.3	8.2	8.6

SACRAMENTO

Elev. 17' 38° 31'N — 121° 30'W **California**

NORMALS, MEANS, EXTREMES

	JAN	FEB	MAR	APR	MAY	JUN	JUL	AUG	SEP	OCT	NOV	DEC	YEAR
TEMPERATURE													
Normal daily maximum	52.6	59.4	64.1	71.0	79.7	87.4	93.3	91.7	87.6	77.7	63.2	53.2	73.4
Normal daily minimum	37.9	41.2	42.4	45.3	50.1	55.1	57.9	57.6	55.8	50.0	42.8	37.9	47.8
Normal monthly	45.3	50.3	53.3	58.2	64.9	71.3	75.6	74.7	71.7	63.9	53.0	45.6	60.6
Extreme highest	70	76	86	92	105	115	114	108	108	101	87	72	115
Extreme highest date	1976	1985	1966	1951	1984	1961	1972	1978	1955	1970	1960	1967	1961
Extreme lowest	23	26	26	32	36	41	48	49	43	36	26	20	20
Extreme lowest date	1979	1972	1971	1953	1974	1952	1983	1978	1978	1971	1961	1972	1972
DEGREE DAYS BASE 65° F													
Heating	611	412	366	229	83	21	0	0	7	82	360	601	2772
Cooling	0	0	0	25	80	207	329	301	208	48	0	0	1198
% OF POSSIBLE SUNSHINE	44	62	72	81	89	93	97	96	93	85	63	46	77
AVERAGE SKY COVER													
Sunrise - Sunset	7.1	6.3	5.5	4.6	3.4	2.2	1.1	1.5	1.8	3.3	5.8	6.9	4.1
NUMBER OF DAYS (Sunrise-Sunset)													
Clear	6.3	7.7	10.4	12.6	17.8	21.7	26.9	25.6	23.5	19.1	9.6	7.4	188.7
Partly cloudy	5.9	6.9	8.2	9.2	8.2	5.8	3.1	4.0	4.1	6.2	6.8	5.8	74.2
Cloudy	18.8	13.6	12.4	8.2	5.1	2.5	1.0	1.5	2.3	5.7	13.6	17.8	102.3
Precipitation .01" or more	10.1	8.7	8.5	5.5	2.7	1.1	0.3	0.4	1.3	3.3	7.2	9.2	58.2
Snow, Ice pellets 1.0" or more	0.0	*	0.0	0.0	0.0	0.0	0.0	0.0	0.0	0.0	0.0	0.0	*
Thunderstorms	0.4	0.5	0.8	0.8	0.4	0.2	0.2	0.1	0.5	0.3	0.3	0.2	4.6
Fog, Visibility 1/4 mile or less	10.2	5.4	1.5	0.4	0.2	0.0	0.0	0.1	0.2	1.5	5.7	9.5	34.6
Temperature Maximum:													
90° and above	0.0	0.0	0.0	0.3	5.2	11.8	22.4	19.3	12.3	2.3	0.0	0.0	73.6
32° and below	*	0.0	0.0	0.0	0.0	0.0	0.0	0.0	0.0	0.0	0.0	*	0.1
Temperature Minimum:													
32° and below	6.5	1.5	0.6	*	0.0	0.0	0.0	0.0	0.0	0.0	1.3	6.3	16.3
0° and below	0.0	0.0	0.0	0.0	0.0	0.0	0.0	0.0	0.0	0.0	0.0	0.0	0.0
RELATIVE HUMIDITY (%)													
Morning	90	87	84	81	80	78	76	77	77	79	87	90	82
Afternoon	71	61	53	44	35	31	28	29	32	39	60	71	46
PRECIPITATION (inches)													
Water Equivalent													
Normal	4.0	2.8	2.0	1.3	0.3	0.1	0.0	0.0	0.2	0.8	2.2	2.9	17.1
Maximum monthly	9.1	8.7	7.1	4.7	3.1	0.6	0.7	0.6	1.8	7.5	7.4	12.6	12.6
Date	1978	1962	1982	1941	1948	1953	1974	1976	1982	1962	1970	1955	1955
Minimum monthly	0.1	0.1	0.1	0.0	T	0.0	0.0	0.0	0.0	0.0	0.0	0.1	0.0
Date	1984	1964	1966	1949	1982	1981	1983	1982	1980	1966	1959	1956	1983
Maximum in 24 hrs	3.4	2.5	2.3	2.2	0.7	0.6	0.7	0.6	1.5	5.5	2.9	3.6	5.5
Date	1967	1958	1982	1958	1957	1953	1974	1965	1959	1962	1970	1955	1962
SNOW, ICE PELLETS													
Maximum monthly	T	2.0	T	0.0	0.0	0.0	0.0	0.0	0.0	0.0	0.0	T	2.0
Date	1974	1976	1982	—	—	—	—	—	—	—	—	1972	1976
Maximum in 24 hrs	T	2.0	T	0.0	0.0	0.0	0.0	0.0	0.0	0.0	0.0	T	2.0
Date	1974	1976	1982	—	—	—	—	—	—	—	—	1972	1976
WIND (Resultant)													
Mean speed (mph)	7.4	7.7	8.8	8.9	9.3	9.8	9.0	8.6	7.6	6.6	6.2	6.8	8.1

SAN DIEGO

Elev. 13' **32° 44'N — 117° 10'W** **California**

NORMALS, MEANS, EXTREMES

	JAN	FEB	MAR	APR	MAY	JUN	JUL	AUG	SEP	OCT	NOV	DEC	YEAR
TEMPERATURE													
Normal daily maximum	65.2	66.4	65.9	67.8	68.6	71.3	75.6	77.6	76.8	74.6	69.9	66.1	70.5
Normal daily minimum	48.4	50.3	52.1	54.5	58.2	61.2	64.9	66.8	65.1	60.3	53.6	48.7	57.0
Normal monthly	56.8	58.4	59.0	61.2	63.4	66.3	70.3	72.2	71.0	67.5	61.8	57.4	63.7
Extreme highest	88	88	93	92	96	101	95	98	111	107	97	88	111
Extreme highest date	1953	1954	1978	1960	1953	1979	1985	1955	1963	1961	1976	1963	1963
Extreme lowest	29	36	39	41	48	51	55	57	51	43	38	34	29
Extreme lowest date	1949	1949	1971	1945	1967	1967	1948	1944	1948	1971	1964	1978	1949
DEGREE DAYS BASE 65° F													
Heating	258	196	193	124	71	40	5	0	7	32	118	240	1284
Cooling	0	11	7	10	21	79	170	226	187	109	22	0	842
% OF POSSIBLE SUNSHINE	71	72	70	67	58	57	69	69	68	68	74	72	68
AVERAGE SKY COVER													
Sunrise - Sunset	5.1	5.2	5.2	5.2	5.7	5.5	4.5	4.1	4.2	4.3	4.2	4.7	4.8
NUMBER OF DAYS (Sunrise-Sunset)													
Clear	12.4	10.6	11.2	10.3	8.5	9.2	13.3	15.1	14.9	14.1	14.5	13.6	147.7
Partly cloudy	7.5	7.5	9.4	10.1	11.4	11.8	12.8	11.4	9.3	9.5	7.8	7.7	116.2
Cloudy	11.1	10.1	10.4	9.6	11.1	9.0	4.8	4.5	5.8	7.4	7.7	9.7	101.3
Precipitation .01" or more	6.8	5.9	7.1	4.7	2.2	1.0	0.3	0.5	1.2	2.4	4.7	5.7	42.6
Snow, Ice pellets 1.0" or more	0.0	0.0	0.0	0.0	0.0	0.0	0.0	0.0	0.0	0.0	0.0	0.0	0.0
Thunderstorms	0.2	0.3	0.4	0.1	0.2	0.1	0.1	0.2	0.3	0.3	0.3	0.4	2.9
Fog, Visibility 1/4 mile or less	3.2	2.8	1.5	1.3	0.6	0.8	0.6	0.7	2.3	3.3	3.8	4.4	25.5
Temperature Maximum:													
90° and above	0.0	0.0	0.1	0.1	0.1	0.5	0.3	0.2	1.5	1.0	0.2	0.0	4.1
32° and below	0.0	0.0	0.0	0.0	0.0	0.0	0.0	0.0	0.0	0.0	0.0	0.0	0.0
Temperature Minimum:													
32° and below	*	0.0	0.0	0.0	0.0	0.0	0.0	0.0	0.0	0.0	0.0	0.0	*
0° and below	0.0	0.0	0.0	0.0	0.0	0.0	0.0	0.0	0.0	0.0	0.0	0.0	0.0
RELATIVE HUMIDITY (%)													
Morning	70	73	74	75	77	81	81	81	79	75	73	71	76
Afternoon	56	58	59	59	64	66	65	66	65	62	62	58	62
PRECIPITATION (inches)													
Water Equivalent													
Normal	2.1	1.4	1.6	0.7	0.2	0.0	0.0	0.1	0.1	0.3	1.1	1.3	9.3
Maximum monthly	6.2	5.4	6.5	3.5	1.7	0.3	0.1	2.1	1.9	2.9	5.8	7.6	7.6
Date	1943	1976	1983	1965	1977	1972	1984	1977	1963	1941	1965	1943	1943
Minimum monthly	T	0.0	T	T	0.0	0.0	0.0	0.0	0.0	0.0	0.0	0.0	0.0
Date	1976	1967	1972	1966	1952	1981	1982	1981	1979	1967	1980	1979	1982
Maximum in 24 hrs	2.6	2.6	2.4	1.4	1.5	0.2	0.1	2.1	0.9	1.2	2.4	3.0	3.0
Date	1978	1979	1952	1965	1977	1972	1984	1977	1963	1941	1944	1945	1945
SNOW, ICE PELLETS													
Maximum monthly	T	0.0	T	0.0	0.0	0.0	0.0	0.0	0.0	0.0	T	T	T
Date	1949	—	1985	—	—	—	—	—	—	—	1985	1967	1985
Maximum in 24 hrs	T	0.0	T	0.0	0.0	0.0	0.0	0.0	0.0	0.0	T	T	T
Date	1949	—	1985	—	—	—	—	—	—	—	1985	1967	1985
WIND (Resultant)													
Mean speed (mph)	5.8	6.4	7.4	7.8	7.8	7.7	7.3	7.2	7.0	6.5	5.8	5.5	6.8

SAN FRANCISCO

Elev. 8' 37° 37'N — 122° 23'W **California**

NORMALS, MEANS, EXTREMES

	JAN	FEB	MAR	APR	MAY	JUN	JUL	AUG	SEP	OCT	NOV	DEC	YEAR
TEMPERATURE													
Normal daily maximum	55.5	59.0	60.6	63.0	66.3	69.6	71.0	71.8	73.4	70.0	62.7	56.3	64.9
Normal daily minimum	41.5	44.1	44.9	46.6	49.3	52.0	53.3	54.2	54.3	51.2	46.3	42.2	48.3
Normal monthly	48.5	51.6	52.8	54.8	57.8	60.8	62.2	63.0	63.9	60.6	54.5	49.3	56.6
Extreme highest	72	78	85	92	97	106	104	98	103	97	85	75	106
Extreme highest date	1948	1930	1952	1981	1984	1961	1931	1968	1971	1980	1967	1958	1961
Extreme lowest	24	25	30	31	36	41	43	42	38	34	25	20	20
Extreme lowest date	1928	1929	1929	1929	1929	1932	1928	1935	1929	1929	1931	1932	1932
DEGREE DAYS BASE 65° F													
Heating	512	375	378	306	226	139	103	89	80	148	315	490	3161
Cooling	0	0	0	0	0	13	16	27	47	12	0	0	115
% OF POSSIBLE SUNSHINE	na	na	na	na	na	na	na	na	na	na	na	na	na
AVERAGE SKY COVER													
Sunrise - Sunset	6.2	6.2	5.7	5.1	4.4	3.7	3.0	3.3	3.2	4.0	5.6	6.0	4.7
NUMBER OF DAYS (Sunrise-Sunset)													
Clear	8.6	7.9	9.8	11.2	13.9	16.1	20.6	19.1	18.2	15.6	10.9	9.2	161.0
Partly cloudy	7.7	7.4	8.6	9.2	9.7	8.7	7.5	8.6	8.1	9.0	8.4	7.7	100.6
Cloudy	14.7	13.0	12.6	9.6	7.4	5.2	3.0	3.3	3.7	6.5	10.7	14.1	103.7
Precipitation .01" or more	10.7	9.7	9.8	6.0	2.7	1.1	0.3	0.5	1.0	3.7	7.2	9.8	62.5
Snow, Ice pellets 1.0" or more	*	0.0	0.0	0.0	0.0	0.0	0.0	0.0	0.0	0.0	0.0	*	*
Thunderstorms	0.4	0.3	0.2	0.2	0.1	0.1	0.1	0.1	0.2	0.2	0.2	0.2	2.3
Fog, Visibility 1/4 mile or less	3.7	2.7	0.4	0.1	0.1	*	*	0.2	0.7	1.5	2.4	3.6	15.6
Temperature Maximum:													
90° and above	0.0	0.0	0.0	*	0.4	0.9	0.8	0.3	1.6	0.3	0.0	0.0	4.3
32° and below	0.0	0.0	0.0	0.0	0.0	0.0	0.0	0.0	0.0	0.0	0.0	0.0	0.0
Temperature Minimum:													
32° and below	1.4	*	*	0.0	0.0	0.0	0.0	0.0	0.0	0.0	0.0	0.9	2.3
0° and below	0.0	0.0	0.0	0.0	0.0	0.0	0.0	0.0	0.0	0.0	0.0	0.0	0.0
RELATIVE HUMIDITY (%)													
Morning	86	84	81	81	83	84	86	86	82	81	83	85	84
Afternoon	66	65	63	60	60	59	59	61	58	59	64	68	62
PRECIPITATION (inches)													
Water Equivalent													
Normal	4.6	3.2	2.6	1.5	0.3	0.1	0.0	0.0	0.1	1.0	2.3	3.5	19.7
Maximum monthly	10.4	9.5	9.0	6.3	3.8	0.8	0.3	0.6	2.3	7.3	7.9	12.3	12.3
Date	1967	1958	1958	1958	1957	1967	1977	1976	1959	1962	1973	1955	1955
Minimum monthly	0.3	T	T	T	T	0.0	0.0	T	T	T	0.0	0.2	0.0
Date	1948	1953	1934	1977	1984	1928	1930	1983	1980	1978	1929	1975	1930
Maximum in 24 hrs	5.7	2.3	2.4	2.6	1.5	0.8	0.3	0.3	2.3	3.7	2.3	3.3	5.7
Date	1982	1945	1982	1958	1957	1967	1977	1976	1959	1962	1973	1955	1982
SNOW, ICE PELLETS													
Maximum monthly	1.5	T	T	0.0	0.0	0.0	0.0	0.0	0.0	0.0	0.0	1.0	1.5
Date	1962	1983	1983	—	—	—	—	—	—	—	—	1932	1962
Maximum in 24 hrs	1.5	T	T	0.0	0.0	0.0	0.0	0.0	0.0	0.0	0.0	1.0	1.5
Date	1962	1983	1983	—	—	—	—	—	—	—	—	1932	1962
WIND (Resultant)													
Mean speed (mph)	7.1	8.5	10.4	12.1	13.3	13.9	13.6	12.8	11.0	9.4	7.4	6.9	10.5

SANTA MARIA

Elev. 236'   34° 54'N — 120° 27'W   ## California

NORMALS, MEANS, EXTREMES

	JAN	FEB	MAR	APR	MAY	JUN	JUL	AUG	SEP	OCT	NOV	DEC	YEAR
TEMPERATURE													
Normal daily maximum	62.8	64.2	63.9	65.6	67.3	69.9	72.1	72.8	74.2	73.3	68.9	64.6	68.3
Normal daily minimum	38.8	40.3	40.9	42.7	46.2	49.6	52.4	53.2	51.8	47.6	42.1	38.3	45.3
Normal monthly	50.8	52.3	52.4	54.2	56.8	59.8	62.3	63.0	63.0	60.5	55.5	51.5	56.8
Extreme highest	86	87	88	97	100	102	104	103	103	103	93	90	104
Extreme highest date	1976	1943	1951	1947	1970	1976	1985	1962	1978	1950	1956	1958	1985
Extreme lowest	20	22	24	31	31	36	43	43	36	26	25	20	20
Extreme lowest date	1976	1971	1971	1984	1964	1962	1964	1973	1948	1971	1958	1978	1978
DEGREE DAYS BASE 65° F													
Heating	440	356	391	324	254	161	97	85	83	152	289	422	3054
Cooling	0	0	0	0	0	0	14	26	23	13	0	0	76
% OF POSSIBLE SUNSHINE	na	na	na	na	na	na	na	na	na	na	na	na	na
AVERAGE SKY COVER													
Sunrise - Sunset	5.0	5.1	4.9	4.5	4.4	3.8	3.4	3.5	3.6	3.6	4.1	4.6	4.2
NUMBER OF DAYS (Sunrise-Sunset)													
Clear	12.6	11.5	12.4	13.2	14.2	15.6	17.1	17.0	16.3	17.1	15.0	14.0	176.0
Partly cloudy	7.3	6.5	8.7	8.9	9.7	10.4	12.2	12.3	10.0	8.7	7.3	7.3	109.2
Cloudy	11.0	10.3	9.9	8.0	7.0	3.9	1.7	1.7	3.7	5.2	7.8	9.8	80.1
Precipitation .01" or more	7.3	7.3	8.0	4.8	1.8	0.8	0.3	0.4	1.3	2.4	5.4	6.5	46.3
Snow, Ice pellets 1.0" or more	0.0	0.0	0.0	0.0	0.0	0.0	0.0	0.0	0.0	0.0	0.0	0.0	0.0
Thunderstorms	0.2	0.1	0.3	0.2	0.2	*	0.2	0.3	0.4	0.1	0.1	0.1	2.3
Fog, Visibility 1/4 mile or less	4.6	4.4	4.7	5.8	6.3	6.7	7.7	9.9	12.3	12.0	6.5	5.8	86.7
Temperature Maximum:													
90° and above	0.0	0.0	0.0	0.3	0.5	0.8	0.4	0.3	1.9	1.5	0.1	0.0	5.8
32° and below	0.0	0.0	0.0	0.0	0.0	0.0	0.0	0.0	0.0	0.0	0.0	0.0	0.0
Temperature Minimum:													
32° and below	6.4	3.3	2.0	0.6	0.1	0.0	0.0	0.0	0.0	0.2	1.8	6.2	20.7
0° and below	0.0	0.0	0.0	0.0	0.0	0.0	0.0	0.0	0.0	0.0	0.0	0.0	0.0
RELATIVE HUMIDITY (%)													
Morning	81	84	86	88	91	92	88	93	91	85	78	79	86
Afternoon	59	61	63	60	60	60	59	61	61	60	61	59	60
PRECIPITATION (inches)													
Water Equivalent													
Normal	2.4	2.6	1.8	1.1	0.2	0.0	0.0	0.0	0.2	0.4	1.3	1.8	12.3
Maximum monthly	7.0	9.6	5.5	4.2	2.4	0.2	0.6	0.8	3.0	2.0	4.7	4.8	9.6
Date	1969	1962	1981	1958	1977	1957	1950	1976	1976	1960	1965	1955	1962
Minimum monthly	T	T	T	T	0.0	T	0.0	0.0	T	T	0.0	0.1	0.0
Date	1976	1953	1959	1973	1978	1985	1982	1971	1981	1978	1959	1963	1982
Maximum in 24 hrs	2.5	2.6	2.5	1.6	1.3	0.2	0.6	0.8	1.7	2.0	1.9	3.1	3.1
Date	1943	1978	1978	1960	1977	1957	1950	1976	1976	1960	1965	1974	1974
SNOW, ICE PELLETS													
Maximum monthly	T	T	0.0	0.0	0.0	0.0	0.0	0.0	0.0	0.0	T	0.0	T
Date	1962	1962	—	—	—	—	—	—	—	—	1975	—	1975
Maximum in 24 hrs	T	T	0.0	0.0	0.0	0.0	0.0	0.0	0.0	0.0	T	0.0	T
Date	1962	1962	—	—	—	—	—	—	—	—	1975	—	1975
WIND (Resultant)													
Mean speed (mph)	6.7	7.2	8.3	8.0	8.3	7.9	6.5	6.2	5.9	6.2	6.6	6.4	7.0

STOCKTON

Elev. 22'   37° 54'N — 121° 15'W   **California**

NORMALS, MEANS, EXTREMES

	JAN	FEB	MAR	APR	MAY	JUN	JUL	AUG	SEP	OCT	NOV	DEC	YEAR
TEMPERATURE													
Normal daily maximum	52.8	59.9	65.3	72.4	81.1	89.0	95.0	93.1	88.7	78.6	64.1	53.5	74.5
Normal daily minimum	37.5	40.6	42.0	45.6	51.5	57.1	60.9	60.4	57.4	50.5	42.4	37.5	48.6
Normal monthly	45.2	50.3	53.7	59.0	66.3	73.1	78.0	76.8	73.1	64.6	53.3	45.5	61.5
Extreme highest	71	78	87	100	107	111	114	109	108	101	84	71	114
Extreme highest date	1981	1977	1966	1981	1984	1961	1972	1983	1979	1980	1966	1959	1972
Extreme lowest	19	25	27	32	38	45	50	50	43	33	25	21	19
Extreme lowest date	1963	1985	1971	1976	1964	1971	1981	1968	1982	1972	1985	1965	1963
DEGREE DAYS BASE 65° F													
Heating	614	412	350	206	52	8	0	0	0	76	351	605	2674
Cooling	0	0	0	26	92	251	403	366	247	63	0	0	1448
% OF POSSIBLE SUNSHINE	na	na	na	na	na	na	na	na	na	na	na	na	na
AVERAGE SKY COVER													
Sunrise - Sunset	7.4	6.5	5.7	4.8	3.4	2.2	1.2	1.4	1.8	3.3	5.9	7.1	4.2
NUMBER OF DAYS (Sunrise-Sunset)													
Clear	5.2	7.0	10.0	12.2	17.8	21.9	26.9	25.9	23.4	19.0	9.0	6.4	184.7
Partly cloudy	6.4	6.5	8.5	8.5	8.3	5.6	3.1	3.6	4.4	6.0	8.1	6.5	75.4
Cloudy	19.4	14.9	12.7	9.3	4.9	2.6	1.0	1.5	2.2	6.0	12.9	18.1	105.5
Precipitation .01" or more	8.9	8.3	8.3	5.5	2.3	0.7	0.3	0.4	1.0	3.1	6.9	6.4	52.1
Snow, Ice pellets 1.0" or more	0.0	0.0	0.0	0.0	0.0	0.0	0.0	0.0	0.0	0.0	0.0	0.0	0.0
Thunderstorms	0.2	0.3	0.3	0.7	0.2	0.3	0.2	0.2	0.4	0.2	0.1	0.1	3.1
Fog, Visibility 1/4 mile or less	12.0	7.5	1.6	0.4	0.1	*	0.0	*	0.1	2.0	7.9	11.4	43.0
Temperature Maximum:													
90° and above	0.0	0.0	0.0	0.6	6.8	15.3	24.9	22.3	13.5	2.9	0.0	0.0	86.3
32° and below	0.1	0.0	0.0	0.0	0.0	0.0	0.0	0.0	0.0	0.0	0.0	*	0.1
Temperature Minimum:													
32° and below	8.2	2.7	1.0	0.1	0.0	0.0	0.0	0.0	0.0	0.0	1.7	8.6	22.1
0° and below	0.0	0.0	0.0	0.0	0.0	0.0	0.0	0.0	0.0	0.0	0.0	0.0	0.0
RELATIVE HUMIDITY (%)													
Morning	90	88	83	78	74	69	65	67	69	75	85	91	78
Afternoon	70	61	51	40	32	28	26	27	30	38	58	72	44
PRECIPITATION (inches)													
Water Equivalent													
Normal	3.0	2.0	1.8	1.3	0.3	0.0	0.0	0.0	0.2	0.6	1.7	2.4	13.7
Maximum monthly	7.0	6.0	6.4	3.5	1.9	0.6	0.6	0.8	3.0	2.9	6.2	8.0	8.0
Date	1967	1962	1982	1958	1948	1964	1974	1975	1959	1945	1972	1955	1955
Minimum monthly	0.1	0.0	T	0.0	0.0	0.0	0.0	0.0	0.0	0.0	T	0.0	0.0
Date	1976	1964	1956	1949	1982	1981	1983	1982	1980	1978	1959	1963	1983
Maximum in 24 hrs	3.0	2.2	1.7	1.5	1.2	0.5	0.5	0.8	2.6	1.5	2.2	3.0	3.0
Date	1967	1945	1968	1958	1948	1964	1974	1975	1959	1964	1950	1955	1967
SNOW, ICE PELLETS													
Maximum monthly	0.0	0.3	T	T	0.0	0.0	0.0	0.0	0.0	0.0	0.0	T	0.3
Date	—	1976	1976	1970	—	—	—	—	—	—	—	1972	1976
Maximum in 24 hrs	0.0	0.3	T	T	0.0	0.0	0.0	0.0	0.0	0.0	0.0	T	0.3
Date	—	1976	1976	1970	—	—	—	—	—	—	—	1972	1976
WIND (Resultant)													
Mean speed (mph)	6.7	6.9	7.7	8.3	9.2	9.2	8.2	7.7	7.1	6.4	5.8	6.2	7.4

ALAMOSA

Elev. 7536'   **37° 27'N — 105° 52'W**   ## Colorado

NORMALS, MEANS, EXTREMES

	JAN	FEB	MAR	APR	MAY	JUN	JUL	AUG	SEP	OCT	NOV	DEC	YEAR
TEMPERATURE													
Normal daily maximum	34.2	40.1	48.0	57.8	67.7	78.1	82.0	79.3	73.6	62.9	47.1	36.1	58.9
Normal daily minimum	-2.3	5.4	15.1	23.5	33.1	41.4	48.0	45.4	36.1	24.6	11.3	0.3	23.4
Normal monthly	16.0	22.8	31.6	40.7	50.4	59.8	65.0	62.4	54.9	43.8	29.2	17.9	41.2
Extreme highest	62	64	73	79	85	91	93	90	87	81	71	61	93
Extreme highest date	1971	1951	1971	1981	1984	1954	1971	1977	1977	1979	1980	1958	1971
Extreme lowest	-50	-35	-20	-6	11	25	34	29	15	-10	-30	-42	-50
Extreme lowest date	1948	1948	1964	1973	1967	1974	1968	1964	1985	1945	1952	1978	1948
DEGREE DAYS BASE 65° F													
Heating	1519	1182	1035	732	453	165	40	100	303	657	1074	1457	8717
Cooling	0	0	0	0	0	9	40	20	0	0	0	0	69
% OF POSSIBLE SUNSHINE	na	na	na	na	na	na	na	na	na	na	na	na	na
AVERAGE SKY COVER													
Sunrise - Sunset	4.7	4.7	5.1	5.1	5.3	3.9	5.1	4.8	3.8	3.7	4.2	4.4	4.6
NUMBER OF DAYS (Sunrise-Sunset)													
Clear	12.8	11.3	10.5	9.8	9.1	13.8	8.8	10.9	15.5	16.7	14.4	14.0	147.6
Partly cloudy	10.1	9.7	11.4	12.5	14.2	12.2	16.7	13.6	9.6	8.2	9.0	9.7	137.0
Cloudy	8.0	7.2	9.1	7.7	7.7	4.0	5.5	6.5	4.9	6.1	6.6	7.3	80.6
Precipitation .01" or more	4.0	4.2	5.1	5.0	6.1	5.2	9.5	10.3	6.0	4.6	3.8	3.9	67.5
Snow, Ice pellets 1.0" or more	1.7	1.7	2.2	1.5	0.5	0.0	0.0	0.0	0.1	1.0	1.4	1.8	11.9
Thunderstorms	0.0	0.2	0.2	1.2	6.3	5.9	12.2	12.4	5.0	1.1	0.1	0.0	44.3
Fog, Visibility 1/4 mile or less	3.2	1.8	1.3	0.7	0.6	0.4	0.5	0.9	1.3	0.6	1.6	3.2	16.1
Temperature Maximum:													
90° and above	0.0	0.0	0.0	0.0	0.0	0.2	0.6	*	0.0	0.0	0.0	0.0	0.9
32° and below	12.3	6.3	1.9	0.1	0.0	0.0	0.0	0.0	0.0	0.1	3.1	10.5	34.2
Temperature Minimum:													
32° and below	30.9	28.3	30.6	26.5	13.6	2.0	0.0	0.2	8.0	26.0	29.7	31.0	226.6
0° and below	18.1	9.5	1.7	0.1	0.0	0.0	0.0	0.0	0.0	0.1	3.8	15.3	48.5
RELATIVE HUMIDITY (%)													
Morning	78	78	74	71	73	75	84	85	81	76	78	77	78
Afternoon	59	50	37	30	28	25	36	38	33	34	48	58	40
PRECIPITATION (inches)													
Water Equivalent													
Normal	0.2	0.2	0.3	0.5	0.7	0.5	1.2	1.1	0.7	0.6	0.3	0.3	7.1
Maximum monthly	0.7	1.4	1.4	1.6	1.8	2.5	3.5	3.2	1.9	2.3	1.2	1.5	3.5
Date	1979	1963	1973	1947	1973	1969	1968	1967	1959	1969	1957	1964	1968
Minimum monthly	T	T	T	T	0.0	T	0.1	0.2	T	T	T	T	T
Date	1981	1954	1955	1972	1975	1980	1979	1980	1956	1983	1950	1980	1983
Maximum in 24 hrs	0.4	1.1	1.0	1.3	0.8	1.0	1.5	0.9	1.8	1.2	0.7	0.9	1.8
Date	1956	1963	1962	1952	1967	1969	1971	1981	1959	1969	1985	1964	1959
SNOW, ICE PELLETS													
Maximum monthly	13.8	16.0	29.2	16.4	13.5	0.2	T	0.0	4.2	20.3	19.8	27.7	29.2
Date	1979	1963	1973	1947	1978	1983	1981	—	1961	1969	1972	1967	1973
Maximum in 24 hrs	7.6	11.5	14.0	10.0	8.4	0.2	T	0.0	4.2	15.5	9.2	15.8	15.8
Date	1960	1963	1962	1957	1973	1983	1981	—	1961	1969	1985	1967	1967
WIND (Resultant)													
Mean speed (mph)	6.3	6.1	10.2	11.9	12.1	10.2	8.6	8.1	8.2	7.7	7.1	5.9	8.5

COLORADO SPRINGS Elev. 6145' 38° 49'N — 104° 43'W Colorado

NORMALS, MEANS, EXTREMES

	JAN	FEB	MAR	APR	MAY	JUN	JUL	AUG	SEP	OCT	NOV	DEC	YEAR
TEMPERATURE													
Normal daily maximum	41.4	45.3	49.3	59.5	68.9	79.9	84.9	82.3	74.9	64.6	50.4	43.9	62.1
Normal daily minimum	16.2	19.6	23.8	32.9	42.5	51.5	57.4	55.6	47.2	37.0	25.0	18.9	35.6
Normal monthly	28.8	32.5	36.6	46.2	55.7	65.7	71.2	69.0	61.1	50.8	37.7	31.4	48.9
Extreme highest	72	76	81	83	93	100	100	99	94	86	78	77	100
Extreme highest date	1974	1963	1971	1981	1984	1954	1954	1954	1960	1979	1981	1955	1954
Extreme lowest	-26	-27	-11	-3	21	32	42	43	22	5	-8	-17	-27
Extreme lowest date	1951	1951	1956	1959	1954	1951	1952	1978	1985	1969	1976	1983	1951
DEGREE DAYS BASE 65° F													
Heating	1122	910	880	564	296	78	8	25	162	440	819	1042	6346
Cooling	0	0	0	0	8	99	200	149	45	0	0	0	501
% OF POSSIBLE SUNSHINE	na	na	na	na	na	na	na	na	na	na	na	na	na
AVERAGE SKY COVER													
Sunrise - Sunset	5.3	5.5	5.9	5.8	6.1	4.9	5.1	5.0	4.2	4.3	5.1	5.1	5.2
NUMBER OF DAYS (Sunrise-Sunset)													
Clear	11.2	9.4	8.8	8.1	6.8	10.5	9.3	10.5	14.6	15.3	11.6	12.1	128.4
Partly cloudy	8.5	8.1	8.9	10.3	12.2	12.2	14.9	12.7	8.1	7.4	7.9	8.1	119.1
Cloudy	11.3	10.8	13.2	11.5	12.0	7.3	6.8	7.9	7.3	8.4	10.5	10.8	117.7
Precipitation .01" or more	5.0	4.5	7.5	7.5	10.4	9.2	13.4	11.8	6.6	5.1	4.1	4.4	89.6
Snow, Ice pellets 1.0" or more	1.5	1.5	2.9	1.6	0.4	*	0.0	0.0	0.2	0.7	1.6	1.7	12.1
Thunderstorms	0.0	*	0.4	2.4	8.5	11.0	16.5	13.5	4.7	0.8	0.1	0.0	57.9
Fog, Visibility 1/4 mile or less	2.3	2.3	2.5	2.0	2.0	0.8	0.5	0.8	2.1	1.9	2.5	2.0	21.8
Temperature Maximum:													
90° and above	0.0	0.0	0.0	0.0	0.1	3.9	8.8	3.4	0.5	0.0	0.0	0.0	16.7
32° and below	7.8	5.3	4.1	0.8	0.0	0.0	0.0	0.0	*	0.3	3.3	6.6	28.2
Temperature Minimum:													
32° and below	30.2	26.7	26.4	13.2	2.3	0.0	0.0	0.0	1.0	8.7	24.0	29.2	161.8
0° and below	3.3	1.2	0.4	0.0	0.0	0.0	0.0	0.0	0.0	0.0	0.1	2.0	7.0
RELATIVE HUMIDITY (%)													
Morning	57	57	60	61	65	65	67	69	66	57	60	55	62
Afternoon	46	38	38	33	36	34	39	41	37	36	45	47	39
PRECIPITATION (inches)													
Water Equivalent													
Normal	0.2	0.3	0.7	1.3	2.2	2.0	2.8	2.6	1.3	0.7	0.5	0.3	15.4
Maximum monthly	1.1	0.7	2.3	5.9	5.6	8.0	5.2	5.9	4.2	5.0	2.2	1.0	8.0
Date	1956	1960	1979	1957	1957	1965	1968	1976	1976	1984	1957	1979	1965
Minimum monthly	T	0.0	0.0	0.0	0.3	0.1	0.9	0.1	T	0.0	T	T	T
Date	1964	1950	1966	1964	1974	1968	1959	1962	1953	1980	1965	1970	1970
Maximum in 24 hrs	0.7	0.4	1.1	2.4	2.5	3.0	3.0	3.7	1.7	1.6	1.4	0.6	3.7
Date	1956	1957	1977	1957	1955	1954	1951	1976	1959	1960	1979	1981	1976
SNOW, ICE PELLETS													
Maximum monthly	12.7	11.5	23.2	42.7	19.4	1.1	0.0	0.0	27.9	25.9	19.1	18.2	42.7
Date	1956	1971	1984	1957	1978	1975	—	—	1959	1984	1979	1983	1957
Maximum in 24 hrs	8.4	7.0	13.3	18.0	17.4	1.1	0.0	0.0	17.1	14.6	14.5	9.6	18.0
Date	1971	1971	1964	1957	1978	1975	—	—	1959	1984	1972	1979	1957
WIND (Resultant)													
Mean speed (mph)	9.5	10.2	11.3	11.8	11.3	10.6	9.4	9.0	9.5	9.7	9.5	9.6	10.1

DENVER

Elev. 5282' **39° 45'N — 104° 52'W** ## Colorado

NORMALS, MEANS, EXTREMES

	JAN	FEB	MAR	APR	MAY	JUN	JUL	AUG	SEP	OCT	NOV	DEC	YEAR
TEMPERATURE													
Normal daily maximum	43.1	46.9	51.2	61.0	70.7	81.6	88.0	85.8	77.5	66.8	52.4	46.1	64.3
Normal daily minimum	15.9	20.2	24.7	33.7	43.6	52.4	58.7	57.0	47.7	36.9	25.1	18.9	36.2
Normal monthly	29.5	33.6	38.0	47.4	57.2	67.0	73.4	71.4	62.6	51.9	38.8	32.5	50.2
Extreme highest	73	76	84	85	96	104	104	101	97	88	79	75	104
Extreme highest date	1982	1963	1971	1960	1942	1936	1939	1938	1960	1947	1941	1980	1939
Extreme lowest	-25	-30	-11	-2	22	30	43	41	17	3	-8	-21	-30
Extreme lowest date	1963	1936	1943	1975	1954	1951	1972	1964	1985	1969	1950	1983	1936
DEGREE DAYS BASE 65° F													
Heating	1101	879	837	528	253	74	0	0	135	414	789	1004	6014
Cooling	0	0	0	0	11	134	261	203	63	8	0	0	680
% OF POSSIBLE SUNSHINE	71	71	70	67	64	71	71	73	74	72	64	67	70
AVERAGE SKY COVER													
Sunrise - Sunset	5.6	5.8	6.1	6.0	6.2	5.0	4.9	4.9	4.4	4.5	5.4	5.4	5.4
NUMBER OF DAYS (Sunrise-Sunset)													
Clear	10.0	8.1	7.8	6.9	6.1	9.6	9.1	10.0	13.5	13.5	10.3	10.6	115.5
Partly cloudy	9.2	8.8	10.3	10.7	12.1	12.3	15.9	13.8	8.9	9.0	9.4	9.8	130.2
Cloudy	11.7	11.4	12.8	12.5	12.8	8.1	6.1	7.3	7.6	8.5	10.2	10.6	119.5
Precipitation .01" or more	5.8	5.7	8.6	8.8	10.6	8.8	9.2	8.6	6.2	5.3	5.3	5.2	88.3
Snow, Ice pellets 1.0" or more	2.3	2.4	3.7	2.5	0.5	0.0	0.0	0.0	0.3	1.2	2.5	2.3	17.7
Thunderstorms	0.0	*	0.2	1.5	6.3	9.8	11.1	8.2	3.4	0.9	0.1	0.0	41.4
Fog, Visibility 1/4 mile or less	1.2	1.6	1.0	0.8	0.5	0.4	0.4	0.6	0.6	0.7	1.2	1.0	10.1
Temperature Maximum:													
90° and above	0.0	0.0	0.0	0.0	0.3	5.9	15.2	9.3	2.2	0.0	0.0	0.0	32.9
32° and below	6.9	4.2	3.0	0.5	0.0	0.0	0.0	0.0	*	0.3	2.5	5.1	22.6
Temperature Minimum:													
32° and below	30.0	26.4	25.4	12.0	1.7	0.0	0.0	0.0	1.0	8.7	24.7	29.1	158.9
0° and below	4.3	1.7	0.5	*	0.0	0.0	0.0	0.0	0.0	0.0	0.2	2.7	9.5
RELATIVE HUMIDITY (%)													
Morning	64	66	67	67	70	69	68	69	68	64	69	64	67
Afternoon	49	43	41	35	38	35	34	35	34	35	49	51	40
PRECIPITATION (inches)													
Water Equivalent													
Normal	0.5	0.6	1.2	1.8	2.4	1.5	1.9	1.5	1.2	0.9	0.8	0.5	15.3
Maximum monthly	1.4	1.6	4.5	4.1	7.3	4.6	6.4	5.8	4.6	4.1	2.9	2.8	7.3
Date	1948	1960	1983	1942	1957	1967	1965	1979	1961	1969	1946	1973	1957
Minimum monthly	0.0	0.0	0.1	0.0	0.0	0.0	0.1	0.0	T	0.0	0.0	0.0	T
Date	1952	1970	1945	1963	1974	1980	1939	1960	1944	1962	1949	1977	1944
Maximum in 24 hrs	1.0	1.0	2.7	3.2	3.5	3.1	2.4	3.4	2.4	1.7	1.2	2.0	3.5
Date	1962	1953	1983	1967	1973	1970	1965	1951	1936	1947	1975	1982	1973
SNOW, ICE PELLETS													
Maximum monthly	23.7	18.3	30.5	28.3	13.6	0.3	0.0	0.0	21.3	31.2	39.1	30.8	39.1
Date	1948	1960	1983	1935	1950	1951	—	—	1936	1969	1946	1973	1946
Maximum in 24 hrs	12.4	9.5	18.0	17.3	10.7	0.3	0.0	0.0	19.4	12.4	15.9	23.6	23.6
Date	1962	1953	1983	1957	1950	1951	—	—	1936	1969	1983	1982	1982
WIND (Resultant)													
Mean speed (mph)	8.7	9.0	9.8	10.2	9.4	8.9	8.4	8.1	8.0	7.9	8.4	8.7	8.8

GRAND JUNCTION

Elev. 4843'   39° 07'N — 108° 32'W   **Colorado**

NORMALS, MEANS, EXTREMES

	JAN	FEB	MAR	APR	MAY	JUN	JUL	AUG	SEP	OCT	NOV	DEC	YEAR
TEMPERATURE													
Normal daily maximum	35.7	44.5	54.1	65.2	76.2	87.9	94.0	90.3	81.9	68.7	51.0	38.7	65.7
Normal daily minimum	15.2	22.4	29.7	38.2	48.0	56.6	63.8	61.5	52.2	41.1	28.2	17.9	39.6
Normal monthly	25.5	33.5	41.9	51.7	62.1	72.3	78.9	75.9	67.1	54.9	39.6	28.3	52.6
Extreme highest	60	68	81	85	95	103	105	103	98	88	75	64	105
Extreme highest date	1971	1981	1971	1969	1956	1981	1976	1969	1977	1963	1977	1980	1976
Extreme lowest	-23	-14	5	11	26	34	46	43	29	18	-2	-12	-23
Extreme lowest date	1963	1951	1948	1975	1970	1976	1982	1968	1978	1975	1976	1978	1963
DEGREE DAYS BASE 65° F													
Heating	1225	882	716	403	148	19	0	0	65	325	762	1138	5683
Cooling	0	0	0	0	58	238	431	338	128	12	0	0	1205
% OF POSSIBLE SUNSHINE	60	64	63	69	72	80	78	76	79	73	63	60	70
AVERAGE SKY COVER													
Sunrise - Sunset	6.2	6.2	6.2	5.8	5.5	3.9	4.2	4.3	3.6	4.2	5.4	5.9	5.1
NUMBER OF DAYS (Sunrise-Sunset)													
Clear	9.0	7.6	8.2	8.5	9.7	15.1	13.7	14.0	16.5	14.9	10.8	9.5	137.6
Partly cloudy	7.3	7.1	8.3	9.1	10.7	9.4	11.9	11.1	8.0	7.9	7.1	7.7	105.7
Cloudy	14.7	13.5	14.5	12.4	10.5	5.5	5.4	5.9	5.4	8.2	11.9	13.8	121.8
Precipitation .01" or more	7.2	6.0	7.8	6.3	6.2	4.2	5.0	6.5	5.7	5.5	5.5	6.3	72.3
Snow, Ice pellets 1.0" or more	2.6	1.2	1.3	0.3	0.1	0.0	0.0	0.0	*	0.2	1.0	2.1	8.8
Thunderstorms	0.1	0.3	0.8	1.9	4.3	4.8	7.6	7.6	5.1	1.5	0.4	0.1	34.3
Fog, Visibility 1/4 mile or less	3.0	1.9	0.6	0.1	*	0.0	0.0	0.0	0.0	0.1	0.8	1.8	8.4
Temperature Maximum:													
90° and above	0.0	0.0	0.0	0.0	1.5	13.7	25.2	20.4	4.5	0.0	0.0	0.0	65.3
32° and below	11.6	2.4	0.2	0.0	0.0	0.0	0.0	0.0	0.0	0.0	0.8	7.0	22.0
Temperature Minimum:													
32° and below	30.2	25.4	17.1	7.1	0.5	0.0	0.0	0.0	0.2	3.1	20.2	29.3	133.1
0° and below	3.9	0.6	0.0	0.0	0.0	0.0	0.0	0.0	0.0	0.0	*	1.1	5.6
RELATIVE HUMIDITY (%)													
Morning	77	70	63	56	53	45	49	50	52	58	70	76	60
Afternoon	63	46	36	28	25	20	22	23	26	34	47	60	36
PRECIPITATION (inches)													
Water Equivalent													
Normal	0.6	0.5	0.7	0.7	0.7	0.4	0.4	0.9	0.7	0.8	0.6	0.5	8.0
Maximum monthly	2.4	1.5	2.0	1.9	1.7	2.0	1.9	3.4	2.8	3.4	2.0	1.8	3.4
Date	1957	1948	1979	1965	1957	1969	1983	1957	1982	1972	1983	1951	1957
Minimum monthly	T	T	0.0	0.0	T	T	0.0	0.0	T	0.0	0.0	0.0	0.0
Date	1961	1972	1972	1958	1970	1980	1972	1956	1953	1952	1976	1976	1952
Maximum in 24 hrs	0.6	0.5	0.9	1.3	1.1	1.5	1.4	1.2	1.3	1.2	0.8	1.1	1.5
Date	1956	1980	1983	1965	1983	1969	1974	1953	1965	1957	1983	1951	1969
SNOW, ICE PELLETS													
Maximum monthly	33.7	18.4	14.9	14.3	5.0	0.0	0.0	0.0	3.1	6.1	12.1	19.0	33.7
Date	1957	1948	1948	1975	1979	—	—	—	1965	1975	1964	1983	1957
Maximum in 24 hrs	9.1	8.6	6.1	8.9	5.0	0.0	0.0	0.0	3.1	6.1	8.4	6.0	9.1
Date	1957	1948	1948	1975	1979	—	—	—	1965	1975	1954	1967	1957
WIND (Resultant)													
Mean speed (mph)	5.6	6.7	8.4	9.6	9.6	9.8	9.3	9.0	9.0	7.9	6.7	5.9	8.1

PUEBLO

Elev. 4684' **38° 17'N — 104° 31'W** # Colorado

NORMALS, MEANS, EXTREMES

	JAN	FEB	MAR	APR	MAY	JUN	JUL	AUG	SEP	OCT	NOV	DEC	YEAR
TEMPERATURE													
Normal daily maximum	45.2	50.7	55.9	66.5	76.0	87.5	92.2	89.5	81.6	70.7	55.7	48.3	68.3
Normal daily minimum	14.3	19.6	25.2	35.7	46.0	55.0	61.5	59.3	50.3	37.5	24.6	17.2	37.2
Normal monthly	29.8	35.2	40.6	51.1	61.0	71.3	76.9	74.4	66.0	54.1	40.2	32.8	52.8
Extreme highest	78	81	86	90	98	106	106	104	99	92	84	82	106
Extreme highest date	1971	1981	1946	1981	1974	1980	1981	1980	1979	1979	1980	1980	1981
Extreme lowest	-29	-31	-20	2	25	38	44	40	27	14	-14	-23	-31
Extreme lowest date	1948	1951	1948	1975	1954	1951	1945	1968	1985	1975	1976	1978	1951
DEGREE DAYS BASE 65° F													
Heating	1091	834	756	421	163	23	0	0	89	346	744	998	5465
Cooling	0	0	0	0	39	212	369	295	119	8	0	0	1042
% OF POSSIBLE SUNSHINE	75	74	74	74	74	79	78	78	80	78	73	72	76
AVERAGE SKY COVER													
Sunrise - Sunset	5.2	5.4	5.5	5.6	5.6	4.5	4.7	4.6	4.0	4.1	4.9	5.0	4.9
NUMBER OF DAYS (Sunrise-Sunset)													
Clear	11.6	9.9	9.9	8.8	8.6	12.5	10.8	11.8	15.5	15.2	12.1	12.0	138.8
Partly cloudy	8.8	7.7	9.3	10.3	11.5	11.1	14.8	12.6	8.3	8.2	8.6	9.0	120.3
Cloudy	10.6	10.6	11.8	10.9	10.9	6.4	5.4	6.6	6.2	7.6	9.3	10.0	106.2
Precipitation .01" or more	4.6	4.3	6.1	6.0	8.2	6.8	9.4	8.5	4.6	3.8	3.6	3.6	69.3
Snow, Ice pellets 1.0" or more	1.8	1.4	2.2	0.8	0.2	0.0	0.0	0.0	0.1	0.3	1.2	1.5	9.5
Thunderstorms	*	0.0	0.2	1.6	6.1	7.9	12.0	9.3	2.9	0.5	0.1	0.0	40.4
Fog, Visibility 1/4 mile or less	1.0	1.2	1.0	0.7	0.3	0.2	0.2	0.3	0.6	0.6	1.1	1.4	8.4
Temperature Maximum:													
90° and above	0.0	0.0	0.0	0.1	2.1	14.5	23.2	18.2	6.9	0.3	0.0	0.0	65.2
32° and below	6.9	2.6	1.4	0.1	0.0	0.0	0.0	0.0	0.0	0.1	1.8	5.4	18.1
Temperature Minimum:													
32° and below	30.2	26.8	23.4	8.5	0.6	0.0	0.0	0.0	0.6	9.3	25.7	29.8	154.7
0° and below	4.0	1.0	0.3	0.0	0.0	0.0	0.0	0.0	0.0	0.0	0.3	2.6	8.1
RELATIVE HUMIDITY (%)													
Morning	66	63	63	65	65	68	72	73	70	66	73	67	68
Afternoon	51	38	34	30	32	27	33	33	32	33	45	50	37
PRECIPITATION (inches)													
Water Equivalent													
Normal	0.2	0.2	0.6	1.0	1.4	1.1	1.8	1.8	0.8	0.7	0.4	0.3	10.8
Maximum monthly	1.4	0.7	2.3	6.1	5.4	4.2	4.8	5.8	2.7	4.9	2.4	0.9	6.1
Date	1948	1947	1979	1942	1957	1961	1985	1955	1976	1957	1957	1979	1942
Minimum monthly	0.0	T	0.0	T	0.3	0.0	0.2	0.0	T	T	T	T	T
Date	1950	1970	1966	1963	1965	1952	1963	1960	1956	1980	1966	1970	1980
Maximum in 24 hrs	0.5	0.4	1.2	2.4	2.5	2.2	1.9	2.9	1.5	3.7	0.9	0.7	3.7
Date	1945	1947	1983	1957	1957	1979	1977	1955	1982	1957	1972	1979	1957
SNOW, ICE PELLETS													
Maximum monthly	20.0	14.4	22.4	21.2	4.8	0.0	0.0	0.0	14.0	12.6	29.3	15.3	29.3
Date	1948	1965	1948	1957	1946	—	—	—	1959	1972	1946	1967	1946
Maximum in 24 hrs	7.3	5.9	10.9	16.8	5.6	0.0	0.0	0.0	9.5	12.6	16.3	8.7	16.8
Date	1956	1965	1972	1957	1954	—	—	—	1959	1972	1946	1961	1957
WIND (Resultant)													
Mean speed (mph)	8.0	8.6	9.8	10.5	9.8	9.4	8.7	8.0	8.0	7.5	7.6	7.9	8.7

BRIDGEPORT

Elev. 7' 41° 10'N — 73° 08'W **Connecticut**

NORMALS, MEANS, EXTREMES

	JAN	FEB	MAR	APR	MAY	JUN	JUL	AUG	SEP	OCT	NOV	DEC	YEAR
TEMPERATURE													
Normal daily maximum	36.5	37.9	45.5	57.2	67.1	76.4	82.1	81.1	74.5	64.5	52.8	41.0	59.7
Normal daily minimum	22.5	23.3	30.9	40.0	49.8	59.3	65.9	65.0	57.8	47.4	38.1	27.3	43.9
Normal monthly	29.5	30.6	38.2	48.6	58.5	67.9	74.0	73.1	66.2	56.0	45.5	34.2	51.8
Extreme highest	65	67	74	86	92	96	103	98	99	85	78	65	103
Extreme highest date	1974	1976	1985	1977	1969	1974	1957	1953	1953	1959	1975	1971	1957
Extreme lowest	-7	-5	4	18	31	41	51	44	36	26	16	-4	-7
Extreme lowest date	1984	1963	1967	1982	1966	1967	1982	1982	1963	1972	1972	1980	1984
DEGREE DAYS BASE 65° F													
Heating	1101	963	831	492	220	20	0	0	49	285	585	955	5501
Cooling	0	0	0	0	18	107	279	251	85	6	0	0	746
% OF POSSIBLE SUNSHINE	na	na	na	na	na	na	na	na	na	na	na	na	na
AVERAGE SKY COVER													
Sunrise - Sunset	6.2	6.2	6.4	6.3	6.5	6.0	5.9	5.8	5.6	5.4	6.3	6.3	6.1
NUMBER OF DAYS (Sunrise-Sunset)													
Clear	8.7	8.2	7.8	7.4	6.6	7.8	7.6	8.7	9.6	10.8	8.1	8.5	99.8
Partly cloudy	7.6	6.9	8.5	8.6	10.0	9.8	12.1	10.7	9.1	8.2	7.6	7.5	106.5
Cloudy	14.7	13.2	14.6	14.0	14.4	12.4	11.2	11.6	11.3	12.1	14.3	15.1	158.9
Precipitation .01" or more	10.6	9.5	11.3	10.5	11.1	9.4	8.2	9.2	8.4	7.1	10.1	11.4	116.9
Snow, Ice pellets 1.0" or more	2.2	1.9	1.3	0.2	0.0	0.0	0.0	0.0	0.0	0.0	0.2	1.6	7.4
Thunderstorms	0.1	0.3	0.9	1.7	2.8	3.8	5.0	4.1	1.9	0.8	0.3	0.1	21.8
Fog, Visibility 1/4 mile or less	3.2	2.8	3.4	3.1	4.3	3.7	1.9	1.1	1.2	1.5	1.5	1.9	29.5
Temperature Maximum:													
90° and above	0.0	0.0	0.0	0.0	0.1	0.9	3.0	1.5	0.5	0.0	0.0	0.0	5.9
32° and below	11.4	7.4	1.2	0.1	0.0	0.0	0.0	0.0	0.0	0.0	0.2	4.7	24.8
Temperature Minimum:													
32° and below	26.5	23.2	17.1	3.9	0.1	0.0	0.0	0.0	0.0	1.1	7.0	21.0	99.8
0° and below	0.6	0.2	0.0	0.0	0.0	0.0	0.0	0.0	0.0	0.0	0.0	0.1	0.9
RELATIVE HUMIDITY (%)													
Morning	69	67	69	70	79	83	82	83	83	77	75	72	76
Afternoon	61	59	57	54	60	62	60	62	62	60	61	62	60
PRECIPITATION (inches)													
Water Equivalent													
Normal	3.2	3.0	3.9	3.7	3.4	2.9	3.4	3.6	3.2	3.3	3.7	3.7	41.5
Maximum monthly	11.2	6.6	9.4	10.7	8.1	17.7	12.8	13.2	7.4	10.7	10.2	7.8	17.7
Date	1979	1972	1953	1983	1984	1972	1971	1952	1960	1955	1972	1972	1972
Minimum monthly	0.4	1.0	0.6	0.6	0.7	0.0	0.4	0.7	0.4	0.3	0.3	0.3	0.0
Date	1970	1980	1981	1985	1955	1949	1979	1981	1959	1963	1976	1955	1949
Maximum in 24 hrs	4.5	2.3	4.6	3.3	3.2	6.8	5.9	3.9	4.6	4.2	4.0	3.6	6.8
Date	1979	1969	1977	1980	1968	1972	1971	1955	1960	1972	1954	1968	1972
SNOW, ICE PELLETS													
Maximum monthly	26.2	24.0	21.8	6.0	T	0.0	0.0	0.0	0.0	T	5.4	16.2	26.2
Date	1965	1967	1967	1982	1977	—	—	—	—	1979	1953	1963	1965
Maximum in 24 hrs	16.7	16.7	11.1	6.0	T	0.0	0.0	0.0	0.0	T	5.4	7.8	16.7
Date	1978	1969	1967	1982	1977	—	—	—	—	1979	1953	1966	1978
WIND (Resultant)													
Mean speed (mph)	13.2	13.6	13.5	13.0	11.6	10.5	10.0	10.1	11.2	11.9	12.7	13.0	12.0

HARTFORD

Elev. 169'   41° 56'N — 72° 41'W   ## Connecticut

NORMALS, MEANS, EXTREMES

	JAN	FEB	MAR	APR	MAY	JUN	JUL	AUG	SEP	OCT	NOV	DEC	YEAR
TEMPERATURE													
Normal daily maximum	33.6	36.3	45.5	60.0	71.4	80.1	84.8	82.6	74.8	63.9	50.6	37.3	60.1
Normal daily minimum	16.7	18.8	28.0	37.6	47.3	57.0	61.9	60.0	51.7	40.9	32.5	20.9	39.5
Normal monthly	25.2	27.6	36.8	48.8	59.4	68.6	73.4	71.3	63.3	52.4	41.6	29.1	49.8
Extreme highest	65	73	87	96	97	100	102	101	99	91	81	74	102
Extreme highest date	1967	1985	1977	1976	1979	1964	1966	1975	1983	1963	1974	1984	1966
Extreme lowest	-26	-21	-6	9	28	37	44	36	30	17	12	-14	-26
Extreme lowest date	1961	1961	1967	1970	1985	1964	1962	1965	1979	1978	1972	1980	1961
DEGREE DAYS BASE 65° F													
Heating	1234	1047	874	486	197	20	0	8	102	391	702	1113	6174
Cooling	0	0	0	0	24	128	260	203	51	0	0	0	666
% OF POSSIBLE SUNSHINE	57	58	56	56	58	60	64	63	60	57	47	49	57
AVERAGE SKY COVER													
Sunrise - Sunset	6.4	6.5	6.8	6.7	6.8	6.7	6.4	6.3	6.1	6.0	6.9	6.8	6.5
NUMBER OF DAYS (Sunrise-Sunset)													
Clear	7.7	6.5	6.4	6.5	5.3	5.5	5.9	6.3	8.3	9.0	5.6	6.7	79.7
Partly cloudy	8.2	8.0	8.4	8.6	9.9	10.4	12.1	11.1	9.2	8.9	8.4	7.5	110.8
Cloudy	15.0	13.8	16.2	14.8	15.8	14.0	13.0	13.6	12.5	13.1	16.0	16.8	174.7
Precipitation .01" or more	10.7	10.4	11.5	11.0	11.5	11.3	9.6	9.9	9.4	8.3	11.2	12.3	127.1
Snow, Ice pellets 1.0" or more	3.0	2.7	2.5	0.5	*	0.0	0.0	0.0	0.0	*	0.5	3.5	12.8
Thunderstorms	0.1	0.2	0.7	1.2	2.4	4.1	4.5	4.3	2.3	0.9	0.4	0.1	21.2
Fog, Visibility 1/4 mile or less	2.2	2.6	2.3	1.3	1.8	2.5	1.9	2.5	3.4	3.9	2.3	3.0	29.8
Temperature Maximum:													
90° and above	0.0	0.0	0.0	0.3	1.1	3.7	8.0	4.7	1.5	*	0.0	0.0	19.2
32° and below	14.9	9.4	2.0	0.1	0.0	0.0	0.0	0.0	0.0	0.0	0.0	0.5	10.0	36.8
Temperature Minimum:													
32° and below	29.1	25.5	21.7	8.7	0.8	0.0	0.0	0.0	0.4	6.3	16.2	27.1	135.7
0° and below	3.3	1.8	*	0.0	0.0	0.0	0.0	0.0	0.0	0.0	0.0	1.2	6.3
RELATIVE HUMIDITY (%)													
Morning	68	68	68	68	75	80	81	84	85	80	75	73	75
Afternoon	56	54	51	44	47	51	50	53	54	51	56	60	52
PRECIPITATION (inches)													
Water Equivalent													
Normal	3.5	3.1	4.1	4.0	3.3	3.3	3.0	4.0	3.9	3.5	4.0	4.1	44.3
Maximum monthly	9.6	7.2	6.8	9.9	11.5	13.6	8.2	21.8	9.0	11.6	8.5	8.3	21.8
Date	1978	1981	1983	1983	1984	1982	1960	1955	1975	1955	1972	1969	1955
Minimum monthly	0.3	0.9	0.2	1.3	0.7	0.7	1.0	0.5	1.2	0.3	0.5	0.7	0.2
Date	1981	1980	1981	1966	1959	1971	1983	1981	1984	1963	1976	1955	1981
Maximum in 24 hrs	2.5	2.1	2.5	3.0	2.9	6.1	3.4	12.1	5.2	4.4	2.3	3.1	12.1
Date	1979	1965	1979	1979	1984	1982	1960	1955	1960	1959	1955	1973	1955
SNOW, ICE PELLETS													
Maximum monthly	37.0	32.2	43.3	14.3	1.3	0.0	0.0	0.0	0.0	1.7	8.6	35.4	43.3
Date	1978	1969	1956	1982	1977	—	—	—	—	1979	1980	1969	1956
Maximum in 24 hrs	14.7	21.0	14.0	14.1	1.3	0.0	0.0	0.0	0.0	1.7	8.6	13.9	21.0
Date	1978	1983	1956	1982	1977	—	—	—	—	1979	1980	1969	1983
WIND (Resultant)													
Mean speed (mph)	9.0	9.4	10.0	10.1	8.9	8.1	7.5	7.1	7.2	7.7	8.4	8.6	8.5

WILMINGTON

Elev. 74'   39° 40'N — 75° 36'W   **Delaware**

NORMALS, MEANS, EXTREMES

	JAN	FEB	MAR	APR	MAY	JUN	JUL	AUG	SEP	OCT	NOV	DEC	YEAR
TEMPERATURE													
Normal daily maximum	39.2	41.8	50.9	63.0	72.7	81.2	85.6	84.1	77.8	66.7	54.8	43.6	63.5
Normal daily minimum	23.2	24.6	32.6	41.8	51.7	61.2	66.3	65.4	58.0	45.9	36.4	27.3	44.5
Normal monthly	31.2	33.2	41.8	52.4	62.2	71.2	76.0	74.8	67.9	56.3	45.6	35.5	54.0
Extreme highest	75	78	86	94	95	99	102	101	100	91	85	74	102
Extreme highest date	1950	1985	1948	1985	1962	1952	1966	1955	1983	1951	1950	1984	1966
Extreme lowest	-14	-6	2	18	30	41	50	43	36	24	14	-7	-14
Extreme lowest date	1985	1979	1984	1982	1978	1972	1979	1982	1974	1976	1955	1983	1985
DEGREE DAYS BASE 65° F													
Heating	1048	890	719	378	130	6	0	0	36	282	582	915	4986
Cooling	0	0	0	0	43	192	341	304	123	12	0	0	1015
% OF POSSIBLE SUNSHINE	na	na	na	na	na	na	na	na	na	na	na	na	na
AVERAGE SKY COVER													
Sunrise - Sunset	6.6	6.4	6.5	6.4	6.6	6.0	5.9	5.8	5.6	5.5	6.3	6.5	6.2
NUMBER OF DAYS (Sunrise-Sunset)													
Clear	7.4	7.3	7.5	7.3	6.3	7.6	8.0	9.0	10.1	10.6	7.7	7.7	96.5
Partly cloudy	7.2	7.0	8.2	8.4	10.1	10.7	11.3	10.2	8.2	8.0	8.2	7.4	104.8
Cloudy	16.5	14.0	15.3	14.3	14.6	11.7	11.7	11.7	11.7	12.3	14.1	15.9	164.0
Precipitation .01" or more	10.9	9.4	11.2	10.9	11.6	9.8	9.2	9.1	7.9	7.7	9.6	9.9	117.2
Snow, Ice pellets 1.0" or more	2.2	1.5	1.0	0.1	0.0	0.0	0.0	0.0	0.0	*	0.2	0.9	5.8
Thunderstorms	0.2	0.3	1.2	2.3	4.4	5.9	6.2	6.1	2.3	0.9	0.6	0.2	30.5
Fog, Visibility 1/4 mile or less	4.2	3.8	2.9	2.1	2.5	2.0	1.8	2.7	2.6	4.0	3.6	3.8	36.1
Temperature Maximum:													
90° and above	0.0	0.0	0.0	0.1	0.6	3.6	7.8	5.1	1.9	*	0.0	0.0	19.1
32° and below	7.8	4.6	0.8	0.0	0.0	0.0	0.0	0.0	0.0	0.0	0.1	4.0	17.3
Temperature Minimum:													
32° and below	25.9	22.1	15.3	3.2	0.1	0.0	0.0	0.0	0.0	1.6	10.5	22.3	100.9
0° and below	0.5	0.2	0.0	0.0	0.0	0.0	0.0	0.0	0.0	0.0	0.0	0.1	0.8
RELATIVE HUMIDITY (%)													
Morning	73	72	71	72	79	82	82	84	84	82	77	75	78
Afternoon	60	57	53	50	53	54	54	56	55	54	56	59	55
PRECIPITATION (inches)													
Water Equivalent													
Normal	3.1	2.9	3.8	3.3	3.2	3.5	3.9	4.0	3.5	2.8	3.3	3.5	41.3
Maximum monthly	8.4	7.0	6.8	6.8	7.3	7.4	7.5	12.0	9.5	6.4	7.8	7.9	12.0
Date	1978	1979	1983	1983	1983	1972	1958	1955	1960	1971	1972	1969	1955
Minimum monthly	0.5	0.8	0.8	0.3	0.2	0.4	0.1	0.2	0.8	0.2	0.4	0.1	0.1
Date	1981	1980	1966	1985	1964	1954	1955	1972	1970	1963	1976	1955	1955
Maximum in 24 hrs	2.1	2.2	3.1	2.5	2.4	4.3	6.2	4.1	5.6	3.8	3.8	2.2	6.2
Date	1978	1966	1978	1961	1985	1972	1952	1971	1960	1966	1956	1969	1952
SNOW, ICE PELLETS													
Maximum monthly	17.2	27.5	20.3	2.6	T	0.0	0.0	0.0	0.0	2.5	11.9	21.5	27.5
Date	1966	1979	1958	1982	1963	—	—	—	—	1979	1953	1966	1979
Maximum in 24 hrs	11.2	16.5	15.6	1.5	T	0.0	0.0	0.0	0.0	2.5	11.9	12.4	16.5
Date	1966	1979	1958	1982	1963	—	—	—	—	1979	1953	1966	1979
WIND (Resultant)													
Mean speed (mph)	10.0	10.5	11.3	10.6	9.1	8.4	7.8	7.5	7.9	8.3	9.3	9.4	9.2

WASHINGTON
Elev. 10'   38° 51'N — 77° 02   **D.C.**

NORMALS, MEANS, EXTREMES

	JAN	FEB	MAR	APR	MAY	JUN	JUL	AUG	SEP	OCT	NOV	DEC	YEAR
TEMPERATURE													
Normal daily maximum	42.9	45.9	55.0	67.1	75.9	84.0	87.9	86.4	80.1	68.9	57.4	46.6	66.5
Normal daily minimum	27.5	29.0	36.6	46.2	56.1	65.0	69.9	68.7	62.0	49.7	39.9	31.2	48.5
Normal monthly	35.2	37.5	45.8	56.7	66.0	74.5	78.9	77.6	71.1	59.3	48.7	38.9	57.5
Extreme highest	79	82	89	95	97	101	103	101	101	94	86	75	103
Extreme highest date	1950	1948	1945	1976	1969	1952	1980	1983	1980	1954	1974	1984	1980
Extreme lowest	-5	4	11	24	34	47	55	51	39	29	16	1	-5
Extreme lowest date	1982	1961	1943	1982	1947	1972	1943	1963	1963	1969	1955	1942	1982
DEGREE DAYS BASE 65° F													
Heating	924	770	595	257	68	0	0	0	13	197	489	809	4122
Cooling	0	0	0	8	99	285	431	391	196	20	0	0	1430
% OF POSSIBLE SUNSHINE	48	52	55	58	59	64	64	63	63	58	51	47	57
AVERAGE SKY COVER													
Sunrise - Sunset	6.6	6.4	6.5	6.3	6.3	5.9	6.0	5.8	5.6	5.5	6.1	6.5	6.1
NUMBER OF DAYS (Sunrise-Sunset)													
Clear	7.7	7.6	7.4	7.2	7.3	7.8	7.7	9.2	10.1	10.9	8.3	8.4	99.5
Partly cloudy	7.1	6.6	8.6	8.9	9.8	10.9	11.9	10.0	8.3	7.4	7.8	6.6	103.9
Cloudy	16.2	14.1	15.1	13.9	13.9	11.3	11.4	11.8	11.6	12.7	13.9	15.9	161.8
Precipitation .01" or more	10.3	8.7	11.0	9.7	11.2	9.5	9.8	9.3	7.6	7.4	8.3	9.1	111.8
Snow, Ice pellets 1.0" or more	1.6	1.4	0.8	0.0	0.0	0.0	0.0	0.0	0.0	0.0	0.1	0.8	4.7
Thunderstorms	0.2	0.2	1.2	2.5	4.5	5.7	6.5	5.2	2.1	1.1	0.5	0.1	29.6
Fog, Visibility 1/4 mile or less	1.9	1.6	0.9	0.8	0.4	0.2	0.2	0.1	0.4	1.3	1.3	1.9	11.0
Temperature Maximum:													
90° and above	0.0	0.0	0.0	0.4	1.3	7.4	13.1	10.1	4.3	*	0.0	0.0	36.7
32° and below	5.3	2.3	0.2	0.0	0.0	0.0	0.0	0.0	0.0	0.0	*	1.9	9.7
Temperature Minimum:													
32° and below	23.0	18.9	8.0	0.9	0.0	0.0	0.0	0.0	0.0	0.5	4.2	15.6	71.2
0° and below	0.1	0.0	0.0	0.0	0.0	0.0	0.0	0.0	0.0	0.0	0.0	0.0	0.1
RELATIVE HUMIDITY (%)													
Morning	66	65	64	65	73	76	76	79	78	76	70	68	71
Afternoon	54	52	49	47	52	53	53	55	55	53	53	56	53
PRECIPITATION (inches)													
Water Equivalent													
Normal	2.7	2.6	3.4	2.9	3.4	3.3	3.8	4.4	3.2	2.9	2.8	3.1	39.0
Maximum monthly	7.1	5.7	7.4	6.8	10.6	11.5	11.0	14.3	12.3	8.1	6.7	6.5	14.3
Date	1978	1961	1953	1983	1953	1972	1945	1955	1975	1942	1963	1969	1955
Minimum monthly	0.3	0.4	0.6	0.0	1.0	1.2	0.9	0.5	0.2	T	0.2	0.2	T
Date	1955	1978	1945	1985	1963	1976	1966	1962	1967	1963	1981	1955	1963
Maximum in 24 hrs	2.1	1.9	3.4	3.0	4.3	7.1	4.6	6.3	5.3	4.9	2.6	2.8	7.1
Date	1976	1983	1958	1970	1953	1972	1970	1955	1975	1955	1971	1977	1972
SNOW, ICE PELLETS													
Maximum monthly	21.3	30.6	17.1	0.6	T	0.0	0.0	0.0	0.0	0.3	6.9	16.2	30.6
Date	1966	1979	1960	1972	1963	—	—	—	—	1979	1967	1962	1979
Maximum in 24 hrs	13.8	18.7	7.9	0.6	T	0.0	0.0	0.0	0.0	0.3	6.9	11.4	18.7
Date	1966	1979	1960	1972	1963	—	—	—	—	1979	1967	1957	1979
WIND (Resultant)													
Mean speed (mph)	10.0	10.3	10.9	10.4	9.1	8.7	8.2	8.0	8.2	8.6	9.3	9.5	9.3

APALACHICOLA

Elev. 19'   29° 44'N — 85° 02'W   **Florida**

NORMALS, MEANS, EXTREMES

	JAN	FEB	MAR	APR	MAY	JUN	JUL	AUG	SEP	OCT	NOV	DEC	YEAR
TEMPERATURE													
Normal daily maximum	60.5	62.4	68.0	75.1	81.7	86.6	88.0	88.0	85.3	78.2	69.2	63.0	75.5
Normal daily minimum	45.1	46.9	53.4	60.7	67.3	72.9	75.0	74.7	72.3	62.1	52.7	47.0	60.8
Normal monthly	52.8	54.7	60.7	67.9	74.5	79.8	81.5	81.4	78.8	70.2	61.0	55.0	68.2
Extreme highest	79	80	85	90	96	101	102	99	96	93	87	82	102
Extreme highest date	1957	1957	1982	1967	1953	1930	1932	1956	1932	1941	1935	1931	1932
Extreme lowest	9	21	22	37	47	48	63	66	50	39	24	13	9
Extreme lowest date	1985	1951	1980	1977	1981	1984	1981	1985	1967	1977	1950	1962	1985
DEGREE DAYS BASE 65° F													
Heating	401	311	168	30	0	0	0	0	0	24	154	320	1408
Cooling	23	23	35	117	295	444	512	508	417	185	34	10	2603
% OF POSSIBLE SUNSHINE	59	62	65	74	78	72	64	64	66	74	67	57	67
AVERAGE SKY COVER													
Sunrise - Sunset	5.7	5.5	5.6	4.8	4.6	5.2	6.1	5.9	5.5	4.0	4.5	5.7	5.3
NUMBER OF DAYS (Sunrise-Sunset)													
Clear	10.2	9.8	10.6	12.3	12.9	9.4	6.4	7.2	9.8	16.1	13.6	10.0	128.4
Partly cloudy	7.6	6.8	8.3	8.9	10.4	12.8	13.0	13.0	9.7	7.7	7.6	7.7	113.5
Cloudy	4.1	11.6	12.0	8.8	7.7	7.8	11.6	10.8	10.5	7.3	8.8	13.3	114.3
Precipitation .01" or more	8.9	8.5	7.8	5.6	5.5	9.6	14.7	13.7	11.2	5.5	6.2	8.2	105.4
Snow, Ice pellets 1.0" or more	0.0	*	0.0	0.0	0.0	0.0	0.0	0.0	0.0	0.0	0.0	0.0	*
Thunderstorms	1.6	2.4	3.8	3.4	4.9	9.8	16.3	15.7	9.8	1.7	1.5	1.6	72.4
Fog, Visibility 1/4 mile or less	6.2	4.6	5.4	2.5	0.9	0.3	0.1	0.1	0.1	0.6	2.1	4.3	27.2
Temperature Maximum:													
90° and above	0.0	0.0	0.0	*	0.6	5.3	7.3	7.0	3.0	0.1	0.0	0.0	23.3
32° and below	*	0.0	0.0	0.0	0.0	0.0	0.0	0.0	0.0	0.0	0.0	*	*
Temperature Minimum:													
32° and below	3.1	1.5	0.3	0.0	0.0	0.0	0.0	0.0	0.0	0.0	0.3	1.7	6.9
0° and below	0.0	0.0	0.0	0.0	0.0	0.0	0.0	0.0	0.0	0.0	0.0	0.0	0.0
RELATIVE HUMIDITY (%)													
Morning	83	83	86	86	86	86	87	87	86	84	83	84	85
Afternoon	66	65	65	65	65	67	71	76	69	63	63	68	67
PRECIPITATION (inches)													
Water Equivalent													
Normal	3.5	3.6	4.0	3.2	2.9	4.8	7.0	7.5	8.6	3.1	2.8	3.5	54.9
Maximum monthly	8.2	9.1	14.3	12.1	8.7	18.3	18.0	21.0	22.5	12.0	9.0	7.8	22.5
Date	1964	1960	1959	1983	1974	1965	1984	1970	1946	1959	1947	1953	1946
Minimum monthly	0.0	0.3	0.7	0.0	0.2	0.3	0.7	1.8	0.6	0.0	0.0	0.3	0.0
Date	1957	1938	1939	1942	1983	1977	1976	1951	1972	1935	1931	1955	1935
Maximum in 24 hrs	3.9	3.7	8.1	7.7	7.0	5.3	6.7	5.6	11.7	6.3	5.8	4.1	11.7
Date	1985	1940	1948	1964	1959	1949	1975	1950	1932	1965	1930	1931	1932
SNOW, ICE PELLETS													
Maximum monthly	0.4	1.2	T	0.0	0.0	0.0	0.0	0.0	0.0	0.0	0.0	T	1.2
Date	1977	1958	1980	—	—	—	—	—	—	—	—	1952	1958
Maximum in 24 hrs	0.4	1.2	T	0.0	0.0	0.0	0.0	0.0	0.0	0.0	0.0	T	1.2
Date	1977	1958	1980	—	—	—	—	—	—	—	—	1952	1958
WIND (Resultant)													
Mean speed (mph)	8.3	8.7	9.0	8.6	7.7	7.2	6.5	6.5	7.9	8.0	8.0	8.0	7.9

DAYTONA BEACH   Elev. 29'   29° 11'N — 81° 03'W   Florida

NORMALS, MEANS, EXTREMES

	JAN	FEB	MAR	APR	MAY	JUN	JUL	AUG	SEP	OCT	NOV	DEC	YEAR
TEMPERATURE													
Normal daily maximum	68.4	69.3	74.6	80.0	84.8	87.8	89.6	89.0	86.9	81.2	74.8	69.8	79.7
Normal daily minimum	47.4	48.2	53.6	59.1	65.3	70.5	72.5	72.8	72.1	65.1	55.5	49.2	60.9
Normal monthly	57.9	58.8	64.1	69.6	75.1	79.2	81.1	80.9	79.5	73.2	65.2	59.5	70.3
Extreme highest	86	89	91	96	100	102	102	99	99	95	89	86	102
Extreme highest date	1985	1985	1977	1968	1953	1944	1981	1956	1944	1959	1948	1978	1981
Extreme lowest	15	24	26	35	44	52	60	65	52	41	27	19	15
Extreme lowest date	1985	1958	1980	1950	1971	1984	1981	1984	1956	1954	1950	1983	1985
DEGREE DAYS BASE 65° F													
Heating	264	214	116	14	0	0	0	0	0	0	83	209	900
Cooling	44	41	88	152	313	426	499	493	435	259	89	39	2878
% OF POSSIBLE SUNSHINE	na	na	na	na	na	na	na	na	na	na	na	na	na
AVERAGE SKY COVER													
Sunrise - Sunset	5.7	5.7	5.6	5.1	5.4	6.2	6.3	6.2	6.4	5.6	5.2	5.8	5.8
NUMBER OF DAYS (Sunrise-Sunset)													
Clear	9.4	8.8	9.5	10.4	9.9	5.8	4.1	4.5	4.9	9.4	10.2	9.3	96.3
Partly cloudy	9.5	8.2	9.9	10.8	11.4	12.5	14.6	15.7	12.9	10.7	10.1	9.0	135.4
Cloudy	12.1	11.2	11.6	8.8	9.7	11.7	12.3	10.8	12.2	10.9	9.7	12.7	133.6
Precipitation .01" or more	6.9	7.8	7.7	5.7	8.4	12.3	13.5	13.8	13.2	10.6	7.2	7.4	114.5
Snow, Ice pellets 1.0" or more	0.0	0.0	0.0	0.0	0.0	0.0	0.0	0.0	0.0	0.0	0.0	0.0	0.0
Thunderstorms	1.0	1.8	3.2	3.6	8.1	13.2	17.3	15.6	8.5	3.2	1.1	1.2	77.9
Fog, Visibility 1/4 mile or less	5.4	3.3	3.3	1.9	1.6	1.0	1.1	1.4	0.7	1.5	2.8	4.7	28.8
Temperature Maximum:													
90° and above	0.0	0.0	0.2	1.6	5.1	10.6	16.0	13.7	5.9	0.7	0.0	0.0	53.8
32° and below	0.0	0.0	0.0	0.0	0.0	0.0	0.0	0.0	0.0	0.0	0.0	0.0	0.0
Temperature Minimum:													
32° and below	2.5	1.2	0.3	0.0	0.0	0.0	0.0	0.0	0.0	0.0	0.2	1.6	5.8
0° and below	0.0	0.0	0.0	0.0	0.0	0.0	0.0	0.0	0.0	0.0	0.0	0.0	0.0
RELATIVE HUMIDITY (%)													
Morning	85	83	83	83	85	88	89	90	88	85	85	85	86
Afternoon	59	57	55	54	57	63	65	67	67	63	60	60	61
PRECIPITATION (inches)													
Water Equivalent													
Normal	2.3	3.1	2.9	2.2	3.3	6.4	5.5	6.3	6.6	4.6	2.5	2.2	48.4
Maximum monthly	7.1	9.1	7.7	7.1	12.3	15.1	14.5	19.8	15.2	13.0	10.9	11.9	19.8
Date	1979	1960	1953	1949	1976	1966	1944	1953	1979	1950	1972	1983	1953
Minimum monthly	0.1	0.2	0.2	T	0.0	1.0	1.0	2.0	0.4	0.1	T	0.0	T
Date	1950	1944	1956	1967	1965	1981	1976	1963	1972	1967	1967	1956	1967
Maximum in 24 hrs	3.6	4.3	5.7	4.0	4.2	6.2	3.9	4.7	6.3	9.2	5.8	5.2	9.2
Date	1977	1971	1953	1982	1947	1966	1967	1974	1964	1953	1979	1983	1953
SNOW, ICE PELLETS													
Maximum monthly	T	T	0.0	0.0	0.0	0.0	0.0	0.0	0.0	0.0	0.0	T	T
Date	1977	1951	—	—	—	—	—	—	—	—	—	1962	1977
Maximum in 24 hrs	T	T	0.0	0.0	0.0	0.0	0.0	0.0	0.0	0.0	0.0	T	T
Date	1977	1951	—	—	—	—	—	—	—	—	—	1962	1977
WIND (Resultant)													
Mean speed (mph)	9.0	9.8	10.0	9.7	9.0	8.2	7.5	7.2	8.6	9.3	8.7	8.6	8.8

FORT MYERS

Elev. 15'   26° 35'N — 81° 52'W   **Florida**

NORMALS, MEANS, EXTREMES

	JAN	FEB	MAR	APR	MAY	JUN	JUL	AUG	SEP	OCT	NOV	DEC	YEAR
TEMPERATURE													
Normal daily maximum	74.3	75.1	79.8	84.5	88.7	90.1	91.0	91.2	89.6	85.2	80.0	75.6	83.8
Normal daily minimum	52.5	53.1	57.8	61.7	67.0	72.0	74.1	74.4	73.8	67.7	59.5	53.7	63.9
Normal monthly	63.4	64.1	68.8	73.1	77.9	81.1	82.6	82.8	81.7	76.5	69.8	64.7	73.9
Extreme highest	88	92	93	95	99	103	101	100	96	94	91	90	103
Extreme highest date	1982	1962	1980	1946	1953	1981	1942	1942	1980	1941	1979	1978	1981
Extreme lowest	28	30	33	39	50	60	66	65	63	45	34	26	26
Extreme lowest date	1981	1958	1980	1950	1945	1984	1950	1957	1956	1957	1970	1962	1962
DEGREE DAYS BASE 65° F													
Heating	150	120	39	0	0	0	0	0	0	0	25	107	441
Cooling	100	94	156	243	400	483	546	552	501	357	169	98	3699
% OF POSSIBLE SUNSHINE	na	na	na	na	na	na	na	na	na	na	na	na	na
AVERAGE SKY COVER													
Sunrise - Sunset	5.0	5.0	4.9	4.6	5.0	6.1	6.5	6.4	6.3	5.1	4.7	4.9	5.4
NUMBER OF DAYS (Sunrise-Sunset)													
Clear	11.0	10.3	11.3	11.1	9.4	4.7	1.9	2.3	3.8	10.8	11.9	11.3	100.0
Partly cloudy	11.5	10.9	12.2	13.2	14.8	15.8	18.3	18.4	15.2	12.6	11.5	11.6	166.0
Cloudy	8.4	7.0	7.5	5.7	6.8	9.5	10.8	10.3	11.0	7.6	6.6	8.1	99.3
Precipitation .01" or more	5.4	5.8	5.3	4.6	7.9	14.7	18.1	17.8	15.7	7.9	4.4	4.9	112.3
Snow, Ice pellets 1.0" or more	0.0	0.0	0.0	0.0	0.0	0.0	0.0	0.0	0.0	0.0	0.0	0.0	0.0
Thunderstorms	0.7	1.4	2.1	2.6	7.2	15.5	22.7	21.3	13.8	3.9	0.8	0.8	92.8
Fog, Visibility 1/4 mile or less	4.6	3.0	3.0	1.7	1.0	0.4	*	*	0.2	0.6	2.2	3.7	20.6
Temperature Maximum:													
90° and above	0.0	0.1	0.6	3.0	13.5	18.9	24.0	24.3	17.7	4.8	0.2	0.1	107.3
32° and below	0.0	0.0	0.0	0.0	0.0	0.0	0.0	0.0	0.0	0.0	0.0	0.0	0.0
Temperature Minimum:													
32° and below	0.6	0.1	0.0	0.0	0.0	0.0	0.0	0.0	0.0	0.0	0.0	0.2	0.9
0° and below	0.0	0.0	0.0	0.0	0.0	0.0	0.0	0.0	0.0	0.0	0.0	0.0	0.0
RELATIVE HUMIDITY (%)													
Morning	85	84	84	84	85	88	89	88	88	87	87	87	86
Afternoon	57	55	52	48	50	59	60	61	62	57	56	56	56
PRECIPITATION (inches)													
Water Equivalent													
Normal	1.8	2.0	2.8	1.5	4.1	8.7	8.5	8.5	8.5	3.8	1.3	1.5	53.6
Maximum monthly	7.4	10.8	18.5	7.6	10.3	20.1	15.2	16.7	16.6	12.0	3.8	5.4	20.1
Date	1979	1983	1970	1941	1968	1974	1941	1981	1969	1959	1972	1940	1974
Minimum monthly	0.0	T	0.0	T	0.3	1.9	2.2	3.9	2.3	0.0	T	0.0	0.0
Date	1950	1944	1974	1970	1962	1980	1964	1963	1972	1963	1944	1984	1950
Maximum in 24 hrs	2.6	2.6	7.9	3.8	5.3	6.6	4.0	6.7	9.3	10.8	3.3	3.0	10.8
Date	1983	1969	1970	1943	1980	1959	1965	1967	1962	1951	1960	1969	1951
WIND (Resultant)													
Mean speed (mph)	8.5	9.1	9.4	9.0	8.2	7.4	6.8	6.8	7.7	8.5	8.3	8.1	8.2

GAINESVILLE

Elev. 138' 29° 41'N — 82° 16'W **Florida**

NORMALS, MEANS, EXTREMES

	JAN	FEB	MAR	APR	MAY	JUN	JUL	AUG	SEP	OCT	NOV	DEC	YEAR
TEMPERATURE													
Normal daily maximum	66.7	68.5	75.1	81.1	86.6	89.5	90.5	90.5	87.8	81.1	73.9	68.1	80.0
Normal daily minimum	42.5	43.7	49.7	55.7	62.5	68.4	71.0	71.1	69.2	59.4	49.8	43.9	57.2
Normal monthly	54.6	56.1	62.4	68.4	74.6	79.0	80.8	80.8	78.5	70.3	61.9	56.0	68.6
Extreme highest	83	83	87	90	97	102	95	96	95	90	85	81	102
Extreme highest date	1985	1985	1985	1985	1985	1985	1984	1984	1985	1985	1985	1985	1985
Extreme lowest	10	26	30	40	47	50	65	62	62	48	33	19	10
Extreme lowest date	1985	1985	1984	1985	1984	1984	1985	1984	1985	1984	1984	1985	1985
DEGREE DAYS BASE 65° F													
Heating	358	279	144	20	0	0	0	0	0	15	141	302	1259
Cooling	35	30	63	122	298	420	488	488	405	179	48	23	2599
NUMBER OF DAYS (Sunrise-Sunset)													
Precipitation .01" or more	9.0	7.0	6.0	8.0	6.5	13.5	17.0	16.5	16.0	11.0	10.0	4.5	125.0
Snow, Ice pellets 1.0" or more	0.0	0.0	0.0	0.0	0.0	0.0	0.0	0.0	0.0	0.0	0.0	0.0	0.0
Thunderstorms	0.5	2.5	1.5	4.0	7.0	11.0	20.5	17.5	7.0	6.5	2.0	0.5	80.5
Fog, Visibility 1/4 mile or less	5.0	2.0	4.0	1.5	2.0	3.0	2.5	2.0	2.5	5.0	5.5	7.5	42.5
Temperature Maximum:													
90° and above	0.0	0.0	0.0	1.0	9.0	17.5	17.5	17.0	9.5	0.5	0.0	0.0	72.0
32° and below	0.5	0.0	0.0	0.0	0.0	0.0	0.0	0.0	0.0	0.0	0.0	0.0	0.5
Temperature Minimum:													
32° and below	7.0	4.5	1.5	0.0	0.0	0.0	0.0	0.0	0.0	0.0	0.0	5.5	18.5
0° and below	0.0	0.0	0.0	0.0	0.0	0.0	0.0	0.0	0.0	0.0	0.0	0.0	0.0
RELATIVE HUMIDITY (%)													
Morning	84	86	90	91	87	92	94	94	93	92	92	92	91
Afternoon	57	51	55	58	48	59	62	63	66	62	63	60	59
PRECIPITATION (inches)													
Water Equivalent													
Normal	3.2	3.9	3.5	2.9	4.1	6.3	6.9	8.0	5.5	2.4	2.0	3.2	52.3
Maximum monthly	1.2	4.8	3.1	4.0	5.4	7.1	8.8	15.8	4.0	4.6	2.9	1.5	15.8
Date	1984	1984	1984	1985	1984	1985	1984	1985	1985	1985	1984	1985	1985
Minimum monthly	1.1	1.6	1.5	2.6	3.7	3.8	7.0	3.1	3.5	0.8	1.7	0.2	0.2
Date	1985	1985	1985	1984	1985	1984	1985	1984	1984	1984	1985	1984	1984
Maximum in 24 hrs	0.5	1.9	1.3	2.6	3.4	1.8	1.6	2.8	1.4	1.1	1.1	0.7	3.4
Date	1985	1984	1984	1985	1985	1985	1984	1985	1984	1985	1984	1985	1985
WIND (Resultant)													
Mean speed (mph)	7.6	7.1	7.4	7.5	6.6	6.2	5.0	5.8	7.2	6.3	6.6	5.2	6.5

JACKSONVILLE   Elev. 26'   30° 30'N — 81° 42'W   Florida

NORMALS, MEANS, EXTREMES

	JAN	FEB	MAR	APR	MAY	JUN	JUL	AUG	SEP	OCT	NOV	DEC	YEAR
TEMPERATURE													
Normal daily maximum	64.6	66.8	73.3	79.7	85.2	88.9	90.7	90.2	86.9	79.7	72.4	66.3	78.7
Normal daily minimum	41.7	43.3	49.3	55.7	63.0	69.1	71.8	71.8	69.4	59.2	49.2	43.2	57.2
Normal monthly	53.2	55.1	61.3	67.7	74.1	79.0	81.3	81.0	78.2	69.5	60.8	54.8	68.0
Extreme highest	85	88	91	95	100	103	105	102	100	96	88	84	105
Extreme highest date	1947	1962	1974	1968	1967	1954	1942	1954	1944	1951	1961	1981	1942
Extreme lowest	7	19	23	35	45	47	61	63	48	36	21	11	7
Extreme lowest date	1985	1943	1980	1975	1973	1984	1972	1984	1981	1977	1970	1983	1985
DEGREE DAYS BASE 65° F													
Heating	396	302	166	21	0	0	0	0	0	21	164	332	1402
Cooling	30	25	51	102	282	420	505	496	396	160	38	15	2520
% OF POSSIBLE SUNSHINE	58	62	67	71	69	63	61	60	55	57	60	57	62
AVERAGE SKY COVER													
Sunrise - Sunset	5.9	5.8	5.8	5.2	5.5	6.2	6.4	6.2	6.5	5.6	5.3	6.0	5.9
NUMBER OF DAYS (Sunrise-Sunset)													
Clear	9.2	8.9	9.2	10.1	9.3	5.7	4.7	5.1	5.3	9.8	10.9	9.3	97.4
Partly cloudy	8.3	7.4	9.4	10.4	11.9	13.1	14.4	15.3	11.8	9.4	8.4	8.1	127.7
Cloudy	13.5	11.9	12.5	9.5	9.8	11.2	12.0	10.7	12.9	11.9	10.7	13.6	140.2
Precipitation .01" or more	7.8	7.8	8.0	6.6	8.3	12.0	14.7	14.4	13.1	8.7	6.3	7.9	115.6
Snow, Ice pellets 1.0" or more	0.0	*	0.0	0.0	0.0	0.0	0.0	0.0	0.0	0.0	0.0	0.0	*
Thunderstorms	0.8	1.3	3.0	3.6	6.6	10.4	15.5	12.8	6.6	2.0	0.7	1.0	64.2
Fog, Visibility 1/4 mile or less	5.3	3.4	3.3	2.7	2.9	1.1	1.0	1.6	1.7	3.3	5.5	5.6	37.5
Temperature Maximum:													
90° and above	0.0	0.0	0.1	1.5	8.0	16.1	23.1	20.7	10.3	1.1	0.0	0.0	80.8
32° and below	*	0.0	0.0	0.0	0.0	0.0	0.0	0.0	0.0	0.0	0.0	*	*
Temperature Minimum:													
32° and below	5.7	3.5	0.8	0.0	0.0	0.0	0.0	0.0	0.0	0.0	1.0	4.1	15.1
0° and below	0.0	0.0	0.0	0.0	0.0	0.0	0.0	0.0	0.0	0.0	0.0	0.0	0.0
RELATIVE HUMIDITY (%)													
Morning	84	82	82	84	85	87	88	90	90	89	87	86	86
Afternoon	57	53	50	48	50	57	58	60	63	58	56	58	56
PRECIPITATION (inches)													
Water Equivalent													
Normal	3.0	3.4	3.7	3.3	4.9	5.3	6.5	7.1	7.2	3.4	1.9	2.5	52.7
Maximum monthly	7.2	8.8	10.1	11.6	10.4	12.9	16.2	16.2	19.3	13.4	7.8	7.0	19.3
Date	1964	1970	1973	1973	1966	1967	1960	1968	1949	1956	1947	1945	1949
Minimum monthly	0.0	0.5	0.1	0.1	0.6	2.1	1.9	1.9	1.0	0.1	T	0.0	T
Date	1950	1962	1945	1942	1953	1950	1977	1942	1961	1942	1970	1956	1970
Maximum in 24 hrs	3.0	6.2	7.1	8.2	5.4	5.9	10.0	7.9	10.1	6.6	5.4	3.7	10.1
Date	1963	1970	1970	1973	1975	1968	1966	1968	1950	1956	1969	1983	1950
SNOW, ICE PELLETS													
Maximum monthly	T	1.5	T	0.0	0.0	0.0	0.0	0.0	0.0	0.0	0.0	T	1.5
Date	1985	1958	1980	—	—	—	—	—	—	—	—	1962	1958
Maximum in 24 hrs	T	1.5	T	0.0	0.0	0.0	0.0	0.0	0.0	0.0	0.0	T	1.5
Date	1985	1958	1980	—	—	—	—	—	—	—	—	1962	1958
WIND (Resultant)													
Mean speed (mph)	8.3	9.2	9.2	8.8	8.2	8.0	7.2	6.9	7.8	8.2	7.9	8.0	8.1

KEY WEST Elev. 4'   24° 33'N — 81° 45'W   Florida

NORMALS, MEANS, EXTREMES

	JAN	FEB	MAR	APR	MAY	JUN	JUL	AUG	SEP	OCT	NOV	DEC	YEAR
TEMPERATURE													
Normal daily maximum	71.8	74.8	78.6	82.0	84.9	87.3	88.9	88.9	86.5	84.4	79.6	75.2	81.9
Normal daily minimum	65.6	65.3	69.5	73.4	76.2	78.5	80.0	79.6	78.6	75.8	71.4	66.8	73.4
Normal monthly	68.7	70.1	74.1	77.7	80.6	82.9	84.5	84.3	82.6	80.1	75.5	71.0	77.7
Extreme highest	85	85	87	89	91	94	95	95	94	93	88	86	95
Extreme highest date	1960	1984	1977	1965	1953	1952	1951	1957	1951	1962	1964	1978	1957
Extreme lowest	41	47	49	55	66	68	69	68	69	60	49	44	41
Extreme lowest date	1981	1958	1980	1950	1960	1961	1952	1952	1985	1957	1959	1985	1981
DEGREE DAYS BASE 65° F													
Heating	49	37	6	0	0	0	0	0	0	0	0	22	114
Cooling	164	180	288	381	484	537	605	598	528	468	315	208	4756
% OF POSSIBLE SUNSHINE	73	76	82	83	80	74	76	75	70	70	69	70	75
AVERAGE SKY COVER													
Sunrise - Sunset	5.1	4.8	4.5	4.4	5.2	6.2	6.4	6.4	6.7	5.7	5.0	5.1	5.5
NUMBER OF DAYS (Sunrise-Sunset)													
Clear	10.8	11.1	13.4	13.5	9.7	5.0	3.3	3.0	2.6	8.2	10.5	10.5	101.6
Partly cloudy	11.7	10.2	11.6	11.3	13.7	14.6	16.9	17.2	15.3	12.8	11.5	11.9	158.8
Cloudy	8.5	6.9	6.0	5.2	7.7	10.4	10.8	10.8	12.1	10.0	8.0	8.6	104.9
Precipitation .01" or more	6.4	5.8	4.9	4.7	7.6	11.7	12.5	14.6	15.7	11.6	6.8	7.0	109.3
Snow, Ice pellets 1.0" or more	0.0	0.0	0.0	0.0	0.0	0.0	0.0	0.0	0.0	0.0	0.0	0.0	0.0
Thunderstorms	0.9	1.2	1.7	1.8	4.2	9.6	13.0	14.2	11.0	4.3	1.1	1.0	63.9
Fog, Visibility 1/4 mile or less	0.3	0.2	0.0	0.0	0.0	0.0	0.0	0.0	*	0.1	0.1	0.3	1.0
Temperature Maximum:													
90° and above	0.0	0.0	0.0	0.0	0.6	6.6	13.9	15.0	6.2	0.5	0.0	0.0	42.9
32° and below	0.0	0.0	0.0	0.0	0.0	0.0	0.0	0.0	0.0	0.0	0.0	0.0	0.0
Temperature Minimum:													
32° and below	0.0	0.0	0.0	0.0	0.0	0.0	0.0	0.0	0.0	0.0	0.0	0.0	0.0
0° and below	0.0	0.0	0.0	0.0	0.0	0.0	0.0	0.0	0.0	0.0	0.0	0.0	0.0
RELATIVE HUMIDITY (%)													
Morning	80	78	77	76	77	78	77	78	79	80	80	80	78
Afternoon	69	67	66	64	65	68	66	67	70	69	69	69	67
PRECIPITATION (inches)													
Water Equivalent													
Normal	1.7	1.9	1.3	1.4	3.2	5.0	3.6	4.8	6.5	4.7	3.2	1.7	39.4
Maximum monthly	17.6	4.4	6.5	12.8	12.9	14.4	11.6	11.3	18.4	21.5	27.6	4.9	27.6
Date	1983	1965	1983	1948	1960	1972	1970	1945	1963	1969	1980	1983	1980
Minimum monthly	0.0	0.0	T	0.0	0.1	0.5	0.5	2.2	1.7	0.7	0.1	0.0	0.0
Date	1960	1948	1971	1959	1945	1985	1961	1969	1951	1972	1961	1981	1959
Maximum in 24 hrs	10.3	2.5	3.1	6.5	8.8	6.1	3.0	3.9	6.6	8.4	23.2	4.6	23.2
Date	1983	1966	1968	1985	1960	1982	1970	1977	1963	1971	1980	1959	1980
WIND (Resultant)													
Mean speed (mph)	12.0	12.2	12.5	12.6	10.7	9.6	9.7	9.5	9.9	11.2	12.0	12.0	11.2

MIAMI

Elev. 7'   25° 49'N — 80° 17'W   **Florida**

NORMALS, MEANS, EXTREMES

	JAN	FEB	MAR	APR	MAY	JUN	JUL	AUG	SEP	OCT	NOV	DEC	YEAR
TEMPERATURE													
Normal daily maximum	75.0	75.8	79.3	82.4	85.1	87.3	88.7	89.2	87.8	84.2	79.8	76.2	82.6
Normal daily minimum	59.2	59.7	64.1	68.2	71.9	74.6	76.2	76.5	75.7	71.6	65.8	60.8	68.7
Normal monthly	67.1	67.8	71.7	75.3	78.5	81.0	82.5	82.9	81.8	77.9	72.8	68.5	75.6
Extreme highest	88	89	92	96	94	98	98	98	95	95	89	87	98
Extreme highest date	1984	1982	1977	1971	1985	1985	1983	1954	1954	1980	1958	1978	1985
Extreme lowest	30	32	32	46	53	60	69	68	68	51	39	33	30
Extreme lowest date	1985	1947	1980	1971	1945	1984	1985	1950	1983	1943	1950	1983	1985
DEGREE DAYS BASE 65° F													
Heating	76	62	14	0	0	0	0	0	0	0	5	42	199
Cooling	141	140	222	309	419	480	539	552	504	400	239	150	4095
% OF POSSIBLE SUNSHINE	68	66	77	77	70	74	76	75	72	71	66	66	72
AVERAGE SKY COVER													
Sunrise - Sunset	5.3	5.3	5.3	5.3	5.8	6.7	6.6	6.6	6.8	6.0	5.4	5.3	5.9
NUMBER OF DAYS (Sunrise-Sunset)													
Clear	9.8	8.6	8.9	8.3	6.1	3.3	2.5	2.4	2.3	6.4	8.2	9.4	76.5
Partly cloudy	12.9	12.0	14.1	14.8	15.0	14.3	17.1	17.8	14.8	13.8	13.8	12.7	172.8
Cloudy	8.3	7.7	8.0	6.9	9.9	12.4	11.4	10.8	12.9	10.8	8.0	8.8	116.1
Precipitation .01" or more	6.5	6.0	5.7	6.0	10.3	14.9	15.8	17.1	17.5	14.5	8.3	6.5	129.2
Snow, Ice pellets 1.0" or more	0.0	0.0	0.0	0.0	0.0	0.0	0.0	0.0	0.0	0.0	0.0	0.0	0.0
Thunderstorms	0.8	1.3	1.6	2.6	7.0	12.3	14.5	15.6	11.7	4.7	1.2	0.8	74.0
Fog, Visibility 1/4 mile or less	1.4	0.9	0.7	0.7	0.4	0.0	0.1	0.1	0.1	0.2	1.0	0.9	6.4
Temperature Maximum:													
90° and above	0.0	0.0	0.2	1.1	2.8	7.7	11.7	10.5	6.4	0.8	0.0	0.0	41.1
32° and below	0.0	0.0	0.0	0.0	0.0	0.0	0.0	0.0	0.0	0.0	0.0	0.0	0.0
Temperature Minimum:													
32° and below	0.1	0.0	*	0.0	0.0	0.0	0.0	0.0	0.0	0.0	0.0	0.0	0.2
0° and below	0.0	0.0	0.0	0.0	0.0	0.0	0.0	0.0	0.0	0.0	0.0	0.0	0.0
RELATIVE HUMIDITY (%)													
Morning	80	79	77	75	79	83	82	83	85	82	81	79	80
Afternoon	59	57	56	55	60	66	63	65	67	64	61	59	61
PRECIPITATION (inches)													
Water Equivalent													
Normal	2.0	2.0	1.8	3.0	6.5	9.1	5.9	7.0	8.0	7.1	2.7	1.8	57.5
Maximum monthly	6.6	8.0	7.2	17.2	18.5	22.3	13.5	16.8	24.4	21.0	13.1	6.3	24.4
Date	1969	1983	1949	1979	1968	1968	1947	1943	1960	1952	1959	1958	1960
Minimum monthly	0.0	0.0	0.0	0.0	0.4	1.8	1.7	1.6	2.6	1.2	0.0	0.1	0.0
Date	1951	1944	1956	1981	1965	1945	1963	1954	1951	1977	1970	1968	1944
Maximum in 24 hrs	2.6	5.7	7.0	16.2	11.5	8.2	4.5	6.9	7.5	9.9	7.9	4.3	16.2
Date	1973	1966	1949	1979	1977	1977	1952	1964	1960	1948	1959	1964	1979
WIND (Resultant)													
Mean speed (mph)	9.4	10.1	10.4	10.6	9.5	8.2	7.9	7.8	8.2	9.3	9.6	9.2	9.2

NORMALS, MEANS, EXTREMES

	JAN	FEB	MAR	APR	MAY	JUN	JUL	AUG	SEP	OCT	NOV	DEC	YEAR
TEMPERATURE													
Normal daily maximum	71.7	72.9	78.3	83.6	88.3	90.6	91.7	91.6	89.7	84.4	78.2	73.1	82.8
Normal daily minimum	49.3	50.0	55.3	60.3	66.2	71.2	73.0	73.4	72.5	65.4	56.8	50.9	62.0
Normal monthly	60.5	61.5	66.8	72.0	77.3	80.9	82.4	82.5	81.1	74.9	67.5	62.0	72.4
Extreme highest	87	90	92	96	102	100	100	100	97	95	89	90	102
Extreme highest date	1963	1962	1970	1968	1945	1985	1961	1980	1977	1962	1980	1978	1945
Extreme lowest	19	28	25	39	49	53	64	64	56	43	29	20	19
Extreme lowest date	1985	1970	1980	1954	1945	1984	1981	1957	1956	1957	1950	1983	1985
DEGREE DAYS BASE 65° F													
Heating	212	172	68	0	0	0	0	0	0	0	47	157	656
Cooling	73	74	124	214	381	477	539	543	483	307	122	64	3401
% OF POSSIBLE SUNSHINE	na	na	na	na	na	na	na	na	na	na	na	na	na
AVERAGE SKY COVER													
Sunrise - Sunset	5.6	5.6	5.5	5.2	5.4	6.4	6.5	6.4	6.5	5.5	5.0	5.6	5.8
NUMBER OF DAYS (Sunrise-Sunset)													
Clear	9.4	8.8	9.4	10.0	9.0	4.6	3.2	3.1	3.8	9.5	10.9	10.1	91.8
Partly cloudy	10.5	8.7	10.4	11.5	13.1	14.0	16.7	17.1	14.3	11.5	10.2	9.2	147.1
Cloudy	11.1	10.7	11.2	8.5	8.8	11.4	11.1	10.8	11.8	10.1	9.0	11.8	126.3
Precipitation .01" or more	6.2	7.1	7.4	5.5	8.6	13.7	17.3	15.9	13.7	8.6	5.4	6.0	115.3
Snow, Ice pellets 1.0" or more	0.0	0.0	0.0	0.0	0.0	0.0	0.0	0.0	0.0	0.0	0.0	0.0	0.0
Thunderstorms	1.0	1.5	2.8	3.4	7.9	14.4	19.4	17.2	9.6	2.6	0.9	1.2	82.0
Fog, Visibility 1/4 mile or less	5.7	3.3	2.7	1.4	1.7	0.9	0.5	1.0	1.3	1.8	2.8	4.6	27.7
Temperature Maximum:													
90° and above	0.0	0.0	0.5	4.4	11.1	19.2	25.0	25.1	17.4	3.2	0.0	*	106.0
32° and below	0.0	0.0	0.0	0.0	0.0	0.0	0.0	0.0	0.0	0.0	0.0	0.0	0.0
Temperature Minimum:													
32° and below	1.9	0.5	0.2	0.0	0.0	0.0	0.0	0.0	0.0	0.0	0.1	0.6	3.3
0° and below	0.0	0.0	0.0	0.0	0.0	0.0	0.0	0.0	0.0	0.0	0.0	0.0	0.0
RELATIVE HUMIDITY (%)													
Morning	84	83	84	83	85	88	89	91	90	87	87	86	86
Afternoon	56	52	50	47	50	57	59	60	61	56	55	57	55
PRECIPITATION (inches)													
Water Equivalent													
Normal	2.1	2.8	3.2	2.1	3.9	7.3	7.7	6.3	5.6	2.8	1.7	1.8	47.8
Maximum monthly	6.4	8.3	10.5	6.2	10.3	18.2	19.5	16.1	15.8	14.5	6.5	5.3	19.5
Date	1979	1983	1960	1982	1976	1968	1960	1972	1945	1950	1980	1983	1960
Minimum monthly	0.1	0.1	0.1	0.1	0.4	1.9	3.5	2.9	0.4	0.3	0.0	T	T
Date	1950	1944	1956	1977	1961	1948	1981	1980	1972	1967	1967	1944	1944
Maximum in 24 hrs	3.4	4.3	5.0	5.0	3.1	8.4	8.1	5.2	9.6	7.7	4.0	3.6	9.6
Date	1979	1970	1960	1984	1980	1945	1960	1949	1945	1950	1951	1969	1945
SNOW, ICE PELLETS													
Maximum monthly	T	0.0	0.0	0.0	0.0	0.0	0.0	0.0	0.0	0.0	0.0	0.0	T
Date	1977	—	—	—	—	—	—	—	—	—	—	—	1977
Maximum in 24 hrs	T	0.0	0.0	0.0	0.0	0.0	0.0	0.0	0.0	0.0	0.0	0.0	T
Date	1977	—	—	—	—	—	—	—	—	—	—	—	1977
WIND (Resultant)													
Mean speed (mph)	9.0	9.7	9.9	9.4	8.8	8.1	7.4	7.2	7.8	8.7	8.7	8.6	8.6

NORMALS, MEANS, EXTREMES

	JAN	FEB	MAR	APR	MAY	JUN	JUL	AUG	SEP	OCT	NOV	DEC	YEAR
TEMPERATURE													
Normal daily maximum	60.6	63.6	69.2	76.7	83.7	89.0	90.1	89.6	86.6	79.3	69.4	63.2	76.8
Normal daily minimum	42.7	44.8	51.4	59.3	66.3	72.1	74.4	73.9	70.9	59.5	49.8	44.4	59.1
Normal monthly	51.7	54.2	60.3	68.0	75.0	80.6	82.3	81.8	78.8	69.4	59.6	53.8	67.9
Extreme highest	80	82	85	89	96	100	106	100	98	92	85	81	106
Extreme highest date	1975	1972	1974	1985	1964	1985	1980	1972	1980	1973	1973	1978	1980
Extreme lowest	5	19	22	37	48	56	61	63	43	37	25	11	5
Extreme lowest date	1985	1970	1980	1973	1979	1984	1967	1967	1967	1982	1976	1983	1985
DEGREE DAYS BASE 65° F													
Heating	445	327	184	29	0	0	0	0	0	35	192	359	1571
Cooling	33	24	42	119	310	468	536	521	411	171	33	12	2680
% OF POSSIBLE SUNSHINE	48	53	61	63	67	67	57	58	60	71	64	49	60
AVERAGE SKY COVER													
Sunrise - Sunset	6.5	5.7	6.1	5.6	5.5	5.4	6.3	6.1	5.3	4.6	5.1	6.1	5.7
NUMBER OF DAYS (Sunrise-Sunset)													
Clear	7.6	9.2	8.5	9.5	9.5	7.8	4.4	5.5	9.9	13.3	11.9	9.3	106.5
Partly cloudy	6.9	7.2	8.5	8.8	10.8	14.5	15.9	14.9	10.5	9.1	7.5	6.4	120.8
Cloudy	16.5	11.9	14.1	11.7	10.7	7.7	10.7	10.6	9.5	8.7	10.6	15.4	137.9
Precipitation .01" or more	10.0	9.1	9.6	6.2	7.5	9.8	13.8	13.0	8.3	5.0	7.3	9.7	109.4
Snow, Ice pellets 1.0" or more	0.1	*	0.0	0.0	0.0	0.0	0.0	0.0	0.0	0.0	0.0	0.0	0.1
Thunderstorms	1.6	2.7	4.5	3.9	5.4	10.5	15.4	14.8	6.3	2.1	1.9	1.6	70.7
Fog, Visibility 1/4 mile or less	6.2	4.8	6.6	3.9	2.0	0.5	0.6	0.2	0.6	1.9	4.0	4.5	35.8
Temperature Maximum:													
90° and above	0.0	0.0	0.0	0.0	2.0	13.1	16.8	14.3	8.0	0.3	0.0	0.0	54.5
32° and below	0.2	0.0	0.0	0.0	0.0	0.0	0.0	0.0	0.0	0.0	0.0	*	0.2
Temperature Minimum:													
32° and below	7.5	4.2	0.8	0.0	0.0	0.0	0.0	0.0	0.0	0.0	0.8	4.4	17.6
0° and below	0.0	0.0	0.0	0.0	0.0	0.0	0.0	0.0	0.0	0.0	0.0	0.0	0.0
RELATIVE HUMIDITY (%)													
Morning	79	77	80	82	84	83	85	86	83	80	81	80	82
Afternoon	63	58	59	57	59	59	64	66	61	56	59	64	60
PRECIPITATION (inches)													
Water Equivalent													
Normal	4.4	4.9	5.6	4.4	3.8	5.7	7.1	7.0	6.7	3.5	3.4	4.1	61.1
Maximum monthly	13.4	11.6	12.9	15.5	8.3	17.6	20.3	13.0	11.5	14.8	6.5	9.5	20.3
Date	1978	1966	1979	1964	1969	1978	1979	1967	1975	1985	1975	1982	1979
Minimum monthly	0.6	1.0	0.8	0.6	0.3	0.8	1.6	3.1	0.3	0.0	0.3	0.5	0.0
Date	1981	1980	1967	1971	1965	1979	1970	1972	1984	1978	1981	1980	1978
Maximum in 24 hrs	5.4	4.7	11.1	7.5	4.7	6.7	5.1	5.6	10.0	4.9	3.5	4.5	11.1
Date	1978	1982	1979	1964	1970	1970	1975	1984	1967	1967	1975	1964	1979
SNOW, ICE PELLETS													
Maximum monthly	2.5	1.9	T	0.0	0.0	0.0	0.0	0.0	0.0	0.0	0.0	T	2.5
Date	1977	1973	1980	—	—	—	—	—	—	—	—	1963	1977
Maximum in 24 hrs	1.5	1.9	T	0.0	0.0	0.0	0.0	0.0	0.0	0.0	0.0	T	1.9
Date	1977	1973	1980	—	—	—	—	—	—	—	—	1963	1973
WIND (Resultant)													
Mean speed (mph)	9.1	9.4	9.7	9.5	8.6	7.5	6.9	6.6	7.7	8.0	8.3	8.9	8.3

TALLAHASSEE   Elev. 55'   30° 23'N — 84° 22'W   Florida

NORMALS, MEANS, EXTREMES

	JAN	FEB	MAR	APR	MAY	JUN	JUL	AUG	SEP	OCT	NOV	DEC	YEAR
TEMPERATURE													
Normal daily maximum	63.4	65.9	72.7	80.0	86.0	90.1	90.9	90.6	87.8	80.4	71.5	65.3	78.7
Normal daily minimum	39.9	41.2	47.7	54.0	62.0	68.8	71.5	71.6	68.8	56.4	46.0	40.7	55.7
Normal monthly	51.7	53.6	60.2	67.0	74.0	79.5	81.2	81.1	78.3	68.4	58.8	53.0	67.2
Extreme highest	82	85	90	95	98	103	103	100	99	93	88	84	103
Extreme highest date	1972	1962	1967	1968	1962	1985	1980	1980	1962	1985	1961	1971	1985
Extreme lowest	6	14	20	29	34	46	57	61	40	30	13	10	6
Extreme lowest date	1985	1971	1980	1971	1971	1984	1967	1969	1967	1973	1970	1962	1985
DEGREE DAYS BASE 65° F													
Heating	441	341	191	48	0	0	0	0	0	38	210	383	1652
Cooling	25	22	42	111	279	435	502	499	399	143	24	11	2492
% OF POSSIBLE SUNSHINE	na	na	na	na	na	na	na	na	na	na	na	na	na
AVERAGE SKY COVER													
Sunrise - Sunset	6.3	5.9	6.0	5.4	5.6	5.9	6.5	6.1	5.9	4.7	5.1	5.9	5.8
NUMBER OF DAYS (Sunrise-Sunset)													
Clear	8.5	8.5	8.5	9.7	8.3	6.0	3.1	4.6	7.3	13.5	11.2	9.0	98.3
Partly cloudy	7.0	7.5	9.0	10.7	12.8	14.2	16.8	16.1	12.2	8.2	8.4	8.2	131.0
Cloudy	15.3	12.3	13.4	9.6	9.9	9.8	11.1	10.3	10.6	9.3	10.4	13.8	135.8
Precipitation .01" or more	9.9	8.9	9.0	6.7	8.6	12.1	16.9	14.8	9.4	5.1	6.6	8.4	116.3
Snow, Ice pellets 1.0" or more	0.0	0.0	0.0	0.0	0.0	0.0	0.0	0.0	0.0	0.0	0.0	0.0	0.0
Thunderstorms	1.7	1.9	4.2	3.7	8.2	12.9	19.8	16.9	8.4	2.1	1.4	1.9	82.9
Fog, Visibility 1/4 mile or less	7.1	5.0	6.0	4.9	4.8	2.9	2.3	1.8	1.8	2.7	5.3	6.2	50.7
Temperature Maximum:													
90° and above	0.0	0.0	*	1.3	7.3	19.2	22.2	21.1	14.2	1.4	0.0	0.0	86.8
32° and below	0.1	0.0	0.0	0.0	0.0	0.0	0.0	0.0	0.0	0.0	0.0	*	0.1
Temperature Minimum:													
32° and below	11.4	8.3	3.0	0.1	0.0	0.0	0.0	0.0	0.0	0.2	4.4	10.0	37.3
0° and below	0.0	0.0	0.0	0.0	0.0	0.0	0.0	0.0	0.0	0.0	0.0	0.0	0.0
RELATIVE HUMIDITY (%)													
Morning	85	84	86	88	89	90	93	93	90	88	88	87	88
Afternoon	59	54	52	48	51	55	62	63	59	53	55	58	56
PRECIPITATION (inches)													
Water Equivalent													
Normal	4.6	5.0	5.6	4.1	5.1	6.5	8.7	7.3	6.4	3.1	3.3	4.5	64.5
Maximum monthly	11.6	11.5	13.5	13.1	11.6	12.6	20.1	15.7	15.9	11.7	10.4	12.6	20.1
Date	1975	1964	1973	1973	1976	1965	1964	1977	1969	1976	1976	1964	1964
Minimum monthly	0.4	1.2	1.2	0.5	T	2.0	2.3	2.4	0.1	T	0.8	0.8	T
Date	1969	1976	1967	1972	1965	1977	1983	1983	1972	1961	1971	1980	1965
Maximum in 24 hrs	3.7	6.0	7.1	4.7	4.5	6.7	8.9	3.3	9.4	5.9	4.9	9.2	9.4
Date	1976	1981	1962	1964	1979	1966	1964	1961	1969	1964	1976	1964	1969
SNOW, ICE PELLETS													
Maximum monthly	T	0.4	T	0.0	0.0	0.0	0.0	0.0	0.0	0.0	0.0	T	0.4
Date	1985	1973	1980	—	—	—	—	—	—	—	—	1976	1973
Maximum in 24 hrs	T	0.4	T	0.0	0.0	0.0	0.0	0.0	0.0	0.0	0.0	T	0.4
Date	1985	1973	1980	—	—	—	—	—	—	—	—	1976	1973
WIND (Resultant)													
Mean speed (mph)	7.1	7.6	7.9	7.2	6.4	6.0	5.3	5.2	6.1	6.4	6.3	6.5	6.5

TAMPA

Elev. 19'   27° 58'N — 82° 32'W   **Florida**

NORMALS, MEANS, EXTREMES

	JAN	FEB	MAR	APR	MAY	JUN	JUL	AUG	SEP	OCT	NOV	DEC	YEAR
TEMPERATURE													
Normal daily maximum	70.0	71.0	76.2	81.9	87.1	89.5	90.0	90.3	88.9	83.7	76.9	71.6	81.4
Normal daily minimum	49.5	50.4	56.1	61.1	67.2	72.3	74.2	74.2	72.8	65.1	56.4	50.9	62.5
Normal monthly	59.8	60.7	66.2	71.5	77.2	80.9	82.1	82.3	80.9	74.4	66.7	61.3	72.0
Extreme highest	84	88	91	93	98	99	97	98	96	94	90	86	99
Extreme highest date	1975	1971	1949	1975	1975	1985	1964	1975	1972	1959	1971	1978	1985
Extreme lowest	21	24	29	40	49	53	63	67	57	40	23	18	18
Extreme lowest date	1985	1958	1980	1971	1971	1984	1970	1973	1981	1964	1970	1962	1962
DEGREE DAYS BASE 65° F													
Heating	228	186	87	0	0	0	0	0	0	0	65	173	739
Cooling	66	68	124	202	375	477	533	533	477	295	116	58	3324
% OF POSSIBLE SUNSHINE	64	66	71	74	75	67	61	60	61	65	65	62	66
AVERAGE SKY COVER													
Sunrise - Sunset	5.6	5.5	5.4	5.0	5.2	6.1	6.8	6.6	6.4	5.2	5.0	5.5	5.7
NUMBER OF DAYS (Sunrise-Sunset)													
Clear	9.6	9.1	10.4	10.9	10.4	5.5	2.1	2.8	4.5	11.2	11.8	10.2	98.4
Partly cloudy	9.9	9.1	10.1	11.1	12.1	13.9	16.1	16.4	13.8	10.6	9.4	9.6	142.0
Cloudy	11.5	10.1	10.5	8.0	8.5	10.6	12.7	11.8	11.9	9.0	8.9	11.4	124.9
Precipitation .01" or more	6.4	6.8	6.7	4.7	6.3	11.5	15.7	16.8	13.1	6.9	5.4	6.4	106.6
Snow, Ice pellets 1.0" or more	0.0	0.0	0.0	0.0	0.0	0.0	0.0	0.0	0.0	0.0	0.0	0.0	0.0
Thunderstorms	1.0	1.6	2.5	2.7	5.7	13.5	21.4	20.9	12.0	3.0	1.2	1.3	86.9
Fog, Visibility 1/4 mile or less	5.7	2.9	2.8	1.2	0.5	0.3	0.1	0.2	0.4	1.2	2.7	4.4	22.4
Temperature Maximum:													
90° and above	0.0	0.0	0.0	0.6	7.5	14.9	19.3	20.1	13.6	1.8	*	0.0	77.8
32° and below	0.0	0.0	0.0	0.0	0.0	0.0	0.0	0.0	0.0	0.0	0.0	0.0	0.0
Temperature Minimum:													
32° and below	2.3	0.8	0.1	0.0	0.0	0.0	0.0	0.0	0.0	0.0	0.1	1.0	4.2
0° and below	0.0	0.0	0.0	0.0	0.0	0.0	0.0	0.0	0.0	0.0	0.0	0.0	0.0
RELATIVE HUMIDITY (%)													
Morning	84	83	82	82	81	84	85	87	86	85	85	84	84
Afternoon	59	56	55	51	53	60	63	64	62	57	57	59	58
PRECIPITATION (inches)													
Water Equivalent													
Normal	2.1	3.0	3.4	1.8	3.3	5.2	7.3	7.6	6.2	2.3	1.8	2.1	46.7
Maximum monthly	8.0	7.9	12.6	6.5	17.6	13.7	20.5	18.5	13.9	7.3	6.1	6.6	20.5
Date	1948	1963	1959	1957	1979	1974	1960	1949	1979	1952	1963	1950	1960
Minimum monthly	T	0.2	0.0	T	0.1	1.8	1.6	2.3	1.2	0.1	T	0.0	T
Date	1950	1950	1956	1981	1973	1951	1981	1952	1972	1979	1960	1984	1981
Maximum in 24 hrs	3.2	3.6	5.2	3.7	11.8	5.5	12.1	5.3	4.9	2.9	4.2	3.2	12.1
Date	1953	1981	1960	1951	1979	1974	1960	1949	1985	1985	1963	1969	1960
SNOW, ICE PELLETS													
Maximum monthly	0.2	T	T	0.0	0.0	0.0	0.0	0.0	0.0	0.0	0.0	0.0	0.2
Date	1977	1951	1980	—	—	—	—	—	—	—	—	—	1977
Maximum in 24 hrs	0.2	T	T	0.0	0.0	0.0	0.0	0.0	0.0	0.0	0.0	0.0	0.2
Date	1977	1951	1980	—	—	—	—	—	—	—	—	—	1977
WIND (Resultant)													
Mean speed (mph)	8.7	9.4	9.6	9.5	8.9	8.1	7.3	7.1	8.0	8.6	8.5	8.6	8.5

VERO BEACH

Elev. 24'　　27° 39'N — 80° 25'W　　**Florida**

NORMALS, MEANS, EXTREMES

	JAN	FEB	MAR	APR	MAY	JUN	JUL	AUG	SEP	OCT	NOV	DEC	YEAR
TEMPERATURE													
Normal daily maximum	72.2	72.8	77.3	81.2	85.2	87.9	89.7	89.9	87.9	83.3	77.9	73.4	81.6
Normal daily minimum	51.6	52.2	57.1	62.2	67.0	70.9	72.4	72.9	72.4	67.1	59.8	53.3	63.2
Normal monthly	61.9	62.5	67.2	71.7	76.1	79.4	81.1	81.4	80.2	75.2	68.9	63.4	72.4
Extreme highest	83	86	87	88	93	95	93	95	91	94	89	84	95
Extreme highest date	1985	1985	1984	1984	1984	1985	1985	1985	1985	1985	1985	1985	1985
Extreme lowest	21	31	36	46	56	57	69	64	65	57	44	28	21
Extreme lowest date	1985	1985	1984	1985	1984	1984	1984	1984	1984	1984	1984	1985	1985
DEGREE DAYS BASE 65° F													
Heating	166	149	55	0	0	0	0	0	0	0	28	124	522
Cooling	70	82	123	204	347	432	499	508	456	316	145	75	3257
NUMBER OF DAYS (Sunrise-Sunset)													
Precipitation .01" or more	7.0	6.5	5.5	8.5	8.5	12.5	15.5	11.5	17.0	12.0	13.5	8.0	126.0
Snow, Ice pellets 1.0" or more	0.0	0.0	0.0	0.0	0.0	0.0	0.0	0.0	0.0	0.0	0.0	0.0	0.0
Thunderstorms	0.5	1.0	2.0	5.5	7.5	12.0	13.5	18.0	9.0	3.5	2.0	0.0	74.5
Fog, Visibility 1/4 mile or less	3.0	2.0	1.0	2.0	1.0	0.0	0.0	0.0	0.5	0.5	0.5	2.0	12.5
Temperature Maximum:													
90° and above	0.0	0.0	0.0	0.0	2.0	9.5	6.0	12.5	1.5	2.5	0.0	0.0	34.0
32° and below	0.0	0.0	0.0	0.0	0.0	0.0	0.0	0.0	0.0	0.0	0.0	0.0	0.0
Temperature Minimum:													
32° and below	1.5	1.0	0.0	0.0	0.0	0.0	0.0	0.0	0.0	0.0	0.0	0.5	3.0
0° and below	0.0	0.0	0.0	0.0	0.0	0.0	0.0	0.0	0.0	0.0	0.0	0.0	0.0
RELATIVE HUMIDITY (%)													
Morning	80	79	77	78	80	83	88	88	87	81	84	79	82
Afternoon	57	55	52	55	58	63	66	66	67	63	63	58	60
PRECIPITATION (inches)													
Water Equivalent													
Normal	2.4	2.8	3.0	2.5	4.3	6.5	5.7	5.3	7.9	5.9	2.5	1.9	51.4
Maximum monthly	1.5	4.7	2.4	4.6	5.7	5.4	6.0	6.6	9.7	3.5	11.7	2.1	11.7
Date	1984	1984	1984	1985	1984	1985	1985	1985	1985	1985	1984	1985	1984
Minimum monthly	1.1	0.3	1.3	0.8	3.2	4.5	3.2	3.7	9.5	1.6	2.2	1.7	0.3
Date	1985	1985	1985	1984	1985	1984	1984	1984	1984	1984	1985	1984	1985
Maximum in 24 hrs	0.4	1.8	0.9	1.7	1.3	1.1	2.4	2.0	1.9	1.0	4.3	1.5	4.3
Date	1985	1984	1985	1985	1984	1985	1985	1985	1985	1985	1984	1985	1984
Date	1984	1984	1984	1984	1984	1984	1984	1984	1984	1984	1984	1984	—
Date	1984	1984	1984	1984	1984	1984	1984	1984	1984	1984	1984	1984	—
WIND (Resultant)													
Mean speed (mph)	9.8	9.2	9.5	9.4	8.8	7.6	6.6	6.5	8.6	8.5	8.7	7.8	8.4

WEST PALM BEACH

Elev. 15'   26° 41'N — 80° 07'W   **Florida**

NORMALS, MEANS, EXTREMES

	JAN	FEB	MAR	APR	MAY	JUN	JUL	AUG	SEP	OCT	NOV	DEC	YEAR
TEMPERATURE													
Normal daily maximum	74.5	75.3	79.3	82.5	85.7	88.1	89.7	90.1	88.4	84.4	79.6	75.7	82.8
Normal daily minimum	55.9	56.2	60.8	65.1	69.5	72.7	74.2	74.8	74.3	70.1	63.5	58.2	66.3
Normal monthly	65.2	65.8	70.1	73.8	77.6	80.4	82.0	82.5	81.4	77.3	71.6	67.0	74.5
Extreme highest	89	90	94	99	96	98	101	98	97	95	91	90	101
Extreme highest date	1942	1949	1977	1971	1971	1980	1942	1963	1937	1959	1941	1941	1942
Extreme lowest	27	32	30	45	53	61	66	65	66	46	36	30	27
Extreme lowest date	1977	1978	1980	1971	1940	1984	1937	1957	1938	1968	1950	1983	1977
DEGREE DAYS BASE 65° F													
Heating	92	86	18	0	0	0	0	0	0	0	9	57	262
Cooling	99	108	176	264	391	462	527	543	492	381	207	119	3769
% OF POSSIBLE SUNSHINE	na	na	na	na	na	na	na	na	na	na	na	na	na
AVERAGE SKY COVER													
Sunrise - Sunset	5.7	5.7	5.6	5.4	5.8	6.7	6.6	6.6	6.9	6.2	5.7	5.6	6.0
NUMBER OF DAYS (Sunrise-Sunset)													
Clear	8.1	7.7	8.0	8.4	7.3	4.2	3.4	2.6	2.4	6.0	7.2	8.6	73.8
Partly cloudy	11.3	10.8	13.3	13.2	13.4	13.2	13.9	16.5	13.8	13.9	13.2	12.1	158.6
Cloudy	11.7	9.7	9.7	8.4	10.4	12.7	13.7	11.9	13.8	11.1	9.7	10.3	132.9
Precipitation .01" or more	7.4	7.1	7.2	6.7	11.2	14.1	14.8	16.2	17.2	13.2	8.8	8.0	131.8
Snow, Ice pellets 1.0" or more	0.0	0.0	0.0	0.0	0.0	0.0	0.0	0.0	0.0	0.0	0.0	0.0	0.0
Thunderstorms	0.9	1.3	2.2	3.6	7.9	12.7	15.9	16.1	11.3	4.5	1.4	0.9	78.6
Fog, Visibility 1/4 mile or less	1.6	1.1	1.0	1.0	0.2	0.2	*	0.1	0.2	0.4	0.6	1.3	7.6
Temperature Maximum:													
90° and above	0.0	0.0	0.4	1.8	3.6	9.2	16.6	18.0	8.8	1.8	*	0.0	60.2
32° and below	0.0	0.0	0.0	0.0	0.0	0.0	0.0	0.0	0.0	0.0	0.0	0.0	0.0
Temperature Minimum:													
32° and below	0.6	*	0.1	0.0	0.0	0.0	0.0	0.0	0.0	0.0	0.0	*	0.8
0° and below	0.0	0.0	0.0	0.0	0.0	0.0	0.0	0.0	0.0	0.0	0.0	0.0	0.0
RELATIVE HUMIDITY (%)													
Morning	80	79	77	76	79	84	84	83	84	80	80	79	80
Afternoon	58	56	55	54	59	66	64	64	66	62	60	59	60
PRECIPITATION (inches)													
Water Equivalent													
Normal	2.7	2.6	2.6	3.2	6.0	7.9	6.0	5.7	9.2	7.7	3.3	2.2	59.7
Maximum monthly	11.0	8.7	16.7	18.2	15.2	17.9	17.7	13.5	24.8	18.7	14.6	8.7	24.8
Date	1983	1983	1982	1942	1976	1966	1941	1950	1960	1965	1982	1949	1960
Minimum monthly	0.2	0.2	0.3	0.0	0.3	1.0	1.2	2.1	2.7	1.2	0.2	0.0	0.0
Date	1960	1948	1956	1967	1967	1952	1961	1955	1939	1972	1970	1968	1967
Maximum in 24 hrs	6.3	4.7	8.8	15.2	7.0	9.2	5.8	5.8	8.7	9.5	7.6	5.2	15.2
Date	1957	1966	1982	1942	1958	1945	1972	1949	1960	1965	1984	1955	1942
SNOW, ICE PELLETS													
Maximum monthly	T	0.0	0.0	0.0	0.0	0.0	0.0	0.0	0.0	0.0	0.0	0.0	T
Date	1977	—	—	—	—	—	—	—	—	—	—	—	1977
Maximum in 24 hrs	T	0.0	0.0	0.0	0.0	0.0	0.0	0.0	0.0	0.0	0.0	0.0	T
Date	1977	—	—	—	—	—	—	—	—	—	—	—	1977
WIND (Resultant)													
Mean speed (mph)	9.8	10.4	10.7	10.8	9.7	8.1	7.5	7.6	8.6	10.0	10.0	9.9	9.4

ATHENS

Elev. 802'   33° 57'N — 83° 19'W   # Georgia

NORMALS, MEANS, EXTREMES

	JAN	FEB	MAR	APR	MAY	JUN	JUL	AUG	SEP	OCT	NOV	DEC	YEAR
TEMPERATURE													
Normal daily maximum	52.2	55.9	63.6	73.6	80.7	86.8	89.3	88.8	82.9	73.6	63.3	54.7	72.1
Normal daily minimum	32.6	34.2	41.0	49.7	58.1	65.2	68.9	68.2	62.9	50.5	40.9	34.7	50.6
Normal monthly	42.4	45.1	52.3	61.7	69.4	76.0	79.1	78.5	72.9	62.1	52.1	44.7	61.3
Extreme highest	80	79	88	90	97	104	104	107	99	98	86	79	107
Extreme highest date	1975	1982	1974	1981	1962	1954	1977	1983	1957	1954	1961	1984	1983
Extreme lowest	-4	5	11	27	37	45	55	54	36	24	7	2	-4
Extreme lowest date	1985	1958	1980	1950	1971	1972	1967	1968	1967	1952	1950	1962	1985
DEGREE DAYS BASE 65° F													
Heating	701	557	402	130	30	0	0	0	0	129	387	629	2965
Cooling	0	0	12	31	167	330	440	419	242	39	0	0	1680
% OF POSSIBLE SUNSHINE	na	na	na	na	na	na	na	na	na	na	na	na	na
AVERAGE SKY COVER													
Sunrise - Sunset	6.2	5.9	6.0	5.4	5.7	5.7	6.1	5.6	5.5	4.7	5.2	5.9	5.6
NUMBER OF DAYS (Sunrise-Sunset)													
Clear	8.8	8.8	9.2	10.1	8.9	7.9	6.3	8.1	9.5	13.6	11.8	9.9	113.0
Partly cloudy	7.0	6.3	7.3	8.4	10.2	11.9	12.8	12.7	9.4	7.3	6.0	6.3	105.6
Cloudy	15.2	13.1	14.5	11.5	11.9	10.1	11.9	10.2	11.1	10.1	12.2	14.8	146.6
Precipitation .01" or more	11.5	9.3	10.8	8.6	8.7	9.1	11.2	8.9	7.5	6.6	8.1	10.3	110.5
Snow, Ice pellets 1.0" or more	0.3	0.3	0.1	0.0	0.0	0.0	0.0	0.0	0.0	0.0	0.1	0.1	0.9
Thunderstorms	1.2	1.3	3.3	4.0	6.2	9.0	12.0	8.4	3.3	1.0	1.0	0.6	51.3
Fog, Visibility 1/4 mile or less	5.1	4.1	3.5	2.3	2.6	1.5	2.5	3.4	3.2	2.7	3.7	4.9	39.3
Temperature Maximum:													
90° and above	0.0	0.0	0.0	0.1	3.2	11.4	15.8	13.9	5.3	0.2	0.0	0.0	49.9
32° and below	0.7	0.2	*	0.0	0.0	0.0	0.0	0.0	0.0	0.0	*	0.3	1.3
Temperature Minimum:													
32° and below	15.3	11.6	5.6	0.5	0.0	0.0	0.0	0.0	0.0	0.4	5.8	14.0	53.2
0° and below	0.1	0.0	0.0	0.0	0.0	0.0	0.0	0.0	0.0	0.0	0.0	0.0	0.1
RELATIVE HUMIDITY (%)													
Morning	75	71	72	73	81	84	87	88	86	83	78	76	80
Afternoon	58	55	52	50	54	56	60	60	59	55	54	57	56
PRECIPITATION (inches)													
Water Equivalent													
Normal	4.8	4.1	5.8	4.0	4.7	4.0	5.1	3.6	3.5	2.7	3.3	4.0	50.1
Maximum monthly	9.4	9.2	10.9	9.5	11.3	13.2	10.5	7.4	7.0	7.7	14.9	8.4	14.9
Date	1960	1961	1964	1964	1959	1967	1964	1961	1970	1964	1948	1945	1948
Minimum monthly	0.6	0.7	1.1	0.6	0.5	0.8	0.9	0.0	0.5	T	0.3	1.0	T
Date	1981	1978	1985	1950	1951	1958	1947	1951	1954	1963	1950	1965	1963
Maximum in 24 hrs	3.8	3.5	4.4	3.8	5.5	9.9	4.1	3.0	5.3	4.7	4.0	4.3	9.9
Date	1969	1981	1964	1979	1959	1967	1964	1969	1956	1964	1948	1972	1967
SNOW, ICE PELLETS													
Maximum monthly	5.1	4.7	8.7	0.0	0.0	0.0	0.0	0.0	0.0	0.0	2.2	3.0	8.7
Date	1982	1979	1983	—	—	—	—	—	—	—	1968	1971	1983
Maximum in 24 hrs	5.0	4.0	8.7	0.0	0.0	0.0	0.0	0.0	0.0	0.0	2.2	3.0	8.7
Date	1948	1952	1983	—	—	—	—	—	—	—	1968	1971	1983
WIND (Resultant)													
Mean speed (mph)	8.5	9.0	8.9	8.5	7.2	6.7	6.3	5.7	6.4	6.8	7.4	8.0	7.4

ATLANTA

Elev. 1010'   33° 39'N — 84° 25'W   **Georgia**

NORMALS, MEANS, EXTREMES

	JAN	FEB	MAR	APR	MAY	JUN	JUL	AUG	SEP	OCT	NOV	DEC	YEAR
TEMPERATURE													
Normal daily maximum	51.2	55.3	63.2	73.2	79.8	85.6	87.9	87.6	82.3	72.9	62.6	54.1	71.3
Normal daily minimum	32.6	34.5	41.7	50.4	58.7	65.9	69.2	68.7	63.6	51.4	41.3	34.8	51.1
Normal monthly	41.9	44.9	52.5	61.8	69.3	75.8	78.6	78.2	73.0	62.2	52.0	44.5	61.2
Extreme highest	79	79	85	91	95	101	105	102	98	95	84	77	105
Extreme highest date	1949	1980	1982	1980	1953	1952	1980	1980	1954	1954	1961	1971	1980
Extreme lowest	-8	5	10	26	37	46	53	56	36	28	3	0	-8
Extreme lowest date	1985	1958	1960	1973	1971	1956	1967	1964	1967	1976	1950	1983	1985
DEGREE DAYS BASE 65° F													
Heating	716	563	400	133	37	5	0	0	7	130	394	636	3021
Cooling	0	0	12	37	170	329	422	409	247	44	0	0	1670
% OF POSSIBLE SUNSHINE	49	54	58	66	68	67	62	65	64	67	59	51	61
AVERAGE SKY COVER													
Sunrise - Sunset	6.4	6.2	6.2	5.6	5.6	5.8	6.3	5.8	5.5	4.6	5.4	6.2	5.8
NUMBER OF DAYS (Sunrise-Sunset)													
Clear	8.4	8.0	8.9	9.9	9.2	7.5	5.7	7.5	9.8	13.9	11.6	9.4	109.8
Partly cloudy	6.4	6.3	7.3	8.2	10.4	12.2	13.3	13.1	9.8	7.2	6.0	6.4	106.6
Cloudy	16.3	13.9	14.8	11.9	11.4	10.3	12.0	10.5	10.4	9.8	12.3	15.2	148.8
Precipitation .01" or more	11.6	10.1	11.6	9.1	9.2	9.9	12.1	9.4	7.5	6.5	8.3	10.2	115.3
Snow, Ice pellets 1.0" or more	0.2	0.2	0.1	0.0	0.0	0.0	0.0	0.0	0.0	0.0	*	0.1	0.6
Thunderstorms	1.2	1.9	3.8	4.2	6.1	8.6	10.3	8.1	3.0	1.1	0.9	0.8	49.8
Fog, Visibility 1/4 mile or less	5.0	3.3	2.8	1.5	1.4	1.0	1.6	1.8	1.9	2.3	3.0	4.5	29.9
Temperature Maximum:													
90° and above	0.0	0.0	0.0	*	0.8	6.8	10.3	7.3	2.8	0.0	0.0	0.0	28.0
32° and below	1.8	0.3	*	0.0	0.0	0.0	0.0	0.0	0.0	0.0	*	0.4	2.7
Temperature Minimum:													
32° and below	17.6	14.0	5.5	0.5	0.0	0.0	0.0	0.0	0.0	0.3	5.4	13.9	57.1
0° and below	0.3	0.0	0.0	0.0	0.0	0.0	0.0	0.0	0.0	0.0	0.0	*	0.3
RELATIVE HUMIDITY (%)													
Morning	74	69	69	70	78	81	85	85	83	78	76	74	77
Afternoon	60	54	51	50	54	57	61	61	60	54	55	58	56
PRECIPITATION (inches)													
Water Equivalent													
Normal	4.9	4.4	5.9	4.4	4.0	3.4	4.7	3.4	3.1	2.5	3.4	4.2	48.6
Maximum monthly	10.8	12.7	11.6	11.8	8.3	7.5	11.2	8.6	7.5	7.5	15.7	9.9	15.7
Date	1936	1961	1980	1979	1980	1939	1948	1967	1983	1966	1948	1961	1948
Minimum monthly	0.8	0.7	1.8	1.4	0.3	0.7	0.7	0.5	0.0	T	0.4	0.6	T
Date	1981	1978	1985	1950	1936	1984	1980	1976	1984	1963	1939	1979	1963
Maximum in 24 hrs	3.9	5.6	5.0	5.5	5.1	3.4	5.4	5.0	5.4	3.9	4.1	3.8	5.6
Date	1973	1961	1976	1979	1948	1943	1948	1940	1956	1985	1935	1961	1961
SNOW, ICE PELLETS													
Maximum monthly	8.3	4.4	7.9	T	0.0	0.0	0.0	0.0	0.0	0.0	1.0	2.5	8.3
Date	1940	1979	1983	1971	—	—	—	—	—	—	1968	1963	1940
Maximum in 24 hrs	8.3	4.2	7.9	T	0.0	0.0	0.0	0.0	0.0	0.0	1.0	2.2	8.3
Date	1940	1979	1983	1971	—	—	—	—	—	—	1968	1963	1940
WIND (Resultant)													
Mean speed (mph)	10.6	10.9	10.9	10.1	8.6	8.0	7.5	7.2	8.0	8.5	9.1	9.9	9.1

AUGUSTA

Elev. 136'   33° 22'N — 81° 58'W   ## Georgia

NORMALS, MEANS, EXTREMES

	JAN	FEB	MAR	APR	MAY	JUN	JUL	AUG	SEP	OCT	NOV	DEC	YEAR
TEMPERATURE													
Normal daily maximum	56.7	60.1	67.6	76.8	83.7	89.1	91.4	90.9	85.6	76.9	67.5	59.2	75.5
Normal daily minimum	33.2	35.0	42.0	49.5	58.3	65.6	69.6	68.9	63.5	50.1	40.3	34.6	50.9
Normal monthly	45.0	47.6	54.8	63.2	71.0	77.4	80.5	79.9	74.6	63.5	53.9	46.9	63.2
Extreme highest	80	86	88	93	99	105	107	108	101	97	90	82	108
Extreme highest date	1985	1962	1985	1980	1964	1952	1980	1983	1957	1954	1961	1982	1983
Extreme lowest	-1	9	12	26	35	47	55	54	36	22	15	5	-1
Extreme lowest date	1985	1973	1980	1982	1971	1984	1951	1968	1967	1952	1970	1981	1985
DEGREE DAYS BASE 65° F													
Heating	626	495	332	92	17	0	0	0	0	107	338	561	2568
Cooling	6	5	16	38	203	372	484	462	288	61	0	0	1935
% OF POSSIBLE SUNSHINE	na	na	na	na	na	na	na	na	na	na	na	na	na
AVERAGE SKY COVER													
Sunrise - Sunset	6.2	5.9	6.0	5.4	5.8	5.9	6.2	5.7	5.7	4.8	5.2	5.9	5.7
NUMBER OF DAYS (Sunrise-Sunset)													
Clear	9.4	9.1	8.9	10.5	8.6	7.6	5.7	7.7	9.2	13.8	11.8	10.3	112.6
Partly cloudy	5.8	6.1	8.1	8.0	10.6	11.5	13.3	13.6	9.3	7.3	6.2	6.2	106.1
Cloudy	15.9	13.0	14.0	11.5	11.7	10.9	12.1	9.7	11.5	9.9	12.0	14.5	146.6
Precipitation .01" or more	10.1	9.1	10.4	8.1	9.2	9.1	11.7	9.9	7.5	5.9	6.9	9.2	107.1
Snow, Ice pellets 1.0" or more	0.1	0.2	*	0.0	0.0	0.0	0.0	0.0	0.0	0.0	0.0	*	0.4
Thunderstorms	0.8	1.6	2.7	4.0	6.5	9.4	12.9	9.9	3.8	1.3	0.7	0.7	54.3
Fog, Visibility 1/4 mile or less	2.9	2.3	1.5	1.5	1.3	1.3	1.6	3.0	3.0	2.7	3.2	3.7	28.1
Temperature Maximum:													
90° and above	0.0	0.0	0.0	0.8	4.6	13.9	21.1	17.7	8.4	0.6	0.0	0.0	67.0
32° and below	0.6	*	*	0.0	0.0	0.0	0.0	0.0	0.0	0.0	0.0	*	0.8
Temperature Minimum:													
32° and below	17.0	13.6	5.5	0.6	0.0	0.0	0.0	0.0	0.0	0.6	7.5	14.0	58.8
0° and below	*	0.0	0.0	0.0	0.0	0.0	0.0	0.0	0.0	0.0	0.0	0.0	*
RELATIVE HUMIDITY (%)													
Morning	78	75	76	79	85	86	87	89	89	87	84	80	83
Afternoon	54	49	48	46	50	52	55	56	54	49	50	53	51
PRECIPITATION (inches)													
Water Equivalent													
Normal	3.9	4.0	4.9	3.3	3.7	3.8	4.4	3.9	3.5	2.0	2.0	3.2	43.0
Maximum monthly	8.4	7.6	11.9	8.4	9.6	7.2	11.4	9.9	9.5	6.9	7.7	8.6	11.9
Date	1960	1961	1980	1961	1979	1973	1967	1964	1975	1959	1985	1981	1980
Minimum monthly	0.7	0.6	0.8	0.6	0.4	0.6	1.4	0.6	0.3	T	0.0	0.3	T
Date	1981	1968	1968	1970	1951	1984	1983	1980	1984	1953	1960	1955	1953
Maximum in 24 hrs	3.6	3.6	5.3	3.9	4.4	5.0	3.7	5.9	4.9	2.7	3.8	3.1	5.9
Date	1960	1985	1967	1955	1981	1981	1979	1964	1969	1985	1985	1970	1964
SNOW, ICE PELLETS													
Maximum monthly	1.5	14.0	1.1	0.0	0.0	0.0	0.0	0.0	0.0	0.0	T	0.9	14.0
Date	1982	1973	1980	—	—	—	—	—	—	—	1968	1958	1973
Maximum in 24 hrs	1.5	13.7	1.1	0.0	0.0	0.0	0.0	0.0	0.0	0.0	T	0.9	13.7
Date	1982	1973	1980	—	—	—	—	—	—	—	1968	1958	1973
WIND (Resultant)													
Mean speed (mph)	7.1	7.7	8.0	7.6	6.5	6.1	5.9	5.4	5.6	5.8	6.1	6.6	6.5

COLUMBUS

Elev. 385' 32° 31'N — 84° 57'W **Georgia**

NORMALS, MEANS, EXTREMES

	JAN	FEB	MAR	APR	MAY	JUN	JUL	AUG	SEP	OCT	NOV	DEC	YEAR
TEMPERATURE													
Normal daily maximum	56.9	60.6	68.0	77.4	83.8	89.4	91.1	90.8	86.0	77.0	67.0	59.5	75.6
Normal daily minimum	35.4	37.0	43.9	51.9	60.2	67.6	71.0	70.5	65.9	53.1	42.7	37.2	53.0
Normal monthly	46.2	48.8	56.0	64.7	72.0	78.5	81.1	80.7	76.0	65.1	54.9	48.4	64.3
Extreme highest	83	83	89	92	97	104	104	102	99	96	86	82	104
Extreme highest date	1949	1962	1982	1970	1962	1978	1977	1983	1957	1954	1961	1977	1978
Extreme lowest	-2	11	16	28	39	44	59	57	38	24	10	4	-2
Extreme lowest date	1985	1973	1980	1950	1963	1956	1967	1952	1967	1952	1950	1962	1985
DEGREE DAYS BASE 65° F													
Heating	593	460	299	84	9	0	0	0	0	83	313	515	2356
Cooling	10	7	20	75	226	405	496	487	330	86	10	0	2152
% OF POSSIBLE SUNSHINE	na	na	na	na	na	na	na	na	na	na	na	na	na
AVERAGE SKY COVER													
Sunrise - Sunset	6.5	6.2	6.2	5.4	5.6	5.7	6.4	5.6	5.6	4.6	5.3	6.0	5.8
NUMBER OF DAYS (Sunrise-Sunset)													
Clear	8.1	8.3	8.7	10.2	9.5	8.3	5.3	8.2	10.1	14.3	11.7	9.8	112.4
Partly cloudy	6.2	6.0	7.1	8.2	10.2	11.7	13.0	13.2	8.5	6.7	6.2	6.1	102.9
Cloudy	16.7	14.0	15.2	11.6	11.4	10.0	12.7	9.7	11.4	10.0	12.2	15.2	150.0
Precipitation .01" or more	10.3	9.7	10.6	8.0	8.4	9.4	13.5	10.4	7.8	5.3	7.7	9.7	110.5
Snow, Ice pellets 1.0" or more	0.1	0.1	*	0.0	0.0	0.0	0.0	0.0	0.0	0.0	0.0	0.0	0.2
Thunderstorms	1.3	2.2	3.9	4.6	6.9	8.4	13.4	9.2	3.6	1.1	1.0	1.4	57.0
Fog, Visibility 1/4 mile or less	3.7	2.2	1.4	1.2	1.0	0.5	1.2	0.8	0.8	1.1	2.1	2.8	18.5
Temperature Maximum:													
90° and above	0.0	0.0	0.0	0.3	6.2	16.5	20.4	20.3	10.0	0.7	0.0	0.0	74.3
32° and below	0.3	0.1	0.0	0.0	0.0	0.0	0.0	0.0	0.0	0.0	0.0	0.1	0.4
Temperature Minimum:													
32° and below	13.7	9.7	3.9	0.2	0.0	0.0	0.0	0.0	0.0	0.3	5.1	11.8	44.7
0° and below	*	0.0	0.0	0.0	0.0	0.0	0.0	0.0	0.0	0.0	0.0	0.0	*
RELATIVE HUMIDITY (%)													
Morning	79	76	78	79	84	83	87	88	87	84	84	81	83
Afternoon	60	54	52	48	51	53	59	57	57	52	54	58	55
PRECIPITATION (inches)													
Water Equivalent													
Normal	4.5	4.5	5.9	4.5	4.4	4.1	5.5	4.0	3.5	2.0	3.0	4.7	51.0
Maximum monthly	10.2	9.4	12.5	11.6	8.4	10.8	13.2	10.0	6.9	8.0	12.4	9.3	13.2
Date	1947	1961	1952	1953	1959	1967	1971	1977	1951	1964	1948	1953	1971
Minimum monthly	0.8	1.2	1.3	0.8	0.2	1.2	1.7	0.9	0.2	0.0	0.3	0.4	0.0
Date	1954	1951	1985	1967	1962	1979	1957	1956	1984	1963	1956	1955	1963
Maximum in 24 hrs	4.2	5.7	5.3	5.7	4.6	3.8	5.3	6.8	4.2	5.6	4.8	4.4	6.8
Date	1978	1981	1966	1981	1957	1959	1955	1977	1971	1964	1977	1970	1977
SNOW, ICE PELLETS													
Maximum monthly	2.0	14.0	1.0	T	0.0	0.0	0.0	0.0	0.0	0.0	T	T	14.0
Date	1982	1973	1980	1971	—	—	—	—	—	—	1975	1981	1973
Maximum in 24 hrs	1.4	14.0	1.0	T	0.0	0.0	0.0	0.0	0.0	0.0	T	T	14.0
Date	1977	1973	1980	1971	—	—	—	—	—	—	1975	1981	1973
WIND (Resultant)													
Mean speed (mph)	7.3	7.9	8.0	7.3	6.6	6.0	5.6	5.3	6.4	6.5	6.5	6.9	6.7

MACON

Elev. 354'   32° 42'N — 83° 39'W   # Georgia

NORMALS, MEANS, EXTREMES

	JAN	FEB	MAR	APR	MAY	JUN	JUL	AUG	SEP	OCT	NOV	DEC	YEAR
TEMPERATURE													
Normal daily maximum	57.6	61.1	68.6	78.2	85.0	90.4	92.2	91.9	86.8	78.0	68.1	60.2	76.5
Normal daily minimum	35.5	37.4	44.2	52.3	60.3	67.3	70.6	70.0	65.1	52.3	42.5	37.1	52.9
Normal monthly	46.6	49.3	56.4	65.3	72.7	78.9	81.4	81.0	76.0	65.2	55.3	48.7	64.7
Extreme highest	84	85	95	94	99	106	108	105	102	100	88	82	108
Extreme highest date	1949	1962	1949	1970	1967	1954	1980	1980	1980	1954	1961	1972	1980
Extreme lowest	-6	9	14	31	40	46	54	55	35	26	10	5	-6
Extreme lowest date	1985	1973	1980	1983	1971	1972	1967	1952	1967	1952	1950	1962	1985
DEGREE DAYS BASE 65° F													
Heating	580	452	287	60	10	0	0	0	0	86	299	505	2279
Cooling	10	9	24	69	249	417	508	496	335	92	8	0	2217
% OF POSSIBLE SUNSHINE	55	59	64	70	71	70	65	70	65	69	63	57	65
AVERAGE SKY COVER													
Sunrise - Sunset	6.3	6.0	6.0	5.4	5.7	5.8	6.4	5.7	5.8	4.6	5.1	5.9	5.7
NUMBER OF DAYS (Sunrise-Sunset)													
Clear	8.5	8.5	8.9	10.9	9.1	7.9	5.2	8.7	8.8	14.1	12.1	9.8	112.6
Partly cloudy	6.9	6.8	7.9	7.5	10.5	11.3	12.5	11.9	9.9	6.8	6.3	6.8	105.1
Cloudy	15.6	13.0	14.2	11.6	11.4	10.8	13.3	10.4	11.4	10.1	11.6	14.4	147.6
Precipitation .01" or more	10.4	9.7	10.8	7.6	9.1	9.6	13.1	10.3	7.9	5.8	7.1	9.3	110.6
Snow, Ice pellets 1.0" or more	0.2	0.2	*	0.0	0.0	0.0	0.0	0.0	0.0	0.0	0.0	0.0	0.4
Thunderstorms	1.1	2.0	3.3	4.3	6.4	8.6	13.2	9.4	3.5	0.8	0.9	1.0	54.5
Fog, Visibility 1/4 mile or less	4.0	2.5	2.0	0.9	0.8	0.9	1.0	1.6	2.0	1.8	3.2	3.9	24.7
Temperature Maximum:													
90° and above	0.0	0.0	*	1.1	6.1	17.0	22.0	20.6	11.4	1.1	0.0	0.0	79.4
32° and below	0.4	*	*	0.0	0.0	0.0	0.0	0.0	0.0	0.0	0.0	*	0.5
Temperature Minimum:													
32° and below	14.6	11.2	4.2	0.2	0.0	0.0	0.0	0.0	0.0	0.5	5.4	11.1	47.2
0° and below	*	0.0	0.0	0.0	0.0	0.0	0.0	0.0	0.0	0.0	0.0	0.0	*
RELATIVE HUMIDITY (%)													
Morning	78	76	77	78	83	85	87	89	89	85	82	80	82
Afternoon	59	54	52	49	51	53	58	59	58	52	53	56	55
PRECIPITATION (inches)													
Water Equivalent													
Normal	4.2	4.5	5.1	3.5	3.7	3.8	4.4	3.6	3.2	1.9	2.3	4.0	44.8
Maximum monthly	8.3	9.3	11.9	8.4	11.7	9.0	13.6	7.0	8.8	9.3	6.9	10.3	13.6
Date	1964	1983	1980	1964	1957	1965	1984	1973	1953	1959	1983	1972	1984
Minimum monthly	0.6	0.5	1.2	0.5	0.3	0.9	1.2	1.1	0.3	0.0	0.4	0.5	0.0
Date	1954	1976	1985	1972	1956	1954	1952	1980	1984	1963	1956	1955	1963
Maximum in 24 hrs	4.4	5.1	3.9	3.6	5.3	4.9	2.6	2.9	4.6	5.3	2.9	4.5	5.3
Date	1962	1981	1970	1955	1976	1965	1965	1959	1956	1970	1983	1972	1976
SNOW, ICE PELLETS													
Maximum monthly	3.7	16.5	1.1	0.0	0.0	0.0	0.0	0.0	0.0	0.0	0.2	0.5	16.5
Date	1955	1973	1980	—	—	—	—	—	—	—	1950	1963	1973
Maximum in 24 hrs	3.7	16.5	1.1	0.0	0.0	0.0	0.0	0.0	0.0	0.0	0.2	0.5	16.5
Date	1955	1973	1980	—	—	—	—	—	—	—	1950	1963	1973
WIND (Resultant)													
Mean speed (mph)	8.3	8.9	9.4	8.8	7.7	7.3	6.9	6.4	7.0	6.9	7.2	7.8	7.7

SAVANNAH
Elev. 46' 32° 08'N — 81° 12'W **Georgia**

NORMALS, MEANS, EXTREMES

	JAN	FEB	MAR	APR	MAY	JUN	JUL	AUG	SEP	OCT	NOV	DEC	YEAR
TEMPERATURE													
Normal daily maximum	60.3	63.1	69.9	77.8	84.2	88.6	90.8	90.1	85.6	77.8	69.5	62.5	76.7
Normal daily minimum	37.9	40.0	46.8	54.1	62.3	68.5	71.5	71.4	67.6	55.9	45.5	39.4	55.1
Normal monthly	49.1	51.6	58.4	66.0	73.3	78.6	81.2	80.8	76.6	66.9	57.5	51.0	65.9
Extreme highest	84	86	91	95	100	104	104	104	98	94	89	83	104
Extreme highest date	1957	1962	1974	1967	1953	1985	1980	1954	1983	1954	1961	1971	1985
Extreme lowest	3	14	20	32	39	51	61	61	43	28	15	9	3
Extreme lowest date	1985	1958	1980	1962	1963	1984	1972	1966	1967	1952	1970	1983	1985
DEGREE DAYS BASE 65° F													
Heating	507	387	243	42	0	0	0	0	0	58	240	444	1921
Cooling	17	12	38	72	261	408	502	490	348	117	15	10	2290
% OF POSSIBLE SUNSHINE	55	58	62	70	67	65	62	62	57	63	62	55	62
AVERAGE SKY COVER													
Sunrise - Sunset	6.1	6.0	6.0	5.5	5.8	6.1	6.6	6.2	6.3	5.1	5.3	6.0	5.9
NUMBER OF DAYS (Sunrise-Sunset)													
Clear	9.4	8.6	8.9	10.4	9.1	6.8	4.7	5.9	6.4	12.1	11.3	9.4	103.0
Partly cloudy	6.1	6.2	8.6	8.5	9.8	11.0	13.5	13.7	10.9	8.0	6.8	7.1	110.3
Cloudy	15.5	13.5	13.5	11.1	12.1	12.2	12.8	11.5	12.7	10.9	11.8	14.4	152.0
Precipitation .01" or more	9.2	8.8	9.4	6.8	8.9	11.1	14.3	12.4	10.1	6.1	6.3	8.2	111.4
Snow, Ice pellets 1.0" or more	*	0.1	0.0	0.0	0.0	0.0	0.0	0.0	0.0	0.0	0.0	0.0	0.1
Thunderstorms	1.0	1.2	3.0	3.6	7.5	9.9	15.1	12.1	5.8	1.4	0.5	0.6	61.7
Fog, Visibility 1/4 mile or less	4.7	2.9	3.3	2.6	3.4	2.4	1.4	2.1	3.8	3.7	5.1	4.6	39.9
Temperature Maximum:													
90° and above	0.0	0.0	0.1	1.4	4.6	12.8	20.1	16.8	6.8	0.4	0.0	0.0	63.0
32° and below	0.3	0.0	*	0.0	0.0	0.0	0.0	0.0	0.0	0.0	0.0	*	0.4
Temperature Minimum:													
32° and below	11.5	8.1	2.2	0.0	0.0	0.0	0.0	0.0	0.0	*	2.8	8.3	33.0
0° and below	0.0	0.0	0.0	0.0	0.0	0.0	0.0	0.0	0.0	0.0	0.0	0.0	0.0
RELATIVE HUMIDITY (%)													
Morning	77	75	77	79	84	86	88	89	88	85	83	79	83
Afternoon	54	49	48	46	52	55	59	61	60	54	51	54	54
PRECIPITATION (inches)													
Water Equivalent													
Normal	3.0	3.1	3.8	3.1	4.6	5.6	7.3	6.6	5.1	2.2	1.8	2.7	49.7
Maximum monthly	8.8	7.9	9.5	7.7	10.0	14.3	20.1	14.9	13.4	8.5	4.9	5.8	20.1
Date	1984	1964	1959	1961	1957	1963	1964	1971	1953	1959	1972	1977	1964
Minimum monthly	0.5	1.1	0.1	0.7	0.5	0.8	1.3	1.0	0.3	0.0	0.1	0.1	0.0
Date	1985	1968	1955	1969	1953	1954	1972	1980	1972	1963	1966	1984	1963
Maximum in 24 hrs	3.5	3.4	4.6	5.6	5.6	4.0	6.3	7.0	6.8	3.5	5.0	3.4	7.0
Date	1984	1964	1959	1976	1976	1963	1957	1971	1979	1959	1969	1964	1971
SNOW, ICE PELLETS													
Maximum monthly	2.0	3.6	T	0.0	0.0	0.0	0.0	0.0	0.0	0.0	0.0	T	3.6
Date	1977	1968	1983	—	—	—	—	—	—	—	—	1980	1968
Maximum in 24 hrs	1.3	3.6	T	0.0	0.0	0.0	0.0	0.0	0.0	0.0	0.0	T	3.6
Date	1977	1968	1983	—	—	—	—	—	—	—	—	1980	1968
WIND (Resultant)													
Mean speed (mph)	8.5	9.2	9.2	8.7	7.7	7.4	7.0	6.6	7.3	7.4	7.5	7.9	7.9

HILO

Elev. 27' 19° 43'N — 155° 04'W # Hawaii

NORMALS, MEANS, EXTREMES

	JAN	FEB	MAR	APR	MAY	JUN	JUL	AUG	SEP	OCT	NOV	DEC	YEAR
TEMPERATURE													
Normal daily maximum	79.5	79.0	79.0	79.7	81.0	82.5	82.8	83.3	83.6	83.0	80.9	79.5	81.2
Normal daily minimum	63.2	63.2	63.9	64.9	66.1	67.1	68.0	68.4	68.0	67.5	66.3	64.3	65.9
Normal monthly	71.4	71.1	71.5	72.3	73.6	74.8	75.4	75.9	75.8	75.3	73.6	71.9	73.5
Extreme highest	91	92	93	89	94	90	89	93	92	91	90	93	94
Extreme highest date	1979	1968	1972	1978	1966	1969	1980	1950	1951	1979	1985	1980	1966
Extreme lowest	54	53	54	56	58	60	62	63	61	62	58	55	53
Extreme lowest date	1980	1962	1983	1949	1947	1946	1970	1955	1970	1985	1985	1977	1962
DEGREE DAYS BASE 65° F													
Heating	0	0	0	0	0	0	0	0	0	0	0	0	0
Cooling	198	176	202	222	267	294	322	338	324	319	258	214	3134
% OF POSSIBLE SUNSHINE	48	45	40	35	37	43	42	42	44	39	35	38	41
AVERAGE SKY COVER													
Sunrise - Sunset	6.3	6.7	7.6	8.1	7.9	7.5	7.6	7.4	7.0	7.3	7.2	6.8	7.3
NUMBER OF DAYS (Sunrise-Sunset)													
Clear	6.5	4.9	2.5	1.1	1.1	1.7	1.4	1.5	3.2	2.7	3.6	5.3	35.5
Partly cloudy	11.4	10.0	10.0	8.1	10.3	10.8	11.7	11.7	11.9	11.6	10.7	10.6	128.8
Cloudy	13.1	13.4	18.6	20.8	19.6	17.5	17.9	17.7	14.9	16.7	15.8	15.1	201.0
Precipitation .01" or more	16.9	17.7	23.6	25.4	25.4	24.1	27.3	26.6	23.4	24.2	22.9	21.3	278.7
Snow, Ice pellets 1.0" or more	0.0	0.0	0.0	0.0	0.0	0.0	0.0	0.0	0.0	0.0	0.0	0.0	0.0
Thunderstorms	1.0	1.3	1.5	0.9	0.6	0.1	0.2	0.2	0.2	1.0	1.1	0.7	8.7
Fog, Visibility 1/4 mile or less	0.0	0.0	0.0	0.0	0.0	0.0	0.0	0.0	0.0	0.0	0.0	0.0	0.0
Temperature Maximum:													
90° and above	0.1	0.1	*	0.0	0.1	*	0.0	0.1	0.2	0.3	*	0.1	0.8
32° and below	0.0	0.0	0.0	0.0	0.0	0.0	0.0	0.0	0.0	0.0	0.0	0.0	0.0
Temperature Minimum:													
32° and below	0.0	0.0	0.0	0.0	0.0	0.0	0.0	0.0	0.0	0.0	0.0	0.0	0.0
0° and below	0.0	0.0	0.0	0.0	0.0	0.0	0.0	0.0	0.0	0.0	0.0	0.0	0.0
RELATIVE HUMIDITY (%)													
Morning	83	84	86	88	88	87	88	88	87	87	86	85	86
Afternoon	66	66	67	69	68	65	68	69	68	69	70	69	68
PRECIPITATION (inches)													
Water Equivalent													
Normal	9.4	13.4	13.5	13.1	9.4	6.1	8.6	10.0	6.6	10.0	14.8	12.8	128.
Maximum monthly	32.2	45.5	49.9	31.9	25.0	15.5	28.5	26.4	13.7	26.1	27.0	50.8	50.8
Date	1979	1979	1980	1963	1964	1943	1982	1957	1980	1951	1959	1954	1954
Minimum monthly	0.3	0.8	0.8	2.9	1.1	1.8	3.8	2.6	1.5	2.4	2.3	0.2	0.2
Date	1953	1983	1972	1962	1945	1985	1975	1971	1974	1962	1983	1980	1980
Maximum in 24 hrs	9.9	22.3	17.0	11.0	10.2	4.2	7.1	9.6	6.6	8.8	15.5	10.5	22.3
Date	1949	1979	1980	1971	1965	1978	1982	1970	1981	1951	1959	1946	1979
WIND (Resultant)													
Mean speed (mph)	7.4	7.7	7.6	7.3	7.2	7.0	6.8	6.7	6.7	6.6	6.7	7.2	7.1

HONOLULU

Elev. 7'   21° 20'N — 157° 56'W   **Hawaii**

NORMALS, MEANS, EXTREMES

	JAN	FEB	MAR	APR	MAY	JUN	JUL	AUG	SEP	OCT	NOV	DEC	YEAR
TEMPERATURE													
Normal daily maximum	79.9	80.4	81.4	82.7	84.8	86.2	87.1	88.3	88.2	86.7	83.9	81.4	84.2
Normal daily minimum	65.3	65.3	67.3	68.7	70.2	71.9	73.1	73.6	72.9	72.2	69.2	66.5	69.7
Normal monthly	72.6	72.9	74.4	75.7	77.5	79.1	80.1	81.0	80.6	79.5	76.6	74.0	77.0
Extreme highest	87	88	88	89	90	91	92	93	93	94	90	89	94
Extreme highest date	1978	1984	1983	1978	1979	1982	1985	1984	1985	1984	1983	1983	1984
Extreme lowest	53	53	55	57	60	65	67	67	66	64	58	54	53
Extreme lowest date	1972	1983	1976	1985	1985	1982	1981	1984	1985	1981	1972	1962	1983
DEGREE DAYS BASE 65° F													
Heating	0	0	0	0	0	0	0	0	0	0	0	0	0
Cooling	236	221	291	321	388	423	468	496	468	450	348	279	4389
% OF POSSIBLE SUNSHINE	62	64	68	66	68	70	73	75	75	68	61	59	67
AVERAGE SKY COVER													
Sunrise - Sunset	5.5	5.7	5.9	6.2	6.0	5.7	5.3	5.3	5.2	5.7	5.7	5.5	5.6
NUMBER OF DAYS (Sunrise-Sunset)													
Clear	9.1	7.4	7.2	5.4	6.4	5.7	7.6	7.9	8.1	7.4	7.1	8.3	87.5
Partly cloudy	13.1	12.6	14.0	14.0	15.1	17.3	18.1	16.8	16.0	15.1	13.7	13.3	179.1
Cloudy	8.8	8.3	9.7	10.6	9.5	7.0	5.3	6.3	5.9	8.5	9.3	9.4	98.5
Precipitation .01" or more	10.1	9.3	9.1	9.3	7.3	5.9	7.4	6.4	7.1	8.9	9.3	10.0	100.1
Snow, Ice pellets 1.0" or more	0.0	0.0	0.0	0.0	0.0	0.0	0.0	0.0	0.0	0.0	0.0	0.0	0.0
Thunderstorms	0.8	1.2	0.8	0.6	0.4	0.1	0.1	*	0.3	0.8	0.8	0.7	6.6
Fog, Visibility 1/4 mile or less	0.0	0.0	0.0	0.0	0.0	0.0	0.0	0.0	0.0	0.0	0.0	0.0	0.0
Temperature Maximum:													
90° and above	0.0	0.0	0.0	0.0	0.1	1.0	2.9	7.8	7.6	2.9	0.1	0.0	22.4
32° and below	0.0	0.0	0.0	0.0	0.0	0.0	0.0	0.0	0.0	0.0	0.0	0.0	0.0
Temperature Minimum:													
32° and below	0.0	0.0	0.0	0.0	0.0	0.0	0.0	0.0	0.0	0.0	0.0	0.0	0.0
0° and below	0.0	0.0	0.0	0.0	0.0	0.0	0.0	0.0	0.0	0.0	0.0	0.0	0.0
RELATIVE HUMIDITY (%)													
Morning	82	79	76	75	74	73	73	73	74	74	79	80	76
Afternoon	63	59	58	57	54	53	52	53	52	55	59	61	56
PRECIPITATION (inches)													
Water Equivalent													
Normal	3.7	2.7	3.4	1.4	1.2	0.4	0.5	0.6	0.6	1.8	3.2	3.4	23.4
Maximum monthly	14.7	13.6	20.7	8.9	7.2	2.4	2.0	3.0	2.7	11.1	14.7	12.0	20.7
Date	1949	1955	1951	1963	1965	1971	1970	1959	1947	1978	1965	1955	1951
Minimum monthly	0.2	0.0	0.0	0.0	0.0	T	0.0	T	0.0	0.1	0.0	0.0	T
Date	1984	1983	1957	1960	1949	1959	1950	1974	1977	1957	1962	1976	1974
Maximum in 24 hrs	6.7	6.8	17.0	4.2	3.4	2.2	1.0	2.3	1.4	7.5	9.1	8.1	17.0
Date	1963	1955	1958	1972	1965	1967	1967	1959	1963	1978	1954	1955	1958
WIND (Resultant)													
Mean speed (mph)	9.7	10.5	11.6	12.0	12.1	12.8	13.5	13.2	11.5	10.8	10.8	10.6	11.6

KAHULUI

Elev. 48' 20° 54'N — 156° 26'W **Hawaii**

NORMALS, MEANS, EXTREMES

	JAN	FEB	MAR	APR	MAY	JUN	JUL	AUG	SEP	OCT	NOV	DEC	YEAR
TEMPERATURE													
Normal daily maximum	79.5	79.7	81.1	82.2	84.5	85.9	86.5	87.4	87.6	86.4	83.5	81.0	83.8
Normal daily minimum	63.4	63.4	64.8	66.2	67.0	68.7	70.4	70.9	69.8	69.1	67.5	65.3	67.2
Normal monthly	71.5	71.6	73.0	74.2	75.8	77.3	78.5	79.2	78.7	77.8	75.5	73.2	75.5
Extreme highest	89	88	90	91	92	93	94	96	95	96	93	90	96
Extreme highest date	1981	1981	1984	1981	1978	1981	1984	1983	1968	1973	1984	1983	1983
Extreme lowest	48	50	55	54	57	58	58	61	60	58	55	52	48
Extreme lowest date	1969	1973	1983	1985	1985	1985	1965	1976	1975	1964	1985	1983	1969
DEGREE DAYS BASE 65° F													
Heating	0	0	0	0	0	0	0	0	0	0	0	0	0
Cooling	202	185	248	276	335	369	419	440	411	397	315	254	3851
% OF POSSIBLE SUNSHINE	65	65	64	64	70	74	72	73	76	70	65	65	69
AVERAGE SKY COVER													
Sunrise - Sunset	4.8	5.1	5.4	6.1	5.4	4.9	4.7	4.7	4.7	5.1	5.0	4.9	5.1
NUMBER OF DAYS (Sunrise-Sunset)													
Clear	12.8	10.7	10.3	7.1	9.4	10.7	10.9	12.2	11.9	11.0	11.1	12.2	130.3
Partly cloudy	10.1	10.0	11.5	11.8	13.5	13.0	14.9	13.4	12.6	12.4	10.8	11.1	145.1
Cloudy	8.1	7.6	9.1	11.1	8.1	6.3	5.3	5.4	5.4	7.6	8.1	7.7	89.9
Precipitation .01" or more	10.5	10.0	11.1	10.5	5.4	4.3	6.1	6.1	5.1	7.0	9.8	10.7	96.7
Snow, Ice pellets 1.0" or more	0.0	0.0	0.0	0.0	0.0	0.0	0.0	0.0	0.0	0.0	0.0	0.0	0.0
Thunderstorms	0.9	0.7	0.5	0.5	0.3	0.0	0.1	0.1	*	0.3	0.4	0.4	4.3
Fog, Visibility 1/4 mile or less	0.0	0.0	0.0	0.0	0.0	0.0	0.0	0.0	0.0	0.0	0.0	0.0	0.0
Temperature Maximum:													
90° and above	0.0	0.0	0.1	0.1	1.4	2.5	4.0	6.8	7.4	5.0	1.1	*	28.5
32° and below	0.0	0.0	0.0	0.0	0.0	0.0	0.0	0.0	0.0	0.0	0.0	0.0	0.0
Temperature Minimum:													
32° and below	0.0	0.0	0.0	0.0	0.0	0.0	0.0	0.0	0.0	0.0	0.0	0.0	0.0
0° and below	0.0	0.0	0.0	0.0	0.0	0.0	0.0	0.0	0.0	0.0	0.0	0.0	0.0
RELATIVE HUMIDITY (%)													
Morning	85	83	81	81	82	80	80	79	80	80	81	82	81
Afternoon	63	61	59	58	55	53	54	54	54	56	59	61	57
PRECIPITATION (inches)													
Water Equivalent													
Normal	4.2	3.2	3.0	1.1	0.6	0.2	0.4	0.5	0.3	0.8	2.2	2.8	19.8
Maximum monthly	14.4	8.3	10.9	3.8	2.6	2.5	1.1	1.5	1.1	5.6	9.2	9.4	14.4
Date	1980	1972	1967	1977	1963	1967	1960	1982	1965	1985	1965	1955	1980
Minimum monthly	0.1	0.0	0.0	0.0	T	0.0	0.0	0.0	0.0	T	0.1	0.0	0.0
Date	1977	1983	1957	1955	1972	1957	1973	1973	1972	1984	1980	1975	1957
Maximum in 24 hrs	7.0	4.9	5.4	2.2	1.9	2.3	0.7	1.2	1.1	4.8	5.4	5.8	7.0
Date	1980	1972	1967	1977	1968	1967	1960	1982	1965	1985	1965	1955	1980
WIND (Resultant)													
Mean speed (mph)	10.8	11.1	12.3	13.3	13.2	14.7	15.6	14.8	12.9	12.0	11.8	11.3	12.8

LIHUE

Elev. 103' 21° 59'N — 159° 21'W **Hawaii**

NORMALS, MEANS, EXTREMES

	JAN	FEB	MAR	APR	MAY	JUN	JUL	AUG	SEP	OCT	NOV	DEC	YEAR
TEMPERATURE													
Normal daily maximum	77.8	78.0	78.1	79.2	81.2	83.0	83.8	84.6	84.7	83.2	80.8	78.8	81.1
Normal daily minimum	64.6	64.7	65.9	67.6	69.7	71.8	72.9	73.5	72.9	71.4	69.7	66.9	69.3
Normal monthly	71.2	71.4	72.0	73.4	75.5	77.4	78.4	79.1	78.8	77.3	75.3	72.9	75.2
Extreme highest	85	86	87	88	88	89	89	90	89	90	87	86	90
Extreme highest date	1981	1982	1963	1981	1981	1969	1981	1981	1981	1957	1980	1981	1981
Extreme lowest	50	52	51	56	59	62	62	66	65	62	57	52	50
Extreme lowest date	1969	1962	1955	1958	1954	1979	1979	1979	1981	1981	1958	1953	1969
DEGREE DAYS BASE 65° F													
Heating	0	0	0	0	0	0	0	0	0	0	0	0	0
Cooling	200	184	220	252	326	372	415	437	417	381	309	245	3758
% OF POSSIBLE SUNSHINE	52	54	53	52	57	61	62	64	66	57	49	47	56
AVERAGE SKY COVER													
Sunrise - Sunset	5.9	6.0	6.7	7.1	6.7	6.5	6.5	6.3	5.7	6.2	6.5	6.2	6.3
NUMBER OF DAYS (Sunrise-Sunset)													
Clear	7.9	6.3	4.2	2.7	2.9	3.2	2.6	3.4	5.1	5.3	4.0	5.8	53.4
Partly cloudy	12.3	12.1	13.9	13.3	15.8	16.3	18.3	18.0	17.5	14.9	13.9	13.5	179.9
Cloudy	10.8	9.9	12.9	14.0	12.2	10.5	10.1	9.6	7.4	10.8	12.2	11.6	132.0
Precipitation .01" or more	15.2	13.8	16.9	17.5	16.0	16.5	19.4	17.7	16.0	17.9	17.5	16.9	201.4
Snow, Ice pellets 1.0" or more	0.0	0.0	0.0	0.0	0.0	0.0	0.0	0.0	0.0	0.0	0.0	0.0	0.0
Thunderstorms	1.2	0.8	1.1	0.5	0.7	0.1	0.1	0.1	0.4	1.1	1.0	0.9	8.0
Fog, Visibility 1/4 mile or less	0.0	0.0	0.0	0.0	0.0	0.0	0.0	0.0	0.0	0.0	0.0	0.0	0.0
Temperature Maximum:													
90° and above	0.0	0.0	0.0	0.0	0.0	0.0	0.0	0.1	0.0	*	0.0	0.0	0.1
32° and below	0.0	0.0	0.0	0.0	0.0	0.0	0.0	0.0	0.0	0.0	0.0	0.0	0.0
Temperature Minimum:													
32° and below	0.0	0.0	0.0	0.0	0.0	0.0	0.0	0.0	0.0	0.0	0.0	0.0	0.0
0° and below	0.0	0.0	0.0	0.0	0.0	0.0	0.0	0.0	0.0	0.0	0.0	0.0	0.0
RELATIVE HUMIDITY (%)													
Morning	83	81	81	81	81	80	79	80	80	82	82	81	81
Afternoon	67	66	66	67	66	65	65	66	65	67	69	68	66
PRECIPITATION (inches)													
Water Equivalent													
Normal	6.2	3.6	4.5	3.2	2.9	1.6	2.0	1.8	2.2	4.5	5.5	5.4	44.0
Maximum monthly	17.5	10.5	14.5	10.6	12.5	4.5	8.8	8.1	10.8	18.0	18.4	22.9	22.9
Date	1956	1979	1951	1972	1977	1978	1954	1959	1980	1982	1955	1968	1968
Minimum monthly	0.8	T	0.3	0.9	0.4	0.4	0.7	0.7	0.4	1.0	0.5	0.5	T
Date	1983	1983	1957	1953	1968	1975	1956	1984	1975	1963	1963	1985	1983
Maximum in 24 hrs	11.0	7.2	6.3	6.5	6.7	2.1	5.0	5.4	7.1	8.4	11.2	11.5	11.5
Date	1956	1954	1962	1972	1977	1971	1954	1959	1980	1978	1955	1968	1968
WIND (Resultant)													
Mean speed (mph)	10.5	11.3	12.2	12.7	12.2	12.6	13.2	12.7	11.3	11.1	11.8	11.4	11.9

BOISE

Elev. 2838'   43° 34'N — 116° 13'W   **Idaho**

NORMALS, MEANS, EXTREMES

	JAN	FEB	MAR	APR	MAY	JUN	JUL	AUG	SEP	OCT	NOV	DEC	YEAR
TEMPERATURE													
Normal daily maximum	37.1	44.3	51.8	60.8	70.8	79.8	90.6	87.3	77.6	64.6	49.0	39.3	62.8
Normal daily minimum	22.6	27.9	30.9	36.4	44.0	51.8	58.5	56.7	48.7	39.1	30.5	24.6	39.3
Normal monthly	29.9	36.1	41.4	48.6	57.4	65.8	74.6	72.0	63.2	51.9	39.8	32.0	51.0
Extreme highest	63	69	81	92	98	109	111	110	102	91	73	65	111
Extreme highest date	1953	1977	1978	1946	1966	1940	1960	1961	1945	1963	1975	1964	1960
Extreme lowest	-17	-12	6	19	22	31	40	37	23	11	-3	-23	-23
Extreme lowest date	1950	1985	1971	1968	1982	1984	1983	1980	1970	1971	1985	1972	1972
DEGREE DAYS BASE 65° F													
Heating	1088	809	732	492	253	83	0	23	134	406	759	1023	5802
Cooling	0	0	0	0	17	107	298	240	80	0	0	0	742
% OF POSSIBLE SUNSHINE	39	50	62	67	71	75	87	85	80	67	44	38	64
AVERAGE SKY COVER													
Sunrise - Sunset	7.7	7.3	6.9	6.4	5.8	4.8	2.8	3.3	3.6	5.1	7.0	7.6	5.7
NUMBER OF DAYS (Sunrise-Sunset)													
Clear	4.5	4.3	6.1	6.7	8.5	11.6	20.7	18.5	16.8	11.9	6.1	4.7	120.4
Partly cloudy	4.8	6.5	7.2	8.7	9.9	10.2	7.1	8.0	7.1	8.3	6.2	5.6	89.6
Cloudy	21.7	17.5	17.8	14.6	12.4	8.3	3.2	4.5	6.1	10.8	17.6	20.7	155.2
Precipitation .01" or more	12.2	10.5	9.7	8.1	7.9	6.3	2.4	2.7	3.8	6.3	10.2	11.7	91.7
Snow, Ice pellets 1.0" or more	2.5	1.3	0.5	0.3	*	0.0	0.0	0.0	0.0	0.1	1.0	2.3	8.0
Thunderstorms	*	0.3	0.6	0.9	2.8	2.8	2.8	2.4	1.6	0.6	0.3	0.1	15.2
Fog, Visibility 1/4 mile or less	5.6	3.0	0.7	0.3	0.2	0.2	0.0	0.0	0.1	0.5	2.9	5.8	19.4
Temperature Maximum:													
90° and above	0.0	0.0	0.0	*	1.0	4.7	18.7	15.0	3.1	0.1	0.0	0.0	42.6
32° and below	10.4	2.7	0.2	0.0	0.0	0.0	0.0	0.0	0.0	0.0	0.9	6.7	21.0
Temperature Minimum:													
32° and below	26.0	20.8	18.3	8.4	1.7	*	0.0	0.0	0.5	5.7	17.8	25.0	124.1
0° and below	1.8	0.3	0.0	0.0	0.0	0.0	0.0	0.0	0.0	0.0	0.1	1.0	3.3
RELATIVE HUMIDITY (%)													
Morning	80	79	74	70	69	67	54	52	59	67	77	81	69
Afternoon	70	60	45	36	34	30	22	23	30	40	61	71	44
PRECIPITATION (inches)													
Water Equivalent													
Normal	1.6	1.0	1.0	1.1	1.2	0.9	0.2	0.4	0.5	0.7	1.2	1.3	11.7
Maximum monthly	3.8	2.6	2.7	3.0	4.0	3.4	1.6	2.3	2.5	2.2	2.4	4.2	4.2
Date	1970	1975	1981	1955	1942	1941	1982	1968	1959	1956	1973	1983	1983
Minimum monthly	0.1	0.1	0.1	0.0	0.0	0.0	0.0	T	T	T	0.1	0.0	0.0
Date	1949	1964	1944	1949	1940	1966	1947	1980	1974	1978	1976	1976	1947
Maximum in 24 hrs	1.4	1.0	1.6	1.2	1.5	2.2	0.9	1.6	1.7	0.7	0.8	1.1	2.2
Date	1953	1951	1981	1969	1942	1958	1960	1979	1976	1947	1971	1955	1958
SNOW, ICE PELLETS													
Maximum monthly	21.4	25.2	11.9	8.0	4.0	T	T	0.0	0.0	2.7	18.6	26.2	26.2
Date	1964	1949	1951	1967	1964	1954	1970	—	—	1971	1985	1983	1983
Maximum in 24 hrs	8.5	13.0	6.4	7.2	4.0	T	T	0.0	0.0	1.7	6.5	6.7	13.0
Date	1950	1949	1952	1969	1964	1954	1970	—	—	1971	1964	1983	1949
WIND (Resultant)													
Mean speed (mph)	8.1	9.2	10.1	10.1	9.5	9.1	8.4	8.2	8.3	8.4	8.5	8.3	8.9

LEWISTON
Elev. 1413' 46° 23'N — 117° 01'W **Idaho**

NORMALS, MEANS, EXTREMES

	JAN	FEB	MAR	APR	MAY	JUN	JUL	AUG	SEP	OCT	NOV	DEC	YEAR
TEMPERATURE													
Normal daily maximum	38.6	46.3	52.7	61.6	70.7	79.0	89.5	87.3	77.6	63.1	47.6	41.5	63.0
Normal daily minimum	25.6	30.6	33.0	38.7	45.9	52.8	58.6	57.4	49.6	40.4	32.6	28.2	41.1
Normal monthly	32.1	38.5	42.9	50.2	58.3	65.9	74.1	72.4	63.6	51.8	40.1	34.9	52.0
Extreme highest	66	66	76	97	100	107	110	115	103	89	74	63	115
Extreme highest date	1953	1977	1964	1977	1983	1973	1967	1961	1950	1980	1975	1965	1961
Extreme lowest	-22	-15	2	20	23	34	41	42	28	16	-3	-22	-22
Extreme lowest date	1950	1950	1955	1966	1954	1951	1955	1980	1965	1971	1955	1968	1968
DEGREE DAYS BASE 65° F													
Heating	1020	742	685	444	225	74	0	21	129	409	747	933	5429
Cooling	0	0	0	0	17	101	286	251	87	0	0	0	742
% OF POSSIBLE SUNSHINE	na	na	na	na	na	na	na	na	na	na	na	na	na
AVERAGE SKY COVER													
Sunrise - Sunset	8.3	8.2	7.6	7.3	6.7	6.1	3.3	3.9	4.7	6.3	8.2	8.5	6.6
NUMBER OF DAYS (Sunrise-Sunset)													
Clear	2.8	2.7	4.3	4.5	6.4	8.3	18.6	16.4	13.0	8.2	2.7	2.7	90.5
Partly cloudy	4.3	4.5	6.2	6.4	8.6	8.6	7.0	7.6	7.5	7.4	5.5	3.8	77.2
Cloudy	23.8	21.1	20.5	19.1	16.1	13.2	5.3	7.1	9.5	15.4	21.8	24.6	197.5
Precipitation .01" or more	11.8	9.8	10.5	9.8	9.3	8.3	4.3	4.5	5.6	8.0	10.3	11.7	103.9
Snow, Ice pellets 1.0" or more	2.0	0.9	0.5	*	0.0	0.0	0.0	0.0	0.0	0.1	0.5	1.7	5.7
Thunderstorms	0.0	0.1	0.1	0.7	2.5	3.6	3.7	3.2	1.2	0.4	0.1	0.0	15.6
Fog, Visibility 1/4 mile or less	3.9	3.5	1.2	0.2	0.4	0.1	0.0	0.0	0.1	2.1	4.1	5.4	21.1
Temperature Maximum:													
90° and above	0.0	0.0	0.0	0.1	1.1	4.4	16.6	14.2	3.3	0.0	0.0	0.0	39.6
32° and below	8.2	1.9	0.2	0.0	0.0	0.0	0.0	0.0	0.0	0.0	1.3	5.0	16.5
Temperature Minimum:													
32° and below	22.3	16.3	13.2	4.1	0.3	0.0	0.0	0.0	0.2	3.3	12.6	20.3	92.5
0° and below	1.6	0.2	0.0	0.0	0.0	0.0	0.0	0.0	0.0	0.0	0.2	0.5	2.4
RELATIVE HUMIDITY (%)													
Morning	81	80	77	75	76	74	61	59	68	80	83	82	75
Afternoon	72	63	50	42	40	36	24	25	32	50	70	75	48
PRECIPITATION (inches)													
Water Equivalent													
Normal	1.3	0.9	1.0	1.1	1.4	1.4	0.5	0.7	0.7	1.0	1.1	1.3	12.7
Maximum monthly	3.5	1.6	2.7	3.2	4.8	4.7	2.1	2.1	2.3	2.7	2.7	3.2	4.8
Date	1970	1974	1972	1978	1948	1950	1964	1956	1947	1950	1973	1964	1948
Minimum monthly	0.2	0.2	0.2	0.0	0.2	0.2	T	T	T	T	0.2	0.1	T
Date	1985	1964	1969	1956	1964	1973	1953	1969	1975	1978	1976	1970	1978
Maximum in 24 hrs	1.3	0.9	0.9	1.0	1.6	1.7	1.4	1.3	1.7	1.1	0.9	1.1	1.7
Date	1956	1959	1981	1978	1948	1950	1964	1960	1955	1950	1973	1958	1955
SNOW, ICE PELLETS													
Maximum monthly	26.1	14.9	9.7	1.1	T	0.0	0.0	0.0	0.0	2.5	14.4	18.7	26.1
Date	1957	1956	1955	1972	1984	—	—	—	—	1971	1961	1968	1957
Maximum in 24 hrs	12.8	7.5	5.4	1.0	T	0.0	0.0	0.0	0.0	1.3	8.3	8.4	12.8
Date	1966	1956	1955	1947	1984	—	—	—	—	1971	1961	1968	1966

POCATELLO

Elev. 4454' 42° 55'N — 112° 36'W **Idaho**

NORMALS, MEANS, EXTREMES

	JAN	FEB	MAR	APR	MAY	JUN	JUL	AUG	SEP	OCT	NOV	DEC	YEAR
TEMPERATURE													
Normal daily maximum	32.4	38.6	45.8	56.8	67.7	77.6	88.6	86.0	75.7	62.8	45.6	35.3	59.4
Normal daily minimum	15.1	20.4	25.2	32.3	40.3	47.3	53.8	51.7	42.7	33.3	24.8	17.9	33.7
Normal monthly	23.8	29.5	35.5	44.6	54.0	62.5	71.2	68.9	59.2	48.1	35.2	26.6	46.6
Extreme highest	57	62	73	85	93	99	102	104	98	88	71	59	104
Extreme highest date	1974	1982	1978	1977	1954	1974	1976	1969	1976	1979	1975	1980	1969
Extreme lowest	-30	-33	-12	15	20	30	34	32	19	10	-13	-28	-33
Extreme lowest date	1962	1985	1985	1970	1972	1968	1981	1969	1985	1971	1955	1972	1985
DEGREE DAYS BASE 65° F													
Heating	1277	994	915	612	348	128	0	32	209	524	894	1190	7123
Cooling	0	0	0	0	7	53	197	153	35	0	0	0	445
% OF POSSIBLE SUNSHINE	38	52	61	65	67	74	83	80	79	70	46	38	63
AVERAGE SKY COVER													
Sunrise - Sunset	8.1	7.6	7.1	6.7	6.2	5.0	3.4	3.8	4.0	5.1	7.2	7.9	6.0
NUMBER OF DAYS (Sunrise-Sunset)													
Clear	2.7	3.8	5.1	6.3	7.5	11.5	17.7	15.5	15.3	12.1	5.3	3.4	106.2
Partly cloudy	6.4	6.2	8.0	9.9	9.9	9.6	8.9	10.6	8.1	8.5	7.3	6.4	98.0
Cloudy	21.8	18.3	17.8	15.7	13.6	8.9	4.4	4.9	6.7	10.4	17.4	21.2	161.1
Precipitation .01" or more	12.2	10.2	10.3	8.0	9.1	7.1	4.1	4.7	4.8	5.3	9.0	11.3	96.1
Snow, Ice pellets 1.0" or more	3.2	2.1	2.2	1.3	0.1	0.0	0.0	0.0	0.1	0.5	1.8	3.1	14.4
Thunderstorms	0.1	0.1	0.4	0.7	3.4	4.5	5.6	5.2	2.6	0.5	0.1	0.1	23.4
Fog, Visibility 1/4 mile or less	4.3	3.3	1.7	0.5	0.3	0.1	*	0.0	0.1	0.3	1.8	4.1	16.4
Temperature Maximum:													
90° and above	0.0	0.0	0.0	0.0	0.0	3.5	15.0	12.4	1.8	0.0	0.0	0.0	32.7
32° and below	14.1	8.0	2.4	*	0.0	0.0	0.0	0.0	0.0	0.2	4.3	12.8	41.8
Temperature Minimum:													
32° and below	27.5	25.6	25.9	17.0	4.6	0.3	0.0	*	3.2	15.5	23.1	27.8	170.6
0° and below	5.4	2.2	0.3	0.0	0.0	0.0	0.0	0.0	0.0	0.0	0.7	4.0	12.5
RELATIVE HUMIDITY (%)													
Morning	78	78	76	69	69	71	64	61	65	70	76	78	71
Afternoon	70	62	51	39	34	32	24	23	28	37	59	70	44
PRECIPITATION (inches)													
Water Equivalent													
Normal	1.1	0.8	0.9	1.1	1.2	1.0	0.4	0.6	0.6	0.9	0.9	0.9	10.8
Maximum monthly	3.2	2.0	2.9	3.3	3.2	3.3	2.2	3.9	3.4	2.5	2.8	3.3	3.9
Date	1980	1984	1983	1963	1980	1967	1984	1968	1982	1956	1983	1983	1968
Minimum monthly	0.2	0.1	0.1	0.0	0.1	0.0	T	T	T	0.0	0.0	0.2	0.0
Date	1961	1970	1965	1977	1969	1974	1963	1958	1964	1952	1976	1976	1952
Maximum in 24 hrs	0.9	0.6	0.9	1.2	1.6	1.0	0.9	1.1	1.1	1.8	0.8	0.9	1.8
Date	1970	1983	1983	1976	1970	1960	1965	1972	1982	1976	1969	1983	1976
SNOW, ICE PELLETS													
Maximum monthly	28.1	20.1	16.6	15.5	5.5	0.2	0.0	0.0	2.0	12.6	27.5	33.7	33.7
Date	1950	1984	1985	1976	1983	1981	—	—	1965	1971	1985	1983	1983
Maximum in 24 hrs	10.1	6.4	8.4	10.0	5.2	0.2	0.0	0.0	2.0	8.0	7.3	9.5	10.1
Date	1950	1984	1985	1976	1983	1981	—	—	1965	1980	1985	1982	1950
WIND (Resultant)													
Mean speed (mph)	10.8	10.7	11.3	11.7	10.6	10.2	9.1	8.9	9.1	9.3	10.2	10.1	10.2

CAIRO

Elev. 314'   37° 00'N — 89° 10'W   **Illinois**

NORMALS, MEANS, EXTREMES

	JAN	FEB	MAR	APR	MAY	JUN	JUL	AUG	SEP	OCT	NOV	DEC	YEAR
TEMPERATURE													
Normal daily maximum	41.9	46.8	56.4	69.2	78.5	87.0	89.8	87.9	81.4	70.9	56.6	46.3	67.7
Normal daily minimum	27.3	31.0	39.5	51.0	60.0	68.2	72.1	70.0	63.1	51.2	40.2	32.1	50.5
Normal monthly	34.6	38.9	48.0	60.1	69.3	77.6	81.0	79.0	72.3	61.1	48.4	39.2	59.1
Extreme highest	75	77	83	90	98	104	104	103	103	92	82	79	104
Extreme highest date	1950	1981	1985	1980	1953	1954	1980	1964	1954	1963	1955	1982	1980
Extreme lowest	-12	-5	6	28	38	51	54	53	40	27	5	-4	-12
Extreme lowest date	1985	1951	1960	1982	1978	1956	1947	1965	1983	1981	1950	1983	1985
DEGREE DAYS BASE 65° F													
Heating	942	731	540	177	46	0	0	0	12	170	495	800	3913
Cooling	0	0	13	30	179	378	496	431	231	49	0	0	1807
% OF POSSIBLE SUNSHINE	44	51	55	62	65	72	74	75	69	67	52	44	61
AVERAGE SKY COVER													
Sunrise - Sunset	6.6	6.3	6.2	6.1	6.1	5.6	5.6	5.0	5.0	4.5	5.9	6.5	5.8
NUMBER OF DAYS (Sunrise-Sunset)													
Clear	7.8	7.7	8.7	7.8	8.2	8.3	8.5	11.5	11.9	14.8	9.1	8.4	112.8
Partly cloudy	6.3	6.4	7.6	8.8	9.5	11.5	12.7	11.2	8.6	6.8	7.5	6.7	103.6
Cloudy	17.0	14.2	14.6	13.4	13.3	10.2	9.8	8.3	9.5	9.4	13.4	15.9	148.9
Precipitation .01" or more	9.9	9.2	11.9	11.2	11.2	9.0	8.8	7.9	7.5	7.4	8.8	9.7	112.6
Snow, Ice pellets 1.0" or more	1.3	0.8	0.6	*	0.0	0.0	0.0	0.0	0.0	0.0	0.1	0.5	3.3
Thunderstorms	1.4	1.7	3.6	5.3	7.0	8.8	8.3	6.2	3.8	2.5	1.9	1.0	51.5
Fog, Visibility 1/4 mile or less	1.1	0.9	0.3	0.3	0.3	*	0.1	0.3	0.5	0.9	1.3	0.9	6.9
Temperature Maximum:													
90° and above	0.0	0.0	0.0	*	2.3	11.1	17.2	13.1	4.0	0.1	0.0	0.0	47.8
32° and below	6.8	3.2	0.5	0.0	0.0	0.0	0.0	0.0	0.0	0.0	0.4	3.3	14.2
Temperature Minimum:													
32° and below	21.2	15.0	7.0	0.2	0.0	0.0	0.0	0.0	0.0	0.1	6.1	16.7	66.4
0° and below	0.3	*	0.0	0.0	0.0	0.0	0.0	0.0	0.0	0.0	0.0	0.1	0.4
Afternoon	67	64	59	54	57	57	59	59	57	53	58	66	59
PRECIPITATION (inches)													
Water Equivalent													
Normal	3.4	3.4	4.9	4.4	4.9	4.3	3.9	3.9	3.5	2.5	3.9	4.1	47.6
Maximum monthly	14.9	8.8	12.6	9.4	11.1	10.2	9.2	11.6	9.3	7.8	13.0	11.3	14.9
Date	1950	1950	1964	1966	1946	1951	1972	1978	1965	1984	1957	1978	1950
Minimum monthly	0.3	0.5	1.1	0.9	1.9	0.7	0.3	0.1	0.4	T	0.7	0.6	T
Date	1943	1947	1966	1949	1948	1952	1983	1983	1953	1964	1954	1955	1964
Maximum in 24 hrs	6.0	4.7	6.5	4.6	6.1	5.9	3.9	7.5	6.2	2.9	4.3	4.8	7.5
Date	1949	1950	1964	1985	1967	1961	1984	1952	1965	1967	1957	1978	1952
SNOW, ICE PELLETS													
Maximum monthly	21.8	8.9	20.3	1.0	0.0	0.0	0.0	0.0	0.0	T	5.2	10.5	21.8
Date	1978	1960	1960	1971	—	—	—	—	—	1949	1958	1969	1978
Maximum in 24 hrs	13.6	5.8	9.8	1.0	0.0	0.0	0.0	0.0	0.0	T	5.2	6.9	13.6
Date	1978	1944	1970	1971	—	—	—	—	—	1949	1958	1969	1978
WIND (Resultant)													
Mean speed (mph)	9.8	9.8	10.6	10.2	8.2	7.4	6.5	6.2	7.0	7.3	9.1	9.3	8.5

CHICAGO

Elev. 658'   41° 59'N — 87° 54'W   **Illinois**

NORMALS, MEANS, EXTREMES

	JAN	FEB	MAR	APR	MAY	JUN	JUL	AUG	SEP	OCT	NOV	DEC	YEAR
TEMPERATURE													
Normal daily maximum	29.2	33.9	44.3	58.8	70.0	79.4	83.3	82.1	75.5	64.1	48.2	35.0	58.7
Normal daily minimum	13.6	18.1	27.6	38.8	48.1	57.7	62.7	61.7	53.9	42.9	31.4	20.3	39.7
Normal monthly	21.4	26.0	36.0	48.8	59.1	68.6	73.0	71.9	64.7	53.5	39.8	27.7	49.2
Extreme highest	61	71	87	91	93	99	102	99	99	91	78	71	102
Extreme highest date	1967	1976	1981	1980	1977	1983	1980	1983	1985	1963	1978	1982	1980
Extreme lowest	-27	-17	-8	7	24	36	40	41	28	17	1	-25	-27
Extreme lowest date	1985	1967	1962	1982	1966	1972	1965	1965	1974	1981	1976	1983	1985
DEGREE DAYS BASE 65° F													
Heating	1352	1092	899	486	224	38	0	9	75	368	756	1156	6455
Cooling	0	0	0	0	41	146	252	223	66	12	0	0	740
% OF POSSIBLE SUNSHINE	45	44	50	47	60	69	68	64	57	49	33	43	52
AVERAGE SKY COVER													
Sunrise - Sunset	6.8	6.8	7.3	6.8	6.3	6.0	5.5	5.7	5.8	6.0	7.2	7.2	6.5
NUMBER OF DAYS (Sunrise-Sunset)													
Clear	7.0	6.1	4.7	6.2	7.1	7.1	8.8	8.9	8.8	8.5	5.8	5.8	84.9
Partly cloudy	5.9	6.3	8.7	7.7	9.8	11.5	12.9	11.3	9.8	9.0	6.4	6.0	105.4
Cloudy	18.0	15.9	17.6	16.1	14.0	11.3	9.3	10.7	11.4	13.4	17.9	19.1	175.0
Precipitation .01" or more	11.3	9.6	12.7	12.6	11.0	10.2	9.8	9.1	9.6	9.2	10.2	11.6	127.0
Snow, Ice pellets 1.0" or more	3.4	2.5	2.2	0.5	0.0	0.0	0.0	0.0	0.0	0.1	0.7	2.7	12.1
Thunderstorms	0.3	0.4	2.1	4.4	4.8	6.6	6.1	5.7	4.6	1.7	1.1	0.7	38.6
Fog, Visibility 1/4 mile or less	1.4	1.9	2.3	0.9	1.4	0.6	0.6	0.8	0.5	1.0	1.6	2.2	15.2
Temperature Maximum:													
90° and above	0.0	0.0	0.0	*	0.9	3.3	5.9	4.3	1.9	0.1	0.0	0.0	16.4
32° and below	19.1	13.3	4.5	0.1	0.0	0.0	0.0	0.0	0.0	0.0	2.0	12.1	51.1
Temperature Minimum:													
32° and below	29.1	25.0	21.5	7.8	1.0	0.0	0.0	0.0	0.3	4.7	17.0	26.5	132.7
0° and below	7.4	3.3	0.3	0.0	0.0	0.0	0.0	0.0	0.0	0.0	0.0	3.0	14.0
RELATIVE HUMIDITY (%)													
Morning	75	75	76	72	73	75	79	81	81	76	77	78	77
Afternoon	67	66	61	55	54	55	57	57	58	56	64	70	60
PRECIPITATION (inches)													
Water Equivalent													
Normal	1.6	1.3	2.5	3.6	3.1	4.0	3.6	3.5	3.3	2.2	2.0	2.1	33.3
Maximum monthly	4.1	3.4	5.9	7.6	7.1	7.9	8.3	8.5	11.4	6.5	8.2	8.5	11.4
Date	1965	1985	1976	1983	1970	1967	1982	1980	1961	1969	1985	1982	1961
Minimum monthly	0.1	0.1	0.6	0.9	1.6	1.5	1.1	0.5	0.0	0.1	0.6	0.2	0.0
Date	1981	1969	1981	1971	1967	1982	1977	1969	1979	1964	1976	1962	1979
Maximum in 24 hrs	2.0	1.9	2.3	2.7	3.4	3.0	2.8	3.5	3.0	4.6	2.8	4.5	4.6
Date	1960	1985	1985	1983	1981	1967	1962	1975	1978	1969	1985	1982	1969
SNOW, ICE PELLETS													
Maximum monthly	34.3	21.5	24.7	11.1	1.6	0.0	0.0	0.0	T	6.6	10.4	35.3	35.3
Date	1979	1967	1965	1975	1966	—	—	—	1967	1967	1959	1978	1978
Maximum in 24 hrs	18.1	9.7	10.6	10.9	1.6	0.0	0.0	0.0	T	6.6	5.8	11.0	18.1
Date	1967	1981	1970	1975	1966	—	—	—	1967	1967	1975	1969	1967
WIND (Resultant)													
Mean speed (mph)	11.6	11.4	11.8	12.0	10.5	9.1	8.1	8.0	8.8	9.9	10.9	10.9	10.3

MOLINE

Elev. 582' 41° 27'N — 90° 31'W **Illinois**

NORMALS, MEANS, EXTREMES

	JAN	FEB	MAR	APR	MAY	JUN	JUL	AUG	SEP	OCT	NOV	DEC	YEAR
TEMPERATURE													
Normal daily maximum	28.0	33.7	44.8	61.1	72.5	82.1	85.4	83.6	76.2	64.8	48.0	34.3	59.5
Normal daily minimum	11.0	16.4	26.5	39.6	50.1	59.9	64.3	62.1	53.2	42.1	30.0	18.4	39.5
Normal monthly	19.5	25.1	35.7	50.4	61.3	71.0	74.9	72.9	64.7	53.5	39.0	26.4	49.5
Extreme highest	65	71	83	92	104	104	105	106	100	92	80	69	106
Extreme highest date	1950	1976	1945	1980	1934	1934	1940	1936	1939	1963	1933	1970	1936
Extreme lowest	-27	-25	-19	7	26	39	46	40	24	16	-9	-22	-27
Extreme lowest date	1979	1979	1960	1982	1966	1972	1971	1934	1942	1952	1976	1963	1979
DEGREE DAYS BASE 65° F													
Heating	1411	1117	908	438	177	20	0	5	75	370	780	1197	6498
Cooling	0	0	0	0	62	200	307	250	66	14	0	0	899
% OF POSSIBLE SUNSHINE	48	50	50	53	56	62	68	67	63	58	42	41	55
AVERAGE SKY COVER													
Sunrise - Sunset	6.6	6.4	6.8	6.6	6.3	6.0	5.3	5.3	5.2	5.3	6.7	6.8	6.1
NUMBER OF DAYS (Sunrise-Sunset)													
Clear	7.9	7.3	6.4	6.5	7.5	7.2	10.2	10.2	11.9	11.6	7.4	6.9	101.0
Partly cloudy	6.9	6.5	8.0	8.8	9.1	10.7	11.8	11.0	7.8	7.7	6.9	6.2	101.2
Cloudy	16.2	14.5	16.5	14.8	14.5	12.2	9.0	9.8	10.3	11.7	15.8	17.8	163.0
Precipitation .01" or more	9.3	7.9	11.2	10.9	12.1	10.3	9.5	8.7	8.7	7.6	8.2	9.3	113.8
Snow, Ice pellets 1.0" or more	2.7	2.1	1.9	0.3	0.0	0.0	0.0	0.0	0.0	0.1	0.8	2.3	10.1
Thunderstorms	0.3	0.5	2.2	4.5	6.7	8.4	8.4	7.0	4.5	2.5	1.3	0.8	47.1
Fog, Visibility 1/4 mile or less	2.3	2.0	2.0	0.7	0.8	0.6	0.8	2.1	1.7	2.0	1.3	1.8	18.0
Temperature Maximum:													
90° and above	0.0	0.0	0.0	0.1	1.2	5.0	7.9	5.9	1.9	0.1	0.0	0.0	22.1
32° and below	19.7	12.8	3.8	0.2	0.0	0.0	0.0	0.0	0.0	0.0	2.1	13.6	52.3
Temperature Minimum:													
32° and below	29.7	25.3	21.1	7.2	0.7	0.0	0.0	0.0	0.2	5.4	18.4	27.2	135.2
0° and below	9.2	4.6	0.2	0.0	0.0	0.0	0.0	0.0	0.0	0.0	0.2	4.0	18.2
RELATIVE HUMIDITY (%)													
Morning	71	73	74	72	75	77	82	84	82	76	75	76	76
Afternoon	64	63	60	55	53	53	57	58	57	55	63	69	59
PRECIPITATION (inches)													
Water Equivalent													
Normal	1.6	1.3	2.7	3.9	4.2	4.3	4.8	3.7	3.7	2.7	1.9	1.9	37.1
Maximum monthly	4.3	2.8	7.4	11.3	11.4	8.8	11.3	9.3	14.1	9.4	6.4	4.9	14.1
Date	1974	1985	1973	1973	1974	1974	1969	1965	1970	1941	1934	1982	1970
Minimum monthly	0.3	0.1	0.3	0.6	0.5	1.0	1.0	0.3	0.0	0.0	0.2	0.2	0.0
Date	1961	1933	1958	1946	1928	1963	1955	1971	1979	1964	1933	1929	1964
Maximum in 24 hrs	2.0	1.9	2.4	5.8	3.6	5.0	5.4	4.6	6.2	4.8	2.7	3.3	6.2
Date	1960	1948	1985	1973	1970	1967	1963	1951	1961	1954	1961	1942	1961
SNOW, ICE PELLETS													
Maximum monthly	26.7	19.3	19.8	13.0	0.3	0.0	0.0	0.0	0.1	6.6	15.6	21.7	26.7
Date	1979	1975	1972	1982	1935	—	—	—	1942	1967	1974	1978	1979
Maximum in 24 hrs	16.4	10.1	11.0	8.2	0.3	0.0	0.0	0.0	0.1	6.5	8.5	9.0	16.4
Date	1971	1975	1972	1970	1935	—	—	—	1942	1967	1975	1978	1971
WIND (Resultant)													
Mean speed (mph)	10.9	11.0	12.1	12.3	10.4	9.3	7.7	7.3	8.3	9.3	10.8	10.7	10.0

PEORIA

Elev. 652' 40° 40'N — 89° 41'W **Illinois**

NORMALS, MEANS, EXTREMES

	JAN	FEB	MAR	APR	MAY	JUN	JUL	AUG	SEP	OCT	NOV	DEC	YEAR
TEMPERATURE													
Normal daily maximum	29.7	35.2	46.5	61.9	72.5	82.1	85.5	83.4	76.7	64.8	48.5	35.4	60.2
Normal daily minimum	13.3	18.4	28.1	40.6	50.6	60.2	64.6	62.7	54.5	42.9	30.9	20.2	40.6
Normal monthly	21.5	26.8	37.3	51.3	61.6	71.2	75.1	73.1	65.6	53.9	39.7	27.8	50.4
Extreme highest	68	72	83	89	92	100	103	102	100	90	81	71	103
Extreme highest date	1950	1976	1985	1952	1985	1971	1940	1983	1953	1963	1950	1982	1940
Extreme lowest	-25	-18	-10	14	25	39	47	43	26	19	-2	-18	-25
Extreme lowest date	1977	1979	1960	1982	1966	1945	1972	1950	1942	1972	1977	1983	1977
DEGREE DAYS BASE 65° F													
Heating	1349	1070	859	411	176	22	0	5	64	361	756	1153	6226
Cooling	0	0	0	0	71	208	314	256	82	17	0	0	948
% OF POSSIBLE SUNSHINE	46	50	51	54	59	66	68	67	65	61	44	41	56
AVERAGE SKY COVER													
Sunrise - Sunset	6.8	6.7	7.0	6.8	6.4	6.1	5.4	5.5	5.1	5.3	6.7	7.0	6.2
NUMBER OF DAYS (Sunrise-Sunset)													
Clear	7.4	7.0	6.1	6.2	7.0	7.1	9.3	10.1	11.3	11.1	7.0	6.6	96.3
Partly cloudy	5.9	5.6	7.3	8.0	9.5	10.5	12.0	10.4	8.6	7.8	6.2	5.7	97.5
Cloudy	17.8	15.6	17.6	15.8	14.5	12.3	9.7	10.5	10.1	12.1	16.8	18.6	171.5
Precipitation .01" or more	9.4	8.4	11.0	11.8	11.6	9.8	8.7	8.2	8.5	7.7	9.0	9.9	114.0
Snow, Ice pellets 1.0" or more	2.3	1.6	1.5	0.4	0.0	0.0	0.0	0.0	0.0	*	0.6	2.0	8.4
Thunderstorms	0.6	0.7	2.6	5.2	6.7	8.6	7.9	6.8	5.1	2.5	1.3	0.7	48.6
Fog, Visibility 1/4 mile or less	3.0	2.8	2.4	1.0	0.9	0.6	1.0	1.5	1.3	1.6	2.2	3.4	21.5
Temperature Maximum:													
90° and above	0.0	0.0	0.0	0.0	0.4	4.2	7.3	4.8	1.9	*	0.0	0.0	18.7
32° and below	18.7	12.0	4.2	0.2	0.0	0.0	0.0	0.0	0.0	0.0	1.7	13.3	50.0
Temperature Minimum:													
32° and below	29.6	25.3	20.3	5.9	0.5	0.0	0.0	0.0	0.1	4.2	17.0	26.7	129.6
0° and below	7.2	3.3	0.3	0.0	0.0	0.0	0.0	0.0	0.0	0.0	0.1	3.0	13.8
RELATIVE HUMIDITY (%)													
Morning	77	78	76	72	75	76	81	83	82	78	79	81	78
Afternoon	68	67	63	56	57	56	59	61	59	58	66	72	62
PRECIPITATION (inches)													
Water Equivalent													
Normal	1.6	1.4	2.8	3.8	3.8	3.8	3.9	3.3	3.6	2.5	1.9	2.0	34.8
Maximum monthly	8.1	5.1	6.9	8.6	7.9	11.6	8.4	8.6	13.0	10.8	7.6	6.3	13.0
Date	1965	1942	1973	1947	1957	1974	1958	1965	1961	1941	1985	1949	1961
Minimum monthly	0.2	0.3	0.3	0.7	1.0	0.9	0.5	0.7	0.0	0.0	0.4	0.3	0.0
Date	1956	1947	1958	1971	1964	1971	1945	1984	1979	1964	1953	1962	1979
Maximum in 24 hrs	4.4	1.9	3.3	5.0	3.6	4.4	3.5	4.3	4.1	3.7	2.4	3.3	5.0
Date	1965	1954	1944	1950	1956	1974	1953	1955	1961	1969	1946	1949	1950
SNOW, ICE PELLETS													
Maximum monthly	24.7	12.8	16.9	13.4	0.1	0.0	0.0	0.0	0.0	1.8	9.1	21.7	24.7
Date	1979	1975	1960	1982	1966	—	—	—	—	1967	1974	1977	1979
Maximum in 24 hrs	12.2	7.6	9.0	6.1	0.1	0.0	0.0	0.0	0.0	1.8	7.2	10.2	12.2
Date	1979	1944	1946	1982	1966	—	—	—	—	1967	1951	1973	1979
WIND (Resultant)													
Mean speed (mph)	11.2	11.3	12.2	12.1	10.2	9.1	7.9	7.7	8.6	9.5	11.0	10.9	10.1

ROCKFORD

Elev. 724'   42° 12'N — 89° 06'W   **Illinois**

NORMALS, MEANS, EXTREMES

	JAN	FEB	MAR	APR	MAY	JUN	JUL	AUG	SEP	OCT	NOV	DEC	YEAR
TEMPERATURE													
Normal daily maximum	26.6	31.8	42.5	58.5	70.6	80.1	83.7	81.9	74.6	63.0	46.3	32.6	57.7
Normal daily minimum	9.8	14.9	25.1	37.3	47.6	57.6	62.2	60.6	52.0	41.0	28.7	17.0	37.8
Normal monthly	18.2	23.4	33.8	47.9	59.1	68.9	73.0	71.3	63.3	52.0	37.5	24.8	47.8
Extreme highest	60	68	81	91	95	99	103	101	102	90	76	66	103
Extreme highest date	1967	1976	1981	1980	1975	1954	1955	1953	1953	1971	1961	1984	1955
Extreme lowest	-27	-22	-11	5	24	38	43	41	27	15	-10	-24	-27
Extreme lowest date	1982	1985	1962	1982	1966	1972	1967	1958	1984	1952	1977	1983	1982
DEGREE DAYS BASE 65° F													
Heating	1448	1165	967	513	227	34	5	11	99	412	825	1246	6952
Cooling	0	0	0	0	44	151	253	206	48	12	0	0	714
% OF POSSIBLE SUNSHINE	na	na	na	na	na	na	na	na	na	na	na	na	na
AVERAGE SKY COVER													
Sunrise - Sunset	6.7	6.5	6.9	6.7	6.3	6.0	5.5	5.7	5.4	5.7	7.0	7.1	6.3
NUMBER OF DAYS (Sunrise-Sunset)													
Clear	7.4	7.6	5.9	6.5	7.5	7.2	9.4	8.8	10.1	10.2	6.7	6.9	94.2
Partly cloudy	6.9	5.8	8.1	7.7	9.2	10.8	12.3	10.9	8.7	7.5	5.7	5.5	99.0
Cloudy	16.7	14.9	17.0	15.7	14.3	12.0	9.3	11.3	11.2	13.3	17.7	18.6	172.1
Precipitation .01" or more	9.4	7.9	11.1	11.8	11.3	10.3	9.7	9.1	9.0	8.6	8.8	10.3	117.3
Snow, Ice pellets 1.0" or more	2.8	2.2	2.2	0.4	*	0.0	0.0	0.0	0.0	0.1	0.9	2.9	11.5
Thunderstorms	0.1	0.5	1.8	4.4	5.5	7.9	7.9	6.3	4.8	2.5	1.1	0.4	43.4
Fog, Visibility 1/4 mile or less	2.5	2.5	2.5	1.2	1.1	0.6	1.3	2.0	1.7	2.3	2.5	2.9	22.9
Temperature Maximum:													
90° and above	0.0	0.0	0.0	*	0.5	2.3	5.4	3.3	1.1	*	0.0	0.0	12.8
32° and below	20.5	14.5	5.2	0.2	0.0	0.0	0.0	0.0	0.0	0.0	3.0	14.9	58.3
Temperature Minimum:													
32° and below	29.5	26.1	23.5	9.2	1.4	0.0	0.0	0.0	0.5	6.3	19.5	27.5	143.6
0° and below	10.1	5.5	0.4	0.0	0.0	0.0	0.0	0.0	0.0	0.0	0.3	4.0	20.2
RELATIVE HUMIDITY (%)													
Morning	77	78	78	75	76	78	83	86	85	81	80	81	80
Afternoon	69	66	62	56	54	55	56	59	58	57	66	73	61
PRECIPITATION (inches)													
Water Equivalent													
Normal	1.4	1.1	2.5	4.2	3.7	4.5	4.5	3.7	3.7	2.9	2.3	1.9	36.7
Maximum monthly	4.6	2.6	5.6	9.9	6.9	9.9	11.8	9.2	10.6	8.3	5.5	5.0	11.8
Date	1960	1971	1961	1973	1974	1967	1952	1965	1961	1969	1985	1971	1952
Minimum monthly	0.1	0.0	0.5	1.1	1.4	1.4	1.1	0.6	0.0	0.0	0.3	0.3	0.0
Date	1961	1969	1958	1985	1961	1957	1981	1970	1979	1952	1976	1976	1952
Maximum in 24 hrs	2.8	1.7	2.5	5.5	3.6	4.1	5.0	4.2	5.5	5.2	3.2	2.2	5.5
Date	1960	1966	1976	1973	1977	1969	1952	1972	1961	1954	1961	1971	1961
SNOW, ICE PELLETS													
Maximum monthly	26.1	19.5	22.7	7.7	1.0	0.0	0.0	0.0	0.0	2.2	14.7	25.1	26.1
Date	1979	1960	1964	1982	1966	—	—	—	—	1967	1951	1978	1979
Maximum in 24 hrs	9.9	10.9	10.4	6.7	T	0.0	0.0	0.0	0.0	2.2	9.5	8.5	10.9
Date	1979	1960	1972	1970	1976	—	—	—	—	1967	1951	1978	1960
WIND (Resultant)													
Mean speed (mph)	10.5	10.6	11.6	11.9	10.6	9.4	8.1	7.8	8.6	9.5	10.4	10.5	10.0

SPRINGFIELD

Elev. 588'   39° 50'N — 89° 40'W   **Illinois**

NORMALS, MEANS, EXTREMES

	JAN	FEB	MAR	APR	MAY	JUN	JUL	AUG	SEP	OCT	NOV	DEC	YEAR
TEMPERATURE													
Normal daily maximum	32.8	38.0	48.9	64.0	74.6	84.1	87.1	84.7	79.3	67.5	51.2	38.4	62.6
Normal daily minimum	16.3	20.9	30.3	42.6	52.5	62.0	65.9	63.7	55.8	44.4	32.9	23.0	42.5
Normal monthly	24.6	29.5	39.6	53.3	63.6	73.1	76.5	74.2	67.6	56.0	42.1	30.7	52.5
Extreme highest	71	74	87	88	95	103	112	103	101	93	83	74	112
Extreme highest date	1950	1972	1981	1980	1967	1954	1954	1964	1984	1954	1950	1984	1954
Extreme lowest	-21	-22	-12	19	28	40	48	43	32	17	-3	-18	-22
Extreme lowest date	1985	1963	1960	1982	1966	1966	1975	1964	1984	1952	1964	1983	1963
DEGREE DAYS BASE 65° F													
Heating	1252	994	787	354	149	13	0	0	48	307	687	1063	5654
Cooling	0	0	0	6	106	256	357	289	126	25	0	0	1165
% OF POSSIBLE SUNSHINE	47	51	50	56	64	68	72	71	69	63	49	43	59
AVERAGE SKY COVER													
Sunrise - Sunset	6.8	6.5	7.0	6.6	6.1	5.8	5.4	5.3	5.0	5.2	6.4	6.9	6.1
NUMBER OF DAYS (Sunrise-Sunset)													
Clear	7.3	7.7	6.4	7.0	8.0	8.5	10.4	11.1	12.3	12.1	8.1	7.1	105.8
Partly cloudy	6.2	5.5	7.0	7.8	9.3	9.4	10.4	9.6	7.8	7.2	6.3	6.0	92.7
Cloudy	17.5	15.0	17.6	15.2	13.7	12.1	10.2	10.3	10.0	11.7	15.5	17.9	166.9
Precipitation .01" or more	9.3	8.8	12.0	11.7	10.5	10.1	8.8	8.5	8.2	7.6	9.2	10.1	114.7
Snow, Ice pellets 1.0" or more	2.0	1.9	1.5	0.3	0.0	0.0	0.0	0.0	0.0	0.0	0.6	1.6	7.9
Thunderstorms	0.5	0.8	2.6	5.6	6.7	8.3	8.6	7.1	4.7	2.3	1.5	0.6	49.2
Fog, Visibility 1/4 mile or less	2.6	2.7	2.1	0.7	0.9	0.3	0.7	1.1	1.1	1.2	1.6	2.6	17.4
Temperature Maximum:													
90° and above	0.0	0.0	0.0	0.0	1.5	7.5	10.7	6.5	3.3	0.2	0.0	0.0	29.7
32° and below	15.9	9.8	2.8	*	0.0	0.0	0.0	0.0	0.0	0.0	1.1	10.2	39.7
Temperature Minimum:													
32° and below	28.5	23.7	17.7	4.3	0.2	0.0	0.0	0.0	*	3.4	14.7	25.3	117.7
0° and below	5.4	2.5	0.2	0.0	0.0	0.0	0.0	0.0	0.0	0.0	*	2.0	10.1
RELATIVE HUMIDITY (%)													
Morning	77	78	77	73	75	77	80	84	82	76	78	80	78
Afternoon	69	68	64	57	54	54	57	60	56	55	65	72	61
PRECIPITATION (inches)													
Water Equivalent													
Normal	1.5	1.7	3.1	3.9	3.3	3.7	3.5	3.2	3.0	2.5	1.9	2.0	33.7
Maximum monthly	5.6	4.4	7.8	9.9	6.3	8.8	10.7	8.3	7.7	6.1	6.9	8.9	10.7
Date	1949	1951	1973	1964	1974	1960	1981	1981	1970	1955	1985	1982	1981
Minimum monthly	0.3	0.5	0.6	0.7	0.9	0.2	0.9	0.6	T	0.1	0.4	0.1	T
Date	1961	1958	1956	1971	1969	1959	1974	1984	1979	1964	1949	1955	1979
Maximum in 24 hrs	2.7	1.8	2.8	4.4	2.4	4.7	4.4	4.7	5.1	3.5	2.4	6.1	6.1
Date	1975	1976	1972	1979	1975	1958	1981	1956	1959	1973	1964	1982	1982
SNOW, ICE PELLETS													
Maximum monthly	21.1	14.9	20.3	7.3	T	0.0	0.0	0.0	0.0	0.1	9.2	22.7	22.7
Date	1977	1960	1960	1980	1966	—	—	—	—	1967	1951	1973	1973
Maximum in 24 hrs	8.8	10.3	8.2	6.1	T	0.0	0.0	0.0	0.0	0.1	8.0	10.9	10.9
Date	1964	1965	1978	1980	1966	—	—	—	—	1967	1951	1973	1973
WIND (Resultant)													
Mean speed (mph)	12.8	12.7	13.8	13.5	11.5	10.0	8.5	8.0	9.2	10.5	12.6	12.7	11.3

EVANSVILLE

Elev. 381'   38° 03'N — 87° 32'W   **Indiana**

NORMALS, MEANS, EXTREMES

	JAN	FEB	MAR	APR	MAY	JUN	JUL	AUG	SEP	OCT	NOV	DEC	YEAR
TEMPERATURE													
Normal daily maximum	39.3	44.2	54.5	67.6	76.8	85.9	88.8	87.3	81.4	70.0	55.1	44.0	66.2
Normal daily minimum	21.9	25.5	34.6	45.4	54.3	63.2	67.4	65.0	57.4	44.5	35.0	27.2	45.1
Normal monthly	30.6	34.9	44.6	56.5	65.6	74.6	78.1	76.2	69.4	57.3	45.1	35.6	55.7
Extreme highest	76	79	84	90	95	104	105	102	103	94	83	77	105
Extreme highest date	1943	1962	1981	1967	1975	1954	1954	1983	1954	1953	1961	1982	1954
Extreme lowest	-21	-23	-9	24	28	41	47	46	31	21	-3	-9	-23
Extreme lowest date	1977	1951	1960	1972	1963	1966	1947	1964	1942	1952	1950	1963	1951
DEGREE DAYS BASE 65° F													
Heating	1066	843	640	267	100	6	0	0	40	259	597	911	4729
Cooling	0	0	8	12	119	294	406	347	172	20	0	0	1378
% OF POSSIBLE SUNSHINE	43	49	54	59	65	72	74	75	70	65	49	41	60
AVERAGE SKY COVER													
Sunrise - Sunset	7.1	6.7	6.8	6.5	6.1	5.7	5.5	5.1	5.1	5.0	6.4	7.0	6.1
NUMBER OF DAYS (Sunrise-Sunset)													
Clear	6.7	6.8	6.5	6.6	8.4	8.2	8.9	11.1	11.4	12.4	7.9	6.6	101.6
Partly cloudy	5.4	6.2	7.9	8.5	8.8	11.2	12.5	11.3	8.5	7.7	6.8	6.1	100.8
Cloudy	18.9	15.2	16.6	15.0	13.8	10.6	9.6	8.7	10.0	10.9	15.3	18.3	162.8
Precipitation .01" or more	10.4	9.1	12.1	11.8	11.1	9.8	9.4	7.6	7.3	7.4	9.5	10.5	115.9
Snow, Ice pellets 1.0" or more	1.5	1.1	0.7	0.1	0.0	0.0	0.0	0.0	0.0	0.0	0.3	0.7	4.4
Thunderstorms	1.0	1.2	3.7	5.1	6.3	7.6	7.6	5.3	3.4	1.9	1.5	0.6	45.2
Fog, Visibility 1/4 mile or less	2.5	1.4	1.0	0.5	0.6	0.6	0.6	1.0	1.4	1.6	1.3	2.0	14.3
Temperature Maximum:													
90° and above	0.0	0.0	0.0	*	2.0	9.1	15.1	10.5	3.9	0.3	0.0	0.0	40.9
32° and below	11.2	6.4	0.8	0.0	0.0	0.0	0.0	0.0	0.0	0.0	0.5	5.4	24.3
Temperature Minimum:													
32° and below	26.0	21.1	13.3	2.3	0.2	0.0	0.0	0.0	0.0	3.0	11.8	22.0	99.7
0° and below	2.7	1.5	0.1	0.0	0.0	0.0	0.0	0.0	0.0	0.0	0.0	0.7	4.9
RELATIVE HUMIDITY (%)													
Morning	74	74	75	73	79	79	82	84	84	79	76	77	78
Afternoon	66	64	61	55	55	54	56	58	57	53	62	68	59
PRECIPITATION (inches)													
Water Equivalent													
Normal	2.9	3.0	4.5	4.0	4.3	3.5	3.9	3.0	2.6	2.4	3.3	3.4	41.5
Maximum monthly	13.5	7.2	12.8	10.2	12.8	9.3	9.6	8.4	9.8	8.3	8.4	8.2	13.5
Date	1950	1956	1964	1983	1981	1943	1958	1977	1945	1941	1957	1982	1950
Minimum monthly	0.5	0.2	0.8	1.1	0.9	0.8	0.1	0.1	0.5	0.0	0.9	0.5	0.0
Date	1981	1947	1941	1959	1965	1978	1974	1943	1953	1964	1965	1976	1964
Maximum in 24 hrs	3.7	3.1	5.6	3.9	6.0	3.2	4.0	3.7	3.4	3.0	2.6	2.2	6.0
Date	1982	1945	1964	1955	1961	1971	1978	1977	1945	1976	1957	1982	1961
SNOW, ICE PELLETS													
Maximum monthly	21.3	11.3	20.2	8.6	0.0	0.0	0.0	0.0	0.0	T	6.9	10.4	21.3
Date	1977	1948	1960	1971	—	—	—	—	—	1957	1958	1973	1977
Maximum in 24 hrs	8.7	8.7	10.6	8.6	0.0	0.0	0.0	0.0	0.0	T	6.9	7.0	10.6
Date	1978	1966	1960	1971	—	—	—	—	—	1957	1958	1963	1960
WIND (Resultant)													
Mean speed (mph)	9.4	9.5	10.3	9.9	8.1	7.3	6.3	5.9	6.5	7.0	8.7	9.1	8.2

FORT WAYNE

Elev. 791' 41° 00'N — 85° 12'W **Indiana**

NORMALS, MEANS, EXTREMES

	JAN	FEB	MAR	APR	MAY	JUN	JUL	AUG	SEP	OCT	NOV	DEC	YEAR
TEMPERATURE													
Normal daily maximum	30.8	34.5	45.2	59.7	70.9	80.5	84.1	82.3	76.0	63.9	48.2	36.0	59.3
Normal daily minimum	15.8	18.3	28.0	38.7	48.9	58.7	62.5	60.5	53.3	42.0	31.9	21.9	40.0
Normal monthly	23.3	26.4	36.6	49.2	59.9	69.6	73.3	71.4	64.7	53.0	40.1	29.0	49.7
Extreme highest	69	69	80	87	92	100	103	101	100	90	79	71	103
Extreme highest date	1950	1954	1983	1985	1977	1953	1954	1962	1953	1951	1950	1982	1954
Extreme lowest	-22	-18	-10	7	27	38	44	38	29	20	-1	-16	-22
Extreme lowest date	1985	1982	1967	1982	1966	1956	1967	1965	1951	1952	1958	1983	1985
DEGREE DAYS BASE 65° F													
Heating	1293	1081	880	474	212	27	0	7	99	384	747	1116	6320
Cooling	0	0	0	0	54	165	260	205	90	12	0	0	786
% OF POSSIBLE SUNSHINE	45	50	53	59	67	72	74	73	67	62	41	38	58
AVERAGE SKY COVER													
Sunrise - Sunset	7.5	7.2	7.3	6.9	6.4	6.1	5.8	5.7	5.6	5.8	7.4	7.7	6.6
NUMBER OF DAYS (Sunrise-Sunset)													
Clear	4.6	4.7	4.6	5.6	6.7	6.4	8.1	8.5	9.0	9.8	4.9	4.2	77.2
Partly cloudy	6.4	6.9	7.7	7.4	9.7	11.5	12.3	11.8	9.4	7.8	6.6	6.2	103.8
Cloudy	20.0	16.6	18.7	17.0	14.6	12.1	10.6	10.6	11.6	13.4	18.5	20.6	184.3
Precipitation .01" or more	12.2	10.5	13.3	13.5	11.6	10.2	9.7	9.0	8.7	8.6	10.7	12.8	130.9
Snow, Ice pellets 1.0" or more	2.5	2.3	1.6	0.4	0.0	0.0	0.0	0.0	0.0	*	1.2	2.2	10.2
Thunderstorms	0.4	0.7	2.6	4.3	5.1	7.0	6.6	5.8	3.7	1.6	0.9	0.4	39.2
Fog, Visibility 1/4 mile or less	2.6	2.4	1.9	0.9	0.8	0.6	0.9	1.8	1.6	1.9	1.5	2.8	19.9
Temperature Maximum:													
90° and above	0.0	0.0	0.0	0.0	0.5	3.1	5.8	3.6	1.3	0.0	0.0	0.0	14.3
32° and below	17.8	12.9	4.2	0.1	0.0	0.0	0.0	0.0	0.0	0.0	1.5	12.0	48.5
Temperature Minimum:													
32° and below	29.0	24.7	20.7	8.5	0.9	0.0	0.0	0.0	0.1	4.7	15.8	25.5	129.8
0° and below	5.9	3.7	0.3	0.0	0.0	0.0	0.0	0.0	0.0	0.0	0.0	2.1	12.1
RELATIVE HUMIDITY (%)													
Morning	77	76	77	73	75	76	80	83	83	79	80	80	78
Afternoon	71	68	65	57	55	54	55	58	57	58	68	74	62
PRECIPITATION (inches)													
Water Equivalent													
Normal	2.0	1.9	2.9	3.5	3.4	3.6	3.3	3.2	2.5	2.5	2.5	2.4	34.4
Maximum monthly	9.7	4.4	5.2	7.1	6.8	8.2	6.3	7.6	6.7	9.2	5.7	5.4	9.7
Date	1950	1950	1955	1957	1952	1958	1951	1975	1972	1954	1982	1967	1950
Minimum monthly	0.3	0.3	0.7	1.2	1.0	1.1	0.4	0.4	0.3	0.1	0.6	0.4	0.1
Date	1966	1978	1981	1962	1977	1966	1974	1969	1979	1964	1976	1962	1964
Maximum in 24 hrs	2.6	1.9	2.1	2.6	3.2	3.7	3.4	4.0	4.6	2.9	2.5	2.1	4.6
Date	1950	1959	1953	1963	1968	1959	1955	1957	1950	1947	1982	1966	1950
SNOW, ICE PELLETS													
Maximum monthly	29.5	16.9	19.5	11.7	T	0.0	0.0	0.0	0.0	1.4	14.1	20.3	29.5
Date	1982	1980	1964	1961	1966	—	—	—	—	1974	1950	1973	1982
Maximum in 24 hrs	10.8	7.7	13.6	6.4	T	0.0	0.0	0.0	0.0	1.4	7.0	11.1	13.6
Date	1982	1952	1964	1957	1966	—	—	—	—	1974	1950	1973	1964
WIND (Resultant)													
Mean speed (mph)	11.6	11.3	12.1	11.8	10.2	9.2	8.1	7.6	8.4	9.2	10.9	11.3	10.1

INDIANAPOLIS   Elev. 792'   39° 44'N — 86° 16'W   Indiana

NORMALS, MEANS, EXTREMES

	JAN	FEB	MAR	APR	MAY	JUN	JUL	AUG	SEP	OCT	NOV	DEC	YEAR
TEMPERATURE													
Normal daily maximum	34.2	38.5	49.3	63.1	73.4	82.3	85.2	83.7	77.9	66.1	50.8	39.2	62.0
Normal daily minimum	17.8	21.1	30.7	41.7	51.5	60.9	64.9	62.7	55.3	43.4	32.8	23.7	42.2
Normal monthly	26.0	29.8	40.0	52.4	62.5	71.6	75.1	73.2	66.6	54.8	41.8	31.5	52.1
Extreme highest	71	74	85	89	93	102	104	100	100	90	81	74	104
Extreme highest date	1950	1972	1981	1970	1965	1954	1954	1941	1954	1954	1950	1982	1954
Extreme lowest	-22	-21	-7	16	28	39	44	41	28	17	-2	-17	-22
Extreme lowest date	1985	1982	1980	1940	1966	1956	1942	1965	1942	1942	1958	1983	1985
DEGREE DAYS BASE 65° F													
Heating	1209	983	775	382	158	15	0	0	63	330	696	1039	5650
Cooling	0	0	0	0	80	213	313	257	111	14	0	0	988
% OF POSSIBLE SUNSHINE	41	50	50	54	60	66	67	69	66	61	42	39	55
AVERAGE SKY COVER													
Sunrise - Sunset	7.3	6.9	7.2	6.9	6.5	6.2	5.8	5.6	5.4	5.5	7.0	7.4	6.5
NUMBER OF DAYS (Sunrise-Sunset)													
Clear	5.9	5.7	5.6	5.9	7.1	7.0	8.5	9.1	10.8	11.1	6.5	5.1	88.4
Partly cloudy	6.0	6.4	7.1	7.3	9.0	10.6	12.6	11.9	8.6	7.4	6.7	6.2	99.9
Cloudy	19.1	16.1	18.3	16.7	14.9	12.3	9.9	10.0	10.6	12.4	16.8	19.7	177.0
Precipitation .01" or more	11.9	10.1	13.1	12.3	12.3	10.0	9.2	8.7	7.7	8.0	10.1	11.8	125.1
Snow, Ice pellets 1.0" or more	2.1	2.0	1.3	0.1	0.0	0.0	0.0	0.0	0.0	*	0.6	1.8	7.9
Thunderstorms	0.8	0.8	2.8	4.6	6.5	7.5	7.7	6.3	3.7	1.8	1.0	0.5	43.9
Fog, Visibility 1/4 mile or less	3.4	2.5	1.8	0.6	0.8	0.7	1.2	1.8	1.4	1.3	1.7	2.9	20.4
Temperature Maximum:													
90° and above	0.0	0.0	0.0	0.0	0.6	3.4	6.7	3.9	1.9	0.0	0.0	0.0	16.6
32° and below	14.8	9.5	2.7	*	0.0	0.0	0.0	0.0	0.0	0.0	0.9	9.1	37.0
Temperature Minimum:													
32° and below	28.0	23.9	17.6	5.4	0.4	0.0	0.0	0.0	0.0	4.0	14.7	25.1	119.0
0° and below	4.8	2.3	0.3	0.0	0.0	0.0	0.0	0.0	0.0	0.0	0.0	1.9	9.3
RELATIVE HUMIDITY (%)													
Morning	78	77	75	72	77	79	84	86	85	80	80	80	79
Afternoon	70	67	63	56	56	57	60	62	59	57	67	73	62
PRECIPITATION (inches)													
Water Equivalent													
Normal	2.6	2.4	3.6	3.6	3.6	3.9	4.3	3.4	2.7	2.5	3.0	3.0	39.1
Maximum monthly	12.6	5.3	10.7	8.0	10.1	9.7	11.0	8.3	6.0	8.3	8.5	6.7	12.6
Date	1950	1971	1963	1964	1943	1942	1979	1980	1955	1941	1985	1957	1950
Minimum monthly	0.2	0.3	1.0	0.9	1.4	1.0	0.9	0.6	0.2	0.1	0.8	0.4	0.1
Date	1944	1978	1941	1976	1964	1967	1941	1964	1963	1963	1976	1976	1963
Maximum in 24 hrs	3.4	2.5	3.0	2.5	3.5	3.8	4.3	4.7	3.0	3.9	3.0	2.2	4.7
Date	1950	1977	1963	1961	1961	1963	1979	1976	1961	1959	1955	1971	1976
SNOW, ICE PELLETS													
Maximum monthly	30.6	18.0	10.5	4.0	T	0.0	0.0	0.0	0.0	1.2	8.3	27.5	30.6
Date	1978	1979	1975	1940	1966	—	—	—	—	1962	1966	1973	1978
Maximum in 24 hrs	12.2	12.5	5.6	3.1	T	0.0	0.0	0.0	0.0	1.2	8.2	11.5	12.5
Date	1978	1965	1948	1953	1966	—	—	—	—	1962	1966	1973	1965
WIND (Resultant)													
Mean speed (mph)	11.0	10.8	11.7	11.3	9.5	8.5	7.4	7.1	7.9	8.8	10.4	10.5	9.6

SOUTH BEND   Elev. 773'   41° 42'N — 86° 19'W   Indiana

NORMALS, MEANS, EXTREMES

	JAN	FEB	MAR	APR	MAY	JUN	JUL	AUG	SEP	OCT	NOV	DEC	YEAR
TEMPERATURE													
Normal daily maximum	30.4	34.1	44.3	58.6	69.9	79.5	82.7	81.0	74.6	63.1	47.8	35.7	58.5
Normal daily minimum	15.9	18.6	27.7	38.4	48.1	58.1	62.3	60.8	53.7	43.4	32.8	22.5	40.2
Normal monthly	23.2	26.4	36.0	48.5	59.0	68.8	72.5	70.9	64.2	53.3	40.3	29.1	49.3
Extreme highest	68	69	85	91	95	100	101	100	99	92	82	70	101
Extreme highest date	1950	1976	1981	1942	1942	1953	1941	1947	1953	1963	1950	1982	1941
Extreme lowest	-22	-17	-13	11	24	35	44	40	29	23	-7	-16	-22
Extreme lowest date	1943	1951	1943	1972	1968	1972	1972	1965	1942	1981	1950	1960	1943
DEGREE DAYS BASE 65° F													
Heating	1296	1081	899	495	230	35	6	17	88	376	741	1113	6377
Cooling	0	0	0	0	47	149	239	200	64	11	0	0	710
% OF POSSIBLE SUNSHINE	na	na	na	na	na	na	na	na	na	na	na	na	na
AVERAGE SKY COVER													
Sunrise - Sunset	8.0	7.7	7.5	6.9	6.4	6.1	5.6	5.7	5.8	6.1	7.8	8.2	6.8
NUMBER OF DAYS (Sunrise-Sunset)													
Clear	3.4	3.6	4.5	5.7	6.6	6.9	8.5	8.6	9.0	8.7	3.5	2.9	72.0
Partly cloudy	5.9	5.5	7.2	7.9	9.7	10.5	12.7	12.3	8.9	8.2	6.3	5.5	100.4
Cloudy	21.7	19.1	19.3	16.4	14.7	12.6	9.8	10.1	12.1	14.1	20.2	22.6	192.9
Precipitation .01" or more	15.7	12.5	14.2	13.4	11.4	10.7	9.4	9.3	9.0	9.8	12.6	15.3	143.4
Snow, Ice pellets 1.0" or more	6.1	5.1	3.0	0.7	0.0	0.0	0.0	0.0	*	0.3	2.5	5.7	23.5
Thunderstorms	0.3	0.5	2.4	4.6	5.2	8.3	7.4	6.4	4.2	1.9	1.0	0.5	42.6
Fog, Visibility 1/4 mile or less	2.6	2.2	2.0	1.2	1.5	1.2	1.2	2.2	2.0	2.3	2.0	3.2	23.7
Temperature Maximum:													
90° and above	0.0	0.0	0.0	0.0	0.5	2.4	4.4	2.8	0.8	0.0	0.0	0.0	11.0
32° and below	17.7	12.8	4.3	0.2	0.0	0.0	0.0	0.0	0.0	0.0	1.6	10.4	47.0
Temperature Minimum:													
32° and below	28.4	24.0	19.9	7.4	0.7	0.0	0.0	0.0	0.0	2.7	13.9	24.7	121.7
0° and below	4.3	2.8	0.1	0.0	0.0	0.0	0.0	0.0	0.0	0.0	0.0	1.2	8.4
RELATIVE HUMIDITY (%)													
Morning	79	78	77	73	75	77	81	84	83	79	80	81	79
Afternoon	73	69	63	57	54	56	57	59	60	61	69	76	63
PRECIPITATION (inches)													
Water Equivalent													
Normal	2.4	1.9	3.0	4.0	2.8	3.9	3.6	3.9	3.2	3.2	2.8	2.9	38.1
Maximum monthly	5.2	5.2	7.9	9.2	6.7	9.0	7.4	8.3	9.0	9.7	6.7	5.5	9.7
Date	1959	1976	1976	1947	1981	1968	1982	1979	1977	1954	1985	1965	1954
Minimum monthly	0.4	0.5	0.5	0.5	1.1	1.1	0.0	0.3	0.0	0.4	1.3	0.6	0.0
Date	1945	1969	1958	1971	1961	1971	1946	1950	1979	1950	1962	1943	1979
Maximum in 24 hrs	2.8	2.6	2.3	3.1	2.9	4.7	3.3	3.7	3.0	3.1	1.9	3.3	4.7
Date	1960	1954	1972	1947	1976	1968	1962	1966	1977	1954	1950	1965	1968
SNOW, ICE PELLETS													
Maximum monthly	86.1	35.1	33.9	14.0	0.6	0.0	0.0	0.0	1.2	8.6	30.3	41.9	86.1
Date	1978	1958	1960	1982	1966	—	—	—	1942	1962	1977	1962	1978
Maximum in 24 hrs	16.7	10.3	14.8	8.7	0.6	0.0	0.0	0.0	1.0	5.4	17.5	13.7	17.5
Date	1978	1967	1960	1982	1966	—	—	—	1942	1962	1977	1981	1977
WIND (Resultant)													
Mean speed (mph)	12.0	11.5	12.2	11.9	10.5	9.3	8.2	7.8	8.7	9.7	11.2	11.5	10.4

DES MOINES

Elev. 938' 41° 32'N — 93° 39'W **Iowa**

NORMALS, MEANS, EXTREMES

	JAN	FEB	MAR	APR	MAY	JUN	JUL	AUG	SEP	OCT	NOV	DEC	YEAR
TEMPERATURE													
Normal daily maximum	27.0	33.2	44.2	61.0	72.6	81.8	86.2	84.0	75.7	65.0	47.6	33.7	59.3
Normal daily minimum	10.1	15.8	26.0	39.9	51.6	61.4	66.3	63.7	54.4	43.3	29.5	17.6	40.0
Normal monthly	18.6	24.5	35.1	50.5	62.1	71.6	76.3	73.9	65.1	54.2	38.6	25.7	49.7
Extreme highest	62	73	84	93	98	101	105	108	101	95	76	69	108
Extreme highest date	1981	1972	1978	1980	1967	1985	1955	1983	1939	1963	1980	1984	1983
Extreme lowest	-24	-20	-22	9	30	38	47	40	26	14	-3	-19	-24
Extreme lowest date	1970	1958	1962	1975	1967	1945	1971	1950	1942	1972	1964	1983	1970
DEGREE DAYS BASE 65° F													
Heating	1438	1134	927	435	156	17	0	0	80	357	792	1218	6554
Cooling	0	0	0	0	66	215	354	279	83	22	0	0	1019
% OF POSSIBLE SUNSHINE	51	54	54	55	61	68	72	70	65	61	49	45	59
AVERAGE SKY COVER													
Sunrise - Sunset	6.6	6.5	6.9	6.6	6.4	5.8	5.2	5.2	5.1	5.3	6.5	6.8	6.1
NUMBER OF DAYS (Sunrise-Sunset)													
Clear	7.8	7.5	6.6	6.9	7.4	8.1	10.5	10.8	12.0	11.6	7.4	6.9	103.4
Partly cloudy	7.0	5.9	7.2	7.8	8.5	10.6	11.3	10.5	7.2	7.2	7.1	6.6	96.8
Cloudy	16.2	14.9	17.1	15.2	15.1	11.4	9.2	9.8	10.8	12.3	15.6	17.6	165.1
Precipitation .01" or more	7.6	7.2	10.2	10.5	11.2	10.8	9.1	9.2	8.5	7.6	6.9	7.9	106.6
Snow, Ice pellets 1.0" or more	2.5	2.2	2.1	0.6	0.0	0.0	0.0	0.0	0.0	0.1	0.8	2.3	10.7
Thunderstorms	0.3	0.5	2.0	4.4	7.2	9.5	8.4	7.4	5.2	2.9	1.1	0.4	49.3
Fog, Visibility 1/4 mile or less	2.0	2.4	1.9	0.9	0.8	0.6	0.6	1.2	1.2	1.4	1.9	2.6	17.6
Temperature Maximum:													
90° and above	0.0	0.0	0.0	0.2	0.6	4.0	10.0	7.3	2.0	0.2	0.0	0.0	24.3
32° and below	19.4	13.3	5.3	0.3	0.0	0.0	0.0	0.0	0.0	0.0	3.4	14.7	56.3
Temperature Minimum:													
32° and below	30.2	25.4	21.3	6.3	0.2	0.0	0.0	0.0	0.3	4.3	18.0	28.7	134.6
0° and below	9.3	4.0	0.3	0.0	0.0	0.0	0.0	0.0	0.0	0.0	0.2	3.9	17.8
RELATIVE HUMIDITY (%)													
Morning	74	76	73	70	70	72	75	78	78	73	75	77	74
Afternoon	67	66	61	56	55	56	57	58	59	56	64	70	60
PRECIPITATION (inches)													
Water Equivalent													
Normal	1.0	1.1	2.2	3.2	3.9	4.1	3.2	4.1	3.0	2.1	1.5	1.0	30.8
Maximum monthly	4.3	2.9	5.3	7.7	7.5	14.1	10.5	13.6	10.1	7.2	6.5	3.4	14.1
Date	1960	1951	1961	1976	1960	1947	1958	1977	1961	1941	1983	1982	1947
Minimum monthly	0.0	0.1	0.3	0.2	1.2	1.1	0.0	0.2	0.4	0.0	0.0	0.1	0.0
Date	1954	1968	1981	1985	1949	1963	1975	1984	1950	1952	1969	1976	1969
Maximum in 24 hrs	2.9	1.7	2.4	3.8	2.7	5.5	5.1	6.1	4.4	2.8	3.3	1.6	6.1
Date	1960	1961	1945	1974	1954	1947	1958	1975	1961	1947	1952	1982	1975
SNOW, ICE PELLETS													
Maximum monthly	19.8	21.3	18.8	15.6	0.2	0.0	0.0	0.0	T	7.4	13.5	23.9	23.9
Date	1942	1962	1948	1982	1944	—	—	—	1985	1980	1968	1961	1961
Maximum in 24 hrs	19.8	12.1	8.5	10.4	0.2	0.0	0.0	0.0	T	7.4	11.8	11.0	19.8
Date	1942	1950	1957	1973	1944	—	—	—	1985	1980	1968	1961	1942
WIND (Resultant)													
Mean speed (mph)	11.7	11.6	12.9	13.0	11.3	10.3	8.9	8.7	9.5	10.4	11.5	11.5	10.9

DUBUQUE

Elev. 1056'   **42° 24'N — 90° 42'W**   **Iowa**

NORMALS, MEANS, EXTREMES

	JAN	FEB	MAR	APR	MAY	JUN	JUL	AUG	SEP	OCT	NOV	DEC	YEAR
TEMPERATURE													
Normal daily maximum	23.7	29.6	40.6	57.3	69.0	78.1	82.0	80.0	72.1	61.1	44.2	30.2	55.7
Normal daily minimum	7.4	12.9	23.3	37.0	47.8	57.2	61.7	59.8	51.1	40.6	27.3	15.1	36.8
Normal monthly	15.6	21.3	32.0	47.2	58.4	67.7	71.9	69.9	61.6	50.9	35.8	22.7	46.2
Extreme highest	56	61	78	93	90	96	99	99	97	89	73	64	99
Extreme highest date	1981	1984	1981	1980	1967	1971	1955	1984	1955	1953	1978	1970	1984
Extreme lowest	-28	-27	-20	11	24	36	44	42	28	13	-17	-25	-28
Extreme lowest date	1970	1979	1962	1973	1966	1972	1984	1967	1984	1952	1977	1983	1970
DEGREE DAYS BASE 65° F													
Heating	1531	1224	1023	534	235	42	11	18	124	446	876	1311	7375
Cooling	0	0	0	0	31	123	225	170	22	9	0	0	580
% OF POSSIBLE SUNSHINE	na	na	na	na	na	na	na	na	na	na	na	na	na
AVERAGE SKY COVER													
Sunrise - Sunset	6.8	6.5	6.9	6.8	6.5	6.4	5.8	5.6	5.5	5.6	6.9	7.0	6.4
NUMBER OF DAYS (Sunrise-Sunset)													
Clear	7.1	7.5	6.1	6.3	6.8	6.4	8.0	9.4	10.5	10.3	6.7	6.7	91.9
Partly cloudy	6.7	6.1	7.9	7.5	8.6	10.6	12.5	10.5	8.0	8.0	5.9	6.3	98.5
Cloudy	17.2	14.7	17.0	16.2	15.6	13.0	10.5	11.1	11.6	12.7	17.4	18.0	174.9
Precipitation .01" or more	9.2	7.9	11.0	11.3	11.5	10.5	9.9	9.1	8.9	8.7	8.3	10.1	116.5
Snow, Ice pellets 1.0" or more	2.9	2.7	3.0	0.8	*	0.0	0.0	0.0	0.0	0.1	1.1	3.4	14.2
Thunderstorms	0.3	0.2	1.8	3.9	5.9	7.1	7.4	7.0	3.5	3.0	1.4	0.3	41.6
Fog, Visibility 1/4 mile or less	3.1	2.9	3.3	1.9	1.8	0.9	1.5	1.8	1.4	2.5	2.7	3.6	27.4
Temperature Maximum:													
90° and above	0.0	0.0	0.0	0.1	0.1	1.1	4.1	2.4	0.6	0.0	0.0	0.0	8.3
32° and below	23.2	16.7	6.3	0.4	0.0	0.0	0.0	0.0	0.0	0.0	4.9	19.2	70.7
Temperature Minimum:													
32° and below	30.7	26.9	23.3	9.0	0.9	0.0	0.0	0.0	0.5	6.4	20.6	29.9	148.2
0° and below	11.6	6.2	0.6	0.0	0.0	0.0	0.0	0.0	0.0	0.0	0.3	5.3	24.1
Afternoon	66	65	62	56	57	60	59	60	61	59	65	71	62
PRECIPITATION (inches)													
Water Equivalent													
Normal	1.4	1.3	2.9	4.1	4.4	4.1	4.3	4.4	4.1	2.8	2.4	1.8	38.5
Maximum monthly	6.0	3.6	6.5	7.6	9.4	10.4	12.2	9.6	15.4	8.5	10.6	4.1	15.4
Date	1960	1953	1959	1964	1962	1969	1961	1981	1965	1967	1961	1982	1965
Minimum monthly	0.3	0.1	0.3	0.8	1.0	1.0	1.0	0.0	0.0	T	0.3	0.3	T
Date	1964	1958	1958	1985	1981	1985	1967	1969	1979	1964	1955	1975	1964
Maximum in 24 hrs	3.7	2.2	2.3	2.6	4.6	3.6	6.2	3.9	8.8	2.5	5.0	2.3	8.8
Date	1960	1953	1959	1964	1962	1966	1961	1970	1967	1959	1961	1971	1967
SNOW, ICE PELLETS													
Maximum monthly	29.3	25.1	30.2	19.8	3.1	0.0	0.0	0.0	0.0	1.5	12.3	26.4	30.2
Date	1979	1975	1959	1973	1966	—	—	—	—	1976	1971	1977	1959
Maximum in 24 hrs	11.8	11.9	15.5	14.6	3.1	0.0	0.0	0.0	0.0	1.5	8.0	15.0	15.5
Date	1971	1962	1959	1973	1966	—	—	—	—	1976	1971	1985	1959

SIOUX CITY Elev. 1095' 42° 24'N — 96° 23'W Iowa

NORMALS, MEANS, EXTREMES

	JAN	FEB	MAR	APR	MAY	JUN	JUL	AUG	SEP	OCT	NOV	DEC	YEAR
TEMPERATURE													
Normal daily maximum	26.0	33.0	43.5	61.5	73.1	82.0	86.5	84.2	75.4	64.9	46.9	32.7	59.1
Normal daily minimum	6.3	13.3	24.0	37.9	49.8	59.7	64.6	62.3	53.6	40.0	25.8	13.9	37.6
Normal monthly	16.2	23.2	33.8	49.7	61.5	70.9	75.6	73.3	64.5	52.5	36.4	23.3	48.4
Extreme highest	70	71	91	97	102	106	107	104	102	93	81	68	107
Extreme highest date	1981	1981	1968	1980	1967	1946	1955	1955	1976	1963	1978	1984	1955
Extreme lowest	-26	-26	-22	-2	25	38	42	37	24	13	-9	-21	-26
Extreme lowest date	1970	1962	1960	1975	1976	1950	1971	1950	1945	1972	1959	1983	1970
DEGREE DAYS BASE 65° F													
Heating	1513	1170	967	463	159	24	0	8	94	398	858	1293	6947
Cooling	0	0	0	0	51	201	333	266	79	10	0	0	940
% OF POSSIBLE SUNSHINE	58	57	58	60	63	68	74	71	66	63	52	51	62
AVERAGE SKY COVER													
Sunrise - Sunset	6.4	6.5	6.8	6.5	6.4	5.7	4.9	4.9	5.1	5.2	6.6	6.6	6.0
NUMBER OF DAYS (Sunrise-Sunset)													
Clear	8.2	7.0	6.6	6.7	6.8	8.4	11.4	11.9	11.8	11.8	7.3	7.2	105.2
Partly cloudy	7.7	6.9	7.7	8.7	9.8	11.0	11.7	10.9	7.5	7.7	7.2	7.3	104.1
Cloudy	15.1	14.3	16.7	14.6	14.4	10.6	7.8	8.2	10.5	11.4	15.5	16.4	155.8
Precipitation .01" or more	6.8	6.6	9.0	9.7	11.4	10.9	8.8	8.9	8.1	6.5	5.5	6.8	98.9
Snow, Ice pellets 1.0" or more	2.0	1.9	2.4	0.5	*	0.0	0.0	0.0	0.0	0.2	1.0	2.1	10.1
Thunderstorms	0.1	0.4	1.2	3.5	6.9	8.9	8.3	7.5	4.9	2.0	0.4	0.2	44.2
Fog, Visibility 1/4 mile or less	2.3	2.8	2.1	0.6	0.6	0.5	0.6	1.4	1.3	1.6	2.3	2.7	18.8
Temperature Maximum:													
90° and above	0.0	0.0	*	0.5	1.1	4.5	9.6	6.2	1.7	0.2	0.0	0.0	23.8
32° and below	19.9	13.7	6.1	0.2	0.0	0.0	0.0	0.0	0.0	0.0	3.8	16.5	60.2
Temperature Minimum:													
32° and below	30.7	27.2	23.5	7.8	0.8	0.0	0.0	0.0	0.6	6.7	22.2	30.2	149.5
0° and below	11.2	5.4	1.0	*	0.0	0.0	0.0	0.0	0.0	0.0	0.4	5.4	23.5
RELATIVE HUMIDITY (%)													
Morning	75	78	77	70	70	74	77	81	80	74	77	78	76
Afternoon	68	67	63	53	54	57	58	60	59	55	63	71	61
PRECIPITATION (inches)													
Water Equivalent													
Normal	0.6	0.9	1.7	2.2	3.4	3.9	3.3	3.1	2.5	1.7	0.9	0.7	25.3
Maximum monthly	2.4	2.6	4.9	6.7	8.4	8.7	10.3	7.7	9.6	5.3	4.1	2.2	10.3
Date	1949	1971	1983	1984	1959	1967	1972	1951	1965	1979	1948	1982	1972
Minimum monthly	0.1	0.1	0.2	0.4	0.6	0.7	0.4	0.1	0.0	T	0.0	0.0	T
Date	1948	1985	1968	1942	1955	1976	1985	1971	1950	1958	1967	1943	1958
Maximum in 24 hrs	1.0	2.1	1.6	1.7	2.5	3.8	5.5	4.2	2.9	4.5	3.4	1.1	5.5
Date	1982	1971	1983	1958	1972	1957	1972	1961	1965	1979	1948	1959	1972
SNOW, ICE PELLETS													
Maximum monthly	29.1	21.3	26.2	9.7	4.0	0.0	0.0	0.0	0.4	8.0	16.5	20.6	29.1
Date	1982	1962	1962	1983	1945	—	—	—	1961	1982	1983	1968	1982
Maximum in 24 hrs	17.4	9.9	12.4	6.8	4.0	0.0	0.0	0.0	0.4	8.0	12.4	9.0	17.4
Date	1982	1984	1983	1957	1945	—	—	—	1961	1982	1983	1968	1982
WIND (Resultant)													
Mean speed (mph)	11.4	11.3	12.4	13.3	11.9	10.8	9.2	9.1	9.8	10.4	11.3	11.0	11.0

WATERLOO

Elev. 868'   42° 33'N — 92° 24'W   **Iowa**

NORMALS, MEANS, EXTREMES

	JAN	FEB	MAR	APR	MAY	JUN	JUL	AUG	SEP	OCT	NOV	DEC	YEAR
TEMPERATURE													
Normal daily maximum	23.2	29.5	40.5	58.2	70.5	80.1	83.4	81.6	73.4	62.3	44.7	30.1	56.5
Normal daily minimum	4.7	10.7	22.2	36.0	47.5	57.6	61.8	59.2	49.8	38.8	25.6	13.0	35.6
Normal monthly	14.0	20.1	31.4	47.1	59.0	68.9	72.6	70.4	61.6	50.6	35.2	21.6	46.0
Extreme highest	58	66	84	100	94	102	103	100	98	95	79	65	103
Extreme highest date	1981	1981	1967	1980	1967	1985	1955	1983	1955	1963	1950	1973	1955
Extreme lowest	-31	-29	-34	-4	25	38	42	38	22	13	-17	-27	-34
Extreme lowest date	1970	1962	1962	1982	1971	1964	1984	1967	1967	1952	1977	1963	1962
DEGREE DAYS BASE 65° F													
Heating	1581	1257	1042	537	222	34	8	23	137	457	894	1345	7537
Cooling	0	0	0	0	36	151	244	190	35	11	0	0	667
% OF POSSIBLE SUNSHINE	na	na	na	na	na	na	na	na	na	na	na	na	na
AVERAGE SKY COVER													
Sunrise - Sunset	6.5	6.7	7.0	6.8	6.5	6.1	5.6	5.7	5.7	6.0	7.1	7.0	6.4
NUMBER OF DAYS (Sunrise-Sunset)													
Clear	7.6	6.8	6.3	6.0	6.7	6.8	9.0	9.3	9.9	9.2	5.3	7.0	90.1
Partly cloudy	7.2	6.4	7.0	7.6	10.0	11.1	11.8	10.6	8.0	7.7	7.0	5.6	100.1
Cloudy	16.2	15.0	17.7	16.3	14.2	12.0	10.3	11.1	12.0	14.0	17.7	18.3	174.9
Precipitation .01" or more	7.3	6.5	9.1	9.7	11.2	9.9	9.2	8.3	8.4	7.1	6.8	7.5	101.0
Snow, Ice pellets 1.0" or more	2.1	2.2	2.1	0.5	0.0	0.0	0.0	0.0	0.0	*	0.8	2.3	10.0
Thunderstorms	0.1	0.3	1.4	3.8	6.5	7.7	7.5	6.9	4.6	2.5	0.5	0.2	42.1
Fog, Visibility 1/4 mile or less	2.0	2.4	2.8	1.4	1.1	0.6	0.8	1.8	1.7	1.2	2.0	2.8	20.7
Temperature Maximum:													
90° and above	0.0	0.0	0.0	0.1	0.7	3.0	5.6	4.1	1.4	0.2	0.0	0.0	15.2
32° and below	22.7	16.0	7.6	0.4	0.0	0.0	0.0	0.0	0.0	0.0	4.4	18.6	69.7
Temperature Minimum:													
32° and below	30.7	27.1	25.0	11.2	1.6	0.0	0.0	0.0	1.0	9.2	22.0	29.6	157.3
0° and below	13.4	7.9	1.4	*	0.0	0.0	0.0	0.0	0.0	0.0	0.4	7.1	30.3
RELATIVE HUMIDITY (%)													
Morning	75	77	79	75	76	79	84	85	84	78	79	79	79
Afternoon	68	68	66	56	55	56	58	59	59	57	66	71	62
PRECIPITATION (inches)													
Water Equivalent													
Normal	0.8	1.0	2.2	3.5	4.1	4.3	4.7	3.6	3.4	2.3	1.6	1.1	33.1
Maximum monthly	2.7	3.5	5.4	8.1	7.2	8.6	12.6	8.0	11.3	5.4	4.6	3.7	12.6
Date	1949	1971	1961	1964	1970	1980	1968	1968	1965	1984	1961	1982	1968
Minimum monthly	0.1	0.0	0.2	0.9	1.4	0.8	0.4	0.3	0.4	T	T	0.2	T
Date	1962	1969	1981	1971	1977	1955	1954	1955	1953	1952	1954	1962	1954
Maximum in 24 hrs	1.6	1.5	1.9	2.8	3.6	4.3	9.3	5.2	3.5	2.6	2.6	1.7	9.3
Date	1971	1976	1966	1979	1980	1980	1968	1966	1978	1961	1959	1982	1968
SNOW, ICE PELLETS													
Maximum monthly	18.1	24.3	20.1	10.3	0.3	0.0	0.0	0.0	0.0	1.2	11.7	20.1	24.3
Date	1982	1962	1959	1973	1966	—	—	—	—	1982	1971	1961	1962
Maximum in 24 hrs	14.8	8.8	12.2	6.2	T	0.0	0.0	0.0	0.0	1.2	8.5	12.3	14.8
Date	1971	1981	1959	1973	1976	—	—	—	—	1982	1972	1985	1971
WIND (Resultant)													
Mean speed (mph)	11.6	11.6	12.4	13.0	11.3	10.1	8.6	8.4	9.2	10.2	11.2	11.3	10.7

CONCORDIA

Elev. 1470'   39° 33'N — 97° 39'W   **Kansas**

NORMALS, MEANS, EXTREMES

	JAN	FEB	MAR	APR	MAY	JUN	JUL	AUG	SEP	OCT	NOV	DEC	YEAR
TEMPERATURE													
Normal daily maximum	35.0	41.7	51.3	64.8	74.8	85.2	90.9	89.2	79.8	69.1	52.0	40.8	64.6
Normal daily minimum	14.7	20.1	28.4	40.9	51.7	61.7	67.0	65.4	55.6	44.2	30.2	20.7	41.7
Normal monthly	24.9	30.9	39.9	52.9	63.3	73.5	79.0	77.3	67.7	56.7	41.1	30.8	53.1
Extreme highest	71	86	87	92	99	109	109	108	104	96	84	82	109
Extreme highest date	1981	1972	1972	1965	1967	1980	1980	1983	1976	1963	1980	1964	1980
Extreme lowest	-17	-15	-7	14	26	41	48	45	29	17	-4	-16	-17
Extreme lowest date	1985	1979	1978	1975	1967	1964	1972	1964	1984	1972	1976	1983	1985
DEGREE DAYS BASE 65° F													
Heating	1243	955	778	367	137	16	0	0	65	277	717	1060	5615
Cooling	0	0	0	0	84	271	438	381	146	20	0	0	1340
% OF POSSIBLE SUNSHINE	63	63	62	64	69	77	79	76	70	69	59	58	67
AVERAGE SKY COVER													
Sunrise - Sunset	5.8	5.8	6.2	6.0	5.9	5.2	4.5	4.6	4.8	5.0	5.8	5.9	5.5
NUMBER OF DAYS (Sunrise-Sunset)													
Clear	10.3	9.3	9.2	9.5	8.8	10.3	13.6	13.0	12.9	13.1	9.9	9.9	129.8
Partly cloudy	6.9	6.7	6.7	7.1	9.3	10.2	10.3	10.1	7.1	6.3	6.4	6.8	94.0
Cloudy	13.8	12.3	15.1	13.3	12.9	9.5	7.0	8.0	10.0	11.6	13.7	14.3	141.5
Precipitation .01" or more	5.7	4.7	7.7	9.8	10.5	9.4	8.7	8.6	8.0	6.2	5.2	4.6	89.2
Snow, Ice pellets 1.0" or more	2.0	1.7	1.5	0.4	0.0	0.0	0.0	0.0	0.0	*	0.6	1.5	7.7
Thunderstorms	0.3	0.5	1.6	5.9	8.4	10.5	10.3	9.1	6.6	2.8	1.0	0.2	57.2
Fog, Visibility 1/4 mile or less	2.4	2.5	1.7	1.2	0.9	0.5	0.3	0.8	1.3	1.4	2.1	2.1	17.3
Temperature Maximum:													
90° and above	0.0	0.0	0.0	0.1	1.3	8.6	18.6	14.2	5.0	0.7	0.0	0.0	48.6
32° and below	13.3	8.3	2.2	0.1	0.0	0.0	0.0	0.0	0.0	0.0	2.1	9.3	35.3
Temperature Minimum:													
32° and below	29.3	24.5	19.5	5.0	0.2	0.0	0.0	0.0	0.1	3.0	18.0	28.6	128.3
0° and below	5.0	2.1	0.2	0.0	0.0	0.0	0.0	0.0	0.0	0.0	0.2	1.8	9.3
RELATIVE HUMIDITY (%)													
Morning	76	75	72	72	76	76	70	72	75	71	76	76	74
Afternoon	66	63	57	55	57	56	50	54	56	53	62	65	58
PRECIPITATION (inches)													
Water Equivalent													
Normal	0.6	0.8	1.8	2.2	3.9	4.2	3.3	3.3	3.0	1.8	1.0	0.7	27.1
Maximum monthly	1.8	2.5	7.3	5.9	9.7	14.1	10.1	10.7	8.4	4.8	4.8	3.6	14.1
Date	1983	1971	1973	1984	1970	1967	1971	1977	1973	1979	1971	1984	1967
Minimum monthly	0.0	0.0	0.0	0.8	0.2	1.2	0.1	0.3	0.5	0.2	0.0	T	T
Date	1964	1974	1968	1966	1966	1980	1984	1971	1974	1965	1965	1976	1976
Maximum in 24 hrs	0.8	1.2	2.0	2.0	5.1	5.4	3.9	4.5	3.1	4.1	3.2	2.6	5.4
Date	1985	1966	1979	1984	1970	1967	1971	1968	1973	1979	1971	1984	1967
SNOW, ICE PELLETS													
Maximum monthly	13.7	20.6	9.2	6.1	T	0.0	0.0	0.0	T	4.6	10.1	16.7	20.6
Date	1979	1971	1971	1983	1967	—	—	—	1985	1970	1972	1983	1971
Maximum in 24 hrs	9.3	13.2	7.5	3.8	T	0.0	0.0	0.0	T	4.6	7.3	12.5	13.2
Date	1985	1965	1975	1970	1967	—	—	—	1985	1970	1983	1966	1965
WIND (Resultant)													
Mean speed (mph)	12.1	12.6	13.9	14.2	12.3	12.0	11.6	11.3	11.6	11.9	11.8	12.1	12.3

DODGE CITY

Elev. 2582' 37° 46'N — 99° 58'W **Kansas**

NORMALS, MEANS, EXTREMES

	JAN	FEB	MAR	APR	MAY	JUN	JUL	AUG	SEP	OCT	NOV	DEC	YEAR
TEMPERATURE													
Normal daily maximum	41.1	47.2	55.0	67.4	76.2	87.2	92.5	90.8	81.5	71.0	54.5	45.3	67.5
Normal daily minimum	17.9	22.7	29.2	41.1	52.0	62.0	67.4	65.7	56.6	44.4	30.4	22.1	42.6
Normal monthly	29.5	35.0	42.1	54.3	64.1	74.6	80.0	78.3	69.1	57.7	42.5	33.7	55.1
Extreme highest	78	85	93	94	102	108	109	107	106	96	91	86	109
Extreme highest date	1967	1972	1946	1956	1967	1985	1978	1983	1947	1968	1980	1955	1978
Extreme lowest	-13	-15	-15	15	26	41	47	47	29	20	0	-10	-15
Extreme lowest date	1984	1951	1948	1975	1967	1954	1952	1950	1985	1957	1958	1983	1951
DEGREE DAYS BASE 65° F													
Heating	1101	840	710	331	124	14	0	0	43	251	675	970	5059
Cooling	0	0	0	10	96	302	465	412	166	28	0	0	1479
% OF POSSIBLE SUNSHINE	66	65	64	67	68	75	78	77	74	72	65	64	70
AVERAGE SKY COVER													
Sunrise - Sunset	5.6	5.7	6.0	5.7	5.8	4.9	4.6	4.5	4.4	4.4	5.2	5.5	5.2
NUMBER OF DAYS (Sunrise-Sunset)													
Clear	10.7	9.2	9.1	9.2	9.1	11.6	12.4	13.7	14.0	14.5	11.4	11.3	136.1
Partly cloudy	7.4	7.7	8.2	8.9	9.9	10.7	11.8	10.2	7.3	7.6	7.7	7.1	104.4
Cloudy	12.9	11.4	13.7	11.9	12.0	7.8	6.7	7.1	8.7	9.0	11.0	12.6	124.7
Precipitation .01" or more	4.8	4.7	7.0	7.1	10.2	8.3	8.4	8.3	6.1	4.9	4.2	4.2	78.3
Snow, Ice pellets 1.0" or more	1.5	1.2	1.6	0.3	0.0	0.0	0.0	0.0	0.0	0.1	0.7	1.0	6.3
Thunderstorms	0.2	0.5	1.3	3.9	8.5	10.1	10.5	9.0	4.6	2.0	0.6	0.2	51.3
Fog, Visibility 1/4 mile or less	2.8	3.3	3.4	1.7	1.5	0.7	0.6	0.9	1.7	2.2	2.3	2.7	23.9
Temperature Maximum:													
90° and above	0.0	0.0	*	0.5	2.7	13.4	23.0	19.3	8.3	1.4	*	0.0	68.5
32° and below	9.4	5.5	2.3	0.1	0.0	0.0	0.0	0.0	0.0	0.1	2.0	6.6	26.1
Temperature Minimum:													
32° and below	29.2	23.6	18.7	4.9	0.3	0.0	0.0	0.0	0.1	2.8	16.9	28.0	124.5
0° and below	2.8	1.1	*	0.0	0.0	0.0	0.0	0.0	0.0	0.0	0.0	1.0	5.0
RELATIVE HUMIDITY (%)													
Morning	72	71	68	67	71	67	61	65	69	67	72	72	69
Afternoon	59	56	51	47	50	46	43	46	49	46	54	57	50
PRECIPITATION (inches)													
Water Equivalent													
Normal	0.4	0.5	1.4	1.8	3.2	3.0	3.0	2.5	1.8	1.2	0.7	0.5	20.6
Maximum monthly	1.9	2.0	8.8	6.2	8.6	7.9	9.1	7.4	6.8	4.8	3.7	2.4	9.1
Date	1949	1971	1973	1976	1951	1951	1962	1977	1973	1968	1971	1984	1962
Minimum monthly	T	0.0	0.0	0.0	0.4	0.1	0.1	0.6	0.0	T	T	T	T
Date	1961	1970	1966	1963	1985	1952	1946	1970	1980	1952	1966	1957	1966
Maximum in 24 hrs	1.1	1.1	2.5	4.6	5.5	3.2	4.1	3.1	3.2	4.5	2.4	2.0	5.5
Date	1945	1948	1973	1978	1978	1944	1944	1974	1959	1968	1971	1984	1978
SNOW, ICE PELLETS													
Maximum monthly	10.3	16.5	24.0	9.0	0.9	0.0	0.0	0.0	T	3.8	13.2	10.8	24.0
Date	1979	1978	1970	1983	1978	—	—	—	1985	1976	1948	1942	1970
Maximum in 24 hrs	8.8	10.3	12.8	7.4	0.9	0.0	0.0	0.0	T	3.8	6.7	6.6	12.8
Date	1971	1971	1970	1983	1978	—	—	—	1985	1976	1948	1958	1970
WIND (Resultant)													
Mean speed (mph)	13.5	14.0	15.6	15.5	14.5	14.3	13.0	12.7	13.7	13.5	13.7	13.5	14.0

GOODLAND
Elev. 3654' 39° 22'N — 101° 42'W **Kansas**

NORMALS, MEANS, EXTREMES

	JAN	FEB	MAR	APR	MAY	JUN	JUL	AUG	SEP	OCT	NOV	DEC	YEAR
TEMPERATURE													
Normal daily maximum	40.6	45.6	51.1	63.2	72.8	84.4	90.6	88.2	79.2	68.0	51.6	43.4	64.9
Normal daily minimum	13.8	18.2	23.2	34.2	45.0	55.2	61.3	59.0	49.3	37.0	24.5	17.1	36.5
Normal monthly	27.2	31.9	37.2	48.7	58.9	69.8	76.0	73.6	64.3	52.5	38.1	30.3	50.7
Extreme highest	79	81	89	92	99	109	111	110	105	96	87	83	111
Extreme highest date	1951	1970	1963	1950	1962	1936	1940	1947	1939	1926	1927	1964	1940
Extreme lowest	-26	-22	-20	0	21	31	42	38	19	10	-12	-19	-26
Extreme lowest date	1959	1982	1960	1936	1967	1951	1952	1964	1985	1925	1925	1961	1959
DEGREE DAYS BASE 65° F													
Heating	1172	927	862	489	215	43	0	0	114	394	807	1076	6099
Cooling	0	0	0	0	26	190	345	274	93	6	0	0	934
% OF POSSIBLE SUNSHINE	na	na	na	na	na	na	na	na	na	na	na	na	na
AVERAGE SKY COVER													
Sunrise - Sunset	5.6	5.6	5.9	5.7	5.8	4.6	4.3	4.2	4.1	4.2	5.1	5.3	5.0
NUMBER OF DAYS (Sunrise-Sunset)													
Clear	11.6	9.7	9.5	9.3	9.3	12.1	13.7	13.5	14.4	15.3	12.1	12.1	142.5
Partly cloudy	9.0	9.0	9.8	9.8	11.1	11.7	12.2	12.2	8.8	8.3	8.5	8.6	119.0
Cloudy	10.4	9.6	11.7	11.0	10.6	6.2	5.1	5.3	6.8	7.4	9.3	10.3	103.7
Precipitation .01" or more	4.6	4.5	6.5	7.4	9.8	9.3	8.6	7.6	5.5	4.4	4.2	4.0	76.5
Snow, Ice pellets 1.0" or more	2.0	1.7	3.1	1.1	0.1	0.0	0.0	0.0	0.1	0.4	1.4	1.9	11.9
Thunderstorms	*	0.4	0.7	2.5	7.7	10.5	11.7	8.9	4.2	1.4	0.3	0.1	48.2
Fog, Visibility 1/4 mile or less	2.5	3.0	3.8	2.6	2.7	1.5	1.4	2.1	2.3	2.0	2.8	2.0	28.6
Temperature Maximum:													
90° and above	0.0	0.0	0.0	0.0	0.6	7.9	17.4	15.2	6.1	0.3	0.0	0.0	47.4
32° and below	8.8	5.4	3.1	0.2	0.0	0.0	0.0	0.0	0.0	0.2	3.4	7.0	28.1
Temperature Minimum:													
32° and below	29.8	26.6	24.6	10.6	1.4	0.0	0.0	0.0	0.9	7.6	24.1	29.7	155.4
0° and below	4.9	1.7	0.3	0.0	0.0	0.0	0.0	0.0	0.0	0.0	0.3	2.4	9.6
RELATIVE HUMIDITY (%)													
Morning	77	76	79	79	84	82	81	81	78	75	78	74	79
Afternoon	62	52	49	43	48	41	39	40	40	45	60	60	48
PRECIPITATION (inches)													
Water Equivalent													
Normal	0.3	0.3	1.0	1.1	2.9	2.7	2.4	1.9	1.4	0.9	0.6	0.4	16.3
Maximum monthly	1.2	2.0	3.6	5.6	8.2	9.4	10.1	6.0	5.3	4.9	2.6	2.9	10.1
Date	1960	1939	1981	1944	1981	1982	1985	1933	1973	1930	1946	1924	1985
Minimum monthly	0.0	T	0.0	T	0.3	0.1	0.3	0.1	0.0	T	T	T	0.0
Date	1933	1970	1929	1963	1927	1976	1924	1964	1922	1939	1959	1981	1933
Maximum in 24 hrs	1.0	1.7	1.6	3.1	3.4	3.8	3.7	2.7	2.6	2.8	1.4	1.5	3.8
Date	1944	1939	1981	1981	1972	1974	1985	1935	1940	1930	1975	1924	1974
SNOW, ICE PELLETS													
Maximum monthly	18.1	25.4	27.4	22.0	4.1	0.0	0.0	0.0	5.6	17.6	23.3	17.3	27.4
Date	1979	1960	1980	1984	1950	—	—	—	1985	1979	1983	1979	1980
Maximum in 24 hrs	12.4	11.2	15.2	8.5	4.1	0.0	0.0	0.0	5.6	12.0	15.1	11.7	15.2
Date	1981	1984	1940	1984	1950	—	—	—	1985	1979	1983	1979	1940
WIND (Resultant)													
Mean speed (mph)	12.4	12.5	14.1	14.6	13.4	12.8	11.9	11.6	12.1	11.8	11.8	11.9	12.6

TOPEKA

Elev. 877' 39° 04'N — 95° 38'W **Kansas**

NORMALS, MEANS, EXTREMES

	JAN	FEB	MAR	APR	MAY	JUN	JUL	AUG	SEP	OCT	NOV	DEC	YEAR
TEMPERATURE													
Normal daily maximum	36.3	43.0	53.2	66.5	76.0	84.6	89.6	88.5	80.7	69.9	53.8	41.8	65.3
Normal daily minimum	15.7	21.9	30.4	42.7	53.2	63.1	67.5	65.6	56.2	44.1	31.5	21.8	42.8
Normal monthly	26.0	32.5	41.8	54.6	64.6	73.9	78.6	77.1	68.5	57.0	42.7	31.8	54.1
Extreme highest	73	84	88	94	97	107	110	110	109	96	85	73	110
Extreme highest date	1967	1972	1966	1953	1975	1953	1980	1984	1947	1963	1980	1984	1984
Extreme lowest	-20	-23	-7	10	26	44	43	45	29	19	2	-17	-23
Extreme lowest date	1974	1979	1978	1975	1963	1985	1972	1956	1984	1976	1976	1983	1979
DEGREE DAYS BASE 65° F													
Heating	1206	910	719	321	117	14	5	0	53	276	669	1029	5319
Cooling	0	0	0	9	105	281	427	372	158	28	0	0	1380
% OF POSSIBLE SUNSHINE	55	54	54	56	59	64	69	69	65	62	53	51	59
AVERAGE SKY COVER													
Sunrise - Sunset	6.2	6.4	6.7	6.4	6.3	5.9	5.2	5.0	5.0	5.0	5.9	6.2	5.8
NUMBER OF DAYS (Sunrise-Sunset)													
Clear	9.2	7.8	7.2	7.5	7.2	8.0	10.9	11.9	12.1	12.8	9.8	8.8	113.3
Partly cloudy	6.3	6.4	7.3	7.8	9.7	10.4	10.7	10.3	7.6	6.8	6.5	6.7	96.7
Cloudy	15.5	14.0	16.5	14.6	14.1	11.6	9.4	8.8	10.3	11.4	13.6	15.5	155.3
Precipitation .01" or more	6.3	6.2	8.8	10.0	11.4	10.4	8.6	8.1	7.5	6.8	6.1	6.4	96.6
Snow, Ice pellets 1.0" or more	2.0	1.4	1.3	0.2	0.0	0.0	0.0	0.0	0.0	0.0	0.4	1.7	7.1
Thunderstorms	0.3	0.7	2.3	5.8	9.2	10.4	8.7	7.9	6.1	3.6	1.3	0.4	56.7
Fog, Visibility 1/4 mile or less	1.9	1.8	1.2	0.9	0.9	0.6	0.5	1.1	1.1	1.5	1.1	1.9	14.4
Temperature Maximum:													
90° and above	0.0	0.0	0.0	0.1	0.7	6.0	15.6	13.2	5.0	0.5	0.0	0.0	41.2
32° and below	12.3	7.6	1.7	*	0.0	0.0	0.0	0.0	0.0	0.0	1.3	7.5	30.4
Temperature Minimum:													
32° and below	29.2	22.9	16.8	4.1	0.2	0.0	0.0	0.0	0.2	4.0	16.4	26.9	120.7
0° and below	4.6	2.2	0.1	0.0	0.0	0.0	0.0	0.0	0.0	0.0	0.0	1.4	8.4
RELATIVE HUMIDITY (%)													
Morning	75	74	72	73	78	80	77	78	82	77	78	77	77
Afternoon	65	62	57	56	58	61	58	59	58	55	61	65	60
PRECIPITATION (inches)													
Water Equivalent													
Normal	0.8	1.0	2.1	3.0	3.9	5.1	4.0	3.6	3.4	2.8	1.7	1.3	33.3
Maximum monthly	5.2	3.4	8.4	8.1	9.3	15.2	12.0	11.1	12.7	7.2	6.2	4.3	15.2
Date	1949	1971	1973	1967	1982	1967	1950	1977	1973	1980	1964	1973	1967
Minimum monthly	0.0	0.1	0.1	0.6	0.4	0.5	0.5	0.2	0.6	0.0	T	0.0	T
Date	1954	1963	1966	1963	1966	1980	1983	1971	1952	1952	1954	1979	1954
Maximum in 24 hrs	1.1	2.3	2.5	3.5	3.6	5.5	4.1	4.4	4.0	4.1	4.6	2.6	5.5
Date	1982	1971	1947	1967	1978	1967	1951	1962	1977	1985	1964	1980	1967
SNOW, ICE PELLETS													
Maximum monthly	20.1	22.4	22.1	6.8	0.0	0.0	0.0	0.0	0.0	0.8	9.4	18.8	22.4
Date	1979	1971	1960	1970	—	—	—	—	—	1970	1972	1983	1971
Maximum in 24 hrs	11.3	15.2	8.4	7.6	0.0	0.0	0.0	0.0	0.0	0.8	7.4	9.0	15.2
Date	1985	1971	1960	1970	—	—	—	—	—	1970	1975	1973	1971
WIND (Resultant)													
Mean speed (mph)	10.1	10.5	12.3	12.3	10.8	10.1	8.7	8.6	8.9	9.3	10.0	10.1	10.1

WICHITA

Elev. 1321' 37° 39'N — 97° 25'W **Kansas**

NORMALS, MEANS, EXTREMES

	JAN	FEB	MAR	APR	MAY	JUN	JUL	AUG	SEP	OCT	NOV	DEC	YEAR
TEMPERATURE													
Normal daily maximum	39.8	46.1	55.8	68.1	77.1	87.4	92.9	91.5	82.0	71.2	55.1	44.6	67.6
Normal daily minimum	19.4	24.1	32.4	44.5	54.6	64.7	69.8	67.9	59.2	46.9	33.5	24.2	45.1
Normal monthly	29.6	35.1	44.1	56.3	65.9	76.1	81.4	79.7	70.6	59.1	44.3	34.4	56.4
Extreme highest	75	84	89	96	100	110	113	110	105	95	85	83	113
Extreme highest date	1967	1976	1956	1972	1967	1980	1954	1984	1985	1979	1980	1955	1954
Extreme lowest	-12	-21	-2	15	31	43	51	48	31	21	1	-10	-21
Extreme lowest date	1962	1982	1960	1975	1976	1969	1975	1967	1984	1976	1975	1983	1982
DEGREE DAYS BASE 65° F													
Heating	1097	837	656	275	89	7	0	0	37	219	621	949	4787
Cooling	0	0	8	14	117	340	508	456	205	36	0	0	1684
% OF POSSIBLE SUNSHINE	59	60	61	63	65	69	76	75	68	65	58	58	65
AVERAGE SKY COVER													
Sunrise - Sunset	6.0	6.0	6.3	6.0	6.0	5.4	4.7	4.5	4.9	4.9	5.6	5.9	5.5
NUMBER OF DAYS (Sunrise-Sunset)													
Clear	10.1	8.3	8.8	8.7	8.3	9.6	12.8	13.7	13.1	13.0	10.5	9.9	126.8
Partly cloudy	6.1	7.1	7.1	8.1	10.0	10.5	10.6	9.8	6.8	7.2	6.3	7.0	96.6
Cloudy	14.8	12.8	15.1	13.3	12.7	9.9	7.6	7.5	10.2	10.8	13.2	14.1	141.9
Precipitation .01" or more	5.6	5.2	7.8	8.0	10.6	9.3	7.5	7.1	7.7	6.3	5.0	5.8	85.8
Snow, Ice pellets 1.0" or more	1.4	1.2	0.6	0.1	0.0	0.0	0.0	0.0	0.0	0.0	0.4	1.1	4.7
Thunderstorms	0.3	0.7	2.6	5.7	9.1	10.2	7.8	7.3	6.2	3.5	1.2	0.3	54.8
Fog, Visibility 1/4 mile or less	2.9	3.0	1.4	0.8	0.8	0.4	0.2	0.2	1.1	1.3	2.1	3.1	17.1
Temperature Maximum:													
90° and above	0.0	0.0	0.0	0.3	2.1	11.5	21.7	20.2	7.6	1.0	0.0	0.0	64.3
32° and below	10.0	5.8	1.4	0.1	0.0	0.0	0.0	0.0	0.0	*	0.8	5.2	23.4
Temperature Minimum:													
32° and below	28.9	23.0	15.5	2.8	0.1	0.0	0.0	0.0	*	1.3	14.5	26.6	112.8
0° and below	2.1	0.8	0.1	0.0	0.0	0.0	0.0	0.0	0.0	0.0	0.0	0.6	3.6
RELATIVE HUMIDITY (%)													
Morning	76	75	70	70	76	74	67	67	72	73	75	76	73
Afternoon	63	60	55	52	55	53	48	49	54	53	58	62	55
PRECIPITATION (inches)													
Water Equivalent													
Normal	0.6	0.8	2.0	2.3	3.9	4.0	3.6	2.8	3.4	2.4	1.4	0.9	28.6
Maximum monthly	2.7	2.1	9.1	5.5	8.8	10.4	9.2	7.9	9.4	6.1	5.8	4.7	10.4
Date	1973	1975	1973	1976	1977	1957	1962	1960	1973	1959	1964	1984	1957
Minimum monthly	0.0	0.0	0.0	0.2	0.5	0.9	0.0	0.3	0.0	T	T	0.0	T
Date	1961	1963	1971	1963	1973	1954	1975	1976	1956	1958	1954	1955	1958
Maximum in 24 hrs	1.7	1.5	2.6	2.4	4.7	4.9	3.8	3.7	3.0	5.0	4.3	2.6	5.0
Date	1980	1973	1961	1969	1963	1965	1983	1959	1968	1985	1964	1984	1985
SNOW, ICE PELLETS													
Maximum monthly	18.5	16.7	16.5	4.6	0.0	0.0	0.0	0.0	0.0	0.1	7.1	13.8	18.5
Date	1962	1971	1970	1979	—	—	—	—	—	1960	1972	1983	1962
Maximum in 24 hrs	13.0	11.9	13.5	4.6	0.0	0.0	0.0	0.0	0.0	0.1	6.8	9.0	13.5
Date	1962	1971	1970	1979	—	—	—	—	—	1960	1984	1983	1970
WIND (Resultant)													
Mean speed (mph)	12.2	12.8	14.2	14.2	12.5	12.2	11.1	11.1	11.6	12.0	12.1	12.2	12.3

LEXINGTON

Elev. 966'   38° 02N — 84° 36W   # Kentucky

NORMALS, MEANS, EXTREMES

	JAN	FEB	MAR	APR	MAY	JUN	JUL	AUG	SEP	OCT	NOV	DEC	YEAR
TEMPERATURE													
Normal daily maximum	39.8	43.7	53.7	65.8	74.9	82.6	85.9	85.0	79.3	67.6	54.1	44.4	64.7
Normal daily minimum	23.1	25.4	34.1	44.3	53.6	61.8	65.9	64.8	58.1	45.9	35.7	27.8	45.0
Normal monthly	31.5	34.6	43.9	55.1	64.3	72.2	75.9	74.9	68.7	56.8	44.9	36.1	54.9
Extreme highest	76	76	83	88	92	101	103	103	103	91	81	75	103
Extreme highest date	1950	1945	1945	1962	1962	1954	1954	1983	1954	1959	1961	1982	1983
Extreme lowest	-21	-15	-2	18	26	39	47	42	35	20	-3	-10	-21
Extreme lowest date	1963	1951	1960	1982	1966	1966	1972	1965	1965	1976	1950	1983	1963
DEGREE DAYS BASE 65° F													
Heating	1039	851	661	306	121	10	0	0	47	280	603	896	4814
Cooling	0	0	7	9	96	226	341	307	158	26	0	0	1170
AVERAGE SKY COVER													
Sunrise - Sunset	7.3	7.0	7.1	6.7	6.3	6.0	5.8	5.5	5.3	5.2	6.7	7.2	6.3
NUMBER OF DAYS													
(Sunrise-Sunset)													
Clear	5.7	6.1	5.5	6.2	7.2	7.3	7.8	9.4	10.8	11.9	7.0	6.0	90.9
Partly cloudy	5.9	5.5	7.6	8.5	10.1	11.4	12.6	12.0	8.5	7.1	6.5	5.9	101.7
Cloudy	19.4	16.6	18.0	15.3	13.7	11.4	10.6	9.5	10.8	11.9	16.5	19.1	172.7
Precipitation .01" or more	12.6	11.2	13.1	12.5	11.9	10.8	11.1	9.2	8.0	8.0	10.8	11.5	130.7
Snow, Ice pellets 1.0" or more	2.0	1.5	0.8	*	0.0	0.0	0.0	0.0	0.0	0.0	0.5	0.8	5.5
Thunderstorms	0.7	1.0	3.0	4.1	6.5	8.3	9.5	6.8	3.2	1.5	1.0	0.4	45.8
Fog, Visibility 1/4 mile or less	2.6	2.1	1.3	0.7	1.0	1.0	1.4	1.8	2.2	1.9	1.4	1.9	19.4
Temperature Maximum:													
90° and above	0.0	0.0	0.0	0.0	0.1	2.9	6.3	5.3	2.0	0.0	0.0	0.0	16.7
32° and below	11.0	6.5	1.0	0.0	0.0	0.0	0.0	0.0	0.0	0.0	0.6	4.5	23.4
Temperature Minimum:													
32° and below	24.5	20.9	13.8	3.5	0.1	0.0	0.0	0.0	0.0	2.4	11.2	20.1	96.4
0° and below	2.1	0.8	0.1	0.0	0.0	0.0	0.0	0.0	0.0	0.0	0.0	0.2	3.2
RELATIVE HUMIDITY (%)													
Morning	76	75	71	69	76	79	82	83	82	77	76	77	77
Afternoon	69	64	58	54	56	57	59	59	58	57	63	68	60
PRECIPITATION (inches)													
Water Equivalent													
Normal	3.5	3.2	4.8	4.0	4.2	4.2	4.9	3.9	3.2	2.2	3.3	3.7	45.6
Maximum monthly	16.6	7.6	10.3	9.3	10.8	11.6	10.6	11.1	9.6	6.1	6.8	9.9	16.6
Date	1950	1955	1975	1970	1983	1960	1958	1974	1979	1983	1951	1978	1950
Minimum monthly	0.3	0.6	0.9	0.7	1.2	1.3	1.8	0.5	0.2	0.3	0.4	0.6	0.2
Date	1981	1978	1966	1946	1965	1966	1951	1984	1959	1963	1976	1965	1959
Maximum in 24 hrs	2.9	3.4	3.8	4.3	3.2	5.8	4.7	3.5	4.3	3.2	2.5	3.7	5.8
Date	1951	1976	1952	1948	1983	1960	1978	1968	1979	1962	1957	1978	1960
SNOW, ICE PELLETS													
Maximum monthly	21.9	16.4	17.7	2.9	0.0	0.0	0.0	0.0	0.0	0.2	9.7	10.7	21.9
Date	1978	1960	1960	1961	—	—	—	—	—	1972	1950	1967	1978
Maximum in 24 hrs	9.4	7.3	9.5	2.9	0.0	0.0	0.0	0.0	0.0	0.2	7.5	7.8	9.5
Date	1966	1971	1947	1961	—	—	—	—	—	1972	1966	1967	1947
WIND (Resultant)													
Mean speed (mph)	11.1	11.0	11.5	11.0	9.0	8.1	7.4	7.0	7.7	8.4	10.2	10.9	9.4

LOUISVILLE Elev. 477' 38° 11N — 85° 44W # Kentucky

NORMALS, MEANS, EXTREMES

	JAN	FEB	MAR	APR	MAY	JUN	JUL	AUG	SEP	OCT	NOV	DEC	YEAR
TEMPERATURE													
Normal daily maximum	40.8	45.0	54.9	67.5	76.2	84.0	87.6	86.7	80.6	69.2	55.5	45.4	66.1
Normal daily minimum	24.1	26.8	35.2	45.6	54.6	63.3	67.5	66.1	59.1	46.2	36.6	28.9	46.2
Normal monthly	32.5	35.9	45.1	56.6	65.4	73.7	77.6	76.4	69.9	57.7	46.1	37.2	56.1
Extreme highest	77	77	86	91	95	102	105	101	104	92	84	76	105
Extreme highest date	1950	1972	1981	1960	1959	1952	1954	1964	1954	1959	1958	1982	1954
Extreme lowest	-20	-19	-1	22	31	42	50	49	33	23	-1	-9	-20
Extreme lowest date	1963	1951	1960	1982	1966	1966	1972	1965	1949	1952	1950	1960	1963
DEGREE DAYS BASE 65° F													
Heating	1008	815	624	264	98	5	0	0	32	250	567	862	4525
Cooling	0	0	7	12	110	266	391	353	179	24	0	0	1342
% OF POSSIBLE SUNSHINE	42	48	49	55	61	66	66	67	66	61	46	40	56
AVERAGE SKY COVER													
Sunrise - Sunset	7.4	6.9	7.0	6.6	6.2	5.9	5.8	5.3	5.3	5.3	6.6	7.2	6.3
NUMBER OF DAYS													
(Sunrise-Sunset)													
Clear	5.7	5.9	5.8	6.1	7.7	7.6	7.4	10.1	10.5	11.5	7.3	6.4	91.9
Partly cloudy	5.8	6.4	7.6	9.0	9.4	11.3	13.1	11.6	9.1	7.8	6.1	5.8	103.1
Cloudy	19.5	15.9	17.6	14.9	13.9	11.1	10.6	9.3	10.4	11.7	16.3	18.7	170.0
Precipitation .01" or more	11.6	10.4	13.2	11.9	11.6	10.0	10.5	8.6	7.7	7.5	10.2	11.3	124.6
Snow, Ice pellets 1.0" or more	1.8	1.2	0.7	0.1	0.0	0.0	0.0	0.0	0.0	0.0	0.3	0.7	4.9
Thunderstorms	0.8	1.1	3.1	4.4	6.5	7.3	8.3	6.8	3.2	1.7	1.4	0.6	45.1
Fog, Visibility 1/4 mile or less	1.0	0.9	0.5	0.2	0.2	0.4	0.6	0.9	1.1	1.6	0.8	0.7	9.0
Temperature Maximum:													
90° and above	0.0	0.0	0.0	0.0	0.3	5.1	10.2	8.5	3.0	0.0	0.0	0.0	27.1
32° and below	10.2	5.5	0.6	0.0	0.0	0.0	0.0	0.0	0.0	0.0	0.4	4.3	21.0
Temperature Minimum:													
32° and below	25.2	20.6	12.0	2.2	0.2	0.0	0.0	0.0	0.0	1.6	9.2	20.5	91.4
0° and below	1.6	0.3	0.0	0.0	0.0	0.0	0.0	0.0	0.0	0.0	0.0	0.2	2.2
RELATIVE HUMIDITY (%)													
Morning	72	72	70	68	76	80	81	82	83	79	75	73	76
Afternoon	65	61	58	53	55	57	58	59	59	56	61	65	59
PRECIPITATION (inches)													
Water Equivalent													
Normal	3.3	3.2	4.7	4.1	4.1	3.6	4.1	3.3	3.3	2.6	3.4	3.4	43.5
Maximum monthly	11.3	8.3	14.9	11.1	10.5	10.1	10.0	8.7	10.4	6.4	9.1	7.6	14.9
Date	1950	1956	1964	1970	1983	1960	1979	1974	1979	1983	1957	1978	1964
Minimum monthly	0.4	0.7	1.0	0.7	1.3	0.4	0.9	0.2	0.2	0.6	0.7	0.6	0.2
Date	1981	1978	1966	1976	1977	1984	1983	1953	1953	1964	1976	1976	1953
Maximum in 24 hrs	2.7	2.8	6.9	4.8	4.6	5.1	5.4	3.0	4.9	3.2	3.5	2.7	6.9
Date	1982	1975	1964	1970	1961	1960	1979	1970	1979	1977	1948	1978	1964
SNOW, ICE PELLETS													
Maximum monthly	28.4	13.1	22.9	1.6	0.0	0.0	0.0	0.0	0.0	T	13.2	9.3	28.4
Date	1978	1948	1960	1973	—	—	—	—	—	1980	1966	1961	1978
Maximum in 24 hrs	14.1	11.0	12.1	1.6	0.0	0.0	0.0	0.0	0.0	T	13.0	5.0	14.1
Date	1978	1966	1968	1973	—	—	—	—	—	1980	1966	1961	1978
WIND (Resultant)													
Mean speed (mph)	9.6	9.6	10.3	9.9	8.1	7.4	6.7	6.4	6.8	7.2	8.9	9.3	8.4

BATON ROUGE
Elev. 64'   30° 32'N — 91° 08'W   **Louisiana**

NORMALS, MEANS, EXTREMES

	JAN	FEB	MAR	APR	MAY	JUN	JUL	AUG	SEP	OCT	NOV	DEC	YEAR
TEMPERATURE													
Normal daily maximum	61.1	64.5	71.6	79.2	85.2	90.6	91.4	90.8	87.4	80.1	70.1	63.8	78.0
Normal daily minimum	40.5	42.7	49.4	57.5	64.3	70.0	72.8	72.0	68.3	56.3	47.2	42.3	57.0
Normal monthly	50.8	53.6	60.5	68.4	74.8	80.3	82.1	81.4	77.9	68.2	58.7	53.1	67.5
Extreme highest	82	85	91	92	98	103	101	102	97	94	86	85	103
Extreme highest date	1957	1962	1963	1952	1953	1954	1960	1962	1963	1952	1971	1982	1954
Extreme lowest	9	20	20	37	44	53	58	59	43	32	21	11	9
Extreme lowest date	1985	1958	1980	1975	1954	1984	1967	1967	1967	1957	1976	1983	1985
DEGREE DAYS BASE 65° F													
Heating	466	342	187	32	0	0	0	0	0	48	218	380	1673
Cooling	26	23	47	134	304	459	530	508	387	147	29	11	2605
% OF POSSIBLE SUNSHINE	na	na	na	na	na	na	na	na	na	na	na	na	na
AVERAGE SKY COVER													
Sunrise - Sunset	6.8	6.3	6.3	6.1	5.8	5.5	6.3	5.8	5.5	4.5	5.7	6.2	5.9
NUMBER OF DAYS (Sunrise-Sunset)													
Clear	7.1	7.7	7.5	7.5	8.2	7.6	4.9	6.9	9.1	14.2	9.6	8.9	99.3
Partly cloudy	6.2	6.3	8.9	9.0	11.6	14.3	15.3	14.7	10.9	8.6	8.0	6.8	120.6
Cloudy	17.7	14.3	14.6	13.5	11.3	8.1	10.8	9.4	9.9	8.2	12.4	15.3	145.4
Precipitation .01" or more	9.6	8.9	8.9	7.1	8.0	9.2	13.2	12.0	9.0	5.4	7.3	9.5	108.1
Snow, Ice pellets 1.0" or more	0.0	0.1	0.0	0.0	0.0	0.0	0.0	0.0	0.0	0.0	0.0	0.0	0.1
Thunderstorms	1.9	3.3	4.1	4.9	5.8	8.9	14.9	12.5	6.7	2.3	2.2	2.4	69.9
Fog, Visibility 1/4 mile or less	4.6	3.3	2.9	3.1	2.8	1.1	1.7	1.6	3.0	4.0	4.4	4.0	36.5
Temperature Maximum:													
90° and above	0.0	0.0	*	0.3	5.1	19.0	23.7	21.1	10.5	1.7	0.0	0.0	81.4
32° and below	0.3	*	0.0	0.0	0.0	0.0	0.0	0.0	0.0	0.0	0.0	0.1	0.4
Temperature Minimum:													
32° and below	9.9	5.7	1.2	0.0	0.0	0.0	0.0	0.0	0.0	0.0	1.8	6.7	25.3
0° and below	0.0	0.0	0.0	0.0	0.0	0.0	0.0	0.0	0.0	0.0	0.0	0.0	0.0
RELATIVE HUMIDITY (%)													
Morning	81	78	79	82	84	85	86	88	87	85	85	82	84
Afternoon	65	59	57	56	56	58	62	62	61	55	59	63	59
PRECIPITATION (inches)													
Water Equivalent													
Normal	4.5	4.9	4.5	5.5	4.8	3.1	7.0	5.0	4.4	2.6	3.9	4.9	55.7
Maximum monthly	9.9	14.5	12.7	14.8	10.7	12.2	10.9	13.3	13.9	14.4	10.3	15.9	15.9
Date	1966	1966	1973	1980	1953	1983	1963	1977	1977	1984	1977	1982	1982
Minimum monthly	1.1	0.7	0.5	0.3	0.6	0.1	2.0	1.3	0.0	T	0.2	1.9	T
Date	1971	1962	1955	1976	1963	1979	1962	1980	1953	1978	1967	1978	1978
Maximum in 24 hrs	4.0	4.7	6.0	12.0	4.9	3.9	4.2	6.2	6.3	8.3	4.6	8.2	12.0
Date	1975	1979	1973	1967	1954	1962	1969	1983	1973	1964	1973	1982	1967
SNOW, ICE PELLETS													
Maximum monthly	0.6	1.8	T	0.0	0.0	0.0	0.0	0.0	0.0	0.0	T	T	1.8
Date	1973	1973	1980	—	—	—	—	—	—	—	1976	1983	1973
Maximum in 24 hrs	0.5	1.8	T	0.0	0.0	0.0	0.0	0.0	0.0	0.0	T	T	1.8
Date	1973	1973	1980	—	—	—	—	—	—	—	1976	1983	1973
WIND (Resultant)													
Mean speed (mph)	9.0	9.4	9.5	8.9	7.8	6.7	5.9	5.6	6.7	6.7	7.8	8.3	7.7

LAKE CHARLES

Elev. 9'   30° 07'N — 93° 13'W   **Louisiana**

NORMALS, MEANS, EXTREMES

	JAN	FEB	MAR	APR	MAY	JUN	JUL	AUG	SEP	OCT	NOV	DEC	YEAR
TEMPERATURE													
Normal daily maximum	60.8	64.0	70.5	77.8	84.1	89.4	91.0	90.8	87.5	80.8	70.5	64.0	77.6
Normal daily minimum	42.2	44.5	50.8	58.9	65.6	71.4	73.5	72.8	68.9	57.7	48.9	43.8	58.3
Normal monthly	51.5	54.3	60.7	68.4	74.9	80.4	82.3	81.8	78.2	69.3	59.7	53.9	67.9
Extreme highest	80	83	86	92	96	98	102	100	96	92	87	82	102
Extreme highest date	1982	1972	1974	1965	1984	1969	1980	1980	1964	1977	1978	1978	1980
Extreme lowest	15	22	25	34	49	56	61	61	47	36	23	13	13
Extreme lowest date	1985	1981	1980	1971	1978	1984	1967	1967	1967	1980	1976	1983	1983
DEGREE DAYS BASE 65° F													
Heating	442	324	184	29	0	0	0	0	0	45	204	351	1579
Cooling	24	24	51	131	307	462	536	521	396	178	45	7	2682
% OF POSSIBLE SUNSHINE	53	56	67	73	82	83	84	83	85	74	61	55	71
AVERAGE SKY COVER													
Sunrise - Sunset	7.0	6.2	6.7	6.5	5.9	5.3	6.2	5.8	5.4	4.7	5.5	6.4	6.0
NUMBER OF DAYS (Sunrise-Sunset)													
Clear	6.9	8.5	6.7	6.4	7.8	8.7	5.7	6.7	9.5	13.0	10.3	8.2	98.4
Partly cloudy	5.3	5.5	8.3	8.6	11.8	13.4	14.1	15.0	10.8	9.3	7.9	7.3	117.4
Cloudy	18.8	14.2	16.0	15.0	11.5	8.0	11.2	9.3	9.7	8.7	11.8	15.5	149.5
Precipitation .01" or more	9.1	7.7	7.8	6.5	7.4	7.4	10.4	10.7	9.0	6.2	7.3	8.7	98.3
Snow, Ice pellets 1.0" or more	0.1	0.0	0.0	0.0	0.0	0.0	0.0	0.0	0.0	0.0	0.0	0.0	0.1
Thunderstorms	3.0	2.8	4.0	4.1	7.2	8.9	14.0	14.0	8.5	3.1	2.7	2.8	75.0
Fog, Visibility 1/4 mile or less	8.5	5.7	6.4	3.7	1.8	0.7	0.5	0.8	2.4	5.6	6.3	7.3	49.6
Temperature Maximum:													
90° and above	0.0	0.0	0.0	0.1	2.1	14.1	22.7	21.0	9.4	0.7	0.0	0.0	70.0
32° and below	0.1	*	0.0	0.0	0.0	0.0	0.0	0.0	0.0	0.0	0.0	0.1	0.2
Temperature Minimum:													
32° and below	6.2	3.1	0.6	0.0	0.0	0.0	0.0	0.0	0.0	0.0	1.0	4.1	15.0
0° and below	0.0	0.0	0.0	0.0	0.0	0.0	0.0	0.0	0.0	0.0	0.0	0.0	0.0
RELATIVE HUMIDITY (%)													
Morning	86	84	86	87	89	90	91	91	90	88	87	86	88
Afternoon	69	63	62	61	62	62	64	64	63	57	60	66	63
PRECIPITATION (inches)													
Water Equivalent													
Normal	4.2	3.8	3.0	4.0	5.1	4.1	5.5	5.3	5.2	3.4	3.7	5.0	53.0
Maximum monthly	12.6	6.7	9.0	10.9	20.7	14.4	13.1	17.3	19.9	17.2	7.3	13.2	20.7
Date	1974	1985	1980	1973	1980	1981	1979	1962	1973	1970	1974	1967	1980
Minimum monthly	0.7	0.8	0.2	0.5	0.3	0.8	0.4	0.7	1.0	T	0.1	2.0	T
Date	1971	1962	1971	1978	1978	1969	1962	1976	1962	1963	1967	1975	1963
Maximum in 24 hrs	3.6	3.2	4.9	5.5	16.8	7.0	6.3	14.1	11.2	7.2	3.5	6.8	16.8
Date	1972	1963	1973	1973	1980	1981	1979	1962	1979	1970	1966	1971	1980
SNOW, ICE PELLETS													
Maximum monthly	4.0	0.3	T	0.0	0.0	0.0	0.0	0.0	0.0	0.0	T	T	4.0
Date	1973	1968	1968	—	—	—	—	—	—	—	1976	1985	1973
Maximum in 24 hrs	4.0	0.3	T	0.0	0.0	0.0	0.0	0.0	0.0	0.0	T	T	4.0
Date	1973	1968	1968	—	—	—	—	—	—	—	1976	1985	1973
WIND (Resultant)													
Mean speed (mph)	10.1	10.4	10.6	10.3	8.9	7.6	6.4	6.1	7.3	7.7	9.0	9.5	8.7

NEW ORLEANS   Elev. 4'   29° 59'N — 90° 15'W   Louisiana

NORMALS, MEANS, EXTREMES

	JAN	FEB	MAR	APR	MAY	JUN	JUL	AUG	SEP	OCT	NOV	DEC	YEAR
TEMPERATURE													
Normal daily maximum	61.8	64.6	71.2	78.6	84.5	89.5	90.7	90.2	86.8	79.4	70.1	64.4	77.7
Normal daily minimum	43.0	44.8	51.6	58.8	65.3	70.9	73.5	73.1	70.1	59.0	49.9	44.8	58.7
Normal monthly	52.4	54.7	61.4	68.7	74.9	80.2	82.1	81.7	78.5	69.2	60.0	54.6	68.2
Extreme highest	83	85	89	91	96	100	101	102	101	92	86	84	102
Extreme highest date	1982	1972	1982	1948	1953	1954	1981	1980	1980	1977	1979	1978	1980
Extreme lowest	14	19	25	32	41	50	60	60	42	35	24	14	14
Extreme lowest date	1985	1970	1980	1971	1960	1984	1967	1968	1967	1968	1970	1983	1985
DEGREE DAYS BASE 65° F													
Heating	423	318	171	25	0	0	0	0	0	31	186	336	1490
Cooling	32	30	59	136	307	459	530	518	405	161	36	13	2686
% OF POSSIBLE SUNSHINE	48	52	57	63	62	67	61	61	63	66	55	54	59
AVERAGE SKY COVER													
Sunrise - Sunset	6.7	6.2	6.3	5.8	5.5	5.3	6.4	5.8	5.4	4.4	5.2	6.2	5.8
NUMBER OF DAYS (Sunrise-Sunset)													
Clear	6.7	7.8	7.6	7.8	9.5	9.2	4.9	7.4	9.9	14.6	10.7	8.2	104.6
Partly cloudy	7.4	6.6	8.4	10.7	11.2	12.6	14.4	13.9	10.3	7.9	8.0	7.6	119.0
Cloudy	16.8	13.8	15.0	11.5	10.2	8.2	11.7	9.7	9.8	8.5	11.2	15.2	141.6
Precipitation .01" or more	10.1	9.1	9.0	7.1	7.6	10.3	14.7	13.3	9.8	5.8	7.2	10.0	113.7
Snow, Ice pellets 1.0" or more	0.0	*	0.0	0.0	0.0	0.0	0.0	0.0	0.0	0.0	0.0	*	0.1
Thunderstorms	1.7	2.8	4.0	4.2	5.8	9.1	15.1	12.9	6.8	1.9	1.7	2.3	68.4
Fog, Visibility 1/4 mile or less	6.4	4.3	4.0	1.9	0.9	0.2	0.1	0.1	0.2	1.8	3.9	5.0	28.9
Temperature Maximum:													
90° and above	0.0	0.0	0.0	0.1	3.4	16.4	20.2	19.5	8.6	0.8	0.0	0.0	69.0
32° and below	0.2	0.0	0.0	0.0	0.0	0.0	0.0	0.0	0.0	0.0	0.0	0.1	0.3
Temperature Minimum:													
32° and below	5.4	3.1	0.6	*	0.0	0.0	0.0	0.0	0.0	0.0	0.8	3.9	13.7
0° and below	0.0	0.0	0.0	0.0	0.0	0.0	0.0	0.0	0.0	0.0	0.0	0.0	0.0
RELATIVE HUMIDITY (%)													
Morning	82	81	81	84	85	86	88	88	86	84	84	83	84
Afternoon	66	63	60	60	60	62	66	66	65	59	61	66	63
PRECIPITATION (inches)													
Water Equivalent													
Normal	4.9	5.2	4.7	4.5	5.0	4.6	6.7	6.0	5.8	2.6	4.0	5.2	59.7
Maximum monthly	13.6	12.5	19.0	16.1	14.3	12.2	13.0	16.1	16.7	13.2	14.5	10.7	19.0
Date	1978	1983	1948	1980	1959	1975	1982	1977	1971	1985	1947	1967	1948
Minimum monthly	0.5	1.0	0.2	0.2	0.9	0.2	1.9	1.6	0.2	0.0	0.2	1.4	0.0
Date	1968	1962	1955	1976	1949	1979	1981	1980	1953	1978	1949	1958	1978
Maximum in 24 hrs	6.0	5.6	7.8	7.9	9.8	4.1	4.3	4.8	6.5	4.5	8.7	5.7	9.8
Date	1978	1961	1948	1980	1959	1953	1966	1975	1971	1985	1975	1982	1959
SNOW, ICE PELLETS													
Maximum monthly	0.4	2.0	T	0.0	0.0	0.0	0.0	0.0	0.0	0.0	T	2.7	2.7
Date	1985	1958	1980	—	—	—	—	—	—	—	1950	1963	1963
Maximum in 24 hrs	0.4	2.0	T	0.0	0.0	0.0	0.0	0.0	0.0	0.0	T	2.7	2.7
Date	1985	1958	1980	—	—	—	—	—	—	—	1950	1963	1963
WIND (Resultant)													
Mean speed (mph)	9.4	9.8	9.9	9.4	8.1	6.8	6.1	5.9	7.3	7.5	8.6	9.0	8.2

SHREVEPORT

Elev. 254' 32° 28'N — 93° 49'W **Louisiana**

NORMALS, MEANS, EXTREMES

	JAN	FEB	MAR	APR	MAY	JUN	JUL	AUG	SEP	OCT	NOV	DEC	YEAR
TEMPERATURE													
Normal daily maximum	55.8	60.6	68.1	76.7	83.5	90.1	93.3	93.2	87.7	78.9	66.8	59.2	76.2
Normal daily minimum	36.2	39.0	45.8	54.6	62.4	69.4	72.5	71.5	66.5	54.5	44.5	38.2	54.6
Normal monthly	46.0	49.8	57.0	65.7	73.0	79.8	82.9	82.4	77.1	66.7	55.7	48.7	65.4
Extreme highest	84	89	92	91	95	101	106	107	103	97	88	84	107
Extreme highest date	1972	1977	1974	1955	1977	1953	1980	1962	1980	1954	1984	1955	1962
Extreme lowest	3	12	20	32	42	52	58	58	42	31	16	6	3
Extreme lowest date	1962	1978	1980	1975	1960	1977	1972	1956	1984	1980	1976	1983	1962
DEGREE DAYS BASE 65° F													
Heating	597	438	282	69	9	0	0	0	0	76	293	505	2269
Cooling	8	12	34	90	257	444	555	539	363	128	14	0	2444
% OF POSSIBLE SUNSHINE	48	55	56	56	62	70	73	72	68	67	59	53	62
AVERAGE SKY COVER													
Sunrise - Sunset	6.7	6.2	6.4	6.3	6.0	5.3	5.3	5.1	5.1	4.8	5.4	6.1	5.7
NUMBER OF DAYS (Sunrise-Sunset)													
Clear	7.6	8.3	8.1	7.5	8.2	9.2	10.4	10.7	11.5	13.2	11.1	9.3	114.8
Partly cloudy	5.4	5.4	6.3	7.6	10.3	12.4	11.5	12.2	8.9	7.7	6.1	6.5	100.4
Cloudy	18.0	14.6	16.6	14.9	12.6	8.4	9.1	8.0	9.5	10.2	12.8	15.2	150.0
Precipitation .01" or more	9.5	7.9	9.4	8.9	8.8	7.4	7.8	6.6	6.6	6.5	8.3	8.8	96.6
Snow, Ice pellets 1.0" or more	0.3	0.2	0.1	0.0	0.0	0.0	0.0	0.0	0.0	0.0	*	0.1	0.7
Thunderstorms	1.8	2.6	5.0	5.9	7.0	6.8	7.9	6.5	3.9	2.7	2.8	2.1	55.0
Fog, Visibility 1/4 mile or less	3.6	2.2	1.5	1.2	0.8	0.5	0.3	0.5	1.1	2.5	2.6	3.0	19.6
Temperature Maximum:													
90° and above	0.0	0.0	*	0.1	4.2	17.8	25.3	25.0	13.8	2.5	0.0	0.0	88.7
32° and below	1.2	0.2	0.0	0.0	0.0	0.0	0.0	0.0	0.0	0.0	0.0	0.4	1.8
Temperature Minimum:													
32° and below	13.1	8.2	2.5	*	0.0	0.0	0.0	0.0	0.0	0.1	3.1	10.2	37.2
0° and below	0.0	0.0	0.0	0.0	0.0	0.0	0.0	0.0	0.0	0.0	0.0	0.0	0.0
RELATIVE HUMIDITY (%)													
Morning	77	75	75	79	83	83	82	82	82	81	80	79	80
Afternoon	64	59	57	57	59	58	57	56	57	54	58	62	58
PRECIPITATION (inches)													
Water Equivalent													
Normal	4.0	3.4	3.7	4.7	4.7	3.5	3.5	2.5	3.2	2.6	3.7	3.8	43.8
Maximum monthly	10.0	8.5	7.2	11.1	11.7	12.3	9.4	6.8	9.5	12.0	9.4	10.0	12.3
Date	1974	1983	1969	1957	1967	1961	1972	1955	1968	1984	1957	1982	1961
Minimum monthly	0.2	0.9	0.5	1.0	1.2	0.8	0.1	0.3	0.1	0.0	0.7	0.5	0.0
Date	1971	1954	1966	1971	1962	1967	1964	1985	1956	1963	1967	1981	1963
Maximum in 24 hrs	3.1	3.5	3.6	7.1	5.2	4.3	4.3	4.6	5.3	3.8	5.9	3.3	7.1
Date	1979	1965	1979	1953	1978	1983	1972	1955	1961	1957	1969	1965	1953
SNOW, ICE PELLETS													
Maximum monthly	5.9	4.4	4.0	0.0	0.0	0.0	0.0	0.0	0.0	0.0	1.3	5.4	5.9
Date	1978	1985	1965	—	—	—	—	—	—	—	1980	1983	1978
Maximum in 24 hrs	5.6	4.4	4.0	0.0	0.0	0.0	0.0	0.0	0.0	0.0	1.3	5.4	5.6
Date	1982	1985	1965	—	—	—	—	—	—	—	1980	1983	1982
WIND (Resultant)													
Mean speed (mph)	9.4	9.8	10.3	9.9	8.4	7.6	7.2	6.9	7.4	7.5	8.6	9.1	8.5

CARIBOU

Elev. 624'   46° 52'N — 68° 01'W   **Maine**

NORMALS, MEANS, EXTREMES

	JAN	FEB	MAR	APR	MAY	JUN	JUL	AUG	SEP	OCT	NOV	DEC	YEAR
TEMPERATURE													
Normal daily maximum	19.9	22.9	33.5	45.8	60.7	71.0	75.7	73.1	63.9	51.7	38.0	23.9	48.3
Normal daily minimum	1.4	3.0	15.1	28.8	39.7	49.6	54.5	51.8	43.2	34.5	24.2	7.5	29.4
Normal monthly	10.7	13.0	24.3	37.3	50.2	60.3	65.1	62.5	53.6	43.1	31.1	15.7	38.9
Extreme highest	51	52	73	80	96	96	95	95	91	79	68	58	96
Extreme highest date	1983	1981	1962	1942	1977	1944	1955	1975	1945	1968	1956	1950	1977
Extreme lowest	-32	-41	-20	-2	18	30	36	34	23	14	-3	-26	-41
Extreme lowest date	1976	1955	1967	1964	1974	1958	1969	1982	1980	1972	1978	1975	1955
DEGREE DAYS BASE 65° F													
Heating	1686	1456	1262	831	459	150	86	120	342	679	1017	1528	9616
Cooling	0	0	0	0	0	12	92	43	0	0	0	0	147
% OF POSSIBLE SUNSHINE	na	na	na	na	na	na	na	na	na	na	na	na	na
AVERAGE SKY COVER													
Sunrise - Sunset	6.9	6.9	6.9	7.3	7.3	7.3	7.1	6.8	6.8	7.2	8.0	7.4	7.2
NUMBER OF DAYS (Sunrise-Sunset)													
Clear	6.8	5.9	6.5	5.0	4.0	3.3	3.0	4.3	5.5	4.8	2.9	5.3	57.3
Partly cloudy	7.0	6.2	7.1	7.0	9.0	9.8	12.9	11.7	9.2	7.9	6.1	6.7	100.5
Cloudy	17.3	16.1	17.4	18.0	18.0	16.9	15.1	15.0	15.3	18.3	21.0	19.0	207.4
Precipitation .01" or more	14.4	12.5	12.9	13.0	13.4	13.6	14.0	13.0	12.3	12.3	14.2	14.7	160.2
Snow, Ice pellets 1.0" or more	6.1	5.9	5.0	2.7	0.3	0.0	0.0	0.0	0.0	0.5	3.3	6.5	30.2
Thunderstorms	*	0.0	0.1	0.5	1.9	4.3	6.7	4.1	1.3	1.0	*	0.0	20.1
Fog, Visibility 1/4 mile or less	2.0	1.6	1.7	2.2	1.0	1.6	2.6	2.3	3.2	2.3	3.7	2.7	26.9
Temperature Maximum:													
90° and above	0.0	0.0	0.0	0.0	0.1	0.5	1.0	0.5	*	0.0	0.0	0.0	2.1
32° and below	26.5	22.8	13.2	1.9	*	0.0	0.0	0.0	0.0	0.4	9.0	23.7	97.5
Temperature Minimum:													
32° and below	30.7	27.9	29.2	22.1	5.5	0.2	0.0	0.0	3.0	14.2	24.8	30.2	187.9
0° and below	16.2	12.6	4.1	*	0.0	0.0	0.0	0.0	0.0	0.0	0.2	10.0	43.1
RELATIVE HUMIDITY (%)													
Morning	74	75	76	79	79	84	84	89	89	86	85	79	82
Afternoon	66	63	61	57	53	56	58	59	60	62	72	71	62
PRECIPITATION (inches)													
Water Equivalent													
Normal	2.3	2.1	2.4	2.5	2.8	3.1	4.0	3.9	3.5	3.1	3.2	3.1	36.5
Maximum monthly	5.1	4.1	5.1	5.2	6.2	7.1	6.8	12.0	8.1	6.3	8.1	7.9	12.0
Date	1978	1955	1953	1973	1947	1940	1957	1981	1954	1970	1983	1973	1981
Minimum monthly	0.1	0.2	0.6	0.5	0.4	0.8	1.7	0.9	0.8	0.6	0.4	0.7	0.1
Date	1944	1978	1965	1967	1982	1983	1977	1957	1968	1955	1939	1963	1944
Maximum in 24 hrs	1.4	1.3	1.7	2.1	2.2	2.3	2.9	6.8	6.2	4.0	2.2	2.8	6.8
Date	1977	1955	1984	1958	1948	1957	1957	1981	1954	1970	1983	1973	1981
SNOW, ICE PELLETS													
Maximum monthly	41.4	41.0	47.1	36.4	10.9	T	0.0	0.0	T	12.1	34.9	59.9	59.9
Date	1978	1960	1955	1982	1967	1980	—	—	1981	1963	1974	1972	1972
Maximum in 24 hrs	15.6	18.2	28.6	21.1	5.8	T	0.0	0.0	T	9.4	15.5	14.7	28.6
Date	1961	1952	1984	1982	1967	1980	—	—	1981	1963	1974	1972	1984
WIND (Resultant)													
Mean speed (mph)	12.4	12.0	12.9	11.7	11.4	10.4	9.8	9.3	10.4	10.9	11.1	11.5	11.2

PORTLAND

Elev. 43' **43° 39'N — 70° 19'W** ## Maine

NORMALS, MEANS, EXTREMES

	JAN	FEB	MAR	APR	MAY	JUN	JUL	AUG	SEP	OCT	NOV	DEC	YEAR
TEMPERATURE													
Normal daily maximum	31.0	33.1	40.5	52.5	63.4	72.8	78.9	77.5	69.6	59.0	47.1	34.9	55.0
Normal daily minimum	11.9	12.9	23.7	33.0	42.1	51.4	57.3	55.8	47.7	37.9	29.6	16.7	35.0
Normal monthly	21.5	23.0	32.1	42.8	52.8	62.1	68.1	66.7	58.7	48.5	38.4	25.8	45.0
Extreme highest	64	64	86	85	92	97	99	103	95	88	74	69	103
Extreme highest date	1950	1957	1946	1957	1979	1941	1977	1975	1983	1963	1974	1982	1975
Extreme lowest	-26	-39	-21	8	23	33	40	33	23	15	5	-21	-39
Extreme lowest date	1971	1943	1950	1954	1956	1944	1965	1965	1941	1976	1940	1963	1943
DEGREE DAYS BASE 65° F													
Heating	1349	1176	1020	666	378	107	22	54	201	515	798	1215	7501
Cooling	0	0	0	0	0	23	118	104	9	0	0	0	254
% OF POSSIBLE SUNSHINE	56	59	56	55	55	59	64	64	62	58	48	52	57
AVERAGE SKY COVER													
Sunrise - Sunset	6.1	6.0	6.4	6.6	6.7	6.4	6.2	5.9	5.7	5.7	6.6	6.2	6.2
NUMBER OF DAYS (Sunrise-Sunset)													
Clear	10.2	8.8	8.7	7.7	6.5	7.3	7.4	9.2	10.6	10.6	7.5	9.2	103.7
Partly cloudy	6.4	7.1	7.1	7.2	9.5	9.7	11.4	10.7	7.8	7.7	7.1	7.3	99.1
Cloudy	14.4	12.4	15.2	15.1	15.0	13.0	12.2	11.1	11.7	12.6	15.4	14.5	162.5
Precipitation .01" or more	11.1	10.1	11.3	11.8	12.6	11.4	9.5	9.4	8.3	9.0	11.6	11.6	127.7
Snow, Ice pellets 1.0" or more	4.6	3.9	3.4	0.8	0.1	0.0	0.0	0.0	0.0	0.1	1.0	3.8	17.7
Thunderstorms	*	0.1	0.4	0.6	1.9	4.1	4.4	3.5	1.6	0.6	0.4	0.1	17.6
Fog, Visibility 1/4 mile or less	1.9	2.1	3.4	3.0	5.6	5.5	6.5	5.6	5.5	4.9	3.8	2.1	50.0
Temperature Maximum:													
90° and above	0.0	0.0	0.0	0.0	0.1	1.1	1.9	1.5	0.4	0.0	0.0	0.0	5.0
32° and below	17.4	12.3	4.4	0.1	0.0	0.0	0.0	0.0	0.0	0.0	0.8	12.0	47.0
Temperature Minimum:													
32° and below	29.9	26.8	26.1	14.3	2.6	0.0	0.0	0.0	1.1	9.2	19.4	28.8	158.2
0° and below	6.4	4.4	0.7	0.0	0.0	0.0	0.0	0.0	0.0	0.0	0.0	2.9	14.5
RELATIVE HUMIDITY (%)													
Morning	75	74	75	79	84	88	89	89	89	85	82	78	82
Afternoon	61	59	58	54	58	61	59	59	60	59	63	62	59
PRECIPITATION (inches)													
Water Equivalent													
Normal	3.7	3.5	3.9	3.9	3.2	3.0	2.8	2.8	3.2	3.8	4.7	4.5	43.5
Maximum monthly	11.9	7.1	9.9	9.9	9.6	6.7	7.4	8.3	9.8	12.2	13.5	9.6	13.5
Date	1979	1981	1953	1973	1984	1982	1976	1946	1954	1962	1983	1969	1983
Minimum monthly	0.7	0.8	0.8	0.7	0.4	0.7	0.6	0.2	0.3	0.2	0.9	0.9	0.2
Date	1970	1978	1965	1941	1965	1941	1965	1947	1948	1947	1976	1955	1947
Maximum in 24 hrs	3.5	3.4	3.4	5.2	3.2	5.5	2.6	4.1	7.4	7.7	3.9	3.8	7.7
Date	1977	1981	1951	1973	1984	1967	1979	1946	1954	1962	1983	1969	1962
SNOW, ICE PELLETS													
Maximum monthly	62.4	61.2	46.6	15.9	7.0	0.0	0.0	0.0	T	3.8	15.6	54.8	62.4
Date	1979	1969	1956	1982	1945	—	—	—	1959	1969	1972	1970	1979
Maximum in 24 hrs	27.1	21.5	15.5	15.9	7.0	0.0	0.0	0.0	T	3.6	11.1	22.8	27.1
Date	1979	1969	1984	1982	1945	—	—	—	1959	1969	1972	1970	1979
WIND (Resultant)													
Mean speed (mph)	9.2	9.4	10.0	10.0	9.1	8.2	7.6	7.4	7.7	8.3	8.7	9.0	8.7

BALTIMORE

Elev. 148'　　39° 11'N — 76° 40'W　　**Maryland**

NORMALS, MEANS, EXTREMES

	JAN	FEB	MAR	APR	MAY	JUN	JUL	AUG	SEP	OCT	NOV	DEC	YEAR
TEMPERATURE													
Normal daily maximum	41.0	43.7	53.1	65.1	74.2	82.9	87.1	85.5	79.1	67.7	55.9	45.1	65.0
Normal daily minimum	24.3	25.7	33.4	42.9	52.5	61.5	66.5	65.7	58.6	46.1	36.6	27.9	45.1
Normal monthly	32.7	34.7	43.3	54.0	63.4	72.2	76.8	75.6	68.9	56.9	46.3	36.5	55.1
Extreme highest	75	79	87	94	98	100	102	105	100	92	83	77	105
Extreme highest date	1975	1985	1979	1960	1962	1959	1980	1983	1983	1954	1974	1984	1983
Extreme lowest	-7	-3	6	20	32	40	51	48	35	25	13	0	-7
Extreme lowest date	1984	1979	1960	1965	1966	1972	1979	1952	1963	1969	1955	1983	1984
DEGREE DAYS BASE 65° F													
Heating	1001	848	673	334	115	0	0	0	29	261	561	884	4706
Cooling	0	0	0	0	66	221	366	329	146	10	0	0	1138
% OF POSSIBLE SUNSHINE	51	56	55	57	56	62	64	62	60	58	51	48	57
AVERAGE SKY COVER													
Sunrise - Sunset	6.2	6.2	6.3	6.1	6.2	5.7	5.6	5.6	5.3	5.3	6.0	6.3	5.9
NUMBER OF DAYS (Sunrise-Sunset)													
Clear	8.5	8.1	7.5	7.9	7.8	8.3	9.4	9.6	10.9	11.9	8.5	8.5	106.9
Partly cloudy	7.4	6.9	9.0	8.9	10.1	11.3	11.9	10.7	8.5	7.7	8.0	7.1	107.6
Cloudy	15.1	13.3	14.5	13.2	13.1	10.3	9.7	10.7	10.5	11.5	13.4	15.4	150.7
Precipitation .01" or more	10.5	8.9	11.0	11.0	11.0	9.4	9.0	9.7	7.3	7.5	9.0	9.2	113.2
Snow, Ice pellets 1.0" or more	2.0	1.9	1.4	*	0.0	0.0	0.0	0.0	0.0	0.0	0.3	1.0	6.7
Thunderstorms	0.3	0.2	0.9	2.4	3.9	5.6	6.0	5.3	1.9	0.9	0.3	0.1	27.7
Fog, Visibility 1/4 mile or less	3.3	3.5	2.7	1.9	1.8	1.0	0.9	1.1	1.5	2.8	2.6	3.7	27.0
Temperature Maximum:													
90° and above	0.0	0.0	0.0	0.4	1.2	5.9	10.8	7.9	3.5	0.1	0.0	0.0	30.0
32° and below	6.6	4.0	0.6	0.0	0.0	0.0	0.0	0.0	0.0	0.0	0.1	3.6	14.9
Temperature Minimum:													
32° and below	25.5	21.2	14.4	3.1	*	0.0	0.0	0.0	0.0	1.7	11.0	21.1	97.9
0° and below	0.5	0.1	0.0	0.0	0.0	0.0	0.0	0.0	0.0	0.0	0.0	0.1	0.6
RELATIVE HUMIDITY (%)													
Morning	68	67	66	67	76	81	81	83	82	79	73	71	75
Afternoon	57	54	51	48	52	53	53	55	55	54	55	57	54
PRECIPITATION (inches)													
Water Equivalent													
Normal	3.0	2.9	3.7	3.3	3.4	3.7	3.8	4.6	3.4	3.1	3.1	3.4	41.8
Maximum monthly	7.8	7.1	6.8	8.1	7.1	9.9	8.1	18.3	8.6	8.0	7.6	7.4	18.3
Date	1979	1979	1983	1952	1960	1972	1960	1955	1975	1976	1952	1969	1955
Minimum monthly	0.2	0.5	0.9	0.3	0.4	0.1	0.3	0.7	0.2	T	0.3	0.2	T
Date	1955	1978	1966	1985	1964	1954	1955	1951	1967	1963	1981	1955	1963
Maximum in 24 hrs	3.1	3.2	3.1	2.8	3.6	5.2	5.8	7.8	6.0	3.4	3.4	3.3	7.8
Date	1976	1983	1958	1952	1960	1972	1952	1955	1985	1955	1952	1977	1955
SNOW, ICE PELLETS													
Maximum monthly	21.4	33.1	21.6	0.7	T	0.0	0.0	0.0	0.0	0.3	8.4	20.4	33.1
Date	1966	1979	1960	1985	1963	—	—	—	—	1979	1967	1966	1979
Maximum in 24 hrs	12.1	22.8	13.0	0.7	T	0.0	0.0	0.0	0.0	0.3	8.4	14.1	22.8
Date	1966	1983	1962	1985	1963	—	—	—	—	1979	1967	1960	1983
WIND (Resultant)													
Mean speed (mph)	9.8	10.4	11.0	10.7	9.2	8.5	7.9	7.8	8.1	8.7	9.3	9.3	9.2

BOSTON

Elev. 15'   42° 22'N — 71° 02'W   **Massachusetts**

NORMALS, MEANS, EXTREMES

	JAN	FEB	MAR	APR	MAY	JUN	JUL	AUG	SEP	OCT	NOV	DEC	YEAR
TEMPERATURE													
Normal daily maximum	36.4	37.7	45.0	56.6	67.0	76.6	81.8	79.8	72.3	62.5	51.6	40.3	59.0
Normal daily minimum	22.8	23.7	31.8	40.8	50.0	59.3	65.1	63.9	56.9	47.1	38.7	27.1	43.9
Normal monthly	29.6	30.7	38.4	48.7	58.5	68.0	73.5	71.9	64.6	54.8	45.2	33.7	51.5
Extreme highest	63	70	81	94	95	100	102	102	100	90	77	73	102
Extreme highest date	1974	1985	1977	1976	1979	1952	1977	1975	1953	1963	1974	1984	1977
Extreme lowest	-12	-4	6	16	34	45	54	47	38	28	17	-7	-12
Extreme lowest date	1957	1961	1984	1982	1956	1982	1985	1965	1965	1976	1978	1980	1957
DEGREE DAYS BASE 65° F													
Heating	1097	960	825	489	218	25	0	6	80	329	594	970	5593
Cooling	0	0	0	0	17	115	266	220	68	13	0	0	699
% OF POSSIBLE SUNSHINE	53	57	57	57	59	63	66	65	64	60	50	52	59
AVERAGE SKY COVER													
Sunrise - Sunset	6.2	6.1	6.4	6.5	6.5	6.2	6.1	5.7	5.5	5.6	6.4	6.2	6.1
NUMBER OF DAYS (Sunrise-Sunset)													
Clear	9.3	8.4	7.8	7.2	6.4	6.8	6.9	9.2	10.4	10.8	8.0	8.7	100.0
Partly cloudy	6.6	6.8	8.0	8.3	10.0	10.5	12.5	10.8	8.3	7.9	7.2	7.4	104.2
Cloudy	15.1	13.1	15.2	14.4	14.6	12.7	11.6	11.0	11.3	12.2	14.8	14.9	161.0
Precipitation .01" or more	11.6	10.6	11.9	11.2	11.6	10.6	9.1	9.9	8.6	8.9	11.0	11.7	126.7
Snow, Ice pellets 1.0" or more	3.2	2.6	2.1	0.3	0.0	0.0	0.0	0.0	0.0	0.0	0.4	2.2	10.9
Thunderstorms	0.1	0.2	0.5	1.0	2.3	3.6	4.3	3.7	1.7	0.6	0.4	0.2	18.7
Fog, Visibility 1/4 mile or less	1.7	1.7	2.0	1.5	2.8	1.9	2.2	1.9	1.9	2.1	1.9	1.4	23.2
Temperature Maximum:													
90° and above	0.0	0.0	0.0	*	0.4	2.8	5.5	3.1	1.0	0.0	0.0	0.0	12.9
32° and below	12.5	8.0	1.9	*	0.0	0.0	0.0	0.0	0.0	0.0	0.3	5.5	28.2
Temperature Minimum:													
32° and below	26.4	23.1	16.6	2.8	0.0	0.0	0.0	0.0	0.0	0.7	6.8	21.7	98.1
0° and below	0.6	0.4	0.0	0.0	0.0	0.0	0.0	0.0	0.0	0.0	0.0	0.2	1.2
RELATIVE HUMIDITY (%)													
Morning	64	64	66	67	73	77	76	79	79	75	72	68	72
Afternoon	57	56	57	53	59	59	56	59	60	58	60	60	58
PRECIPITATION (inches)													
Water Equivalent													
Normal	3.9	3.7	4.1	3.7	3.5	2.9	2.6	3.6	3.4	3.3	4.2	4.4	43.8
Maximum monthly	10.5	7.8	11.0	7.8	13.3	13.2	8.1	17.0	8.3	8.6	8.8	9.7	17.0
Date	1979	1984	1953	1958	1954	1982	1959	1955	1954	1962	1983	1969	1955
Minimum monthly	0.7	0.8	0.6	1.2	0.5	0.4	0.5	0.8	0.3	0.9	0.6	0.9	0.3
Date	1980	1980	1981	1966	1964	1953	1952	1972	1957	1967	1976	1980	1957
Maximum in 24 hrs	2.7	2.6	4.1	2.3	5.7	4.1	2.4	8.4	5.6	4.2	3.3	4.1	8.4
Date	1979	1969	1968	1983	1954	1984	1959	1955	1954	1962	1955	1969	1955
SNOW, ICE PELLETS													
Maximum monthly	35.9	41.3	31.2	13.3	0.5	0.0	0.0	0.0	0.0	0.2	10.0	27.9	41.3
Date	1978	1969	1956	1982	1977	—	—	—	—	1979	1938	1970	1969
Maximum in 24 hrs	21.0	23.6	17.7	13.2	0.5	0.0	0.0	0.0	0.0	0.2	8.0	13.0	23.6
Date	1978	1978	1960	1982	1977	—	—	—	—	1979	1940	1960	1978
WIND (Resultant)													
Mean speed (mph)	13.9	13.8	13.8	13.2	12.1	11.3	10.9	10.6	11.1	11.9	12.8	13.5	12.4

WORCESTER   Elev. 986'   42° 16'N — 71° 52'W   Massachusetts

NORMALS, MEANS, EXTREMES

	JAN	FEB	MAR	APR	MAY	JUN	JUL	AUG	SEP	OCT	NOV	DEC	YEAR
TEMPERATURE													
Normal daily maximum	30.9	32.9	41.1	54.5	65.9	74.4	79.0	77.0	69.4	59.3	46.9	34.7	55.5
Normal daily minimum	15.6	16.6	25.2	35.4	45.5	54.8	60.7	59.0	51.3	41.3	32.0	20.1	38.1
Normal monthly	23.3	24.8	33.2	45.0	55.7	64.6	69.9	68.0	60.4	50.3	39.5	27.4	46.8
Extreme highest	60	67	80	91	92	93	94	96	91	85	78	70	96
Extreme highest date	1974	1985	1977	1976	1962	1956	1964	1975	1983	1963	1982	1984	1975
Extreme lowest	-19	-12	-4	11	28	37	46	38	30	20	9	-13	-19
Extreme lowest date	1957	1967	1967	1982	1970	1980	1963	1965	1957	1969	1972	1962	1957
DEGREE DAYS BASE 65° F													
Heating	1293	1126	989	600	296	68	10	22	159	456	765	1166	6950
Cooling	0	0	0	0	8	56	162	115	18	0	0	0	359
% OF POSSIBLE SUNSHINE	na	na	na	na	na	na	na	na	na	na	na	na	na
AVERAGE SKY COVER													
Sunrise - Sunset	6.1	6.2	6.6	6.5	6.7	6.5	6.3	6.0	5.8	5.8	6.7	6.5	6.3
NUMBER OF DAYS (Sunrise-Sunset)													
Clear	8.9	7.6	7.4	7.0	6.1	5.9	6.1	7.6	9.1	10.0	7.0	7.5	90.1
Partly cloudy	7.9	7.1	7.9	8.7	9.6	10.9	12.1	11.4	8.7	8.4	7.5	7.8	108.2
Cloudy	14.2	13.6	15.7	14.3	15.3	13.2	12.8	12.0	12.2	12.6	15.4	15.7	167.0
Precipitation .01" or more	11.5	10.9	12.0	11.2	12.0	11.1	9.8	10.2	9.1	8.6	11.7	12.9	131.0
Snow, Ice pellets 1.0" or more	4.3	3.7	3.2	1.0	0.1	0.0	0.0	0.0	0.0	0.2	0.8	3.8	17.1
Thunderstorms	*	0.1	0.7	1.2	3.0	4.2	5.3	4.1	1.5	1.0	0.5	0.1	21.6
Fog, Visibility 1/4 mile or less	5.7	5.6	7.6	7.0	7.1	8.0	6.3	6.2	8.2	7.2	7.9	7.0	83.8
Temperature Maximum:													
90° and above	0.0	0.0	0.0	*	0.1	0.7	1.3	0.5	*	0.0	0.0	0.0	2.7
32° and below	18.5	13.7	5.7	0.2	0.0	0.0	0.0	0.0	0.0	0.0	1.7	13.6	53.4
Temperature Minimum:													
32° and below	29.7	26.8	25.8	11.5	0.7	0.0	0.0	0.0	0.1	5.0	16.5	27.9	144.0
0° and below	3.4	2.0	0.1	0.0	0.0	0.0	0.0	0.0	0.0	0.0	0.0	0.9	6.4
RELATIVE HUMIDITY (%)													
Morning	69	68	68	67	72	78	78	81	83	78	76	73	74
Afternoon	58	57	54	49	51	56	57	59	61	56	61	62	57
PRECIPITATION (inches)													
Water Equivalent													
Normal	3.8	3.2	4.1	3.9	3.8	3.4	3.5	4.4	4.2	4.2	4.4	4.2	47.6
Maximum monthly	11.1	8.3	7.9	8.5	9.9	12.1	8.1	7.3	13.1	8.5	10.4	9.8	13.1
Date	1979	1981	1972	1983	1984	1982	1959	1979	1974	1962	1972	1973	1974
Minimum monthly	0.8	0.7	0.7	1.2	0.8	0.7	1.0	1.0	0.8	1.4	0.6	1.0	0.6
Date	1970	1980	1981	1985	1959	1979	1957	1981	1957	1963	1976	1980	1976
Maximum in 24 hrs	2.9	2.4	3.8	2.3	3.0	3.2	3.8	3.9	4.7	3.7	2.9	2.6	4.7
Date	1978	1973	1968	1959	1967	1982	1985	1985	1960	1959	1972	1973	1960
SNOW, ICE PELLETS													
Maximum monthly	44.0	45.2	36.5	15.1	12.7	0.0	0.0	0.0	0.0	7.5	20.7	32.1	45.2
Date	1966	1962	1958	1982	1977	—	—	—	—	1979	1971	1970	1962
Maximum in 24 hrs	18.7	24.0	16.6	14.9	12.7	0.0	0.0	0.0	0.0	7.5	14.8	15.6	24.0
Date	1961	1962	1960	1982	1977	—	—	—	—	1979	1971	1961	1962
WIND (Resultant)													
Mean speed (mph)	12.0	11.8	11.6	11.3	10.2	9.0	8.5	8.3	8.7	9.4	10.2	10.9	10.2

ALPENA

Elev. 689'   **45° 04'N — 83° 34'W**   # Michigan

NORMALS, MEANS, EXTREMES

	JAN	FEB	MAR	APR	MAY	JUN	JUL	AUG	SEP	OCT	NOV	DEC	YEAR
TEMPERATURE													
Normal daily maximum	26.2	28.1	36.9	51.1	64.4	74.2	79.0	76.8	68.1	57.5	42.8	30.9	53.0
Normal daily minimum	8.5	7.8	16.7	29.4	38.6	48.1	53.0	52.1	45.0	36.6	27.3	16.0	31.6
Normal monthly	17.4	18.0	26.8	40.3	51.5	61.2	66.0	64.5	56.6	47.1	35.1	23.5	42.3
Extreme highest	52	65	73	89	94	98	102	95	94	88	76	65	102
Extreme highest date	1973	1984	1977	1985	1962	1983	1983	1965	1983	1971	1978	1982	1983
Extreme lowest	-28	-37	-27	0	20	28	34	30	26	16	-1	-18	-37
Extreme lowest date	1963	1979	1962	1965	1966	1966	1965	1982	1965	1966	1976	1985	1979
DEGREE DAYS BASE 65° F													
Heating	1476	1316	1184	741	419	137	51	91	256	555	897	1287	8410
Cooling	0	0	0	0	0	23	82	75	0	0	0	0	180
% OF POSSIBLE SUNSHINE	38	44	53	54	59	63	67	60	52	44	30	27	49
AVERAGE SKY COVER													
Sunrise - Sunset	7.8	7.4	6.8	6.7	6.3	6.0	5.6	5.8	6.6	7.0	8.2	8.4	6.9
NUMBER OF DAYS (Sunrise-Sunset)													
Clear	3.1	4.3	6.2	6.8	7.2	7.4	8.0	8.9	6.0	5.3	2.5	1.7	67.2
Partly cloudy	7.5	7.2	8.0	7.5	9.8	10.9	13.2	10.8	10.0	8.5	6.2	6.0	105.6
Cloudy	20.4	16.8	16.8	15.7	14.0	11.7	9.8	11.3	14.0	17.3	21.3	23.3	192.4
Precipitation .01" or more	14.2	11.3	12.5	11.6	11.8	11.0	9.8	11.0	12.4	11.8	13.2	16.0	146.6
Snow, Ice pellets 1.0" or more	6.8	4.8	4.0	1.5	0.1	0.0	0.0	0.0	0.0	0.3	2.3	6.7	26.4
Thunderstorms	0.1	*	0.8	2.5	3.8	5.7	6.8	6.1	3.9	1.4	0.3	0.2	31.6
Fog, Visibility 1/4 mile or less	1.2	1.7	2.7	2.3	2.4	2.6	2.2	3.2	2.6	3.3	2.4	1.4	28.0
Temperature Maximum:													
90° and above	0.0	0.0	0.0	0.0	0.4	1.5	2.4	1.1	0.4	0.0	0.0	0.0	5.7
32° and below	23.0	18.7	9.6	0.9	0.0	0.0	0.0	0.0	0.0	*	3.8	17.8	73.8
Temperature Minimum:													
32° and below	30.5	27.5	28.3	19.2	7.7	0.8	0.0	0.1	2.4	11.3	21.9	28.9	178.6
0° and below	8.9	8.5	3.4	*	0.0	0.0	0.0	0.0	0.0	0.0	*	3.3	24.2
RELATIVE HUMIDITY (%)													
Morning	79	77	78	76	79	85	85	89	88	84	82	82	82
Afternoon	70	66	62	54	51	53	53	58	62	61	69	74	61
PRECIPITATION (inches)													
Water Equivalent													
Normal	1.6	1.3	1.9	2.5	2.8	3.1	3.1	3.1	2.9	1.9	2.2	1.9	28.7
Maximum monthly	3.3	3.1	4.4	4.1	8.2	8.3	7.1	5.9	6.6	4.7	7.4	4.4	8.3
Date	1978	1971	1976	1980	1983	1969	1975	1984	1968	1969	1966	1971	1969
Minimum monthly	0.1	0.1	0.6	1.1	1.0	1.0	0.9	0.9	0.2	0.6	0.7	0.6	0.1
Date	1961	1982	1974	1978	1966	1985	1966	1970	1979	1971	1962	1976	1982
Maximum in 24 hrs	1.8	1.2	1.3	1.2	2.5	2.6	3.1	3.1	3.0	1.7	1.9	1.6	3.1
Date	1978	1977	1971	1965	1973	1969	1974	1968	1968	1985	1966	1971	1968
SNOW, ICE PELLETS													
Maximum monthly	43.5	33.4	35.8	12.3	3.7	0.0	0.0	0.0	T	4.3	30.5	46.3	46.3
Date	1978	1967	1971	1980	1974	—	—	—	1984	1969	1966	1970	1970
Maximum in 24 hrs	16.3	13.7	17.3	8.0	3.7	0.0	0.0	0.0	T	3.8	16.1	12.4	17.3
Date	1978	1981	1985	1973	1974	—	—	—	1984	1969	1966	1970	1985
WIND (Resultant)													
Mean speed (mph)	8.7	8.2	8.9	9.1	8.2	7.4	6.9	6.5	6.9	7.6	8.2	8.4	7.9

DETROIT
Elev. 633' 42° 14'N — 83° 20'W **Michigan**

NORMALS, MEANS, EXTREMES

	JAN	FEB	MAR	APR	MAY	JUN	JUL	AUG	SEP	OCT	NOV	DEC	YEAR
TEMPERATURE													
Normal daily maximum	30.6	33.5	43.4	57.7	69.4	79.0	83.1	81.5	74.4	62.5	47.6	35.4	58.2
Normal daily minimum	16.1	18.0	26.5	36.9	46.7	56.3	60.7	59.4	52.2	41.2	31.4	21.6	38.9
Normal monthly	23.4	25.8	35.0	47.3	58.1	67.7	71.9	70.5	63.3	51.9	39.5	28.5	48.5
Extreme highest	62	65	77	89	92	99	102	97	98	91	77	68	102
Extreme highest date	1965	1976	1977	1977	1977	1971	1977	1964	1976	1963	1968	1982	1977
Extreme lowest	-21	-15	-4	10	25	36	41	38	29	17	9	-10	-21
Extreme lowest date	1984	1985	1978	1982	1966	1972	1965	1982	1974	1974	1969	1983	1984
DEGREE DAYS BASE 65° F													
Heating	1290	1098	930	528	247	36	5	12	106	414	765	1132	6563
Cooling	0	0	0	0	33	117	219	183	55	8	0	0	615
% OF POSSIBLE SUNSHINE	40	46	51	55	61	67	70	69	61	50	34	30	53
AVERAGE SKY COVER													
Sunrise - Sunset	7.6	7.2	7.2	6.7	6.4	5.8	5.5	5.7	6.1	6.3	7.6	7.9	6.7
NUMBER OF DAYS (Sunrise-Sunset)													
Clear	4.2	4.9	5.5	6.3	6.4	7.8	9.4	8.6	8.4	7.7	4.0	3.3	76.6
Partly cloudy	6.6	6.8	7.3	7.4	10.6	11.2	12.1	11.4	9.3	8.8	6.6	6.4	104.6
Cloudy	20.1	16.5	18.2	16.3	13.9	11.0	9.5	11.0	12.3	14.6	19.3	21.3	184.0
Precipitation .01" or more	13.0	11.1	13.3	12.6	11.1	10.5	9.2	9.2	9.6	9.2	11.6	13.9	134.3
Snow, Ice pellets 1.0" or more	3.2	2.9	2.2	0.7	0.0	0.0	0.0	0.0	0.0	*	1.3	3.2	13.4
Thunderstorms	0.1	0.5	1.7	3.6	4.0	6.0	5.9	5.5	3.9	1.1	0.6	0.4	33.2
Fog, Visibility 1/4 mile or less	2.3	2.4	2.4	1.0	0.6	0.8	0.7	1.6	1.6	2.6	2.2	3.1	21.3
Temperature Maximum:													
90° and above	0.0	0.0	0.0	0.0	0.3	2.6	4.7	2.6	1.0	0.1	0.0	0.0	11.2
32° and below	18.1	13.3	4.6	0.2	0.0	0.0	0.0	0.0	0.0	0.0	1.3	12.3	49.9
Temperature Minimum:													
32° and below	29.5	25.4	23.1	10.0	0.9	0.0	0.0	0.0	0.1	5.0	17.1	26.3	137.5
0° and below	4.0	2.4	0.1	0.0	0.0	0.0	0.0	0.0	0.0	0.0	0.0	1.4	7.9
RELATIVE HUMIDITY (%)													
Morning	78	77	76	74	76	79	81	83	83	80	79	79	79
Afternoon	69	65	61	55	53	54	53	56	57	57	66	71	60
PRECIPITATION (inches)													
Water Equivalent													
Normal	1.8	1.6	2.5	3.1	2.7	3.4	3.1	3.2	2.2	2.1	2.3	2.5	30.9
Maximum monthly	3.6	3.8	4.4	5.4	5.8	6.6	6.0	7.8	5.8	4.8	5.6	6.0	7.8
Date	1965	1985	1973	1961	1968	1960	1969	1975	1961	1967	1982	1965	1975
Minimum monthly	0.2	0.1	0.8	0.9	1.1	1.0	0.5	0.7	0.4	0.3	0.7	0.4	0.1
Date	1961	1969	1981	1971	1965	1984	1974	1982	1960	1964	1976	1960	1969
Maximum in 24 hrs	1.7	1.4	1.6	1.9	2.8	2.8	3.1	3.2	2.1	2.5	2.2	3.7	3.7
Date	1967	1981	1985	1965	1968	1983	1966	1964	1981	1985	1982	1965	1965
SNOW, ICE PELLETS													
Maximum monthly	29.6	17.4	16.1	9.0	T	0.0	0.0	0.0	0.0	2.9	11.8	34.9	34.9
Date	1978	1962	1965	1982	1976	—	—	—	—	1980	1966	1974	1974
Maximum in 24 hrs	10.0	10.3	9.2	7.4	T	0.0	0.0	0.0	0.0	2.9	5.6	19.2	19.2
Date	1982	1965	1973	1982	1976	—	—	—	—	1980	1977	1974	1974
WIND (Resultant)													
Mean speed (mph)	11.7	11.4	11.8	11.7	10.1	9.1	8.4	8.2	8.7	9.6	10.9	11.4	10.2

FLINT

Elev. 771'   42° 58'N — 83° 45'W   **Michigan**

NORMALS, MEANS, EXTREMES

	JAN	FEB	MAR	APR	MAY	JUN	JUL	AUG	SEP	OCT	NOV	DEC	YEAR
TEMPERATURE													
Normal daily maximum	28.6	31.3	39.6	55.9	67.6	77.0	81.2	79.4	72.0	60.6	46.2	33.9	56.1
Normal daily minimum	14.0	15.3	24.5	35.7	45.2	54.8	58.9	57.5	50.4	40.6	31.3	20.4	37.4
Normal monthly	21.3	23.3	32.1	45.8	56.4	65.9	70.1	68.5	61.2	50.6	38.8	27.2	46.7
Extreme highest	60	63	77	85	90	96	99	97	93	89	76	67	99
Extreme highest date	1965	1984	1963	1985	1962	1971	1977	1965	1983	1963	1978	1982	1977
Extreme lowest	-25	-22	-12	6	22	33	40	37	27	19	6	-11	-25
Extreme lowest date	1976	1967	1978	1982	1966	1966	1965	1982	1957	1974	1976	1976	1976
DEGREE DAYS BASE 65° F													
Heating	1355	1168	1020	576	288	67	9	28	144	455	786	1172	7068
Cooling	0	0	0	0	21	94	167	136	30	8	0	0	456
% OF POSSIBLE SUNSHINE	na	na	na	na	na	na	na	na	na	na	na	na	na
AVERAGE SKY COVER													
Sunrise - Sunset	7.8	7.4	7.3	6.9	6.6	6.2	5.8	5.9	6.3	6.6	8.0	8.2	6.9
NUMBER OF DAYS (Sunrise-Sunset)													
Clear	3.4	4.0	5.1	6.1	6.0	6.1	7.7	8.2	7.1	7.4	2.7	2.7	66.4
Partly cloudy	6.7	6.9	7.1	7.0	9.7	12.0	13.1	11.6	10.3	9.0	6.3	5.9	105.5
Cloudy	20.9	17.4	18.8	16.9	15.3	12.0	10.2	11.2	12.6	14.6	21.0	22.4	193.3
Precipitation .01" or more	12.8	11.2	12.8	12.4	10.9	10.2	9.3	9.2	9.8	9.1	12.2	13.4	133.2
Snow, Ice pellets 1.0" or more	3.6	3.2	2.6	0.6	0.0	0.0	0.0	0.0	0.0	*	1.2	3.3	14.5
Thunderstorms	0.2	0.2	1.3	2.6	4.1	6.2	6.3	5.8	3.5	1.4	0.8	0.3	32.5
Fog, Visibility 1/4 mile or less	1.6	1.6	1.6	0.8	1.0	0.9	1.1	2.1	1.9	2.3	1.6	1.9	18.5
Temperature Maximum:													
90° and above	0.0	0.0	0.0	0.0	0.0	0.9	2.2	1.2	0.6	0.0	0.0	0.0	4.9
32° and below	19.3	14.8	5.5	0.5	0.0	0.0	0.0	0.0	0.0	0.0	2.1	13.2	55.5
Temperature Minimum:													
32° and below	29.3	25.4	23.0	10.4	1.8	0.0	0.0	0.0	0.1	5.5	15.8	25.9	137.1
0° and below	4.7	3.6	0.6	0.0	0.0	0.0	0.0	0.0	0.0	0.0	0.0	1.6	10.6
RELATIVE HUMIDITY (%)													
Morning	77	76	75	73	75	79	81	84	85	80	80	79	79
Afternoon	71	67	63	56	55	57	56	57	60	60	68	73	62
PRECIPITATION (inches)													
Water Equivalent													
Normal	1.5	1.4	2.1	3.0	2.7	3.2	2.8	3.3	2.3	2.1	2.2	2.0	29.2
Maximum monthly	3.5	5.2	4.3	5.9	7.3	5.8	7.9	11.0	8.6	4.2	4.9	4.6	11.0
Date	1947	1954	1948	1947	1945	1949	1957	1975	1950	1954	1973	1971	1975
Minimum monthly	0.0	0.1	0.2	0.6	0.9	0.9	0.7	0.4	0.3	0.3	0.6	0.4	0.0
Date	1945	1969	1958	1942	1958	1952	1978	1969	1979	1944	1980	1969	1945
Maximum in 24 hrs	1.8	2.8	2.3	2.8	2.2	3.5	3.7	4.4	6.0	3.1	2.1	1.7	6.0
Date	1967	1954	1948	1976	1974	1943	1957	1968	1950	1981	1952	1971	1950
SNOW, ICE PELLETS													
Maximum monthly	28.5	19.7	19.4	17.3	0.6	0.0	0.0	0.0	T	2.6	16.2	24.9	28.5
Date	1976	1965	1965	1975	1961	—	—	—	1975	1967	1951	1951	1976
Maximum in 24 hrs	19.8	11.3	12.6	16.7	0.5	0.0	0.0	0.0	T	2.6	13.4	9.7	19.8
Date	1967	1965	1973	1975	1961	—	—	—	1975	1967	1951	1970	1967
WIND (Resultant)													
Mean speed (mph)	11.8	11.4	12.0	11.7	10.2	9.0	8.2	7.8	8.9	9.8	11.2	11.4	10.3

NORMALS, MEANS, EXTREMES

	JAN	FEB	MAR	APR	MAY	JUN	JUL	AUG	SEP	OCT	NOV	DEC	YEAR
TEMPERATURE													
Normal daily maximum	29.0	31.7	41.6	56.9	69.4	78.9	83.0	81.1	73.4	61.4	46.0	33.8	57.2
Normal daily minimum	14.9	15.6	24.5	35.6	45.5	55.3	59.8	58.1	50.8	40.4	30.9	20.7	37.7
Normal monthly	22.0	23.7	33.1	46.3	57.5	67.1	71.4	69.6	62.1	50.9	38.5	27.3	47.4
Extreme highest	62	67	77	88	92	96	97	100	93	87	77	67	100
Extreme highest date	1967	1976	1981	1970	1978	1971	1966	1964	1973	1975	1975	1982	1964
Extreme lowest	-21	-19	-8	3	22	33	41	39	28	18	5	-18	-21
Extreme lowest date	1979	1973	1978	1982	1966	1972	1983	1976	1974	1974	1977	1983	1979
DEGREE DAYS BASE 65° F													
Heating	1333	1156	989	561	262	54	12	23	130	443	795	1169	6927
Cooling	0	0	0	0	29	117	210	165	43	6	0	0	570
% OF POSSIBLE SUNSHINE	30	40	44	51	55	61	64	61	54	44	28	22	46
AVERAGE SKY COVER													
Sunrise - Sunset	8.4	7.7	7.5	6.8	6.5	6.2	5.7	5.8	6.4	7.0	8.2	8.7	7.1
NUMBER OF DAYS (Sunrise-Sunset)													
Clear	2.5	3.6	4.4	6.5	6.5	6.3	8.5	8.6	7.2	5.6	3.1	1.9	64.8
Partly cloudy	4.7	6.0	6.9	6.9	9.6	11.6	12.2	10.8	9.1	8.2	5.2	4.0	95.3
Cloudy	23.8	18.7	19.7	16.7	14.8	12.0	10.2	11.6	13.7	17.1	21.7	25.1	205.2
Precipitation .01" or more	16.3	11.7	13.0	13.1	10.8	10.1	9.1	9.4	10.0	10.9	13.3	16.7	144.5
Snow, Ice pellets 1.0" or more	6.9	3.8	3.2	0.9	0.0	0.0	0.0	0.0	0.0	0.1	2.7	6.0	23.5
Thunderstorms	0.3	0.3	1.8	3.7	3.9	6.0	6.2	5.5	4.0	1.4	1.5	0.5	35.2
Fog, Visibility 1/4 mile or less	2.0	2.2	2.5	2.0	1.5	1.4	1.4	2.4	2.3	2.5	2.6	3.7	26.6
Temperature Maximum:													
90° and above	0.0	0.0	0.0	0.0	0.5	1.9	4.9	2.5	0.5	0.0	0.0	0.0	10.1
32° and below	20.1	15.3	5.8	0.5	0.0	0.0	0.0	0.0	0.0	0.0	2.5	14.4	58.6
Temperature Minimum:													
32° and below	29.6	26.0	23.9	12.1	2.4	0.0	0.0	0.0	0.3	5.9	17.6	27.5	145.3
0° and below	4.3	3.2	0.5	0.0	0.0	0.0	0.0	0.0	0.0	0.0	0.0	1.4	9.3
RELATIVE HUMIDITY (%)													
Morning	80	78	77	75	76	80	82	85	85	81	81	81	80
Afternoon	72	68	64	58	53	55	55	58	61	62	70	75	63
PRECIPITATION (inches)													
Water Equivalent													
Normal	1.9	1.5	2.4	3.5	3.0	3.8	3.0	3.4	3.1	2.8	2.9	2.5	34.3
Maximum monthly	4.3	3.2	5.1	6.1	8.2	8.2	6.4	7.3	9.5	6.3	7.8	6.6	9.5
Date	1975	1985	1974	1981	1981	1967	1969	1975	1981	1969	1966	1971	1981
Minimum monthly	0.4	0.3	1.0	2.1	1.0	0.6	0.8	0.1	T	0.6	1.5	0.6	T
Date	1981	1969	1968	1984	1971	1984	1976	1969	1979	1964	1976	1969	1979
Maximum in 24 hrs	1.8	1.5	1.7	2.0	5.4	3.2	2.5	2.3	3.1	2.0	2.6	2.7	5.4
Date	1975	1985	1985	1976	1981	1972	1969	1980	1981	1969	1966	1982	1981
SNOW, ICE PELLETS													
Maximum monthly	45.5	21.3	36.0	12.4	0.1	0.0	0.0	0.0	T	8.4	16.6	34.8	45.5
Date	1979	1985	1965	1982	1976	—	—	—	1967	1967	1966	1983	1979
Maximum in 24 hrs	16.1	9.1	13.2	9.8	0.1	0.0	0.0	0.0	T	8.4	8.3	15.1	16.1
Date	1978	1985	1970	1975	1976	—	—	—	1967	1967	1965	1970	1978
WIND (Resultant)													
Mean speed (mph)	11.4	10.6	11.1	11.1	9.7	8.8	8.2	7.8	8.4	9.4	10.3	10.8	9.8

NORMALS, MEANS, EXTREMES

	JAN	FEB	MAR	APR	MAY	JUN	JUL	AUG	SEP	OCT	NOV	DEC	YEAR
TEMPERATURE													
Normal daily maximum	25.2	28.0	37.3	52.6	65.8	74.8	78.9	76.5	68.0	56.7	41.8	29.9	53.0
Normal daily minimum	8.7	8.0	17.5	31.2	41.5	50.8	55.0	53.8	46.5	37.5	27.9	15.8	32.8
Normal monthly	17.0	18.0	27.4	41.9	53.7	62.8	67.0	65.2	57.3	47.1	34.9	22.9	42.9
Extreme highest	53	59	67	86	89	93	96	92	92	85	70	63	96
Extreme highest date	1973	1984	1977	1980	1978	1971	1977	1975	1985	1971	1978	1982	1977
Extreme lowest	-26	-34	-23	3	21	29	33	29	24	16	0	-21	-34
Extreme lowest date	1981	1979	1967	1982	1966	1972	1965	1982	1976	1969	1976	1976	1979
DEGREE DAYS BASE 65° F													
Heating	1488	1316	1166	693	364	129	42	89	242	561	903	1305	8298
Cooling	0	0	0	0	14	63	104	95	11	6	0	0	293
% OF POSSIBLE SUNSHINE	na	na	na	na	na	na	na	na	na	na	na	na	na
AVERAGE SKY COVER													
Sunrise - Sunset	8.0	7.4	7.1	6.7	6.5	6.1	5.7	5.8	6.5	7.1	8.3	8.4	7.0
NUMBER OF DAYS (Sunrise-Sunset)													
Clear	2.9	4.5	5.8	6.7	7.1	6.5	8.0	8.8	6.1	5.4	2.5	2.4	66.5
Partly cloudy	6.7	6.3	6.7	7.0	9.7	11.5	13.1	10.5	9.7	7.9	5.1	5.5	99.3
Cloudy	21.5	17.5	18.6	16.4	14.3	12.0	10.0	11.8	14.2	17.8	22.5	23.1	199.5
Precipitation .01" or more	15.1	11.6	12.5	12.0	10.6	11.0	9.2	9.6	11.7	11.6	13.1	15.5	143.6
Snow, Ice pellets 1.0" or more	6.6	4.9	3.8	1.7	0.1	0.0	0.0	0.0	0.0	0.2	3.2	6.0	26.5
Thunderstorms	0.1	0.1	0.9	2.4	4.4	6.0	6.4	6.2	4.4	1.7	0.6	0.3	33.6
Fog, Visibility 1/4 mile or less	2.0	1.8	2.5	1.6	1.2	1.3	2.2	3.9	3.7	3.4	3.0	3.3	29.8
Temperature Maximum:													
90° and above	0.0	0.0	0.0	0.0	0.0	0.5	1.1	0.3	*	0.0	0.0	0.0	2.0
32° and below	24.9	18.9	9.4	1.0	0.0	0.0	0.0	0.0	0.0	0.0	5.5	20.0	79.7
Temperature Minimum:													
32° and below	30.8	27.7	27.7	18.0	5.4	0.3	0.0	*	1.5	9.6	22.1	29.6	172.9
0° and below	9.6	8.7	3.1	0.0	0.0	0.0	0.0	0.0	0.0	0.0	*	3.2	24.8
RELATIVE HUMIDITY (%)													
Morning	83	81	80	77	78	84	84	88	88	85	86	86	83
Afternoon	72	70	65	56	51	55	55	60	63	65	74	77	64
PRECIPITATION (inches)													
Water Equivalent													
Normal	1.4	1.3	1.8	2.5	2.5	3.1	2.8	2.9	2.7	2.2	2.2	1.8	27.9
Maximum monthly	3.1	3.3	5.6	4.5	5.9	6.6	4.9	7.1	6.7	5.4	4.8	4.4	7.1
Date	1974	1971	1976	1967	1983	1969	1975	1975	1978	1969	1966	1971	1975
Minimum monthly	0.6	0.2	0.8	1.2	0.4	0.9	0.8	0.8	0.0	0.4	0.7	0.6	0.0
Date	1977	1982	1968	1968	1966	1977	1979	1969	1979	1971	1976	1976	1979
Maximum in 24 hrs	1.3	1.4	2.1	1.3	1.9	2.5	3.8	3.1	2.5	1.5	1.8	1.7	3.8
Date	1974	1971	1976	1971	1973	1969	1984	1981	1985	1970	1966	1971	1984
SNOW, ICE PELLETS													
Maximum monthly	38.0	23.6	28.7	11.6	2.3	0.0	T	0.0	0.1	4.4	18.9	30.4	38.0
Date	1982	1971	1971	1979	1979	—	1970	—	1967	1980	1968	1968	1982
Maximum in 24 hrs	15.4	8.5	11.7	7.6	2.3	0.0	T	0.0	0.1	3.5	14.4	13.2	15.4
Date	1978	1974	1970	1979	1979	—	1970	—	1967	1980	1981	1980	1978
WIND (Resultant)													
Mean speed (mph)	10.1	9.2	9.3	9.8	9.0	8.0	7.6	7.2	8.0	9.1	9.9	9.6	8.9

LANSING
Elev. 841' 42° 47'N — 84° 36'W # Michigan

NORMALS, MEANS, EXTREMES

	JAN	FEB	MAR	APR	MAY	JUN	JUL	AUG	SEP	OCT	NOV	DEC	YEAR
TEMPERATURE													
Normal daily maximum	29.0	31.7	41.7	56.8	69.1	78.5	82.6	80.9	73.2	61.3	46.3	34.0	57.1
Normal daily minimum	14.1	14.9	24.2	35.6	45.3	55.1	58.9	57.3	50.0	40.0	30.6	20.1	37.2
Normal monthly	21.6	23.3	33.0	46.2	57.2	66.8	70.8	69.1	61.6	50.7	38.5	27.1	47.1
Extreme highest	66	64	78	86	94	96	99	100	97	89	77	66	100
Extreme highest date	1967	1984	1963	1980	1977	1964	1977	1964	1973	1963	1975	1982	1964
Extreme lowest	-29	-24	-15	-2	19	30	37	35	26	15	4	-17	-29
Extreme lowest date	1981	1967	1978	1982	1966	1966	1972	1976	1976	1966	1976	1976	1981
DEGREE DAYS BASE 65° F													
Heating	1345	1168	992	561	269	58	12	25	132	452	795	1178	6987
Cooling	0	0	0	0	28	112	192	156	33	9	0	0	530
% OF POSSIBLE SUNSHINE	36	44	48	53	62	66	70	66	59	51	31	29	51
AVERAGE SKY COVER													
Sunrise - Sunset	7.9	7.4	7.3	6.8	6.4	6.0	5.5	5.6	6.0	6.3	7.8	8.2	6.8
NUMBER OF DAYS (Sunrise-Sunset)													
Clear	3.0	4.2	5.1	6.4	6.8	7.2	8.8	9.0	8.3	7.5	3.9	2.8	73.0
Partly cloudy	6.8	6.9	7.5	7.1	10.0	11.7	12.9	11.5	9.2	8.8	5.9	5.5	104.0
Cloudy	21.1	17.2	18.4	16.5	14.1	11.1	9.3	10.5	12.5	14.7	20.3	22.6	188.3
Precipitation .01" or more	15.2	12.1	13.7	12.6	10.8	10.4	9.6	9.5	9.8	8.9	12.5	15.1	140.3
Snow, Ice pellets 1.0" or more	3.7	3.0	2.8	0.8	0.0	0.0	0.0	0.0	0.0	0.1	1.7	3.8	16.0
Thunderstorms	0.2	0.2	1.5	3.0	3.9	6.4	6.2	5.7	3.8	1.3	1.0	0.5	33.8
Fog, Visibility 1/4 mile or less	1.8	1.8	2.3	1.0	1.0	1.2	1.2	2.5	2.1	2.6	2.0	2.5	21.9
Temperature Maximum:													
90° and above	0.0	0.0	0.0	0.0	0.4	2.0	4.3	2.5	1.0	0.0	0.0	0.0	10.2
32° and below	20.0	15.1	5.9	0.5	0.0	0.0	0.0	0.0	0.0	0.0	2.8	14.0	58.3
Temperature Minimum:													
32° and below	29.6	26.3	24.5	12.6	2.7	0.1	0.0	0.0	0.7	7.7	18.0	26.8	149.0
0° and below	6.0	4.9	1.0	*	0.0	0.0	0.0	0.0	0.0	0.0	0.0	2.3	14.3
RELATIVE HUMIDITY (%)													
Morning	82	81	80	77	78	81	85	88	88	84	84	84	83
Afternoon	76	70	66	59	55	57	56	58	62	64	72	77	64
PRECIPITATION (inches)													
Water Equivalent													
Normal	1.7	1.5	2.3	2.8	2.5	3.5	2.7	3.0	2.5	2.1	2.3	2.2	29.5
Maximum monthly	3.6	4.2	4.3	5.1	4.9	7.9	5.0	9.8	8.0	4.9	4.6	4.7	9.8
Date	1950	1954	1974	1981	1952	1968	1959	1975	1981	1959	1966	1949	1975
Minimum monthly	0.3	0.2	0.9	1.0	0.6	0.3	0.5	0.1	T	0.2	0.5	0.3	T
Date	1981	1969	1960	1982	1977	1984	1965	1969	1979	1956	1962	1960	1979
Maximum in 24 hrs	1.5	2.4	1.5	2.5	2.7	4.3	2.1	3.7	3.4	3.4	1.5	1.6	4.3
Date	1949	1954	1954	1975	1981	1963	1972	1975	1981	1981	1973	1970	1963
SNOW, ICE PELLETS													
Maximum monthly	34.0	21.3	19.8	17.0	0.3	0.0	0.0	0.0	T	7.5	16.8	27.8	34.0
Date	1978	1973	1971	1970	1954	—	—	—	1967	1967	1966	1951	1978
Maximum in 24 hrs	20.4	9.0	15.5	17.0	0.3	0.0	0.0	0.0	T	7.5	11.0	15.1	20.4
Date	1967	1965	1973	1970	1954	—	—	—	1967	1967	1951	1970	1967
WIND (Resultant)													
Mean speed (mph)	11.9	11.2	11.5	11.5	10.1	9.1	8.1	7.6	8.4	9.4	10.7	11.4	10.1

MARQUETTE

Elev. 677' 46° 32'N — 87° 33'W ## Michigan

NORMALS, MEANS, EXTREMES

	JAN	FEB	MAR	APR	MAY	JUN	JUL	AUG	SEP	OCT	NOV	DEC	YEAR
TEMPERATURE													
Normal daily maximum	20.1	23.8	33.2	47.4	61.5	70.4	75.3	73.3	63.9	53.4	36.5	24.6	48.6
Normal daily minimum	4.1	4.8	13.2	27.4	38.9	48.8	53.8	51.8	44.1	35.2	23.6	11.2	29.7
Normal monthly	12.1	14.3	23.2	37.4	50.2	59.6	64.6	62.6	54.0	44.3	30.1	17.9	39.2
Extreme highest	46	61	61	92	89	89	95	93	92	76	67	59	95
Extreme highest date	1981	1981	1981	1980	1980	1980	1983	1983	1983	1983	1981	1982	1983
Extreme lowest	-25	-34	-23	-5	17	29	38	34	25	14	-4	-28	-34
Extreme lowest date	1982	1979	1982	1979	1983	1982	1985	1984	1981	1984	1985	1983	1979
DEGREE DAYS BASE 65° F													
Heating	1640	1420	1296	828	469	179	86	123	330	642	1047	1460	9520
Cooling	0	0	0	0	10	17	73	48	0	0	0	0	148
% OF POSSIBLE SUNSHINE	31	33	43	49	54	56	67	56	44	39	27	25	44
NUMBER OF DAYS (Sunrise-Sunset)													
Clear	0.0	0.0	0.0	0.0	0.0	0.0	0.0	0.0	0.0	0.0	0.0	0.0	0.0
Precipitation .01" or more	19.6	14.6	15.9	12.3	11.4	13.0	9.4	11.4	14.4	14.9	15.7	19.4	172.0
Snow, Ice pellets 1.0" or more	11.9	7.3	7.7	4.0	0.1	0.0	0.0	0.0	0.0	2.1	5.6	8.9	47.6
Thunderstorms	0.0	0.1	0.3	1.0	2.3	6.6	6.6	5.4	4.1	2.0	0.0	0.0	28.4
Fog, Visibility 1/4 mile or less	0.6	2.3	3.0	3.1	2.6	1.7	2.6	5.1	4.7	4.0	1.3	2.3	33.3
Temperature Maximum:													
90° and above	0.0	0.0	0.0	0.1	0.0	0.0	1.3	0.1	0.3	0.0	0.0	0.0	1.9
32° and below	28.3	19.7	14.4	2.7	0.0	0.0	0.0	0.0	0.0	0.7	9.3	24.3	99.4
Temperature Minimum:													
32° and below	31.0	27.9	29.3	22.3	8.9	0.3	0.0	0.0	2.4	16.3	26.6	30.4	195.3
0° and below	13.0	11.9	4.7	0.3	0.0	0.0	0.0	0.0	0.0	0.0	0.7	8.4	39.0
PRECIPITATION (inches)													
Water Equivalent													
Normal	2.0	1.8	2.8	3.6	3.9	3.8	3.2	3.2	3.9	3.2	2.9	2.4	37.1
Maximum monthly	3.8	3.6	6.0	6.5	6.4	6.6	4.6	4.7	6.9	7.5	5.7	4.3	7.5
Date	1982	1984	1979	1985	1983	1981	1982	1985	1980	1979	1985	1981	1979
Minimum monthly	1.2	0.5	0.5	1.8	0.7	1.2	0.5	1.4	2.0	2.0	1.9	1.5	0.5
Date	1984	1982	1980	1979	1984	1982	1981	1979	1979	1984	1980	1979	1980
Maximum in 24 hrs	1.1	2.0	2.3	3.0	3.4	2.3	2.6	1.9	2.0	3.6	2.3	2.4	3.6
Date	1982	1983	1984	1985	1983	1979	1985	1980	1983	1985	1983	1985	1985
SNOW, ICE PELLETS													
Maximum monthly	68.8	51.4	59.1	29.2	1.4	0.0	0.0	0.0	0.1	18.6	31.6	82.6	82.6
Date	1982	1985	1985	1982	1980	—	—	—	1980	1979	1983	1981	1981
Maximum in 24 hrs	12.7	20.6	24.9	20.0	1.2	0.0	0.0	0.0	0.1	9.0	13.7	25.8	25.8
Date	1982	1983	1984	1985	1980	—	—	—	1980	1979	1983	1985	1985

MUSKEGON

Elev. 625' 43° 10'N — 86° 15'W **Michigan**

NORMALS, MEANS, EXTREMES

	JAN	FEB	MAR	APR	MAY	JUN	JUL	AUG	SEP	OCT	NOV	DEC	YEAR
TEMPERATURE													
Normal daily maximum	28.9	30.9	40.4	54.6	66.6	76.1	80.3	78.7	71.2	59.7	45.6	34.0	55.6
Normal daily minimum	17.2	17.3	25.2	35.8	45.4	54.8	59.9	59.0	51.7	42.2	32.7	22.6	38.7
Normal monthly	23.1	24.1	32.8	45.2	56.0	65.5	70.1	68.9	61.5	51.0	39.2	28.3	47.1
Extreme highest	63	62	80	86	93	97	95	99	95	83	76	64	99
Extreme highest date	1950	1976	1981	1970	1962	1953	1966	1964	1954	1971	1961	1982	1964
Extreme lowest	-13	-14	-10	1	22	31	40	36	28	21	-14	-15	-15
Extreme lowest date	1948	1973	1943	1982	1947	1972	1945	1979	1984	1980	1950	1976	1976
DEGREE DAYS BASE 65° F													
Heating	1299	1145	998	594	297	76	10	22	132	440	774	1138	6925
Cooling	0	0	0	0	18	91	169	143	24	6	0	0	451
% OF POSSIBLE SUNSHINE	na	na	na	na	na	na	na	na	na	na	na	na	na
AVERAGE SKY COVER													
Sunrise - Sunset	8.9	8.1	7.3	6.6	6.1	5.7	5.0	5.2	5.7	6.4	8.4	8.8	6.9
NUMBER OF DAYS (Sunrise-Sunset)													
Clear	1.5	3.0	5.2	6.8	8.0	8.8	11.5	10.9	9.3	7.7	2.6	1.5	76.9
Partly cloudy	3.3	4.8	7.1	7.4	9.1	10.1	11.0	10.7	9.1	8.2	4.4	3.7	88.9
Cloudy	26.2	20.5	18.8	15.8	13.9	11.1	8.5	9.4	11.6	15.1	22.9	25.7	199.5
Precipitation .01" or more	17.3	13.8	13.6	12.0	11.0	9.6	8.1	8.5	10.0	10.2	13.9	16.2	144.2
Snow, Ice pellets 1.0" or more	10.0	5.8	3.9	0.8	0.0	0.0	0.0	0.0	0.0	0.2	3.1	7.7	31.4
Thunderstorms	0.2	0.4	1.6	3.5	4.5	6.4	6.2	6.2	4.9	2.3	1.1	0.4	37.8
Fog, Visibility 1/4 mile or less	1.5	1.8	2.1	2.0	2.4	2.0	1.5	2.2	1.6	2.4	1.9	1.4	22.9
Temperature Maximum:													
90° and above	0.0	0.0	0.0	0.0	*	0.6	0.9	0.4	0.0	0.0	0.0	0.0	2.0
32° and below	19.9	16.0	6.1	0.4	0.0	0.0	0.0	0.0	0.0	0.0	2.1	14.4	59.0
Temperature Minimum:													
32° and below	29.5	26.2	23.8	11.4	2.0	*	0.0	0.0	0.2	4.7	15.1	26.9	140.0
0° and below	2.0	2.2	0.4	0.0	0.0	0.0	0.0	0.0	0.0	0.0	0.0	0.5	5.0
RELATIVE HUMIDITY (%)													
Morning	80	78	75	72	73	78	81	85	84	79	78	80	79
Afternoon	75	71	64	57	54	57	59	62	64	64	70	76	64
PRECIPITATION (inches)													
Water Equivalent													
Normal	2.3	1.6	2.5	3.1	2.5	2.5	2.4	3.1	2.9	2.7	2.8	2.6	31.5
Maximum monthly	4.5	3.0	6.5	7.1	5.6	5.4	6.6	9.8	8.5	6.5	6.6	5.4	9.8
Date	1982	1960	1976	1947	1984	1967	1952	1975	1961	1969	1985	1949	1975
Minimum monthly	0.4	0.3	0.5	0.8	1.0	0.1	0.4	0.1	0.1	0.3	1.1	0.9	0.1
Date	1956	1982	1958	1942	1961	1959	1951	1969	1979	1944	1962	1960	1969
Maximum in 24 hrs	1.6	1.3	2.3	2.3	2.1	3.1	2.5	3.7	3.6	3.2	2.2	3.0	3.7
Date	1974	1957	1976	1963	1955	1967	1959	1975	1965	1954	1985	1982	1975
SNOW, ICE PELLETS													
Maximum monthly	102.4	45.8	35.7	20.4	0.4	0.0	0.0	0.0	T	4.9	21.5	82.6	102.4
Date	1982	1981	1965	1982	1954	—	—	—	1983	1967	1951	1963	1982
Maximum in 24 hrs	22.0	17.5	9.9	12.2	0.4	0.0	0.0	0.0	T	4.7	9.1	20.1	22.0
Date	1982	1965	1961	1982	1954	—	—	—	1983	1967	1964	1963	1982
WIND (Resultant)													
Mean speed (mph)	12.5	11.7	12.0	11.9	10.1	9.4	8.7	8.5	9.4	10.8	11.8	12.1	10.7

SAULT STE. MARIE

Elev. 718' 46° 28'N — 84° 22'W **Michigan**

NORMALS, MEANS, EXTREMES

	JAN	FEB	MAR	APR	MAY	JUN	JUL	AUG	SEP	OCT	NOV	DEC	YEAR
TEMPERATURE													
Normal daily maximum	21.2	23.1	32.3	47.1	61.0	70.1	75.1	73.4	64.2	53.6	39.0	26.6	48.9
Normal daily minimum	5.4	5.3	15.4	29.0	38.3	46.7	51.9	52.4	45.3	36.9	26.4	12.7	30.5
Normal monthly	13.3	14.2	23.9	38.1	49.7	58.4	63.5	62.9	54.8	45.3	32.7	19.7	39.7
Extreme highest	45	47	75	83	89	93	97	98	95	80	66	60	98
Extreme highest date	1973	1984	1946	1976	1975	1983	1975	1947	1976	1968	1978	1982	1947
Extreme lowest	-36	-35	-24	-2	18	26	36	29	25	16	-10	-25	-36
Extreme lowest date	1982	1979	1943	1982	1966	1982	1985	1982	1981	1981	1976	1980	1982
DEGREE DAYS BASE 65° F													
Heating	1603	1420	1274	807	480	210	101	123	306	611	966	1404	9305
Cooling	0	0	0	0	6	12	55	58	0	0	0	0	131
% OF POSSIBLE SUNSHINE	36	46	54	54	57	58	63	58	45	40	24	27	47
AVERAGE SKY COVER													
Sunrise - Sunset	7.9	7.4	6.9	6.7	6.5	6.3	5.8	6.1	7.1	7.3	8.5	8.3	7.1
NUMBER OF DAYS (Sunrise-Sunset)													
Clear	3.8	4.6	6.5	6.5	7.0	6.8	8.6	7.6	4.7	5.1	1.9	3.2	66.3
Partly cloudy	5.7	5.8	6.8	7.6	8.5	9.8	10.7	10.8	8.7	6.8	4.8	4.4	90.3
Cloudy	21.5	17.8	17.7	15.9	15.5	13.4	11.6	12.6	16.6	19.1	23.4	23.4	208.6
Precipitation .01" or more	19.1	15.0	13.1	11.4	11.2	11.6	10.0	10.7	13.3	13.2	17.3	19.8	165.7
Snow, Ice pellets 1.0" or more	9.2	6.2	4.5	1.7	0.2	0.0	0.0	0.0	*	0.8	5.0	9.4	37.1
Thunderstorms	0.1	0.1	0.7	1.5	3.1	6.0	5.8	5.3	4.2	1.9	0.5	0.1	29.3
Fog, Visibility 1/4 mile or less	1.6	2.0	3.2	2.8	3.0	3.8	4.7	5.9	6.0	5.0	3.0	2.8	43.9
Temperature Maximum:													
90° and above	0.0	0.0	0.0	0.0	0.0	0.1	0.6	0.5	0.1	0.0	0.0	0.0	1.3
32° and below	26.5	22.5	14.4	1.9	0.0	0.0	0.0	0.0	0.0	0.2	7.1	22.1	94.7
Temperature Minimum:													
32° and below	30.7	28.0	29.3	21.6	7.3	0.6	0.0	*	1.8	9.4	22.5	29.8	181.0
0° and below	11.8	9.3	3.4	*	0.0	0.0	0.0	0.0	0.0	0.0	0.2	5.8	30.5
RELATIVE HUMIDITY (%)													
Morning	81	81	81	80	80	88	89	91	91	88	85	84	85
Afternoon	75	72	68	61	56	62	62	63	67	67	75	78	67
PRECIPITATION (inches)													
Water Equivalent													
Normal	2.2	1.6	2.0	2.3	2.9	3.2	3.0	3.4	3.9	2.8	3.2	2.5	33.4
Maximum monthly	4.5	3.7	4.9	5.1	7.4	7.3	6.0	9.4	7.7	6.3	5.7	5.1	9.4
Date	1982	1971	1976	1954	1970	1969	1956	1974	1970	1979	1966	1984	1974
Minimum monthly	0.5	0.5	0.6	0.6	0.8	0.6	0.8	0.5	0.8	0.1	0.8	0.7	0.1
Date	1961	1978	1958	1949	1980	1962	1981	1947	1943	1963	1962	1954	1963
Maximum in 24 hrs	1.3	1.1	1.8	2.6	5.1	5.0	2.7	5.9	2.4	2.0	1.8	1.3	5.9
Date	1950	1977	1976	1954	1970	1970	1965	1974	1984	1979	1963	1971	1974
SNOW, ICE PELLETS													
Maximum monthly	71.0	41.3	34.7	25.8	4.6	T	0.0	0.0	2.7	12.5	34.2	69.3	71.0
Date	1982	1972	1964	1982	1947	1951	—	—	1956	1943	1976	1980	1982
Maximum in 24 hrs	14.2	12.6	11.9	11.5	4.6	T	0.0	0.0	2.7	10.1	14.3	12.5	14.3
Date	1972	1968	1964	1979	1947	1951	—	—	1956	1943	1943	1984	1943
WIND (Resultant)													
Mean speed (mph)	9.9	9.6	10.2	10.5	9.9	8.7	7.9	7.9	8.7	9.3	9.9	9.8	9.3

DULUTH

Elev. 1428' 46° 50'N — 92° 11'W **Minnesota**

NORMALS, MEANS, EXTREMES

	JAN	FEB	MAR	APR	MAY	JUN	JUL	AUG	SEP	OCT	NOV	DEC	YEAR
TEMPERATURE													
Normal daily maximum	15.5	21.7	31.9	47.6	61.3	70.5	76.4	73.6	63.6	53.0	35.2	21.8	47.7
Normal daily minimum	-2.9	2.2	13.9	28.9	39.3	48.2	54.3	52.8	44.3	35.4	21.2	5.8	28.6
Normal monthly	6.3	12.0	22.9	38.3	50.3	59.4	65.4	63.2	54.0	44.2	28.2	13.8	38.1
Extreme highest	52	55	78	88	90	93	97	97	95	86	70	55	97
Extreme highest date	1942	1976	1946	1952	1969	1980	1947	1947	1976	1953	1978	1962	1947
Extreme lowest	-39	-32	-28	-5	17	27	36	33	22	8	-23	-34	-39
Extreme lowest date	1972	1970	1962	1975	1967	1972	1967	1976	1942	1976	1964	1983	1972
DEGREE DAYS BASE 65° F													
Heating	1820	1484	1305	801	456	179	71	115	334	645	1104	1587	9901
Cooling	0	0	0	0	0	11	80	59	0	0	0	0	150
% OF POSSIBLE SUNSHINE	49	52	55	55	56	58	66	60	51	46	35	40	52
AVERAGE SKY COVER													
Sunrise - Sunset	6.7	6.6	6.8	6.9	6.6	6.7	6.0	6.1	6.7	6.8	7.7	7.3	6.7
NUMBER OF DAYS (Sunrise-Sunset)													
Clear	7.2	7.3	7.1	5.9	6.1	5.0	7.0	7.4	6.1	6.5	4.4	5.9	75.9
Partly cloudy	7.1	6.0	7.1	7.8	9.5	10.9	13.3	11.9	8.7	7.8	5.7	6.0	101.9
Cloudy	16.6	14.9	16.8	16.2	15.5	14.1	10.7	11.6	15.3	16.7	19.9	19.1	187.5
Precipitation .01" or more	11.9	10.0	11.0	10.5	12.3	12.7	11.4	11.4	11.6	9.6	11.0	11.6	134.9
Snow, Ice pellets 1.0" or more	4.6	3.7	4.0	1.9	0.3	0.0	0.0	0.0	0.0	0.3	2.9	4.2	21.9
Thunderstorms	0.1	*	0.7	1.5	3.6	7.0	8.2	7.3	3.8	1.3	0.4	0.1	34.1
Fog, Visibility 1/4 mile or less	2.2	2.3	3.5	3.6	5.6	6.8	5.2	6.8	5.8	4.9	3.7	3.1	53.6
Temperature Maximum:													
90° and above	0.0	0.0	0.0	0.0	0.1	0.1	0.8	0.6	0.2	0.0	0.0	0.0	1.8
32° and below	28.7	22.9	15.9	2.2	0.0	0.0	0.0	0.0	0.0	0.5	12.3	26.6	109.0
Temperature Minimum:													
32° and below	31.0	28.0	29.2	20.4	5.3	0.4	0.0	0.0	2.6	11.3	25.2	30.8	184.2
0° and below	18.5	13.1	5.0	0.1	0.0	0.0	0.0	0.0	0.0	0.0	1.6	12.7	51.0
RELATIVE HUMIDITY (%)													
Morning	73	72	73	71	70	79	80	83	83	77	78	77	76
Afternoon	69	65	64	57	53	59	58	63	64	63	70	74	63
PRECIPITATION (inches)													
Water Equivalent													
Normal	1.2	0.9	1.7	2.1	3.1	3.9	3.9	4.1	3.2	2.2	1.6	1.2	29.6
Maximum monthly	4.7	2.3	5.1	5.8	7.6	7.5	8.4	10.3	6.6	7.5	5.0	3.7	10.3
Date	1969	1971	1965	1948	1962	1944	1949	1972	1980	1949	1983	1968	1972
Minimum monthly	0.1	0.2	0.2	0.4	0.1	1.1	0.9	0.7	0.1	0.1	0.1	0.1	0.1
Date	1961	1968	1959	1980	1976	1956	1947	1970	1952	1944	1976	1979	1944
Maximum in 24 hrs	1.7	1.3	2.3	2.2	3.2	4.0	3.4	5.7	3.7	2.9	2.6	2.1	5.7
Date	1975	1965	1977	1954	1979	1958	1974	1978	1972	1973	1968	1950	1978
SNOW, ICE PELLETS													
Maximum monthly	46.8	31.5	45.5	31.5	8.1	0.2	0.0	T	0.7	8.1	37.7	44.3	46.8
Date	1969	1955	1965	1950	1954	1945	—	1949	1985	1966	1983	1950	1969
Maximum in 24 hrs	14.7	17.0	19.4	11.6	4.3	0.2	0.0	T	0.7	7.9	16.6	25.4	25.4
Date	1982	1948	1965	1983	1954	1945	—	1949	1985	1966	1983	1950	1950
WIND (Resultant)													
Mean speed (mph)	11.8	11.4	12.0	12.7	11.9	10.7	9.6	9.5	10.6	11.3	11.8	11.3	11.2

NORMALS, MEANS, EXTREMES

	JAN	FEB	MAR	APR	MAY	JUN	JUL	AUG	SEP	OCT	NOV	DEC	YEAR
TEMPERATURE													
Normal daily maximum	11.1	19.5	32.0	49.1	63.9	73.3	78.5	75.4	64.1	52.8	32.9	17.8	47.5
Normal daily minimum	-11.0	-4.9	8.9	27.1	38.6	49.0	53.7	50.9	41.6	32.8	16.9	-1.4	25.2
Normal monthly	0.1	7.3	20.5	38.1	51.3	61.2	66.1	63.2	52.9	42.8	24.9	8.2	36.4
Extreme highest	48	53	76	93	95	98	98	95	95	88	73	57	98
Extreme highest date	1973	1958	1946	1952	1964	1956	1975	1955	1976	1963	1975	1939	1975
Extreme lowest	-46	-44	-38	-14	11	23	35	30	20	7	-32	-41	-46
Extreme lowest date	1968	1966	1962	1954	1967	1964	1972	1982	1965	1976	1985	1955	1968
DEGREE DAYS BASE 65° F													
Heating	2012	1613	1380	804	439	155	67	116	366	688	1203	1761	10604
Cooling	0	0	0	0	14	41	101	60	0	0	0	0	216
% OF POSSIBLE SUNSHINE	na	na	na	na	na	na	na	na	na	na	na	na	na
AVERAGE SKY COVER													
Sunrise - Sunset	6.6	6.2	6.5	6.5	6.6	6.8	6.1	6.1	6.9	7.2	8.0	7.2	6.7
NUMBER OF DAYS (Sunrise-Sunset)													
Clear	7.7	8.1	8.2	6.9	6.7	4.6	6.7	7.3	5.7	6.2	3.7	6.4	78.0
Partly cloudy	7.6	6.3	7.6	8.5	9.1	11.0	13.5	11.5	8.8	6.9	5.2	5.8	101.8
Cloudy	15.7	13.8	15.2	14.6	15.2	14.5	10.8	12.3	15.5	17.8	21.1	18.8	185.5
Precipitation .01" or more	11.9	9.3	10.1	9.2	11.5	13.0	11.3	11.6	11.6	9.8	11.0	11.8	132.3
Snow, Ice pellets 1.0" or more	3.5	2.9	2.9	1.6	0.3	0.0	0.0	0.0	0.1	0.6	3.2	3.6	18.8
Thunderstorms	0.0	0.0	0.3	0.9	3.3	6.8	8.6	7.1	3.6	1.0	0.1	0.0	31.6
Fog, Visibility 1/4 mile or less	0.8	1.2	1.1	0.9	0.9	0.8	1.4	2.2	1.9	1.4	1.2	1.4	15.3
Temperature Maximum:													
90° and above	0.0	0.0	0.0	0.1	0.2	0.6	2.0	1.0	0.2	0.0	0.0	0.0	4.1
32° and below	29.2	23.9	15.2	2.0	0.2	0.0	0.0	0.0	0.0	0.8	15.2	27.3	113.8
Temperature Minimum:													
32° and below	31.0	28.2	29.8	22.1	7.7	0.4	0.0	0.1	4.4	15.3	28.0	30.8	197.8
0° and below	22.1	17.3	8.6	0.3	0.0	0.0	0.0	0.0	0.0	0.0	3.6	16.7	68.5
RELATIVE HUMIDITY (%)													
Morning	72	71	72	70	72	81	84	87	87	81	83	78	78
Afternoon	68	64	61	53	50	57	57	60	64	63	74	73	62
PRECIPITATION (inches)													
Water Equivalent													
Normal	0.8	0.7	1.1	1.6	2.4	3.6	3.8	2.9	3.1	1.7	1.2	0.9	24.3
Maximum monthly	3.0	1.8	3.0	3.1	6.6	8.1	9.5	11.2	7.3	4.8	3.4	1.6	11.2
Date	1975	1955	1966	1985	1985	1941	1966	1942	1961	1971	1977	1960	1942
Minimum monthly	0.1	0.1	0.1	0.3	0.2	0.7	1.0	0.9	0.2	0.2	0.1	0.1	0.1
Date	1973	1968	1969	1944	1976	1961	1941	1956	1952	1944	1939	1940	1973
Maximum in 24 hrs	1.5	1.1	1.8	1.5	2.4	3.8	4.8	4.8	3.3	2.6	1.5	1.2	4.8
Date	1975	1946	1957	1979	1950	1964	1966	1942	1973	1979	1977	1960	1966
SNOW, ICE PELLETS													
Maximum monthly	43.0	25.8	31.5	23.0	13.4	0.3	0.0	T	1.9	8.5	29.7	22.6	43.0
Date	1975	1955	1951	1950	1954	1969	—	1978	1942	1981	1965	1942	1975
Maximum in 24 hrs	17.7	11.4	17.0	13.9	7.7	0.3	0.0	T	1.5	5.9	12.0	8.6	17.7
Date	1975	1955	1966	1950	1954	1969	—	1978	1951	1981	1947	1953	1975
WIND (Resultant)													
Mean speed (mph)	8.9	8.8	9.4	10.2	9.6	8.6	7.8	7.7	8.8	9.5	9.5	8.9	9.0

MINNEAPOLIS-ST.PAUL   Elev. 834'   44° 53'N — 93° 13'W   Minnesota

NORMALS, MEANS, EXTREMES

	JAN	FEB	MAR	APR	MAY	JUN	JUL	AUG	SEP	OCT	NOV	DEC	YEAR
TEMPERATURE													
Normal daily maximum	19.9	26.4	37.5	56.0	69.4	78.5	83.4	80.9	71.0	59.7	41.1	26.7	54.2
Normal daily minimum	2.4	8.5	20.8	36.0	47.6	57.7	62.7	60.3	50.2	39.4	25.3	11.7	35.2
Normal monthly	11.2	17.5	29.2	46.0	58.5	68.1	73.1	70.6	60.6	49.6	33.2	19.2	44.7
Extreme highest	58	60	83	95	96	102	104	102	98	89	75	63	104
Extreme highest date	1944	1981	1968	1980	1978	1985	1941	1947	1976	1953	1944	1982	1941
Extreme lowest	-34	-28	-32	2	18	34	43	39	26	15	-17	-29	-34
Extreme lowest date	1970	1965	1962	1962	1967	1945	1972	1967	1974	1972	1964	1983	1970
DEGREE DAYS BASE 65° F													
Heating	1668	1330	1110	570	238	41	12	16	160	488	954	1420	8007
Cooling	0	0	0	0	36	134	263	190	28	11	0	0	662
% OF POSSIBLE SUNSHINE	52	58	55	57	60	64	72	68	61	55	39	41	57
AVERAGE SKY COVER													
Sunrise - Sunset	6.3	6.3	6.7	6.6	6.4	6.1	5.2	5.3	5.6	5.8	7.1	7.0	6.2
NUMBER OF DAYS (Sunrise-Sunset)													
Clear	8.5	7.8	7.0	6.8	7.1	7.4	10.5	10.3	10.0	10.1	5.4	6.2	97.2
Partly cloudy	7.3	6.8	7.6	7.9	9.1	10.1	11.5	11.0	8.5	7.3	6.8	6.4	100.4
Cloudy	15.2	13.6	16.4	15.3	14.8	12.4	9.0	9.6	11.5	13.6	17.7	18.3	167.6
Precipitation .01" or more	8.9	7.5	10.4	10.1	11.4	12.0	9.7	9.9	9.6	8.1	8.3	9.1	114.9
Snow, Ice pellets 1.0" or more	3.3	2.6	3.1	0.8	0.1	0.0	0.0	0.0	*	0.1	1.9	3.1	15.1
Thunderstorms	*	0.2	0.9	2.6	5.3	7.6	7.6	6.5	4.1	1.9	0.6	0.2	37.6
Fog, Visibility 1/4 mile or less	1.2	1.3	1.2	0.4	0.6	0.6	0.4	0.6	0.9	1.1	1.2	1.4	10.9
Temperature Maximum:													
90° and above	0.0	0.0	0.0	0.2	0.6	2.3	6.4	3.9	1.0	0.0	0.0	0.0	14.5
32° and below	24.8	18.4	9.7	0.4	0.0	0.0	0.0	0.0	0.0	0.0	6.7	22.3	82.4
Temperature Minimum:													
32° and below	30.8	27.1	25.8	11.2	1.2	0.0	0.0	0.0	0.6	7.2	22.3	29.7	155.8
0° and below	15.0	8.6	2.1	0.0	0.0	0.0	0.0	0.0	0.0	0.0	0.6	8.4	34.7
RELATIVE HUMIDITY (%)													
Morning	71	73	72	67	67	73	74	76	79	75	76	75	73
Afternoon	66	65	62	53	52	55	54	56	60	59	66	70	60
PRECIPITATION (inches)													
Water Equivalent													
Normal	0.8	0.8	1.7	2.0	3.2	4.0	3.5	3.6	2.5	1.8	1.2	0.8	26.3
Maximum monthly	3.6	2.1	4.7	5.4	8.0	7.9	7.1	9.3	7.5	5.6	5.1	4.2	9.3
Date	1967	1981	1965	1975	1962	1975	1955	1977	1942	1971	1940	1982	1977
Minimum monthly	0.1	0.0	0.3	0.5	0.6	1.0	0.5	0.4	0.4	0.0	0.0	T	T
Date	1959	1964	1958	1952	1967	1973	1975	1946	1940	1952	1939	1943	1943
Maximum in 24 hrs	1.2	1.1	1.6	2.2	3.0	2.9	4.1	7.3	3.5	2.9	2.9	2.4	7.3
Date	1967	1966	1965	1975	1965	1984	1949	1977	1942	1966	1940	1982	1977
SNOW, ICE PELLETS													
Maximum monthly	46.4	26.5	40.0	21.8	3.0	0.0	0.0	0.0	1.7	3.7	30.4	33.2	46.4
Date	1982	1962	1951	1983	1946	—	—	—	1942	1959	1983	1969	1982
Maximum in 24 hrs	18.5	9.3	14.7	13.6	3.0	0.0	0.0	0.0	1.7	3.0	16.2	16.5	18.5
Date	1982	1939	1985	1983	1946	—	—	—	1942	1977	1940	1982	1982
WIND (Resultant)													
Mean speed (mph)	10.4	10.5	11.4	12.3	11.2	10.5	9.3	9.2	9.9	10.5	10.9	10.4	10.5

Elev. 1297'　　　43° 55'N — 92° 30'W　　　

NORMALS, MEANS, EXTREMES

	JAN	FEB	MAR	APR	MAY	JUN	JUL	AUG	SEP	OCT	NOV	DEC	YEAR
TEMPERATURE													
Normal daily maximum	19.7	26.2	36.7	54.9	68.2	77.6	81.4	79.1	70.3	59.2	41.1	26.3	53.4
Normal daily minimum	1.9	7.7	19.2	34.3	45.6	55.5	59.9	57.6	48.1	38.1	24.1	10.7	33.6
Normal monthly	10.8	17.0	28.0	44.6	56.9	66.6	70.7	68.4	59.2	48.7	32.6	18.5	43.5
Extreme highest	55	63	78	91	92	101	102	96	95	88	73	62	102
Extreme highest date	1981	1981	1978	1980	1980	1985	1976	1964	1978	1976	1978	1982	1976
Extreme lowest	-32	-29	-31	5	21	36	42	37	23	13	-20	-33	-33
Extreme lowest date	1970	1979	1962	1982	1967	1972	1967	1964	1967	1972	1977	1983	1983
DEGREE DAYS BASE 65° F													
Heating	1680	1344	1147	612	277	59	18	26	188	512	972	1442	8277
Cooling	0	0	0	0	26	107	194	131	14	7	0	0	479
AVERAGE SKY COVER													
Sunrise - Sunset	6.5	6.6	6.9	6.9	6.4	6.2	5.5	5.7	5.9	6.3	7.4	7.2	6.5
NUMBER OF DAYS (Sunrise-Sunset)													
Clear	7.7	7.2	6.3	5.8	6.7	6.6	9.1	8.9	9.2	8.1	5.1	5.7	86.4
Partly cloudy	7.0	6.1	7.3	7.7	9.0	10.8	11.8	11.1	7.3	7.8	5.7	6.4	97.9
Cloudy	16.3	14.9	17.4	16.5	15.3	12.7	10.1	11.0	13.5	15.1	19.2	18.9	180.9
Precipitation .01" or more	8.8	7.8	10.4	11.6	11.7	11.4	9.7	9.8	10.9	8.8	8.6	9.4	119.0
Snow, Ice pellets 1.0" or more	2.9	2.4	3.4	1.2	0.0	0.0	0.0	0.0	0.0	0.2	1.6	3.2	14.8
Thunderstorms	0.1	0.2	1.2	3.2	6.1	7.6	7.5	6.8	5.1	2.2	0.7	0.2	41.0
Fog, Visibility 1/4 mile or less	3.0	2.9	4.2	2.5	1.8	1.2	1.4	2.4	2.9	2.4	3.8	4.4	33.0
Temperature Maximum:													
90° and above	0.0	0.0	0.0	0.1	0.4	1.5	3.2	1.6	0.4	0.0	0.0	0.0	7.2
32° and below	25.0	18.2	10.1	0.7	0.0	0.0	0.0	0.0	0.0	0.1	7.2	22.7	84.1
Temperature Minimum:													
32° and below	30.8	27.4	26.5	13.0	2.0	0.0	0.0	0.0	0.9	9.2	22.9	30.2	162.8
0° and below	15.3	9.7	2.3	0.0	0.0	0.0	0.0	0.0	0.0	0.0	0.9	9.1	37.3
RELATIVE HUMIDITY (%)													
Morning	77	79	79	76	75	79	83	85	84	78	81	81	80
Afternoon	73	72	69	61	57	58	59	61	63	60	70	76	65
PRECIPITATION (inches)													
Water Equivalent													
Normal	0.7	0.6	1.7	2.5	3.4	4.1	3.8	3.8	3.0	2.0	1.3	0.8	28.2
Maximum monthly	2.5	2.2	3.3	4.2	8.4	8.3	12.3	9.5	8.0	6.0	4.6	2.8	12.3
Date	1967	1971	1966	1973	1982	1967	1978	1979	1978	1970	1975	1982	1978
Minimum monthly	0.0	0.0	0.4	1.0	1.1	0.9	1.0	1.1	0.3	0.2	0.0	0.2	0.0
Date	1961	1964	1978	1966	1963	1985	1975	1970	1975	1965	1967	1967	1964
Maximum in 24 hrs	1.4	1.0	2.0	1.8	2.6	2.4	7.4	3.2	6.0	2.8	2.2	1.3	7.4
Date	1967	1984	1966	1968	1980	1967	1981	1962	1978	1966	1975	1982	1981
SNOW, ICE PELLETS													
Maximum monthly	27.3	19.1	25.2	16.4	0.3	0.0	0.0	0.0	0.8	5.4	22.5	30.6	30.6
Date	1982	1962	1985	1983	1967	—	—	—	1961	1979	1985	1969	1969
Maximum in 24 hrs	15.4	9.3	11.3	7.2	0.3	0.0	0.0	0.0	0.8	5.4	6.8	9.0	15.4
Date	1982	1983	1966	1962	1967	—	—	—	1961	1979	1983	1985	1982
WIND (Resultant)													
Mean speed (mph)	14.5	13.7	14.2	14.5	13.2	12.4	10.8	10.6	11.7	13.0	13.4	13.7	13.0

SAINT CLOUD

Elev. 1028'   45° 33'N — 94° 04'W   **Minnesota**

NORMALS, MEANS, EXTREMES

	JAN	FEB	MAR	APR	MAY	JUN	JUL	AUG	SEP	OCT	NOV	DEC	YEAR
TEMPERATURE													
Normal daily maximum	17.4	24.5	35.8	54.1	68.3	76.9	81.8	79.2	69.0	58.0	38.8	24.2	52.3
Normal daily minimum	-3.3	2.8	15.5	31.8	43.3	53.1	57.7	55.4	45.7	35.5	20.8	6.2	30.4
Normal monthly	7.1	13.7	25.7	43.0	55.8	65.0	69.8	67.3	57.4	46.8	29.8	15.2	41.4
Extreme highest	55	55	79	96	97	98	103	103	98	90	74	60	103
Extreme highest date	1942	1961	1968	1980	1969	1985	1940	1947	1978	1953	1978	1982	1947
Extreme lowest	-43	-35	-32	-3	19	33	40	33	18	5	-20	-41	-43
Extreme lowest date	1977	1951	1962	1975	1967	1951	1972	1974	1974	1976	1964	1983	1977
DEGREE DAYS BASE 65° F													
Heating	1798	1436	1218	660	305	78	26	40	240	564	1056	1544	8965
Cooling	0	0	0	0	20	78	175	112	12	0	0	0	397
% OF POSSIBLE SUNSHINE	na	na	na	na	na	na	na	na	na	na	na	na	na
AVERAGE SKY COVER													
Sunrise - Sunset	6.4	6.1	6.7	6.7	6.4	6.0	5.2	5.2	5.7	6.0	7.1	7.1	6.2
NUMBER OF DAYS (Sunrise-Sunset)													
Clear	7.9	8.1	6.8	6.8	6.8	6.7	10.1	10.6	9.7	9.9	5.5	6.4	95.2
Partly cloudy	7.9	7.0	7.3	7.4	9.4	10.8	11.9	11.0	8.8	7.8	6.3	6.7	102.2
Cloudy	15.1	13.1	16.9	15.8	14.8	12.5	9.0	9.5	11.5	13.3	18.2	17.9	167.6
Precipitation .01" or more	8.8	7.0	9.0	9.4	11.4	11.7	9.6	9.7	8.8	7.5	7.9	8.9	109.6
Snow, Ice pellets 1.0" or more	2.9	2.3	3.1	0.8	*	0.0	0.0	0.0	*	0.1	2.1	2.9	14.3
Thunderstorms	0.0	*	0.5	2.0	4.8	7.8	7.5	7.4	3.6	1.5	0.3	0.0	35.5
Fog, Visibility 1/4 mile or less	1.6	1.9	1.3	0.5	1.0	1.0	1.3	2.5	1.8	2.4	1.7	2.6	19.6
Temperature Maximum:													
90° and above	0.0	0.0	0.0	*	0.3	1.7	4.2	3.4	0.8	*	0.0	0.0	10.6
32° and below	26.3	20.2	11.5	0.8	0.0	0.0	0.0	0.0	0.0	0.2	9.2	23.7	91.8
Temperature Minimum:													
32° and below	31.0	28.0	28.4	16.7	3.1	0.0	0.0	0.0	2.0	11.7	26.1	30.6	177.5
0° and below	18.3	13.1	4.6	*	0.0	0.0	0.0	0.0	0.0	0.0	1.9	9.0	47.0
RELATIVE HUMIDITY (%)													
Morning	76	76	78	75	74	82	85	85	85	79	80	79	80
Afternoon	69	66	64	53	50	55	55	58	59	59	67	71	61
PRECIPITATION (inches)													
Water Equivalent													
Normal	0.8	0.7	1.4	2.2	3.2	4.5	3.3	4.3	2.7	2.0	1.2	0.8	27.7
Maximum monthly	2.5	2.7	3.4	5.3	8.0	9.5	8.0	7.5	9.4	6.1	3.7	2.0	9.5
Date	1969	1951	1965	1954	1962	1983	1955	1956	1985	1971	1977	1969	1983
Minimum monthly	0.0	0.0	0.1	0.3	0.3	1.3	0.2	0.4	0.0	0.0	0.0	0.0	0.0
Date	1942	1964	1959	1959	1948	1964	1975	1950	1952	1952	1941	1943	1943
Maximum in 24 hrs	0.9	1.8	1.8	3.1	3.7	4.0	2.2	4.6	5.3	3.2	2.2	1.3	5.3
Date	1949	1951	1957	1954	1979	1983	1972	1956	1985	1950	1977	1984	1985
SNOW, ICE PELLETS													
Maximum monthly	29.9	21.6	51.7	11.1	3.2	0.0	0.0	0.0	1.8	4.1	26.9	25.4	51.7
Date	1975	1971	1965	1950	1971	—	—	—	1942	1959	1940	1968	1965
Maximum in 24 hrs	9.4	12.2	14.5	6.3	3.2	0.0	0.0	0.0	1.8	3.6	11.4	10.2	14.5
Date	1975	1951	1985	1953	1971	—	—	—	1942	1969	1975	1968	1985
WIND (Resultant)													
Mean speed (mph)	8.2	7.8	9.0	9.8	8.9	8.2	7.0	6.4	7.1	7.8	8.3	7.7	8.0

JACKSON

Elev. 291'   32° 19'N — 90° 05'W   **Mississippi**

NORMALS, MEANS, EXTREMES

	JAN	FEB	MAR	APR	MAY	JUN	JUL	AUG	SEP	OCT	NOV	DEC	YEAR
TEMPERATURE													
Normal daily maximum	56.5	60.9	68.4	77.3	84.1	90.5	92.5	92.1	87.6	78.6	67.5	60.0	76.3
Normal daily minimum	34.9	37.2	44.2	52.9	60.8	67.9	71.3	70.2	65.1	51.4	42.3	37.1	52.9
Normal monthly	45.7	49.1	56.3	65.1	72.5	79.2	81.9	81.2	76.4	65.0	54.9	48.6	64.6
Extreme highest	82	84	89	92	99	103	106	102	104	92	88	84	106
Extreme highest date	1972	1977	1982	1970	1964	1969	1980	1981	1980	1981	1971	1978	1980
Extreme lowest	2	11	15	30	38	47	51	55	35	30	17	7	2
Extreme lowest date	1985	1970	1980	1971	1971	1984	1967	1966	1967	1980	1976	1983	1985
DEGREE DAYS BASE 65° F													
Heating	611	462	303	77	9	0	0	0	0	98	316	513	2389
Cooling	13	17	34	80	241	426	524	502	342	98	13	0	2290
% OF POSSIBLE SUNSHINE	47	55	59	63	63	70	65	64	61	66	55	49	60
AVERAGE SKY COVER													
Sunrise - Sunset	6.6	6.0	6.3	5.8	5.7	5.3	5.7	5.5	5.3	4.6	5.6	6.2	5.7
NUMBER OF DAYS (Sunrise-Sunset)													
Clear	7.8	8.5	8.5	9.1	8.7	9.7	7.5	8.9	10.4	14.8	10.2	9.0	113.0
Partly cloudy	6.0	6.2	7.4	7.3	10.7	11.9	13.3	13.0	9.2	6.3	7.2	6.5	105.0
Cloudy	17.2	13.5	15.1	13.6	11.6	8.4	10.1	9.1	10.5	9.9	12.6	15.6	147.3
Precipitation .01" or more	11.0	8.9	10.5	8.8	9.3	8.0	10.5	9.7	8.4	6.2	8.3	9.9	109.5
Snow, Ice pellets 1.0" or more	0.2	0.1	*	0.0	0.0	0.0	0.0	0.0	0.0	0.0	0.0	0.0	0.4
Thunderstorms	1.8	2.5	6.2	5.7	6.8	7.9	12.5	10.5	5.0	2.0	2.2	3.0	66.0
Fog, Visibility 1/4 mile or less	3.6	2.3	1.8	1.6	1.0	0.7	1.3	1.7	1.9	2.1	2.7	2.9	23.4
Temperature Maximum:													
90° and above	0.0	0.0	0.0	0.1	4.3	18.2	23.8	21.8	11.1	0.9	0.0	0.0	80.2
32° and below	1.0	0.2	0.0	0.0	0.0	0.0	0.0	0.0	0.0	0.0	*	0.3	1.5
Temperature Minimum:													
32° and below	15.7	12.4	4.0	0.3	0.0	0.0	0.0	0.0	0.0	0.5	6.1	12.2	51.2
0° and below	0.0	0.0	0.0	0.0	0.0	0.0	0.0	0.0	0.0	0.0	0.0	0.0	0.0
RELATIVE HUMIDITY (%)													
Morning	84	82	82	84	87	87	90	90	90	89	87	84	86
Afternoon	65	59	57	56	56	56	59	59	59	54	58	63	58
PRECIPITATION (inches)													
Water Equivalent													
Normal	5.0	4.4	5.8	5.8	4.8	2.9	4.4	3.7	3.5	2.6	4.1	5.4	52.8
Maximum monthly	14.1	8.3	15.1	15.5	10.8	7.4	13.2	7.4	9.6	9.1	9.9	17.7	17.7
Date	1979	1979	1976	1983	1967	1975	1979	1979	1965	1970	1977	1982	1982
Minimum monthly	0.8	1.4	2.0	1.2	0.7	0.3	1.5	1.4	0.5	0.0	0.5	0.9	0.0
Date	1969	1976	1966	1965	1977	1973	1974	1980	1969	1963	1985	1980	1963
Maximum in 24 hrs	5.6	3.4	3.8	8.4	3.2	3.2	5.3	4.4	5.8	6.9	4.3	6.7	8.4
Date	1979	1974	1964	1979	1966	1979	1981	1985	1965	1975	1983	1982	1979
SNOW, ICE PELLETS													
Maximum monthly	6.3	3.6	5.3	T	0.0	0.0	0.0	0.0	0.0	0.0	0.2	3.1	6.3
Date	1982	1968	1968	1983	—	—	—	—	—	—	1976	1963	1982
Maximum in 24 hrs	6.0	3.6	5.3	T	0.0	0.0	0.0	0.0	0.0	0.0	0.2	1.8	6.0
Date	1982	1968	1968	1983	—	—	—	—	—	—	1976	1963	1982
WIND (Resultant)													
Mean speed (mph)	8.7	8.7	9.3	8.5	7.2	6.3	5.9	5.7	6.5	6.6	7.5	8.5	7.4

MERIDIAN

Elev. 290'   32° 20'N — 88° 45'W   **Mississippi**

NORMALS, MEANS, EXTREMES

	JAN	FEB	MAR	APR	MAY	JUN	JUL	AUG	SEP	OCT	NOV	DEC	YEAR
TEMPERATURE													
Normal daily maximum	56.7	61.1	68.6	77.7	84.2	90.4	92.5	92.1	87.2	77.8	67.3	60.0	76.3
Normal daily minimum	34.2	36.5	43.1	51.4	59.3	66.4	70.0	69.1	64.2	50.0	40.8	36.0	51.8
Normal monthly	45.5	48.8	55.9	64.6	71.8	78.4	81.3	80.6	75.7	63.9	54.1	48.0	64.0
Extreme highest	83	85	90	91	99	103	107	104	103	97	87	82	107
Extreme highest date	1950	1982	1974	1970	1951	1969	1980	1980	1980	1954	1946	1982	1980
Extreme lowest	0	8	15	29	38	42	55	53	34	24	16	4	0
Extreme lowest date	1962	1951	1980	1950	1971	1984	1967	1952	1967	1952	1976	1962	1962
DEGREE DAYS BASE 65° F													
Heating	616	464	312	85	17	0	0	0	5	118	335	527	2479
Cooling	12	10	30	73	224	402	505	484	326	84	8	0	2158
% OF POSSIBLE SUNSHINE	na	na	na	na	na	na	na	na	na	na	na	na	na
AVERAGE SKY COVER													
Sunrise - Sunset	6.7	6.2	6.3	5.8	5.7	5.5	6.1	5.4	5.5	4.6	5.5	6.2	5.8
NUMBER OF DAYS (Sunrise-Sunset)													
Clear	7.5	7.7	8.4	9.1	8.9	8.7	5.7	9.2	10.6	14.4	10.5	9.1	109.4
Partly cloudy	6.5	6.5	7.4	8.2	11.0	12.7	15.7	13.2	8.8	7.2	7.1	6.9	111.1
Cloudy	17.0	14.1	15.2	12.7	11.2	8.7	9.7	8.6	11.0	9.4	12.5	15.1	145.2
Precipitation .01" or more	10.6	8.9	10.0	8.6	8.2	8.1	11.2	9.2	7.6	5.4	7.5	9.6	104.8
Snow, Ice pellets 1.0" or more	0.2	0.1	*	0.0	0.0	0.0	0.0	0.0	0.0	0.0	0.0	0.1	0.4
Thunderstorms	1.7	2.6	4.8	5.5	6.3	7.2	11.6	8.5	3.9	1.5	2.0	2.0	57.6
Fog, Visibility 1/4 mile or less	2.8	2.2	2.0	2.4	1.9	1.3	1.9	1.9	1.9	2.5	3.3	2.9	26.8
Temperature Maximum:													
90° and above	0.0	0.0	*	0.1	3.8	15.9	23.4	21.8	11.0	0.6	0.0	0.0	76.7
32° and below	0.4	0.1	0.0	0.0	0.0	0.0	0.0	0.0	0.0	0.0	0.0	0.1	0.7
Temperature Minimum:													
32° and below	16.4	12.9	5.3	0.3	0.0	0.0	0.0	0.0	0.0	0.4	6.3	13.0	54.6
0° and below	0.0	0.0	0.0	0.0	0.0	0.0	0.0	0.0	0.0	0.0	0.0	0.0	0.0
RELATIVE HUMIDITY (%)													
Morning	82	80	82	86	88	88	90	90	88	88	86	82	86
Afternoon	60	55	53	52	55	54	58	58	57	52	54	58	56
PRECIPITATION (inches)													
Water Equivalent													
Normal	4.9	4.5	6.6	5.4	4.2	3.4	5.3	3.3	3.5	2.5	3.4	5.6	53.3
Maximum monthly	12.1	12.8	16.4	16.8	9.7	7.8	15.2	8.5	10.2	10.6	13.9	14.7	16.8
Date	1947	1961	1976	1964	1980	1961	1959	1960	1957	1970	1948	1973	1964
Minimum monthly	1.5	1.6	1.2	1.0	0.2	0.7	1.0	0.7	0.1	0.0	0.3	1.1	0.0
Date	1981	1947	1955	1976	1951	1968	1952	1951	1982	1963	1956	1980	1963
Maximum in 24 hrs	4.5	5.6	7.0	6.3	5.8	2.6	6.9	3.7	4.6	6.0	4.5	8.1	8.1
Date	1972	1961	1979	1964	1952	1974	1959	1985	1979	1970	1957	1973	1973
SNOW, ICE PELLETS													
Maximum monthly	5.8	3.1	1.5	0.0	0.0	0.0	0.0	0.0	0.0	0.0	T	17.6	17.6
Date	1948	1960	1968	—	—	—	—	—	—	—	1976	1963	1963
Maximum in 24 hrs	4.7	3.1	1.5	0.0	0.0	0.0	0.0	0.0	0.0	0.0	T	15.0	15.0
Date	1948	1960	1968	—	—	—	—	—	—	—	1976	1963	1963
WIND (Resultant)													
Mean speed (mph)	7.1	7.3	7.9	7.1	5.9	5.0	4.7	4.5	5.3	5.1	6.0	6.8	6.1

TUPELO
Elev. 349'   34° 16'N — 88° 46'W   **Mississippi**

NORMALS, MEANS, EXTREMES

	JAN	FEB	MAR	APR	MAY	JUN	JUL	AUG	SEP	OCT	NOV	DEC	YEAR
TEMPERATURE													
Normal daily maximum	51.1	56.4	64.6	75.4	82.7	89.7	92.5	92.0	86.0	76.0	63.1	54.8	73.7
Normal daily minimum	31.2	33.5	40.6	49.8	58.0	65.6	69.4	68.2	62.2	48.5	39.1	33.3	50.0
Normal monthly	41.2	45.0	52.6	62.6	70.4	77.7	81.0	80.1	74.1	62.3	51.1	44.1	61.8
Extreme highest	67	74	83	86	91	97	908	100	96	87	81	77	908
Extreme highest date	1984	1985	1985	1985	1985	1985	1983	1983	1984	1984	1985	1984	1983
Extreme lowest	-6	10	23	34	45	49	61	59	44	37	25	11	-6
Extreme lowest date	1985	1985	1984	1985	1984	1984	1985	1985	1985	1985	1984	1985	1985
DEGREE DAYS BASE 65° F													
Heating	738	563	403	125	33	0	0	0	8	149	421	648	3088
Cooling	0	0	19	53	201	381	493	468	281	65	0	0	1961
% OF POSSIBLE SUNSHINE	56	56	56	68	76	72	68	62	69	49	53	51	61
AVERAGE SKY COVER													
Sunrise - Sunset	6.1	6.3	6.7	5.4	5.6	5.0	4.8	5.2	4.3	6.5	6.3	6.5	5.7
NUMBER OF DAYS (Sunrise-Sunset)													
Clear	10.5	7.5	7.0	11.5	8.5	8.5	13.7	10.3	13.7	7.7	8.3	7.0	114.2
Partly cloudy	5.5	9.0	8.0	5.5	13.0	16.0	9.3	11.7	9.0	7.7	6.3	8.3	109.3
Cloudy	15.0	12.0	16.0	13.0	9.5	5.5	8.0	9.0	7.3	15.7	15.3	15.7	142.0
Precipitation .01" or more	10.0	11.0	10.5	11.5	10.5	8.0	7.7	6.3	6.0	9.0	8.0	10.3	108.8
Snow, Ice pellets 1.0" or more	1.0	1.0	0.5	0.0	0.0	0.0	0.0	0.0	0.0	0.0	0.0	0.7	3.2
Thunderstorms	0.5	1.5	4.0	7.5	6.0	7.0	8.0	8.0	4.7	4.3	2.7	3.0	57.2
Fog, Visibility 1/4 mile or less	2.5	2.5	2.5	1.0	0.0	0.5	1.0	2.7	0.3	4.7	2.0	1.3	21.0
Temperature Maximum:													
90° and above	0.0	0.0	0.0	0.0	2.5	19.0	21.3	18.0	8.0	0.0	0.0	0.0	68.8
32° and below	3.5	1.5	0.0	0.0	0.0	0.0	0.0	0.0	0.0	0.0	0.0	4.0	9.0
Temperature Minimum:													
32° and below	25.5	13.0	3.5	0.0	0.0	0.0	0.0	0.0	0.0	0.0	6.0	15.7	63.7
0° and below	1.0	0.0	0.0	0.0	0.0	0.0	0.0	0.0	0.0	0.0	0.0	0.3	1.3
RELATIVE HUMIDITY (%)													
Morning	76	72	72	76	80	78	82	89	81	86	79	77	79
Afternoon	65	58	58	52	54	49	54	61	54	65	64	62	58
PRECIPITATION (inches)													
Water Equivalent													
Normal	5.6	4.6	6.9	5.6	5.2	3.7	4.5	2.8	3.6	2.9	4.6	5.6	56.1
Maximum monthly	3.7	5.1	3.5	5.8	8.4	3.0	3.0	6.2	2.8	7.9	7.0	13.6	13.6
Date	1985	1985	1984	1984	1984	1985	1983	1985	1985	1984	1983	1983	1983
Minimum monthly	2.8	3.3	2.1	4.9	5.3	.0.5	1.9	0.5	1.3	3.6	1.5	1.5	0.5
Date	1984	1984	1985	1985	1985	1984	1984	1983	1984	1983	1985	1984	1984
Maximum in 24 hrs	1.4	1.7	1.0	2.4	4.1	0.8	1.5	3.6	2.3	3.2	2.5	7.1	7.1
Date	1984	1985	1984	1985	1984	1985	1983	1985	1983	1985	1983	1983	1983
SNOW, ICE PELLETS													
Maximum monthly	3.7	5.3	1.7	0.0	0.0	0.0	0.0	0.0	0.0	0.0	0.0	2.2	5.3
Date	1985	1985	1984	—	—	—	—	—	—	—	—	1983	1985
Maximum in 24 hrs	2.8	3.1	1.7	0.0	0.0	0.0	0.0	0.0	0.0	0.0	0.0	1.9	3.1
Date	1985	1985	1984	—	—	—	—	—	—	—	—	1983	1985
WIND (Resultant)													
Mean speed (mph)	5.5	6.3	6.7	6.1	6.3	4.6	4.3	4.4	5.8	4.8	6.4	6.1	5.6

COLUMBIA

Elev. 887' 38° 49'N — 92° 13'W **Missouri**

NORMALS, MEANS, EXTREMES

	JAN	FEB	MAR	APR	MAY	JUN	JUL	AUG	SEP	OCT	NOV	DEC	YEAR
TEMPERATURE													
Normal daily maximum	36.3	41.6	51.6	65.4	74.5	83.3	88.6	87.2	79.7	68.4	53.1	41.3	64.3
Normal daily minimum	18.6	23.4	31.8	44.2	53.7	62.5	66.9	64.8	57.0	45.7	33.9	24.5	43.9
Normal monthly	27.5	32.5	41.7	54.8	64.1	72.9	77.8	76.0	68.4	57.1	43.5	32.9	54.1
Extreme highest	66	82	85	90	90	101	111	110	101	93	83	71	111
Extreme highest date	1970	1972	1985	1972	1979	1980	1980	1984	1971	1981	1978	1984	1980
Extreme lowest	-19	-15	-5	19	29	44	48	50	32	22	5	-19	-19
Extreme lowest date	1982	1979	1978	1975	1976	1983	1975	1979	1984	1972	1976	1983	1983
DEGREE DAYS BASE 65° F													
Heating	1163	910	722	316	120	13	0	0	47	275	645	995	5206
Cooling	0	0	0	10	92	250	397	341	149	30	0	0	1269
% OF POSSIBLE SUNSHINE	51	50	50	55	60	66	71	66	61	58	48	45	57
AVERAGE SKY COVER													
Sunrise - Sunset	6.5	6.6	7.0	6.5	6.4	6.0	5.2	5.4	5.6	5.7	6.5	6.8	6.2
NUMBER OF DAYS (Sunrise-Sunset)													
Clear	8.3	6.8	6.3	7.6	7.5	7.7	11.2	9.9	10.2	10.9	8.2	7.3	101.8
Partly cloudy	6.4	6.3	6.4	6.8	7.2	9.9	10.0	10.3	7.8	6.6	6.1	6.2	89.8
Cloudy	16.4	15.3	18.4	15.6	16.3	12.4	9.8	10.8	12.1	13.4	15.8	17.5	173.6
Precipitation .01" or more	7.7	8.4	11.3	11.5	12.4	8.9	7.3	7.8	8.8	9.7	9.6	9.4	112.7
Snow, Ice pellets 1.0" or more	2.2	2.1	1.2	0.3	0.0	0.0	0.0	0.0	0.0	0.0	0.8	1.5	8.1
Thunderstorms	0.4	1.0	3.5	5.6	8.1	7.9	7.7	7.1	5.4	3.4	2.0	1.0	53.1
Fog, Visibility 1/4 mile or less	2.3	2.7	2.6	1.3	1.3	1.3	1.0	1.8	1.8	1.9	1.8	3.2	22.9
Temperature Maximum:													
90° and above	0.0	0.0	0.0	0.1	0.1	3.8	15.7	12.5	5.1	0.1	0.0	0.0	37.3
32° and below	14.1	8.0	1.3	0.0	0.0	0.0	0.0	0.0	0.0	0.0	1.4	7.8	32.6
Temperature Minimum:													
32° and below	28.3	21.6	14.9	3.4	0.1	0.0	0.0	0.0	0.1	1.6	13.4	24.9	108.2
0° and below	3.8	1.6	0.8	0.0	0.0	0.0	0.0	0.0	0.0	0.0	0.0	1.6	7.7
RELATIVE HUMIDITY (%)													
Morning	75	75	72	70	79	81	80	80	80	77	77	77	77
Afternoon	66	65	60	56	60	60	55	56	58	58	64	68	61
PRECIPITATION (inches)													
Water Equivalent													
Normal	1.5	1.8	3.1	3.8	4.4	3.7	3.5	2.9	3.6	3.3	2.0	1.9	36.0
Maximum monthly	3.5	6.1	10.0	9.0	9.8	10.2	12.1	8.9	8.9	6.1	10.4	6.9	12.1
Date	1974	1985	1973	1983	1970	1985	1981	1982	1970	1976	1985	1982	1981
Minimum monthly	0.2	0.3	0.7	1.3	3.3	0.3	0.2	0.2	0.4	1.2	0.5	0.5	0.2
Date	1970	1970	1971	1971	1979	1980	1976	1976	1979	1974	1969	1976	1976
Maximum in 24 hrs	1.8	2.8	2.3	3.1	3.3	3.0	5.0	3.9	2.8	2.5	2.9	2.8	5.0
Date	1985	1985	1978	1984	1983	1985	1984	1975	1984	1976	1983	1982	1984
SNOW, ICE PELLETS													
Maximum monthly	23.5	17.5	18.0	7.1	0.0	0.0	0.0	0.0	0.0	0.1	8.3	17.8	23.5
Date	1979	1978	1978	1980	—	—	—	—	—	1976	1971	1973	1979
Maximum in 24 hrs	6.1	12.1	8.0	7.1	0.0	0.0	0.0	0.0	0.0	0.1	8.1	11.2	12.1
Date	1978	1978	1978	1980	—	—	—	—	—	1976	1975	1973	1978
WIND (Resultant)													
Mean speed (mph)	10.8	11.0	11.9	11.5	9.1	8.6	8.1	7.9	8.5	9.4	10.4	10.8	9.8

KANSAS CITY

Elev. 742'   39° 17'N — 94° 43'W   **Missouri**

NORMALS, MEANS, EXTREMES

	JAN	FEB	MAR	APR	MAY	JUN	JUL	AUG	SEP	OCT	NOV	DEC	YEAR
TEMPERATURE													
Normal daily maximum	34.5	41.1	51.3	65.1	74.6	83.3	88.5	86.8	78.6	67.9	52.1	40.1	63.7
Normal daily minimum	17.2	23.0	31.7	44.4	54.6	63.8	68.5	66.5	58.1	47.0	34.0	23.7	44.4
Normal monthly	25.9	32.1	41.5	54.8	64.6	73.6	78.5	76.7	68.4	57.5	43.1	31.9	54.0
Extreme highest	68	76	82	90	92	105	107	109	98	92	82	70	109
Extreme highest date	1981	1981	1978	1980	1985	1980	1974	1984	1984	1976	1980	1980	1984
Extreme lowest	-17	-19	-10	12	30	43	52	50	33	21	1	-21	-21
Extreme lowest date	1982	1982	1978	1975	1976	1983	1973	1973	1984	1972	1976	1983	1983
DEGREE DAYS BASE 65° F													
Heating	1212	921	729	314	112	12	0	0	42	258	657	1026	5283
Cooling	0	0	0	8	99	270	423	363	144	26	0	0	1333
% OF POSSIBLE SUNSHINE	59	56	58	64	64	69	74	67	65	59	48	51	61
AVERAGE SKY COVER													
Sunrise - Sunset	6.0	6.3	6.8	6.3	6.3	5.5	4.4	4.9	5.1	5.1	6.2	6.2	5.8
NUMBER OF DAYS (Sunrise-Sunset)													
Clear	9.7	7.6	6.3	8.3	7.8	9.5	14.2	12.5	12.0	12.2	8.5	9.3	117.9
Partly cloudy	6.1	6.6	7.7	6.4	8.6	9.9	9.3	10.2	7.8	7.3	6.4	6.2	92.5
Cloudy	15.2	14.0	17.0	15.3	14.5	10.6	7.5	8.4	10.2	11.5	15.2	15.5	154.8
Precipitation .01" or more	8.0	6.9	10.9	11.2	11.2	10.5	7.2	8.9	7.8	8.2	7.8	7.8	106.7
Snow, Ice pellets 1.0" or more	2.5	1.8	1.1	0.5	0.0	0.0	0.0	0.0	0.0	0.0	0.4	1.4	7.6
Thunderstorms	0.2	0.6	2.2	5.5	8.6	9.8	6.9	7.6	5.6	3.6	1.4	0.6	52.6
Fog, Visibility 1/4 mile or less	2.0	2.8	2.8	1.1	1.4	0.5	0.4	1.4	1.7	1.8	2.3	3.2	21.3
Temperature Maximum:													
90° and above	0.0	0.0	0.0	0.1	0.2	4.2	16.5	12.0	4.0	0.2	0.0	0.0	37.2
32° and below	14.8	9.4	2.2	0.2	0.0	0.0	0.0	0.0	0.0	0.0	2.5	9.0	37.9
Temperature Minimum:													
32° and below	28.8	21.5	14.4	3.3	0.1	0.0	0.0	0.0	0.0	1.8	13.3	26.7	110.0
0° and below	5.5	2.6	0.2	0.0	0.0	0.0	0.0	0.0	0.0	0.0	0.0	2.1	10.5
RELATIVE HUMIDITY (%)													
Morning	72	73	72	70	76	78	74	77	78	73	74	74	74
Afternoon	64	64	61	57	59	59	56	59	59	57	63	65	60
PRECIPITATION (inches)													
Water Equivalent													
Normal	1.0	1.1	2.4	3.2	4.4	4.6	4.3	3.5	4.1	3.1	1.6	1.3	35.1
Maximum monthly	2.6	2.6	9.0	6.8	10.0	7.4	8.7	9.5	11.3	7.6	3.9	5.4	11.3
Date	1982	1985	1973	1984	1974	1981	1973	1982	1977	1977	1985	1980	1977
Minimum monthly	0.1	0.3	1.1	1.0	2.2	2.1	0.2	0.7	1.1	0.3	0.2	0.0	0.0
Date	1984	1981	1974	1980	1984	1974	1975	1984	1974	1978	1976	1979	1979
Maximum in 24 hrs	1.8	1.3	1.7	4.6	4.2	2.6	4.1	6.1	8.8	4.9	2.0	3.6	8.8
Date	1982	1985	1973	1975	1974	1976	1981	1982	1977	1973	1973	1980	1977
SNOW, ICE PELLETS													
Maximum monthly	14.2	12.7	11.4	7.2	0.0	0.0	0.0	0.0	0.0	T	7.1	13.2	14.2
Date	1977	1982	1978	1983	—	—	—	—	—	1980	1975	1983	1977
Maximum in 24 hrs	7.6	9.3	7.2	4.0	0.0	0.0	0.0	0.0	0.0	T	6.1	8.3	9.3
Date	1985	1978	1978	1983	—	—	—	—	—	1980	1975	1978	1978
WIND (Resultant)													
Mean speed (mph)	11.1	11.5	12.5	12.5	10.2	9.9	8.9	9.0	9.5	10.4	11.2	11.3	10.7

NORMALS, MEANS, EXTREMES

	JAN	FEB	MAR	APR	MAY	JUN	JUL	AUG	SEP	OCT	NOV	DEC	YEAR
TEMPERATURE													
Normal daily maximum	37.6	43.1	53.4	67.1	76.4	85.2	89.0	87.4	80.7	69.1	54.0	42.6	65.5
Normal daily minimum	19.9	24.5	33.0	45.1	54.7	64.3	68.8	66.6	58.6	46.7	35.1	25.7	45.3
Normal monthly	28.8	33.8	43.2	56.1	65.6	74.8	78.9	77.0	69.7	57.9	44.6	34.2	55.4
Extreme highest	76	85	89	92	92	98	107	107	104	94	82	76	107
Extreme highest date	1970	1972	1985	1970	1978	1971	1980	1984	1984	1963	1978	1970	1984
Extreme lowest	-18	-10	-5	22	31	43	51	47	36	23	1	-13	-18
Extreme lowest date	1985	1979	1960	1975	1976	1969	1972	1965	1974	1976	1964	1983	1985
DEGREE DAYS BASE 65° F													
Heating	1122	874	676	279	110	12	0	0	40	258	612	955	4938
Cooling	0	0	0	12	128	306	431	372	181	38	0	0	1468
% OF POSSIBLE SUNSHINE	52	53	53	56	61	66	70	65	64	59	46	42	57
AVERAGE SKY COVER													
Sunrise - Sunset	6.7	6.5	6.8	6.5	6.2	6.0	5.5	5.4	5.1	5.1	6.2	6.8	6.1
NUMBER OF DAYS (Sunrise-Sunset)													
Clear	7.5	7.0	6.5	7.0	7.6	7.4	9.5	10.4	11.7	12.2	8.8	7.1	102.8
Partly cloudy	6.4	6.4	8.0	8.2	9.6	10.8	11.6	11.0	8.1	7.7	6.7	6.7	101.3
Cloudy	17.1	14.8	16.5	14.9	13.8	11.7	9.8	9.6	10.2	11.1	14.5	17.2	161.2
Precipitation .01" or more	8.6	8.2	11.6	11.4	10.8	9.4	8.4	7.8	7.9	8.4	9.4	9.4	111.3
Snow, Ice pellets 1.0" or more	2.0	1.6	1.0	0.3	0.0	0.0	0.0	0.0	0.0	0.0	0.5	1.2	6.6
Thunderstorms	0.7	0.8	3.2	5.9	6.6	7.1	6.9	6.3	3.8	2.4	1.6	0.6	45.9
Fog, Visibility 1/4 mile or less	2.2	1.5	1.7	0.5	0.5	0.3	0.3	0.4	0.6	0.9	0.9	1.8	11.6
Temperature Maximum:													
90° and above	0.0	0.0	0.0	0.2	1.2	7.3	14.5	11.6	4.4	0.3	0.0	0.0	39.4
32° and below	12.7	7.3	1.4	0.0	0.0	0.0	0.0	0.0	0.0	0.0	0.7	7.2	29.3
Temperature Minimum:													
32° and below	27.6	21.9	14.0	2.9	0.1	0.0	0.0	0.0	0.0	1.8	11.7	23.4	103.6
0° and below	2.7	0.6	*	0.0	0.0	0.0	0.0	0.0	0.0	0.0	0.0	1.1	4.4
RELATIVE HUMIDITY (%)													
Morning	79	78	76	72	76	78	77	80	82	78	79	81	78
Afternoon	67	64	60	56	56	57	56	57	59	57	64	69	60
PRECIPITATION (inches)													
Water Equivalent													
Normal	1.7	2.1	3.2	3.5	3.5	3.7	3.6	2.5	2.7	2.3	2.5	2.2	33.9
Maximum monthly	5.3	4.1	6.6	9.0	7.2	9.4	10.7	6.4	8.8	7.1	9.9	7.8	10.7
Date	1975	1974	1978	1970	1961	1985	1981	1970	1984	1984	1985	1982	1981
Minimum monthly	0.2	0.2	1.0	0.9	1.0	0.4	0.6	0.0	T	0.2	0.4	0.3	T
Date	1970	1963	1966	1977	1972	1959	1970	1971	1979	1975	1969	1958	1979
Maximum in 24 hrs	2.4	2.5	2.9	4.9	2.9	3.2	3.4	2.6	2.9	2.6	3.7	4.0	4.9
Date	1975	1959	1977	1979	1974	1960	1982	1974	1984	1983	1985	1982	1979
SNOW, ICE PELLETS													
Maximum monthly	23.9	12.9	22.3	6.5	T	0.0	0.0	0.0	0.0	T	11.3	26.3	26.3
Date	1977	1961	1960	1971	1944	—	—	—	—	1967	1951	1973	1973
Maximum in 24 hrs	13.9	8.3	10.0	6.1	T	0.0	0.0	0.0	0.0	T	10.3	12.0	13.9
Date	1982	1966	1958	1971	1944	—	—	—	—	1967	1951	1973	1982
WIND (Resultant)													
Mean speed (mph)	10.6	10.9	11.9	11.5	9.5	8.8	7.9	7.7	8.1	8.8	10.0	10.4	9.7

SPRINGFIELD

Elev. 1268'   37° 14'N — 93° 23'W   **Missouri**

NORMALS, MEANS, EXTREMES

	JAN	FEB	MAR	APR	MAY	JUN	JUL	AUG	SEP	OCT	NOV	DEC	YEAR
TEMPERATURE													
Normal daily maximum	42.2	47.1	56.1	68.3	76.5	84.9	89.8	89.3	81.6	70.8	56.2	46.4	67.4
Normal daily minimum	20.8	25.3	33.0	44.0	53.1	61.9	66.2	64.7	57.3	45.5	33.9	25.9	44.3
Normal monthly	31.5	36.2	44.6	56.2	64.8	73.4	78.0	77.0	69.5	58.2	45.1	36.2	55.9
Extreme highest	76	81	87	93	93	101	113	106	104	93	80	77	113
Extreme highest date	1950	1972	1974	1963	1972	1954	1954	1984	1947	1981	1980	1948	1954
Extreme lowest	-13	-17	-3	18	30	42	44	44	31	21	4	-10	-17
Extreme lowest date	1985	1979	1948	1957	1970	1966	1972	1967	1984	1952	1959	1983	1979
DEGREE DAYS BASE 65° F													
Heating	1039	806	640	279	107	14	0	0	43	242	597	893	4660
Cooling	0	0	7	15	101	266	403	372	178	32	0	0	1374
% OF POSSIBLE SUNSHINE	50	53	56	60	62	66	72	72	69	64	54	48	61
AVERAGE SKY COVER													
Sunrise - Sunset	6.4	6.4	6.5	6.2	6.1	5.6	5.0	4.9	4.9	4.9	5.8	6.4	5.8
NUMBER OF DAYS (Sunrise-Sunset)													
Clear	8.1	7.6	7.4	8.3	7.7	8.7	11.8	11.9	12.1	13.4	10.1	8.4	115.5
Partly cloudy	7.0	6.1	7.7	7.6	9.9	10.3	10.6	10.6	7.8	6.5	6.6	6.5	97.2
Cloudy	15.9	14.5	15.9	14.1	13.4	11.0	8.7	8.5	10.1	11.1	13.3	16.1	152.6
Precipitation .01" or more	8.3	8.3	10.4	10.8	10.9	9.8	7.7	8.5	8.1	7.9	8.4	8.6	107.6
Snow, Ice pellets 1.0" or more	1.6	1.2	1.0	0.1	0.0	0.0	0.0	0.0	0.0	0.0	0.4	1.1	5.4
Thunderstorms	0.8	1.3	3.8	6.4	8.2	9.1	7.5	8.0	5.5	3.4	2.0	1.2	56.8
Fog, Visibility 1/4 mile or less	3.5	2.7	1.6	0.9	1.1	1.1	1.0	1.0	1.4	1.8	1.9	2.7	20.6
Temperature Maximum:													
90° and above	0.0	0.0	0.0	*	0.4	6.2	17.4	15.3	4.5	0.4	0.0	0.0	44.2
32° and below	8.2	4.5	0.9	0.0	0.0	0.0	0.0	0.0	0.0	0.0	0.5	4.9	19.0
Temperature Minimum:													
32° and below	26.6	20.9	13.7	3.3	0.3	0.0	0.0	0.0	*	2.4	12.7	23.0	103.0
0° and below	2.7	0.8	*	0.0	0.0	0.0	0.0	0.0	0.0	0.0	0.0	0.9	4.5
RELATIVE HUMIDITY (%)													
Morning	73	73	72	72	80	84	82	80	82	77	76	75	77
Afternoon	61	59	56	55	58	60	55	54	58	54	59	62	58
PRECIPITATION (inches)													
Water Equivalent													
Normal	1.6	2.1	3.4	4.0	4.3	4.6	3.5	2.8	4.2	3.2	2.8	2.5	39.4
Maximum monthly	6.7	5.3	9.0	10.1	10.5	11.3	18.7	8.6	11.3	8.7	12.2	8.8	18.7
Date	1950	1955	1973	1983	1957	1975	1958	1982	1975	1967	1985	1982	1958
Minimum monthly	0.0	0.3	0.5	0.8	1.5	0.5	0.3	0.5	0.2	0.4	0.2	0.1	0.0
Date	1961	1947	1956	1955	1969	1952	1953	1955	1952	1963	1976	1950	1961
Maximum in 24 hrs	3.9	3.7	4.0	3.8	3.5	4.8	6.8	3.4	4.7	5.4	4.5	4.5	6.8
Date	1950	1966	1974	1970	1979	1975	1958	1976	1962	1949	1985	1982	1958
SNOW, ICE PELLETS													
Maximum monthly	23.1	19.2	23.9	7.1	0.0	0.0	0.0	0.0	0.0	0.6	19.5	14.5	23.9
Date	1979	1980	1970	1971	—	—	—	—	—	1951	1951	1983	1970
Maximum in 24 hrs	9.1	16.1	15.7	6.9	0.0	0.0	0.0	0.0	0.0	0.6	12.5	7.5	16.1
Date	1978	1980	1970	1971	—	—	—	—	—	1951	1951	1966	1980
WIND (Resultant)													
Mean speed (mph)	11.8	12.1	13.1	12.5	10.6	9.8	8.6	8.7	9.5	10.3	11.4	11.8	10.8

BILLINGS

Elev. 3567'   45° 48'N — 108° 32'W   **Montana**

NORMALS, MEANS, EXTREMES

	JAN	FEB	MAR	APR	MAY	JUN	JUL	AUG	SEP	OCT	NOV	DEC	YEAR
TEMPERATURE													
Normal daily maximum	29.9	37.9	44.0	55.9	66.4	76.3	86.6	84.3	72.3	61.0	44.4	36.0	57.9
Normal daily minimum	11.8	18.8	23.6	33.2	43.3	51.6	58.0	56.2	46.5	37.5	25.5	18.2	35.4
Normal monthly	20.9	28.4	33.8	44.6	54.9	64.0	72.3	70.3	59.4	49.3	35.0	27.1	46.6
Extreme highest	68	72	79	92	96	105	106	105	103	90	77	69	106
Extreme highest date	1953	1961	1978	1939	1936	1984	1937	1961	1983	1963	1983	1980	1937
Extreme lowest	-30	-38	-19	-5	14	32	41	40	22	2	-22	-32	-38
Extreme lowest date	1937	1936	1951	1936	1954	1969	1972	1939	1984	1984	1959	1983	1936
DEGREE DAYS BASE 65° F													
Heating	1367	1025	967	612	318	111	9	27	214	487	900	1175	7212
Cooling	0	0	0	0	0	81	235	191	46	0	0	0	553
% OF POSSIBLE SUNSHINE	48	54	61	60	60	64	76	75	68	61	46	44	60
AVERAGE SKY COVER													
Sunrise - Sunset	7.1	7.2	7.2	7.1	6.6	5.9	4.2	4.3	5.2	5.8	6.8	6.8	6.2
NUMBER OF DAYS (Sunrise-Sunset)													
Clear	5.4	4.0	4.4	4.3	5.4	7.1	13.9	13.7	10.3	9.3	5.8	5.8	89.5
Partly cloudy	7.8	8.3	8.8	8.7	10.6	11.8	12.1	11.0	9.6	9.4	7.8	8.5	114.6
Cloudy	17.7	16.0	17.8	17.0	14.9	11.1	5.0	6.2	10.1	12.3	16.4	16.6	161.2
Precipitation .01" or more	8.1	7.5	9.1	9.3	11.0	11.1	7.2	6.5	7.1	6.4	6.1	6.8	96.1
Snow, Ice pellets 1.0" or more	3.5	2.5	3.5	2.2	0.4	*	0.0	0.0	0.5	1.2	2.2	2.8	18.8
Thunderstorms	*	*	0.1	1.1	4.1	7.2	7.6	5.7	1.8	0.2	0.0	*	28.1
Fog, Visibility 1/4 mile or less	1.4	2.3	1.9	2.5	1.3	0.7	0.3	0.3	1.2	1.9	2.3	1.7	17.8
Temperature Maximum:													
90° and above	0.0	0.0	0.0	*	0.3	3.3	12.9	11.1	1.9	*	0.0	0.0	29.7
32° and below	14.8	7.7	5.2	0.8	0.0	0.0	0.0	0.0	*	0.7	5.6	12.2	47.0
Temperature Minimum:													
32° and below	27.7	23.8	24.2	13.2	1.7	0.1	0.0	0.0	1.7	8.1	21.9	27.6	150.0
0° and below	9.2	2.9	1.3	0.0	0.0	0.0	0.0	0.0	0.0	0.0	1.3	4.9	19.6
RELATIVE HUMIDITY (%)													
Morning	65	65	68	67	69	71	63	61	65	63	66	65	66
Afternoon	57	51	46	40	42	40	31	30	38	42	54	58	44
PRECIPITATION (inches)													
Water Equivalent													
Normal	0.9	0.7	1.0	1.9	2.3	2.0	0.8	1.0	1.2	1.1	0.8	0.8	15.0
Maximum monthly	2.3	1.7	2.7	4.4	7.7	7.6	3.1	3.5	4.9	3.8	2.3	2.0	7.7
Date	1972	1978	1954	1955	1981	1944	1958	1965	1941	1971	1978	1973	1981
Minimum monthly	0.0	0.0	0.1	0.0	0.5	0.2	0.0	0.0	0.0	0.0	T	0.0	T
Date	1941	1977	1936	1962	1937	1961	1976	1955	1964	1948	1954	1957	1954
Maximum in 24 hrs	1.4	0.6	1.0	3.1	2.8	2.7	1.8	2.4	2.1	1.9	1.3	0.9	3.1
Date	1972	1952	1973	1978	1952	1937	1958	1965	1966	1974	1959	1978	1978
SNOW, ICE PELLETS													
Maximum monthly	27.7	22.4	27.6	42.3	15.6	2.0	0.0	0.0	9.3	23.1	25.2	28.8	42.3
Date	1963	1978	1935	1955	1981	1950	—	—	1984	1949	1978	1955	1955
Maximum in 24 hrs	16.6	9.0	10.5	23.7	15.3	2.0	0.0	0.0	7.5	11.2	15.3	13.7	23.7
Date	1972	1944	1964	1955	1981	1950	—	—	1983	1980	1959	1978	1955
WIND (Resultant)													
Mean speed (mph)	13.0	12.4	11.5	11.6	10.9	10.3	9.6	9.6	10.3	11.1	12.1	13.1	11.3

GLASGOW

Elev. 2284' 48° 13'N — 106° 37'W **Montana**

NORMALS, MEANS, EXTREMES

	JAN	FEB	MAR	APR	MAY	JUN	JUL	AUG	SEP	OCT	NOV	DEC	YEAR
TEMPERATURE													
Normal daily maximum	17.7	25.5	36.6	54.2	67.0	75.8	84.1	82.7	70.5	58.7	39.5	26.4	53.2
Normal daily minimum	-1.3	6.3	15.7	30.7	42.1	51.0	56.7	54.9	44.2	33.6	18.8	7.3	30.0
Normal monthly	8.2	15.9	26.2	42.5	54.6	63.4	70.4	68.8	57.4	46.2	29.2	16.9	41.6
Extreme highest	55	62	75	91	99	99	104	108	103	88	75	59	108
Extreme highest date	1968	1984	1966	1980	1980	1980	1984	1983	1983	1970	1975	1979	1983
Extreme lowest	-47	-37	-27	-3	20	33	41	37	20	-5	-26	-38	-47
Extreme lowest date	1969	1982	1960	1975	1976	1979	1977	1956	1985	1984	1985	1977	1969
DEGREE DAYS BASE 65° F													
Heating	1761	1375	1203	675	332	113	23	50	260	583	1074	1491	8940
Cooling	0	0	0	0	10	65	190	168	32	0	0	0	465
% OF POSSIBLE SUNSHINE	na	na	na	na	na	na	na	na	na	na	na	na	na
AVERAGE SKY COVER													
Sunrise - Sunset	7.1	7.2	6.9	6.9	6.6	5.9	4.5	4.7	5.6	6.2	7.0	7.2	6.3
NUMBER OF DAYS (Sunrise-Sunset)													
Clear	5.5	4.7	5.4	5.4	5.6	7.0	12.8	12.3	9.2	7.8	6.0	4.6	86.3
Partly cloudy	7.3	7.3	9.1	8.3	10.5	11.9	12.4	11.0	9.3	8.6	7.0	8.3	111.0
Cloudy	18.2	16.2	16.5	16.4	14.9	11.1	5.9	7.7	11.5	14.6	17.0	18.1	168.0
Precipitation .01" or more	8.6	6.8	7.2	7.0	9.6	10.6	7.8	7.2	6.4	4.9	6.1	8.5	90.7
Snow, Ice pellets 1.0" or more	2.2	1.4	1.2	0.8	0.1	0.0	0.0	0.0	0.1	0.5	1.2	1.6	9.2
Thunderstorms	0.0	0.0	0.1	0.5	3.6	7.2	7.7	5.7	1.5	0.2	*	0.0	26.4
Fog, Visibility 1/4 mile or less	2.1	2.3	1.9	0.7	0.3	0.3	*	0.1	0.2	0.6	1.8	2.7	12.8
Temperature Maximum:													
90° and above	0.0	0.0	0.0	*	0.6	2.1	9.4	9.0	1.6	0.0	0.0	0.0	22.8
32° and below	23.5	16.8	9.1	0.9	0.0	0.0	0.0	0.0	0.0	0.8	9.2	20.7	81.1
Temperature Minimum:													
32° and below	30.9	27.6	28.2	15.6	2.8	0.0	0.0	0.0	2.2	12.6	27.3	30.9	178.1
0° and below	16.4	9.8	3.3	0.1	0.0	0.0	0.0	0.0	0.0	0.1	2.4	10.7	42.7
RELATIVE HUMIDITY (%)													
Morning	73	77	79	75	73	76	72	69	72	74	78	77	75
Afternoon	70	71	59	43	40	40	33	32	39	47	63	73	51
PRECIPITATION (inches)													
Water Equivalent													
Normal	0.4	0.3	0.4	0.8	1.7	2.4	1.6	1.4	0.8	0.5	0.3	0.3	11.5
Maximum monthly	1.2	0.7	0.9	1.9	3.7	5.3	5.1	5.7	4.1	1.7	1.2	1.0	5.7
Date	1969	1979	1974	1969	1982	1963	1962	1985	1978	1975	1958	1982	1985
Minimum monthly	T	0.0	0.0	0.0	0.0	0.0	0.0	0.0	0.0	T	T	0.0	T
Date	1973	1985	1957	1956	1958	1985	1984	1983	1960	1965	1969	1959	1973
Maximum in 24 hrs	0.3	0.2	0.4	1.1	2.0	2.4	3.9	4.9	1.9	1.2	0.3	0.3	4.9
Date	1969	1982	1964	1969	1974	1972	1962	1985	1978	1981	1981	1982	1985
SNOW, ICE PELLETS													
Maximum monthly	24.2	15.9	14.8	13.7	10.7	0.0	0.0	0.0	2.2	7.0	17.2	13.9	24.2
Date	1971	1979	1967	1970	1983	—	—	—	1983	1975	1958	1972	1971
Maximum in 24 hrs	8.8	4.7	5.0	8.4	10.1	0.0	0.0	0.0	2.1	5.3	4.7	7.0	10.1
Date	1971	1979	1967	1970	1983	—	—	—	1983	1975	1985	1972	1983
WIND (Resultant)													
Mean speed (mph)	10.2	10.4	11.4	12.6	11.9	11.0	10.5	10.9	11.0	10.6	9.4	9.8	10.8

GREAT FALLS

Elev. 3663'   47° 29'N — 111° 22'W   **Montana**

NORMALS, MEANS, EXTREMES

	JAN	FEB	MAR	APR	MAY	JUN	JUL	AUG	SEP	OCT	NOV	DEC	YEAR
TEMPERATURE													
Normal daily maximum	28.2	36.5	41.7	54.0	65.3	74.3	84.2	82.0	70.5	59.5	43.5	34.7	56.2
Normal daily minimum	9.2	16.8	21.1	31.3	41.1	49.4	54.4	53.0	44.2	36.2	24.5	16.6	33.2
Normal monthly	18.7	26.7	31.4	42.7	53.2	61.9	69.3	67.5	57.4	47.9	34.0	25.7	44.7
Extreme highest	62	67	78	89	93	99	105	106	98	91	76	69	106
Extreme highest date	1981	1981	1978	1980	1980	1976	1973	1969	1980	1943	1975	1939	1969
Extreme lowest	-37	-35	-29	-6	15	31	40	35	21	-9	-25	-43	-43
Extreme lowest date	1969	1939	1951	1975	1954	1950	1980	1939	1985	1984	1985	1968	1968
DEGREE DAYS BASE 65° F													
Heating	1435	1072	1042	669	369	141	20	66	268	536	930	1218	7766
Cooling	0	0	0	0	0	48	153	144	40	6	0	0	391
% OF POSSIBLE SUNSHINE	49	55	66	61	62	64	80	76	67	60	46	44	61
AVERAGE SKY COVER													
Sunrise - Sunset	7.3	7.4	7.4	7.3	7.0	6.6	4.3	4.8	5.7	6.4	7.1	7.3	6.5
NUMBER OF DAYS (Sunrise-Sunset)													
Clear	5.4	4.0	4.1	4.0	4.7	5.4	13.6	12.5	9.5	7.0	4.9	4.8	79.9
Partly cloudy	6.1	6.5	8.8	8.0	9.7	10.6	11.5	10.6	9.2	8.9	7.5	7.7	105.1
Cloudy	19.5	17.7	18.1	17.9	16.6	14.0	6.0	7.9	11.3	15.0	17.6	18.6	180.2
Precipitation .01" or more	9.2	7.8	9.3	8.9	11.4	12.0	7.3	7.6	7.3	5.8	7.1	7.7	101.5
Snow, Ice pellets 1.0" or more	3.5	2.8	3.5	2.1	0.5	0.1	0.0	0.0	0.5	1.1	2.6	3.1	19.8
Thunderstorms	*	0.1	0.2	0.7	3.4	6.7	7.2	6.0	1.4	0.3	*	*	26.0
Fog, Visibility 1/4 mile or less	1.1	1.5	2.0	1.6	0.8	0.6	0.3	0.3	0.7	1.2	2.0	1.0	13.0
Temperature Maximum:													
90° and above	0.0	0.0	0.0	0.0	0.1	2.0	8.5	8.0	1.8	0.0	0.0	0.0	20.5
32° and below	14.6	8.1	6.6	1.6	0.0	0.0	0.0	0.0	*	1.0	5.4	12.8	50.1
Temperature Minimum:													
32° and below	27.4	23.9	25.8	16.0	3.6	0.1	0.0	0.0	2.9	10.8	21.5	26.6	158.4
0° and below	11.3	4.6	2.7	0.1	0.0	0.0	0.0	0.0	0.0	0.1	2.4	7.4	28.6
RELATIVE HUMIDITY (%)													
Morning	67	67	67	66	68	69	64	63	66	63	64	66	66
Afternoon	61	55	49	40	40	39	29	30	37	43	55	61	45
PRECIPITATION (inches)													
Water Equivalent													
Normal	1.0	0.7	0.9	1.4	2.5	2.7	1.1	1.3	1.0	0.8	0.7	0.8	15.2
Maximum monthly	2.0	2.1	2.1	4.6	8.1	5.3	4.3	4.9	3.5	3.4	2.2	1.9	8.1
Date	1969	1958	1967	1975	1953	1965	1955	1985	1941	1975	1955	1977	1953
Minimum monthly	T	0.0	0.1	0.0	0.6	0.5	0.0	0.0	0.1	T	0.0	T	T
Date	1944	1950	1960	1981	1950	1960	1959	1969	1962	1965	1954	1954	1965
Maximum in 24 hrs	0.7	0.8	1.1	2.4	3.4	2.7	2.4	2.0	1.8	1.1	0.9	0.8	3.4
Date	1966	1951	1977	1951	1980	1964	1983	1985	1982	1954	1946	1972	1980
SNOW, ICE PELLETS													
Maximum monthly	22.6	26.1	23.4	35.4	8.6	11.1	T	T	10.4	16.6	22.1	25.0	35.4
Date	1969	1958	1982	1967	1983	1950	1966	1985	1984	1975	1955	1945	1967
Maximum in 24 hrs	10.2	11.0	11.0	16.8	8.6	11.0	T	T	6.1	8.3	10.8	9.8	16.8
Date	1984	1951	1977	1973	1983	1950	1966	1985	1954	1957	1946	1945	1973
WIND (Resultant)													
Mean speed (mph)	15.2	14.5	13.1	13.0	11.5	11.2	10.2	10.3	11.4	13.4	14.6	15.6	12.8

HAVRE

Elev. 2584'   48° 33'N — 109° 46'W   **Montana**

NORMALS, MEANS, EXTREMES

	JAN	FEB	MAR	APR	MAY	JUN	JUL	AUG	SEP	OCT	NOV	DEC	YEAR
TEMPERATURE													
Normal daily maximum	21.5	30.3	39.8	55.3	67.8	76.4	85.4	83.6	71.6	60.0	41.5	29.6	55.3
Normal daily minimum	0.4	8.8	16.9	30.1	41.2	49.1	53.8	52.0	42.0	31.8	17.9	8.0	29.3
Normal monthly	11.0	19.6	28.4	42.7	54.5	62.8	69.6	67.8	56.8	45.9	29.7	18.8	42.3
Extreme highest	63	68	75	91	98	105	106	111	101	90	78	65	111
Extreme highest date	1968	1981	1977	1980	1980	1984	1975	1961	1967	1980	1975	1962	1961
Extreme lowest	-52	-35	-28	-14	24	31	39	36	18	-16	-30	-50	-52
Extreme lowest date	1969	1982	1978	1975	1967	1979	1981	1981	1984	1984	1985	1983	1969
DEGREE DAYS BASE 65° F													
Heating	1674	1271	1135	669	333	131	21	64	279	592	1059	1432	8660
Cooling	0	0	0	0	8	65	163	151	33	0	0	0	420
% OF POSSIBLE SUNSHINE	50	61	69	70	73	76	85	82	74	65	50	46	67
AVERAGE SKY COVER													
Sunrise - Sunset	7.4	7.2	7.2	7.1	6.6	6.2	4.2	4.7	5.7	6.5	7.1	7.4	6.4
NUMBER OF DAYS (Sunrise-Sunset)													
Clear	4.4	4.9	4.8	4.4	5.7	6.7	14.4	13.0	9.1	7.6	5.1	4.6	84.8
Partly cloudy	7.0	6.7	8.0	8.9	10.9	11.0	10.5	10.2	8.5	7.8	7.6	7.1	103.9
Cloudy	19.5	16.6	18.3	16.8	14.5	12.4	6.2	7.9	12.4	15.7	17.4	19.4	176.9
Precipitation .01" or more	9.0	6.0	7.7	7.8	10.0	9.6	7.4	6.9	7.0	5.1	5.4	7.9	89.6
Snow, Ice pellets 1.0" or more	2.7	2.1	2.1	2.0	0.2	0.0	0.0	0.0	0.1	0.8	1.8	3.0	15.0
Thunderstorms	0.0	0.0	0.0	0.6	2.8	5.1	5.6	5.3	1.2	0.2	0.0	0.0	20.9
Fog, Visibility 1/4 mile or less	0.4	1.1	1.3	1.1	0.5	0.1	0.1	0.1	0.4	0.8	1.6	0.9	8.3
Temperature Maximum:													
90° and above	0.0	0.0	0.0	*	0.3	3.6	10.5	10.5	2.1	*	0.0	0.0	27.1
32° and below	18.6	11.9	7.2	1.0	0.0	0.0	0.0	0.0	0.0	0.9	7.7	16.6	63.9
Temperature Minimum:													
32° and below	29.7	26.5	27.6	16.7	3.3	0.1	0.0	0.0	3.9	16.0	26.6	29.6	180.0
0° and below	15.4	8.0	4.1	0.3	0.0	0.0	0.0	0.0	0.0	0.2	3.7	11.0	42.8
RELATIVE HUMIDITY (%)													
Morning	74	77	78	74	73	75	71	68	72	74	75	75	74
Afternoon	70	64	54	40	37	35	28	28	35	45	61	70	47
PRECIPITATION (inches)													
Water Equivalent													
Normal	0.5	0.4	0.5	1.0	1.6	2.1	1.2	1.1	0.9	0.5	0.4	0.5	11.1
Maximum monthly	2.3	1.0	2.0	2.5	4.9	4.7	4.0	3.5	3.1	2.0	1.2	2.0	4.9
Date	1971	1979	1977	1967	1974	1965	1983	1974	1985	1980	1978	1977	1974
Minimum monthly	T	0.0	0.0	0.0	0.2	0.1	0.0	T	0.0	0.0	T	0.0	T
Date	1973	1976	1973	1981	1967	1985	1967	1967	1969	1965	1969	1962	1973
Maximum in 24 hrs	0.5	0.3	1.8	1.6	2.1	2.2	2.5	2.3	1.7	1.2	0.4	0.7	2.5
Date	1971	1973	1977	1973	1983	1970	1983	1968	1978	1980	1978	1977	1983
SNOW, ICE PELLETS													
Maximum monthly	41.4	18.6	30.1	32.8	30.6	T	0.0	0.0	6.2	10.5	18.9	25.1	41.4
Date	1971	1978	1977	1975	1982	1969	—	—	1982	1984	1978	1977	1971
Maximum in 24 hrs	11.7	6.2	26.9	16.2	23.5	T	0.0	0.0	6.2	8.5	6.6	6.1	26.9
Date	1971	1973	1977	1967	1982	1969	—	—	1982	1981	1978	1977	1977
WIND (Resultant)													
Mean speed (mph)	10.3	10.0	9.9	10.9	10.2	9.6	9.1	9.0	9.6	9.8	9.6	10.2	9.9

HELENA

Elev. 3828'   46° 36'N — 112° 00'W   **Montana**

NORMALS, MEANS, EXTREMES

	JAN	FEB	MAR	APR	MAY	JUN	JUL	AUG	SEP	OCT	NOV	DEC	YEAR
TEMPERATURE													
Normal daily maximum	28.1	36.2	42.5	54.7	64.9	73.1	83.6	81.3	70.3	58.6	42.3	33.3	55.7
Normal daily minimum	8.1	15.7	20.6	29.8	39.5	47.0	52.2	50.3	40.8	31.5	20.4	13.5	30.8
Normal monthly	18.1	26.0	31.6	42.3	52.2	60.1	67.9	65.8	55.6	45.1	31.4	23.4	43.3
Extreme highest	62	68	77	85	90	98	102	105	99	85	70	64	105
Extreme highest date	1953	1950	1978	1980	1966	1941	1981	1969	1967	1963	1953	1980	1969
Extreme lowest	-42	-31	-30	1	17	30	36	32	18	-3	-39	-38	-42
Extreme lowest date	1957	1956	1955	1954	1954	1969	1971	1956	1970	1972	1959	1964	1957
DEGREE DAYS BASE 65° F													
Heating	1454	1092	1035	681	397	179	41	77	308	617	1008	1287	8176
Cooling	0	0	0	0	0	32	131	105	26	0	0	0	294
% OF POSSIBLE SUNSHINE	46	54	60	59	61	62	78	74	67	60	44	41	59
AVERAGE SKY COVER													
Sunrise - Sunset	7.5	7.4	7.4	7.2	6.9	6.4	4.0	4.5	5.4	6.2	7.2	7.5	6.5
NUMBER OF DAYS (Sunrise-Sunset)													
Clear	4.7	4.1	3.8	3.8	4.8	5.6	14.8	13.2	10.0	8.1	4.7	4.0	81.6
Partly cloudy	5.9	6.5	8.3	8.7	9.8	11.0	10.8	10.8	8.8	8.6	7.4	6.9	103.6
Cloudy	20.4	17.7	19.0	17.5	16.4	13.3	5.4	7.0	11.2	14.3	17.9	20.1	180.0
Precipitation .01" or more	8.2	6.4	8.6	8.0	11.0	11.5	7.3	7.5	6.8	5.8	7.0	8.0	96.2
Snow, Ice pellets 1.0" or more	2.8	1.9	2.4	1.4	0.3	*	0.0	0.0	0.5	0.7	1.7	2.5	14.2
Thunderstorms	0.1	0.1	0.1	0.9	4.2	7.6	9.1	8.0	1.9	0.4	0.1	*	32.4
Fog, Visibility 1/4 mile or less	1.6	1.3	0.8	0.2	0.2	*	*	0.1	0.2	0.4	1.4	1.9	8.2
Temperature Maximum:													
90° and above	0.0	0.0	0.0	0.0	*	1.4	7.5	6.9	1.1	0.0	0.0	0.0	17.0
32° and below	15.1	7.9	4.5	0.5	0.0	0.0	0.0	0.0	0.0	0.6	5.9	14.8	49.3
Temperature Minimum:													
32° and below	29.3	26.6	27.5	18.9	4.0	0.1	0.0	0.0	3.9	17.4	27.3	29.5	184.3
0° and below	9.2	4.1	1.6	0.0	0.0	0.0	0.0	0.0	0.0	0.1	1.9	6.4	23.5
RELATIVE HUMIDITY (%)													
Morning	69	71	71	69	70	71	66	66	72	73	74	71	70
Afternoon	62	54	46	38	37	38	29	31	36	42	58	65	45
PRECIPITATION (inches)													
Water Equivalent													
Normal	0.6	0.4	0.6	1.0	1.7	2.0	1.0	1.1	0.8	0.6	0.5	0.6	11.3
Maximum monthly	2.7	1.1	1.6	3.0	6.0	4.7	3.8	4.2	3.3	2.6	1.5	1.4	6.0
Date	1969	1959	1982	1975	1981	1944	1975	1974	1965	1975	1950	1977	1981
Minimum monthly	0.0	0.0	0.0	0.1	0.2	0.0	0.0	0.1	0.0	0.0	0.0	0.0	0.0
Date	1944	1961	1959	1977	1979	1985	1973	1981	1972	1978	1969	1976	1978
Maximum in 24 hrs	0.7	0.5	1.0	1.2	2.3	1.7	2.2	1.8	1.6	0.8	0.8	0.5	2.3
Date	1969	1953	1957	1951	1981	1979	1983	1974	1980	1954	1959	1982	1981
SNOW, ICE PELLETS													
Maximum monthly	35.6	19.7	21.6	20.6	12.7	2.7	T	0.0	13.7	11.0	32.9	22.8	35.6
Date	1969	1959	1955	1967	1967	1969	1972	—	1965	1969	1959	1967	1969
Maximum in 24 hrs	11.5	8.6	8.7	12.9	12.5	2.7	T	0.0	13.3	7.4	21.5	10.7	21.5
Date	1969	1959	1955	1960	1967	1969	1972	—	1957	1969	1959	1941	1959
WIND (Resultant)													
Mean speed (mph)	6.8	7.5	8.5	9.3	8.9	8.6	7.9	7.5	7.5	7.2	7.1	6.9	7.8

KALISPELL

Elev. 2965'   48° 18'N — 114° 16'W   **Montana**

NORMALS, MEANS, EXTREMES

	JAN	FEB	MAR	APR	MAY	JUN	JUL	AUG	SEP	OCT	NOV	DEC	YEAR
TEMPERATURE													
Normal daily maximum	27.4	35.0	42.1	54.6	64.8	72.1	82.1	80.3	69.2	55.3	39.0	31.5	54.4
Normal daily minimum	11.2	17.5	21.6	30.5	38.1	44.5	47.9	46.7	38.6	29.6	22.7	16.9	30.5
Normal monthly	19.3	26.3	31.9	42.6	51.5	58.3	65.0	63.5	53.9	42.5	30.9	24.2	42.5
Extreme highest	53	56	71	84	89	96	104	105	99	82	65	57	105
Extreme highest date	1953	1981	1966	1977	1966	1955	1960	1961	1967	1979	1975	1979	1961
Extreme lowest	-38	-36	-29	10	19	28	31	31	16	-3	-28	-35	-38
Extreme lowest date	1950	1950	1960	1951	1954	1973	1971	1969	1970	1984	1959	1968	1950
DEGREE DAYS BASE 65° F													
Heating	1417	1084	1026	672	419	218	66	128	345	698	1023	1265	8361
Cooling	0	0	0	0	0	17	66	82	12	0	0	0	177
% OF POSSIBLE SUNSHINE	na	na	na	na	na	na	na	na	na	na	na	na	na
AVERAGE SKY COVER													
Sunrise - Sunset	8.7	8.3	7.8	7.5	6.9	6.5	4.1	4.7	5.6	7.0	8.4	8.9	7.0
NUMBER OF DAYS (Sunrise-Sunset)													
Clear	2.0	2.1	3.5	4.0	5.4	6.7	14.9	13.0	10.1	6.1	2.1	1.7	71.6
Partly cloudy	3.6	4.5	6.3	6.3	8.8	9.3	9.5	8.9	7.5	6.7	5.1	3.3	79.8
Cloudy	25.3	21.6	21.3	19.7	16.8	14.1	6.6	9.1	12.3	18.2	22.8	26.0	213.8
Precipitation .01" or more	15.6	11.8	11.4	9.3	11.0	12.2	6.6	8.3	8.3	9.1	12.3	15.6	131.6
Snow, Ice pellets 1.0" or more	6.1	3.9	2.1	0.8	0.3	0.0	0.0	0.0	*	0.6	2.6	5.4	22.0
Thunderstorms	0.0	0.1	0.3	0.8	2.7	5.2	5.4	5.3	2.0	0.4	0.1	0.0	22.1
Fog, Visibility 1/4 mile or less	4.6	4.4	2.3	0.5	1.0	0.8	0.7	0.9	2.3	4.7	4.6	4.7	31.6
Temperature Maximum:													
90° and above	0.0	0.0	0.0	0.0	0.0	1.0	6.6	6.3	0.3	0.0	0.0	0.0	14.3
32° and below	18.0	8.5	3.5	*	0.0	0.0	0.0	0.0	0.0	0.3	6.3	16.7	53.3
Temperature Minimum:													
32° and below	29.5	25.7	27.6	19.0	6.3	0.6	0.2	0.2	6.0	21.9	25.7	28.7	191.4
0° and below	7.6	2.8	1.2	0.0	0.0	0.0	0.0	0.0	0.0	*	0.8	4.5	17.0
RELATIVE HUMIDITY (%)													
Morning	79	81	78	76	78	83	82	80	82	83	82	82	81
Afternoon	74	68	54	43	43	46	35	35	43	53	71	77	54
PRECIPITATION (inches)													
Water Equivalent													
Normal	1.6	1.0	0.8	1.0	1.7	2.2	0.9	1.4	1.1	0.9	1.2	1.5	15.9
Maximum monthly	3.1	1.9	1.8	2.3	3.9	4.7	2.7	3.7	3.9	2.9	4.4	4.2	4.7
Date	1970	1981	1950	1978	1980	1966	1950	1976	1985	1951	1959	1964	1966
Minimum monthly	0.2	0.4	0.3	0.2	0.4	0.4	0.0	T	0.1	0.0	0.2	0.3	T
Date	1985	1967	1965	1968	1950	1977	1953	1955	1952	1953	1969	1954	1955
Maximum in 24 hrs	1.0	0.6	0.7	1.7	1.4	2.7	1.2	1.7	1.2	0.7	0.9	1.3	2.7
Date	1982	1961	1981	1951	1980	1982	1977	1976	1959	1957	1959	1964	1982
SNOW, ICE PELLETS													
Maximum monthly	34.8	21.2	14.8	8.1	8.9	0.3	0.0	0.0	3.1	11.1	39.0	49.7	49.7
Date	1970	1975	1977	1961	1964	1962	—	—	1968	1984	1959	1951	1951
Maximum in 24 hrs	11.8	7.2	7.6	10.0	7.5	0.3	0.0	0.0	3.0	6.2	10.1	15.4	15.4
Date	1982	1979	1953	1951	1964	1962	—	—	1968	1951	1959	1951	1951
WIND (Resultant)													
Mean speed (mph)	6.0	6.1	7.3	8.2	7.7	7.3	6.7	6.6	6.5	5.3	5.6	5.7	6.6

MILES CITY

Elev. 2629'   46° 26'N — 105° 52'W   **Montana**

NORMALS, MEANS, EXTREMES

	JAN	FEB	MAR	APR	MAY	JUN	JUL	AUG	SEP	OCT	NOV	DEC	YEAR
TEMPERATURE													
Normal daily maximum	24.3	32.6	42.6	57.1	69.2	79.2	88.9	86.6	73.8	61.3	42.7	31.5	57.5
Normal daily minimum	3.9	11.6	20.0	32.7	44.2	53.5	60.3	57.9	46.4	35.5	21.3	11.4	33.2
Normal monthly	14.1	22.1	31.3	44.9	56.7	66.4	74.6	72.3	60.1	48.4	32.0	21.5	45.4
Extreme highest	62	67	83	92	99	104	109	110	106	93	75	69	110
Extreme highest date	1953	1980	1943	1980	1980	1961	1980	1949	1983	1963	1965	1939	1949
Extreme lowest	-37	-37	-27	6	15	32	41	35	20	0	-25	-38	-38
Extreme lowest date	1969	1939	1947	1982	1954	1951	1945	1966	1942	1984	1985	1983	1983
DEGREE DAYS BASE 65° F													
Heating	1578	1201	1045	603	271	86	10	28	215	515	990	1349	7891
Cooling	0	0	0	0	17	128	308	255	68	0	0	0	776
% OF POSSIBLE SUNSHINE	na	na	na	na	na	na	na	na	na	na	na	na	na
AVERAGE SKY COVER													
Sunrise - Sunset	6.8	7.0	6.9	6.8	6.5	5.5	4.0	4.0	5.1	5.4	6.6	6.5	5.9
NUMBER OF DAYS (Sunrise-Sunset)													
Clear	6.0	5.1	4.6	5.4	5.9	7.7	14.5	15.1	10.1	11.8	6.5	6.9	99.6
Partly cloudy	7.9	8.2	8.4	7.9	9.8	10.7	12.6	11.2	9.8	8.4	7.3	7.7	109.8
Cloudy	17.1	15.0	18.1	16.7	15.3	11.6	3.9	4.8	10.1	10.8	16.2	16.4	155.8
Precipitation .01" or more	8.1	6.8	7.5	7.9	10.6	11.4	7.8	6.5	6.6	5.6	5.8	7.2	91.8
Snow, Ice pellets 1.0" or more	2.1	1.8	2.1	1.3	0.1	*	0.0	0.0	0.0	0.3	1.8	2.4	12.2
Thunderstorms	0.0	*	0.1	0.7	4.0	7.8	7.3	6.1	1.8	0.2	*	*	28.1
Fog, Visibility 1/4 mile or less	1.4	1.9	1.2	0.7	0.7	0.3	0.1	0.1	0.6	0.7	1.2	1.9	10.7
Temperature Maximum:													
90° and above	0.0	0.0	0.0	0.1	1.1	4.2	15.6	13.5	3.1	0.1	0.0	0.0	37.7
32° and below	18.0	12.4	6.9	0.6	*	0.0	0.0	0.0	0.0	0.4	6.8	15.7	61.0
Temperature Minimum:													
32° and below	30.5	27.3	27.0	14.1	2.2	0.1	0.0	0.0	1.7	10.8	26.2	30.4	170.3
0° and below	12.4	7.1	3.0	0.0	0.0	0.0	0.0	0.0	0.0	*	2.1	7.2	31.8
RELATIVE HUMIDITY (%)													
Morning	75	79	80	76	76	77	68	65	72	75	78	77	75
Afternoon	70	67	56	44	43	40	31	29	38	47	63	72	50
PRECIPITATION (inches)													
Water Equivalent													
Normal	0.5	0.5	0.5	1.3	2.3	2.7	1.5	1.2	1.0	0.9	0.6	0.6	14.1
Maximum monthly	1.7	1.3	1.8	4.2	6.8	9.7	4.5	4.0	4.6	6.3	2.1	1.7	9.7
Date	1971	1959	1950	1973	1978	1944	1948	1951	1941	1971	1978	1968	1944
Minimum monthly	0.0	0.0	0.0	0.0	0.2	0.7	0.1	T	T	T	0.0	0.0	T
Date	1981	1985	1959	1983	1958	1979	1971	1967	1960	1965	1953	1957	1967
Maximum in 24 hrs	0.4	0.7	0.6	1.3	2.3	2.7	2.2	1.6	2.6	1.3	1.1	0.5	2.7
Date	1944	1952	1944	1947	1955	1964	1985	1943	1941	1953	1957	1941	1964
SNOW, ICE PELLETS													
Maximum monthly	17.2	19.0	17.8	16.6	12.0	2.0	0.0	0.0	7.1	12.6	19.4	18.0	19.4
Date	1971	1949	1967	1967	1983	1950	—	—	1972	1949	1977	1968	1977
Maximum in 24 hrs	7.5	6.5	5.6	10.5	2.0	2.0	0.0	0.0	2.2	3.8	8.0	7.0	10.5
Date	1964	1952	1985	1947	1953	1950	—	—	1984	1946	1964	1958	1947
WIND (Resultant)													
Mean speed (mph)	9.6	9.7	10.7	11.8	11.1	10.3	9.7	9.8	10.0	9.9	9.7	9.8	10.2

NORMALS, MEANS, EXTREMES

	JAN	FEB	MAR	APR	MAY	JUN	JUL	AUG	SEP	OCT	NOV	DEC	YEAR
TEMPERATURE													
Normal daily maximum	28.8	36.4	44.4	56.5	65.8	74.0	84.8	82.7	71.3	57.0	40.4	31.8	56.2
Normal daily minimum	13.7	19.8	23.8	31.3	38.4	45.1	49.5	48.3	40.1	31.2	23.2	17.9	31.9
Normal monthly	21.3	28.1	34.1	43.9	52.1	59.6	67.2	65.5	55.7	44.1	31.8	24.9	44.0
Extreme highest	59	60	75	86	92	98	105	105	99	85	66	60	105
Extreme highest date	1953	1967	1978	1977	1956	1955	1973	1961	1967	1980	1983	1956	1973
Extreme lowest	-33	-27	-13	14	21	31	31	32	20	0	-23	-30	-33
Extreme lowest date	1957	1982	1955	1951	1985	1984	1971	1980	1985	1971	1955	1983	1957
DEGREE DAYS BASE 65° F													
Heating	1355	1033	958	633	400	180	29	75	289	648	996	1243	7839
Cooling	0	0	0	0	0	18	97	91	10	0	0	0	216
% OF POSSIBLE SUNSHINE	31	41	51	54	57	59	80	75	67	53	34	28	53
AVERAGE SKY COVER													
Sunrise - Sunset	8.4	8.2	7.9	7.5	7.0	6.4	3.8	4.5	5.5	6.8	8.2	8.6	6.9
NUMBER OF DAYS (Sunrise-Sunset)													
Clear	2.6	2.5	3.3	3.8	5.3	6.4	16.1	13.9	9.8	6.4	2.6	1.9	74.5
Partly cloudy	3.9	4.4	5.8	6.7	8.4	9.0	9.9	9.1	8.5	7.2	4.6	4.0	81.5
Cloudy	24.5	21.3	21.8	19.5	17.2	14.6	5.1	8.0	11.8	17.4	22.8	25.2	209.2
Precipitation .01" or more	14.3	10.8	11.6	10.0	11.6	11.5	6.9	7.2	7.7	8.1	11.4	13.1	124.3
Snow, Ice pellets 1.0" or more	4.4	2.1	2.0	0.7	0.3	0.0	0.0	0.0	0.0	0.3	2.1	4.0	15.9
Thunderstorms	*	*	*	0.5	3.4	5.2	6.3	6.1	2.0	0.3	*	0.0	23.9
Fog, Visibility 1/4 mile or less	4.8	3.9	1.3	0.2	0.2	0.3	0.2	0.5	1.1	3.4	4.5	6.4	27.0
Temperature Maximum:													
90° and above	0.0	0.0	0.0	0.0	0.1	2.2	9.2	9.1	0.9	0.0	0.0	0.0	21.4
32° and below	16.8	6.9	2.5	0.0	0.0	0.0	0.0	0.0	0.0	0.2	6.0	17.4	49.8
Temperature Minimum:													
32° and below	29.4	26.1	26.3	18.0	5.8	0.2	*	*	4.4	18.3	26.2	29.4	184.2
0° and below	5.5	1.6	0.3	0.0	0.0	0.0	0.0	0.0	0.0	*	0.4	3.2	11.0
RELATIVE HUMIDITY (%)													
Morning	85	85	84	80	81	83	77	75	84	86	87	87	83
Afternoon	77	67	52	42	43	43	31	31	40	51	71	80	52
PRECIPITATION (inches)													
Water Equivalent													
Normal	1.4	0.8	0.8	1.0	1.6	1.8	0.8	0.9	1.0	0.8	0.8	1.2	13.2
Maximum monthly	2.9	1.8	1.6	2.4	7.3	4.1	3.0	3.2	3.6	3.5	2.5	3.1	7.3
Date	1969	1972	1972	1956	1980	1958	1946	1985	1985	1975	1973	1964	1980
Minimum monthly	0.1	0.1	0.2	0.0	0.2	0.3	0.0	T	0.0	0.0	0.2	0.2	T
Date	1981	1973	1953	1977	1963	1961	1985	1967	1979	1978	1976	1976	1967
Maximum in 24 hrs	0.8	1.0	0.6	1.6	1.9	1.6	1.4	1.4	1.3	1.4	0.8	0.9	1.9
Date	1948	1975	1972	1951	1980	1964	1946	1947	1954	1946	1973	1964	1980
SNOW, ICE PELLETS													
Maximum monthly	42.5	20.1	13.4	8.2	8.1	T	0.0	0.0	0.4	5.4	17.7	31.6	42.5
Date	1963	1975	1955	1970	1978	1973	—	—	1983	1973	1947	1964	1963
Maximum in 24 hrs	11.3	14.4	6.9	6.9	8.1	T	0.0	0.0	0.4	5.4	6.2	9.6	14.4
Date	1980	1975	1977	1950	1978	1973	—	—	1983	1973	1961	1955	1975
WIND (Resultant)													
Mean speed (mph)	5.2	5.6	6.7	7.5	7.3	7.0	6.8	6.6	6.0	5.0	5.0	4.8	6.1

GRAND ISLAND
Elev. 1841'   40° 58N — 98° 19W   **Nebraska**

NORMALS, MEANS, EXTREMES

	JAN	FEB	MAR	APR	MAY	JUN	JUL	AUG	SEP	OCT	NOV	DEC	YEAR
TEMPERATURE													
Normal daily maximum	31.2	38.1	47.1	62.3	73.0	83.6	88.8	86.9	77.1	66.7	49.4	37.3	61.8
Normal daily minimum	9.9	16.2	24.7	37.8	49.1	59.2	64.4	62.3	51.5	39.4	25.7	16.0	38.0
Normal monthly	20.6	27.2	35.9	50.1	61.1	71.4	76.6	74.6	64.3	53.1	37.6	26.7	49.9
Extreme highest	72	77	90	94	101	107	109	110	104	96	82	76	110
Extreme highest date	1981	1972	1978	1964	1967	1970	1954	1983	1947	1947	1980	1964	1983
Extreme lowest	-28	-19	-21	7	23	38	42	40	23	16	-11	-23	-28
Extreme lowest date	1963	1979	1960	1975	1967	1954	1971	1950	1984	1981	1976	1983	1963
DEGREE DAYS BASE 65° F													
Heating	1376	1058	902	447	169	27	7	6	104	377	822	1187	6482
Cooling	0	0	0	0	49	219	366	303	83	8	0	0	1028
AVERAGE SKY COVER													
Sunrise - Sunset	6.1	6.3	6.4	6.1	6.0	5.1	4.4	4.5	4.6	4.8	6.0	6.0	5.5
NUMBER OF DAYS													
(Sunrise-Sunset)													
Clear	9.0	7.2	7.9	8.0	7.8	10.3	12.8	13.2	13.5	13.5	9.4	9.5	122.2
Partly cloudy	8.0	7.5	7.8	8.4	9.4	10.1	11.1	10.3	7.3	7.7	7.4	7.4	102.4
Cloudy	14.0	13.6	15.4	13.5	13.6	9.6	7.1	7.5	9.0	9.8	13.2	14.1	140.5
Precipitation .01" or more	5.2	6.0	7.5	9.2	10.9	9.9	8.7	7.8	7.1	5.0	4.7	4.6	86.6
Snow, Ice pellets 1.0" or more	2.0	2.2	2.0	0.6	*	0.0	0.0	0.0	*	0.1	1.0	1.7	9.6
Thunderstorms	*	0.2	1.2	3.8	7.7	10.0	9.0	8.0	5.3	2.0	0.5	0.1	47.9
Fog, Visibility 1/4 mile or less	1.9	2.3	1.8	1.3	0.8	0.6	0.7	1.0	1.2	1.6	2.1	2.3	17.8
Temperature Maximum:													
90° and above	0.0	0.0	*	0.5	1.8	7.6	14.4	11.9	3.6	0.3	0.0	0.0	40.2
32° and below	16.3	10.5	4.6	0.1	0.0	0.0	0.0	0.0	0.0	0.0	3.2	13.0	47.7
Temperature Minimum:													
32° and below	30.6	26.8	23.4	7.2	0.7	0.0	0.0	0.0	0.5	6.3	22.5	30.1	148.2
0° and below	8.7	3.7	0.5	0.0	0.0	0.0	0.0	0.0	0.0	0.0	0.4	3.8	17.0
RELATIVE HUMIDITY (%)													
Morning	74	75	73	71	73	73	73	76	78	73	76	75	74
Afternoon	64	62	57	51	52	51	52	52	54	49	57	63	55
PRECIPITATION (inches)													
Water Equivalent													
Normal	0.5	0.8	1.5	2.6	3.7	3.7	2.7	2.5	2.5	1.0	0.8	0.6	23.3
Maximum monthly	1.6	3.3	5.5	7.3	8.8	13.9	9.6	8.7	9.0	4.4	3.7	2.1	13.9
Date	1960	1971	1973	1984	1982	1967	1950	1977	1965	1946	1983	1968	1967
Minimum monthly	13.9	0.0	0.0	0.3	0.4	0.5	0.6	0.5	0.1	0.0	0.0	0.0	0.0
Date	1961	1974	1967	1946	1964	1978	1970	1940	1939	1958	1939	1943	1958
Maximum in 24 hrs	1.3	2.2	3.1	3.3	3.0	4.5	5.4	4.1	5.8	2.7	1.9	1.2	5.8
Date	1947	1971	1979	1964	1985	1967	1950	1977	1977	1968	1973	1968	1977
SNOW, ICE PELLETS													
Maximum monthly	16.1	21.5	20.5	9.0	4.5	0.0	0.0	0.0	3.8	6.6	17.1	26.0	26.0
Date	1960	1969	1984	1984	1947	—	—	—	1985	1980	1983	1973	1973
Maximum in 24 hrs	8.3	15.0	12.2	5.5	4.5	0.0	0.0	0.0	3.8	6.6	11.2	12.0	15.0
Date	1960	1984	1984	1984	1947	—	—	—	1985	1980	1983	1968	1984
WIND (Resultant)													
Mean speed (mph)	11.8	12.0	13.6	14.2	12.7	12.0	10.7	10.6	11.1	11.4	11.9	11.8	12.0

LINCOLN

Elev. 1150'   40° 51N — 96° 45W   **Nebraska**

NORMALS, MEANS, EXTREMES

	JAN	FEB	MAR	APR	MAY	JUN	JUL	AUG	SEP	OCT	NOV	DEC	YEAR
TEMPERATURE													
Normal daily maximum	30.4	37.5	47.7	63.6	74.4	84.3	89.5	87.2	78.0	67.4	50.0	37.2	62.3
Normal daily minimum	8.9	15.4	25.1	38.6	49.9	60.2	65.6	63.4	52.9	40.6	26.9	16.0	38.6
Normal monthly	19.7	26.5	36.4	51.1	62.2	72.3	77.6	75.3	65.5	54.0	38.5	26.6	50.4
Extreme highest	72	84	87	91	93	105	106	107	101	93	82	68	107
Extreme highest date	1981	1972	1978	1972	1983	1974	1983	1983	1975	1975	1980	1976	1983
Extreme lowest	-33	-24	-19	3	25	39	42	45	26	12	-5	-27	-33
Extreme lowest date	1974	1979	1978	1975	1976	1978	1972	1978	1984	1972	1976	1983	1974
DEGREE DAYS BASE 65° F													
Heating	1404	1078	887	417	151	16	5	0	79	353	795	1190	6375
Cooling	0	0	0	0	64	235	396	323	94	12	0	0	1124
% OF POSSIBLE SUNSHINE	57	57	56	59	62	70	73	72	66	63	54	52	62
AVERAGE SKY COVER													
Sunrise - Sunset	6.2	6.3	6.5	6.3	6.1	5.4	4.8	4.9	5.0	5.4	6.3	6.5	5.8
NUMBER OF DAYS													
(Sunrise-Sunset)													
Clear	9.2	8.0	7.8	8.1	8.0	9.7	12.3	11.9	12.4	11.3	8.2	7.9	114.8
Partly cloudy	6.2	6.3	7.5	7.7	9.9	10.0	10.3	10.3	7.3	7.5	7.1	7.4	97.6
Cloudy	15.6	13.9	15.7	14.1	13.0	10.4	8.3	8.9	10.3	12.2	14.6	15.8	152.9
Precipitation .01" or more	6.5	5.2	8.8	9.9	11.2	7.9	8.1	8.6	7.8	7.1	5.9	5.5	92.6
Snow, Ice pellets 1.0" or more	2.2	2.0	1.9	0.5	0.0	0.0	0.0	0.0	0.0	0.1	1.0	1.9	9.6
Thunderstorms	0.1	0.2	1.7	4.9	7.0	7.9	8.1	7.5	5.1	2.6	0.7	0.4	46.4
Fog, Visibility 1/4 mile or less	0.9	1.7	2.1	0.4	0.4	0.4	0.1	0.6	0.4	1.2	1.7	1.7	11.6
Temperature Maximum:													
90° and above	0.0	0.0	0.0	0.1	0.6	7.8	17.1	12.3	4.5	0.2	0.0	0.0	42.6
32° and below	17.3	11.3	2.7	0.1	0.0	0.0	0.0	0.0	0.0	0.0	3.4	13.1	47.9
Temperature Minimum:													
32° and below	30.7	26.4	21.5	7.0	0.8	0.0	0.0	0.0	0.6	5.9	21.2	30.1	144.2
0° and below	9.1	4.7	0.6	0.0	0.0	0.0	0.0	0.0	0.0	0.0	0.2	4.4	19.1
RELATIVE HUMIDITY (%)													
Morning	76	80	77	74	77	75	73	78	79	75	79	78	77
Afternoon	66	67	62	56	57	54	52	57	56	54	62	66	59
PRECIPITATION (inches)													
Water Equivalent													
Normal	0.6	1.0	1.9	2.8	3.8	3.8	3.2	3.4	2.9	1.6	0.9	0.6	26.9
Maximum monthly	1.5	1.2	6.6	7.2	7.9	7.6	6.9	8.5	7.5	5.2	3.8	3.4	8.5
Date	1975	1984	1973	1978	1984	1983	1985	1982	1973	1979	1981	1984	1982
Minimum monthly	0.1	0.0	0.4	1.0	2.0	0.6	0.3	0.0	0.2	0.0	0.0	0.0	0.0
Date	1981	1977	1972	1983	1980	1976	1983	1976	1974	1975	1976	1976	1975
Maximum in 24 hrs	0.7	0.8	1.8	2.3	3.3	4.2	4.6	2.9	3.5	4.2	1.9	2.2	4.6
Date	1975	1984	1979	1974	1984	1985	1985	1982	1977	1979	1977	1984	1985
SNOW, ICE PELLETS													
Maximum monthly	14.6	13.8	17.0	7.2	0.0	0.0	0.0	0.0	0.8	3.3	8.6	19.8	19.8
Date	1975	1978	1984	1983	—	—	—	—	1985	1980	1983	1973	1973
Maximum in 24 hrs	8.0	7.7	8.3	4.2	0.0	0.0	0.0	0.0	0.8	3.3	7.7	10.4	10.4
Date	1975	1978	1977	1979	—	—	—	—	1985	1980	1972	1973	1973
WIND (Resultant)													
Mean speed (mph)	10.1	10.5	11.9	12.7	10.5	10.1	9.8	9.6	9.8	10.1	10.2	10.3	10.5

NORFOLK

Elev. 1544' 41° 59N — 97° 26W **Nebraska**

NORMALS, MEANS, EXTREMES

	JAN	FEB	MAR	APR	MAY	JUN	JUL	AUG	SEP	OCT	NOV	DEC	YEAR
TEMPERATURE													
Normal daily maximum	27.8	34.2	43.8	60.5	72.2	82.4	87.4	85.0	75.5	64.7	47.1	34.1	59.6
Normal daily minimum	6.9	13.3	23.2	36.9	48.8	58.9	64.2	61.9	51.0	38.8	24.8	13.7	36.9
Normal monthly	17.4	23.8	33.5	48.7	60.5	70.7	75.8	73.5	63.3	51.8	36.0	23.9	48.2
Extreme highest	71	73	87	95	103	106	113	107	101	95	82	71	113
Extreme highest date	1981	1946	1968	1980	1967	1946	1954	1983	1971	1963	1945	1962	1954
Extreme lowest	-27	-26	-20	2	24	38	42	40	26	13	-15	-22	-27
Extreme lowest date	1974	1981	1960	1975	1976	1964	1971	1967	1984	1972	1964	1983	1974
DEGREE DAYS BASE 65° F													
Heating	1476	1154	977	489	181	27	6	9	125	417	870	1274	7005
Cooling	0	0	0	0	45	198	341	269	74	8	0	0	935
AVERAGE SKY COVER													
Sunrise - Sunset	6.2	6.3	6.7	6.3	6.1	5.4	4.7	4.7	4.8	5.0	6.2	6.3	5.7
NUMBER OF DAYS													
(Sunrise-Sunset)													
Clear	8.8	7.6	7.2	7.7	7.6	10.0	12.3	12.6	12.9	12.5	8.5	8.5	116.3
Partly cloudy	7.5	6.9	7.8	8.2	10.0	10.1	11.6	10.4	7.4	7.6	7.4	7.6	102.4
Cloudy	14.8	13.7	16.1	14.1	13.5	9.9	7.1	8.0	9.7	10.9	14.1	14.9	146.6
Precipitation .01" or more	5.7	5.6	8.0	9.1	11.1	9.9	8.7	8.5	7.7	5.6	5.0	5.5	90.0
Snow, Ice pellets 1.0" or more	1.9	2.0	2.2	0.6	*	0.0	0.0	0.0	*	0.2	1.2	1.9	10.0
Thunderstorms	*	0.2	0.9	3.9	8.0	10.0	9.5	9.7	3.9	2.6	0.6	0.1	49.3
Fog, Visibility 1/4 mile or less	1.2	2.1	1.6	0.7	0.6	0.7	0.7	1.2	0.9	1.1	1.6	1.5	13.8
Temperature Maximum:													
90° and above	0.0	0.0	0.0	0.4	1.2	6.6	11.9	10.0	3.6	0.3	0.0	0.0	34.0
32° and below	17.6	12.6	6.7	0.2	0.0	0.0	0.0	0.0	0.0	0.0	3.8	14.2	55.1
Temperature Minimum:													
32° and below	30.8	27.2	24.9	9.6	1.0	0.0	0.0	0.0	0.7	7.1	23.6	30.5	155.4
0° and below	10.1	5.0	0.9	0.0	0.0	0.0	0.0	0.0	0.0	0.0	0.6	4.5	21.1
RELATIVE HUMIDITY (%)													
Morning	70	74	76	70	72	72	74	80	75	74	77	76	74
Afternoon	64	64	61	50	51	52	53	54	52	50	58	65	56
PRECIPITATION (inches)													
Water Equivalent													
Normal	0.5	0.8	1.5	2.2	3.7	4.3	3.2	2.6	2.0	1.3	0.7	0.6	23.7
Maximum monthly	2.3	3.1	5.1	7.4	8.6	12.2	9.1	5.5	8.1	4.5	3.9	2.2	12.2
Date	1949	1971	1973	1984	1977	1967	1950	1951	1970	1968	1983	1982	1967
Minimum monthly	0.1	0.0	0.0	0.2	1.0	0.8	0.3	0.5	0.3	0.3	0.0	0.0	0.0
Date	1970	1949	1967	1969	1948	1978	1954	1971	1956	1958	1980	1958	1958
Maximum in 24 hrs	1.3	2.4	2.4	1.9	4.1	5.5	3.4	2.8	3.8	2.7	1.5	1.3	5.5
Date	1982	1971	1981	1985	1973	1974	1952	1978	1970	1968	1975	1981	1974
SNOW, ICE PELLETS													
Maximum monthly	16.4	22.8	20.8	13.2	2.7	0.0	0.0	0.0	1.1	3.1	22.6	19.1	22.8
Date	1982	1984	1960	1984	1947	—	—	—	1985	1982	1983	1968	1984
Maximum in 24 hrs	12.8	22.5	9.7	9.7	2.7	0.0	0.0	0.0	1.1	3.1	14.6	12.1	22.5
Date	1982	1984	1966	1984	1947	—	—	—	1985	1982	1983	1978	1984
WIND (Resultant)													
Mean speed (mph)	12.6	12.1	13.4	13.7	11.8	10.8	10.0	9.9	10.9	11.2	11.9	12.4	11.7

NORMALS, MEANS, EXTREMES

	JAN	FEB	MAR	APR	MAY	JUN	JUL	AUG	SEP	OCT	NOV	DEC	YEAR
TEMPERATURE													
Normal daily maximum	34.2	40.5	47.8	61.5	71.5	81.6	87.8	86.4	77.3	66.7	49.4	39.3	62.0
Normal daily minimum	8.3	14.1	21.5	33.6	44.8	55.0	60.6	58.3	46.5	33.7	20.5	12.5	34.1
Normal monthly	21.3	27.3	34.7	47.6	58.2	68.3	74.2	72.4	61.9	50.2	35.0	25.9	48.1
Extreme highest	70	79	86	94	97	107	112	105	102	91	82	75	112
Extreme highest date	1981	1962	1968	1980	1953	1952	1954	1954	1979	1978	1980	1980	1954
Extreme lowest	-23	-22	-22	7	20	29	40	35	17	11	-13	-34	-34
Extreme lowest date	1979	1981	1962	1975	1976	1969	1952	1976	1984	1969	1976	1983	1983
DEGREE DAYS BASE 65° F													
Heating	1355	1056	939	522	235	59	8	9	151	463	900	1212	6909
Cooling	0	0	0	0	24	158	294	239	58	0	0	0	773
% OF POSSIBLE SUNSHINE	60	59	60	62	63	69	75	73	70	68	59	60	65
AVERAGE SKY COVER													
Sunrise - Sunset	6.2	6.3	6.6	6.3	6.4	5.2	4.7	4.7	4.6	4.9	5.9	5.9	5.6
NUMBER OF DAYS													
(Sunrise-Sunset)													
Clear	8.3	6.9	7.3	7.2	6.7	10.4	12.1	12.0	13.1	12.9	9.2	9.4	115.4
Partly cloudy	8.5	7.8	7.6	9.1	10.4	10.9	12.2	11.7	8.5	8.5	8.1	8.2	111.4
Cloudy	14.2	13.6	16.1	13.7	13.9	8.7	6.7	7.4	8.4	9.6	12.7	13.5	138.5
Precipitation .01" or more	5.2	5.3	7.0	8.3	10.7	9.5	9.8	7.6	6.6	4.9	4.7	4.5	84.0
Snow, Ice pellets 1.0" or more	1.7	1.6	1.9	0.9	0.1	0.0	0.0	0.0	*	0.4	1.1	1.5	9.2
Thunderstorms	0.1	0.1	0.8	2.7	6.7	10.1	10.3	8.5	4.3	1.1	0.2	0.0	44.9
Fog, Visibility 1/4 mile or less	1.3	1.9	2.0	0.9	0.7	0.8	1.0	1.7	1.9	2.0	2.4	1.5	18.1
Temperature Maximum:													
90° and above	0.0	0.0	0.0	0.2	0.8	5.2	13.1	11.2	3.9	0.2	0.0	0.0	34.7
32° and below	14.3	8.5	4.3	0.3	*	0.0	0.0	0.0	0.0	0.1	4.1	11.4	43.1
Temperature Minimum:													
32° and below	31.0	28.0	27.4	12.7	2.6	*	0.0	0.0	2.7	14.5	27.9	30.9	177.7
0° and below	9.6	3.6	0.7	0.0	0.0	0.0	0.0	0.0	0.0	0.0	0.7	5.0	19.6
RELATIVE HUMIDITY (%)													
Morning	76	75	73	71	73	74	72	74	73	71	75	76	74
Afternoon	63	58	53	48	50	52	50	50	48	46	55	61	53
PRECIPITATION (inches)													
Water Equivalent													
Normal	0.4	0.5	1.1	1.8	3.3	3.7	2.9	1.9	1.6	0.9	0.5	0.4	19.4
Maximum monthly	1.1	1.9	2.8	5.0	8.0	6.8	7.0	5.3	6.0	2.9	2.8	1.2	8.0
Date	1960	1978	1977	1984	1962	1965	1979	1957	1963	1969	1979	1977	1962
Minimum monthly	8.0	0.0	0.0	0.1	0.7	0.3	0.4	0.0	0.0	0.0	0.0	0.0	0.0
Date	1964	1954	1967	1954	1966	1952	1955	1967	1953	1955	1974	1976	1964
Maximum in 24 hrs	0.6	1.1	2.2	2.4	2.9	3.8	3.1	2.9	2.5	1.3	1.4	0.7	3.8
Date	1960	1971	1959	1971	1962	1965	1964	1957	1963	1982	1979	1978	1965
SNOW, ICE PELLETS													
Maximum monthly	17.1	20.6	21.9	14.5	3.6	0.0	0.0	0.0	3.1	15.7	17.5	14.1	21.9
Date	1976	1978	1980	1984	1967	—	—	—	1985	1969	1979	1973	1980
Maximum in 24 hrs	11.9	9.7	15.1	8.5	2.3	0.0	0.0	0.0	3.1	8.8	8.8	8.6	15.1
Date	1976	1955	1980	1984	1967	—	—	—	1985	1969	1979	1968	1980
WIND (Resultant)													
Mean speed (mph)	9.3	10.0	11.7	12.8	11.7	10.5	9.6	9.4	9.8	9.6	9.6	9.2	10.3

OMAHA

Elev. 977' **41° 18N — 95° 54W** # Nebraska

NORMALS, MEANS, EXTREMES

	JAN	FEB	MAR	APR	MAY	JUN	JUL	AUG	SEP	OCT	NOV	DEC	YEAR
TEMPERATURE													
Normal daily maximum	30.2	37.3	47.7	64.0	74.7	84.2	88.5	86.2	77.5	67.0	50.3	36.9	62.0
Normal daily minimum	10.2	17.1	26.9	40.3	51.8	61.7	66.8	64.2	54.0	42.0	28.6	17.4	40.1
Normal monthly	20.2	27.2	37.3	52.2	63.3	73.0	77.7	75.2	65.8	54.5	39.5	27.2	51.1
Extreme highest	69	78	89	93	99	105	114	110	104	96	80	72	114
Extreme highest date	1944	1972	1968	1965	1939	1953	1936	1936	1939	1938	1980	1939	1936
Extreme lowest	-23	-21	-16	5	27	38	44	43	25	13	-9	-21	-23
Extreme lowest date	1982	1981	1948	1975	1980	1983	1972	1967	1984	1972	1964	1983	1982
DEGREE DAYS BASE 65° F													
Heating	1389	1058	859	390	130	16	0	0	73	342	765	1172	6194
Cooling	0	0	0	6	77	256	394	320	97	16	0	0	1166
AVERAGE SKY COVER													
Sunrise - Sunset	6.1	6.3	6.6	6.3	6.2	5.6	4.8	4.7	4.8	4.7	6.0	6.4	5.7
NUMBER OF DAYS													
(Sunrise-Sunset)													
Clear	8.9	7.4	7.0	7.3	7.4	8.5	11.7	12.8	12.7	13.3	8.9	8.1	114.0
Partly cloudy	7.9	7.5	8.1	8.7	9.8	11.2	12.4	10.1	7.4	8.1	7.6	7.4	106.1
Cloudy	14.2	13.3	15.9	14.1	13.8	10.3	6.9	8.1	10.0	9.6	13.5	15.4	145.2
Precipitation .01" or more	6.5	6.6	8.7	9.5	11.5	10.6	8.9	9.1	8.4	6.4	5.3	6.2	97.7
Snow, Ice pellets 1.0" or more	2.5	1.9	2.2	0.4	*	0.0	0.0	0.0	0.0	0.1	0.8	1.9	9.8
Thunderstorms	0.1	0.4	1.4	4.0	7.4	9.4	8.0	7.8	5.2	2.5	0.8	0.2	47.3
Fog, Visibility 1/4 mile or less	1.9	2.0	1.5	0.5	0.8	0.4	0.5	1.5	1.4	1.5	1.6	2.0	15.5
Temperature Maximum:													
90° and above	0.0	0.0	0.0	0.2	1.4	7.0	13.8	9.4	3.0	0.3	0.0	0.0	35.1
32° and below	16.0	10.2	3.8	0.1	0.0	0.0	0.0	0.0	0.0	0.0	2.6	12.5	45.2
Temperature Minimum:													
32° and below	30.1	26.1	21.6	6.3	0.5	0.0	0.0	0.0	0.5	5.5	19.8	29.2	139.7
0° and below	8.1	3.6	0.5	0.0	0.0	0.0	0.0	0.0	0.0	0.0	0.2	3.4	15.9
RELATIVE HUMIDITY (%)													
Morning	76	77	73	69	73	76	77	79	81	76	77	77	76
Afternoon	66	64	58	53	54	55	56	58	59	56	63	68	59
PRECIPITATION (inches)													
Water Equivalent													
Normal	0.7	0.9	1.9	2.9	4.3	4.0	3.6	4.1	3.5	2.0	1.3	0.7	30.3
Maximum monthly	3.7	2.9	5.9	6.4	10.3	10.8	9.6	9.1	13.7	4.9	4.7	5.4	13.7
Date	1949	1965	1973	1951	1959	1947	1958	1959	1965	1961	1983	1984	1965
Minimum monthly	0.0	0.0	0.1	0.2	0.5	1.0	0.3	0.6	0.4	0.4	0.0	0.0	0.0
Date	1943	1981	1956	1936	1948	1972	1983	1984	1953	1952	1976	1943	1952
Maximum in 24 hrs	1.5	2.2	1.4	2.5	3.5	3.4	3.3	3.4	6.4	3.1	2.5	3.0	6.4
Date	1967	1954	1959	1938	1964	1942	1958	1959	1965	1968	1948	1984	1965
SNOW, ICE PELLETS													
Maximum monthly	25.7	25.4	27.2	8.6	2.0	0.0	0.0	0.0	T	7.2	12.0	19.9	27.2
Date	1936	1965	1948	1945	1945	—	—	—	1985	1941	1957	1969	1948
Maximum in 24 hrs	13.1	18.3	13.0	8.6	2.0	T	0.0	0.0	T	7.2	8.7	10.2	18.3
Date	1949	1965	1948	1945	1945	1985	—	—	1985	1941	1957	1969	1965
WIND (Resultant)													
Mean speed (mph)	10.9	11.2	12.3	12.8	11.0	10.2	8.9	8.9	9.5	9.8	10.8	10.7	10.6

SCOTTSBLUFF

Elev. 3957'   41° 52N — 103° 36W   **Nebraska**

NORMALS, MEANS, EXTREMES

	JAN	FEB	MAR	APR	MAY	JUN	JUL	AUG	SEP	OCT	NOV	DEC	YEAR
TEMPERATURE													
Normal daily maximum	37.2	43.4	48.8	60.3	70.8	81.7	89.2	86.7	77.5	66.0	49.8	40.8	62.7
Normal daily minimum	11.2	16.7	22.3	32.5	43.6	53.3	59.2	56.5	45.6	34.3	22.0	14.8	34.3
Normal monthly	24.2	30.1	35.6	46.4	57.2	67.5	74.2	71.6	61.6	50.2	35.9	27.8	48.5
Extreme highest	74	77	87	89	95	105	109	104	101	92	78	77	109
Extreme highest date	1982	1962	1943	1981	1969	1954	1973	1980	1948	1967	1980	1980	1973
Extreme lowest	-32	-28	-27	-8	15	30	40	39	19	9	-13	-27	-32
Extreme lowest date	1963	1962	1948	1975	1983	1969	1959	1944	1985	1969	1947	1983	1963
DEGREE DAYS BASE 65° F													
Heating	1265	977	911	558	254	69	6	5	172	459	873	1153	6702
Cooling	0	0	0	0	13	144	291	210	70	0	0	0	728
AVERAGE SKY COVER													
Sunrise - Sunset	6.2	6.2	6.6	6.4	6.4	5.2	4.3	4.4	4.3	4.8	6.0	6.0	5.6
NUMBER OF DAYS													
(Sunrise-Sunset)													
Clear	8.4	7.5	6.6	6.9	6.2	10.1	13.7	13.5	14.5	13.3	8.6	8.6	117.7
Partly cloudy	8.2	8.0	9.5	8.8	10.6	11.1	11.7	11.2	7.5	7.7	8.0	8.6	110.8
Cloudy	14.4	12.8	14.9	14.4	14.2	8.8	5.6	6.4	8.0	10.0	13.4	13.8	136.8
Precipitation .01" or more	5.6	4.8	7.5	8.6	11.6	11.2	8.6	6.6	6.7	4.7	4.6	5.3	85.9
Snow, Ice pellets 1.0" or more	2.1	1.7	2.8	1.6	0.4	0.0	0.0	0.0	0.1	0.7	1.7	2.0	13.0
Thunderstorms	0.0	0.0	0.3	1.7	7.2	11.3	10.7	8.0	4.0	0.8	0.1	*	44.0
Fog, Visibility 1/4 mile or less	0.9	0.8	1.5	0.6	0.7	0.6	0.4	0.5	0.8	0.9	1.2	1.1	10.0
Temperature Maximum:													
90° and above	0.0	0.0	0.0	0.0	1.1	7.2	16.8	13.4	4.4	0.1	0.0	0.0	43.0
32° and below	9.9	5.9	3.3	0.3	0.0	0.0	0.0	0.0	*	0.3	3.8	8.4	31.9
Temperature Minimum:													
32° and below	29.5	27.0	26.7	12.7	1.8	0.1	0.0	0.0	1.9	12.4	26.4	30.0	168.6
0° and below	7.0	3.2	0.8	0.1	0.0	0.0	0.0	0.0	0.0	0.0	1.0	4.3	16.4
RELATIVE HUMIDITY (%)													
Morning	73	73	74	75	77	79	79	80	78	74	75	74	76
Afternoon	58	47	43	40	41	39	37	38	36	39	52	58	44
PRECIPITATION (inches)													
Water Equivalent													
Normal	0.4	0.3	0.9	1.4	2.6	2.9	1.9	0.9	1.0	0.7	0.5	0.5	14.5
Maximum monthly	1.2	1.1	2.6	3.8	6.2	8.3	4.8	2.5	4.2	3.0	1.7	1.5	8.3
Date	1978	1978	1961	1984	1962	1947	1978	1979	1973	1969	1983	1978	1947
Minimum monthly	8.3	8.3	0.1	0.2	0.2	0.5	0.0	0.0	0.0	0.0	0.0	0.0	0.0
Date	1961	1954	1966	1962	1966	1950	1946	1973	1953	1956	1943	1949	1961
Maximum in 24 hrs	0.9	0.5	1.6	1.4	2.3	3.7	2.5	1.3	3.2	1.3	1.1	0.9	3.7
Date	1976	1978	1974	1943	1955	1953	1948	1974	1951	1948	1979	1975	1953
SNOW, ICE PELLETS													
Maximum monthly	23.7	15.3	23.5	18.0	7.5	0.1	0.0	0.0	5.1	21.6	18.5	18.1	23.7
Date	1949	1978	1980	1957	1967	1951	—	—	1985	1969	1983	1985	1949
Maximum in 24 hrs	11.2	6.6	15.0	9.9	3.7	0.1	0.0	0.0	4.8	8.5	8.4	10.9	15.0
Date	1976	1978	1974	1970	1979	1951	—	—	1985	1969	1979	1975	1974
WIND (Resultant)													
Mean speed (mph)	10.6	11.2	12.3	12.7	11.7	10.4	9.2	9.0	9.4	9.6	10.1	10.5	10.6

ELKO

Elev. 5050' 40° 50'N — 115° 47'W **Nevada**

NORMALS, MEANS, EXTREMES

	JAN	FEB	MAR	APR	MAY	JUN	JUL	AUG	SEP	OCT	NOV	DEC	YEAR
TEMPERATURE													
Normal daily maximum	36.6	42.6	48.9	58.2	68.5	79.2	90.4	87.8	78.8	66.3	49.4	38.3	62.1
Normal daily minimum	13.2	19.4	23.0	28.6	36.1	43.3	49.8	47.3	38.0	28.7	21.2	13.9	30.2
Normal monthly	24.9	31.0	36.0	43.4	52.3	61.3	70.1	67.6	58.4	47.5	35.3	26.1	46.1
Extreme highest	63	67	77	86	92	104	107	107	99	88	78	64	107
Extreme highest date	1981	1981	1966	1981	1977	1981	1981	1978	1950	1980	1980	1940	1981
Extreme lowest	-43	-37	-9	-2	10	23	30	24	9	8	-12	-38	-43
Extreme lowest date	1937	1933	1952	1936	1965	1976	1932	1932	1934	1958	1931	1932	1937
DEGREE DAYS BASE 65° F													
Heating	1240	952	899	648	396	166	19	58	230	543	891	1206	7248
Cooling	0	0	0	0	6	52	178	138	32	0	0	0	406
% OF POSSIBLE SUNSHINE	na	na	na	na	na	na	na	na	na	na	na	na	na
AVERAGE SKY COVER													
Sunrise - Sunset	6.7	6.6	6.8	6.5	5.9	4.4	3.4	3.4	3.3	4.4	6.1	6.5	5.3
NUMBER OF DAYS (Sunrise-Sunset)													
Clear	6.7	6.2	6.3	6.4	8.2	13.0	17.4	17.9	18.5	14.0	8.6	7.5	130.8
Partly cloudy	7.8	7.3	8.2	9.2	10.3	9.5	9.7	8.9	6.6	8.0	6.9	6.9	99.3
Cloudy	16.6	14.7	16.5	14.3	12.5	7.4	3.9	4.2	4.9	9.1	14.5	16.6	135.1
Precipitation .01" or more	9.2	8.7	8.9	7.4	7.9	5.8	3.5	3.6	3.8	4.9	7.0	8.7	79.2
Snow, Ice pellets 1.0" or more	3.3	2.0	2.3	1.2	0.3	0.0	0.0	0.0	*	0.4	1.7	3.5	14.7
Thunderstorms	0.2	0.3	0.3	0.8	3.3	3.6	4.8	4.6	2.0	0.5	0.2	0.1	20.7
Fog, Visibility 1/4 mile or less	1.6	0.7	0.4	0.2	0.4	0.1	0.1	0.1	0.1	0.3	0.5	1.2	5.6
Temperature Maximum:													
90° and above	0.0	0.0	0.0	0.0	0.3	5.7	20.4	15.0	3.5	0.0	0.0	0.0	45.0
32° and below	9.1	3.7	0.8	0.1	0.0	0.0	0.0	0.0	0.0	0.1	1.5	8.8	24.0
Temperature Minimum:													
32° and below	28.6	25.4	25.6	20.3	6.9	0.8	0.0	*	5.5	19.6	24.0	28.8	185.5
0° and below	4.2	1.5	0.1	0.0	0.0	0.0	0.0	0.0	0.0	0.0	0.3	4.0	10.2
RELATIVE HUMIDITY (%)													
Morning	77	78	76	72	70	67	56	56	62	68	75	76	69
Afternoon	59	52	42	35	30	25	20	21	24	30	48	60	37
PRECIPITATION (inches)													
Water Equivalent													
Normal	1.1	0.8	0.8	0.7	1.0	0.9	0.3	0.5	0.4	0.5	0.8	0.9	9.3
Maximum monthly	3.3	2.9	2.3	2.1	4.0	2.6	2.3	4.6	3.2	2.7	2.7	4.2	4.6
Date	1956	1932	1975	1963	1971	1963	1950	1970	1978	1938	1942	1983	1970
Minimum monthly	0.0	0.0	0.1	0.1	T	T	0.0	T	T	T	T	T	0.0
Date	1961	1967	1977	1949	1974	1974	1963	1969	1951	1958	1959	1976	1963
Maximum in 24 hrs	1.2	0.8	1.0	1.1	1.7	1.8	1.0	4.1	2.3	1.3	1.3	1.6	4.1
Date	1951	1936	1975	1943	1971	1968	1950	1970	1978	1939	1950	1950	1970
SNOW, ICE PELLETS													
Maximum monthly	27.4	26.1	23.2	15.6	11.3	T	T	T	2.0	5.6	16.8	33.2	33.2
Date	1950	1932	1967	1975	1971	1982	1950	1949	1982	1984	1985	1983	1983
Maximum in 24 hrs	16.7	9.1	13.8	10.0	8.6	T	T	T	2.0	5.2	9.0	9.2	16.7
Date	1951	1949	1967	1975	1971	1982	1950	1949	1982	1963	1965	1955	1951
WIND (Resultant)													
Mean speed (mph)	5.3	5.8	6.7	7.2	6.9	6.7	6.2	5.9	5.4	5.1	5.2	5.2	6.0

ELY

Elev. 6253' 39° 17'N — 114° 51'W **Nevada**

NORMALS, MEANS, EXTREMES

	JAN	FEB	MAR	APR	MAY	JUN	JUL	AUG	SEP	OCT	NOV	DEC	YEAR
TEMPERATURE													
Normal daily maximum	39.0	42.6	47.3	56.2	66.5	77.5	86.8	84.2	76.0	64.0	49.2	40.9	60.9
Normal daily minimum	9.7	15.0	19.4	25.7	33.6	40.4	48.1	46.6	37.3	28.0	18.5	11.0	27.8
Normal monthly	24.4	28.8	33.4	41.0	50.1	59.0	67.5	65.4	56.7	46.0	33.9	26.0	44.3
Extreme highest	68	66	73	78	89	99	100	97	93	84	75	67	100
Extreme highest date	1951	1977	1966	1985	1984	1954	1985	1981	1950	1967	1975	1958	1985
Extreme lowest	-27	-25	-13	-5	7	18	30	24	15	-3	-15	-28	-28
Extreme lowest date	1949	1949	1952	1982	1950	1976	1983	1960	1968	1971	1985	1972	1972
DEGREE DAYS BASE 65° F													
Heating	1259	1014	980	723	462	196	10	64	261	589	933	1209	7700
Cooling	0	0	0	0	0	16	88	76	12	0	0	0	192
% OF POSSIBLE SUNSHINE	67	67	70	69	72	80	80	81	82	75	66	65	73
AVERAGE SKY COVER													
Sunrise - Sunset	6.2	6.4	6.4	6.1	5.9	4.3	3.9	3.8	3.3	4.3	5.8	6.0	5.2
NUMBER OF DAYS (Sunrise-Sunset)													
Clear	8.6	6.9	7.6	7.7	7.7	13.2	14.9	14.8	17.3	14.4	9.7	8.8	131.6
Partly cloudy	7.6	6.9	8.3	9.0	11.4	10.3	11.3	11.7	7.7	8.2	8.1	7.9	108.4
Cloudy	14.7	14.4	15.1	13.3	12.0	6.5	4.9	4.4	4.9	8.4	12.2	14.3	125.1
Precipitation .01" or more	6.9	7.0	8.5	7.4	7.2	4.8	5.5	5.3	4.5	5.0	5.1	6.4	73.7
Snow, Ice pellets 1.0" or more	2.5	2.4	3.2	2.1	0.9	0.1	0.0	0.0	0.1	0.8	1.4	2.6	16.1
Thunderstorms	0.2	0.3	0.4	1.2	4.1	4.6	8.3	8.0	3.3	1.4	0.3	0.2	32.3
Fog, Visibility 1/4 mile or less	0.3	0.2	0.3	0.3	0.1	*	0.0	*	0.1	0.2	0.3	0.4	2.4
Temperature Maximum:													
90° and above	0.0	0.0	0.0	0.0	0.0	2.2	9.8	5.3	0.5	0.0	0.0	0.0	17.7
32° and below	7.9	4.5	2.2	0.4	*	0.0	0.0	0.0	0.0	0.2	2.6	6.4	24.1
Temperature Minimum:													
32° and below	30.6	27.5	29.5	24.6	13.2	3.6	0.1	0.5	7.8	22.5	28.1	30.5	218.5
0° and below	7.4	3.9	1.3	0.1	0.0	0.0	0.0	0.0	0.0	*	1.3	4.7	18.8
RELATIVE HUMIDITY (%)													
Morning	71	74	72	68	66	59	52	56	59	65	70	71	65
Afternoon	55	50	43	34	31	23	22	23	24	32	46	55	37
PRECIPITATION (inches)													
Water Equivalent													
Normal	0.7	0.6	0.9	0.9	1.0	0.8	0.6	0.6	0.7	0.5	0.6	0.7	9.0
Maximum monthly	1.9	2.1	2.4	3.4	3.2	3.5	2.1	2.5	4.9	3.6	1.8	2.1	4.9
Date	1952	1969	1952	1978	1977	1963	1984	1983	1982	1981	1960	1966	1982
Minimum monthly	T	0.0	0.0	0.1	T	T	T	T	T	0.0	T	T	0.0
Date	1948	1972	1972	1966	1948	1978	1948	1985	1953	1952	1959	1976	1952
Maximum in 24 hrs	0.9	1.5	0.8	1.0	1.4	1.5	1.2	0.9	2.8	1.3	1.2	1.1	2.8
Date	1952	1969	1954	1947	1955	1963	1952	1984	1982	1976	1960	1966	1982
SNOW, ICE PELLETS													
Maximum monthly	24.8	20.0	24.8	24.5	12.1	5.6	0.0	0.0	6.3	12.1	17.3	22.3	24.8
Date	1967	1976	1958	1963	1975	1939	—	—	1982	1981	1985	1968	1967
Maximum in 24 hrs	13.1	10.4	10.6	10.7	8.0	5.6	0.0	0.0	2.9	7.3	12.9	12.7	13.1
Date	1943	1956	1954	1970	1975	1939	—	—	1982	1954	1978	1970	1943
WIND (Resultant)													
Mean speed (mph)	10.3	10.4	10.8	11.0	10.7	10.6	10.3	10.5	10.4	10.1	10.0	10.0	10.4

LAS VEGAS

Elev. 2162'   36° 05'N — 115° 10'W   **Nevada**

NORMALS, MEANS, EXTREMES

	JAN	FEB	MAR	APR	MAY	JUN	JUL	AUG	SEP	OCT	NOV	DEC	YEAR
TEMPERATURE													
Normal daily maximum	56.0	62.4	68.3	77.2	87.4	98.6	104.5	101.9	94.7	81.5	66.0	57.1	79.6
Normal daily minimum	33.0	37.7	42.3	49.8	59.0	68.6	75.9	73.9	65.6	53.5	41.2	33.6	52.8
Normal monthly	44.5	50.1	55.3	63.5	73.2	83.6	90.2	87.9	80.2	67.5	53.6	45.4	66.2
Extreme highest	77	82	91	99	109	115	116	116	113	103	85	77	116
Extreme highest date	1975	1981	1966	1981	1951	1970	1985	1979	1950	1978	1980	1980	1985
Extreme lowest	8	18	23	31	40	49	61	56	46	26	21	15	8
Extreme lowest date	1963	1985	1971	1975	1964	1955	1984	1968	1965	1971	1952	1968	1963
DEGREE DAYS BASE 65° F													
Heating	632	417	313	131	22	0	0	0	0	63	346	608	2532
Cooling	0	0	12	86	279	558	784	713	453	144	0	0	3029
% OF POSSIBLE SUNSHINE	77	81	83	87	88	93	87	88	91	87	80	78	85
AVERAGE SKY COVER													
Sunrise - Sunset	4.7	4.7	4.5	3.6	3.3	2.1	2.9	2.5	2.0	2.7	3.9	4.5	3.5
NUMBER OF DAYS (Sunrise-Sunset)													
Clear	14.0	12.5	13.8	16.6	18.5	22.4	19.5	21.5	22.6	20.6	15.6	14.6	212.1
Partly cloudy	6.2	7.1	8.9	7.5	7.9	5.1	8.1	6.6	5.1	6.3	7.4	6.8	83.0
Cloudy	10.8	8.7	8.2	5.9	4.7	2.5	3.4	2.8	2.4	4.2	7.0	9.6	70.2
Precipitation .01" or more	3.0	2.6	2.9	1.8	1.3	0.7	2.7	3.0	1.8	1.7	2.1	2.5	26.1
Snow, Ice pellets 1.0" or more	0.3	0.0	0.0	0.0	0.0	0.0	0.0	0.0	0.0	0.0	0.1	*	0.4
Thunderstorms	*	0.2	0.3	0.4	0.9	1.0	4.4	4.2	1.7	0.5	0.2	*	14.0
Fog, Visibility 1/4 mile or less	0.2	0.1	0.1	0.0	0.0	0.0	0.0	0.0	*	*	0.1	0.2	0.7
Temperature Maximum:													
90° and above	0.0	0.0	*	2.6	15.4	25.4	30.5	29.8	22.0	5.5	0.0	0.0	131.3
32° and below	0.2	0.0	0.0	0.0	0.0	0.0	0.0	0.0	0.0	0.0	0.0	*	0.2
Temperature Minimum:													
32° and below	13.4	4.6	1.5	0.1	0.0	0.0	0.0	0.0	0.0	0.2	2.3	11.5	33.5
0° and below	0.0	0.0	0.0	0.0	0.0	0.0	0.0	0.0	0.0	0.0	0.0	0.0	0.0
RELATIVE HUMIDITY (%)													
Morning	55	50	44	35	31	24	29	35	34	38	46	55	40
Afternoon	31	26	22	15	13	10	15	17	17	19	27	33	20
PRECIPITATION (inches)													
Water Equivalent													
Normal	0.5	0.4	0.4	0.2	0.2	0.0	0.4	0.5	0.3	0.2	0.4	0.3	4.1
Maximum monthly	2.4	2.4	1.8	2.4	0.9	0.8	2.4	2.5	1.5	1.1	2.2	1.6	2.5
Date	1949	1976	1973	1965	1969	1967	1984	1957	1963	1972	1965	1984	1957
Minimum monthly	T	0.0	0.0	0.0	0.0	0.0	0.0	0.0	0.0	0.0	0.0	0.0	0.0
Date	1984	1977	1972	1962	1970	1982	1981	1980	1971	1979	1980	1981	1982
Maximum in 24 hrs	1.0	1.1	1.1	0.9	0.8	0.7	1.3	2.5	1.0	0.7	1.7	0.9	2.5
Date	1952	1976	1952	1965	1969	1967	1984	1957	1963	1976	1960	1977	1957
SNOW, ICE PELLETS													
Maximum monthly	16.7	0.3	0.1	T	0.0	0.0	0.0	0.0	0.0	T	4.0	2.0	16.7
Date	1949	1979	1976	1970	—	—	—	—	—	1956	1964	1967	1949
Maximum in 24 hrs	9.0	6.9	0.1	T	0.0	0.0	0.0	0.0	0.0	T	4.0	2.0	9.0
Date	1974	1979	1976	1970	—	—	—	—	—	1956	1964	1967	1974
WIND (Resultant)													
Mean speed (mph)	7.4	8.5	10.2	11.0	11.0	11.0	10.1	9.5	8.9	8.1	7.6	7.2	9.2

RENO

Elev. 4404' 39° 30'N — 119° 47'W **Nevada**

NORMALS, MEANS, EXTREMES

	JAN	FEB	MAR	APR	MAY	JUN	JUL	AUG	SEP	OCT	NOV	DEC	YEAR
TEMPERATURE													
Normal daily maximum	44.8	51.1	55.8	63.3	72.3	81.8	91.3	88.7	81.4	70.0	55.6	46.2	66.9
Normal daily minimum	19.5	23.5	25.4	29.4	36.9	43.0	47.7	45.2	38.9	30.5	23.8	18.9	31.9
Normal monthly	32.2	37.3	40.6	46.4	54.6	62.4	69.5	67.0	60.2	50.3	39.7	32.6	49.4
Extreme highest	70	74	83	89	95	101	104	105	101	91	77	70	105
Extreme highest date	1967	1967	1966	1981	1970	1985	1980	1983	1950	1980	1980	1969	1983
Extreme lowest	-16	-12	-2	13	18	25	33	24	20	8	1	-16	-16
Extreme lowest date	1949	1962	1945	1956	1964	1954	1976	1962	1965	1971	1958	1972	1972
DEGREE DAYS BASE 65° F													
Heating	1017	773	756	558	333	124	16	59	171	456	759	1008	6030
Cooling	0	0	0	0	11	46	156	117	27	0	0	0	357
% OF POSSIBLE SUNSHINE	66	68	75	80	82	85	92	93	92	83	71	64	79
AVERAGE SKY COVER													
Sunrise - Sunset	6.3	6.3	6.0	5.6	4.9	3.6	2.3	2.3	2.6	4.0	5.8	6.2	4.7
NUMBER OF DAYS (Sunrise-Sunset)													
Clear	8.6	6.8	8.2	8.9	12.2	16.7	22.3	22.2	20.8	15.6	9.2	8.2	159.8
Partly cloudy	7.1	7.6	9.2	10.0	9.7	7.6	6.2	6.3	5.6	7.7	7.8	7.8	92.5
Cloudy	15.3	13.8	13.5	11.2	9.1	5.7	2.5	2.6	3.6	7.7	13.0	15.1	113.0
Precipitation .01" or more	6.1	5.8	6.4	4.1	4.3	3.1	2.3	2.3	2.4	3.0	5.1	6.1	51.1
Snow, Ice pellets 1.0" or more	2.1	1.6	1.6	0.6	0.3	0.0	0.0	0.0	*	0.2	0.8	1.4	8.4
Thunderstorms	0.0	*	0.1	0.3	2.0	2.6	3.5	3.0	1.2	0.6	0.0	0.0	13.2
Fog, Visibility 1/4 mile or less	2.2	0.8	0.3	0.1	0.1	0.0	*	0.1	0.1	0.2	0.7	2.9	7.5
Temperature Maximum:													
90° and above	0.0	0.0	0.0	0.0	1.2	7.0	21.1	16.5	4.8	0.1	0.0	0.0	50.8
32° and below	3.4	0.3	*	0.0	0.0	0.0	0.0	0.0	0.0	0.0	0.5	3.9	8.1
Temperature Minimum:													
32° and below	27.9	25.2	25.4	19.6	6.7	0.7	0.0	0.2	4.5	19.1	24.0	27.9	181.2
0° and below	1.0	*	*	0.0	0.0	0.0	0.0	0.0	0.0	0.0	0.0	1.0	2.1
RELATIVE HUMIDITY (%)													
Morning	78	74	70	67	67	66	65	68	70	74	75	77	71
Afternoon	51	40	34	28	25	22	19	20	22	28	43	52	32
PRECIPITATION (inches)													
Water Equivalent													
Normal	1.2	0.9	0.7	0.4	0.7	0.3	0.3	0.2	0.3	0.3	0.6	1.2	7.4
Maximum monthly	4.1	3.6	2.0	2.0	2.8	1.3	1.0	1.6	2.3	2.1	3.0	5.2	5.2
Date	1969	1962	1952	1958	1963	1965	1971	1965	1982	1945	1983	1955	1955
Minimum monthly	T	T	0.0	T	T	0.0	0.0	0.0	0.0	T	0.0	0.0	0.0
Date	1966	1967	1972	1985	1985	1959	1951	1957	1974	1966	1959	1976	1974
Maximum in 24 hrs	2.3	1.5	1.2	1.6	1.2	0.7	0.8	0.9	0.9	1.5	1.3	2.1	2.3
Date	1943	1962	1943	1958	1963	1969	1949	1965	1982	1962	1981	1955	1943
SNOW, ICE PELLETS													
Maximum monthly	20.0	23.5	29.0	7.5	14.1	0.2	0.0	0.0	1.5	5.1	16.5	25.6	29.0
Date	1956	1969	1952	1958	1964	1970	—	—	1982	1971	1985	1971	1952
Maximum in 24 hrs	12.0	13.9	16.9	7.3	9.0	0.2	0.0	0.0	1.5	3.7	15.4	14.9	16.9
Date	1956	1959	1952	1958	1962	1970	—	—	1982	1971	1985	1971	1952
WIND (Resultant)													
Mean speed (mph)	5.6	6.1	7.7	8.2	7.8	7.5	6.9	6.4	5.7	5.3	5.4	5.2	6.5

WINNEMUCCA

Elev. 4298' 40° 54'N — 117° 48'W **Nevada**

NORMALS, MEANS, EXTREMES

	JAN	FEB	MAR	APR	MAY	JUN	JUL	AUG	SEP	OCT	NOV	DEC	YEAR
TEMPERATURE													
Normal daily maximum	42.3	48.7	53.6	61.8	72.0	81.8	92.7	89.7	80.8	68.5	53.2	43.9	65.8
Normal daily minimum	17.2	22.6	23.8	28.8	37.4	45.1	51.2	47.6	38.3	28.9	22.2	17.0	31.7
Normal monthly	29.8	35.7	38.7	45.3	54.7	63.5	72.0	68.7	59.6	48.7	37.7	30.5	48.7
Extreme highest	68	74	81	90	96	105	106	108	103	91	77	67	108
Extreme highest date	1971	1981	1972	1981	1977	1974	1979	1983	1950	1980	1980	1980	1983
Extreme lowest	-24	-28	-3	6	12	23	29	28	12	7	-8	-34	-34
Extreme lowest date	1963	1985	1971	1972	1953	1954	1983	1960	1958	1970	1985	1972	1972
DEGREE DAYS BASE 65° F													
Heating	1091	820	815	591	334	126	0	42	193	505	819	1073	6409
Cooling	0	0	0	0	14	81	222	157	31	0	0	0	505
% OF POSSIBLE SUNSHINE	49	54	57	64	70	76	85	84	81	73	53	49	66
AVERAGE SKY COVER													
Sunrise - Sunset	7.0	6.9	6.7	6.4	5.7	4.5	2.8	3.0	3.2	4.5	6.3	6.6	5.3
NUMBER OF DAYS (Sunrise-Sunset)													
Clear	6.3	5.9	6.8	6.7	9.0	13.7	20.2	19.3	18.4	14.2	8.1	7.6	136.1
Partly cloudy	6.6	6.4	7.4	9.0	9.6	8.6	7.0	7.6	6.4	7.4	6.9	6.5	89.4
Cloudy	18.1	16.0	16.9	14.3	12.4	7.7	3.8	4.1	5.2	9.4	15.0	17.0	139.8
Precipitation .01" or more	8.3	6.8	7.6	6.2	6.2	5.5	2.3	2.7	3.3	4.6	7.4	8.7	69.5
Snow, Ice pellets 1.0" or more	1.9	1.3	1.8	0.8	0.3	0.0	0.0	0.0	0.0	0.1	1.0	1.8	9.0
Thunderstorms	*	0.2	0.2	0.7	2.5	2.9	3.3	3.5	1.8	0.5	0.1	0.1	15.8
Fog, Visibility 1/4 mile or less	1.9	0.4	0.1	0.1	*	0.1	0.0	*	0.1	0.2	0.3	1.1	4.4
Temperature Maximum:													
90° and above	0.0	0.0	0.0	*	1.1	8.1	22.6	18.4	5.4	0.1	0.0	0.0	55.7
32° and below	5.6	1.1	0.4	0.0	0.0	0.0	0.0	0.0	0.0	0.0	0.6	3.8	11.4
Temperature Minimum:													
32° and below	28.1	24.5	26.3	20.6	8.1	1.5	0.1	0.2	6.3	21.0	24.8	28.1	189.6
0° and below	3.7	0.6	0.1	0.0	0.0	0.0	0.0	0.0	0.0	0.0	0.5	2.2	7.1
RELATIVE HUMIDITY (%)													
Morning	77	75	71	66	63	57	46	47	53	63	74	78	64
Afternoon	57	47	38	29	26	22	15	16	20	29	46	58	34
PRECIPITATION (inches)													
Water Equivalent													
Normal	0.8	0.6	0.6	0.8	0.8	0.9	0.1	0.3	0.3	0.5	0.7	0.8	7.8
Maximum monthly	2.7	2.1	1.6	2.9	2.8	2.8	1.7	1.7	1.5	2.1	2.6	3.6	3.6
Date	1956	1962	1952	1978	1957	1958	1984	1979	1976	1951	1950	1983	1983
Minimum monthly	0.0	0.0	0.0	0.0	T	T	0.0	0.0	0.0	T	T	0.0	0.0
Date	1966	1967	1959	1959	1985	1981	1963	1969	1974	1978	1959	1976	1974
Maximum in 24 hrs	0.7	0.7	0.6	1.0	1.3	1.7	0.8	0.7	0.8	1.6	1.5	0.9	1.7
Date	1980	1960	1979	1958	1984	1958	1984	1958	1976	1951	1950	1969	1958
SNOW, ICE PELLETS													
Maximum monthly	16.5	13.8	23.4	12.0	5.4	T	0.0	0.0	0.2	7.4	19.6	17.5	23.4
Date	1950	1969	1952	1964	1965	1954	—	—	1971	1984	1985	1971	1952
Maximum in 24 hrs	7.4	9.9	9.0	7.2	4.3	T	0.0	0.0	0.2	4.9	5.7	8.4	9.9
Date	1983	1959	1982	1971	1971	1954	—	—	1971	1984	1985	1955	1959
WIND (Resultant)													
Mean speed (mph)	7.5	7.9	8.5	8.7	8.6	8.5	8.3	7.8	7.6	7.3	7.2	7.3	7.9

CONCORD

Elev. 342' 43° 12'N — 71° 30'W **New Hampshire**

NORMALS, MEANS, EXTREMES

	JAN	FEB	MAR	APR	MAY	JUN	JUL	AUG	SEP	OCT	NOV	DEC	YEAR
TEMPERATURE													
Normal daily maximum	30.8	33.2	41.9	56.5	68.9	77.7	82.6	80.1	71.9	61.0	47.2	34.4	57.2
Normal daily minimum	9.0	11.0	22.2	31.6	41.4	51.6	56.4	54.5	46.2	35.5	27.3	14.5	33.4
Normal monthly	19.9	22.1	32.1	44.1	55.2	64.7	69.5	67.3	59.1	48.3	37.3	24.5	45.3
Extreme highest	68	66	85	95	97	98	102	101	98	90	80	68	102
Extreme highest date	1950	1957	1977	1976	1962	1980	1966	1975	1953	1963	1950	1982	1966
Extreme lowest	-33	-37	-16	8	21	30	35	29	21	10	-1	-22	-37
Extreme lowest date	1984	1943	1967	1969	1966	1972	1965	1965	1947	1972	1972	1951	1943
DEGREE DAYS BASE 65° F													
Heating	1398	1198	1020	627	314	67	20	39	191	521	831	1256	7482
Cooling	0	0	0	0	10	58	160	111	14	0	0	0	353
% OF POSSIBLE SUNSHINE	52	55	52	53	54	58	63	60	56	54	42	47	54
AVERAGE SKY COVER													
Sunrise - Sunset	6.1	6.1	6.4	6.5	6.6	6.3	6.1	5.9	5.9	5.9	6.8	6.4	6.2
NUMBER OF DAYS (Sunrise-Sunset)													
Clear	9.3	7.6	7.7	7.3	6.4	6.3	6.8	7.9	9.0	9.5	6.3	7.8	91.8
Partly cloudy	7.1	7.8	8.1	8.2	9.7	11.8	12.6	11.8	9.0	8.8	7.5	8.0	110.5
Cloudy	14.5	12.8	15.2	14.6	15.0	11.9	11.5	11.3	12.0	12.7	16.1	15.2	162.9
Precipitation .01" or more	10.8	9.7	11.0	11.5	12.0	10.8	9.8	9.7	8.8	8.6	11.4	11.0	125.0
Snow, Ice pellets 1.0" or more	4.5	4.0	3.1	0.6	*	0.0	0.0	0.0	0.0	*	1.3	4.1	17.7
Thunderstorms	*	0.1	0.3	0.9	2.5	4.5	5.4	3.8	1.9	0.6	0.1	*	20.0
Fog, Visibility 1/4 mile or less	2.1	1.8	2.9	1.9	3.2	3.8	5.4	7.0	9.2	6.6	3.6	2.7	50.0
Temperature Maximum:													
90° and above	0.0	0.0	0.0	0.2	0.9	2.4	4.9	2.6	0.6	0.0	0.0	0.0	11.4
32° and below	19.3	13.4	4.6	0.3	0.0	0.0	0.0	0.0	0.0	0.1	1.8	13.7	53.1
Temperature Minimum:													
32° and below	30.5	27.1	25.8	17.7	5.9	0.3	0.0	0.1	2.2	14.0	21.1	29.2	173.7
0° and below	10.8	7.4	1.4	0.0	0.0	0.0	0.0	0.0	0.0	0.0	0.2	5.6	25.4
RELATIVE HUMIDITY (%)													
Morning	74	72	73	74	82	88	89	90	90	85	81	78	81
Afternoon	59	56	53	45	47	53	51	53	55	53	60	63	54
PRECIPITATION (inches)													
Water Equivalent													
Normal	2.7	2.4	2.9	3.0	2.9	2.9	2.9	3.2	3.1	3.1	3.6	3.4	36.5
Maximum monthly	8.0	7.7	7.8	5.8	9.5	10.1	5.9	6.8	7.7	8.7	7.3	7.5	10.1
Date	1979	1981	1953	1983	1984	1944	1967	1973	1960	1962	1983	1973	1944
Minimum monthly	0.4	0.6	0.8	1.0	0.6	0.6	0.9	0.9	0.4	0.5	0.7	0.5	0.4
Date	1970	1978	1981	1985	1965	1979	1955	1944	1948	1947	1976	1943	1970
Maximum in 24 hrs	2.1	2.2	2.2	2.1	2.5	4.4	2.5	3.7	4.1	4.2	2.8	3.3	4.4
Date	1979	1981	1974	1945	1984	1944	1971	1973	1960	1962	1947	1969	1944
SNOW, ICE PELLETS													
Maximum monthly	42.3	49.8	38.3	15.3	5.0	0.0	0.0	0.0	0.0	2.1	18.4	38.1	49.8
Date	1979	1969	1956	1982	1945	—	—	—	—	1969	1971	1956	1969
Maximum in 24 hrs	19.0	14.2	14.4	13.9	5.0	0.0	0.0	0.0	0.0	2.1	9.5	14.6	19.0
Date	1944	1972	1984	1982	1945	—	—	—	—	1969	1961	1946	1944
WIND (Resultant)													
Mean speed (mph)	7.3	7.9	8.3	7.9	7.0	6.4	5.7	5.3	5.5	5.9	6.6	7.0	6.7

GORHAM (MT. WASHINGTON) Elev. 6262' 44° 16'N — 71° 18'W New Hampshire

NORMALS, MEANS, EXTREMES

	JAN	FEB	MAR	APR	MAY	JUN	JUL	AUG	SEP	OCT	NOV	DEC	YEAR
TEMPERATURE													
Normal daily maximum	13.4	13.1	19.1	28.9	40.7	50.7	54.4	52.7	46.3	36.5	26.9	17.0	33.3
Normal daily minimum	-3.3	-3.4	4.7	15.9	28.1	38.4	42.9	41.5	34.9	24.5	13.8	1.2	19.9
Normal monthly	5.1	4.9	11.9	22.4	34.4	44.6	48.7	47.1	40.6	30.5	20.4	9.1	26.6
Extreme highest	44	43	48	60	66	71	71	72	67	59	52	45	72
Extreme highest date	1950	1981	1946	1976	1977	1933	1953	1975	1960	1938	1982	1982	1975
Extreme lowest	-47	-46	-38	-20	-2	8	25	20	11	-5	-20	-46	-47
Extreme lowest date	1934	1943	1950	1954	1966	1945	1982	1976	1942	1939	1958	1933	1934
DEGREE DAYS BASE 65° F													
Heating	1857	1686	1643	1278	949	612	505	555	732	1070	1341	1733	13961
Cooling	0	0	0	0	0	0	0	0	0	0	0	0	0
% OF POSSIBLE SUNSHINE	32	34	34	35	36	32	31	31	36	39	29	29	33
AVERAGE SKY COVER													
Sunrise - Sunset	7.7	7.6	7.8	7.7	7.7	8.1	8.2	7.9	7.4	7.0	7.9	8.0	7.8
NUMBER OF DAYS (Sunrise-Sunset)													
Clear	4.8	4.5	4.3	4.2	3.6	2.4	1.5	2.8	4.6	6.4	3.6	4.2	47.0
Partly cloudy	5.3	5.1	5.6	6.0	7.3	6.6	7.6	8.1	6.5	6.1	5.2	5.1	74.4
Cloudy	20.9	18.6	21.1	19.9	20.2	21.0	21.9	20.1	18.9	18.5	21.2	21.7	243.9
Precipitation .01" or more	19.1	17.7	19.2	18.0	17.2	16.0	16.5	15.6	15.0	15.0	19.3	20.3	209.1
Snow, Ice pellets 1.0" or more	11.3	10.2	10.8	7.8	3.0	0.5	*	*	0.6	3.8	8.5	11.5	68.0
Thunderstorms	0.2	0.1	0.3	0.9	1.7	3.6	4.4	2.8	1.0	0.5	0.3	0.1	16.0
Fog, Visibility 1/4 mile or less	26.2	24.7	27.3	24.8	24.1	25.9	27.3	27.5	25.9	25.5	26.8	27.5	313.6
Temperature Maximum:													
90° and above	0.0	0.0	0.0	0.0	0.0	0.0	0.0	0.0	0.0	0.0	0.0	0.0	0.0
32° and below	29.0	26.5	26.4	18.6	6.4	0.8	*	0.2	2.1	10.2	20.3	27.1	167.6
Temperature Minimum:													
32° and below	31.0	28.0	30.7	28.3	20.1	6.5	1.5	3.1	12.0	23.1	28.2	30.8	243.2
0° and below	18.2	16.2	11.1	2.2	0.1	0.0	0.0	0.0	0.0	0.2	3.8	14.0	65.8
RELATIVE HUMIDITY (%)													
Morning	82	82	86	86	86	91	93	92	86	84	85	85	87
Afternoon	83	83	84	84	81	84	87	87	85	81	84	84	84
PRECIPITATION (inches)													
Water Equivalent													
Normal	7.3	8.0	8.1	7.0	6.4	7.0	6.9	7.6	7.1	6.7	8.5	8.9	89.9
Maximum monthly	18.2	25.5	15.9	14.6	18.8	16.0	15.5	13.1	14.0	13.4	19.5	17.9	25.5
Date	1958	1969	1977	1974	1984	1973	1969	1955	1938	1959	1983	1973	1969
Minimum monthly	1.2	0.9	2.1	2.1	1.7	2.4	2.6	2.7	2.7	0.7	2.3	1.4	0.7
Date	1981	1980	1946	1959	1951	1979	1955	1947	1948	1947	1939	1955	1947
Maximum in 24 hrs	3.7	10.3	3.9	8.3	4.6	6.5	7.3	5.2	5.3	7.0	6.0	8.6	10.3
Date	1975	1970	1962	1984	1967	1973	1969	1955	1985	1959	1968	1969	1970
SNOW, ICE PELLETS													
Maximum monthly	94.6	172.8	98.0	89.3	52.2	8.1	1.1	2.5	7.8	34.4	86.6	103.7	172.8
Date	1978	1969	1970	1975	1967	1959	1957	1965	1949	1969	1968	1968	1969
Maximum in 24 hrs	24.0	49.3	27.4	25.4	22.2	4.4	1.1	2.5	5.9	17.0	25.0	37.5	49.3
Date	1978	1969	1969	1974	1967	1965	1957	1965	1949	1969	1968	1968	1969
WIND (Resultant)													
Mean speed (mph)	45.7	44.2	41.9	36.7	29.6	27.3	25.3	24.9	28.6	33.5	38.9	44.5	35.1

ATLANTIC CITY
Elev. 64'   39° 27'N — 74° 34'W   **New Jersey**

NORMALS, MEANS, EXTREMES

	JAN	FEB	MAR	APR	MAY	JUN	JUL	AUG	SEP	OCT	NOV	DEC	YEAR
TEMPERATURE													
Normal daily maximum	40.6	42.4	50.3	61.6	71.0	79.6	84.0	82.5	76.7	66.1	55.4	45.0	62.9
Normal daily minimum	22.9	23.9	31.6	40.4	49.9	58.8	64.8	63.5	56.4	44.8	35.8	26.6	43.3
Normal monthly	31.8	33.2	41.0	51.0	60.5	69.2	74.4	73.0	66.6	55.5	45.6	35.8	53.1
Extreme highest	78	75	87	94	99	106	104	102	99	90	84	75	106
Extreme highest date	1967	1985	1945	1969	1969	1969	1966	1948	1983	1959	1950	1984	1969
Extreme lowest	-10	-11	5	12	25	37	46	40	32	23	11	-7	-11
Extreme lowest date	1977	1979	1984	1969	1966	1980	1965	1976	1969	1969	1964	1950	1979
DEGREE DAYS BASE 65° F													
Heating	1029	890	744	420	165	26	0	0	27	298	582	905	5086
Cooling	0	0	0	0	26	152	291	248	75	0	0	0	792
% OF POSSIBLE SUNSHINE	49	52	53	55	54	58	60	63	60	56	48	44	54
AVERAGE SKY COVER													
Sunrise - Sunset	6.3	6.3	6.3	6.2	6.4	6.1	6.2	6.0	5.7	5.5	6.2	6.4	6.1
NUMBER OF DAYS (Sunrise-Sunset)													
Clear	8.4	7.7	7.7	7.4	6.4	6.9	7.3	7.4	10.0	10.2	7.7	8.1	95.3
Partly cloudy	7.8	6.9	8.1	9.4	10.6	11.0	10.8	11.5	8.3	8.5	8.7	7.6	109.2
Cloudy	14.7	13.6	15.2	13.2	14.0	12.1	13.0	12.1	11.7	12.3	13.6	15.4	160.7
Precipitation .01" or more	10.8	9.7	10.8	10.7	10.4	8.9	8.6	8.6	7.4	7.2	9.3	9.6	112.1
Snow, Ice pellets 1.0" or more	1.7	1.4	0.6	0.1	0.0	0.0	0.0	0.0	0.0	0.0	0.1	1.6	4.6
Thunderstorms	0.2	0.5	0.9	2.2	3.4	4.5	5.7	5.4	1.9	0.7	0.4	0.2	26.0
Fog, Visibility 1/4 mile or less	3.1	3.4	3.6	3.4	4.6	4.4	4.1	3.6	3.4	4.8	3.5	2.8	44.6
Temperature Maximum:													
90° and above	0.0	0.0	0.0	0.2	0.4	3.0	6.4	5.0	1.6	0.0	0.0	0.0	16.7
32° and below	8.6	5.5	0.6	0.0	0.0	0.0	0.0	0.0	0.0	0.0	0.1	3.0	17.8
Temperature Minimum:													
32° and below	26.2	21.8	17.0	6.3	0.4	0.0	0.0	0.0	0.1	3.4	12.4	21.6	109.1
0° and below	1.0	0.6	0.0	0.0	0.0	0.0	0.0	0.0	0.0	0.0	0.0	0.3	1.9
RELATIVE HUMIDITY (%)													
Morning	75	76	75	77	83	87	86	88	87	86	81	76	81
Afternoon	59	56	55	51	56	57	56	57	57	56	58	58	56
PRECIPITATION (inches)													
Water Equivalent													
Normal	3.4	3.3	4.0	3.2	3.0	2.7	4.0	4.7	2.8	3.0	3.7	3.6	41.9
Maximum monthly	7.7	5.9	6.8	7.9	11.5	6.3	13.0	11.9	6.2	7.5	9.6	7.3	13.0
Date	1948	1958	1953	1952	1948	1970	1959	1967	1966	1943	1972	1969	1959
Minimum monthly	0.2	0.8	0.6	0.8	0.4	0.1	0.5	0.3	0.4	0.1	0.6	0.6	0.1
Date	1955	1980	1945	1976	1957	1954	1983	1943	1970	1963	1976	1955	1954
Maximum in 24 hrs	2.8	2.5	2.6	3.3	4.1	2.9	6.4	6.4	3.9	2.9	3.9	2.7	6.4
Date	1944	1966	1979	1952	1959	1952	1959	1966	1954	1958	1953	1951	1959
SNOW, ICE PELLETS													
Maximum monthly	15.9	35.2	17.6	3.2	T	0.0	0.0	0.0	0.0	T	7.8	8.6	35.2
Date	1961	1967	1969	1965	1977	—	—	—	—	1980	1967	1960	1967
Maximum in 24 hrs	14.4	17.1	11.5	3.2	T	0.0	0.0	0.0	0.0	T	7.8	7.5	17.1
Date	1964	1979	1969	1965	1977	—	—	—	—	1980	1967	1960	1979
WIND (Resultant)													
Mean speed (mph)	11.3	11.6	12.1	11.9	10.4	9.3	8.6	8.2	8.6	9.1	10.6	10.8	10.2

NEWARK

Elev. 7'   **40° 42'N — 74° 10'W**   **New Jersey**

NORMALS, MEANS, EXTREMES

	JAN	FEB	MAR	APR	MAY	JUN	JUL	AUG	SEP	OCT	NOV	DEC	YEAR
TEMPERATURE													
Normal daily maximum	38.2	40.3	49.1	61.3	71.6	80.6	85.6	84.0	76.9	66.0	54.0	42.3	62.5
Normal daily minimum	24.2	25.3	33.3	42.9	53.0	62.4	67.9	67.0	59.4	48.3	39.0	28.6	45.9
Normal monthly	31.2	32.8	41.2	52.1	62.3	71.5	76.8	75.5	68.2	57.2	46.5	35.5	54.2
Extreme highest	74	76	89	93	98	102	105	103	105	92	85	72	105
Extreme highest date	1950	1949	1945	1976	1962	1952	1966	1948	1953	1949	1950	1982	1966
Extreme lowest	-8	-7	6	16	33	43	52	45	35	28	15	-1	-8
Extreme lowest date	1985	1943	1943	1982	1947	1945	1945	1982	1947	1969	1955	1980	1985
DEGREE DAYS BASE 65° F													
Heating	1045	902	738	387	140	0	0	0	36	254	555	915	4972
Cooling	0	0	0	0	56	199	366	326	132	12	0	0	1091
% OF POSSIBLE SUNSHINE	na	na	na	na	na	na	na	na	na	na	na	na	na
AVERAGE SKY COVER													
Sunrise - Sunset	6.4	6.3	6.3	6.3	6.5	6.2	6.2	6.0	5.7	5.5	6.3	6.4	6.2
NUMBER OF DAYS (Sunrise-Sunset)													
Clear	8.0	7.4	7.8	7.3	6.3	7.0	6.7	7.9	9.8	10.7	7.7	8.1	94.8
Partly cloudy	7.7	7.6	8.6	9.0	10.7	10.6	12.3	11.5	8.9	8.5	8.3	7.9	111.5
Cloudy	15.3	13.3	14.7	13.7	14.0	12.4	12.0	11.6	11.3	11.7	14.0	15.0	159.0
Precipitation .01" or more	11.1	9.5	11.5	10.8	12.0	10.2	9.8	9.1	8.3	7.8	10.3	11.0	121.4
Snow, Ice pellets 1.0" or more	2.2	1.9	1.3	0.2	0.0	0.0	0.0	0.0	0.0	0.0	0.2	1.5	7.3
Thunderstorms	0.2	0.2	1.0	1.6	3.7	4.8	5.8	4.6	2.2	1.0	0.4	0.2	25.7
Fog, Visibility 1/4 mile or less	2.3	1.9	1.5	1.1	1.8	1.2	0.5	0.6	0.9	2.0	2.0	1.8	17.7
Temperature Maximum:													
90° and above	0.0	0.0	0.0	0.2	0.9	3.8	8.1	6.3	1.6	0.0	0.0	0.0	20.7
32° and below	11.1	6.0	1.1	0.1	0.0	0.0	0.0	0.0	0.0	0.0	0.1	3.9	22.1
Temperature Minimum:													
32° and below	24.6	20.7	12.4	2.0	0.0	0.0	0.0	0.0	0.0	0.7	6.1	19.1	85.5
0° and below	0.7	0.3	0.0	0.0	0.0	0.0	0.0	0.0	0.0	0.0	0.0	0.1	1.0
RELATIVE HUMIDITY (%)													
Morning	71	69	66	64	72	73	72	76	77	76	73	73	72
Afternoon	59	55	51	47	51	53	51	54	55	54	57	60	54
PRECIPITATION (inches)													
Water Equivalent													
Normal	3.1	3.0	4.1	3.5	3.5	2.9	3.8	4.3	3.6	3.0	3.5	3.4	42.3
Maximum monthly	10.1	4.9	11.1	11.1	10.2	6.4	8.6	11.8	10.2	8.2	11.5	9.4	11.8
Date	1979	1979	1983	1983	1984	1975	1984	1955	1944	1943	1977	1983	1955
Minimum monthly	0.4	1.2	1.1	0.9	0.5	0.0	0.8	0.5	0.9	0.2	0.5	0.2	0.0
Date	1981	1968	1981	1963	1964	1949	1966	1964	1951	1963	1976	1955	1949
Maximum in 24 hrs	3.5	2.4	2.6	3.7	4.2	2.3	3.4	7.8	5.2	3.0	7.2	2.7	7.8
Date	1979	1961	1978	1984	1979	1973	1971	1971	1971	1973	1977	1983	1971
SNOW, ICE PELLETS													
Maximum monthly	27.4	26.1	26.0	13.8	T	0.0	0.0	0.0	0.0	0.3	3.1	29.1	29.1
Date	1978	1979	1956	1982	1977	—	—	—	—	1952	1967	1947	1947
Maximum in 24 hrs	17.8	20.0	17.6	12.8	T	0.0	0.0	0.0	0.0	0.3	3.1	26.0	26.0
Date	1978	1961	1956	1982	1977	—	—	—	—	1952	1967	1947	1947
WIND (Resultant)													
Mean speed (mph)	11.3	11.6	12.0	11.4	10.0	9.4	8.9	8.7	9.0	9.4	10.2	10.8	10.2

ALBUQUERQUE
Elev. 5311' **35° 03'N — 106° 37'W** **New Mexico**

NORMALS, MEANS, EXTREMES

	JAN	FEB	MAR	APR	MAY	JUN	JUL	AUG	SEP	OCT	NOV	DEC	YEAR
TEMPERATURE													
Normal daily maximum	47.2	52.9	60.7	70.6	79.9	90.6	92.8	89.4	83.0	71.7	57.2	48.0	70.3
Normal daily minimum	22.3	25.9	31.7	39.5	48.6	58.4	64.7	62.8	54.9	43.1	30.7	23.2	42.1
Normal monthly	34.8	39.4	46.2	55.1	64.3	74.5	78.8	76.1	69.0	57.4	44.0	35.6	56.2
Extreme highest	69	75	85	89	98	105	105	101	100	91	77	72	105
Extreme highest date	1971	1972	1971	1965	1951	1980	1980	1979	1979	1979	1975	1958	1980
Extreme lowest	-17	-5	8	19	28	40	52	52	37	25	-7	3	-17
Extreme lowest date	1971	1951	1948	1980	1975	1980	1985	1968	1971	1980	1976	1974	1971
DEGREE DAYS BASE 65° F													
Heating	936	717	583	302	81	0	0	0	12	242	630	911	4414
Cooling	0	0	0	0	59	285	428	344	132	6	0	0	1254
% OF POSSIBLE SUNSHINE	72	73	73	77	80	83	76	76	79	79	77	72	76
AVERAGE SKY COVER													
Sunrise - Sunset	4.9	4.9	5.1	4.5	4.1	3.3	4.5	4.3	3.6	3.5	4.0	4.6	4.3
NUMBER OF DAYS (Sunrise-Sunset)													
Clear	12.9	11.3	11.2	12.8	14.7	17.9	12.0	13.8	16.8	17.5	15.1	13.9	170.0
Partly cloudy	7.8	7.8	10.0	9.4	10.2	8.6	14.3	12.4	7.7	7.6	7.7	7.5	111.2
Cloudy	10.3	9.2	9.7	7.7	6.1	3.6	4.7	4.8	5.5	5.9	7.2	9.5	84.1
Precipitation .01" or more	3.9	4.0	4.5	3.3	4.3	3.7	8.8	9.3	5.7	4.8	3.3	4.0	59.8
Snow, Ice pellets 1.0" or more	1.0	0.8	0.7	0.2	*	0.0	0.0	0.0	0.0	0.0	0.4	0.9	4.1
Thunderstorms	0.1	0.3	0.9	1.5	3.8	4.9	11.2	11.0	4.7	2.4	0.6	0.2	41.7
Fog, Visibility 1/4 mile or less	1.2	1.0	0.6	0.2	*	*	0.1	*	0.1	0.3	0.6	1.4	5.6
Temperature Maximum:													
90° and above	0.0	0.0	0.0	0.0	2.6	17.4	24.0	16.9	4.3	0.2	0.0	0.0	65.3
32° and below	2.5	0.6	0.2	0.0	0.0	0.0	0.0	0.0	0.0	0.0	0.2	1.5	5.0
Temperature Minimum:													
32° and below	28.9	23.5	16.8	5.0	0.3	0.0	0.0	0.0	0.0	2.2	16.3	28.5	121.6
0° and below	0.5	0.0	0.0	0.0	0.0	0.0	0.0	0.0	0.0	0.0	0.1	0.0	0.6
RELATIVE HUMIDITY (%)													
Morning	71	65	56	48	48	45	60	65	62	62	65	70	60
Afternoon	41	32	25	18	18	17	27	30	31	30	36	43	29
PRECIPITATION (inches)													
Water Equivalent													
Normal	0.4	0.4	0.5	0.4	0.4	0.5	1.3	1.5	0.8	0.8	0.3	0.5	8.1
Maximum monthly	1.3	1.4	2.1	1.9	3.0	1.7	3.3	3.3	1.9	3.0	1.4	1.8	3.3
Date	1978	1948	1973	1942	1941	1967	1968	1967	1940	1972	1940	1959	1968
Minimum monthly	T	T	T	T	T	T	0.0	T	T	0.0	0.0	0.0	0.0
Date	1970	1984	1966	1972	1945	1975	1980	1962	1957	1952	1949	1981	1981
Maximum in 24 hrs	0.8	0.5	1.1	1.6	1.1	1.6	1.7	1.7	1.9	1.8	0.7	1.3	1.9
Date	1962	1981	1973	1969	1969	1952	1961	1980	1955	1969	1940	1958	1955
SNOW, ICE PELLETS													
Maximum monthly	9.5	8.2	13.9	8.1	1.0	0.0	0.0	0.0	T	0.9	9.3	14.7	14.7
Date	1973	1964	1973	1973	1979	—	—	—	1971	1979	1940	1959	1959
Maximum in 24 hrs	5.1	4.2	10.7	6.6	1.0	0.0	0.0	0.0	T	0.9	5.5	14.2	14.2
Date	1973	1946	1973	1973	1979	—	—	—	1971	1979	1946	1958	1958
WIND (Resultant)													
Mean speed (mph)	8.1	8.8	10.2	11.1	10.5	10.0	9.1	8.2	8.6	8.3	7.9	7.7	9.0

CLAYTON

Elev. 4969'   36° 27'N — 103° 09'W   **New Mexico**

NORMALS, MEANS, EXTREMES

	JAN	FEB	MAR	APR	MAY	JUN	JUL	AUG	SEP	OCT	NOV	DEC	YEAR
TEMPERATURE													
Normal daily maximum	47.4	50.6	56.3	65.9	74.5	84.4	87.8	85.6	78.4	69.2	55.8	49.6	67.1
Normal daily minimum	18.6	22.1	26.4	36.0	45.8	55.3	60.5	58.9	51.2	40.1	27.7	21.5	38.7
Normal monthly	33.0	36.4	41.4	51.0	60.2	69.9	74.2	72.3	64.8	54.7	41.8	35.6	52.9
Extreme highest	78	81	85	91	95	104	102	102	99	90	85	83	104
Extreme highest date	1956	1963	1971	1965	1984	1968	1964	1944	1948	1979	1980	1955	1968
Extreme lowest	-21	-17	-11	9	23	37	45	45	26	17	-10	-14	-21
Extreme lowest date	1959	1951	1948	1945	1967	1964	1958	1964	1985	1969	1976	1983	1959
DEGREE DAYS BASE 65° F													
Heating	992	801	732	420	177	25	0	0	80	327	699	915	5168
Cooling	0	0	0	0	25	172	288	230	74	8	0	0	797
% OF POSSIBLE SUNSHINE	na	na	na	na	na	na	na	na	na	na	na	na	na
AVERAGE SKY COVER													
Sunrise - Sunset	5.1	5.0	5.3	5.0	5.1	4.1	4.8	4.3	3.8	3.6	4.4	4.6	4.6
NUMBER OF DAYS (Sunrise-Sunset)													
Clear	12.5	11.2	11.3	11.7	11.4	13.5	12.3	15.0	17.2	17.8	14.8	13.9	162.5
Partly cloudy	7.0	7.3	8.8	8.8	9.3	10.4	11.9	9.7	6.0	6.6	6.0	7.0	98.7
Cloudy	11.5	9.6	10.9	9.5	10.4	6.2	6.8	6.3	6.8	6.6	9.2	10.1	103.9
Precipitation .01" or more	3.5	3.4	4.8	5.2	8.1	7.8	10.3	8.7	5.4	3.9	3.3	2.9	67.3
Snow, Ice pellets 1.0" or more	1.5	1.2	1.6	0.6	0.1	0.0	0.0	0.0	0.1	0.3	0.9	1.2	7.5
Thunderstorms	0.1	0.3	0.7	2.2	8.3	10.5	13.4	11.4	5.3	1.2	0.3	0.1	53.8
Fog, Visibility 1/4 mile or less	0.7	1.4	2.1	1.0	0.9	0.6	0.6	0.3	0.8	0.7	0.9	0.8	10.9
Temperature Maximum:													
90° and above	0.0	0.0	0.0	0.1	1.0	8.7	13.5	9.5	2.9	0.1	0.0	0.0	35.6
32° and below	4.8	3.2	1.9	0.2	0.0	0.0	0.0	0.0	0.0	0.2	1.5	3.4	15.2
Temperature Minimum:													
32° and below	29.4	24.9	23.3	9.5	0.9	0.0	0.0	0.0	0.3	4.9	20.8	28.1	142.1
0° and below	1.5	0.5	0.2	0.0	0.0	0.0	0.0	0.0	0.0	0.0	0.1	0.6	2.8
RELATIVE HUMIDITY (%)													
Morning	64	65	65	65	71	71	76	77	73	64	64	63	68
Afternoon	47	42	37	31	36	35	41	42	40	40	47	52	41
PRECIPITATION (inches)													
Water Equivalent													
Normal	0.2	0.2	0.5	1.0	2.2	1.7	2.5	2.4	1.4	0.7	0.4	0.2	14.1
Maximum monthly	1.0	1.0	2.3	4.6	6.7	4.5	7.7	5.7	5.2	4.5	2.0	1.1	7.7
Date	1960	1948	1957	1944	1949	1950	1950	1981	1960	1984	1978	1960	1950
Minimum monthly	T	T	0.0	0.0	0.2	0.1	0.6	0.2	T	T	T	0.0	0.0
Date	1970	1950	1966	1974	1974	1955	1946	1983	1956	1980	1966	1957	1957
Maximum in 24 hrs	0.7	0.7	0.9	2.4	4.6	2.8	2.6	4.4	3.4	3.9	1.5	0.7	4.6
Date	1960	1953	1959	1980	1954	1984	1982	1963	1960	1965	1961	1947	1954
SNOW, ICE PELLETS													
Maximum monthly	12.0	9.5	16.0	10.9	8.0	0.0	0.0	0.0	5.0	8.0	14.8	11.0	16.0
Date	1983	1978	1984	1955	1978	—	—	—	1984	1984	1961	1978	1984
Maximum in 24 hrs	7.2	7.5	9.0	10.9	7.6	0.0	0.0	0.0	5.0	6.0	12.7	8.1	12.7
Date	1983	1953	1973	1955	1978	—	—	—	1984	1984	1961	1958	1961
WIND (Resultant)													
Mean speed (mph)	11.7	11.7	12.6	14.5	12.6	12.4	10.6	9.6	11.5	11.0	11.9	12.3	11.8

ROSWELL

Elev. 3612'   33° 39'N — 104° 52'W   **New Mexico**

NORMALS, MEANS, EXTREMES

	JAN	FEB	MAR	APR	MAY	JUN	JUL	AUG	SEP	OCT	NOV	DEC	YEAR
TEMPERATURE													
Normal daily maximum	55.4	60.4	67.7	76.9	85.0	93.1	93.7	91.3	84.9	75.8	63.1	56.7	75.3
Normal daily minimum	27.4	31.4	37.9	46.8	55.6	64.8	69.0	67.0	59.6	47.5	35.0	28.2	47.5
Normal monthly	41.4	45.9	52.8	61.9	70.3	79.0	81.4	79.2	72.3	61.7	49.1	42.5	61.4
Extreme highest	82	84	90	92	101	109	105	104	100	95	86	81	109
Extreme highest date	1975	1979	1978	1978	1978	1981	1980	1980	1983	1979	1980	1981	1981
Extreme lowest	-9	3	18	23	34	51	59	57	42	25	4	-8	-9
Extreme lowest date	1979	1985	1980	1973	1975	1983	1973	1976	1973	1980	1976	1978	1979
DEGREE DAYS BASE 65° F													
Heating	732	535	386	134	11	0	0	0	10	143	477	698	3126
Cooling	0	0	8	41	176	420	508	440	229	41	0	0	1863
% OF POSSIBLE SUNSHINE	60	68	75	77	80	83	77	73	72	77	73	71	74
AVERAGE SKY COVER													
Sunrise - Sunset	5.3	4.7	4.4	4.2	4.3	3.5	4.6	4.5	4.8	3.6	3.9	4.2	4.3
NUMBER OF DAYS (Sunrise-Sunset)													
Clear	11.3	12.1	14.2	14.3	13.4	17.2	11.1	12.8	12.8	18.1	15.8	14.9	168.1
Partly cloudy	8.8	7.8	9.1	8.9	11.8	9.9	14.7	12.2	7.9	5.9	7.1	9.0	113.0
Cloudy	10.9	8.3	7.7	6.8	5.8	2.9	5.2	6.0	9.3	7.0	7.1	7.1	84.1
Precipitation .01" or more	4.8	3.3	2.6	3.1	3.8	4.8	5.5	7.2	7.2	4.5	3.0	3.3	53.0
Snow, Ice pellets 1.0" or more	1.1	1.0	0.3	0.3	0.0	0.0	0.0	0.0	0.0	0.1	0.7	0.9	4.4
Thunderstorms	0.2	0.0	0.5	2.0	4.4	6.6	7.2	7.5	3.9	2.0	0.5	0.0	34.8
Fog, Visibility 1/4 mile or less	3.3	2.8	0.5	0.2	0.5	0.2	0.2	0.2	0.8	2.2	2.8	2.2	15.8
Temperature Maximum:													
90° and above	0.0	0.0	0.1	0.2	7.5	20.9	24.5	21.2	9.2	1.0	0.0	0.0	84.5
32° and below	3.0	0.7	0.1	0.0	0.0	0.0	0.0	0.0	0.0	0.0	0.5	2.2	6.5
Temperature Minimum:													
32° and below	24.8	18.2	6.9	2.2	0.0	0.0	0.0	0.0	0.0	1.1	11.2	25.0	89.5
0° and below	0.3	0.0	0.0	0.0	0.0	0.0	0.0	0.0	0.0	0.0	0.0	0.3	0.6
RELATIVE HUMIDITY (%)													
Morning	71	65	56	53	59	63	67	72	75	70	67	66	65
Afternoon	43	33	24	23	25	26	32	37	42	37	40	40	34
PRECIPITATION (inches)													
Water Equivalent													
Normal	0.2	0.2	0.2	0.3	0.7	0.9	1.3	2.1	1.7	0.9	0.3	0.2	9.7
Maximum monthly	0.8	1.0	1.4	2.4	3.3	4.5	6.2	6.4	6.5	3.8	1.5	1.6	6.5
Date	1980	1975	1973	1985	1981	1981	1981	1974	1980	1974	1984	1982	1980
Minimum monthly	0.0	T	0.0	0.0	T	0.0	0.0	0.0	0.3	0.1	T	T	0.0
Date	1984	1984	1980	1980	1978	1974	1974	1980	1985	1979	1980	1976	1980
Maximum in 24 hrs	0.6	0.3	1.4	2.2	1.7	3.0	4.9	3.9	2.7	1.6	1.3	0.6	4.9
Date	1982	1975	1973	1985	1981	1981	1981	1977	1980	1983	1984	1982	1981
SNOW, ICE PELLETS													
Maximum monthly	7.3	7.5	4.8	5.3	T	0.0	0.0	0.0	0.0	4.2	12.3	8.0	12.3
Date	1980	1973	1984	1983	1978	1973	1973	1973	1973	1976	1980	1982	1980
Maximum in 24 hrs	7.3	5.4	4.8	4.0	T	T	0.0	0.0	0.0	3.1	6.3	5.0	7.3
Date	1980	1979	1984	1983	1985	1985	1973	1973	1973	1976	1980	1978	1980
WIND (Resultant)													
Mean speed (mph)	7.9	8.6	10.5	10.4	9.8	9.6	8.5	7.8	8.1	8.0	7.8	7.6	8.7

ALBANY

Elev. 275'   42° 45'N — 73° 48'W   **New York**

NORMALS, MEANS, EXTREMES

	JAN	FEB	MAR	APR	MAY	JUN	JUL	AUG	SEP	OCT	NOV	DEC	YEAR
TEMPERATURE													
Normal daily maximum	30.2	32.7	42.5	57.6	69.5	78.3	83.2	80.7	72.8	61.5	47.8	34.6	57.6
Normal daily minimum	11.9	14.0	24.6	35.5	45.4	55.0	59.6	57.6	49.6	39.4	30.8	18.2	36.8
Normal monthly	21.1	23.4	33.6	46.6	57.5	66.7	71.4	69.2	61.2	50.5	39.3	26.4	47.2
Extreme highest	62	67	85	92	94	99	100	99	100	89	82	71	100
Extreme highest date	1974	1976	1977	1976	1981	1952	1953	1955	1953	1963	1950	1984	1953
Extreme lowest	-28	-21	-21	10	26	36	40	34	24	16	5	-22	-28
Extreme lowest date	1971	1973	1948	1965	1968	1980	1978	1982	1947	1969	1972	1969	1971
DEGREE DAYS BASE 65° F													
Heating	1361	1165	973	552	252	38	7	15	149	450	771	1194	6927
Cooling	0	0	0	0	19	89	206	145	35	0	0	0	494
% OF POSSIBLE SUNSHINE	45	51	53	53	55	59	64	60	57	51	36	38	52
AVERAGE SKY COVER													
Sunrise - Sunset	7.0	6.9	7.0	6.9	6.9	6.5	6.2	6.2	6.0	6.3	7.5	7.4	6.7
NUMBER OF DAYS (Sunrise-Sunset)													
Clear	5.5	5.4	6.0	5.8	5.2	5.3	6.1	6.9	7.8	7.7	3.7	4.9	70.2
Partly cloudy	8.1	7.4	7.9	8.1	9.2	11.1	12.9	11.6	10.0	9.3	7.8	6.8	110.2
Cloudy	17.4	15.4	17.1	16.1	16.6	13.6	12.0	12.5	12.2	14.0	18.5	19.3	184.8
Precipitation .01" or more	12.4	10.6	12.1	12.2	13.1	11.2	10.2	10.1	9.5	8.7	11.9	12.5	134.4
Snow, Ice pellets 1.0" or more	3.9	3.3	2.7	0.7	0.1	0.0	0.0	0.0	0.0	*	1.1	4.0	15.8
Thunderstorms	0.1	0.2	0.5	1.3	3.6	5.6	6.7	4.7	2.4	0.9	0.3	0.1	26.4
Fog, Visibility 1/4 mile or less	1.1	0.9	1.2	0.8	1.4	1.3	1.4	2.6	3.8	4.5	1.7	1.8	22.5
Temperature Maximum:													
90° and above	0.0	0.0	0.0	0.1	0.3	1.6	3.6	1.7	0.5	0.0	0.0	0.0	7.6
32° and below	18.7	13.1	4.0	0.3	0.0	0.0	0.0	0.0	0.0	0.0	1.3	11.8	49.0
Temperature Minimum:													
32° and below	29.7	26.0	24.5	13.4	2.3	0.0	0.0	0.0	0.6	8.9	18.0	27.7	150.9
0° and below	7.6	4.6	0.5	0.0	0.0	0.0	0.0	0.0	0.0	0.0	0.0	2.5	15.1
RELATIVE HUMIDITY (%)													
Morning	76	73	71	70	78	83	84	87	87	82	79	78	79
Afternoon	63	59	54	48	53	56	55	58	59	57	63	66	58
PRECIPITATION (inches)													
Water Equivalent													
Normal	2.3	2.2	3.0	2.9	3.3	3.2	3.0	3.3	3.2	2.9	3.0	3.0	35.7
Maximum monthly	6.4	5.0	5.9	7.9	8.9	7.3	6.9	7.3	7.8	8.8	8.0	6.7	8.9
Date	1978	1981	1977	1983	1953	1973	1975	1950	1960	1955	1972	1973	1953
Minimum monthly	0.4	0.3	0.2	1.1	1.0	0.6	0.4	0.7	0.4	0.2	0.9	0.6	0.2
Date	1980	1968	1981	1963	1980	1964	1968	1947	1964	1963	1978	1958	1963
Maximum in 24 hrs	1.9	1.5	2.1	2.2	2.1	3.4	2.7	4.5	3.6	2.7	2.0	4.0	4.5
Date	1978	1975	1977	1968	1968	1952	1960	1971	1960	1976	1959	1948	1971
SNOW, ICE PELLETS													
Maximum monthly	40.8	34.5	34.7	17.7	1.6	0.0	0.0	0.0	0.0	2.0	24.6	57.5	57.5
Date	1978	1962	1956	1982	1977	—	—	—	—	1952	1972	1969	1969
Maximum in 24 hrs	21.2	17.9	17.0	17.5	1.6	0.0	0.0	0.0	0.0	2.0	21.9	18.3	21.9
Date	1983	1958	1984	1982	1977	—	—	—	—	1952	1971	1966	1971
WIND (Resultant)													
Mean speed (mph)	9.8	10.3	10.7	10.6	9.0	8.2	7.5	7.0	7.4	8.0	9.0	9.3	8.9

BUFFALO

Elev. 705'   42° 56'N — 78° 44'W   **New York**

NORMALS, MEANS, EXTREMES

	JAN	FEB	MAR	APR	MAY	JUN	JUL	AUG	SEP	OCT	NOV	DEC	YEAR
TEMPERATURE													
Normal daily maximum	30.0	31.4	40.4	54.4	65.9	75.6	80.2	78.2	71.4	60.2	47.0	35.0	55.8
Normal daily minimum	17.0	17.5	25.6	36.3	46.3	56.4	61.2	59.6	52.7	42.7	33.6	22.5	39.3
Normal monthly	23.5	24.5	33.0	45.4	56.1	66.0	70.7	68.9	62.1	51.5	40.3	28.8	47.5
Extreme highest	72	65	81	88	90	95	94	99	98	87	80	74	99
Extreme highest date	1950	1981	1945	1985	1977	1957	1968	1948	1953	1951	1961	1982	1948
Extreme lowest	-16	-20	-7	12	26	35	43	38	32	20	9	-10	-20
Extreme lowest date	1982	1961	1984	1982	1947	1945	1945	1982	1963	1965	1971	1980	1961
DEGREE DAYS BASE 65° F													
Heating	1287	1134	992	588	294	53	9	25	130	423	741	1122	6798
Cooling	0	0	0	0	18	83	186	146	43	0	0	0	476
% OF POSSIBLE SUNSHINE	32	38	45	52	58	65	68	64	59	50	29	26	49
AVERAGE SKY COVER													
Sunrise - Sunset	8.4	8.2	7.6	7.1	6.8	6.2	6.0	6.2	6.3	6.7	8.3	8.5	7.2
NUMBER OF DAYS (Sunrise-Sunset)													
Clear	1.4	2.0	3.7	4.9	5.6	6.3	7.0	6.8	6.5	6.5	2.1	1.2	53.9
Partly cloudy	6.2	5.6	7.4	8.2	9.6	11.6	13.0	11.8	10.0	8.3	5.4	6.1	103.2
Cloudy	23.5	20.7	19.9	16.9	15.7	12.1	11.0	12.4	13.5	16.2	22.5	23.7	208.1
Precipitation .01" or more	20.2	16.9	16.2	14.3	12.5	10.3	9.8	10.6	10.8	11.4	15.9	19.9	169.0
Snow, Ice pellets 1.0" or more	7.5	5.5	3.8	1.0	*	0.0	0.0	0.0	0.0	0.1	3.1	6.2	27.3
Thunderstorms	0.1	0.2	1.2	2.4	2.9	5.0	5.6	6.1	3.7	1.5	1.1	0.5	30.5
Fog, Visibility 1/4 mile or less	1.6	1.7	2.5	2.4	2.5	1.3	0.9	0.9	1.0	1.5	1.4	1.3	19.0
Temperature Maximum:													
90° and above	0.0	0.0	0.0	0.0	*	0.6	1.2	0.3	*	0.0	0.0	0.0	2.2
32° and below	18.7	15.8	7.4	0.7	0.0	0.0	0.0	0.0	0.0	0.0	2.0	12.8	57.5
Temperature Minimum:													
32° and below	28.9	25.7	24.4	11.0	0.7	0.0	0.0	0.0	*	3.3	14.0	25.9	134.0
0° and below	2.5	1.7	0.2	0.0	0.0	0.0	0.0	0.0	0.0	0.0	0.0	0.6	5.0
RELATIVE HUMIDITY (%)													
Morning	78	79	78	75	76	79	79	83	82	80	80	80	79
Afternoon	73	70	67	58	56	57	54	58	60	60	70	74	63
PRECIPITATION (inches)													
Water Equivalent													
Normal	3.0	2.4	2.9	3.0	2.8	2.7	2.9	4.1	3.3	2.9	3.6	3.4	37.5
Maximum monthly	6.8	5.8	5.5	5.9	6.3	6.8	6.4	10.6	8.9	9.1	9.7	8.0	10.6
Date	1982	1960	1976	1961	1953	1984	1963	1977	1977	1954	1985	1977	1977
Minimum monthly	1.0	0.8	1.2	1.2	1.2	0.1	0.9	1.1	0.7	0.3	1.4	0.6	0.1
Date	1946	1968	1967	1946	1965	1955	1972	1948	1964	1963	1944	1943	1955
Maximum in 24 hrs	2.5	2.3	2.1	1.7	2.0	3.0	3.3	3.8	4.9	3.4	2.5	2.1	4.9
Date	1982	1954	1954	1977	1957	1968	1963	1963	1979	1945	1949	1945	1979
SNOW, ICE PELLETS													
Maximum monthly	68.3	54.2	29.2	15.0	2.0	T	0.0	0.0	T	3.1	31.3	68.4	68.4
Date	1977	1958	1959	1975	1945	1980	—	—	1956	1972	1976	1985	1985
Maximum in 24 hrs	25.3	19.4	15.8	6.8	2.0	T	0.0	0.0	T	2.5	19.9	24.3	25.3
Date	1982	1984	1954	1975	1945	1980	—	—	1956	1972	1955	1945	1982
WIND (Resultant)													
Mean speed (mph)	14.3	13.8	13.5	12.8	11.5	11.0	10.4	9.8	10.4	11.2	12.7	13.4	12.1

ISLIP

Elev. 84'   40° 47'N — 73° 06'W   **New York**

NORMALS, MEANS, EXTREMES

	JAN	FEB	MAR	APR	MAY	JUN	JUL	AUG	SEP	OCT	NOV	DEC	YEAR
TEMPERATURE													
Extreme highest	56	63	74	82	84	92	89	90	91	76	68	65	92
Extreme highest date	1985	1985	1985	1985	1985	1984	1985	1984	1985	1985	1985	1984	1984
Extreme lowest	-7	11	11	27	36	46	58	56	45	28	26	8	-7
Extreme lowest date	1984	1985	1984	1985	1985	1984	1985	1985	1984	1985	1984	1985	1984
NUMBER OF DAYS (Sunrise-Sunset)													
Precipitation .01" or more	11.5	8.0	11.5	9.5	12.0	12.5	8.5	6.5	5.5	6.5	11.5	11.5	115.0
Snow, Ice pellets 1.0" or more	4.0	1.5	2.5	0.0	0.0	0.0	0.0	0.0	0.0	0.0	0.0	1.0	9.0
Thunderstorms	0.0	1.5	0.0	2.5	3.5	6.5	5.5	4.0	1.5	0.5	0.0	0.0	25.5
Fog, Visibility 1/4 mile or less	2.5	5.5	2.0	4.0	3.5	2.5	2.0	2.5	2.0	6.5	3.5	4.0	40.5
Temperature Maximum:													
90° and above	0.0	0.0	0.0	0.0	0.0	1.5	0.0	0.5	1.5	0.0	0.0	0.0	3.5
32° and below	13.5	5.0	2.5	0.0	0.0	0.0	0.0	0.0	0.0	0.0	0.0	2.5	23.5
Temperature Minimum:													
32° and below	29.0	18.0	17.5	3.0	0.0	0.0	0.0	0.0	0.0	1.0	6.5	20.0	95.0
0° and below	1.5	0.0	0.0	0.0	0.0	0.0	0.0	0.0	0.0	0.0	0.0	0.0	1.5
RELATIVE HUMIDITY (%)													
Morning	76	79	70	78	84	83	89	88	84	82	80	76	81
Afternoon	69	69	57	54	58	60	63	63	56	61	63	59	61
Maximum monthly	2.6	5.5	5.5	4.8	9.4	6.3	8.3	3.8	5.0	2.4	6.1	2.3	9.4
Date	1984	1984	1984	1984	1984	1985	1984	1985	1984	1984	1985	1984	1984
Minimum monthly	1.3	2.0	2.3	1.7	4.1	5.1	3.4	0.4	0.8	1.3	1.6	0.9	0.4
Date	1985	1985	1985	1985	1985	1984	1985	1984	1985	1985	1984	1985	1984
Maximum in 24 hrs	0.6	2.3	2.4	1.7	2.2	1.8	2.6	2.1	2.2	0.8	2.0	0.7	2.6
Date	1984	1984	1984	1984	1984	1984	1984	1985	1984	1984	1985	1984	1984
SNOW, ICE PELLETS													
Maximum monthly	13.5	8.7	13.0	T	0.0	0.0	0.0	0.0	0.0	0.0	T	4.7	13.5
Date	1985	1985	1984	1985	1984	1984	1984	1984	1984	1984	1984	1985	1984	1985
Maximum in 24 hrs	6.0	3.5	5.0	T	0.0	0.0	0.0	0.0	0.0	0.0	T	4.0	6.0
Date	1984	1985	1984	1985	1984	1984	1984	1984	1984	1984	1985	1984	1984
WIND (Resultant)													
Mean speed (mph)	9.2	10.5	11.8	10.7	10.2	8.4	8.2	7.2	7.9	8.4	10.3	8.9	9.3

NORMALS, MEANS, EXTREMES

	JAN	FEB	MAR	APR	MAY	JUN	JUL	AUG	SEP	OCT	NOV	DEC	YEAR
TEMPERATURE													
Normal daily maximum	37.5	39.1	46.6	58.3	67.7	76.9	82.7	81.7	75.2	64.7	53.2	41.8	60.5
Normal daily minimum	25.1	25.9	33.2	42.3	51.7	61.0	67.2	66.3	59.2	48.7	39.6	29.6	45.8
Normal monthly	31.3	32.5	39.9	50.3	59.7	69.0	75.0	74.0	67.2	56.7	46.4	35.7	53.1
Extreme highest	65	67	77	90	99	99	104	100	98	84	77	70	104
Extreme highest date	1974	1976	1985	1977	1969	1964	1966	1983	1983	1967	1982	1982	1966
Extreme lowest	-2	-2	7	20	34	45	55	46	40	25	19	2	-2
Extreme lowest date	1985	1963	1967	1982	1966	1967	1979	1965	1963	1961	1976	1983	1985
DEGREE DAYS BASE 65° F													
Heating	1045	910	775	441	192	23	0	0	47	270	558	908	5169
Cooling	0	0	0	0	28	143	310	279	113	13	0	0	886
% OF POSSIBLE SUNSHINE	na	na	na	na	na	na	na	na	na	na	na	na	na
AVERAGE SKY COVER													
Sunrise - Sunset	6.1	6.1	6.2	6.0	6.2	6.0	5.9	5.8	5.4	5.4	6.2	6.3	6.0
NUMBER OF DAYS (Sunrise-Sunset)													
Clear	8.4	7.9	7.9	8.2	6.9	7.3	7.5	7.5	10.1	10.8	7.9	7.7	98.1
Partly cloudy	8.6	7.6	9.4	9.3	11.4	11.0	12.6	13.1	9.6	9.1	8.3	8.2	118.3
Cloudy	14.0	12.8	13.7	12.5	12.7	11.7	10.9	10.4	10.4	11.0	13.7	15.1	148.9
Precipitation .01" or more	10.3	9.6	11.3	10.3	11.3	9.9	8.9	9.0	8.1	7.5	10.0	11.4	117.7
Snow, Ice pellets 1.0" or more	2.6	2.0	1.2	0.1	0.0	0.0	0.0	0.0	0.0	0.0	0.1	1.1	7.1
Thunderstorms	0.1	0.3	1.0	1.6	2.8	3.8	4.4	4.8	1.7	1.1	0.4	0.1	22.3
Fog, Visibility 1/4 mile or less	2.7	2.7	3.7	2.7	4.3	3.9	2.5	1.3	1.1	2.3	2.2	2.6	32.1
Temperature Maximum:													
90° and above	0.0	0.0	0.0	*	0.3	1.8	4.1	3.0	0.9	0.0	0.0	0.0	10.2
32° and below	10.1	6.0	1.0	*	0.0	0.0	0.0	0.0	0.0	0.0	*	4.1	21.3
Temperature Minimum:													
32° and below	24.1	20.7	11.7	1.6	0.0	0.0	0.0	0.0	0.0	0.4	4.3	17.7	80.4
0° and below	0.2	0.1	0.0	0.0	0.0	0.0	0.0	0.0	0.0	0.0	0.0	0.0	0.3
RELATIVE HUMIDITY (%)													
Morning	68	68	68	70	77	80	78	79	80	76	73	71	74
Afternoon	59	58	56	55	59	61	59	59	59	56	59	61	58
PRECIPITATION (inches)													
Water Equivalent													
Normal	2.9	3.2	3.9	3.7	3.4	2.9	3.5	4.1	3.5	2.9	3.7	3.6	41.7
Maximum monthly	8.3	5.4	8.1	9.5	8.5	9.2	8.4	17.4	9.6	6.4	9.5	6.1	17.4
Date	1979	1960	1980	1983	1984	1984	1969	1955	1975	1958	1972	1969	1955
Minimum monthly	0.2	1.0	0.9	1.1	0.3	T	0.4	0.4	0.7	0.0	0.3	0.8	T
Date	1956	1980	1981	1963	1955	1949	1954	1972	1951	1963	1976	1985	1949
Maximum in 24 hrs	3.2	2.8	2.4	3.3	2.8	6.2	5.9	6.5	5.8	3.4	4.0	2.4	6.5
Date	1979	1958	1977	1980	1968	1984	1984	1955	1960	1972	1972	1974	1955
SNOW, ICE PELLETS													
Maximum monthly	20.1	25.3	21.1	8.2	T	0.0	0.0	0.0	0.0	0.5	2.1	16.4	25.3
Date	1978	1961	1960	1982	1967	—	—	—	—	1962	1967	1960	1961
Maximum in 24 hrs	14.2	21.7	8.1	8.0	T	0.0	0.0	0.0	0.0	0.5	2.1	8.2	21.7
Date	1978	1983	1967	1982	1967	—	—	—	—	1962	1967	1960	1983
WIND (Resultant)													
Mean speed (mph)	13.6	13.9	14.0	13.4	11.9	10.9	10.6	10.3	10.6	11.2	12.5	13.0	12.2

ROCHESTER

Elev. 547'   43° 07'N — 77° 40'W   **New York**

NORMALS, MEANS, EXTREMES

	JAN	FEB	MAR	APR	MAY	JUN	JUL	AUG	SEP	OCT	NOV	DEC	YEAR
TEMPERATURE													
Normal daily maximum	30.8	32.2	41.2	56.0	67.7	77.7	82.3	80.1	72.8	61.5	48.0	35.5	57.2
Normal daily minimum	16.3	16.7	25.3	36.1	46.0	55.7	60.3	58.7	51.6	41.8	33.2	22.3	38.7
Normal monthly	23.6	24.5	33.3	46.1	56.9	66.7	71.3	69.4	62.2	51.7	40.6	28.9	47.9
Extreme highest	74	67	84	93	94	100	98	99	99	91	81	72	100
Extreme highest date	1950	1947	1945	1970	1974	1953	1978	1948	1953	1951	1950	1982	1953
Extreme lowest	-16	-19	-6	13	26	35	42	36	28	20	5	-16	-19
Extreme lowest date	1957	1979	1980	1982	1979	1949	1963	1965	1947	1972	1971	1942	1979
DEGREE DAYS BASE 65° F													
Heating	1283	1137	983	570	274	41	10	23	132	412	732	1116	6713
Cooling	0	0	0	0	23	92	205	163	48	0	0	0	531
% OF POSSIBLE SUNSHINE	36	41	49	54	59	66	69	66	60	49	30	30	51
AVERAGE SKY COVER													
Sunrise - Sunset	8.2	8.0	7.4	6.7	6.6	6.0	5.7	5.9	6.1	6.6	8.2	8.4	7.0
NUMBER OF DAYS (Sunrise-Sunset)													
Clear	2.0	2.2	4.4	6.2	5.9	7.2	8.2	7.8	7.2	6.7	2.2	2.0	62.0
Partly cloudy	6.8	6.8	8.3	8.2	9.7	10.9	12.6	11.6	10.7	8.3	6.2	5.5	105.5
Cloudy	22.1	19.3	18.4	15.6	15.4	11.8	10.3	11.6	12.1	16.0	21.6	23.6	197.7
Precipitation .01" or more	17.6	15.7	14.7	13.2	12.0	10.4	9.5	10.0	10.6	11.3	14.9	17.7	157.5
Snow, Ice pellets 1.0" or more	7.4	6.8	4.1	1.0	*	0.0	0.0	0.0	0.0	*	1.9	6.3	27.7
Thunderstorms	0.1	0.1	0.9	2.1	3.6	5.2	6.4	5.7	3.0	1.0	0.4	0.2	28.9
Fog, Visibility 1/4 mile or less	1.0	0.6	1.4	1.1	1.1	1.2	0.6	0.9	1.3	1.8	0.7	1.1	12.7
Temperature Maximum:													
90° and above	0.0	0.0	0.0	*	0.3	1.7	4.5	2.0	0.7	0.0	0.0	0.0	9.3
32° and below	17.9	14.5	6.6	0.5	0.0	0.0	0.0	0.0	0.0	0.0	1.5	10.9	52.0
Temperature Minimum:													
32° and below	28.8	25.2	23.2	11.1	1.1	0.0	0.0	0.0	*	4.2	14.6	25.5	133.7
0° and below	3.5	2.4	0.3	0.0	0.0	0.0	0.0	0.0	0.0	0.0	0.0	0.7	6.8
RELATIVE HUMIDITY (%)													
Morning	76	77	76	75	78	82	82	86	87	82	80	80	80
Afternoon	69	67	63	55	54	56	53	57	61	61	69	74	62
PRECIPITATION (inches)													
Water Equivalent													
Normal	2.3	2.3	2.5	2.6	2.5	2.7	2.4	3.2	2.6	2.5	2.6	2.5	31.2
Maximum monthly	5.7	5.0	5.4	4.9	6.6	6.7	9.7	6.0	6.3	7.8	6.9	5.0	9.7
Date	1978	1950	1942	1944	1974	1980	1947	1984	1977	1955	1985	1944	1947
Minimum monthly	0.8	0.7	0.4	1.2	0.3	0.2	0.9	0.7	0.2	0.2	0.4	0.6	0.2
Date	1946	1968	1958	1971	1977	1963	1955	1951	1960	1963	1976	1958	1963
Maximum in 24 hrs	1.6	2.4	2.2	1.9	3.8	2.8	2.9	2.3	3.5	2.9	3.1	1.6	3.8
Date	1966	1950	1942	1943	1974	1950	1947	1968	1979	1980	1945	1978	1974
SNOW, ICE PELLETS													
Maximum monthly	60.4	64.8	40.3	20.2	2.0	0.0	0.0	T	T	1.4	17.6	46.1	64.8
Date	1978	1958	1959	1979	1945	—	—	1965	1956	1960	1983	1981	1958
Maximum in 24 hrs	18.2	22.8	17.6	8.3	2.0	0.0	0.0	T	T	1.4	11.2	19.1	22.8
Date	1966	1978	1959	1979	1945	—	—	1965	1956	1960	1953	1978	1978
WIND (Resultant)													
Mean speed (mph)	11.8	11.5	11.2	10.8	9.3	8.6	8.0	7.7	8.1	8.8	10.2	10.9	9.7

SYRACUSE

Elev. 410' 43° 07'N — 76° 07'W **New York**

NORMALS, MEANS, EXTREMES

	JAN	FEB	MAR	APR	MAY	JUN	JUL	AUG	SEP	OCT	NOV	DEC	YEAR
TEMPERATURE													
Normal daily maximum	30.6	32.2	41.4	56.2	67.9	77.2	81.6	79.6	72.3	60.9	47.9	35.3	56.9
Normal daily minimum	15.0	15.8	25.2	36.0	46.0	55.4	60.3	58.9	51.8	41.7	33.3	21.3	38.4
Normal monthly	22.8	24.0	33.3	46.1	57.0	66.3	71.0	69.3	62.1	51.3	40.6	28.3	47.7
Extreme highest	70	69	85	89	96	98	97	97	97	87	81	70	98
Extreme highest date	1967	1981	1977	1962	1977	1953	1962	1965	1953	1963	1950	1966	1953
Extreme lowest	-26	-26	-16	9	25	35	45	40	28	19	5	-22	-26
Extreme lowest date	1966	1979	1950	1972	1966	1966	1976	1965	1965	1976	1976	1980	1979
DEGREE DAYS BASE 65° F													
Heating	1308	1148	983	567	269	47	12	25	133	425	732	1138	6787
Cooling	0	0	0	0	21	86	195	158	46	0	0	0	506
% OF POSSIBLE SUNSHINE	34	39	46	51	54	59	64	59	53	44	25	25	46
AVERAGE SKY COVER													
Sunrise - Sunset	8.1	7.9	7.5	6.8	6.6	6.2	5.8	6.2	6.2	6.7	8.3	8.4	7.1
NUMBER OF DAYS (Sunrise-Sunset)													
Clear	2.7	2.8	4.5	6.4	6.0	7.3	7.9	6.9	6.9	6.6	2.3	2.3	62.6
Partly cloudy	6.4	6.2	6.8	6.8	10.0	10.4	12.2	11.2	10.4	7.8	5.4	4.7	98.4
Cloudy	21.9	19.3	19.8	16.8	15.0	12.3	10.9	12.9	12.7	16.7	22.3	24.0	204.3
Precipitation .01" or more	19.0	15.8	17.0	14.1	13.0	11.0	10.7	10.9	10.9	11.8	16.3	19.2	169.6
Snow, Ice pellets 1.0" or more	8.6	7.4	5.2	1.1	0.1	0.0	0.0	0.0	0.0	0.2	2.8	7.7	33.1
Thunderstorms	0.2	0.2	0.8	1.9	3.1	5.6	6.3	5.6	2.6	1.0	0.6	0.1	27.9
Fog, Visibility 1/4 mile or less	0.7	0.7	0.8	0.6	0.7	0.6	0.4	0.8	0.9	1.2	0.6	0.8	8.7
Temperature Maximum:													
90° and above	0.0	0.0	0.0	0.0	0.4	1.2	3.5	1.5	0.4	0.0	0.0	0.0	6.9
32° and below	18.1	14.1	5.9	0.4	0.0	0.0	0.0	0.0	0.0	0.0	1.5	11.7	51.6
Temperature Minimum:													
32° and below	28.9	25.3	23.8	12.3	1.0	0.0	0.0	0.0	0.1	5.0	14.3	26.2	136.8
0° and below	5.0	3.0	0.7	0.0	0.0	0.0	0.0	0.0	0.0	0.0	0.0	1.5	10.2
RELATIVE HUMIDITY (%)													
Morning	76	76	76	74	78	83	84	87	86	82	80	80	80
Afternoon	68	65	61	53	55	57	56	60	62	61	68	72	62
PRECIPITATION (inches)													
Water Equivalent													
Normal	2.6	2.6	3.1	3.3	3.1	3.6	3.7	3.7	3.2	3.1	3.4	3.2	39.1
Maximum monthly	5.7	5.3	6.8	8.1	7.4	12.3	9.5	8.4	8.8	8.2	6.7	5.5	12.3
Date	1978	1951	1955	1976	1976	1972	1974	1956	1975	1955	1972	1983	1972
Minimum monthly	1.0	0.8	1.0	1.2	0.7	1.1	0.9	1.3	0.7	0.2	1.2	1.7	0.2
Date	1970	1978	1981	1985	1977	1962	1969	1980	1964	1963	1978	1958	1963
Maximum in 24 hrs	1.4	1.9	1.3	2.8	3.1	3.8	4.0	4.2	4.1	3.6	2.0	2.1	4.2
Date	1958	1961	1974	1976	1969	1972	1974	1954	1975	1955	1967	1952	1954
SNOW, ICE PELLETS													
Maximum monthly	72.2	72.6	40.3	16.4	1.2	0.0	0.0	0.0	0.0	4.4	25.9	52.5	72.6
Date	1978	1958	1984	1983	1973	—	—	—	—	1952	1976	1969	1958
Maximum in 24 hrs	24.5	21.4	14.7	7.1	1.2	0.0	0.0	0.0	0.0	2.4	12.1	15.6	24.5
Date	1966	1961	1971	1975	1973	—	—	—	—	1974	1973	1978	1966
WIND (Resultant)													
Mean speed (mph)	10.9	11.0	11.1	10.9	9.3	8.5	8.3	7.9	8.5	9.1	10.3	10.6	9.7

ASHEVILLE

Elev. 2140' 35° 26'N — 82° 33'W **North Carolina**

NORMALS, MEANS, EXTREMES

	JAN	FEB	MAR	APR	MAY	JUN	JUL	AUG	SEP	OCT	NOV	DEC	YEAR
TEMPERATURE													
Normal daily maximum	47.5	50.6	58.4	68.6	75.6	81.4	84.0	83.5	77.9	68.7	58.6	50.3	67.1
Normal daily minimum	26.0	27.6	34.4	42.7	51.0	58.2	62.4	61.6	55.8	43.3	34.2	28.2	43.8
Normal monthly	36.8	39.1	46.4	55.7	63.3	69.8	73.2	72.6	66.9	56.0	46.4	39.3	55.4
Extreme highest	78	77	83	89	91	96	96	100	92	85	81	78	100
Extreme highest date	1975	1977	1985	1972	1969	1969	1983	1983	1975	1981	1974	1971	1983
Extreme lowest	-16	-2	9	23	29	35	46	43	30	21	8	-7	-16
Extreme lowest date	1985	1967	1980	1985	1971	1966	1967	1968	1967	1976	1970	1983	1985
DEGREE DAYS BASE 65° F													
Heating	874	725	577	283	114	23	0	0	57	286	558	797	4294
Cooling	0	0	0	0	61	167	254	239	114	7	0	0	842
% OF POSSIBLE SUNSHINE	56	61	62	66	61	64	58	54	56	60	58	58	60
AVERAGE SKY COVER													
Sunrise - Sunset	6.0	5.8	6.0	5.6	6.1	6.1	6.5	6.3	6.2	5.3	5.5	5.8	5.9
NUMBER OF DAYS (Sunrise-Sunset)													
Clear	9.7	9.4	8.8	9.9	7.8	6.3	4.6	5.2	7.0	11.8	10.7	10.7	101.8
Partly cloudy	7.0	6.3	8.7	8.7	9.5	12.2	13.5	13.7	10.3	7.8	7.2	6.8	111.9
Cloudy	14.2	12.6	13.5	11.4	13.7	11.5	13.0	12.1	12.7	11.4	12.1	13.5	151.6
Precipitation .01" or more	10.3	9.3	11.3	9.2	11.9	11.3	12.5	12.0	9.3	8.2	9.2	9.5	123.9
Snow, Ice pellets 1.0" or more	1.6	1.5	0.9	0.1	0.0	0.0	0.0	0.0	0.0	0.0	0.2	0.5	4.8
Thunderstorms	0.4	0.8	2.3	3.2	7.4	8.0	9.2	8.9	3.4	1.0	0.7	0.3	45.7
Fog, Visibility 1/4 mile or less	4.0	3.0	2.2	2.6	5.4	8.1	10.3	14.9	12.1	8.5	4.4	4.8	80.5
Temperature Maximum:													
90° and above	0.0	0.0	0.0	0.0	*	1.8	3.8	2.3	0.3	0.0	0.0	0.0	8.2
32° and below	3.8	1.6	0.3	0.0	0.0	0.0	0.0	0.0	0.0	0.0	0.1	0.9	6.6
Temperature Minimum:													
32° and below	24.0	21.3	13.7	4.1	0.3	0.0	0.0	0.0	*	3.8	13.4	20.8	101.4
0° and below	0.6	*	0.0	0.0	0.0	0.0	0.0	0.0	0.0	0.0	0.0	0.1	0.8
RELATIVE HUMIDITY (%)													
Morning	81	78	79	78	90	94	95	97	96	92	86	83	87
Afternoon	60	56	54	51	58	60	65	64	64	58	57	59	59
PRECIPITATION (inches)													
Water Equivalent													
Normal	3.4	3.6	5.1	3.8	4.1	4.2	4.4	4.7	3.9	3.2	3.2	3.5	47.7
Maximum monthly	7.4	7.0	9.8	7.2	8.8	6.5	9.9	11.2	9.1	7.0	7.7	8.4	11.2
Date	1978	1982	1975	1979	1973	1972	1982	1967	1977	1971	1979	1973	1967
Minimum monthly	0.4	0.4	0.7	0.2	1.5	1.4	0.6	0.5	0.1	0.3	1.1	0.1	0.1
Date	1981	1978	1985	1976	1985	1985	1978	1981	1984	1978	1981	1965	1984
Maximum in 24 hrs	2.9	3.4	5.1	3.0	4.9	3.5	4.0	4.1	3.4	2.9	4.0	2.6	5.1
Date	1978	1982	1968	1973	1973	1972	1969	1967	1975	1977	1977	1973	1968
SNOW, ICE PELLETS													
Maximum monthly	17.6	25.5	13.0	3.0	T	0.0	0.0	0.0	0.0	T	9.6	16.3	25.5
Date	1966	1969	1969	1982	1979	—	—	—	—	1977	1968	1971	1969
Maximum in 24 hrs	8.0	11.7	10.9	3.0	T	0.0	0.0	0.0	0.0	T	5.7	16.3	16.3
Date	1983	1969	1969	1982	1979	—	—	—	—	1977	1968	1971	1971
WIND (Resultant)													
Mean speed (mph)	9.8	9.6	9.5	8.8	7.1	6.1	5.8	5.4	5.6	6.7	8.2	8.9	7.6

CAPE HATTERAS

Elev. 7' 35° 16'N — 75° 33'W **North Carolina**

NORMALS, MEANS, EXTREMES

	JAN	FEB	MAR	APR	MAY	JUN	JUL	AUG	SEP	OCT	NOV	DEC	YEAR
TEMPERATURE													
Normal daily maximum	52.6	53.5	58.8	67.2	74.1	80.5	84.4	84.4	80.5	71.7	63.6	56.4	69.0
Normal daily minimum	37.6	37.7	43.3	51.1	59.7	67.5	71.9	72.0	67.9	58.1	48.3	40.9	54.7
Normal monthly	45.1	45.6	51.1	59.2	66.9	74.0	78.2	78.2	74.2	64.9	56.0	48.7	61.8
Extreme highest	75	76	79	89	88	95	95	94	92	86	81	77	95
Extreme highest date	1985	1971	1977	1985	1962	1978	1969	1968	1978	1959	1971	1982	1978
Extreme lowest	6	14	19	26	39	44	54	56	45	32	22	12	6
Extreme lowest date	1985	1958	1967	1972	1971	1966	1972	1979	1970	1979	1967	1983	1985
DEGREE DAYS BASE 65° F													
Heating	617	543	437	186	37	0	0	0	0	76	276	510	2682
Cooling	0	0	6	12	96	270	409	409	276	72	6	0	1556
% OF POSSIBLE SUNSHINE	49	53	60	66	62	62	62	63	62	58	56	48	58
AVERAGE SKY COVER													
Sunrise - Sunset	6.1	6.0	6.0	5.4	6.0	6.2	6.6	6.1	5,6	5.5	5.4	5.9	5.9
NUMBER OF DAYS (Sunrise-Sunset)													
Clear	9.3	9.0	9.8	10.3	8.3	7.2	6.3	7.9	9.5	10.9	10.5	10.0	108.7
Partly cloudy	6.8	5.4	7.1	8.6	9.5	10.4	9.8	10.2	9.4	7.7	7.9	7.1	100.0
Cloudy	14.9	13.9	14.2	11.1	13.2	12.4	15.0	12.9	11.0	12.5	11.6	13.9	156.5
Precipitation .01" or more	11.0	10.4	10.5	8.4	10.5	9.2	11.9	10.4	8.9	9.4	9.0	9.6	119.2
Snow, Ice pellets 1.0" or more	0.2	0.3	0.1	0.0	0.0	0.0	0.0	0.0	0.0	0.0	0.0	*	0.7
Thunderstorms	0.8	1.5	2.0	3.1	5.4	5.1	8.6	7.4	3.4	2.0	1.5	1.0	41.9
Fog, Visibility 1/4 mile or less	2.7	2.8	2.5	1.3	1.2	0.3	0.2	0.4	0.3	0.8	1.3	2.4	15.9
Temperature Maximum:													
90° and above	0.0	0.0	0.0	0.0	0.0	0.6	1.3	1.6	0.4	0.0	0.0	0.0	3.9
32° and below	0.9	0.4	0.0	0.0	0.0	0.0	0.0	0.0	0.0	0.0	0.0	0.2	1.5
Temperature Minimum:													
32° and below	11.3	9.7	3.7	0.4	0.0	0.0	0.0	0.0	0.0	*	1.3	6.7	33.1
0° and below	0.0	0.0	0.0	0.0	0.0	0.0	0.0	0.0	0.0	0.0	0.0	0.0	0.0
RELATIVE HUMIDITY (%)													
Morning	78	79	79	81	86	87	89	88	85	82	81	79	83
Afternoon	68	64	62	59	65	68	70	69	67	66	64	66	66
PRECIPITATION (inches)													
Water Equivalent													
Normal	4.7	4.1	3.9	3.2	4.0	4.2	5.3	6.1	5.7	4.8	4.8	4.4	55.7
Maximum monthly	9.7	8.4	9.2	7.1	11.4	10.8	9.9	11.7	12.7	15.0	16.2	8.6	16.2
Date	1979	1983	1983	1962	1972	1962	1965	1976	1979	1985	1985	1962	1985
Minimum monthly	1.7	1.4	0.9	0.5	0.6	0.3	0.4	0.9	0.7	0.5	1.2	0.6	0.3
Date	1981	1976	1967	1976	1962	1978	1958	1983	1978	1984	1973	1985	1978
Maximum in 24 hrs	5.0	2.9	2.9	5.6	3.5	6.6	5.5	8.1	5.4	7.6	7.6	3.5	8.1
Date	1979	1970	1982	1963	1984	1962	1967	1962	1979	1983	1985	1979	1962
SNOW, ICE PELLETS													
Maximum monthly	3.5	4.4	8.5	0.0	0.0	0.0	0.0	0.0	0.0	0.0	T	2.5	8.5
Date	1962	1978	1960	—	—	—	—	—	—	—	1970	1970	1960
Maximum in 24 hrs	3.5	4.4	7.3	0.0	0.0	0.0	0.0	0.0	0.0	0.0	T	2.5	7.3
Date	1962	1978	1980	—	—	—	—	—	—	—	1970	1970	1980
WIND (Resultant)													
Mean speed (mph)	12.4	12.6	12.2	12.1	11.1	10.8	10.3	9.7	10.8	11.4	11.2	11.7	11.4

CHARLOTTE

Elev. 737'   35° 13'N — 80° 56'W   **North Carolina**

NORMALS, MEANS, EXTREMES

	JAN	FEB	MAR	APR	MAY	JUN	JUL	AUG	SEP	OCT	NOV	DEC	YEAR
TEMPERATURE													
Normal daily maximum	50.3	53.6	61.6	72.1	79.1	85.2	88.3	87.6	81.7	71.7	61.7	52.6	70.5
Normal daily minimum	30.7	32.1	39.1	48.4	57.2	64.7	68.7	68.2	62.3	49.6	39.7	32.6	49.4
Normal monthly	40.5	42.9	50.4	60.3	68.2	75.0	78.5	77.9	72.0	60.7	50.7	42.6	60.0
Extreme highest	78	81	90	93	100	103	103	103	104	98	85	77	104
Extreme highest date	1952	1977	1945	1960	1941	1954	1952	1983	1954	1954	1961	1971	1954
Extreme lowest	-5	5	4	24	32	45	53	53	39	24	11	2	-5
Extreme lowest date	1985	1958	1980	1960	1963	1972	1961	1965	1967	1962	1950	1962	1985
DEGREE DAYS BASE 65° F													
Heating	760	619	459	155	50	0	0	0	10	166	429	694	3342
Cooling	0	0	7	14	149	304	419	400	220	33	0	0	1546
% OF POSSIBLE SUNSHINE	56	60	63	69	68	70	67	69	67	67	60	58	65
AVERAGE SKY COVER													
Sunrise - Sunset	6.2	6.0	6.0	5.6	6.1	6.0	6.2	5.8	5.7	4.8	5.4	5.9	5.8
NUMBER OF DAYS (Sunrise-Sunset)													
Clear	9.2	8.8	9.2	9.8	8.0	7.4	6.5	7.7	9.4	13.2	11.7	10.4	111.3
Partly cloudy	6.4	6.3	8.2	8.7	9.9	11.2	11.4	12.7	9.3	7.5	6.4	6.0	104.1
Cloudy	15.3	13.1	13.6	11.5	13.1	11.5	13.1	10.6	11.3	10.3	11.9	14.6	149.9
Precipitation .01" or more	10.1	9.6	11.2	8.8	9.7	9.8	11.4	9.4	7.1	6.8	7.6	9.5	111.2
Snow, Ice pellets 1.0" or more	0.7	0.5	0.3	0.0	0.0	0.0	0.0	0.0	0.0	0.0	*	0.2	1.7
Thunderstorms	0.5	0.9	1.8	3.0	5.7	7.6	9.8	7.1	3.0	1.2	0.6	0.4	41.7
Fog, Visibility 1/4 mile or less	3.7	2.8	2.4	1.4	1.0	1.1	1.1	1.5	2.1	2.0	3.0	4.2	26.5
Temperature Maximum:													
90° and above	0.0	0.0	0.0	0.3	1.8	6.0	11.5	10.0	4.0	0.0	0.0	0.0	33.6
32° and below	1.9	0.4	*	0.0	0.0	0.0	0.0	0.0	0.0	0.0	0.0	0.4	2.8
Temperature Minimum:													
32° and below	19.9	16.8	8.0	1.2	*	0.0	0.0	0.0	0.0	0.9	7.2	16.1	70.2
0° and below	0.1	0.0	0.0	0.0	0.0	0.0	0.0	0.0	0.0	0.0	0.0	0.0	0.1
RELATIVE HUMIDITY (%)													
Morning	72	67	69	69	78	81	84	84	83	80	76	74	76
Afternoon	56	52	50	47	53	56	58	58	57	54	53	57	54
PRECIPITATION (inches)													
Water Equivalent													
Normal	3.8	3.8	4.8	3.2	3.6	3.5	3.9	3.7	3.5	2.7	2.8	3.4	43.1
Maximum monthly	7.4	7.5	8.7	7.6	12.4	8.2	9.1	9.9	10.8	8.3	8.6	7.4	12.4
Date	1962	1979	1980	1958	1975	1961	1941	1948	1945	1976	1985	1983	1975
Minimum monthly	0.4	0.7	0.5	0.3	0.1	0.6	0.5	0.6	0.0	T	0.4	0.4	T
Date	1981	1978	1985	1976	1941	1954	1983	1972	1954	1953	1973	1965	1953
Maximum in 24 hrs	3.5	2.9	3.8	3.2	3.6	3.7	3.0	4.5	4.7	5.3	3.2	2.8	5.3
Date	1962	1973	1977	1962	1975	1949	1949	1978	1959	1976	1985	1972	1976
SNOW, ICE PELLETS													
Maximum monthly	11.7	14.9	19.3	0.1	0.0	0.0	0.0	0.0	0.0	0.0	2.5	7.5	19.3
Date	1962	1979	1960	1982	—	—	—	—	—	—	1968	1971	1960
Maximum in 24 hrs	10.2	12.0	10.3	0.1	0.0	0.0	0.0	0.0	0.0	0.0	2.5	7.5	12.0
Date	1965	1969	1983	1982	—	—	—	—	—	—	1968	1971	1969
WIND (Resultant)													
Mean speed (mph)	7.9	8.4	8.9	8.8	7.5	6.9	6.6	6.4	6.7	7.0	7.2	7.4	7.5

GREENSBORO — North Carolina

Elev. 897'   36° 04'N — 79° 47'W

NORMALS, MEANS, EXTREMES

	JAN	FEB	MAR	APR	MAY	JUN	JUL	AUG	SEP	OCT	NOV	DEC	YEAR
TEMPERATURE													
Normal daily maximum	47.6	50.8	59.3	70.7	77.9	84.2	87.4	86.2	80.4	70.1	59.9	50.4	68.7
Normal daily minimum	27.3	29.0	36.5	45.9	55.0	62.6	66.9	66.3	59.3	46.7	37.1	29.9	46.9
Normal monthly	37.5	39.9	47.9	58.3	66.5	73.4	77.2	76.3	69.9	58.4	48.5	40.2	57.8
Extreme highest	78	81	90	94	98	102	102	101	100	95	85	78	102
Extreme highest date	1975	1977	1945	1930	1941	1954	1977	1932	1954	1954	1974	1971	1977
Extreme lowest	-8	-4	5	21	32	42	48	47	35	20	10	0	-8
Extreme lowest date	1985	1936	1960	1943	1963	1977	1933	1946	1942	1962	1970	1962	1985
DEGREE DAYS BASE 65° F													
Heating	853	703	533	215	73	0	0	0	12	221	495	769	3874
Cooling	0	0	6	14	120	259	378	350	159	17	0	0	1303
% OF POSSIBLE SUNSHINE	52	57	60	64	65	65	62	63	63	65	59	55	61
AVERAGE SKY COVER													
Sunrise - Sunset	6.2	6.0	6.0	5.7	5.9	5.9	6.2	5.9	5.5	4.7	5.4	6.0	5.8
NUMBER OF DAYS (Sunrise-Sunset)													
Clear	8.9	8.7	9.1	9.5	8.2	6.7	6.4	7.5	10.1	13.6	11.3	10.2	110.1
Partly cloudy	6.8	6.5	8.1	8.5	10.8	12.6	12.5	12.5	8.7	7.3	6.7	6.3	107.5
Cloudy	15.3	13.0	13.8	11.9	11.9	10.7	12.1	11.0	11.2	10.1	12.0	14.5	147.6
Precipitation .01" or more	10.3	9.7	11.2	9.5	10.4	10.5	12.4	10.7	7.7	7.1	8.3	9.4	117.0
Snow, Ice pellets 1.0" or more	0.9	0.7	0.5	0.0	0.0	0.0	0.0	0.0	0.0	0.0	*	0.4	2.6
Thunderstorms	0.5	0.8	1.9	3.2	6.7	8.3	10.8	8.3	3.2	1.1	0.4	0.2	45.5
Fog, Visibility 1/4 mile or less	4.8	3.3	2.8	1.7	1.9	1.4	1.9	2.2	2.9	2.6	3.2	4.1	32.8
Temperature Maximum:													
90° and above	0.0	0.0	0.0	0.4	1.2	5.4	10.1	8.2	2.3	0.0	0.0	0.0	27.6
32° and below	3.0	1.0	0.1	0.0	0.0	0.0	0.0	0.0	0.0	0.0	*	0.9	5.1
Temperature Minimum:													
32° and below	22.8	19.8	10.4	2.1	0.0	0.0	0.0	0.0	0.0	1.5	9.9	18.3	84.9
0° and below	0.2	0.0	0.0	0.0	0.0	0.0	0.0	0.0	0.0	0.0	0.0	0.0	0.2
RELATIVE HUMIDITY (%)													
Morning	75	70	70	71	82	85	88	88	87	84	77	76	79
Afternoon	56	51	51	48	55	57	60	60	58	56	53	56	55
PRECIPITATION (inches)													
Water Equivalent													
Normal	3.5	3.3	3.8	3.1	3.3	3.9	4.2	4.1	3.6	3.1	2.5	3.3	42.4
Maximum monthly	8.2	7.0	8.7	6.1	8.3	7.9	12.7	12.5	13.2	9.6	8.2	6.4	13.2
Date	1937	1929	1975	1936	1982	1965	1984	1939	1947	1959	1985	1973	1947
Minimum monthly	0.6	0.7	0.6	0.5	0.3	0.3	0.9	0.7	T	0.2	0.3	0.3	T
Date	1981	1978	1985	1942	1936	1933	1953	1972	1985	1963	1981	1955	1985
Maximum in 24 hrs	3.0	3.0	3.0	2.7	3.1	4.9	4.4	4.4	7.4	6.2	3.3	3.6	7.4
Date	1936	1934	1932	1944	1978	1972	1944	1949	1947	1954	1962	1958	1947
SNOW, ICE PELLETS													
Maximum monthly	22.9	16.3	21.3	T	0.0	0.0	0.0	0.0	0.0	0.0	5.9	14.3	22.9
Date	1966	1979	1960	1983	—	—	—	—	—	—	1968	1930	1966
Maximum in 24 hrs	14.0	9.3	11.1	T	0.0	0.0	0.0	0.0	0.0	0.0	5.0	14.3	14.3
Date	1940	1979	1960	1983	—	—	—	—	—	—	1968	1930	1930
WIND (Resultant)													
Mean speed (mph)	8.1	8.6	9.1	8.8	7.6	6.9	6.5	6.2	6.6	7.0	7.5	7.6	7.5

RALEIGH

Elev. 416'   35° 52'N — 78° 47'W   **North Carolina**

NORMALS, MEANS, EXTREMES

	JAN	FEB	MAR	APR	MAY	JUN	JUL	AUG	SEP	OCT	NOV	DEC	YEAR
TEMPERATURE													
Normal daily maximum	50.1	52.8	61.0	72.3	79.0	85.2	88.2	87.1	81.6	71.6	61.8	52.7	70.3
Normal daily minimum	29.1	30.3	37.7	46.5	55.3	62.6	67.1	66.8	60.4	47.7	38.1	31.2	47.7
Normal monthly	39.6	41.6	49.4	59.4	67.2	73.9	77.7	77.0	71.0	59.7	50.0	42.0	59.0
Extreme highest	79	84	92	95	97	104	105	101	104	98	88	79	105
Extreme highest date	1952	1977	1945	1980	1953	1954	1952	1983	1954	1954	1950	1978	1952
Extreme lowest	-9	5	11	23	31	38	48	46	37	19	11	4	-9
Extreme lowest date	1985	1971	1980	1985	1977	1977	1975	1965	1983	1962	1970	1983	1985
DEGREE DAYS BASE 65° F													
Heating	787	655	496	181	53	0	0	0	9	187	450	713	3531
Cooling	0	0	9	16	121	270	394	372	189	23	0	0	1394
% OF POSSIBLE SUNSHINE	54	59	62	64	60	61	61	61	60	61	59	55	60
AVERAGE SKY COVER													
Sunrise - Sunset	6.1	5.9	5.9	5.6	6.0	5.8	6.1	5.9	5.6	5.1	5.3	5.8	5.7
NUMBER OF DAYS (Sunrise-Sunset)													
Clear	9.2	8.9	9.5	9.8	8.2	7.7	7.3	7.8	10.1	12.6	11.7	10.3	113.0
Partly cloudy	6.9	6.3	7.6	8.9	10.1	11.8	11.7	12.4	8.8	7.1	7.3	6.8	105.6
Cloudy	14.8	13.1	13.9	11.3	12.8	10.5	12.0	10.8	11.2	11.3	11.0	13.9	146.6
Precipitation .01" or more	10.0	9.6	10.3	8.9	10.3	9.2	11.2	9.8	7.5	7.1	8.2	9.0	111.3
Snow, Ice pellets 1.0" or more	1.0	0.7	0.4	*	0.0	0.0	0.0	0.0	0.0	0.0	0.1	0.3	2.4
Thunderstorms	0.5	0.8	1.9	3.3	6.3	7.1	10.4	8.0	3.6	1.5	0.7	0.3	44.5
Fog, Visibility 1/4 mile or less	3.6	2.8	2.2	1.6	2.5	2.1	2.9	3.4	3.5	3.8	3.3	3.6	35.3
Temperature Maximum:													
90° and above	0.0	0.0	0.0	0.6	1.1	5.9	10.9	9.7	3.1	0.0	0.0	0.0	31.2
32° and below	2.5	0.5	0.1	0.0	0.0	0.0	0.0	0.0	0.0	0.0	*	0.7	3.9
Temperature Minimum:													
32° and below	21.5	18.1	10.0	2.3	*	0.0	0.0	0.0	0.0	1.5	10.0	17.1	80.7
0° and below	0.2	0.0	0.0	0.0	0.0	0.0	0.0	0.0	0.0	0.0	0.0	0.0	0.2
RELATIVE HUMIDITY (%)													
Morning	73	69	71	73	84	87	88	89	88	85	78	75	80
Afternoon	55	51	49	45	54	57	59	60	59	54	52	55	54
PRECIPITATION (inches)													
Water Equivalent													
Normal	3.5	3.4	3.6	2.9	3.6	3.6	4.3	4.4	3.2	2.7	2.8	3.1	41.7
Maximum monthly	7.5	6.0	7.7	6.1	7.6	9.3	10.0	10.4	12.9	7.5	8.2	6.6	12.9
Date	1954	1983	1983	1978	1974	1973	1945	1955	1945	1971	1948	1983	1945
Minimum monthly	0.8	1.0	1.0	0.2	0.9	0.5	0.8	0.8	0.2	0.4	0.6	0.2	0.2
Date	1981	1968	1985	1976	1964	1981	1953	1950	1985	1963	1973	1965	1985
Maximum in 24 hrs	3.1	3.2	3.7	4.0	4.4	3.4	3.8	5.2	5.1	4.1	4.7	3.1	5.2
Date	1984	1973	1983	1978	1957	1967	1952	1955	1944	1954	1963	1958	1955
SNOW, ICE PELLETS													
Maximum monthly	14.4	17.2	14.0	1.8	0.0	0.0	0.0	0.0	0.0	0.0	2.6	10.6	17.2
Date	1955	1979	1960	1983	—	—	—	—	—	—	1975	1958	1979
Maximum in 24 hrs	9.0	10.4	9.3	1.8	0.0	0.0	0.0	0.0	0.0	0.0	2.6	9.1	10.4
Date	1966	1979	1969	1983	—	—	—	—	—	—	1975	1958	1979
WIND (Resultant)													
Mean speed (mph)	8.6	8.9	9.4	9.0	7.6	6.9	6.6	6.3	6.8	7.1	7.7	8.0	7.7

WILMINGTON
Elev. 30'   34° 16'N — 77° 54'W   **North Carolina**

NORMALS, MEANS, EXTREMES

	JAN	FEB	MAR	APR	MAY	JUN	JUL	AUG	SEP	OCT	NOV	DEC	YEAR
TEMPERATURE													
Normal daily maximum	55.9	58.1	64.8	74.3	80.9	86.1	89.3	88.6	83.9	75.2	66.8	59.1	73.6
Normal daily minimum	35.3	36.6	43.3	51.8	60.4	67.1	71.3	70.8	65.7	53.7	43.9	37.2	53.1
Normal monthly	45.6	47.4	54.1	63.1	70.7	76.6	80.3	79.7	74.8	64.5	55.4	48.2	63.3
Extreme highest	82	85	89	95	98	104	102	102	98	95	87	81	104
Extreme highest date	1975	1962	1974	1967	1953	1952	1977	1954	1975	1954	1974	1984	1952
Extreme lowest	5	11	9	30	40	48	59	55	44	27	20	9	5
Extreme lowest date	1985	1958	1980	1983	1981	1983	1972	1982	1981	1962	1970	1983	1985
DEGREE DAYS BASE 65° F													
Heating	607	498	350	94	10	0	0	0	0	94	295	521	2469
Cooling	6	5	12	37	187	348	474	456	294	78	7	0	1904
% OF POSSIBLE SUNSHINE	57	59	63	70	67	66	63	63	62	64	65	60	63
AVERAGE SKY COVER													
Sunrise - Sunset	6.0	5.9	5.8	5.3	5.9	6.1	6.5	6.2	6.0	5.1	5.0	5.7	5.8
NUMBER OF DAYS (Sunrise-Sunset)													
Clear	9.8	9.4	9.9	11.0	8.4	7.1	5.6	7.1	8.4	12.6	12.3	10.6	112.2
Partly cloudy	6.3	5.9	7.9	7.9	10.4	10.9	12.0	12.0	9.6	7.2	7.3	7.0	104.5
Cloudy	14.9	13.0	13.2	11.1	12.2	12.0	13.4	11.9	11.9	11.2	10.4	13.4	148.5
Precipitation .01" or more	10.5	9.6	10.3	8.0	9.7	10.0	13.2	11.9	9.4	7.2	7.6	9.1	116.4
Snow, Ice pellets 1.0" or more	0.2	0.2	0.1	0.0	0.0	0.0	0.0	0.0	0.0	0.0	0.0	0.1	0.6
Thunderstorms	0.4	1.1	2.2	3.1	5.4	7.4	11.1	9.0	3.9	1.2	0.7	0.6	46.1
Fog, Visibility 1/4 mile or less	2.6	1.7	2.3	1.6	1.9	1.7	0.8	1.3	2.6	2.8	2.8	2.8	24.8
Temperature Maximum:													
90° and above	0.0	0.0	0.0	0.9	2.1	7.6	15.2	13.0	4.5	0.1	0.0	0.0	43.4
32° and below	0.6	0.1	*	0.0	0.0	0.0	0.0	0.0	0.0	0.0	0.0	*	0.8
Temperature Minimum:													
32° and below	14.5	11.7	3.8	0.3	0.0	0.0	0.0	0.0	0.0	0.1	3.3	10.7	44.3
0° and below	0.0	0.0	0.0	0.0	0.0	0.0	0.0	0.0	0.0	0.0	0.0	0.0	0.0
RELATIVE HUMIDITY (%)													
Morning	78	76	79	79	87	88	89	91	90	87	83	79	84
Afternoon	56	52	52	48	56	60	64	64	62	57	53	56	57
PRECIPITATION (inches)													
Water Equivalent													
Normal	3.6	3.4	4.0	2.9	4.2	5.6	7.4	6.6	5.7	2.9	3.1	3.4	53.3
Maximum monthly	7.0	8.7	8.0	8.2	9.1	12.8	15.1	14.0	18.9	9.8	7.8	6.5	18.9
Date	1964	1983	1983	1961	1956	1962	1966	1981	1984	1964	1972	1982	1984
Minimum monthly	1.0	1.0	0.9	0.3	1.1	0.8	1.6	1.6	1.0	0.1	0.4	0.4	0.1
Date	1981	1976	1967	1957	1983	1984	1961	1968	1981	1953	1973	1955	1953
Maximum in 24 hrs	3.0	3.2	3.3	3.5	4.9	7.7	5.6	5.1	8.2	4.3	4.8	3.8	8.2
Date	1982	1983	1960	1961	1963	1966	1966	1981	1958	1964	1969	1980	1958
SNOW, ICE PELLETS													
Maximum monthly	2.9	12.5	6.6	0.0	0.0	0.0	0.0	0.0	0.0	0.0	T	4.0	12.5
Date	1965	1973	1980	—	—	—	—	—	—	—	1976	1970	1973
Maximum in 24 hrs	2.8	11.7	5.7	0.0	0.0	0.0	0.0	0.0	0.0	0.0	T	4.0	11.7
Date	1965	1973	1980	—	—	—	—	—	—	—	1976	1970	1973
WIND (Resultant)													
Mean speed (mph)	9.2	10.0	10.3	10.5	9.4	8.5	8.0	7.5	8.0	8.2	8.2	8.6	8.9

BISMARCK

Elev. 1647' 46° 46'N — 100° 45'W **North Dakota**

NORMALS, MEANS, EXTREMES

	JAN	FEB	MAR	APR	MAY	JUN	JUL	AUG	SEP	OCT	NOV	DEC	YEAR
TEMPERATURE													
Normal daily maximum	17.5	25.2	36.4	54.2	67.7	76.8	84.4	83.3	71.4	59.3	39.4	25.9	53.5
Normal daily minimum	-4.2	3.7	15.6	30.8	42.0	51.8	56.4	54.2	43.2	32.8	17.7	4.8	29.1
Normal monthly	6.7	14.5	26.0	42.5	54.9	64.3	70.4	68.8	57.3	46.1	28.6	15.4	41.3
Extreme highest	62	68	81	93	98	100	109	109	105	95	75	65	109
Extreme highest date	1981	1958	1946	1980	1941	1961	1973	1941	1959	1963	1978	1979	1973
Extreme lowest	-44	-39	-31	-12	15	30	35	33	11	5	-30	-43	-44
Extreme lowest date	1950	1982	1948	1975	1967	1969	1971	1982	1974	1960	1985	1967	1950
DEGREE DAYS BASE 65° F													
Heating	1807	1414	1209	675	324	100	18	57	255	586	1092	1538	9075
Cooling	0	0	0	0	10	79	186	174	24	0	0	0	473
% OF POSSIBLE SUNSHINE	54	54	59	59	62	64	75	72	65	58	44	47	59
AVERAGE SKY COVER													
Sunrise - Sunset	6.7	6.9	7.0	6.8	6.5	6.1	4.8	4.9	5.5	5.9	6.9	6.8	6.2
NUMBER OF DAYS (Sunrise-Sunset)													
Clear	6.9	5.3	5.4	5.8	6.3	7.3	11.6	11.7	10.2	9.5	6.3	6.6	93.0
Partly cloudy	7.6	7.7	8.4	8.7	10.5	10.5	12.7	11.1	8.8	7.7	6.9	6.9	107.4
Cloudy	16.6	15.3	17.1	15.5	14.3	12.2	6.7	8.2	11.0	13.8	16.8	17.4	164.9
Precipitation .01" or more	7.8	6.8	8.1	8.1	9.8	11.8	8.8	8.5	7.0	5.8	6.1	7.9	96.4
Snow, Ice pellets 1.0" or more	2.6	2.0	2.4	1.2	0.3	0.0	0.0	0.0	0.1	0.4	1.8	2.1	12.9
Thunderstorms	0.0	*	0.1	1.0	3.7	8.7	9.4	7.9	2.6	0.6	*	0.0	34.1
Fog, Visibility 1/4 mile or less	1.0	1.5	1.5	0.8	0.4	0.5	0.7	0.7	0.7	1.1	1.3	1.4	11.6
Temperature Maximum:													
90° and above	0.0	0.0	0.0	0.1	0.5	2.0	7.8	8.5	1.9	0.1	0.0	0.0	20.8
32° and below	23.9	17.3	10.8	0.8	0.1	0.0	0.0	0.0	0.0	0.5	8.9	21.8	84.1
Temperature Minimum:													
32° and below	30.8	28.1	28.7	17.5	4.1	0.1	0.0	0.0	2.8	14.3	28.2	31.0	185.6
0° and below	18.6	11.2	4.2	0.2	0.0	0.0	0.0	0.0	0.0	0.0	2.5	13.3	50.0
RELATIVE HUMIDITY (%)													
Morning	73	76	77	72	70	78	74	71	73	72	77	77	74
Afternoon	67	67	63	52	48	53	47	45	49	52	63	70	56
PRECIPITATION (inches)													
Water Equivalent													
Normal	0.5	0.4	0.7	1.5	2.2	3.0	2.0	1.6	1.3	0.8	0.5	0.5	15.3
Maximum monthly	1.2	1.2	3.1	5.4	5.1	8.2	5.2	5.0	6.9	4.3	2.5	0.9	8.2
Date	1969	1979	1975	1975	1965	1947	1969	1944	1977	1982	1944	1967	1947
Minimum monthly	0.0	0.0	0.0	T	0.2	0.5	0.1	0.0	0.0	0.0	T	T	T
Date	1940	1985	1981	1952	1984	1974	1968	1971	1948	1968	1963	1944	1963
Maximum in 24 hrs	0.6	0.7	1.3	1.9	2.5	3.2	2.3	2.6	3.0	1.8	0.9	0.5	3.2
Date	1952	1958	1950	1964	1985	1947	1969	1965	1977	1980	1944	1960	1947
SNOW, ICE PELLETS													
Maximum monthly	25.0	25.6	31.1	18.7	10.3	T	0.0	0.0	5.0	7.6	24.2	17.2	31.1
Date	1982	1979	1975	1984	1950	1969	—	—	1984	1946	1985	1977	1975
Maximum in 24 hrs	7.9	8.9	15.5	11.9	11.0	T	0.0	0.0	4.8	4.9	9.4	7.6	15.5
Date	1952	1979	1966	1984	1967	1969	—	—	1984	1946	1985	1950	1966
WIND (Resultant)													
Mean speed (mph)	10.0	9.9	11.0	12.1	11.8	10.5	9.2	9.5	10.0	10.1	10.0	9.5	10.3

FARGO
Elev. 896' 46° 54'N — 96° 48'W # North Dakota

NORMALS, MEANS, EXTREMES

	JAN	FEB	MAR	APR	MAY	JUN	JUL	AUG	SEP	OCT	NOV	DEC	YEAR
TEMPERATURE													
Normal daily maximum	13.7	20.5	33.2	52.5	68.1	76.9	82.7	81.1	69.8	57.7	37.0	21.3	51.2
Normal daily minimum	-5.1	1.5	14.8	31.6	43.0	53.5	58.4	56.4	45.7	34.9	19.4	4.0	29.8
Normal monthly	4.3	11.0	24.0	42.1	55.6	65.2	70.6	68.8	57.8	46.3	28.2	12.7	40.5
Extreme highest	52	66	78	100	98	99	102	106	102	93	73	57	106
Extreme highest date	1981	1958	1967	1980	1964	1959	1980	1976	1959	1963	1978	1962	1976
Extreme lowest	-35	-34	-23	-7	20	30	36	33	19	7	-24	-32	-35
Extreme lowest date	1977	1962	1980	1975	1966	1969	1967	1982	1965	1976	1985	1967	1977
DEGREE DAYS BASE 65° F													
Heating	1882	1512	1271	687	311	86	17	36	236	580	1104	1621	9343
Cooling	0	0	0	0	19	92	191	154	20	0	0	0	476
% OF POSSIBLE SUNSHINE	50	56	57	59	60	60	71	68	59	55	40	43	57
AVERAGE SKY COVER													
Sunrise - Sunset	6.7	6.7	7.0	6.7	6.4	6.2	5.0	5.2	5.8	6.2	7.2	7.0	6.3
NUMBER OF DAYS (Sunrise-Sunset)													
Clear	6.6	6.2	5.4	6.4	6.8	6.5	10.5	10.6	8.7	8.7	5.4	6.1	87.9
Partly cloudy	7.6	7.3	8.9	8.7	9.8	10.9	13.3	11.7	9.1	8.2	6.4	7.4	109.1
Cloudy	16.8	14.8	16.7	15.0	14.4	12.6	7.2	8.7	12.2	14.1	18.2	17.5	168.2
Precipitation .01" or more	8.7	7.0	7.9	8.2	10.0	10.7	9.5	9.0	8.0	6.6	6.0	8.1	99.6
Snow, Ice pellets 1.0" or more	2.4	1.6	2.2	1.1	*	0.0	0.0	0.0	0.0	0.3	1.7	2.2	11.6
Thunderstorms	0.0	*	0.3	1.3	3.7	7.4	8.6	6.8	3.0	1.0	0.1	*	32.2
Fog, Visibility 1/4 mile or less	0.7	1.7	1.8	0.6	0.4	0.6	0.7	1.1	0.8	1.0	1.4	1.8	12.6
Temperature Maximum:													
90° and above	0.0	0.0	0.0	0.1	0.4	1.6	5.2	5.4	1.3	*	0.0	0.0	14.0
32° and below	28.0	21.9	13.5	1.3	*	0.0	0.0	0.0	0.0	0.5	10.3	25.8	101.5
Temperature Minimum:													
32° and below	31.0	28.2	27.9	16.5	4.5	*	0.0	0.0	1.9	12.3	26.7	30.8	179.8
0° and below	19.9	13.2	5.0	0.2	0.0	0.0	0.0	0.0	0.0	0.0	2.1	14.0	54.3
RELATIVE HUMIDITY (%)													
Morning	73	76	80	74	68	76	78	76	78	76	79	77	76
Afternoon	70	72	71	59	50	57	55	55	58	60	70	74	63
PRECIPITATION (inches)													
Water Equivalent													
Normal	0.5	0.4	0.8	1.9	2.2	3.0	3.3	2.6	1.8	1.2	0.7	0.6	19.5
Maximum monthly	1.3	1.7	2.2	4.2	7.3	9.4	8.4	8.5	6.1	7.0	4.5	2.1	9.4
Date	1950	1979	1983	1942	1977	1975	1952	1944	1957	1982	1977	1951	1975
Minimum monthly	0.0	0.0	0.0	0.0	0.4	0.5	0.4	0.1	0.1	0.0	0.0	0.0	0.0
Date	1961	1954	1958	1980	1976	1972	1950	1984	1974	1952	1967	1958	1980
Maximum in 24 hrs	0.8	1.2	1.1	1.9	4.1	4.0	3.9	4.7	3.9	3.2	1.9	0.8	4.7
Date	1980	1946	1950	1963	1977	1975	1952	1943	1957	1982	1977	1960	1943
SNOW, ICE PELLETS													
Maximum monthly	30.0	19.5	18.7	12.8	1.0	0.0	0.0	0.0	0.6	8.1	24.3	20.3	30.0
Date	1982	1979	1975	1970	1950	—	—	—	1942	1951	1985	1951	1982
Maximum in 24 hrs	17.4	11.2	10.4	8.6	1.0	0.0	0.0	0.0	0.6	7.8	12.6	8.0	17.4
Date	1982	1951	1975	1970	1950	—	—	—	1942	1951	1977	1967	1982
WIND (Resultant)													
Mean speed (mph)	12.8	12.6	13.2	14.1	13.1	11.8	10.6	11.1	12.0	12.8	13.0	12.3	12.4

WILLISTON

Elev. 1900' 48° 11'N — 103° 38'W **North Dakota**

NORMALS, MEANS, EXTREMES

	JAN	FEB	MAR	APR	MAY	JUN	JUL	AUG	SEP	OCT	NOV	DEC	YEAR
TEMPERATURE													
Normal daily maximum	17.5	25.6	36.3	54.0	67.5	76.5	84.0	82.5	70.2	58.2	38.1	25.5	53.0
Normal daily minimum	-4.3	3.5	14.3	29.6	41.5	51.1	56.0	53.7	43.0	32.0	17.0	4.3	28.5
Normal monthly	6.6	14.6	25.3	41.8	54.5	63.8	70.0	68.1	56.6	45.1	27.6	14.9	40.7
Extreme highest	53	58	78	92	106	103	109	107	104	93	73	58	109
Extreme highest date	1981	1984	1978	1980	1980	1979	1980	1983	1983	1963	1981	1979	1980
Extreme lowest	-40	-41	-28	-15	17	30	34	35	17	0	-24	-50	-50
Extreme lowest date	1966	1962	1962	1975	1980	1969	1967	1982	1974	1984	1985	1983	1983
DEGREE DAYS BASE 65° F													
Heating	1810	1411	1231	696	335	108	23	58	277	617	1122	1553	9241
Cooling	0	0	0	0	10	72	178	155	25	0	0	0	440
% OF POSSIBLE SUNSHINE	52	57	61	61	63	67	76	75	65	59	44	48	61
AVERAGE SKY COVER													
Sunrise - Sunset	6.9	7.0	6.6	6.7	6.5	6.0	4.7	4.9	5.7	6.2	6.8	6.8	6.2
NUMBER OF DAYS (Sunrise-Sunset)													
Clear	5.5	4.9	7.0	5.8	5.8	6.9	11.5	11.5	9.1	8.6	6.6	6.3	89.5
Partly cloudy	8.7	7.5	8.4	9.1	11.2	11.6	12.7	11.5	8.6	7.8	7.3	7.2	111.8
Cloudy	16.8	15.9	15.6	15.1	14.0	11.5	6.8	8.0	12.3	14.6	16.0	17.5	163.9
Precipitation .01" or more	8.5	6.5	7.6	7.7	9.6	10.3	8.5	7.0	7.0	5.4	6.2	8.5	92.7
Snow, Ice pellets 1.0" or more	2.3	1.8	2.0	1.6	0.1	0.0	0.0	0.0	0.2	0.5	1.7	2.8	13.0
Thunderstorms	0.0	0.0	0.1	0.7	2.8	7.4	8.2	5.9	2.0	0.0	0.0	0.0	27.2
Fog, Visibility 1/4 mile or less	0.7	1.1	1.0	1.0	0.3	0.3	0.3	0.1	0.6	1.1	1.5	1.2	9.2
Temperature Maximum:													
90° and above	0.0	0.0	0.0	0.1	0.9	2.1	8.6	9.2	1.8	*	0.0	0.0	22.7
32° and below	23.6	16.7	10.4	1.0	0.0	0.0	0.0	0.0	0.0	0.8	10.0	21.5	84.0
Temperature Minimum:													
32° and below	30.8	27.9	29.3	18.3	4.1	0.2	0.0	0.0	3.0	15.3	28.6	31.0	188.5
0° and below	18.2	11.5	4.3	0.1	0.0	0.0	0.0	0.0	0.0	*	3.6	14.2	52.1
RELATIVE HUMIDITY (%)													
Morning	77	79	79	71	67	71	66	64	69	73	79	80	73
Afternoon	72	71	65	52	47	50	45	44	51	55	68	73	58
PRECIPITATION (inches)													
Water Equivalent													
Normal	0.5	0.5	0.5	1.2	1.8	2.6	1.8	1.4	1.3	0.7	0.5	0.5	13.8
Maximum monthly	1.4	1.4	2.2	3.3	7.3	5.9	6.2	3.3	3.0	3.5	1.1	1.4	7.3
Date	1967	1967	1975	1967	1965	1964	1963	1968	1973	1971	1975	1982	1965
Minimum monthly	0.0	0.0	0.0	0.0	0.1	0.8	0.4	0.0	0.1	T	0.0	0.0	T
Date	1973	1983	1966	1983	1980	1983	1976	1971	1963	1965	1969	1979	1965
Maximum in 24 hrs	0.5	0.4	0.9	2.0	2.0	2.2	5.0	2.4	2.2	2.2	0.8	0.8	5.0
Date	1980	1962	1985	1967	1965	1964	1963	1972	1971	1971	1974	1982	1963
SNOW, ICE PELLETS													
Maximum monthly	24.3	16.5	30.9	22.2	15.5	0.0	0.0	0.0	4.0	14.2	14.1	15.2	30.9
Date	1982	1972	1975	1970	1983	—	—	—	1984	1985	1975	1978	1975
Maximum in 24 hrs	8.4	4.3	9.7	12.1	14.6	0.0	0.0	0.0	4.0	10.5	7.9	10.1	14.6
Date	1976	1962	1985	1984	1983	—	—	—	1984	1985	1975	1978	1983
WIND (Resultant)													
Mean speed (mph)	9.9	9.8	10.4	11.3	11.3	10.2	9.4	9.7	10.1	10.2	9.2	9.8	10.1

AKRON

Elev. 1208' 40° 55'N — 81° 26'W # Ohio

NORMALS, MEANS, EXTREMES

	JAN	FEB	MAR	APR	MAY	JUN	JUL	AUG	SEP	OCT	NOV	DEC	YEAR
TEMPERATURE													
Normal daily maximum	32.9	35.6	45.8	59.2	69.8	78.7	82.3	80.9	74.3	62.6	48.9	37.5	59.0
Normal daily minimum	17.2	18.8	27.5	38.0	47.7	56.8	61.0	59.9	53.2	42.4	33.0	23.0	39.9
Normal monthly	25.1	27.2	36.7	48.6	58.8	67.8	71.7	70.4	63.8	52.5	41.0	30.3	49.5
Extreme highest	70	68	79	85	92	100	100	98	99	86	80	76	100
Extreme highest date	1950	1961	1977	1985	1978	1952	1980	1953	1953	1952	1961	1982	1980
Extreme lowest	-24	-13	-3	10	24	32	43	41	32	20	-1	-15	-24
Extreme lowest date	1985	1979	1980	1964	1966	1972	1979	1982	1956	1952	1958	1983	1985
DEGREE DAYS BASE 65° F													
Heating	1237	1058	877	492	228	37	0	14	108	394	720	1076	6241
Cooling	0	0	0	0	36	121	208	181	72	7	0	0	625
% OF POSSIBLE SUNSHINE	na	na	na	na	na	na	na	na	na	na	na	na	na
AVERAGE SKY COVER													
Sunrise - Sunset	8.0	7.7	7.5	7.1	6.7	6.2	5.9	5.9	5.8	6.0	7.7	8.1	6.9
NUMBER OF DAYS (Sunrise-Sunset)													
Clear	3.1	3.5	4.3	4.9	6.3	6.6	7.1	7.8	8.9	9.2	4.1	2.8	68.5
Partly cloudy	5.9	6.0	6.6	7.5	9.2	11.2	13.0	11.9	9.1	7.6	6.2	5.7	99.9
Cloudy	22.1	18.7	20.1	17.6	15.5	12.2	10.9	11.3	12.0	14.2	19.7	22.5	196.8
Precipitation .01" or more	16.1	14.5	16.2	14.2	12.9	10.9	10.9	9.8	9.2	10.1	13.7	15.6	154.0
Snow, Ice pellets 1.0" or more	4.1	3.1	2.8	0.7	*	0.0	0.0	0.0	0.0	0.2	1.4	2.9	15.1
Thunderstorms	0.3	0.4	2.2	3.9	5.6	7.4	8.0	6.2	3.5	1.4	0.7	0.3	39.8
Fog, Visibility 1/4 mile or less	2.9	2.8	2.2	1.5	1.6	1.5	1.7	2.6	2.3	2.3	2.0	3.1	26.6
Temperature Maximum:													
90° and above	0.0	0.0	0.0	0.0	0.1	1.5	3.2	1.3	0.5	0.0	0.0	0.0	6.5
32° and below	15.7	11.4	3.6	0.2	0.0	0.0	0.0	0.0	0.0	0.0	1.4	9.0	41.3
Temperature Minimum:													
32° and below	28.4	23.8	21.2	9.2	1.0	*	0.0	0.0	0.0	3.4	14.2	24.5	125.7
0° and below	3.7	2.3	0.1	0.0	0.0	0.0	0.0	0.0	0.0	0.0	0.0	0.7	6.8
RELATIVE HUMIDITY (%)													
Morning	75	74	71	68	73	78	81	83	82	76	75	75	76
Afternoon	68	64	60	53	54	56	56	59	59	57	65	69	60
PRECIPITATION (inches)													
Water Equivalent													
Normal	2.5	2.1	3.3	3.2	3.5	3.2	4.0	3.3	2.9	2.2	2.5	2.6	35.9
Maximum monthly	8.7	5.2	8.8	6.4	9.6	7.0	11.4	8.1	7.8	8.4	9.3	4.8	11.4
Date	1950	1956	1964	1981	1956	1970	1958	1974	1979	1954	1985	1951	1958
Minimum monthly	0.7	0.4	1.0	0.9	1.0	1.0	1.5	0.4	0.2	0.4	0.6	0.3	0.2
Date	1961	1978	1958	1971	1977	1967	1965	1970	1960	1953	1976	1955	1960
Maximum in 24 hrs	2.9	2.5	3.2	1.9	3.1	2.8	4.1	3.0	6.3	2.7	2.6	1.6	6.3
Date	1959	1959	1964	1957	1985	1970	1958	1975	1979	1954	1985	1974	1979
SNOW, ICE PELLETS													
Maximum monthly	37.5	21.1	20.9	15.8	3.2	0.0	0.0	0.0	T	6.8	22.3	29.4	37.5
Date	1978	1984	1960	1961	1966	—	—	—	1965	1952	1950	1974	1978
Maximum in 24 hrs	10.9	12.3	10.7	5.9	3.2	0.0	0.0	0.0	T	3.9	7.4	17.9	17.9
Date	1966	1984	1973	1961	1966	—	—	—	1965	1952	1950	1974	1974
WIND (Resultant)													
Mean speed (mph)	11.6	11.2	11.6	11.0	9.2	8.4	7.6	7.3	8.0	9.1	10.9	11.4	9.8

CINCINNATI

Elev. 869'   39°03N — 84° 40W   **Ohio**

NORMALS, MEANS, EXTREMES

	JAN	FEB	MAR	APR	MAY	JUN	JUL	AUG	SEP	OCT	NOV	DEC	YEAR
TEMPERATURE													
Normal daily maximum	37.3	41.2	51.5	64.5	74.2	82.3	85.8	84.8	78.7	66.7	52.6	41.9	63.5
Normal daily minimum	20.4	23.0	32.0	42.4	51.7	60.5	64.9	63.3	56.3	43.9	34.1	25.7	43.2
Normal monthly	28.9	32.1	41.8	53.5	63.0	71.4	75.4	74.1	67.5	55.3	43.4	33.8	53.3
Extreme highest	69	73	83	89	93	97	101	102	98	88	80	75	102
Extreme highest date	1967	1972	1981	1976	1962	1971	1983	1962	1964	1963	1982	1982	1962
Extreme lowest	-25	-11	-11	17	27	39	47	43	33	16	1	-12	-25
Extreme lowest date	1977	1982	1980	1964	1963	1972	1963	1965	1983	1962	1976	1983	1977
DEGREE DAYS BASE 65° F													
Heating	1119	921	719	350	143	12	0	0	52	316	648	967	5247
Cooling	0	0	0	5	81	204	322	282	127	16	0	0	1037
% OF POSSIBLE SUNSHINE	35	47	39	55	56	62	66	65	75	44	35	35	51
AVERAGE SKY COVER													
Sunrise - Sunset	7.5	7.3	7.4	7.0	6.7	6.2	6.1	5.8	5.6	5.7	7.1	7.5	6.6
NUMBER OF DAYS													
(Sunrise-Sunset)													
Clear	5.0	5.3	5.0	5.6	5.9	6.9	7.4	8.1	9.8	10.5	6.1	5.1	80.4
Partly cloudy	6.3	5.7	6.8	7.5	9.5	10.3	11.7	12.0	8.9	7.2	5.9	5.9	97.6
Cloudy	19.8	17.3	19.2	16.9	15.6	12.8	11.9	10.9	11.4	13.3	18.1	20.0	187.2
Precipitation .01" or more	12.2	11.0	13.3	12.6	11.5	10.6	10.0	9.0	7.8	8.3	11.0	12.2	129.5
Snow, Ice pellets 1.0" or more	2.4	1.8	1.3	0.2	0.0	0.0	0.0	0.0	0.0	*	0.6	1.2	7.4
Thunderstorms	0.7	0.9	2.4	4.2	5.7	7.1	8.3	7.5	3.2	1.4	1.1	0.4	42.9
Fog, Visibility 1/4 mile or less	2.5	2.1	1.6	0.9	1.2	1.4	2.0	2.9	3.8	2.9	1.8	2.6	25.6
Temperature Maximum:													
90° and above	0.0	0.0	0.0	0.0	0.4	4.2	7.5	4.9	2.2	0.0	0.0	0.0	19.1
32° and below	13.4	8.4	1.4	0.0	0.0	0.0	0.0	0.0	0.0	0.0	0.7	6.6	30.5
Temperature Minimum:													
32° and below	26.8	23.2	16.4	4.5	0.3	0.0	0.0	0.0	0.0	3.2	13.0	22.1	109.5
0° and below	3.7	2.0	0.1	0.0	0.0	0.0	0.0	0.0	0.0	0.0	0.0	1.1	7.0
RELATIVE HUMIDITY (%)													
Morning	75	74	73	71	77	80	83	84	82	77	75	76	77
Afternoon	68	64	60	54	55	56	57	58	57	56	64	69	60
PRECIPITATION (inches)													
Water Equivalent													
Normal	3.1	2.7	3.9	3.5	3.8	4.0	4.2	2.9	2.9	2.5	3.1	3.0	40.1
Maximum monthly	9.4	6.7	12.1	7.1	9.4	7.3	8.3	7.7	8.6	8.6	7.5	6.4	12.1
Date	1950	1955	1964	1970	1968	1977	1962	1982	1979	1983	1985	1978	1964
Minimum monthly	0.5	0.2	1.1	1.0	1.1	0.9	1.1	0.3	0.1	0.2	0.4	0.5	0.1
Date	1981	1978	1960	1971	1964	1965	1951	1953	1963	1963	1949	1976	1963
Maximum in 24 hrs	4.3	2.3	5.2	2.7	3.7	3.4	3.4	3.1	4.5	4.4	3.3	2.9	5.2
Date	1959	1950	1964	1950	1956	1974	1953	1957	1979	1985	1948	1948	1964
SNOW, ICE PELLETS													
Maximum monthly	31.5	13.3	13.0	3.7	T	0.0	0.0	0.0	0.0	1.7	12.1	12.5	31.5
Date	1978	1971	1968	1977	1966	—	—	—	—	1962	1966	1960	1978
Maximum in 24 hrs	8.1	9.3	9.8	3.6	T	0.0	0.0	0.0	0.0	1.7	9.0	7.3	9.8
Date	1978	1966	1968	1977	1966	—	—	—	—	1962	1966	1984	1968
WIND (Resultant)													
Mean speed (mph)	10.7	10.4	11.1	10.7	8.7	7.9	7.2	6.8	7.4	8.2	9.6	10.3	9.1

CLEVELAND   Elev. 777'   41° 25'N — 81° 52'W   Ohio

NORMALS, MEANS, EXTREMES

	JAN	FEB	MAR	APR	MAY	JUN	JUL	AUG	SEP	OCT	NOV	DEC	YEAR
TEMPERATURE													
Normal daily maximum	32.5	34.8	44.8	57.9	68.5	78.0	81.7	80.3	74.2	62.7	49.3	37.5	58.5
Normal daily minimum	18.5	19.9	28.4	38.3	47.9	57.2	61.4	60.5	54.0	43.6	34.3	24.6	40.7
Normal monthly	25.5	27.4	36.6	48.1	58.2	67.6	71.6	70.4	64.1	53.2	41.8	31.1	49.6
Extreme highest	73	69	83	88	92	101	103	102	101	90	82	77	103
Extreme highest date	1950	1961	1945	1942	1959	1944	1941	1948	1953	1946	1950	1982	1941
Extreme lowest	-19	-15	-5	10	25	31	41	38	32	22	3	-11	-19
Extreme lowest date	1963	1963	1984	1964	1966	1972	1968	1982	1942	1969	1976	1976	1963
DEGREE DAYS BASE 65° F													
Heating	1225	1053	880	507	244	33	8	11	99	371	696	1051	6178
Cooling	0	0	0	0	33	111	213	178	72	5	0	0	612
% OF POSSIBLE SUNSHINE	31	37	44	52	58	65	67	63	60	53	31	26	49
AVERAGE SKY COVER													
Sunrise - Sunset	8.3	7.9	7.6	7.0	6.6	6.1	5.6	5.7	5.9	6.2	8.0	8.4	6.9
NUMBER OF DAYS (Sunrise-Sunset)													
Clear	2.8	3.1	4.4	5.2	6.0	6.7	8.6	8.7	8.5	8.3	3.1	2.4	67.7
Partly cloudy	4.8	5.5	6.5	7.9	10.1	11.3	11.9	11.1	9.4	7.9	5.9	4.9	97.3
Cloudy	23.5	19.7	20.2	16.9	14.9	12.0	10.5	11.2	12.1	14.8	21.0	23.7	200.2
Precipitation .01" or more	16.5	14.3	15.6	14.2	13.0	10.9	10.1	9.7	9.8	10.9	14.5	16.4	155.9
Snow, Ice pellets 1.0" or more	4.3	3.9	3.1	0.7	*	0.0	0.0	0.0	0.0	0.2	1.8	4.2	18.3
Thunderstorms	0.1	0.5	1.8	3.7	5.0	6.9	6.4	5.3	3.4	1.5	1.0	0.3	35.9
Fog, Visibility 1/4 mile or less	1.5	1.6	1.8	1.2	1.3	0.6	0.5	1.0	0.5	1.0	0.6	1.1	12.7
Temperature Maximum:													
90° and above	0.0	0.0	0.0	0.0	0.2	1.6	3.4	1.7	0.7	0.0	0.0	0.0	7.5
32° and below	16.9	13.3	5.2	0.3	0.0	0.0	0.0	0.0	0.0	0.0	1.1	10.5	47.3
Temperature Minimum:													
32° and below	28.4	24.4	21.1	9.4	1.0	*	0.0	0.0	0.0	2.6	12.8	24.6	124.3
0° and below	3.6	2.4	0.1	0.0	0.0	0.0	0.0	0.0	0.0	0.0	0.0	0.8	6.8
RELATIVE HUMIDITY (%)													
Morning	75	75	74	72	76	79	81	83	81	76	75	75	77
Afternoon	70	68	63	56	57	57	57	60	60	59	66	70	62
PRECIPITATION (inches)													
Water Equivalent													
Normal	2.4	2.2	2.9	3.3	3.3	3.4	3.3	3.3	2.9	2.4	2.7	2.7	35.4
Maximum monthly	7.0	4.6	6.0	6.6	6.0	9.0	6.4	8.9	6.7	9.5	8.8	5.6	9.5
Date	1950	1950	1954	1961	1947	1972	1969	1975	1981	1954	1985	1951	1954
Minimum monthly	0.3	0.4	0.7	1.1	1.0	1.1	1.2	0.5	0.7	0.6	0.8	0.7	0.3
Date	1961	1978	1958	1946	1963	1967	1982	1969	1964	1952	1976	1958	1961
Maximum in 24 hrs	2.3	2.3	2.7	2.2	3.7	4.0	2.8	3.0	2.3	3.4	2.7	2.0	4.0
Date	1959	1959	1948	1961	1955	1972	1969	1947	1979	1954	1985	1974	1972
SNOW, ICE PELLETS													
Maximum monthly	42.8	27.1	26.3	14.5	2.1	0.0	0.0	0.0	T	8.0	22.3	30.3	42.8
Date	1978	1984	1954	1943	1974	—	—	—	1976	1962	1950	1962	1978
Maximum in 24 hrs	10.5	11.5	14.9	11.6	2.1	0.0	0.0	0.0	T	6.7	15.0	12.2	15.0
Date	1978	1984	1954	1982	1974	—	—	—	1976	1962	1950	1974	1950
WIND (Resultant)													
Mean speed (mph)	12.4	12.1	12.4	11.8	10.2	9.4	8.7	8.4	9.1	10.0	11.9	12.3	10.7

COLUMBUS

Elev. 813'   40° 00'N — 82° 53'W   **Ohio**

NORMALS, MEANS, EXTREMES

	JAN	FEB	MAR	APR	MAY	JUN	JUL	AUG	SEP	OCT	NOV	DEC	YEAR
TEMPERATURE													
Normal daily maximum	34.7	38.1	49.3	62.3	72.6	81.3	84.4	83.0	76.9	65.0	50.7	39.4	61.5
Normal daily minimum	19.4	21.5	30.6	40.5	50.2	59.0	63.2	61.7	54.6	42.8	33.5	24.7	41.8
Normal monthly	27.1	29.8	40.0	51.4	61.4	70.2	73.8	72.4	65.8	53.9	42.1	32.1	51.6
Extreme highest	74	73	85	89	94	102	100	101	100	90	80	76	102
Extreme highest date	1950	1957	1945	1948	1941	1944	1955	1983	1951	1951	1950	1982	1944
Extreme lowest	-19	-13	-6	14	25	35	43	39	31	20	5	-12	-19
Extreme lowest date	1985	1977	1984	1982	1966	1972	1972	1965	1963	1962	1976	1983	1985
DEGREE DAYS BASE 65° F													
Heating	1175	986	775	408	178	19	0	5	78	355	687	1020	5686
Cooling	0	0	0	0	66	175	273	235	102	11	0	0	862
% OF POSSIBLE SUNSHINE	36	42	44	51	56	60	60	60	61	55	37	30	49
AVERAGE SKY COVER													
Sunrise - Sunset	7.8	7.5	7.4	7.0	6.6	6.2	6.0	5.9	5.6	5.7	7.4	7.8	6.7
NUMBER OF DAYS (Sunrise-Sunset)													
Clear	4.2	4.0	4.9	5.4	6.0	6.3	6.6	7.1	9.5	10.3	4.9	3.9	73.0
Partly cloudy	6.3	6.2	6.7	7.9	10.4	11.3	13.4	12.9	9.1	7.3	6.6	6.1	104.2
Cloudy	20.5	18.0	19.5	16.7	14.6	12.5	11.0	11.1	11.5	13.3	18.4	20.9	188.1
Precipitation .01" or more	13.3	11.5	14.0	12.9	12.7	11.0	10.8	9.4	8.3	8.8	11.5	12.7	136.8
Snow, Ice pellets 1.0" or more	3.0	2.1	1.5	0.2	0.0	0.0	0.0	0.0	0.0	*	0.8	1.9	9.6
Thunderstorms	0.4	0.5	2.2	4.1	6.4	8.0	8.1	6.4	3.0	1.2	0.9	0.3	41.4
Fog, Visibility 1/4 mile or less	2.0	1.6	1.1	0.6	0.9	1.1	1.2	1.8	1.8	1.5	1.3	1.5	16.5
Temperature Maximum:													
90° and above	0.0	0.0	0.0	0.0	0.5	3.2	5.3	3.0	1.4	0.0	0.0	0.0	13.4
32° and below	14.8	10.1	3.0	0.1	0.0	0.0	0.0	0.0	0.0	0.0	1.2	9.2	38.4
Temperature Minimum:													
32° and below	27.5	23.9	18.9	6.8	0.7	0.0	0.0	0.0	0.1	3.9	14.0	23.9	119.8
0° and below	3.3	1.7	0.2	0.0	0.0	0.0	0.0	0.0	0.0	0.0	0.0	0.8	6.0
RELATIVE HUMIDITY (%)													
Morning	74	73	69	69	76	80	82	84	82	78	77	76	77
Afternoon	67	64	57	52	54	55	56	58	57	55	64	69	59
PRECIPITATION (inches)													
Water Equivalent													
Normal	2.7	2.1	3.2	3.4	3.7	4.0	4.0	3.7	2.7	1.9	2.6	2.6	36.9
Maximum monthly	8.2	4.6	9.5	6.3	9.1	9.7	9.4	8.6	6.7	5.2	10.6	5.0	10.6
Date	1950	1981	1964	1964	1968	1958	1958	1979	1979	1954	1985	1951	1985
Minimum monthly	0.5	0.2	0.6	0.6	0.9	0.7	0.4	0.5	0.5	0.1	0.6	0.4	0.1
Date	1944	1978	1941	1971	1977	1984	1940	1951	1963	1963	1976	1955	1963
Maximum in 24 hrs	4.8	2.1	3.4	2.3	2.7	2.9	3.8	3.7	4.8	1.8	2.4	1.7	4.8
Date	1959	1975	1964	1957	1968	1958	1969	1972	1979	1965	1985	1978	1979
SNOW, ICE PELLETS													
Maximum monthly	34.4	16.4	13.5	7.1	T	0.0	0.0	0.0	T	1.3	15.2	17.3	34.4
Date	1978	1979	1962	1973	1966	—	—	—	1967	1962	1950	1960	1978
Maximum in 24 hrs	7.5	8.9	8.6	6.3	T	0.0	0.0	0.0	T	1.3	8.2	8.7	8.9
Date	1978	1971	1962	1973	1966	—	—	—	1967	1962	1950	1960	1971
WIND (Resultant)													
Mean speed (mph)	10.3	10.1	10.7	10.1	8.5	7.6	6.9	6.5	6.7	7.7	9.5	9.9	8.7

DAYTON

Elev. 995'   39° 54'N — 84° 12'W   **Ohio**

NORMALS, MEANS, EXTREMES

	JAN	FEB	MAR	APR	MAY	JUN	JUL	AUG	SEP	OCT	NOV	DEC	YEAR
TEMPERATURE													
Normal daily maximum	34.5	38.0	48.6	62.0	72.4	81.6	84.9	83.4	77.1	65.1	50.5	39.3	61.5
Normal daily minimum	18.8	21.2	30.3	41.0	51.2	60.4	64.3	62.6	55.5	43.9	33.7	24.3	42.3
Normal monthly	26.7	29.6	39.5	51.5	61.8	71.0	74.6	73.0	66.3	54.5	42.1	31.8	51.9
Extreme highest	71	71	82	89	93	99	102	100	101	89	79	72	102
Extreme highest date	1950	1976	1981	1962	1962	1944	1954	1964	1954	1951	1975	1982	1954
Extreme lowest	-24	-16	-7	15	27	40	44	40	32	21	-2	-15	-24
Extreme lowest date	1985	1951	1980	1972	1947	1972	1972	1965	1974	1962	1958	1983	1985
DEGREE DAYS BASE 65° F													
Heating	1190	991	791	405	171	15	0	0	68	342	687	1029	5689
Cooling	0	0	0	0	72	195	301	252	110	17	0	0	947
% OF POSSIBLE SUNSHINE	41	45	49	53	60	67	68	68	66	59	41	37	55
AVERAGE SKY COVER													
Sunrise - Sunset	7.6	7.3	7.4	7.0	6.7	6.2	5.8	5.7	5.5	5.6	7.3	7.6	6.6
NUMBER OF DAYS (Sunrise-Sunset)													
Clear	4.8	5.2	4.6	5.5	6.0	6.6	7.7	8.6	9.7	10.6	5.2	4.3	79.0
Partly cloudy	6.1	5.9	7.3	7.3	9.5	10.3	12.5	11.8	9.0	7.6	6.8	6.5	100.6
Cloudy	20.1	17.2	19.0	17.2	15.5	13.1	10.8	10.5	11.2	12.8	18.0	20.2	185.7
Precipitation .01" or more	13.0	10.8	13.0	12.8	12.1	10.4	10.1	9.5	8.1	8.7	11.3	12.1	131.9
Snow, Ice pellets 1.0" or more	2.6	1.9	1.7	0.2	0.0	0.0	0.0	0.0	0.0	*	0.6	2.0	9.0
Thunderstorms	0.5	0.5	2.5	4.4	6.2	7.4	7.2	6.1	3.1	1.4	0.8	0.3	40.4
Fog, Visibility 1/4 mile or less	3.6	2.7	1.9	0.8	1.2	1.0	1.3	1.8	1.6	1.6	1.9	3.3	23.0
Temperature Maximum:													
90° and above	0.0	0.0	0.0	0.0	0.4	3.6	7.0	3.5	1.4	0.0	0.0	0.0	15.9
32° and below	14.9	9.8	2.6	0.1	0.0	0.0	0.0	0.0	0.0	0.0	0.9	7.6	35.9
Temperature Minimum:													
32° and below	27.7	23.6	18.8	6.0	0.4	0.0	0.0	0.0	*	3.5	14.0	23.5	117.5
0° and below	3.6	2.1	0.2	0.0	0.0	0.0	0.0	0.0	0.0	0.0	0.0	0.9	6.9
RELATIVE HUMIDITY (%)													
Morning	74	74	74	71	73	76	78	81	80	76	76	77	76
Afternoon	69	66	62	55	54	54	55	57	57	57	66	71	60
PRECIPITATION (inches)													
Water Equivalent													
Normal	2.5	2.1	3.0	3.4	3.6	3.8	3.3	3.1	2.3	2.0	2.6	2.5	34.7
Maximum monthly	9.8	4.5	7.6	6.6	7.7	10.8	7.2	8.0	5.6	5.5	8.0	5.0	10.8
Date	1950	1950	1964	1947	1957	1958	1955	1974	1965	1983	1985	1951	1958
Minimum monthly	0.3	0.1	1.0	0.5	1.5	0.3	0.4	0.3	0.2	0.1	0.4	0.3	0.1
Date	1981	1947	1966	1962	1964	1962	1974	1967	1963	1944	1949	1955	1944
Maximum in 24 hrs	4.3	2.7	2.8	3.1	2.9	3.7	3.2	3.6	2.6	2.3	2.9	1.7	4.3
Date	1959	1959	1964	1977	1968	1981	1955	1974	1981	1983	1955	1945	1959
SNOW, ICE PELLETS													
Maximum monthly	40.2	17.5	13.8	4.9	T	0.0	0.0	0.0	0.0	2.0	12.7	15.6	40.2
Date	1978	1979	1984	1974	1966	—	—	—	—	1962	1950	1960	1978
Maximum in 24 hrs	12.2	7.7	11.3	4.7	T	0.0	0.0	0.0	0.0	2.0	10.0	7.6	12.2
Date	1978	1984	1968	1974	1966	—	—	—	—	1962	1950	1974	1978
WIND (Resultant)													
Mean speed (mph)	11.7	11.6	12.1	11.7	9.8	9.0	8.0	7.5	8.2	9.0	11.1	11.4	10.1

MANSFIELD

Elev. 1295' **40° 49'N — 82° 31'W** **Ohio**

NORMALS, MEANS, EXTREMES

	JAN	FEB	MAR	APR	MAY	JUN	JUL	AUG	SEP	OCT	NOV	DEC	YEAR
TEMPERATURE													
Normal daily maximum	32.2	35.0	45.4	58.8	69.3	78.4	82.1	80.7	74.4	62.8	48.5	36.8	58.7
Normal daily minimum	17.4	19.2	27.9	38.4	48.2	57.5	61.8	60.5	53.8	43.0	33.0	22.9	40.3
Normal monthly	24.8	27.1	36.7	48.6	58.8	68.0	72.0	70.6	64.1	52.9	40.8	29.9	49.5
Extreme highest	63	67	76	85	92	97	96	95	93	85	78	73	97
Extreme highest date	1972	1961	1983	1960	1962	1971	1965	1964	1964	1963	1968	1982	1971
Extreme lowest	-22	-11	-6	8	25	38	44	40	34	20	2	-14	-22
Extreme lowest date	1985	1982	1980	1982	1966	1980	1965	1965	1974	1976	1976	1983	1985
DEGREE DAYS BASE 65° F													
Heating	1246	1058	877	492	231	35	0	10	105	381	726	1088	6249
Cooling	0	0	0	0	39	125	220	184	78	6	0	0	652
% OF POSSIBLE SUNSHINE	na	na	na	na	na	na	na	na	na	na	na	na	na
AVERAGE SKY COVER													
Sunrise - Sunset	7.9	7.6	7.6	7.0	6.6	6.0	5.8	5.9	5.9	6.1	7.7	8.1	6.9
NUMBER OF DAYS (Sunrise-Sunset)													
Clear	3.7	3.7	4.5	5.3	6.6	6.9	7.3	8.0	8.7	8.9	4.0	3.4	71.0
Partly cloudy	6.3	6.5	6.8	7.6	9.5	11.6	13.4	11.1	8.8	7.8	5.8	5.2	100.4
Cloudy	21.1	18.2	19.7	17.0	14.9	11.5	10.2	11.9	12.5	14.3	20.2	22.4	193.9
Precipitation .01" or more	12.9	12.0	14.8	13.2	12.9	10.7	9.6	9.8	8.9	9.5	12.6	13.9	140.8
Snow, Ice pellets 1.0" or more	3.8	3.7	2.3	0.5	*	0.0	0.0	0.0	0.0	0.0	1.0	3.0	14.4
Thunderstorms	0.2	0.5	2.3	4.0	5.2	6.7	7.1	6.2	3.4	0.9	0.9	0.2	37.6
Fog, Visibility 1/4 mile or less	2.6	2.8	3.6	1.8	2.3	1.5	1.5	2.7	2.2	2.5	2.5	4.2	30.1
Temperature Maximum:													
90° and above	0.0	0.0	0.0	0.0	0.0	1.0	3.2	1.2	0.6	0.0	0.0	0.0	5.9
32° and below	17.6	12.5	4.6	0.3	0.0	0.0	0.0	0.0	0.0	0.0	1.6	11.2	47.6
Temperature Minimum:													
32° and below	28.4	24.0	20.6	8.5	0.9	0.0	0.0	0.0	0.0	3.3	14.5	25.0	125.1
0° and below	4.2	2.6	0.3	0.0	0.0	0.0	0.0	0.0	0.0	0.0	0.0	1.1	8.1
RELATIVE HUMIDITY (%)													
Morning	78	77	76	72	76	81	82	83	82	77	79	79	79
Afternoon	71	68	62	56	57	58	57	60	60	59	67	74	62
PRECIPITATION (inches)													
Water Equivalent													
Normal	2.2	1.8	3.0	3.5	3.7	3.4	3.7	3.2	3.0	1.9	2.6	2.4	34.8
Maximum monthly	4.5	4.2	7.0	6.5	6.5	10.0	8.0	7.6	6.8	4.8	12.8	4.7	12.8
Date	1982	1961	1964	1964	1985	1981	1969	1974	1972	1978	1985	1978	1985
Minimum monthly	0.4	0.2	1.1	0.7	1.5	1.2	0.9	0.6	0.7	0.4	0.7	0.7	0.2
Date	1981	1978	1960	1971	1961	1984	1975	1970	1963	1963	1976	1976	1978
Maximum in 24 hrs	1.7	2.7	2.4	2.3	2.3	3.7	5.0	3.8	4.1	1.8	2.3	1.8	5.0
Date	1979	1961	1964	1979	1965	1978	1969	1972	1979	1983	1985	1978	1969
SNOW, ICE PELLETS													
Maximum monthly	42.1	19.1	14.8	13.4	1.4	0.0	0.0	0.0	T	0.6	7.4	18.0	42.1
Date	1978	1984	1963	1982	1966	—	—	—	1970	1962	1980	1962	1978
Maximum in 24 hrs	12.0	10.0	7.5	6.4	1.4	0.0	0.0	0.0	T	0.6	3.2	12.3	12.3
Date	1968	1985	1960	1982	1966	—	—	—	1970	1962	1966	1974	1974
WIND (Resultant)													
Mean speed (mph)	13.4	12.6	12.5	12.3	10.3	9.9	8.4	8.4	9.0	10.6	11.9	12.7	11.0

TOLEDO

Elev. 669'   41° 36'N — 83° 48'W   **Ohio**

NORMALS, MEANS, EXTREMES

	JAN	FEB	MAR	APR	MAY	JUN	JUL	AUG	SEP	OCT	NOV	DEC	YEAR
TEMPERATURE													
Normal daily maximum	30.7	34.0	44.6	59.1	70.5	79.9	83.4	81.8	75.1	63.3	47.9	35.5	58.8
Normal daily minimum	15.5	17.5	26.1	36.5	46.6	56.0	60.2	58.4	51.2	40.1	30.6	20.6	38.3
Normal monthly	23.1	25.8	35.4	47.8	58.6	68.0	71.8	70.1	63.2	51.7	39.3	28.1	48.5
Extreme highest	62	68	80	88	95	99	101	98	98	91	78	68	101
Extreme highest date	1967	1957	1963	1977	1962	1971	1977	1964	1978	1963	1968	1982	1977
Extreme lowest	-20	-14	-6	8	25	32	43	34	26	15	2	-15	-20
Extreme lowest date	1984	1982	1984	1982	1974	1972	1972	1982	1974	1976	1958	1983	1984
DEGREE DAYS BASE 65° F													
Heating	1299	1098	918	516	237	39	0	16	113	419	771	1144	6570
Cooling	0	0	0	0	38	129	215	174	59	7	0	0	622
% OF POSSIBLE SUNSHINE	42	47	50	53	60	64	67	63	61	55	38	34	53
AVERAGE SKY COVER													
Sunrise - Sunset	7.5	7.3	7.3	6.9	6.4	6.0	5.7	5.7	5.9	6.1	7.6	7.9	6.7
NUMBER OF DAYS (Sunrise-Sunset)													
Clear	4.5	4.6	4.8	5.9	6.3	6.7	7.7	8.1	8.7	8.4	3.7	3.1	72.6
Partly cloudy	6.8	6.9	7.2	7.7	10.9	12.0	13.5	12.2	9.4	8.6	7.1	6.5	108.7
Cloudy	19.7	16.7	19.0	16.4	13.8	11.3	9.8	10.7	12.0	14.0	19.2	21.4	183.9
Precipitation .01" or more	13.6	11.1	13.5	12.7	12.1	10.3	9.4	9.1	10.0	9.0	11.7	14.4	136.9
Snow, Ice pellets 1.0" or more	2.9	2.5	2.1	0.6	0.0	0.0	0.0	0.0	0.0	0.0	1.2	2.8	12.1
Thunderstorms	0.1	0.5	2.0	4.0	5.0	7.4	7.1	6.3	3.8	1.1	0.7	0.2	38.2
Fog, Visibility 1/4 mile or less	1.5	2.0	1.6	0.9	0.8	0.9	0.8	1.9	1.7	2.2	1.7	2.2	18.1
Temperature Maximum:													
90° and above	0.0	0.0	0.0	0.0	0.6	3.3	4.6	2.9	1.3	*	0.0	0.0	12.7
32° and below	18.6	13.2	4.7	0.2	0.0	0.0	0.0	0.0	0.0	0.0	2.2	12.5	51.3
Temperature Minimum:													
32° and below	29.6	25.9	23.3	11.1	1.7	*	0.0	0.0	0.4	6.5	17.7	26.6	142.9
0° and below	4.7	3.2	0.2	0.0	0.0	0.0	0.0	0.0	0.0	0.0	0.0	1.8	9.9
RELATIVE HUMIDITY (%)													
Morning	75	74	75	76	78	82	84	88	87	81	81	81	80
Afternoon	69	66	62	55	53	54	55	59	58	57	67	74	61
PRECIPITATION (inches)													
Water Equivalent													
Normal	1.9	1.8	2.6	3.0	2.9	3.4	3.2	3.1	2.5	1.9	2.4	2.5	31.7
Maximum monthly	4.6	4.4	5.7	6.1	5.1	8.4	6.7	8.4	8.1	3.7	6.8	6.8	8.4
Date	1965	1976	1985	1977	1968	1981	1969	1965	1972	1981	1982	1967	1981
Minimum monthly	0.2	0.2	0.5	0.8	0.9	1.4	0.6	0.4	0.5	0.2	0.5	0.5	0.2
Date	1961	1969	1958	1962	1964	1984	1974	1976	1963	1964	1976	1958	1969
Maximum in 24 hrs	1.7	1.6	2.6	3.4	1.9	3.2	4.3	2.4	3.9	1.9	3.1	3.5	4.3
Date	1959	1981	1985	1977	1970	1978	1969	1972	1972	1981	1982	1967	1969
SNOW, ICE PELLETS													
Maximum monthly	30.8	14.4	15.0	12.0	T	0.0	0.0	0.0	T	0.9	17.9	24.2	30.8
Date	1978	1967	1977	1957	1984	—	—	—	1967	1980	1966	1977	1978
Maximum in 24 hrs	10.4	7.7	7.8	9.8	T	0.0	0.0	0.0	T	0.9	8.3	13.9	13.9
Date	1978	1981	1977	1957	1984	—	—	—	1967	1980	1966	1974	1974
WIND (Resultant)													
Mean speed (mph)	10.9	10.6	11.0	10.9	9.6	8.4	7.3	7.1	7.6	8.7	10.1	10.5	9.4

YOUNGSTOWN   Elev. 1178'   41° 16'N — 80° 40'W   Ohio

NORMALS, MEANS, EXTREMES

	JAN	FEB	MAR	APR	MAY	JUN	JUL	AUG	SEP	OCT	NOV	DEC	YEAR
TEMPERATURE													
Normal daily maximum	31.4	33.8	44.0	57.9	68.6	77.5	81.2	79.8	73.2	61.4	47.7	36.0	57.7
Normal daily minimum	16.9	18.0	26.5	36.9	46.0	55.1	59.0	58.2	51.5	41.5	32.7	22.6	38.7
Normal monthly	24.2	25.9	35.3	47.4	57.3	66.3	70.1	69.0	62.4	51.5	40.2	29.3	48.2
Extreme highest	71	67	80	87	92	99	100	97	99	87	80	76	100
Extreme highest date	1950	1961	1977	1976	1962	1952	1954	1953	1954	1953	1961	1982	1954
Extreme lowest	-20	-14	-10	11	24	30	42	32	29	20	1	-12	-20
Extreme lowest date	1985	1979	1980	1950	1970	1972	1968	1982	1957	1969	1976	1983	1985
DEGREE DAYS BASE 65° F													
Heating	1265	1095	921	528	267	57	7	19	130	423	744	1104	6560
Cooling	0	0	0	0	28	96	166	143	52	0	0	0	485
% OF POSSIBLE SUNSHINE	na	na	na	na	na	na	na	na	na	na	na	na	na
AVERAGE SKY COVER													
Sunrise - Sunset	8.3	7.9	7.7	7.2	6.7	6.2	6.0	6.0	6.1	6.3	7.9	8.4	7.0
NUMBER OF DAYS (Sunrise-Sunset)													
Clear	2.8	3.2	4.3	5.0	6.1	6.5	7.1	7.5	8.0	8.4	3.3	2.5	64.5
Partly cloudy	5.1	5.4	6.2	7.4	8.5	11.2	13.0	11.8	9.8	7.5	5.5	5.4	97.2
Cloudy	23.0	19.7	20.5	17.6	16.4	12.3	10.9	11.7	12.2	15.1	21.2	23.2	203.6
Precipitation .01" or more	17.0	14.9	16.0	14.4	13.0	11.5	10.4	10.1	10.1	10.7	14.8	17.6	160.6
Snow, Ice pellets 1.0" or more	4.3	3.8	3.3	0.8	*	0.0	0.0	0.0	0.0	0.2	1.6	4.5	18.6
Thunderstorms	0.3	0.4	1.7	3.4	4.5	6.8	6.7	5.6	3.2	1.2	0.7	0.3	34.7
Fog, Visibility 1/4 mile or less	2.3	2.2	1.9	1.6	2.0	2.3	2.7	3.5	3.2	2.0	2.1	2.8	28.5
Temperature Maximum:													
90° and above	0.0	0.0	0.0	0.0	0.1	1.3	2.7	2.0	0.5	0.0	0.0	0.0	6.6
32° and below	16.5	12.3	5.6	0.3	0.0	0.0	0.0	0.0	0.0	*	2.4	12.7	49.8
Temperature Minimum:													
32° and below	28.3	25.2	22.6	10.9	1.6	*	0.0	*	0.1	4.2	15.9	25.7	134.5
0° and below	3.1	2.3	0.2	0.0	0.0	0.0	0.0	0.0	0.0	0.0	0.0	0.9	6.5
RELATIVE HUMIDITY (%)													
Morning	79	78	77	75	78	83	84	86	85	80	79	80	80
Afternoon	72	68	64	56	54	56	55	57	58	58	67	73	62
PRECIPITATION (inches)													
Water Equivalent													
Normal	2.6	2.2	3.2	3.4	3.2	3.5	4.0	3.4	3.1	2.6	2.8	2.7	37.3
Maximum monthly	7.6	5.2	6.2	6.4	9.8	6.9	7.4	7.8	6.1	8.5	9.1	5.5	9.8
Date	1950	1950	1964	1957	1946	1957	1958	1956	1945	1954	1985	1971	1946
Minimum monthly	0.7	0.6	1.3	1.0	0.7	1.3	1.5	0.5	0.2	0.4	0.9	0.8	0.2
Date	1985	1978	1960	1982	1977	1952	1957	1969	1960	1953	1976	1958	1960
Maximum in 24 hrs	2.7	2.7	2.4	1.7	2.8	3.1	3.8	2.8	4.0	4.3	3.0	2.2	4.3
Date	1959	1959	1954	1957	1946	1983	1967	1980	1979	1954	1985	1979	1954
SNOW, ICE PELLETS													
Maximum monthly	36.0	22.7	23.2	12.2	5.4	0.0	0.0	0.0	T	7.4	30.6	23.0	36.0
Date	1978	1967	1965	1961	1966	—	—	—	1983	1962	1950	1963	1978
Maximum in 24 hrs	17.5	13.4	10.7	6.4	5.4	0.0	0.0	0.0	T	4.9	20.7	14.8	20.7
Date	1948	1984	1983	1961	1966	—	—	—	1983	1962	1950	1944	1950
WIND (Resultant)													
Mean speed (mph)	11.8	11.4	11.6	11.1	9.7	8.7	7.9	7.5	8.3	9.4	11.1	11.6	10.0

NORMALS, MEANS, EXTREMES

	JAN	FEB	MAR	APR	MAY	JUN	JUL	AUG	SEP	OCT	NOV	DEC	YEAR
TEMPERATURE													
Normal daily maximum	46.6	52.2	61.0	71.7	79.0	87.6	93.5	92.8	84.7	74.3	59.9	50.7	71.2
Normal daily minimum	25.2	29.4	37.1	48.6	57.7	66.3	70.6	69.4	61.9	50.2	37.6	29.1	48.6
Normal monthly	35.9	40.8	49.1	60.2	68.4	77.0	82.1	81.1	73.3	62.3	48.8	39.9	59.9
Extreme highest	79	84	93	100	104	105	108	110	102	96	87	86	110
Extreme highest date	1967	1981	1967	1972	1985	1980	1980	1980	1985	1972	1980	1955	1980
Extreme lowest	-4	-3	3	20	37	47	53	51	37	22	11	-3	-4
Extreme lowest date	1959	1979	1960	1957	1981	1954	1971	1956	1985	1957	1959	1983	1959
DEGREE DAYS BASE 65° F													
Heating	902	678	506	184	41	0	0	0	15	145	486	778	3735
Cooling	0	0	13	40	147	360	530	499	264	61	0	0	1914
% OF POSSIBLE SUNSHINE	59	60	63	66	67	74	79	79	72	69	60	59	67
AVERAGE SKY COVER													
Sunrise - Sunset	5.9	5.8	5.9	5.7	5.8	5.0	4.4	4.3	4.6	4.6	5.1	5.5	5.2
NUMBER OF DAYS (Sunrise-Sunset)													
Clear	10.3	9.1	9.6	9.5	8.9	10.8	14.5	14.9	13.6	14.3	11.9	11.7	139.3
Partly cloudy	6.1	6.9	8.0	7.7	9.8	10.5	9.4	9.6	8.0	6.9	6.7	6.1	95.8
Cloudy	14.6	12.2	13.4	12.7	12.2	8.6	7.1	6.5	8.4	9.8	11.3	13.2	130.1
Precipitation .01" or more	5.5	6.3	7.2	7.8	10.0	8.5	6.4	6.4	6.7	6.4	5.2	5.3	81.7
Snow, Ice pellets 1.0" or more	0.9	1.0	0.4	0.0	0.0	0.0	0.0	0.0	0.0	0.0	0.2	0.6	3.1
Thunderstorms	0.5	1.4	3.0	5.5	9.1	8.7	6.2	6.3	4.5	3.1	1.3	0.6	50.1
Fog, Visibility 1/4 mile or less	4.0	3.3	1.9	1.0	0.6	0.4	0.3	0.3	0.8	1.6	2.1	3.3	19.6
Temperature Maximum:													
90° and above	0.0	0.0	0.2	0.3	1.7	11.4	22.9	22.8	9.4	1.0	0.0	0.0	69.5
32° and below	6.2	2.6	0.1	0.0	0.0	0.0	0.0	0.0	0.0	0.0	0.1	2.5	11.4
Temperature Minimum:													
32° and below	23.8	17.7	8.0	1.2	0.0	0.0	0.0	0.0	0.0	0.6	8.7	20.8	80.6
0° and below	0.5	0.2	0.0	0.0	0.0	0.0	0.0	0.0	0.0	0.0	0.0	0.2	0.8
RELATIVE HUMIDITY (%)													
Morning	73	72	68	69	76	76	70	70	74	72	74	72	72
Afternoon	60	57	53	52	57	56	49	49	54	52	56	58	54
PRECIPITATION (inches)													
Water Equivalent													
Normal	0.9	1.2	2.0	2.9	5.5	3.8	3.0	2.4	3.4	2.7	1.5	1.2	30.8
Maximum monthly	5.6	3.7	7.1	10.7	12.0	9.9	8.4	6.7	9.6	13.1	5.4	8.1	13.1
Date	1949	1985	1948	1947	1982	1979	1959	1966	1970	1983	1964	1984	1983
Minimum monthly	T	T	T	0.6	0.3	0.6	T	0.2	T	T	T	0.0	T
Date	1976	1947	1940	1971	1942	1952	1983	1978	1948	1958	1949	1955	1983
Maximum in 24 hrs	3.1	2.2	3.4	3.8	5.6	4.5	5.7	3.3	7.6	8.9	2.0	2.5	8.9
Date	1982	1978	1944	1970	1970	1985	1981	1966	1970	1983	1961	1984	1983
SNOW, ICE PELLETS													
Maximum monthly	17.3	12.0	13.9	0.7	0.0	0.0	0.0	0.0	0.0	T	7.5	8.2	17.3
Date	1949	1978	1968	1957	—	—	—	—	—	1967	1972	1960	1949
Maximum in 24 hrs	8.0	6.1	8.4	0.7	0.0	0.0	0.0	0.0	0.0	T	5.5	5.7	8.4
Date	1944	1979	1948	1957	—	—	—	—	—	1967	1972	1984	1948
WIND (Resultant)													
Mean speed (mph)	12.9	13.3	14.6	14.5	12.7	12.3	10.9	10.6	11.2	12.0	12.4	12.6	12.5

TULSA

Elev. 650' 36° 12'N — 95° 54'W **Oklahoma**

NORMALS, MEANS, EXTREMES

	JAN	FEB	MAR	APR	MAY	JUN	JUL	AUG	SEP	OCT	NOV	DEC	YEAR
TEMPERATURE													
Normal daily maximum	45.6	51.9	60.8	72.4	79.7	87.9	93.9	93.0	85.0	74.9	60.2	50.3	71.3
Normal daily minimum	24.8	29.5	37.7	49.5	58.5	67.5	72.4	70.3	62.5	50.3	38.1	29.3	49.2
Normal monthly	35.2	40.7	49.3	61.0	69.1	77.7	83.2	81.7	73.8	62.6	49.2	39.8	60.3
Extreme highest	79	86	96	102	96	103	112	110	109	98	87	80	112
Extreme highest date	1950	1962	1974	1972	1985	1953	1954	1970	1939	1979	1945	1966	1954
Extreme lowest	-8	-7	-3	22	35	49	51	52	35	26	10	-3	-8
Extreme lowest date	1947	1979	1948	1957	1961	1954	1971	1967	1984	1952	1976	1963	1947
DEGREE DAYS BASE 65° F													
Heating	924	680	500	168	40	0	0	0	18	146	474	781	3731
Cooling	0	0	14	45	167	381	564	518	282	72	0	0	2043
% OF POSSIBLE SUNSHINE	52	55	56	57	58	65	73	72	65	64	56	53	61
AVERAGE SKY COVER													
Sunrise - Sunset	6.0	5.8	6.0	6.0	6.0	5.4	4.6	4.4	4.8	4.7	5.3	5.8	5.4
NUMBER OF DAYS (Sunrise-Sunset)													
Clear	9.1	8.9	8.9	8.1	8.1	9.0	12.8	13.6	12.6	13.4	11.3	10.2	126.1
Partly cloudy	7.2	6.5	8.2	8.8	10.3	11.4	10.9	10.6	8.1	7.6	6.8	7.4	103.8
Cloudy	14.7	12.9	13.9	13.0	12.6	9.6	7.3	6.8	9.2	10.0	11.9	13.4	135.4
Precipitation .01" or more	6.3	7.0	8.2	8.9	10.6	8.9	6.4	6.7	7.1	6.7	6.2	6.6	89.6
Snow, Ice pellets 1.0" or more	1.4	1.0	0.4	*	0.0	0.0	0.0	0.0	0.0	0.0	0.2	0.6	3.5
Thunderstorms	0.7	1.3	3.3	6.1	9.1	8.4	5.8	6.2	5.0	3.1	1.4	0.8	51.3
Fog, Visibility 1/4 mile or less	2.0	1.7	0.9	0.2	0.4	0.3	0.2	0.1	0.6	1.0	1.2	1.6	10.1
Temperature Maximum:													
90° and above	0.0	0.0	0.3	0.7	2.2	12.8	24.4	22.2	9.9	1.8	0.0	0.0	74.3
32° and below	6.4	2.5	0.3	0.0	0.0	0.0	0.0	0.0	0.0	0.0	0.1	3.2	12.5
Temperature Minimum:													
32° and below	24.8	17.9	8.7	0.6	0.0	0.0	0.0	0.0	0.0	0.3	7.8	20.4	80.5
0° and below	0.7	0.1	0.0	0.0	0.0	0.0	0.0	0.0	0.0	0.0	0.0	0.3	1.1
RELATIVE HUMIDITY (%)													
Morning	72	70	68	69	78	79	72	73	79	76	75	74	74
Afternoon	60	56	53	52	58	59	53	53	58	53	58	60	56
PRECIPITATION (inches)													
Water Equivalent													
Normal	1.3	1.7	3.1	4.1	5.1	4.5	3.5	3.0	4.3	3.4	2.5	1.8	38.7
Maximum monthly	6.6	5.7	11.9	9.2	18.0	11.1	10.8	7.4	18.8	16.5	7.5	8.7	18.8
Date	1949	1985	1973	1947	1943	1948	1961	1942	1971	1941	1946	1984	1971
Minimum monthly	T	0.4	0.0	0.5	1.3	0.5	0.0	0.2	T	T	0.0	0.1	T
Date	1943	1947	1971	1950	1945	1963	1954	1945	1984	1952	1949	1950	1952
Maximum in 24 hrs	2.2	4.3	2.6	4.5	9.2	5.0	7.5	4.1	6.3	5.8	5.1	3.2	9.2
Date	1946	1985	1969	1964	1984	1941	1963	1942	1940	1983	1974	1984	1984
SNOW, ICE PELLETS													
Maximum monthly	12.7	10.1	11.8	1.7	0.0	0.0	0.0	0.0	0.0	T	5.6	9.9	12.7
Date	1979	1960	1968	1957	—	—	—	—	—	1967	1972	1958	1979
Maximum in 24 hrs	9.0	6.3	9.8	1.7	0.0	0.0	0.0	0.0	0.0	T	4.0	8.8	9.8
Date	1944	1944	1968	1957	—	—	—	—	—	1967	1972	1954	1968
WIND (Resultant)													
Mean speed (mph)	10.6	11.0	12.2	12.2	10.7	10.1	9.1	8.9	9.2	9.8	10.3	10.4	10.4

NORMALS, MEANS, EXTREMES

	JAN	FEB	MAR	APR	MAY	JUN	JUL	AUG	SEP	OCT	NOV	DEC	YEAR
TEMPERATURE													
Normal daily maximum	46.8	50.6	51.9	55.5	60.2	63.9	67.9	68.6	67.8	61.4	53.5	48.8	58.1
Normal daily minimum	35.4	37.1	36.9	39.7	44.1	49.2	52.2	52.6	49.2	44.3	39.7	37.3	43.1
Normal monthly	41.1	43.9	44.4	47.6	52.2	56.6	60.1	60.6	58.5	52.9	46.6	43.1	50.6
Extreme highest	65	72	73	83	87	93	100	96	95	85	71	64	100
Extreme highest date	1961	1968	1979	1956	1985	1955	1961	1981	1972	1980	1970	1980	1961
Extreme lowest	11	19	22	29	30	37	39	39	33	26	15	6	6
Extreme lowest date	1980	1979	1971	1968	1954	1980	1971	1973	1983	1971	1955	1972	1972
DEGREE DAYS BASE 65° F													
Heating	741	591	639	522	397	252	158	143	199	375	552	679	5248
Cooling	0	0	0	0	0	0	7	7	0	0	0	0	14
% OF POSSIBLE SUNSHINE	na	na	na	na	na	na	na	na	na	na	na	na	na
AVERAGE SKY COVER													
Sunrise - Sunset	8.4	8.3	8.1	7.9	7.6	7.7	6.7	6.6	6.3	7.2	8.0	8.4	7.6
NUMBER OF DAYS (Sunrise-Sunset)													
Clear	2.9	2.9	3.0	3.2	3.0	3.2	5.7	6.4	8.2	5.4	3.3	2.5	49.5
Partly cloudy	3.8	3.5	5.0	6.0	8.7	7.2	10.2	9.5	7.2	6.6	5.1	4.3	77.1
Cloudy	24.3	21.8	23.0	20.8	19.3	19.6	15.1	15.2	14.6	19.0	21.7	24.3	238.6
Precipitation .01" or more	21.8	19.7	20.5	18.4	15.0	13.3	7.2	8.4	10.8	16.4	20.3	22.8	194.6
Snow, Ice pellets 1.0" or more	0.8	0.1	0.3	*	0.0	0.0	0.0	0.0	0.0	0.0	0.1	0.4	1.7
Thunderstorms	0.6	0.3	0.5	0.6	0.3	0.3	0.4	0.4	0.9	1.0	1.1	1.0	7.3
Fog, Visibility 1/4 mile or less	3.9	2.9	2.5	2.2	1.7	1.5	2.0	4.2	5.6	6.8	3.8	4.0	41.1
Temperature Maximum:													
90° and above	0.0	0.0	0.0	0.0	0.0	0.1	0.1	0.1	0.2	0.0	0.0	0.0	0.5
32° and below	0.7	0.0	0.0	0.0	0.0	0.0	0.0	0.0	0.0	0.0	0.2	0.6	1.6
Temperature Minimum:													
32° and below	9.9	6.3	6.4	2.1	0.1	0.0	0.0	0.0	0.0	0.5	4.8	8.1	38.1
0° and below	0.0	0.0	0.0	0.0	0.0	0.0	0.0	0.0	0.0	0.0	0.0	0.0	0.0
RELATIVE HUMIDITY (%)													
Morning	86	87	87	88	89	90	89	91	90	89	87	86	88
Afternoon	78	74	71	69	70	71	69	70	70	73	77	80	73
PRECIPITATION (inches)													
Water Equivalent													
Normal	11.2	7.8	7.2	4.6	2.8	2.4	1.0	1.5	3.1	6.2	9.8	11.5	69.6
Maximum monthly	18.9	21.8	13.4	8.0	6.6	5.4	4.3	5.2	6.9	12.5	16.7	16.5	21.8
Date	1954	1961	1956	1955	1960	1954	1983	1968	1978	1975	1983	1955	1961
Minimum monthly	0.6	2.6	0.9	1.3	0.3	0.7	0.0	0.0	0.0	1.0	1.4	2.6	0.0
Date	1985	1973	1965	1956	1982	1965	1960	1970	1975	1978	1976	1985	1960
Maximum in 24 hrs	5.1	2.8	2.6	2.2	1.8	2.4	1.9	1.6	2.6	3.7	3.4	3.6	5.1
Date	1982	1961	1956	1965	1979	1968	1974	1968	1953	1982	1959	1974	1982
SNOW, ICE PELLETS													
Maximum monthly	26.3	4.0	6.7	1.1	T	0.0	0.0	0.0	T	T	4.6	19.0	26.3
Date	1969	1962	1966	1975	1985	—	—	—	1972	1984	1985	1964	1969
Maximum in 24 hrs	10.8	4.0	5.9	1.0	T	0.0	0.0	0.0	T	T	4.3	7.2	10.8
Date	1971	1962	1960	1975	1985	—	—	—	1972	1984	1985	1964	1971
WIND (Resultant)													
Mean speed (mph)	9.0	8.9	8.9	8.6	8.4	8.4	8.6	7.9	7.5	7.6	8.6	9.1	8.5

BURNS

Elev. 4151'　　　43° 35'N — 119° 03'W　　　**Oregon**

NORMALS, MEANS, EXTREMES

	JAN	FEB	MAR	APR	MAY	JUN	JUL	AUG	SEP	OCT	NOV	DEC	YEAR
TEMPERATURE													
Extreme highest	53	54	60	81	90	92	100	97	93	86	67	54	100
Extreme highest date	1981	1983	1981	1981	1983	1981	1980	1983	1981	1980	1980	1981	1980
Extreme lowest	-27	-10	16	16	22	23	28	28	20	7	2	-19	-27
Extreme lowest date	1982	1982	1981	1981	1982	1980	1981	1980	1983	1980	1982	1983	1982
DEGREE DAYS BASE 65° F													
Heating	1163	882	884	657	405	177	18	48	215	530	882	1163	7024
Cooling	0	0	0	0	5	42	155	116	32	0	0	0	350
% OF POSSIBLE SUNSHINE	na	na	na	na	na	na	na	na	na	na	na	na	na
AVERAGE SKY COVER													
Sunrise - Sunset	8.0	7.4	7.5	6.4	5.6	5.7	3.0	3.7	3.9	6.1	7.6	7.9	6.1
NUMBER OF DAYS (Sunrise-Sunset)													
Clear	2.7	4.0	5.3	6.0	8.3	8.0	20.7	16.0	15.0	8.7	4.7	3.3	102.7
Partly cloudy	7.0	6.0	4.0	10.3	11.7	11.7	6.0	9.7	7.7	7.7	4.3	5.7	91.7
Cloudy	21.3	18.0	21.7	13.7	11.0	10.3	4.3	5.3	7.3	14.7	21.0	22.0	170.7
Precipitation .01" or more	11.3	12.0	14.3	9.0	8.3	9.3	2.7	6.3	4.7	8.0	15.7	16.3	118.0
Snow, Ice pellets 1.0" or more	3.3	1.0	1.3	0.3	0.0	0.0	0.0	0.0	0.0	0.0	2.3	6.3	14.7
Temperature Maximum:													
90° and above	0.0	0.0	0.0	0.0	0.3	0.7	3.7	8.0	1.3	0.0	0.0	0.0	14.0
32° and below	10.0	7.0	0.0	0.0	0.0	0.0	0.0	0.0	0.0	0.0	4.0	12.0	33.0
Temperature Minimum:													
32° and below	30.0	25.3	26.7	22.3	11.7	2.7	0.3	0.3	7.7	23.0	26.0	30.7	206.7
0° and below	4.3	2.0	0.0	0.0	0.0	0.0	0.0	0.0	0.0	0.0	0.0	4.0	10.3
RELATIVE HUMIDITY (%)													
Morning	9	9	9	8	9	8	7	6	6	8	9	9	8
PRECIPITATION (inches)													
Water Equivalent													
Normal	1.5	0.9	0.8	0.6	0.7	0.5	0.2	0.4	0.4	0.7	1.1	1.5	10.1
Maximum monthly	1.1	2.1	3.6	1.1	2.1	0.9	1.0	0.7	1.0	1.4	2.6	3.8	3.8
Date	1982	1983	1983	1983	1981	1982	1983	1983	1982	1982	1981	1981	1981
Minimum monthly	0.7	0.9	0.6	0.5	0.6	0.3	0.2	0.0	0.0	0.8	0.5	1.3	0.0
Date	1981	1981	1980	1980	1982	1983	1981	1980	1983	1980	1980	1980	1980
Maximum in 24 hrs	0.3	0.6	0.6	0.5	0.8	0.4	0.8	0.1	0.5	0.8	0.6	0.6	0.8
Date	1982	1982	1983	1982	1983	1982	1983	1983	1982	1982	1981	1983	1982
SNOW, ICE PELLETS													
Maximum monthly	13.8	7.2	8.3	3.2	1.4	0.6	0.0	0.0	0.0	0.3	17.4	26.8	26.8
Date	1982	1983	1983	1982	1983	1981	—	—	—	1980	1983	1983	1983
Maximum in 24 hrs	3.9	2.5	4.5	1.7	0.7	0.6	0.0	0.0	0.0	0.3	7.0	6.5	7.0
Date	1982	1983	1983	1980	1983	1981	—	—	—	1980	1983	1981	1983

NORMALS, MEANS, EXTREMES

	JAN	FEB	MAR	APR	MAY	JUN	JUL	AUG	SEP	OCT	NOV	DEC	YEAR
TEMPERATURE													
Normal daily maximum	46.3	51.4	55.0	60.5	67.2	74.2	82.6	81.3	76.4	64.6	52.8	47.3	63.3
Normal daily minimum	33.8	35.5	36.5	38.7	42.9	48.0	51.0	51.1	47.7	42.0	37.8	35.3	41.7
Normal monthly	40.1	43.5	45.8	49.6	55.1	61.1	66.8	66.2	62.1	53.3	45.3	41.3	52.5
Extreme highest	67	71	77	86	92	100	105	108	101	94	76	68	108
Extreme highest date	1975	1968	1978	1957	1983	1961	1961	1981	1944	1980	1975	1979	1981
Extreme lowest	-4	-3	20	27	28	32	39	38	32	19	12	-12	-12
Extreme lowest date	1957	1950	1956	1983	1954	1976	1973	1969	1983	1971	1978	1972	1972
DEGREE DAYS BASE 65° F													
Heating	772	602	595	462	307	145	44	57	126	363	591	735	4799
Cooling	0	0	0	0	0	28	100	94	39	0	0	0	261
% OF POSSIBLE SUNSHINE	na	na	na	na	na	na	na	na	na	na	na	na	na
AVERAGE SKY COVER													
Sunrise - Sunset	8.5	8.4	8.0	7.5	6.8	6.3	3.8	4.6	5.1	7.1	8.4	8.9	6.9
NUMBER OF DAYS (Sunrise-Sunset)													
Clear	2.2	2.3	3.0	4.0	5.8	7.4	16.3	13.7	11.8	4.7	1.6	1.5	74.1
Partly cloudy	4.0	4.6	6.0	7.1	8.6	8.0	7.9	8.8	8.3	8.8	5.6	3.8	81.4
Cloudy	24.8	21.4	22.0	19.0	16.5	14.7	6.8	8.5	9.9	17.6	22.7	25.7	209.7
Precipitation .01" or more	17.5	15.3	16.6	12.6	10.0	6.9	2.2	3.9	6.0	11.5	16.4	18.6	137.7
Snow, Ice pellets 1.0" or more	1.2	0.1	0.3	0.0	0.0	0.0	0.0	0.0	0.0	0.0	0.1	0.5	2.2
Thunderstorms	0.2	0.1	0.2	0.5	0.8	0.7	0.5	0.6	0.5	0.2	0.2	0.2	4.7
Fog, Visibility 1/4 mile or less	8.6	6.5	3.7	2.2	1.3	0.9	0.4	0.9	4.6	11.4	9.5	9.2	59.1
Temperature Maximum:													
90° and above	0.0	0.0	0.0	0.0	0.1	1.2	6.3	4.7	2.3	*	0.0	0.0	14.7
32° and below	1.8	0.2	0.0	0.0	0.0	0.0	0.0	0.0	0.0	0.0	0.2	0.8	3.0
Temperature Minimum:													
32° and below	15.3	9.6	7.3	2.9	0.5	*	0.0	0.0	0.1	2.2	7.6	11.4	56.9
0° and below	0.1	*	0.0	0.0	0.0	0.0	0.0	0.0	0.0	0.0	0.0	0.1	0.2
RELATIVE HUMIDITY (%)													
Morning	91	92	91	90	91	90	87	88	89	94	93	92	91
Afternoon	80	72	64	57	53	49	38	40	43	63	78	84	60
PRECIPITATION (inches)													
Water Equivalent													
Normal	8.3	5.1	5.1	2.7	1.9	1.2	0.2	0.9	1.4	3.4	6.8	8.4	46.0
Maximum monthly	14.8	12.2	12.4	6.8	4.4	4.7	2.6	5.7	3.4	12.6	20.4	20.9	20.9
Date	1964	1983	1974	1982	1960	1952	1947	1968	1978	1950	1973	1964	1964
Minimum monthly	0.3	0.8	0.7	0.4	0.2	T	0.0	0.0	T	0.2	1.2	1.2	0.0
Date	1985	1964	1965	1985	1982	1951	1967	1967	1975	1978	1956	1976	1967
Maximum in 24 hrs	4.8	4.8	2.4	2.2	2.3	2.3	1.3	1.9	1.6	3.8	4.5	5.1	5.1
Date	1974	1984	1963	1971	1972	1952	1947	1983	1981	1955	1960	1981	1981
SNOW, ICE PELLETS													
Maximum monthly	47.1	4.8	10.8	T	T	T	0.0	0.0	T	T	6.0	10.2	47.1
Date	1969	1949	1951	1985	1984	1981	—	—	1971	1984	1955	1964	1969
Maximum in 24 hrs	22.9	2.5	4.9	T	T	T	0.0	0.0	T	T	5.0	6.3	22.9
Date	1969	1971	1951	1985	1984	1981	—	—	1971	1984	1955	1972	1969
WIND (Resultant)													
Mean speed (mph)	7.9	7.9	8.4	7.7	7.4	7.4	8.0	7.5	7.4	6.6	7.3	7.7	7.6

MEDFORD

Elev. 1298' 42° 22'N — 122° 52'W **Oregon**

NORMALS, MEANS, EXTREMES

	JAN	FEB	MAR	APR	MAY	JUN	JUL	AUG	SEP	OCT	NOV	DEC	YEAR
TEMPERATURE													
Normal daily maximum	45.0	52.9	57.1	63.8	72.2	81.0	90.7	88.8	82.8	68.7	52.6	44.2	66.7
Normal daily minimum	30.2	31.9	33.9	36.8	42.7	49.3	54.2	53.4	47.4	39.6	34.5	31.2	40.4
Normal monthly	37.6	42.4	45.5	50.3	57.5	65.2	72.5	71.1	65.1	54.2	43.6	37.7	53.5
Extreme highest	71	77	86	92	100	109	115	114	107	99	75	72	115
Extreme highest date	1981	1968	1930	1947	1941	1961	1946	1981	1955	1980	1970	1962	1946
Extreme lowest	-3	6	16	21	28	31	38	39	29	18	10	-6	-6
Extreme lowest date	1930	1950	1956	1936	1968	1952	1976	1962	1950	1971	1978	1972	1972
DEGREE DAYS BASE 65° F													
Heating	849	633	605	441	245	85	6	19	92	335	642	846	4798
Cooling	0	0	0	0	12	91	239	208	95	0	0	0	645
% OF POSSIBLE SUNSHINE	na	na	na	na	na	na	na	na	na	na	na	na	na
AVERAGE SKY COVER													
Sunrise - Sunset	8.2	7.7	7.3	6.7	5.7	4.7	2.1	2.5	3.3	5.6	7.8	8.6	5.9
NUMBER OF DAYS (Sunrise-Sunset)													
Clear	2.6	3.4	5.2	5.9	9.3	12.6	23.3	21.5	17.7	10.0	3.6	1.9	117.1
Partly cloudy	4.9	5.7	6.5	8.4	8.8	8.3	5.2	5.8	6.6	8.4	5.9	4.0	78.3
Cloudy	23.5	19.1	19.3	15.6	12.8	9.2	2.6	3.7	5.7	12.6	20.6	25.1	169.9
Precipitation .01" or more	13.5	11.4	11.7	9.2	8.1	5.3	1.5	2.1	4.2	7.9	12.3	14.5	101.6
Snow, Ice pellets 1.0" or more	1.2	0.5	0.3	0.1	0.0	0.0	0.0	0.0	0.0	*	0.1	0.5	2.7
Thunderstorms	*	0.2	0.2	0.8	1.7	1.8	1.5	1.2	0.9	0.2	*	*	8.6
Fog, Visibility 1/4 mile or less	11.8	5.8	1.6	0.4	0.3	0.2	*	0.1	0.5	4.6	10.5	13.5	49.4
Temperature Maximum:													
90° and above	0.0	0.0	0.0	0.0	1.7	7.5	18.3	16.5	8.1	0.8	0.0	0.0	53.0
32° and below	1.2	0.0	0.0	0.0	0.0	0.0	0.0	0.0	0.0	0.0	*	2.2	3.4
Temperature Minimum:													
32° and below	20.2	15.2	12.3	7.4	1.0	0.0	0.0	0.0	0.2	4.5	10.5	16.1	87.3
0° and below	*	0.0	0.0	0.0	0.0	0.0	0.0	0.0	0.0	0.0	0.0	0.2	0.2
RELATIVE HUMIDITY (%)													
Morning	90	88	86	84	82	78	73	74	79	87	91	90	84
Afternoon	72	59	50	45	39	33	26	28	31	46	69	76	48
PRECIPITATION (inches)													
Water Equivalent													
Normal	3.4	2.1	1.8	1.0	1.1	0.6	0.2	0.4	0.7	1.6	2.8	3.4	19.8
Maximum monthly	6.6	5.6	5.5	3.0	4.5	3.4	1.6	2.8	4.2	9.1	8.6	12.7	12.7
Date	1936	1983	1957	1965	1945	1931	1966	1976	1977	1950	1942	1964	1964
Minimum monthly	0.1	0.2	0.2	0.1	T	0.0	0.0	0.0	0.0	T	0.0	0.3	0.0
Date	1984	1964	1969	1949	1982	1951	1970	1981	1974	1936	1936	1976	1981
Maximum in 24 hrs	3.1	2.9	1.6	1.0	1.6	1.9	1.0	1.1	3.0	2.9	2.9	3.7	3.7
Date	1943	1956	1972	1965	1956	1931	1966	1945	1977	1950	1953	1964	1964
SNOW, ICE PELLETS													
Maximum monthly	22.6	11.6	8.1	4.2	T	0.0	0.0	0.0	0.0	1.3	11.4	12.2	22.6
Date	1930	1956	1956	1953	1984	—	—	—	—	1956	1955	1972	1930
Maximum in 24 hrs	9.3	5.2	7.9	4.2	T	0.0	0.0	0.0	0.0	1.3	8.5	4.2	9.3
Date	1971	1956	1956	1953	1984	—	—	—	—	1956	1977	1964	1971
WIND (Resultant)													
Mean speed (mph)	4.1	4.6	5.3	5.7	5.7	5.9	5.8	5.3	4.5	3.7	3.6	3.6	4.8

PENDLETON

Elev. 1482'   45° 41'N — 118° 51'W   **Oregon**

NORMALS, MEANS, EXTREMES

	JAN	FEB	MAR	APR	MAY	JUN	JUL	AUG	SEP	OCT	NOV	DEC	YEAR
TEMPERATURE													
Normal daily maximum	39.4	46.9	53.4	61.4	70.6	79.6	88.9	85.9	77.1	63.7	48.7	42.5	63.2
Normal daily minimum	26.3	31.8	34.4	39.2	46.1	52.9	58.6	57.5	50.5	41.3	33.4	29.5	41.8
Normal monthly	32.9	39.4	43.9	50.3	58.4	66.3	73.8	71.7	63.8	52.5	41.1	36.0	52.5
Extreme highest	68	69	79	91	99	108	110	113	102	92	77	67	113
Extreme highest date	1974	1982	1964	1977	1936	1961	1939	1961	1955	1980	1975	1980	1961
Extreme lowest	-22	-18	10	18	25	36	42	40	30	11	-12	-19	-22
Extreme lowest date	1957	1950	1955	1936	1954	1966	1971	1980	1970	1935	1985	1983	1957
DEGREE DAYS BASE 65° F													
Heating	998	717	654	441	220	75	7	27	120	388	717	899	5263
Cooling	0	0	0	0	16	111	280	235	84	0	0	0	726
% OF POSSIBLE SUNSHINE	na	na	na	na	na	na	na	na	na	na	na	na	na
AVERAGE SKY COVER													
Sunrise - Sunset	8.4	8.1	7.3	6.8	6.1	5.4	2.9	3.4	4.2	5.8	7.8	8.3	6.2
NUMBER OF DAYS (Sunrise-Sunset)													
Clear	2.4	2.6	4.9	5.5	7.6	9.7	19.9	18.2	14.7	9.9	3.6	2.6	101.8
Partly cloudy	5.3	5.5	7.4	9.3	10.7	10.1	7.5	7.7	8.0	7.8	6.4	4.6	90.2
Cloudy	23.3	20.1	18.7	15.2	12.7	10.2	3.6	5.1	7.3	13.3	19.9	23.8	173.3
Precipitation .01" or more	12.5	11.0	10.7	9.0	7.8	6.7	2.6	3.2	4.5	7.6	11.3	13.0	99.9
Snow, Ice pellets 1.0" or more	2.7	1.0	0.3	0.1	0.0	0.0	0.0	0.0	0.0	*	0.6	1.4	6.2
Thunderstorms	0.0	*	0.2	0.7	1.8	1.9	1.8	2.1	1.1	0.3	0.1	*	10.0
Fog, Visibility 1/4 mile or less	7.2	4.6	1.7	0.3	0.3	0.1	0.0	*	0.3	1.1	6.1	8.1	29.8
Temperature Maximum:													
90° and above	0.0	0.0	0.0	*	0.8	4.5	14.7	10.5	2.7	*	0.0	0.0	33.3
32° and below	9.7	2.7	0.2	0.0	0.0	0.0	0.0	0.0	0.0	0.0	2.2	7.0	21.8
Temperature Minimum:													
32° and below	21.3	15.6	9.7	2.6	0.1	0.0	0.0	0.0	0.1	2.5	12.8	18.8	83.5
0° and below	1.9	0.6	0.0	0.0	0.0	0.0	0.0	0.0	0.0	0.0	0.1	0.5	3.1
RELATIVE HUMIDITY (%)													
Morning	81	79	73	71	69	66	54	54	62	73	80	81	70
Afternoon	75	65	49	41	37	32	23	26	33	47	70	78	48
PRECIPITATION (inches)													
Water Equivalent													
Normal	1.7	1.1	1.0	0.9	1.0	0.7	0.3	0.5	0.5	0.9	1.4	1.6	12.2
Maximum monthly	3.9	3.0	2.8	2.7	3.0	2.7	1.2	2.5	2.3	2.7	3.7	4.6	4.6
Date	1970	1940	1983	1978	1962	1947	1948	1977	1941	1947	1973	1973	1973
Minimum monthly	0.2	0.0	0.2	0.0	0.0	0.1	T	0.0	T	T	0.0	0.2	0.0
Date	1949	1964	1941	1956	1964	1940	1967	1969	1974	1978	1939	1965	1969
Maximum in 24 hrs	1.2	1.0	1.3	1.0	1.5	1.4	1.1	1.4	1.2	1.8	1.3	1.2	1.8
Date	1956	1959	1983	1978	1972	1947	1948	1977	1981	1982	1971	1978	1982
SNOW, ICE PELLETS													
Maximum monthly	41.6	15.8	4.9	2.2	T	0.0	0.0	0.0	0.0	3.2	14.9	26.6	41.6
Date	1950	1936	1971	1975	1978	—	—	—	—	1973	1985	1983	1950
Maximum in 24 hrs	13.3	9.7	4.0	2.2	T	0.0	0.0	0.0	0.0	3.2	8.0	9.9	13.3
Date	1950	1949	1970	1975	1978	—	—	—	—	1973	1977	1948	1950
WIND (Resultant)													
Mean speed (mph)	8.1	8.7	9.7	10.3	9.9	10.1	9.2	8.9	8.7	7.9	7.8	8.1	9.0

PORTLAND

Elev. 21' 45° 36'N — 122° 36'W **Oregon**

NORMALS, MEANS, EXTREMES

	JAN	FEB	MAR	APR	MAY	JUN	JUL	AUG	SEP	OCT	NOV	DEC	YEAR
TEMPERATURE													
Normal daily maximum	44.3	50.4	54.5	60.2	66.9	72.7	79.5	78.6	74.2	63.9	52.3	46.4	62.0
Normal daily minimum	33.5	36.0	37.4	40.6	46.4	52.2	55.8	55.8	51.1	44.6	38.6	35.4	44.0
Normal monthly	38.9	43.2	46.0	50.4	56.7	62.5	67.7	67.2	62.7	54.3	45.5	40.9	53.0
Extreme highest	62	70	80	87	100	100	107	107	101	90	73	64	107
Extreme highest date	1984	1968	1947	1957	1983	1982	1965	1981	1944	1980	1975	1980	1981
Extreme lowest	-2	-3	19	29	29	39	43	44	34	26	13	6	-3
Extreme lowest date	1950	1950	1955	1955	1954	1966	1955	1980	1965	1971	1985	1964	1950
DEGREE DAYS BASE 65° F													
Heating	809	610	592	438	263	118	35	51	111	332	585	747	4691
Cooling	0	0	0	0	6	43	119	122	42	0	0	0	332
% OF POSSIBLE SUNSHINE	27	37	47	53	58	55	70	66	61	42	29	22	47
AVERAGE SKY COVER													
Sunrise - Sunset	8.4	8.3	8.1	7.7	7.2	6.8	4.7	5.2	5.6	7.2	8.2	8.7	7.2
NUMBER OF DAYS (Sunrise-Sunset)													
Clear	2.9	2.5	3.2	3.8	4.8	6.2	13.1	11.1	10.0	5.3	3.1	2.0	67.9
Partly cloudy	3.5	3.6	4.4	5.8	7.3	7.4	8.8	9.5	8.0	7.0	4.1	3.1	72.4
Cloudy	24.6	22.1	23.4	20.4	19.0	16.5	9.1	10.4	12.0	18.7	22.9	25.9	225.0
Precipitation .01" or more	18.2	16.4	17.1	14.0	11.6	9.5	3.7	5.1	7.9	12.9	17.9	19.0	153.3
Snow, Ice pellets 1.0" or more	1.2	0.2	0.1	0.0	*	0.0	0.0	0.0	0.0	0.0	0.2	0.5	2.3
Thunderstorms	*	0.1	0.5	0.8	1.4	0.9	0.8	1.0	0.7	0.4	0.3	*	7.1
Fog, Visibility 1/4 mile or less	4.3	3.7	2.3	1.1	0.2	0.1	0.1	0.2	3.0	7.6	6.2	4.9	33.6
Temperature Maximum:													
90° and above	0.0	0.0	0.0	0.0	0.2	1.2	3.6	3.4	1.5	*	0.0	0.0	10.0
32° and below	2.6	0.3	*	0.0	0.0	0.0	0.0	0.0	0.0	0.0	0.3	0.8	4.0
Temperature Minimum:													
32° and below	13.6	8.2	5.1	1.1	0.1	0.0	0.0	0.0	0.0	0.6	5.5	9.4	43.6
0° and below	*	*	0.0	0.0	0.0	0.0	0.0	0.0	0.0	0.0	0.0	0.0	*
RELATIVE HUMIDITY (%)													
Morning	86	86	86	86	85	84	82	83	87	90	88	87	86
Afternoon	76	68	60	55	53	49	45	46	49	63	74	79	60
PRECIPITATION (inches)													
Water Equivalent													
Normal	6.1	3.9	3.6	2.3	2.0	1.4	0.4	1.1	1.6	3.0	5.1	6.4	37.3
Maximum monthly	12.8	9.4	7.5	4.7	4.5	4.0	2.6	4.5	3.9	8.0	11.5	11.1	12.8
Date	1953	1949	1957	1955	1945	1984	1983	1968	1982	1947	1942	1968	1953
Minimum monthly	0.0	0.7	1.1	0.5	0.4	0.0	0.0	T	T	0.3	0.7	1.3	0.0
Date	1985	1964	1965	1956	1982	1951	1967	1970	1975	1978	1976	1976	1967
Maximum in 24 hrs	2.6	2.0	1.8	1.4	1.4	1.8	1.0	1.5	2.3	2.1	2.6	2.5	2.6
Date	1974	1982	1943	1962	1968	1958	1978	1977	1982	1941	1973	1977	1973
SNOW, ICE PELLETS													
Maximum monthly	41.4	13.2	12.9	T	0.6	T	0.0	0.0	T	0.2	8.2	15.7	41.4
Date	1950	1949	1951	1985	1953	1981	—	—	1949	1950	1955	1968	1950
Maximum in 24 hrs	10.6	3.2	7.7	T	0.5	T	0.0	0.0	T	0.2	7.4	8.0	10.6
Date	1950	1962	1951	1985	1953	1981	—	—	1949	1950	1977	1964	1950
WIND (Resultant)													
Mean speed (mph)	10.0	9.1	8.3	7.4	7.0	7.1	7.6	7.1	6.5	6.5	8.7	9.6	7.9

SALEM

Elev. 196' **44° 55'N — 123° 00'W** **Oregon**

NORMALS, MEANS, EXTREMES

	JAN	FEB	MAR	APR	MAY	JUN	JUL	AUG	SEP	OCT	NOV	DEC	YEAR
TEMPERATURE													
Normal daily maximum	45.7	51.1	54.6	60.3	67.3	73.9	82.2	81.2	76.2	64.5	52.6	47.0	63.1
Normal daily minimum	32.8	34.3	35.0	37.4	42.3	47.8	50.3	50.7	47.0	41.4	36.8	34.4	40.9
Normal monthly	39.3	42.7	44.8	48.9	54.8	60.9	66.3	66.0	61.6	53.0	44.7	40.7	52.0
Extreme highest	65	72	80	88	100	102	108	108	103	93	72	66	108
Extreme highest date	1984	1968	1947	1957	1983	1982	1941	1981	1944	1970	1970	1980	1981
Extreme lowest	-10	-4	12	23	25	32	37	36	26	23	9	-12	-12
Extreme lowest date	1950	1950	1971	1968	1954	1976	1962	1980	1972	1971	1955	1972	1972
DEGREE DAYS BASE 65° F													
Heating	797	624	626	483	316	152	46	65	131	372	609	753	4974
Cooling	0	0	0	0	0	29	87	93	29	0	0	0	238
% OF POSSIBLE SUNSHINE	na	na	na	na	na	na	na	na	na	na	na	na	na
AVERAGE SKY COVER													
Sunrise - Sunset	8.3	8.2	7.9	7.4	6.9	6.4	4.1	4.7	5.1	6.9	8.1	8.7	6.9
NUMBER OF DAYS (Sunrise-Sunset)													
Clear	2.8	3.0	3.5	4.2	5.8	7.0	15.1	13.5	11.2	5.8	2.9	2.0	76.7
Partly cloudy	4.6	4.8	6.1	7.2	7.7	8.1	8.6	8.6	8.4	8.3	5.2	3.7	81.3
Cloudy	23.6	20.5	21.4	16.6	17.5	14.9	7.3	8.9	10.4	17.0	21.9	25.3	207.3
Precipitation .01" or more	18.0	16.4	17.1	13.7	10.8	8.0	3.0	4.2	7.1	12.8	17.9	19.2	148.2
Snow, Ice pellets 1.0" or more	1.0	0.2	0.2	0.0	0.0	0.0	0.0	0.0	0.0	0.0	0.1	0.5	2.1
Thunderstorms	0.1	0.1	0.2	0.5	0.9	0.5	0.8	0.8	0.9	0.4	0.2	0.1	5.4
Fog, Visibility 1/4 mile or less	6.6	4.2	2.1	0.7	0.4	0.1	*	0.3	2.0	6.9	6.7	7.2	37.4
Temperature Maximum:													
90° and above	0.0	0.0	0.0	0.0	0.1	1.8	6.1	5.7	2.0	0.1	0.0	0.0	15.8
32° and below	1.4	*	0.0	0.0	0.0	0.0	0.0	0.0	0.0	0.0	0.3	1.3	3.0
Temperature Minimum:													
32° and below	14.6	11.7	10.6	6.9	1.1	*	0.0	0.0	0.3	3.3	8.6	12.5	69.6
0° and below	0.0	0.0	0.0	0.0	0.0	0.0	0.0	0.0	0.0	0.0	0.0	0.2	0.2
RELATIVE HUMIDITY (%)													
Morning	86	87	87	87	86	86	85	86	87	90	90	87	87
Afternoon	75	69	61	57	53	50	40	41	46	61	76	80	59
PRECIPITATION (inches)													
Water Equivalent													
Normal	7.0	4.5	4.3	2.4	1.9	1.2	0.3	0.7	1.5	3.3	5.7	7.1	40.3
Maximum monthly	15.4	12.3	8.5	5.1	4.5	4.1	2.6	4.1	3.9	11.1	15.2	12.4	15.4
Date	1953	1949	1983	1955	1942	1984	1983	1968	1971	1947	1973	1964	1953
Minimum monthly	0.2	0.7	0.8	0.3	0.1	0.0	0.0	T	0.0	0.3	0.8	1.2	0.0
Date	1985	1964	1965	1939	1947	1951	1967	1984	1975	1978	1939	1976	1975
Maximum in 24 hrs	3.0	3.1	3.0	2.2	1.8	1.7	1.2	1.2	1.8	2.8	2.8	2.7	3.1
Date	1972	1949	1943	1971	1963	1985	1983	1943	1951	1955	1950	1964	1949
SNOW, ICE PELLETS													
Maximum monthly	32.8	8.4	10.9	0.1	T	0.0	0.0	0.0	T	T	6.1	14.6	32.8
Date	1950	1962	1951	1972	1984	—	—	—	1981	1974	1977	1972	1950
Maximum in 24 hrs	10.8	5.4	8.5	0.1	T	0.0	0.0	0.0	T	T	6.1	9.4	10.8
Date	1943	1962	1960	1972	1984	—	—	—	1981	1974	1977	1972	1943
WIND (Resultant)													
Mean speed (mph)	8.1	7.7	7.9	7.1	6.5	6.5	6.5	6.2	6.1	6.1	7.4	8.0	7.0

NORMALS, MEANS, EXTREMES

	JAN	FEB	MAR	APR	MAY	JUN	JUL	AUG	SEP	OCT	NOV	DEC	YEAR
TEMPERATURE													
Normal daily maximum	34.9	37.8	47.6	61.0	71.1	80.1	84.6	82.4	75.3	64.2	51.3	39.2	60.8
Normal daily minimum	19.5	20.9	29.2	39.0	48.8	58.3	63.0	61.6	54.1	42.6	33.6	23.8	41.2
Normal monthly	27.2	29.4	38.4	50.0	60.0	69.2	73.8	72.0	64.7	53.4	42.5	31.5	51.0
Extreme highest	72	76	86	93	97	100	105	100	99	90	81	72	105
Extreme highest date	1950	1985	1945	1976	1962	1966	1966	1955	1980	1951	1950	1984	1966
Extreme lowest	-12	-7	-1	16	28	39	48	43	30	22	11	-8	-12
Extreme lowest date	1961	1967	1967	1982	1947	1972	1976	1982	1947	1969	1976	1950	1961
DEGREE DAYS BASE 65° F													
Heating	1172	1000	822	450	190	12	0	6	85	364	675	1039	5815
Cooling	0	0	0	0	35	138	273	226	79	0	0	0	751
% OF POSSIBLE SUNSHINE	35	50	45	53	0.0	0.0	40	47	59	45	42	35	0.0
AVERAGE SKY COVER													
Sunrise - Sunset	6.7	6.4	6.4	6.4	6.5	6.0	5.9	5.8	5.7	5.6	6.6	6.7	6.2
NUMBER OF DAYS (Sunrise-Sunset)													
Clear	6.9	7.1	7.5	6.9	6.6	7.2	8.3	8.7	9.4	10.5	6.6	7.0	92.7
Partly cloudy	8.2	7.9	8.6	9.2	10.7	11.3	12.1	11.1	9.0	8.7	8.1	7.5	112.5
Cloudy	16.0	13.3	14.8	14.0	13.7	11.5	10.7	11.1	11.5	11.9	15.3	16.5	160.1
Precipitation .01" or more	11.0	9.6	11.4	11.3	12.3	10.6	10.1	9.8	8.9	8.0	10.1	11.0	124.1
Snow, Ice pellets 1.0" or more	2.4	2.2	1.5	0.3	0.0	0.0	0.0	0.0	0.0	*	0.5	2.0	8.9
Thunderstorms	0.2	0.3	0.8	2.2	4.4	6.0	7.0	6.1	3.1	1.0	0.7	0.1	32.0
Fog, Visibility 1/4 mile or less	2.7	2.5	2.5	1.5	2.0	1.2	1.0	1.8	2.7	3.0	2.7	3.0	26.6
Temperature Maximum:													
90° and above	0.0	0.0	0.0	0.1	0.5	3.5	6.7	3.9	1.2	*	0.0	0.0	16.0
32° and below	11.8	7.7	1.5	*	0.0	0.0	0.0	0.0	0.0	0.0	0.0	0.3	7.4	28.9
Temperature Minimum:													
32° and below	28.2	25.0	20.4	6.5	0.3	0.0	0.0	0.0	0.1	3.6	14.2	25.8	124.0
0° and below	1.4	0.6	*	0.0	0.0	0.0	0.0	0.0	0.0	0.0	0.0	0.4	2.5
RELATIVE HUMIDITY (%)													
Morning	74	73	71	71	77	81	82	85	86	83	79	77	78
Afternoon	62	59	54	50	52	54	52	55	57	56	60	63	56
PRECIPITATION (inches)													
Water Equivalent													
Normal	3.3	3.0	3.8	3.9	3.5	3.4	4.1	4.4	4.0	3.0	3.7	3.7	44.3
Maximum monthly	8.4	5.4	7.2	10.0	10.6	8.5	10.4	12.1	8.7	6.8	9.6	7.8	12.1
Date	1979	1971	1953	1952	1984	1972	1969	1955	1985	1955	1972	1973	1955
Minimum monthly	0.6	1.0	0.9	0.6	0.0	0.3	0.4	0.9	0.9	0.1	0.6	0.3	0.0
Date	1981	1980	1981	1985	1964	1949	1955	1980	1967	1963	1976	1955	1964
Maximum in 24 hrs	2.4	2.0	3.0	2.5	3.3	3.5	4.5	5.8	7.8	2.9	3.4	2.8	7.8
Date	1949	1966	1952	1968	1984	1967	1969	1982	1985	1955	1972	1983	1985
SNOW, ICE PELLETS													
Maximum monthly	24.1	29.5	30.5	13.4	T	0.0	0.0	0.0	0.0	1.4	7.8	28.4	30.5
Date	1966	1983	1958	1982	1977	—	—	—	—	1972	1967	1966	1958
Maximum in 24 hrs	16.0	25.2	17.5	11.4	T	0.0	0.0	0.0	0.0	1.4	6.4	13.3	25.2
Date	1961	1983	1958	1982	1977	—	—	—	—	1972	1968	1966	1983
WIND (Resultant)													
Mean speed (mph)	10.7	11.1	11.7	11.0	9.1	8.1	7.2	6.8	7.3	8.2	9.7	10.1	9.2

AVOCA

Elev. 930' **41° 20'N — 75° 44'W** # Pennsylvania

NORMALS, MEANS, EXTREMES

	JAN	FEB	MAR	APR	MAY	JUN	JUL	AUG	SEP	OCT	NOV	DEC	YEAR
TEMPERATURE													
Normal daily maximum	32.1	34.4	44.1	58.2	69.1	77.8	82.1	80.0	72.7	61.4	48.2	36.3	58.0
Normal daily minimum	18.2	19.2	28.1	38.4	48.1	56.9	61.4	60.0	52.8	42.0	33.6	23.1	40.1
Normal monthly	25.2	26.8	36.1	48.3	58.6	67.4	71.8	70.0	62.8	51.7	40.9	29.7	49.1
Extreme highest	67	71	83	92	93	97	101	94	95	84	80	67	101
Extreme highest date	1967	1985	1977	1976	1962	1964	1966	1983	1983	1959	1982	1984	1966
Extreme lowest	-14	-16	-4	14	27	34	43	38	30	19	9	-7	-16
Extreme lowest date	1985	1979	1967	1982	1974	1972	1979	1982	1974	1972	1976	1980	1979
DEGREE DAYS BASE 65° F													
Heating	1234	1070	896	501	227	34	7	10	117	417	723	1094	6330
Cooling	0	0	0	0	29	106	218	165	51	0	0	0	569
% OF POSSIBLE SUNSHINE	43	47	49	53	56	60	62	60	55	51	36	35	51
AVERAGE SKY COVER													
Sunrise - Sunset	7.5	7.3	7.2	6.8	6.7	6.2	6.1	6.1	6.1	6.3	7.6	7.8	6.8
NUMBER OF DAYS (Sunrise-Sunset)													
Clear	4.2	4.4	5.2	6.4	5.8	7.0	6.3	6.9	7.2	8.0	3.8	3.8	69.0
Partly cloudy	7.3	6.9	7.5	7.4	9.6	10.9	12.8	11.9	10.0	8.4	6.6	6.5	105.9
Cloudy	19.5	16.9	18.3	16.2	15.6	12.2	11.9	12.2	12.8	14.6	19.5	20.7	190.4
Precipitation .01" or more	12.2	11.1	13.1	12.3	12.8	11.9	11.3	10.8	9.5	9.5	12.1	13.2	139.8
Snow, Ice pellets 1.0" or more	3.3	2.9	2.8	0.7	*	0.0	0.0	0.0	0.0	*	0.9	2.6	13.3
Thunderstorms	0.1	0.3	1.0	2.2	3.6	6.0	7.1	5.0	2.7	1.0	0.4	0.2	29.5
Fog, Visibility 1/4 mile or less	2.0	2.0	2.1	1.5	1.3	1.2	1.5	1.9	2.6	2.2	1.9	2.4	22.7
Temperature Maximum:													
90° and above	0.0	0.0	0.0	0.1	0.3	1.7	2.8	1.7	0.5	0.0	0.0	0.0	7.0
32° and below	16.6	12.1	3.9	0.2	0.0	0.0	0.0	0.0	0.0	0.0	1.3	11.2	45.3
Temperature Minimum:													
32° and below	28.4	24.8	22.1	8.9	0.8	0.0	0.0	0.0	0.2	4.2	13.8	25.5	128.6
0° and below	2.3	1.5	0.1	0.0	0.0	0.0	0.0	0.0	0.0	0.0	0.0	0.6	4.5
RELATIVE HUMIDITY (%)													
Morning	72	71	69	66	72	79	80	83	83	78	75	75	75
Afternoon	66	64	59	52	52	56	56	58	60	59	65	68	60
PRECIPITATION (inches)													
Water Equivalent													
Normal	2.2	2.0	2.6	3.0	3.1	3.4	3.3	3.4	3.3	2.7	2.9	2.5	35.0
Maximum monthly	6.4	8.0	4.8	9.5	7.3	7.2	6.8	5.2	7.8	8.1	7.6	6.5	9.5
Date	1979	1981	1977	1983	1972	1982	1969	1965	1985	1976	1972	1983	1983
Minimum monthly	0.3	0.3	0.4	1.1	0.7	0.2	1.2	1.2	0.8	0.0	0.8	0.3	0.0
Date	1980	1968	1981	1975	1959	1966	1972	1980	1964	1963	1976	1958	1963
Maximum in 24 hrs	1.8	3.1	2.2	3.8	2.5	3.6	2.3	3.1	6.5	3.2	2.9	2.8	6.5
Date	1978	1981	1964	1983	1972	1973	1969	1966	1985	1976	1972	1983	1985
SNOW, ICE PELLETS													
Maximum monthly	28.8	22.0	29.7	26.7	2.4	0.0	0.0	0.0	T	4.4	22.5	33.9	33.9
Date	1978	1964	1967	1983	1977	—	—	—	1956	1962	1971	1969	1969
Maximum in 24 hrs	20.1	13.3	15.5	12.2	2.4	0.0	0.0	0.0	T	4.4	20.5	12.4	20.5
Date	1964	1961	1960	1983	1977	—	—	—	1956	1962	1971	1969	1971
WIND (Resultant)													
Mean speed (mph)	9.0	9.1	9.4	9.6	8.6	7.9	7.3	7.0	7.4	7.9	8.6	8.9	8.4

ERIE

Elev. 731' 42° 05'N — 80° 11'W **Pennsylvania**

NORMALS, MEANS, EXTREMES

	JAN	FEB	MAR	APR	MAY	JUN	JUL	AUG	SEP	OCT	NOV	DEC	YEAR
TEMPERATURE													
Normal daily maximum	30.9	32.2	41.1	53.7	64.6	74.0	78.2	77.0	71.0	60.1	47.1	35.7	55.5
Normal daily minimum	18.0	17.7	25.8	36.1	45.4	55.2	59.9	59.4	53.1	43.2	34.3	24.2	39.4
Normal monthly	24.5	25.0	33.5	44.9	55.0	64.6	69.1	68.2	62.1	51.7	40.7	30.0	47.4
Extreme highest	65	67	79	85	89	92	94	92	94	88	80	75	94
Extreme highest date	1985	1957	1977	1958	1975	1964	1968	1978	1959	1963	1961	1982	1968
Extreme lowest	-16	-17	-9	12	26	32	44	37	33	24	7	-6	-17
Extreme lowest date	1985	1979	1980	1982	1970	1972	1963	1982	1974	1975	1976	1983	1979
DEGREE DAYS BASE 65° F													
Heating	1256	1120	977	603	323	80	17	28	130	420	729	1085	6768
Cooling	0	0	0	0	13	68	144	127	43	7	0	0	402
% OF POSSIBLE SUNSHINE	na	na	na	na	na	na	na	na	na	na	na	na	na
AVERAGE SKY COVER													
Sunrise - Sunset	8.6	8.0	7.5	6.8	6.4	5.7	5.5	5.8	6.2	6.7	8.4	9.0	7.1
NUMBER OF DAYS (Sunrise-Sunset)													
Clear	1.7	2.5	4.5	5.9	6.8	8.2	8.8	8.7	6.9	6.4	2.5	1.3	64.3
Partly cloudy	4.2	6.1	7.2	7.8	10.3	11.3	12.6	11.1	9.6	7.9	4.3	3.3	95.6
Cloudy	25.1	19.7	19.3	16.3	13.9	10.5	9.7	11.2	13.5	16.7	23.2	26.4	205.4
Precipitation .01" or more	18.6	14.9	15.3	13.9	12.0	10.2	9.5	10.9	10.7	12.4	16.2	19.1	163.6
Snow, Ice pellets 1.0" or more	7.8	4.9	3.5	0.8	0.0	0.0	0.0	0.0	0.0	0.2	2.5	6.8	26.5
Thunderstorms	0.2	0.5	1.5	3.0	4.0	6.0	6.7	7.0	4.2	2.4	1.7	0.4	37.5
Fog, Visibility 1/4 mile or less	1.0	1.6	2.7	1.8	2.0	0.9	0.4	0.5	0.3	0.4	0.9	0.8	13.4
Temperature Maximum:													
90° and above	0.0	0.0	0.0	0.0	0.0	0.4	0.5	0.2	0.1	0.0	0.0	0.0	1.1
32° and below	18.2	14.9	7.7	0.6	0.0	0.0	0.0	0.0	0.0	0.0	1.6	10.6	53.4
Temperature Minimum:													
32° and below	28.5	25.2	23.7	11.9	1.3	0.1	0.0	0.0	0.0	2.1	12.1	25.0	129.7
0° and below	2.6	2.3	0.3	0.0	0.0	0.0	0.0	0.0	0.0	0.0	0.0	0.4	5.6
RELATIVE HUMIDITY (%)													
Morning	75	77	75	72	77	80	81	82	81	75	75	76	77
Afternoon	73	71	66	61	63	65	64	65	66	64	69	73	67
PRECIPITATION (inches)													
Water Equivalent													
Normal	2.4	2.1	2.9	3.4	3.2	3.7	3.2	3.8	3.8	3.3	3.7	3.2	39.3
Maximum monthly	4.5	5.2	6.7	7.1	5.8	7.7	7.7	11.0	10.6	9.8	10.4	5.6	11.0
Date	1959	1981	1976	1961	1984	1957	1970	1977	1977	1954	1985	1977	1977
Minimum monthly	0.8	0.5	0.6	1.6	1.4	0.8	0.6	0.5	1.4	1.1	1.5	1.3	0.5
Date	1981	1978	1960	1975	1962	1963	1978	1959	1960	1963	1978	1960	1978
Maximum in 24 hrs	1.5	2.1	1.8	2.5	2.2	2.8	3.2	3.5	6.1	4.3	3.6	2.3	6.1
Date	1959	1961	1965	1977	1969	1957	1970	1980	1979	1954	1985	1979	1979
SNOW, ICE PELLETS													
Maximum monthly	62.4	32.1	26.8	17.2	0.1	0.0	0.0	0.0	0.0	4.0	36.3	59.9	62.4
Date	1978	1972	1971	1957	1963	—	—	—	—	1954	1967	1985	1978
Maximum in 24 hrs	12.7	17.8	12.0	10.0	0.2	0.0	0.0	0.0	0.0	2.3	23.0	13.1	23.0
Date	1985	1979	1965	1957	1963	—	—	—	—	1974	1956	1983	1956
WIND (Resultant)													
Mean speed (mph)	13.3	12.2	12.2	11.7	10.0	9.6	9.0	9.0	9.9	11.2	13.0	13.6	11.2

HARRISBURG

Elev. 338' 40° 13'N — 76° 51'W **Pennsylvania**

NORMALS, MEANS, EXTREMES

	JAN	FEB	MAR	APR	MAY	JUN	JUL	AUG	SEP	OCT	NOV	DEC	YEAR
TEMPERATURE													
Normal daily maximum	36.7	39.5	49.6	62.9	73.0	81.8	86.2	84.4	77.2	65.4	52.4	40.6	62.5
Normal daily minimum	22.1	23.5	31.5	41.5	51.0	60.5	65.3	64.2	56.6	44.6	35.4	26.2	43.5
Normal monthly	29.4	31.5	40.6	52.2	62.0	71.2	75.8	74.3	66.9	55.0	43.9	33.4	53.0
Extreme highest	73	75	86	93	97	100	107	101	102	97	84	75	107
Extreme highest date	1950	1985	1945	1985	1942	1966	1966	1944	1953	1941	1950	1984	1966
Extreme lowest	-9	-5	5	19	31	40	49	45	30	23	13	-8	-9
Extreme lowest date	1985	1979	1984	1982	1966	1980	1945	1976	1963	1969	1955	1960	1985
DEGREE DAYS BASE 65° F													
Heating	1104	938	756	384	150	12	0	0	58	320	633	980	5335
Cooling	0	0	0	0	57	198	335	291	115	10	0	0	1006
% OF POSSIBLE SUNSHINE	49	55	57	59	60	64	69	68	63	57	46	45	58
AVERAGE SKY COVER													
Sunrise - Sunset	6.7	6.5	6.6	6.5	6.5	6.1	6.0	5.9	5.7	5.8	6.8	6.9	6.3
NUMBER OF DAYS (Sunrise-Sunset)													
Clear	6.9	6.8	7.0	6.4	6.1	6.7	7.3	8.3	9.0	9.9	6.2	6.2	86.8
Partly cloudy	7.4	7.2	8.2	8.7	10.2	11.1	11.4	10.7	9.4	7.9	8.1	7.6	107.8
Cloudy	16.7	14.3	15.9	14.9	14.7	12.2	12.3	12.0	11.5	13.3	15.7	17.2	170.6
Precipitation .01" or more	10.9	10.3	12.1	12.4	13.6	11.0	9.1	10.0	7.1	9.9	10.6	10.4	127.4
Snow, Ice pellets 1.0" or more	3.0	2.6	1.3	0.6	0.0	0.0	0.0	0.0	0.0	0.0	0.3	1.9	9.6
Thunderstorms	0.2	0.2	1.1	2.3	5.2	6.3	7.0	5.3	2.9	0.8	0.5	0.2	31.9
Fog, Visibility 1/4 mile or less	2.3	2.3	1.7	1.0	0.9	0.6	0.6	0.8	1.6	2.7	1.8	2.4	18.8
Temperature Maximum:													
90° and above	0.0	0.0	0.0	0.3	1.0	4.6	8.7	6.1	2.0	0.1	0.0	0.0	22.7
32° and below	9.8	6.1	1.4	0.0	0.0	0.0	0.0	0.0	0.0	0.0	0.2	5.4	23.0
Temperature Minimum:													
32° and below	26.5	23.1	17.3	3.6	0.1	0.0	0.0	0.0	0.1	1.9	10.9	22.9	106.3
0° and below	0.7	0.2	0.0	0.0	0.0	0.0	0.0	0.0	0.0	0.0	0.0	0.2	1.1
RELATIVE HUMIDITY (%)													
Morning	69	68	67	67	73	79	79	82	80	79	73	70	74
Afternoon	58	55	52	49	52	53	52	55	55	55	57	58	54
PRECIPITATION (inches)													
Water Equivalent													
Normal	2.9	2.7	3.5	3.1	3.6	3.6	3.3	3.2	3.6	2.7	3.2	3.2	39.0
Maximum monthly	8.0	5.9	5.4	7.9	6.2	8.1	4.6	4.1	6.6	4.2	6.2	7.5	8.1
Date	1979	1981	1980	1983	1985	1982	1981	1981	1979	1983	1985	1983	1982
Minimum monthly	0.4	0.8	1.0	0.4	1.8	2.5	0.9	1.5	1.0	1.3	0.9	0.7	0.4
Date	1981	1980	1981	1985	1981	1980	1983	1980	1980	1985	1981	1980	1981
Maximum in 24 hrs	2.0	1.8	1.8	1.2	2.9	2.2	1.9	1.6	3.0	2.1	2.1	0.8	3.0
Date	1979	1985	1980	1980	1984	1984	1981	1981	1979	1980	1984	1979	1979
SNOW, ICE PELLETS													
Maximum monthly	18.8	28.8	14.9	10.2	0.0	0.0	0.0	0.0	0.0	T	4.0	12.5	28.8
Date	1982	1983	1984	1982	—	—	—	—	—	1982	1980	1981	1983
Maximum in 24 hrs	3.5	14.2	7.0	2.6	0.0	0.0	0.0	0.0	0.0	T	4.0	5.6	14.2
Date	1984	1979	1984	1985	—	—	—	—	—	1979	1980	1981	1979
WIND (Resultant)													
Mean speed (mph)	8.4	9.1	9.7	9.2	7.7	6.8	6.3	5.9	6.1	6.5	7.8	8.1	7.6

PHILADELPHIA   Elev. 5'   39° 53'N — 75° 15'W   Pennsylvania

NORMALS, MEANS, EXTREMES

	JAN	FEB	MAR	APR	MAY	JUN	JUL	AUG	SEP	OCT	NOV	DEC	YEAR
TEMPERATURE													
Normal daily maximum	38.6	41.1	50.5	63.2	73.0	81.7	86.1	84.6	77.8	66.5	54.5	43.0	63.4
Normal daily minimum	23.8	25.0	33.1	42.6	52.5	61.5	66.8	66.0	58.6	46.5	37.1	28.0	45.1
Normal monthly	31.2	33.1	41.8	52.9	62.8	71.6	76.5	75.3	68.2	56.5	45.8	35.5	54.3
Extreme highest	74	74	87	94	96	100	104	101	100	96	81	72	104
Extreme highest date	1950	1985	1945	1976	1962	1964	1966	1955	1953	1941	1974	1984	1966
Extreme lowest	-7	-4	7	19	28	44	51	45	35	25	15	1	-7
Extreme lowest date	1984	1961	1984	1982	1966	1984	1966	1965	1963	1969	1976	1983	1984
DEGREE DAYS BASE 65° F													
Heating	1048	893	719	363	127	0	0	0	33	273	576	915	4947
Cooling	0	0	0	0	59	202	357	319	129	9	0	0	1075
% OF POSSIBLE SUNSHINE	50	53	55	56	56	62	62	62	60	59	52	49	56
AVERAGE SKY COVER													
Sunrise - Sunset	6.6	6.3	6.4	6.4	6.5	6.2	6.0	5.9	5.6	5.6	6.3	6.5	6.2
NUMBER OF DAYS (Sunrise-Sunset)													
Clear	7.4	7.2	7.6	7.1	6.2	6.9	7.2	8.3	9.8	10.5	7.2	7.5	93.0
Partly cloudy	7.5	7.3	8.1	8.9	10.4	11.3	11.8	11.0	9.0	8.4	8.9	8.4	111.0
Cloudy	16.1	13.7	15.3	14.0	14.4	11.8	12.1	11.6	11.2	12.2	13.8	15.0	161.2
Precipitation .01" or more	11.0	9.2	11.1	10.7	11.4	10.2	9.2	9.1	7.9	7.6	9.4	10.1	116.9
Snow, Ice pellets 1.0" or more	2.0	1.6	1.1	0.1	0.0	0.0	0.0	0.0	0.0	*	0.2	0.9	6.0
Thunderstorms	0.2	0.3	1.0	2.0	4.3	5.4	5.6	5.2	2.3	0.7	0.5	0.2	27.5
Fog, Visibility 1/4 mile or less	2.8	2.4	1.8	1.3	1.4	1.2	0.9	1.1	1.6	3.4	2.5	2.7	23.0
Temperature Maximum:													
90° and above	0.0	0.0	0.0	0.4	0.5	3.5	7.5	5.8	2.0	0.0	0.0	0.0	19.7
32° and below	9.7	6.0	1.0	0.0	0.0	0.0	0.0	0.0	0.0	0.0	*	4.4	21.2
Temperature Minimum:													
32° and below	26.5	22.7	14.5	2.8	*	0.0	0.0	0.0	0.0	1.6	9.0	21.4	98.4
0° and below	0.5	0.2	0.0	0.0	0.0	0.0	0.0	0.0	0.0	0.0	0.0	0.0	0.7
RELATIVE HUMIDITY (%)													
Morning	70	68	68	68	76	80	81	82	82	80	75	72	75
Afternoon	59	56	53	48	53	54	54	55	55	54	56	59	55
PRECIPITATION (inches)													
Water Equivalent													
Normal	3.1	2.8	3.8	3.4	3.1	3.9	3.8	4.1	3.4	2.8	3.3	3.4	41.4
Maximum monthly	8.8	6.4	7.0	8.1	7.4	7.8	8.3	9.7	8.7	5.2	9.0	7.3	9.7
Date	1978	1979	1980	1983	1948	1973	1969	1955	1960	1943	1972	1983	1955
Minimum monthly	0.4	0.9	0.6	0.5	0.4	0.1	0.6	0.4	0.4	0.0	0.3	0.2	0.0
Date	1955	1980	1966	1985	1964	1949	1957	1964	1968	1963	1976	1955	1963
Maximum in 24 hrs	2.7	1.9	2.3	2.7	3.1	4.6	4.2	5.6	5.4	3.8	3.9	2.0	5.6
Date	1979	1966	1968	1970	1984	1973	1969	1971	1960	1980	1977	1978	1971
SNOW, ICE PELLETS													
Maximum monthly	23.4	27.6	13.4	4.3	T	0.0	0.0	0.0	0.0	2.1	8.8	18.8	27.6
Date	1978	1979	1958	1971	1963	—	—	—	—	1979	1953	1966	1979
Maximum in 24 hrs	13.2	21.3	10.0	4.3	T	0.0	0.0	0.0	0.0	2.1	8.7	14.6	21.3
Date	1961	1983	1958	1971	1963	—	—	—	—	1979	1953	1960	1983
WIND (Resultant)													
Mean speed (mph)	10.3	11.0	11.4	10.9	9.6	8.7	8.0	7.8	8.2	8.8	9.6	10.0	9.5

PITTSBURGH

Elev. 747'　　40° 30'N — 80° 13'W　　# Pennsylvania

NORMALS, MEANS, EXTREMES

	JAN	FEB	MAR	APR	MAY	JUN	JUL	AUG	SEP	OCT	NOV	DEC	YEAR
TEMPERATURE													
Normal daily maximum	34.1	36.8	47.6	60.7	70.8	79.1	82.7	81.1	74.8	62.9	49.8	38.4	59.9
Normal daily minimum	19.2	20.7	29.4	39.4	48.5	57.1	61.3	60.1	53.3	42.1	33.3	24.3	40.7
Normal monthly	26.7	28.8	38.5	50.1	59.7	68.1	72.0	70.6	64.1	52.5	41.6	31.4	50.3
Extreme highest	69	69	80	87	91	96	99	97	97	87	82	74	99
Extreme highest date	1985	1954	1977	1970	1962	1971	1954	1953	1954	1959	1961	1982	1954
Extreme lowest	-18	-12	-1	14	26	34	42	39	31	16	-1	-12	-18
Extreme lowest date	1985	1979	1980	1982	1970	1972	1963	1982	1959	1965	1958	1983	1985
DEGREE DAYS BASE 65° F													
Heating	1187	1014	822	447	201	28	0	13	101	393	702	1042	5950
Cooling	0	0	0	0	37	121	222	186	74	5	0	0	645
% OF POSSIBLE SUNSHINE	33	38	44	48	52	57	59	56	58	52	38	29	47
AVERAGE SKY COVER													
Sunrise - Sunset	8.1	7.8	7.6	7.2	6.9	6.4	6.3	6.3	6.1	6.3	7.7	8.2	7.1
NUMBER OF DAYS (Sunrise-Sunset)													
Clear	2.9	3.4	4.1	4.5	5.2	5.2	5.3	6.3	7.7	7.9	3.9	2.6	59.0
Partly cloudy	6.0	5.8	6.8	8.2	9.2	11.6	13.2	11.8	10.3	8.5	6.2	5.8	103.4
Cloudy	22.1	19.0	20.1	17.4	16.6	13.2	12.5	12.9	12.0	14.6	19.9	22.6	202.9
Precipitation .01" or more	16.5	14.1	16.1	13.5	12.3	11.5	10.8	9.8	9.2	10.6	13.2	16.5	154.1
Snow, Ice pellets 1.0" or more	3.9	3.0	2.3	0.4	0.1	0.0	0.0	0.0	0.0	0.1	1.1	2.7	13.6
Thunderstorms	0.1	0.3	1.8	3.3	5.0	6.7	7.0	5.6	3.1	1.3	0.6	0.3	35.3
Fog, Visibility 1/4 mile or less	1.4	1.2	1.0	0.9	1.2	1.1	1.7	2.1	2.4	1.8	1.5	1.7	17.8
Temperature Maximum:													
90° and above	0.0	0.0	0.0	0.0	0.2	1.4	2.5	1.2	0.7	0.0	0.0	0.0	6.1
32° and below	15.5	11.1	4.0	0.1	0.0	0.0	0.0	0.0	0.0	0.0	1.4	10.4	42.5
Temperature Minimum:													
32° and below	27.5	24.2	19.8	8.4	1.0	0.0	0.0	0.0	0.0	3.9	14.4	24.7	124.0
0° and below	2.8	1.7	0.1	0.0	0.0	0.0	0.0	0.0	0.0	0.0	*	0.8	5.4
RELATIVE HUMIDITY (%)													
Morning	72	70	69	66	72	77	80	82	81	76	75	74	75
Afternoon	65	62	58	50	52	52	53	56	56	54	62	67	57
PRECIPITATION (inches)													
Water Equivalent													
Normal	2.8	2.4	3.5	3.2	3.5	3.3	3.8	3.3	2.8	2.4	2.3	2.5	36.3
Maximum monthly	6.2	5.9	6.1	7.6	6.3	8.2	7.4	7.5	5.4	8.2	11.0	5.2	11.0
Date	1978	1956	1967	1964	1968	1981	1958	1975	1972	1954	1985	1978	1985
Minimum monthly	0.7	0.5	1.1	0.4	1.2	0.9	1.8	0.7	0.2	0.1	0.9	0.4	0.1
Date	1981	1969	1969	1971	1965	1967	1965	1957	1985	1963	1976	1955	1963
Maximum in 24 hrs	1.4	2.3	2.0	2.1	2.4	1.9	2.9	3.0	2.2	3.5	1.9	1.7	3.5
Date	1982	1975	1964	1964	1971	1955	1971	1956	1975	1954	1985	1978	1954
SNOW, ICE PELLETS													
Maximum monthly	40.2	24.2	21.3	7.2	3.1	0.0	0.0	0.0	0.0	1.8	11.0	21.2	40.2
Date	1978	1972	1960	1985	1966	—	—	—	—	1972	1958	1974	1978
Maximum in 24 hrs	14.0	12.3	14.7	4.8	3.1	0.0	0.0	0.0	0.0	1.8	10.5	12.5	14.7
Date	1966	1960	1962	1985	1966	—	—	—	—	1972	1958	1974	1962
WIND (Resultant)													
Mean speed (mph)	10.7	10.6	10.9	10.5	8.9	8.0	7.3	6.9	7.4	8.4	9.8	10.4	9.1

WILLIAMSPORT

Elev. 524'   **41° 15'N — 76° 55'W**   # Pennsylvania

NORMALS, MEANS, EXTREMES

	JAN	FEB	MAR	APR	MAY	JUN	JUL	AUG	SEP	OCT	NOV	DEC	YEAR
TEMPERATURE													
Normal daily maximum	34.1	36.8	46.8	60.6	71.2	79.7	83.7	82.0	74.5	63.0	49.6	38.1	60.0
Normal daily minimum	18.3	19.5	28.4	38.5	48.0	56.8	61.3	60.3	53.2	41.6	33.2	23.3	40.2
Normal monthly	26.2	28.2	37.6	49.6	59.6	68.3	72.5	71.2	63.9	52.3	41.4	30.7	50.1
Extreme highest	69	71	86	92	95	102	100	100	102	91	83	67	102
Extreme highest date	1967	1985	1977	1976	1969	1952	1966	1955	1953	1951	1950	1984	1953
Extreme lowest	-17	-13	-1	15	28	36	43	38	28	20	8	-15	-17
Extreme lowest date	1977	1971	1984	1982	1966	1945	1965	1965	1947	1972	1976	1950	1977
DEGREE DAYS BASE 65° F													
Heating	1203	1030	849	462	196	30	0	7	101	398	708	1063	6047
Cooling	0	0	0	0	29	129	237	196	68	0	0	0	659
% OF POSSIBLE SUNSHINE	na	na	na	na	na	na	na	na	na	na	na	na	na
AVERAGE SKY COVER													
Sunrise - Sunset	7.3	7.0	6.9	6.7	6.7	6.3	6.2	6.3	6.5	6.4	7.5	7.5	6.8
NUMBER OF DAYS (Sunrise-Sunset)													
Clear	5.0	5.5	6.0	6.4	5.6	6.3	6.2	5.7	5.9	7.2	4.2	4.2	68.2
Partly cloudy	7.6	6.8	7.8	7.8	10.1	11.8	13.2	13.3	11.1	9.1	6.6	6.9	112.1
Cloudy	18.4	16.0	17.2	15.9	15.3	12.0	11.6	12.0	13.0	14.7	19.2	19.9	185.0
Precipitation .01" or more	12.2	11.3	12.9	13.2	13.5	11.8	11.5	11.0	9.7	10.0	12.4	12.8	142.2
Snow, Ice pellets 1.0" or more	3.2	3.1	2.1	0.3	0.0	0.0	0.0	0.0	0.0	*	0.9	2.6	12.2
Thunderstorms	0.2	0.3	1.0	1.8	4.0	6.9	7.7	6.2	3.2	0.9	0.5	0.3	33.0
Fog, Visibility 1/4 mile or less	1.3	1.3	1.3	1.2	2.3	2.9	3.5	4.6	7.9	6.1	3.0	1.9	37.2
Temperature Maximum:													
90° and above	0.0	0.0	0.0	0.2	0.6	2.8	5.2	2.8	0.9	*	0.0	0.0	12.5
32° and below	13.3	8.2	2.0	*	0.0	0.0	0.0	0.0	0.0	0.0	0.7	8.0	32.3
Temperature Minimum:													
32° and below	28.0	24.8	21.5	7.8	0.7	0.0	0.0	0.0	0.2	4.3	14.8	25.6	127.7
0° and below	2.5	1.4	0.1	0.0	0.0	0.0	0.0	0.0	0.0	0.0	0.0	0.8	4.7
RELATIVE HUMIDITY (%)													
Morning	74	73	73	73	80	87	88	90	90	86	80	77	81
Afternoon	62	58	54	49	52	54	55	58	59	57	62	64	57
PRECIPITATION (inches)													
Water Equivalent													
Normal	2.8	2.8	3.6	3.5	3.6	3.8	3.9	3.2	3.5	3.2	3.6	3.2	41.2
Maximum monthly	8.2	8.4	5.9	7.0	9.4	16.8	8.3	7.6	10.0	8.1	8.0	7.3	16.8
Date	1978	1981	1980	1983	1946	1972	1958	1955	1975	1976	1972	1973	1972
Minimum monthly	0.5	0.5	0.8	0.9	0.8	0.6	0.9	0.9	0.5	0.1	0.8	0.8	0.1
Date	1985	1968	1981	1946	1964	1966	1955	1951	1964	1963	1976	1955	1963
Maximum in 24 hrs	2.4	2.7	2.5	2.7	4.1	8.6	2.5	3.4	4.6	4.3	3.4	3.2	8.6
Date	1978	1971	1964	1977	1946	1972	1958	1950	1975	1955	1956	1983	1972
SNOW, ICE PELLETS													
Maximum monthly	38.1	34.3	29.5	13.8	0.2	0.0	0.0	0.0	0.0	1.0	13.7	35.5	38.1
Date	1978	1972	1967	1982	1977	—	—	—	—	1977	1953	1969	1978
Maximum in 24 hrs	23.1	20.4	13.9	8.8	0.2	0.0	0.0	0.0	0.0	1.0	12.1	16.5	23.1
Date	1964	1972	1967	1982	1977	—	—	—	—	1977	1953	1969	1964
WIND (Resultant)													
Mean speed (mph)	9.2	9.2	9.5	9.4	8.0	7.0	6.4	6.0	6.2	6.8	8.2	8.7	7.9

BLOCK ISLAND
Elev. 110' 41° 10'N — 71° 35'W **Rhode Island**

NORMALS, MEANS, EXTREMES

	JAN	FEB	MAR	APR	MAY	JUN	JUL	AUG	SEP	OCT	NOV	DEC	YEAR
TEMPERATURE													
Normal daily maximum	37.2	36.9	42.8	51.8	60.7	69.8	76.0	75.8	69.7	60.8	51.5	41.9	56.2
Normal daily minimum	25.0	25.1	31.4	38.9	47.6	56.9	63.6	63.8	57.9	48.9	40.2	29.6	44.1
Normal monthly	31.1	31.0	37.1	45.4	54.2	63.4	69.8	69.8	63.8	54.9	45.9	35.8	50.2
Extreme highest	57	62	74	92	82	90	91	91	87	77	70	64	92
Extreme highest date	1962	1976	1977	1976	1969	1952	1972	1973	1983	1967	1956	1953	1976
Extreme lowest	-2	-2	8	18	34	41	51	45	42	30	20	-4	-4
Extreme lowest date	1968	1961	1967	1982	1972	1967	1979	1982	1973	1976	1957	1962	1962
DEGREE DAYS BASE 65° F													
Heating	1051	952	865	588	335	83	7	5	75	316	573	905	5755
Cooling	0	0	0	0	0	35	155	154	39	0	0	0	383
% OF POSSIBLE SUNSHINE	na	na	na	na	na	na	na	na	na	na	na	na	na
AVERAGE SKY COVER													
Sunrise - Sunset	6.5	6.0	5.8	6.3	6.2	6.3	6.8	6.6	5.9	5.4	6.6	6.2	6.2
NUMBER OF DAYS (Sunrise-Sunset)													
Clear	8.0	7.9	9.0	8.1	7.2	8.5	7.1	7.4	9.9	11.4	6.6	6.7	97.8
Partly cloudy	8.6	7.9	8.5	8.4	10.8	9.8	10.9	10.9	9.2	7.7	9.8	10.2	112.7
Cloudy	14.4	12.5	13.5	13.5	13.1	11.7	13.0	12.6	10.9	11.9	13.6	14.1	154.8
Precipitation .01" or more	10.2	9.3	10.8	10.1	10.0	8.6	7.2	8.0	7.3	7.6	10.3	11.4	110.8
Snow, Ice pellets 1.0" or more	1.7	1.6	1.7	0.2	0.0	0.0	0.0	0.0	0.0	0.0	0.1	1.2	6.4
Thunderstorms	0.2	0.3	0.3	1.4	1.8	1.9	3.9	3.6	1.4	1.1	0.4	0.1	16.4
Fog, Visibility 1/4 mile or less	3.6	3.7	4.7	8.2	10.1	10.0	12.4	10.7	5.4	3.7	3.2	3.1	78.8
Temperature Maximum:													
90° and above	0.0	0.0	0.0	*	0.0	*	0.1	0.1	0.0	0.0	0.0	0.0	0.2
32° and below	9.4	7.1	1.4	*	0.0	0.0	0.0	0.0	0.0	0.0	0.1	4.1	22.1
Temperature Minimum:													
32° and below	24.3	21.4	16.1	2.7	0.0	0.0	0.0	0.0	0.0	0.2	4.6	17.6	86.9
0° and below	0.1	0.1	0.0	0.0	0.0	0.0	0.0	0.0	0.0	0.0	0.0	0.1	0.4
Afternoon	65	65	65	65	67	69	72	71	70	66	65	65	67
PRECIPITATION (inches)													
Water Equivalent													
Normal	3.5	3.3	3.9	3.5	3.3	2.2	2.7	4.0	3.5	3.2	3.9	4.3	41.9
Maximum monthly	6.7	6.8	8.5	9.2	6.0	8.6	6.1	9.7	11.5	8.7	8.0	8.1	11.5
Date	1958	1971	1959	1983	1984	1982	1959	1954	1961	1955	1969	1967	1961
Minimum monthly	0.2	0.8	1.1	0.8	0.7	T	0.3	0.1	0.3	0.8	0.8	0.8	T
Date	1970	1980	1966	1985	1955	1957	1952	1984	1971	1952	1984	1955	1957
Maximum in 24 hrs	4.0	2.8	3.6	2.7	3.6	4.3	3.6	4.8	8.5	6.6	3.9	4.3	8.5
Date	1962	1972	1968	1983	1984	1981	1978	1953	1960	1955	1969	1967	1960
SNOW, ICE PELLETS													
Maximum monthly	30.0	16.9	24.1	2.0	0.0	0.0	0.0	0.0	0.0	T	2.5	10.4	30.0
Date	1978	1961	1956	1973	—	—	—	—	—	1970	1955	1963	1978
Maximum in 24 hrs	21.7	16.9	11.5	2.0	0.0	0.0	0.0	0.0	0.0	T	2.5	6.3	21.7
Date	1978	1961	1960	1973	—	—	—	—	—	1970	1955	1960	1978
WIND (Resultant)													
Mean speed (mph)	10.3	12.9	13.4	10.3	10.5	10.0	13.1	6.8	5.9	7.9	12.3	6.6	10.0

PROVIDENCE
Elev. 51' 41° 44'N — 71° 26'W **Rhode Island**

NORMALS, MEANS, EXTREMES

	JAN	FEB	MAR	APR	MAY	JUN	JUL	AUG	SEP	OCT	NOV	DEC	YEAR
TEMPERATURE													
Normal daily maximum	36.4	37.7	45.5	57.5	67.6	76.6	81.7	80.3	73.1	63.2	51.9	40.5	59.3
Normal daily minimum	20.0	20.9	29.2	38.3	47.6	57.0	63.3	61.9	53.8	43.1	34.8	24.1	41.2
Normal monthly	28.2	29.3	37.4	47.9	57.6	66.8	72.5	71.1	63.5	53.2	43.4	32.3	50.3
Extreme highest	66	72	78	98	94	96	100	104	100	86	78	70	104
Extreme highest date	1974	1985	1977	1976	1964	1980	1980	1975	1983	1979	1974	1984	1975
Extreme lowest	-13	-7	1	14	29	41	49	40	33	20	14	-10	-13
Extreme lowest date	1976	1979	1967	1954	1956	1980	1979	1965	1980	1976	1972	1980	1976
DEGREE DAYS BASE 65° F													
Heating	1141	1000	856	513	239	31	0	6	94	366	648	1014	5908
Cooling	0	0	0	0	10	85	235	195	49	0	0	0	574
% OF POSSIBLE SUNSHINE	57	57	57	57	57	60	64	60	61	60	50	52	58
AVERAGE SKY COVER													
Sunrise - Sunset	6.2	6.3	6.6	6.5	6.7	6.3	6.3	6.2	5.8	5.5	6.3	6.2	6.2
NUMBER OF DAYS (Sunrise-Sunset)													
Clear	9.9	7.9	8.6	7.9	6.7	6.9	7.2	8.3	9.7	11.0	8.4	8.3	100.8
Partly cloudy	6.7	7.5	7.6	8.2	10.0	10.2	12.0	10.5	8.3	7.9	6.7	7.8	103.4
Cloudy	14.4	12.8	14.9	13.8	14.3	12.8	11.8	12.3	12.1	12.1	14.9	14.8	161.0
Precipitation .01" or more	11.1	10.1	11.8	10.9	11.4	10.8	8.7	9.5	8.2	8.3	11.0	12.3	124.2
Snow, Ice pellets 1.0" or more	2.8	2.3	2.0	0.3	*	0.0	0.0	0.0	0.0	0.1	0.3	2.2	10.0
Thunderstorms	0.2	0.2	0.6	1.3	2.7	3.7	4.3	3.8	1.7	1.0	0.8	0.2	20.3
Fog, Visibility 1/4 mile or less	2.0	2.1	2.1	2.0	2.3	2.2	1.9	1.4	1.8	3.2	2.2	1.9	25.1
Temperature Maximum:													
90° and above	0.0	0.0	0.0	0.1	0.6	1.9	3.7	2.2	1.0	0.0	0.0	0.0	9.6
32° and below	12.5	8.1	1.4	*	0.0	0.0	0.0	0.0	0.0	0.0	0.3	6.2	28.5
Temperature Minimum:													
32° and below	28.2	24.2	19.8	6.0	0.2	0.0	0.0	0.0	0.0	3.8	12.3	24.7	119.2
0° and below	1.6	0.7	0.0	0.0	0.0	0.0	0.0	0.0	0.0	0.0	0.0	0.4	2.7
RELATIVE HUMIDITY (%)													
Morning	68	67	68	69	77	82	81	83	83	79	75	72	75
Afternoon	56	54	53	47	52	56	55	56	55	53	57	58	54
PRECIPITATION (inches)													
Water Equivalent													
Normal	4.0	3.7	4.2	3.9	3.4	2.7	3.0	4.0	3.5	3.7	4.2	4.4	45.3
Maximum monthly	11.6	7.2	8.8	12.7	8.3	11.0	8.0	11.1	7.9	11.8	11.0	10.7	12.7
Date	1979	1984	1983	1983	1984	1982	1976	1955	1961	1962	1983	1969	1983
Minimum monthly	0.5	1.1	0.5	1.4	0.7	0.3	1.0	0.7	0.7	1.6	0.8	0.5	0.3
Date	1970	1980	1981	1966	1964	1957	1970	1984	1959	1969	1976	1955	1957
Maximum in 24 hrs	3.3	3.1	4.5	4.4	5.1	5.0	4.8	6.7	4.8	6.6	4.1	3.8	6.7
Date	1962	1978	1968	1983	1984	1984	1976	1979	1961	1962	1983	1969	1979
SNOW, ICE PELLETS													
Maximum monthly	28.7	30.9	31.6	7.6	7.0	0.0	0.0	0.0	0.0	2.5	4.1	19.8	31.6
Date	1965	1962	1956	1982	1977	—	—	—	—	1979	1980	1963	1956
Maximum in 24 hrs	10.8	27.6	16.9	7.6	7.0	0.0	0.0	0.0	0.0	2.5	4.1	11.9	27.6
Date	1978	1978	1960	1982	1977	—	—	—	—	1979	1980	1981	1978
WIND (Resultant)													
Mean speed (mph)	11.3	11.6	12.2	12.2	10.9	10.0	9.5	9.3	9.4	9.6	10.5	10.9	10.6

CHARLESTON

Elev. 40'   32° 54'N — 80° 02'W   **South Carolina**

NORMALS, MEANS, EXTREMES

	JAN	FEB	MAR	APR	MAY	JUN	JUL	AUG	SEP	OCT	NOV	DEC	YEAR
TEMPERATURE													
Normal daily maximum	58.8	61.2	68.0	76.0	82.9	87.0	89.4	88.8	84.6	76.8	68.7	61.4	75.3
Normal daily minimum	36.9	38.4	45.3	52.5	61.4	68.0	71.6	71.2	66.7	54.7	44.6	38.5	54.2
Normal monthly	47.9	49.8	56.7	64.3	72.2	77.5	80.5	80.0	75.7	65.8	56.7	50.0	64.7
Extreme highest	83	86	90	93	98	103	101	102	99	94	88	83	103
Extreme highest date	1950	1962	1974	1985	1953	1944	1977	1954	1944	1954	1961	1972	1944
Extreme lowest	6	12	15	29	36	50	58	56	42	27	15	8	6
Extreme lowest date	1985	1973	1980	1944	1963	1972	1952	1979	1967	1976	1950	1962	1985
DEGREE DAYS BASE 65° F													
Heating	543	434	286	69	6	0	0	0	0	76	262	471	2147
Cooling	13	9	29	48	229	378	481	465	321	101	13	6	2093
% OF POSSIBLE SUNSHINE	58	62	67	71	71	68	67	65	63	66	63	59	65
AVERAGE SKY COVER													
Sunrise - Sunset	6.2	5.9	6.0	5.4	6.0	6.3	6.6	6.2	6.2	5.2	5.1	5.9	5.9
NUMBER OF DAYS (Sunrise-Sunset)													
Clear	9.0	9.1	9.1	11.2	7.9	6.2	4.9	5.9	6.6	11.5	12.4	9.7	103.5
Partly cloudy	6.5	6.5	8.3	7.7	10.9	11.3	12.2	13.1	10.7	8.4	6.4	7.1	109.2
Cloudy	15.5	12.6	13.6	11.1	12.2	12.5	13.9	12.0	12.6	11.1	11.2	14.2	152.5
Precipitation .01" or more	9.7	8.9	10.3	7.3	9.2	10.8	13.7	12.3	9.3	6.0	6.9	8.5	113.0
Snow, Ice pellets 1.0" or more	0.0	0.1	*	0.0	0.0	0.0	0.0	0.0	0.0	0.0	0.0	*	0.2
Thunderstorms	0.7	1.1	2.3	2.7	6.9	9.8	13.2	11.0	5.1	1.3	0.7	0.6	55.5
Fog, Visibility 1/4 mile or less	4.2	2.0	2.4	2.1	2.1	1.7	0.8	1.4	1.7	2.8	3.7	3.6	28.6
Temperature Maximum:													
90° and above	0.0	0.0	*	0.7	3.8	10.8	15.3	13.9	5.0	0.3	0.0	0.0	49.8
32° and below	0.2	0.1	*	0.0	0.0	0.0	0.0	0.0	0.0	0.0	0.0	0.1	0.3
Temperature Minimum:													
32° and below	11.4	8.3	3.0	0.2	0.0	0.0	0.0	0.0	0.0	0.1	3.5	9.5	36.0
0° and below	0.0	0.0	0.0	0.0	0.0	0.0	0.0	0.0	0.0	0.0	0.0	0.0	0.0
RELATIVE HUMIDITY (%)													
Morning	80	78	81	83	88	89	90	91	90	88	84	82	85
Afternoon	55	51	50	49	54	59	63	63	62	56	52	55	56
PRECIPITATION (inches)													
Water Equivalent													
Normal	3.3	3.3	4.3	2.5	4.4	6.5	7.3	6.5	4.9	2.9	2.1	3.1	51.5
Maximum monthly	6.6	6.3	11.1	9.5	9.2	27.2	18.4	16.9	17.3	9.1	7.3	7.0	27.2
Date	1966	1983	1983	1958	1957	1973	1964	1974	1945	1959	1972	1953	1973
Minimum monthly	0.6	0.3	0.9	0.0	0.6	0.9	1.7	0.7	0.5	0.0	0.4	0.6	0.0
Date	1950	1947	1963	1972	1944	1970	1972	1980	1971	1943	1966	1984	1972
Maximum in 24 hrs	2.4	3.2	6.6	4.1	6.2	10.1	5.8	5.7	8.8	5.7	5.2	3.4	10.1
Date	1983	1944	1959	1958	1967	1973	1960	1964	1945	1944	1969	1978	1973
SNOW, ICE PELLETS													
Maximum monthly	1.0	7.1	2.0	T	0.0	0.0	0.0	0.0	0.0	0.0	T	3.8	7.1
Date	1977	1973	1969	1985	—	—	—	—	—	—	1950	1980	1973
Maximum in 24 hrs	0.8	5.9	2.0	T	0.0	0.0	0.0	0.0	0.0	0.0	T	3.8	5.9
Date	1966	1973	1969	1985	—	—	—	—	—	—	1950	1980	1973
WIND (Resultant)													
Mean speed (mph)	9.2	10.0	10.1	9.8	8.7	8.4	7.9	7.4	7.9	8.1	8.1	8.6	8.7

COLUMBIA

Elev. 213'   33° 57'N — 81° 07'W   South Carolina

NORMALS, MEANS, EXTREMES

	JAN	FEB	MAR	APR	MAY	JUN	JUL	AUG	SEP	OCT	NOV	DEC	YEAR
TEMPERATURE													
Normal daily maximum	56.2	59.5	67.1	77.0	83.8	89.2	91.9	91.0	85.5	76.5	67.1	58.8	75.3
Normal daily minimum	33.2	34.6	41.9	50.5	59.1	66.1	70.1	69.4	63.9	50.3	40.6	34.7	51.2
Normal monthly	44.7	47.1	54.5	63.8	71.5	77.7	81.0	80.2	74.7	63.4	53.9	46.8	63.3
Extreme highest	84	84	91	94	101	107	107	107	101	101	90	83	107
Extreme highest date	1975	1977	1974	1970	1953	1954	1952	1983	1954	1954	1961	1978	1983
Extreme lowest	-1	5	4	26	34	44	54	53	40	23	12	4	-1
Extreme lowest date	1985	1973	1980	1983	1963	1984	1951	1969	1967	1952	1970	1958	1985
DEGREE DAYS BASE 65° F													
Heating	637	508	346	87	22	0	0	0	0	123	339	567	2629
Cooling	8	6	20	51	223	381	496	471	297	74	6	0	2033
% OF POSSIBLE SUNSHINE	57	61	65	69	68	68	67	67	66	66	64	60	65
AVERAGE SKY COVER													
Sunrise - Sunset	6.1	5.8	5.9	5.2	5.7	5.8	6.2	5.7	5.6	4.8	5.0	5.7	5.6
NUMBER OF DAYS (Sunrise-Sunset)													
Clear	9.4	9.1	9.2	11.4	9.7	8.1	6.5	8.5	9.6	13.6	12.6	10.6	118.4
Partly cloudy	6.1	6.6	8.1	7.6	9.9	11.4	12.6	12.8	9.0	7.1	6.3	6.2	103.6
Cloudy	15.5	12.6	13.7	10.9	11.4	10.5	11.9	9.7	11.4	10.3	11.2	14.2	143.3
Precipitation .01" or more	10.1	9.6	10.6	8.2	9.0	9.5	11.8	10.5	7.4	6.1	7.1	9.2	109.1
Snow, Ice pellets 1.0" or more	0.2	0.2	0.1	0.0	0.0	0.0	0.0	0.0	0.0	0.0	0.0	*	0.5
Thunderstorms	0.7	1.5	2.7	3.7	6.4	9.1	12.8	9.9	3.9	1.4	0.8	0.3	53.1
Fog, Visibility 1/4 mile or less	2.9	2.2	1.7	1.3	1.5	1.5	1.7	2.5	2.8	2.8	3.0	3.6	27.6
Temperature Maximum:													
90° and above	0.0	0.0	0.1	1.9	4.9	13.7	20.3	16.2	8.4	0.5	0.0	0.0	65.9
32° and below	0.6	0.1	0.1	0.0	0.0	0.0	0.0	0.0	0.0	0.0	0.0	0.1	0.9
Temperature Minimum:													
32° and below	17.4	14.6	6.5	1.1	0.0	0.0	0.0	0.0	0.0	1.0	8.5	13.9	63.0
0° and below	0.1	0.0	0.0	0.0	0.0	0.0	0.0	0.0	0.0	0.0	0.0	0.0	0.1
RELATIVE HUMIDITY (%)													
Morning	78	76	76	77	85	87	87	91	90	88	84	80	83
Afternoon	55	49	48	44	50	53	56	57	56	52	50	54	52
PRECIPITATION (inches)													
Water Equivalent													
Normal	4.3	3.9	5.1	3.5	3.8	4.4	5.3	5.5	4.2	2.5	2.5	3.5	49.1
Maximum monthly	9.2	8.6	10.8	6.8	8.8	14.8	13.8	16.7	8.7	12.0	7.2	8.5	16.7
Date	1978	1961	1973	1979	1967	1973	1959	1949	1953	1959	1957	1981	1949
Minimum monthly	0.8	0.8	0.5	0.8	0.2	1.2	0.5	1.0	0.0	T	0.4	0.3	T
Date	1981	1976	1985	1976	1951	1955	1977	1976	1985	1963	1973	1955	1963
Maximum in 24 hrs	2.8	3.6	3.5	3.6	5.5	5.4	5.8	7.6	6.2	5.4	2.5	3.1	7.6
Date	1968	1962	1960	1956	1967	1973	1959	1949	1953	1964	1976	1970	1949
SNOW, ICE PELLETS													
Maximum monthly	3.5	16.0	4.1	0.0	0.0	0.0	0.0	0.0	0.0	0.0	T	9.1	16.0
Date	1982	1973	1980	—	—	—	—	—	—	—	1976	1958	1973
Maximum in 24 hrs	3.3	15.7	4.1	0.0	0.0	0.0	0.0	0.0	0.0	0.0	T	8.8	15.7
Date	1982	1973	1980	—	—	—	—	—	—	—	1976	1958	1973
WIND (Resultant)													
Mean speed (mph)	7.2	7.6	8.2	8.3	7.0	6.6	6.3	5.8	6.2	6.2	6.4	6.7	6.9

GREENVILLE

Elev. 821'   34° 51'N — 82° 23'W   **South Carolina**

NORMALS, MEANS, EXTREMES

	JAN	FEB	MAR	APR	MAY	JUN	JUL	AUG	SEP	OCT	NOV	DEC	YEAR
TEMPERATURE													
Normal daily maximum	51.0	54.5	62.5	72.6	79.7	85.4	88.2	87.5	81.7	72.2	62.1	53.5	70.9
Normal daily minimum	31.2	32.6	39.4	48.3	56.9	64.2	68.2	67.4	61.7	49.1	39.6	33.2	49.3
Normal monthly	41.1	43.6	51.0	60.5	68.3	74.8	78.2	77.5	71.7	60.7	50.9	43.4	60.1
Extreme highest	79	79	88	91	97	100	101	103	96	88	85	76	103
Extreme highest date	1975	1982	1967	1980	1967	1985	1983	1983	1975	1981	1974	1984	1983
Extreme lowest	-6	8	11	25	33	40	54	52	36	25	12	5	-6
Extreme lowest date	1966	1967	1980	1983	1971	1972	1979	1968	1967	1976	1970	1985	1966
DEGREE DAYS BASE 65° F													
Heating	741	599	442	154	41	0	0	0	7	162	423	670	3239
Cooling	0	0	8	19	143	297	409	388	208	29	0	0	1501
% OF POSSIBLE SUNSHINE	56	61	65	66	61	61	59	61	63	65	60	56	61
AVERAGE SKY COVER													
Sunrise - Sunset	5.8	5.6	5.6	5.4	5.8	5.8	6.2	5.6	5.5	4.6	5.1	5.7	5.6
NUMBER OF DAYS (Sunrise-Sunset)													
Clear	11.0	10.5	10.3	10.9	8.8	8.3	6.1	8.7	10.0	14.0	12.7	11.5	122.8
Partly cloudy	5.9	5.6	8.0	8.1	9.7	11.1	12.9	12.2	8.9	6.8	6.0	5.7	100.9
Cloudy	14.2	12.2	12.7	11.0	12.5	10.6	12.0	10.0	11.1	10.2	11.3	13.8	141.5
Precipitation .01" or more	11.0	9.3	11.3	9.0	11.4	10.1	12.3	9.7	8.1	7.4	8.7	10.0	118.2
Snow, Ice pellets 1.0" or more	0.8	0.7	0.3	0.0	0.0	0.0	0.0	0.0	0.0	0.0	*	0.1	2.0
Thunderstorms	0.5	0.7	2.7	2.9	6.3	6.4	10.0	6.7	3.1	0.9	0.7	0.6	41.7
Fog, Visibility 1/4 mile or less	4.7	3.3	3.2	2.3	1.7	1.3	2.3	3.0	2.2	1.9	3.6	5.2	34.7
Temperature Maximum:													
90° and above	0.0	0.0	0.0	0.2	1.4	6.7	11.3	8.6	2.6	0.0	0.0	0.0	30.7
32° and below	1.4	0.3	*	0.0	0.0	0.0	0.0	0.0	0.0	0.0	0.0	0.3	2.0
Temperature Minimum:													
32° and below	19.4	16.3	7.3	1.0	0.0	0.0	0.0	0.0	0.0	0.7	7.2	15.3	67.1
0° and below	0.1	0.0	0.0	0.0	0.0	0.0	0.0	0.0	0.0	0.0	0.0	0.0	0.1
RELATIVE HUMIDITY (%)													
Morning	72	69	69	70	79	82	85	86	85	82	76	74	77
Afternoon	55	51	49	48	53	55	59	59	58	53	53	55	54
PRECIPITATION (inches)													
Water Equivalent													
Normal	4.2	4.3	5.8	4.3	4.2	4.7	4.0	3.6	4.3	3.4	3.2	3.9	50.5
Maximum monthly	7.1	7.4	11.3	11.3	8.8	9.5	13.5	7.5	11.6	10.2	7.5	8.4	13.5
Date	1979	1971	1980	1964	1972	1969	1984	1967	1975	1964	1985	1983	1984
Minimum monthly	0.2	0.5	1.1	0.6	1.0	1.2	0.8	1.1	0.2	0.2	1.3	0.3	0.2
Date	1981	1978	1985	1976	1965	1981	1977	1963	1978	1974	1973	1965	1974
Maximum in 24 hrs	3.3	3.5	4.4	3.7	3.5	4.8	3.8	4.4	6.2	4.5	2.8	3.0	6.2
Date	1982	1984	1963	1963	1972	1980	1964	1967	1973	1977	1964	1972	1973
SNOW, ICE PELLETS													
Maximum monthly	9.1	12.3	9.3	0.1	0.0	0.0	0.0	0.0	0.0	0.0	1.9	11.4	12.3
Date	1966	1979	1983	1983	—	—	—	—	—	—	1968	1971	1979
Maximum in 24 hrs	5.7	8.2	9.3	0.1	0.0	0.0	0.0	0.0	0.0	0.0	1.9	11.4	11.4
Date	1965	1979	1983	1983	—	—	—	—	—	—	1968	1971	1971
WIND (Resultant)													
Mean speed (mph)	7.2	7.8	8.0	7.7	6.8	6.3	5.8	5.5	5.9	6.4	6.5	7.2	6.8

ABERDEEN

Elev. 1296'   45° 27'N — 98° 26'W   **South Dakota**

NORMALS, MEANS, EXTREMES

	JAN	FEB	MAR	APR	MAY	JUN	JUL	AUG	SEP	OCT	NOV	DEC	YEAR
TEMPERATURE													
Normal daily maximum	18.9	26.1	37.9	56.5	69.6	78.6	85.3	84.4	73.4	61.3	41.0	26.5	55.0
Normal daily minimum	-2.2	5.3	17.5	32.6	43.9	54.0	58.9	56.5	45.5	34.1	19.4	6.4	31.0
Normal monthly	8.4	15.7	27.7	44.6	56.8	66.3	72.1	70.5	59.5	47.7	30.2	16.5	43.0
Extreme highest	60	62	82	97	96	103	110	112	103	96	78	62	112
Extreme highest date	1981	1976	1963	1980	1969	1963	1966	1965	1970	1963	1975	1969	1965
Extreme lowest	-35	-37	-29	-2	19	33	39	35	20	11	-27	39	-39
Extreme lowest date	1972	1971	1962	1975	1961	1964	1971	1965	1965	1976	1964	1967	1967
DEGREE DAYS BASE 65° F													
Heating	1758	1380	1156	612	274	73	16	20	197	536	1044	1504	8570
Cooling	0	0	0	0	19	112	236	190	32	0	0	0	589
% OF POSSIBLE SUNSHINE	na	na	na	na	na	na	na	na	na	na	na	na	na
AVERAGE SKY COVER													
Sunrise - Sunset	6.4	6.8	6.9	6.8	6.4	5.8	4.7	4.8	5.3	5.9	6.9	6.8	6.1
NUMBER OF DAYS (Sunrise-Sunset)													
Clear	8.1	6.4	6.3	6.6	7.1	8.4	11.8	11.8	10.6	9.9	6.2	7.2	100.5
Partly cloudy	7.2	6.2	7.4	7.1	10.1	10.2	12.7	10.9	8.3	7.7	6.8	6.6	101.2
Cloudy	15.8	15.6	17.3	16.4	13.8	11.4	6.5	8.2	11.1	13.3	16.9	17.2	163.6
Precipitation .01" or more	6.6	5.7	7.1	8.2	9.6	10.4	8.3	7.9	6.2	5.1	5.5	6.3	86.9
Snow, Ice pellets 1.0" or more	2.6	2.1	2.1	0.9	0.1	0.0	0.0	0.0	0.0	0.3	1.6	2.0	11.7
Thunderstorms	0.0	0.0	0.4	1.9	4.9	9.6	9.0	6.1	2.9	1.4	0.0	0.0	36.1
Fog, Visibility 1/4 mile or less	1.6	2.1	2.4	1.4	0.5	0.9	0.9	0.9	1.1	1.1	2.5	2.9	18.3
Temperature Maximum:													
90° and above	0.0	0.0	0.0	0.2	0.3	2.7	9.5	9.0	2.2	0.2	0.0	0.0	24.0
32° and below	24.4	17.3	10.7	0.3	0.0	0.0	0.0	0.0	0.0	0.1	8.1	21.9	82.8
Temperature Minimum:													
32° and below	30.9	27.9	27.2	15.1	3.4	0.0	0.0	0.0	2.3	13.3	27.3	30.9	178.1
0° and below	17.3	10.0	3.3	*	0.0	0.0	0.0	0.0	0.0	0.0	2.1	12.0	44.8
RELATIVE HUMIDITY (%)													
Morning	73	76	79	75	72	77	75	72	74	74	80	80	76
Afternoon	69	70	68	56	52	57	52	50	52	56	68	72	60
PRECIPITATION (inches)													
Water Equivalent													
Normal	0.4	0.6	0.9	1.9	2.5	3.2	2.4	1.9	1.5	1.0	0.6	0.4	17.7
Maximum monthly	2.2	2.0	3.4	5.1	6.3	8.8	7.7	6.6	4.5	5.1	2.3	1.8	8.8
Date	1937	1952	1977	1953	1949	1939	1972	1942	1941	1982	1977	1935	1939
Minimum monthly	0.0	0.0	0.0	0.3	0.2	0.3	0.3	0.0	0.0	0.0	T	T	0.0
Date	1961	1932	1971	1952	1948	1974	1975	1947	1979	1952	1980	1943	1952
Maximum in 24 hrs	1.1	1.0	3.0	2.2	3.8	5.2	3.4	2.7	2.6	2.3	1.3	0.9	5.2
Date	1939	1958	1937	1938	1949	1978	1983	1930	1967	1982	1977	1935	1978
SNOW, ICE PELLETS													
Maximum monthly	26.2	25.1	27.9	24.4	2.0	0.0	0.0	0.0	0.1	5.5	24.7	18.5	27.9
Date	1937	1969	1975	1970	1943	—	—	—	1965	1970	1936	1935	1975
Maximum in 24 hrs	10.0	14.3	13.0	15.0	2.0	0.0	0.0	0.0	0.1	5.0	9.0	8.0	15.0
Date	1937	1951	1937	1970	1943	—	—	—	1965	1932	1953	1935	1970
WIND (Resultant)													
Mean speed (mph)	11.3	11.4	12.4	13.2	12.3	10.5	9.4	10.3	10.7	11.2	10.9	10.8	11.2

HURON

Elev. 1281'   44° 23'N — 98° 13'W   **South Dakota**

NORMALS, MEANS, EXTREMES

	JAN	FEB	MAR	APR	MAY	JUN	JUL	AUG	SEP	OCT	NOV	DEC	YEAR
TEMPERATURE													
Normal daily maximum	21.9	28.6	39.4	57.7	70.2	80.3	87.3	85.5	74.7	62.2	43.2	29.0	56.7
Normal daily minimum	0.4	7.6	19.2	33.5	44.2	55.0	60.5	58.4	46.9	35.5	21.1	9.0	32.6
Normal monthly	11.2	18.1	29.3	45.6	57.2	67.7	73.9	72.0	60.8	48.9	32.2	19.0	44.6
Extreme highest	63	71	89	97	99	106	112	110	106	102	77	62	112
Extreme highest date	1944	1958	1943	1980	1959	1979	1966	1965	1970	1963	1962	1969	1966
Extreme lowest	-35	-39	-24	-2	17	32	37	36	19	9	-21	-30	-39
Extreme lowest date	1970	1962	1960	1975	1976	1964	1971	1964	1974	1976	1964	1985	1962
DEGREE DAYS BASE 65° F													
Heating	1668	1313	1104	582	259	62	15	14	171	505	984	1426	8103
Cooling	0	0	0	0	20	143	294	231	45	5	0	0	738
% OF POSSIBLE SUNSHINE	58	60	59	60	65	69	77	74	68	63	52	50	63
AVERAGE SKY COVER													
Sunrise - Sunset	6.6	6.7	7.0	6.6	6.3	5.7	4.6	4.7	5.1	5.5	6.6	6.8	6.0
NUMBER OF DAYS (Sunrise-Sunset)													
Clear	8.0	6.4	5.7	6.3	7.3	8.7	12.3	12.4	11.8	10.8	7.0	7.2	103.9
Partly cloudy	7.5	7.6	7.7	8.7	9.8	11.2	12.3	11.2	8.2	8.4	7.5	7.1	107.2
Cloudy	15.5	14.3	17.6	15.0	13.9	10.2	6.4	7.3	10.0	11.8	15.4	16.8	154.2
Precipitation .01" or more	6.3	6.6	8.3	9.0	10.1	10.9	8.7	8.3	6.9	5.9	5.9	5.8	92.7
Snow, Ice pellets 1.0" or more	2.2	2.6	2.5	0.8	0.1	0.0	0.0	0.0	0.0	0.2	1.6	1.9	12.0
Thunderstorms	*	*	0.4	2.5	5.4	8.8	9.5	8.0	3.9	1.5	0.1	*	40.2
Fog, Visibility 1/4 mile or less	1.7	1.8	2.0	0.7	0.7	0.5	0.7	1.0	1.0	1.1	1.5	2.1	14.7
Temperature Maximum:													
90° and above	0.0	0.0	0.0	0.2	0.5	3.7	12.3	10.2	3.0	0.2	0.0	0.0	30.1
32° and below	21.7	15.4	7.9	0.3	0.0	0.0	0.0	0.0	0.0	0.1	6.3	19.2	70.8
Temperature Minimum:													
32° and below	30.8	27.4	26.2	13.3	2.8	*	0.0	0.0	1.6	11.1	26.1	30.8	170.2
0° and below	15.3	9.0	2.5	*	0.0	0.0	0.0	0.0	0.0	0.0	1.3	9.2	37.4
RELATIVE HUMIDITY (%)													
Morning	74	78	80	77	76	81	78	78	79	76	78	77	78
Afternoon	67	69	66	55	54	57	52	52	54	55	64	69	60
PRECIPITATION (inches)													
Water Equivalent													
Normal	0.4	0.7	1.2	1.9	2.7	3.3	2.2	2.0	1.3	1.3	0.6	0.5	18.6
Maximum monthly	1.9	3.8	5.8	5.3	7.6	11.4	5.1	5.4	3.5	6.4	3.0	1.5	11.4
Date	1975	1962	1977	1968	1962	1984	1982	1956	1965	1946	1947	1968	1984
Minimum monthly	0.0	0.0	0.1	0.2	0.5	0.6	0.4	0.1	0.1	T	T	T	T
Date	1942	1968	1939	1981	1940	1950	1941	1976	1952	1952	1939	1943	1952
Maximum in 24 hrs	1.5	2.1	2.8	2.4	3.4	5.4	2.3	4.1	2.6	4.2	2.0	1.2	5.4
Date	1944	1962	1985	1970	1945	1967	1985	1956	1950	1961	1972	1949	1967
SNOW, ICE PELLETS													
Maximum monthly	27.7	39.9	33.9	12.8	1.6	0.0	0.0	0.0	T	7.3	32.7	26.0	39.9
Date	1975	1962	1975	1970	1954	—	—	—	1965	1976	1985	1968	1962
Maximum in 24 hrs	12.3	17.5	18.3	8.9	1.6	0.0	0.0	0.0	T	5.0	10.0	10.7	18.3
Date	1982	1962	1985	1957	1954	—	—	—	1965	1970	1953	1955	1985
WIND (Resultant)													
Mean speed (mph)	11.5	11.5	12.5	13.6	12.4	11.3	10.5	10.7	11.4	11.4	11.8	11.2	11.6

RAPID CITY Elev. 3162' 44° 03'N — 103° 04'W South Dakota

NORMALS, MEANS, EXTREMES

	JAN	FEB	MAR	APR	MAY	JUN	JUL	AUG	SEP	OCT	NOV	DEC	YEAR
TEMPERATURE													
Normal daily maximum	32.4	37.4	44.2	57.0	68.1	77.9	86.5	85.7	75.4	63.2	46.7	37.4	59.3
Normal daily minimum	9.2	14.6	21.0	32.1	43.0	52.5	58.7	57.0	46.4	36.1	23.0	14.8	34.0
Normal monthly	20.8	26.0	32.6	44.6	55.6	65.2	72.6	71.4	60.9	49.7	34.9	26.1	46.7
Extreme highest	74	74	82	92	98	106	110	106	104	94	77	75	110
Extreme highest date	1953	1954	1946	1980	1969	1961	1973	1947	1978	1963	1965	1965	1973
Extreme lowest	-27	-22	-17	1	18	31	39	38	18	10	-19	-27	-27
Extreme lowest date	1950	1971	1962	1975	1950	1951	1959	1966	1985	1972	1959	1983	1983
DEGREE DAYS BASE 65° F													
Heating	1370	1092	1004	612	298	101	21	24	188	482	903	1206	7301
Cooling	0	0	0	0	7	107	257	223	65	8	0	0	667
% OF POSSIBLE SUNSHINE	55	59	61	60	58	62	72	73	68	65	54	53	62
AVERAGE SKY COVER													
Sunrise - Sunset	6.5	6.5	6.7	6.6	6.4	5.6	4.4	4.3	4.5	5.0	6.2	6.2	5.7
NUMBER OF DAYS (Sunrise-Sunset)													
Clear	7.6	6.1	6.3	5.8	6.5	8.9	13.1	13.9	13.3	12.5	7.7	8.0	109.7
Partly cloudy	7.6	8.5	9.0	9.4	11.0	11.3	12.6	11.7	8.6	7.8	8.6	8.1	114.3
Cloudy	15.9	13.7	15.6	14.7	13.5	9.8	5.3	5.4	8.1	10.7	13.7	14.9	141.3
Precipitation .01" or more	6.8	7.1	8.7	9.3	11.9	12.5	9.2	7.9	6.4	4.9	5.7	6.1	96.4
Snow, Ice pellets 1.0" or more	1.3	2.3	2.6	1.9	0.2	*	0.0	0.0	0.1	0.4	1.7	1.7	12.3
Thunderstorms	0.0	0.0	0.1	1.1	5.8	10.8	11.8	8.9	3.4	0.5	*	*	42.3
Fog, Visibility 1/4 mile or less	1.5	1.9	2.5	1.7	0.9	1.1	0.6	0.6	0.4	0.6	1.9	2.1	15.7
Temperature Maximum:													
90° and above	0.0	0.0	0.0	*	0.5	3.0	11.3	11.5	3.5	0.2	0.0	0.0	30.0
32° and below	13.5	10.0	7.0	0.8	*	0.0	0.0	0.0	0.0	0.3	5.2	11.0	48.0
Temperature Minimum:													
32° and below	30.1	26.9	27.5	14.7	2.7	0.1	0.0	0.0	1.7	10.1	24.5	29.9	168.3
0° and below	8.6	4.4	2.1	0.0	0.0	0.0	0.0	0.0	0.0	0.0	1.1	4.3	20.5
RELATIVE HUMIDITY (%)													
Morning	68	71	74	72	74	77	73	70	67	65	68	68	71
Afternoon	64	61	54	45	46	48	41	37	38	45	58	65	50
PRECIPITATION (inches)													
Water Equivalent													
Normal	0.4	0.6	1.0	1.9	2.6	3.2	2.1	1.4	1.0	0.8	0.5	0.4	16.2
Maximum monthly	1.7	2.4	3.0	5.1	7.3	7.0	6.1	4.8	3.9	3.8	2.2	1.6	7.3
Date	1944	1953	1945	1967	1946	1968	1969	1982	1946	1982	1985	1975	1946
Minimum monthly	0.0	0.0	0.1	0.2	0.3	0.6	0.6	0.1	0.0	T	0.0	0.0	T
Date	1952	1985	1981	1954	1966	1973	1965	1943	1975	1960	1945	1957	1960
Maximum in 24 hrs	1.2	1.0	2.1	3.0	3.4	4.0	2.5	2.6	2.1	2.4	1.0	1.0	4.0
Date	1944	1953	1945	1946	1965	1963	1944	1982	1966	1982	1944	1975	1963
SNOW, ICE PELLETS													
Maximum monthly	24.0	23.7	30.7	30.6	11.6	3.6	0.0	0.0	2.0	10.2	33.6	17.9	33.6
Date	1949	1953	1950	1970	1950	1951	—	—	1970	1971	1985	1975	1985
Maximum in 24 hrs	16.3	10.0	14.9	16.0	13.4	3.6	0.0	0.0	2.0	7.6	9.4	9.8	16.3
Date	1944	1953	1973	1970	1967	1951	—	—	1970	1971	1977	1975	1944
WIND (Resultant)													
Mean speed (mph)	10.8	11.1	12.7	13.3	12.3	10.8	10.1	10.3	11.1	11.2	10.8	10.5	11.3

SIOUX FALLS

Elev. 1418' 43° 34'N — 96° 44'W **South Dakota**

NORMALS, MEANS, EXTREMES

	JAN	FEB	MAR	APR	MAY	JUN	JUL	AUG	SEP	OCT	NOV	DEC	YEAR
TEMPERATURE													
Normal daily maximum	22.9	29.3	40.1	58.1	70.5	80.3	86.2	83.9	73.5	62.1	43.7	29.3	56.7
Normal daily minimum	1.9	8.9	20.6	34.6	45.7	56.3	61.8	59.7	48.5	36.7	22.3	10.1	33.9
Normal monthly	12.4	19.1	30.4	46.4	58.1	68.3	74.0	71.8	61.0	49.4	33.0	19.7	45.3
Extreme highest	66	70	87	94	100	101	108	108	104	94	76	61	108
Extreme highest date	1981	1982	1968	1962	1967	1974	1947	1973	1976	1963	1978	1984	1973
Extreme lowest	-36	-31	-23	5	17	33	38	34	22	9	-17	-26	-36
Extreme lowest date	1970	1962	1948	1982	1967	1969	1971	1950	1974	1972	1964	1983	1970
DEGREE DAYS BASE 65° F													
Heating	1631	1285	1073	561	240	52	14	15	161	489	960	1404	7885
Cooling	0	0	0	0	29	154	293	226	41	6	0	0	749
% OF POSSIBLE SUNSHINE	na	na	na	na	na	na	na	na	na	na	na	na	na
AVERAGE SKY COVER													
Sunrise - Sunset	6.4	6.6	6.9	6.5	6.3	5.7	4.8	4.9	5.1	5.5	6.6	6.7	6.0
NUMBER OF DAYS (Sunrise-Sunset)													
Clear	8.1	6.9	6.1	7.0	7.3	8.6	11.7	12.0	11.7	11.2	7.1	7.3	104.9
Partly cloudy	7.8	6.7	7.6	8.2	9.9	11.2	12.1	10.4	7.9	7.5	7.3	7.0	103.5
Cloudy	15.2	14.7	17.3	14.9	13.8	10.3	7.3	8.6	10.4	12.3	15.7	16.7	156.9
Precipitation .01" or more	6.2	6.5	8.7	9.2	10.4	11.0	9.3	8.9	8.1	6.2	6.0	6.3	96.8
Snow, Ice pellets 1.0" or more	2.1	2.2	2.6	0.6	0.0	0.0	0.0	0.0	0.0	0.1	1.5	2.1	11.2
Thunderstorms	0.0	0.1	0.8	2.9	5.9	9.0	9.3	8.1	5.5	2.0	0.4	0.1	44.0
Fog, Visibility 1/4 mile or less	2.5	3.0	2.8	1.0	0.7	0.6	0.6	1.1	1.3	1.7	2.8	3.7	21.6
Temperature Maximum:													
90° and above	0.0	0.0	0.0	0.3	0.5	3.5	10.6	7.9	1.7	0.0	0.0	0.0	24.6
32° and below	22.5	15.7	8.2	0.4	0.0	0.0	0.0	0.0	0.0	*	6.5	19.8	73.1
Temperature Minimum:													
32° and below	30.9	27.5	26.0	12.1	2.4	0.0	0.0	0.0	1.5	11.3	25.2	30.7	167.6
0° and below	14.6	8.5	1.8	0.0	0.0	0.0	0.0	0.0	0.0	0.0	1.4	8.1	34.4
RELATIVE HUMIDITY (%)													
Morning	74	78	79	74	71	75	74	77	78	75	79	79	76
Afternoon	67	68	64	56	53	56	53	55	57	56	65	71	60
PRECIPITATION (inches)													
Water Equivalent													
Normal	0.5	0.9	1.5	2.3	3.2	3.7	2.7	3.1	2.7	1.5	0.9	0.7	24.1
Maximum monthly	1.7	4.0	3.6	5.7	7.2	8.4	7.7	9.0	6.3	5.7	2.9	2.6	9.0
Date	1969	1962	1977	1984	1965	1984	1948	1975	1966	1973	1983	1968	1975
Minimum monthly	0.0	0.0	0.1	0.1	0.6	1.0	0.2	0.5	0.2	T	0.0	0.0	T
Date	1958	1985	1967	1969	1981	1976	1947	1970	1956	1952	1980	1979	1952
Maximum in 24 hrs	1.6	2.0	1.9	2.6	3.9	4.3	3.0	4.5	4.0	4.5	1.6	1.4	4.5
Date	1960	1962	1956	1953	1972	1957	1982	1975	1966	1973	1972	1955	1975
SNOW, ICE PELLETS													
Maximum monthly	19.6	48.4	31.5	18.4	0.2	0.0	0.0	0.0	0.9	5.1	21.9	41.1	48.4
Date	1969	1962	1951	1983	1954	—	—	—	1985	1970	1985	1968	1962
Maximum in 24 hrs	11.8	26.0	18.9	9.0	0.2	0.0	0.0	0.0	0.9	5.0	11.8	16.6	26.0
Date	1960	1962	1956	1957	1954	—	—	—	1985	1970	1979	1968	1962
WIND (Resultant)													
Mean speed (mph)	11.0	11.1	12.5	13.3	11.9	10.7	9.7	9.8	10.3	10.8	11.5	10.7	11.1

BRISTOL

Elev. 1507' 36° 29'N — 82° 24'W **Tennessee**

NORMALS, MEANS, EXTREMES

	JAN	FEB	MAR	APR	MAY	JUN	JUL	AUG	SEP	OCT	NOV	DEC	YEAR
TEMPERATURE													
Normal daily maximum	44.5	48.4	57.6	68.3	76.3	82.9	85.5	85.2	80.4	69.5	57.3	48.1	67.0
Normal daily minimum	25.5	27.4	34.9	43.8	52.5	60.1	64.3	63.4	57.2	44.7	35.1	28.3	44.8
Normal monthly	35.0	37.9	46.3	56.1	64.4	71.5	74.9	74.3	68.8	57.1	46.2	38.2	55.9
Extreme highest	79	80	85	88	92	97	102	98	100	90	81	78	102
Extreme highest date	1950	1977	1954	1957	1969	1952	1952	1983	1954	1954	1974	1951	1952
Extreme lowest	-21	-5	-2	21	30	38	45	47	34	20	5	-9	-21
Extreme lowest date	1985	1958	1980	1982	1963	1966	1947	1979	1983	1962	1950	1962	1985
DEGREE DAYS BASE 65° F													
Heating	930	759	580	273	111	10	0	0	35	263	564	831	4356
Cooling	0	0	0	6	93	205	307	288	149	18	0	0	1066
% OF POSSIBLE SUNSHINE	na	na	na	na	na	na	na	na	na	na	na	na	na
AVERAGE SKY COVER													
Sunrise - Sunset	7.2	6.8	6.8	6.3	6.2	6.0	6.3	5.9	5.5	5.2	6.3	6.8	6.3
NUMBER OF DAYS (Sunrise-Sunset)													
Clear	5.9	5.9	6.6	7.5	6.9	6.1	5.6	6.9	9.9	12.3	8.6	6.9	89.1
Partly cloudy	6.8	7.0	7.8	8.7	10.6	12.4	12.5	13.8	9.9	8.1	7.1	7.2	111.9
Cloudy	18.3	15.4	16.6	13.8	13.5	11.5	12.8	10.4	10.2	10.6	14.3	16.9	164.3
Precipitation .01" or more	14.1	11.9	13.2	11.2	11.6	11.1	12.2	10.5	7.9	8.1	10.6	11.4	133.4
Snow, Ice pellets 1.0" or more	1.8	1.3	0.7	*	0.0	0.0	0.0	0.0	0.0	0.0	0.2	1.0	5.0
Thunderstorms	0.3	0.9	2.0	3.4	6.4	8.4	9.6	7.5	3.6	1.0	0.5	0.2	43.6
Fog, Visibility 1/4 mile or less	3.4	2.6	1.3	1.6	3.4	3.7	4.9	7.3	5.4	4.9	2.7	3.1	44.4
Temperature Maximum:													
90° and above	0.0	0.0	0.0	0.0	0.3	2.3	4.1	2.8	2.0	0.0	0.0	0.0	11.5
32° and below	6.2	3.3	0.4	0.0	0.0	0.0	0.0	0.0	0.0	0.0	0.3	2.9	13.0
Temperature Minimum:													
32° and below	23.8	20.4	13.8	3.6	0.1	0.0	0.0	0.0	0.0	2.6	12.6	20.6	97.6
0° and below	1.1	0.3	*	0.0	0.0	0.0	0.0	0.0	0.0	0.0	0.0	0.2	1.7
RELATIVE HUMIDITY (%)													
Morning	76	73	71	71	82	86	88	89	87	83	79	77	80
Afternoon	63	58	52	49	55	57	62	61	57	54	57	62	57
PRECIPITATION (inches)													
Water Equivalent													
Normal	3.5	3.4	4.2	3.4	3.6	3.4	4.1	3.2	3.0	2.5	2.9	3.5	41.2
Maximum monthly	9.1	7.2	9.5	5.8	9.7	6.6	9.7	7.0	7.0	5.6	5.9	6.7	9.7
Date	1957	1956	1955	1970	1950	1957	1949	1966	1972	1959	1948	1961	1949
Minimum monthly	1.3	0.7	1.3	0.2	1.3	1.1	0.7	0.8	0.5	0.0	1.0	0.2	0.0
Date	1981	1968	1985	1976	1966	1980	1957	1954	1985	1963	1953	1965	1963
Maximum in 24 hrs	2.3	1.8	3.3	2.6	3.2	3.1	2.9	3.0	3.6	3.6	2.5	2.9	3.6
Date	1950	1954	1973	1977	1984	1954	1946	1982	1972	1964	1957	1969	1964
SNOW, ICE PELLETS													
Maximum monthly	22.1	20.4	27.9	5.6	T	0.0	0.0	0.0	0.0	T	18.1	12.9	27.9
Date	1966	1979	1960	1983	1963	—	—	—	—	1977	1952	1963	1960
Maximum in 24 hrs	9.7	10.7	13.0	5.6	T	0.0	0.0	0.0	0.0	T	16.2	9.6	16.2
Date	1955	1969	1960	1983	1963	—	—	—	—	1977	1952	1969	1952
WIND (Resultant)													
Mean speed (mph)	6.6	6.8	7.4	7.1	5.3	4.8	4.2	3.9	4.3	4.7	5.7	6.0	5.6

CHATTANOOGA   Elev. 665'   35° 02'N — 85° 12'W   Tennessee

NORMALS, MEANS, EXTREMES

	JAN	FEB	MAR	APR	MAY	JUN	JUL	AUG	SEP	OCT	NOV	DEC	YEAR
TEMPERATURE													
Normal daily maximum	48.2	52.6	60.9	72.6	79.8	86.4	89.3	88.8	83.0	72.3	60.3	51.4	70.5
Normal daily minimum	29.2	31.2	38.6	47.5	55.7	63.8	68.1	67.4	61.5	47.7	37.5	31.5	48.3
Normal monthly	38.7	41.9	49.8	60.1	67.8	75.1	78.7	78.1	72.3	60.0	48.9	41.5	59.4
Extreme highest	78	79	87	93	99	104	106	105	102	94	84	78	106
Extreme highest date	1949	1977	1963	1942	1941	1952	1952	1947	1954	1954	1961	1951	1952
Extreme lowest	-10	1	8	26	34	41	51	50	36	22	4	-2	-10
Extreme lowest date	1985	1958	1960	1973	1971	1972	1972	1946	1967	1952	1950	1983	1985
DEGREE DAYS BASE 65° F													
Heating	815	644	478	171	56	6	0	0	11	190	483	729	3583
Cooling	0	0	7	24	142	309	425	406	230	35	0	0	1578
% OF POSSIBLE SUNSHINE	43	49	52	60	65	65	61	62	64	62	53	44	57
AVERAGE SKY COVER													
Sunrise - Sunset	6.7	6.5	6.4	5.9	5.8	5.7	6.0	5.7	5.4	4.9	5.7	6.6	5.9
NUMBER OF DAYS (Sunrise-Sunset)													
Clear	7.3	7.6	7.9	9.0	8.9	8.1	6.7	8.3	10.0	13.1	10.3	8.0	105.4
Partly cloudy	6.5	6.0	7.6	8.1	10.3	11.9	12.9	12.9	9.7	7.7	6.7	6.4	106.6
Cloudy	17.2	14.7	15.5	12.9	11.8	10.0	11.3	9.8	10.3	10.1	13.0	16.7	153.2
Precipitation .01" or more	11.7	10.5	12.1	9.7	10.1	10.5	11.9	9.9	7.7	6.8	8.8	10.8	120.5
Snow, Ice pellets 1.0" or more	0.8	0.5	0.2	*	0.0	0.0	0.0	0.0	0.0	0.0	*	0.3	1.9
Thunderstorms	1.2	1.8	3.7	4.7	7.2	9.4	11.4	9.3	3.8	1.4	1.2	0.6	55.5
Fog, Visibility 1/4 mile or less	3.1	1.7	1.8	1.7	2.4	2.1	2.1	2.8	3.8	6.1	4.0	3.3	34.9
Temperature Maximum:													
90° and above	0.0	0.0	0.0	0.1	2.6	10.4	15.9	13.8	4.8	0.3	0.0	0.0	47.9
32° and below	2.1	1.0	0.1	0.0	0.0	0.0	0.0	0.0	0.0	0.0	*	0.8	4.0
Temperature Minimum:													
32° and below	19.6	15.6	9.1	1.5	0.0	0.0	0.0	0.0	0.0	1.2	10.2	17.8	75.0
0° and below	0.2	0.0	0.0	0.0	0.0	0.0	0.0	0.0	0.0	0.0	0.0	*	0.2
RELATIVE HUMIDITY (%)													
Morning	79	77	76	77	86	88	88	89	89	88	82	81	83
Afternoon	62	57	53	49	53	54	57	57	56	53	56	62	56
PRECIPITATION (inches)													
Water Equivalent													
Normal	5.2	4.6	6.3	4.5	4.0	3.3	4.5	3.4	4.3	2.9	4.1	5.1	52.6
Maximum monthly	12.2	11.0	16.3	11.9	9.2	9.4	11.7	7.5	14.1	9.9	13.5	13.6	16.3
Date	1947	1944	1980	1964	1979	1949	1979	1975	1977	1949	1948	1961	1980
Minimum monthly	1.1	0.6	1.1	0.4	0.5	0.8	0.2	0.5	0.3	0.2	0.9	0.8	0.2
Date	1961	1941	1967	1942	1941	1968	1957	1963	1941	1963	1953	1965	1957
Maximum in 24 hrs	4.4	3.9	6.5	3.3	3.4	4.8	5.7	3.7	6.6	3.5	4.5	5.2	6.6
Date	1949	1958	1973	1983	1979	1949	1979	1941	1977	1977	1948	1942	1977
SNOW, ICE PELLETS													
Maximum monthly	8.4	10.4	10.1	1.0	T	0.0	0.0	0.0	0.0	T	2.8	9.1	10.4
Date	1966	1960	1960	1971	1944	—	—	—	—	1954	1950	1963	1960
Maximum in 24 hrs	8.4	8.7	6.0	1.0	T	0.0	0.0	0.0	0.0	T	2.8	8.9	8.9
Date	1966	1960	1960	1971	1944	—	—	—	—	1954	1950	1963	1963
WIND (Resultant)													
Mean speed (mph)	7.1	7.5	8.0	7.5	6.0	5.4	5.1	4.6	4.9	5.0	6.1	6.5	6.2

KNOXVILLE

Elev. 980'   35° 49'N — 83° 59'W   Tennessee

NORMALS, MEANS, EXTREMES

	JAN	FEB	MAR	APR	MAY	JUN	JUL	AUG	SEP	OCT	NOV	DEC	YEAR
TEMPERATURE													
Normal daily maximum	46.9	51.2	60.1	71.0	78.3	84.6	87.2	86.9	81.7	70.9	59.1	50.3	69.0
Normal daily minimum	29.5	31.7	39.3	48.2	56.5	64.0	68.0	67.1	61.2	48.1	38.4	31.9	48.7
Normal monthly	38.2	41.5	49.7	59.6	67.4	74.3	77.6	77.0	71.5	59.5	48.8	41.1	58.8
Extreme highest	77	83	86	92	94	102	103	102	103	91	84	80	103
Extreme highest date	1950	1977	1963	1942	1962	1944	1952	1944	1954	1953	1948	1982	1954
Extreme lowest	-24	-2	1	23	34	43	51	49	36	25	5	-6	-24
Extreme lowest date	1985	1958	1980	1985	1963	1956	1961	1946	1967	1962	1950	1983	1985
DEGREE DAYS BASE 65° F													
Heating	831	658	483	181	63	0	0	0	14	201	486	741	3658
Cooling	0	0	8	19	137	283	391	372	209	30	0	0	1449
% OF POSSIBLE SUNSHINE	40	47	52	62	63	64	62	62	60	60	49	40	55
AVERAGE SKY COVER													
Sunrise - Sunset	7.1	6.7	6.7	6.1	6.1	5.8	6.0	5.6	5.6	5.0	6.2	6.7	6.1
NUMBER OF DAYS (Sunrise-Sunset)													
Clear	6.1	6.6	7.1	8.0	8.0	7.5	6.6	8.7	9.5	12.3	8.8	7.1	96.1
Partly cloudy	6.6	6.1	7.5	8.7	9.7	12.6	12.9	11.9	9.6	7.8	6.6	6.8	106.8
Cloudy	18.3	15.5	16.4	13.3	13.3	10.0	11.5	10.5	10.9	10.9	14.7	17.1	162.3
Precipitation .01" or more	12.4	11.3	12.8	11.1	11.0	10.3	11.5	9.7	8.3	7.7	10.0	10.8	127.0
Snow, Ice pellets 1.0" or more	1.4	1.1	0.5	0.1	0.0	0.0	0.0	0.0	0.0	0.0	0.2	0.6	3.9
Thunderstorms	0.8	1.4	3.2	4.2	6.5	8.2	9.7	6.8	3.0	1.4	1.0	0.5	46.8
Fog, Visibility 1/4 mile or less	3.0	1.7	1.6	1.1	2.3	2.1	2.1	3.4	4.0	4.9	3.0	2.6	31.8
Temperature Maximum:													
90° and above	0.0	0.0	0.0	0.0	0.8	4.1	9.0	6.9	2.6	0.0	0.0	0.0	23.4
32° and below	3.8	1.4	0.1	0.0	0.0	0.0	0.0	0.0	0.0	0.0	0.1	1.4	6.8
Temperature Minimum:													
32° and below	20.6	17.2	8.3	1.4	0.0	0.0	0.0	0.0	0.0	0.6	7.7	17.3	73.1
0° and below	0.5	*	0.0	0.0	0.0	0.0	0.0	0.0	0.0	0.0	0.0	0.1	0.7
RELATIVE HUMIDITY (%)													
Morning	77	73	71	71	82	86	87	88	87	84	79	77	80
Afternoon	64	59	55	52	57	59	62	61	60	56	59	63	59
PRECIPITATION (inches)													
Water Equivalent													
Normal	4.6	4.1	5.4	3.8	3.7	3.9	4.3	3.0	2.9	2.7	3.7	4.5	47.2
Maximum monthly	11.7	9.3	10.4	7.2	10.9	7.5	10.0	8.8	8.6	6.6	10.3	11.6	11.7
Date	1954	1944	1975	1970	1974	1969	1967	1942	1944	1949	1948	1961	1954
Minimum monthly	1.0	0.7	1.9	0.3	0.7	0.2	0.7	0.7	0.4	T	0.9	0.4	T
Date	1981	1968	1985	1976	1970	1944	1957	1954	1985	1963	1942	1965	1963
Maximum in 24 hrs	3.8	2.8	4.8	3.6	3.4	3.5	4.6	3.2	5.0	2.4	4.0	4.8	5.0
Date	1946	1956	1973	1977	1984	1972	1942	1959	1944	1961	1948	1969	1944
SNOW, ICE PELLETS													
Maximum monthly	15.1	23.3	20.2	7.0	T	0.0	0.0	0.0	0.0	T	18.2	12.2	23.3
Date	1962	1960	1960	1971	1945	—	—	—	—	1962	1952	1963	1960
Maximum in 24 hrs	12.0	17.5	12.1	7.0	T	0.0	0.0	0.0	0.0	T	18.2	8.9	18.2
Date	1962	1960	1942	1971	1945	—	—	—	—	1962	1952	1969	1952
WIND (Resultant)													
Mean speed (mph)	8.0	8.4	8.9	8.8	7.1	6.6	6.1	5.6	5.7	5.8	6.9	7.4	7.1

MEMPHIS

Elev. 258'   35° 03'N — 90° 00'W   **Tennessee**

NORMALS, MEANS, EXTREMES

	JAN	FEB	MAR	APR	MAY	JUN	JUL	AUG	SEP	OCT	NOV	DEC	YEAR
TEMPERATURE													
Normal daily maximum	48.3	53.0	61.4	72.9	81.0	88.4	91.5	90.3	84.3	74.5	61.4	52.3	71.6
Normal daily minimum	30.9	34.1	41.9	52.2	60.9	68.9	72.6	70.8	64.1	51.3	41.1	34.3	51.9
Normal monthly	39.6	43.6	51.7	62.6	71.0	78.7	82.1	80.6	74.2	62.9	51.3	43.3	61.8
Extreme highest	78	81	85	91	99	104	108	105	103	95	85	81	108
Extreme highest date	1972	1962	1963	1952	1977	1954	1980	1943	1954	1954	1955	1982	1980
Extreme lowest	-4	-11	12	29	38	48	52	48	36	25	9	-13	-13
Extreme lowest date	1985	1951	1943	1944	1944	1966	1947	1946	1949	1952	1950	1963	1963
DEGREE DAYS BASE 65° F													
Heating	787	602	433	126	25	0	0	0	9	137	415	673	3207
Cooling	0	0	20	54	211	411	530	484	285	72	0	0	2067
% OF POSSIBLE SUNSHINE	50	54	56	64	69	74	74	75	69	70	58	50	64
AVERAGE SKY COVER													
Sunrise - Sunset	6.8	6.4	6.5	6.0	5.9	5.3	5.3	5.0	5.0	4.6	5.6	6.4	5.7
NUMBER OF DAYS (Sunrise-Sunset)													
Clear	7.9	7.8	8.0	8.8	8.7	10.1	10.4	11.8	12.5	14.3	10.1	8.8	119.2
Partly cloudy	5.9	5.8	6.6	7.1	9.7	11.1	11.8	11.4	7.7	7.1	6.4	5.9	96.5
Cloudy	17.2	14.7	16.4	14.1	12.6	8.8	8.8	7.8	9.9	9.6	13.6	16.3	149.5
Precipitation .01" or more	10.1	9.5	11.0	10.4	9.2	8.3	8.7	8.0	7.1	6.2	8.6	9.7	106.8
Snow, Ice pellets 1.0" or more	0.9	0.6	0.3	0.0	0.0	0.0	0.0	0.0	0.0	0.0	*	0.2	1.9
Thunderstorms	1.9	2.3	4.7	6.6	6.7	7.2	8.2	6.3	3.4	1.9	2.3	1.6	53.1
Fog, Visibility 1/4 mile or less	2.2	1.3	0.8	0.3	0.2	0.2	0.3	0.4	0.7	1.1	1.3	1.8	10.6
Temperature Maximum:													
90° and above	0.0	0.0	0.0	*	3.0	14.5	21.5	18.1	7.5	0.6	0.0	0.0	65.2
32° and below	3.5	1.2	0.2	0.0	0.0	0.0	0.0	0.0	0.0	0.0	0.1	1.3	6.3
Temperature Minimum:													
32° and below	18.5	12.8	5.4	0.3	0.0	0.0	0.0	0.0	0.0	0.4	6.0	14.6	57.9
0° and below	0.1	*	0.0	0.0	0.0	0.0	0.0	0.0	0.0	0.0	0.0	0.1	0.2
RELATIVE HUMIDITY (%)													
Morning	75	73	71	71	76	78	79	80	80	77	74	74	76
Afternoon	63	59	56	54	55	56	57	57	56	51	56	61	57
PRECIPITATION (inches)													
Water Equivalent													
Normal	4.6	4.3	5.4	5.7	5.0	3.5	4.0	3.7	3.6	2.3	4.1	4.8	51.5
Maximum monthly	12.2	9.3	12.0	12.2	11.5	6.8	8.8	9.6	7.6	7.7	9.5	13.8	13.8
Date	1951	1956	1975	1955	1953	1951	1959	1978	1958	1984	1983	1982	1982
Minimum monthly	0.8	1.1	1.5	2.0	0.8	0.0	0.4	0.4	0.1	T	0.7	1.0	T
Date	1961	1980	1966	1965	1977	1953	1954	1953	1953	1963	1965	1955	1963
Maximum in 24 hrs	3.8	3.6	5.9	4.3	4.9	4.7	4.7	4.0	4.6	3.4	4.7	5.4	5.9
Date	1974	1966	1975	1985	1958	1980	1980	1978	1957	1981	1983	1978	1975
SNOW, ICE PELLETS													
Maximum monthly	12.4	8.3	17.3	T	0.0	0.0	0.0	0.0	0.0	0.0	1.5	14.3	17.3
Date	1985	1985	1968	1971	—	—	—	—	—	—	1976	1963	1968
Maximum in 24 hrs	8.1	5.8	16.1	T	0.0	0.0	0.0	0.0	0.0	0.0	1.2	14.3	16.1
Date	1985	1960	1968	1971	—	—	—	—	—	—	1976	1963	1968
WIND (Resultant)													
Mean speed (mph)	10.3	10.3	11.1	10.6	8.9	8.0	7.5	7.0	7.5	7.8	9.2	9.9	9.0

NASHVILLE

Elev. 590'   36° 07'N — 86° 41'W   Tennessee

NORMALS, MEANS, EXTREMES

	JAN	FEB	MAR	APR	MAY	JUN	JUL	AUG	SEP	OCT	NOV	DEC	YEAR
TEMPERATURE													
Normal daily maximum	46.3	50.7	59.6	71.2	79.2	86.7	89.8	89.0	83.2	72.3	59.2	50.4	69.8
Normal daily minimum	27.8	30.1	38.3	48.1	56.9	64.8	69.0	67.8	61.3	48.0	38.0	31.3	48.5
Normal monthly	37.1	40.4	49.0	59.7	68.1	75.8	79.4	78.4	72.3	60.2	48.6	40.9	59.1
Extreme highest	78	84	86	90	97	106	107	104	105	94	84	79	107
Extreme highest date	1972	1962	1982	1980	1941	1952	1952	1954	1954	1953	1971	1982	1952
Extreme lowest	-17	-13	2	23	34	42	51	47	36	26	-1	-7	-17
Extreme lowest date	1985	1951	1980	1982	1976	1966	1947	1946	1983	1952	1950	1962	1985
DEGREE DAYS BASE 65° F													
Heating	865	689	510	186	55	0	0	0	19	193	492	747	3756
Cooling	0	0	14	24	151	328	446	415	238	45	0	0	1661
% OF POSSIBLE SUNSHINE	41	47	51	58	61	66	63	64	63	62	50	42	56
AVERAGE SKY COVER													
Sunrise - Sunset	7.1	6.7	6.6	6.1	6.0	5.6	5.7	5.3	5.2	4.9	6.1	6.7	6.0
NUMBER OF DAYS (Sunrise-Sunset)													
Clear	6.3	6.9	7.5	8.2	8.3	8.3	8.1	10.1	10.8	12.6	8.8	7.3	103.1
Partly cloudy	6.2	6.0	6.8	8.4	9.9	12.4	13.0	11.8	8.8	8.3	6.8	6.8	105.1
Cloudy	18.5	15.4	16.7	13.5	12.8	9.3	9.9	9.0	10.4	10.0	14.4	17.0	157.0
Precipitation .01" or more	11.3	10.7	12.2	11.0	10.7	9.4	10.2	8.9	7.8	7.0	9.4	10.9	119.5
Snow, Ice pellets 1.0" or more	1.4	1.2	0.5	*	0.0	0.0	0.0	0.0	0.0	0.0	0.1	0.6	3.8
Thunderstorms	1.3	1.7	4.2	5.5	7.4	8.3	9.9	7.8	3.7	1.6	1.6	1.2	54.1
Fog, Visibility 1/4 mile or less	2.6	1.3	1.1	0.5	1.0	0.9	1.2	1.7	1.9	2.1	1.7	1.8	17.6
Temperature Maximum:													
90° and above	0.0	0.0	0.0	0.1	0.9	9.1	16.0	10.9	5.2	0.2	0.0	0.0	42.2
32° and below	5.9	2.5	0.2	0.0	0.0	0.0	0.0	0.0	0.0	0.0	0.2	1.9	10.6
Temperature Minimum:													
32° and below	22.8	17.7	9.4	1.6	0.0	0.0	0.0	0.0	0.0	1.1	8.3	17.0	77.8
0° and below	1.0	0.3	0.0	0.0	0.0	0.0	0.0	0.0	0.0	0.0	0.0	0.1	1.4
RELATIVE HUMIDITY (%)													
Morning	75	73	71	72	82	84	86	86	86	81	77	76	79
Afternoon	64	59	54	52	56	55	58	59	59	55	60	63	58
PRECIPITATION (inches)													
Water Equivalent													
Normal	4.4	4.0	5.5	4.4	4.5	3.7	3.8	3.4	3.7	2.5	3.5	4.6	48.4
Maximum monthly	13.9	10.3	12.3	8.4	11.0	9.3	7.7	8.3	11.4	6.1	9.0	13.6	13.9
Date	1950	1956	1975	1984	1983	1960	1950	1942	1979	1959	1945	1978	1950
Minimum monthly	1.1	0.6	1.3	1.1	0.6	0.7	0.7	0.6	0.2	T	0.5	0.9	T
Date	1970	1968	1966	1948	1941	1952	1954	1968	1956	1963	1949	1985	1963
Maximum in 24 hrs	4.4	4.0	4.6	3.2	4.2	4.9	3.5	5.3	6.6	3.7	3.7	5.1	6.6
Date	1946	1948	1975	1979	1984	1960	1950	1963	1979	1975	1973	1978	1979
SNOW, ICE PELLETS													
Maximum monthly	18.8	18.9	16.1	1.1	0.0	0.0	0.0	0.0	0.0	T	9.2	13.2	18.9
Date	1948	1979	1960	1971	—	—	—	—	—	1954	1950	1963	1979
Maximum in 24 hrs	7.5	8.3	8.8	1.1	0.0	0.0	0.0	0.0	0.0	T	9.2	10.2	10.2
Date	1966	1979	1951	1971	—	—	—	—	—	1954	1950	1963	1963
WIND (Resultant)													
Mean speed (mph)	9.2	9.3	10.0	9.5	7.7	7.1	6.4	6.1	6.4	6.7	8.4	9.0	8.0

ABILENE

Elev. 1784' 32° 25'N — 99° 41'W **Texas**

NORMALS, MEANS, EXTREMES

	JAN	FEB	MAR	APR	MAY	JUN	JUL	AUG	SEP	OCT	NOV	DEC	YEAR
TEMPERATURE													
Normal daily maximum	55.5	60.3	68.6	77.6	84.1	91.8	95.4	94.5	87.1	77.6	64.8	58.4	76.3
Normal daily minimum	31.2	35.5	42.6	52.8	60.8	69.0	72.7	71.7	64.9	54.1	42.0	34.3	52.6
Normal monthly	43.4	47.9	55.6	65.2	72.5	80.4	84.1	83.1	76.0	65.9	53.4	46.4	64.5
Extreme highest	89	90	97	99	107	109	110	109	106	103	92	89	110
Extreme highest date	1943	1940	1974	1948	1967	1980	1978	1943	1952	1979	1980	1955	1978
Extreme lowest	-9	-7	7	25	36	47	55	55	35	28	14	2	-9
Extreme lowest date	1947	1985	1943	1973	1979	1964	1940	1961	1942	1957	1976	1983	1947
DEGREE DAYS BASE 65° F													
Heating	673	479	321	98	11	0	0	0	10	91	361	577	2621
Cooling	0	0	29	104	244	465	592	561	340	119	13	0	2467
% OF POSSIBLE SUNSHINE	62	65	69	71	70	78	79	77	69	71	68	65	70
AVERAGE SKY COVER													
Sunrise - Sunset	5.7	5.6	5.4	5.2	5.4	4.5	4.4	4.4	4.5	4.4	4.8	5.2	5.0
NUMBER OF DAYS (Sunrise-Sunset)													
Clear	10.7	10.2	11.2	11.5	10.2	12.9	14.4	14.5	14.0	14.7	13.5	12.1	149.8
Partly cloudy	6.4	6.2	7.4	7.7	10.2	10.3	9.8	9.8	7.8	7.0	6.0	6.5	95.1
Cloudy	13.9	11.9	12.4	10.8	10.6	6.8	6.8	6.8	8.2	9.3	10.5	12.4	120.3
Precipitation .01" or more	5.1	5.1	4.6	6.3	7.9	6.0	4.7	5.4	5.9	5.6	4.4	4.3	65.4
Snow, Ice pellets 1.0" or more	0.7	0.5	0.2	0.0	0.0	0.0	0.0	0.0	0.0	0.0	0.2	0.3	1.9
Thunderstorms	0.5	1.2	2.8	5.2	7.9	5.9	4.7	5.2	3.2	2.8	1.3	0.7	41.5
Fog, Visibility 1/4 mile or less	1.3	1.3	0.6	0.4	0.5	0.1	*	*	0.3	0.7	1.0	1.0	7.2
Temperature Maximum:													
90° and above	0.0	0.0	0.5	2.3	7.3	20.0	26.5	25.0	12.5	2.2	0.1	0.0	96.5
32° and below	2.3	0.8	*	0.0	0.0	0.0	0.0	0.0	0.0	0.0	0.1	1.1	4.4
Temperature Minimum:													
32° and below	17.9	12.4	4.4	0.5	0.0	0.0	0.0	0.0	0.0	0.1	4.9	14.1	54.2
0° and below	*	*	0.0	0.0	0.0	0.0	0.0	0.0	0.0	0.0	0.0	0.0	0.1
RELATIVE HUMIDITY (%)													
Morning	67	66	61	63	68	64	57	60	67	67	69	66	65
Afternoon	55	53	48	46	51	49	44	47	53	52	53	52	50
PRECIPITATION (inches)													
Water Equivalent													
Normal	0.9	0.9	1.0	2.3	3.2	2.5	2.1	2.4	3.0	2.3	1.3	0.8	23.2
Maximum monthly	4.3	2.8	5.1	6.8	13.1	9.6	7.1	8.1	11.0	10.6	4.6	3.0	13.1
Date	1968	1940	1979	1966	1957	1961	1968	1969	1974	1981	1968	1984	1957
Minimum monthly	T	0.0	0.0	T	0.1	0.0	T	T	T	0.0	0.0	T	0.0
Date	1967	1962	1963	1961	1956	1954	1970	1943	1956	1952	1949	1972	1952
Maximum in 24 hrs	2.1	1.7	2.2	3.7	2.8	3.6	3.7	6.3	6.7	6.0	2.4	2.3	6.7
Date	1961	1940	1977	1957	1969	1959	1960	1978	1961	1981	1975	1946	1961
SNOW, ICE PELLETS													
Maximum monthly	13.5	8.4	7.3	T	0.0	0.0	0.0	0.0	0.0	T	8.1	7.8	13.5
Date	1973	1956	1970	1980	—	—	—	—	—	1980	1968	1983	1973
Maximum in 24 hrs	7.5	4.5	6.1	T	0.0	0.0	0.0	0.0	0.0	T	5.3	4.2	7.5
Date	1973	1979	1970	1980	—	—	—	—	—	1980	1976	1946	1973
WIND (Resultant)													
Mean speed (mph)	11.9	12.7	14.1	14.1	13.1	13.0	10.9	10.5	10.6	11.1	11.7	11.9	12.1

AMARILLO

Elev. 3604' **35° 14'N — 101° 42'W** **Texas**

NORMALS, MEANS, EXTREMES

	JAN	FEB	MAR	APR	MAY	JUN	JUL	AUG	SEP	OCT	NOV	DEC	YEAR
TEMPERATURE													
Normal daily maximum	49.1	53.1	60.8	71.0	79.1	88.2	91.4	89.6	82.4	72.7	58.7	51.8	70.7
Normal daily minimum	21.7	26.1	32.0	42.0	51.9	61.5	66.2	64.5	56.9	45.5	32.1	24.8	43.8
Normal monthly	35.4	39.6	46.4	56.5	65.5	74.9	78.8	77.1	69.7	59.1	45.4	38.3	57.2
Extreme highest	81	88	94	98	102	108	105	106	102	95	87	81	108
Extreme highest date	1950	1963	1971	1965	1953	1953	1981	1944	1983	1954	1980	1955	1953
Extreme lowest	-11	-14	-3	14	28	42	53	49	30	21	0	-7	-14
Extreme lowest date	1984	1951	1948	1945	1954	1955	1950	1956	1984	1980	1976	1983	1951
DEGREE DAYS BASE 65° F													
Heating	918	711	577	271	92	6	0	0	25	215	588	828	4231
Cooling	0	0	0	16	108	303	428	372	166	35	0	0	1428
% OF POSSIBLE SUNSHINE	68	69	71	73	72	77	78	77	73	74	71	67	73
AVERAGE SKY COVER													
Sunrise - Sunset	5.2	5.2	5.3	5.0	5.1	4.3	4.5	4.3	4.1	4.0	4.4	4.9	4.7
NUMBER OF DAYS (Sunrise-Sunset)													
Clear	12.3	10.5	11.4	11.7	11.0	13.1	13.0	14.7	15.3	16.2	14.5	12.9	156.7
Partly cloudy	7.3	7.7	8.7	8.8	10.4	11.2	12.4	10.1	7.2	7.0	6.8	7.6	105.1
Cloudy	11.4	10.0	10.9	9.6	9.5	5.7	5.6	6.2	7.5	7.9	8.8	10.5	103.4
Precipitation .01" or more	4.1	4.4	4.7	5.0	8.2	8.2	8.3	8.3	5.8	5.0	3.3	3.8	69.0
Snow, Ice pellets 1.0" or more	1.4	1.1	0.7	0.2	0.0	0.0	0.0	0.0	0.0	0.1	0.5	0.8	4.8
Thunderstorms	0.1	0.5	1.5	3.4	8.5	9.4	9.5	8.8	4.0	2.5	0.6	0.2	49.1
Fog, Visibility 1/4 mile or less	3.4	4.2	3.3	2.0	2.0	0.7	0.5	0.7	2.1	2.4	2.8	2.8	26.9
Temperature Maximum:													
90° and above	0.0	0.0	0.1	0.8	4.8	13.2	22.0	17.0	7.0	1.1	0.0	0.0	65.9
32° and below	5.0	2.7	0.8	*	0.0	0.0	0.0	0.0	0.0	*	0.8	3.5	12.9
Temperature Minimum:													
32° and below	27.5	22.0	14.9	3.3	0.1	0.0	0.0	0.0	0.2	1.8	14.2	26.5	110.6
0° and below	1.3	0.3	0.0	0.0	0.0	0.0	0.0	0.0	0.0	0.0	*	0.4	2.0
RELATIVE HUMIDITY (%)													
Morning	65	64	58	55	62	64	60	66	69	64	66	65	63
Afternoon	51	49	42	38	42	44	41	45	49	44	48	48	45
PRECIPITATION (inches)													
Water Equivalent													
Normal	0.4	0.5	0.8	1.0	2.7	3.5	2.7	2.9	1.7	1.3	0.5	0.4	19.1
Maximum monthly	2.3	1.8	3.9	3.7	9.8	10.7	7.5	7.5	5.0	7.6	2.2	4.5	10.7
Date	1968	1948	1973	1942	1951	1965	1960	1974	1950	1941	1961	1959	1965
Minimum monthly	T	T	T	T	0.0	0.0	0.1	0.2	0.0	0.0	T	T	0.0
Date	1976	1943	1950	1964	1984	1953	1946	1983	1977	1952	1960	1976	1952
Maximum in 24 hrs	1.7	1.2	2.2	1.9	6.7	6.1	4.7	4.2	3.4	3.4	1.2	3.1	6.7
Date	1968	1971	1973	1985	1951	1960	1982	1945	1941	1948	1971	1943	1951
SNOW, ICE PELLETS													
Maximum monthly	14.5	17.3	14.7	6.4	0.5	0.0	0.0	0.0	0.3	3.9	13.6	8.5	17.3
Date	1983	1971	1961	1947	1978	—	—	—	1984	1976	1952	1943	1971
Maximum in 24 hrs	9.8	13.5	9.8	5.1	0.5	0.0	0.0	0.0	0.3	3.2	12.2	7.4	13.5
Date	1983	1971	1957	1947	1978	—	—	—	1984	1976	1952	1971	1971
WIND (Resultant)													
Mean speed (mph)	13.0	14.1	15.5	15.5	14.7	14.3	12.6	12.1	13.0	13.0	13.1	13.0	13.7

AUSTIN

Elev. 597'   30° 18'N — 97° 42'W   **Texas**

NORMALS, MEANS, EXTREMES

	JAN	FEB	MAR	APR	MAY	JUN	JUL	AUG	SEP	OCT	NOV	DEC	YEAR
TEMPERATURE													
Normal daily maximum	59.4	64.1	71.7	79.0	84.7	91.6	95.4	95.3	89.3	80.8	69.2	62.8	78.6
Normal daily minimum	38.8	42.2	49.3	58.3	65.1	71.5	73.9	73.7	69.1	58.7	48.1	41.4	57.5
Normal monthly	49.1	53.2	60.5	68.7	74.9	81.6	84.7	84.5	79.2	69.8	58.7	52.1	68.1
Extreme highest	90	93	98	98	100	105	109	106	104	97	91	90	109
Extreme highest date	1971	1954	1971	1982	1984	1980	1954	1984	1985	1979	1951	1955	1954
Extreme lowest	-2	7	18	35	43	53	64	61	41	32	20	10	-2
Extreme lowest date	1949	1951	1948	1973	1954	1970	1970	1967	1942	1957	1976	1983	1949
DEGREE DAYS BASE 65° F													
Heating	505	347	203	41	0	0	0	0	0	37	221	406	1760
Cooling	12	16	63	152	307	498	611	605	426	186	32	6	2914
% OF POSSIBLE SUNSHINE	49	52	55	54	58	69	76	75	67	64	56	51	61
AVERAGE SKY COVER													
Sunrise - Sunset	6.3	6.0	6.1	6.3	6.1	5.2	4.7	4.7	5.0	4.8	5.3	5.9	5.5
NUMBER OF DAYS (Sunrise-Sunset)													
Clear	8.9	8.5	8.5	7.7	6.8	8.3	11.8	11.7	10.8	12.5	11.2	10.2	116.9
Partly cloudy	5.9	6.4	8.0	7.3	11.4	15.0	13.5	13.8	10.8	9.2	6.8	6.0	114.0
Cloudy	16.2	13.4	14.6	15.0	12.8	6.8	5.7	5.5	8.4	9.2	12.1	14.8	134.3
Precipitation .01" or more	7.9	7.7	7.2	7.5	8.7	6.2	4.8	5.2	7.1	6.6	7.0	7.0	82.8
Snow, Ice pellets 1.0" or more	0.2	0.2	*	0.0	0.0	0.0	0.0	0.0	0.0	0.0	0.1	0.0	0.5
Thunderstorms	0.8	2.0	3.2	4.7	6.9	4.7	3.9	4.8	4.0	2.8	1.6	1.2	40.8
Fog, Visibility 1/4 mile or less	4.5	3.1	2.7	1.4	1.0	0.5	0.3	0.4	0.8	2.1	2.8	4.3	23.6
Temperature Maximum:													
90° and above	*	*	0.7	1.5	6.3	20.7	27.7	28.2	16.4	3.5	0.0	0.0	105.0
32° and below	0.8	0.2	0.0	0.0	0.0	0.0	0.0	0.0	0.0	0.0	0.0	0.3	1.2
Temperature Minimum:													
32° and below	9.7	5.0	1.0	0.0	0.0	0.0	0.0	0.0	0.0	0.0	1.0	5.8	22.5
0° and below	0.0	0.0	0.0	0.0	0.0	0.0	0.0	0.0	0.0	0.0	0.0	0.0	0.0
RELATIVE HUMIDITY (%)													
Morning	72	71	71	75	80	79	74	73	78	75	76	73	75
Afternoon	60	58	56	58	60	56	50	50	56	55	58	59	56
PRECIPITATION (inches)													
Water Equivalent													
Normal	1.6	2.4	1.6	3.1	4.1	3.0	1.8	2.2	3.6	3.3	2.2	2.0	31.5
Maximum monthly	7.9	6.3	6.0	9.9	9.9	14.9	10.5	8.9	8.1	12.3	7.9	5.9	14.9
Date	1968	1958	1983	1957	1965	1981	1979	1974	1942	1960	1946	1944	1981
Minimum monthly	0.0	0.2	T	0.0	0.8	T	0.0	0.0	0.0	T	T	T	0.0
Date	1971	1954	1972	1984	1960	1967	1962	1952	1947	1952	1970	1950	1962
Maximum in 24 hrs	3.4	3.7	2.6	3.8	5.6	6.5	5.4	4.6	6.7	7.2	5.0	4.0	7.2
Date	1965	1958	1980	1942	1979	1964	1961	1945	1973	1960	1974	1953	1960
SNOW, ICE PELLETS													
Maximum monthly	7.5	6.0	2.0	0.0	0.0	0.0	0.0	0.0	0.0	0.0	2.0	T	7.5
Date	1985	1966	1965	—	—	—	—	—	—	—	1980	1983	1985
Maximum in 24 hrs	7.0	6.0	2.0	0.0	0.0	0.0	0.0	0.0	0.0	0.0	2.0	T	7.0
Date	1944	1966	1965	—	—	—	—	—	—	—	1980	1983	1944
WIND (Resultant)													
Mean speed (mph)	9.8	10.2	10.9	10.6	9.7	9.3	8.4	7.9	8.0	8.1	9.0	9.2	9.2

BROWNSVILLE

Elev. 19'   25° 54'N — 97° 26'W   **Texas**

NORMALS, MEANS, EXTREMES

	JAN	FEB	MAR	APR	MAY	JUN	JUL	AUG	SEP	OCT	NOV	DEC	YEAR
TEMPERATURE													
Normal daily maximum	69.7	72.5	77.5	83.2	87.0	90.5	92.6	92.8	89.8	84.4	77.0	71.9	82.4
Normal daily minimum	50.8	53.0	59.5	66.6	71.3	74.7	75.6	75.4	73.1	66.1	58.3	52.6	64.8
Normal monthly	60.3	62.8	68.5	74.9	79.2	82.6	84.1	84.1	81.5	75.3	67.7	62.3	73.6
Extreme highest	93	94	106	102	102	101	102	102	104	96	94	94	106
Extreme highest date	1971	1982	1984	1984	1974	1942	1939	1962	1947	1977	1969	1977	1984
Extreme lowest	19	22	32	38	52	60	68	63	55	44	33	20	19
Extreme lowest date	1962	1951	1980	1980	1970	1975	1937	1967	1942	1939	1976	1983	1962
DEGREE DAYS BASE 65° F													
Heating	216	135	53	0	0	0	0	0	0	0	55	150	609
Cooling	70	73	164	297	440	528	592	592	492	322	136	66	3772
% OF POSSIBLE SUNSHINE	42	48	52	57	64	73	80	76	67	64	51	43	60
AVERAGE SKY COVER													
Sunrise - Sunset	6.9	6.5	6.8	6.6	6.1	5.2	4.8	5.0	5.3	4.9	5.7	6.6	5.9
NUMBER OF DAYS (Sunrise-Sunset)													
Clear	6.3	7.1	6.3	5.1	6.0	8.4	11.3	10.5	9.2	11.4	9.3	7.0	97.9
Partly cloudy	6.9	6.1	8.0	10.6	14.3	15.8	14.3	14.0	13.1	12.4	9.3	7.8	132.4
Cloudy	17.7	15.1	16.7	14.3	10.7	5.8	5.4	6.6	7.7	7.2	11.4	16.2	135.0
Precipitation .01" or more	7.6	6.2	4.3	3.7	4.8	5.6	4.9	6.9	10.2	6.5	5.7	6.5	73.0
Snow, Ice pellets 1.0" or more	0.0	0.0	0.0	0.0	0.0	0.0	0.0	0.0	0.0	0.0	0.0	0.0	0.0
Thunderstorms	0.6	0.7	0.6	2.3	3.5	2.7	2.7	4.5	4.6	2.0	0.9	0.5	25.4
Fog, Visibility 1/4 mile or less	5.9	4.6	3.6	2.4	1.0	0.2	0.1	0.2	0.3	0.7	2.9	5.4	27.4
Temperature Maximum:													
90° and above	0.2	0.2	1.6	4.0	10.6	22.9	26.4	27.2	18.1	5.9	0.4	0.1	117.5
32° and below	0.0	0.0	0.0	0.0	0.0	0.0	0.0	0.0	0.0	0.0	0.0	0.1	0.1
Temperature Minimum:													
32° and below	1.4	0.4	0.1	0.0	0.0	0.0	0.0	0.0	0.0	0.0	0.0	0.6	2.5
0° and below	0.0	0.0	0.0	0.0	0.0	0.0	0.0	0.0	0.0	0.0	0.0	0.0	0.0
RELATIVE HUMIDITY (%)													
Morning	86	85	85	84	86	86	85	85	86	85	84	85	85
Afternoon	68	62	60	59	60	59	55	56	61	60	60	64	60
PRECIPITATION (inches)													
Water Equivalent													
Normal	1.2	1.5	0.5	1.5	2.1	2.7	1.5	2.8	5.2	3.5	1.4	1.1	25.4
Maximum monthly	5.1	10.2	4.2	6.6	9.1	13.0	9.4	9.5	20.1	17.1	6.2	9.4	20.1
Date	1945	1958	1941	1977	1982	1942	1976	1975	1984	1958	1957	1940	1984
Minimum monthly	T	T	T	T	T	0.0	T	0.0	0.0	0.3	0.0	T	T
Date	1956	1954	1971	1984	1978	1955	1982	1974	1959	1961	1949	1969	1984
Maximum in 24 hrs	2.9	4.9	2.5	5.2	4.5	8.1	4.2	5.4	12.1	6.6	3.6	5.6	12.1
Date	1958	1958	1981	1977	1969	1942	1976	1980	1967	1954	1957	1940	1967
SNOW, ICE PELLETS													
Maximum monthly	T	T	T	0.0	0.0	0.0	0.0	0.0	0.0	0.0	T	T	T
Date	1985	1973	1943	—	—	—	—	—	—	—	1976	1966	1985
Maximum in 24 hrs	T	T	T	0.0	0.0	0.0	0.0	0.0	0.0	0.0	T	T	T
Date	1985	1973	1943	—	—	—	—	—	—	—	1976	1966	1985
WIND (Resultant)													
Mean speed (mph)	11.5	12.1	13.5	14.0	13.2	12.3	11.4	10.4	9.5	9.6	10.7	10.8	11.6

CORPUS CHRISTI   Elev. 41'   27° 46'N — 97° 30'W   Texas

NORMALS, MEANS, EXTREMES

	JAN	FEB	MAR	APR	MAY	JUN	JUL	AUG	SEP	OCT	NOV	DEC	YEAR
TEMPERATURE													
Normal daily maximum	66.5	69.9	76.1	82.1	86.7	91.2	94.2	94.1	90.1	83.9	75.1	69.3	81.6
Normal daily minimum	46.1	48.7	55.7	63.9	69.5	74.1	75.6	75.8	72.8	64.1	54.9	48.8	62.5
Normal monthly	56.3	59.3	65.9	73.0	78.1	82.7	84.9	85.0	81.5	74.0	65.0	59.1	72.1
Extreme highest	91	98	101	102	103	101	104	103	103	98	95	91	104
Extreme highest date	1971	1940	1984	1984	1984	1980	1939	1962	1977	1950	1949	1977	1939
Extreme lowest	14	18	24	33	47	58	64	64	50	40	29	14	14
Extreme lowest date	1962	1951	1980	1980	1970	1975	1967	1967	1942	1964	1969	1983	1983
DEGREE DAYS BASE 65° F													
Heating	310	209	97	7	0	0	0	0	0	11	116	220	970
Cooling	40	50	125	247	406	531	617	620	495	290	116	37	3574
% OF POSSIBLE SUNSHINE	45	51	55	57	61	74	82	78	69	68	57	47	62
AVERAGE SKY COVER													
Sunrise - Sunset	6.8	6.4	6.7	6.7	6.4	5.2	4.8	4.9	5.2	4.7	5.7	6.5	5.8
NUMBER OF DAYS (Sunrise-Sunset)													
Clear	6.9	7.6	6.7	5.6	5.7	8.9	10.8	11.3	10.0	12.5	9.3	8.1	103.3
Partly cloudy	6.9	6.0	7.5	9.2	12.3	14.6	14.5	12.8	11.9	10.3	8.7	6.6	121.2
Cloudy	17.2	14.7	16.8	15.2	13.0	6.6	5.7	6.9	8.2	8.2	12.0	16.3	140.7
Precipitation .01" or more	8.2	6.9	5.6	4.8	6.4	5.8	4.8	5.8	9.1	6.8	5.8	6.6	76.5
Snow, Ice pellets 1.0" or more	*	*	0.0	0.0	0.0	0.0	0.0	0.0	0.0	0.0	0.0	0.0	0.1
Thunderstorms	0.8	1.1	1.4	2.3	4.6	3.3	2.8	3.8	4.8	2.4	1.1	0.8	29.2
Fog, Visibility 1/4 mile or less	5.9	5.0	4.1	2.6	1.0	0.2	0.2	0.2	0.3	1.1	3.5	5.3	29.4
Temperature Maximum:													
90° and above	0.1	*	1.0	1.7	4.7	18.6	27.1	26.5	16.2	5.0	0.1	0.1	101.1
32° and below	0.0	*	0.0	0.0	0.0	0.0	0.0	0.0	0.0	0.0	0.0	0.1	0.2
Temperature Minimum:													
32° and below	3.5	1.5	0.3	0.0	0.0	0.0	0.0	0.0	0.0	0.0	0.3	1.4	7.0
0° and below	0.0	0.0	0.0	0.0	0.0	0.0	0.0	0.0	0.0	0.0	0.0	0.0	0.0
RELATIVE HUMIDITY (%)													
Morning	85	84	84	86	89	89	87	86	86	86	85	83	86
Afternoon	69	65	62	63	66	63	57	59	63	61	62	64	63
PRECIPITATION (inches)													
Water Equivalent													
Normal	1.6	1.5	0.8	1.9	3.0	3.3	1.9	3.5	6.1	3.1	1.5	1.4	30.1
Maximum monthly	10.7	8.1	4.8	8.0	9.3	13.3	11.9	14.7	20.3	11.0	8.5	7.8	20.3
Date	1958	1982	1974	1956	1968	1973	1976	1980	1967	1981	1947	1960	1967
Minimum monthly	0.0	T	T	T	T	0.0	0.0	0.1	0.4	0.0	T	0.0	0.0
Date	1971	1976	1971	1984	1961	1980	1957	1952	1981	1952	1949	1950	1957
Maximum in 24 hrs	6.3	4.8	2.6	7.1	4.6	5.6	4.6	8.9	8.7	7.2	3.4	3.8	8.9
Date	1958	1982	1945	1956	1968	1978	1981	1980	1967	1960	1947	1960	1980
SNOW, ICE PELLETS													
Maximum monthly	1.2	1.1	T	0.0	0.0	0.0	0.0	0.0	0.0	0.0	T	T	1.2
Date	1940	1973	1962	—	—	—	—	—	—	—	1979	1983	1940
Maximum in 24 hrs	1.1	1.1	T	0.0	0.0	0.0	0.0	0.0	0.0	0.0	T	T	1.1
Date	1940	1973	1962	—	—	—	—	—	—	—	1979	1983	1973
WIND (Resultant)													
Mean speed (mph)	12.1	13.0	14.1	14.4	12.9	11.9	11.5	10.9	10.3	10.2	11.5	11.4	12.0

DALLAS-FORT WORTH   Elev. 551'   32° 54'N — 97° 02'W   Texas

NORMALS, MEANS, EXTREMES

	JAN	FEB	MAR	APR	MAY	JUN	JUL	AUG	SEP	OCT	NOV	DEC	YEAR
TEMPERATURE													
Normal daily maximum	54.0	59.1	67.2	76.8	84.4	93.2	97.8	97.3	89.7	79.5	66.2	58.1	76.9
Normal daily minimum	33.9	37.8	44.9	55.0	62.9	70.8	74.7	73.7	67.5	56.3	44.9	37.4	55.0
Normal monthly	44.0	48.5	56.1	65.9	73.7	82.0	86.3	85.5	78.6	67.9	55.6	47.8	66.0
Extreme highest	88	88	96	95	103	113	110	108	106	102	89	88	113
Extreme highest date	1969	1959	1974	1972	1985	1980	1980	1964	1985	1979	1955	1955	1980
Extreme lowest	4	7	15	30	41	51	59	56	43	29	20	5	4
Extreme lowest date	1964	1985	1980	1973	1978	1964	1972	1967	1984	1980	1959	1983	1964
DEGREE DAYS BASE 65° F													
Heating	651	469	313	85	0	0	0	0	0	56	300	533	2407
Cooling	0	7	37	112	275	510	660	636	408	146	18	0	2809
% OF POSSIBLE SUNSHINE	53	56	58	64	65	72	80	78	73	59	58	58	65
AVERAGE SKY COVER													
Sunrise - Sunset	6.1	5.7	5.9	6.0	5.8	4.8	4.2	4.2	4.7	4.7	5.2	5.5	5.2
NUMBER OF DAYS (Sunrise-Sunset)													
Clear	9.8	9.9	9.6	8.7	8.4	11.2	15.3	15.2	13.0	13.4	12.1	11.5	138.2
Partly cloudy	5.7	5.7	7.5	8.0	10.9	11.5	9.3	10.0	8.5	7.5	6.0	6.3	97.0
Cloudy	15.5	12.7	13.9	13.3	11.7	7.3	6.4	5.8	8.4	10.0	11.9	13.2	130.1
Precipitation .01" or more	7.0	6.4	7.3	8.1	8.6	5.9	4.8	4.6	6.8	6.1	5.7	6.0	77.5
Snow, Ice pellets 1.0" or more	0.7	0.4	0.1	0.0	0.0	0.0	0.0	0.0	0.0	0.0	*	0.1	1.3
Thunderstorms	0.9	1.7	4.2	6.0	7.3	5.8	4.8	4.5	3.5	2.8	1.6	1.0	44.1
Fog, Visibility 1/4 mile or less	2.7	1.7	1.1	0.7	0.4	0.1	0.0	*	0.1	0.9	1.5	2.5	11.7
Temperature Maximum:													
90° and above	0.0	0.0	0.2	0.6	3.8	19.6	27.8	26.9	14.2	2.6	0.0	0.0	95.8
32° and below	1.9	0.7	0.0	0.0	0.0	0.0	0.0	0.0	0.0	0.0	0.0	0.8	3.4
Temperature Minimum:													
32° and below	16.0	10.0	2.7	0.1	0.0	0.0	0.0	0.0	0.0	*	2.5	10.0	41.3
0° and below	0.0	0.0	0.0	0.0	0.0	0.0	0.0	0.0	0.0	0.0	0.0	0.0	0.0
RELATIVE HUMIDITY (%)													
Morning	73	71	71	73	79	73	66	67	74	74	74	73	72
Afternoon	61	59	57	57	60	55	48	50	56	55	57	59	56
PRECIPITATION (inches)													
Water Equivalent													
Normal	1.6	1.9	2.4	3.6	4.2	2.5	2.0	1.7	3.3	2.4	1.7	1.6	29.4
Maximum monthly	3.6	6.2	6.3	12.1	13.6	7.8	11.1	6.8	9.5	14.1	6.2	6.9	14.1
Date	1968	1965	1968	1957	1982	1981	1973	1970	1964	1981	1964	1971	1981
Minimum monthly	0.1	0.1	0.1	0.5	0.9	0.4	0.0	T	0.0	T	0.2	0.1	T
Date	1976	1963	1972	1983	1977	1964	1965	1980	1984	1975	1970	1981	1980
Maximum in 24 hrs	2.3	4.0	4.3	4.5	4.8	3.1	3.7	4.0	4.7	5.9	2.8	3.1	5.9
Date	1975	1965	1977	1957	1965	1966	1975	1976	1965	1959	1964	1971	1959
SNOW, ICE PELLETS													
Maximum monthly	12.1	13.5	2.5	0.0	0.0	0.0	0.0	0.0	0.0	0.0	5.0	2.6	13.5
Date	1964	1978	1962	—	—	—	—	—	—	—	1976	1963	1978
Maximum in 24 hrs	12.1	7.5	2.5	0.0	0.0	0.0	0.0	0.0	0.0	0.0	4.8	2.5	12.1
Date	1964	1978	1962	—	—	—	—	—	—	—	1976	1963	1964
WIND (Resultant)													
Mean speed (mph)	11.1	11.9	13.0	12.7	11.1	10.8	9.5	9.0	9.4	9.7	10.7	11.1	10.8

EL PASO

Elev. 3918'   **31° 48'N — 106° 24'W**   # Texas

NORMALS, MEANS, EXTREMES

	JAN	FEB	MAR	APR	MAY	JUN	JUL	AUG	SEP	OCT	NOV	DEC	YEAR
TEMPERATURE													
Normal daily maximum	57.9	62.7	69.6	78.7	87.1	95.9	95.3	93.0	87.5	78.5	65.7	58.2	77.5
Normal daily minimum	30.4	34.1	40.5	48.5	56.6	65.7	69.6	67.5	60.6	48.7	37.0	30.6	49.2
Normal monthly	44.2	48.4	55.1	63.6	71.9	80.8	82.5	80.3	74.1	63.6	51.4	44.4	63.3
Extreme highest	80	83	88	98	104	111	112	108	104	96	87	80	112
Extreme highest date	1970	1972	1971	1965	1951	1978	1979	1980	1982	1979	1983	1973	1979
Extreme lowest	-8	8	14	23	31	48	57	56	41	25	1	5	-8
Extreme lowest date	1962	1985	1971	1983	1967	1979	1985	1973	1945	1970	1976	1953	1962
DEGREE DAYS BASE 65° F													
Heating	645	465	318	93	0	0	0	0	0	96	408	639	2664
Cooling	0	0	11	51	218	474	543	474	273	52	0	0	2096
% OF POSSIBLE SUNSHINE	77	82	85	87	89	89	80	81	82	83	82	78	83
AVERAGE SKY COVER													
Sunrise - Sunset	4.7	4.1	4.3	3.6	3.2	2.8	4.5	4.2	3.5	3.2	3.5	4.2	3.8
NUMBER OF DAYS (Sunrise-Sunset)													
Clear	13.9	14.0	14.8	16.5	18.8	20.0	12.3	14.0	17.7	19.0	17.3	15.3	193.4
Partly cloudy	7.4	7.4	8.0	8.0	7.9	7.2	13.0	12.3	7.2	6.6	6.4	7.5	99.0
Cloudy	9.8	6.8	8.1	5.5	4.3	2.8	5.7	4.7	5.2	5.4	6.3	8.3	72.9
Precipitation .01" or more	4.1	2.8	2.4	1.7	2.1	3.3	7.5	7.4	5.2	4.2	2.7	3.6	47.0
Snow, Ice pellets 1.0" or more	0.5	0.3	*	0.1	0.0	0.0	0.0	0.0	0.0	*	0.3	0.4	1.8
Thunderstorms	0.2	0.4	0.4	1.0	2.6	4.5	10.2	10.0	4.0	1.9	0.3	0.2	35.8
Fog, Visibility 1/4 mile or less	0.7	0.2	0.1	*	*	0.0	0.0	0.0	0.1	0.2	0.3	0.5	2.2
Temperature Maximum:													
90° and above	0.0	0.0	0.0	1.8	12.9	26.1	27.4	24.1	11.8	1.6	0.0	0.0	105.8
32° and below	0.4	0.1	0.0	0.0	0.0	0.0	0.0	0.0	0.0	0.0	0.1	0.1	0.7
Temperature Minimum:													
32° and below	18.8	12.3	4.9	0.9	*	0.0	0.0	0.0	0.0	0.3	7.4	18.5	63.2
0° and below	0.1	0.0	0.0	0.0	0.0	0.0	0.0	0.0	0.0	0.0	0.0	0.0	0.1
RELATIVE HUMIDITY (%)													
Morning	65	55	46	39	41	44	61	64	67	63	61	64	56
Afternoon	36	26	21	16	16	18	28	32	34	30	33	36	27
PRECIPITATION (inches)													
Water Equivalent													
Normal	0.3	0.4	0.3	0.1	0.2	0.5	1.6	1.2	1.4	0.7	0.3	0.3	7.8
Maximum monthly	1.8	1.6	2.2	1.4	1.9	3.1	5.5	5.5	6.6	4.3	1.6	2.6	6.6
Date	1949	1973	1958	1983	1941	1984	1968	1984	1974	1945	1961	1982	1974
Minimum monthly	0.0	0.0	T	0.0	0.0	T	0.0	T	T	0.0	0.0	0.0	0.0
Date	1967	1943	1982	1978	1962	1980	1978	1962	1959	1952	1964	1955	1978
Maximum in 24 hrs	0.6	0.8	1.7	1.0	1.2	1.4	2.6	2.3	2.5	1.7	1.1	1.0	2.6
Date	1960	1956	1941	1966	1941	1966	1968	1984	1958	1945	1943	1946	1968
SNOW, ICE PELLETS													
Maximum monthly	8.3	8.9	7.3	16.5	0.0	0.0	0.0	0.0	0.0	1.0	12.7	18.2	18.2
Date	1949	1956	1958	1983	—	—	—	—	—	1980	1976	1982	1982
Maximum in 24 hrs	4.8	7.2	7.3	8.8	0.0	0.0	0.0	0.0	0.0	1.0	7.8	7.1	8.8
Date	1981	1956	1958	1983	—	—	—	—	—	1980	1961	1951	1983
WIND (Resultant)													
Mean speed (mph)	8.6	9.4	11.4	11.4	10.6	9.5	8.4	7.9	7.8	7.7	8.1	8.1	9.1

GALVESTON

Elev. 7'   29° 18'N — 94° 48'W   **Texas**

NORMALS, MEANS, EXTREMES

	JAN	FEB	MAR	APR	MAY	JUN	JUL	AUG	SEP	OCT	NOV	DEC	YEAR
TEMPERATURE													
Normal daily maximum	59.2	60.9	66.4	73.3	79.8	85.1	87.3	87.5	84.6	77.6	68.3	62.3	74.4
Normal daily minimum	47.9	50.2	56.5	64.9	71.6	77.2	79.1	78.8	75.4	67.7	57.6	51.2	64.8
Normal monthly	53.6	55.6	61.5	69.1	75.7	81.2	83.2	83.2	80.0	72.7	63.0	56.8	69.6
Extreme highest	77	83	85	92	94	99	101	100	96	94	85	80	101
Extreme highest date	1969	1932	1879	1953	1984	1918	1932	1924	1927	1952	1886	1918	1932
Extreme lowest	11	8	26	38	52	57	66	67	52	41	26	14	8
Extreme lowest date	1886	1899	1980	1938	1954	1903	1910	1966	1942	1925	1911	1983	1899
DEGREE DAYS BASE 65° F													
Heating	376	282	160	19	0	0	0	0	0	10	139	267	1253
Cooling	23	18	48	142	332	486	564	564	450	248	79	13	2967
% OF POSSIBLE SUNSHINE	48	51	55	60	67	75	72	71	68	71	59	49	62
NUMBER OF DAYS (Sunrise-Sunset)													
Precipitation .01" or more	10.0	8.6	7.8	6.3	6.1	6.5	8.5	9.1	9.3	6.5	7.7	9.8	96.2
Snow, Ice pellets 1.0" or more	*	*	0.0	0.0	0.0	0.0	0.0	0.0	0.0	0.0	0.0	0.0	*
Temperature Maximum:													
90° and above	0.0	0.0	0.0	*	0.1	1.3	3.8	5.2	1.6	0.1	0.0	0.0	12.2
32° and below	0.1	0.1	0.0	0.0	0.0	0.0	0.0	0.0	0.0	0.0	0.0	*	0.2
Temperature Minimum:													
32° and below	2.0	0.8	0.1	0.0	0.0	0.0	0.0	0.0	0.0	0.0	0.1	0.7	3.7
0° and below	0.0	0.0	0.0	0.0	0.0	0.0	0.0	0.0	0.0	0.0	0.0	0.0	0.0
RELATIVE HUMIDITY (%)													
Morning	83	82	84	85	83	80	80	78	78	75	81	82	81
Afternoon	77	74	74	75	73	70	70	69	68	65	72	76	72
PRECIPITATION (inches)													
Water Equivalent													
Normal	2.9	2.3	2.1	2.6	3.3	3.4	3.7	4.4	5.8	2.6	3.2	3.6	40.2
Maximum monthly	10.3	8.2	9.4	11.0	10.7	15.4	18.7	19.0	26.0	17.7	16.1	10.2	26.0
Date	1899	1881	1973	1904	1975	1919	1900	1915	1885	1871	1940	1887	1885
Minimum monthly	0.0	0.0	0.0	T	T	T	T	0.0	0.0	T	0.0	0.2	0.0
Date	1909	1954	1953	1984	1978	1907	1962	1902	1924	1952	1903	1889	1902
Maximum in 24 hrs	5.3	6.5	8.1	9.2	7.7	12.5	14.3	10.8	11.6	14.1	9.0	5.4	14.3
Date	1923	1952	1973	1904	1975	1961	1900	1981	1961	1901	1940	1964	1900
SNOW, ICE PELLETS													
Maximum monthly	2.5	15.4	T	0.0	0.0	0.0	0.0	0.0	0.0	0.0	0.0	0.2	15.4
Date	1973	1895	1932	—	—	—	—	—	—	—	—	1924	1895
Maximum in 24 hrs	2.5	15.4	T	0.0	0.0	0.0	0.0	0.0	0.0	0.0	0.0	0.2	15.4
Date	1973	1895	1932	—	—	—	—	—	—	—	—	1924	1895
WIND (Resultant)													
Mean speed (mph)	11.6	11.8	11.9	12.1	11.5	10.7	9.8	9.4	10.1	10.3	11.2	11.3	11.0

HOUSTON

Elev. 96' **29° 58'N — 95° 21'W** # Texas

NORMALS, MEANS, EXTREMES

	JAN	FEB	MAR	APR	MAY	JUN	JUL	AUG	SEP	OCT	NOV	DEC	YEAR
TEMPERATURE													
Normal daily maximum	61.9	65.7	72.1	79.0	85.1	90.9	93.6	93.1	88.7	81.9	71.6	65.2	79.1
Normal daily minimum	40.8	43.2	49.8	58.3	64.7	70.2	72.5	72.1	68.1	57.5	48.6	42.7	57.4
Normal monthly	51.4	54.5	61.0	68.7	74.9	80.6	83.1	82.6	78.4	69.7	60.1	54.0	68.2
Extreme highest	84	85	90	92	95	103	104	107	102	94	89	83	107
Extreme highest date	1975	1982	1974	1981	1978	1980	1980	1980	1985	1981	1978	1978	1980
Extreme lowest	12	20	22	31	44	52	62	62	48	33	19	11	11
Extreme lowest date	1982	1985	1980	1973	1978	1970	1972	1970	1975	1976	1976	1983	1983
DEGREE DAYS BASE 65° F													
Heating	442	314	175	32	0	0	0	0	0	36	201	349	1549
Cooling	20	20	51	143	307	468	561	546	402	181	54	8	2761
% OF POSSIBLE SUNSHINE	43	50	47	51	58	64	66	64	62	59	52	55	56
AVERAGE SKY COVER													
Sunrise - Sunset	7.0	6.3	6.9	6.6	6.1	5.5	5.7	5.6	5.6	5.3	5.6	6.5	6.1
NUMBER OF DAYS (Sunrise-Sunset)													
Clear	7.6	7.8	6.3	7.3	7.1	8.8	7.4	6.8	8.9	10.8	9.9	8.4	96.9
Partly cloudy	5.3	6.1	6.6	6.6	10.8	12.4	15.4	16.1	10.6	8.8	7.4	5.8	111.6
Cloudy	18.2	14.4	18.2	16.2	13.2	8.8	8.1	8.1	10.6	11.5	12.6	16.9	156.8
Precipitation .01" or more	10.3	7.6	9.9	7.1	8.2	7.8	9.6	9.7	9.6	8.1	8.6	8.4	104.9
Snow, Ice pellets 1.0" or more	0.1	0.2	0.0	0.0	0.0	0.0	0.0	0.0	0.0	0.0	0.0	0.0	0.3
Thunderstorms	1.8	1.4	3.8	3.6	6.8	6.9	10.8	10.8	7.0	3.9	2.6	1.9	61.1
Fog, Visibility 1/4 mile or less	5.6	4.1	3.5	3.2	1.7	0.8	0.3	0.6	1.5	3.3	4.1	4.8	33.4
Temperature Maximum:													
90° and above	0.0	0.0	0.1	0.4	4.4	19.1	26.5	25.9	13.4	2.4	0.0	0.0	92.1
32° and below	0.3	0.1	0.0	0.0	0.0	0.0	0.0	0.0	0.0	0.0	0.0	0.3	0.6
Temperature Minimum:													
32° and below	8.8	5.4	1.3	0.1	0.0	0.0	0.0	0.0	0.0	0.0	1.8	5.6	22.8
0° and below	0.0	0.0	0.0	0.0	0.0	0.0	0.0	0.0	0.0	0.0	0.0	0.0	0.0
RELATIVE HUMIDITY (%)													
Morning	83	83	83	86	87	87	87	89	90	89	86	83	86
Afternoon	64	60	60	59	59	59	58	59	61	57	59	61	60
PRECIPITATION (inches)													
Water Equivalent													
Normal	3.2	3.2	2.6	4.2	4.6	4.0	3.3	3.6	4.9	3.6	3.3	3.6	44.7
Maximum monthly	7.6	5.3	8.5	10.9	14.3	13.4	8.1	9.4	11.3	16.0	8.9	7.3	16.0
Date	1974	1985	1972	1976	1970	1973	1979	1983	1976	1984	1982	1971	1984
Minimum monthly	0.3	0.3	1.2	0.4	0.7	0.2	1.4	1.1	0.8	0.0	1.5	0.6	0.0
Date	1971	1976	1971	1983	1977	1970	1971	1985	1975	1978	1970	1973	1978
Maximum in 24 hrs	2.5	2.2	7.4	8.1	5.1	6.6	3.9	6.8	7.9	9.3	3.6	3.4	9.3
Date	1984	1985	1972	1976	1981	1973	1973	1981	1976	1984	1981	1971	1984
SNOW, ICE PELLETS													
Maximum monthly	2.0	2.8	0.0	0.0	0.0	0.0	0.0	0.0	0.0	0.0	T	0.0	2.8
Date	1973	1973	—	—	—	—	—	—	—	—	1979	—	1973
Maximum in 24 hrs	2.0	1.4	0.0	0.0	0.0	0.0	0.0	0.0	0.0	0.0	T	0.0	2.0
Date	1973	1980	—	—	—	—	—	—	—	—	1979	—	1973
WIND (Resultant)													
Mean speed (mph)	8.2	8.7	9.5	9.3	8.2	7.7	6.8	6.1	6.9	6.9	7.8	8.1	7.8

LUBBOCK

Elev. 3254'   33° 39'N — 101° 49'W   **Texas**

NORMALS, MEANS, EXTREMES

	JAN	FEB	MAR	APR	MAY	JUN	JUL	AUG	SEP	OCT	NOV	DEC	YEAR
TEMPERATURE													
Normal daily maximum	53.3	57.3	65.1	74.8	82.8	90.8	91.9	90.1	83.6	74.7	62.1	55.5	73.5
Normal daily minimum	24.3	27.9	35.2	45.8	55.2	64.3	67.6	65.7	58.7	47.3	34.8	27.4	46.2
Normal monthly	38.8	42.6	50.2	60.3	69.0	77.6	79.8	77.9	71.2	61.0	48.5	41.5	59.8
Extreme highest	83	87	94	96	104	108	108	108	106	103	98	86	81	108
Extreme highest date	1972	1979	1971	1972	1947	1980	1983	1966	1948	1979	1980	1958	1983
Extreme lowest	-16	-8	2	22	30	44	51	52	33	23	-1	0	-16
Extreme lowest date	1963	1960	1948	1948	1967	1947	1952	1956	1983	1980	1957	1983	1963
DEGREE DAYS BASE 65° F													
Heating	812	627	470	178	33	0	0	0	15	157	495	729	3516
Cooling	0	0	11	37	157	378	459	400	201	33	0	0	1676
% OF POSSIBLE SUNSHINE	64	69	72	74	73	78	78	80	72	73	68	66	72
AVERAGE SKY COVER													
Sunrise - Sunset	5.3	5.0	5.1	4.8	4.9	4.1	4.4	4.2	4.3	3.9	4.4	4.8	4.6
NUMBER OF DAYS (Sunrise-Sunset)													
Clear	12.5	11.2	11.6	12.8	11.4	13.6	14.1	15.5	14.7	16.5	14.6	13.5	162.1
Partly cloudy	6.4	7.4	8.7	8.3	11.3	10.9	11.0	9.7	7.8	6.7	7.1	7.1	102.4
Cloudy	12.1	9.7	10.6	8.9	8.4	5.4	5.9	5.8	7.5	7.8	8.4	10.3	100.7
Precipitation .01" or more	3.8	3.9	3.9	4.4	7.4	6.9	6.8	6.5	5.6	5.2	3.4	3.7	61.6
Snow, Ice pellets 1.0" or more	0.8	1.0	0.5	0.1	0.0	0.0	0.0	0.0	0.0	0.1	0.3	0.5	3.3
Thunderstorms	0.1	0.5	1.8	3.4	8.6	9.0	7.3	6.9	4.1	2.8	0.8	0.2	45.6
Fog, Visibility 1/4 mile or less	2.9	2.8	1.6	1.0	1.2	0.3	0.2	0.3	1.1	1.7	2.5	1.7	17.3
Temperature Maximum:													
90° and above	0.0	0.0	0.1	1.6	8.1	18.3	22.0	19.4	8.9	0.9	0.0	0.0	79.1
32° and below	3.3	1.2	0.4	0.0	0.0	0.0	0.0	0.0	0.0	0.0	0.2	1.5	6.7
Temperature Minimum:													
32° and below	25.8	19.6	11.1	2.0	0.1	0.0	0.0	0.0	0.0	0.9	12.0	23.8	95.3
0° and below	0.4	0.1	0.0	0.0	0.0	0.0	0.0	0.0	0.0	0.0	*	0.1	0.6
RELATIVE HUMIDITY (%)													
Morning	66	63	56	54	61	62	61	64	68	67	65	65	63
Afternoon	50	49	41	40	43	44	47	48	51	48	47	47	46
PRECIPITATION (inches)													
Water Equivalent													
Normal	0.3	0.5	0.9	1.0	2.5	2.8	2.3	2.2	2.0	1.8	0.5	0.4	17.7
Maximum monthly	4.0	2.5	3.2	3.4	7.8	7.9	7.2	8.8	6.6	10.8	2.6	1.9	10.8
Date	1949	1961	1958	1957	1949	1967	1976	1966	1974	1983	1968	1982	1983
Minimum monthly	0.0	T	T	0.1	0.1	0.3	T	0.0	T	0.0	0.0	T	0.0
Date	1967	1955	1972	1961	1962	1973	1970	1960	1954	1952	1960	1973	1967
Maximum in 24 hrs	1.5	2.1	1.8	2.1	5.1	5.7	3.2	3.7	2.8	5.8	1.5	1.1	5.8
Date	1983	1961	1973	1982	1949	1967	1985	1966	1965	1983	1968	1959	1983
SNOW, ICE PELLETS													
Maximum monthly	25.3	16.8	14.3	5.3	0.0	0.0	0.0	0.0	0.0	7.5	21.4	9.9	25.3
Date	1983	1956	1958	1983	—	—	—	—	—	1976	1980	1960	1983
Maximum in 24 hrs	16.3	12.1	10.0	4.5	0.0	0.0	0.0	0.0	0.0	4.7	10.8	6.3	16.3
Date	1983	1961	1969	1983	—	—	—	—	—	1976	1980	1960	1983
WIND (Resultant)													
Mean speed (mph)	12.1	13.4	14.8	14.9	14.2	13.7	11.2	9.9	10.5	11.1	11.6	11.9	12.4

MIDLAND-ODESSA

Elev. 2851' 31° 57'N — 102° 11'W **Texas**

NORMALS, MEANS, EXTREMES

	JAN	FEB	MAR	APR	MAY	JUN	JUL	AUG	SEP	OCT	NOV	DEC	YEAR
TEMPERATURE													
Normal daily maximum	57.6	62.1	69.8	78.8	86.0	93.0	94.2	93.1	86.4	77.7	65.5	59.7	77.0
Normal daily minimum	29.7	33.3	40.2	49.4	58.2	66.6	69.2	68.0	61.9	51.1	39.0	32.2	49.9
Normal monthly	43.7	47.7	55.0	64.1	72.1	79.8	81.7	80.6	74.2	64.4	52.3	46.0	63.4
Extreme highest	84	87	95	99	107	109	106	107	107	100	88	85	109
Extreme highest date	1974	1950	1971	1972	1953	1951	1983	1964	1953	1979	1963	1954	1951
Extreme lowest	-8	-11	9	20	34	47	53	56	40	27	13	6	-11
Extreme lowest date	1962	1985	1980	1973	1970	1983	1978	1967	1983	1980	1976	1983	1985
DEGREE DAYS BASE 65° F													
Heating	660	484	329	102	8	0	0	0	7	94	385	589	2658
Cooling	0	0	19	75	228	444	518	484	283	75	0	0	2126
% OF POSSIBLE SUNSHINE	64	69	71	75	78	78	84	78	80	66	72	67	74
AVERAGE SKY COVER													
Sunrise - Sunset	5.2	4.9	4.9	4.6	4.6	3.9	4.4	4.3	4.3	3.9	4.3	4.7	4.5
NUMBER OF DAYS (Sunrise-Sunset)													
Clear	12.5	11.6	13.1	13.6	13.5	15.1	13.6	14.3	14.5	16.8	14.7	14.2	167.4
Partly cloudy	6.3	7.0	7.6	7.7	9.3	9.4	10.8	10.5	7.7	6.2	6.5	6.3	95.4
Cloudy	12.2	9.6	10.3	8.7	8.2	5.5	6.6	6.2	7.8	8.0	8.8	10.5	102.5
Precipitation .01" or more	3.8	3.8	2.5	3.4	5.7	4.9	5.2	5.4	5.5	4.8	3.1	3.1	51.1
Snow, Ice pellets 1.0" or more	0.7	0.5	0.1	0.0	0.0	0.0	0.0	0.0	0.0	0.0	0.2	0.3	1.8
Thunderstorms	0.1	0.4	1.1	2.9	6.6	5.8	6.1	5.9	3.6	2.5	0.6	0.4	36.0
Fog, Visibility 1/4 mile or less	3.4	2.8	0.9	0.5	0.5	0.1	0.1	0.1	0.6	1.3	2.6	2.9	15.6
Temperature Maximum:													
90° and above	0.0	0.0	0.3	2.9	11.2	21.0	26.4	22.6	11.3	1.9	0.0	0.0	97.5
32° and below	1.6	0.3	*	0.0	0.0	0.0	0.0	0.0	0.0	0.0	0.1	0.9	3.0
Temperature Minimum:													
32° and below	19.9	13.9	5.6	0.7	0.0	0.0	0.0	0.0	0.0	0.1	6.1	17.1	63.5
0° and below	*	0.1	0.0	0.0	0.0	0.0	0.0	0.0	0.0	0.0	0.0	0.0	0.1
RELATIVE HUMIDITY (%)													
Morning	64	62	53	52	60	59	55	59	68	71	69	64	61
Afternoon	48	44	35	34	38	41	40	43	50	47	46	44	43
PRECIPITATION (inches)													
Water Equivalent													
Normal	0.4	0.5	0.5	0.8	2.0	1.4	1.7	1.6	2.0	1.4	0.6	0.4	13.7
Maximum monthly	3.6	1.7	2.8	2.8	4.9	3.9	7.7	4.4	9.7	5.9	2.3	2.8	9.7
Date	1949	1969	1970	1949	1959	1949	1975	1974	1980	1985	1968	1979	1980
Minimum monthly	0.0	0.0	T	0.0	0.0	0.0	T	0.1	0.0	0.0	0.0	T	0.0
Date	1967	1971	1984	1964	1953	1951	1983	1967	1979	1952	1950	1958	1967
Maximum in 24 hrs	1.1	1.2	2.2	1.6	4.7	2.5	5.9	2.4	2.7	3.5	2.1	1.5	5.9
Date	1958	1965	1970	1979	1968	1969	1961	1965	1980	1985	1975	1979	1961
SNOW, ICE PELLETS													
Maximum monthly	9.0	3.9	5.9	0.5	0.0	0.0	0.0	0.0	0.0	T	7.2	6.4	9.0
Date	1985	1973	1970	1983	—	—	—	—	—	1980	1980	1982	1985
Maximum in 24 hrs	6.8	3.9	5.0	0.5	0.0	0.0	0.0	0.0	0.0	T	5.7	3.5	6.8
Date	1974	1985	1970	1983	—	—	—	—	—	1980	1980	1982	1974
WIND (Resultant)													
Mean speed (mph)	10.3	11.3	12.8	12.9	12.4	12.3	10.6	10.0	10.2	10.1	10.2	10.1	11.1

SAN ANTONIO   Elev. 788'   29° 32'N — 98° 28'W   Texas

NORMALS, MEANS, EXTREMES

	JAN	FEB	MAR	APR	MAY	JUN	JUL	AUG	SEP	OCT	NOV	DEC	YEAR
TEMPERATURE													
Normal daily maximum	61.7	66.3	73.7	80.3	85.5	91.8	94.9	94.6	89.3	81.5	70.7	64.6	79.6
Normal daily minimum	39.0	42.4	49.8	58.8	65.5	72.0	74.3	73.7	69.4	58.9	48.2	41.4	57.8
Normal monthly	50.4	54.4	61.8	69.6	75.5	81.9	84.6	84.2	79.4	70.2	59.5	53.0	68.7
Extreme highest	89	92	100	100	101	105	106	106	103	98	91	90	106
Extreme highest date	1971	1959	1971	1984	1967	1980	1954	1962	1985	1979	1962	1955	1962
Extreme lowest	0	6	19	33	43	53	62	61	41	33	21	9	0
Extreme lowest date	1949	1951	1980	1983	1984	1964	1967	1966	1942	1980	1976	1983	1949
DEGREE DAYS BASE 65° F													
Heating	463	319	178	28	0	0	0	0	0	41	199	378	1606
Cooling	10	19	78	166	326	507	608	595	432	202	34	6	2983
% OF POSSIBLE SUNSHINE	48	52	57	55	56	67	74	73	67	63	55	50	60
AVERAGE SKY COVER													
Sunrise - Sunset	6.3	6.1	6.2	6.4	6.4	5.5	5.0	4.9	5.2	5.0	5.5	5.9	5.7
NUMBER OF DAYS (Sunrise-Sunset)													
Clear	8.9	8.4	8.4	7.3	6.2	7.0	9.2	10.4	9.5	11.6	10.7	9.9	107.5
Partly cloudy	6.2	6.0	7.3	7.4	11.3	15.4	15.3	14.6	12.2	9.8	6.9	6.1	118.4
Cloudy	15.9	13.9	15.3	15.2	13.5	7.7	6.5	6.0	8.3	9.6	12.5	15.0	139.3
Precipitation .01" or more	8.1	7.7	7.1	7.5	8.3	6.0	4.3	5.3	7.1	6.5	6.5	7.3	81.5
Snow, Ice pellets 1.0" or more	0.1	0.1	0.0	0.0	0.0	0.0	0.0	0.0	0.0	0.0	0.0	0.0	0.2
Thunderstorms	0.9	1.4	2.4	4.0	6.5	4.3	3.4	4.2	4.0	2.6	1.8	0.8	36.3
Fog, Visibility 1/4 mile or less	5.3	3.1	2.5	1.4	0.7	0.1	0.1	*	0.2	1.5	3.0	4.7	22.7
Temperature Maximum:													
90° and above	0.0	0.1	0.9	2.2	8.4	21.6	28.3	28.0	16.8	4.1	0.1	*	110.4
32° and below	0.3	0.1	0.0	0.0	0.0	0.0	0.0	0.0	0.0	0.0	0.0	0.1	0.5
Temperature Minimum:													
32° and below	8.7	5.0	1.5	0.0	0.0	0.0	0.0	0.0	0.0	0.0	1.9	6.0	23.1
0° and below	*	0.0	0.0	0.0	0.0	0.0	0.0	0.0	0.0	0.0	0.0	0.0	*
RELATIVE HUMIDITY (%)													
Morning	76	75	72	76	81	80	75	74	77	77	76	76	76
Afternoon	59	57	54	56	59	56	51	51	55	54	55	57	55
PRECIPITATION (inches)													
Water Equivalent													
Normal	1.5	1.8	1.3	2.7	3.6	3.0	1.9	2.6	3.7	2.8	2.3	1.3	29.1
Maximum monthly	8.5	6.4	4.1	9.3	11.2	10.4	8.1	11.1	15.7	9.5	6.0	4.5	15.7
Date	1968	1965	1957	1957	1972	1973	1942	1974	1946	1942	1977	1965	1946
Minimum monthly	0.0	0.0	0.0	0.1	0.1	0.0	T	0.0	0.0	T	T	0.0	0.0
Date	1971	1954	1961	1984	1961	1967	1984	1952	1947	1952	1966	1950	1952
Maximum in 24 hrs	3.1	2.3	2.3	4.8	6.5	6.1	6.9	5.5	7.2	5.2	4.8	2.8	7.2
Date	1968	1965	1945	1977	1972	1951	1958	1950	1973	1942	1977	1944	1973
SNOW, ICE PELLETS													
Maximum monthly	15.9	3.5	T	0.0	0.0	0.0	0.0	0.0	0.0	0.0	0.3	0.2	15.9
Date	1985	1966	1978	—	—	—	—	—	—	—	1957	1964	1985
Maximum in 24 hrs	13.2	3.5	T	0.0	0.0	0.0	0.0	0.0	0.0	0.0	0.3	0.2	13.2
Date	1985	1966	1978	—	—	—	—	—	—	—	1957	1964	1985
WIND (Resultant)													
Mean speed (mph)	9.2	9.8	10.6	10.6	10.2	10.2	9.3	8.6	8.6	8.6	8.9	8.7	9.5

VICTORIA

Elev. 104'   28° 51'N — 96° 55'W

Texas

NORMALS, MEANS, EXTREMES

	JAN	FEB	MAR	APR	MAY	JUN	JUL	AUG	SEP	OCT	NOV	DEC	YEAR
TEMPERATURE													
Normal daily maximum	63.6	67.1	73.8	80.2	85.6	90.8	93.7	93.7	89.3	82.8	73.0	66.7	80.0
Normal daily minimum	43.1	45.9	52.8	61.5	67.7	73.1	75.2	74.7	70.9	61.0	51.5	45.4	60.2
Normal monthly	53.4	56.5	63.3	70.9	76.7	82.0	84.5	84.2	80.1	71.9	62.3	56.1	70.1
Extreme highest	88	90	95	98	101	100	104	107	102	95	92	88	107
Extreme highest date	1971	1962	1984	1963	1964	1980	1964	1962	1985	1962	1963	1964	1962
Extreme lowest	14	19	21	35	49	59	62	63	49	36	24	14	14
Extreme lowest date	1982	1985	1980	1980	1978	1984	1967	1967	1984	1980	1976	1983	1983
DEGREE DAYS BASE 65° F													
Heating	386	268	140	18	0	0	0	0	0	20	150	291	1273
Cooling	27	30	87	195	363	510	605	595	453	234	69	16	3184
% OF POSSIBLE SUNSHINE	na	na	na	na	na	na	na	na	na	na	na	na	na
AVERAGE SKY COVER													
Sunrise - Sunset	7.0	6.4	7.0	7.1	6.7	5.8	5.7	5.8	5.7	5.2	5.7	6.8	6.2
NUMBER OF DAYS (Sunrise-Sunset)													
Clear	6.5	7.6	6.2	5.3	4.9	6.0	6.6	6.6	7.9	11.1	9.7	7.3	85.6
Partly cloudy	6.5	5.9	6.8	7.3	11.1	15.1	15.6	15.3	12.2	10.0	7.3	5.9	118.9
Cloudy	18.0	14.7	18.0	17.4	15.0	8.9	8.8	9.2	10.0	10.0	13.0	17.9	160.8
Precipitation .01" or more	8.1	6.5	6.9	6.0	7.2	7.2	7.6	8.8	10.2	6.8	6.5	7.9	89.5
Snow, Ice pellets 1.0" or more	0.1	*	0.0	0.0	0.0	0.0	0.0	0.0	0.0	0.0	0.0	0.0	0.1
Thunderstorms	0.9	1.5	2.4	3.2	5.9	5.4	6.6	9.0	7.9	4.0	1.8	1.0	49.3
Fog, Visibility 1/4 mile or less	7.0	5.2	5.1	4.3	1.9	0.6	0.1	0.3	1.2	3.1	5.9	6.4	41.1
Temperature Maximum:													
90° and above	0.0	*	0.3	0.8	5.3	20.0	27.3	27.6	16.3	4.0	0.1	0.0	101.9
32° and below	0.2	*	0.0	0.0	0.0	0.0	0.0	0.0	0.0	0.0	0.0	0.2	0.4
Temperature Minimum:													
32° and below	6.0	2.6	0.5	0.0	0.0	0.0	0.0	0.0	0.0	0.0	0.7	3.1	12.9
0° and below	0.0	0.0	0.0	0.0	0.0	0.0	0.0	0.0	0.0	0.0	0.0	0.0	0.0
RELATIVE HUMIDITY (%)													
Morning	84	83	83	84	87	87	87	86	87	86	86	84	85
Afternoon	65	60	59	60	61	59	56	57	61	57	59	63	60
PRECIPITATION (inches)													
Water Equivalent													
Normal	1.8	2.2	1.3	2.6	4.4	4.5	2.5	3.3	6.2	3.3	2.2	2.1	36.9
Maximum monthly	5.2	5.4	5.5	9.4	14.0	12.6	10.4	7.3	19.0	10.1	8.6	6.9	19.0
Date	1979	1969	1985	1969	1968	1973	1983	1974	1978	1981	1982	1975	1978
Minimum monthly	0.0	0.2	0.1	0.0	1.0	T	0.0	0.3	1.1	0.3	0.0	0.3	T
Date	1971	1974	1971	1984	1971	1980	1982	1965	1982	1964	1981	1972	1980
Maximum in 24 hrs	3.6	2.6	2.6	8.5	8.4	9.3	4.2	6.1	8.5	5.0	6.6	6.1	9.3
Date	1980	1969	1985	1969	1972	1977	1983	1964	1967	1981	1982	1975	1977
SNOW, ICE PELLETS													
Maximum monthly	2.1	1.0	0.0	0.0	0.0	0.0	0.0	0.0	0.0	0.0	0.2	T	2.1
Date	1985	1973	—	—	—	—	—	—	—	—	1976	1969	1985
Maximum in 24 hrs	2.1	1.0	0.0	0.0	0.0	0.0	0.0	0.0	0.0	0.0	0.2	T	2.1
Date	1985	1973	—	—	—	—	—	—	—	—	1976	1969	1985
WIND (Resultant)													
Mean speed (mph)	10.6	11.0	11.7	11.9	10.7	9.6	8.8	8.3	8.6	8.9	9.8	10.2	10.0

WACO

Elev. 501'   31° 37'N — 97° 13'W   **Texas**

NORMALS, MEANS, EXTREMES

	JAN	FEB	MAR	APR	MAY	JUN	JUL	AUG	SEP	OCT	NOV	DEC	YEAR
TEMPERATURE													
Normal daily maximum	56.6	61.6	69.5	77.6	84.2	92.1	96.5	96.7	89.7	80.3	67.9	60.3	77.8
Normal daily minimum	35.7	39.4	46.6	56.5	64.2	71.5	75.2	74.5	68.6	57.2	46.1	38.5	56.2
Normal monthly	46.2	50.5	58.1	67.1	74.2	81.8	85.9	85.6	79.2	68.8	57.0	49.4	67.0
Extreme highest	88	90	100	101	102	109	108	112	106	101	92	91	112
Extreme highest date	1971	1954	1971	1963	1985	1980	1957	1969	1985	1979	1948	1955	1969
Extreme lowest	-5	4	15	27	37	52	61	60	40	29	17	7	-5
Extreme lowest date	1949	1985	1948	1975	1981	1964	1970	1967	1983	1980	1976	1983	1949
DEGREE DAYS BASE 65° F													
Heating	591	415	257	71	0	0	0	0	0	46	265	481	2126
Cooling	8	9	43	134	288	507	648	639	426	164	25	0	2891
% OF POSSIBLE SUNSHINE	na	na	na	na	na	na	na	na	na	na	na	na	na
AVERAGE SKY COVER													
Sunrise - Sunset	6.3	6.0	5.9	6.1	6.0	4.9	4.4	4.3	4.8	4.7	5.2	5.7	5.4
NUMBER OF DAYS (Sunrise-Sunset)													
Clear	9.0	9.0	9.6	8.6	8.2	10.6	14.0	13.8	12.9	13.1	11.7	10.8	131.2
Partly cloudy	6.2	5.8	6.8	7.0	10.2	12.2	10.5	11.6	8.9	8.2	5.9	5.9	99.2
Cloudy	15.8	13.5	14.6	14.4	12.6	7.2	6.5	5.6	8.3	9.7	12.4	14.4	134.9
Precipitation .01" or more	7.3	7.2	7.4	7.5	8.6	6.0	4.3	5.0	6.3	5.9	6.4	5.9	77.7
Snow, Ice pellets 1.0" or more	0.3	0.2	*	0.0	0.0	0.0	0.0	0.0	0.0	0.0	0.0	*	0.6
Thunderstorms	1.2	2.5	3.8	5.5	7.7	5.4	4.1	4.4	3.9	3.0	2.0	1.4	44.8
Fog, Visibility 1/4 mile or less	2.9	2.2	1.1	0.8	0.5	0.2	*	0.0	0.2	0.9	1.9	2.6	13.4
Temperature Maximum:													
90° and above	0.0	0.0	0.5	1.0	6.7	22.1	28.1	28.5	16.8	3.4	0.0	0.0	107.2
32° and below	1.1	0.2	0.0	0.0	0.0	0.0	0.0	0.0	0.0	0.0	0.0	0.5	1.8
Temperature Minimum:													
32° and below	13.8	8.3	2.0	0.1	0.0	0.0	0.0	0.0	0.0	*	2.1	9.3	35.7
0° and below	0.0	0.0	0.0	0.0	0.0	0.0	0.0	0.0	0.0	0.0	0.0	0.0	0.0
RELATIVE HUMIDITY (%)													
Morning	77	75	74	75	78	74	67	67	75	76	77	76	74
Afternoon	64	60	59	60	61	54	48	48	55	56	59	61	57
PRECIPITATION (inches)													
Water Equivalent													
Normal	1.6	2.0	1.9	3.7	4.7	2.5	1.7	1.9	3.1	3.0	2.2	1.9	30.9
Maximum monthly	5.8	4.5	6.8	13.3	15.0	12.0	8.5	8.9	7.2	10.5	6.2	7.0	15.0
Date	1961	1944	1945	1957	1965	1961	1971	1974	1970	1984	1952	1960	1965
Minimum monthly	0.0	0.1	0.0	0.1	0.7	0.2	T	T	0.0	0.0	0.1	0.0	0.0
Date	1971	1972	1956	1983	1945	1953	1963	1952	1956	1952	1970	1950	1956
Maximum in 24 hrs	2.2	3.0	3.0	5.0	7.1	4.2	4.4	4.8	4.5	5.7	4.2	3.1	7.1
Date	1961	1977	1946	1957	1953	1947	1973	1958	1957	1974	1952	1945	1953
SNOW, ICE PELLETS													
Maximum monthly	7.0	4.8	1.0	0.0	0.0	0.0	0.0	0.0	0.0	0.0	0.8	2.0	7.0
Date	1949	1966	1962	—	—	—	—	—	—	—	1980	1946	1949
Maximum in 24 hrs	7.0	4.8	1.0	0.0	0.0	0.0	0.0	0.0	0.0	0.0	0.8	2.0	7.0
Date	1949	1966	1962	—	—	—	—	—	—	—	1980	1946	1949
WIND (Resultant)													
Mean speed (mph)	11.6	12.0	13.1	12.9	11.9	11.7	10.7	9.9	9.6	10.0	10.8	11.2	11.3

WICHITA FALLS

Elev. 994'   33° 58'N — 98° 29'W   **Texas**

NORMALS, MEANS, EXTREMES

	JAN	FEB	MAR	APR	MAY	JUN	JUL	AUG	SEP	OCT	NOV	DEC	YEAR
TEMPERATURE													
Normal daily maximum	52.3	58.0	66.7	76.8	84.1	93.2	98.5	97.3	88.7	78.2	64.4	56.2	76.2
Normal daily minimum	28.2	32.6	39.9	50.6	59.4	68.2	72.5	71.2	63.7	52.0	39.6	31.6	50.8
Normal monthly	40.3	45.3	53.3	63.7	71.8	80.7	85.5	84.3	76.2	65.1	52.0	43.9	63.5
Extreme highest	87	92	100	102	105	117	114	113	108	102	89	88	117
Extreme highest date	1969	1979	1971	1972	1985	1980	1980	1964	1977	1979	1965	1954	1980
Extreme lowest	-5	-8	9	24	36	51	54	54	38	25	14	1	-8
Extreme lowest date	1966	1985	1965	1975	1979	1983	1970	1962	1984	1957	1950	1983	1985
DEGREE DAYS BASE 65° F													
Heating	766	552	388	118	18	0	0	0	14	105	396	654	3011
Cooling	0	0	26	79	229	471	639	598	350	108	6	0	2506
% OF POSSIBLE SUNSHINE	na	na	na	na	na	na	na	na	na	na	na	na	na
AVERAGE SKY COVER													
Sunrise - Sunset	5.7	5.5	5.6	5.4	5.3	4.5	4.2	4.0	4.2	4.3	4.8	5.3	4.9
NUMBER OF DAYS (Sunrise-Sunset)													
Clear	10.7	9.8	10.7	11.0	10.8	13.0	14.6	15.8	15.1	15.0	12.9	12.3	151.6
Partly cloudy	6.5	6.6	7.6	7.4	9.3	10.5	9.6	9.3	7.2	7.3	6.5	6.2	94.0
Cloudy	13.8	11.9	12.7	11.6	10.9	6.5	6.7	5.9	7.8	8.8	10.6	12.4	119.6
Precipitation .01" or more	5.0	5.4	5.9	6.6	8.9	6.4	5.2	5.3	6.0	5.9	4.6	4.8	70.0
Snow, Ice pellets 1.0" or more	0.8	0.7	0.3	0.0	0.0	0.0	0.0	0.0	0.0	0.0	0.1	0.3	2.2
Thunderstorms	0.9	1.5	3.2	5.5	9.4	7.1	5.6	5.5	3.8	3.3	1.6	0.8	48.3
Fog, Visibility 1/4 mile or less	2.3	2.3	1.1	0.8	0.5	0.2	*	0.1	0.5	1.0	1.5	2.1	12.4
Temperature Maximum:													
90° and above	0.0	*	0.9	2.4	8.4	21.0	28.5	27.0	14.6	3.9	0.0	0.0	106.9
32° and below	4.0	1.5	0.1	0.0	0.0	0.0	0.0	0.0	0.0	0.0	*	1.7	7.4
Temperature Minimum:													
32° and below	22.4	15.1	6.4	0.7	0.0	0.0	0.0	0.0	0.0	0.2	6.0	17.9	68.7
0° and below	0.1	*	0.0	0.0	0.0	0.0	0.0	0.0	0.0	0.0	0.0	0.0	0.2
RELATIVE HUMIDITY (%)													
Morning	73	73	69	72	76	74	65	67	76	74	76	74	72
Afternoon	57	55	50	49	52	50	42	45	53	52	54	56	51
PRECIPITATION (inches)													
Water Equivalent													
Normal	0.9	1.0	1.8	2.9	4.3	2.8	2.0	2.1	3.4	2.6	1.4	1.2	26.7
Maximum monthly	4.4	3.4	3.8	8.5	13.2	8.3	11.8	7.6	10.2	7.8	5.6	5.0	13.2
Date	1968	1945	1973	1957	1982	1945	1950	1971	1980	1972	1957	1984	1982
Minimum monthly	T	0.1	T	0.3	0.0	0.2	T	T	T	T	0.0	0.0	0.0
Date	1976	1976	1956	1980	1966	1980	1943	1943	1983	1952	1949	1950	1949
Maximum in 24 hrs	2.0	3.0	2.6	4.0	5.7	5.3	3.9	4.6	6.2	5.6	2.5	2.4	6.2
Date	1968	1981	1978	1967	1975	1985	1950	1971	1980	1959	1968	1984	1980
SNOW, ICE PELLETS													
Maximum monthly	11.9	11.8	6.5	0.8	0.0	0.0	0.0	0.0	0.0	T	3.9	7.1	11.9
Date	1966	1978	1947	1973	—	—	—	—	—	1967	1957	1983	1966
Maximum in 24 hrs	8.1	4.5	5.2	0.8	0.0	0.0	0.0	0.0	0.0	T	3.9	5.6	8.1
Date	1985	1958	1958	1973	—	—	—	—	—	1967	1957	1983	1985
WIND (Resultant)													
Mean speed (mph)	11.4	12.0	13.5	13.4	12.3	12.2	11.0	10.4	10.7	10.7	11.4	11.3	11.7

MILFORD

Elev. 5028' 38° 26'N — 113° 01'W **Utah**

NORMALS, MEANS, EXTREMES

	JAN	FEB	MAR	APR	MAY	JUN	JUL	AUG	SEP	OCT	NOV	DEC	YEAR
TEMPERATURE													
Normal daily maximum	39.4	45.3	52.7	62.2	73.1	84.8	92.9	89.9	81.2	67.8	51.5	41.5	65.2
Normal daily minimum	13.4	18.8	23.6	30.4	38.6	46.8	55.6	54.2	43.9	32.6	22.0	14.8	32.9
Normal monthly	26.4	32.1	38.2	46.3	55.9	65.8	74.3	72.1	62.6	50.2	36.8	28.2	49.0
Extreme highest	66	73	78	87	94	105	104	102	98	90	76	65	105
Extreme highest date	1975	1963	1972	1959	1967	1970	1985	1958	1950	1963	1965	1979	1970
Extreme lowest	-28	-27	-14	9	17	24	38	34	23	-2	-13	-32	-32
Extreme lowest date	1949	1949	1966	1975	1975	1976	1982	1968	1984	1971	1958	1972	1972
DEGREE DAYS BASE 65° F													
Heating	1197	921	831	561	295	68	0	9	126	456	846	1141	6451
Cooling	0	0	0	0	13	92	288	229	54	0	0	0	676
% OF POSSIBLE SUNSHINE	56	64	60	68	73	83	77	81	81	75	62	60	70
AVERAGE SKY COVER													
Sunrise - Sunset	6.1	6.1	5.9	5.4	5.0	3.4	3.8	3.7	3.1	3.7	5.3	5.8	4.8
NUMBER OF DAYS (Sunrise-Sunset)													
Clear	8.8	7.3	9.2	10.0	11.3	17.4	15.6	16.2	18.6	16.7	10.8	9.8	151.5
Partly cloudy	8.1	8.4	8.3	9.4	10.3	7.7	10.4	10.2	7.3	7.1	7.8	8.0	102.9
Cloudy	14.1	12.5	13.5	10.6	9.4	4.9	5.0	4.7	4.1	7.2	11.4	13.2	110.8
Precipitation .01" or more	7.0	6.6	8.4	6.2	5.5	3.2	5.2	5.8	3.9	4.4	4.7	5.9	66.8
Snow, Ice pellets 1.0" or more	2.7	2.2	3.3	1.8	0.5	0.0	0.0	0.0	0.1	0.5	1.4	2.3	14.9
Thunderstorms	0.1	0.3	0.4	1.5	3.4	2.9	8.8	9.8	3.9	1.3	0.3	0.1	32.8
Fog, Visibility 1/4 mile or less	1.4	1.2	0.5	0.2	0.2	0.0	0.0	0.1	0.1	0.1	1.3	1.8	6.7
Temperature Maximum:													
90° and above	0.0	0.0	0.0	0.0	0.6	9.7	23.9	18.0	4.7	*	0.0	0.0	56.9
32° and below	8.3	3.8	0.9	*	0.0	0.0	0.0	0.0	0.0	0.1	1.6	6.4	21.1
Temperature Minimum:													
32° and below	29.9	26.3	26.9	18.5	5.9	0.6	0.0	0.0	2.5	15.5	25.8	29.8	181.8
0° and below	5.4	2.1	0.4	0.0	0.0	0.0	0.0	0.0	0.0	*	0.5	3.1	11.6
Afternoon	60	54	37	28	23	17	20	21	20	28	46	60	35
PRECIPITATION (inches)													
Water Equivalent													
Normal	0.6	0.7	0.9	0.9	0.7	0.4	0.6	0.7	0.6	0.7	0.6	0.6	8.5
Maximum monthly	1.8	1.6	2.0	2.2	2.2	2.4	1.7	3.7	3.6	2.6	2.2	2.4	3.7
Date	1980	1976	1981	1973	1981	1967	1985	1984	1982	1972	1978	1966	1984
Minimum monthly	0.0	0.0	0.0	0.0	T	T	0.0	0.0	T	0.0	0.0	0.0	0.0
Date	1972	1972	1972	1955	1963	1979	1958	1957	1979	1952	1956	1976	1972
Maximum in 24 hrs	0.8	0.7	1.1	1.0	1.3	1.1	1.2	1.7	1.5	1.2	1.0	1.0	1.7
Date	1954	1953	1953	1973	1981	1982	1985	1984	1982	1951	1963	1972	1984
SNOW, ICE PELLETS													
Maximum monthly	29.8	18.8	29.4	24.4	11.4	0.0	0.0	0.0	8.4	17.4	14.0	30.6	30.6
Date	1949	1971	1985	1973	1975	—	—	—	1965	1971	1963	1972	1972
Maximum in 24 hrs	11.8	9.2	20.4	11.2	8.6	0.0	0.0	0.0	6.7	6.4	8.5	16.3	20.4
Date	1957	1971	1985	1973	1975	—	—	—	1965	1971	1978	1949	1985

SALT LAKE CITY
Elev. 4221'   40° 46'N — 111° 58'W   **Utah**

NORMALS, MEANS, EXTREMES

	JAN	FEB	MAR	APR	MAY	JUN	JUL	AUG	SEP	OCT	NOV	DEC	YEAR
TEMPERATURE													
Normal daily maximum	37.4	43.7	51.5	61.1	72.4	83.3	93.2	90.0	80.0	66.7	50.2	38.9	64.0
Normal daily minimum	19.7	24.4	29.9	37.2	45.2	53.3	61.8	59.7	50.0	39.3	29.2	21.6	39.3
Normal monthly	28.6	34.1	40.7	49.2	58.8	68.3	77.5	74.9	65.0	53.0	39.7	30.3	51.7
Extreme highest	62	69	78	85	93	104	107	104	100	89	75	67	107
Extreme highest date	1982	1972	1960	1985	1984	1979	1960	1979	1979	1963	1967	1969	1960
Extreme lowest	-22	-30	2	14	25	35	40	37	27	16	-14	-21	-30
Extreme lowest date	1949	1933	1966	1936	1965	1962	1968	1965	1965	1971	1955	1932	1933
DEGREE DAYS BASE 65° F													
Heating	1128	865	753	474	220	53	0	0	97	377	759	1076	5802
Cooling	0	0	0	0	28	152	388	311	97	5	0	0	981
% OF POSSIBLE SUNSHINE	45	54	63	67	72	79	83	83	82	72	53	42	66
AVERAGE SKY COVER													
Sunrise - Sunset	7.3	7.1	6.7	6.3	5.7	4.3	3.6	3.6	3.6	4.6	6.2	7.2	5.5
NUMBER OF DAYS (Sunrise-Sunset)													
Clear	5.5	5.2	7.0	7.0	9.2	13.7	16.8	15.7	16.9	14.1	8.6	6.2	125.9
Partly cloudy	6.6	7.0	8.3	9.3	10.4	10.0	9.8	10.8	8.0	7.8	7.2	6.5	101.8
Cloudy	18.8	16.1	15.7	13.7	11.4	6.3	4.4	4.5	5.1	9.1	14.2	18.3	137.5
Precipitation .01" or more	9.9	8.8	9.9	9.5	8.0	5.5	4.6	5.6	5.3	6.4	7.6	9.3	90.5
Snow, Ice pellets 1.0" or more	4.1	3.2	3.1	1.4	0.2	0.0	0.0	0.0	0.1	0.3	2.0	3.9	18.3
Thunderstorms	0.2	0.7	1.3	2.1	5.0	5.5	7.0	7.9	4.2	2.0	0.5	0.3	36.8
Fog, Visibility 1/4 mile or less	4.2	2.3	0.4	0.1	*	0.0	0.0	0.0	0.0	*	0.9	3.6	11.5
Temperature Maximum:													
90° and above	0.0	0.0	0.0	0.0	0.7	8.7	24.3	19.3	3.5	0.0	0.0	0.0	56.6
32° and below	10.8	3.9	0.7	0.0	0.0	0.0	0.0	0.0	0.0	*	0.6	8.7	24.8
Temperature Minimum:													
32° and below	27.1	22.8	17.3	7.3	0.8	0.0	0.0	0.0	0.4	5.4	17.7	27.1	126.1
0° and below	2.0	0.3	0.0	0.0	0.0	0.0	0.0	0.0	0.0	0.0	0.0	0.6	3.0
RELATIVE HUMIDITY (%)													
Morning	78	77	71	67	65	60	52	55	62	69	74	78	67
Afternoon	69	59	47	39	33	26	21	23	29	41	59	71	43
PRECIPITATION (inches)													
Water Equivalent													
Normal	1.3	1.3	1.7	2.2	1.4	0.9	0.7	0.9	0.8	1.1	1.2	1.3	15.3
Maximum monthly	3.1	3.2	3.9	4.9	4.7	2.9	2.5	3.6	7.0	3.9	2.6	4.3	7.0
Date	1940	1936	1983	1944	1977	1947	1982	1968	1982	1981	1985	1983	1982
Minimum monthly	0.0	0.1	0.1	0.4	T	0.0	T	T	T	0.0	0.0	0.0	0.0
Date	1961	1946	1956	1981	1934	1946	1963	1944	1951	1952	1939	1976	1952
Maximum in 24 hrs	1.3	1.0	1.8	2.4	2.0	1.8	2.3	1.9	2.3	1.7	1.1	1.8	2.4
Date	1953	1958	1944	1957	1942	1948	1962	1932	1982	1984	1954	1972	1957
SNOW, ICE PELLETS													
Maximum monthly	32.3	27.9	41.9	26.4	7.5	T	0.0	0.0	4.0	20.4	27.2	35.2	41.9
Date	1937	1969	1977	1974	1975	1984	—	—	1971	1984	1985	1972	1977
Maximum in 24 hrs	10.7	8.8	15.4	16.2	6.4	T	0.0	0.0	4.0	18.4	11.0	18.1	18.4
Date	1980	1984	1944	1974	1975	1984	—	—	1971	1984	1930	1972	1984
WIND (Resultant)													
Mean speed (mph)	7.6	8.2	9.3	9.6	9.4	9.4	9.5	9.7	9.1	8.5	7.9	7.5	8.8

BURLINGTON

Elev. 332'   44° 28'N — 73° 09'W   # Vermont

NORMALS, MEANS, EXTREMES

	JAN	FEB	MAR	APR	MAY	JUN	JUL	AUG	SEP	OCT	NOV	DEC	YEAR
TEMPERATURE													
Normal daily maximum	25.4	27.3	37.7	52.6	66.4	75.9	80.5	77.6	68.8	57.0	43.6	30.3	53.6
Normal daily minimum	7.7	8.8	20.8	32.7	44.0	54.0	58.6	56.6	48.7	38.7	29.6	14.9	34.6
Normal monthly	16.6	18.1	29.3	42.7	55.2	65.0	69.6	67.1	58.8	47.9	36.6	22.6	44.1
Extreme highest	63	62	84	91	93	96	99	101	94	85	75	65	101
Extreme highest date	1950	1981	1946	1976	1977	1946	1977	1944	1945	1949	1948	1982	1944
Extreme lowest	-30	-30	-20	2	24	33	39	35	25	15	-2	-26	-30
Extreme lowest date	1957	1979	1948	1972	1966	1965	1962	1976	1963	1972	1958	1980	1979
DEGREE DAYS BASE 65° F													
Heating	1500	1313	1110	669	326	64	23	50	202	530	852	1314	7953
Cooling	0	0	0	0	22	61	165	115	16	0	0	0	379
% OF POSSIBLE SUNSHINE	41	47	50	49	55	58	64	60	54	48	30	32	49
AVERAGE SKY COVER													
Sunrise - Sunset	7.6	7.3	7.2	7.1	7.0	6.8	6.4	6.4	6.5	6.9	8.3	8.1	7.1
NUMBER OF DAYS (Sunrise-Sunset)													
Clear	4.3	4.4	5.6	5.1	5.0	4.8	5.3	6.0	6.0	6.1	2.5	2.8	57.8
Partly cloudy	6.6	6.4	6.8	7.5	9.1	10.7	13.0	11.7	9.9	7.9	5.1	5.8	100.7
Cloudy	20.1	17.5	18.6	17.3	17.0	14.5	12.7	13.3	14.0	17.0	22.3	22.4	206.7
Precipitation .01" or more	14.3	11.6	13.1	12.4	13.4	12.5	11.9	12.4	11.6	11.4	14.1	15.0	153.7
Snow, Ice pellets 1.0" or more	5.2	4.7	3.7	1.2	0.1	0.0	0.0	0.0	0.0	*	2.0	5.4	22.2
Thunderstorms	*	0.0	0.3	0.9	2.4	5.2	6.3	5.4	2.2	0.6	0.3	*	23.8
Fog, Visibility 1/4 mile or less	0.9	1.1	1.2	1.3	0.9	1.1	0.8	1.4	2.5	2.0	1.3	1.2	15.7
Temperature Maximum:													
90° and above	0.0	0.0	0.0	0.1	0.6	1.1	2.5	0.9	*	0.0	0.0	0.0	5.2
32° and below	22.8	18.2	9.3	0.6	0.0	0.0	0.0	0.0	0.0	*	4.7	17.3	73.0
Temperature Minimum:													
32° and below	29.9	26.4	25.9	16.0	3.0	0.0	0.0	0.0	0.6	8.6	18.9	27.6	156.9
0° and below	11.0	8.4	2.2	0.0	0.0	0.0	0.0	0.0	0.0	0.0	0.0	4.7	26.3
RELATIVE HUMIDITY (%)													
Morning	69	71	72	73	76	81	82	84	85	79	77	75	77
Afternoon	63	63	59	54	51	56	53	57	62	62	67	69	60
PRECIPITATION (inches)													
Water Equivalent													
Normal	1.8	1.7	2.2	2.7	2.9	3.6	3.4	3.8	3.2	2.8	2.8	2.4	33.6
Maximum monthly	4.6	5.3	3.5	6.5	6.3	7.6	6.1	11.5	8.1	6.2	6.8	5.9	11.5
Date	1978	1981	1972	1983	1983	1973	1972	1955	1945	1959	1983	1973	1955
Minimum monthly	0.4	0.2	0.3	0.9	0.2	1.0	1.2	0.7	0.8	0.5	0.6	0.6	0.2
Date	1981	1978	1965	1966	1977	1949	1979	1957	1948	1963	1952	1960	1978
Maximum in 24 hrs	1.5	1.9	1.6	2.1	2.2	2.8	2.6	3.5	3.2	2.1	1.8	2.6	3.5
Date	1978	1981	1971	1968	1955	1972	1985	1955	1983	1983	1959	1950	1955
SNOW, ICE PELLETS													
Maximum monthly	42.4	34.3	33.1	21.3	3.9	0.0	0.0	0.0	T	5.1	19.2	56.7	56.7
Date	1978	1958	1971	1983	1966	—	—	—	1963	1969	1971	1970	1970
Maximum in 24 hrs	14.5	16.5	15.6	15.6	3.5	0.0	0.0	0.0	T	5.1	10.1	17.0	17.0
Date	1961	1966	1971	1983	1966	—	—	—	1963	1969	1958	1978	1978
WIND (Resultant)													
Mean speed (mph)	9.5	9.2	9.4	9.3	8.8	8.3	7.9	7.4	8.1	8.6	9.5	9.8	8.8

LYNCHBURG

Elev. 921'   37° 20'N — 79° 12'W   ## Virginia

NORMALS, MEANS, EXTREMES

	JAN	FEB	MAR	APR	MAY	JUN	JUL	AUG	SEP	OCT	NOV	DEC	YEAR
TEMPERATURE													
Normal daily maximum	44.4	47.1	56.2	68.1	75.8	82.5	86.1	85.0	78.8	68.1	57.2	47.5	66.4
Normal daily minimum	25.9	27.6	35.1	44.6	53.2	60.6	65.1	64.5	57.9	46.1	36.7	29.1	45.5
Normal monthly	35.2	37.4	45.7	56.4	64.5	71.6	75.6	74.8	68.4	57.1	47.0	38.3	56.0
Extreme highest	76	79	87	92	93	100	103	102	101	93	83	78	103
Extreme highest date	1952	1985	1945	1985	1969	1945	1954	1983	1954	1951	1974	1984	1954
Extreme lowest	-10	0	7	20	31	40	50	45	36	21	8	-4	-10
Extreme lowest date	1985	1965	1965	1985	1966	1977	1963	1965	1983	1969	1970	1983	1985
DEGREE DAYS BASE 65° F													
Heating	927	773	598	263	97	7	0	0	32	258	540	828	4323
Cooling	0	0	0	5	81	205	332	304	134	13	0	0	1074
% OF POSSIBLE SUNSHINE	51	56	59	61	63	66	62	62	61	60	55	52	59
AVERAGE SKY COVER													
Sunrise - Sunset	6.1	6.0	6.0	5.8	6.0	5.7	5.9	5.6	5.4	4.9	5.5	5.8	5.7
NUMBER OF DAYS (Sunrise-Sunset)													
Clear	9.1	8.7	8.7	8.7	8.2	8.0	7.9	9.1	10.6	13.3	10.6	10.4	113.3
Partly cloudy	7.0	7.1	9.1	9.0	10.3	11.8	11.3	11.4	8.7	6.8	7.2	6.7	106.4
Cloudy	14.9	12.5	13.2	12.3	12.5	10.2	11.8	10.5	10.7	10.9	12.2	13.9	145.6
Precipitation .01" or more	11.2	9.4	11.1	9.8	11.4	10.0	11.4	10.1	8.0	7.9	9.1	9.5	118.9
Snow, Ice pellets 1.0" or more	1.6	1.6	0.8	0.1	0.0	0.0	0.0	0.0	0.0	*	0.2	1.0	5.4
Thunderstorms	0.3	0.4	1.2	2.9	6.4	7.1	9.3	7.8	3.5	0.9	0.5	0.1	40.5
Fog, Visibility 1/4 mile or less	3.9	3.9	2.7	2.6	3.5	2.3	2.6	3.4	3.7	2.6	3.8	3.9	39.0
Temperature Maximum:													
90° and above	0.0	0.0	0.0	0.4	0.5	4.0	7.6	6.7	2.6	0.0	0.0	0.0	21.9
32° and below	5.5	2.5	0.2	0.0	0.0	0.0	0.0	0.0	0.0	0.0	0.1	2.1	10.5
Temperature Minimum:													
32° and below	23.8	21.0	12.5	3.0	0.2	0.0	0.0	0.0	0.0	2.5	10.4	19.5	92.8
0° and below	0.6	*	0.0	0.0	0.0	0.0	0.0	0.0	0.0	0.0	0.0	*	0.7
Afternoon	53	49	48	45	52	55	58	57	56	53	51	54	53
PRECIPITATION (inches)													
Water Equivalent													
Normal	3.0	2.9	3.6	2.9	3.6	3.4	3.8	3.6	3.2	3.3	2.9	3.1	39.9
Maximum monthly	7.9	5.7	9.2	6.6	9.0	8.5	10.3	11.3	9.2	11.4	8.7	7.1	11.4
Date	1978	1972	1975	1983	1971	1972	1984	1952	1979	1976	1985	1973	1976
Minimum monthly	0.4	0.5	0.7	0.2	1.3	0.6	1.1	0.9	0.0	0.3	0.9	0.3	0.0
Date	1981	1978	1966	1976	1957	1980	1977	1963	1978	1974	1960	1965	1978
Maximum in 24 hrs	2.2	2.8	2.4	3.6	3.4	6.2	4.8	4.4	3.7	4.9	2.6	3.0	6.2
Date	1978	1984	1975	1978	1960	1972	1984	1967	1979	1954	1951	1948	1972
SNOW, ICE PELLETS													
Maximum monthly	31.8	19.2	24.9	4.8	0.0	0.0	0.0	0.0	0.0	2.4	11.6	17.9	31.8
Date	1966	1979	1960	1971	—	—	—	—	—	1979	1968	1966	1966
Maximum in 24 hrs	10.9	14.6	13.4	4.8	0.0	0.0	0.0	0.0	0.0	2.4	6.7	12.7	14.6
Date	1966	1983	1969	1971	—	—	—	—	—	1979	1968	1969	1983
WIND (Resultant)													
Mean speed (mph)	8.8	8.8	9.3	9.2	7.7	6.9	6.6	6.3	6.9	7.4	7.9	7.9	7.8

NORFOLK
Elev. 24' 36° 54'N — 76° 12'W **Virginia**

NORMALS, MEANS, EXTREMES

	JAN	FEB	MAR	APR	MAY	JUN	JUL	AUG	SEP	OCT	NOV	DEC	YEAR
TEMPERATURE													
Normal daily maximum	48.1	49.9	57.5	68.2	75.7	83.2	86.9	85.7	80.2	69.8	60.8	51.9	68.2
Normal daily minimum	31.7	32.3	39.4	48.1	57.2	65.3	69.9	69.6	64.2	52.8	43.0	35.0	50.7
Normal monthly	39.9	41.1	48.5	58.2	66.5	74.3	78.4	77.7	72.2	61.3	51.9	43.5	59.4
Extreme highest	78	81	88	97	97	101	103	104	99	95	86	80	104
Extreme highest date	1970	1976	1985	1960	1956	1964	1952	1980	1983	1954	1974	1978	1980
Extreme lowest	-3	8	18	28	36	45	54	49	45	27	20	7	-3
Extreme lowest date	1985	1965	1980	1982	1966	1967	1979	1982	1967	1976	1950	1983	1985
DEGREE DAYS BASE 65° F													
Heating	778	669	512	219	53	0	0	0	9	146	393	667	3446
Cooling	0	0	0	15	96	282	415	394	225	31	0	0	1458
% OF POSSIBLE SUNSHINE	56	59	63	65	65	68	64	65	64	59	58	57	62
AVERAGE SKY COVER													
Sunrise - Sunset	6.2	6.1	6.1	5.8	6.1	5.8	6.0	5.7	5.7	5.5	5.5	6.0	5.9
NUMBER OF DAYS (Sunrise-Sunset)													
Clear	9.2	8.6	9.0	8.9	7.9	7.6	7.6	8.3	9.3	11.4	10.7	9.4	107.9
Partly cloudy	6.4	6.0	7.4	9.2	9.7	11.5	11.6	11.9	9.5	7.0	7.9	7.3	105.3
Cloudy	15.4	13.7	14.6	11.8	13.4	10.8	11.8	10.9	11.2	12.6	11.4	14.4	152.0
Precipitation .01" or more	10.4	10.0	11.0	9.9	9.9	9.0	11.3	10.3	7.8	7.8	8.0	9.1	114.5
Snow, Ice pellets 1.0" or more	0.8	0.7	0.3	*	0.0	0.0	0.0	0.0	0.0	0.0	0.0	0.4	2.2
Thunderstorms	0.4	0.6	1.8	2.7	4.9	5.7	8.5	7.1	2.7	1.4	0.5	0.4	36.7
Fog, Visibility 1/4 mile or less	2.2	2.7	1.8	1.4	1.9	1.2	0.6	1.2	1.3	2.4	2.0	2.3	21.1
Temperature Maximum:													
90° and above	0.0	0.0	0.0	0.5	1.3	6.3	11.0	8.7	3.0	0.1	0.0	0.0	30.8
32° and below	2.8	1.3	0.2	0.0	0.0	0.0	0.0	0.0	0.0	0.0	0.0	1.0	5.3
Temperature Minimum:													
32° and below	17.3	14.5	6.0	0.4	0.0	0.0	0.0	0.0	0.0	0.2	3.2	13.6	55.1
0° and below	*	0.0	0.0	0.0	0.0	0.0	0.0	0.0	0.0	0.0	0.0	0.0	*
RELATIVE HUMIDITY (%)													
Morning	72	72	71	72	80	83	84	86	84	82	76	73	78
Afternoon	59	56	53	49	56	57	59	61	61	60	56	58	57
PRECIPITATION (inches)													
Water Equivalent													
Normal	3.7	3.2	3.8	2.8	3.7	3.4	5.1	5.3	4.3	3.4	2.8	3.1	45.2
Maximum monthly	6.4	6.2	7.8	7.2	10.1	9.7	13.7	11.1	13.8	10.1	7.0	6.1	13.8
Date	1979	1983	1978	1984	1979	1963	1975	1967	1979	1971	1951	1983	1979
Minimum monthly	1.0	0.8	1.3	0.4	1.4	0.3	0.7	0.7	0.3	0.5	0.4	0.7	0.3
Date	1981	1950	1967	1985	1965	1954	1983	1975	1958	1984	1965	1985	1958
Maximum in 24 hrs	3.8	2.7	3.1	2.9	3.4	6.8	5.6	11.4	6.7	4.3	3.3	2.7	11.4
Date	1967	1983	1958	1984	1980	1963	1969	1964	1959	1971	1952	1983	1964
SNOW, ICE PELLETS													
Maximum monthly	14.2	18.9	13.7	1.2	0.0	0.0	0.0	0.0	0.0	0.0	0.6	14.7	18.9
Date	1966	1980	1980	1964	—	—	—	—	—	—	1950	1958	1980
Maximum in 24 hrs	9.1	12.4	9.9	1.2	0.0	0.0	0.0	0.0	0.0	0.0	0.6	11.4	12.4
Date	1973	1980	1980	1964	—	—	—	—	—	—	1950	1958	1980
WIND (Resultant)													
Mean speed (mph)	11.5	11.9	12.4	11.8	10.4	9.6	8.9	8.8	9.6	10.4	10.6	11.0	10.6

RICHMOND
Elev. 164'   **37° 30'N — 77° 20'W**   # Virginia

NORMALS, MEANS, EXTREMES

	JAN	FEB	MAR	APR	MAY	JUN	JUL	AUG	SEP	OCT	NOV	DEC	YEAR
TEMPERATURE													
Normal daily maximum	46.7	49.6	58.5	70.6	77.9	84.8	88.4	87.1	81.0	70.5	60.5	50.2	68.8
Normal daily minimum	26.5	28.1	35.8	45.1	54.2	62.2	67.2	66.4	59.3	46.7	37.3	29.6	46.5
Normal monthly	36.6	38.9	47.2	57.9	66.1	73.5	77.8	76.8	70.2	58.6	48.9	39.9	57.7
Extreme highest	80	83	93	96	100	104	105	102	103	99	86	80	105
Extreme highest date	1950	1932	1938	1985	1941	1952	1977	1983	1954	1941	1974	1971	1977
Extreme lowest	-12	-10	11	23	31	40	51	46	35	21	10	-1	-12
Extreme lowest date	1940	1936	1960	1985	1956	1967	1965	1934	1974	1962	1933	1942	1940
DEGREE DAYS BASE 65° F													
Heating	880	731	552	226	65	0	0	0	24	221	483	778	3960
Cooling	0	0	0	13	99	258	397	366	180	23	0	0	1336
% OF POSSIBLE SUNSHINE	53	58	60	65	65	68	66	66	64	60	58	53	61
AVERAGE SKY COVER													
Sunrise - Sunset	6.4	6.1	6.3	6.1	6.3	6.1	6.2	6.0	5.7	5.5	5.7	6.2	6.0
NUMBER OF DAYS (Sunrise-Sunset)													
Clear	8.3	8.7	8.1	8.0	7.0	6.6	7.0	7.5	9.5	11.3	9.6	9.5	100.9
Partly cloudy	6.8	6.2	8.2	9.3	10.2	12.0	11.4	11.6	8.5	7.2	7.7	6.4	105.5
Cloudy	16.0	13.4	14.7	12.7	13.8	11.4	12.6	11.9	12.0	12.6	12.7	15.1	158.8
Precipitation .01" or more	10.3	9.1	10.8	9.2	10.8	9.5	11.1	9.9	7.9	7.4	8.3	8.8	113.1
Snow, Ice pellets 1.0" or more	1.4	1.1	0.7	0.1	0.0	0.0	0.0	0.0	0.0	0.0	0.1	0.6	4.0
Thunderstorms	0.2	0.4	1.5	2.5	5.5	6.6	8.7	6.8	3.1	1.0	0.5	0.3	37.1
Fog, Visibility 1/4 mile or less	2.8	2.1	1.7	1.7	1.9	1.6	2.3	2.6	3.1	3.4	2.3	2.9	28.2
Temperature Maximum:													
90° and above	0.0	0.0	0.1	0.9	2.7	9.3	13.4	11.0	4.6	0.4	0.0	0.0	42.3
32° and below	3.3	1.5	0.2	0.0	0.0	0.0	0.0	0.0	0.0	0.0	*	1.7	6.7
Temperature Minimum:													
32° and below	21.6	18.9	10.2	2.2	0.1	0.0	0.0	0.0	0.0	1.8	10.2	20.3	85.2
0° and below	0.4	0.1	0.0	0.0	0.0	0.0	0.0	0.0	0.0	0.0	0.0	*	0.5
RELATIVE HUMIDITY (%)													
Morning	77	74	73	74	83	87	88	90	90	87	80	77	82
Afternoon	57	52	49	45	51	54	57	57	56	53	51	55	53
PRECIPITATION (inches)													
Water Equivalent													
Normal	3.2	3.1	3.5	2.9	3.5	3.6	5.1	5.0	3.5	3.7	3.2	3.3	44.0
Maximum monthly	7.9	5.9	8.6	5.9	8.8	9.2	18.8	14.1	10.9	9.3	7.6	7.0	18.8
Date	1978	1979	1984	1984	1972	1938	1945	1955	1975	1971	1959	1973	1945
Minimum monthly	0.6	0.4	0.9	0.6	0.8	0.3	0.5	0.5	0.2	0.3	0.3	0.4	0.2
Date	1981	1978	1966	1963	1965	1980	1983	1943	1978	1963	1965	1980	1978
Maximum in 24 hrs	3.3	2.6	2.5	2.6	3.0	4.6	5.7	8.7	4.0	6.5	4.0	3.1	8.7
Date	1962	1979	1984	1978	1981	1963	1969	1955	1985	1961	1956	1958	1955
SNOW, ICE PELLETS													
Maximum monthly	28.5	21.4	19.7	2.0	0.0	0.0	0.0	0.0	0.0	T	7.3	12.5	28.5
Date	1940	1983	1960	1940	—	—	—	—	—	1979	1953	1958	1940
Maximum in 24 hrs	21.6	16.8	12.1	2.0	0.0	0.0	0.0	0.0	0.0	T	7.3	7.5	21.6
Date	1940	1983	1962	1940	—	—	—	—	—	1979	1953	1966	1940
WIND (Resultant)													
Mean speed (mph)	8.0	8.6	9.0	8.8	7.7	7.2	6.7	6.3	6.5	6.9	7.4	7.6	7.6

ROANOKE

Elev. 1149'   37° 19'N — 79° 58'W   **Virginia**

NORMALS, MEANS, EXTREMES

	JAN	FEB	MAR	APR	MAY	JUN	JUL	AUG	SEP	OCT	NOV	DEC	YEAR
TEMPERATURE													
Normal daily maximum	44.8	48.0	56.9	68.2	76.4	83.0	86.7	85.5	79.4	68.6	57.4	47.8	66.9
Normal daily minimum	26.2	27.8	35.3	44.3	53.0	60.1	64.6	63.8	57.0	44.9	36.3	28.7	45.2
Normal monthly	35.5	37.9	46.1	56.3	64.7	71.6	75.7	74.7	68.2	56.8	46.9	38.3	56.0
Extreme highest	78	80	86	95	96	100	104	105	101	93	83	76	105
Extreme highest date	1952	1985	1968	1957	1962	1959	1954	1983	1954	1951	1950	1984	1983
Extreme lowest	-11	1	10	20	31	39	48	43	34	22	9	-4	-11
Extreme lowest date	1985	1970	1980	1985	1966	1977	1983	1965	1983	1976	1950	1983	1985
DEGREE DAYS BASE 65° F													
Heating	915	759	586	268	99	12	0	0	38	267	543	828	4315
Cooling	0	0	0	7	89	210	332	301	134	12	0	0	1085
% OF POSSIBLE SUNSHINE	na	na	na	na	na	na	na	na	na	na	na	na	na
AVERAGE SKY COVER													
Sunrise - Sunset	6.3	6.2	6.3	6.0	6.1	6.0	6.1	5.8	5.6	5.2	5.9	6.1	6.0
NUMBER OF DAYS (Sunrise-Sunset)													
Clear	8.3	7.9	7.8	8.6	7.5	7.2	6.6	7.9	9.8	12.6	8.9	8.8	101.9
Partly cloudy	7.7	7.2	9.0	8.7	10.4	11.5	12.8	12.6	8.8	7.1	8.6	8.1	112.5
Cloudy	15.0	13.1	14.2	12.7	13.1	11.3	11.6	10.6	11.4	11.3	12.5	14.1	150.9
Precipitation .01" or more	10.3	9.5	11.2	10.1	11.9	10.1	11.7	10.7	8.2	7.8	9.0	8.8	119.3
Snow, Ice pellets 1.0" or more	1.8	1.9	1.1	0.1	0.0	0.0	0.0	0.0	0.0	*	0.6	1.2	6.6
Thunderstorms	0.1	0.3	1.1	2.9	6.1	6.6	8.5	7.1	2.6	1.1	0.3	0.1	36.8
Fog, Visibility 1/4 mile or less	2.9	2.8	1.9	1.2	1.8	1.1	1.5	1.5	2.5	2.2	2.2	2.5	24.0
Temperature Maximum:													
90° and above	0.0	0.0	0.0	0.4	0.6	4.7	9.0	7.4	2.6	0.0	0.0	0.0	24.8
32° and below	5.6	3.0	0.2	0.0	0.0	0.0	0.0	0.0	0.0	0.0	0.2	2.4	11.4
Temperature Minimum:													
32° and below	23.9	20.6	12.6	2.5	0.1	0.0	0.0	0.0	0.0	2.5	10.5	19.7	92.4
0° and below	0.5	0.0	0.0	0.0	0.0	0.0	0.0	0.0	0.0	0.0	0.0	0.1	0.6
RELATIVE HUMIDITY (%)													
Morning	67	64	63	63	76	83	84	86	86	80	72	69	74
Afternoon	53	49	48	46	52	54	55	56	56	54	52	54	52
PRECIPITATION (inches)													
Water Equivalent													
Normal	2.8	3.1	3.6	3.0	3.5	3.3	3.4	3.9	3.1	3.4	2.5	2.9	39.1
Maximum monthly	6.1	7.1	7.8	7.9	8.4	7.5	7.8	9.5	9.1	9.7	12.3	7.1	12.3
Date	1978	1960	1975	1983	1950	1972	1949	1984	1979	1976	1985	1948	1985
Minimum monthly	0.2	0.5	0.4	0.4	1.2	1.4	0.4	1.1	0.4	0.2	0.4	0.1	0.1
Date	1981	1968	1966	1976	1951	1960	1977	1965	1968	1963	1960	1965	1965
Maximum in 24 hrs	2.7	2.6	3.0	5.5	3.9	3.9	2.7	5.2	3.8	6.4	6.6	3.4	6.6
Date	1968	1984	1983	1978	1973	1972	1966	1985	1979	1968	1985	1948	1985
SNOW, ICE PELLETS													
Maximum monthly	41.2	27.6	30.3	7.3	T	0.0	0.0	0.0	T	1.0	13.8	22.6	41.2
Date	1966	1960	1960	1971	1963	—	—	—	1953	1957	1968	1966	1966
Maximum in 24 hrs	13.7	18.4	17.4	7.3	T	0.0	0.0	0.0	T	1.0	10.0	16.4	18.4
Date	1966	1983	1960	1971	1963	—	—	—	1953	1957	1968	1969	1983
WIND (Resultant)													
Mean speed (mph)	9.8	10.0	10.5	10.0	8.0	7.0	6.7	6.2	6.2	7.0	8.5	8.9	8.2

Elev. 40'   37° 56'N — 75° 29'W   **Virginia**

NORMALS, MEANS, EXTREMES

	JAN	FEB	MAR	APR	MAY	JUN	JUL	AUG	SEP	OCT	NOV	DEC	YEAR
TEMPERATURE													
Extreme highest	72	79	83	90	92	93	101	100	96	87	79	73	101
Extreme highest date	1985	1976	1985	1985	1977	1981	1977	1977	1983	1977	1982	1984	1977
Extreme lowest	0	15	14	27	37	48	55	51	46	33	22	8	0
Extreme lowest date	1985	1981	1980	1985	1985	1984	1984	1982	1983	1980	1984	1983	1985
DEGREE DAYS BASE 65° F													
Heating	905	781	654	342	124	11	0	0	24	220	480	781	4322
Cooling	0	0	0	0	37	179	332	326	177	37	0	0	1088
% OF POSSIBLE SUNSHINE	na	na	na	na	na	na	na	na	na	na	na	na	na
AVERAGE SKY COVER													
Sunrise - Sunset	0.0	0.0	0.0	6.3	6.8	5.6	5.1	6.0	0.0	0.0	0.0	0.0	0.0
NUMBER OF DAYS (Sunrise-Sunset)													
Clear	0.0	0.0	0.0	7.0	3.0	9.3	10.0	8.0	0.0	0.0	0.0	0.0	0.0
Partly cloudy	0.0	0.0	0.0	10.0	13.0	11.0	11.0	9.0	0.0	0.0	0.0	0.0	0.0
Cloudy	0.0	0.0	0.0	13.0	15.0	9.7	10.0	14.0	0.0	0.0	0.0	0.0	0.0
Precipitation .01" or more	11.5	9.8	10.5	9.4	10.1	8.6	10.6	7.9	7.8	7.9	8.9	10.4	113.3
Snow, Ice pellets 1.0" or more	1.1	1.1	0.5	0.1	0.0	0.0	0.0	0.0	0.0	0.0	0.1	0.3	3.2
Thunderstorms	0.0	0.0	2.0	4.0	4.0	4.0	0.0	0.0	0.0	0.0	0.0	0.0	0.0
Fog, Visibility 1/4 mile or less	4.0	7.0	2.0	5.0	1.0	1.0	0.0	0.0	0.0	0.0	0.0	0.0	0.0
Temperature Maximum:													
90° and above	0.0	0.0	0.0	0.3	0.2	1.4	3.8	3.4	0.9	0.0	0.0	0.0	10.0
32° and below	5.5	3.2	0.3	0.0	0.0	0.0	0.0	0.0	0.0	0.0	0.1	1.8	10.8
Temperature Minimum:													
32° and below	22.9	17.8	8.4	1.3	0.0	0.0	0.0	0.0	0.0	0.5	5.3	16.1	72.3
0° and below	0.3	0.0	0.0	0.0	0.0	0.0	0.0	0.0	0.0	0.0	0.0	0.0	0.3
Afternoon	65	64	63	60	68	69	68	70	66	64	64	64	65
PRECIPITATION (inches)													
Water Equivalent													
Normal	3.1	3.2	3.6	2.7	3.5	3.6	3.7	4.3	3.3	3.3	2.8	3.3	40.7
Maximum monthly	6.7	5.8	6.4	4.9	8.0	4.6	6.3	8.6	6.8	5.6	5.2	8.7	8.7
Date	1979	1979	1975	1983	1979	1977	1978	1985	1975	1980	1985	1977	1977
Minimum monthly	2.8	3.0	3.0	0.4	4.2	1.1	2.1	1.9	1.4	1.2	2.0	0.8	0.4
Date	1985	1985	1985	1985	1985	1984	1985	1984	1984	1984	1984	1985	1985
Maximum in 24 hrs	1.6	2.1	3.3	2.1	2.8	2.8	3.9	4.2	4.3	2.5	2.4	5.1	5.1
Date	1979	1975	1979	1978	1984	1979	1979	1985	1985	1978	1977	1977	1977
SNOW, ICE PELLETS													
Maximum monthly	9.1	13.4	6.5	2.0	0.0	0.0	0.0	0.0	0.0	0.0	3.0	3.5	13.4
Date	1985	1979	1980	1983	1974	1974	1974	1974	1974	1974	1976	1981	1979
Maximum in 24 hrs	5.2	5.8	5.6	2.0	0.0	0.0	0.0	0.0	0.0	0.0	3.0	3.4	5.8
Date	1980	1982	1980	1983	1974	1974	1974	1974	1974	1974	1976	1982	1982

OLYMPIA

Elev. 195'   46° 58'N — 122° 54'W   **Washington**

NORMALS, MEANS, EXTREMES

	JAN	FEB	MAR	APR	MAY	JUN	JUL	AUG	SEP	OCT	NOV	DEC	YEAR
TEMPERATURE													
Normal daily maximum	43.6	49.1	52.5	58.7	65.7	70.8	77.2	76.2	71.0	60.8	50.3	45.1	60.1
Normal daily minimum	30.8	32.5	32.8	35.8	40.5	46.0	48.7	48.8	45.1	39.4	34.8	32.8	39.0
Normal monthly	37.2	40.8	42.7	47.3	53.1	58.4	63.0	62.5	58.1	50.1	42.6	39.0	49.5
Extreme highest	63	72	76	85	96	101	103	104	96	89	74	64	104
Extreme highest date	1942	1968	1969	1947	1983	1942	1941	1981	1981	1980	1949	1958	1981
Extreme lowest	-8	-1	13	23	25	30	35	33	25	20	-1	-7	-8
Extreme lowest date	1979	1972	1955	1975	1954	1976	1962	1973	1972	1971	1955	1983	1979
DEGREE DAYS BASE 65° F													
Heating	862	678	691	531	369	208	101	115	214	462	672	806	5709
Cooling	0	0	0	0	0	10	39	38	7	0	0	0	94
% OF POSSIBLE SUNSHINE	na	na	na	na	na	na	na	na	na	na	na	na	na
AVERAGE SKY COVER													
Sunrise - Sunset	8.7	8.4	8.1	7.7	7.2	6.9	5.3	5.9	6.2	7.7	8.5	8.8	7.5
NUMBER OF DAYS (Sunrise-Sunset)													
Clear	2.1	2.0	2.5	2.8	4.2	5.2	10.3	8.7	7.5	2.9	1.5	1.6	51.4
Partly cloudy	3.7	4.5	6.6	7.6	8.9	8.5	10.3	9.9	9.4	8.0	5.4	3.5	86.3
Cloudy	25.2	21.8	21.9	19.5	17.9	16.4	10.5	12.4	13.0	20.1	23.1	25.9	227.6
Precipitation .01" or more	19.4	17.7	17.8	14.7	10.7	9.3	4.8	5.9	8.8	14.3	19.2	21.0	163.6
Snow, Ice pellets 1.0" or more	2.6	0.9	0.7	*	0.0	0.0	0.0	0.0	0.0	0.0	0.4	1.2	5.7
Thunderstorms	*	0.2	0.2	0.5	0.7	0.6	0.4	0.9	0.7	0.5	0.3	0.1	5.2
Fog, Visibility 1/4 mile or less	9.5	8.2	7.6	5.2	3.4	2.4	3.4	6.0	9.8	14.3	11.2	9.8	90.9
Temperature Maximum:													
90° and above	0.0	0.0	0.0	0.0	0.1	0.6	2.6	2.5	0.6	0.0	0.0	0.0	6.3
32° and below	1.5	*	0.0	0.0	0.0	0.0	0.0	0.0	0.0	0.0	0.3	1.4	3.2
Temperature Minimum:													
32° and below	16.1	13.3	14.1	9.3	2.4	0.2	0.0	0.0	0.8	5.6	11.0	15.5	88.3
0° and below	0.2	*	0.0	0.0	0.0	0.0	0.0	0.0	0.0	0.0	0.1	0.2	0.5
RELATIVE HUMIDITY (%)													
Morning	91	91	90	90	89	90	90	90	92	93	92	91	91
Afternoon	80	71	62	57	54	55	50	51	56	68	79	84	64
PRECIPITATION (inches)													
Water Equivalent													
Normal	8.5	5.7	4.8	3.1	1.8	1.4	0.7	1.3	2.3	4.6	7.5	8.7	50.9
Maximum monthly	19.8	13.1	10.1	5.8	5.8	6.4	3.0	5.4	7.5	10.0	15.5	14.3	19.8
Date	1953	1961	1950	1972	1948	1946	1983	1968	1978	1967	1962	1970	1953
Minimum monthly	0.2	1.7	0.4	0.3	0.1	0.0	T	0.0	T	0.7	1.3	2.2	0.0
Date	1985	1973	1965	1956	1947	1945	1984	1946	1975	1978	1976	1944	1946
Maximum in 24 hrs	3.3	4.9	3.9	2.3	1.5	1.9	1.5	1.3	2.4	3.6	4.3	3.8	4.9
Date	1972	1951	1972	1965	1948	1985	1979	1977	1978	1981	1962	1956	1951
SNOW, ICE PELLETS													
Maximum monthly	58.7	17.7	20.6	2.2	T	T	0.0	0.0	T	T	14.8	21.4	58.7
Date	1969	1949	1951	1972	1985	1976	—	—	1972	1975	1978	1968	1969
Maximum in 24 hrs	20.5	10.1	9.1	1.8	T	T	0.0	0.0	T	T	14.5	11.9	20.5
Date	1972	1980	1966	1972	1985	1976	—	—	1972	1975	1978	1974	1972
WIND (Resultant)													
Mean speed (mph)	7.1	7.2	7.4	7.4	6.8	6.7	6.2	5.9	5.7	5.9	6.7	7.4	6.7

SEATTLE

Elev. 400'   47° 27'N — 122° 18'W   **Washington**

NORMALS, MEANS, EXTREMES

	JAN	FEB	MAR	APR	MAY	JUN	JUL	AUG	SEP	OCT	NOV	DEC	YEAR
TEMPERATURE													
Normal daily maximum	43.9	48.8	51.1	56.8	64.0	69.2	75.2	73.9	68.7	59.5	50.3	45.6	58.9
Normal daily minimum	34.3	36.8	37.2	40.5	46.0	51.1	54.3	54.3	51.2	45.3	39.3	36.3	43.9
Normal monthly	39.1	42.8	44.2	48.7	55.0	60.2	64.8	64.1	60.0	52.4	44.8	41.0	51.4
Extreme highest	64	70	72	85	93	96	98	99	94	82	74	63	99
Extreme highest date	1981	1968	1947	1976	1963	1955	1979	1981	1981	1980	1949	1980	1981
Extreme lowest	0	1	11	29	28	38	43	44	35	28	6	6	0
Extreme lowest date	1950	1950	1955	1975	1954	1952	1954	1955	1972	1949	1955	1968	1950
DEGREE DAYS BASE 65° F													
Heating	803	622	645	489	313	169	76	97	169	388	606	744	5121
Cooling	0	0	0	0	0	25	70	70	19	0	0	0	184
% OF POSSIBLE SUNSHINE	25	37	49	52	56	54	65	64	59	43	29	21	46
AVERAGE SKY COVER													
Sunrise - Sunset	8.5	8.3	7.9	7.7	7.1	7.0	5.3	5.8	6.2	7.5	8.3	8.7	7.4
NUMBER OF DAYS (Sunrise-Sunset)													
Clear	2.6	2.5	3.1	2.8	4.4	5.0	10.5	8.8	7.6	3.9	2.7	2.1	56.0
Partly cloudy	3.9	4.1	5.8	7.2	9.1	7.6	9.9	9.7	8.7	7.3	4.3	3.6	81.2
Cloudy	24.4	21.6	22.0	19.9	17.5	17.3	10.3	12.6	13.7	19.7	23.0	25.4	227.6
Precipitation .01" or more	18.6	16.1	17.1	13.9	10.2	9.3	5.0	6.6	9.4	13.5	17.9	19.7	157.2
Snow, Ice pellets 1.0" or more	1.8	0.5	0.5	*	0.0	0.0	0.0	0.0	0.0	*	0.4	1.0	4.2
Thunderstorms	0.2	0.3	0.6	0.9	0.9	0.7	0.7	0.8	0.8	0.3	0.6	0.4	7.2
Fog, Visibility 1/4 mile or less	5.8	3.4	2.3	1.1	0.9	0.8	1.8	2.9	5.6	7.8	6.0	6.4	44.8
Temperature Maximum:													
90° and above	0.0	0.0	0.0	0.0	0.2	0.3	1.2	1.2	0.2	0.0	0.0	0.0	3.0
32° and below	1.3	*	0.0	0.0	0.0	0.0	0.0	0.0	0.0	0.0	0.3	1.2	2.8
Temperature Minimum:													
32° and below	10.3	4.9	3.3	0.3	0.0	0.0	0.0	0.0	0.0	0.2	4.1	8.7	31.9
0° and below	0.0	0.0	0.0	0.0	0.0	0.0	0.0	0.0	0.0	0.0	0.0	0.0	0.0
RELATIVE HUMIDITY (%)													
Morning	80	80	81	83	82	81	81	83	86	86	83	82	82
Afternoon	74	67	62	57	54	53	49	51	58	67	74	77	62
PRECIPITATION (inches)													
Water Equivalent													
Normal	6.0	4.2	3.5	2.4	1.5	1.3	0.7	1.2	2.0	3.4	5.6	6.3	38.6
Maximum monthly	12.9	9.1	8.4	4.1	4.7	3.9	2.3	4.5	5.9	8.9	9.6	11.8	12.9
Date	1953	1961	1950	1978	1948	1946	1983	1975	1978	1947	1963	1979	1953
Minimum monthly	0.5	1.5	0.5	0.3	0.3	0.1	T	0.0	T	0.7	0.7	1.3	T
Date	1985	1977	1965	1956	1947	1951	1960	1974	1975	1972	1976	1978	1975
Maximum in 24 hrs	2.4	3.4	2.8	1.8	1.8	2.0	0.8	1.7	2.2	3.7	3.4	2.6	3.7
Date	1967	1951	1972	1965	1969	1985	1981	1968	1978	1981	1959	1979	1981
SNOW, ICE PELLETS													
Maximum monthly	57.2	13.1	18.2	2.3	T	0.0	T	0.0	T	2.0	17.5	22.1	57.2
Date	1950	1949	1951	1972	1974	—	1980	—	1972	1971	1985	1968	1950
Maximum in 24 hrs	21.4	7.2	5.6	2.3	T	0.0	T	0.0	T	2.0	9.4	13.0	21.4
Date	1950	1962	1951	1972	1974	—	1980	—	1972	1971	1946	1968	1950
WIND (Resultant)													
Mean speed (mph)	9.8	9.6	9.9	9.6	9.0	8.7	8.3	7.9	8.1	8.6	9.2	9.7	9.0

SPOKANE

Elev. 2357' 47° 38'N — 117° 32'W **Washington**

NORMALS, MEANS, EXTREMES

	JAN	FEB	MAR	APR	MAY	JUN	JUL	AUG	SEP	OCT	NOV	DEC	YEAR
TEMPERATURE													
Normal daily maximum	31.3	39.0	46.2	56.7	66.1	74.0	84.0	81.7	72.4	58.3	41.4	34.2	57.1
Normal daily minimum	20.0	25.7	29.0	34.9	42.5	49.3	55.3	54.3	46.5	36.7	28.5	23.7	37.2
Normal monthly	25.7	32.4	37.6	45.8	54.3	61.7	69.7	68.0	59.5	47.5	35.0	29.0	47.2
Extreme highest	59	61	71	90	94	100	103	108	96	86	67	56	108
Extreme highest date	1971	1958	1960	1977	1983	1973	1967	1961	1950	1980	1975	1980	1961
Extreme lowest	-22	-17	-3	17	24	33	37	35	24	11	-21	-25	-25
Extreme lowest date	1979	1979	1955	1966	1954	1984	1981	1965	1985	1984	1985	1968	1968
DEGREE DAYS BASE 65° F													
Heating	1218	913	849	576	339	140	17	63	209	539	903	1116	6882
Cooling	0	0	0	0	8	41	162	159	41	0	0	0	411
% OF POSSIBLE SUNSHINE	26	38	53	60	63	66	80	77	70	52	28	21	53
AVERAGE SKY COVER													
Sunrise - Sunset	8.2	8.0	7.4	7.1	6.6	6.1	3.7	4.2	4.9	6.4	8.0	8.5	6.6
NUMBER OF DAYS (Sunrise-Sunset)													
Clear	3.2	3.2	4.3	4.5	5.6	7.2	16.8	15.2	11.9	7.7	3.2	2.8	85.6
Partly cloudy	4.2	4.9	7.8	8.3	10.4	10.4	8.4	8.4	8.4	7.8	5.1	3.8	88.0
Cloudy	23.5	20.1	18.9	17.2	15.0	12.4	5.8	7.4	9.8	15.6	21.6	24.4	191.7
Precipitation .01" or more	14.2	11.7	11.3	8.5	9.2	7.8	4.1	5.1	5.8	7.9	12.6	15.4	113.7
Snow, Ice pellets 1.0" or more	5.4	2.9	1.6	0.2	*	0.0	0.0	0.0	0.0	0.2	2.1	5.1	17.5
Thunderstorms	*	*	0.2	0.6	1.4	2.9	2.1	2.3	0.7	0.3	0.1	0.0	10.6
Fog, Visibility 1/4 mile or less	9.4	7.3	2.8	1.3	0.9	0.5	0.2	0.3	0.9	4.4	8.8	12.2	48.8
Temperature Maximum:													
90° and above	0.0	0.0	0.0	*	0.2	2.0	9.3	7.3	0.8	0.0	0.0	0.0	19.6
32° and below	15.3	4.2	1.0	0.0	0.0	0.0	0.0	0.0	0.0	0.1	4.4	13.8	38.7
Temperature Minimum:													
32° and below	26.7	22.2	21.0	11.5	1.7	0.0	0.0	0.0	0.9	9.5	20.3	26.2	140.0
0° and below	2.9	0.5	0.0	0.0	0.0	0.0	0.0	0.0	0.0	0.0	0.3	1.9	5.6
RELATIVE HUMIDITY (%)													
Morning	84	84	80	76	76	74	63	62	71	79	87	87	77
Afternoon	78	69	55	44	41	36	26	28	35	49	75	82	52
PRECIPITATION (inches)													
Water Equivalent													
Normal	2.4	1.6	1.3	1.0	1.3	1.2	0.5	0.7	0.7	1.0	2.0	2.4	16.7
Maximum monthly	4.9	3.9	3.7	3.0	5.7	3.0	1.8	1.8	2.0	4.0	5.1	5.1	5.7
Date	1959	1961	1950	1948	1948	1964	1983	1976	1959	1950	1973	1964	1948
Minimum monthly	0.3	0.4	0.3	0.0	0.2	0.1	T	T	0.0	0.0	0.2	0.6	T
Date	1985	1967	1965	1956	1982	1960	1973	1969	1975	1965	1976	1976	1973
Maximum in 24 hrs	1.4	1.1	0.9	1.0	1.6	2.0	0.9	1.0	1.1	0.9	1.4	1.6	2.0
Date	1954	1963	1950	1982	1948	1964	1983	1959	1973	1955	1960	1951	1964
SNOW, ICE PELLETS													
Maximum monthly	56.9	28.5	15.3	6.6	3.5	T	0.0	0.0	0.0	6.1	24.7	42.0	56.9
Date	1950	1975	1962	1964	1967	1954	—	—	—	1957	1955	1964	1950
Maximum in 24 hrs	13.0	8.9	5.3	4.9	3.5	T	0.0	0.0	0.0	6.1	9.0	12.1	13.0
Date	1950	1975	1970	1964	1967	1954	—	—	—	1957	1973	1951	1950
WIND (Resultant)													
Mean speed (mph)	8.6	9.1	9.5	9.9	9.0	9.0	8.3	8.1	8.2	8.1	8.4	8.6	8.7

WALLA WALLA   Elev. 949'   46° 02'N — 118° 20'W   Washington

NORMALS, MEANS, EXTREMES

	JAN	FEB	MAR	APR	MAY	JUN	JUL	AUG	SEP	OCT	NOV	DEC	YEAR
TEMPERATURE													
Normal daily maximum	40.1	47.3	54.3	62.2	70.9	79.3	88.8	86.0	77.3	64.0	49.0	43.0	63.5
Normal daily minimum	28.4	33.9	37.3	42.4	49.3	55.8	62.2	61.2	53.6	44.5	35.9	31.4	44.7
Normal monthly	34.3	40.6	45.8	52.3	60.1	67.6	75.5	73.6	65.5	54.3	42.5	37.2	54.1
Extreme highest	71	71	79	93	99	106	112	113	103	90	80	73	113
Extreme highest date	1968	1963	1960	1977	1983	1961	1928	1961	1955	1980	1975	1921	1961
Extreme lowest	-16	-14	13	19	28	41	46	45	26	15	-5	-14	-16
Extreme lowest date	1957	1950	1955	1936	1954	1984	1971	1918	1926	1935	1985	1919	1957
DEGREE DAYS BASE 65° F													
Heating	952	680	595	381	175	54	0	16	85	332	675	862	4807
Cooling	0	0	0	0	23	132	326	282	100	0	0	0	863
% OF POSSIBLE SUNSHINE	22	34	50	60	66	71	85	82	72	58	30	18	54
AVERAGE SKY COVER													
Sunrise - Sunset	8.7	8.0	7.1	6.5	5.9	5.1	2.8	3.3	4.3	5.8	8.2	8.8	6.2
NUMBER OF DAYS (Sunrise-Sunset)													
Clear	2.2	3.3	5.9	7.4	9.4	12.0	20.9	20.0	14.8	10.8	3.8	2.1	112.7
Partly cloudy	4.8	5.7	8.3	9.8	10.7	9.8	7.0	6.8	7.8	7.2	5.8	4.2	88.0
Cloudy	24.0	19.2	16.8	12.7	10.9	8.2	3.1	4.1	7.4	12.9	20.4	24.7	164.6
Precipitation .01" or more	13.4	11.5	11.5	9.4	8.5	6.9	2.6	3.5	5.4	8.4	11.9	14.1	107.0
Snow, Ice pellets 1.0" or more	2.5	1.1	0.5	*	0.0	0.0	0.0	0.0	0.0	0.1	0.7	1.8	6.6
Thunderstorms	*	0.1	0.4	0.8	1.7	2.2	2.0	2.1	1.4	0.4	0.1	0.0	11.2
Fog, Visibility 1/4 mile or less	3.3	2.0	0.4	0.0	*	0.0	0.0	0.0	*	0.4	3.0	5.2	14.3
Temperature Maximum:													
90° and above	0.0	0.0	0.0	0.1	1.0	4.8	15.4	12.4	2.7	*	0.0	0.0	36.5
32° and below	9.9	2.5	0.2	0.0	0.0	0.0	0.0	0.0	0.0	*	2.0	7.3	21.9
Temperature Minimum:													
32° and below	19.4	12.0	5.0	0.5	*	0.0	0.0	0.0	*	0.9	9.3	17.5	64.6
0° and below	0.7	0.3	0.0	0.0	0.0	0.0	0.0	0.0	0.0	0.0	*	0.5	1.5
PRECIPITATION (inches)													
Water Equivalent													
Normal	2.1	1.4	1.4	1.3	1.4	0.9	0.3	0.7	0.8	1.4	1.8	2.1	15.9
Maximum monthly	5.8	3.9	4.1	3.6	4.1	3.0	1.7	2.9	4.5	4.2	4.1	4.3	5.8
Date	1970	1940	1983	1917	1957	1941	1966	1977	1927	1950	1973	1964	1970
Minimum monthly	0.3	0.1	0.3	0.1	T	0.0	0.0	T	T	0.0	0.0	0.2	0.0
Date	1949	1920	1965	1956	1924	1919	1953	1974	1943	1917	1936	1965	1953
Maximum in 24 hrs	1.4	1.3	1.3	1.5	1.9	2.0	1.1	1.5	1.3	3.0	1.4	1.4	3.0
Date	1948	1970	1983	1915	1971	1923	1940	1977	1927	1980	1932	1971	1980
SNOW, ICE PELLETS													
Maximum monthly	31.3	33.4	6.2	4.0	T	0.0	0.0	0.0	0.0	3.5	19.9	21.9	33.4
Date	1969	1916	1944	1929	1908	—	—	—	—	1973	1921	1968	1916
Maximum in 24 hrs	8.7	14.0	6.0	4.0	T	0.0	0.0	0.0	0.0	3.5	12.1	12.1	14.0
Date	1966	1916	1944	1929	1968	—	—	—	—	1973	1921	1968	1916
WIND (Resultant)													
Mean speed (mph)	5.1	5.5	6.2	6.1	5.7	5.5	5.4	5.1	4.7	4.5	4.8	5.2	5.3

YAKIMA

Elev. 1052'   **46° 34'N — 120° 32'W**   # Washington

NORMALS, MEANS, EXTREMES

	JAN	FEB	MAR	APR	MAY	JUN	JUL	AUG	SEP	OCT	NOV	DEC	YEAR
TEMPERATURE													
Normal daily maximum	36.7	46.0	54.5	63.5	72.5	79.9	87.8	85.6	77.5	64.5	48.1	39.4	63.0
Normal daily minimum	19.7	26.1	29.2	34.7	42.1	49.1	53.0	51.5	44.3	35.1	28.2	23.6	36.4
Normal monthly	28.2	36.1	41.9	49.1	57.3	64.5	70.4	68.6	60.9	49.8	38.2	31.5	49.7
Extreme highest	68	69	80	92	101	103	108	110	100	86	72	67	110
Extreme highest date	1977	1947	1960	1977	1983	1961	1971	1971	1949	1980	1975	1980	1971
Extreme lowest	-21	-25	-1	20	25	30	34	35	24	11	-13	-17	-25
Extreme lowest date	1950	1950	1960	1985	1954	1984	1971	1960	1985	1971	1985	1964	1950
DEGREE DAYS BASE 65° F													
Heating	1141	809	716	474	254	101	18	46	161	468	804	1039	6031
Cooling	0	0	0	0	16	86	186	158	38	0	0	0	484
% OF POSSIBLE SUNSHINE	na	na	na	na	na	na	na	na	na	na	na	na	na
AVERAGE SKY COVER													
Sunrise - Sunset	7.8	7.5	6.8	6.4	5.8	5.3	3.0	3.5	4.2	5.9	7.4	7.9	5.9
NUMBER OF DAYS (Sunrise-Sunset)													
Clear	4.5	4.3	6.3	6.3	8.5	10.5	19.2	17.6	14.5	9.1	4.9	4.0	109.7
Partly cloudy	5.1	5.9	8.1	9.5	10.5	9.6	7.7	7.8	8.1	8.2	6.0	5.4	91.9
Cloudy	21.4	18.0	16.7	14.2	12.0	10.0	4.2	5.6	7.4	13.7	19.0	21.5	163.6
Precipitation .01" or more	9.5	7.3	6.3	4.4	5.0	4.7	2.1	3.0	3.2	5.3	8.6	9.8	69.1
Snow, Ice pellets 1.0" or more	2.8	1.2	0.6	0.0	0.0	0.0	0.0	0.0	0.0	0.1	0.7	2.7	8.1
Thunderstorms	0.0	*	0.1	0.4	1.1	1.7	1.5	1.3	0.7	0.1	0.0	0.0	6.8
Fog, Visibility 1/4 mile or less	4.6	2.4	0.4	0.1	0.1	0.0	0.0	0.0	0.1	0.7	3.6	6.7	18.6
Temperature Maximum:													
90° and above	0.0	0.0	0.0	*	1.3	4.4	14.1	10.5	2.2	0.0	0.0	0.0	32.5
32° and below	10.8	2.4	0.1	0.0	0.0	0.0	0.0	0.0	0.0	0.0	1.8	7.9	23.1
Temperature Minimum:													
32° and below	27.9	23.6	20.6	12.3	2.8	0.1	0.0	0.0	1.1	10.6	21.1	27.7	147.8
0° and below	2.7	0.6	*	0.0	0.0	0.0	0.0	0.0	0.0	0.0	0.2	0.8	4.4
RELATIVE HUMIDITY (%)													
Morning	82	82	76	71	69	69	68	70	76	80	84	84	76
Afternoon	71	58	41	32	30	31	25	28	32	43	63	74	44
PRECIPITATION (inches)													
Water Equivalent													
Normal	1.4	0.7	0.6	0.5	0.4	0.6	0.1	0.3	0.3	0.4	0.9	1.3	7.9
Maximum monthly	3.6	2.4	2.6	1.6	2.7	2.1	0.7	2.1	1.0	2.2	2.8	4.1	4.1
Date	1970	1961	1957	1963	1948	1948	1966	1975	1982	1950	1973	1964	1964
Minimum monthly	0.0	T	0.0	T	0.0	0.0	T	0.0	T	0.0	T	0.0	0.0
Date	1985	1971	1973	1985	1964	1970	1980	1955	1975	1978	1976	1976	1978
Maximum in 24 hrs	1.3	0.8	0.6	1.2	0.7	1.5	0.6	1.4	0.8	1.0	1.0	1.5	1.5
Date	1963	1961	1976	1974	1951	1982	1963	1975	1954	1982	1955	1977	1977
SNOW, ICE PELLETS													
Maximum monthly	26.6	16.5	10.8	T	T	0.0	0.0	0.0	0.0	2.4	21.2	37.5	37.5
Date	1950	1949	1971	1983	1984	—	—	—	—	1973	1955	1964	1964
Maximum in 24 hrs	13.6	5.8	7.4	T	T	0.0	0.0	0.0	0.0	2.4	11.2	14.0	14.0
Date	1963	1956	1951	1983	1984	—	—	—	—	1973	1984	1964	1964
WIND (Resultant)													
Mean speed (mph)	5.6	6.3	7.9	8.6	8.4	8.2	7.7	7.3	7.3	6.6	5.7	5.2	7.1

BECKLEY

Elev. 2504'   37° 47'N — 81° 07'W   **West Virginia**

NORMALS, MEANS, EXTREMES

	JAN	FEB	MAR	APR	MAY	JUN	JUL	AUG	SEP	OCT	NOV	DEC	YEAR
TEMPERATURE													
Normal daily maximum	38.6	41.4	50.5	62.2	70.5	76.5	79.6	78.7	73.3	62.9	51.3	42.1	60.6
Normal daily minimum	21.6	23.2	31.4	40.8	49.2	55.9	59.8	59.0	52.9	41.7	33.0	25.3	41.1
Normal monthly	30.1	32.3	41.0	51.5	59.9	66.2	69.7	68.9	63.1	52.3	42.2	33.7	50.9
Extreme highest	69	74	80	86	85	90	90	90	89	81	75	73	90
Extreme highest date	1985	1977	1985	1976	1974	1964	1980	1965	1973	1969	1974	1971	1980
Extreme lowest	-22	-10	-5	11	23	32	41	36	30	18	4	-15	-22
Extreme lowest date	1985	1970	1980	1985	1966	1972	1972	1965	1983	1976	1970	1983	1985
DEGREE DAYS BASE 65° F													
Heating	1082	916	744	405	186	57	11	14	110	398	684	970	5577
Cooling	0	0	0	0	28	93	157	135	53	0	0	0	466
% OF POSSIBLE SUNSHINE	na	na	na	na	na	na	na	na	na	na	na	na	na
AVERAGE SKY COVER													
Sunrise - Sunset	7.6	7.5	7.6	7.1	7.1	7.2	7.2	6.9	6.6	6.2	7.2	7.6	7.2
NUMBER OF DAYS (Sunrise-Sunset)													
Clear	4.8	4.6	4.7	5.1	5.2	3.6	3.2	4.2	6.6	8.8	5.4	4.5	60.7
Partly cloudy	5.4	5.8	5.9	7.3	8.5	10.4	11.4	11.3	9.0	7.4	6.7	6.0	94.9
Cloudy	20.9	17.9	20.5	17.6	17.3	16.0	16.4	15.5	14.4	14.8	18.0	20.5	209.7
Precipitation .01" or more	16.3	14.5	15.2	14.4	13.5	12.3	13.7	11.6	10.5	10.3	12.7	14.7	159.7
Snow, Ice pellets 1.0" or more	6.1	5.4	3.0	0.4	0.0	0.0	0.0	0.0	0.0	0.2	1.3	3.3	19.6
Thunderstorms	0.3	0.5	2.1	3.8	6.3	8.4	10.5	7.6	3.1	0.8	0.5	0.2	44.2
Fog, Visibility 1/4 mile or less	4.7	3.4	3.6	2.0	3.0	3.7	5.1	6.2	6.0	4.0	3.0	3.4	48.2
Temperature Maximum:													
90° and above	0.0	0.0	0.0	0.0	0.0	*	0.1	0.1	0.0	0.0	0.0	0.0	0.2
32° and below	11.5	7.6	2.4	*	0.0	0.0	0.0	0.0	0.0	0.0	2.0	6.0	29.5
Temperature Minimum:													
32° and below	25.7	22.2	16.8	6.7	1.1	*	0.0	0.0	0.1	5.2	14.4	21.8	114.0
0° and below	2.7	1.4	0.1	0.0	0.0	0.0	0.0	0.0	0.0	0.0	0.0	0.5	4.6
RELATIVE HUMIDITY (%)													
Morning	78	76	73	70	79	87	90	91	90	83	77	77	81
Afternoon	68	64	59	51	54	59	63	64	63	58	61	67	61
PRECIPITATION (inches)													
Water Equivalent													
Normal	3.4	3.1	4.1	3.5	3.8	3.8	4.4	3.6	3.3	2.5	2.8	3.2	42.1
Maximum monthly	6.3	6.0	9.1	6.2	7.1	7.0	9.6	5.9	8.2	5.8	6.3	6.1	9.6
Date	1974	1972	1975	1977	1985	1969	1982	1977	1964	1976	1985	1969	1982
Minimum monthly	0.5	0.9	1.7	0.2	1.0	1.4	2.9	1.7	0.5	0.1	0.9	0.5	0.1
Date	1983	1968	1966	1976	1977	1978	1964	1976	1985	1963	1965	1965	1963
Maximum in 24 hrs	2.2	2.0	2.2	3.7	2.5	2.4	2.6	2.5	5.3	2.5	2.5	1.9	5.3
Date	1974	1984	1967	1977	1985	1983	1984	1980	1964	1974	1985	1969	1964
SNOW, ICE PELLETS													
Maximum monthly	35.5	30.8	20.4	8.2	T	0.0	0.0	0.0	T	3.2	13.1	22.1	35.5
Date	1977	1964	1981	1971	1976	—	—	—	1967	1973	1974	1963	1977
Maximum in 24 hrs	9.5	14.4	9.5	8.2	T	0.0	0.0	0.0	T	3.2	7.0	13.8	14.4
Date	1971	1983	1980	1971	1976	—	—	—	1967	1973	1968	1967	1983
WIND (Resultant)													
Mean speed (mph)	10.8	10.9	11.5	10.8	9.1	7.8	7.0	6.6	7.3	8.7	9.9	10.8	9.3

CHARLESTON

Elev. 939'   38° 22'N — 81° 36'W   ## West Virginia

NORMALS, MEANS, EXTREMES

	JAN	FEB	MAR	APR	MAY	JUN	JUL	AUG	SEP	OCT	NOV	DEC	YEAR
TEMPERATURE													
Normal daily maximum	41.8	45.4	55.4	67.3	76.0	82.5	85.2	84.2	78.7	67.7	55.6	45.9	65.5
Normal daily minimum	23.9	25.8	34.1	43.3	51.8	59.4	63.8	63.1	56.4	44.0	35.0	27.8	44.0
Normal monthly	32.9	35.6	44.8	55.3	63.9	71.0	74.5	73.7	67.6	55.9	45.3	36.9	54.8
Extreme highest	79	78	87	92	93	98	102	100	102	92	85	80	102
Extreme highest date	1950	1977	1954	1985	1985	1953	1954	1953	1953	1951	1948	1982	1954
Extreme lowest	-15	-6	0	19	26	33	46	41	34	17	6	-10	-15
Extreme lowest date	1985	1968	1980	1982	1966	1972	1963	1965	1983	1962	1950	1983	1985
DEGREE DAYS BASE 65° F													
Heating	995	823	626	298	125	16	0	0	51	301	591	871	4697
Cooling	0	0	0	7	91	196	295	270	129	19	0	0	1007
% OF POSSIBLE SUNSHINE	na	na	na	na	na	na	na	na	na	na	na	na	na
AVERAGE SKY COVER													
Sunrise - Sunset	7.8	7.5	7.4	6.9	6.6	6.5	6.6	6.4	6.1	6.1	7.2	7.5	6.9
NUMBER OF DAYS (Sunrise-Sunset)													
Clear	3.5	4.3	4.4	5.8	5.8	4.7	4.2	4.8	6.7	8.7	5.2	4.6	62.7
Partly cloudy	6.8	6.1	7.8	7.7	10.2	13.0	13.3	14.5	11.3	9.2	7.1	6.6	113.6
Cloudy	20.7	17.8	18.8	16.5	15.0	12.2	13.5	11.7	12.0	13.1	17.8	19.8	188.9
Precipitation .01" or more	15.6	13.6	15.2	13.9	13.2	11.3	12.9	11.0	9.2	9.7	12.0	14.0	151.5
Snow, Ice pellets 1.0" or more	3.4	2.6	1.5	0.1	0.0	0.0	0.0	0.0	0.0	*	0.8	1.7	10.2
Thunderstorms	0.5	0.8	2.2	4.2	6.6	7.8	9.6	7.0	2.9	1.1	0.6	0.3	43.8
Fog, Visibility 1/4 mile or less	4.4	3.3	2.8	2.8	7.8	12.4	15.9	19.4	16.8	11.2	4.7	4.0	105.6
Temperature Maximum:													
90° and above	0.0	0.0	0.0	0.3	1.1	4.8	7.6	4.9	2.4	0.1	0.0	0.0	21.3
32° and below	7.8	4.7	0.9	0.0	0.0	0.0	0.0	0.0	0.0	0.0	0.6	4.5	18.5
Temperature Minimum:													
32° and below	23.4	20.0	14.6	4.8	0.4	0.0	0.0	0.0	0.0	3.3	12.9	21.0	100.5
0° and below	1.1	0.3	*	0.0	0.0	0.0	0.0	0.0	0.0	0.0	0.0	0.2	1.7
RELATIVE HUMIDITY (%)													
Morning	74	72	68	67	79	86	90	91	89	83	75	75	79
Afternoon	63	59	53	47	50	54	60	58	55	53	56	61	56
PRECIPITATION (inches)													
Water Equivalent													
Normal	3.4	3.1	4.0	3.5	3.6	3.3	5.3	4.1	3.0	2.6	2.9	3.2	42.4
Maximum monthly	9.1	6.8	6.8	6.4	6.5	7.0	13.5	10.4	7.6	6.4	8.4	8.0	13.5
Date	1950	1956	1967	1965	1968	1982	1961	1958	1971	1983	1985	1978	1961
Minimum monthly	1.0	0.6	1.4	0.5	0.8	0.7	2.1	0.6	0.6	0.0	0.6	0.4	0.0
Date	1981	1968	1969	1976	1977	1966	1974	1957	1959	1963	1965	1965	1963
Maximum in 24 hrs	1.9	2.4	2.8	2.7	3.3	2.2	5.6	4.1	2.4	2.4	2.4	2.4	5.6
Date	1961	1951	1967	1948	1982	1962	1961	1958	1956	1961	1985	1978	1961
SNOW, ICE PELLETS													
Maximum monthly	39.5	21.8	18.3	5.9	0.2	0.0	0.0	0.0	0.0	2.8	25.8	18.6	39.5
Date	1978	1964	1960	1959	1963	—	—	—	—	1961	1950	1962	1978
Maximum in 24 hrs	15.8	11.2	9.9	5.5	0.2	0.0	0.0	0.0	0.0	2.8	15.1	11.2	15.8
Date	1978	1983	1954	1959	1963	—	—	—	—	1961	1950	1967	1978
WIND (Resultant)													
Mean speed (mph)	7.6	7.6	8.4	7.8	6.2	5.6	5.1	4.4	4.8	5.2	6.7	7.2	6.4

ELKINS

Elev. 1948'   38° 53'N — 79° 51'W   **West Virginia**

NORMALS, MEANS, EXTREMES

	JAN	FEB	MAR	APR	MAY	JUN	JUL	AUG	SEP	OCT	NOV	DEC	YEAR
TEMPERATURE													
Normal daily maximum	39.0	41.6	50.9	62.2	71.3	77.9	80.7	79.6	74.4	63.8	52.0	42.7	61.3
Normal daily minimum	17.6	19.1	27.3	36.0	44.8	52.4	57.0	56.3	49.7	37.1	29.1	21.6	37.3
Normal monthly	28.3	30.4	39.1	49.1	58.1	65.2	68.9	68.0	62.1	50.5	40.6	32.2	49.3
Extreme highest	76	72	84	88	88	93	95	95	97	86	80	76	97
Extreme highest date	1950	1985	1954	1976	1979	1952	1954	1948	1953	1951	1958	1951	1953
Extreme lowest	-24	-22	-15	3	20	25	39	34	27	11	0	-17	-24
Extreme lowest date	1984	1977	1978	1985	1978	1977	1963	1965	1963	1952	1958	1983	1984
DEGREE DAYS BASE 65° F													
Heating	1138	969	803	477	233	69	11	19	127	450	732	1017	6045
Cooling	0	0	0	0	19	75	132	112	40	0	0	0	378
% OF POSSIBLE SUNSHINE	26	39	39	47	50	51	42	38	59	38	34	31	41
AVERAGE SKY COVER													
Sunrise - Sunset	8.0	7.8	7.6	7.3	7.1	7.1	7.2	7.0	6.7	6.4	7.4	7.8	7.3
NUMBER OF DAYS (Sunrise-Sunset)													
Clear	3.2	3.6	4.0	4.3	4.4	3.2	2.6	2.5	4.6	7.6	4.7	4.1	48.6
Partly cloudy	5.8	5.8	6.7	7.7	9.5	11.3	12.6	13.8	11.8	7.8	6.4	5.5	104.6
Cloudy	22.0	18.9	20.3	18.0	17.2	15.6	15.9	14.7	13.9	13.0	19.0	21.4	209.8
Precipitation .01" or more	18.1	15.5	17.1	15.1	14.5	13.2	13.7	11.9	10.4	10.7	13.6	16.5	170.2
Snow, Ice pellets 1.0" or more	6.3	6.0	3.5	0.9	0.0	0.0	0.0	0.0	0.0	0.1	2.2	4.3	23.4
Thunderstorms	0.2	0.5	2.0	4.1	6.2	7.8	10.0	7.7	3.3	1.3	0.7	0.4	44.3
Fog, Visibility 1/4 mile or less	2.0	1.8	1.7	1.9	5.2	10.8	13.1	16.9	14.7	9.6	3.1	2.0	82.8
Temperature Maximum:													
90° and above	0.0	0.0	0.0	0.0	0.0	0.3	0.6	0.4	0.3	0.0	0.0	0.0	1.6
32° and below	10.2	7.1	2.8	0.2	0.0	0.0	0.0	0.0	0.0	*	2.1	6.7	29.2
Temperature Minimum:													
32° and below	26.8	23.8	21.9	11.9	2.8	0.1	0.0	0.0	0.8	9.8	19.8	25.8	143.4
0° and below	3.6	2.4	0.3	0.0	0.0	0.0	0.0	0.0	0.0	0.0	*	1.3	7.6
RELATIVE HUMIDITY (%)													
Morning	81	78	82	81	85	95	97	97	96	91	84	85	88
Afternoon	66	61	57	52	54	59	62	64	62	55	60	66	60
PRECIPITATION (inches)													
Water Equivalent													
Normal	3.3	2.8	3.6	3.7	3.8	4.3	4.6	4.2	3.2	2.9	2.6	3.3	42.8
Maximum monthly	6.0	5.6	8.8	6.9	7.6	8.3	9.3	10.4	6.2	8.4	11.0	6.7	11.0
Date	1949	1972	1963	1972	1967	1981	1958	1980	1971	1954	1985	1978	1985
Minimum monthly	1.0	0.7	1.3	1.0	1.4	1.6	1.9	1.0	0.3	0.3	1.1	0.9	0.3
Date	1967	1978	1957	1971	1970	1960	1974	1976	1985	1963	1976	1965	1963
Maximum in 24 hrs	1.8	1.7	2.9	2.0	2.0	2.4	2.7	3.2	2.6	3.6	5.1	2.2	5.1
Date	1971	1984	1963	1966	1985	1974	1985	1969	1967	1985	1985	1970	1985
SNOW, ICE PELLETS													
Maximum monthly	54.1	29.5	33.5	8.0	0.7	0.0	0.0	0.0	0.0	3.9	14.8	34.9	54.1
Date	1985	1964	1971	1985	1963	—	—	—	—	1979	1976	1969	1985
Maximum in 24 hrs	18.7	12.8	8.3	5.6	0.7	0.0	0.0	0.0	0.0	3.6	12.4	17.8	18.7
Date	1971	1983	1971	1985	1963	—	—	—	—	1979	1970	1967	1971
WIND (Resultant)													
Mean speed (mph)	7.3	8.0	8.2	7.9	6.7	4.9	4.3	4.1	4.4	5.0	6.9	6.9	6.2

HUNTINGTON

Elev. 827'   38° 22'N — 82° 33'W   # West Virginia

NORMALS, MEANS, EXTREMES

	JAN	FEB	MAR	APR	MAY	JUN	JUL	AUG	SEP	OCT	NOV	DEC	YEAR
TEMPERATURE													
Normal daily maximum	41.1	45.0	55.2	67.2	75.7	82.6	85.6	84.4	78.7	67.6	55.2	45.2	65.3
Normal daily minimum	24.5	26.6	35.0	44.4	52.8	60.7	65.1	64.0	57.2	44.9	35.9	28.5	45.0
Normal monthly	32.8	35.8	45.1	55.8	64.3	71.7	75.4	74.2	68.0	56.3	45.6	36.9	55.1
Extreme highest	74	79	85	92	92	95	100	100	97	86	82	80	100
Extreme highest date	1967	1977	1973	1985	1963	1980	1983	1983	1983	1962	1979	1982	1983
Extreme lowest	-16	-6	-2	20	27	40	46	43	31	16	8	-9	-16
Extreme lowest date	1985	1970	1980	1985	1966	1977	1968	1965	1983	1962	1964	1983	1985
DEGREE DAYS BASE 65° F													
Heating	998	818	617	293	125	17	0	0	62	293	582	871	4676
Cooling	0	0	0	17	103	218	322	285	152	24	0	0	1121
% OF POSSIBLE SUNSHINE	na	na	na	na	na	na	na	na	na	na	na	na	na
AVERAGE SKY COVER													
Sunrise - Sunset	7.6	7.6	7.5	7.1	6.9	6.8	6.9	6.8	6.5	6.2	7.4	7.7	7.1
NUMBER OF DAYS (Sunrise-Sunset)													
Clear	4.3	4.4	4.1	5.1	5.6	4.3	4.0	4.2	6.3	8.6	4.9	4.5	60.4
Partly cloudy	6.8	5.7	7.3	7.7	9.3	11.3	11.9	12.8	9.8	7.8	6.2	5.6	102.0
Cloudy	19.9	18.2	19.6	17.2	16.2	14.4	15.0	14.0	13.9	14.6	18.9	20.9	202.8
Precipitation .01" or more	13.8	12.8	14.3	12.8	12.3	10.9	11.9	9.7	8.5	9.5	11.6	12.9	141.0
Snow, Ice pellets 1.0" or more	3.1	2.4	1.2	0.0	0.0	0.0	0.0	0.0	0.0	0.0	0.4	1.0	8.1
Thunderstorms	0.3	0.6	2.7	4.3	6.3	7.0	9.2	7.1	2.2	1.1	0.9	0.3	42.0
Fog, Visibility 1/4 mile or less	2.9	3.0	2.1	1.4	4.1	6.5	10.2	10.9	9.9	6.3	3.5	3.0	63.9
Temperature Maximum:													
90° and above	0.0	0.0	0.0	0.1	0.5	3.8	6.5	5.1	1.8	0.0	0.0	0.0	17.8
32° and below	10.2	6.1	1.0	0.0	0.0	0.0	0.0	0.0	0.0	0.0	0.4	5.0	22.7
Temperature Minimum:													
32° and below	24.5	21.0	13.5	3.8	0.3	0.0	0.0	0.0	*	3.2	11.3	20.2	97.9
0° and below	1.8	0.4	*	0.0	0.0	0.0	0.0	0.0	0.0	0.0	0.0	0.3	2.5
RELATIVE HUMIDITY (%)													
Morning	73	71	67	66	78	86	88	89	89	81	74	74	78
Afternoon	66	62	55	49	53	57	61	60	60	55	60	66	59
PRECIPITATION (inches)													
Water Equivalent													
Normal	3.2	2.8	4.0	3.4	3.9	3.5	4.4	3.7	3.0	2.4	2.8	3.1	40.7
Maximum monthly	6.3	5.6	7.5	6.5	9.2	7.6	8.5	6.8	5.6	5.7	7.4	8.6	9.2
Date	1978	1962	1963	1966	1974	1979	1962	1979	1966	1983	1985	1978	1974
Minimum monthly	0.6	0.5	1.1	0.7	0.9	0.4	1.3	0.6	0.3	T	0.7	0.3	T
Date	1981	1968	1966	1976	1965	1966	1974	1962	1985	1963	1976	1965	1963
Maximum in 24 hrs	2.6	2.4	3.4	2.2	2.6	3.4	4.2	2.9	2.7	2.9	2.2	3.3	4.2
Date	1974	1966	1967	1978	1974	1979	1962	1964	1964	1985	1973	1978	1962
SNOW, ICE PELLETS													
Maximum monthly	30.3	21.2	11.0	0.8	T	0.0	0.0	0.0	0.0	0.4	4.6	13.2	30.3
Date	1978	1985	1971	1974	1963	—	—	—	—	1974	1969	1967	1978
Maximum in 24 hrs	11.6	11.2	7.9	0.6	T	0.0	0.0	0.0	0.0	0.4	4.4	6.7	11.6
Date	1978	1985	1971	1974	1963	—	—	—	—	1974	1969	1967	1978
WIND (Resultant)													
Mean speed (mph)	7.7	7.6	8.1	7.8	6.2	5.6	5.1	4.9	5.1	5.8	7.0	7.5	6.5

GREEN BAY
Elev. 682'   44° 29'N — 88° 08'W   # Wisconsin

NORMALS, MEANS, EXTREMES

	JAN	FEB	MAR	APR	MAY	JUN	JUL	AUG	SEP	OCT	NOV	DEC	YEAR
TEMPERATURE													
Normal daily maximum	22.5	26.9	37.0	53.7	66.6	76.2	80.9	78.7	69.8	58.5	42.0	28.5	53.4
Normal daily minimum	5.4	8.7	20.1	33.6	43.5	53.1	58.1	56.3	47.9	38.2	26.3	13.0	33.7
Normal monthly	14.0	17.8	28.6	43.7	55.1	64.7	69.5	67.5	58.9	48.4	34.2	20.8	43.6
Extreme highest	50	55	73	89	91	97	99	99	95	88	72	62	99
Extreme highest date	1961	1981	1967	1980	1959	1971	1977	1955	1955	1963	1953	1970	1977
Extreme lowest	-31	-26	-29	7	21	32	40	38	24	15	-9	-27	-31
Extreme lowest date	1951	1971	1962	1954	1966	1958	1965	1967	1949	1966	1976	1983	1951
DEGREE DAYS BASE 65° F													
Heating	1581	1322	1128	639	325	91	17	39	192	515	924	1370	8143
Cooling	0	0	0	0	18	82	156	116	9	0	0	0	381
% OF POSSIBLE SUNSHINE	48	52	53	52	60	64	66	63	55	48	37	39	53
AVERAGE SKY COVER													
Sunrise - Sunset	6.6	6.5	6.6	6.8	6.4	6.0	5.6	5.8	6.0	6.4	7.4	7.1	6.4
NUMBER OF DAYS (Sunrise-Sunset)													
Clear	8.0	7.2	7.2	6.3	6.9	7.4	8.5	8.8	8.1	7.3	5.0	6.4	87.2
Partly cloudy	6.3	6.5	7.6	7.7	9.6	11.1	12.1	10.5	9.7	8.4	6.4	6.0	101.9
Cloudy	16.7	14.6	16.2	16.0	14.5	11.5	10.4	11.7	12.2	15.3	18.6	18.6	176.2
Precipitation .01" or more	10.3	8.3	10.9	11.0	11.2	10.6	9.7	10.4	10.2	8.8	9.3	10.9	121.7
Snow, Ice pellets 1.0" or more	3.7	2.7	2.8	0.8	*	0.0	0.0	0.0	0.0	0.1	1.4	3.2	14.7
Thunderstorms	0.1	0.2	1.2	2.4	4.1	6.9	6.6	5.8	4.1	1.9	0.6	0.2	34.0
Fog, Visibility 1/4 mile or less	1.7	2.6	2.6	2.2	1.5	1.4	1.1	2.5	2.0	2.8	2.4	2.4	25.2
Temperature Maximum:													
90° and above	0.0	0.0	0.0	0.0	*	1.4	2.9	1.3	0.2	0.0	0.0	0.0	5.8
32° and below	24.5	19.2	8.4	0.5	0.0	0.0	0.0	0.0	0.0	0.0	4.7	20.3	77.5
Temperature Minimum:													
32° and below	30.7	27.5	26.8	14.2	2.8	0.0	0.0	0.0	0.6	7.8	21.9	29.4	161.5
0° and below	12.7	7.8	1.4	0.0	0.0	0.0	0.0	0.0	0.0	0.0	0.3	6.5	28.6
RELATIVE HUMIDITY (%)													
Morning	75	76	77	75	75	80	82	86	86	81	81	79	79
Afternoon	69	68	66	59	55	58	57	61	63	62	70	73	63
PRECIPITATION (inches)													
Water Equivalent													
Normal	1.1	1.0	1.9	2.7	3.1	3.1	3.2	3.1	3.1	2.1	1.7	1.4	28.0
Maximum monthly	2.6	3.5	4.6	5.5	8.2	8.4	6.5	9.0	7.8	5.0	4.9	3.1	9.0
Date	1950	1953	1977	1953	1973	1967	1950	1975	1965	1954	1985	1971	1975
Minimum monthly	0.1	0.0	0.3	0.9	0.5	0.3	0.8	0.9	0.2	T	0.1	0.1	T
Date	1981	1969	1978	1963	1981	1976	1981	1955	1976	1952	1976	1960	1952
Maximum in 24 hrs	1.1	1.7	1.4	2.0	3.2	2.6	2.9	4.6	2.9	3.6	2.3	1.5	4.6
Date	1980	1966	1979	1981	1973	1969	1959	1975	1964	1954	1985	1959	1975
SNOW, ICE PELLETS													
Maximum monthly	28.0	20.6	22.2	11.8	2.6	0.0	0.0	0.0	T	1.7	16.5	27.0	28.0
Date	1982	1962	1972	1977	1960	—	—	—	1965	1959	1985	1977	1982
Maximum in 24 hrs	8.8	9.2	10.1	10.2	2.2	0.0	0.0	0.0	T	1.6	8.2	11.1	11.1
Date	1982	1959	1964	1977	1960	—	—	—	1965	1959	1977	1985	1985
WIND (Resultant)													
Mean speed (mph)	11.1	10.7	11.1	11.6	10.4	9.3	8.3	8.0	9.1	10.0	11.1	10.8	10.1

LA CROSSE

Elev. 651'   43° 52'N — 91° 15'W   **Wisconsin**

NORMALS, MEANS, EXTREMES

	JAN	FEB	MAR	APR	MAY	JUN	JUL	AUG	SEP	OCT	NOV	DEC	YEAR
TEMPERATURE													
Normal daily maximum	23.0	29.4	40.0	57.5	70.2	79.1	83.5	81.4	72.0	60.8	43.1	29.2	55.8
Normal daily minimum	5.0	9.9	21.8	36.9	48.5	57.8	62.4	60.3	51.2	41.0	27.4	13.8	36.3
Normal monthly	14.0	19.7	30.9	47.2	59.4	68.5	73.0	70.9	61.6	50.9	35.3	21.5	46.1
Extreme highest	57	64	80	93	94	98	104	103	100	93	75	64	104
Extreme highest date	1981	1981	1978	1980	1967	1985	1980	1955	1978	1963	1978	1982	1980
Extreme lowest	-37	-36	-28	7	26	37	33	40	28	15	-9	-30	-37
Extreme lowest date	1951	1971	1962	1982	1971	1978	1982	1965	1967	1972	1977	1983	1951
DEGREE DAYS BASE 65° F													
Heating	1581	1268	1057	534	216	37	10	14	135	448	891	1349	7540
Cooling	0	0	0	0	42	142	258	197	33	11	0	0	683
% OF POSSIBLE SUNSHINE	na	na	na	na	na	na	na	na	na	na	na	na	na
AVERAGE SKY COVER													
Sunrise - Sunset	6.7	6.2	6.7	6.7	6.5	6.2	5.6	5.7	5.8	5.7	7.1	7.1	6.3
NUMBER OF DAYS (Sunrise-Sunset)													
Clear	7.4	7.9	7.4	6.8	6.9	7.3	9.8	9.5	9.1	10.8	5.8	6.8	95.4
Partly cloudy	6.9	7.1	7.1	7.1	9.1	10.4	10.9	10.6	8.9	6.9	6.1	5.8	96.8
Cloudy	16.7	13.2	16.5	16.1	15.0	12.3	10.4	10.9	11.9	13.4	18.1	18.5	173.0
Precipitation .01" or more	8.1	7.1	9.9	9.9	11.4	11.0	9.9	9.7	9.7	7.8	7.5	8.8	110.8
Snow, Ice pellets 1.0" or more	3.0	2.4	2.8	0.5	0.0	0.0	0.0	0.0	0.0	*	1.1	2.9	12.8
Thunderstorms	0.1	0.3	1.3	2.9	5.5	7.9	7.4	7.0	4.7	2.2	0.6	0.3	40.2
Fog, Visibility 1/4 mile or less	1.1	1.5	1.6	0.6	0.6	1.2	1.7	3.7	3.4	2.0	1.4	1.2	20.0
Temperature Maximum:													
90° and above	0.0	0.0	0.0	0.1	0.7	3.2	6.5	4.4	1.3	0.1	0.0	0.0	16.2
32° and below	23.1	15.8	6.9	0.2	0.0	0.0	0.0	0.0	0.0	0.0	5.0	18.9	69.9
Temperature Minimum:													
32° and below	30.7	27.1	26.2	9.9	0.8	0.0	0.0	0.0	0.3	5.7	21.1	29.4	151.2
0° and below	12.2	7.3	1.3	0.0	0.0	0.0	0.0	0.0	0.0	0.0	0.4	5.9	27.2
RELATIVE HUMIDITY (%)													
Morning	76	78	78	74	75	82	81	88	88	79	80	79	80
Afternoon	67	65	62	53	52	56	57	60	62	59	67	72	61
PRECIPITATION (inches)													
Water Equivalent													
Normal	0.9	0.8	1.9	3.0	3.6	4.1	3.8	3.7	3.4	2.0	1.5	1.0	30.2
Maximum monthly	2.8	2.5	3.8	7.3	8.8	9.5	9.1	9.8	10.5	5.0	3.7	2.5	10.5
Date	1967	1959	1951	1973	1960	1968	1978	1980	1965	1984	1983	1971	1965
Minimum monthly	0.1	0.0	0.3	0.6	1.0	1.5	0.1	0.5	0.4	0.0	T	0.3	T
Date	1981	1969	1978	1966	1958	1979	1967	1976	1952	1952	1976	1962	1976
Maximum in 24 hrs	1.3	1.0	1.6	3.8	2.7	3.9	3.7	3.9	2.2	2.1	2.3	0.9	3.9
Date	1967	1966	1966	1954	1960	1967	1952	1962	1968	1966	1958	1965	1967
SNOW, ICE PELLETS													
Maximum monthly	29.7	31.0	33.5	17.0	0.8	0.0	0.0	0.0	T	1.4	13.0	26.6	33.5
Date	1979	1959	1959	1973	1960	—	—	—	1985	1959	1957	1968	1959
Maximum in 24 hrs	8.7	10.9	15.7	7.3	0.8	0.0	0.0	0.0	T	1.2	11.0	9.1	15.7
Date	1963	1959	1959	1952	1960	—	—	—	1985	1959	1957	1966	1959
WIND (Resultant)													
Mean speed (mph)	8.6	8.5	9.2	10.4	9.5	8.4	7.6	7.4	8.2	9.2	9.6	8.7	8.8

MADISON

Elev. 858'   43° 08'N — 89° 20'W   # Wisconsin

NORMALS, MEANS, EXTREMES

	JAN	FEB	MAR	APR	MAY	JUN	JUL	AUG	SEP	OCT	NOV	DEC	YEAR
TEMPERATURE													
Normal daily maximum	24.5	30.0	40.8	57.5	69.8	78.8	82.8	80.6	72.3	61.1	44.1	30.6	56.1
Normal daily minimum	6.7	11.0	21.5	34.1	44.2	53.8	58.3	56.3	47.8	37.8	26.0	14.1	34.3
Normal monthly	15.6	20.5	31.2	45.8	57.0	66.3	70.6	68.5	60.1	49.5	35.1	22.4	45.2
Extreme highest	55	61	82	94	93	97	104	101	99	90	76	62	104
Extreme highest date	1981	1981	1981	1980	1975	1953	1976	1947	1953	1976	1964	1984	1976
Extreme lowest	-37	-28	-29	0	19	31	36	35	25	14	-11	-25	-37
Extreme lowest date	1951	1985	1962	1982	1978	1972	1965	1968	1974	1952	1947	1983	1951
DEGREE DAYS BASE 65° F													
Heating	1531	1246	1048	576	273	58	12	29	161	490	897	1321	7642
Cooling	0	0	0	0	25	97	185	137	14	9	0	0	467
% OF POSSIBLE SUNSHINE	48	51	53	51	58	64	68	66	61	54	39	39	54
AVERAGE SKY COVER													
Sunrise - Sunset	6.7	6.6	6.9	6.8	6.5	6.1	5.7	5.7	5.7	6.0	7.2	7.2	6.4
NUMBER OF DAYS (Sunrise-Sunset)													
Clear	7.6	7.2	6.4	6.4	6.7	7.2	9.3	9.4	9.6	9.5	5.7	6.2	91.0
Partly cloudy	6.3	5.8	7.7	7.6	9.6	10.2	11.2	10.6	8.5	7.4	6.1	6.1	97.0
Cloudy	17.1	15.2	16.9	16.1	14.7	12.7	10.5	11.1	11.9	14.1	18.3	18.7	177.3
Precipitation .01" or more	10.2	7.9	11.1	11.4	11.4	10.6	9.5	9.5	9.2	8.7	9.1	9.9	118.5
Snow, Ice pellets 1.0" or more	2.7	2.3	2.7	0.7	0.0	0.0	0.0	0.0	0.0	0.0	1.2	3.3	12.9
Thunderstorms	0.2	0.3	1.9	3.6	5.2	7.4	7.4	6.8	4.7	2.0	0.9	0.4	40.9
Fog, Visibility 1/4 mile or less	2.3	2.0	2.7	1.3	1.4	0.8	1.2	2.2	1.7	1.9	2.1	2.9	22.3
Temperature Maximum:													
90° and above	0.0	0.0	0.0	*	0.3	2.8	4.6	2.7	0.7	0.1	0.0	0.0	11.3
32° and below	22.3	15.7	6.5	0.4	0.0	0.0	0.0	0.0	0.0	*	3.8	17.8	66.4
Temperature Minimum:													
32° and below	30.2	27.1	26.1	14.3	3.5	*	0.0	0.0	1.3	9.6	21.6	29.1	162.8
0° and below	12.0	7.2	1.5	*	0.0	0.0	0.0	0.0	0.0	0.0	0.2	6.0	26.9
RELATIVE HUMIDITY (%)													
Morning	77	77	78	76	77	81	84	87	88	82	83	82	81
Afternoon	69	66	63	56	54	56	56	59	61	59	68	73	62
PRECIPITATION (inches)													
Water Equivalent													
Normal	1.1	1.0	2.1	3.1	3.3	3.8	3.7	3.8	3.0	2.2	1.8	1.5	30.8
Maximum monthly	2.4	2.7	5.0	7.1	6.2	9.9	10.9	9.4	9.5	5.6	5.1	3.6	10.9
Date	1974	1953	1973	1973	1960	1978	1950	1980	1941	1984	1985	1982	1950
Minimum monthly	0.1	0.0	0.2	0.9	0.6	0.8	1.3	0.7	0.1	0.0	0.1	0.2	0.0
Date	1981	1958	1978	1946	1981	1973	1946	1948	1979	1952	1976	1960	1952
Maximum in 24 hrs	1.2	1.5	2.5	2.8	3.6	3.6	5.2	2.9	3.5	2.7	2.3	1.7	5.2
Date	1960	1981	1973	1975	1966	1963	1950	1965	1961	1984	1985	1985	1950
SNOW, ICE PELLETS													
Maximum monthly	26.9	20.9	25.4	17.4	0.7	0.0	0.0	0.0	T	0.9	18.3	24.6	26.9
Date	1979	1975	1959	1973	1966	—	—	—	1965	1967	1985	1977	1979
Maximum in 24 hrs	11.6	10.3	13.6	12.9	0.7	0.0	0.0	0.0	T	0.9	9.0	16.0	16.0
Date	1971	1950	1971	1973	1966	—	—	—	1965	1967	1985	1970	1970
WIND (Resultant)													
Mean speed (mph)	10.5	10.4	11.2	11.4	10.1	9.1	8.1	7.9	8.7	9.6	10.7	10.2	9.8

MILWAUKEE

Elev. 672'   42° 57'N — 87° 54'W   **Wisconsin**

NORMALS, MEANS, EXTREMES

	JAN	FEB	MAR	APR	MAY	JUN	JUL	AUG	SEP	OCT	NOV	DEC	YEAR
TEMPERATURE													
Normal daily maximum	26.0	30.1	39.2	53.5	64.8	75.0	79.8	78.4	71.2	59.9	44.7	32.0	54.6
Normal daily minimum	11.3	15.8	24.9	35.6	44.7	54.7	61.1	60.2	52.5	41.9	29.9	18.2	37.6
Normal monthly	18.7	23.0	32.1	44.6	54.8	64.9	70.5	69.3	61.9	50.9	37.3	25.1	46.1
Extreme highest	62	65	81	91	92	99	101	100	98	89	77	63	101
Extreme highest date	1944	1976	1945	1980	1975	1953	1955	1955	1953	1963	1950	1982	1955
Extreme lowest	-26	-19	-10	12	21	33	40	44	28	18	-5	-20	-26
Extreme lowest date	1982	1951	1962	1982	1966	1945	1965	1982	1974	1981	1950	1983	1982
DEGREE DAYS BASE 65° F													
Heating	1435	1176	1020	612	334	84	11	25	117	444	831	1237	7326
Cooling	0	0	0	0	18	81	182	158	24	7	0	0	470
% OF POSSIBLE SUNSHINE	44	47	50	53	59	64	70	66	59	54	40	38	54
AVERAGE SKY COVER													
Sunrise - Sunset	6.8	6.8	6.9	6.7	6.3	6.0	5.3	5.4	5.6	5.8	7.2	7.2	6.3
NUMBER OF DAYS (Sunrise-Sunset)													
Clear	7.3	6.6	6.0	6.4	7.0	7.6	10.2	10.3	9.6	9.4	5.7	6.2	92.2
Partly cloudy	6.2	5.9	7.9	8.0	10.1	10.4	11.3	10.6	9.2	8.6	6.0	5.9	99.9
Cloudy	17.6	15.7	17.1	15.6	14.0	12.0	9.5	10.1	11.2	13.0	18.3	18.9	173.2
Precipitation .01" or more	11.2	9.6	11.9	12.0	12.0	10.9	9.5	9.1	9.0	8.8	10.0	11.2	125.1
Snow, Ice pellets 1.0" or more	3.7	2.6	2.7	0.5	0.0	0.0	0.0	0.0	0.0	*	1.0	3.3	13.8
Thunderstorms	0.3	0.4	1.4	3.5	4.5	6.6	6.4	5.7	3.9	1.6	1.0	0.4	35.8
Fog, Visibility 1/4 mile or less	2.1	2.0	3.1	3.0	3.2	2.5	1.1	1.7	1.2	2.2	2.3	2.2	26.7
Temperature Maximum:													
90° and above	0.0	0.0	0.0	*	0.1	1.6	3.7	2.1	0.6	0.0	0.0	0.0	8.1
32° and below	21.5	16.0	6.8	0.6	0.0	0.0	0.0	0.0	0.0	0.0	2.6	16.1	63.6
Temperature Minimum:													
32° and below	30.0	26.2	23.7	10.4	1.2	0.0	0.0	0.0	0.1	4.2	18.5	28.2	142.4
0° and below	8.4	3.8	0.2	0.0	0.0	0.0	0.0	0.0	0.0	0.0	0.1	3.4	15.9
RELATIVE HUMIDITY (%)													
Morning	74	74	75	75	75	78	80	84	83	79	78	78	78
Afternoon	68	67	65	61	60	61	60	63	63	63	67	72	64
PRECIPITATION (inches)													
Water Equivalent													
Normal	1.6	1.3	2.5	3.3	2.6	3.5	3.5	3.0	2.8	2.2	1.9	2.0	30.9
Maximum monthly	4.0	3.1	6.9	7.3	5.8	8.2	7.6	7.0	9.8	6.4	7.1	4.3	9.8
Date	1960	1974	1976	1973	1983	1954	1964	1960	1941	1959	1985	1971	1941
Minimum monthly	0.3	0.0	0.3	0.8	0.9	0.8	0.9	0.4	0.0	0.1	0.6	0.2	0.0
Date	1981	1969	1968	1942	1977	1965	1946	1948	1979	1956	1949	1976	1979
Maximum in 24 hrs	1.7	1.6	2.5	3.1	3.1	3.1	4.3	4.0	5.2	2.6	2.1	2.2	5.2
Date	1985	1960	1960	1976	1978	1950	1959	1953	1941	1959	1943	1982	1941
SNOW, ICE PELLETS													
Maximum monthly	33.6	42.0	26.7	15.8	0.4	0.0	0.0	0.0	T	4.0	16.1	27.9	42.0
Date	1979	1974	1965	1973	1960	—	—	—	1960	1976	1977	1978	1974
Maximum in 24 hrs	12.8	16.7	11.2	11.6	0.4	0.0	0.0	0.0	T	4.0	10.6	12.4	16.7
Date	1962	1960	1961	1973	1960	—	—	—	1960	1976	1977	1978	1960
WIND (Resultant)													
Mean speed (mph)	12.8	12.5	13.1	13.0	11.7	10.5	9.6	9.4	10.6	11.4	12.5	12.4	11.6

CASPER

Elev. 5338'   **42° 55'N — 106° 28'W**   # Wyoming

NORMALS, MEANS, EXTREMES

	JAN	FEB	MAR	APR	MAY	JUN	JUL	AUG	SEP	OCT	NOV	DEC	YEAR
TEMPERATURE													
Normal daily maximum	32.5	37.4	43.4	54.9	66.2	78.1	87.1	84.8	74.2	61.0	43.9	35.6	58.3
Normal daily minimum	11.9	16.3	20.2	29.3	38.9	47.6	54.7	52.8	42.5	33.2	21.9	15.7	32.1
Normal monthly	22.2	26.9	31.8	42.1	52.6	62.9	70.9	68.8	58.4	47.1	32.9	25.7	45.2
Extreme highest	60	68	73	81	92	101	104	102	96	85	71	61	104
Extreme highest date	1971	1982	1966	1980	1984	1970	1954	1979	1983	1957	1983	1980	1954
Extreme lowest	-40	-27	-21	-4	16	28	30	33	16	-3	-21	-39	-40
Extreme lowest date	1972	1982	1965	1966	1953	1969	1972	1977	1983	1971	1985	1983	1972
DEGREE DAYS BASE 65° F													
Heating	1327	1067	1026	687	384	131	16	31	240	552	963	1218	7642
Cooling	0	0	0	0	0	68	199	148	42	0	0	0	457
% OF POSSIBLE SUNSHINE	na	na	na	na	na	na	na	na	na	na	na	na	na
AVERAGE SKY COVER													
Sunrise - Sunset	6.7	6.6	6.8	6.8	6.7	5.4	4.3	4.5	4.6	5.3	6.3	6.4	5.9
NUMBER OF DAYS (Sunrise-Sunset)													
Clear	6.6	6.0	6.0	5.5	5.2	9.6	13.8	13.3	13.3	11.5	7.1	7.6	105.5
Partly cloudy	7.6	8.4	8.7	8.8	10.8	10.9	11.0	10.6	8.6	7.9	8.7	8.1	110.2
Cloudy	16.8	13.9	16.3	15.7	15.0	9.5	6.1	7.1	8.1	11.6	14.2	15.3	149.5
Precipitation .01" or more	7.5	7.9	9.5	10.3	10.8	8.4	7.9	5.4	6.4	6.5	6.8	7.5	95.1
Snow, Ice pellets 1.0" or more	3.6	3.4	4.5	3.7	1.0	0.1	0.0	0.0	0.4	1.8	3.1	3.1	24.7
Thunderstorms	0.0	*	0.2	1.2	6.1	8.1	9.0	6.5	2.8	0.5	0.1	0.0	34.5
Fog, Visibility 1/4 mile or less	0.7	0.7	1.0	1.5	1.0	0.5	0.4	0.3	0.7	0.9	0.9	0.6	9.1
Temperature Maximum:													
90° and above	0.0	0.0	0.0	0.0	0.1	3.2	12.6	10.8	1.4	0.0	0.0	0.0	28.0
32° and below	13.8	8.5	4.7	1.3	0.1	0.0	0.0	0.0	0.2	0.8	6.1	13.2	48.7
Temperature Minimum:													
32° and below	29.2	26.5	27.4	19.2	7.4	0.4	*	0.0	4.5	15.9	25.2	28.6	184.5
0° and below	7.5	3.3	1.6	0.2	0.0	0.0	0.0	0.0	0.0	0.1	2.1	5.6	20.4
RELATIVE HUMIDITY (%)													
Morning	69	69	73	75	78	76	70	67	67	68	70	69	71
Afternoon	62	56	48	42	41	33	26	25	30	41	56	62	44
PRECIPITATION (inches)													
Water Equivalent													
Normal	0.5	0.5	0.9	1.5	2.1	1.2	1.0	0.6	0.7	0.8	0.6	0.5	11.4
Maximum monthly	1.1	1.0	2.4	3.9	6.4	4.1	3.0	2.6	3.4	2.4	2.7	3.7	6.4
Date	1984	1955	1954	1974	1978	1982	1951	1979	1982	1962	1983	1982	1978
Minimum monthly	T	0.1	0.2	0.2	0.3	0.0	0.1	0.0	0.0	T	0.0	0.0	T
Date	1952	1957	1953	1952	1966	1956	1971	1950	1956	1965	1965	1952	1965
Maximum in 24 hrs	0.5	0.4	1.0	3.0	2.6	2.3	2.0	1.7	2.0	2.4	1.2	1.6	3.0
Date	1972	1977	1958	1974	1978	1982	1983	1979	1973	1962	1983	1982	1974
SNOW, ICE PELLETS													
Maximum monthly	22.1	23.8	36.2	56.3	24.6	3.0	0.0	T	11.5	13.1	37.1	62.8	62.8
Date	1980	1952	1975	1973	1978	1969	—	1964	1982	1971	1983	1982	1982
Maximum in 24 hrs	9.7	10.4	14.6	16.5	14.1	3.0	0.0	T	6.8	8.2	14.3	31.1	31.1
Date	1972	1952	1954	1973	1950	1969	—	1964	1982	1970	1983	1982	1982
WIND (Resultant)													
Mean speed (mph)	16.4	15.3	14.0	12.8	11.7	11.1	10.1	10.5	11.1	12.2	14.4	16.2	13.0

NORMALS, MEANS, EXTREMES

	JAN	FEB	MAR	APR	MAY	JUN	JUL	AUG	SEP	OCT	NOV	DEC	YEAR
TEMPERATURE													
Normal daily maximum	37.3	40.7	43.6	54.0	64.6	75.4	83.1	80.8	72.1	61.0	46.5	40.4	58.3
Normal daily minimum	14.8	17.9	20.6	29.6	39.7	48.5	54.6	52.8	43.7	34.0	23.1	18.2	33.1
Normal monthly	26.1	29.3	32.1	41.8	52.2	62.0	68.9	66.8	57.9	47.5	34.8	29.3	45.7
Extreme highest	66	71	73	82	90	100	100	96	93	83	73	69	100
Extreme highest date	1982	1962	1967	1981	1969	1954	1939	1979	1960	1967	1954	1939	1954
Extreme lowest	-29	-34	-21	-8	16	25	38	36	8	2	-14	-28	-34
Extreme lowest date	1984	1936	1943	1975	1947	1951	1952	1975	1985	1935	1983	1983	1936
DEGREE DAYS BASE 65° F													
Heating	1206	1000	1020	696	397	139	24	37	235	543	906	1107	7310
Cooling	0	0	0	0	0	49	145	93	22	0	0	0	309
% OF POSSIBLE SUNSHINE	62	66	66	61	60	65	68	67	70	69	60	60	65
AVERAGE SKY COVER													
Sunrise - Sunset	5.8	6.2	6.3	6.5	6.7	5.5	5.0	5.1	4.6	4.7	5.6	5.8	5.6
NUMBER OF DAYS (Sunrise-Sunset)													
Clear	8.8	7.0	7.1	5.9	4.6	8.2	9.6	9.8	13.3	12.8	9.6	9.2	105.8
Partly cloudy	9.6	9.2	9.8	10.4	12.2	12.6	15.1	13.3	8.5	9.2	9.1	9.2	128.1
Cloudy	13.0	12.0	13.9	13.7	14.2	9.2	6.3	7.8	8.3	9.0	11.3	12.8	131.8
Precipitation .01" or more	5.9	6.0	9.4	9.6	11.8	10.8	10.7	9.6	7.3	5.5	5.9	5.5	98.0
Snow, Ice pellets 1.0" or more	2.1	1.9	3.6	2.5	0.9	0.1	0.0	0.0	0.3	1.2	2.4	1.8	16.8
Thunderstorms	0.0	0.1	0.2	2.1	7.6	11.1	13.3	10.5	4.3	0.8	*	0.0	50.1
Fog, Visibility 1/4 mile or less	0.9	1.8	3.0	3.0	3.0	2.1	1.1	1.3	1.9	2.1	1.9	1.4	23.4
Temperature Maximum:													
90° and above	0.0	0.0	0.0	0.0	*	1.1	5.3	2.3	0.3	0.0	0.0	0.0	9.1
32° and below	9.6	7.1	5.5	1.5	*	0.0	0.0	0.0	0.2	0.7	4.2	8.6	37.3
Temperature Minimum:													
32° and below	29.0	26.4	27.8	18.1	3.4	0.0	0.0	0.0	2.3	12.0	24.7	28.4	172.1
0° and below	4.8	2.4	1.2	0.2	0.0	0.0	0.0	0.0	0.0	0.0	0.6	3.0	12.2
RELATIVE HUMIDITY (%)													
Morning	57	60	64	66	70	70	69	68	65	60	60	57	64
Afternoon	50	46	46	41	43	41	38	37	38	40	49	52	43
PRECIPITATION (inches)													
Water Equivalent													
Normal	0.4	0.4	0.9	1.2	2.3	2.0	1.8	1.3	1.0	0.6	0.5	0.3	13.3
Maximum monthly	2.7	2.1	2.9	5.0	5.6	5.3	5.0	6.6	4.5	3.5	2.4	1.6	6.6
Date	1949	1953	1983	1942	1981	1955	1973	1985	1973	1942	1979	1937	1985
Minimum monthly	T	T	0.1	0.3	0.1	0.0	0.5	0.0	0.1	0.0	T	0.0	T
Date	1952	1983	1966	1946	1974	1980	1969	1944	1953	1964	1965	1959	1983
Maximum in 24 hrs	1.4	1.6	1.8	1.9	2.0	2.6	3.4	6.0	2.7	1.7	1.6	1.1	6.0
Date	1949	1953	1946	1984	1942	1955	1973	1985	1973	1947	1979	1979	1985
SNOW, ICE PELLETS													
Maximum monthly	35.5	19.9	31.9	31.8	30.4	8.7	0.0	0.0	7.4	21.3	31.1	21.3	35.5
Date	1980	1953	1983	1984	1943	1947	—	—	1985	1969	1979	1958	1980
Maximum in 24 hrs	12.0	14.0	15.6	17.4	15.0	8.7	0.0	0.0	5.8	6.9	19.8	11.7	19.8
Date	1980	1953	1973	1984	1942	1947	—	—	1985	1982	1979	1979	1979
WIND (Resultant)													
Mean speed (mph)	15.2	14.9	14.5	14.3	12.6	11.4	10.3	10.3	11.2	12.2	13.2	14.9	12.9

NORMALS, MEANS, EXTREMES

	JAN	FEB	MAR	APR	MAY	JUN	JUL	AUG	SEP	OCT	NOV	DEC	YEAR
TEMPERATURE													
Normal daily maximum	31.3	37.7	44.2	54.7	65.5	76.5	86.0	83.7	73.1	60.3	42.6	35.0	57.6
Normal daily minimum	7.7	13.5	19.9	29.8	39.6	48.0	55.4	53.4	43.6	33.3	18.9	11.3	31.2
Normal monthly	19.5	25.6	32.1	42.3	52.6	62.3	70.7	68.6	58.4	46.8	30.8	23.2	44.4
Extreme highest	63	68	76	82	91	100	101	101	94	85	70	64	101
Extreme highest date	1971	1951	1966	1962	1954	1954	1954	1979	1983	1963	1980	1980	1979
Extreme lowest	-37	-28	-16	-2	18	25	39	35	10	0	-18	-37	-37
Extreme lowest date	1963	1949	1960	1973	1954	1951	1983	1962	1965	1971	1985	1983	1983
DEGREE DAYS BASE 65° F													
Heating	1407	1100	1020	681	384	142	12	32	241	564	1026	1296	7905
Cooling	0	0	0	0	0	61	192	143	40	0	0	0	436
% OF POSSIBLE SUNSHINE	66	68	71	68	65	72	76	76	73	70	61	64	69
AVERAGE SKY COVER													
Sunrise - Sunset	6.1	6.1	6.2	6.2	6.4	5.1	4.2	4.3	4.3	4.9	5.9	5.7	5.5
NUMBER OF DAYS (Sunrise-Sunset)													
Clear	7.6	6.7	7.2	5.9	6.1	10.1	13.6	13.1	13.8	11.9	7.9	9.3	113.3
Partly cloudy	10.3	10.1	9.9	10.5	11.1	11.0	11.8	12.1	8.9	9.3	9.9	9.9	124.8
Cloudy	13.1	11.5	13.8	13.6	13.5	8.9	5.6	5.8	7.3	9.8	12.3	11.8	127.0
Precipitation .01" or more	4.6	5.2	7.5	8.4	9.2	6.4	5.8	4.5	5.3	4.9	5.1	4.6	71.5
Snow, Ice pellets 1.0" or more	2.6	2.9	4.4	4.3	1.5	0.2	0.0	0.0	0.8	2.2	3.0	2.7	24.6
Thunderstorms	0.0	0.0	0.2	0.8	4.5	7.3	9.5	6.9	2.9	0.4	*	0.0	32.4
Fog, Visibility 1/4 mile or less	0.9	0.6	0.2	0.2	0.1	0.1	0.0	0.1	0.2	0.2	0.7	0.8	3.9
Temperature Maximum:													
90° and above	0.0	0.0	0.0	0.0	0.1	2.1	10.1	6.6	0.9	0.0	0.0	0.0	19.8
32° and below	15.2	8.9	4.4	0.7	0.1	0.0	0.0	0.0	0.1	0.6	6.7	13.4	50.1
Temperature Minimum:													
32° and below	30.5	27.8	28.6	18.7	5.2	0.3	0.0	0.0	3.1	14.1	27.7	30.6	186.6
0° and below	8.5	4.1	1.3	*	0.0	0.0	0.0	0.0	0.0	0.1	1.9	5.3	21.3
RELATIVE HUMIDITY (%)													
Morning	67	68	66	66	67	62	55	54	59	64	69	68	64
Afternoon	60	54	47	40	38	33	28	27	33	41	57	61	43
PRECIPITATION (inches)													
Water Equivalent													
Normal	0.4	0.6	1.1	2.2	2.6	1.4	0.7	0.4	0.8	1.2	0.7	0.5	13.1
Maximum monthly	1.6	2.1	3.3	5.4	6.0	6.8	2.5	2.3	4.6	3.5	3.3	1.6	6.8
Date	1949	1955	1977	1957	1957	1947	1977	1979	1973	1971	1983	1985	1947
Minimum monthly	T	T	0.3	0.7	0.2	T	0.0	T	0.0	0.1	0.0	0.0	T
Date	1952	1970	1960	1982	1984	1971	1963	1970	1979	1958	1949	1954	1971
Maximum in 24 hrs	0.8	0.8	1.2	2.1	2.7	3.5	2.1	1.0	2.2	1.7	1.3	1.2	3.5
Date	1963	1955	1977	1971	1964	1947	1977	1979	1973	1966	1983	1985	1947
SNOW, ICE PELLETS													
Maximum monthly	26.5	43.8	52.0	66.0	33.9	18.4	0.0	0.0	32.9	39.9	48.7	28.0	66.0
Date	1962	1955	1977	1973	1975	1947	—	—	1982	1971	1983	1985	1973
Maximum in 24 hrs	13.8	19.8	20.3	21.9	20.8	18.4	0.0	0.0	16.9	19.4	23.1	20.5	23.1
Date	1980	1955	1973	1967	1975	1947	—	—	1982	1966	1958	1985	1958
WIND (Resultant)													
Mean speed (mph)	6.0	6.1	7.1	7.9	7.9	7.9	7.7	7.5	7.0	6.1	5.6	5.8	6.9

SHERIDAN

Elev. 3964'   44° 46'N — 106° 58'W   # Wyoming

NORMALS, MEANS, EXTREMES

	JAN	FEB	MAR	APR	MAY	JUN	JUL	AUG	SEP	OCT	NOV	DEC	YEAR
TEMPERATURE													
Normal daily maximum	31.8	38.0	44.1	55.6	66.2	75.9	86.0	84.5	73.3	61.9	45.3	36.9	58.3
Normal daily minimum	7.3	14.1	19.7	29.4	39.7	47.6	53.8	52.1	42.0	32.1	19.7	12.3	30.8
Normal monthly	19.6	26.1	31.9	42.5	53.0	61.8	69.9	68.3	57.7	47.0	32.5	24.6	44.6
Extreme highest	70	76	77	87	95	100	106	106	103	91	78	72	106
Extreme highest date	1974	1982	1978	1946	1960	1984	1983	1983	1983	1963	1975	1981	1983
Extreme lowest	-35	-31	-23	-2	13	27	35	34	6	1	-25	-37	-37
Extreme lowest date	1963	1949	1965	1975	1954	1951	1971	1966	1984	1971	1959	1983	1983
DEGREE DAYS BASE 65° F													
Heating	1411	1089	1026	675	372	149	34	45	255	558	975	1252	7841
Cooling	0	0	0	0	0	53	186	147	33	0	0	0	419
% OF POSSIBLE SUNSHINE	55	58	61	59	59	64	75	74	67	62	53	53	62
AVERAGE SKY COVER													
Sunrise - Sunset	6.9	7.0	6.9	6.8	6.7	5.7	4.2	4.3	4.9	5.6	6.6	6.7	6.0
NUMBER OF DAYS (Sunrise-Sunset)													
Clear	5.7	4.8	4.9	5.3	5.6	7.8	13.8	13.9	11.8	10.2	6.1	6.2	96.2
Partly cloudy	8.0	8.1	9.4	9.0	10.6	11.7	12.2	10.9	9.1	8.7	8.2	7.8	113.8
Cloudy	17.2	15.3	16.7	15.6	14.8	10.5	5.0	6.3	9.1	12.0	15.6	17.0	155.3
Precipitation .01" or more	9.0	8.6	10.8	10.8	11.7	11.2	7.2	6.5	7.6	7.4	7.7	8.9	107.3
Snow, Ice pellets 1.0" or more	3.7	3.7	4.4	2.9	0.5	*	0.0	0.0	0.5	1.2	2.8	3.8	23.6
Thunderstorms	0.0	*	0.0	0.7	4.8	9.4	9.5	7.3	2.6	0.3	*	0.0	34.6
Fog, Visibility 1/4 mile or less	0.8	0.9	0.7	0.4	0.4	0.4	0.1	0.1	0.2	0.5	0.7	0.7	5.7
Temperature Maximum:													
90° and above	0.0	0.0	0.0	0.0	0.2	2.1	10.5	11.0	2.3	0.0	0.0	0.0	26.1
32° and below	14.3	7.9	4.6	0.8	0.0	0.0	0.0	0.0	*	0.4	5.4	13.1	46.6
Temperature Minimum:													
32° and below	30.3	27.4	28.0	19.2	5.6	0.3	0.0	0.0	3.8	16.9	28.0	30.0	189.5
0° and below	11.0	4.3	1.4	*	0.0	0.0	0.0	0.0	0.0	0.0	2.2	7.8	26.8
RELATIVE HUMIDITY (%)													
Morning	69	70	72	72	75	77	72	68	70	69	72	70	71
Afternoon	63	59	49	43	46	45	33	30	38	45	60	64	48
PRECIPITATION (inches)													
Water Equivalent													
Normal	0.7	0.7	1.0	2.0	2.4	2.2	0.9	0.9	1.1	1.1	0.8	0.6	14.9
Maximum monthly	1.7	2.6	3.2	4.8	6.8	9.5	3.7	3.0	3.0	3.1	2.2	2.0	9.5
Date	1972	1955	1946	1963	1978	1944	1958	1968	1951	1971	1942	1955	1944
Minimum monthly	0.0	0.0	0.1	0.1	0.3	0.2	0.0	T	0.0	0.0	0.1	0.2	T
Date	1983	1977	1978	1980	1958	1971	1959	1970	1964	1965	1981	1979	1970
Maximum in 24 hrs	1.0	1.1	2.2	3.8	2.0	3.4	2.2	1.7	1.5	1.9	0.8	0.8	3.8
Date	1972	1955	1946	1948	1956	1944	1948	1943	1982	1974	1978	1980	1948
SNOW, ICE PELLETS													
Maximum monthly	26.3	35.0	36.8	39.6	12.5	4.0	0.0	0.0	21.0	14.8	25.8	27.6	39.6
Date	1977	1955	1954	1955	1979	1969	—	—	1984	1971	1964	1955	1955
Maximum in 24 hrs	13.5	11.0	13.3	26.7	10.9	4.0	0.0	0.0	12.9	8.4	12.0	11.7	26.7
Date	1972	1955	1946	1955	1979	1969	—	—	1984	1977	1942	1980	1955
WIND (Resultant)													
Mean speed (mph)	7.6	7.9	9.0	9.9	9.1	8.1	7.3	7.4	7.6	7.6	7.7	7.6	8.1

V. State Weather Risk Profiles

Alabama

PHENOMENON	RISK	COMMENTS
Cold, blizzards	Low	
Heat, drought	Moderate	
Earthquake	Moderate	Primarily Northeast area
Volcano	Low	None reported
Flood	Moderate	
Land sink, slide	Low	Some sinkholes reported
Hurricane	High	Baldwin and Mobile counties.
Tornado	High	All counties
Hail	Low	
Tsunami, tidal wave	Moderate	Southern coast only

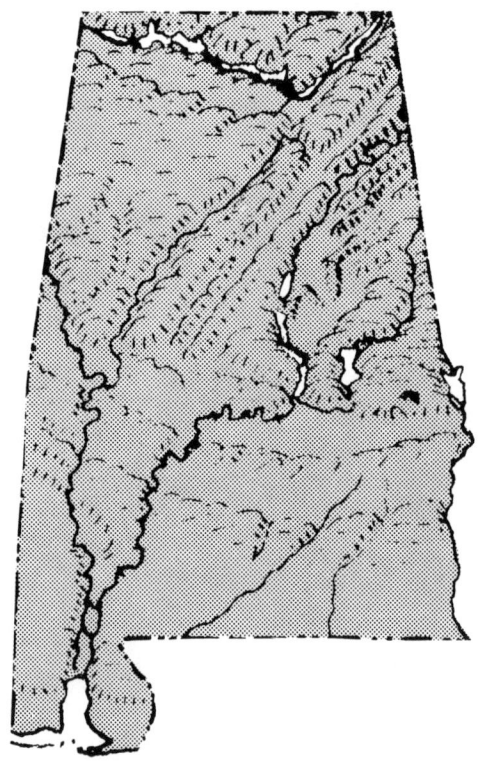

Alaska

PHENOMENON	RISK	COMMENTS
Cold, blizzards	High	Northern and interior areas
Heat, drought	Low	
Earthquake	High	City of Anchorage severly damaged 1964
Volcano	High	Active sites generally follow Aleutian chain
Flood	Low	
Land sink, slide	Low	
Hurricane	Low	
Tornado	Low	
Hail	Low	
Tsunami, tidal wave	High	Often associated with earthquakes-coastal zone

Arizona		
PHENOMENON	**RISK**	**COMMENTS**
Cold, blizzards	Moderate	Nothern area, higher elevations
Heat, drought	High	Southern area, desert
Earthquake	High	Most of state
Volcano	Moderate	None active, numerous old cones and craters
Flood	High	Flash floods
Land sink, slide	Low	
Hurricane	None	
Tornado	Moderate	
Hail	Low	
Tsunami, tidal wave	None	

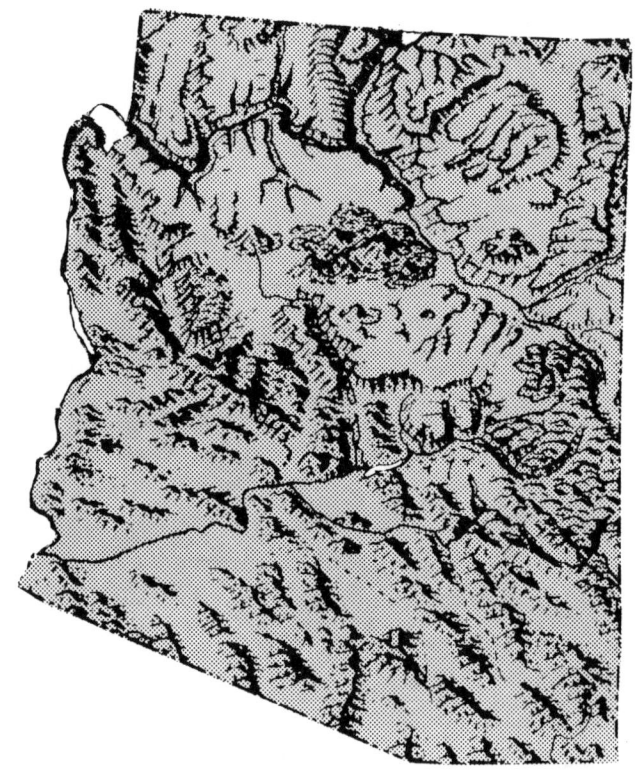

Arkansas

PHENOMENON	RISK	COMMENTS
Cold, blizzards	Low	
Heat, drought	High	
Earthquake	High	Northeast, along Mississippi River basin
Volcano	Low	
Flood	Moderate	
Land sink, slide	Low	
Hurricane	None	
Tornado	High	
Hail	Moderate	
Tsunami, tidal wave	None	

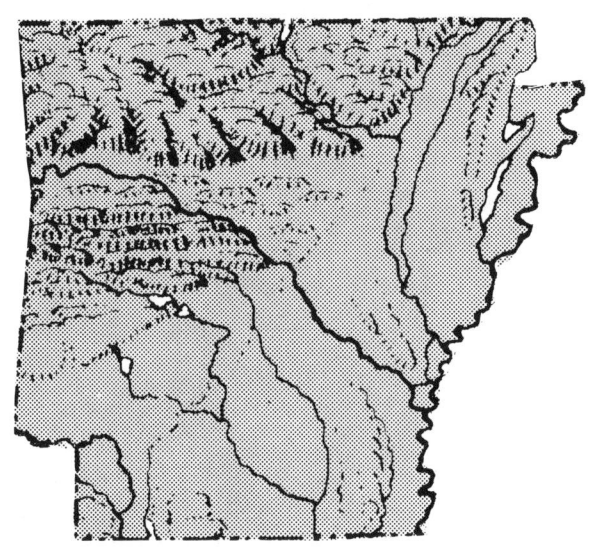

California

PHENOMENON	RISK	COMMENTS
Cold, blizzards	Moderate	Higher elevations, Sierras
Heat, drought	High	Central valley, southern desert
Earthquake	High	Numerous faults, major recent activity
Volcano	High	Two active sites, numerous old sites
Flood	Moderate	
Land sink, slide	High	Coastal range
Hurricane	None	Heavy rains in south may result from Pacific storms
Tornado	Low	
Hail	Low	
Tsunami, tidal wave	High	Low areas along coast

Colorado

PHENOMENON	RISK	COMMENTS
Cold, blizzards	High	
Heat, drought	High	
Earthquake	Low	
Volcano	Moderate	Old lava flows visible SW sector
Flood	Low	
Land sink, slide	Low	
Hurricane	None	
Tornado	Moderate	
Hail	High	Wheat crop suffers annual losses in Eastern plains
Tsunami, tidal wave	None	

Connecticut

PHENOMENON	RISK	COMMENTS
Cold, blizzards	Low	
Heat, drought	Low	
Earthquake	Moderate	Northeast corner
Volcano	Low	None reported
Flood	High	Conn. River valley
Land sink, slide	Low	
Hurricane	High	Southern coast
Tornado	Low	
Hail	Low	
Tsunami, tidal wave	Moderate	Low areas along coast

Delaware		
PHENOMENON	**RISK**	**COMMENTS**
Cold, blizzards	Low	
Heat, drought	Low	
Earthquake	Low	History nil
Volcano	Low	None reported
Flood	Low	
Land sink, slide	Low	
Hurricane	High	Coastal zone
Tornado	Low	
Hail	Low	
Tsunami, tidal wave	Moderate	Low areas along shore

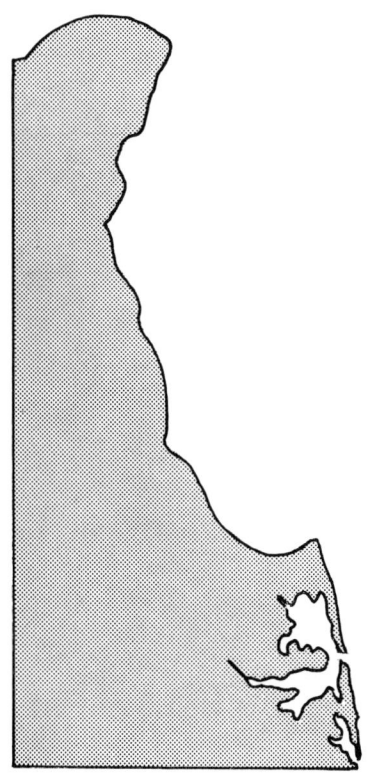

Florida

PHENOMENON	RISK	COMMENTS
Cold, blizzards	Low	
Heat, drought	Low	
Earthquake	Low	Risk rated nil over most of state
Volcano	Low	None reported
Flood	High	Areas throughout state
Land sink, slide	Low	Sinkholes reported
Hurricane	High	Extensive coastline, history of many storms
Tornado	High	Throughout state
Hail	Low	
Tsunami, tidal wave	Moderate	Coastal areas

Georgia

PHENOMENON	RISK	COMMENTS
Cold, blizzards	Low	
Heat, drought	Moderate	
Earthquake	Moderate	Northern counties and Savannah River basin
Volcano	Low	None reported
Flood	Low	
Land sink, slide	Low	
Hurricane	High	Coastal zone
Tornado	High	All counties
Hail	Low	
Tsunami, tidal wave	Moderate	Low coastal areas

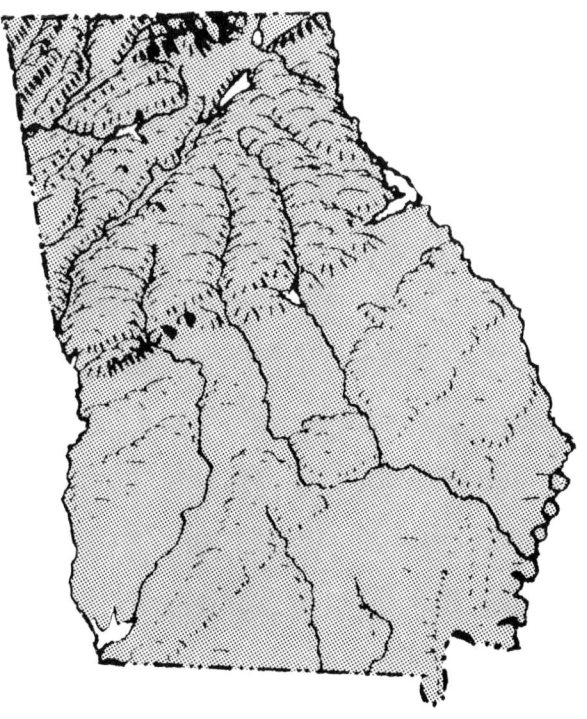

Hawaii

PHENOMENON	RISK	COMMENTS
Cold, blizzards	Low	
Heat, drought	Low	
Earthquake	High	
Volcano	High	Active sites plus history of eruptions
Flood	Low	
Land sink, slide	Low	
Hurricane	High	Occasional damage from Pacific typhoon
Tornado	Low	
Hail	Low	
Tsunami, tidal wave	High	Low coastal zones

Idaho

PHENOMENON	RISK	COMMENTS
Cold, blizzards	High	
Heat, drought	High	
Earthquake	High	Major risk Southeast moderate risk elsewhere
Volcano	Moderate	Old lava flows; received ash from Mt. St. Helens
Flood	Low	
Land sink, slide	Low	
Hurricane	Low	
Tornado	Low	
Hail	High	Southern Valley
Tsunami, tidal wave	Low	

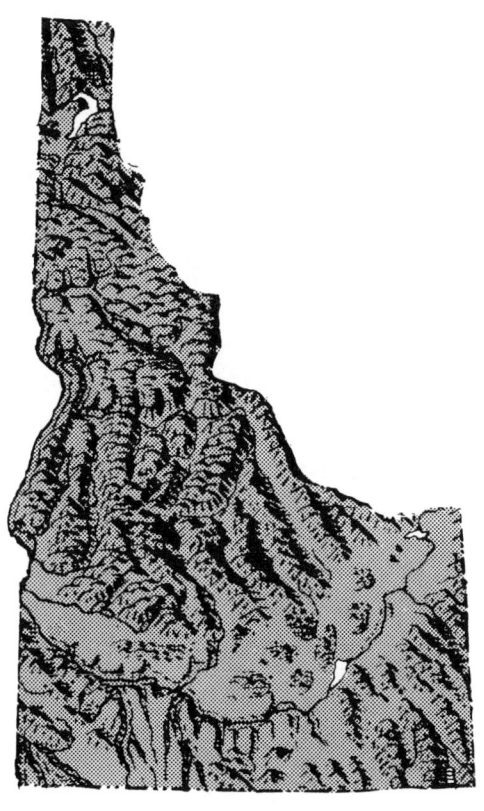

Illinois

PHENOMENON	RISK	COMMENTS
Cold, blizzards	Moderate	
Heat, drought	Moderate	
Earthquake	High	Southern counties
Volcano	Low	
Flood	High	Major river basins
Land sink, slide	High	
Hurricane	Low	
Tornado	High	All counties
Hail	Moderate	
Tsunami, tidal wave	Low	

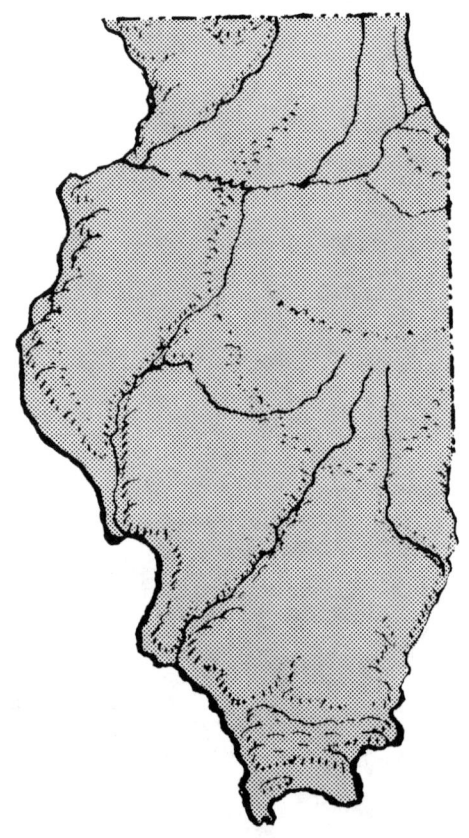

Indiana

PHENOMENON	RISK	COMMENTS
Cold, blizzards	Moderate	
Heat, drought	Moderate	
Earthquake	Moderate	Southern counties
Volcano	Low	None reported
Flood	Moderate	River Bsin
Land sink, slide	Low	
Hurricane	Low	
Tornado	High	All counties
Hail	Moderate	
Tsunami, tidal wave	Low	

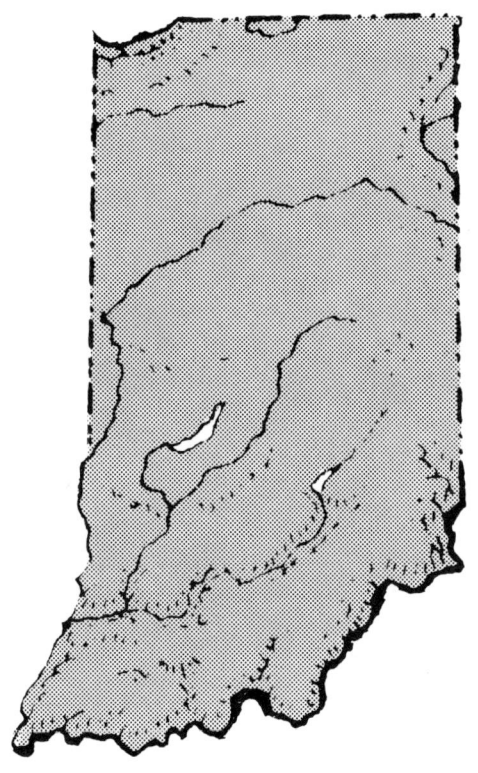

Iowa

PHENOMENON	RISK	COMMENTS
Cold, blizzards	Moderate	All counties
Heat, drought	High	All counties
Earthquake	Low	
Volcano	Low	
Flood	High	River basin
Land sink, slide	Low	
Hurricane	Low	
Tornado	High	All counties
Hail	High	All counties
Tsunami, tidal wave	Low	

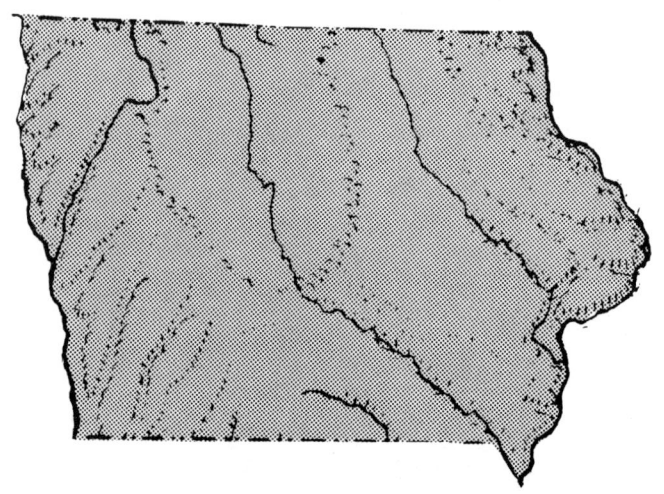

Kansas

PHENOMENON	RISK	COMMENTS
Cold, blizzards	Moderate	All counties
Heat, drought	High	All counties
Earthquake	Moderate	East-central counties
Volcano	Low	
Flood	Moderate	River basins
Land sink, slide	Low	
Hurricane	Low	
Tornado	High	All counties
Hail	High	All counties
Tsunami, tidal wave	Low	

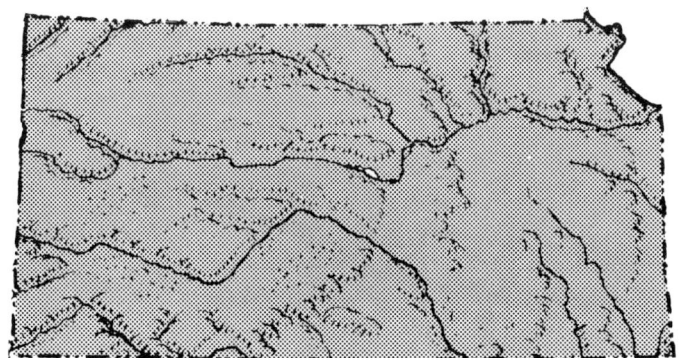

Kentucky

PHENOMENON	RISK	COMMENTS
Cold, blizzards	Moderate	
Heat, drought	Moderate	
Earthquake	High	High risk Southwest, 1980 quake centered central Kentucky, 5.1 Richter
Volcano	Low	
Flood	Low	
Land sink, slide	Low	
Hurricane	Low	
Tornado	Moderate	
Hail	Moderate	
Tsunami, tidal wave	Low	

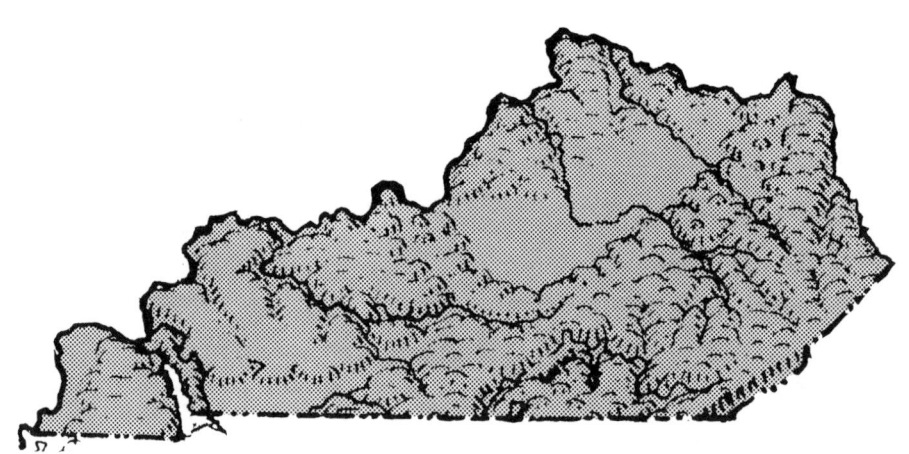

Louisiana

PHENOMENON	RISK	COMMENTS
Cold, blizzards	Low	
Heat, drought	Moderate	
Earthquake	Low	
Volcano	Low	
Flood	High	Major river basins
Land sink, slide	Low	
Hurricane	High	Coastal zones, history of damage
Tornado	Moderate	All counties
Hail	Low	
Tsunami, tidal wave	Moderate	Low coastal areas

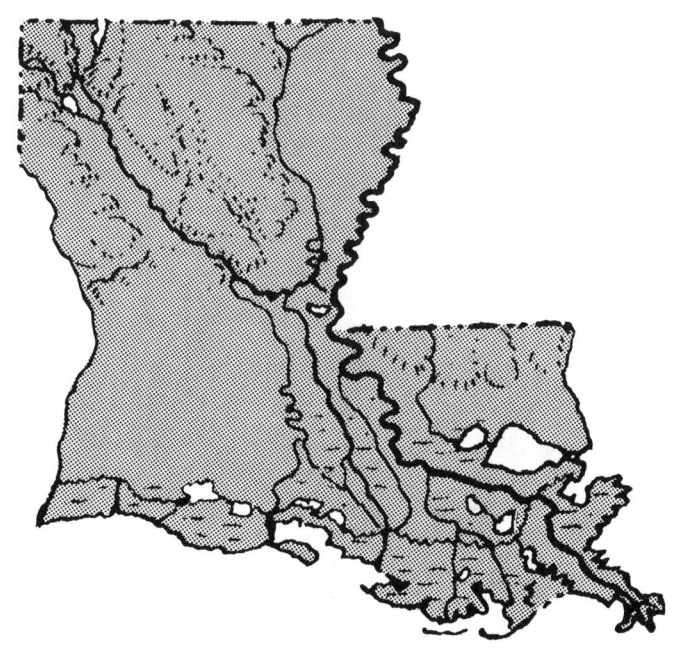

Maine		
PHENOMENON	**RISK**	**COMMENTS**
Cold, blizzards	Moderate	North, interior
Heat, drought	Low	
Earthquake	Moderate	Major risk north, moderate risk west
Volcano	Low	None reported
Flood	High	River basins
Land sink, slide	Low	
Hurricane	High	Coastal zone
Tornado	Low	
Hail	Low	
Tsunami, tidal wave	Moderate	Low coastal areas

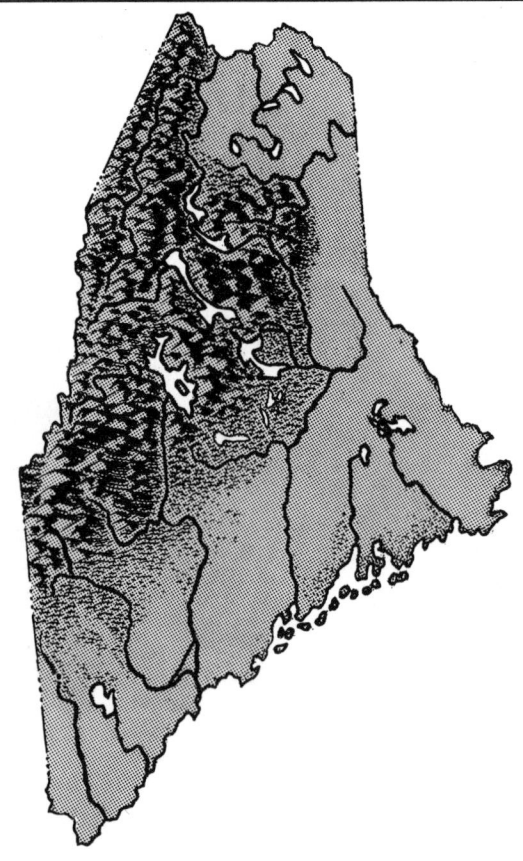

Maryland

PHENOMENON	RISK	COMMENTS
Cold, blizzards	Moderate	
Heat, drought	Low	
Earthquake	Moderate	Western highlands
Volcano	Low	None reported
Flood	Low	
Land sink, slide	Low	
Hurricane	High	Eastern shore
Tornado	Low	
Hail	Low	
Tsunami, tidal wave	Moderate	Low coastal areas

Massachusetts

PHENOMENON	RISK	COMMENTS
Cold, blizzards	Low	
Heat, drought	Low	
Earthquake	High	High risk eastern area, moderate risk central
Volcano	Low	None reported
Flood	High	River basins
Land sink, slide	Low	
Hurricane	High	Coastal zones, Cape Cod
Tornado	Low	
Hail	Low	
Tsunami, tidal wave	Moderate	Low coastal areas

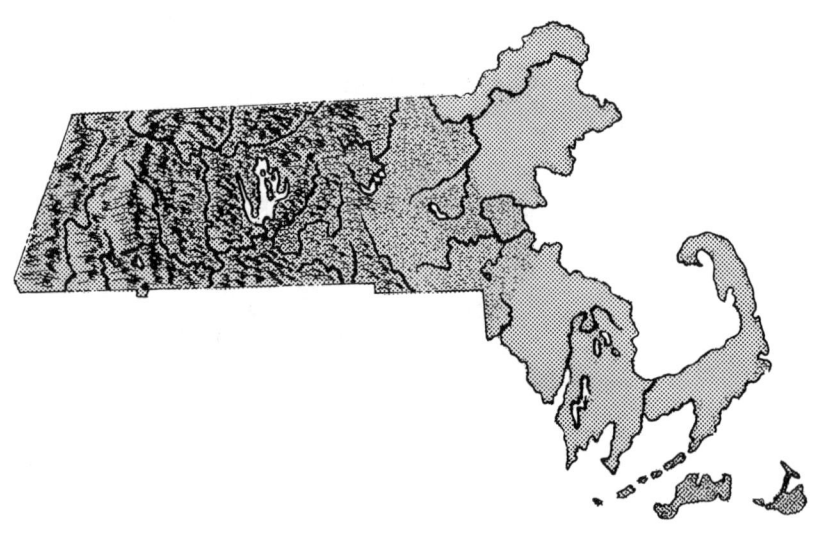

Michigan

PHENOMENON	RISK	COMMENTS
Cold, blizzards	High	Upper peninsula
Heat, drought	Moderate	
Earthquake	Low	
Volcano	Low	None reported
Flood	Moderate	
Land sink, slide	Low	
Hurricane	Low	
Tornado	Moderate	
Hail	Moderate	
Tsunami, tidal wave	Low	

Minnesota

PHENOMENON	RISK	COMMENTS
Cold, blizzards	High	All counties
Heat, drought	Moderate	
Earthquake	Low	
Volcano	Low	
Flood	Moderate	Major river basins
Land sink, slide	Moderate	
Hurricane	Low	
Tornado	High	
Hail	Moderate	
Tsunami, tidal wave	Low	

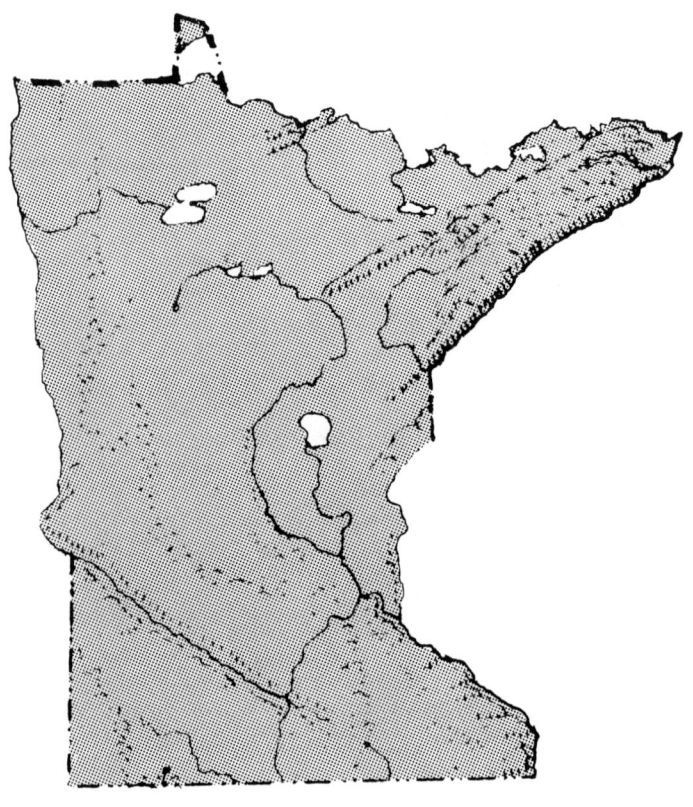

Mississippi

PHENOMENON	RISK	COMMENTS
Cold, blizzards	Low	
Heat, drought	Moderate	
Earthquake	Moderate	Northwest
Volcano	Low	None reported
Flood	Moderate	River basins
Land sink, slide	Low	
Hurricane	High	Coastal zone, history of heavy damage
Tornado	High	All counties
Hail	Low	
Tsunami, tidal wave	Moderate	Low coastal areas

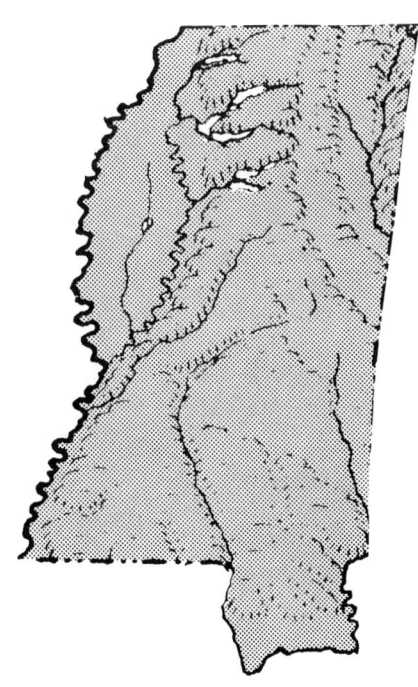

Missouri

PHENOMENON	RISK	COMMENTS
Cold, blizzards	Moderate	
Heat, drought	High	
Earthquake	High	Southeast corner, history of major quake
Volcano	Low	None reported
Flood	Moderate	
Land sink, slide	Moderate	
Hurricane	Low	
Tornado	High	
Hail	Moderate	
Tsunami, tidal wave	Low	

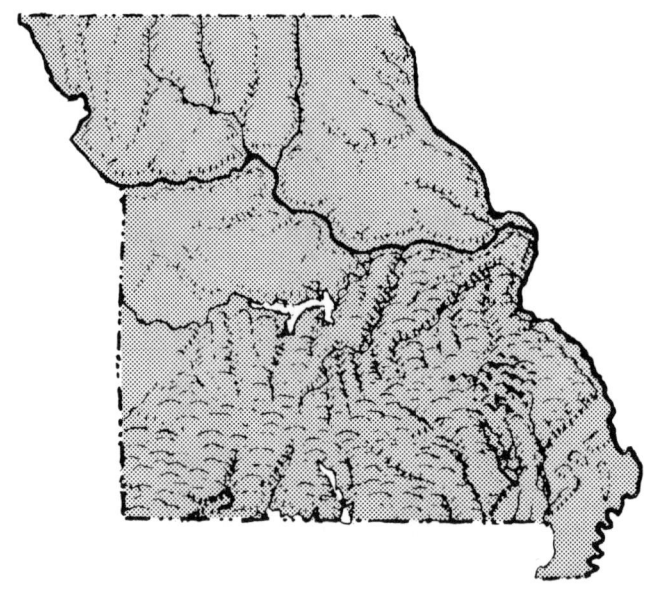

Montana

PHENOMENON	RISK	COMMENTS
Cold, blizzards	High	All counties
Heat, drought	Moderate	
Earthquake	High	Southwest area
Volcano	Moderate	Southwest area
Flood	Moderate	
Land sink, slide	Low	
Hurricane	Low	
Tornado	Moderate	
Hail	Moderate	
Tsunami, tidal wave	Low	

Nebraska

PHENOMENON	RISK	COMMENTS
Cold, blizzards	Moderate	
Heat, drought	High	
Earthquake	Moderate	Southeast corner
Volcano	Low	None reported
Flood	Low	
Land sink, slide	Low	
Hurricane	Low	
Tornado	High	All counties
Hail	High	All counties
Tsunami, tidal wave	Low	

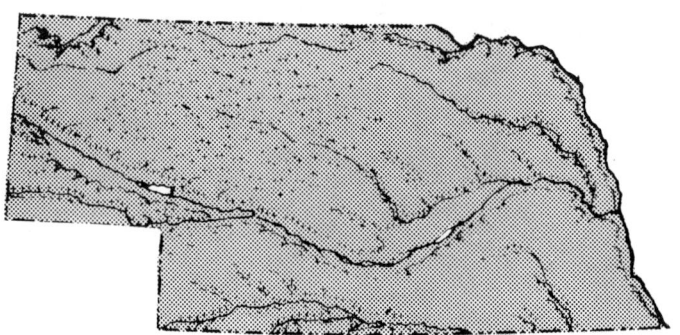

Nevada

PHENOMENON	RISK	COMMENTS
Cold, blizzards	High	
Heat, drought	High	
Earthquake	High	Western area-high risk; East-moderate
Volcano	Moderate	No active sites
Flood	High	Flash flooding
Land sink, slide	Low	
Hurricane	Low	
Tornado	Low	
Hail		
Tsunami, tidal wave	Low	

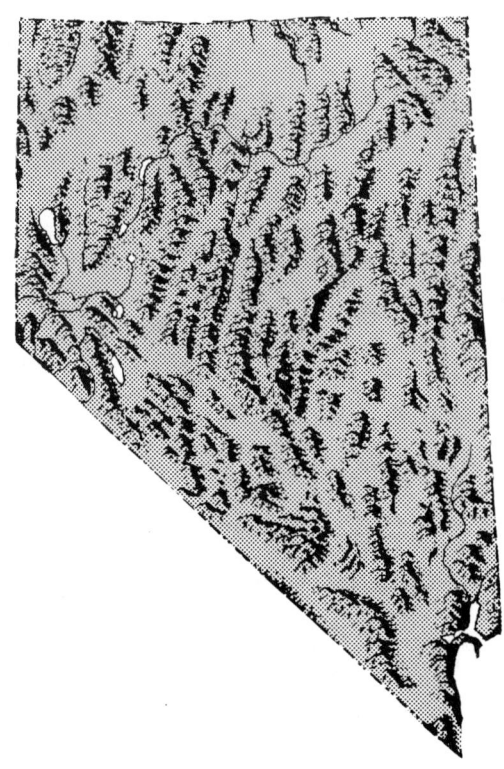

New Hampshire

PHENOMENON	RISK	COMMENTS
Cold, blizzards	Moderate	North interior
Heat, drought	Low	
Earthquake	Moderate	Greater risk southeast
Volcano	Low	
Flood	High	River basin
Land sink, slide	Low	
Hurricane	High	Coastal zone
Tornado	Low	
Hail	Low	
Tsunami, tidal wave	Moderate	Low coastal areas

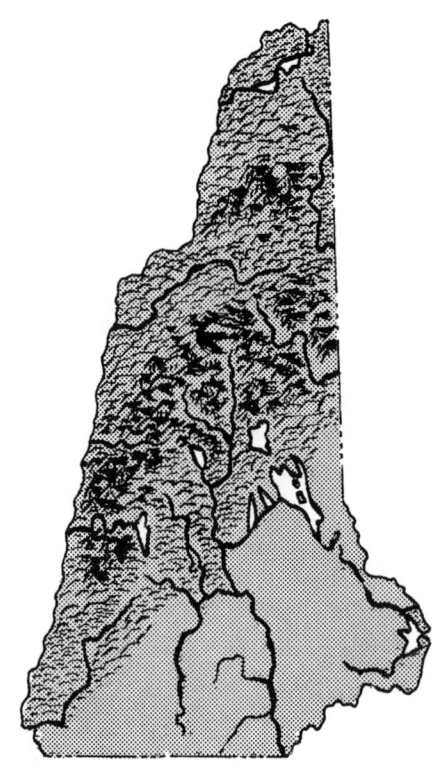

New Jersey

PHENOMENON	RISK	COMMENTS
Cold, blizzards	Low	
Heat, drought	Low	
Earthquake	Low	
Volcano	Low	
Flood	High	
Land sink, slide	Low	
Hurricane	High	Coastal zone
Tornado	Low	
Hail	Low	
Tsunami, tidal wave	Moderate	Low coastal areas

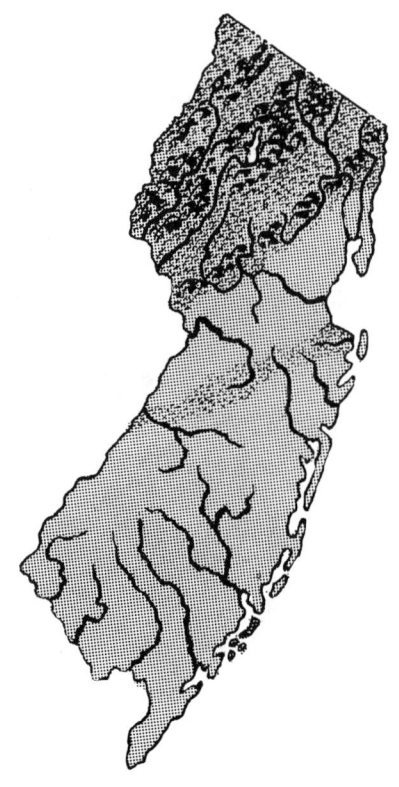

New Mexico

PHENOMENON	RISK	COMMENTS
Cold, blizzards	High	North, high elevations
Heat, drought	Moderate	Southern desert
Earthquake	Moderate	Western counties
Volcano	Moderate	No active sites; numerous craters, cones, lava flows
Flood	Low	
Land sink, slide	Low	
Hurricane	Low	
Tornado	Moderate	
Hail	High	
Tsunami, tidal wave	Low	

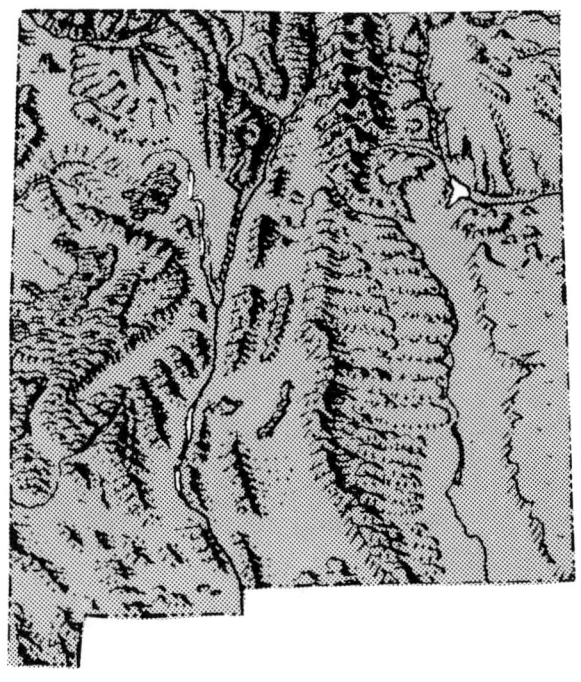

New York

PHENOMENON	RISK	COMMENTS
Cold, blizzards	High	St. Lawrence Valley, northwest and mountains
Heat, drought	Low	
Earthquake	High	High risk northwest; moderate central area
Volcano	Low	None reported
Flood	Moderate	River basins
Land sink, slide	High	
Hurricane	High	Coastal zones, Long Island
Tornado	Moderate	
Hail	Low	
Tsunami, tidal wave	Moderate	Low coastal areas

North Carolina

PHENOMENON	RISK	COMMENTS
Cold, blizzards	Low	
Heat, drought	Low	
Earthquake	Moderate	Western counties
Volcano	Low	
Flood	Low	
Land sink, slide	Low	
Hurricane	High	Coastal zones
Tornado	Moderate	
Hail	Low	
Tsunami, tidal wave	Moderate	Low coastal areas

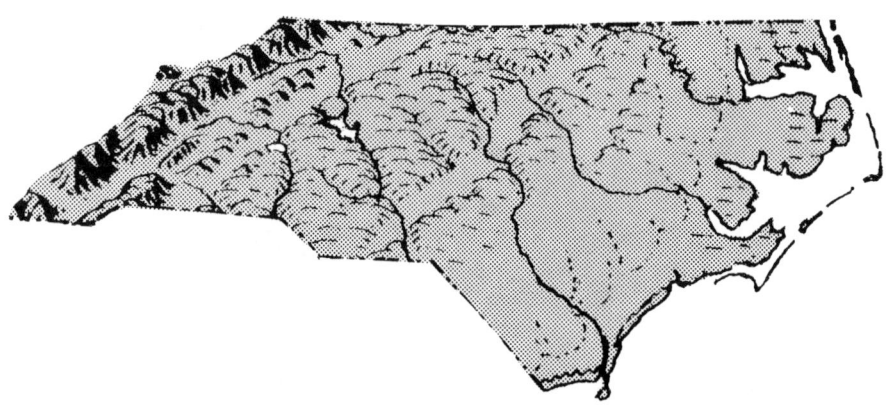

North Dakota

PHENOMENON	RISK	COMMENTS
Cold, blizzards	High	All counties
Heat, drought	High	All counties
Earthquake	Low	
Volcano	Low	
Flood	High	River basins
Land sink, slide	Low	
Hurricane	Low	
Tornado	Low	
Hail	Moderate	
Tsunami, tidal wave	Low	

Ohio

PHENOMENON	RISK	COMMENTS
Cold, blizzards	Moderate	
Heat, drought	Moderate	
Earthquake	Moderate	Southwest sector
Volcano	Low	
Flood	Low	
Land sink, slide	High	
Hurricane	Low	
Tornado	Moderate	
Hail	Moderate	
Tsunami, tidal wave	Low	

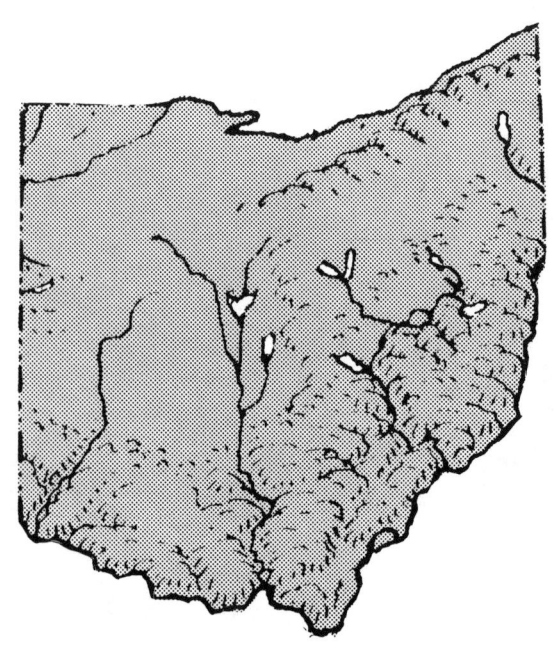

Oklahoma

PHENOMENON	RISK	COMMENTS
Cold, blizzards	Low	
Heat, drought	High	All counties
Earthquake	Moderate	North central area
Volcano	Low	
Flood	High	River basins
Land sink, slide	Low	
Hurricane	Low	
Tornado	High	All counties
Hail	High	All counties
Tsunami, tidal wave	Low	

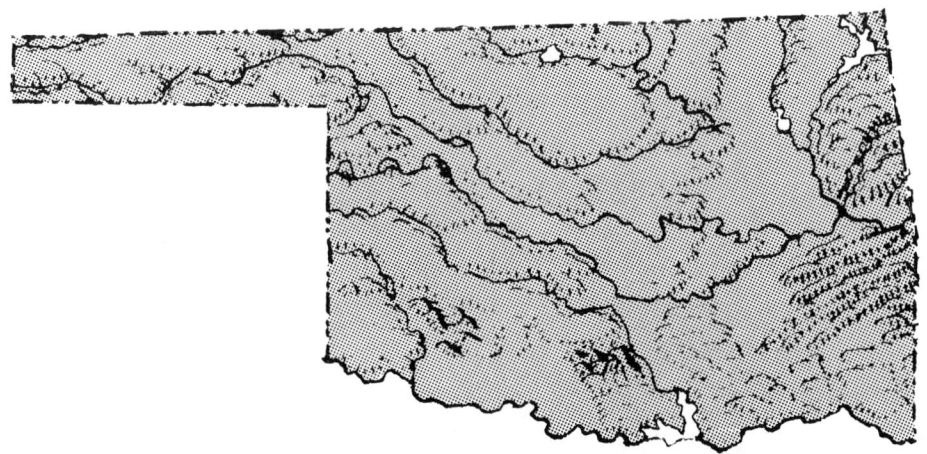

Oregon

PHENOMENON	RISK	COMMENTS
Cold, blizzards	High	
Heat, drought	High	Eastern counties
Earthquake	Moderate	Recent quakes centered Mt. Hood
Volcano	High	Received ash from Mt. St. Helens, several inactive cones
Flood	Low	
Land sink, slide	Low	
Hurricane	Low	
Tornado	Low	
Hail	Low	
Tsunami, tidal wave	High	Low areas along coast

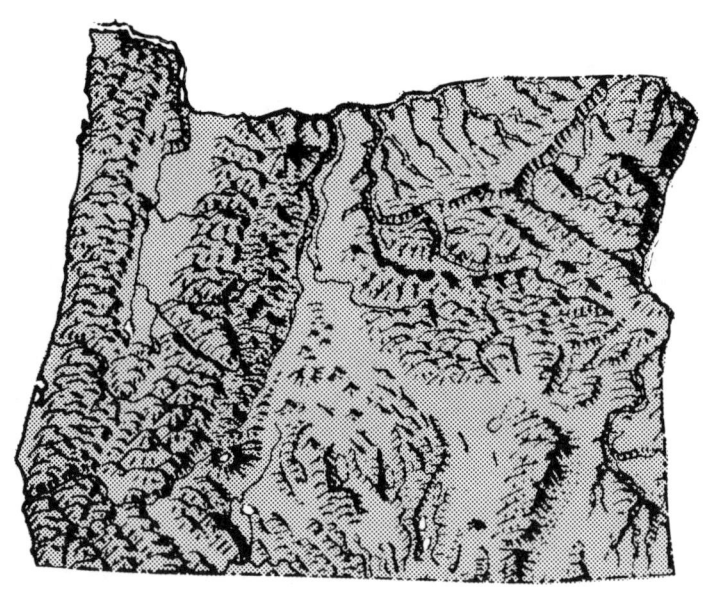

Pennsylvania

PHENOMENON	RISK	COMMENTS
Cold, blizzards	Moderate	
Heat, drought	Low	
Earthquake	Low	
Volcano	Low	
Flood	Moderate	
Land sink, slide	High	
Hurricane	Low	
Tornado	Moderate	
Hail	Low	
Tsunami, tidal wave	Low	

Rhode Island

PHENOMENON	RISK	COMMENTS
Cold, blizzards	Low	
Heat, drought	Low	
Earthquake	Moderate	
Volcano	Low	
Flood	Moderate	
Land sink, slide	Low	
Hurricane	High	Southern coastal zone
Tornado	Low	
Hail	Low	
Tsunami, tidal wave	Moderate	

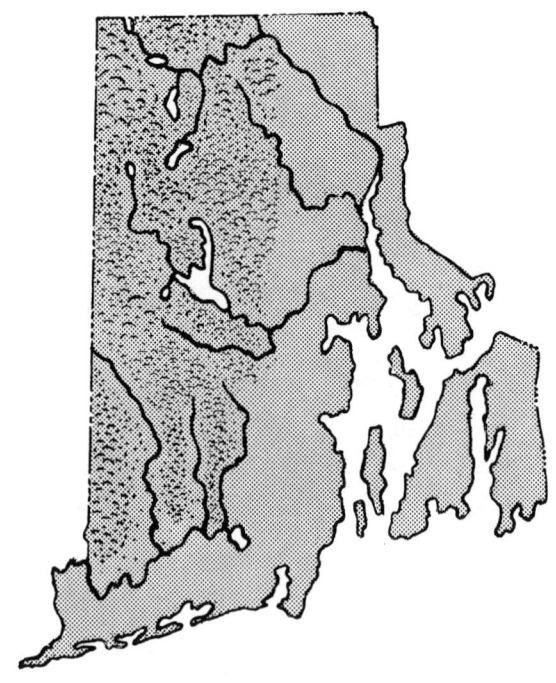

South Carolina		
PHENOMENON	**RISK**	**COMMENTS**
Cold, blizzards	Low	
Heat, drought	Low	
Earthquake	High	High risk southeast, moderate elsewhere
Volcano	Low	
Flood	Low	
Land sink, slide	Low	
Hurricane	High	Coastal zone, recent history of damage
Tornado	Moderate	All counties
Hail	Low	
Tsunami, tidal wave	Moderate	Low coastal areas

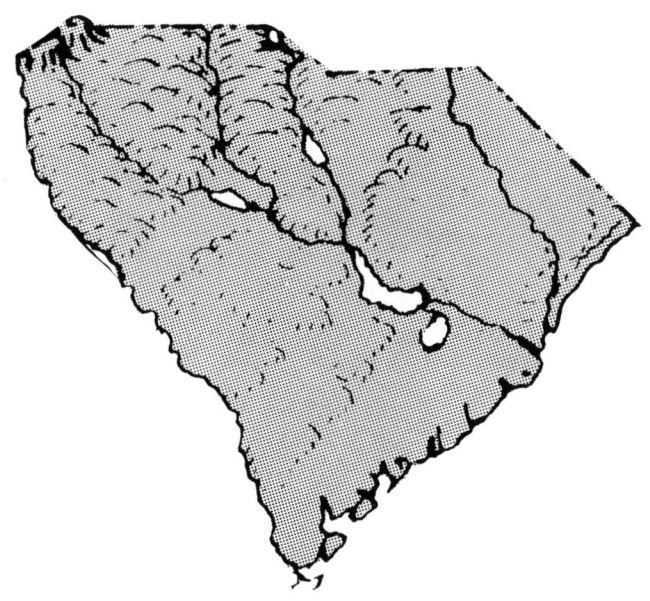

South Dakota

PHENOMENON	RISK	COMMENTS
Cold, blizzards	High	All counties
Heat, drought	High	All counties
Earthquake	Low	
Volcano	Low	
Flood	Moderate	
Land sink, slide	Low	
Hurricane	Low	
Tornado	High	All counties
Hail	Moderate	
Tsunami, tidal wave	Low	

Tennessee

PHENOMENON	RISK	COMMENTS
Cold, blizzards	Low	
Heat, drought	Moderate	
Earthquake	High	High risk west, moderate east
Volcano	Low	
Flood	Low	
Land sink, slide	Low	
Hurricane	Low	
Tornado	Moderate	
Hail	Moderate	
Tsunami, tidal wave	Low	

Texas

PHENOMENON	RISK	COMMENTS
Cold, blizzards	Low	
Heat, drought	High	Destructive heat wave 1980
Earthquake	Moderate	Minimal risk except Big Bend area in southwest
Volcano	Moderate	
Flood	High	River basins
Land sink, slide	Moderate	
Hurricane	High	Gulf coastal zone
Tornado	High	All areas
Hail	High	Greatest risk northwest
Tsunami, tidal wave	Moderate	Low coastal areas

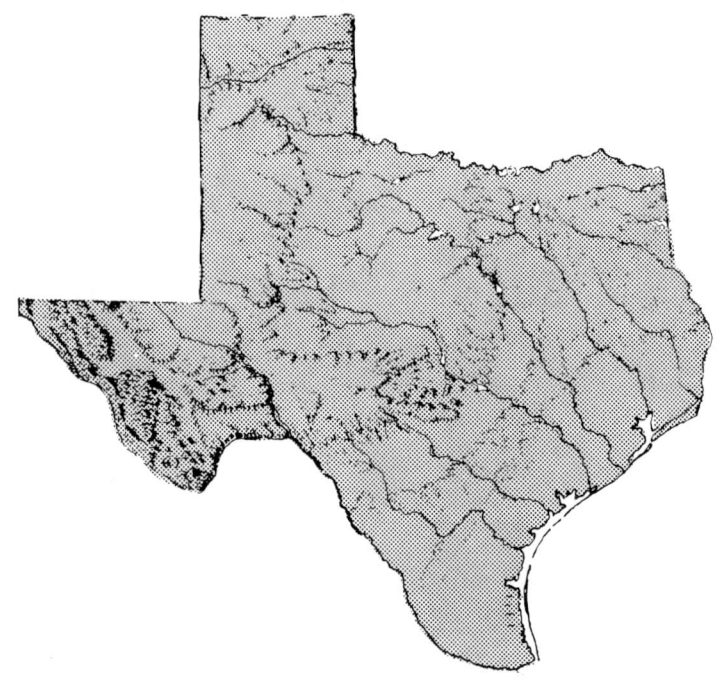

Utah		
PHENOMENON	**RISK**	**COMMENTS**
Cold, blizzards	High	Higher elevations
Heat, drought	Moderate	
Earthquake	High	High risk west, minimal east
Volcano	Moderate	
Flood	Moderate	
Land sink, slide	Low	
Hurricane	Low	
Tornado	Low	
Hail	High	
Tsunami, tidal wave	Low	

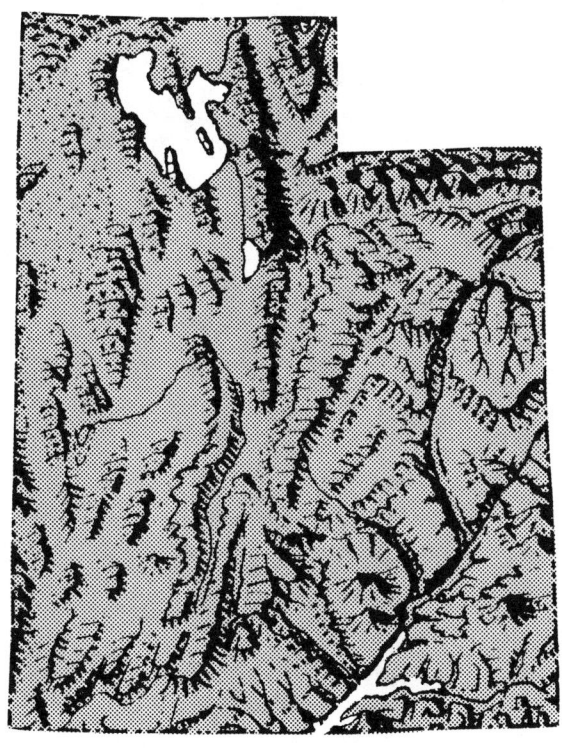

Vermont

PHENOMENON	RISK	COMMENTS
Cold, blizzards	High	
Heat, drought	Low	
Earthquake	Moderate	
Volcano	Low	
Flood	High	River basins
Land sink, slide	Low	
Hurricane	Low	
Tornado	Low	
Hail	Low	
Tsunami, tidal wave	Low	

Virginia

PHENOMENON	RISK	COMMENTS
Cold, blizzards	Low	
Heat, drought	Low	
Earthquake	Moderate	Central and western areas
Volcano	Low	
Flood	High	River basins
Land sink, slide	Low	
Hurricane	High	Coastal zone
Tornado	Moderate	
Hail	Low	
Tsunami, tidal wave	Moderate	Low coastal areas

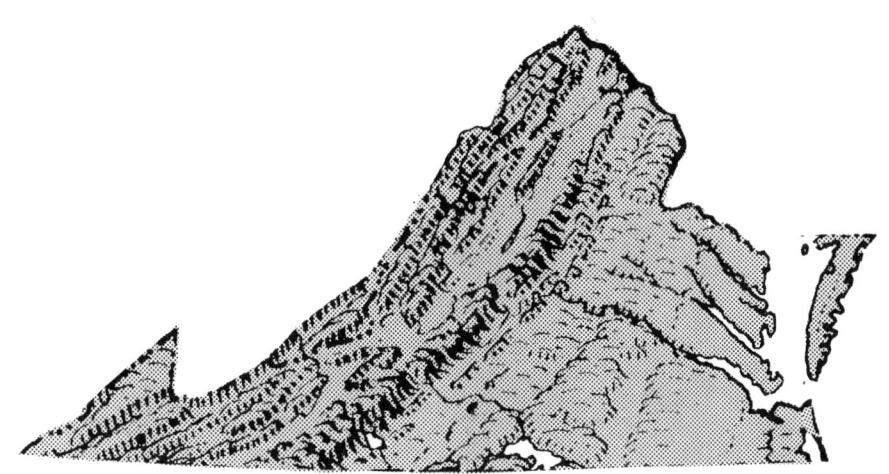

Washington

PHENOMENON	RISK	COMMENTS
Cold, blizzards	Moderate	High elevations
Heat, drought	High	Eastern area
Earthquake	High	Highest risk Puget Sound, moderate all counties
Volcano	High	Mt. St. Helens major eruptions 1980
Flood	Low	
Land sink, slide	Low	
Hurricane	Low	
Tornado	Low	
Hail	Low	
Tsunami, tidal wave	High	Low coastal areas

West Virginia

PHENOMENON	RISK	COMMENTS
Cold, blizzards	Moderate	
Heat, drought	Low	
Earthquake	Moderate	Southeast only
Volcano	Low	
Flood	Low	
Land sink, slide	Low	
Hurricane	Low	
Tornado	Low	
Hail	Low	
Tsunami, tidal wave	Low	

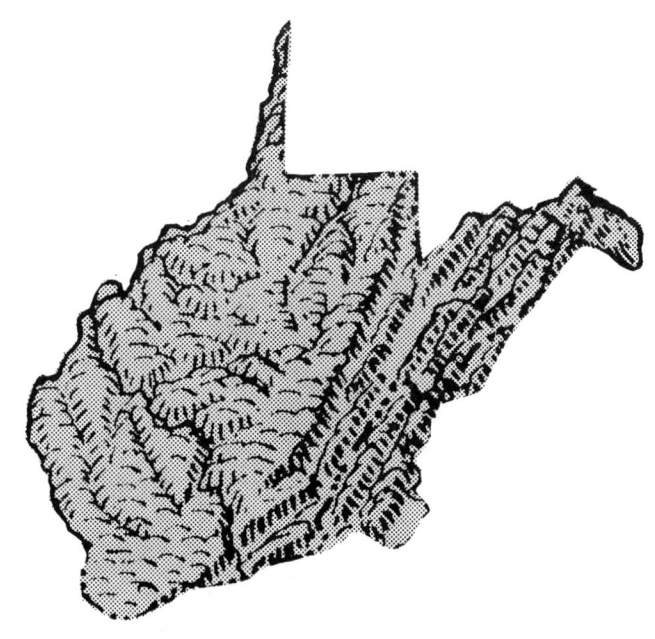

Wisconsin

PHENOMENON	RISK	COMMENTS
Cold, blizzards	High	All counties
Heat, drought	Moderate	
Earthquake	Low	
Volcano	Low	
Flood	Low	
Land sink, slide	Low	
Hurricane	Low	
Tornado	High	All counties
Hail	Moderate	
Tsunami, tidal wave	Low	

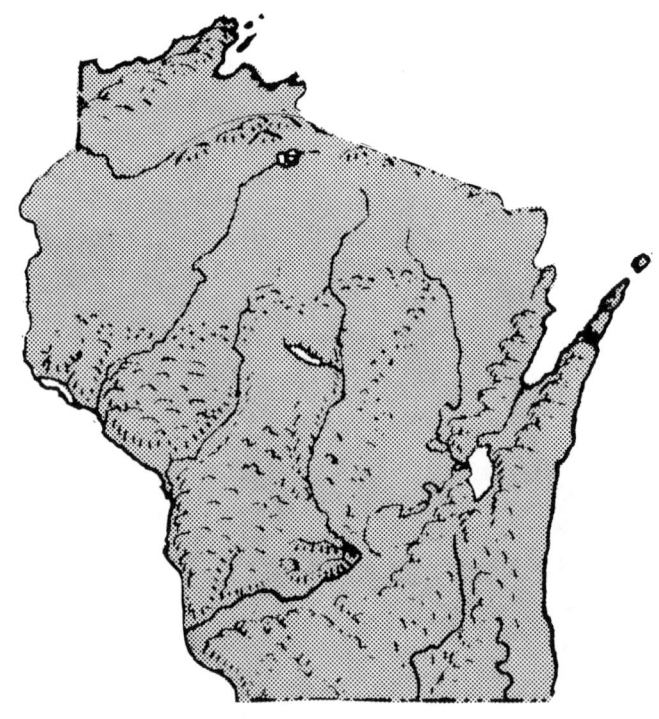

Wyoming

PHENOMENON	RISK	COMMENTS
Cold, blizzards	High	All counties
Heat, drought	Moderate	
Earthquake	High	Western counties
Volcano	Moderate	No active sites
Flood	Low	
Land sink, slide	Low	
Hurricane	Low	
Tornado	Moderate	
Hail	High	
Tsunami, tidal wave	Low	

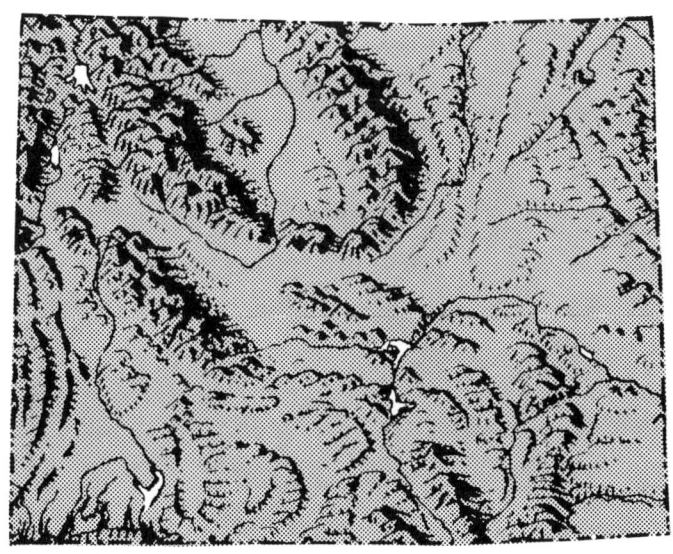

VI. Weather Summaries for Principal Cities of the World

Cities included in this chapter were selected largely on the basis of population. When possible, we included cities in diverse areas of each country to show the effect of terrain, elevation and bodies of water on weather patterns.

Most summaries are based on 30-year periods of observation ending in 1987. In a few instances, weather stations at large population centers may have been moved, and the period of observation will be less than 30 years. In no instance, however, are data presented for less than 10 years.

Temperature data in this chapter have been rounded to make the tables easier to read. Both U.S. Customary System and metric system are included.

SHKODER   Albania

	JAN	FEB	MAR	APR	MAY	JUN	JUL	AUG	SEP	OCT	NOV	DEC	YEAR
TEMPERATURE													
Daily Average Min.°C......................2	1	5	9	13	17	19	19	16	11	8	4	10
Daily Average Min.°F 35	35	41	48	55	62	66	66	60	52	47	40	51
Daily Average Max.°C 9	10	14	18	23	27	31	31	27	21	15	11	20
Daily Average Max.°F...................47	49	56	65	73	81	87	88	80	70	59	52	68
Monthly Average °C........................5	6	9	14	18	22	25	25	21	16	11	7	15
Monthly Average °F 41	43	49	57	65	72	77	77	70	60	52	45	59
RELATIVE HUMIDITY (%)	77	77	76	75	73	66	61	59	68	77	85	80	73
PRECIPITATION													
Monthly Average mm 259	224	189	183	124	71	44	69	181	207	285	305	2141.0
Monthly Average Inches 10.2	8.8	7.4	7.2	4.8	2.7	1.7	2.7	7.1	8.1	11.2	12.0	83.9
Days of 1mm or More 11	11	10	9	6	6	3	4	7	8	13	15	103

TIRANA   Albania

	JAN	FEB	MAR	APR	MAY	JUN	JUL	AUG	SEP	OCT	NOV	DEC	YEAR
TEMPERATURE													
Daily Average Min.°C......................2	2	5	8	12	16	17	17	14	10	8	5	10
Daily Average Min.°F 36	36	41	47	53	60	63	62	58	50	47	40	49
Daily Average Max.°C 12	12	15	18	23	28	31	31	27	23	17	14	21
Daily Average Max.°F...................53	54	59	65	74	82	87	89	81	73	63	56	70
Monthly Average °C........................6	8	10	13	18	22	24	24	20	16	12	8	15
Monthly Average °F 44	46	49	56	64	71	75	74	68	60	53	47	59
RELATIVE HUMIDITY (%)	58	54	53	54	56	49	42	39	45	49	63	63	52
PRECIPITATION													
Monthly Average mm 154	145	115	95	105	68	38	41	66	107	174	163	1271.0
Monthly Average Inches 6.0	5.7	4.5	3.7	4.1	2.6	1.4	1.6	2.5	4.2	6.8	6.4	49.5
Days of 1mm or More 12	9	8	10	8	7	4	4	5	6	11	15	99

VALONA   Albania

	JAN	FEB	MAR	APR	MAY	JUN	JUL	AUG	SEP	OCT	NOV	DEC	YEAR
TEMPERATURE													
Daily Average Min.°C......................6	6	8	10	14	17	19	19	16	14	11	8	12
Daily Average Min.°F 42	42	46	51	57	63	66	66	61	57	53	46	54
Daily Average Max.°C 13	14	16	19	23	27	30	30	27	23	19	15	21
Daily Average Max.°F...................56	56	60	66	74	81	85	87	81	74	66	59	70
Monthly Average °C........................9	10	11	15	19	22	24	24	22	18	14	11	17
Monthly Average °F 48	50	53	58	65	72	76	76	71	64	58	52	62
RELATIVE HUMIDITY (%)	56	54	57	55	56	51	48	46	50	54	62	60	54
PRECIPITATION													
Monthly Average mm 140	107	82	62	54	26	14	23	51	103	164	152	978.0
Monthly Average Inches 5.5	4.2	3.2	2.4	2.1	1.0	0.5	0.9	2.0	4.0	6.4	5.9	38.1
Days of 1mm or More 12	9	6	7	5	3	1	3	4	6	11	14	81

BECHAR

Algeria

	JAN	FEB	MAR	APR	MAY	JUN	JUL	AUG	SEP	OCT	NOV	DEC	YEAR
Elevation 772 m. (2532 ft.)					31°37'N—2°14'W								
TEMPERATURE													
Daily Average Min.°C	4	6	10	13	18	23	27	26	22	15	10	5	15
Daily Average Min.°F	39	43	50	56	65	73	80	79	71	59	49	40	59
Daily Average Max.°C	16	19	22	26	31	36	40	39	34	27	21	16	27
Daily Average Max.°F	61	65	72	78	87	97	104	102	93	81	70	61	81
Monthly Average °C	10	12	16	20	25	29	33	33	28	21	15	10	21
Monthly Average °F	50	54	60	67	76	85	92	91	83	70	59	50	70
RELATIVE HUMIDITY (%)	43	34	28	25	21	19	15	17	24	31	40	45	29
PRECIPITATION													
Monthly Average mm	9	7	9	13	5	8	0	4	7	12	11	12	97.0
Monthly Average Inches	0.3	0.2	0.3	0.5	0.1	0.3	0.0	0.1	0.2	0.4	0.4	0.4	3.2
Days of 1mm or More	1	1	1	1	1	0	0	0	1	1	1	1	9

CONSTANTINE

Algeria

	JAN	FEB	MAR	APR	MAY	JUN	JUL	AUG	SEP	OCT	NOV	DEC	YEAR
Elevation 694 m. (2276 ft.)					36°17'N—6°37'E								
TEMPERATURE													
Daily Average Min.°C	2	2	4	6	9	14	16	17	14	10	6	3	9
Daily Average Min.°F	36	35	39	43	49	56	61	62	58	50	42	37	47
Daily Average Max.°C	12	13	17	19	24	29	34	34	30	23	17	13	22
Daily Average Max.°F	53	56	63	66	76	85	93	93	85	73	63	56	72
Monthly Average °C	7	7	9	12	16	21	24	25	21	16	11	7	15
Monthly Average °F	44	45	48	53	61	70	75	77	69	60	52	45	58
RELATIVE HUMIDITY (%)	71	63	60	58	52	45	39	41	47	58	64	72	56
PRECIPITATION													
Monthly Average mm	90	65	69	38	36	18	7	7	32	50	28	90	530.0
Monthly Average Inches	3.5	2.5	2.7	1.4	1.4	0.7	0.2	0.2	1.2	1.9	1.1	3.5	20.3
Days of 1mm or More	10	10	10	6	4	2	1	1	4	7	5	9	69

EL GOLEA

Algeria

	JAN	FEB	MAR	APR	MAY	JUN	JUL	AUG	SEP	OCT	NOV	DEC	YEAR
Elevation 398 m. (1305 ft.)					30°34'N—2°52'E								
TEMPERATURE													
Daily Average Min.°C	3	5	9	13	18	23	26	25	22	15	9	5	15
Daily Average Min.°F	37	42	48	56	64	73	78	78	72	60	48	41	58
Daily Average Max.°C	17	20	24	28	33	39	41	41	36	29	23	17	29
Daily Average Max.°F	63	69	76	83	92	102	106	105	97	85	73	63	84
Monthly Average °C	10	12	16	20	26	31	33	33	29	22	15	10	21
Monthly Average °F	49	54	61	69	78	88	92	91	83	71	59	50	71
RELATIVE HUMIDITY (%)	44	34	29	25	22	19	18	17	27	32	38	45	29
PRECIPITATION													
Monthly Average mm	7	1	7	2	0	0	0	0	1	3	5	15	41.0
Monthly Average Inches	0.2	0.0	0.2	0.0	0.0	0.0	0.0	0.0	0.0	0.1	0.1	0.5	1.1
Days of 1mm or More	0	0	0	0	0	0	0	0	0	0	0	1	1

IN AMENAS
Algeria

Elevation 562 m. (1843 ft.) 28°5'N—9°30'E

	JAN	FEB	MAR	APR	MAY	JUN	JUL	AUG	SEP	OCT	NOV	DEC	YEAR
TEMPERATURE													
Monthly Average °C	10	13	16	23	27	32	32	31	29	23	16	11	22
Monthly Average °F	50	56	61	73	81	89	89	88	84	73	61	51	71
PRECIPITATION													
Monthly Average mm	2	1	6	3	1	0	0	1	0	6	1	4	25.0
Monthly Average Inches	0.0	0.0	0.2	0.1	0.0	0.0	0.0	0.0	0.0	0.2	0.0	0.1	0.6
Days of 1mm or More	0	0	0	0	0	0	0	0	0	0	0	0	0

TAMANRASSET
Algeria

Elevation 1378 m. (4520 ft.) 22°47'N—5°31'E

	JAN	FEB	MAR	APR	MAY	JUN	JUL	AUG	SEP	OCT	NOV	DEC	YEAR
TEMPERATURE													
Daily Average Min.°C	5	8	10	14	18	22	22	22	20	16	11	7	15
Daily Average Min.°F	41	46	51	58	65	71	72	71	68	61	52	44	58
Daily Average Max.°C	20	23	26	29	32	35	35	34	32	29	25	21	28
Daily Average Max.°F	68	73	78	84	90	94	94	93	90	84	77	69	83
Monthly Average °C	13	15	19	22	26	29	28	28	27	23	18	14	22
Monthly Average °F	55	60	66	72	79	84	83	83	80	73	64	57	71
RELATIVE HUMIDITY (%)	18	15	14	14	14	16	15	18	18	20	20	19	17
PRECIPITATION													
Monthly Average mm	0	7	1	3	6	9	5	11	8	5	4	3	62.0
Monthly Average Inches	0.0	0.2	0.0	0.1	0.2	0.3	0.1	0.4	0.3	0.1	0.1	0.1	1.9
Days of 1mm or More	0	0	0	0	0	0	1	1	1	0	0	0	3

LUANDA
Angola

Elevation 44 m. (144 ft.) 8°49'S—13°13'E

	JAN	FEB	MAR	APR	MAY	JUN	JUL	AUG	SEP	OCT	NOV	DEC	YEAR
TEMPERATURE													
Daily Average Min.°C	24	24	24	24	23	20	18	18	20	22	23	23	22
Daily Average Min.°F	74	75	76	75	73	68	65	65	67	71	74	74	71
Daily Average Max.°C	30	30	31	30	29	26	24	24	25	27	29	29	28
Daily Average Max.°F	85	87	87	86	83	78	74	74	77	81	83	84	82
Extreme Monthly Min.°C	21	21	21	21	18	15	14	14	17	18	20	19	14
Extreme Monthly Min.°F	69	70	70	70	64	59	58	58	62	65	68	67	58
Extreme Monthly Max.°C	33	35	35	34	36	32	29	28	29	32	37	34	36
Extreme Monthly Max.°F	91	95	95	94	97	89	85	83	84	89	98	94	98
Monthly Average °C	26	27	27	27	25	22	20	20	22	24	25	25	24
Monthly Average °F	79	80	81	80	77	71	69	69	71	75	77	78	76
RELATIVE HUMIDITY (%)	73	71	73	77	77	75	77	77	76	76	76	73	75
PRECIPITATION													
Monthly Average mm	42	30	120	150	35	0	0	0	3	9	41	27	457.0
Monthly Average Inches	1.6	1.1	4.7	5.9	1.3	0.0	0.0	0.0	0.1	0.3	1.6	1.0	17.6
Days of 1mm or More	2	3	6	8	0	0	0	0	0	1	4	2	26

LUBANGO

Angola

	Elevation 1763 m. (5783 ft.)				14°54'S—13°31'E								
	JAN	FEB	MAR	APR	MAY	JUN	JUL	AUG	SEP	OCT	NOV	DEC	YEAR
TEMPERATURE													
Daily Average Min.°C	13	13	13	13	10	7	8	11	13	13	13	13	12
Daily Average Min.°F	55	55	56	55	50	45	46	51	56	56	56	56	53
Daily Average Max.°C	25	24	24	25	25	24	24	26	28	28	26	25	25
Daily Average Max.°F	76	76	76	77	76	74	76	79	83	82	79	78	78
Monthly Average °C	19	19	19	19	18	15	16	18	20	20	20	19	18
Monthly Average °F	66	66	66	65	64	60	60	64	69	69	67	67	65
RELATIVE HUMIDITY (%)	59	54	63	53	34	25	22	19	21	37	49	52	41
PRECIPITATION													
Monthly Average mm	132	143	190	89	8	0	0	0	4	66	119	131	882.0
Monthly Average Inches	5.1	5.6	7.4	3.5	0.3	0.0	0.0	0.0	0.1	2.5	4.6	5.1	34.2
Days of 1mm or More	12	10	16	9	0	0	0	0	0	6	11	13	77

MAVINGA

Angola

	Elevation 1188 m. (3897 ft.)				15°50'S—20°21'E								
	JAN	FEB	MAR	APR	MAY	JUN	JUL	AUG	SEP	OCT	NOV	DEC	YEAR
TEMPERATURE													
Daily Average Min.°C	18	17	16	13	8	4	3	6	11	15	17	17	12
Daily Average Min.°F	64	63	61	55	46	39	38	42	51	59	62	62	53
Daily Average Max.°C	29	28	29	29	28	26	26	29	32	33	30	29	29
Daily Average Max.°F	84	83	84	84	82	78	79	84	90	92	86	85	84
Monthly Average °C	23	23	22	22	19	16	15	18	22	24	23	23	21
Monthly Average °F	73	73	72	71	66	60	59	65	72	76	74	74	70
RELATIVE HUMIDITY (%)	57	60	58	43	33	28	23	19	18	27	48	55	39
PRECIPITATION													
Monthly Average mm	204	183	142	39	4	0	0	0	2	32	88	150	844.0
Monthly Average Inches	8.0	7.2	5.5	1.5	0.1	0.0	0.0	0.0	0.0	1.2	3.4	5.9	32.8
Days of 1mm or More	15	14	11	4	0	0	0	0	0	3	10	13	70

BAHIA BLANCA

Argentina

	Elevation 29 m. (95 ft.)				38°43'S—62°16'W								
	JAN	FEB	MAR	APR	MAY	JUN	JUL	AUG	SEP	OCT	NOV	DEC	YEAR
TEMPERATURE													
Daily Average Min.°C	17	16	14	11	7	4	4	4	7	9	12	15	10
Daily Average Min.°F	62	60	57	51	45	39	39	40	44	48	54	59	50
Daily Average Max.°C	31	29	26	22	17	14	14	16	18	22	26	29	22
Daily Average Max.°F	88	84	79	71	63	57	57	60	65	71	78	85	72
Monthly Average °C	23	22	19	15	11	8	8	9	11	14	18	21	15
Monthly Average °F	74	72	66	58	52	46	46	48	53	58	65	70	59
RELATIVE HUMIDITY (%)	41	41	46	50	56	64	56	54	45	40	38	35	47
PRECIPITATION													
Monthly Average mm	59	67	90	64	36	29	29	22	44	67	59	66	632.0
Monthly Average Inches	2.3	2.6	3.5	2.5	1.4	1.1	1.1	0.8	1.7	2.6	2.3	2.5	24.4
Days of 1mm or More	6	4	6	5	4	3	4	3	4	7	6	6	58

BUENOS AIRES Argentina

		JAN	FEB	MAR	APR	MAY	JUN	JUL	AUG	SEP	OCT	NOV	DEC	YEAR
Elevation 25 m. (82 ft.)							34°35'S—58°29'W							
TEMPERATURE														
Daily Average Min.°C	17	17	16	12	8	5	6	6	8	10	13	16	11
Daily Average Min.°F	63	63	60	53	47	41	42	43	46	50	56	61	52
Daily Average Max.°C	29	28	26	22	18	14	14	16	17	21	24	28	21
Daily Average Max.°F	85	83	79	72	64	57	57	60	64	69	76	82	71
Extreme Monthly Min.°C	6	4	4	-2	-4	-5	-6	-3	-2	-2	2	4	-5
Extreme Monthly Min.°F	43	40	39	28	25	23	22	27	28	28	36	39	22
Extreme Monthly Max.°C	40	39	37	36	29	25	29	31	30	33	35	39	40
Extreme Monthly Max.°F	104	103	99	97	84	77	84	87	86	91	95	102	104
Monthly Average °C	24	23	21	18	14	11	11	12	14	17	20	23	17
Monthly Average °F	76	74	70	64	58	52	52	54	58	63	68	73	63
RELATIVE HUMIDITY (%)	61	63	69	71	74	78	79	74	68	65	60	62	69
PRECIPITATION														
Monthly Average mm	118	110	123	97	78	67	76	68	78	121	109	97	1142.0
Monthly Average Inches	4.6	4.3	4.8	3.8	3.0	2.6	2.9	2.6	3.0	4.7	4.2	3.8	44.3
Days of 1mm or More	7	5	6	6	5	5	5	5	5	7	6	6	68

CORDOBA Argentina

		JAN	FEB	MAR	APR	MAY	JUN	JUL	AUG	SEP	OCT	NOV	DEC	YEAR
Elevation 423 m. (1388 ft.)							31°22'S—64°15'W							
TEMPERATURE														
Daily Average Min.°C	16	16	14	11	7	3	3	4	7	11	13	16	10
Daily Average Min.°F	61	60	58	51	44	38	38	40	45	51	56	60	50
Daily Average Max.°C	31	30	28	24	21	18	18	21	23	25	28	30	25
Daily Average Max.°F	88	86	82	75	69	64	65	69	73	77	82	86	76
Monthly Average °C	23	22	20	17	14	10	11	12	15	18	21	23	17
Monthly Average °F	74	72	68	63	58	51	51	54	59	65	69	73	63
RELATIVE HUMIDITY (%)	47	48	54	50	47	46	42	37	38	42	45	47	45
PRECIPITATION														
Monthly Average mm	127	121	118	51	19	11	14	13	39	73	107	141	834.0
Monthly Average Inches	5.0	4.7	4.6	2.0	0.7	0.4	0.5	0.5	1.5	2.8	4.2	5.5	32.4
Days of 1mm or More	9	7	8	5	2	2	1	1	3	5	7	9	59

MENDOZA Argentina

		JAN	FEB	MAR	APR	MAY	JUN	JUL	AUG	SEP	OCT	NOV	DEC	YEAR
Elevation 800 m. (2656 ft.)							32°53'S—68°49'W							
TEMPERATURE														
Daily Average Min.°C	16	15	13	8	5	2	2	3	7	10	12	14	9
Daily Average Min.°F	60	59	55	47	41	36	35	38	44	50	54	58	48
Daily Average Max.°C	32	31	28	23	18	15	15	17	21	24	28	31	24
Daily Average Max.°F	90	87	82	73	65	59	59	63	69	76	83	88	75
Extreme Monthly Min.°C	5	5	-2	-1	-5	-9	-9	-5	-4	0	2	2	-9
Extreme Monthly Min.°F	41	41	29	30	23	15	16	23	25	32	36	36	15
Extreme Monthly Max.°C	43	41	37	33	30	30	28	33	34	36	41	42	42
Extreme Monthly Max.°F	109	105	99	91	86	86	83	92	93	97	106	108	109
Monthly Average °C	25	23	20	16	11	8	8	10	13	18	22	24	17
Monthly Average °F	77	74	68	61	53	46	46	50	56	64	71	75	62
RELATIVE HUMIDITY (%)	42	44	47	50	52	50	48	42	33	34	34	37	43
PRECIPITATION														
Monthly Average mm	36	28	29	12	5	4	9	3	8	13	16	24	187.0
Monthly Average Inches	1.4	1.1	1.1	0.4	0.1	0.1	0.3	0.1	0.3	0.5	0.6	0.9	6.9
Days of 1mm or More	3	3	3	2	1	1	1	0	1	2	2	3	22

TUCUMAN

Argentina

	JAN	FEB	MAR	APR	MAY	JUN	JUL	AUG	SEP	OCT	NOV	DEC	YEAR
Elevation 481 m. (1578 ft.)					26°49'S—65°13'W								
TEMPERATURE													
Monthly Average °C	25	24	22	18	15	12	12	14	17	20	22	25	19
Monthly Average °F	77	75	71	65	60	54	54	58	63	68	72	76	66
PRECIPITATION													
Monthly Average mm	184	154	161	57	27	18	9	7	11	76	107	150	961.0
Monthly Average Inches	7.2	6.0	6.3	2.2	1.0	0.7	0.3	0.2	0.4	2.9	4.2	5.9	37.3
Days of 1mm or More	0	0	0	0	0	0	0	0	0	0	0	0	0

ADELAIDE

Australia

	JAN	FEB	MAR	APR	MAY	JUN	JUL	AUG	SEP	OCT	NOV	DEC	YEAR
Elevation 43 m. (140 ft.)					34°56'S—138°35'E								
TEMPERATURE													
Daily Average Min.°C	16	17	15	13	10	8	7	8	9	11	13	15	12
Daily Average Min.°F	61	62	59	55	50	47	45	46	48	51	55	59	53
Daily Average Max.°C	30	30	27	23	19	16	15	17	19	23	26	28	23
Daily Average Max.°F	86	86	81	73	66	61	59	62	66	73	79	83	73
Extreme Monthly Min.°F	45	45	44	40	37	33	32	32	33	36	41	43	32
Extreme Monthly Max.°C	48	46	44	37	32	24	23	29	33	39	45	46	47
Extreme Monthly Max.°F	118	114	111	99	89	76	74	85	91	103	113	115	118
Monthly Average °C	22	22	20	17	14	12	11	12	13	16	18	20	16
Monthly Average °F	71	71	68	62	57	53	52	53	56	60	65	68	61
RELATIVE HUMIDITY (%)	31	32	36	45	56	65	63	57	52	42	36	32	43
PRECIPITATION													
Monthly Average mm	17	21	20	39	57	44	63	49	43	38	23	22	436.0
Monthly Average Inches	0.6	0.8	0.7	1.5	2.2	1.7	2.4	1.9	1.6	1.4	0.9	0.8	16.5
Days of 1mm or More	3	2	3	6	9	8	11	11	9	6	4	3	75

ALICE SPRINGS

Australia

	JAN	FEB	MAR	APR	MAY	JUN	JUL	AUG	SEP	OCT	NOV	DEC	YEAR
Elevation 580 m. (1901 ft.)					23°38'S—133°35'E								
TEMPERATURE													
Daily Average Min.°C	21	21	17	12	8	5	4	6	9	14	18	20	13
Daily Average Min.°F	70	69	63	54	46	41	39	43	49	58	64	68	55
Daily Average Max.°C	36	35	32	27	23	19	19	23	27	31	34	36	29
Daily Average Max.°F	97	95	90	81	73	67	67	73	81	88	93	96	83
Monthly Average °C	29	28	25	20	16	12	12	14	18	22	26	28	21
Monthly Average °F	84	82	77	69	60	54	53	58	65	72	79	82	70
RELATIVE HUMIDITY (%)	23	24	25	28	32	35	31	25	22	21	21	22	26
PRECIPITATION													
Monthly Average mm	41	40	42	16	18	14	15	10	11	20	27	33	287.0
Monthly Average Inches	1.6	1.5	1.6	0.6	0.7	0.5	0.5	0.3	0.4	0.7	1.0	1.2	10.6
Days of 1mm or More	4	3	2	1	2	1	1	1	2	2	4	3	26

BRISBANE Australia

	JAN	FEB	MAR	APR	MAY	JUN	JUL	AUG	SEP	OCT	NOV	DEC	YEAR
Elevation 42 m. (137 ft.)					27°28'S—153°2'E								
TEMPERATURE													
Daily Average Min.°C	21	20	19	16	13	11	9	10	13	16	18	19	16
Daily Average Min.°F	69	68	66	61	56	51	49	50	55	60	64	67	60
Daily Average Max.°C	29	29	28	26	23	21	20	22	24	27	28	29	26
Daily Average Max.°F	85	85	82	79	74	69	68	71	76	80	82	85	78
Extreme Monthly Min.°C	15	14	11	7	5	3	2	3	5	6	9	13	2
Extreme Monthly Min.°F	59	58	52	44	41	37	36	37	41	43	48	56	36
Extreme Monthly Max.°C	43	41	37	35	32	32	28	31	35	38	41	41	43
Extreme Monthly Max.°F	110	106	99	95	90	89	83	88	95	101	106	106	110
Monthly Average °C	25	25	24	22	19	16	15	16	18	21	23	24	21
Monthly Average °F	77	77	75	71	66	61	59	61	65	69	73	76	69
RELATIVE HUMIDITY (%)	59	60	60	56	55	54	51	49	51	53	57	56	55
PRECIPITATION													
Monthly Average mm	172	167	139	73	89	75	63	44	34	105	115	133	1209.0
Monthly Average Inches	6.7	6.5	5.4	2.8	3.5	2.9	2.4	1.7	1.3	4.1	4.5	5.2	47.0
Days of 1mm or More	10	10	9	6	8	4	4	5	4	7	7	9	83

CANBERRA Australia

	JAN	FEB	MAR	APR	MAY	JUN	JUL	AUG	SEP	OCT	NOV	DEC	YEAR
Elevation 560 m. (1837 ft.)					35°20'S—149°15'E								
TEMPERATURE													
Daily Average Min.°C	13	13	11	7	3	1	1	2	3	6	9	12	7
Daily Average Min.°F	55	55	51	44	37	34	33	35	38	43	48	53	44
Daily Average Max.°C	10	10	24	19	16	12	11	13	16	20	24	27	17
Daily Average Max.°F	82	82	76	67	60	53	52	55	61	68	75	80	68
Extreme Monthly Min.°C	3	1	-1	-3	-7	-8	-10	-8	-4	-3	-2	0	-10
Extreme Monthly Min.°F	38	33	31	27	19	18	14	18	24	27	28	32	14
Extreme Monthly Max.°C	43	39	37	33	23	19	18	23	28	34	37	39	42
Extreme Monthly Max.°F	109	103	99	91	73	66	65	73	83	94	98	103	109
Monthly Average °C	20	20	18	13	9	6	5	7	9	13	16	18	13
Monthly Average °F	69	68	64	56	48	43	42	44	49	55	60	65	55
RELATIVE HUMIDITY (%)	35	39	42	51	57	64	63	59	50	45	51	36	48
PRECIPITATION													
Monthly Average mm	60	58	50	44	41	31	40	49	57	71	63	53	617.0
Monthly Average Inches	2.3	2.2	1.9	1.7	1.6	1.2	1.5	1.9	2.2	2.7	2.4	2.0	23.6
Days of 1mm or More	5	5	5	4	5	4	5	7	7	8	7	5	67

DARWIN Australia

	JAN	FEB	MAR	APR	MAY	JUN	JUL	AUG	SEP	OCT	NOV	DEC	YEAR
Elevation 29 m. (95 ft.)					12°28'S—130°50'E								
TEMPERATURE													
Monthly Average °C	28	28	28	28	27	25	25	26	28	29	29	29	28
Monthly Average °F	83	82	83	83	81	77	76	79	82	84	85	84	82
PRECIPITATION													
Monthly Average mm	448	346	330	90	25	1	0	5	17	73	127	223	1685.0
Monthly Average Inches	17.6	13.6	12.9	3.5	0.9	0.0	0.0	0.1	0.6	2.8	5.0	8.7	65.7
Days of 1mm or More	19	18	17	6	2	0	0	0	2	5	9	13	91

HOBART   Australia

Elevation 54 m. (177 ft.)						49°53'S—147°20'E							
	JAN	FEB	MAR	APR	MAY	JUN	JUL	AUG	SEP	OCT	NOV	DEC	YEAR
TEMPERATURE													
Daily Average Min.°C	12	12	11	9	7	5	4	5	6	8	9	11	8
Daily Average Min.°F	53	53	51	48	44	41	40	41	43	46	48	51	47
Daily Average Max.°C	22	22	20	17	14	12	11	25	15	17	19	21	18
Daily Average Max.°F	71	71	68	63	58	53	52	55	59	63	66	69	62
Extreme Monthly Min.°C	4	4	2	1	-2	-2	-2	-1	-1	0	2	3	-2
Extreme Monthly Min.°F	40	39	35	33	29	29	28	30	30	32	35	38	28
Extreme Monthly Max.°C	41	40	37	31	26	21	19	22	28	33	37	41	40
Extreme Monthly Max.°F	105	104	99	87	78	69	66	72	82	92	98	105	105
Monthly Average °C	17	16	15	13	10	9	8	9	10	12	13	15	12
Monthly Average °F	62	62	60	56	50	47	46	48	50	54	56	59	54
RELATIVE HUMIDITY (%)	53	56	56	61	63	70	69	61	58	56	54	54	58
PRECIPITATION													
Monthly Average mm	36	49	41	54	53	48	54	59	65	54	57	53	623.0
Monthly Average Inches	1.4	1.9	1.6	2.1	2.0	1.8	2.1	2.3	2.5	2.1	2.2	2.0	24.0
Days of 1mm or More	0	0	0	0	0	0	0	0	0	0	0	0	0

LORD HOWE ISLAND   Australia

Elevation 5 m. (15 ft.)						31°31'S—159°7'E							
	JAN	FEB	MAR	APR	MAY	JUN	JUL	AUG	SEP	OCT	NOV	DEC	YEAR
TEMPERATURE													
Daily Average Min.°C	19	19	19	17	16	14	13	13	13	15	16	18	16
Daily Average Min.°F	67	67	66	63	60	57	55	55	56	59	61	64	61
Daily Average Max.°C	26	26	25	23	21	19	18	19	20	21	23	24	22
Daily Average Max.°F	78	78	77	74	70	67	65	66	68	70	73	76	72
Monthly Average °C	23	23	22	21	19	17	16	16	17	18	19	21	19
Monthly Average °F	73	73	72	69	66	63	61	61	62	64	67	70	67
RELATIVE HUMIDITY (%)	71.	68	69	70	70	70	70	68	69	71	72	72	70
PRECIPITATION													
Monthly Average mm	92	109	115	113	150	160	160	140	128	108	156	105	1536.0
Monthly Average Inches	3.6	4.2	4.5	4.4	5.9	6.3	6.3	5.5	5.0	4.2	6.1	4.1	60.1
Days of 1mm or More	7	8	10	12	15	18	17	16	12	10	9	7	141

MELBOURNE   Australia

Elevation 35 m. (115 ft.)						37°49'S—144°58'E							
	JAN	FEB	MAR	APR	MAY	JUN	JUL	AUG	SEP	OCT	NOV	DEC	YEAR
TEMPERATURE													
Daily Average Min.°C	14	14	13	11	8	7	6	6	8	9	11	12	10
Daily Average Min.°F	57	57	55	51	47	44	42	43	46	48	51	54	50
Daily Average Max.°C	26	26	24	20	17	14	13	15	17	19	22	24	20
Daily Average Max.°F	78	78	75	68	62	56	56	59	63	67	71	75	67
Extreme Monthly Min.°C	6	4	3	2	-1	-2	-3	-2	-1	0	3	4	-2
Extreme Monthly Min.°F	42	40	37	35	30	28	27	28	31	32	37	40	27
Extreme Monthly Max.°C	46	43	42	35	29	22	21	25	32	37	41	44	45
Extreme Monthly Max.°F	114	110	107	95	84	72	69	77	89	98	106	111	114
Monthly Average °C	21	21	19	16	13	11	10	11	13	15	17	19	15
Monthly Average °F	69	69	66	61	55	51	50	52	55	59	62	66	60
RELATIVE HUMIDITY (%)	48	50	51	56	62	67	65	60	55	52	52	51	56
PRECIPITATION													
Monthly Average mm	46	51	44	53	72	39	46	59	58	68	59	55	650.0
Monthly Average Inches	1.8	2.0	1.7	2.0	2.8	1.5	1.8	2.3	2.2	2.6	2.3	2.1	25.1
Days of 1mm or More	0	0	0	0	0	0	0	0	0	0	0	0	0

NORFOLK ISLAND — Australia

	JAN	FEB	MAR	APR	MAY	JUN	JUL	AUG	SEP	OCT	NOV	DEC	YEAR
Elevation 181 m. (325 ft.)					29°4'S—167°59'E								
TEMPERATURE													
Daily Average Min.°C	19	20	19	18	16	16	14	13	14	16	22	18	17
Daily Average Min.°F	67	68	67	65	61	60	57	56	57	60	62	65	62
Daily Average Max.°C	26	25	24	23	21	19	18	18	19	21	22	24	22
Daily Average Max.°F	78	77	76	73	69	67	65	65	67	69	72	75	71
Monthly Average °C	22	22	22	20	18	17	17	16	16	17	19	19	19
Monthly Average °F	71	72	71	68	65	63	62	60	61	63	66	69	66
RELATIVE HUMIDITY (%)	71	71	75	76	73	76	75	72	72	73	72	75	73
PRECIPITATION													
Monthly Average mm	91	104	111	123	112	160	128	116	98	87	83	77	1290.0
Monthly Average Inches	3.5	4.0	4.3	4.8	4.4	6.3	5.0	4.5	3.8	3.4	3.2	3.0	50.2
Days of 1mm or More	8	8	10	11	11	14	14	14	10	9	7	7	123

PERTH — Australia

	JAN	FEB	MAR	APR	MAY	JUN	JUL	AUG	SEP	OCT	NOV	DEC	YEAR
Elevation 60 m. (196 ft.)					31°57'S—115°51'E								
TEMPERATURE													
Daily Average Min.°C	17	17	16	14	12	10	9	9	10	12	14	16	13
Daily Average Min.°F	63	63	61	57	53	50	48	48	50	53	57	61	55
Daily Average Max.°C	29	29	27	24	21	18	17	18	19	21	24	27	23
Daily Average Max.°F	85	85	81	76	69	64	63	64	67	70	76	81	73
Extreme Monthly Min.°C	9	9	8	4	1	2	1	2	4	4	6	9	1
Extreme Monthly Min.°F	49	48	46	39	34	35	34	35	39	40	42	48	34
Extreme Monthly Max.°C	43	44	41	38	32	28	24	28	33	35	41	42	44
Extreme Monthly Max.°F	110	112	106	100	90	82	76	82	91	95	105	108	112
Monthly Average °C	24	25	22	19	16	14	13	13	15	17	19	22	18
Monthly Average °F	76	76	72	66	61	58	56	56	59	62	67	72	65
RELATIVE HUMIDITY (%)	44	43	45	49	58	63	63	61	58	55	49	47	53
PRECIPITATION													
Monthly Average mm	10	16	15	44	116	177	177	116	66	55	18	9	819.0
Monthly Average Inches	0.3	0.6	0.5	1.7	4.5	6.9	6.9	4.5	2.5	2.1	0.7	0.3	31.5
Days of 1mm or More	0	0	0	0	0	0	0	0	0	0	0	0	0

ROCKHAMPTON — Australia

	JAN	FEB	MAR	APR	MAY	JUN	JUL	AUG	SEP	OCT	NOV	DEC	YEAR
Elevation 11 m. (37 ft.)					23°24'S—150°30'E								
TEMPERATURE													
Daily Average Min.°C	22	22	21	18	14	12	10	12	15	18	19	22	17
Daily Average Min.°F	72	72	70	65	58	53	50	53	59	64	67	71	63
Daily Average Max.°C	32	32	31	29	26	23	23	25	28	30	32	32	28
Daily Average Max.°F	89	89	87	84	79	74	73	77	82	86	89	90	83
Monthly Average °C	26	26	25	23	19	17	16	17	20	23	25	26	22
Monthly Average °F	79	79	78	74	67	62	60	63	68	73	77	79	72
RELATIVE HUMIDITY (%)	55	54	54	51	49	51	46	42	42	44	46	50	49
PRECIPITATION													
Monthly Average mm	170	153	85	40	46	31	28	25	23	41	76	111	829.0
Monthly Average Inches	6.6	6.0	3.3	1.5	1.8	1.2	1.1	0.9	0.9	1.6	2.9	4.3	32.1
Days of 1mm or More	8	8	6	4	4	3	3	3	3	4	5	9	60

SYDNEY
Australia

Elevation 42 m. (138 ft.)   33°52'S—151°12'E

	JAN	FEB	MAR	APR	MAY	JUN	JUL	AUG	SEP	OCT	NOV	DEC	YEAR
TEMPERATURE													
Daily Average Min.°C	18	18	17	14	11	9	8	9	11	13	16	17	13
Daily Average Min.°F	65	65	63	58	52	48	46	48	51	56	60	63	56
Daily Average Max.°C	26	26	24	22	19	16	16	17	19	22	23	25	21
Daily Average Max.°F	78	78	76	71	66	61	60	63	67	71	74	77	70
Extreme Monthly Min.°C	11	9	9	7	4	2	2	3	5	6	8	9	2
Extreme Monthly Min.°F	51	49	49	45	40	36	36	37	41	42	46	48	36
Extreme Monthly Max.°C	46	42	39	33	30	27	26	28	33	37	39	42	45
Extreme Monthly Max.°F	114	108	103	91	86	80	78	82	92	99	103	107	114
Monthly Average °C	22	22	21	19	16	14	13	14	15	18	20	21	18
Monthly Average °F	72	72	71	67	60	56	55	56	59	64	67	70	64
RELATIVE HUMIDITY (%)	64	65	65	64	63	62	60	56	55	57	60	62	61
PRECIPITATION													
Monthly Average mm	127	152	167	78	100	134	58	78	57	94	100	89	1234.0
Monthly Average Inches	5.0	5.9	6.5	3.0	3.9	5.2	2.2	3.0	2.2	3.7	3.9	3.5	48.0
Days of 1mm or More	8	8	7	6	5	10	4	7	7	8	8	8	86

GRAZ
Austria

Elevation 377 m. (1237 ft.)   47°4'N—15°30'E

	JAN	FEB	MAR	APR	MAY	JUN	JUL	AUG	SEP	OCT	NOV	DEC	YEAR
TEMPERATURE													
Daily Average Min.°C	-5	-4	0	5	9	13	14	14	11	6	1	-2	5
Daily Average Min.°F	23	25	32	41	49	55	58	56	51	42	35	28	41
Daily Average Max.°C	1	4	9	15	19	23	25	24	20	14	7	2	14
Daily Average Max.°F	33	39	48	59	67	73	77	75	69	58	45	36	56
Monthly Average °C	-4	-1	4	9	14	17	19	18	14	9	3	-2	8
Monthly Average °F	26	30	39	48	57	63	65	64	57	47	38	29	47
RELATIVE HUMIDITY (%)	71	63	53	49	53	54	53	54	57	64	72	76	60
PRECIPITATION													
Monthly Average mm	32	36	51	50	81	119	120	111	75	58	62	40	835.0
Monthly Average Inches	1.2	1.4	2.0	1.9	3.1	4.6	4.7	4.3	2.9	2.2	2.4	1.5	32.2
Days of 1mm or More	7	6	7	7	10	11	10	10	6	5	7	5	91

INNSBRUCK
Austria

Elevation 582 m. (1909 ft.)   47°18'N—11°24'E

	JAN	FEB	MAR	APR	MAY	JUN	JUL	AUG	SEP	OCT	NOV	DEC	YEAR
TEMPERATURE													
Daily Average Min.°C	-7	-5	0	4	8	11	13	12	10	5	0	-4	4
Daily Average Min.°F	20	24	32	39	46	52	55	54	49	40	32	24	39
Daily Average Max.°C	1	4	11	16	20	24	25	24	21	15	8	2	14
Daily Average Max.°F	34	40	51	60	68	74	77	75	69	58	46	36	57
Extreme Monthly Min.°C	-26	-27	-17	-7	-8	-1	4	3	-1	-8	-15	-25	-26
Extreme Monthly Min.°F	-15	-16	2	19	18	31	40	38	30	18	5	-13	-16
Extreme Monthly Max.°C	15	16	25	28	33	36	36	34	31	24	23	18	36
Extreme Monthly Max.°F	59	60	77	83	91	97	97	94	87	76	73	64	97
Monthly Average °C	-2	0	4	9	13	16	18	17	14	9	3	-1	8
Monthly Average °F	28	33	40	48	56	61	64	63	58	48	38	30	47
RELATIVE HUMIDITY (%)	67	58	46	43	43	48	52	52	53	55	65	70	54
PRECIPITATION													
Monthly Average mm	49	36	47	59	91	106	124	119	82	56	59	53	881.0
Monthly Average Inches	1.9	1.4	1.8	2.3	3.5	4.1	4.8	4.6	3.2	2.2	2.3	2.0	34.1
Days of 1mm or More	9	7	8	9	11	13	13	13	9	6	8	8	114

SALZBURG   Austria

	JAN	FEB	MAR	APR	MAY	JUN	JUL	AUG	SEP	OCT	NOV	DEC	YEAR
Elevation 446 m. (1463 ft.)					47°48'N—13°0'E								
TEMPERATURE													
Daily Average Min.°C	-6	-5	-1	4	8	11	13	13	10	5	1	-4	4
Daily Average Min.°F	22	23	30	38	46	52	55	55	49	40	33	26	39
Daily Average Max.°C	2	4	9	14	19	22	24	23	20	14	8	3	13
Daily Average Max.°F	35	39	49	57	65	71	74	74	68	57	46	37	56
Monthly Average °C	-2	0	4	8	13	16	18	17	14	9	4	0	8
Monthly Average °F	29	32	39	47	55	61	64	63	58	48	39	32	47
RELATIVE HUMIDITY (%)	75	69	61	58	59	59	60	61	63	68	75	79	66
PRECIPITATION													
Monthly Average mm	66	58	64	81	130	166	154	153	84	67	71	69	1163.0
Monthly Average Inches	2.5	2.2	2.5	3.1	5.1	6.5	6.0	6.0	3.3	2.6	2.7	2.7	45.2
Days of 1mm or More	10	9	11	12	13	14	14	13	9	8	10	11	134

VIENNA   Austria

	JAN	FEB	MAR	APR	MAY	JUN	JUL	AUG	SEP	OCT	NOV	DEC	YEAR
Elevation 212 m. (695 ft.)					48°18'N—16°24'E								
TEMPERATURE													
Daily Average Min.°C	-4	-3	1	6	10	14	15	15	11	7	3	-1	6
Daily Average Min.°F	25	28	34	42	50	56	60	58	53	44	37	30	43
Daily Average Max.°C	1	3	8	15	19	23	25	24	20	14	7	3	13
Daily Average Max.°F	34	38	47	58	67	73	76	75	68	56	45	37	56
Extreme Monthly Min.°C	-22	-26	-16	-8	-3	4	7	6	-1	-9	-14	-20	-25
Extreme Monthly Min.°F	-8	-14	3	18	27	39	45	42	31	16	6	-4	-14
Extreme Monthly Max.°C	17	19	23	28	33	36	37	36	31	28	22	19	36
Extreme Monthly Max.°F	62	67	74	83	92	97	98	97	88	82	71	66	98
Monthly Average °C	-1	1	5	10	15	18	20	19	15	10	5	1	10
Monthly Average °F	30	34	41	50	58	64	67	66	60	50	41	34	50
RELATIVE HUMIDITY (%)	72	66	57	49	52	55	54	54	56	64	74	76	61
PRECIPITATION													
Monthly Average mm	39	39	42	48	59	80	66	60	40	44	49	47	613.0
Monthly Average Inches	1.5	1.5	1.6	1.8	2.3	3.1	2.5	2.3	1.5	1.7	1.9	1.8	23.5
Days of 1mm or More	8	7	7	7	8	9	9	8	6	5	8	7	89

Bahrain

	JAN	FEB	MAR	APR	MAY	JUN	JUL	AUG	SEP	OCT	NOV	DEC	YEAR
Elevation 5 m. (18 ft.)					26°12'N—50°30'E								
TEMPERATURE													
Daily Average Min.°C	14	15	17	21	26	28	29	29	27	24	21	16	22
Daily Average Min.°F	57	59	63	70	78	82	85	85	81	75	69	60	72
Daily Average Max.°C	20	21	24	29	33	36	37	38	36	32	28	22	30
Daily Average Max.°F	68	70	75	84	92	96	99	100	96	90	82	71	85
Monthly Average °C	17	18	21	26	30	32	34	34	33	29	24	19	27
Monthly Average °F	63	65	71	78	86	90	93	94	91	84	76	67	80
RELATIVE HUMIDITY (%)	71	70	70	66	63	64	67	65	64	66	70	77	68
PRECIPITATION													
Monthly Average mm	20	16	11	9	1	0	0	0	0	1	4	12	74.0
Monthly Average Inches	0.7	0.6	0.4	0.3	0.0	0.0	0.0	0.0	0.0	0.0	0.1	0.4	2.5
Days of 1mm or More	2	2	2	1	0	0	0	0	0	0	0	1	8

BOGRA
Bangladesh

Elevation 20 m. (65 ft.)   24°51'N—89°22'E

	JAN	FEB	MAR	APR	MAY	JUN	JUL	AUG	SEP	OCT	NOV	DEC	YEAR
TEMPERATURE													
Monthly Average °C	18	21	25	29	29	29	29	29	29	27	23	19	26
Monthly Average °F	65	69	78	85	85	84	84	84	84	81	74	67	78
PRECIPITATION													
Monthly Average mm	13	10	27	57	166	300	356	322	255	155	13	1	1675.0
Monthly Average Inches	0.5	0.3	1.0	2.2	6.5	11.8	14.0	12.6	10.0	6.1	0.5	0.0	65.5
Days of 1mm or More	0	1	2	4	9	14	17	16	12	6	0	0	81

SEAWELL AIRPORT
Barbados

Elevation 56 m. (183 ft.)   13°6'N—59°37'W

	JAN	FEB	MAR	APR	MAY	JUN	JUL	AUG	SEP	OCT	NOV	DEC	YEAR
TEMPERATURE													
Monthly Average °C	25	25	26	26	27	27	27	27	27	27	27	26	27
Monthly Average °F	78	78	79	80	81	81	81	81	81	81	80	79	80
PRECIPITATION													
Monthly Average mm	58	42	37	52	57	87	129	148	128	166	128	96	1128.0
Monthly Average Inches	2.2	1.6	1.4	2.0	2.2	3.4	5.0	5.8	5.0	6.5	5.0	3.7	43.8
Days of 1mm or More	10	8	7	7	8	11	15	15	14	15	13	12	135

BRUSSELS/UCCLE
Belgium

Elevation 104 m. (341 ft.)   50°48'N—4°24'E

	JAN	FEB	MAR	APR	MAY	JUN	JUL	AUG	SEP	OCT	NOV	DEC	YEAR
TEMPERATURE													
Daily Average Min.°C	-1	0	2	5	8	11	12	12	11	7	3	0	6
Daily Average Min.°F	30	33	36	41	46	52	54	54	51	45	38	32	43
Daily Average Max.°C	4	7	10	14	18	22	23	22	21	15	9	6	14
Daily Average Max.°F	40	44	51	58	65	72	73	72	69	60	48	42	58
Monthly Average °C	2	3	6	9	13	16	17	17	15	11	6	4	10
Monthly Average °F	36	38	42	48	55	60	63	63	58	52	43	39	50
RELATIVE HUMIDITY (%)	86	81	74	71	65	65	68	69	69	77	85	86	75
PRECIPITATION													
Monthly Average mm	86	68	70	63	68	78	90	73	62	70	80	74	882.0
Monthly Average Inches	3.3	2.6	2.7	2.4	2.6	3.0	3.5	2.8	2.4	2.7	3.1	2.9	34.0
Days of 1mm or More	12	9	12	11	12	11	10	10	9	10	13	12	131

BELIZE CITY
Belize

Elevation 5 m. (16 ft.)   17°31'N—88°11'W

	JAN	FEB	MAR	APR	MAY	JUN	JUL	AUG	SEP	OCT	NOV	DEC	YEAR
TEMPERATURE													
Daily Average Min.°C	19	21	22	23	24	24	24	24	23	22	20	20	22
Daily Average Min.°F	67	69	71	74	75	75	75	75	74	72	68	68	72
Daily Average Max.°C	27	28	29	30	31	31	31	31	31	30	28	27	29
Daily Average Max.°F	81	82	84	86	87	87	87	88	87	86	83	81	85
Monthly Average °C	24	24	26	27	28	28	28	28	28	27	25	24	26
Monthly Average °F	74	76	78	81	82	82	82	82	82	80	77	76	79
RELATIVE HUMIDITY (%)	89	87	87	87	87	87	86	87	87	88	91	90	88
PRECIPITATION													
Monthly Average mm	118	61	60	52	118	246	254	181	239	244	172	160	1905.0
Monthly Average Inches	4.6	2.4	2.3	2.0	4.6	9.6	10.0	7.1	9.4	9.6	6.7	6.3	74.6
Days of 1mm or More	12	6	5	3	7	14	17	16	15	15	13	12	135

COTONOU   Benin

Elevation 4 m. (13 ft.)   6°21'N—2°23'E

	JAN	FEB	MAR	APR	MAY	JUN	JUL	AUG	SEP	OCT	NOV	DEC	YEAR
TEMPERATURE													
Daily Average Min.°C	24	25	26	25	24	23	23	23	24	23	24	24	24
Daily Average Min.°F	75	77	78	77	76	74	74	74	74	74	75	75	75
Daily Average Max.°C	31	32	32	32	31	29	28	28	29	30	31	31	30
Daily Average Max.°F	87	89	90	89	88	84	82	82	83	85	88	88	86
Extreme Monthly Min.°C	19	21	21	21	21	18	20	21	20	22	22	19	18
Extreme Monthly Min.°F	66	70	70	70	70	65	68	69	68	71	71	67	65
Extreme Monthly Max.°C	32	34	34	35	34	33	32	31	32	33	33	33	35
Extreme Monthly Max.°F	90	93	94	95	94	91	89	87	89	91	92	91	95
Monthly Average °C	27	28	29	28	27	26	26	25	26	27	28	27	27
Monthly Average °F	81	83	84	83	81	80	78	78	78	80	82	81	81
RELATIVE HUMIDITY (%)	72	71	71	73	76	81	81	79	79	77	74	71	75
PRECIPITATION													
Monthly Average mm	10	41	72	137	197	358	144	64	90	124	43	16	1296.0
Monthly Average Inches	0.3	1.6	2.8	5.3	7.7	14.0	5.6	2.5	3.5	4.8	1.6	0.6	50.3
Days of 1mm or More	0	2	4	6	11	15	7	4	7	8	3	1	68

KANDI   Benin

Elevation 290 m. (951 ft.)   11°8'N—2°56'E

	JAN	FEB	MAR	APR	MAY	JUN	JUL	AUG	SEP	OCT	NOV	DEC	YEAR
TEMPERATURE													
Daily Average Min.°C	16	19	23	25	24	23	22	22	21	21	18	16	21
Daily Average Min.°F	61	66	73	77	76	73	71	71	70	70	64	60	69
Daily Average Max.°C	34	36	38	38	36	33	30	29	30	34	35	34	34
Daily Average Max.°F	93	97	101	101	96	91	86	85	87	92	95	93	93
Monthly Average °C	25	28	31	31	30	28	26	25	26	27	26	25	27
Monthly Average °F	76	82	87	89	86	82	79	78	78	81	79	76	81
RELATIVE HUMIDITY (%)	21	20	26	39	53	63	72	75	71	55	29	22	45
PRECIPITATION													
Monthly Average mm	0	2	7	40	103	154	195	277	198	34	0	0	1010.0
Monthly Average Inches	0.0	0.0	0.2	1.5	4.0	6.0	7.6	10.9	7.7	1.3	0.0	0.0	39.2
Days of 1mm or More	0	0	1	3	8	10	12	16	13	3	0	0	66

NATITINGOU   Benin

Elevation 461 m. (1512 ft.)   10°19'N—1°23'E

	JAN	FEB	MAR	APR	MAY	JUN	JUL	AUG	SEP	OCT	NOV	DEC	YEAR
TEMPERATURE													
Daily Average Min.°C	19	21	22	23	22	21	21	21	20	20	19	19	21
Daily Average Min.°F	67	69	72	73	72	70	69	69	69	68	65	65	69
Daily Average Max.°C	34	36	37	35	33	31	29	28	29	32	34	34	33
Daily Average Max.°F	94	96	98	95	92	87	83	82	85	89	92	93	91
Monthly Average °C	26	28	29	29	28	26	25	24	25	26	26	26	26
Monthly Average °F	79	83	85	84	82	79	76	76	76	78	78	78	79
RELATIVE HUMIDITY (%)	21	25	36	50	61	68	75	77	72	61	38	23	51
PRECIPITATION													
Monthly Average mm	1	3	28	94	106	141	220	271	270	112	13	4	1263.0
Monthly Average Inches	0.0	0.1	1.1	3.7	4.1	5.5	8.6	10.6	10.6	4.4	0.5	0.1	49.3
Days of 1mm or More	0	0	2	6	9	11	14	18	17	8	0	0	85

CONCEPCION   Bolivia

Elevation 490 m. (1607 ft.)   16°15'S—62°3'W

	JAN	FEB	MAR	APR	MAY	JUN	JUL	AUG	SEP	OCT	NOV	DEC	YEAR
TEMPERATURE													
Daily Average Min.°C	19	19	18	17	15	13	12	13	16	17	19	18	16
Daily Average Min.°F	66	66	65	62	59	56	54	56	61	62	66	65	62
Daily Average Max.°C	29	30	29	30	28	27	27	31	33	31	31	30	30
Daily Average Max.°F	85	86	85	86	83	80	81	87	91	88	88	86	86
Extreme Monthly Min.°F	55	49	54	48	43	45	36	39	40	45	52	47	32
Extreme Monthly Max.°C	36	34	34	34	34	32	34	36	38	37	38	34	38
Extreme Monthly Max.°F	96	93	93	93	93	90	94	97	100	98	101	94	101
Monthly Average °C	25	25	25	24	22	21	21	23	25	27	26	26	24
Monthly Average °F	77	78	77	75	72	70	70	74	78	80	78	79	76
RELATIVE HUMIDITY (%)	63	74	71	65	61	61	55	47	49	58	61	69	61
PRECIPITATION													
Monthly Average mm	182	167	126	91	57	41	35	34	53	90	147	166	1189.0
Monthly Average Inches	7.1	6.5	4.9	3.5	2.2	1.6	1.3	1.3	2.0	3.5	5.7	6.5	46.1
Days of 1mm or More	17	15	11	8	5	3	2	3	4	7	11	13	99

SANTA CRUZ   Bolivia

Elevation 437 m. (1433 ft.)   17°48'S—63°10'W

	JAN	FEB	MAR	APR	MAY	JUN	JUL	AUG	SEP	OCT	NOV	DEC	YEAR
TEMPERATURE													
Monthly Average °C	27	27	26	25	23	20	21	23	25	26	27	27	25
Monthly Average °F	80	80	79	76	73	69	70	73	77	79	81	81	76
PRECIPITATION													
Monthly Average mm	215	133	122	119	98	71	61	52	77	109	146	186	1389.0
Monthly Average Inches	8.4	5.2	4.8	4.6	3.8	2.7	2.4	2.0	3.0	4.2	5.7	7.3	54.1
Days of 1mm or More	12	11	11	7	8	7	6	4	4	7	9	12	98

SUCRE   Bolivia

Elevation 2850 m. (9350 ft.)   19°3'S—65°17'W

	JAN	FEB	MAR	APR	MAY	JUN	JUL	AUG	SEP	OCT	NOV	DEC	YEAR
TEMPERATURE													
Daily Average Min.°C	9	9	9	7	4	3	3	4	7	8	9	9	7
Daily Average Min.°F	48	48	48	45	40	38	37	40	44	46	48	49	44
Daily Average Max.°C	17	17	18	17	17	16	16	18	19	18	19	19	18
Daily Average Max.°F	63	62	64	63	62	61	61	65	67	65	67	66	64
Extreme Monthly Min.°C	4	5	3	3	-2	-3	-4	-1	-2	1	4	5	-3
Extreme Monthly Min.°F	40	41	38	37	29	27	25	30	29	33	40	41	25
Extreme Monthly Max.°C	31	29	31	29	27	27	26	28	27	28	28	29	31
Extreme Monthly Max.°F	88	85	87	84	81	81	78	82	81	83	83	84	88
Monthly Average °C	16	16	16	15	15	14	14	15	16	17	17	17	16
Monthly Average °F	61	60	60	60	60	57	57	59	61	63	63	62	60
RELATIVE HUMIDITY (%)	55	55	54	50	34	31	34	31	38	41	42	41	42
PRECIPITATION													
Monthly Average mm	158	126	116	36	4	3	1	8	19	50	68	128	717.0
Monthly Average Inches	6.2	4.9	4.5	1.4	0.1	0.1	0.0	0.3	0.7	1.9	2.6	5.0	27.7
Days of 1mm or More	15	12	11	4	1	0	0	1	3	6	8	12	73

MAUN   Botswana

Elevation 945 m. (3100 ft.)						19°59'S—23°25'E						
	JAN	FEB	MAR	APR	MAY	JUN	JUL	AUG	SEP	OCT	NOV	DEC	YEAR
TEMPERATURE													
Daily Average Min.°C	19	19	18	15	10	6	6	9	14	19	19	19	14
Daily Average Min.°F	67	66	64	58	49	43	43	49	57	65	67	67	58
Daily Average Max.°C	32	31	31	31	28	25	25	29	32	35	34	32	30
Daily Average Max.°F	89	88	88	87	82	77	78	83	90	94	92	90	87
Monthly Average °C	24	24	23	22	18	16	16	19	23	27	26	25	22
Monthly Average °F	76	75	74	72	65	60	61	66	74	81	78	77	72
RELATIVE HUMIDITY (%)	49	49	44	36	28	27	25	21	19	23	33	44	33
PRECIPITATION													
Monthly Average mm	123	120	68	28	4	1	0	1	3	15	49	82	494.0
Monthly Average Inches	4.8	4.7	2.6	1.1	0.1	0.0	0.0	0.0	0.1	0.5	1.9	3.2	19.0
Days of 1mm or More	10	8	8	3	0	0	0	0	0	2	7	8	46

BELO HORIZONTE   Brazil

Elevation 850 m. (2788 ft.)						19°55'S—43°56'W						
	JAN	FEB	MAR	APR	MAY	JUN	JUL	AUG	SEP	OCT	NOV	DEC	YEAR
TEMPERATURE													
Monthly Average °C	23	23	23	22	20	19	19	20	21	22	22	23	21
Monthly Average °F	73	74	74	71	68	65	65	68	70	72	72	73	70
PRECIPITATION													
Monthly Average mm	316	191	166	63	28	13	41	12	39	120	249	318	1556.0
Monthly Average Inches	12.4	7.5	6.5	2.4	1.1	0.5	1.6	0.4	1.5	4.7	9.8	12.5	60.9
Days of 1mm or More	16	10	12	5	3	1	1	1	4	9	13	17	92

BRASILIA   Brazil

Elevation 1158 m. (3799 ft.)						15°47'S—47°55'W						
	JAN	FEB	MAR	APR	MAY	JUN	JUL	AUG	SEP	OCT	NOV	DEC	YEAR
TEMPERATURE													
Monthly Average °C	21	21	21	21	20	19	18	20	22	22	21	21	21
Monthly Average °F	70	70	71	69	67	65	65	69	71	71	70	70	69
PRECIPITATION													
Monthly Average mm	247	207	188	125	45	6	8	11	48	159	233	238	1515.0
Monthly Average Inches	9.7	8.1	7.4	4.9	1.7	0.2	0.3	0.4	1.8	6.2	9.1	9.3	59.1
Days of 1mm or More	18	14	15	9	3	0	0	1	5	14	16	20	115

MANAUS
Brazil

	JAN	FEB	MAR	APR	MAY	JUN	JUL	AUG	SEP	OCT	NOV	DEC	YEAR
Elevation 44 m. (144 ft.)					3°8'S—60°1'W								
TEMPERATURE													
Daily Average Min.°C	24	24	24	24	24	24	24	24	24	24	24	24	24
Daily Average Min.°F	75	75	75	75	75	75	75	75	75	76	76	75	75
Daily Average Max.°C	31	31	31	31	31	31	32	33	33	33	33	32	32
Daily Average Max.°F	88	88	88	87	88	88	89	91	92	92	91	90	89
Extreme Monthly Min.°C	18	20	19	20	20	18	18	19	20	20	20	19	17
Extreme Monthly Min.°F	65	68	67	68	68	65	64	67	68	68	68	67	63
Extreme Monthly Max.°C	37	38	36	34	35	35	35	37	37	38	37	38	38
Extreme Monthly Max.°F	99	100	97	94	95	95	95	98	99	100	99	101	101
Monthly Average °C	26	26	26	26	26	26	27	27	28	28	27	27	27
Monthly Average °F	79	79	79	79	79	79	80	81	82	82	81	80	80
RELATIVE HUMIDITY (%)	70	71	72	73	72	68	64	59	57	59	63	68	66
PRECIPITATION													
Monthly Average mm	260	256	324	306	235	109	74	55	75	113	177	222	2206.0
Monthly Average Inches	10.2	10.0	12.7	12.0	9.2	4.2	2.9	2.1	2.9	4.4	6.9	8.7	86.2
Days of 1mm or More	18	19	19	19	16	11	9	6	7	8	11	16	159

NATAL
Brazil

	JAN	FEB	MAR	APR	MAY	JUN	JUL	AUG	SEP	OCT	NOV	DEC	YEAR
Elevation 16 m. (52 ft.)					5°46'S—35°12'W								
TEMPERATURE													
Daily Average Min.°C	24	24	24	23	23	22	21	21	22	24	24	25	23
Daily Average Min.°F	76	76	75	73	73	71	69	69	72	75	76	77	74
Daily Average Max.°C	31	30	30	30	29	28	28	28	29	29	30	30	29
Daily Average Max.°F	87	86	86	86	85	83	82	82	84	85	86	86	85
Monthly Average °C	27	27	27	26	26	25	24	24	25	25	26	26	26
Monthly Average °F	80	80	80	79	78	77	75	75	76	78	79	79	78
RELATIVE HUMIDITY (%)	73	72	73	75	77	76	77	75	74	74	73	72	74
PRECIPITATION													
Monthly Average mm	52	107	168	234	192	200	198	87	63	26	24	27	1378.0
Monthly Average Inches	2.0	4.2	6.6	9.2	7.5	7.8	7.7	3.4	2.4	1.0	0.9	1.0	53.7
Days of 1mm or More	6	8	13	15	13	15	16	10	7	4	4	5	116

RECIFE
Brazil

	JAN	FEB	MAR	APR	MAY	JUN	JUL	AUG	SEP	OCT	NOV	DEC	YEAR
Elevation 30 m. (97 ft.)					8°4'S—34°53'W								
TEMPERATURE													
Daily Average Min.°C	25	25	24	24	23	23	22	22	23	24	24	25	24
Daily Average Min.°F	77	77	76	75	74	73	71	71	73	75	76	77	75
Daily Average Max.°C	30	30	30	29	28	28	27	27	28	29	29	29	29
Daily Average Max.°F	86	86	86	85	83	82	80	81	82	84	85	85	84
Extreme Monthly Min.°C	22	21	21	21	21	19	18	18	19	20	21	21	17
Extreme Monthly Min.°F	72	69	69	69	69	66	64	64	66	68	69	70	64
Extreme Monthly Max.°C	34	34	34	34	32	32	31	31	32	33	33	33	34
Extreme Monthly Max.°F	94	93	94	93	90	89	87	88	90	91	91	92	94
Monthly Average °C	27	27	26	26	25	25	24	24	25	26	26	26	26
Monthly Average °F	80	80	79	79	78	76	75	75	76	78	79	79	78
RELATIVE HUMIDITY (%)	69	70	71	73	74	75	75	73	70	67	68	67	71
PRECIPITATION													
Monthly Average mm	96	143	277	297	331	385	357	190	122	54	39	58	2349.0
Monthly Average Inches	3.7	5.6	10.9	11.6	13.0	15.1	14.0	7.4	4.8	2.1	1.5	2.2	91.9
Days of 1mm or More	10	11	17	18	20	20	20	18	12	10	7	8	171

RIO DE JANEIRO   Brazil

Elevation 61 m. (201 ft.)					22°55'S—43°12'W								
	JAN	FEB	MAR	APR	MAY	JUN	JUL	AUG	SEP	OCT	NOV	DEC	YEAR
TEMPERATURE													
Daily Average Min.°C	23	23	22	21	19	18	17	18	18	19	20	22	20
Daily Average Min.°F	73	73	72	69	66	64	63	64	65	66	68	71	68
Daily Average Max.°C	29	29	28	27	25	24	24	24	24	25	26	28	26
Daily Average Max.°F	84	85	83	80	77	76	75	76	75	77	79	82	79
Extreme Monthly Min.°C	16	17	18	16	13	11	11	12	10	14	15	13	10
Extreme Monthly Min.°F	60	63	64	60	56	52	52	53	50	57	59	56	50
Extreme Monthly Max.°C	39	37	36	34	35	32	33	34	38	39	38	39	38
Extreme Monthly Max.°F	102	98	97	94	95	90	91	93	100	102	100	102	102
Monthly Average °C	26	27	26	24	23	22	21	22	22	23	24	25	24
Monthly Average °F	79	80	79	76	73	71	70	71	72	73	75	77	75
RELATIVE HUMIDITY (%)	70	71	74	73	70	69	68	66	72	72	72	72	71
PRECIPITATION													
Monthly Average mm	154	131	142	107	82	52	47	51	61	85	99	154	1165.0
Monthly Average Inches	6.0	5.1	5.5	4.2	3.2	2.0	1.8	2.0	2.4	3.3	3.8	6.0	45.3
Days of 1mm or More	11	8	8	9	6	5	4	5	8	9	10	12	95

SALVADOR   Brazil

Elevation 47 m. (154 ft.)					13°0'S—38°30'W								
	JAN	FEB	MAR	APR	MAY	JUN	JUL	AUG	SEP	OCT	NOV	DEC	YEAR
TEMPERATURE													
Daily Average Min.°C	23	23	23	23	22	22	21	21	21	22	22	23	22
Daily Average Min.°F	74	74	74	74	72	71	69	69	70	71	72	73	72
Daily Average Max.°C	30	30	30	29	28	27	26	26	27	28	29	29	28
Daily Average Max.°F	86	86	86	84	82	80	79	79	81	83	84	84	83
Extreme Monthly Min.°C	20	19	21	20	20	18	18	17	18	19	19	19	16
Extreme Monthly Min.°F	68	66	69	68	68	64	65	62	65	66	67	67	62
Extreme Monthly Max.°C	34	34	35	34	32	31	29	30	31	35	33	33	35
Extreme Monthly Max.°F	94	94	95	94	90	87	85	86	88	95	92	92	95
Monthly Average °C	26	27	27	26	25	24	24	24	24	25	25	26	25
Monthly Average °F	79	80	80	79	77	76	75	75	76	77	78	79	77
RELATIVE HUMIDITY (%)	71	72	73	77	79	79	78	76	74	74	73	72	75
PRECIPITATION													
Monthly Average mm	105	130	144	303	324	247	179	116	98	111	115	110	1982.0
Monthly Average Inches	4.1	5.1	5.6	11.9	12.7	9.7	7.0	4.5	3.8	4.3	4.5	4.3	77.5
Days of 1mm or More	8	13	13	18	20	19	18	15	12	11	10	9	166

SANTAREM   Brazil

Elevation 21 m. (68 ft.)					2°30'S—54°42'W								
	JAN	FEB	MAR	APR	MAY	JUN	JUL	AUG	SEP	OCT	NOV	DEC	YEAR
TEMPERATURE													
Daily Average Min.°C	23	23	23	23	23	22	22	22	23	23	23	23	23
Daily Average Min.°F	73	73	73	73	73	72	71	72	73	73	73	73	73
Daily Average Max.°C	30	29	29	29	29	30	31	32	33	33	33	32	31
Daily Average Max.°F	86	85	85	85	85	86	87	89	91	91	91	89	88
Monthly Average °C	26	25	26	26	26	25	25	26	27	27	27	26	26
Monthly Average °F	78	78	78	78	78	78	78	79	80	80	80	80	79
RELATIVE HUMIDITY (%)	74	80	81	82	83	80	72	65	61	59	61	68	72
PRECIPITATION													
Monthly Average mm	194	258	386	350	283	138	116	55	44	53	88	116	2081.0
Monthly Average Inches	7.6	10.1	15.2	13.7	11.1	5.4	4.5	2.1	1.7	2.0	3.4	4.5	81.3
Days of 1mm or More	16	17	20	19	21	14	11	6	7	3	4	8	146

SAO LUIZ   Brazil

	Elevation 20 m. (667 ft.)				2°32'S—44°17'W								
	JAN	FEB	MAR	APR	MAY	JUN	JUL	AUG	SEP	OCT	NOV	DEC	YEAR
TEMPERATURE													
Daily Average Min.°C	24	23	23	23	23	-16	23	23	24	24	24	24	20
Daily Average Min.°F	75	74	74	74	74	4	73	74	75	75	75	75	69
Daily Average Max.°C	30	29	30	30	31	31	31	31	31	31	31	31	30
Daily Average Max.°F	86	85	86	86	87	88	87	87	87	87	87	87	87
Monthly Average °C	26	25	25	26	26	26	26	26	26	27	27	27	26
Monthly Average °F	79	78	78	79	79	79	78	79	80	80	81	80	79
RELATIVE HUMIDITY (%)	75	76	76	78	75	73	73	73	73	72	71	73	74
PRECIPITATION													
Monthly Average mm	263	366	448	445	279	170	111	35	33	33	9	59	2251.0
Monthly Average Inches	10.3	14.4	17.6	17.5	10.9	6.6	4.3	1.3	1.2	1.2	0.3	2.3	87.9
Days of 1mm or More	14	18	23	22	21	13	9	3	2	2	1	4	132

SAO PAULO   Brazil

	Elevation 795 m. (2608 ft.)				23°32'S—46°37'W								
	JAN	FEB	MAR	APR	MAY	JUN	JUL	AUG	SEP	OCT	NOV	DEC	YEAR
TEMPERATURE													
Monthly Average °C	22	22	21	20	17	16	16	17	18	19	20	21	19
Monthly Average °F	71	72	71	67	63	61	61	63	64	66	68	70	66
PRECIPITATION													
Monthly Average mm	224	224	155	74	75	55	36	48	70	127	151	202	1441.0
Monthly Average Inches	8.8	8.8	6.1	2.9	2.9	2.1	1.4	1.8	2.7	5.0	5.9	7.9	56.3
Days of 1mm or More	15	13	11	7	6	4	4	4	7	9	10	14	104

PLOVDIV   Bulgaria

	Elevation 160 m. (524 ft.)				42°29'N—24°48'E								
	JAN	FEB	MAR	APR	MAY	JUN	JUL	AUG	SEP	OCT	NOV	DEC	YEAR
TEMPERATURE													
Daily Average Min.°C	-3	-2	1	5	10	14	16	15	11	8	3	-2	6
Daily Average Min.°F	26	28	34	41	50	57	61	59	52	46	37	29	43
Daily Average Max.°C	5	7	12	18	23	28	31	30	26	21	12	6	18
Daily Average Max.°F	40	45	54	65	74	82	87	86	78	69	54	43	65
Monthly Average °C	1	3	6	12	17	21	23	23	18	13	8	3	12
Monthly Average °F	33	37	43	54	63	69	73	73	65	55	46	37	54
RELATIVE HUMIDITY (%)	76	67	60	53	53	50	45	46	48	59	69	76	59
PRECIPITATION													
Monthly Average mm	44	29	42	40	73	66	51	28	37	44	51	47	552.0
Monthly Average Inches	1.7	1.1	1.6	1.5	2.8	2.5	2.0	1.1	1.4	1.7	2.0	1.8	21.2
Days of 1mm or More	0	0	0	0	0	0	0	0	0	0	0	0	0

VARNA Bulgaria

	JAN	FEB	MAR	APR	MAY	JUN	JUL	AUG	SEP	OCT	NOV	DEC	YEAR
Elevation 35 m. (115 ft.)					**43°12'N—27°54'E**								
TEMPERATURE													
Daily Average Min.°C	-1	-1	2	7	12	16	19	18	14	11	6	1	9
Daily Average Min.°F	30	30	36	44	53	61	65	64	58	52	43	34	47
Daily Average Max.°C	6	6	11	16	22	26	30	29	26	21	13	7	18
Daily Average Max.°F	42	43	51	60	71	79	86	85	78	69	55	45	64
Extreme Monthly Min.°C	-23	-24	-14	-3	2	7	10	10	3	-2	-8	-14	-24
Extreme Monthly Min.°F	-10	-12	6	27	36	44	50	50	37	29	17	6	-12
Extreme Monthly Max.°C	21	22	26	29	34	36	42	39	34	33	26	21	41
Extreme Monthly Max.°F	69	71	78	85	94	96	107	103	93	91	79	70	107
Monthly Average °C	2	3	6	11	15	20	22	22	19	14	8	5	12
Monthly Average °F	36	38	42	51	59	68	72	71	66	57	46	41	54
RELATIVE HUMIDITY (%)	80	75	70	68	69	67	61	60	62	68	72	79	69
PRECIPITATION													
Monthly Average mm	45	36	30	42	39	47	49	31	25	32	57	76	509.0
Monthly Average Inches	1.7	1.4	1.1	1.6	1.5	1.8	1.9	1.2	0.9	1.2	2.2	2.9	19.4
Days of 1mm or More	6	7	4	6	3	5	5	3	2	4	6	11	62

BOBO DIOULASSO Burkina Faso

	JAN	FEB	MAR	APR	MAY	JUN	JUL	AUG	SEP	OCT	NOV	DEC	YEAR
Elevation 432 m. (1417 ft.)					**11°10'N—4°18'W**								
TEMPERATURE													
Daily Average Min.°C	17	20	23	24	24	22	21	21	21	21	20	17	21
Daily Average Min.°F	63	68	73	75	74	71	70	69	69	70	68	63	69
Daily Average Max.°C	33	35	37	36	34	32	30	30	30	33	34	33	33
Daily Average Max.°F	92	95	98	97	94	90	86	86	86	91	93	92	92
Monthly Average °C	26	28	30	30	29	27	25	25	25	27	27	25	27
Monthly Average °F	78	83	86	86	84	80	77	76	77	80	81	78	81
RELATIVE HUMIDITY (%)	16	19	26	40	54	63	69	74	69	54	34	19	45
PRECIPITATION													
Monthly Average mm	1	3	17	44	95	129	213	272	188	58	9	3	1032.0
Monthly Average Inches	0.0	0.1	0.6	1.7	3.7	5.0	8.3	10.7	7.4	2.2	0.3	0.1	40.1
Days of 1mm or More	0	0	2	4	7	10	12	16	13	5	0	0	69

OUAGADOUGOU Burkina Faso

	JAN	FEB	MAR	APR	MAY	JUN	JUL	AUG	SEP	OCT	NOV	DEC	YEAR
Elevation 304 m. (997 ft.)					**12°21'N—1°31'W**								
TEMPERATURE													
Daily Average Min.°C	16	19	23	26	25	24	22	22	22	23	20	17	21
Daily Average Min.°F	62	66	73	78	78	74	72	71	71	73	68	62	71
Daily Average Max.°C	34	37	39	39	37	34	32	30	32	35	36	34	35
Daily Average Max.°F	93	98	102	102	99	93	89	87	89	96	98	94	95
Extreme Monthly Min.°C	9	12	15	15	19	17	18	14	19	18	16	11	8
Extreme Monthly Min.°F	48	54	59	59	66	63	65	58	66	64	60	51	48
Extreme Monthly Max.°C	45	45	45	47	48	44	41	38	39	47	48	44	47
Extreme Monthly Max.°F	113	113	113	116	118	111	106	101	102	116	118	111	118
Monthly Average °C	24	27	30	33	33	31	28	27	27	29	27	25	29
Monthly Average °F	75	81	87	91	91	87	83	81	81	85	81	76	83
RELATIVE HUMIDITY (%)	14	13	16	28	43	55	64	70	65	46	23	16	38
PRECIPITATION													
Monthly Average mm	0	0	2	8	43	102	157	178	106	26	1	0	623.0
Monthly Average Inches	0.0	0.0	0.0	0.3	1.6	4.0	6.1	7.0	4.1	1.0	0.0	0.0	24.1
Days of 1mm or More	0	0	0	1	4	7	11	13	9	2	0	0	47

AKYAB   Burma

		JAN	FEB	MAR	APR	MAY	JUN	JUL	AUG	SEP	OCT	NOV	DEC	YEAR
Elevation 9 m. (29 ft.)							20°8'N—92°55'E							
TEMPERATURE														
Daily Average Min.°C	15	16	20	24	26	25	25	25	25	24	22	17	22
Daily Average Min.°F	59	61	68	75	78	77	77	77	77	76	71	63	72
Daily Average Max.°C	27	29	31	32	32	30	29	29	30	31	29	27	30
Daily Average Max.°F	81	84	88	90	90	86	84	84	86	87	85	81	86
Monthly Average °C	22	22	26	28	29	27	27	27	27	27	25	22	26
Monthly Average °F	71	72	79	83	84	81	80	80	81	81	78	72	78
RELATIVE HUMIDITY (%)	65	65	70	73	77	87	89	88	86	82	79	73	78
PRECIPITATION														
Monthly Average mm	12	10	41	79	319	1042	956	986	459	226	69	9	4208.0
Monthly Average Inches	0.4	0.3	1.6	3.1	12.5	41.0	37.6	38.8	18.0	8.9	2.7	0.3	165.2
Days of 1mm or More	0	1	1	5	11	25	25	24	16	8	4	0	120

MANDALAY   Burma

		JAN	FEB	MAR	APR	MAY	JUN	JUL	AUG	SEP	OCT	NOV	DEC	YEAR
Elevation 76 m. (249 ft.)							21°59'N—96°6'E							
TEMPERATURE														
Daily Average Min.°C	13	15	19	25	26	26	26	25	24	23	19	14	21
Daily Average Min.°F	55	59	66	77	79	78	78	77	76	73	66	57	70
Daily Average Max.°C	28	31	36	38	37	34	34	33	33	32	29	27	33
Daily Average Max.°F	82	88	97	101	98	93	93	92	91	89	85	80	91
Extreme Monthly Min.°C	7	8	12	18	21	20	22	22	21	17	13	7	6
Extreme Monthly Min.°F	45	47	54	64	69	68	72	71	69	62	56	44	44
Extreme Monthly Max.°C	33	37	42	43	44	42	41	38	39	39	37	32	43
Extreme Monthly Max.°F	91	99	108	110	111	107	106	101	103	102	98	90	111
Monthly Average °C	21	23	28	31	31	30	30	29	29	27	25	21	27
Monthly Average °F	70	74	82	87	88	86	85	84	83	81	76	71	81
RELATIVE HUMIDITY (%)	52	41	31	33	52	64	66	72	74	78	74	66	59
PRECIPITATION														
Monthly Average mm	2	1	6	46	132	116	96	123	142	91	33	8	796.0
Monthly Average Inches	0.0	0.0	0.2	1.8	5.1	4.5	3.7	4.8	5.5	3.5	1.2	0.3	30.6
Days of 1mm or More	0	0	0	4	8	8	8	10	8	5	3	1	55

RANGOON   Burma

		JAN	FEB	MAR	APR	MAY	JUN	JUL	AUG	SEP	OCT	NOV	DEC	YEAR
Elevation 6 m. (18 ft.)							16°46'N—96°11'E							
TEMPERATURE														
Daily Average Min.°C	18	19	22	24	25	24	24	24	24	24	23	19	23
Daily Average Min.°F	65	67	71	76	77	76	76	76	76	76	73	67	73
Daily Average Max.°C	32	33	36	36	33	30	29	29	30	31	31	31	32
Daily Average Max.°F	89	92	96	97	92	86	85	85	86	88	88	88	89
Monthly Average °C	25	26	28	30	29	27	27	27	27	27	27	25	27
Monthly Average °F	77	79	83	86	85	81	80	80	81	81	81	77	81
RELATIVE HUMIDITY (%)	52	52	54	64	76	85	88	88	86	77	72	61	71
PRECIPITATION														
Monthly Average mm	2	1	47	49	345	748	457	500	304	173	40	21	2687.0
Monthly Average Inches	0.0	0.0	1.8	1.9	13.5	29.4	17.9	19.6	11.9	6.8	1.5	0.8	105.1
Days of 1mm or More	0	0	2	4	15	25	24	24	16	10	3	1	124

DOUALA — Cameroon

Elevation 15 m. (49 ft.)					4°5'N—9°42'E								
	JAN	FEB	MAR	APR	MAY	JUN	JUL	AUG	SEP	OCT	NOV	DEC	YEAR
TEMPERATURE													
Daily Average Min.°C	23	24	23	23	23	23	23	22	23	22	23	23	23
Daily Average Min.°F	73	75	74	74	74	73	73	72	73	72	73	73	73
Daily Average Max.°C	31	32	32	32	31	29	27	27	28	30	31	31	30
Daily Average Max.°F	88	89	89	89	88	85	81	81	83	85	87	88	86
Monthly Average °C	27	28	27	27	27	26	25	25	25	26	27	27	26
Monthly Average °F	81	82	81	81	81	79	77	77	77	78	80	81	79
RELATIVE HUMIDITY (%)	68	67	69	69	73	77	83	84	80	75	72	69	74
PRECIPITATION													
Monthly Average mm	59	66	184	230	276	476	692	841	656	429	167	51	4127.0
Monthly Average Inches	2.3	2.5	7.2	9.0	10.8	18.7	27.2	33.1	25.8	16.8	6.5	2.0	161.9
Days of 1mm or More	3	5	11	13	17	20	24	27	25	22	9	4	180

MAROUA — Cameroon

Elevation 405 m. (1328 ft.)					10°28'N—14°16'E								
	JAN	FEB	MAR	APR	MAY	JUN	JUL	AUG	SEP	OCT	NOV	DEC	YEAR
TEMPERATURE													
Daily Average Min.°C	18	20	24	25	24	23	22	21	21	21	20	18	21
Daily Average Min.°F	64	67	74	78	76	73	71	70	70	70	68	65	70
Daily Average Max.°C	33	36	39	40	38	35	32	30	32	35	35	34	35
Daily Average Max.°F	92	96	102	104	100	94	89	86	89	95	96	92	95
Monthly Average °C	24	27	31	32	31	28	26	26	26	28	27	25	28
Monthly Average °F	76	81	87	90	87	83	79	78	79	82	80	77	82
RELATIVE HUMIDITY (%)	17	15	16	21	35	50	61	68	61	38	21	20	35
PRECIPITATION													
Monthly Average mm	0	0	2	23	75	126	205	227	142	32	0	0	832.0
Monthly Average Inches	0.0	0.0	0.0	0.9	2.9	4.9	8.0	8.9	5.5	1.2	0.0	0.0	32.3
Days of 1mm or More	0	0	0	3	5	7	14	15	9	4	0	0	57

YAOUNDE — Cameroon

Elevation 760 m. (2493 ft.)					3°52'N—11°32'E								
	JAN	FEB	MAR	APR	MAY	JUN	JUL	AUG	SEP	OCT	NOV	DEC	YEAR
TEMPERATURE													
Daily Average Min.°C	19	20	19	19	19	19	19	19	19	19	19	19	19
Daily Average Min.°F	66	67	67	67	67	66	66	65	66	65	66	66	66
Daily Average Max.°C	29	30	30	29	28	27	26	26	27	28	28	28	28
Daily Average Max.°F	84	85	85	85	83	81	78	79	81	82	83	83	82
Extreme Monthly Min.°C	14	15	16	15	16	15	16	16	15	15	17	16	13
Extreme Monthly Min.°F	57	59	60	59	60	59	60	60	59	59	62	60	57
Extreme Monthly Max.°C	33	33	33	36	34	32	31	34	31	33	32	32	35
Extreme Monthly Max.°F	91	92	91	96	94	90	87	93	88	91	89	90	96
Monthly Average °C	24	25	24	24	24	23	22	22	23	23	23	24	23
Monthly Average °F	75	76	76	75	75	73	72	72	73	73	74	74	74
RELATIVE HUMIDITY (%)	61	60	63	67	70	73	75	75	73	72	67	64	68
PRECIPITATION													
Monthly Average mm	23	54	139	207	215	191	80	83	234	311	133	32	1702.0
Monthly Average Inches	0.9	2.1	5.4	8.1	8.4	7.5	3.1	3.2	9.2	12.2	5.2	1.2	66.5
Days of 1mm or More	1	3	9	14	15	11	9	10	20	22	9	3	126

CALGARY, ALBERTA

Canada

Elevation 1079 m. (3540 ft.)   **51°6'N—114°1'W**

	JAN	FEB	MAR	APR	MAY	JUN	JUL	AUG	SEP	OCT	NOV	DEC	YEAR
TEMPERATURE													
Daily Average Min.°C	-16	-15	-10	-3	3	7	10	8	4	-1	-8	-12	-3
Daily Average Min.°F	4	6	15	27	38	44	49	46	40	30	18	10	27
Daily Average Max.°C	-4	-3	1	10	16	19	24	22	17	12	3	-1	10
Daily Average Max.°F	24	26	34	49	61	66	75	72	63	53	38	30	49
Extreme Monthly Min.°C	-44	-45	-37	-26	-11	-3	0	-2	-13	-22	-35	-43	-45
Extreme Monthly Min.°F	-48	-49	-35	-14	12	26	32	28	8	-8	-31	-45	-49
Extreme Monthly Max.°C	16	19	24	29	32	35	36	36	32	29	22	19	36
Extreme Monthly Max.°F	61	66	75	85	90	95	97	96	90	85	71	67	97
Monthly Average °C	-11	-7	-4	3	9	13	16	15	11	6	-3	-8	3
Monthly Average °F	12	19	24	38	49	56	62	59	51	42	27	18	38
RELATIVE HUMIDITY (%)	70	70	65	51	45	50	48	47	49	55	65	69	57
PRECIPITATION													
Monthly Average mm	16	19	20	29	49	91	68	55	35	18	15	15	430.0
Monthly Average Inches	0.6	0.7	0.7	1.1	1.9	3.5	2.6	2.1	1.3	0.7	0.5	0.5	16.2
Days of 1mm or More	0	0	0	0	0	0	0	0	0	0	0	0	0

DAWSON, YUKON TERRITORY

Canada

Elevation 324 m. (1062 ft.)   **64°4'N—139°26'W**

	JAN	FEB	MAR	APR	MAY	JUN	JUL	AUG	SEP	OCT	NOV	DEC	YEAR
TEMPERATURE													
Daily Average Min.°C	-31	-28	-22	-9	1	7	9	6	1	-7	-20	-28	-10
Daily Average Min.°F	-25	-19	-7	17	34	44	47	43	34	20	-3	-19	14
Daily Average Max.°C	-24	-19	-8	6	15	21	22	19	12	0	-13	-21	1
Daily Average Max.°F	-11	-3	18	42	59	70	72	66	53	33	8	-7	33
Monthly Average °C	-29	-23	-14	-2	8	14	16	13	6	-3	-17	-25	-5
Monthly Average °F	-19	-9	6	29	46	57	60	55	44	26	2	-13	24
RELATIVE HUMIDITY (%)	80	82	83	61	49	49	55	60	67	83	85	85	70
PRECIPITATION													
Monthly Average mm	19	15	12	8	21	36	52	50	28	26	24	25	316.0
Monthly Average Inches	0.7	0.5	0.4	0.3	0.8	1.4	2.0	1.9	1.1	1.0	0.9	0.9	11.9
Days of 1mm or More	0	0	0	0	0	0	0	0	0	0	0	0	0

EDMONTON, ALBERTA

Canada

Elevation 676 m. (2217 ft.)   **53°34'N—113°31'W**

	JAN	FEB	MAR	APR	MAY	JUN	JUL	AUG	SEP	OCT	NOV	DEC	YEAR
TEMPERATURE													
Daily Average Min.°C	-19	-17	-10	-2	4	8	11	9	5	-1	-9	-14	-3
Daily Average Min.°F	-2	2	13	29	40	47	52	48	40	31	17	6	27
Daily Average Max.°C	-9	-7	0	10	17	20	24	22	17	11	0	-5	8
Daily Average Max.°F	16	20	31	50	63	68	74	71	63	52	32	23	47
Extreme Monthly Min.°C	-49	-49	-40	-26	-12	-4	-2	-3	-11	-26	-42	-43	-49
Extreme Monthly Min.°F	-57	-57	-40	-15	10	25	29	26	12	-15	-44	-46	-57
Extreme Monthly Max.°C	14	17	22	31	34	37	37	36	32	28	23	16	37
Extreme Monthly Max.°F	57	62	72	88	94	99	98	96	90	83	74	61	99
Monthly Average °C	-13	-9	-4	5	11	15	18	16	11	6	-4	-10	4
Monthly Average °F	9	16	25	41	53	60	64	62	52	43	24	13	38
RELATIVE HUMIDITY (%)	80	75	67	49	41	49	51	54	52	56	73	80	61
PRECIPITATION													
Monthly Average mm	22	16	16	20	43	76	88	68	45	19	15	22	450.0
Monthly Average Inches	0.8	0.6	0.6	0.7	1.6	2.9	3.4	2.6	1.7	0.7	0.5	0.8	16.9
Days of 1mm or More	7	5	4	4	7	9	10	8	6	3	4	5	72

KAMLOOPS, BRITISH COLUMBIA   Canada

Elevation 345 m. (1131 ft.)						43°24'N—120°25'W						
	JAN	FEB	MAR	APR	MAY	JUN	JUL	AUG	SEP	OCT	NOV	DEC	YEAR

TEMPERATURE

	JAN	FEB	MAR	APR	MAY	JUN	JUL	AUG	SEP	OCT	NOV	DEC	YEAR
Daily Average Min.°C	-9	-6	-2	3	7	11	13	12	8	3	-2	-5	3
Daily Average Min.°F	16	20	29	37	45	51	55	53	46	38	29	23	37
Daily Average Max.°C	-2	2	9	17	22	25	30	28	23	14	5	1	14
Daily Average Max.°F	29	36	49	62	72	77	85	82	73	57	41	34	58
Monthly Average °C	-6	-1	4	9	14	18	21	20	15	8	2	-3	8
Monthly Average °F	21	30	38	49	58	64	70	67	59	47	35	27	47
RELATIVE HUMIDITY (%)	77	70	52	37	36	38	33	37	42	57	73	78	53

PRECIPITATION

	JAN	FEB	MAR	APR	MAY	JUN	JUL	AUG	SEP	OCT	NOV	DEC	YEAR
Monthly Average mm	28	15	8	12	19	36	25	26	20	18	20	28	255.0
Monthly Average Inches	1.1	0.5	0.3	0.4	0.7	1.4	0.9	1.0	0.7	0.7	0.7	1.1	9.5
Days of 1mm or More	0	0	0	0	0	0	0	0	0	0	0	0	0

LETHBRIDGE, ALBERTA   Canada

Elevation 920 m. (3018 ft.)						49°38'N—112°48'W						
	JAN	FEB	MAR	APR	MAY	JUN	JUL	AUG	SEP	OCT	NOV	DEC	YEAR

TEMPERATURE

	JAN	FEB	MAR	APR	MAY	JUN	JUL	AUG	SEP	OCT	NOV	DEC	YEAR
Daily Average Min.°C	-14	-13	-8	-1	4	8	11	10	6	1	-6	-10	-1
Daily Average Min.°F	7	9	18	30	40	47	52	49	42	34	21	14	30
Daily Average Max.°C	-3	-1	3	12	18	21	27	25	20	14	5	1	12
Daily Average Max.°F	27	29	38	53	64	70	80	77	67	57	41	33	53
Monthly Average °C	-9	-5	-1	6	11	16	18	18	12	8	-1	-6	5
Monthly Average °F	17	23	30	42	52	60	65	64	54	46	29	21	42
RELATIVE HUMIDITY (%)	71	71	63	45	43	48	39	40	44	53	66	71	55

PRECIPITATION

	JAN	FEB	MAR	APR	MAY	JUN	JUL	AUG	SEP	OCT	NOV	DEC	YEAR
Monthly Average mm	20	14	24	37	52	68	45	43	43	16	17	20	399.0
Monthly Average Inches	0.7	0.5	0.9	1.4	2.0	2.6	1.7	1.6	1.6	0.6	0.6	0.7	14.9
Days of 1mm or More	6	3	6	6	7	7	5	5	5	3	4	5	62

MONTREAL, QUEBEC   Canada

Elevation 57 m. (187 ft.)						45°30'N—73°35'W						
	JAN	FEB	MAR	APR	MAY	JUN	JUL	AUG	SEP	OCT	NOV	DEC	YEAR

TEMPERATURE

	JAN	FEB	MAR	APR	MAY	JUN	JUL	AUG	SEP	OCT	NOV	DEC	YEAR
Daily Average Min.°C	-13	-11	-5	2	9	14	17	16	11	6	0	-9	3
Daily Average Min.°F	8	12	22	36	47	58	63	61	53	42	32	16	37
Daily Average Max.°C	-6	-4	2	11	18	23	26	25	20	14	5	-3	11
Daily Average Max.°F	22	25	35	51	65	74	79	77	67	56	42	28	52
Extreme Monthly Min.°C	-33	-33	-29	-17	-5	3	8	6	0	-7	-28	-34	-33
Extreme Monthly Min.°F	-27	-28	-20	2	23	38	46	43	32	20	-18	-29	-29
Extreme Monthly Max.°C	12	11	20	28	34	34	36	36	32	27	21	15	36
Extreme Monthly Max.°F	54	51	68	83	94	94	97	96	90	80	70	59	97
Monthly Average °C	-9	-8	-1	7	14	19	22	20	16	10	3	-6	7
Monthly Average °F	16	18	29	44	56	66	71	69	60	50	37	22	45
RELATIVE HUMIDITY (%)	79	77	76	73	71	74	76	79	83	81	81	79	77

PRECIPITATION

	JAN	FEB	MAR	APR	MAY	JUN	JUL	AUG	SEP	OCT	NOV	DEC	YEAR
Monthly Average mm	79	71	74	76	74	86	92	91	86	78	92	90	989.0
Monthly Average Inches	3.1	2.7	2.9	2.9	2.9	3.3	3.6	3.5	3.3	3.0	3.6	3.5	38.3
Days of 1mm or More	0	0	0	0	0	0	0	0	0	0	0	0	0

MOOSONEE, ONTARIO   Canada

	JAN	FEB	MAR	APR	MAY	JUN	JUL	AUG	SEP	OCT	NOV	DEC	YEAR
Elevation 10 m. (33 ft.)					51°16'N—80°39'W								
TEMPERATURE													
Daily Average Min.°C	-26	-24	-18	-8	0	6	10	9	5	0	-8	-20	-6
Daily Average Min.°F	-15	-12	-1	18	32	43	49	49	41	32	17	-3	21
Daily Average Max.°C	-14	-11	-5	3	11	18	22	21	15	9	-1	-10	5
Daily Average Max.°F	6	12	23	38	52	65	72	69	60	47	30	14	41
Monthly Average °C	-20	-19	-12	-3	6	12	15	14	9	4	-5	-16	-1
Monthly Average °F	-5	-2	10	27	42	53	59	57	49	39	23	3	30
RELATIVE HUMIDITY (%)	79	76	71	65	64	61	61	64	68	69	81	81	70
PRECIPITATION													
Monthly Average mm	35	25	33	41	52	75	101	82	80	72	59	35	690.0
Monthly Average Inches	1.3	0.9	1.2	1.6	2.0	2.9	3.9	3.2	3.1	2.8	2.3	1.3	26.5
Days of 1mm or More	9	6	7	7	8	10	13	11	11	11	10	9	112

PRINCE ALBERT, SASKATCHEWAN   Canada

	JAN	FEB	MAR	APR	MAY	JUN	JUL	AUG	SEP	OCT	NOV	DEC	YEAR
Elevation 431 m. (1414 ft.)					53°13'N—105°41'W								
TEMPERATURE													
Daily Average Min.°C	-25	-23	-16	-4	3	7	11	10	4	-2	-11	-20	-6
Daily Average Min.°F	-13	-9	3	25	37	45	52	49	40	29	12	-4	22
Daily Average Max.°C	-14	-11	-3	8	17	21	25	23	17	10	-3	-10	7
Daily Average Max.°F	7	13	26	47	63	69	77	74	63	50	27	14	44
Monthly Average °C	-21	-17	-10	2	10	14	18	16	10	4	-7	-16	0
Monthly Average °F	-5	2	14	35	49	58	64	61	50	39	19	3	32
RELATIVE HUMIDITY (%)	89	93	91	88	83	86	87	91	92	89	92	93	89
PRECIPITATION													
Monthly Average mm	17	17	18	25	35	60	62	52	34	23	21	21	385.0
Monthly Average Inches	0.6	0.6	0.7	0.9	1.3	2.3	2.4	2.0	1.3	0.9	0.8	0.8	14.6
Days of 1mm or More	0	0	0	0	0	0	0	0	0	0	0	0	0

PRINCE GEORGE, BRITISH COLUMBIA   Canada

	JAN	FEB	MAR	APR	MAY	JUN	JUL	AUG	SEP	OCT	NOV	DEC	YEAR
Elevation 676 m. (2217 ft.)					53°12'N—122°41'W								
TEMPERATURE													
Daily Average Min.°C	-16	-13	-8	-2	2	6	8	6	3	0	-6	-11	-2
Daily Average Min.°F	4	9	18	28	36	43	46	44	38	32	20	13	28
Daily Average Max.°C	-6	2	4	11	17	20	23	21	17	10	1	-3	10
Daily Average Max.°F	21	35	39	51	63	68	73	70	63	50	35	27	50
Extreme Monthly Min.°C	-49	-47	-37	-25	-11	-4	-2	-4	-14	-20	-33	-49	-49
Extreme Monthly Min.°F	-57	-52	-35	-13	12	24	28	25	6	-4	-28	-56	-57
Extreme Monthly Max.°C	12	14	20	30	35	34	38	36	33	29	17	13	38
Extreme Monthly Max.°F	54	58	68	86	95	93	100	96	92	84	62	55	102
Monthly Average °C	-10	-5	-1	5	9	13	15	14	10	5	-3	-8	4
Monthly Average °F	14	22	31	40	49	56	60	58	49	41	26	17	39
RELATIVE HUMIDITY (%)	82	73	63	50	46	51	53	56	58	67	80	84	62
PRECIPITATION													
Monthly Average mm	55	34	34	27	51	64	59	65	64	61	49	50	613.0
Monthly Average Inches	2.1	1.3	1.3	1.0	2.0	2.5	2.3	2.5	2.5	2.4	1.9	1.9	23.7
Days of 1mm or More	10	8	8	6	8	11	9	10	10	10	10	11	111

REGINA, SASKATCHEWAN   Canada

Elevation 574 m. (1883 ft.)						50°27'N—104°37'W						
	JAN	FEB	MAR	APR	MAY	JUN	JUL	AUG	SEP	OCT	NOV	DEC	YEAR

TEMPERATURE	JAN	FEB	MAR	APR	MAY	JUN	JUL	AUG	SEP	OCT	NOV	DEC	YEAR
Daily Average Min.°C	-22	-20	-14	-2	4	8	12	11	5	-2	-11	-17	-4
Daily Average Min.°F	-7	-4	8	29	39	47	53	51	41	29	13	1	25
Daily Average Max.°C	-11	-9	-3	9	18	21	26	25	19	12	0	-7	8
Daily Average Max.°F	12	15	26	48	65	70	80	77	66	54	32	20	47
Extreme Monthly Min.°C	-48	-49	-42	-29	-14	-5	-2	-5	-13	-26	-44	-48	-48
Extreme Monthly Min.°F	-54	-56	-44	-20	7	23	28	23	9	-15	-47	-55	-56
Extreme Monthly Max.°C	9	12	24	32	37	39	42	40	37	31	23	15	41
Extreme Monthly Max.°F	48	53	76	89	99	102	107	104	99	87	73	59	107
Monthly Average °C	-17	-13	-6	4	11	16	19	18	12	5	-5	-13	3
Monthly Average °F	2	9	21	39	52	61	66	65	53	41	22	8	37
RELATIVE HUMIDITY (%)	89	87	83	55	44	51	49	46	50	60	82	88	65
PRECIPITATION													
Monthly Average mm	17	13	15	20	49	69	55	38	37	20	12	16	361.0
Monthly Average Inches	0.6	0.5	0.5	0.7	1.9	2.7	2.1	1.4	1.4	0.7	0.4	0.6	13.5
Days of 1mm or More	4	4	4	4	7	8	7	5	5	3	3	4	58

SAINT JOHN, NEW BRUNSWICK   Canada

Elevation 36 m. (118 ft.)						45°17'N—66°4'W						
	JAN	FEB	MAR	APR	MAY	JUN	JUL	AUG	SEP	OCT	NOV	DEC	YEAR

TEMPERATURE	JAN	FEB	MAR	APR	MAY	JUN	JUL	AUG	SEP	OCT	NOV	DEC	YEAR
Daily Average Min.°C	-11	-10	-6	0	5	9	12	13	10	5	0	-8	2
Daily Average Min.°F	13	13	22	32	41	49	54	55	49	41	32	19	35
Daily Average Max.°C	-2	-1	3	8	14	18	21	21	18	13	7	1	10
Daily Average Max.°F	29	30	37	47	57	64	70	70	64	55	44	33	50
Extreme Monthly Min.°C	-7	-29	-26	-18	-7	-3	1	0	-2	-6	-14	-20	-29
Extreme Monthly Min.°F	19	-21	-14	-1	20	27	33	32	29	22	6	-4	-21
Extreme Monthly Max.°C	15	13	19	22	27	31	32	34	29	31	20	16	33
Extreme Monthly Max.°F	59	56	67	72	81	87	90	93	84	87	68	60	93
Monthly Average °C	-4	-4	-2	1	6	10	15	15	12	7	3	-1	5
Monthly Average °F	25	24	28	34	42	51	60	60	54	45	38	30	41
RELATIVE HUMIDITY (%)	73	69	66	66	66	71	70	70	69	67	76	72	70
PRECIPITATION													
Monthly Average mm	143	153	130	111	98	90	81	111	112	136	159	165	1489.0
Monthly Average Inches	5.6	6.0	5.1	4.3	3.8	3.5	3.1	4.3	4.4	5.3	6.2	6.4	58.0
Days of 1mm or More	0	0	0	0	0	0	0	0	0	0	0	0	0

SEPT-ILES, QUEBEC   Canada

Elevation 58 m. (190 ft.)						50°13'N—66°16'W						
	JAN	FEB	MAR	APR	MAY	JUN	JUL	AUG	SEP	OCT	NOV	DEC	YEAR

TEMPERATURE	JAN	FEB	MAR	APR	MAY	JUN	JUL	AUG	SEP	OCT	NOV	DEC	YEAR
Daily Average Min.°C	-20	-18	-12	-5	1	6	10	9	5	0	-6	-15	-4
Daily Average Min.°F	-4	-1	10	23	35	44	51	49	41	32	21	4	25
Daily Average Max.°C	-8	-6	-1	4	11	17	20	20	15	8	1	-6	6
Daily Average Max.°F	17	21	30	39	51	62	69	67	58	47	35	22	43
Monthly Average °C	-14	-12	-7	0	6	12	15	14	9	3	-3	-11	1
Monthly Average °F	6	10	20	32	43	53	59	57	49	38	27	12	34
RELATIVE HUMIDITY (%)	80	80	79	75	68	67	70	69	69	69	79	79	74
PRECIPITATION													
Monthly Average mm	88	74	80	91	93	98	91	97	109	98	101	103	1123.0
Monthly Average Inches	3.4	2.9	3.1	3.5	3.6	3.8	3.5	3.8	4.2	3.8	3.9	4.0	43.5
Days of 1mm or More	12	8	10	9	10	10	10	10	10	11	10	12	122

TORONTO, ONTARIO   Canada

Elevation 116 m. (381 ft.)   43°40'N—79°24'W

	JAN	FEB	MAR	APR	MAY	JUN	JUL	AUG	SEP	OCT	NOV	DEC	YEAR
TEMPERATURE													
Daily Average Min.°C	-8	-7	-3	3	9	14	17	16	12	7	2	-4	5
Daily Average Min.°F	18	20	26	38	47	57	62	62	54	45	35	24	41
Daily Average Max.°C	-1	0	4	12	18	24	27	26	22	15	7	1	13
Daily Average Max.°F	31	32	39	53	65	76	81	79	71	58	45	34	55
Extreme Monthly Min.°C	-32	-32	-27	-15	-4	-2	4	4	-2	-9	-21	-6	-32
Extreme Monthly Min.°F	-26	-25	-16	5	25	28	39	40	28	16	-5	22	-26
Extreme Monthly Max.°C	14	13	27	32	34	36	41	39	36	29	21	16	40
Extreme Monthly Max.°F	58	55	80	90	93	97	105	102	96	85	70	61	105
Monthly Average °C	-7	-6	-1	6	12	17	20	20	15	9	3	-4	7
Monthly Average °F	19	21	30	43	54	63	69	67	60	48	38	26	45
RELATIVE HUMIDITY (%)	71	67	62	55	55	55	54	56	59	61	67	71	61
PRECIPITATION													
Monthly Average mm	48	45	58	64	65	66	74	82	74	61	70	63	770.0
Monthly Average Inches	1.8	1.7	2.2	2.5	2.5	2.5	2.9	3.2	2.9	2.4	2.7	2.4	29.7
Days of 1mm or More	8	7	8	8	8	8	7	7	8	8	9	9	95

TREPASSEY, NEWFOUNDLAND   Canada

Elevation 128 m. (419 ft.)   47°34'N—52°43'W

	JAN	FEB	MAR	APR	MAY	JUN	JUL	AUG	SEP	OCT	NOV	DEC	YEAR
TEMPERATURE													
Monthly Average °C	-3	-3	-2	1	4	8	12	13	11	7	4	-1	4
Monthly Average °F	27	26	28	34	39	46	53	56	52	45	38	31	40
PRECIPITATION													
Monthly Average mm	133	119	102	109	100	83	101	114	101	131	139	130	1362.0
Monthly Average Inches	5.2	4.6	4.0	4.2	3.9	3.2	3.9	4.4	3.9	5.1	5.4	5.1	52.9
Days of 1mm or More	0	0	0	0	0	0	0	0	0	0	0	0	0

VANCOUVER, BRITISH COLUMBIA   Canada

Elevation 5 m. (17 ft.)   49°11'N—123°10'W

	JAN	FEB	MAR	APR	MAY	JUN	JUL	AUG	SEP	OCT	NOV	DEC	YEAR
TEMPERATURE													
Daily Average Min.°C	0	1	3	5	8	11	13	12	10	7	3	2	6
Daily Average Min.°F	32	34	37	41	47	52	55	54	50	44	38	35	43
Daily Average Max.°C	6	7	10	14	17	20	23	22	19	14	9	7	14
Daily Average Max.°F	42	45	50	57	63	68	73	72	66	57	49	44	57
Extreme Monthly Min.°C	-17	-13	-9	-3	1	2	4	4	-1	-6	-12	-13	-16
Extreme Monthly Min.°F	2	8	15	27	33	35	40	39	30	21	10	8	2
Extreme Monthly Max.°C	15	16	20	26	28	33	33	33	29	25	23	16	33
Extreme Monthly Max.°F	59	61	68	79	83	92	91	92	85	77	74	60	92
Monthly Average °C	3	5	6	9	12	15	17	17	14	10	6	4	10
Monthly Average °F	37	41	43	48	54	59	63	63	57	50	43	38	50
RELATIVE HUMIDITY (%)	85	79	72	65	63	63	62	65	72	80	85	88	73
PRECIPITATION													
Monthly Average mm	154	126	106	73	58	43	35	40	67	118	161	176	1157.0
Monthly Average Inches	6.0	4.9	4.1	2.8	2.2	1.6	1.3	1.5	2.6	4.6	6.3	6.9	44.8
Days of 1mm or More	15	13	13	11	8	6	5	5	7	12	16	17	128

WHITEHORSE, YUKON TERRITORY   Canada

	JAN	FEB	MAR	APR	MAY	JUN	JUL	AUG	SEP	OCT	NOV	DEC	YEAR
Elevation 636 m. (2086 ft.)					60°43'N—135°3'W								

TEMPERATURE

	JAN	FEB	MAR	APR	MAY	JUN	JUL	AUG	SEP	OCT	NOV	DEC	YEAR
Daily Average Min.°C	-21	-18	-13	-5	1	8	8	7	3	-3	-12	-19	-5
Daily Average Min.°F	-7	-1	9	23	34	46	46	44	37	27	10	-2	22
Daily Average Max.°C	-13	-9	-2	5	14	18	20	18	13	5	-5	-11	4
Daily Average Max.°F	9	16	29	42	56	64	68	65	55	40	22	12	40
Extreme Monthly Min.°C	-52	-51	-38	-26	-7	-1	0	-4	-9	-20	-41	-48	-52
Extreme Monthly Min.°F	-62	-59	-36	-14	19	30	32	24	15	-4	-41	-54	-62
Extreme Monthly Max.°C	8	10	12	15	30	32	33	29	27	19	11	8	32
Extreme Monthly Max.°F	47	50	54	59	86	89	91	84	80	66	51	47	91
Monthly Average °C	-19	-13	-8	0	7	12	14	12	7	1	-9	-16	-1
Monthly Average °F	-2	9	18	32	44	53	57	54	45	33	15	3	30
RELATIVE HUMIDITY (%)	82	76	62	47	41	43	47	50	55	64	80	84	61

PRECIPITATION

	JAN	FEB	MAR	APR	MAY	JUN	JUL	AUG	SEP	OCT	NOV	DEC	YEAR
Monthly Average mm	17	12	12	9	13	29	35	38	34	22	17	18	256.0
Monthly Average Inches	0.6	0.4	0.4	0.3	0.5	1.1	1.3	1.4	1.3	0.8	0.6	0.7	9.4
Days of 1mm or More	5	3	3	2	4	6	8	8	7	6	5	5	62

WINNIPEG, MANITOBA   Canada

	JAN	FEB	MAR	APR	MAY	JUN	JUL	AUG	SEP	OCT	NOV	DEC	YEAR
Elevation 240 m. (787 ft.)					49°54'N—97°14'W								

TEMPERATURE

	JAN	FEB	MAR	APR	MAY	JUN	JUL	AUG	SEP	OCT	NOV	DEC	YEAR
Daily Average Min.°C	-22	-21	-13	-2	5	10	14	13	7	1	-9	-17	-3
Daily Average Min.°F	-8	-5	9	29	40	50	56	55	45	34	17	1	27
Daily Average Max.°C	-13	-10	-3	9	18	22	26	25	19	12	-1	-9	8
Daily Average Max.°F	9	13	27	48	64	72	79	77	66	53	30	17	46
Extreme Monthly Min.°C	-44	-44	-39	-28	-12	-6	2	-1	-8	-21	-37	-48	-47
Extreme Monthly Min.°F	-48	-47	-38	-18	11	21	35	30	17	-5	-34	-54	-54
Extreme Monthly Max.°C	8	8	23	32	38	38	42	39	37	30	22	12	42
Extreme Monthly Max.°F	46	47	74	90	100	101	108	103	99	86	71	53	108
Monthly Average °C	-19	-15	-7	4	11	17	20	18	12	6	-5	-14	2
Monthly Average °F	-1	5	19	39	53	62	67	65	54	42	23	6	36
RELATIVE HUMIDITY (%)	83	85	78	58	48	54	55	55	61	66	81	85	67

PRECIPITATION

	JAN	FEB	MAR	APR	MAY	JUN	JUL	AUG	SEP	OCT	NOV	DEC	YEAR
Monthly Average mm	17	15	22	39	62	76	75	78	52	33	22	18	509.0
Monthly Average Inches	0.6	0.5	0.8	1.5	2.4	2.9	2.9	3.0	2.0	1.2	0.8	0.7	19.3
Days of 1mm or More	5	4	4	5	7	8	8	7	7	5	5	4	69

SANTA CRUZ DE TENERIFE   Canary Islands

	JAN	FEB	MAR	APR	MAY	JUN	JUL	AUG	SEP	OCT	NOV	DEC	YEAR
Elevation 46 m. (150 ft.)					28°28'N—16°15'W								

TEMPERATURE

	JAN	FEB	MAR	APR	MAY	JUN	JUL	AUG	SEP	OCT	NOV	DEC	YEAR
Daily Average Min.°C	15	14	15	16	17	19	20	21	20	19	17	16	17
Daily Average Min.°F	58	58	59	60	63	65	68	69	69	67	63	60	63
Daily Average Max.°C	21	21	22	23	24	26	29	29	28	26	24	21	24
Daily Average Max.°F	69	70	72	73	75	79	83	84	82	79	74	69	76
Monthly Average °C	18	18	19	19	20	22	24	25	24	23	21	19	21
Monthly Average °F	64	64	65	67	69	72	76	77	76	73	69	66	70
RELATIVE HUMIDITY (%)	63	61	60	56	57	56	52	54	59	62	63	62	59

PRECIPITATION

	JAN	FEB	MAR	APR	MAY	JUN	JUL	AUG	SEP	OCT	NOV	DEC	YEAR
Monthly Average mm	40	38	26	15	4	1	0	0	7	14	37	46	228.0
Monthly Average Inches	1.5	1.4	1.0	0.5	0.1	0.0	0.0	0.0	0.2	0.5	1.4	1.8	8.4
Days of 1mm or More	5	4	5	3	1	0	0	0	0	4	5	5	32

BANGUI Central African Republic

Elevation 381 m. (1250 ft.)					4°23'N—18°34'E								
	JAN	FEB	MAR	APR	MAY	JUN	JUL	AUG	SEP	OCT	NOV	DEC	YEAR
TEMPERATURE													
Daily Average Min.°C	20	21	22	22	22	22	21	21	21	21	21	19	21
Daily Average Min.°F	67	69	71	71	71	71	70	69	69	69	69	67	69
Daily Average Max.°C	32	34	33	32	31	30	29	29	30	30	31	32	31
Daily Average Max.°F	90	93	91	90	89	87	84	84	86	86	87	89	88
Extreme Monthly Min.°C	14	14	18	18	18	18	18	17	18	18	17	14	13
Extreme Monthly Min.°F	57	57	64	65	65	65	64	62	65	64	63	57	57
Extreme Monthly Max.°C	37	38	38	37	36	35	34	34	34	34	34	36	38
Extreme Monthly Max.°F	98	101	100	99	96	95	94	93	94	94	94	96	101
Monthly Average °C	25	27	27	27	26	25	25	25	25	25	25	25	26
Monthly Average °F	77	80	81	80	79	78	76	76	77	77	77	77	78
RELATIVE HUMIDITY (%)	49	47	57	61	65	68	72	70	68	68	65	52	62
PRECIPITATION													
Monthly Average mm	18	35	102	138	166	158	171	237	194	198	72	27	1516.0
Monthly Average Inches	0.7	1.3	4.0	5.4	6.5	6.2	6.7	9.3	7.6	7.7	2.8	1.0	59.2
Days of 1mm or More	1	3	7	9	11	11	11	14	14	15	7	2	105

BERBERATI Central African Republic

Elevation 583 m. (1912 ft.)					4°15'N—15°47'E								
	JAN	FEB	MAR	APR	MAY	JUN	JUL	AUG	SEP	OCT	NOV	DEC	YEAR
TEMPERATURE													
Daily Average Min.°C	18	19	20	20	20	19	19	19	19	19	19	18	19
Daily Average Min.°F	64	65	68	68	68	67	67	66	66	66	66	64	66
Daily Average Max.°C	31	32	32	31	31	29	28	28	29	30	29	31	30
Daily Average Max.°F	88	90	89	88	87	85	83	83	85	85	85	87	86
Monthly Average °C	24	25	25	25	25	24	23	23	23	24	24	24	24
Monthly Average °F	75	77	78	77	77	75	74	74	74	75	75	75	75
RELATIVE HUMIDITY (%)	50	49	59	64	66	70	72	72	69	68	62	52	63
PRECIPITATION													
Monthly Average mm	17	35	87	132	146	170	142	197	225	231	69	30	1481.0
Monthly Average Inches	0.6	1.3	3.4	5.1	5.7	6.6	5.5	7.7	8.8	9.0	2.7	1.1	57.5
Days of 1mm or More	1	3	7	10	12	12	12	15	16	17	7	2	114

BIRAO Central African Republic

Elevation 465 m. (1525 ft.)					10°17'N—22°47'E								
	JAN	FEB	MAR	APR	MAY	JUN	JUL	AUG	SEP	OCT	NOV	DEC	YEAR
TEMPERATURE													
Daily Average Min.°C	12	14	19	21	23	22	21	21	21	19	14	12	18
Daily Average Min.°F	54	58	66	70	73	71	70	69	69	67	58	53	65
Daily Average Max.°C	35	37	39	39	37	34	31	30	32	33	35	34	35
Daily Average Max.°F	95	98	102	102	99	92	88	87	89	92	95	94	94
Monthly Average °C	24	26	29	30	30	28	26	26	26	27	25	23	27
Monthly Average °F	75	79	85	87	86	82	79	78	79	80	76	74	80
RELATIVE HUMIDITY (%)	16	14	18	24	38	56	66	68	63	49	28	21	38
PRECIPITATION													
Monthly Average mm	0	0	5	21	57	100	174	171	141	34	0	0	703.0
Monthly Average Inches	0.0	0.0	0.1	0.8	2.2	3.9	6.8	6.7	5.5	1.3	0.0	0.0	27.3
Days of 1mm or More	0	0	0	1	5	8	12	14	9	2	0	0	51

BRIA
Central African Republic

Elevation 584 m. (1916 ft.)					6°32'N—21°59'E								
	JAN	FEB	MAR	APR	MAY	JUN	JUL	AUG	SEP	OCT	NOV	DEC	YEAR

TEMPERATURE

	JAN	FEB	MAR	APR	MAY	JUN	JUL	AUG	SEP	OCT	NOV	DEC	YEAR
Daily Average Min.°C	15	16	20	20	20	20	20	20	19	19	17	15	18
Daily Average Min.°F	58	61	67	69	69	67	67	67	67	66	63	58	65
Daily Average Max.°C	34	36	34	33	31	30	29	29	30	31	32	33	32
Daily Average Max.°F	94	96	94	91	89	86	84	84	86	87	90	92	89
Monthly Average °C	24	26	27	26	26	25	24	24	24	24	24	23	25
Monthly Average °F	75	79	80	80	78	76	75	75	75	76	76	74	77
RELATIVE HUMIDITY (%)	29	29	43	55	61	66	68	71	66	63	48	34	53

PRECIPITATION

	JAN	FEB	MAR	APR	MAY	JUN	JUL	AUG	SEP	OCT	NOV	DEC	YEAR
Monthly Average mm	8	14	71	114	166	186	208	248	243	201	32	3	1494.0
Monthly Average Inches	0.3	0.5	2.7	4.4	6.5	7.3	8.1	9.7	9.5	7.9	1.2	0.1	58.2
Days of 1mm or More	0	1	6	8	13	12	17	16	18	15	2	0	108

ABECHE
Chad

Elevation 549 m. (1801 ft.)					13°51'N—20°51'E								
	JAN	FEB	MAR	APR	MAY	JUN	JUL	AUG	SEP	OCT	NOV	DEC	YEAR

TEMPERATURE

	JAN	FEB	MAR	APR	MAY	JUN	JUL	AUG	SEP	OCT	NOV	DEC	YEAR
Daily Average Min.°C	16	18	22	24	25	24	22	21	21	21	19	16	21
Daily Average Min.°F	61	64	71	75	77	75	72	70	69	69	67	62	69
Daily Average Max.°C	36	37	40	41	41	39	35	32	35	38	37	35	37
Daily Average Max.°F	96	98	103	107	106	102	95	90	95	101	98	95	99
Monthly Average °C	25	27	31	33	33	32	28	26	28	29	28	25	29
Monthly Average °F	77	81	87	91	91	89	83	79	82	85	82	78	84
RELATIVE HUMIDITY (%)	16	15	15	18	22	31	49	60	47	25	21	18	28

PRECIPITATION

	JAN	FEB	MAR	APR	MAY	JUN	JUL	AUG	SEP	OCT	NOV	DEC	YEAR
Monthly Average mm	0	0	0	3	18	34	119	206	65	7	0	0	452.0
Monthly Average Inches	0.0	0.0	0.0	0.1	0.7	1.3	4.6	8.1	2.5	0.2	0.0	0.0	17.5
Days of 1mm or More	0	0	0	0	2	5	11	16	7	1	0	0	42

FAYA-LARGEAU
Chad

Elevation 234 m. (767 ft.)					18°0'N—19°10'E								
	JAN	FEB	MAR	APR	MAY	JUN	JUL	AUG	SEP	OCT	NOV	DEC	YEAR

TEMPERATURE

	JAN	FEB	MAR	APR	MAY	JUN	JUL	AUG	SEP	OCT	NOV	DEC	YEAR
Daily Average Min.°C	14	15	19	22	25	26	26	26	26	23	19	15	21
Daily Average Min.°F	57	59	65	72	77	79	78	78	78	73	65	59	70
Daily Average Max.°C	27	30	34	39	41	42	41	40	40	37	32	28	36
Daily Average Max.°F	81	86	94	102	105	108	105	103	103	98	90	83	96
Monthly Average °C	20	22	26	30	33	34	33	33	33	30	24	21	28
Monthly Average °F	69	72	79	86	92	93	92	91	91	86	76	70	83
RELATIVE HUMIDITY (%)	18	14	12	12	13	15	21	26	16	16	17	19	17

PRECIPITATION

	JAN	FEB	MAR	APR	MAY	JUN	JUL	AUG	SEP	OCT	NOV	DEC	YEAR
Monthly Average mm	0	0	0	0	0	1	4	10	0	0	0	0	15.0
Monthly Average Inches	0.0	0.0	0.0	0.0	0.0	0.0	0.1	0.3	0.0	0.0	0.0	0.0	0.4
Days of 1mm or More	0	0	0	0	0	0	0	1	0	0	0	0	1

MOUNDOU Chad

	Elevation 422 m. (1384 ft.)					8°37'N—16°4'E							
	JAN	FEB	MAR	APR	MAY	JUN	JUL	AUG	SEP	OCT	NOV	DEC	YEAR
TEMPERATURE													
Daily Average Min.°C	15	18	22	24	23	22	21	21	21	21	18	15	20
Daily Average Min.°F	58	64	72	74	74	71	70	70	70	70	64	59	68
Daily Average Max.°C	35	38	39	38	35	33	30	30	30	33	35	34	34
Daily Average Max.°F	94	100	103	100	95	91	86	86	87	91	95	94	93
Monthly Average °C	24	27	31	31	29	27	26	25	25	26	26	24	27
Monthly Average °F	76	81	87	87	84	81	78	77	78	80	79	76	80
RELATIVE HUMIDITY (%)	16	12	17	38	47	59	67	69	66	52	28	20	41
PRECIPITATION													
Monthly Average mm	0	0	9	58	98	152	243	308	223	80	3	0	1174.0
Monthly Average Inches	0.0	0.0	0.3	2.2	3.8	5.9	9.5	12.1	8.7	3.1	0.1	0.0	45.7
Days of 1mm or More	0	0	1	5	9	12	16	20	16	7	0	0	86

ANTOFAGASTA Chile

	Elevation 94 m. (308 ft.)					23°42'S—70°24'W							
	JAN	FEB	MAR	APR	MAY	JUN	JUL	AUG	SEP	OCT	NOV	DEC	YEAR
TEMPERATURE													
Daily Average Min.°C	17	17	16	14	13	11	11	11	12	13	14	16	14
Daily Average Min.°F	63	63	61	58	55	52	51	52	53	55	58	60	57
Daily Average Max.°C	24	24	23	21	19	18	17	17	18	19	21	22	20
Daily Average Max.°F	76	76	74	70	67	65	63	62	64	66	69	72	69
Extreme Monthly Min.°C	11	14	13	10	8	6	6	5	7	8	11	11	5
Extreme Monthly Min.°F	52	57	55	50	47	43	43	41	45	47	51	51	41
Extreme Monthly Max.°C	28	29	28	27	24	26	26	24	22	23	24	27	29
Extreme Monthly Max.°F	83	85	83	80	75	78	79	75	72	73	76	80	85
Monthly Average °C	20	20	19	17	15	14	13	14	14	16	17	19	16
Monthly Average °F	68	68	66	62	59	57	56	57	58	60	63	66	62
RELATIVE HUMIDITY (%)	71	70	71	72	73	71	73	73	71	71	71	70	71
PRECIPITATION													
Monthly Average mm	0	0	0	0	0	0	0	0	0	0	0	0	0.0
Monthly Average Inches	0.0	0.0	0.0	0.0	0.0	0.0	0.0	0.0	0.0	0.0	0.0	0.0	0.0
Days of 1mm or More	0	0	0	0	0	0	0	0	0	0	0	0	0

ARICA Chile

	Elevation 29 m. (95 ft.)					18°28'S—70°20'W							
	JAN	FEB	MAR	APR	MAY	JUN	JUL	AUG	SEP	OCT	NOV	DEC	YEAR
TEMPERATURE													
Daily Average Min.°C	18	18	17	16	14	14	12	13	13	14	16	17	15
Daily Average Min.°F	64	65	63	60	58	57	54	55	56	58	60	62	59
Daily Average Max.°C	26	26	25	23	21	19	19	18	19	21	22	24	22
Daily Average Max.°F	78	79	77	74	70	67	66	65	67	69	72	75	72
Monthly Average °C	22	22	21	20	18	17	16	16	16	18	19	21	19
Monthly Average °F	72	72	71	67	64	62	60	60	61	64	66	69	66
RELATIVE HUMIDITY (%)	62	61	63	68	70	73	73	74	73	70	65	61	68
PRECIPITATION													
Monthly Average mm	0	0	0	0	0	0	0	0	0	0	0	0	0.0
Monthly Average Inches	0.0	0.0	0.0	0.0	0.0	0.0	0.0	0.0	0.0	0.0	0.0	0.0	0.0
Days of 1mm or More	0	0	0	0	0	0	0	0	0	0	0	0	0

CONCEPCION   Chile

	Elevation 12 m. (39 ft.)					36°50'S—73°3'W							
	JAN	FEB	MAR	APR	MAY	JUN	JUL	AUG	SEP	OCT	NOV	DEC	YEAR
TEMPERATURE													
Monthly Average °C	16	16	14	12	11	9	9	9	9	12	14	16	12
Monthly Average °F	62	60	57	54	51	48	47	48	49	53	57	60	54
PRECIPITATION													
Monthly Average mm	24	16	32	68	199	242	220	169	101	62	38	34	1205.0
Monthly Average Inches	0.9	0.6	1.2	2.6	7.8	9.5	8.6	6.6	3.9	2.4	1.4	1.3	46.8
Days of 1mm or More	1	2	2	4	12	13	15	10	8	8	1	3	79

PUNTA ARENAS   Chile

	Elevation 8 m. (26 ft.)					53°10'S—70°54'W							
	JAN	FEB	MAR	APR	MAY	JUN	JUL	AUG	SEP	OCT	NOV	DEC	YEAR
TEMPERATURE													
Daily Average Min.°C	7	7	5	4	2	1	-1	1	2	3	4	6	3
Daily Average Min.°F	45	44	41	39	35	33	31	33	35	38	40	43	38
Daily Average Max.°C	14	14	12	10	7	5	4	6	8	11	12	14	10
Daily Average Max.°F	58	58	54	50	45	41	40	42	46	51	54	57	50
Monthly Average °C	10	10	8	6	3	2	1	2	4	6	8	10	6
Monthly Average °F	51	50	47	43	38	35	34	36	39	43	47	50	43
RELATIVE HUMIDITY (%)	68	64	69	73	76	80	79	77	71	65	65	67	71
PRECIPITATION													
Monthly Average mm	33	29	31	43	39	27	36	31	23	22	25	28	367.0
Monthly Average Inches	1.2	1.1	1.2	1.6	1.5	1.0	1.4	1.2	0.9	0.8	0.9	1.1	13.9
Days of 1mm or More	7	6	6	8	7	6	6	6	4	5	6	6	73

SANTIAGO   Chile

	Elevation 520 m. (1706 ft.)					33°27'S—70°42'W							
	JAN	FEB	MAR	APR	MAY	JUN	JUL	AUG	SEP	OCT	NOV	DEC	YEAR
TEMPERATURE													
Daily Average Min.°C	12	11	9	7	5	3	3	4	6	7	9	11	7
Daily Average Min.°F	53	52	49	45	41	37	37	39	42	45	48	51	45
Daily Average Max.°C	29	29	27	23	18	14	15	17	19	22	26	28	22
Daily Average Max.°F	85	84	80	74	65	58	59	62	66	72	78	83	72
Extreme Monthly Min.°C	6	6	3	1	-3	-3	-4	-3	-1	0	3	2	-4
Extreme Monthly Min.°F	43	43	38	33	27	26	24	26	31	32	37	36	24
Extreme Monthly Max.°C	36	37	34	31	31	27	27	29	31	32	36	37	37
Extreme Monthly Max.°F	96	98	94	88	87	80	81	85	88	90	97	99	99
Monthly Average °C	21	20	17	14	11	8	8	9	11	14	17	20	14
Monthly Average °F	69	67	63	57	52	47	46	48	52	57	63	67	57
RELATIVE HUMIDITY (%)	38	40	41	46	58	64	60	58	55	50	41	38	49
PRECIPITATION													
Monthly Average mm	0	0	4	10	45	70	68	44	19	10	7	1	278.0
Monthly Average Inches	0.0	0.0	0.1	0.3	1.7	2.7	2.6	1.7	0.7	0.3	0.2	0.0	10.3
Days of 1mm or More	0	0	0	1	5	5	6	3	3	1	1	0	25

VALDIVA Chile

Elevation 5 m. (16 ft.)					39°48'S—73°14'W									
	JAN	FEB	MAR	APR	MAY	JUN	JJL	AUG	SEP	OCT	NOV	DEC	YEAR
TEMPERATURE														
Daily Average Min.°C	11	11	9	8	6	6	5	4	5	7	8	10	7
Daily Average Min.°F	52	51	49	46	43	42	41	40	41	44	46	50	45
Daily Average Max.°C	23	23	21	17	13	11	11	12	14	17	18	21	17
Daily Average Max.°F	73	73	69	62	56	52	52	54	58	63	65	69	62
Monthly Average °C	16	15	13	11	9	7	7	7	8	10	13	15	11
Monthly Average °F	61	59	56	51	49	45	45	45	47	51	55	59	52
RELATIVE HUMIDITY (%)	64	67	70	77	87	89	89	83	74	71	68	67	76
PRECIPITATION														
Monthly Average mm	62	53	71	157	328	301	353	274	179	123	93	70	2064.0
Monthly Average Inches	2.4	2.0	2.7	6.1	12.9	11.8	13.9	10.7	7.0	4.8	3.6	2.7	80.6
Days of 1mm or More	6	6	7	10	19	18	18	16	13	10	9	6	138

BEIJING China

Elevation 32 m. (104 ft.)					39°55'N—116°25'E									
	JAN	FEB	MAR	APR	MAY	JUN	JUL	AUG	SEP	OCT	NOV	DEC	YEAR
TEMPERATURE														
Monthly Average °C	-5	-2	5	13	20	24	26	25	20	13	4	-2	12
Monthly Average °F	24	28	41	56	68	76	79	76	67	55	39	28	53
PRECIPITATION														
Monthly Average mm	1	6	8	25	28	82	181	237	58	22	7	3	658.0
Monthly Average Inches	0.0	0.2	0.3	0.9	1.1	3.2	7.1	9.3	2.2	0.8	0.2	0.1	25.4
Days of 1mm or More	0	1	2	2	3	7	9	10	4	3	1	2	44

HAMI China

Elevation 739 m. (2424 ft.)					42°47'N—93°32'E									
	JAN	FEB	MAR	APR	MAY	JUN	JUL	AUG	SEP	OCT	NOV	DEC	YEAR
TEMPERATURE														
Monthly Average °C	-11	-5	5	13	20	25	27	25	19	10	0	-8	10
Monthly Average °F	11	23	40	56	68	77	80	77	65	49	31	17	50
PRECIPITATION														
Monthly Average mm	1	1	1	2	3	6	5	5	3	2	1	1	31.0
Monthly Average Inches	0.0	0.0	0.0	0.0	0.1	0.2	0.1	0.1	0.1	0.0	0.0	0.0	0.6
Days of 1mm or More	0	0	0	0	0	1	1	0	1	0	0	0	3

HARBIN

China

Elevation 160 m. (526 ft.)   45°43'N—126°40'E

	JAN	FEB	MAR	APR	MAY	JUN	JUL	AUG	SEP	OCT	NOV	DEC	YEAR
TEMPERATURE													
Daily Average Min.°C	-24	-22	-12	-1	6	13	17	16	8	-2	-12	-21	-3
Daily Average Min.°F	-12	-7	11	30	43	55	62	60	47	29	11	-6	27
Daily Average Max.°C	-12	-8	2	13	21	26	28	27	21	11	0	-10	10
Daily Average Max.°F	10	18	36	55	69	78	82	80	69	51	32	14	50
Monthly Average °C	-20	-16	-5	6	14	20	23	21	14	6	-6	-16	3
Monthly Average °F	-4	3	23	43	57	68	73	70	58	42	21	3	38
RELATIVE HUMIDITY (%)	64	55	45	36	40	50	58	60	49	47	49	61	51
PRECIPITATION													
Monthly Average mm	3	4	10	21	42	86	174	124	57	30	10	4	565.0
Monthly Average Inches	0.1	0.1	0.3	0.8	1.6	3.3	6.8	4.8	2.2	1.1	0.3	0.1	21.5
Days of 1mm or More	0	0	0	0	0	0	0	0	0	0	0	0	0

KASHI

China

Elevation 1291 m. (4235 ft.)   39°29'N—75°59'E

	JAN	FEB	MAR	APR	MAY	JUN	JUL	AUG	SEP	OCT	NOV	DEC	YEAR
TEMPERATURE													
Monthly Average °C	-6	-1	8	15	20	24	26	24	20	12	3	-4	12
Monthly Average °F	21	30	46	60	67	75	79	76	67	54	38	25	53
PRECIPITATION													
Monthly Average mm	2	6	4	5	14	6	7	9	5	2	1	1	62.0
Monthly Average Inches	0.0	0.2	0.1	0.1	0.5	0.2	0.2	0.3	0.1	0.0	0.0	0.0	1.7
Days of 1mm or More	0	0	1	0	1	1	0	1	1	0	0	0	5

KUNMING

China

Elevation 1893 m. (6210 ft.)   25°7'N—102°54'E

	JAN	FEB	MAR	APR	MAY	JUN	JUL	AUG	SEP	OCT	NOV	DEC	YEAR
TEMPERATURE													
Daily Average Min.°C	3	4	7	11	14	17	17	17	15	12	7	3	11
Daily Average Min.°F	37	39	44	51	57	62	62	62	59	53	45	38	51
Daily Average Max.°C	16	18	21	24	26	25	25	25	24	21	18	17	22
Daily Average Max.°F	61	64	70	76	78	77	77	77	75	70	65	62	71
Monthly Average °C	7	9	13	16	18	20	20	19	17	15	11	8	14
Monthly Average °F	45	49	55	61	65	67	67	66	63	59	52	46	58
RELATIVE HUMIDITY (%)	42	41	39	41	51	64	70	72	62	63	63	49	55
PRECIPITATION													
Monthly Average mm	13	13	16	23	85	172	215	204	125	82	38	13	999.0
Monthly Average Inches	0.5	0.5	0.6	0.9	3.3	6.7	8.4	8.0	4.9	3.2	1.4	0.5	38.9
Days of 1mm or More	2	2	3	4	8	14	15	14	12	10	4	2	90

NANNING

China

	JAN	FEB	MAR	APR	MAY	JUN	JUL	AUG	SEP	OCT	NOV	DEC	YEAR
Elevation 73 m. (239 ft.)					22°48'N—108°20'E								
TEMPERATURE													
Monthly Average °C	13	14	18	22	26	28	28	28	27	23	19	15	22
Monthly Average °F	55	56	64	72	79	82	83	82	80	74	65	58	71
PRECIPITATION													
Monthly Average mm	35	51	41	111	181	242	202	227	121	70	50	28	1359.0
Monthly Average Inches	1.3	2.0	1.6	4.3	7.1	9.5	7.9	8.9	4.7	2.7	1.9	1.1	53.0
Days of 1mm or More	6	9	7	9	11	11	12	13	8	7	5	2	100

SHANGHAI

China

	JAN	FEB	MAR	APR	MAY	JUN	JUL	AUG	SEP	OCT	NOV	DEC	YEAR
Elevation 7 m. (23 ft.)					31°12'N—121°26'E								
TEMPERATURE													
Daily Average Min.°C	1	1	4	10	15	19	23	23	19	14	7	2	12
Daily Average Min.°F	33	34	40	50	59	67	74	74	66	57	45	36	53
Daily Average Max.°C	8	8	13	19	25	28	32	32	28	23	17	12	20
Daily Average Max.°F	46	47	55	66	77	82	90	90	82	74	63	53	69
Extreme Monthly Min.°C	-12	-8	-6	-1	3	11	16	16	7	1	-5	-10	-12
Extreme Monthly Min.°F	10	17	21	30	37	51	61	61	44	34	23	14	10
Extreme Monthly Max.°C	23	28	30	34	36	39	40	40	38	33	30	24	40
Extreme Monthly Max.°F	74	83	86	93	96	103	104	104	100	92	86	75	104
Monthly Average °C	3	4	9	14	19	23	28	28	24	18	12	6	16
Monthly Average °F	38	40	47	57	66	74	82	82	75	65	54	43	60
RELATIVE HUMIDITY (%)	58	60	53	58	56	66	66	65	64	53	55	62	60
PRECIPITATION													
Monthly Average mm	40	54	81	109	115	158	121	133	168	61	53	36	1129.0
Monthly Average Inches	1.5	2.1	3.1	4.2	4.5	6.2	4.7	5.2	6.6	2.4	2.0	1.4	43.9
Days of 1mm or More	7	5	11	10	8	10	11	9	8	5	5	3	92

BOGOTA

Colombia

	JAN	FEB	MAR	APR	MAY	JUN	JUL	AUG	SEP	OCT	NOV	DEC	YEAR
Elevation 2547 m. (8354 ft.)					4°36'N—74°5'W								
TEMPERATURE													
Daily Average Min.°C	9	9	10	11	11	11	10	10	9	10	10	9	10
Daily Average Min.°F	48	49	50	51	51	51	50	50	49	50	50	49	50
Daily Average Max.°C	19	20	19	19	19	18	18	18	19	19	19	19	19
Daily Average Max.°F	67	68	67	67	66	65	64	65	66	66	66	66	66
Extreme Monthly Min.°C	4	6	6	7	7	7	7	7	7	6	7	4	4
Extreme Monthly Min.°F	40	42	42	45	45	44	44	44	44	43	44	40	40
Extreme Monthly Max.°C	23	24	24	24	23	22	22	22	23	23	23	23	23
Extreme Monthly Max.°F	74	75	75	75	74	72	72	72	73	73	73	73	75
Monthly Average °C	13	13	14	14	14	13	13	13	13	13	13	13	13
Monthly Average °F	55	55	56	57	57	56	55	55	55	56	56	55	56
RELATIVE HUMIDITY (%)	51	53	54	57	58	56	56	54	54	61	64	56	56
PRECIPITATION													
Monthly Average mm	31	37	52	96	86	66	41	42	59	112	86	46	754.0
Monthly Average Inches	1.2	1.4	2.0	3.7	3.3	2.5	1.6	1.6	2.3	4.4	3.3	1.8	29.1
Days of 1mm or More	4	7	9	12	14	11	8	9	10	13	11	6	114

CALI   Colombia

	JAN	FEB	MAR	APR	MAY	JUN	JUL	AUG	SEP	OCT	NOV	DEC	YEAR
Elevation 964 m. (3162 ft.)				3°27'N—76°31'W									
TEMPERATURE													
Monthly Average °C	24	24	24	23	23	24	24	24	24	23	23	23	24
Monthly Average °F	75	75	75	74	74	75	75	75	75	74	74	74	74
PRECIPITATION													
Monthly Average mm	45	70	115	124	104	52	30	69	70	119	97	57	952.0
Monthly Average Inches	1.7	2.7	4.5	4.8	4.0	2.0	1.1	2.7	2.7	4.6	3.8	2.2	36.8
Days of 1mm or More	5	8	9	11	11	7	4	6	8	13	11	7	100

CARTAGENA   Colombia

	JAN	FEB	MAR	APR	MAY	JUN	JUL	AUG	SEP	OCT	NOV	DEC	YEAR
Elevation 2 m. (6 ft.)				10°25'N—75°32'W									
TEMPERATURE													
Monthly Average °C	27	27	27	28	28	28	28	28	28	28	28	27	28
Monthly Average °F	80	80	81	82	83	83	83	83	83	82	82	80	82
PRECIPITATION													
Monthly Average mm	4	2	5	33	105	110	94	116	129	276	101	29	1004.0
Monthly Average Inches	0.1	0.0	0.1	1.2	4.1	4.3	3.7	4.5	5.0	10.8	3.9	1.1	38.8
Days of 1mm or More	0	0	0	2	6	8	6	7	10	13	6	2	60

BRAZZAVILLE   Congo

	JAN	FEB	MAR	APR	MAY	JUN	JUL	AUG	SEP	OCT	NOV	DEC	YEAR
Elevation 314 m. (1030 ft.)				4°15'S—15°15'E									
TEMPERATURE													
Daily Average Min.°C	21	21	21	22	21	19	17	18	20	21	21	21	20
Daily Average Min.°F	70	70	70	71	70	66	63	65	68	70	70	70	69
Daily Average Max.°C	30	31	31	32	30	28	27	28	30	30	30	30	30
Daily Average Max.°F	86	87	88	89	86	83	80	82	85	86	86	86	85
Monthly Average °C	26	26	26	26	26	23	22	23	25	26	26	25	25
Monthly Average °F	78	79	79	79	78	74	71	73	77	78	78	78	77
RELATIVE HUMIDITY (%)	69	65	64	66	67	67	65	60	60	64	68	70	65
PRECIPITATION													
Monthly Average mm	187	148	189	268	355	5	10	23	39	153	244	166	1787.0
Monthly Average Inches	7.3	5.8	7.4	10.5	13.9	0.1	0.3	0.9	1.5	6.0	9.6	6.5	69.8
Days of 1mm or More	10	8	12	12	9	0	0	1	4	9	16	11	92

IMPFONDO Congo

	JAN	FEB	MAR	APR	MAY	JUN	JUL	AUG	SEP	OCT	NOV	DEC	YEAR
Elevation 326 m. (1069 ft.)					1°37'N—18°4'E								
TEMPERATURE													
Daily Average Min.°C	20	21	21	21	21	21	20	20	20	20	20	20	20
Daily Average Min.°F	68	69	70	70	70	69	68	69	69	69	69	69	69
Daily Average Max.°C	31	32	32	32	31	30	29	29	30	30	30	30	30
Daily Average Max.°F	87	89	89	89	88	86	84	84	85	85	85	87	87
Monthly Average °C	25	26	26	26	26	25	25	25	25	25	25	25	25
Monthly Average °F	78	79	79	79	79	77	76	76	77	77	77	77	78
RELATIVE HUMIDITY (%)	70	66	67	70	72	75	76	75	74	75	75	71	72
PRECIPITATION													
Monthly Average mm	70	96	164	168	160	150	151	165	180	205	186	78	1773.0
Monthly Average Inches	2.7	3.7	6.4	6.6	6.3	5.9	5.9	6.4	7.0	8.0	7.3	3.0	69.2
Days of 1mm or More	5	6	10	11	12	11	10	12	14	17	13	4	125

POINTE NOIRE Congo

	JAN	FEB	MAR	APR	MAY	JUN	JUL	AUG	SEP	OCT	NOV	DEC	YEAR
Elevation 17 m. (55 ft.)					4°49'S—11°54'E								
TEMPERATURE													
Daily Average Min.°C	23	23	23	24	23	19	18	19	21	23	23	23	22
Daily Average Min.°F	74	74	74	74	73	67	64	65	69	73	73	73	71
Daily Average Max.°C	30	30	31	30	29	26	25	25	26	28	29	29	28
Daily Average Max.°F	85	86	87	87	84	79	77	77	79	82	83	84	83
Monthly Average °C	26	27	27	27	26	23	21	22	23	25	26	26	25
Monthly Average °F	79	80	80	80	78	73	70	71	74	77	78	79	77
RELATIVE HUMIDITY (%)	73	72	72	74	74	69	68	68	72	74	76	74	72
PRECIPITATION													
Monthly Average mm	186	195	237	312	203	0	1	1	17	71	212	154	1589.0
Monthly Average Inches	7.3	7.6	9.3	12.2	7.9	0.0	0.0	0.0	0.6	2.7	8.3	6.0	61.9
Days of 1mm or More	11	13	12	9	6	0	0	1	4	10	13	9	88

SOUANKE Congo

	JAN	FEB	MAR	APR	MAY	JUN	JUL	AUG	SEP	OCT	NOV	DEC	YEAR
Elevation 547 m. (1794 ft.)					2°4'N—14°3'E								
TEMPERATURE													
Daily Average Min.°C	18	18	19	19	19	19	19	19	19	19	19	18	19
Daily Average Min.°F	64	65	66	67	67	67	66	65	66	66	66	65	66
Daily Average Max.°C	29	29	30	30	30	28	27	27	28	28	29	29	29
Daily Average Max.°F	83	85	86	86	85	83	80	80	82	83	83	83	83
Monthly Average °C	23	24	24	25	24	23	23	23	23	24	24	23	24
Monthly Average °F	74	75	76	76	76	74	73	73	74	74	75	74	74
RELATIVE HUMIDITY (%)	75	73	71	70	73	77	79	78	76	75	74	74	75
PRECIPITATION													
Monthly Average mm	53	79	182	168	208	114	72	97	230	249	168	53	1673.0
Monthly Average Inches	2.0	3.1	7.1	6.6	8.1	4.4	2.8	3.8	9.0	9.8	6.6	2.0	65.3
Days of 1mm or More	3	6	13	13	13	10	7	9	15	19	13	4	125

RAROTONGA

Cook Islands

Elevation 5 m. (15 ft.)   21°12'S—159°49'W

	JAN	FEB	MAR	APR	MAY	JUN	JUL	AUG	SEP	OCT	NOV	DEC	YEAR
TEMPERATURE													
Daily Average Min.°C	29	29	28	27	26	25	25	25	25	26	27	28	27
Daily Average Min.°F	84	84	83	81	79	77	77	77	77	79	80	82	80
Daily Average Max.°C	22	22	22	22	21	19	18	18	19	20	21	22	20
Daily Average Max.°F	72	72	72	71	69	66	65	65	66	68	69	72	69
Monthly Average °C	26	26	26	25	24	22	22	22	22	23	24	25	24
Monthly Average °F	78	79	79	77	75	72	71	71	72	73	75	77	75
RELATIVE HUMIDITY (%)	75	79	78	77	76	75	70	71	68	71	72	72	74
PRECIPITATION													
Monthly Average mm	250	198	211	200	185	113	96	180	136	101	145	218	2033.0
Monthly Average Inches	9.8	7.7	8.3	7.8	7.2	4.4	3.7	7.0	5.3	3.9	5.7	8.5	79.3
Days of 1mm or More	15	13	14	13	13	9	8	10	9	9	10	12	135

PUNTARENAS

Costa Rica

Elevation 3 m. (9 ft.)   9°58'N—84°50'W

	JAN	FEB	MAR	APR	MAY	JUN	JUL	AUG	SEP	OCT	NOV	DEC	YEAR
TEMPERATURE													
Monthly Average °C	28	28	29	29	28	27	27	27	27	27	27	27	28
Monthly Average °F	82	83	84	84	83	81	81	81	80	80	80	81	82
PRECIPITATION													
Monthly Average mm	5	3	6	42	175	236	199	205	254	245	107	32	1509.0
Monthly Average Inches	0.1	0.1	0.2	1.6	6.8	9.2	7.8	8.0	10.0	9.6	4.2	1.2	58.8
Days of 1mm or More	0	0	0	3	12	14	13	14	18	16	7	2	99

SAN JOSE

Costa Rica

Elevation 1146 m. (3760 ft.)   9°56'N—84°8'W

	JAN	FEB	MAR	APR	MAY	JUN	JUL	AUG	SEP	OCT	NOV	DEC	YEAR
TEMPERATURE													
Daily Average Min.°C	14	14	15	17	17	17	17	16	16	16	16	14	16
Daily Average Min.°F	58	58	59	62	62	62	62	61	61	60	60	58	60
Daily Average Max.°C	24	24	26	26	27	26	25	26	26	25	25	24	25
Daily Average Max.°F	75	76	79	79	80	79	77	78	79	77	77	75	78
Extreme Monthly Min.°C	9	11	10	12	12	14	12	13	13	13	11	9	9
Extreme Monthly Min.°F	49	51	50	53	54	57	54	56	56	55	52	49	49
Extreme Monthly Max.°C	31	31	33	32	31	33	29	29	30	29	29	31	33
Extreme Monthly Max.°F	87	88	91	89	88	92	84	85	86	85	84	87	92
Monthly Average °C	19	19	20	21	21	21	20	20	21	20	20	19	20
Monthly Average °F	66	67	68	69	70	70	69	69	69	69	68	67	68
RELATIVE HUMIDITY (%)	63	57	55	60	70	74	74	73	76	78	71	67	68
PRECIPITATION													
Monthly Average mm	10	9	8	51	225	291	211	256	349	316	127	40	1893.0
Monthly Average Inches	0.3	0.3	0.3	2.0	8.8	11.4	8.3	10.0	13.7	12.4	5.0	1.5	74.0
Days of 1mm or More	1	0	0	3	20	23	19	20	24	24	12	7	153

ABIDJAN
Cote d'Ivoire

	JAN	FEB	MAR	APR	MAY	JUN	JUL	AUG	SEP	OCT	NOV	DEC	YEAR
Elevation 7 m. (22 ft.)					5°15'N—3°56'W								

TEMPERATURE

	JAN	FEB	MAR	APR	MAY	JUN	JUL	AUG	SEP	OCT	NOV	DEC	YEAR
Daily Average Min.°C	23	24	24	24	24	23	23	22	22	23	24	24	23
Daily Average Min.°F	73	75	75	76	75	74	73	71	72	74	75	74	74
Daily Average Max.°C	30	31	31	31	30	29	28	27	28	29	30	30	29
Daily Average Max.°F	87	88	88	88	87	83	82	81	82	84	86	87	85
Extreme Monthly Min.°C	15	18	19	20	20	20	18	-14	18	19	19	17	13
Extreme Monthly Min.°F	59	64	67	68	68	68	64	6	65	67	67	62	56
Extreme Monthly Max.°C	34	35	34	35	34	34	33	31	32	33	34	35	35
Extreme Monthly Max.°F	94	95	93	95	94	93	91	88	90	92	94	95	96
Monthly Average °C	27	27	28	28	27	26	25	24	24	26	27	27	26
Monthly Average °F	80	81	82	82	81	79	77	75	76	78	81	80	79
RELATIVE HUMIDITY (%)	74	74	73	73	76	82	79	80	81	79	75	74	77

PRECIPITATION

	JAN	FEB	MAR	APR	MAY	JUN	JUL	AUG	SEP	OCT	NOV	DEC	YEAR
Monthly Average mm	20	59	100	148	314	607	308	33	62	124	147	82	2004.0
Monthly Average Inches	0.7	2.3	3.9	5.8	12.3	23.9	12.1	1.2	2.4	4.8	5.7	3.2	78.3
Days of 1mm or More	1	3	6	8	14	19	8	5	7	8	11	5	95

BOUAKE
Cote d'Ivoire

	JAN	FEB	MAR	APR	MAY	JUN	JUL	AUG	SEP	OCT	NOV	DEC	YEAR
Elevation 369 m. (1210 ft.)					7°41'N—5°2'W								

TEMPERATURE

	JAN	FEB	MAR	APR	MAY	JUN	JUL	AUG	SEP	OCT	NOV	DEC	YEAR
Daily Average Min.°C	20	21	22	22	22	21	21	20	21	21	21	20	21
Daily Average Min.°F	69	71	71	71	71	70	69	69	69	69	69	69	70
Daily Average Max.°C	33	34	34	33	32	30	28	28	29	30	31	32	31
Daily Average Max.°F	92	93	93	91	89	86	82	82	84	86	88	89	88
Monthly Average °C	27	28	27	27	26	25	24	24	24	25	25	26	26
Monthly Average °F	80	82	81	80	79	76	75	75	76	77	78	78	78
RELATIVE HUMIDITY (%)	49	52	59	64	69	75	77	78	77	74	68	57	67

PRECIPITATION

	JAN	FEB	MAR	APR	MAY	JUN	JUL	AUG	SEP	OCT	NOV	DEC	YEAR
Monthly Average mm	7	39	88	130	125	143	119	105	167	114	31	16	1084.0
Monthly Average Inches	0.2	1.5	3.4	5.1	4.9	5.6	4.6	4.1	6.5	4.4	1.2	0.6	42.1
Days of 1mm or More	0	2	6	8	9	9	8	8	12	8	2	1	73

MAN
Cote d'Ivoire

	JAN	FEB	MAR	APR	MAY	JUN	JUL	AUG	SEP	OCT	NOV	DEC	YEAR
Elevation 340 m. (1115 ft.)					7°24'N—7°31'W								

TEMPERATURE

	JAN	FEB	MAR	APR	MAY	JUN	JUL	AUG	SEP	OCT	NOV	DEC	YEAR
Daily Average Min.°C	17	19	21	21	21	21	20	20	20	20	20	18	20
Daily Average Min.°F	63	66	69	69	69	69	68	68	68	68	67	64	67
Daily Average Max.°C	32	33	32	31	31	29	27	27	28	29	30	31	30
Daily Average Max.°F	89	91	90	88	87	84	81	80	83	85	86	87	86
Monthly Average °C	24	26	26	26	26	25	24	24	24	25	25	23	25
Monthly Average °F	75	78	79	79	78	76	74	74	75	76	76	74	76
RELATIVE HUMIDITY (%)	55	54	63	69	72	78	83	84	80	75	71	61	70

PRECIPITATION

	JAN	FEB	MAR	APR	MAY	JUN	JUL	AUG	SEP	OCT	NOV	DEC	YEAR
Monthly Average mm	15	45	122	155	147	183	168	262	276	136	46	23	1578.0
Monthly Average Inches	0.5	1.7	4.8	6.1	5.7	7.2	6.6	10.3	10.8	5.3	1.8	0.9	61.7
Days of 1mm or More	0	3	8	8	10	13	14	19	17	11	4	1	108

BRATISLAVA   Czechoslovakia

Elevation 132 m. (433 ft.)					48°12'N—17°8'E								
	JAN	FEB	MAR	APR	MAY	JUN	JUL	AUG	SEP	OCT	NOV	DEC	YEAR
TEMPERATURE													
Daily Average Min.°C	-3	-2	1	6	11	14	16	16	12	7	3	0	7
Daily Average Min.°F	27	28	34	44	52	58	61	60	54	44	38	32	44
Daily Average Max.°C	2	4	9	16	21	24	26	26	22	15	8	4	15
Daily Average Max.°F	35	38	49	61	69	75	79	78	72	59	46	39	58
Monthly Average °C	-2	0	4	10	15	18	20	19	15	10	5	1	10
Monthly Average °F	29	32	39	50	58	65	68	66	60	50	41	33	49
RELATIVE HUMIDITY (%)	77	70	58	49	49	50	49	51	52	62	76	80	60
PRECIPITATION													
Monthly Average mm	32	37	39	39	54	77	72	66	34	44	53	51	598.0
Monthly Average Inches	1.2	1.4	1.5	1.5	2.1	3.0	2.8	2.5	1.3	1.7	2.0	2.0	23.0
Days of 1mm or More	0	0	0	0	0	0	0	0	0	0	0	0	0

BRNO   Czechoslovakia

Elevation 242 m. (793 ft.)					49°12'N—16°34'E								
	JAN	FEB	MAR	APR	MAY	JUN	JUL	AUG	SEP	OCT	NOV	DEC	YEAR
TEMPERATURE													
Daily Average Min.°C	-5	-5	-1	4	9	12	14	13	9	4	2	-1	5
Daily Average Min.°F	24	24	30	39	47	53	57	55	49	40	35	30	40
Daily Average Max.°C	1	3	8	15	20	23	25	25	21	14	7	3	14
Daily Average Max.°F	34	37	47	59	68	74	77	76	70	58	45	38	57
Monthly Average °C	-3	-1	4	9	14	17	18	18	14	9	4	-1	9
Monthly Average °F	27	31	38	48	57	62	65	64	58	48	39	31	47
RELATIVE HUMIDITY (%)	77	69	58	49	49	52	52	53	55	63	77	82	61
PRECIPITATION													
Monthly Average mm	25	20	25	30	62	72	66	57	35	32	35	29	488.0
Monthly Average Inches	0.9	0.7	0.9	1.1	2.4	2.8	2.5	2.2	1.3	1.2	1.3	1.1	18.4
Days of 1mm or More	6	5	5	6	9	9	9	7	5	5	7	7	80

KOSICE   Czechoslovakia

Elevation 235 m. (770 ft.)					48°42'N—21°18'E								
	JAN	FEB	MAR	APR	MAY	JUN	JUL	AUG	SEP	OCT	NOV	DEC	YEAR
TEMPERATURE													
Daily Average Min.°C	-7	-6	-2	3	8	12	13	13	9	3	0	-3	4
Daily Average Min.°F	19	22	29	38	47	53	56	55	48	38	33	27	39
Daily Average Max.°C	0	2	8	15	21	24	26	25	21	14	7	3	14
Daily Average Max.°F	33	35	47	60	69	74	78	78	71	58	45	37	57
Monthly Average °C	-4	-2	3	9	14	18	19	19	14	9	4	-1	8
Monthly Average °F	25	29	37	49	57	64	67	65	58	48	39	30	47
RELATIVE HUMIDITY (%)	78	72	59	51	51	55	53	53	53	61	76	82	62
PRECIPITATION													
Monthly Average mm	27	32	29	35	61	86	93	79	45	35	52	40	614.0
Monthly Average Inches	1.0	1.2	1.1	1.3	2.4	3.3	3.6	3.1	1.7	1.3	2.0	1.5	23.5
Days of 1mm or More	0	0	0	0	0	0	0	0	0	0	0	0	0

PRAGUE   Czechoslovakia

Elevation 262 m. (859 ft.)   50°6'N—14°26'E

	JAN	FEB	MAR	APR	MAY	JUN	JUL	AUG	SEP	OCT	NOV	DEC	YEAR
TEMPERATURE													
Daily Average Min.°C	-4	-2	1	4	9	13	14	14	11	7	2	-2	6
Daily Average Min.°F	25	28	33	40	49	55	58	57	52	44	35	29	42
Daily Average Max.°C	1	3	7	13	18	22	23	23	18	12	5	1	12
Daily Average Max.°F	34	38	45	55	65	72	74	73	65	54	41	34	54
Extreme Monthly Min.°C	-27	-24	-15	-6	-1	6	8	7	2	-5	-17	-25	-26
Extreme Monthly Min.°F	-16	-12	5	21	30	42	47	45	35	23	2	-13	-16
Extreme Monthly Max.°C	13	14	22	28	33	35	37	37	32	26	18	16	36
Extreme Monthly Max.°F	55	57	71	83	91	95	98	98	89	78	64	60	98
Monthly Average °C	-3	-1	3	8	13	16	17	17	13	8	3	-1	8
Monthly Average °F	27	30	37	46	55	61	63	62	56	47	38	31	46
RELATIVE HUMIDITY (%)	73	67	55	47	45	46	49	48	51	60	73	78	58
PRECIPITATION													
Monthly Average mm	24	21	27	37	80	70	69	73	38	35	28	26	528.0
Monthly Average Inches	0.9	0.8	1.0	1.4	3.1	2.7	2.7	2.8	1.4	1.3	1.1	1.0	20.2
Days of 1mm or More	7	5	6	7	10	10	9	9	7	5	7	7	89

COPENHAGEN   Denmark

Elevation 9 m. (30 ft.)   55°42'N—12°36'E

	JAN	FEB	MAR	APR	MAY	JUN	JUL	AUG	SEP	OCT	NOV	DEC	YEAR
TEMPERATURE													
Daily Average Min.°C	-2	-3	-1	3	8	11	14	14	11	7	3	1	5
Daily Average Min.°F	28	28	31	38	46	52	57	56	51	44	38	33	42
Daily Average Max.°C	2	2	5	10	16	19	22	21	18	12	7	4	12
Daily Average Max.°F	36	36	41	51	61	67	71	70	64	54	45	40	53
Extreme Monthly Min.°C	-14	-19	-10	-6	-1	3	6	4	-2	-4	-11	-16	-19
Extreme Monthly Min.°F	6	-3	14	21	30	37	42	40	29	24	13	3	-3
Extreme Monthly Max.°C	9	10	17	28	28	31	33	32	29	23	13	12	32
Extreme Monthly Max.°F	49	50	62	82	82	88	91	89	84	74	56	53	91
Monthly Average °C	0	0	2	6	12	16	17	17	14	10	6	2	9
Monthly Average °F	32	32	36	44	53	61	63	63	57	50	42	36	47
RELATIVE HUMIDITY (%)	86	86	77	66	60	61	63	67	70	77	83	87	74
PRECIPITATION													
Monthly Average mm	51	35	38	48	43	52	73	65	58	54	62	61	640.0
Monthly Average Inches	2.0	1.3	1.4	1.8	1.6	2.0	2.8	2.5	2.2	2.1	2.4	2.4	24.5
Days of 1mm or More	11	7	9	8	8	8	8	8	9	9	12	10	107

DJIBOUTI   Djibouti

Elevation 7 m. (22 ft.)   11°34'N—43°9'E

	JAN	FEB	MAR	APR	MAY	JUN	JUL	AUG	SEP	OCT	NOV	DEC	YEAR
TEMPERATURE													
Daily Average Min.°C	22	23	24	26	27	30	31	30	29	26	24	22	26
Daily Average Min.°F	71	73	75	78	81	85	88	86	85	78	75	72	79
Daily Average Max.°C	29	29	30	32	34	38	42	41	38	33	31	29	34
Daily Average Max.°F	83	84	86	89	94	101	107	105	100	92	87	85	93
Monthly Average °C	25	25	27	29	31	33	35	34	32	29	27	26	29
Monthly Average °F	77	78	80	83	87	92	95	94	90	85	80	78	85
RELATIVE HUMIDITY (%)	65	65	65	67	61	48	32	35	48	59	61	62	56
PRECIPITATION													
Monthly Average mm	14	22	19	13	15	0	12	8	5	17	28	23	176.0
Monthly Average Inches	0.5	0.8	0.7	0.5	0.5	0.0	0.4	0.3	0.1	0.6	1.1	0.9	6.4
Days of 1mm or More	1	1	0	1	0	0	1	1	0	1	2	1	9

SANTO DOMINGO · Dominican Republic

Elevation 14 m. (45 ft.)					18°28'N—69°54'W							
	JAN	FEB	MAR	APR	MAY	JUN	JUL	AUG	SEP	OCT	NOV	DEC	YEAR
TEMPERATURE													
Monthly Average °C	24	24	25	26	26	27	27	27	27	27	26	25	26
Monthly Average °F	76	76	77	78	79	80	81	81	81	80	79	77	79
PRECIPITATION													
Monthly Average mm	55	54	51	67	194	146	154	168	186	152	85	73	1385.0
Monthly Average Inches	2.1	2.1	2.0	2.6	7.6	5.7	6.0	6.6	7.3	5.9	3.3	2.8	54.0
Days of 1mm or More	8	7	6	8	11	12	13	13	13	13	10	10	124

POTSDAM · East Germany

Elevation 85 m. (278 ft.)					52°24'N—13°6'E							
	JAN	FEB	MAR	APR	MAY	JUN	JUL	AUG	SEP	OCT	NOV	DEC	YEAR
TEMPERATURE													
Monthly Average °C	-1	0	3	8	13	17	18	17	14	9	4	1	9
Monthly Average °F	30	32	38	46	56	62	64	63	57	49	40	33	47
PRECIPITATION													
Monthly Average mm	44	34	35	45	60	65	55	63	44	41	45	52	583.0
Monthly Average Inches	1.7	1.3	1.3	1.7	2.3	2.5	2.1	2.4	1.7	1.6	1.7	2.0	22.3
Days of 1mm or More	10	7	8	8	10	10	8	8	8	7	9	11	104

GUAYAQUIL · Ecuador

Elevation 4 m. (13 ft.)					2°10'S—79°50'W							
	JAN	FEB	MAR	APR	MAY	JUN	JUL	AUG	SEP	OCT	NOV	DEC	YEAR
TEMPERATURE													
Monthly Average °C	26	26	27	27	26	25	24	24	24	25	25	26	25
Monthly Average °F	79	79	80	80	79	77	75	75	76	76	77	79	78
PRECIPITATION													
Monthly Average mm	206	245	288	175	67	35	0	0	2	2	5	35	1060.0
Monthly Average Inches	8.1	9.6	11.3	6.8	2.6	1.3	0.0	0.0	0.0	0.0	0.1	1.3	41.1
Days of 1mm or More	14	17	16	14	5	2	0	1	0	1	1	4	75

PORTOVIEJO · Ecuador

Elevation 44 m. (144 ft.)					1°3'S—80°27'W							
	JAN	FEB	MAR	APR	MAY	JUN	JUL	AUG	SEP	OCT	NOV	DEC	YEAR
TEMPERATURE													
Monthly Average °C	26	26	26	26	25	24	24	24	24	24	24	25	25
Monthly Average °F	78	79	79	79	78	76	75	75	75	76	76	77	77
PRECIPITATION													
Monthly Average mm	79	100	99	61	38	23	2	2	3	2	4	17	430.0
Monthly Average Inches	3.1	3.9	3.8	2.4	1.4	0.9	0.0	0.0	0.1	0.0	0.1	0.6	16.3
Days of 1mm or More	13	14	14	11	8	4	0	1	1	1	1	5	73

QUITO   Ecuador

		Elevation 2880 m. (9446 ft.)			0°13'S—78°32'W							
	JAN	FEB	MAR	APR	MAY	JUN	JUL	AUG	SEP	OCT	NOV	DEC	YEAR

TEMPERATURE													
Daily Average Min.°C	8	8	8	8	8	7	7	7	7	8	7	8	8
Daily Average Min.°F	46	47	47	47	47	45	44	45	45	46	45	46	46
Daily Average Max.°C	22	22	22	21	21	22	22	23	23	22	22	22	22
Daily Average Max.°F	72	71	71	70	70	71	72	73	73	72	72	72	72
Extreme Monthly Min.°F	37	34	40	40	35	36	33	36	35	32	33	34	32
Extreme Monthly Max.°C	26	27	27	26	26	26	26	28	28	30	27	27	30
Extreme Monthly Max.°F	79	80	80	78	79	78	79	82	83	86	80	81	86
Monthly Average °C	14	14	14	14	14	14	14	14	14	13	13	14	14
Monthly Average °F	56	56	57	56	57	56	56	57	57	56	56	56	56
RELATIVE HUMIDITY (%)	54	59	59	60	60	51	43	40	44	53	53	54	53

PRECIPITATION													
Monthly Average mm	92	107	139	177	104	50	24	29	76	122	108	89	1117.0
Monthly Average Inches	3.6	4.2	5.4	6.9	4.0	1.9	0.9	1.1	2.9	4.8	4.2	3.5	43.4
Days of 1mm or More	10	13	15	17	13	9	6	6	9	14	14	10	136

RIOBAMBA   Ecuador

		Elevation 2754 m. (9035 ft.)			1°40'S—78°38'W							
	JAN	FEB	MAR	APR	MAY	JUN	JUL	AUG	SEP	OCT	NOV	DEC	YEAR

TEMPERATURE													
Monthly Average °C	14	14	14	14	14	12	12	13	13	14	14	14	13
Monthly Average °F	57	57	56	57	57	54	54	55	55	56	57	57	56

PRECIPITATION													
Monthly Average mm	27	40	52	45	25	43	12	11	20	52	50	30	407.0
Monthly Average Inches	1.0	1.5	2.0	1.7	0.9	1.6	0.4	0.4	0.7	2.0	1.9	1.1	15.2
Days of 1mm or More	0	0	0	0	0	0	0	0	0	0	0	0	0

ALEXANDRIA   Egypt

		Elevation 7 m. (23 ft.)			31°12'N—29°57'E							
	JAN	FEB	MAR	APR	MAY	JUN	JUL	AUG	SEP	OCT	NOV	DEC	YEAR

TEMPERATURE													
Daily Average Min.°C	10	10	12	14	17	21	23	25	22	19	16	12	17
Daily Average Min.°F	49	50	53	57	62	70	73	78	71	66	60	53	62
Daily Average Max.°C	19	20	21	24	27	29	30	31	30	28	25	21	25
Daily Average Max.°F	66	67	71	75	80	85	86	87	85	82	76	69	78
Extreme Monthly Min.°C	3	3	7	9	12	15	17	18	16	12	8	3	2
Extreme Monthly Min.°F	38	37	44	49	54	59	63	64	60	54	46	37	37
Extreme Monthly Max.°C	28	33	39	42	44	44	39	40	41	40	35	31	43
Extreme Monthly Max.°F	82	91	103	108	111	111	103	104	106	104	95	88	111
Monthly Average °C	14	14	16	19	21	24	26	27	25	23	19	15	20
Monthly Average °F	57	58	61	65	71	76	79	80	78	73	66	60	69
RELATIVE HUMIDITY (%)	55	54	52	55	56	60	63	61	57	55	56	55	57

PRECIPITATION													
Monthly Average mm	54	27	14	4	1	0	0	0	1	9	33	52	195.0
Monthly Average Inches	2.1	1.0	0.5	0.1	0.0	0.0	0.0	0.0	0.0	0.3	1.2	2.0	7.2
Days of 1mm or More	9	3	2	1	0	0	0	0	0	1	3	7	26

ASWAN   Egypt

		Elevation 194 m. (636 ft.)				23°58'N—32°47'E							
	JAN	FEB	MAR	APR	MAY	JUN	JUL	AUG	SEP	OCT	NOV	DEC	YEAR
TEMPERATURE													
Daily Average Min.°C	9	10	14	18	23	25	26	26	23	21	16	11	18
Daily Average Min.°F	48	50	57	65	73	76	78	78	74	69	60	51	65
Daily Average Max.°C	24	26	30	35	40	42	42	42	40	37	31	26	35
Daily Average Max.°F	75	79	87	96	103	107	107	107	104	98	88	78	94
Extreme Monthly Min.°C	3	3	7	9	12	15	17	18	16	12	8	3	2
Extreme Monthly Min.°F	38	37	44	49	54	59	63	64	60	54	46	37	37
Extreme Monthly Max.°C	28	33	39	42	44	44	39	40	41	40	35	31	43
Extreme Monthly Max.°F	82	91	103	108	111	111	103	104	106	104	95	88	111
Monthly Average °C	16	18	22	27	31	33	34	34	31	28	22	18	26
Monthly Average °F	60	65	72	80	88	91	93	92	89	82	72	64	79
RELATIVE HUMIDITY (%)	26	20	16	14	13	13	16	17	18	20	27	29	19
PRECIPITATION													
Monthly Average mm	0	0	0	0	0	0	0	0	0	0	0	0	0.0
Monthly Average Inches	0.0	0.0	0.0	0.0	0.0	0.0	0.0	0.0	0.0	0.0	0.0	0.0	0.0
Days of 1mm or More	0	0	0	0	0	0	0	0	0	0	0	0	0

CAIRO   Egypt

		Elevation 74 m. (242 ft.)				30°8'N—31°34'E							
	JAN	FEB	MAR	APR	MAY	JUN	JUL	AUG	SEP	OCT	NOV	DEC	YEAR
TEMPERATURE													
Daily Average Min.°C	9	9	12	14	18	20	22	22	20	18	14	10	16
Daily Average Min.°F	48	49	53	58	64	68	71	72	68	64	59	51	60
Daily Average Max.°C	19	21	24	28	32	35	35	35	33	30	26	21	28
Daily Average Max.°F	67	70	76	83	90	95	96	95	91	86	78	70	83
Extreme Monthly Min.°C	2	2	3	6	9	13	16	17	14	11	6	1	1
Extreme Monthly Min.°F	35	35	38	42	49	55	61	63	58	51	42	34	34
Extreme Monthly Max.°C	31	33	38	45	47	47	43	43	42	43	38	31	47
Extreme Monthly Max.°F	88	92	101	113	116	117	109	109	108	109	100	87	117
Monthly Average °C	14	15	18	21	25	27	28	28	26	24	19	15	22
Monthly Average °F	57	60	64	70	77	81	82	82	80	75	67	59	71
RELATIVE HUMIDITY (%)	43	39	33	28	25	27	31	35	37	36	42	46	35
PRECIPITATION													
Monthly Average mm	6	4	4	1	0	0	0	0	0	0	4	10	29.0
Monthly Average Inches	0.2	0.1	0.1	0.0	0.0	0.0	0.0	0.0	0.0	0.0	0.1	0.3	0.8
Days of 1mm or More	1	0	1	0	0	0	0	0	0	0	0	1	3

SIWA   Egypt

		Elevation -13 m. (-43 ft.)				29°12'N—25°29'E							
	JAN	FEB	MAR	APR	MAY	JUN	JUL	AUG	SEP	OCT	NOV	DEC	YEAR
TEMPERATURE													
Daily Average Min.°C	5	6	9	13	17	20	21	21	19	15	10	7	14
Daily Average Min.°F	41	43	48	55	62	68	70	70	66	59	51	44	56
Daily Average Max.°C	20	22	25	30	34	37	38	38	35	31	26	21	30
Daily Average Max.°F	67	71	77	86	93	99	100	100	94	88	79	70	85
Monthly Average °C	12	14	17	22	26	29	30	29	27	23	18	13	22
Monthly Average °F	54	57	63	71	78	84	85	85	81	74	64	56	71
RELATIVE HUMIDITY (%)	42	36	28	26	22	23	25	26	32	34	39	45	31
PRECIPITATION													
Monthly Average mm	1	1	0	2	2	0	0	0	0	0	1	2	9.0
Monthly Average Inches	0.0	0.0	0.0	0.0	0.0	0.0	0.0	0.0	0.0	0.0	0.0	0.0	0.0
Days of 1mm or More	0	0	0	0	0	0	0	0	0	0	0	0	0

SAN SALVADOR   El Salvador

Elevation 699 m. (2293 ft.)						13°42'N—89°13'W						
	JAN	FEB	MAR	APR	MAY	JUN	JUL	AUG	SEP	OCT	NOV	DEC	YEAR

TEMPERATURE	JAN	FEB	MAR	APR	MAY	JUN	JUL	AUG	SEP	OCT	NOV	DEC	YEAR
Daily Average Min.°C	16	16	17	18	19	19	18	19	19	18	17	16	18
Daily Average Min.°F	60	60	62	65	67	66	65	66	66	65	63	61	64
Daily Average Max.°C	32	33	34	34	33	31	32	32	31	31	31	32	32
Daily Average Max.°F	90	92	94	93	91	87	89	89	87	87	87	89	90
Extreme Monthly Min.°C	7	9	7	12	14	13	14	16	12	12	9	8	7
Extreme Monthly Min.°F	45	49	45	54	58	56	58	60	53	54	49	47	45
Extreme Monthly Max.°C	38	39	41	40	39	37	37	37	37	38	39	38	40
Extreme Monthly Max.°F	101	103	105	104	103	98	98	98	99	101	102	101	105
Monthly Average °C	22	23	24	25	24	23	23	23	23	23	22	22	23
Monthly Average °F	72	73	75	76	75	74	74	74	73	73	72	72	73
RELATIVE HUMIDITY (%)	45	43	44	50	60	66	61	62	69	66	56	50	56
PRECIPITATION													
Monthly Average mm	5	3	20	63	153	288	348	319	336	202	33	9	1779.0
Monthly Average Inches	0.1	0.1	0.7	2.4	6.0	11.3	13.7	12.5	13.2	7.9	1.2	0.3	69.4
Days of 1mm or More	0	0	1	4	10	19	19	20	18	13	4	1	109

ADDIS ABABA   Ethiopia

Elevation 2408 m. (7898 ft.)						9°2'N—34°45'E						
	JAN	FEB	MAR	APR	MAY	JUN	JUL	AUG	SEP	OCT	NOV	DEC	YEAR

TEMPERATURE	JAN	FEB	MAR	APR	MAY	JUN	JUL	AUG	SEP	OCT	NOV	DEC	YEAR
Daily Average Min.°C	6	7	9	10	9	10	11	11	10	7	5	5	8
Daily Average Min.°F	42	44	48	50	49	50	51	51	50	44	41	40	47
Daily Average Max.°C	23	24	25	24	25	23	20	20	21	22	23	22	23
Daily Average Max.°F	73	74	76	76	77	73	69	68	70	72	73	72	73
Extreme Monthly Min.°F	35	36	37	40	39	44	45	43	38	36	33	32	32
Extreme Monthly Max.°C	28	30	29	31	33	34	31	29	27	33	27	28	34
Extreme Monthly Max.°F	82	86	84	88	91	94	88	84	81	91	81	82	94
Monthly Average °C	16	17	18	18	18	17	15	15	16	16	16	15	16
Monthly Average °F	61	62	64	65	65	62	60	60	61	61	60	60	62
RELATIVE HUMIDITY (%)	38	47	45	47	39	52	65	67	58	40	40	33	48
PRECIPITATION													
Monthly Average mm	25	41	70	76	94	116	254	268	172	42	10	16	1184.0
Monthly Average Inches	0.9	1.6	2.7	2.9	3.7	4.5	10.0	10.5	6.7	1.6	0.3	0.6	46.0
Days of 1mm or More	3	5	7	9	9	15	24	24	16	4	1	1	118

ASMERA   Ethiopia

Elevation 2325 m. (7627 ft.)						15°17'N—38°55'E						
	JAN	FEB	MAR	APR	MAY	JUN	JUL	AUG	SEP	OCT	NOV	DEC	YEAR

TEMPERATURE	JAN	FEB	MAR	APR	MAY	JUN	JUL	AUG	SEP	OCT	NOV	DEC	YEAR
Daily Average Min.°C	6	7	9	10	11	12	12	12	10	9	9	7	9
Daily Average Min.°F	42	45	48	50	52	53	53	53	50	48	48	44	49
Daily Average Max.°C	23	24	25	25	25	26	20	20	25	22	23	22	23
Daily Average Max.°F	73	75	77	77	78	78	67	67	77	72	73	71	74
Monthly Average °C	14	15	17	17	18	18	16	16	16	15	14	14	16
Monthly Average °F	57	59	62	63	64	65	61	61	61	59	57	57	61
RELATIVE HUMIDITY (%)	35	31	28	31	31	31	64	64	36	48	41	34	39
PRECIPITATION													
Monthly Average mm	3	2	16	36	48	41	189	153	20	18	19	5	550.0
Monthly Average Inches	0.1	0.0	0.6	1.4	1.8	1.6	7.4	6.0	0.7	0.7	0.7	0.1	21.1
Days of 1mm or More	0	0	2	5	6	5	11	12	2	2	1	1	47

STANLEY   Falkland Islands

		JAN	FEB	MAR	APR	MAY	JUN	JUL	AUG	SEP	OCT	NOV	DEC	YEAR
Elevation 2 m. (6 ft.)						51°42'S—57°51'W								
TEMPERATURE														
Daily Average Min.°C	6	5	4	3	1	-1	-1	-1	1	2	3	4	2
Daily Average Min.°F	42	41	40	37	34	31	31	31	33	35	37	39	36
Daily Average Max.°C	13	13	12	9	7	5	4	5	7	9	11	12	9
Daily Average Max.°F	56	55	53	49	44	41	40	41	45	48	52	54	48
Monthly Average °C	9	9	8	6	4	3	2	3	4	5	7	8	6
Monthly Average °F	49	49	47	43	39	37	36	37	39	42	45	47	42
RELATIVE HUMIDITY (%)	78	79	82	86	88	89	89	87	84	80	75	77	83
PRECIPITATION														
Monthly Average mm	73	49	53	52	55	49	46	43	37	38	42	63	600.0
Monthly Average Inches	2.8	1.9	2.0	2.0	2.1	1.9	1.8	1.6	1.4	1.4	1.6	2.4	22.9
Days of 1mm or More	14	10	13	11	12	12	10	10	9	9	10	12	132

IVALO   Finland

		JAN	FEB	MAR	APR	MAY	JUN	JUL	AUG	SEP	OCT	NOV	DEC	YEAR
Elevation 145 m. (475 ft.)						69°4'N—27°6'E								
TEMPERATURE														
Monthly Average °C	-14	-15	-10	-3	4	11	13	11	6	0	-6	-12	-1
Monthly Average °F	6	6	15	27	39	51	55	52	43	32	22	10	30
PRECIPITATION														
Monthly Average mm	19	15	15	16	23	43	65	57	47	42	24	20	386.0
Monthly Average Inches	0.7	0.5	0.5	0.6	0.9	1.6	2.5	2.2	1.8	1.6	0.9	0.7	14.5
Days of 1mm or More	0	0	0	0	0	0	0	0	0	0	0	0	0

JYVASKYLA   Finland

		JAN	FEB	MAR	APR	MAY	JUN	JUL	AUG	SEP	OCT	NOV	DEC	YEAR
Elevation 145 m. (475 ft.)						62°14'N—25°44'E								
TEMPERATURE														
Monthly Average °C	-10	-10	-5	1	9	14	16	14	8	3	-2	-7	3
Monthly Average °F	13	14	23	34	48	57	60	57	47	38	29	19	37
PRECIPITATION														
Monthly Average mm	41	25	30	33	40	54	79	87	64	57	61	47	618.0
Monthly Average Inches	1.6	0.9	1.1	1.2	1.5	2.1	3.1	3.4	2.5	2.2	2.4	1.8	23.8
Days of 1mm or More	10	7	8	7	7	9	11	11	11	11	12	10	114

BORDEAUX   France

Elevation 51 m. (167 ft.)					**44°48'N—0°42'W**								
	JAN	FEB	MAR	APR	MAY	JUN	JUL	AUG	SEP	OCT	NOV	DEC	YEAR
TEMPERATURE													
Daily Average Min.°C	2	2	4	6	9	12	14	14	12	8	5	3	8
Daily Average Min.°F	35	36	40	43	48	54	57	56	54	47	40	37	45
Daily Average Max.°C	9	11	15	17	20	24	25	26	23	18	13	9	18
Daily Average Max.°F	49	51	59	63	69	75	78	78	74	65	55	49	63
Extreme Monthly Min.°C	-12	-12	-6	-6	1	3	6	1	-2	-6	-7	-13	-12
Extreme Monthly Min.°F	10	11	21	22	33	37	42	33	29	22	19	9	9
Extreme Monthly Max.°C	19	26	29	31	35	38	38	39	38	31	25	20	38
Extreme Monthly Max.°F	66	79	84	88	95	101	101	102	100	88	77	68	102
Monthly Average °C	5	7	8	11	14	18	20	19	17	13	9	6	12
Monthly Average °F	42	44	47	52	57	64	68	67	63	56	47	43	54
RELATIVE HUMIDITY (%)	80	73	64	60	60	62	61	60	67	71	80	83	68
PRECIPITATION													
Monthly Average mm	100	78	80	67	80	57	48	60	81	92	96	112	951.0
Monthly Average Inches	3.9	3.0	3.1	2.6	3.1	2.2	1.8	2.3	3.1	3.6	3.7	4.4	36.8
Days of 1mm or More	13	11	12	10	11	8	6	8	9	10	12	12	122

DIJON   France

Elevation 227 m. (744 ft.)					**47°18'N—5°6'E**								
	JAN	FEB	MAR	APR	MAY	JUN	JUL	AUG	SEP	OCT	NOV	DEC	YEAR
TEMPERATURE													
Daily Average Min.°C	-2	-1	2	5	9	12	14	14	11	6	3	0	6
Daily Average Min.°F	29	30	36	41	48	54	57	56	52	44	37	31	43
Daily Average Max.°C	4	7	12	16	20	23	25	25	21	15	9	5	15
Daily Average Max.°F	40	44	54	60	68	73	77	76	70	60	48	41	59
Monthly Average °C	1	3	6	10	14	17	20	19	16	11	5	2	10
Monthly Average °F	35	37	43	49	56	63	67	66	60	51	42	36	51
RELATIVE HUMIDITY (%)	82	75	61	53	55	57	53	56	61	69	79	84	65
PRECIPITATION													
Monthly Average mm	60	52	53	48	80	68	48	71	69	57	63	63	732.0
Monthly Average Inches	2.3	2.0	2.0	1.8	3.1	2.6	1.8	2.7	2.7	2.2	2.4	2.4	28.0
Days of 1mm or More	11	9	10	9	11	9	7	8	8	8	10	10	110

LYON   France

Elevation 201 m. (659 ft.)					**45°42'N—4°57'E**								
	JAN	FEB	MAR	APR	MAY	JUN	JUL	AUG	SEP	OCT	NOV	DEC	YEAR
TEMPERATURE													
Daily Average Min.°C	-1	0	3	6	9	13	15	14	12	7	4	0	7
Daily Average Min.°F	30	31	37	42	49	55	59	58	53	45	38	33	44
Daily Average Max.°C	5	7	13	16	20	24	27	26	23	16	10	6	16
Daily Average Max.°F	42	45	55	61	69	75	80	79	73	61	50	43	61
Extreme Monthly Min.°C	-25	-23	-13	-3	-4	-3	6	4	0	-7	-9	-24	-25
Extreme Monthly Min.°F	-13	-9	8	26	25	26	42	40	32	20	15	-12	-13
Extreme Monthly Max.°C	19	22	26	29	34	38	41	41	37	28	23	18	40
Extreme Monthly Max.°F	66	71	79	85	94	100	105	105	98	82	73	65	105
Monthly Average °C	2	4	7	10	14	18	21	20	17	12	7	3	11
Monthly Average °F	36	39	44	50	58	64	69	67	62	53	44	38	52
RELATIVE HUMIDITY (%)	80	72	60	56	56	55	50	54	60	69	78	80	64
PRECIPITATION													
Monthly Average mm	55	52	66	61	82	78	59	85	82	79	71	61	831.0
Monthly Average Inches	2.1	2.0	2.5	2.4	3.2	3.0	2.3	3.3	3.2	3.1	2.7	2.4	32.2
Days of 1mm or More	10	9	9	9	11	8	6	8	7	8	8	10	103

NANTES
France

Elevation 41 m. (135 ft.)					**47°18'N—1°36'W**								
	JAN	FEB	MAR	APR	MAY	JUN	JUL	AUG	SEP	OCT	NOV	DEC	YEAR
TEMPERATURE													
Daily Average Min.°C	2	2	4	6	9	12	14	13	12	8	5	3	7
Daily Average Min.°F	36	36	40	43	48	53	56	56	53	46	41	37	45
Daily Average Max.°C	8	9	13	15	19	22	24	24	21	16	11	8	16
Daily Average Max.°F	46	48	55	60	65	71	74	75	70	61	52	47	60
Monthly Average °C	5	6	8	10	13	17	19	18	16	13	8	6	12
Monthly Average °F	41	42	46	50	56	62	66	65	61	55	47	43	53
RELATIVE HUMIDITY (%)	84	78	70	62	63	63	61	63	69	75	82	86	71
PRECIPITATION													
Monthly Average mm	84	64	69	47	65	46	46	50	67	81	90	88	797.0
Monthly Average Inches	3.3	2.5	2.7	1.8	2.5	1.8	1.8	1.9	2.6	3.1	3.5	3.4	30.9
Days of 1mm or More	12	10	11	8	11	7	6	7	8	10	11	11	112

NICE
France

Elevation 10 m. (32 ft.)					**43°42'N—7°12'E**								
	JAN	FEB	MAR	APR	MAY	JUN	JUL	AUG	SEP	OCT	NOV	DEC	YEAR
TEMPERATURE													
Daily Average Min.°C	4	5	7	9	13	16	18	18	16	12	8	5	11
Daily Average Min.°F	40	40	44	48	55	61	65	64	61	54	46	41	52
Daily Average Max.°C	13	13	15	17	20	24	27	27	25	21	17	13	19
Daily Average Max.°F	55	56	59	63	69	75	80	80	77	69	62	56	67
Monthly Average °C	8	9	10	13	16	20	23	23	20	16	12	9	15
Monthly Average °F	46	48	51	55	61	68	73	73	68	61	53	48	59
RELATIVE HUMIDITY (%)	62	62	67	69	70	71	69	70	67	65	64	62	67
PRECIPITATION													
Monthly Average mm	82	78	81	61	50	35	16	35	65	114	115	89	821.0
Monthly Average Inches	3.2	3.0	3.1	2.4	1.9	1.3	0.6	1.3	2.5	4.4	4.5	3.5	31.7
Days of 1mm or More	7	6	6	6	5	4	1	3	4	5	7	6	60

PARIS
France

Elevation 75 m. (246 ft.)					**48°48'N—2°18'E**								
	JAN	FEB	MAR	APR	MAY	JUN	JUL	AUG	SEP	OCT	NOV	DEC	YEAR
TEMPERATURE													
Daily Average Min.°C	1	1	4	6	10	13	15	14	12	8	5	2	8
Daily Average Min.°F	34	34	38	43	49	55	58	58	53	46	40	36	46
Daily Average Max.°C	6	7	12	16	20	23	25	24	21	16	10	7	15
Daily Average Max.°F	43	45	54	60	67	73	76	75	70	60	50	44	60
Extreme Monthly Min.°C	-14	-16	-7	-2	1	4	6	6	2	-4	-9	-13	-15
Extreme Monthly Min.°F	7	4	20	28	33	40	43	43	35	25	15	8	4
Extreme Monthly Max.°C	15	18	24	31	33	37	40	36	34	28	21	17	40
Extreme Monthly Max.°F	59	64	75	88	92	98	104	97	94	83	69	62	104
Monthly Average °C	4	5	7	10	14	17	19	18	16	12	7	4	11
Monthly Average °F	38	41	45	51	57	63	66	65	61	54	45	38	52
RELATIVE HUMIDITY (%)	80	73	63	54	55	58	57	61	65	71	79	82	67
PRECIPITATION													
Monthly Average mm	51	44	45	54	57	46	48	56	51	49	70	52	623.0
Monthly Average Inches	2.0	1.7	1.7	2.1	2.2	1.8	1.8	2.2	2.0	1.9	2.7	2.0	24.1
Days of 1mm or More	0	0	0	0	0	0	0	0	0	0	0	0	0

TOULOUSE   France

	JAN	FEB	MAR	APR	MAY	JUN	JUL	AUG	SEP	OCT	NOV	DEC	YEAR
Elevation 152 m. (498 ft.)					43°36'N—1°24'E								

TEMPERATURE	JAN	FEB	MAR	APR	MAY	JUN	JUL	AUG	SEP	OCT	NOV	DEC	YEAR
Daily Average Min.°C	1	1	4	6	9	13	15	15	13	8	5	2	8
Daily Average Min.°F	33	34	39	43	49	55	58	59	55	47	40	36	46
Daily Average Max.°C	9	10	14	17	20	24	27	27	24	18	13	9	18
Daily Average Max.°F	47	50	58	62	69	76	80	80	75	65	55	48	64
Monthly Average °C	5	6	8	11	14	18	21	20	18	14	8	6	13
Monthly Average °F	41	43	47	52	58	65	70	69	65	56	47	42	55
RELATIVE HUMIDITY (%)	80	70	64	61	62	59	57	56	62	68	77	82	67
PRECIPITATION													
Monthly Average mm	54	50	61	56	71	57	43	48	51	51	51	64	657.0
Monthly Average Inches	2.1	1.9	2.4	2.2	2.7	2.2	1.6	1.8	2.0	2.0	2.0	2.5	25.4
Days of 1mm or More	10	9	10	10	10	7	5	6	6	7	8	9	97

CAYENNE   French Guiana

	JAN	FEB	MAR	APR	MAY	JUN	JUL	AUG	SEP	OCT	NOV	DEC	YEAR
Elevation 6 m. (20 ft.)					4°56'N—52°27'W								

TEMPERATURE	JAN	FEB	MAR	APR	MAY	JUN	JUL	AUG	SEP	OCT	NOV	DEC	YEAR
Daily Average Min.°C	23	23	23	24	23	23	23	23	23	23	23	23	23
Daily Average Min.°F	74	74	74	75	74	73	73	73	74	74	74	74	74
Daily Average Max.°C	29	29	29	30	29	31	31	32	33	33	32	30	31
Daily Average Max.°F	84	85	85	86	85	87	88	90	91	91	89	86	87
Monthly Average °C	26	26	26	26	26	26	26	26	26	26	26	26	26
Monthly Average °F	78	78	78	79	78	78	78	79	79	79	79	78	79
RELATIVE HUMIDITY (%)	80	78	80	81	83	79	75	71	69	69	74	79	77
PRECIPITATION													
Monthly Average mm	404	303	350	419	588	450	259	162	70	77	156	347	3585.0
Monthly Average Inches	15.9	11.9	13.7	16.5	23.1	17.7	10.2	6.3	2.7	3.0	6.1	13.6	140.7
Days of 1mm or More	23	19	21	20	25	26	20	15	8	7	13	22	219

TAHITI   French Polynesia

	JAN	FEB	MAR	APR	MAY	JUN	JUL	AUG	SEP	OCT	NOV	DEC	YEAR
Elevation 92 m. (302 ft.)					17°32'S—149°34'W								

TEMPERATURE	JAN	FEB	MAR	APR	MAY	JUN	JUL	AUG	SEP	OCT	NOV	DEC	YEAR
Daily Average Min.°C	32	32	32	32	31	30	30	30	30	31	31	31	31
Daily Average Min.°F	89	89	89	89	87	86	86	86	86	87	88	88	88
Daily Average Max.°C	22	22	22	22	21	21	20	20	21	21	22	22	21
Daily Average Max.°F	72	72	72	72	70	69	68	68	69	70	71	72	70
Monthly Average °C	27	27	27	27	26	25	24	24	25	25	26	26	26
Monthly Average °F	80	80	81	80	79	77	76	76	77	78	79	79	78
RELATIVE HUMIDITY (%)	77	77	78	78	78	79	77	78	76	76	77	78	77
PRECIPITATION													
Monthly Average mm	328	235	180	127	106	63	61	42	50	84	147	282	1705.0
Monthly Average Inches	12.9	9.2	7.0	5.0	4.1	2.4	2.4	1.6	1.9	3.3	5.7	11.1	66.6
Days of 1mm or More	14	12	10	8	7	5	5	4	5	7	10	14	101

PORT AUX FRANCAIS — French Southern Antarctic Lands

				Elevation 29 m. (95 ft.)			49°21'S—70°15'E						
	JAN	FEB	MAR	APR	MAY	JUN	JUL	AUG	SEP	OCT	NOV	DEC	YEAR
TEMPERATURE													
Daily Average Min.°C	4	4	4	3	1	-1	-1	-1	-1	0	1	3	1
Daily Average Min.°F	39	39	39	37	34	31	30	30	31	32	34	37	34
Daily Average Max.°C	11	11	10	9	7	5	5	5	5	7	8	10	8
Daily Average Max.°F	51	52	51	48	44	40	40	41	41	44	46	49	46
Monthly Average °C	7	8	7	6	4	2	2	2	2	3	4	6	4
Monthly Average °F	45	46	45	42	38	36	35	35	36	38	40	42	40
RELATIVE HUMIDITY (%)	68	66	69	73	75	80	79	77	73	71	67	67	72
PRECIPITATION													
Monthly Average mm	51	43	53	66	73	60	67	74	70	58	56	56	727.0
Monthly Average Inches	2.0	1.6	2.0	2.5	2.8	2.3	2.6	2.9	2.7	2.2	2.2	2.2	28.0
Days of 1mm or More	12	7	9	11	11	10	11	11	10	11	9	10	122

LIBREVILLE — Gabon

				Elevation 10 m. (32 ft.)			0°27'N—9°25'E						
	JAN	FEB	MAR	APR	MAY	JUN	JUL	AUG	SEP	OCT	NOV	DEC	YEAR
TEMPERATURE													
Daily Average Min.°C	24	24	24	24	24	23	22	22	23	24	23	24	23
Daily Average Min.°F	75	75	75	75	75	74	72	72	74	74	74	75	74
Daily Average Max.°C	29	30	30	30	29	28	26	27	28	28	28	29	29
Daily Average Max.°F	85	86	86	86	85	82	79	80	82	83	83	84	83
Extreme Monthly Min.°C	17	17	17	18	18	17	17	17	19	19	19	19	16
Extreme Monthly Min.°F	63	63	63	64	64	63	62	63	66	67	67	66	62
Extreme Monthly Max.°C	34	34	36	35	37	35	33	33	33	33	35	33	37
Extreme Monthly Max.°F	94	94	96	95	99	95	92	92	92	92	95	92	99
Monthly Average °C	27	27	27	27	27	25	24	25	25	26	26	26	26
Monthly Average °F	80	81	81	80	80	77	75	76	78	78	79	79	79
RELATIVE HUMIDITY (%)	79	78	78	78	78	74	73	74	77	81	82	80	78
PRECIPITATION													
Monthly Average mm	273	255	382	326	224	36	8	21	97	408	506	345	2881.0
Monthly Average Inches	10.7	10.0	15.0	12.8	8.8	1.4	0.3	0.8	3.8	16.0	19.9	13.5	113.0
Days of 1mm or More	14	12	17	16	13	2	1	3	9	19	19	14	139

SAN CRISTOBAL — Galapagos Islands

				Elevation 6 m. (19 ft.)			7°46'N—72°14'W						
	JAN	FEB	MAR	APR	MAY	JUN	JUL	AUG	SEP	OCT	NOV	DEC	YEAR
TEMPERATURE													
Monthly Average °C	25	26	26	26	25	24	22	22	22	22	23	24	24
Monthly Average °F	77	79	79	79	77	75	72	71	71	72	73	75	75
PRECIPITATION													
Monthly Average mm	65	96	105	64	34	26	5	5	5	6	6	31	448.0
Monthly Average Inches	2.5	3.7	4.1	2.5	1.3	1.0	0.1	0.1	0.1	0.2	0.2	1.2	17.0
Days of 1mm or More	12	12	8	6	5	7	11	11	10	10	7	10	109

ACCRA Ghana

		Elevation 65 m. (213 ft.)					5°36'N—0°10'W						
	JAN	FEB	MAR	APR	MAY	JUN	JUL	AUG	SEP	OCT	NOV	DEC	YEAR
TEMPERATURE													
Daily Average Min.°C	23	24	24	24	23	23	22	21	22	22	23	23	23
Daily Average Min.°F	73	74	75	75	74	73	71	71	71	72	73	74	73
Daily Average Max.°C	32	32	32	32	31	29	27	27	29	30	31	31	30
Daily Average Max.°F	89	90	90	89	88	84	81	81	84	86	88	88	86
Extreme Monthly Min.°C	15	17	20	19	21	20	19	18	20	19	21	17	15
Extreme Monthly Min.°F	59	62	68	67	69	68	66	64	68	67	69	63	59
Extreme Monthly Max.°C	34	38	38	34	35	33	32	32	32	32	33	34	37
Extreme Monthly Max.°F	94	100	100	93	95	92	90	89	89	90	91	94	100
Monthly Average °C	27	28	28	28	27	26	25	25	25	26	27	27	27
Monthly Average °F	81	82	82	82	81	78	77	76	78	79	81	81	80
RELATIVE HUMIDITY (%)	64	65	67	69	72	78	76	75	73	72	70	66	71
PRECIPITATION													
Monthly Average mm	19	35	73	102	134	257	68	23	60	70	40	20	901.0
Monthly Average Inches	0.7	1.3	2.8	4.0	5.2	10.1	2.6	0.9	2.3	2.7	1.5	0.7	34.8
Days of 1mm or More	0	1	4	6	8	14	7	4	5	4	2	1	56

TARAWA Gilbert Islands

		Elevation 4 m. (13 ft.)					1°21'N—172°56'E						
	JAN	FEB	MAR	APR	MAY	JUN	JUL	AUG	SEP	OCT	NOV	DEC	YEAR
TEMPERATURE													
Daily Average Min.°C	26	26	26	26	26	26	25	25	25	26	26	26	25
Daily Average Min.°F	78	78	78	78	78	78	77	77	77	79	78	78	78
Daily Average Max.°C	31	31	31	31	31	31	31	32	32	32	32	31	31
Daily Average Max.°F	88	88	88	88	88	88	88	89	89	90	90	88	88
Monthly Average °C	28	28	28	28	28	28	28	28	28	28	28	28	28
Monthly Average °F	82	82	82	82	83	82	82	82	83	83	83	82	82
RELATIVE HUMIDITY (%)	73	72	73	73	73	72	70	71	70	68	66	73	71
PRECIPITATION													
Monthly Average mm	268	231	221	176	176	164	179	135	102	122	168	202	2144.0
Monthly Average Inches	10.5	9.0	8.7	6.9	6.9	6.4	7.0	5.3	4.0	4.8	6.6	7.9	84.0
Days of 1mm or More	15	11	14	13	13	12	13	11	10	10	9	13	144

ATHENS Greece

		Elevation 107 m. (351 ft.)					37°58'N—24°43'E						
	JAN	FEB	MAR	APR	MAY	JUN	JUL	AUG	SEP	OCT	NOV	DEC	YEAR
TEMPERATURE													
Daily Average Min.°C	6	7	8	11	16	20	23	23	19	15	12	8	14
Daily Average Min.°F	44	44	46	52	61	68	73	73	67	60	53	47	57
Daily Average Max.°C	13	14	16	20	25	30	33	33	29	24	19	15	23
Daily Average Max.°F	55	57	60	68	77	86	92	92	84	75	65	58	73
Extreme Monthly Min.°C	-7	-6	-7	2	6	12	14	15	9	7	-1	-4	-6
Extreme Monthly Min.°F	20	21	20	35	42	54	58	59	48	45	30	24	20
Extreme Monthly Max.°C	21	23	28	33	38	43	41	42	39	35	31	22	42
Extreme Monthly Max.°F	69	73	83	91	101	109	106	107	103	95	87	71	109
Monthly Average °C	10	11	12	16	21	25	28	28	24	20	16	12	19
Monthly Average °F	51	51	54	61	69	77	82	82	76	67	60	54	65
RELATIVE HUMIDITY (%)	62	57	54	48	47	39	34	34	42	52	61	63	49
PRECIPITATION													
Monthly Average mm	48	39	37	25	16	5	5	5	13	62	54	63	372.0
Monthly Average Inches	1.8	1.5	1.4	0.9	0.6	0.1	0.1	0.1	0.5	2.4	2.1	2.4	13.9
Days of 1mm or More	5	5	5	4	2	1	0	0	0	4	5	5	36

CORFU

Greece

		Elevation 25 m. (82 ft.)				39°36'N—19°54'E							
	JAN	FEB	MAR	APR	MAY	JUN	JUL	AUG	SEP	OCT	NOV	DEC	YEAR
TEMPERATURE													
Daily Average Min.°C	6	6	8	10	13	17	19	19	17	14	11	8	12
Daily Average Min.°F	43	43	46	50	56	62	67	67	63	58	51	46	54
Daily Average Max.°C	14	15	16	19	23	28	31	32	28	23	19	16	22
Daily Average Max.°F	57	58	61	66	74	83	89	89	82	74	66	61	72
Monthly Average °C	10	10	12	15	20	24	26	26	23	18	14	11	17
Monthly Average °F	49	50	54	59	67	75	79	79	73	65	58	52	63
RELATIVE HUMIDITY (%)	66	64	63	63	60	54	50	48	58	62	66	68	60
PRECIPITATION													
Monthly Average mm	148	136	100	66	38	12	8	17	83	155	190	205	1158.0
Monthly Average Inches	5.8	5.3	3.9	2.5	1.4	0.4	0.3	0.6	3.2	6.1	7.4	8.0	44.9
Days of 1mm or More	12	11	9	7	4	1	1	1	4	8	10	13	81

LIMNOS

Greece

		Elevation 2 m. (7 ft.)				39°54'N—25°6'E							
	JAN	FEB	MAR	APR	MAY	JUN	JUL	AUG	SEP	OCT	NOV	DEC	YEAR
TEMPERATURE													
Daily Average Min.°C	6	6	7	10	14	18	21	21	18	15	11	8	13
Daily Average Min.°F	42	42	44	50	58	65	69	70	64	58	51	47	55
Daily Average Max.°C	11	12	13	18	23	27	30	30	26	22	16	13	20
Daily Average Max.°F	52	54	56	64	73	81	86	87	79	71	61	56	68
Monthly Average °C	9	9	10	14	19	24	26	26	22	18	14	11	17
Monthly Average °F	48	49	51	58	67	74	79	79	72	64	58	52	62
RELATIVE HUMIDITY (%)	73	68	67	65	64	58	54	52	56	65	71	73	64
PRECIPITATION													
Monthly Average mm	99	57	47	21	24	15	8	11	22	48	60	92	504.0
Monthly Average Inches	3.8	2.2	1.8	0.8	0.9	0.5	0.3	0.4	0.8	1.8	2.3	3.6	19.2
Days of 1mm or More	0	0	0	0	0	0	0	0	0	0	0	0	0

SALONICA

Greece

		Elevation 25 m. (82 ft.)				40°37'N—22°57'E							
	JAN	FEB	MAR	APR	MAY	JUN	JUL	AUG	SEP	OCT	NOV	DEC	YEAR
TEMPERATURE													
Daily Average Min.°C	2	3	5	10	14	18	21	21	17	13	9	4	11
Daily Average Min.°F	35	37	41	49	58	65	70	69	63	55	47	39	52
Daily Average Max.°C	9	12	14	20	25	29	32	32	28	22	16	11	21
Daily Average Max.°F	49	53	58	67	77	85	90	90	82	71	61	53	70
Extreme Monthly Min.°C	-6	-9	-3	-1	6	11	14	14	8	2	-2	-6	-9
Extreme Monthly Min.°F	21	15	26	31	42	52	58	58	47	36	29	22	15
Extreme Monthly Max.°C	17	19	26	30	33	38	42	40	37	33	27	21	41
Extreme Monthly Max.°F	63	67	78	86	91	100	107	104	99	91	81	70	107
Monthly Average °C	5	7	10	14	20	24	26	26	22	16	11	7	16
Monthly Average °F	41	44	49	57	67	76	80	79	71	61	52	45	60
RELATIVE HUMIDITY (%)	71	61	61	58	57	50	48	48	54	62	70	73	59
PRECIPITATION													
Monthly Average mm	40	40	43	38	47	30	24	20	30	43	54	57	466.0
Monthly Average Inches	1.5	1.5	1.6	1.4	1.8	1.1	0.9	0.7	1.1	1.6	2.1	2.2	17.5
Days of 1mm or More	7	6	6	5	5	4	3	2	2	4	6	6	56

NORD   Greenland

	Elevation 2 m. (7 ft.)					81°36'N—16°42'W						
	JAN	FEB	MAR	APR	MAY	JUN	JUL	AUG	SEP	OCT	NOV	DEC	YEAR
TEMPERATURE													
Daily Average Min.°C	-34	-36	-36	-29	-15	-3	1	-1	-12	-22	-28	-32	-21
Daily Average Min.°F	-29	-32	-33	-20	5	27	34	31	11	-8	-19	-25	-5
Daily Average Max.°C	-24	-26	-27	-20	-8	2	7	4	-5	-15	-20	-23	-13
Daily Average Max.°F	-12	-14	-17	-4	17	36	45	39	22	4	-4	-9	9
Monthly Average °C	-30	-30	-31	-24	-11	-1	3	2	-9	-19	-25	-27	-17
Monthly Average °F	-22	-23	-23	-11	13	31	38	35	17	-3	-13	-17	2
RELATIVE HUMIDITY (%)	75	72	70	68	73	79	75	82	84	81	77	76	76
PRECIPITATION													
Monthly Average mm	10	9	10	10	5	9	20	20	23	16	16	13	161.0
Monthly Average Inches	0.3	0.3	0.3	0.3	0.1	0.3	0.7	0.7	0.9	0.6	0.6	0.5	5.6
Days of 1mm or More	5	5	3	3	4	3	6	5	4	5	5	4	52

THULE   Greenland

	Elevation 44 m. (144 ft.)					77°29'N—69°10'W						
	JAN	FEB	MAR	APR	MAY	JUN	JUL	AUG	SEP	OCT	NOV	DEC	YEAR
TEMPERATURE													
Daily Average Min.°C	-25	-26	-28	-21	-8	0	3	4	-3	-9	-17	-22	-13
Daily Average Min.°F	-13	-14	-19	-6	17	32	38	39	26	17	1	-8	9
Daily Average Max.°C	-17	-17	-20	-12	0	8	10	8	1	-4	-12	-16	-6
Daily Average Max.°F	2	1	-4	10	32	46	51	47	34	24	11	3	21
Extreme Monthly Min.°C	-38	-41	-39	-32	-22	-6	-2	-4	-14	-24	-33	-38	-40
Extreme Monthly Min.°F	-37	-41	-38	-26	-8	22	28	24	6	-11	-28	-37	-41
Extreme Monthly Max.°C	2	2	1	3	7	15	15	14	7	10	3	2	17
Extreme Monthly Max.°F	36	36	34	37	44	59	59	57	45	50	38	35	63
Monthly Average °C	-24	-26	-26	-18	-6	3	5	4	-2	-10	-16	-23	-11
Monthly Average °F	-11	-14	-14	0	22	37	42	40	28	14	3	-9	11
RELATIVE HUMIDITY (%)	85	86	87	85	83	92	85	86	85	84	85	85	85
PRECIPITATION													
Monthly Average mm	9	8	4	3	5	6	15	15	13	11	26	5	120.0
Monthly Average Inches	0.3	0.3	0.1	0.1	0.1	0.2	0.5	0.5	0.5	0.4	1.0	0.1	4.1
Days of 1mm or More	0	0	0	0	0	0	0	0	0	0	0	0	0

UPERNAVIK   Greenland

	Elevation 35 m. (115 ft.)					72°48'N—56°6'W						
	JAN	FEB	MAR	APR	MAY	JUN	JUL	AUG	SEP	OCT	NOV	DEC	YEAR
TEMPERATURE													
Daily Average Min.°C	-20	-23	-24	-17	-6	-1	2	3	-1	-6	-11	-16	-10
Daily Average Min.°F	-4	-10	-10	1	21	31	36	37	30	21	13	4	14
Daily Average Max.°C	-13	-16	-15	-8	1	6	10	9	4	-1	-5	-10	-3
Daily Average Max.°F	8	4	6	17	34	43	49	48	39	30	23	14	26
Monthly Average °C	-17	-19	-20	-13	-4	2	5	5	1	-4	-9	-14	-7
Monthly Average °F	1	-2	-5	8	25	35	42	42	34	25	16	7	19
RELATIVE HUMIDITY (%)	71	74	74	79	89	88	87	87	86	87	84	75	82
PRECIPITATION													
Monthly Average mm	12	12	8	10	11	11	29	25	39	30	33	18	238.0
Monthly Average Inches	0.4	0.4	0.3	0.3	0.4	0.4	1.1	0.9	1.5	1.1	1.2	0.7	8.7
Days of 1mm or More	4	6	3	4	4	4	5	8	11	9	12	7	77

PEARLS   Grenada

Elevation 7 m. (22 ft.)					12°3'N—61°45'W								
	JAN	FEB	MAR	APR	MAY	JUN	JUL	AUG	SEP	OCT	NOV	DEC	YEAR
TEMPERATURE													
Monthly Average °C 26	26	27	27	27	27	27	28	28	27	27	27	27	
Monthly Average °F 79	79	80	81	81	81	81	82	82	81	81	80	81	
PRECIPITATION													
Monthly Average mm 123	72	54	68	117	230	200	196	190	245	253	168	1916.0	
Monthly Average Inches 4.8	2.8	2.1	2.6	4.6	9.0	7.8	7.7	7.4	9.6	9.9	6.6	74.9	
Days of 1mm or More 18	13	5	4	4	18	25	17	11	18	19	0	152	

Guam

Elevation 19 m. (62 ft.)					13°24'N—144°38'E								
	JAN	FEB	MAR	APR	MAY	JUN	JUL	AUG	SEP	OCT	NOV	DEC	YEAR
TEMPERATURE													
Daily Average Min.°C 24	23	24	24	25	25	24	24	24	24	25	24	24	
Daily Average Min.°F 75	74	75	76	77	77	76	76	76	76	77	76	76	
Daily Average Max.°C 29	29	29	31	31	31	30	30	30	30	30	29	30	
Daily Average Max.°F 84	84	85	87	88	88	86	86	86	86	86	85	86	
Monthly Average °C 26	26	27	27	28	28	28	27	27	27	27	27	27	
Monthly Average °F 80	80	80	81	82	82	82	81	81	81	81	80	81	
RELATIVE HUMIDITY (%)	72	71	69	67	68	71	75	78	78	78	76	73	73
PRECIPITATION													
Monthly Average mm 109	64	55	88	112	127	233	327	360	311	215	131	2132.0	
Monthly Average Inches 4.2	2.5	2.1	3.4	4.4	5.0	9.1	12.8	14.1	12.2	8.4	5.1	83.3	
Days of 1mm or More 20	18	15	19	19	23	25	24	25	24	23	22	257	

GUATEMALA CITY   Guatemala

Elevation 1480 m. (4855 ft.)					14°37'N—90°31'W								
	JAN	FEB	MAR	APR	MAY	JUN	JUL	AUG	SEP	OCT	NOV	DEC	YEAR
TEMPERATURE													
Daily Average Min.°C 12	12	14	14	16	16	16	16	16	16	14	13	14	
Daily Average Min.°F 53	54	57	58	60	61	60	60	60	60	57	55	58	
Daily Average Max.°C 23	25	27	28	29	27	26	26	26	24	23	22	26	
Daily Average Max.°F 73	77	81	82	84	81	78	79	79	76	74	72	78	
Extreme Monthly Min.°C 5	6	5	8	11	11	11	11	12	10	7	5	5	
Extreme Monthly Min.°F 41	43	41	47	52	52	51	52	54	50	44	41	41	
Extreme Monthly Max.°C 30	29	30	32	32	30	29	28	28	28	28	28	32	
Extreme Monthly Max.°F 86	85	86	90	89	86	84	83	82	82	83	83	90	
Monthly Average °C 17	18	20	20	20	19	19	19	19	18	17	17	18	
Monthly Average °F 62	64	66	68	68	66	66	66	66	65	63	62	65	
RELATIVE HUMIDITY (%)	69	62	51	51	55	70	67	72	71	72	71	70	65
PRECIPITATION													
Monthly Average mm 5	6	8	21	122	246	184	169	237	118	26	6	1148.0	
Monthly Average Inches 0.1	0.2	0.3	0.8	4.8	9.6	7.2	6.6	9.3	4.6	1.0	0.2	44.7	
Days of 1mm or More 1	1	1	3	9	16	15	15	16	11	3	1	92	

CONAKRY

Guinea

	JAN	FEB	MAR	APR	MAY	JUN	JUL	AUG	SEP	OCT	NOV	DEC	YEAR
Elevation 46 m. (151 ft.)				9°34'N—13°37'W									
TEMPERATURE													
Daily Average Min.°C	22	22	23	24	24	23	22	22	22	22	23	23	23
Daily Average Min.°F	72	72	73	75	75	73	72	72	72	72	73	73	73
Daily Average Max.°C	31	31	32	32	31	29	28	27	29	30	31	31	30
Daily Average Max.°F	87	88	89	89	88	85	82	81	83	85	87	88	86
Extreme Monthly Min.°C	18	17	21	20	19	18	19	20	19	18	21	19	17
Extreme Monthly Min.°F	64	63	69	68	66	65	67	68	66	64	69	66	63
Extreme Monthly Max.°C	34	34	36	35	35	33	32	31	32	33	33	34	35
Extreme Monthly Max.°F	94	94	96	95	95	92	89	87	90	91	91	93	95
Monthly Average °C	26	26	27	28	27	26	25	25	25	26	27	26	26
Monthly Average °F	79	80	81	82	81	79	77	77	78	79	80	79	79
RELATIVE HUMIDITY (%)	59	58	58	59	67	78	85	88	82	75	73	65	71
PRECIPITATION													
Monthly Average mm	1	1	8	29	122	423	996	893	564	297	86	12	3432.0
Monthly Average Inches	0.0	0.0	0.3	1.1	4.8	16.6	39.2	35.1	22.2	11.6	3.3	0.4	134.6
Days of 1mm or More	0	0	1	1	9	19	27	26	21	16	5	1	126

KANKAN

Guinea

	JAN	FEB	MAR	APR	MAY	JUN	JUL	AUG	SEP	OCT	NOV	DEC	YEAR
Elevation 377 m. (1237 ft.)				10°23'N—9°18'W									
TEMPERATURE													
Daily Average Min.°C	15	18	22	23	23	21	21	21	21	21	19	15	20
Daily Average Min.°F	58	65	71	74	73	70	69	69	70	69	67	59	68
Daily Average Max.°C	33	35	36	35	33	31	29	28	30	31	32	33	32
Daily Average Max.°F	92	95	97	95	92	87	84	83	85	88	90	91	90
Monthly Average °C	24	28	29	30	28	26	25	25	25	24	26	22	26
Monthly Average °F	75	82	85	86	83	79	78	77	78	76	78	71	79
RELATIVE HUMIDITY (%)	26	29	40	51	63	73	77	78	75	67	53	34	55
PRECIPITATION													
Monthly Average mm	1	6	40	66	139	210	283	333	375	171	46	5	1675.0
Monthly Average Inches	0.0	0.2	1.5	2.5	5.4	8.2	11.1	13.1	14.7	6.7	1.8	0.1	65.3
Days of 1mm or More	0	0	2	4	11	13	16	19	18	10	3	0	96

BISSAU

Guinea-Bissau

	JAN	FEB	MAR	APR	MAY	JUN	JUL	AUG	SEP	OCT	NOV	DEC	YEAR
Elevation 21 m. (69 ft.)				11°52'N—15°35'W									
TEMPERATURE													
Daily Average Min.°C	18	19	20	21	22	23	23	23	23	23	22	19	21
Daily Average Min.°F	64	66	68	69	72	74	73	73	73	73	72	66	71
Daily Average Max.°C	32	33	34	33	33	31	30	29	30	31	32	31	31
Daily Average Max.°F	89	91	92	92	91	88	85	84	86	88	89	88	89
Monthly Average °C	25	26	27	27	28	27	26	26	26	27	27	25	26
Monthly Average °F	77	79	80	80	82	81	79	79	80	81	81	77	80
RELATIVE HUMIDITY (%)	34	36	42	46	55	66	77	81	76	69	58	41	57
PRECIPITATION													
Monthly Average mm	0	0	0	0	22	149	475	628	419	201	32	1	1927.0
Monthly Average Inches	0.0	0.0	0.0	0.0	0.8	5.8	18.7	24.7	16.5	7.9	1.2	0.0	75.6
Days of 1mm or More	0	0	0	0	1	9	19	22	18	10	0	0	79

GEORGETOWN   Guyana

	Elevation 2 m. (6 ft.)					6°50'N—58°12'W							
	JAN	FEB	MAR	APR	MAY	JUN	JUL	AUG	SEP	OCT	NOV	DEC	YEAR
TEMPERATURE													
Daily Average Min.°C	23	23	24	24	24	24	24	24	24	24	24	24	24
Daily Average Min.°F	74	74	75	76	75	75	75	75	76	76	76	75	75
Daily Average Max.°C	29	29	29	29	29	29	29	30	31	31	30	29	29
Daily Average Max.°F	84	84	84	85	85	85	85	86	87	87	86	84	85
Extreme Monthly Min.°C	20	21	21	22	21	21	21	22	21	21	21	21	20
Extreme Monthly Min.°F	68	69	69	71	70	69	70	71	69	70	69	70	68
Extreme Monthly Max.°C	31	32	32	32	32	32	32	32	34	34	33	32	33
Extreme Monthly Max.°F	88	89	89	90	90	89	90	90	93	93	91	90	93
Monthly Average °C	26	26	27	27	27	27	27	27	28	28	27	27	27
Monthly Average °F	79	80	81	81	81	80	80	81	82	82	81	80	81
RELATIVE HUMIDITY (%)	75	72	71	71	75	77	74	73	69	69	69	75	73
PRECIPITATION													
Monthly Average mm	255	132	126	172	289	351	270	205	111	110	202	277	2500.0
Monthly Average Inches	10.0	5.1	4.9	6.7	11.3	13.8	10.6	8.0	4.3	4.3	7.9	10.9	97.8
Days of 1mm or More	17	11	9	12	19	22	20	15	8	9	13	17	172

PORT-AU-PRINCE   Haiti

	Elevation 37 m. (122 ft.)					33°30'N—72°20'W							
	JAN	FEB	MAR	APR	MAY	JUN	JUL	AUG	SEP	OCT	NOV	DEC	YEAR
TEMPERATURE													
Daily Average Min.°C	20	20	21	22	22	23	23	23	23	22	22	21	22
Daily Average Min.°F	68	68	69	71	72	73	74	73	73	72	71	69	71
Daily Average Max.°C	31	31	32	32	32	33	34	34	33	32	31	31	32
Daily Average Max.°F	87	88	89	89	90	92	94	93	91	90	88	87	90
Extreme Monthly Min.°C	17	16	16	16	19	19	19	20	19	19	18	16	15
Extreme Monthly Min.°F	62	61	60	61	66	66	67	68	67	66	64	60	60
Extreme Monthly Max.°C	34	35	37	37	37	37	38	38	37	37	36	34	38
Extreme Monthly Max.°F	93	95	98	98	99	99	101	101	99	98	96	93	101
Monthly Average °C	25	26	26	27	27	28	29	28	28	27	27	26	27
Monthly Average °F	78	78	79	81	81	83	84	83	82	81	80	78	81
RELATIVE HUMIDITY (%)	44	44	45	49	54	50	43	49	54	56	54	48	49
PRECIPITATION													
Monthly Average mm	33	33	67	147	202	83	74	129	146	167	72	42	1195.0
Monthly Average Inches	1.2	1.2	2.6	5.7	7.9	3.2	2.9	5.0	5.7	6.5	2.8	1.6	46.3
Days of 1mm or More	2	4	4	10	9	5	3	8	11	12	6	1	75

TEGUCIGALPA   Honduras

	Elevation 1007 m. (3303 ft.)					14°6'N—87°13'W							
	JAN	FEB	MAR	APR	MAY	JUN	JUL	AUG	SEP	OCT	NOV	DEC	YEAR
TEMPERATURE													
Monthly Average °C	19	20	22	23	23	22	22	22	22	21	20	19	21
Monthly Average °F	67	68	71	74	74	72	71	72	72	71	68	67	71
PRECIPITATION													
Monthly Average mm	7	3	5	29	157	152	88	83	185	132	31	9	881.0
Monthly Average Inches	0.2	0.1	0.1	1.1	6.1	5.9	3.4	3.2	7.2	5.1	1.2	0.3	33.9
Days of 1mm or More	4	1	1	3	11	17	14	15	19	17	9	5	116

Hong Kong

Elevation 33 m. (108 ft.)						22°18'N—114°10'E							
	JAN	FEB	MAR	APR	MAY	JUN	JUL	AUG	SEP	OCT	NOV	DEC	YEAR
TEMPERATURE													
Daily Average Min.°C	13	13	16	19	23	26	26	26	25	23	18	15	20
Daily Average Min.°F	56	55	60	67	74	78	78	78	77	73	65	59	68
Daily Average Max.°C	18	17	19	24	28	29	31	31	29	27	23	20	25
Daily Average Max.°F	64	63	67	75	82	85	87	87	85	81	74	68	77
Monthly Average °C	16	16	19	22	26	28	29	28	28	25	21	17	23
Monthly Average °F	60	61	66	72	79	82	84	83	82	77	71	63	73
RELATIVE HUMIDITY (%)	66	73	74	77	78	77	77	77	72	63	60	63	71
PRECIPITATION													
Monthly Average mm	26	50	70	156	308	407	328	406	312	141	41	29	2274.0
Monthly Average Inches	1.0	1.9	2.7	6.1	12.1	16.0	12.9	15.9	12.2	5.5	1.6	1.1	89.0
Days of 1mm or More	3	5	5	7	11	16	14	14	11	6	3	2	97

BUDAPEST — Hungary

Elevation 130 m. (426 ft.)						47°26'N—19°11'E							
	JAN	FEB	MAR	APR	MAY	JUN	JUL	AUG	SEP	OCT	NOV	DEC	YEAR
TEMPERATURE													
Daily Average Min.°C	-4	-2	2	7	11	15	16	16	12	7	3	-1	7
Daily Average Min.°F	25	28	35	44	52	58	62	60	53	44	38	30	44
Daily Average Max.°C	1	4	10	17	22	26	28	27	23	16	8	4	16
Daily Average Max.°F	34	39	50	62	71	78	82	81	74	61	47	38	60
Extreme Monthly Min.°C	-22	-23	-13	-4	0	3	9	7	1	-9	-13	-19	-23
Extreme Monthly Min.°F	-7	-10	8	24	32	37	48	45	34	15	8	-3	-10
Extreme Monthly Max.°C	15	18	26	30	32	39	38	39	35	31	23	16	39
Extreme Monthly Max.°F	59	64	78	86	90	103	101	102	95	87	73	60	103
Monthly Average °C	-1	2	6	12	17	20	22	21	17	12	6	2	11
Monthly Average °F	31	35	43	53	62	68	71	70	63	53	43	35	52
RELATIVE HUMIDITY (%)	76	68	55	48	49	49	47	47	49	60	76	81	59
PRECIPITATION													
Monthly Average mm	42	36	34	40	60	67	50	52	37	36	62	50	566.0
Monthly Average Inches	1.6	1.4	1.3	1.5	2.3	2.6	1.9	2.0	1.4	1.4	2.4	1.9	21.7
Days of 1mm or More	7	6	6	6	8	8	6	6	5	5	8	8	79

DEBRECHEN — Hungary

Elevation 111 m. (364 ft.)						47°30'N—21°36'E							
	JAN	FEB	MAR	APR	MAY	JUN	JUL	AUG	SEP	OCT	NOV	DEC	YEAR
TEMPERATURE													
Daily Average Min.°C	-6	-4	0	5	10	13	15	14	10	5	2	-2	5
Daily Average Min.°F	21	25	32	41	50	56	59	57	50	41	36	28	41
Daily Average Max.°C	0	3	10	16	22	25	27	27	23	16	9	3	15
Daily Average Max.°F	33	38	50	62	71	77	81	80	73	61	47	38	59
Extreme Monthly Min.°C	-30	-26	-18	-7	-3	-1	5	3	-3	-15	-19	-22	-30
Extreme Monthly Min.°F	-22	-15	0	19	27	31	41	37	27	5	-2	-8	-22
Extreme Monthly Max.°C	14	18	26	33	33	37	38	39	36	29	22	16	38
Extreme Monthly Max.°F	57	64	78	92	91	99	101	102	97	85	71	61	102
Monthly Average °C	-3	0	5	11	16	19	20	20	16	10	5	0	10
Monthly Average °F	27	32	41	51	61	66	69	67	60	51	41	32	50
RELATIVE HUMIDITY (%)	78	71	59	51	52	53	50	50	50	59	75	80	61
PRECIPITATION													
Monthly Average mm	38	29	33	41	57	80	65	61	36	32	47	45	564.0
Monthly Average Inches	1.4	1.1	1.2	1.6	2.2	3.1	2.5	2.4	1.4	1.2	1.8	1.7	21.6
Days of 1mm or More	8	5	6	8	9	10	8	7	4	5	7	7	84

MISKOLC
Hungary

	Elevation 120 m. (393 ft.)					48°6'N—20°48'E							
	JAN	FEB	MAR	APR	MAY	JUN	JUL	AUG	SEP	OCT	NOV	DEC	YEAR
TEMPERATURE													
Daily Average Min.°C	-7	-5	-1	4	9	13	14	14	10	4	1	-3	5
Daily Average Min.°F	20	24	30	40	49	55	57	56	49	40	34	27	40
Daily Average Max.°C	0	3	10	17	22	25	27	27	23	16	8	3	15
Daily Average Max.°F	32	37	49	62	71	77	81	80	73	60	46	37	59
Monthly Average °C	-3	-1	4	10	15	18	20	19	15	9	4	-1	9
Monthly Average °F	26	31	40	50	60	65	68	66	59	49	39	31	49
RELATIVE HUMIDITY (%)	82	75	61	51	53	56	54	53	54	64	79	86	64
PRECIPITATION													
Monthly Average mm	28	26	33	38	64	85	65	65	39	34	46	38	561.0
Monthly Average Inches	1.1	1.0	1.2	1.4	2.5	3.3	2.5	2.5	1.5	1.3	1.8	1.4	21.5
Days of 1mm or More	5	5	6	6	9	9	7	6	5	4	6	6	74

PECS
Hungary

	Elevation 201 m. (659 ft.)					46°0'N—18°12'E							
	JAN	FEB	MAR	APR	MAY	JUN	JUL	AUG	SEP	OCT	NOV	DEC	YEAR
TEMPERATURE													
Daily Average Min.°C	-3	-3	0	6	10	14	16	15	12	7	3	-1	6
Daily Average Min.°F	26	26	32	42	51	56	60	59	53	44	37	29	43
Daily Average Max.°C	2	4	10	17	22	25	28	28	24	17	9	5	16
Daily Average Max.°F	36	40	50	62	71	77	82	82	74	62	48	40	60
Monthly Average °C	-1	1	5	11	16	19	21	20	17	11	6	1	10
Monthly Average °F	29	34	42	51	60	66	69	68	62	52	42	34	51
RELATIVE HUMIDITY (%)	72	67	57	49	51	50	48	46	46	56	70	74	57
PRECIPITATION													
Monthly Average mm	42	33	35	55	62	84	64	62	48	36	59	49	629.0
Monthly Average Inches	1.6	1.2	1.3	2.1	2.4	3.3	2.5	2.4	1.8	1.4	2.3	1.9	24.2
Days of 1mm or More	7	6	6	7	8	9	7	6	5	6	7	7	81

GRIMSEY
Iceland

	Elevation 22 m. (72 ft.)					66°36'N—18°0'W							
	JAN	FEB	MAR	APR	MAY	JUN	JUL	AUG	SEP	OCT	NOV	DEC	YEAR
TEMPERATURE													
Daily Average Min.°C	-3	-3	-3	-2	1	4	6	6	4	2	-1	-2	1
Daily Average Min.°F	27	28	26	29	34	39	42	42	39	36	31	28	33
Daily Average Max.°C	1	1	1	2	5	9	10	10	8	6	3	2	5
Daily Average Max.°F	34	34	34	36	42	48	51	49	47	42	38	35	41
Monthly Average °C	-1	-1	-1	0	3	6	8	8	6	4	1	0	3
Monthly Average °F	31	30	30	32	37	43	46	46	43	39	35	32	37
PRECIPITATION													
Monthly Average mm	54	55	59	45	25	25	43	51	66	63	51	49	586.0
Monthly Average Inches	2.1	2.1	2.3	1.7	0.9	0.9	1.6	2.0	2.5	2.4	2.0	1.9	22.4
Days of 1mm or More	0	0	0	0	0	0	0	0	0	0	0	0	0

HOLAR   Iceland

	JAN	FEB	MAR	APR	MAY	JUN	JUL	AUG	SEP	OCT	NOV	DEC	YEAR
Elevation 17 m. (55 ft.)					64°18'N—15°12'W								
TEMPERATURE													
Daily Average Min.°C	-2	-2	-1	1	3	6	8	7	5	3	0	-2	2
Daily Average Min.°F	29	28	30	33	38	43	46	45	42	37	32	29	36
Daily Average Max.°C	2	3	4	6	9	12	13	13	11	7	4	3	7
Daily Average Max.°F	36	37	39	43	48	54	56	55	51	45	40	37	45
Monthly Average °C	0	1	1	3	6	8	10	10	7	5	1	0	4
Monthly Average °F	32	33	34	38	42	47	50	49	45	41	35	32	40
RELATIVE HUMIDITY (%)	77	76	76	76	73	76	80	79	80	81	76	76	77
PRECIPITATION													
Monthly Average mm	136	131	117	87	83	80	73	97	117	168	120	136	1345.0
Monthly Average Inches	5.3	5.1	4.6	3.4	3.2	3.1	2.8	3.8	4.6	6.6	4.7	5.3	52.5
Days of 1mm or More	14	12	12	9	10	9	9	10	11	14	11	13	134

REYKJAVIK   Iceland

	JAN	FEB	MAR	APR	MAY	JUN	JUL	AUG	SEP	OCT	NOV	DEC	YEAR
Elevation 16 m. (52 ft.)					64°6'N—21°54'W								
TEMPERATURE													
Daily Average Min.°C	-2	-2	-1	1	4	7	9	8	6	3	0	-2	3
Daily Average Min.°F	28	28	30	34	39	45	48	47	43	38	32	29	37
Daily Average Max.°C	2	3	4	6	10	12	14	14	11	7	4	2	7
Daily Average Max.°F	35	37	39	43	50	54	57	56	52	45	39	36	45
Extreme Monthly Min.°C	-15	-16	-14	-11	-7	0	4	1	-3	-10	-12	-16	-15
Extreme Monthly Min.°F	5	4	6	13	19	32	39	34	27	14	10	4	4
Extreme Monthly Max.°C	10	10	14	15	18	21	23	22	20	14	12	12	23
Extreme Monthly Max.°F	50	50	58	59	64	69	74	71	68	58	53	53	74
Monthly Average °C	-1	1	1	3	6	9	11	10	8	5	1	0	4
Monthly Average °F	31	33	33	38	44	48	51	50	46	40	34	32	40
RELATIVE HUMIDITY (%)	80	78	77	68	66	72	72	72	72	77	81	80	75
PRECIPITATION													
Monthly Average mm	71	73	79	59	36	51	49	60	66	88	74	75	781.0
Monthly Average Inches	2.7	2.8	3.1	2.3	1.4	2.0	1.9	2.3	2.5	3.4	2.9	2.9	30.2
Days of 1mm or More	12	12	14	12	9	10	9	11	12	14	12	13	140

AHMADABAD   India

	JAN	FEB	MAR	APR	MAY	JUN	JUL	AUG	SEP	OCT	NOV	DEC	YEAR
Elevation 50 m. (163 ft.)					23°2'N—72°35'E								
TEMPERATURE													
Daily Average Min.°C	14	15	19	23	26	27	26	25	24	22	18	15	22
Daily Average Min.°F	58	59	67	74	79	81	79	77	76	72	65	59	71
Daily Average Max.°C	29	31	36	40	42	38	34	32	34	36	34	30	35
Daily Average Max.°F	85	88	97	104	107	101	93	90	93	97	93	86	95
Extreme Monthly Min.°C	6	10	12	17	21	22	22	23	22	16	14	9	5
Extreme Monthly Min.°F	42	50	53	62	70	72	72	73	71	61	58	49	42
Extreme Monthly Max.°C	35	38	41	43	46	43	40	38	40	39	38	36	45
Extreme Monthly Max.°F	95	100	106	110	114	110	104	100	104	103	101	96	114
Monthly Average °C	20	23	27	31	34	33	30	28	29	28	25	21	27
Monthly Average °F	68	73	81	88	93	91	85	83	84	83	76	71	81
RELATIVE HUMIDITY (%)	47	46	44	49	59	70	81	83	78	56	45	46	59
PRECIPITATION													
Monthly Average mm	2	1	1	1	14	108	253	227	147	21	11	2	788.0
Monthly Average Inches	0.0	0.0	0.0	0.0	0.5	4.2	9.9	8.9	5.7	0.8	0.4	0.0	30.4
Days of 1mm or More	0	0	0	0	0	5	13	13	6	0	0	0	37

BOMBAY   India

Elevation 11 m. (36 ft.)   18°54'N—72°49'E

	JAN	FEB	MAR	APR	MAY	JUN	JUL	AUG	SEP	OCT	NOV	DEC	YEAR
TEMPERATURE													
Daily Average Min.°C	19	19	22	24	27	26	25	24	24	24	23	21	23
Daily Average Min.°F	67	67	72	76	80	79	77	76	76	76	73	69	74
Daily Average Max.°C	28	28	30	32	33	32	29	29	29	32	32	31	30
Daily Average Max.°F	83	83	86	89	91	89	85	85	85	89	89	87	87
Extreme Monthly Min.°C	12	12	17	20	23	21	22	22	22	21	18	13	11
Extreme Monthly Min.°F	53	53	62	68	73	70	72	72	72	70	64	55	53
Extreme Monthly Max.°C	34	36	38	38	36	37	36	32	35	36	36	34	38
Extreme Monthly Max.°F	94	97	101	100	96	99	96	90	95	97	96	94	101
Monthly Average °C	24	25	27	29	30	29	28	27	28	29	28	26	27
Monthly Average °F	76	77	81	84	86	84	82	81	82	84	83	79	81
RELATIVE HUMIDITY (%)	70	71	73	75	74	79	83	83	85	81	73	70	76
PRECIPITATION													
Monthly Average mm	0	0	0	2	7	591	706	464	266	60	15	4	2115.0
Monthly Average Inches	0.0	0.0	0.0	0.0	0.2	23.2	27.8	18.2	10.4	2.3	0.5	0.1	82.7
Days of 1mm or More	0	0	0	0	0	16	25	24	14	3	1	0	83

CALCUTTA   India

Elevation 6 m. (19 ft.)   22°32'N—88°20'E

	JAN	FEB	MAR	APR	MAY	JUN	JUL	AUG	SEP	OCT	NOV	DEC	YEAR
TEMPERATURE													
Daily Average Min.°C	13	15	21	24	25	26	26	26	26	23	18	13	21
Daily Average Min.°F	55	59	69	75	77	79	79	78	78	74	64	55	70
Daily Average Max.°C	27	29	34	36	36	33	32	32	32	32	29	26	31
Daily Average Max.°F	80	84	93	97	96	92	89	89	90	89	84	79	89
Extreme Monthly Min.°C	7	8	10	16	18	21	23	23	22	17	11	7	6
Extreme Monthly Min.°F	44	46	50	61	65	70	73	74	72	63	51	45	44
Extreme Monthly Max.°C	32	37	40	42	42	44	37	36	36	36	33	31	42
Extreme Monthly Max.°F	89	98	104	107	108	111	98	96	97	96	92	87	108
Monthly Average °C	20	23	28	30	31	30	29	29	29	28	25	21	27
Monthly Average °F	68	74	82	87	88	87	85	84	84	82	76	69	80
RELATIVE HUMIDITY (%)	85	82	79	56	77	82	86	88	86	85	79	80	82
PRECIPITATION													
Monthly Average mm	16	24	32	57	113	271	359	348	303	136	19	11	1689.0
Monthly Average Inches	0.6	0.9	1.2	2.2	4.4	10.6	14.1	13.7	11.9	5.3	0.7	0.4	66.0
Days of 1mm or More	1	2	2	4	8	14	19	20	15	7	1	0	93

JODHPUR   India

Elevation 238 m. (780 ft.)   26°18'N—73°1'E

	JAN	FEB	MAR	APR	MAY	JUN	JUL	AUG	SEP	OCT	NOV	DEC	YEAR
TEMPERATURE													
Daily Average Min.°C	9	11	16	21	26	28	27	25	24	18	13	10	19
Daily Average Min.°F	48	52	61	70	79	82	80	77	75	65	55	50	66
Daily Average Max.°C	24	27	32	37	41	40	36	34	34	35	31	26	33
Daily Average Max.°F	76	80	90	99	105	104	97	93	94	95	88	79	92
Monthly Average °C	17	20	25	31	34	34	31	30	30	28	23	19	27
Monthly Average °F	63	68	78	87	93	93	89	86	86	83	74	66	80
RELATIVE HUMIDITY (%)	23	20	15	13	17	30	49	56	41	17	18	24	27
PRECIPITATION													
Monthly Average mm	1	3	8	7	18	38	123	118	61	6	5	1	389.0
Monthly Average Inches	0.0	0.1	0.3	0.2	0.7	1.4	4.8	4.6	2.4	0.2	0.1	0.0	14.8
Days of 1mm or More	0	0	0	0	1	2	7	7	3	0	0	0	20

MADRAS

India

	Elevation 16 m. (52 ft.)						13°4'N—80°15'E						
	JAN	FEB	MAR	APR	MAY	JUN	JUL	AUG	SEP	OCT	NOV	DEC	YEAR
TEMPERATURE													
Daily Average Min.°C	19	20	22	26	28	27	26	26	25	24	22	21	24
Daily Average Min.°F	67	68	72	78	82	81	79	78	77	75	72	69	75
Daily Average Max.°C	29	31	33	35	38	38	36	35	34	32	29	29	33
Daily Average Max.°F	85	88	91	95	101	100	96	95	94	90	85	84	92
Extreme Monthly Min.°C	14	15	17	20	21	21	22	21	21	17	15	14	13
Extreme Monthly Min.°F	57	59	62	68	70	69	71	69	69	62	59	57	57
Extreme Monthly Max.°C	33	37	39	43	45	43	41	40	39	39	34	33	43
Extreme Monthly Max.°F	91	98	102	109	113	110	106	104	102	102	94	91	110
Monthly Average °C	25	26	28	31	33	32	31	30	30	28	26	25	29
Monthly Average °F	76	79	83	88	91	90	87	86	85	82	79	77	84
RELATIVE HUMIDITY (%)	87	83	80	74	63	59	65	71	75	83	86	87	76
PRECIPITATION													
Monthly Average mm	27	14	3	10	29	66	124	149	134	290	383	151	1380.0
Monthly Average Inches	1.0	0.5	0.1	0.3	1.1	2.5	4.8	5.8	5.2	11.4	15.0	5.9	53.6
Days of 1mm or More	2	0	0	1	1	6	10	11	9	11	12	7	70

NEW DELHI

India

	Elevation 216 m. (708 ft.)						28°35'N—77°12'E						
	JAN	FEB	MAR	APR	MAY	JUN	JUL	AUG	SEP	OCT	NOV	DEC	YEAR
TEMPERATURE													
Daily Average Min.°C	7	9	14	20	26	28	27	26	24	18	11	8	18
Daily Average Min.°F	44	49	58	68	79	83	81	79	75	65	52	46	65
Daily Average Max.°C	21	24	31	36	41	39	36	34	34	34	29	23	32
Daily Average Max.°F	70	75	87	97	105	102	96	93	93	93	84	73	89
Extreme Monthly Min.°C	-1	0	7	12	18	19	22	22	18	11	5	1	0
Extreme Monthly Min.°F	31	32	45	53	65	66	71	72	64	51	41	34	31
Extreme Monthly Max.°C	29	32	39	46	46	46	45	40	41	39	34	28	7
Extreme Monthly Max.°F	84	89	103	114	115	115	113	104	105	103	93	83	46
Monthly Average °C	14	17	23	29	32	34	31	30	29	26	21	16	25
Monthly Average °F	57	62	73	84	90	93	88	85	85	79	69	60	77
RELATIVE HUMIDITY (%)	41	35	23	19	20	36	59	64	51	32	31	42	38
PRECIPITATION													
Monthly Average mm	16	14	13	14	23	65	237	254	119	19	5	9	788.0
Monthly Average Inches	0.6	0.5	0.5	0.5	0.9	2.5	9.3	10.0	4.6	0.7	0.1	0.3	30.5
Days of 1mm or More	1	2	2	1	2	5	12	12	6	1	0	1	45

AMBON

Indonesia

	Elevation 12 m. (39 ft.)						3°43'S—128°12'E						
	JAN	FEB	MAR	APR	MAY	JUN	JUL	AUG	SEP	OCT	NOV	DEC	YEAR
TEMPERATURE													
Monthly Average °C	27	27	27	27	27	26	25	25	26	27	27	28	27
Monthly Average °F	81	81	81	81	81	79	78	78	79	80	81	82	80
PRECIPITATION													
Monthly Average mm	94	82	120	125	297	439	435	279	251	103	54	96	2375.0
Monthly Average Inches	3.7	3.2	4.7	4.9	11.6	17.2	17.1	10.9	9.8	4.0	2.1	3.7	92.9
Days of 1mm or More	13	10	14	13	15	21	19	13	11	7	5	11	152

BALIKPAPAN

Indonesia

		JAN	FEB	MAR	APR	MAY	JUN	JUL	AUG	SEP	OCT	NOV	DEC	YEAR
Elevation 7 m. (23 ft.)							1°17'S—116°51'E							
TEMPERATURE														
Daily Average Min.°C	23	23	23	23	23	23	23	23	23	23	23	23	23	23
Daily Average Min.°F	73	73	73	73	73	74	74	73	74	74	74	73	73	73
Daily Average Max.°C	29	30	30	29	29	29	29	28	29	29	29	29	29	29
Daily Average Max.°F	85	86	86	85	85	84	83	84	84	85	85	85	85
Monthly Average °C	27	26	27	27	27	27	27	27	27	27	27	27	27
Monthly Average °F	80	80	80	81	81	80	80	80	81	81	81	80	80
RELATIVE HUMIDITY (%)	74	72	72	74	76	75	75	72	70	71	73	70	73
PRECIPITATION														
Monthly Average mm	229	211	247	211	244	248	248	235	188	152	175	217	2605.0
Monthly Average Inches	9.0	8.3	9.7	8.3	9.6	9.7	9.7	9.2	7.4	5.9	6.8	8.5	102.1
Days of 1mm or More	14	14	14	15	15	15	12	15	11	10	12	17	164

GORONTALO

Indonesia

		JAN	FEB	MAR	APR	MAY	JUN	JUL	AUG	SEP	OCT	NOV	DEC	YEAR
Elevation 2 m. (6 ft.)							0°33'N—123°3'E							
TEMPERATURE														
Monthly Average °C	27	27	27	27	27	27	26	27	27	27	27	27	27
Monthly Average °F	80	80	81	81	81	80	80	80	80	81	81	81	81
PRECIPITATION														
Monthly Average mm	88	98	99	105	151	135	92	53	61	101	100	121	1204.0
Monthly Average Inches	3.4	3.8	3.8	4.1	5.9	5.3	3.6	2.0	2.4	3.9	3.9	4.7	46.8
Days of 1mm or More	16	11	13	16	17	18	13	8	11	12	14	17	166

JAKARTA

Indonesia

		JAN	FEB	MAR	APR	MAY	JUN	JUL	AUG	SEP	OCT	NOV	DEC	YEAR
Elevation 8 m. (26 ft.)							6°11'S—106°50'E							
TEMPERATURE														
Daily Average Min.°C	23	23	23	24	24	23	23	23	23	23	23	23	23
Daily Average Min.°F	74	74	74	75	75	74	73	73	74	74	74	74	74
Daily Average Max.°C	29	29	30	31	31	31	31	31	31	31	30	29	30
Daily Average Max.°F	84	84	86	87	87	87	87	87	88	87	86	85	86
Extreme Monthly Min.°C	21	21	21	21	21	19	19	19	19	21	20	19	18
Extreme Monthly Min.°F	69	69	69	69	70	67	67	67	66	69	68	67	66
Extreme Monthly Max.°C	34	33	33	34	34	34	33	34	36	37	36	34	36
Extreme Monthly Max.°F	93	92	92	94	93	93	92	94	96	98	96	93	98
Monthly Average °C	26	27	27	28	28	27	27	27	28	28	28	27	27
Monthly Average °F	79	80	81	82	82	81	81	81	82	82	82	81	81
RELATIVE HUMIDITY (%)	75	75	73	71	69	67	64	61	62	64	68	71	68
PRECIPITATION														
Monthly Average mm	409	314	223	126	93	60	38	36	38	70	87	163	1657.0
Monthly Average Inches	16.1	12.3	8.7	4.9	3.6	2.3	1.4	1.4	1.4	2.7	3.4	6.4	64.6
Days of 1mm or More	21	15	15	11	10	7	3	3	6	7	9	14	121

KUPANG
Indonesia

Elevation 108 m. (354 ft.)					10°10'S—123°35'E								
	JAN	FEB	MAR	APR	MAY	JUN	JUL	AUG	SEP	OCT	NOV	DEC	YEAR
TEMPERATURE													
Monthly Average °C	27	26	27	27	27	26	26	26	27	28	29	28	27
Monthly Average °F	80	79	80	81	81	79	79	79	81	83	84	82	81
PRECIPITATION													
Monthly Average mm	299	253	158	64	34	12	33	1	2	32	94	197	1179.0
Monthly Average Inches	11.7	9.9	6.2	2.5	1.3	0.4	1.2	0.0	0.0	1.2	3.7	7.7	45.8
Days of 1mm or More	24	20	15	6	2	2	1	0	0	3	10	15	98

MEDAN
Indonesia

Elevation 25 m. (82 ft.)					3°35'N—98°41'E								
	JAN	FEB	MAR	APR	MAY	JUN	JUL	AUG	SEP	OCT	NOV	DEC	YEAR
TEMPERATURE													
Daily Average Min.°C	22	22	22	23	23	22	22	22	22	22	22	22	22
Daily Average Min.°F	71	71	72	73	73	72	72	72	72	72	72	72	72
Daily Average Max.°C	29	31	31	32	32	32	32	32	31	30	30	29	31
Daily Average Max.°F	85	87	88	89	89	89	89	89	88	86	86	85	88
Monthly Average °C	25	26	26	27	27	27	26	26	26	26	26	26	26
Monthly Average °F	78	79	79	80	80	80	79	79	79	79	78	78	79
RELATIVE HUMIDITY (%)	66	61	61	62	63	63	59	61	66	69	69	68	64
PRECIPITATION													
Monthly Average mm	106	65	96	169	189	148	176	198	227	297	252	185	2108.0
Monthly Average Inches	4.1	2.5	3.7	6.6	7.4	5.8	6.9	7.7	8.9	11.6	9.9	7.2	82.3
Days of 1mm or More	10	8	9	12	13	11	14	15	19	22	18	15	166

PALEMBANG
Indonesia

Elevation 10 m. (32 ft.)					2°55'S—104°45'E								
	JAN	FEB	MAR	APR	MAY	JUN	JUL	AUG	SEP	OCT	NOV	DEC	YEAR
TEMPERATURE													
Monthly Average °C	26	26	27	27	27	27	26	27	27	27	27	26	27
Monthly Average °F	79	79	80	81	81	80	79	80	80	81	80	79	80
PRECIPITATION													
Monthly Average mm	279	217	305	309	222	114	121	106	166	205	292	303	2639.0
Monthly Average Inches	10.9	8.5	12.0	12.1	8.7	4.4	4.7	4.1	6.5	8.0	11.5	11.9	103.3
Days of 1mm or More	17	16	20	15	13	9	8	7	9	13	16	17	160

PONTIANAK
Indonesia

Elevation 3 m. (9 ft.)						0°1'S—109°20'E							
	JAN	FEB	MAR	APR	MAY	JUN	JUL	AUG	SEP	OCT	NOV	DEC	YEAR
TEMPERATURE													
Daily Average Min.°C	23	24	24	24	24	24	23	23	24	24	24	24	24
Daily Average Min.°F	74	76	75	75	75	75	74	74	75	75	75	75	75
Daily Average Max.°C	31	32	32	32	32	32	32	32	32	32	31	31	32
Daily Average Max.°F	87	89	89	89	90	90	89	90	90	89	88	87	89
Monthly Average °C	26	26	26	27	27	27	27	27	27	26	26	26	26
Monthly Average °F	79	79	79	80	81	80	80	80	80	79	79	79	80
RELATIVE HUMIDITY (%)	67	65	64	66	66	66	63	62	63	65	68	69	65
PRECIPITATION													
Monthly Average mm	260	221	313	270	264	250	206	201	246	333	373	333	3270.0
Monthly Average Inches	10.2	8.7	12.3	10.6	10.3	9.8	8.1	7.9	9.6	13.1	14.6	13.1	128.3
Days of 1mm or More	16	12	15	18	15	13	13	10	14	20	22	21	189

SURABAYA
Indonesia

Elevation 3 m. (9 ft.)						7°15'S—112°45'E							
	JAN	FEB	MAR	APR	MAY	JUN	JUL	AUG	SEP	OCT	NOV	DEC	YEAR
TEMPERATURE													
Monthly Average °C	27	27	27	28	27	27	27	27	28	29	29	27	27
Monthly Average °F	81	81	81	82	81	81	80	80	82	84	84	81	81
PRECIPITATION													
Monthly Average mm	308	253	223	138	102	52	27	15	14	46	109	217	1504.0
Monthly Average Inches	12.1	9.9	8.7	5.4	4.0	2.0	1.0	0.5	0.5	1.8	4.2	8.5	58.6
Days of 1mm or More	25	19	19	14	10	5	4	1	1	5	9	19	131

TARAKAN
Indonesia

Elevation 12 m. (39 ft.)						3°19'N—117°36'E							
	JAN	FEB	MAR	APR	MAY	JUN	JUL	AUG	SEP	OCT	NOV	DEC	YEAR
TEMPERATURE													
Daily Average Min.°C	23	23	23	24	23	23	23	23	23	23	23	23	23
Daily Average Min.°F	73	73	74	75	74	74	74	74	74	74	74	74	74
Daily Average Max.°C	29	30	30	30	31	30	31	31	31	31	30	30	30
Daily Average Max.°F	85	86	86	86	87	86	87	87	87	87	86	86	86
Monthly Average °C	26	26	26	27	27	27	27	27	27	27	27	27	27
Monthly Average °F	79	79	80	80	81	81	81	81	81	81	81	80	80
RELATIVE HUMIDITY (%)	70	69	70	69	70	69	66	65	66	67	70	71	69
PRECIPITATION													
Monthly Average mm	186	158	177	189	236	188	119	177	201	177	122	167	2097.0
Monthly Average Inches	7.3	6.2	6.9	7.4	9.2	7.4	4.6	6.9	7.9	6.9	4.8	6.5	82.0
Days of 1mm or More	16	16	18	21	20	15	16	14	16	20	16	22	210

TEHRAN   Iran

	JAN	FEB	MAR	APR	MAY	JUN	JUL	AUG	SEP	OCT	NOV	DEC	YEAR
Elevation 1220 m. (4002 ft.)					**35°41'N—51°25'E**								
TEMPERATURE													
Daily Average Min.°C	-3	0	4	9	14	19	22	22	18	12	6	1	11
Daily Average Min.°F	27	32	39	49	58	66	72	71	64	53	43	33	51
Daily Average Max.°C	7	10	15	22	28	34	37	36	32	24	17	11	23
Daily Average Max.°F	45	50	59	71	82	93	99	97	90	76	63	51	73
Extreme Monthly Min.°C	-21	-16	-9	-2	4	11	15	14	8	3	-7	-12	-20
Extreme Monthly Min.°F	-5	4	16	28	39	51	59	57	47	38	19	10	-5
Extreme Monthly Max.°C	18	19	29	33	37	42	43	43	38	32	29	20	42
Extreme Monthly Max.°F	65	67	85	91	99	107	109	109	101	90	84	68	109
Monthly Average °C	3	6	10	16	22	27	30	29	25	18	11	5	17
Monthly Average °F	38	42	50	60	71	80	85	84	77	65	51	41	62
RELATIVE HUMIDITY (%)	77	73	61	54	55	50	51	47	49	53	63	76	59
PRECIPITATION													
Monthly Average mm	33	30	36	34	14	3	1	2	0	12	24	29	218.0
Monthly Average Inches	1.2	1.1	1.4	1.3	0.5	0.1	0.0	0.0	0.0	0.4	0.9	1.1	8.0
Days of 1mm or More	5	4	5	5	3	0	0	0	0	2	3	5	32

BAGHDAD   Iraq

	JAN	FEB	MAR	APR	MAY	JUN	JUL	AUG	SEP	OCT	NOV	DEC	YEAR
Elevation 34 m. (111 ft.)					**33°20'N—44°24'E**								
TEMPERATURE													
Daily Average Min.°C	4	6	9	14	19	23	24	24	21	16	11	6	15
Daily Average Min.°F	39	42	48	57	67	73	76	76	70	61	51	42	59
Daily Average Max.°C	16	18	22	29	36	41	43	43	40	33	25	18	30
Daily Average Max.°F	60	64	71	85	97	105	110	110	104	92	77	64	87
Extreme Monthly Min.°C	-8	-5	-3	3	11	14	17	18	11	4	-2	-7	-7
Extreme Monthly Min.°F	18	23	27	37	51	58	62	64	51	39	29	20	18
Extreme Monthly Max.°C	25	30	32	40	44	48	49	49	47	42	34	26	49
Extreme Monthly Max.°F	77	86	90	104	112	119	121	120	116	107	94	79	121
Monthly Average °C	10	12	17	22	28	33	35	34	31	25	17	11	23
Monthly Average °F	49	54	62	72	82	91	95	93	87	76	62	52	73
RELATIVE HUMIDITY (%)	51	42	36	34	19	13	12	13	15	22	39	52	29
PRECIPITATION													
Monthly Average mm	26	24	30	24	13	0	0	0	0	4	20	22	163.0
Monthly Average Inches	1.0	0.9	1.1	0.9	0.5	0.0	0.0	0.0	0.0	0.1	0.7	0.8	6.0
Days of 1mm or More	5	4	3	3	0	0	0	0	0	1	2	3	21

CORK   Ireland

	JAN	FEB	MAR	APR	MAY	JUN	JUL	AUG	SEP	OCT	NOV	DEC	YEAR
Elevation 15 m. (49 ft.)					**51°54'N—8°12'W**								
TEMPERATURE													
Daily Average Min.°C	2	3	4	5	7	10	12	12	10	7	4	3	7
Daily Average Min.°F	36	37	39	42	45	51	54	53	50	45	40	38	44
Daily Average Max.°C	9	9	11	13	16	19	20	20	18	14	11	9	14
Daily Average Max.°F	47	48	52	56	61	66	68	68	64	58	52	49	57
Extreme Monthly Min.°C	-9	-7	-5	-3	-1	3	6	3	1	-5	-5	-7	-9
Extreme Monthly Min.°F	15	20	23	27	30	37	42	37	34	23	23	19	15
Extreme Monthly Max.°C	16	14	21	22	26	29	28	29	26	23	17	14	29
Extreme Monthly Max.°F	60	58	69	72	79	84	83	85	79	74	62	58	85
Monthly Average °C	5	5	6	8	10	13	15	15	13	10	7	6	9
Monthly Average °F	41	41	43	46	50	55	59	58	55	51	45	43	49
RELATIVE HUMIDITY (%)	89	88	86	81	77	78	80	82	86	90	90	89	85
PRECIPITATION													
Monthly Average mm	132	105	95	67	89	67	62	90	97	120	112	133	1169.0
Monthly Average Inches	5.1	4.1	3.7	2.6	3.5	2.6	2.4	3.5	3.8	4.7	4.4	5.2	45.6
Days of 1mm or More	16	13	13	9	13	10	8	11	12	14	14	16	149

DUBLIN   Ireland

	JAN	FEB	MAR	APR	MAY	JUN	JUL	AUG	SEP	OCT	NOV	DEC	YEAR
Elevation 81 m. (265 ft.)					**53°24'N—6°18'W**								
TEMPERATURE													
Daily Average Min.°C	2	2	3	5	7	9	11	11	10	7	4	3	6
Daily Average Min.°F	35	35	38	40	44	49	52	52	49	45	40	38	43
Daily Average Max.°C	7	8	10	12	14	18	19	19	17	14	10	8	13
Daily Average Max.°F	45	46	49	54	58	64	66	65	62	56	50	47	55
Extreme Monthly Min.°C	-12	-13	-9	-7	-6	-1	2	1	-1	-6	-9	-9	-13
Extreme Monthly Min.°F	10	8	15	19	22	31	35	33	30	22	15	15	8
Extreme Monthly Max.°C	16	17	22	22	27	29	30	27	26	22	19	17	30
Extreme Monthly Max.°F	61	62	72	72	80	84	86	81	79	72	67	63	86
Monthly Average °C	5	5	6	8	11	14	15	15	13	11	7	6	10
Monthly Average °F	41	41	43	47	51	56	59	59	56	51	45	42	49
RELATIVE HUMIDITY (%)	80	86	83	78	76	75	78	81	84	86	88	88	83
PRECIPITATION													
Monthly Average mm	67	49	53	50	58	58	55	72	74	71	68	80	755.0
Monthly Average Inches	2.6	1.9	2.0	1.9	2.2	2.2	2.1	2.8	2.9	2.7	2.6	3.1	29.0
Days of 1mm or More	12	9	10	9	12	10	8	11	10	10	10	12	123

SHANNON AIRPORT   Ireland

	JAN	FEB	MAR	APR	MAY	JUN	JUL	AUG	SEP	OCT	NOV	DEC	YEAR
Elevation 7 m. (22 ft.)					**52°42'N—8°54'W**								
TEMPERATURE													
Daily Average Min.°C	2	2	4	5	7	10	12	12	10	7	5	3	7
Daily Average Min.°F	35	36	38	41	44	50	53	53	50	45	40	38	44
Daily Average Max.°C	8	9	11	13	16	19	19	20	17	14	11	9	14
Daily Average Max.°F	46	48	52	56	61	65	67	67	63	58	51	48	57
Extreme Monthly Min.°C	-11	-7	-8	-3	-2	2	4	3	-1	-3	-7	-6	-11
Extreme Monthly Min.°F	12	19	18	26	29	35	40	37	31	26	20	21	12
Extreme Monthly Max.°C	14	15	18	21	25	28	31	29	24	21	18	16	30
Extreme Monthly Max.°F	57	59	65	69	77	82	87	84	75	70	65	61	87
Monthly Average °C	5	6	7	9	11	14	16	16	14	11	8	6	10
Monthly Average °F	41	42	45	48	52	57	60	60	57	52	46	43	50
RELATIVE HUMIDITY (%)	88	85	80	74	70	71	77	77	82	89	89	89	81
PRECIPITATION													
Monthly Average mm	94	63	67	56	64	64	59	81	84	89	99	105	925.0
Monthly Average Inches	3.7	2.4	2.6	2.2	2.5	2.5	2.3	3.1	3.3	3.5	3.8	4.1	36.0
Days of 1mm or More	15	11	13	11	13	11	10	12	13	14	15	16	154

HAIFA   Israel

	JAN	FEB	MAR	APR	MAY	JUN	JUL	AUG	SEP	OCT	NOV	DEC	YEAR
Elevation 10 m. (33 ft.)					**32°48'N—35°0'E**								
TEMPERATURE													
Daily Average Min.°C	9	10	12	14	18	22	24	24	23	20	16	12	17
Daily Average Min.°F	49	50	53	58	65	71	75	76	74	68	60	53	63
Daily Average Max.°C	18	19	22	25	28	29	31	32	31	29	26	20	26
Daily Average Max.°F	65	67	71	77	83	85	88	90	88	85	78	68	79
Extreme Monthly Min.°C	-2	-3	1	4	10	13	17	18	16	8	7	1	-2
Extreme Monthly Min.°F	29	27	33	40	50	56	63	65	61	47	44	33	27
Extreme Monthly Max.°C	26	31	40	43	44	43	36	37	42	41	36	29	41
Extreme Monthly Max.°F	79	87	104	109	112	109	96	99	107	106	97	85	107
Monthly Average °C	14	14	16	19	22	25	27	28	26	24	20	16	21
Monthly Average °F	58	58	61	66	71	77	80	82	79	75	67	60	69
RELATIVE HUMIDITY (%)	56	56	56	57	59	66	68	69	66	66	56	56	61
PRECIPITATION													
Monthly Average mm	129	69	57	21	6	0	0	0	2	6	86	119	495.0
Monthly Average Inches	5.0	2.7	2.2	0.8	0.2	0.0	0.0	0.0	0.0	0.2	3.3	4.6	19.0
Days of 1mm or More	0	0	0	0	0	0	0	0	0	0	0	0	0

JERUSALEM   Israel

	Elevation 758 m. (2485 ft.)					31°47'N—34°13'E							
	JAN	FEB	MAR	APR	MAY	JUN	JUL	AUG	SEP	OCT	NOV	DEC	YEAR
TEMPERATURE													
Daily Average Min.°C	5	6	8	10	14	16	17	18	17	15	12	7	12
Daily Average Min.°F	41	42	46	50	57	60	63	64	62	59	53	45	54
Daily Average Max.°C	13	13	18	23	27	29	31	31	29	27	21	15	23
Daily Average Max.°F	55	56	65	73	81	85	87	87	85	81	70	59	74
Extreme Monthly Min.°C	-3	-3	-1	2	6	8	10	11	10	8	4	-3	-3
Extreme Monthly Min.°F	26	27	30	36	42	47	50	52	50	47	39	27	26
Extreme Monthly Max.°C	25	27	31	39	39	42	38	39	39	36	31	26	41
Extreme Monthly Max.°F	77	80	87	102	103	107	100	103	103	97	88	79	107
Monthly Average °C	9	9	12	16	19	22	23	23	22	20	15	10	17
Monthly Average °F	47	49	53	60	67	72	73	74	71	67	59	51	62
RELATIVE HUMIDITY (%)	66	58	57	42	33	32	35	36	36	36	50	60	45
PRECIPITATION													
Monthly Average mm	132	130	93	44	5	0	0	0	0	31	62	125	622.0
Monthly Average Inches	5.1	5.1	3.6	1.7	0.1	0.0	0.0	0.0	0.0	1.2	2.4	4.9	24.1
Days of 1mm or More	10	8	8	3	0	0	0	0	0	2	5	8	44

TEL AVIV   Israel

	Elevation 11 m. (36 ft.)					32°18'N—34°54'E							
	JAN	FEB	MAR	APR	MAY	JUN	JUL	AUG	SEP	OCT	NOV	DEC	YEAR
TEMPERATURE													
Monthly Average °C	14	14	15	18	20	24	26	27	25	22	19	15	20
Monthly Average °F	56	57	60	64	69	75	79	80	78	72	66	60	68
PRECIPITATION													
Monthly Average mm	124	68	50	18	1	0	0	0	3	11	103	153	531.0
Monthly Average Inches	4.8	2.6	1.9	0.7	0.0	0.0	0.0	0.0	0.1	0.4	4.0	6.0	20.5
Days of 1mm or More	0	0	0	0	0	0	0	0	0	0	0	0	0

BOLOGNA   Italy

	Elevation 60 m. (197 ft.)					44°30'N—11°18'E							
	JAN	FEB	MAR	APR	MAY	JUN	JUL	AUG	SEP	OCT	NOV	DEC	YEAR
TEMPERATURE													
Daily Average Min.°C	-1	2	5	10	14	18	20	19	17	12	6	2	10
Daily Average Min.°F	31	35	42	49	57	64	67	67	62	53	43	35	50
Daily Average Max.°C	5	8	14	18	23	27	30	30	26	20	19	7	19
Daily Average Max.°F	41	47	56	65	74	81	86	85	79	67	66	45	65
Monthly Average °C	0	4	8	13	18	22	24	23	20	15	8	2	13
Monthly Average °F	33	39	47	56	64	71	75	74	68	58	47	35	56
RELATIVE HUMIDITY (%)	79	72	61	55	57	48	47	49	57	73	80	85	64
PRECIPITATION													
Monthly Average mm	42	35	60	73	67	62	37	50	54	66	92	75	713.0
Monthly Average Inches	1.6	1.3	2.3	2.8	2.6	2.4	1.4	1.9	2.1	2.5	3.6	2.9	27.4
Days of 1mm or More	0	0	0	0	0	0	0	0	0	0	0	0	0

BRINDISI
Italy

	JAN	FEB	MAR	APR	MAY	JUN	JUL	AUG	SEP	OCT	NOV	DEC	YEAR
Elevation 28 m. (92 ft.)					40°38'N—17°56'E								
TEMPERATURE													
Daily Average Min.°C	6	7	8	11	14	18	21	21	18	15	11	8	13
Daily Average Min.°F	43	44	47	51	58	65	70	70	65	59	53	47	56
Daily Average Max.°C	12	13	15	18	22	26	29	29	26	22	18	14	20
Daily Average Max.°F	54	56	58	65	72	79	84	84	79	71	64	58	69
Monthly Average °C	10	10	11	14	18	22	25	25	22	18	14	11	17
Monthly Average °F	49	50	52	57	64	71	76	76	72	65	57	52	62
RELATIVE HUMIDITY (%)	73	68	67	67	67	65	64	62	66	70	72	73	68
PRECIPITATION													
Monthly Average mm	59	66	71	35	26	18	8	27	46	74	75	66	571.0
Monthly Average Inches	2.3	2.5	2.7	1.3	1.0	0.7	0.3	1.0	1.8	2.9	2.9	2.5	21.9
Days of 1mm or More	9	8	7	5	3	2	1	2	4	6	7	7	61

MILAN
Italy

	JAN	FEB	MAR	APR	MAY	JUN	JUL	AUG	SEP	OCT	NOV	DEC	YEAR
Elevation 121 m. (397 ft.)					45°30'N—9°12'E								
TEMPERATURE													
Daily Average Min.°C	0	2	6	10	14	17	20	19	16	11	6	2	10
Daily Average Min.°F	32	35	43	49	57	63	67	66	61	52	43	35	50
Daily Average Max.°C	5	8	13	18	23	27	29	28	24	17	10	6	17
Daily Average Max.°F	40	46	56	65	74	80	84	82	75	63	51	43	63
Monthly Average °C	1	4	8	12	16	21	23	22	18	13	7	2	12
Monthly Average °F	34	38	46	54	62	69	74	71	65	55	44	36	54
RELATIVE HUMIDITY (%)	82	73	65	57	59	56	61	58	63	73	80	89	68
PRECIPITATION													
Monthly Average mm	63	61	87	77	101	77	62	94	72	110	107	71	982.0
Monthly Average Inches	2.4	2.4	3.4	3.0	3.9	3.0	2.4	3.7	2.8	4.3	4.2	2.7	38.2
Days of 1mm or More	7	7	7	7	9	7	5	7	5	7	7	6	81

NAPLES
Italy

	JAN	FEB	MAR	APR	MAY	JUN	JUL	AUG	SEP	OCT	NOV	DEC	YEAR
Elevation 110 m. (361 ft.)					40°54'N—14°18'E								
TEMPERATURE													
Daily Average Min.°C	4	5	6	9	12	16	18	18	16	12	9	6	11
Daily Average Min.°F	40	41	44	48	54	61	65	65	61	54	48	44	52
Daily Average Max.°C	12	13	15	18	22	26	29	29	26	22	17	14	20
Daily Average Max.°F	53	55	59	65	72	79	84	84	79	71	63	56	68
Extreme Monthly Min.°C	-4	-2	-2	4	7	11	12	12	12	5	1	-2	-4
Extreme Monthly Min.°F	24	28	28	40	45	51	53	53	53	41	34	28	24
Extreme Monthly Max.°C	19	20	25	28	33	35	38	37	38	30	25	21	38
Extreme Monthly Max.°F	67	68	77	82	91	95	101	99	100	86	77	69	101
Monthly Average °C	8	9	10	13	17	21	24	23	21	16	12	9	15
Monthly Average °F	46	47	51	56	63	70	74	74	69	61	54	49	59
RELATIVE HUMIDITY (%)	68	67	62	61	63	58	53	53	59	63	68	70	62
PRECIPITATION													
Monthly Average mm	111	99	87	71	51	31	26	46	87	132	160	120	1021.0
Monthly Average Inches	4.3	3.8	3.4	2.7	2.0	1.2	1.0	1.8	3.4	5.1	6.3	4.7	39.7
Days of 1mm or More	10	9	9	8	5	3	2	4	6	8	10	10	84

VENICE   Italy

	JAN	FEB	MAR	APR	MAY	JUN	JUL	AUG	SEP	OCT	NOV	DEC	YEAR
Elevation 1 m. (3 ft.)					45°24'N—12°19'E								
TEMPERATURE													
Daily Average Min.°C	1	2	5	10	14	17	19	18	16	11	7	3	10
Daily Average Min.°F	33	35	41	49	56	63	66	65	61	53	44	37	50
Daily Average Max.°C	6	8	12	17	21	25	27	27	24	19	12	8	17
Daily Average Max.°F	42	46	53	62	70	76	81	80	75	65	53	46	62
Extreme Monthly Min.°C	-6	-7	-3	2	7	9	11	13	9	-1	-2	-4	-6
Extreme Monthly Min.°F	22	20	27	35	44	48	52	55	48	30	28	24	20
Extreme Monthly Max.°C	14	18	21	27	29	32	36	34	33	25	19	17	35
Extreme Monthly Max.°F	58	65	70	80	84	89	96	93	91	77	67	62	96
Monthly Average °C	2	4	8	12	17	21	23	22	19	14	8	3	13
Monthly Average °F	36	40	46	53	62	69	73	72	66	56	46	38	55
RELATIVE HUMIDITY (%)	76	76	68	67	69	65	64	63	64	68	75	79	70
PRECIPITATION													
Monthly Average mm	56	54	63	64	67	75	56	79	67	73	94	68	816.0
Monthly Average Inches	2.2	2.1	2.4	2.5	2.6	2.9	2.2	3.1	2.6	2.8	3.7	2.6	31.7
Days of 1mm or More	7	6	6	7	8	8	5	6	5	6	7	6	77

KINGSTON   Jamaica

	JAN	FEB	MAR	APR	MAY	JUN	JUL	AUG	SEP	OCT	NOV	DEC	YEAR
Elevation 8 m. (25 ft.)					17°56'N—76°47'W								
TEMPERATURE													
Daily Average Min.°C	22	22	23	23	24	25	25	25	25	24	24	23	24
Daily Average Min.°F	72	72	73	74	76	77	77	77	77	76	75	73	75
Daily Average Max.°C	30	29	29	30	31	31	31	31	31	31	31	30	30
Daily Average Max.°F	86	85	85	86	87	88	88	88	88	88	87	86	87
Monthly Average °C	26	26	26	27	28	28	29	29	28	28	27	26	27
Monthly Average °F	78	78	79	80	82	83	84	83	83	82	81	79	81
RELATIVE HUMIDITY (%)	63	65	68	70	74	73	71	73	74	72	67	65	70
PRECIPITATION													
Monthly Average mm	18	17	18	39	78	75	35	81	115	180	74	38	768.0
Monthly Average Inches	0.7	0.6	0.7	1.5	3.0	2.9	1.3	3.1	4.5	7.0	2.9	1.4	29.6
Days of 1mm or More	2	2	2	2	3	4	3	5	5	8	4	2	42

MONTEGO BAY   Jamaica

	JAN	FEB	MAR	APR	MAY	JUN	JUL	AUG	SEP	OCT	NOV	DEC	YEAR
Elevation 8 m. (26 ft.)					18°28'N—77°55'W								
TEMPERATURE													
Monthly Average °C	25	25	25	26	27	27	28	28	27	27	26	25	26
Monthly Average °F	76	76	77	79	80	81	82	82	81	81	79	78	79
PRECIPITATION													
Monthly Average mm	74	54	33	58	110	140	59	93	128	160	105	81	1095.0
Monthly Average Inches	2.9	2.1	1.2	2.2	4.3	5.5	2.3	3.6	5.0	6.3	4.1	3.1	42.6
Days of 1mm or More	10	7	5	7	10	10	7	9	12	13	12	10	112

HIROSHIMA Japan

	JAN	FEB	MAR	APR	MAY	JUN	JUL	AUG	SEP	OCT	NOV	DEC	YEAR
Elevation 30 m. (98 ft.)						34°22'N—132°26'E							
TEMPERATURE													
Daily Average Min.°C	-1	0	3	7	12	17	22	23	19	12	6	2	10
Daily Average Min.°F	31	32	37	45	54	63	72	73	66	53	43	35	50
Daily Average Max.°C	9	9	13	18	22	26	29	32	28	23	17	12	20
Daily Average Max.°F	48	49	55	64	72	78	85	89	82	73	62	53	68
Monthly Average °C	4	5	8	13	18	21	26	27	23	17	12	7	15
Monthly Average °F	39	41	46	56	64	71	78	80	73	63	53	44	59
RELATIVE HUMIDITY (%)	56	54	53	57	61	63	66	60	61	53	56	58	58
PRECIPITATION													
Monthly Average mm	46	60	109	171	154	258	244	121	174	102	70	41	1550.0
Monthly Average Inches	1.8	2.3	4.2	6.7	6.0	10.1	9.6	4.7	6.8	4.0	2.7	1.6	60.5
Days of 1mm or More	5	6	8	10	9	11	10	6	9	6	5	4	89

NAGASAKI Japan

	JAN	FEB	MAR	APR	MAY	JUN	JUL	AUG	SEP	OCT	NOV	DEC	YEAR
Elevation 133 m. (436 ft.)						32°44'N—129°53'E							
TEMPERATURE													
Daily Average Min.°C	2	2	5	10	14	18	23	23	20	14	9	4	12
Daily Average Min.°F	36	36	41	50	57	65	73	74	68	58	49	40	54
Daily Average Max.°C	9	10	14	19	23	26	29	31	27	22	17	12	20
Daily Average Max.°F	49	50	57	66	73	78	85	88	81	72	63	53	68
Extreme Monthly Min.°C	-6	-4	-3	1	6	12	15	17	11	5	1	-3	-5
Extreme Monthly Min.°F	22	24	26	34	42	53	59	63	52	41	33	26	22
Extreme Monthly Max.°C	21	23	24	28	29	34	36	37	34	31	27	24	36
Extreme Monthly Max.°F	70	73	76	82	85	94	96	98	94	87	81	75	98
Monthly Average °C	6	7	10	15	19	22	27	28	24	19	14	9	17
Monthly Average °F	43	45	50	59	66	72	80	82	76	66	57	48	62
RELATIVE HUMIDITY (%)	59	60	56	60	65	70	72	65	67	55	59	63	63
PRECIPITATION													
Monthly Average mm	75	80	111	189	191	312	317	197	186	108	87	71	1924.0
Monthly Average Inches	2.9	3.1	4.3	7.4	7.5	12.2	12.4	7.7	7.3	4.2	3.4	2.7	75.1
Days of 1mm or More	10	9	10	11	10	12	11	8	8	6	8	9	112

OSAKA Japan

	JAN	FEB	MAR	APR	MAY	JUN	JUL	AUG	SEP	OCT	NOV	DEC	YEAR
Elevation 3 m. (10 ft.)						34°39'N—135°26'E							
TEMPERATURE													
Daily Average Min.°C	0	1	3	8	13	18	23	23	19	13	7	3	11
Daily Average Min.°F	32	33	37	47	55	64	73	74	67	55	44	37	51
Daily Average Max.°C	8	9	12	18	23	27	31	32	28	22	17	11	20
Daily Average Max.°F	47	48	54	65	73	80	87	90	83	72	62	52	68
Extreme Monthly Min.°C	-7	-7	-5	-3	3	9	15	14	11	3	-2	-4	-7
Extreme Monthly Min.°F	19	20	23	27	38	48	59	57	51	37	28	24	19
Extreme Monthly Max.°C	19	23	24	29	31	34	37	38	35	33	27	24	38
Extreme Monthly Max.°F	66	73	75	84	88	94	98	101	95	91	80	75	101
Monthly Average °C	5	6	8	15	19	23	27	28	24	18	13	8	16
Monthly Average °F	41	42	47	58	67	73	81	83	76	65	55	46	61
RELATIVE HUMIDITY (%)	56	56	56	56	57	63	63	59	61	58	57	57	58
PRECIPITATION													
Monthly Average mm	45	55	100	145	139	195	157	104	146	111	70	39	1306.0
Monthly Average Inches	1.7	2.1	3.9	5.7	5.4	7.6	6.1	4.0	5.7	4.3	2.7	1.5	50.7
Days of 1mm or More	5	6	8	11	9	11	10	7	9	8	7	5	96

SAPPORO   Japan

Elevation 18 m. (59 ft.)					**43°4'N—141°21'E**								
	JAN	**FEB**	**MAR**	**APR**	**MAY**	**JUN**	**JUL**	**AUG**	**SEP**	**OCT**	**NOV**	**DEC**	**YEAR**
TEMPERATURE													
Daily Average Min.°C...............-12	-11	-7	0	4	10	14	16	11	4	-2	-8	2
Daily Average Min.°F 11	13	20	32	40	50	58	61	51	39	29	18	35
Daily Average Max.°C...............-2	-1	2	11	16	21	24	26	22	16	8	1	12
Daily Average Max.°F...............29	31	36	51	61	69	75	79	71	60	46	33	53
Monthly Average °C.................-5	-4	0	6	12	16	20	22	17	11	4	-2	8
Monthly Average °F 23	25	31	43	54	61	68	71	63	51	40	29	47
RELATIVE HUMIDITY (%)	70	67	66	59	61	68	71	69	67	63	66	68	66
PRECIPITATION													
Monthly Average mm 111	96	81	65	54	65	75	140	139	116	98	96	1136.0
Monthly Average Inches 4.3	3.7	3.1	2.5	2.1	2.5	2.9	5.5	5.4	4.5	3.8	3.7	44.0
Days of 1mm or More 16	14	14	9	8	8	8	9	10	12	13	14	135

TOKYO   Japan

Elevation 6 m. (19 ft.)					**35°41'N—139°46'E**								
	JAN	**FEB**	**MAR**	**APR**	**MAY**	**JUN**	**JUL**	**AUG**	**SEP**	**OCT**	**NOV**	**DEC**	**YEAR**
TEMPERATURE													
Daily Average Min.°C.................-2	-1	2	8	12	17	21	22	19	13	6	1	10
Daily Average Min.°F 29	31	36	46	54	63	70	72	66	55	43	33	50
Daily Average Max.°C.................8	9	12	17	22	24	28	30	26	21	16	11	19
Daily Average Max.°F...............47	48	54	63	71	76	83	86	79	69	60	52	66
Extreme Monthly Min.°C...............-8	-8	-6	-1	2	8	13	16	11	2	-3	-7	-8
Extreme Monthly Min.°F...............17	18	22	30	36	47	55	60	51	36	26	20	17
Extreme Monthly Max.°C.............22	25	25	29	31	34	37	38	36	32	27	23	38
Extreme Monthly Max.°F...............72	77	77	85	88	93	99	101	96	90	81	74	101
Monthly Average °C...................5	6	8	14	19	22	25	27	23	17	12	8	16
Monthly Average °F 41	42	47	57	65	71	78	80	74	63	54	46	60
RELATIVE HUMIDITY (%)	48	48	53	59	62	68	69	66	68	64	58	51	60
PRECIPITATION													
Monthly Average mm 46	58	93	120	135	178	124	132	188	173	89	55	1391.0
Monthly Average Inches 1.8	2.2	3.6	4.7	5.3	7.0	4.8	5.1	7.4	6.8	3.5	2.1	54.3
Days of 1mm or More 4	5	8	10	9	12	9	8	10	8	6	4	93

Johnston Island

Elevation 5 m. (16 ft.)					**16° 44'N — 169° 31'W**								
	JAN	**FEB**	**MAR**	**APR**	**MAY**	**JUN**	**JUL**	**AUG**	**SEP**	**OCT**	**NOV**	**DEC**	**YEAR**
TEMPERATURE													
Monthly Average °C...................25	25	25	25	26	27	27	27	27	27	26	25	26
Monthly Average °F 77	77	77	78	79	80	81	81	81	81	79	78	79
PRECIPITATION													
Monthly Average mm 46	44	64	63	47	24	25	63	55	79	90	80	680.0
Monthly Average Inches 1.8	1.7	2.5	2.4	1.8	0.9	0.9	2.4	2.1	3.1	3.5	3.1	26.2
Days of 1mm or More 6	6	8	7	7	6	7	8	8	10	9	10	92

AMMAN
Jordan

Elevation 777 m. (2548 ft.)   31°57'N—35°57'E

TEMPERATURE	JAN	FEB	MAR	APR	MAY	JUN	JUL	AUG	SEP	OCT	NOV	DEC	YEAR
Daily Average Min.°C	4	4	6	9	14	16	18	18	17	14	10	6	11
Daily Average Min.°F	39	40	43	49	57	61	65	65	62	57	50	42	52
Daily Average Max.°C	12	13	16	23	28	31	32	32	31	27	21	15	23
Daily Average Max.°F	54	56	60	73	83	87	89	90	88	81	70	59	74
Monthly Average °C	8	9	12	16	20	24	25	25	23	20	14	9	17
Monthly Average °F	46	48	53	60	68	74	77	77	74	68	58	48	63
RELATIVE HUMIDITY (%)	56	52	44	34	28	28	30	30	31	31	40	53	38
PRECIPITATION													
Monthly Average mm	62	51	48	21	3	0	0	0	0	8	27	48	268.0
Monthly Average Inches	2.4	2.0	1.8	0.8	0.1	0.0	0.0	0.0	0.0	0.3	1.0	1.8	10.2
Days of 1mm or More	7	7	5	2	0	0	0	0	0	1	3	5	30

PHNOM PENH
Kampuchea

Elevation 10 m. (32 ft.)   11°33'N—104°55'E

TEMPERATURE	JAN	FEB	MAR	APR	MAY	JUN	JUL	AUG	SEP	OCT	NOV	DEC	YEAR
Monthly Average °C	26	28	29	30	29	28	28	28	27	27	27	26	28
Monthly Average °F	79	82	84	85	84	83	82	82	81	81	80	78	82
PRECIPITATION													
Monthly Average mm	7	7	25	70	165	138	131	153	237	265	133	30	1361.0
Monthly Average Inches	0.2	0.2	0.9	2.7	6.4	5.4	5.1	6.0	9.3	10.4	5.2	1.1	52.9
Days of 1mm or More	1	1	0	4	13	14	13	15	17	18	7	2	105

ELDORET
Kenya

Elevation 2073 m. (6799 ft.)   0°31'N—35°17'E

TEMPERATURE	JAN	FEB	MAR	APR	MAY	JUN	JUL	AUG	SEP	OCT	NOV	DEC	YEAR
Daily Average Min.°C	9	9	10	9	10	9	9	9	9	10	10	9	9
Daily Average Min.°F	47	48	49	48	51	48	49	49	47	49	50	49	49
Daily Average Max.°C	25	26	26	25	24	23	21	22	23	24	24	24	24
Daily Average Max.°F	78	79	79	76	74	73	71	71	74	75	75	75	75
Monthly Average °C	17	18	18	18	17	16	16	16	16	17	17	17	17
Monthly Average °F	63	64	65	64	63	61	60	61	61	63	63	63	63
RELATIVE HUMIDITY (%)	35	33	36	47	51	53	60	62	51	46	46	43	47
PRECIPITATION													
Monthly Average mm	29	43	72	154	145	103	140	148	59	38	86	20	1037.0
Monthly Average Inches	1.1	1.6	2.8	6.0	5.7	4.0	5.5	5.8	2.3	1.4	3.3	0.7	40.2
Days of 1mm or More	2	3	6	11	13	10	13	13	7	5	7	2	92

LODWAR   Kenya

	Elevation 513 m. (1683 ft.)					3°7'N—35°37'E							
	JAN	FEB	MAR	APR	MAY	JUN	JUL	AUG	SEP	OCT	NOV	DEC	YEAR
TEMPERATURE													
Daily Average Min.°C	22	23	24	24	25	24	24	24	33	24	24	22	24
Daily Average Min.°F	71	73	75	75	76	75	74	75	91	76	74	72	76
Daily Average Max.°C	35	36	36	35	35	34	33	33	35	35	35	35	35
Daily Average Max.°F	96	97	97	94	95	93	96	92	95	96	94	94	95
Monthly Average °C	29	30	30	30	29	29	28	28	29	30	29	29	29
Monthly Average °F	83	85	86	85	85	84	83	83	85	86	84	84	84
RELATIVE HUMIDITY (%)	31	31	35	42	41	39	40	39	34	34	36	35	36
PRECIPITATION													
Monthly Average mm	13	7	26	55	26	6	21	11	2	10	18	14	209.0
Monthly Average Inches	0.5	0.2	1.0	2.1	1.0	0.2	0.8	0.4	0.0	0.3	0.7	0.5	7.7
Days of 1mm or More	1	1	1	4	2	1	2	1	0	1	2	1	17

MOYALE   Kenya

	Elevation 1107 m. (3631 ft.)					3°32'N—39°3'E							
	JAN	FEB	MAR	APR	MAY	JUN	JUL	AUG	SEP	OCT	NOV	DEC	YEAR
TEMPERATURE													
Daily Average Min.°C	18	19	19	19	18	16	16	16	16	17	18	18	17
Daily Average Min.°F	65	66	66	65	64	61	60	60	62	63	64	64	63
Daily Average Max.°C	30	31	30	27	25	24	24	24	26	26	27	29	27
Daily Average Max.°F	86	88	86	81	77	76	75	76	79	79	81	83	81
Monthly Average °C	25	25	25	23	22	21	20	21	22	22	22	23	23
Monthly Average °F	76	77	77	74	71	69	68	69	71	72	72	74	73
RELATIVE HUMIDITY (%)	36	34	44	63	69	62	61	57	52	59	56	47	53
PRECIPITATION													
Monthly Average mm	18	19	57	191	148	18	16	16	21	123	95	36	758.0
Monthly Average Inches	0.7	0.7	2.2	7.5	5.8	0.7	0.6	0.6	0.8	4.8	3.7	1.4	29.5
Days of 1mm or More	1	1	4	12	10	3	2	2	1	8	9	3	56

NAIROBI   Kenya

	Elevation 1616 m. (5301 ft.)					1°19'N—36°55'E							
	JAN	FEB	MAR	APR	MAY	JUN	JUL	AUG	SEP	OCT	NOV	DEC	YEAR
TEMPERATURE													
Daily Average Min.°C	13	13	14	15	14	12	11	12	12	13	14	14	13
Daily Average Min.°F	55	56	57	59	58	54	53	53	54	56	57	56	56
Daily Average Max.°C	27	28	28	26	25	24	23	23	26	27	25	25	25
Daily Average Max.°F	80	82	82	79	76	75	73	73	78	80	77	78	78
Extreme Monthly Min.°C	8	9	9	11	9	7	6	7	5	7	6	8	5
Extreme Monthly Min.°F	47	48	49	52	48	45	43	44	41	45	43	47	41
Extreme Monthly Max.°C	29	31	30	28	28	27	26	27	28	30	28	28	30
Extreme Monthly Max.°F	84	87	86	82	82	80	79	80	82	86	82	82	87
Monthly Average °C	19	20	21	20	19	18	17	17	19	20	19	19	19
Monthly Average °F	67	68	69	68	66	64	62	63	65	67	67	66	66
RELATIVE HUMIDITY (%)	42	38	43	53	58	54	55	53	44	42	53	50	49
PRECIPITATION													
Monthly Average mm	38	48	68	142	111	25	12	12	17	41	119	76	709.0
Monthly Average Inches	1.4	1.8	2.6	5.5	4.3	0.9	0.4	0.4	0.6	1.6	4.6	2.9	27.0
Days of 1mm or More	3	3	5	10	7	2	1	1	1	4	11	6	54

WAJIR

Kenya

Elevation 244 m. (800 ft.) 1°45'N—40°4'E

	JAN	FEB	MAR	APR	MAY	JUN	JUL	AUG	SEP	OCT	NOV	DEC	YEAR
TEMPERATURE													
Daily Average Min.°C	22	22	24	24	23	21	21	21	21	22	22	22	22
Daily Average Min.°F	71	72	75	74	73	70	69	70	70	72	72	72	72
Daily Average Max.°C	35	36	36	34	33	33	32	32	33	34	33	34	34
Daily Average Max.°F	95	97	97	93	92	91	89	90	91	92	91	92	93
Monthly Average °C	29	29	30	29	28	27	26	27	27	28	28	28	28
Monthly Average °F	83	85	86	84	82	81	79	80	81	82	82	82	82
RELATIVE HUMIDITY (%)	42	41	44	53	52	49	48	46	47	48	53	51	48
PRECIPITATION													
Monthly Average mm	6	5	28	82	39	2	2	1	5	30	77	19	296.0
Monthly Average Inches	0.2	0.1	1.1	3.2	1.5	0.0	0.0	0.0	0.1	1.1	3.0	0.7	11.0
Days of 1mm or More	1	0	2	6	2	0	0	0	0	2	5	2	20

KUWAIT

Kuwait

Elevation 5 m. (16 ft.) 29°21'N—48°0'E

	JAN	FEB	MAR	APR	MAY	JUN	JUL	AUG	SEP	OCT	NOV	DEC	YEAR
TEMPERATURE													
Daily Average Min.°C	9	11	15	20	25	28	30	30	27	23	17	12	21
Daily Average Min.°F	49	51	59	68	77	82	86	86	81	73	62	53	69
Daily Average Max.°C	16	18	22	28	34	37	39	40	38	33	25	18	29
Daily Average Max.°F	61	65	72	83	94	98	103	104	100	91	77	65	84
Extreme Monthly Min.°F	33	36	40	54	60	72	78	68	67	57	43	36	33
Extreme Monthly Max.°C	28	26	32	39	43	48	48	46	47	41	38	26	48
Extreme Monthly Max.°F	82	78	90	103	109	119	118	115	117	105	100	79	119
Monthly Average °C	13	15	19	25	31	36	37	37	33	27	20	14	26
Monthly Average °F	55	59	67	77	88	96	99	98	92	81	68	57	78
RELATIVE HUMIDITY (%)	61	61	61	55	55	49	41	46	51	60	59	65	55
PRECIPITATION													
Monthly Average mm	26	15	11	15	4	0	0	0	0	3	15	22	111.0
Monthly Average Inches	1.0	0.5	0.4	0.5	0.1	0.0	0.0	0.0	0.0	0.1	0.5	0.8	3.9
Days of 1mm or More	5	2	2	1	0	0	0	0	0	1	1	3	15

VIENTIANE

Laos

Elevation 162 m. (531 ft.) 17°58'N—102°36'E

	JAN	FEB	MAR	APR	MAY	JUN	JUL	AUG	SEP	OCT	NOV	DEC	YEAR
TEMPERATURE													
Daily Average Min.°C	14	17	19	23	23	24	24	24	24	21	18	16	21
Daily Average Min.°F	57	63	67	73	73	75	75	75	75	70	65	60	69
Daily Average Max.°C	28	30	33	34	32	32	31	31	31	31	29	28	31
Daily Average Max.°F	83	86	91	93	90	89	87	88	87	87	85	83	87
Extreme Monthly Min.°C	4	8	12	17	21	21	21	21	21	13	11	5	3
Extreme Monthly Min.°F	39	46	54	63	69	70	70	70	70	55	51	41	39
Extreme Monthly Max.°C	35	37	40	39	39	36	34	37	35	34	34	33	40
Extreme Monthly Max.°F	95	98	104	103	102	96	94	98	95	94	94	92	104
Monthly Average °C	21	24	27	29	28	28	28	27	27	26	24	22	26
Monthly Average °F	71	75	80	84	83	82	82	81	81	80	75	72	79
RELATIVE HUMIDITY (%)	77	75	71	74	82	85	87	86	86	82	79	78	80
PRECIPITATION													
Monthly Average mm	6	15	30	87	236	258	258	338	320	70	5	1	1624.0
Monthly Average Inches	0.2	0.5	1.1	3.4	9.2	10.1	10.1	13.3	12.6	2.7	0.1	0.0	63.3
Days of 1mm or More	1	1	3	6	14	16	17	19	14	6	1	0	98

BEIRUT   Lebanon

	JAN	FEB	MAR	APR	MAY	JUN	JUL	AUG	SEP	OCT	NOV	DEC	YEAR
Elevation 34 m. (111 ft.)					33°54'N—35°30'E								
TEMPERATURE													
Daily Average Min.°C	11	11	12	14	18	21	23	23	23	21	16	13	17
Daily Average Min.°F	51	51	54	58	64	69	73	74	73	69	61	55	63
Daily Average Max.°C	17	17	19	22	26	28	31	32	30	27	23	18	24
Daily Average Max.°F	62	63	66	72	78	83	87	89	86	81	73	65	75
Extreme Monthly Min.°C	-1	-1	2	6	10	13	18	17	16	11	5	-1	-1
Extreme Monthly Min.°F	31	30	36	43	50	56	64	62	60	52	41	30	30
Extreme Monthly Max.°C	25	31	36	37	42	40	37	37	37	38	33	29	41
Extreme Monthly Max.°F	77	87	97	99	107	104	98	99	99	101	91	84	107
Monthly Average °C													0
Monthly Average °F													32
RELATIVE HUMIDITY (%)	70	70	69	67	64	61	58	57	57	62	61	69	64
PRECIPITATION													
Monthly Average mm	194	115	106	47	17	1	0	0	8	34	148	147	817.0
Monthly Average Inches	7.6	4.5	4.1	1.8	0.6	0.0	0.0	0.0	0.3	1.3	5.8	5.7	31.7
Days of 1mm or More	0	0	0	0	0	0	0	0	0	0	0	0	0

HARBEL   Liberia

	JAN	FEB	MAR	APR	MAY	JUN	JUL	AUG	SEP	OCT	NOV	DEC	YEAR
Elevation 30 m. (98 ft.)													
TEMPERATURE													
Monthly Average °C	26	27	27	27	26	25	24	24	25	26	26	26	26
Monthly Average °F	79	80	80	80	79	78	76	75	77	78	79	78	78
PRECIPITATION													
Monthly Average mm	35	51	125	154	279	483	569	532	660	386	177	74	3525.0
Monthly Average Inches	1.3	2.0	4.9	6.0	10.9	19.0	22.4	20.9	25.9	15.2	6.9	2.9	138.3
Days of 1mm or More	0	0	0	0	0	0	0	0	0	0	0	0	0

DERNA   Libya

	JAN	FEB	MAR	APR	MAY	JUN	JUL	AUG	SEP	OCT	NOV	DEC	YEAR
Elevation 9 m. (29 ft.)					32°46'N—22°39'E								
TEMPERATURE													
Daily Average Min.°C	11	11	12	14	16	20	22	23	22	19	16	12	16
Daily Average Min.°F	51	52	53	57	61	68	72	74	71	66	61	54	62
Daily Average Max.°C	18	18	20	22	24	28	28	29	28	27	24	19	24
Daily Average Max.°F	64	65	67	71	76	82	83	84	82	80	75	67	75
Monthly Average °C	14	15	16	18	21	24	25	26	25	23	20	16	20
Monthly Average °F	57	59	60	64	69	75	78	79	77	73	67	60	68
RELATIVE HUMIDITY (%)	65	63	62	63	64	65	69	69	67	61	59	62	64
PRECIPITATION													
Monthly Average mm	66	52	31	6	7	0	0	0	4	30	40	64	300.0
Monthly Average Inches	2.5	2.0	1.2	0.2	0.2	0.0	0.0	0.0	0.1	1.1	1.5	2.5	11.3
Days of 1mm or More	0	0	0	0	0	0	0	0	0	0	0	0	0

KUFRA OASIS Libya

		Elevation 382 m. (1253 ft.)				24°11'N—23°19'E							
	JAN	FEB	MAR	APR	MAY	JUN	JUL	AUG	SEP	OCT	NOV	DEC	YEAR
TEMPERATURE													
Monthly Average °C 13	15	19	25	28	31	31	30	28	24	18	14	23
Monthly Average °F 55	59	67	76	83	87	87	87	83	76	65	58	74
PRECIPITATION													
Monthly Average mm 1	0	0	0	0	0	0	0	0	0	0	0	1.0
Monthly Average Inches 0.0	0.0	0.0	0.0	0.0	0.0	0.0	0.0	0.0	0.0	0.0	0.0	0.0
Days of 1mm or More 0	0	0	0	0	0	0	0	0	0	0	0	0

SABHA Libya

		Elevation 444 m. (1456 ft.)				°24'N—77°36'E							
	JAN	FEB	MAR	APR	MAY	JUN	JUL	AUG	SEP	OCT	NOV	DEC	YEAR
TEMPERATURE													
Monthly Average °C 11	14	18	23	28	31	30	30	28	24	18	13	22
Monthly Average °F 52	58	65	74	82	87	87	86	83	75	64	55	72
PRECIPITATION													
Monthly Average mm 1	0	0	0	1	0	0	0	0	2	2	0	6.0
Monthly Average Inches 0.0	0.0	0.0	0.0	0.0	0.0	0.0	0.0	0.0	0.0	0.0	0.0	0.0
Days of 1mm or More 0	0	0	0	0	0	0	0	0	0	0	0	0

TRIPOLI Libya

		Elevation 18 m. (59 ft.)				32°54'N—13°11'E							
	JAN	FEB	MAR	APR	MAY	JUN	JUL	AUG	SEP	OCT	NOV	DEC	YEAR
TEMPERATURE													
Daily Average Min.°C 9	9	11	13	16	19	21	21	20	17	13	10	15
Daily Average Min.°F 47	47	51	55	60	67	71	71	69	63	56	50	59
Daily Average Max.°C 19	19	21	23	26	30	32	32	31	28	25	20	25
Daily Average Max.°F 65	67	69	74	79	85	89	90	87	82	77	68	78
Extreme Monthly Min.°F 34	37	39	43	43	50	60	62	59	50	42	33	33
Extreme Monthly Max.°C 28	33	38	41	43	44	46	44	45	41	36	30	45
Extreme Monthly Max.°F 83	91	101	105	109	112	114	112	113	106	96	86	114
Monthly Average °C 12	13	15	17	20	23	25	26	25	22	18	14	19
Monthly Average °F 53	56	58	63	67	74	77	78	77	72	64	57	66
RELATIVE HUMIDITY (%)	59	57	59	58	59	61	62	62	64	61	57	59	60
PRECIPITATION													
Monthly Average mm 184	108	112	55	16	1	0	0	12	55	112	172	827.0
Monthly Average Inches 7.2	4.2	4.4	2.1	0.6	0.0	0.0	0.0	0.4	2.1	4.4	6.7	32.1
Days of 1mm or More 12	10	10	6	2	0	0	0	0	5	7	13	65

LUXEMBOURG
Luxembourg

	JAN	FEB	MAR	APR	MAY	JUN	JUL	AUG	SEP	OCT	NOV	DEC	YEAR
Elevation 330 m. (1082 ft.)					49°36'N—6°6'E								
TEMPERATURE													
Daily Average Min.°C	-1	-1	1	4	8	11	13	12	10	6	3	0	6
Daily Average Min.°F	29	31	35	40	46	52	55	54	50	43	37	33	42
Daily Average Max.°C	3	4	10	14	18	21	23	22	19	13	7	4	13
Daily Average Max.°F	37	40	49	57	65	70	73	71	66	56	44	39	56
Extreme Monthly Min.°C	-23	-22	-14	-6	-3	-2	3	1	-5	-7	-11	-22	-23
Extreme Monthly Min.°F	-10	-7	7	21	26	29	38	33	23	19	13	-8	-10
Extreme Monthly Max.°C	14	17	23	29	33	37	37	36	33	27	19	14	37
Extreme Monthly Max.°F	57	63	73	85	91	98	99	97	91	80	66	58	99
Monthly Average °C	0	1	4	8	12	15	17	17	14	9	4	1	9
Monthly Average °F	32	34	40	46	54	60	63	62	57	49	39	34	47
RELATIVE HUMIDITY (%)	86	79	62	57	60	61	59	60	69	75	86	91	70
PRECIPITATION													
Monthly Average mm	68	54	65	55	75	71	63	74	63	73	79	77	817.0
Monthly Average Inches	2.6	2.1	2.5	2.1	2.9	2.7	2.4	2.9	2.4	2.8	3.1	3.0	31.5
Days of 1mm or More	13	10	12	10	12	11	9	10	8	10	11	11	127

ANTANANARIVO
Madagascar

	JAN	FEB	MAR	APR	MAY	JUN	JUL	AUG	SEP	OCT	NOV	DEC	YEAR
Elevation 1381 m. (4530 ft.)					18°55'S—47°33'E								
TEMPERATURE													
Daily Average Min.°C	16	16	16	14	12	10	9	9	10	12	14	15	13
Daily Average Min.°F	61	60	60	58	53	50	48	49	51	53	57	60	55
Daily Average Max.°C	25	25	25	24	22	20	19	20	22	25	26	25	23
Daily Average Max.°F	77	78	76	75	72	69	67	68	72	77	78	78	74
Monthly Average °C	21	21	20	19	17	15	14	15	16	19	20	20	18
Monthly Average °F	69	69	68	67	63	59	58	58	62	65	68	69	65
RELATIVE HUMIDITY (%)	65	65	66	60	59	59	58	56	50	49	54	61	59
PRECIPITATION													
Monthly Average mm	276	259	225	70	18	8	11	11	15	71	182	315	1461.0
Monthly Average Inches	10.8	10.2	8.8	2.7	0.7	0.3	0.4	0.4	0.5	2.7	7.1	12.4	57.0
Days of 1mm or More	15	13	12	5	2	1	2	2	1	6	11	16	86

ANTSIRANANA
Madagascar

	JAN	FEB	MAR	APR	MAY	JUN	JUL	AUG	SEP	OCT	NOV	DEC	YEAR
Elevation 105 m. (344 ft.)					12°21'S—49°18'E								
TEMPERATURE													
Daily Average Min.°C	24	24	24	24	23	21	21	20	21	22	23	24	22
Daily Average Min.°F	74	74	75	74	73	70	69	69	70	71	74	74	72
Daily Average Max.°C	31	31	32	32	31	30	29	29	30	30	31	32	31
Daily Average Max.°F	88	88	89	89	88	86	84	84	85	87	89	89	87
Monthly Average °C	26	26	26	26	26	24	24	24	25	26	27	27	26
Monthly Average °F	79	79	80	80	78	76	75	75	76	78	80	80	78
RELATIVE HUMIDITY (%)	70	73	70	63	57	55	53	53	51	50	55	64	59
PRECIPITATION													
Monthly Average mm	322	306	197	42	11	27	18	20	9	19	61	170	1202.0
Monthly Average Inches	12.6	12.0	7.7	1.6	0.4	1.0	0.7	0.7	0.3	0.7	2.4	6.6	46.7
Days of 1mm or More	16	15	12	5	3	3	3	5	2	3	4	11	82

TOLIARAY   Madagascar

	JAN	FEB	MAR	APR	MAY	JUN	JUL	AUG	SEP	OCT	NOV	DEC	YEAR
Elevation 9 m. (29 ft.)					23°23'S—43°44'E								
TEMPERATURE													
Daily Average Min.°C	23	23	22	19	16	14	14	14	16	18	20	22	18
Daily Average Min.°F	73	73	71	67	62	58	56	58	61	64	68	71	65
Daily Average Max.°C	32	33	32	31	29	27	27	28	29	30	30	31	30
Daily Average Max.°F	90	91	89	87	84	81	80	82	84	85	87	88	86
Monthly Average °C	28	28	27	25	23	21	20	21	22	24	25	27	24
Monthly Average °F	82	82	80	77	73	69	69	70	72	75	77	80	76
RELATIVE HUMIDITY (%)	69	67	60	59	57	55	55	52	58	64	65	71	61
PRECIPITATION													
Monthly Average mm	96	88	33	15	16	12	5	6	7	12	22	97	409.0
Monthly Average Inches	3.7	3.4	1.2	0.5	0.6	0.4	0.1	0.2	0.2	0.4	0.8	3.8	15.3
Days of 1mm or More	5	6	3	1	2	2	0	1	1	1	1	5	28

ZOMBA   Malawi

	JAN	FEB	MAR	APR	MAY	JUN	JUL	AUG	SEP	OCT	NOV	DEC	YEAR
Elevation 949 m. (3113 ft.)					15°23'S—35°19'E								
TEMPERATURE													
Daily Average Min.°C	19	19	18	18	14	12	12	13	15	18	19	19	16
Daily Average Min.°F	66	66	65	64	58	54	54	56	59	65	66	66	61
Daily Average Max.°C	27	27	26	25	24	22	22	24	27	30	29	28	26
Daily Average Max.°F	81	80	79	78	75	72	72	76	81	86	85	82	79
Extreme Monthly Min.°C	10	10	10	12	9	5	6	7	8	8	11	11	5
Extreme Monthly Min.°F	50	50	50	53	48	41	43	44	46	47	51	51	41
Extreme Monthly Max.°C	33	33	32	31	32	32	29	32	33	35	35	34	35
Extreme Monthly Max.°F	92	92	89	88	89	90	85	89	91	95	95	94	95
Monthly Average °C	23	23	22	21	19	17	17	19	21	24	24	23	21
Monthly Average °F	73	73	72	71	67	63	63	65	70	75	75	74	70
RELATIVE HUMIDITY (%)	70	71	68	62	59	54	55	47	41	39	50	64	57
PRECIPITATION													
Monthly Average mm	295	265	243	76	24	12	7	5	9	23	130	298	1387.0
Monthly Average Inches	11.6	10.4	9.5	2.9	0.9	0.4	0.2	0.1	0.3	0.9	5.1	11.7	54.0
Days of 1mm or More	0	0	0	0	0	0	0	0	0	0	0	0	0

KUALA LUMPUR   Malaysia

	JAN	FEB	MAR	APR	MAY	JUN	JUL	AUG	SEP	OCT	NOV	DEC	YEAR
Elevation 39 m. (127 ft.)					3°7'N—101°42'E								
TEMPERATURE													
Daily Average Min.°C	22	22	23	23	23	23	22	23	23	23	23	22	23
Daily Average Min.°F	72	72	73	74	74	73	72	73	73	73	73	72	73
Daily Average Max.°C	32	33	33	33	33	33	32	32	32	32	32	32	32
Daily Average Max.°F	90	92	92	91	91	90	90	90	90	89	89	90	90
Extreme Monthly Min.°C	18	20	20	21	21	20	19	20	20	21	21	19	17
Extreme Monthly Min.°F	64	68	68	70	69	68	67	68	68	69	69	66	64
Extreme Monthly Max.°C	36	37	37	36	36	36	36	36	35	35	35	35	36
Extreme Monthly Max.°F	96	98	98	96	97	96	96	96	95	95	95	95	98
Monthly Average °C	26	27	27	27	27	27	27	27	26	26	26	26	27
Monthly Average °F	79	80	80	81	81	80	80	80	79	79	79	79	80
RELATIVE HUMIDITY (%)	60	60	58	63	66	63	63	62	64	65	66	61	63
PRECIPITATION													
Monthly Average mm	153	137	229	269	196	123	133	135	186	276	271	227	2335.0
Monthly Average Inches	6.0	5.3	9.0	10.5	7.7	4.8	5.2	5.3	7.3	10.8	10.6	8.9	91.4
Days of 1mm or More	9	10	14	16	13	9	9	10	12	17	18	15	152

PENANG ## Malaysia

Elevation 5 m. (17 ft.)					5°25'N—100°19'E								
	JAN	FEB	MAR	APR	MAY	JUN	JUL	AUG	SEP	OCT	NOV	DEC	YEAR
TEMPERATURE													
Daily Average Min.°C	23	23	23	24	23	23	23	23	23	23	23	23	23
Daily Average Min.°F	73	73	74	75	74	74	74	73	73	73	73	73	74
Daily Average Max.°C	32	33	33	33	32	32	32	32	31	32	31	32	32
Daily Average Max.°F	90	91	92	91	90	90	90	89	88	89	88	89	90
Monthly Average °C	27	27	28	28	28	27	27	27	26	26	26	27	27
Monthly Average °F	81	81	82	82	82	81	80	80	80	79	80	80	81
RELATIVE HUMIDITY (%)	68	64	64	66	66	67	67	67	69	70	71	68	67
PRECIPITATION													
Monthly Average mm	65	76	141	213	231	176	189	234	339	379	242	110	2395.0
Monthly Average Inches	2.5	2.9	5.5	8.3	9.0	6.9	7.4	9.2	13.3	14.9	9.5	4.3	93.7
Days of 1mm or More	4	5	8	12	14	10	13	14	18	18	15	8	139

GAN ## Maldives

Elevation 2 m. (6 ft.)					3°15'N—73°0'E								
	JAN	FEB	MAR	APR	MAY	JUN	JUL	AUG	SEP	OCT	NOV	DEC	YEAR
TEMPERATURE													
Monthly Average °C	27	28	28	28	28	28	27	27	27	27	27	27	28
Monthly Average °F	81	82	83	83	82	82	81	81	81	81	81	81	82
PRECIPITATION													
Monthly Average mm	201	107	100	200	184	215	168	170	266	252	177	281	2321.0
Monthly Average Inches	7.9	4.2	3.9	7.8	7.2	8.4	6.6	6.6	10.4	9.9	6.9	11.0	90.8
Days of 1mm or More	11	7	8	13	13	11	10	11	13	13	13	15	138

BAMAKO ## Mali

Elevation 332 m. (1089 ft.)					12°38'N—8°1'W								
	JAN	FEB	MAR	APR	MAY	JUN	JUL	AUG	SEP	OCT	NOV	DEC	YEAR
TEMPERATURE													
Daily Average Min.°C	16	19	22	24	25	23	22	22	21	21	18	16	21
Daily Average Min.°F	62	66	72	76	77	73	71	71	71	70	65	61	69
Daily Average Max.°C	33	36	38	39	38	35	32	30	31	34	35	33	35
Daily Average Max.°F	92	98	101	102	100	94	89	87	89	93	94	92	94
Extreme Monthly Min.°C	9	11	14	18	19	18	18	17	17	15	12	8	8
Extreme Monthly Min.°F	48	51	58	65	66	64	64	63	63	59	53	47	47
Extreme Monthly Max.°C	42	47	43	44	46	41	39	36	36	40	43	40	47
Extreme Monthly Max.°F	107	117	109	111	115	105	102	96	97	104	110	104	117
Monthly Average °C													0
Monthly Average °F													32
RELATIVE HUMIDITY (%)	20	16	18	27	42	58	69	74	69	54	32	24	42
PRECIPITATION													
Monthly Average mm	0	0	4	18	56	141	239	317	220	63	6	1	1065.0
Monthly Average Inches	0.0	0.0	0.1	0.7	2.2	5.5	9.4	12.4	8.6	2.4	0.2	0.0	41.5
Days of 1mm or More	0	0	0	0	0	0	0	0	0	0	0	0	0

GAO   Mali

Elevation 258 m. (846 ft.)					16°16'N—0°3'W								
	JAN	**FEB**	**MAR**	**APR**	**MAY**	**JUN**	**JUL**	**AUG**	**SEP**	**OCT**	**NOV**	**DEC**	**YEAR**
TEMPERATURE													
Daily Average Min.°C	14	17	20	24	27	28	26	24	25	24	20	15	22
Daily Average Min.°F	57	62	68	75	81	82	78	76	77	75	67	59	71
Daily Average Max.°C	31	34	38	40	42	41	38	35	37	39	36	32	37
Daily Average Max.°F	88	94	100	105	108	106	100	96	99	102	97	89	99
Monthly Average °C	23	25	29	32	35	35	32	31	32	32	28	24	30
Monthly Average °F	73	78	85	90	96	95	90	88	89	90	82	74	86
RELATIVE HUMIDITY (%)	15	11	9	10	17	27	40	52	40	20	13	15	22
PRECIPITATION													
Monthly Average mm	0	0	0	2	8	23	66	76	30	5	0	0	210.0
Monthly Average Inches	0.0	0.0	0.0	0.0	0.3	0.9	2.5	2.9	1.1	0.1	0.0	0.0	7.8
Days of 1mm or More	0	0	0	0	1	2	6	6	5	0	0	0	20

FORT-DE-FRANCE   Martinique

Elevation 4 m. (13 ft.)					14°37'N—61°5'W								
	JAN	**FEB**	**MAR**	**APR**	**MAY**	**JUN**	**JUL**	**AUG**	**SEP**	**OCT**	**NOV**	**DEC**	**YEAR**
TEMPERATURE													
Daily Average Min.°C	21	21	21	22	23	23	23	23	23	23	22	22	22
Daily Average Min.°F	69	69	69	71	73	74	74	74	74	73	72	71	72
Daily Average Max.°C	28	29	29	30	31	30	30	31	31	31	30	29	30
Daily Average Max.°F	83	84	85	86	87	86	86	87	88	87	86	84	86
Monthly Average °C	24	24	25	25	26	26	26	26	26	26	26	25	25
Monthly Average °F	75	75	76	77	78	79	79	79	79	79	78	76	78
RELATIVE HUMIDITY (%)	77	73	72	71	74	77	78	78	79	80	81	79	77
PRECIPITATION													
Monthly Average mm	68	53	43	66	97	116	160	155	179	161	156	95	1349.0
Monthly Average Inches	2.6	2.0	1.6	2.5	3.8	4.5	6.3	6.1	7.0	6.3	6.1	3.7	52.5
Days of 1mm or More	0	0	0	0	0	0	0	0	0	0	0	0	0

NOUAKCHOTT   Mauritania

Elevation 1 m. (3 ft.)					18°7'N—15°56'W								
	JAN	**FEB**	**MAR**	**APR**	**MAY**	**JUN**	**JUL**	**AUG**	**SEP**	**OCT**	**NOV**	**DEC**	**YEAR**
TEMPERATURE													
Daily Average Min.°C	13	15	16	18	19	22	24	25	25	22	18	14	19
Daily Average Min.°F	56	58	61	64	67	71	75	76	77	72	65	57	67
Daily Average Max.°C	29	31	33	34	34	34	32	33	35	36	34	29	33
Daily Average Max.°F	85	88	92	92	94	94	90	91	94	96	94	85	91
Extreme Monthly Min.°C	7	9	11	12	14	18	21	20	22	17	13	7	6
Extreme Monthly Min.°F	45	49	51	54	58	64	70	68	71	63	56	44	44
Extreme Monthly Max.°C	36	39	41	43	46	46	43	42	44	43	42	37	46
Extreme Monthly Max.°F	96	103	106	109	115	114	109	108	111	109	107	98	115
Monthly Average °C	21	23	25	25	26	27	27	28	29	29	25	22	26
Monthly Average °F	70	73	76	77	78	81	81	83	85	84	78	71	78
RELATIVE HUMIDITY (%)	30	27	29	30	35	45	59	64	55	39	29	31	39
PRECIPITATION													
Monthly Average mm	0	2	2	0	0	0	17	34	27	12	5	1	100.0
Monthly Average Inches	0.0	0.0	0.0	0.0	0.0	0.0	0.6	1.3	1.0	0.4	0.1	0.0	3.4
Days of 1mm or More	0	0	0	0	0	0	1	2	2	0	0	0	5

PLAISANCE AIRPORT　　　　　　　　　　　　　　　Mauritius

	JAN	FEB	MAR	APR	MAY	JUN	JUL	AUG	SEP	OCT	NOV	DEC	YEAR
Elevation 56 m. (183 ft.)				20°17'S—57°33'E									
TEMPERATURE													
Monthly Average °C	26	26	26	25	23	22	21	21	21	22	24	25	23
Monthly Average °F	79	79	78	77	74	71	70	69	70	72	75	77	74
PRECIPITATION													
Monthly Average mm	269	252	241	216	146	100	113	92	60	73	87	175	1824.0
Monthly Average Inches	10.5	9.9	9.4	8.5	5.7	3.9	4.4	3.6	2.3	2.8	3.4	6.8	71.2
Days of 1mm or More	16	16	17	16	14	14	15	15	10	9	8	12	162

ACAPULCO　　　　　　　　　　　　　　　　　　　Mexico

	JAN	FEB	MAR	APR	MAY	JUN	JUL	AUG	SEP	OCT	NOV	DEC	YEAR
Elevation 3 m. (9 ft.)				16°50'N—99°56'W									
TEMPERATURE													
Daily Average Min.°C	22	22	22	23	24	25	25	25	25	25	24	23	24
Daily Average Min.°F	72	72	72	73	76	77	76	77	76	76	74	73	75
Daily Average Max.°C	31	31	31	31	32	32	32	33	32	32	32	31	31
Daily Average Max.°F	87	87	87	87	89	89	90	91	89	89	89	88	89
Monthly Average °C	26	26	26	27	29	29	29	29	28	28	28	27	28
Monthly Average °F	79	79	79	81	83	83	83	83	82	83	82	80	82
RELATIVE HUMIDITY (%)	77	76	74	76	75	77	77	78	81	80	78	78	77
PRECIPITATION													
Monthly Average mm	16	0	4	6	20	262	228	298	403	166	57	8	1468.0
Monthly Average Inches	0.6	0.0	0.1	0.2	0.7	10.3	8.9	11.7	15.8	6.5	2.2	0.3	57.3
Days of 1mm or More	2	0	0	0	2	9	15	14	15	7	1	1	66

CHIHUAHUA　　　　　　　　　　　　　　　　　　Mexico

	JAN	FEB	MAR	APR	MAY	JUN	JUL	AUG	SEP	OCT	NOV	DEC	YEAR
Elevation 1423 m. (4668 ft.)				28°38'N—106°04'W									
TEMPERATURE													
Daily Average Min.°C	2	3	7	11	15	19	18	18	16	11	6	2	11
Daily Average Min.°F	35	38	44	51	59	66	65	65	61	52	43	36	51
Daily Average Max.°C	18	20	24	28	32	34	32	32	29	28	22	19	27
Daily Average Max.°F	64	69	76	83	90	93	90	89	85	82	72	66	80
Monthly Average °C	10	12	15	20	24	26	25	24	22	19	14	10	18
Monthly Average °F	49	53	59	67	74	80	77	76	72	66	57	51	65
RELATIVE HUMIDITY (%)	53	42	36	29	29	38	53	59	60	54	55	56	47
PRECIPITATION													
Monthly Average mm	8	14	5	9	22	37	88	95	79	20	6	11	394.0
Monthly Average Inches	0.3	0.5	0.1	0.3	0.8	1.4	3.4	3.7	3.1	0.7	0.2	0.4	14.9
Days of 1mm or More	1	1	1	2	5	10	13	16	11	5	0	1	66

GUADALAJARA   Mexico

Elevation 1589 m. (5213 ft.)					20°41'N—103°20'W								
	JAN	**FEB**	**MAR**	**APR**	**MAY**	**JUN**	**JUL**	**AUG**	**SEP**	**OCT**	**NOV**	**DEC**	**YEAR**
TEMPERATURE													
Daily Average Min.°C	7	7	9	11	14	16	16	15	15	12	9	7	11
Daily Average Min.°F	44	45	48	51	56	60	60	60	59	54	48	45	53
Daily Average Max.°C	23	25	28	30	32	29	26	26	25	26	25	24	27
Daily Average Max.°F	74	77	82	87	89	85	78	79	78	78	78	75	80
Monthly Average °C	16	17	19	22	24	23	21	21	21	19	18	16	20
Monthly Average °F	60	62	66	71	75	73	70	69	69	67	64	60	67
RELATIVE HUMIDITY (%)	57	52	42	36	41	58	75	76	77	70	62	59	59
PRECIPITATION													
Monthly Average mm	15	10	7	11	25	156	256	204	163	67	13	21	948.0
Monthly Average Inches	0.5	0.3	0.2	0.4	0.9	6.1	10.0	8.0	6.4	2.6	0.5	0.8	36.7
Days of 1mm or More	3	2	0	1	2	17	24	22	19	8	2	2	102

LA PAZ   Mexico

Elevation 18 m. (59 ft.)					24°10'N—110°12'W								
	JAN	**FEB**	**MAR**	**APR**	**MAY**	**JUN**	**JUL**	**AUG**	**SEP**	**OCT**	**NOV**	**DEC**	**YEAR**
TEMPERATURE													
Daily Average Min.°C	13	14	14	17	19	20	24	24	24	21	18	15	19
Daily Average Min.°F	56	56	58	62	65	67	76	76	75	70	65	59	65
Daily Average Max.°C	22	23	26	29	31	33	35	34	33	31	27	24	29
Daily Average Max.°F	71	73	79	84	88	91	95	94	92	89	81	74	84
Extreme Monthly Min.°C	4	3	2	6	10	13	18	18	17	14	10	5	1
Extreme Monthly Min.°F	39	38	35	43	50	56	64	65	62	57	50	41	35
Extreme Monthly Max.°C	32	32	36	38	40	42	41	41	42	39	35	31	42
Extreme Monthly Max.°F	89	90	96	101	104	107	106	106	108	102	95	88	108
Monthly Average °C	17	19	20	22	24	27	29	29	29	26	23	20	24
Monthly Average °F	63	66	67	71	75	80	84	84	84	79	73	67	75
RELATIVE HUMIDITY (%)	69	67	63	63	63	61	62	67	69	66	68	69	66
PRECIPITATION													
Monthly Average mm	16	7	2	0	4	19	19	56	44	20	7	16	210.0
Monthly Average Inches	0.6	0.2	0.0	0.0	0.1	0.7	0.7	2.2	1.7	0.7	0.2	0.6	7.7
Days of 1mm or More	1	1	1	0	0	0	3	6	5	3	0	1	21

MAZATLAN   Mexico

Elevation 78 m. (256 ft.)					23°11'N—106°25'W								
	JAN	**FEB**	**MAR**	**APR**	**MAY**	**JUN**	**JUL**	**AUG**	**SEP**	**OCT**	**NOV**	**DEC**	**YEAR**
TEMPERATURE													
Daily Average Min.°C	16	16	17	18	21	24	25	25	25	24	21	18	21
Daily Average Min.°F	61	61	62	65	70	76	77	77	76	76	70	65	70
Daily Average Max.°C	22	22	23	25	27	29	30	30	30	29	27	24	27
Daily Average Max.°F	72	72	74	77	81	84	86	87	86	85	80	75	80
Extreme Monthly Min.°C	12	11	13	14	15	21	21	20	20	21	17	12	11
Extreme Monthly Min.°F	53	52	55	57	59	70	69	68	68	69	62	54	52
Extreme Monthly Max.°C	25	26	28	31	31	33	33	34	32	32	31	28	33
Extreme Monthly Max.°F	77	79	82	87	87	91	91	93	89	89	87	82	93
Monthly Average °C	20	20	21	22	25	28	29	29	28	27	24	21	24
Monthly Average °F	69	68	69	72	77	82	83	84	83	81	75	70	76
RELATIVE HUMIDITY (%)	77	78	79	79	80	78	80	81	83	79	76	77	79
PRECIPITATION													
Monthly Average mm	38	7	10	1	2	33	197	228	249	80	15	20	880.0
Monthly Average Inches	1.4	0.2	0.3	0.0	0.0	1.2	7.7	8.9	9.8	3.1	0.5	0.7	33.8
Days of 1mm or More	2	1	0	0	0	2	15	14	15	4	1	2	56

MERIDA
Mexico

	Elevation 22 m. (72 ft.)					20°58'N—89°38'W							
	JAN	FEB	MAR	APR	MAY	JUN	JUL	AUG	SEP	OCT	NOV	DEC	YEAR
TEMPERATURE													
Daily Average Min.°C	19	19	20	22	23	23	23	23	23	22	20	19	21
Daily Average Min.°F	66	66	68	71	73	74	74	74	74	72	69	66	70
Daily Average Max.°C	28	29	31	33	33	33	32	32	32	30	28	28	31
Daily Average Max.°F	82	85	88	91	91	91	90	90	89	86	83	82	87
Extreme Monthly Min.°C	12	11	11	14	17	21	18	19	20	17	13	13	10
Extreme Monthly Min.°F	53	51	52	58	63	69	64	67	68	63	56	55	51
Extreme Monthly Max.°C	33	35	37	41	40	39	36	38	36	34	33	33	41
Extreme Monthly Max.°F	92	95	98	106	104	103	97	100	96	94	91	92	106
Monthly Average °C	23	24	26	27	29	28	27	27	27	26	24	23	26
Monthly Average °F	74	75	78	81	84	82	81	81	81	79	75	73	79
RELATIVE HUMIDITY (%)	74	71	67	67	70	77	79	79	81	79	76	76	75
PRECIPITATION													
Monthly Average mm	57	27	18	22	69	143	162	175	181	101	40	29	1024.0
Monthly Average Inches	2.2	1.0	0.7	0.8	2.7	5.6	6.3	6.8	7.1	3.9	1.5	1.1	39.7
Days of 1mm or More	4	3	3	3	5	11	16	16	15	10	7	4	97

MEXICO CITY
Mexico

	Elevation 2309 m. (7534 ft.)					9°24'N—99°11'W							
	JAN	FEB	MAR	APR	MAY	JUN	JUL	AUG	SEP	OCT	NOV	DEC	YEAR
TEMPERATURE													
Daily Average Min.°C	5	6	7	9	10	11	11	11	11	9	6	5	8
Daily Average Min.°F	40	42	45	48	51	52	52	52	51	48	44	41	47
Daily Average Max.°C	21	23	26	27	26	25	23	24	23	22	21	21	24
Daily Average Max.°F	70	74	78	80	80	77	74	74	73	72	71	69	74
Extreme Monthly Min.°C	-3	-2	1	1	6	9	8	9	1	2	2	0	-2
Extreme Monthly Min.°F	27	29	34	33	43	49	47	49	34	35	36	32	27
Extreme Monthly Max.°C	23	27	29	32	32	31	28	27	26	26	25	23	32
Extreme Monthly Max.°F	74	81	84	90	89	87	83	81	78	78	77	73	90
Monthly Average °C	14	15	17	19	19	18	18	18	17	16	15	14	17
Monthly Average °F	57	60	63	65	67	65	64	64	63	61	59	57	62
RELATIVE HUMIDITY (%)	32	29	23	26	34	41	50	55	58	48	38	36	39
PRECIPITATION													
Monthly Average mm	6	3	12	16	48	103	130	124	110	35	11	4	602.0
Monthly Average Inches	0.2	0.1	0.4	0.6	1.8	4.0	5.1	4.8	4.3	1.3	0.4	0.1	23.1
Days of 1mm or More	2	3	0	1	15	20	24	23	23	15	7	2	135

MONTERREY
Mexico

	Elevation 534 m. (1751 ft.)					25°40'N—100°18'W							
	JAN	FEB	MAR	APR	MAY	JUN	JUL	AUG	SEP	OCT	NOV	DEC	YEAR
TEMPERATURE													
Daily Average Min.°C	10	11	14	18	21	22	23	23	21	18	14	10	17
Daily Average Min.°F	49	52	57	64	69	72	73	73	71	64	57	51	63
Daily Average Max.°C	20	23	26	30	31	33	34	33	30	27	23	20	27
Daily Average Max.°F	67	73	79	86	88	92	92	92	86	81	74	67	81
Extreme Monthly Min.°C	-4	-3	-1	6	11	13	16	16	11	7	-1	-1	-3
Extreme Monthly Min.°F	25	26	30	42	51	55	60	60	51	45	30	30	25
Extreme Monthly Max.°C	34	37	38	41	42	41	39	39	38	35	34	34	41
Extreme Monthly Max.°F	94	99	100	105	107	105	102	102	101	95	94	94	107
Monthly Average °C	14	16	20	24	26	27	28	28	26	22	18	15	22
Monthly Average °F	57	61	67	75	79	81	82	82	79	72	65	60	72
RELATIVE HUMIDITY (%)	66	64	55	61	66	62	66	67	73	70	68	66	65
PRECIPITATION													
Monthly Average mm	17	36	15	25	45	69	60	78	176	79	24	14	638.0
Monthly Average Inches	0.6	1.4	0.5	0.9	1.7	2.7	2.3	3.0	6.9	3.1	0.9	0.5	24.5
Days of 1mm or More	7	4	2	7	10	5	4	9	11	8	5	5	77

OAXACA

Mexico

Elevation 1563 m. (5127 ft.)   17°4'N—96°43'W

	JAN	FEB	MAR	APR	MAY	JUN	JUL	AUG	SEP	OCT	NOV	DEC	YEAR
TEMPERATURE													
Daily Average Min.°C	9	10	12	14	14	16	15	15	15	13	10	9	13
Daily Average Min.°F	48	50	54	57	58	60	59	58	59	55	50	48	55
Daily Average Max.°C	28	30	31	32	31	29	28	28	27	28	27	27	29
Daily Average Max.°F	82	85	88	90	89	84	82	83	81	82	81	81	84
Monthly Average °C	18	19	22	23	23	21	21	21	21	20	18	18	20
Monthly Average °F	64	66	71	73	74	71	70	70	69	67	65	64	69
RELATIVE HUMIDITY (%)	60	58	56	55	61	67	68	68	71	66	62	61	63
PRECIPITATION													
Monthly Average mm	4	8	14	20	55	144	89	127	109	52	9	2	633.0
Monthly Average Inches	0.1	0.3	0.5	0.7	2.1	5.6	3.5	5.0	4.2	2.0	0.3	0.0	24.3
Days of 1mm or More	0	1	4	5	7	14	13	17	15	6	3	0	85

SALINA CRUZ

Mexico

Elevation 56 m. (184 ft.)   16°12'N—95°12'W

	JAN	FEB	MAR	APR	MAY	JUN	JUL	AUG	SEP	OCT	NOV	DEC	YEAR
TEMPERATURE													
Daily Average Min.°C	21	21	22	24	25	24	24	24	23	23	22	21	23
Daily Average Min.°F	70	70	72	75	77	75	75	75	74	74	72	70	73
Daily Average Max.°C	30	30	31	32	34	32	32	33	32	31	30	30	31
Daily Average Max.°F	85	86	87	89	92	90	90	91	89	89	87	86	88
Extreme Monthly Min.°C	17	17	17	18	21	19	20	20	20	19	17	17	16
Extreme Monthly Min.°F	62	63	63	65	70	66	68	68	68	66	62	63	62
Extreme Monthly Max.°C	33	33	35	36	37	36	35	36	35	34	34	34	36
Extreme Monthly Max.°F	91	92	95	97	98	97	95	97	95	93	94	93	98
Monthly Average °C	26	26	27	29	30	29	29	29	28	28	27	26	28
Monthly Average °F	78	79	81	84	85	84	84	84	83	82	81	79	82
RELATIVE HUMIDITY (%)	61	63	65	65	65	72	71	71	74	65	58	59	66
PRECIPITATION													
Monthly Average mm	13	7	5	5	68	292	189	203	278	73	36	10	1179.0
Monthly Average Inches	0.5	0.2	0.1	0.1	2.6	11.5	7.4	7.9	10.9	2.8	1.4	0.3	45.7
Days of 1mm or More	3	0	0	0	3	13	12	12	14	6	1	0	64

TAMPICO

Mexico

Elevation 20 m. (66 ft.)   22°12'N—97°51'W

	JAN	FEB	MAR	APR	MAY	JUN	JUL	AUG	SEP	OCT	NOV	DEC	YEAR
TEMPERATURE													
Daily Average Min.°C	15	16	17	20	23	24	24	24	23	21	18	16	20
Daily Average Min.°F	59	61	63	69	73	75	75	75	74	71	64	60	68
Daily Average Max.°C	22	24	26	28	30	31	32	32	31	30	26	24	28
Daily Average Max.°F	72	75	78	83	86	88	89	89	88	85	79	75	82
Monthly Average °C	18	19	22	24	27	27	28	28	27	26	22	20	24
Monthly Average °F	64	67	71	76	80	81	82	83	81	78	71	68	75
RELATIVE HUMIDITY (%)	81	80	79	79	79	79	79	80	79	78	76	79	79
PRECIPITATION													
Monthly Average mm	24	17	17	16	46	155	101	106	219	109	41	43	894.0
Monthly Average Inches	0.9	0.6	0.6	0.6	1.8	6.1	3.9	4.1	8.6	4.2	1.6	1.6	34.6
Days of 1mm or More	5	3	2	2	7	12	6	12	13	6	7	7	82

VERACRUZ   Mexico

			Elevation 16 m. (53 ft.)				19°12'N—96°8'W						
	JAN	FEB	MAR	APR	MAY	JUN	JUL	AUG	SEP	OCT	NOV	DEC	YEAR
TEMPERATURE													
Daily Average Min.°C	19	19	20	23	24	24	24	24	24	23	21	19	22
Daily Average Min.°F	66	67	69	73	76	76	75	75	75	73	69	67	71
Daily Average Max.°C	25	25	27	28	30	31	31	31	31	30	27	26	28
Daily Average Max.°F	77	78	80	83	86	87	87	88	87	85	81	78	83
Extreme Monthly Min.°C	12	13	12	16	20	20	19	21	18	18	13	13	11
Extreme Monthly Min.°F	54	55	53	61	68	68	66	69	65	64	55	55	53
Extreme Monthly Max.°C	30	33	37	36	36	36	33	33	33	33	33	32	36
Extreme Monthly Max.°F	86	91	98	96	96	97	92	92	92	92	92	89	98
Monthly Average °C	21	22	23	26	27	28	27	28	28	27	24	23	25
Monthly Average °F	70	71	74	78	81	82	81	83	82	80	76	73	78
RELATIVE HUMIDITY (%)	87	87	87	86	85	84	85	84	85	84	83	85	85
PRECIPITATION													
Monthly Average mm	25	17	18	22	67	282	411	338	347	146	67	47	1787.0
Monthly Average Inches	0.9	0.6	0.7	0.8	2.6	11.1	16.1	13.3	13.6	5.7	2.6	1.8	69.8
Days of 1mm or More	5	3	5	4	6	15	21	20	21	12	9	9	130

TRUK   Micronesia

			Elevation 2 m. (6 ft.)				7°25'N—151°47'E						
	JAN	FEB	MAR	APR	MAY	JUN	JUL	AUG	SEP	OCT	NOV	DEC	YEAR
TEMPERATURE													
Monthly Average °C	27	27	28	28	28	28	27	27	27	28	28	28	28
Monthly Average °F	81	81	82	82	82	82	81	81	81	82	82	82	82
PRECIPITATION													
Monthly Average mm	224	172	237	290	361	293	361	341	312	349	290	322	3552.0
Monthly Average Inches	8.8	6.7	9.3	11.4	14.2	11.5	14.2	13.4	12.2	13.7	11.4	12.6	139.4
Days of 1mm or More	14	12	14	16	21	20	20	21	18	19	20	18	213

MIDWAY ISLAND   Midway Island

			Elevation 13 m. (42 ft.)				28°13'N—177°22'W						
	JAN	FEB	MAR	APR	MAY	JUN	JUL	AUG	SEP	OCT	NOV	DEC	YEAR
TEMPERATURE													
Monthly Average °C	19	19	19	20	22	24	26	26	26	24	22	20	22
Monthly Average °F	66	66	66	68	71	76	78	79	79	76	72	69	72
PRECIPITATION													
Monthly Average mm	172	111	122	61	101	67	128	155	114	165	113	205	1514.0
Monthly Average Inches	6.7	4.3	4.8	2.4	3.9	2.6	5.0	6.1	4.4	6.4	4.4	8.0	59.0
Days of 1mm or More	15	10	8	6	7	5	10	11	9	11	11	10	113

ULAN-BATOR
Mongolia

Elevation 1325 m. (4347 ft.)				47°55'N—106°50'E									
	JAN	FEB	MAR	APR	MAY	JUN	JUL	AUG	SEP	OCT	NOV	DEC	YEAR
TEMPERATURE													
Daily Average Min.°C	-32	-29	-22	-8	-2	7	11	8	2	-8	-20	-28	-10
Daily Average Min.°F	-26	-21	-/	17	29	44	51	46	35	18	-4	-19	14
Daily Average Max.°C	-19	-13	-4	7	13	21	22	21	14	6	-6	-16	4
Daily Average Max.°F	-2	9	25	44	55	69	71	69	58	43	22	3	39
Extreme Monthly Min.°C	-44	-44	-39	-24	-12	-4	1	-7	-11	-27	-36	-43	-44
Extreme Monthly Min.°F	-47	-48	-39	-11	10	24	34	20	13	-16	-32	-45	-48
Extreme Monthly Max.°C	-6	2	18	24	30	36	33	33	28	23	11	0	36
Extreme Monthly Max.°F	21	35	64	76	86	97	92	91	83	73	52	32	97
Monthly Average °C	-19	-15	-10	-1	8	13	15	14	8	-1	-9	-18	-1
Monthly Average °F	-3	4	15	31	47	56	59	57	46	31	15	-1	30
RELATIVE HUMIDITY (%)	73	66	61	42	40	44	54	49	43	48	57	75	54
PRECIPITATION													
Monthly Average mm	1	5	6	14	24	71	86	82	49	12	10	3	363.0
Monthly Average Inches	0.0	0.1	0.2	0.5	0.9	2.7	3.3	3.2	1.9	0.4	0.3	0.1	13.6
Days of 1mm or More	1	2	1	2	4	6	10	14	2	4	1	0	47

CASABLANCA
Morocco

Elevation 50 m. (164 ft.)				33°35'N—7°39'W									
	JAN	FEB	MAR	APR	MAY	JUN	JUL	AUG	SEP	OCT	NOV	DEC	YEAR
TEMPERATURE													
Daily Average Min.°C	8	9	11	12	15	18	19	20	18	15	12	10	14
Daily Average Min.°F	47	47	51	53	58	64	67	67	65	60	54	49	57
Daily Average Max.°C	17	18	20	21	22	24	26	26	26	24	21	18	22
Daily Average Max.°F	63	64	67	69	72	75	78	80	78	75	70	65	71
Extreme Monthly Min.°C	-1	2	2	5	7	8	12	12	10	8	4	3	0
Extreme Monthly Min.°F	31	35	35	41	45	46	54	53	50	46	40	37	31
Extreme Monthly Max.°C	27	31	37	38	38	36	42	43	43	42	35	29	43
Extreme Monthly Max.°F	81	87	98	100	100	97	108	110	110	107	95	84	110
Monthly Average °C	13	14	15	16	18	20	22	22	22	19	16	13	17
Monthly Average °F	55	56	58	60	64	68	72	72	71	66	60	55	63
RELATIVE HUMIDITY (%)	72	68	68	67	67	69	71	72	70	65	66	71	69
PRECIPITATION													
Monthly Average mm	69	54	51	35	24	6	0	1	7	35	67	92	441.0
Monthly Average Inches	2.7	2.1	2.0	1.3	0.9	0.2	0.0	0.0	0.2	1.3	2.6	3.6	16.9
Days of 1mm or More	8	7	5	5	3	1	0	0	1	5	6	8	49

MARRAKECH
Morocco

Elevation 470 m. (1542 ft.)				31°37'N—8°2'W									
	JAN	FEB	MAR	APR	MAY	JUN	JUL	AUG	SEP	OCT	NOV	DEC	YEAR
TEMPERATURE													
Daily Average Min.°C	5	7	9	12	14	17	20	20	18	15	10	7	13
Daily Average Min.°F	42	44	49	53	58	62	67	68	64	58	51	44	55
Daily Average Max.°C	18	20	23	25	29	33	38	37	33	28	23	19	27
Daily Average Max.°F	64	68	74	78	84	91	100	99	91	83	73	65	81
Extreme Monthly Min.°C	-2	-3	1	2	7	9	12	14	11	4	1	-2	-2
Extreme Monthly Min.°F	28	27	33	36	44	48	54	57	51	40	33	29	28
Extreme Monthly Max.°C	28	31	38	39	44	46	49	47	45	38	35	27	48
Extreme Monthly Max.°F	83	87	100	102	112	114	120	117	113	101	95	81	120
Monthly Average °C	12	13	16	17	20	23	28	27	25	21	16	12	19
Monthly Average °F	53	56	60	63	68	73	82	81	76	69	60	53	66
RELATIVE HUMIDITY (%)	63	59	55	53	47	48	39	40	45	49	59	61	51
PRECIPITATION													
Monthly Average mm	32	36	31	34	23	8	1	2	4	19	37	32	259.0
Monthly Average Inches	1.2	1.4	1.2	1.3	0.9	0.3	0.0	0.0	0.1	0.7	1.4	1.2	9.7
Days of 1mm or More	4	3	4	4	2	0	0	0	1	2	4	4	28

OUARZAZATE   Morocco

		Elevation 1136 m. (3727 ft.)			30°56'N—6°54'W							
	JAN	FEB	MAR	APR	MAY	JUN	JUL	AUG	SEP	OCT	NOV	DEC	YEAR

TEMPERATURE													
Daily Average Min.°C	2	3	7	10	14	17	21	21	17	12	7	3	11
Daily Average Min.°F	35	38	45	50	57	63	69	69	62	54	44	36	52
Daily Average Max.°C	17	19	23	26	30	35	39	40	35	27	21	17	27
Daily Average Max.°F	62	67	73	80	86	95	102	104	94	80	70	62	81
Monthly Average °C	9	12	15	18	21	26	30	29	25	19	13	9	19
Monthly Average °F	49	53	59	64	71	79	85	84	76	67	56	48	66
RELATIVE HUMIDITY (%)	46	36	31	26	24	19	15	19	25	36	45	47	31
PRECIPITATION													
Monthly Average mm	14	12	3	7	9	2	1	4	14	17	15	7	105.0
Monthly Average Inches	0.5	0.4	0.1	0.2	0.3	0.0	0.0	0.1	0.5	0.6	0.5	0.2	3.4
Days of 1mm or More	2	1	0	0	1	0	0	0	2	2	2	1	11

INHAMBANE   Mozambique

		Elevation 15 m. (49 ft.)			23°52'S—35°23'E							
	JAN	FEB	MAR	APR	MAY	JUN	JUL	AUG	SEP	OCT	NOV	DEC	YEAR

TEMPERATURE													
Daily Average Min.°C	23	23	22	21	19	17	16	17	18	20	21	22	20
Daily Average Min.°F	74	74	72	70	65	62	61	62	65	68	70	72	68
Daily Average Max.°C	31	31	30	29	27	26	25	26	27	28	29	30	28
Daily Average Max.°F	88	88	87	85	81	78	78	78	81	83	85	86	83
Monthly Average °C	27	27	26	24	22	20	20	21	22	23	25	26	24
Monthly Average °F	80	80	79	76	72	69	68	69	72	74	76	79	74
RELATIVE HUMIDITY (%)	65	64	62	62	62	62	61	62	63	65	65	65	63
PRECIPITATION													
Monthly Average mm	166	134	121	74	57	57	39	31	40	39	74	172	1004.0
Monthly Average Inches	6.5	5.2	4.7	2.9	2.2	2.2	1.5	1.2	1.5	1.5	2.9	6.7	39.0
Days of 1mm or More	8	9	8	6	6	6	5	3	2	4	5	7	69

PORTO AMELIA   Mozambique

		Elevation 50 m. (164 ft.)			12°58'S—40°30'E							
	JAN	FEB	MAR	APR	MAY	JUN	JUL	AUG	SEP	OCT	NOV	DEC	YEAR

TEMPERATURE													
Daily Average Min.°C	24	24	24	23	21	20	20	20	21	23	24	24	22
Daily Average Min.°F	75	75	75	74	71	68	67	68	70	73	75	76	72
Daily Average Max.°C	31	31	31	31	30	29	29	29	30	30	31	32	30
Daily Average Max.°F	88	88	89	88	87	84	83	84	86	87	88	89	87
Monthly Average °C	27	27	27	26	25	24	23	24	24	26	27	27	26
Monthly Average °F	80	80	80	79	77	75	74	74	76	78	80	81	78
RELATIVE HUMIDITY (%)	74	75	71	68	62	61	59	60	60	64	67	72	66
PRECIPITATION													
Monthly Average mm	148	149	204	119	24	18	12	7	2	11	41	130	865.0
Monthly Average Inches	5.8	5.8	8.0	4.6	0.9	0.7	0.4	0.2	0.0	0.4	1.6	5.1	33.5
Days of 1mm or More	11	10	12	9	2	2	1	0	0	1	3	8	59

QUELIMANE   Mozambique

	Elevation 6 m. (20 ft.)					17°53'S—36°53'E							
	JAN	FEB	MAR	APR	MAY	JUN	JUL	AUG	SEP	OCT	NOV	DEC	YEAR
TEMPERATURE													
Daily Average Min.°C	24	24	23	22	19	17	16	17	19	21	23	23	21
Daily Average Min.°F	74	75	74	71	66	62	61	62	66	70	73	74	69
Daily Average Max.°C	33	33	32	31	29	27	27	28	30	32	33	33	30
Daily Average Max.°F	91	91	89	88	84	81	80	82	86	90	91	91	87
Monthly Average °C	27	27	27	26	23	21	21	22	24	25	27	27	25
Monthly Average °F	81	81	80	78	74	70	69	71	75	78	80	81	77
RELATIVE HUMIDITY (%)	68	68	68	66	64	65	63	61	61	60	63	66	64
PRECIPITATION													
Monthly Average mm	252	239	229	141	76	56	71	30	16	34	86	225	1455.0
Monthly Average Inches	9.9	9.4	9.0	5.5	2.9	2.2	2.7	1.1	0.6	1.3	3.3	8.8	56.7
Days of 1mm or More	11	12	13	9	7	7	8	4	2	2	5	10	90

WINDHOEK   Namibia

	Elevation 1728 m. (5669 ft.)					22°34'S—17°6'E							
	JAN	FEB	MAR	APR	MAY	JUN	JUL	AUG	SEP	OCT	NOV	DEC	YEAR
TEMPERATURE													
Daily Average Min.°C	17	17	15	13	9	7	7	9	12	15	16	17	13
Daily Average Min.°F	63	62	60	55	49	44	44	48	54	58	60	62	55
Daily Average Max.°C	30	29	27	26	23	20	21	24	27	29	30	30	26
Daily Average Max.°F	86	84	81	78	73	68	69	74	81	85	85	87	79
Extreme Monthly Min.°C	9	7	4	2	-2	-3	-3	-4	-1	2	1	3	-3
Extreme Monthly Min.°F	49	44	39	36	29	27	27	25	31	35	33	38	25
Extreme Monthly Max.°C	36	34	34	31	32	26	25	29	33	34	36	36	36
Extreme Monthly Max.°F	97	94	94	87	89	79	77	85	91	93	96	97	97
Monthly Average °C	23	22	21	19	16	13	14	16	20	22	23	24	19
Monthly Average °F	74	71	70	66	61	56	56	61	68	71	73	75	67
RELATIVE HUMIDITY (%)	26	35	36	29	22	21	17	13	11	13	20	21	22
PRECIPITATION													
Monthly Average mm	71	85	73	30	5	2	0	1	2	11	33	31	344.0
Monthly Average Inches	2.7	3.3	2.8	1.1	0.1	0.0	0.0	0.0	0.0	0.4	1.2	1.2	12.8
Days of 1mm or More	9	10	8	4	0	0	0	0	0	1	3	4	39

Nauru

	Elevation 27 m. (87 ft.)					0°32'S—167°3'E							
	JAN	FEB	MAR	APR	MAY	JUN	JUL	AUG	SEP	OCT	NOV	DEC	YEAR
TEMPERATURE													
Daily Average Min.°C	23	24	24	24	24	23	23	23	24	23	23	23	24
Daily Average Min.°F	74	75	75	75	75	74	74	74	75	74	74	74	74
Daily Average Max.°C	31	31	32	32	32	32	32	32	32	32	32	32	32
Daily Average Max.°F	88	88	89	90	90	90	89	89	90	90	90	89	89
Monthly Average °C	28	28	28	28	28	28	28	28	28	28	28	28	28
Monthly Average °F	82	82	82	82	82	82	82	82	82	83	83	82	82
RELATIVE HUMIDITY (%)	74	73	73	71	70	70	71	69	68	68	69	71	71
PRECIPITATION													
Monthly Average mm	283	242	217	200	129	110	142	133	109	103	113	258	2039.0
Monthly Average Inches	11.1	9.5	8.5	7.8	5.0	4.3	5.5	5.2	4.2	4.0	4.4	10.1	79.6
Days of 1mm or More	0	0	0	0	0	0	0	0	0	0	0	0	0

KATMANDU   Nepal

Elevation 1338 m. (4388 ft.)   27°42'N—85°12'E

	JAN	FEB	MAR	APR	MAY	JUN	JUL	AUG	SEP	OCT	NOV	DEC	YEAR
TEMPERATURE													
Daily Average Min.°C	2	4	7	12	16	19	20	20	19	13	7	3	12
Daily Average Min.°F	35	39	45	53	61	67	68	68	66	56	45	37	53
Daily Average Max.°C	18	19	25	28	30	29	29	28	28	27	23	19	25
Daily Average Max.°F	65	67	77	83	86	85	84	83	83	80	74	67	78
Extreme Monthly Min.°C	-2	-1	2	4	10	14	18	17	13	6	-1	-2	-2
Extreme Monthly Min.°F	28	31	35	40	50	58	64	63	56	43	31	29	28
Extreme Monthly Max.°C	25	25	33	35	36	36	33	33	33	33	28	24	36
Extreme Monthly Max.°F	77	77	92	95	96	97	91	92	92	92	83	76	97
Monthly Average °C	10	13	16	20	23	24	24	24	23	20	15	11	19
Monthly Average °F	49	55	62	68	73	75	75	75	74	68	59	52	65
RELATIVE HUMIDITY (%)	89	90	73	68	72	79	86	87	86	88	90	89	83
PRECIPITATION													
Monthly Average mm	17	12	31	38	97	195	373	329	178	45	3	5	1323.0
Monthly Average Inches	0.6	0.4	1.2	1.4	3.8	7.6	14.6	12.9	7.0	1.7	0.1	0.1	51.4
Days of 1mm or More	2	2	4	9	12	18	27	20	24	2	0	1	121

DE BILT   Netherlands

Elevation 3 m. (10 ft.)   52°6'N—5°12'E

	JAN	FEB	MAR	APR	MAY	JUN	JUL	AUG	SEP	OCT	NOV	DEC	YEAR
TEMPERATURE													
Daily Average Min.°C	-1	-1	1	4	8	11	13	13	10	7	3	1	6
Daily Average Min.°F	31	31	34	40	46	51	55	55	50	44	38	33	42
Daily Average Max.°C	4	5	10	13	18	21	22	22	19	14	9	5	14
Daily Average Max.°F	40	42	49	56	64	70	72	71	67	57	48	42	56
Monthly Average °C	2	2	5	8	12	15	17	17	14	10	6	3	9
Monthly Average °F	35	36	41	46	54	59	62	62	58	51	43	37	49
RELATIVE HUMIDITY (%)	82	76	65	61	59	59	64	65	67	72	81	85	70
PRECIPITATION													
Monthly Average mm	68	43	58	52	63	68	77	74	63	75	81	80	802.0
Monthly Average Inches	2.6	1.6	2.2	2.0	2.4	2.6	3.0	2.9	2.4	2.9	3.1	3.1	30.8
Days of 1mm or More	12	8	11	10	10	10	9	10	10	10	13	13	126

KOUMAC   New Caledonia

Elevation 18 m. (59 ft.)   20°33'S—164°17'E

	JAN	FEB	MAR	APR	MAY	JUN	JUL	AUG	SEP	OCT	NOV	DEC	YEAR
TEMPERATURE													
Monthly Average °C	26	26	26	24	23	21	20	20	21	22	24	25	23
Monthly Average °F	79	79	78	75	73	70	68	68	70	72	75	77	74
PRECIPITATION													
Monthly Average mm	157	169	138	68	72	65	54	40	38	40	72	89	1002.0
Monthly Average Inches	6.1	6.6	5.4	2.6	2.8	2.5	2.1	1.5	1.4	1.5	2.8	3.5	38.8
Days of 1mm or More	9	10	9	4	4	5	4	3	3	3	5	6	65

AUCKLAND   New Zealand

		Elevation 26 m. (85 ft.)					36°47'S—174°39'E						
	JAN	FEB	MAR	APR	MAY	JUN	JUL	AUG	SEP	OCT	NOV	DEC	YEAR
TEMPERATURE													
Daily Average Min.°C	16	16	15	13	11	9	8	8	9	11	12	14	12
Daily Average Min.°F	60	60	59	56	51	48	46	46	49	52	54	57	53
Daily Average Max.°C	23	23	22	19	17	14	13	14	16	0	0	0	13
Daily Average Max.°F	73	73	71	67	62	58	56	58	60	63	66	70	65
Extreme Monthly Min.°F	45	47	42	39	36	35	33	34	34	36	41	43	33
Extreme Monthly Max.°C	32	32	30	27	23	21	24	19	22	24	27	32	32
Extreme Monthly Max.°F	90	90	86	81	73	70	76	67	71	75	81	89	90
Monthly Average °C	20	21	19	17	15	12	11	12	13	15	17	18	16
Monthly Average °F	68	69	67	63	58	54	52	53	56	59	63	65	61
RELATIVE HUMIDITY (%)	62	61	65	69	70	73	74	70	68	66	64	64	67
PRECIPITATION													
Monthly Average mm	48	116	87	130	130	118	136	141	92	110	84	95	1287.0
Monthly Average Inches	1.8	4.5	3.4	5.1	5.1	4.6	5.3	5.5	3.6	4.3	3.3	3.7	50.2
Days of 1mm or More	0	0	0	0	0	0	0	0	0	0	0	0	0

CHRISTCHURCH   New Zealand

		Elevation 10 m. (32 ft.)					43°32'S—172°37'E						
	JAN	FEB	MAR	APR	MAY	JUN	JUL	AUG	SEP	OCT	NOV	DEC	YEAR
TEMPERATURE													
Daily Average Min.°C	12	12	10	7	4	2	2	2	4	7	8	11	7
Daily Average Min.°F	53	53	50	45	40	36	35	36	40	44	47	51	44
Daily Average Max.°C	21	21	19	17	13	11	10	11	14	17	19	21	16
Daily Average Max.°F	70	69	66	62	56	51	50	52	57	62	66	69	61
Extreme Monthly Min.°C	1	2	-1	-3	-6	-6	-5	-5	-5	-3	-1	1	-6
Extreme Monthly Min.°F	34	35	30	26	21	22	23	23	23	26	31	33	21
Extreme Monthly Max.°C	36	34	32	28	26	21	21	21	27	31	32	33	35
Extreme Monthly Max.°F	96	94	90	82	78	69	70	70	81	88	90	92	96
Monthly Average °C	17	16	15	12	9	6	6	7	9	11	14	16	12
Monthly Average °F	62	62	59	54	48	43	43	45	49	53	57	60	53
RELATIVE HUMIDITY (%)	59	60	69	71	69	72	76	66	69	60	64	60	66
PRECIPITATION													
Monthly Average mm	48	42	58	55	60	65	68	57	38	43	48	47	629.0
Monthly Average Inches	1.8	1.6	2.2	2.1	2.3	2.5	2.6	2.2	1.4	1.6	1.8	1.8	23.9
Days of 1mm or More	6	5	8	6	7	7	9	7	6	6	6	6	79

WELLINGTON   New Zealand

		Elevation 128 m. (419 ft.)					41°16'S—174°46'E						
	JAN	FEB	MAR	APR	MAY	JUN	JUL	AUG	SEP	OCT	NOV	DEC	YEAR
TEMPERATURE													
Daily Average Min.°C	13	13	12	11	8	7	6	6	8	9	10	12	10
Daily Average Min.°F	56	56	54	51	47	44	42	43	46	48	50	54	49
Daily Average Max.°C	21	21	19	17	14	13	12	12	14	16	17	19	16
Daily Average Max.°F	69	69	67	63	58	55	53	54	57	60	68	67	62
Extreme Monthly Min.°C	4	5	4	2	0	-1	-2	-2	-1	1	2	3	-1
Extreme Monthly Min.°F	39	41	39	36	32	30	29	29	31	34	36	38	29
Extreme Monthly Max.°C	29	31	27	23	22	21	19	19	21	24	27	28	31
Extreme Monthly Max.°F	85	88	81	74	71	69	66	66	69	75	81	83	88
Monthly Average °C	17	17	16	13	11	9	9	9	10	12	13	15	13
Monthly Average °F	62	62	60	56	52	49	47	48	50	53	56	59	55
RELATIVE HUMIDITY (%)	67	71	69	76	77	78	76	74	75	74	69	69	73
PRECIPITATION													
Monthly Average mm	80	66	93	104	126	133	142	129	107	97	85	96	1258.0
Monthly Average Inches	3.1	2.5	3.6	4.0	4.9	5.2	5.5	5.0	4.2	3.8	3.3	3.7	48.8
Days of 1mm or More	7	6	8	9	11	14	14	14	11	11	9	9	123

BLUEFIELDS — Nicaragua

Elevation 12 m. (39 ft.)   12°0'N—83°45'W

	JAN	FEB	MAR	APR	MAY	JUN	JUL	AUG	SEP	OCT	NOV	DEC	YEAR
TEMPERATURE													
Monthly Average °C	25	25	26	27	27	27	26	27	27	26	26	25	26
Monthly Average °F	77	78	79	81	81	80	79	80	80	80	78	77	79
PRECIPITATION													
Monthly Average mm	264	111	80	102	398	465	746	609	298	397	481	423	4374.0
Monthly Average Inches	10.3	4.3	3.1	4.0	15.6	18.3	29.3	23.9	11.7	15.6	18.9	16.6	171.6
Days of 1mm or More	0	0	0	0	0	0	0	0	0	0	0	0	0

MANAGUA — Nicaragua

Elevation 54 m. (177 ft.)   12°9'N—86°17'W

	JAN	FEB	MAR	APR	MAY	JUN	JUL	AUG	SEP	OCT	NOV	DEC	YEAR
TEMPERATURE													
Monthly Average °C	26	27	28	29	29	27	27	27	27	26	27	27	27
Monthly Average °F	79	81	83	84	84	81	81	80	81	80	80	80	81
PRECIPITATION													
Monthly Average mm	2	4	3	3	130	228	147	124	219	315	38	9	1222.0
Monthly Average Inches	0.0	0.1	0.1	0.1	5.1	8.9	5.7	4.8	8.6	12.4	1.4	0.3	47.5
Days of 1mm or More	2	0	0	0	4	17	25	13	10	19	2	0	92

PUERTO CABEZAS — Nicaragua

Elevation 13 m. (42 ft.)   14°2'N—83°23'W

	JAN	FEB	MAR	APR	MAY	JUN	JUL	AUG	SEP	OCT	NOV	DEC	YEAR
TEMPERATURE													
Monthly Average °C	25	25	27	27	27	27	26	27	27	27	26	25	26
Monthly Average °F	77	77	80	81	81	81	79	80	81	81	79	77	80
PRECIPITATION													
Monthly Average mm	165	83	38	51	265	431	477	366	277	334	363	279	3129.0
Monthly Average Inches	6.4	3.2	1.4	2.0	10.4	16.9	18.7	14.4	10.9	13.1	14.2	10.9	122.5
Days of 1mm or More	0	0	0	0	0	0	0	0	0	0	0	0	0

AGADES — Niger

Elevation 498 m. (1633 ft.)   16°19'N—7°59'E

	JAN	FEB	MAR	APR	MAY	JUN	JUL	AUG	SEP	OCT	NOV	DEC	YEAR
TEMPERATURE													
Daily Average Min.°C	11	13	17	22	24	25	24	23	23	20	15	12	19
Daily Average Min.°F	52	56	63	71	76	77	75	73	73	69	60	54	66
Daily Average Max.°C	29	32	36	40	41	42	39	37	39	38	34	30	36
Daily Average Max.°F	85	90	97	103	107	107	103	98	101	100	92	85	97
Monthly Average °C	20	23	27	31	34	34	32	31	32	30	24	21	28
Monthly Average °F	68	73	81	89	92	93	89	88	89	86	75	69	83
RELATIVE HUMIDITY (%)	16	13	12	11	15	20	32	42	26	16	15	17	20
PRECIPITATION													
Monthly Average mm	0	0	0	2	6	10	36	54	8	0	0	0	116.0
Monthly Average Inches	0.0	0.0	0.0	0.0	0.2	0.3	1.4	2.1	0.3	0.0	0.0	0.0	4.3
Days of 1mm or More	0	0	0	0	0	1	5	5	1	0	0	0	12

MARADI — Niger

	Elevation 369 m. (1210 ft.)					13°28'N—7°5'E							
	JAN	FEB	MAR	APR	MAY	JUN	JUL	AUG	SEP	OCT	NOV	DEC	YEAR
TEMPERATURE													
Daily Average Min.°C	13	15	19	23	25	24	22	22	22	19	16	13	19
Daily Average Min.°F	55	59	67	74	77	75	72	71	71	66	60	55	67
Daily Average Max.°C	32	34	38	40	40	37	33	31	33	36	35	32	35
Daily Average Max.°F	89	94	101	105	103	99	92	87	91	97	95	90	95
Monthly Average °C	22	25	29	32	33	30	28	27	28	28	25	22	27
Monthly Average °F	71	77	84	90	91	86	83	81	82	82	78	72	81
RELATIVE HUMIDITY (%)	12	10	10	16	30	43	58	67	59	31	15	13	30
PRECIPITATION													
Monthly Average mm	0	0	0	3	16	67	147	179	71	4	0	0	487.0
Monthly Average Inches	0.0	0.0	0.0	0.1	0.6	2.6	5.7	7.0	2.7	0.1	0.0	0.0	18.8
Days of 1mm or More	0	0	0	0	1	6	9	11	5	0	0	0	32

NIAMEY — Niger

	Elevation 223 m. (731 ft.)					13°29'N—2°10'E							
	JAN	FEB	MAR	APR	MAY	JUN	JUL	AUG	SEP	OCT	NOV	DEC	YEAR
TEMPERATURE													
Daily Average Min.°C	16	18	22	26	27	25	24	23	23	23	19	16	21
Daily Average Min.°F	60	65	72	79	81	77	74	73	73	74	66	61	71
Daily Average Max.°C	33	36	39	41	40	37	34	32	33	37	37	34	36
Daily Average Max.°F	92	97	103	106	104	99	93	89	92	99	98	93	97
Extreme Monthly Min.°C	8	10	11	17	19	19	18	17	19	16	12	14	8
Extreme Monthly Min.°F	47	50	51	62	67	67	64	63	67	61	53	58	47
Extreme Monthly Max.°C	39	43	44	46	46	46	40	38	41	43	43	40	45
Extreme Monthly Max.°F	102	109	112	114	114	114	104	100	105	109	109	104	114
Monthly Average °C	24	28	31	34	34	31	29	28	29	30	28	25	29
Monthly Average °F	76	82	88	93	93	88	84	82	84	87	82	77	84
RELATIVE HUMIDITY (%)	13	11	11	19	34	45	58	68	60	38	18	15	33
PRECIPITATION													
Monthly Average mm	0	0	5	5	44	67	147	175	88	12	0	0	543.0
Monthly Average Inches	0.0	0.0	0.1	0.1	1.7	2.6	5.7	6.8	3.4	0.4	0.0	0.0	20.8
Days of 1mm or More	0	0	0	0	3	5	10	11	7	2	0	0	38

TAHOUA — Niger

	Elevation 387 m. (1269 ft.)					14°54'N—5°15'E							
	JAN	FEB	MAR	APR	MAY	JUN	JUL	AUG	SEP	OCT	NOV	DEC	YEAR
TEMPERATURE													
Daily Average Min.°C	15	17	22	25	27	26	23	23	23	22	19	16	22
Daily Average Min.°F	59	63	71	77	80	78	74	73	73	72	66	61	71
Daily Average Max.°C	32	35	38	41	41	39	35	32	35	38	36	33	36
Daily Average Max.°F	90	94	101	105	105	101	94	90	94	100	96	91	97
Monthly Average °C	23	26	30	33	34	32	30	29	30	31	28	24	29
Monthly Average °F	74	79	86	92	93	90	85	83	85	87	82	75	84
RELATIVE HUMIDITY (%)	13	11	10	13	25	36	49	62	50	23	12	12	26
PRECIPITATION													
Monthly Average mm	0	0	1	5	18	55	106	115	54	2	0	0	356.0
Monthly Average Inches	0.0	0.0	0.0	0.1	0.7	2.1	4.1	4.5	2.1	0.0	0.0	0.0	13.6
Days of 1mm or More	0	0	0	0	2	5	9	9	5	1	0	0	31

ZINDER   Niger

	JAN	FEB	MAR	APR	MAY	JUN	JUL	AUG	SEP	OCT	NOV	DEC	YEAR
Elevation 477 m. (1565 ft.)				13°48'N—9°0'E									

TEMPERATURE

	JAN	FEB	MAR	APR	MAY	JUN	JUL	AUG	SEP	OCT	NOV	DEC	YEAR
Daily Average Min.°C	15	17	21	25	26	25	23	22	23	22	19	15	21
Daily Average Min.°F	59	63	71	76	78	77	73	71	73	72	66	60	70
Daily Average Max.°C	31	33	37	40	40	37	34	31	34	37	34	31	35
Daily Average Max.°F	87	92	99	104	104	99	93	88	94	99	94	88	95
Monthly Average °C	22	25	29	32	33	31	29	27	29	30	26	23	28
Monthly Average °F	71	77	84	90	92	89	84	81	84	85	79	73	82
RELATIVE HUMIDITY (%)	18	15	13	15	26	38	55	64	52	24	18	19	30

PRECIPITATION

	JAN	FEB	MAR	APR	MAY	JUN	JUL	AUG	SEP	OCT	NOV	DEC	YEAR
Monthly Average mm	0	0	0	1	19	38	145	188	56	5	0	0	452.0
Monthly Average Inches	0.0	0.0	0.0	0.0	0.7	1.4	5.7	7.4	2.2	0.1	0.0	0.0	17.5
Days of 1mm or More	0	0	0	0	1	4	8	10	5	0	0	0	28

ENUGU   Nigeria

	JAN	FEB	MAR	APR	MAY	JUN	JUL	AUG	SEP	OCT	NOV	DEC	YEAR
Elevation 140 m. (459 ft.)				6°28'N—7°33'E									

TEMPERATURE

	JAN	FEB	MAR	APR	MAY	JUN	JUL	AUG	SEP	OCT	NOV	DEC	YEAR
Daily Average Min.°C	21	22	23	23	23	22	22	22	22	22	22	20	22
Daily Average Min.°F	69	72	74	74	73	72	72	72	71	71	71	68	71
Daily Average Max.°C	33	34	34	33	32	30	29	29	30	31	32	33	32
Daily Average Max.°F	91	93	93	91	89	86	84	84	85	87	90	91	89
Monthly Average °C	27	28	29	28	27	26	25	25	26	26	27	26	27
Monthly Average °F	80	83	84	83	81	79	78	78	78	79	80	79	80
RELATIVE HUMIDITY (%)	39	39	50	58	65	69	71	69	71	66	57	43	58

PRECIPITATION

	JAN	FEB	MAR	APR	MAY	JUN	JUL	AUG	SEP	OCT	NOV	DEC	YEAR
Monthly Average mm	24	22	75	151	214	246	231	182	302	228	34	15	1724.0
Monthly Average Inches	0.9	0.8	2.9	5.9	8.4	9.6	9.0	7.1	11.8	8.9	1.3	0.5	67.1
Days of 1mm or More	0	1	3	7	13	15	16	15	19	14	1	0	104

KANO   Nigeria

	JAN	FEB	MAR	APR	MAY	JUN	JUL	AUG	SEP	OCT	NOV	DEC	YEAR
Elevation 481 m. (1578 ft.)				12°3'N—8°32'E									

TEMPERATURE

	JAN	FEB	MAR	APR	MAY	JUN	JUL	AUG	SEP	OCT	NOV	DEC	YEAR
Daily Average Min.°C	13	15	19	23	24	23	21	21	21	20	16	13	19
Daily Average Min.°F	55	59	67	74	76	73	70	70	70	67	61	56	66
Daily Average Max.°C	30	33	37	39	37	34	31	29	27	32	33	31	33
Daily Average Max.°F	86	91	98	101	99	94	87	85	81	90	92	87	91
Monthly Average °C	21	24	28	31	31	29	26	25	26	27	24	22	26
Monthly Average °F	70	75	82	87	87	83	79	77	79	80	76	72	79
RELATIVE HUMIDITY (%)	16	13	14	19	33	44	60	68	58	32	17	18	33

PRECIPITATION

	JAN	FEB	MAR	APR	MAY	JUN	JUL	AUG	SEP	OCT	NOV	DEC	YEAR
Monthly Average mm	0	0	0	12	70	114	208	275	121	11	0	0	811.0
Monthly Average Inches	0.0	0.0	0.0	0.4	2.7	4.4	8.1	10.8	4.7	0.4	0.0	0.0	31.5
Days of 1mm or More	0	0	0	1	4	7	14	15	9	1	0	0	51

LAGOS   Nigeria

Elevation 38 m. (124 ft.)   4°24'N—14°24'E

	JAN	FEB	MAR	APR	MAY	JUN	JUL	AUG	SEP	OCT	NOV	DEC	YEAR
TEMPERATURE													
Daily Average Min.°C	23	25	26	25	24	23	23	23	23	23	24	24	24
Daily Average Min.°F	74	77	78	77	76	74	74	73	74	74	75	75	75
Daily Average Max.°C	31	32	32	32	31	29	28	28	28	29	31	31	30
Daily Average Max.°F	88	89	89	89	87	85	83	82	83	85	88	88	86
Extreme Monthly Min.°C	17	19	16	21	21	21	20	19	20	21	21	19	15
Extreme Monthly Min.°F	63	66	60	69	69	69	68	67	68	69	70	66	60
Extreme Monthly Max.°C	35	36	37	37	40	34	34	36	34	36	37	37	40
Extreme Monthly Max.°F	95	96	99	99	104	93	93	96	94	96	99	99	104
Monthly Average °C	27	28	28	28	27	26	25	24	25	26	27	27	26
Monthly Average °F	80	82	82	82	80	78	76	76	77	78	80	80	79
RELATIVE HUMIDITY (%)	65	69	72	72	76	80	80	76	77	76	72	68	74
PRECIPITATION													
Monthly Average mm	26	44	92	149	219	345	225	75	177	176	65	21	1614.0
Monthly Average Inches	1.0	1.7	3.6	5.8	8.6	13.5	8.8	2.9	6.9	6.9	2.5	0.8	63.0
Days of 1mm or More	1	2	6	8	12	17	14	9	11	11	6	1	98

MAIDUGURI   Nigeria

Elevation 354 m. (1161 ft.)   11°51'N—13°5'E

	JAN	FEB	MAR	APR	MAY	JUN	JUL	AUG	SEP	OCT	NOV	DEC	YEAR
TEMPERATURE													
Daily Average Min.°C	12	14	19	23	25	24	22	22	22	20	15	12	19
Daily Average Min.°F	54	58	66	74	77	75	72	71	71	67	60	54	67
Daily Average Max.°C	32	34	38	40	39	36	33	31	33	36	35	32	35
Daily Average Max.°F	90	94	100	105	102	97	91	87	91	97	95	90	95
Monthly Average °C	22	24	28	31	32	30	28	26	27	28	25	22	27
Monthly Average °F	72	76	83	88	90	86	82	79	81	82	77	72	81
RELATIVE HUMIDITY (%)	19	15	13	17	31	40	59	69	58	34	21	23	33
PRECIPITATION													
Monthly Average mm	0	0	0	9	38	74	167	235	102	14	0	0	639.0
Monthly Average Inches	0.0	0.0	0.0	0.3	1.4	2.9	6.5	9.2	4.0	0.5	0.0	0.0	24.8
Days of 1mm or More	0	0	0	0	4	6	11	14	7	1	0	0	43

PORT HARCOURT   Nigeria

Elevation 18 m. (59 ft.)   4°51'N—7°01'E

	JAN	FEB	MAR	APR	MAY	JUN	JUL	AUG	SEP	OCT	NOV	DEC	YEAR
TEMPERATURE													
Daily Average Min.°C	21	22	23	23	23	22	22	22	22	22	22	21	22
Daily Average Min.°F	70	71	73	73	73	72	71	71	72	71	71	70	71
Daily Average Max.°C	32	33	32	32	31	29	28	28	29	30	31	31	30
Daily Average Max.°F	89	91	90	89	88	85	83	83	83	85	87	89	87
Monthly Average °C	26	27	27	27	27	26	25	25	25	26	26	26	26
Monthly Average °F	79	81	81	81	81	78	77	77	78	78	79	79	79
RELATIVE HUMIDITY (%)	60	58	68	71	75	80	82	80	84	79	74	61	73
PRECIPITATION													
Monthly Average mm	31	65	127	190	225	265	363	301	394	271	110	30	2372.0
Monthly Average Inches	1.2	2.5	5.0	7.4	8.8	10.4	14.2	11.8	15.5	10.6	4.3	1.1	92.8
Days of 1mm or More	3	4	8	12	14	17	21	22	21	18	9	3	152

YOLA   Nigeria

		Elevation 174 m. (570 ft.)				9°14'N—12°28'E							
	JAN	FEB	MAR	APR	MAY	JUN	JUL	AUG	SEP	OCT	NOV	DEC	YEAR
TEMPERATURE													
Daily Average Min.°C	17	19	24	25	25	23	22	22	22	22	19	16	21
Daily Average Min.°F	62	67	74	78	76	73	72	72	71	72	66	61	70
Daily Average Max.°C	35	37	39	39	36	32	31	30	31	33	36	35	35
Daily Average Max.°F	95	99	103	101	96	90	88	87	87	92	96	95	94
Monthly Average °C	26	28	32	32	30	28	27	26	26	28	27	25	28
Monthly Average °F	78	83	89	90	86	82	80	79	79	82	80	78	82
RELATIVE HUMIDITY (%)	16	15	19	31	45	60	65	68	68	55	29	20	41
PRECIPITATION													
Monthly Average mm	0	0	8	43	113	154	140	190	216	52	6	0	922.0
Monthly Average Inches	0.0	0.0	0.3	1.6	4.4	6.0	5.5	7.4	8.5	2.0	0.2	0.0	35.9
Days of 1mm or More	0	0	0	5	8	10	11	14	14	4	1	0	67

PYONGYANG   North Korea

		Elevation 29 m. (95 ft.)				39°1'N—125°45'E							
	JAN	FEB	MAR	APR	MAY	JUN	JUL	AUG	SEP	OCT	NOV	DEC	YEAR
TEMPERATURE													
Monthly Average °C	-8	-5	2	10	16	21	24	24	19	12	4	-4	9
Monthly Average °F	17	23	35	49	61	70	76	76	66	53	38	24	49
PRECIPITATION													
Monthly Average mm	11	12	27	50	72	75	263	243	107	41	47	22	970.0
Monthly Average Inches	0.4	0.4	1.0	1.9	2.8	2.9	10.3	9.5	4.2	1.6	1.8	0.8	37.6
Days of 1mm or More	4	3	4	5	8	7	14	13	8	5	8	4	83

BELFAST   Northern Ireland

		Elevation 73 m. (239 ft.)				54°42'N—6°12'W							
	JAN	FEB	MAR	APR	MAY	JUN	JUL	AUG	SEP	OCT	NOV	DEC	YEAR
TEMPERATURE													
Daily Average Min.°C	2	2	3	4	6	9	11	11	9	7	4	3	6
Daily Average Min.°F	35	35	37	39	43	48	52	51	48	44	39	37	42
Daily Average Max.°C	6	7	9	12	15	18	18	18	16	13	9	7	12
Daily Average Max.°F	43	44	49	53	59	64	65	65	61	55	48	44	54
Monthly Average °C	4	4	5	8	10	13	15	14	13	10	6	5	9
Monthly Average °F	39	39	42	46	50	56	58	58	55	50	43	40	48
RELATIVE HUMIDITY (%)	87	80	74	69	66	71	73	75	78	80	85	89	77
PRECIPITATION													
Monthly Average mm	83	55	64	52	60	62	67	74	85	83	79	81	845.0
Monthly Average Inches	3.2	2.1	2.5	2.0	2.3	2.4	2.6	2.9	3.3	3.2	3.1	3.1	32.7
Days of 1mm or More	14	10	13	10	13	11	11	12	13	13	13	14	147

SAIPAN — Northern Mariana Islands

	JAN	FEB	MAR	APR	MAY	JUN	JUL	AUG	SEP	OCT	NOV	DEC	YEAR
Elevation 206 m. (676 ft.)					15°14'N—145°46'E								
TEMPERATURE													
Daily Average Min.°C	22	22	23	23	23	24	23	24	23	24	24	23	23
Daily Average Min.°F	72	72	73	74	74	75	74	75	74	75	75	74	74
Daily Average Max.°C	27	27	28	28	29	29	28	29	28	28	28	28	28
Daily Average Max.°F	81	81	82	83	84	84	83	84	83	83	83	82	83
Monthly Average °C	26	26	26	27	27	28	27	27	27	27	27	26	27
Monthly Average °F	79	78	79	80	81	82	81	81	81	81	81	80	80
RELATIVE HUMIDITY (%)	73	70	71	69	72	71	78	77	79	79	78	75	74
PRECIPITATION													
Monthly Average mm	111	78	79	96	81	126	235	320	358	265	188	127	2064.0
Monthly Average Inches	4.3	3.0	3.1	3.7	3.1	4.9	9.2	12.6	14.0	10.4	7.4	5.0	80.7
Days of 1mm or More	13	14	14	16	15	20	17	19	18	25	17	13	201

BERGEN — Norway

	JAN	FEB	MAR	APR	MAY	JUN	JUL	AUG	SEP	OCT	NOV	DEC	YEAR
Elevation 44 m. (144 ft.)					60°24'N—5°19'E								
TEMPERATURE													
Daily Average Min.°C	-1	-1	0	3	7	10	12	12	10	6	3	1	5
Daily Average Min.°F	31	30	33	37	44	49	54	54	49	43	38	34	42
Daily Average Max.°C	3	3	6	9	14	16	19	19	15	11	8	5	11
Daily Average Max.°F	38	38	43	49	58	61	66	65	59	52	46	41	51
Extreme Monthly Min.°C	-14	-16	-12	-9	-4	2	4	4	-2	-6	-6	-14	-16
Extreme Monthly Min.°F	7	3	10	15	25	35	39	39	28	22	21	6	3
Extreme Monthly Max.°C	13	12	20	25	27	32	32	29	26	20	15	17	31
Extreme Monthly Max.°F	56	54	68	77	81	89	89	85	79	68	59	62	89
Monthly Average °C	1	1	3	6	10	13	14	14	12	9	5	3	8
Monthly Average °F	35	34	38	42	50	55	57	58	53	48	41	37	46
RELATIVE HUMIDITY (%)	77	74	64	66	65	70	73	74	75	75	77	79	73
PRECIPITATION													
Monthly Average mm	171	129	131	102	99	131	140	161	243	262	250	216	2035.0
Monthly Average Inches	6.7	5.0	5.1	4.0	3.8	5.1	5.5	6.3	9.5	10.3	9.8	8.5	79.6
Days of 1mm or More	16	12	14	12	12	13	13	14	18	18	19	17	178

BJORNOYA (BEAR ISLAND) — Norway

	JAN	FEB	MAR	APR	MAY	JUN	JUL	AUG	SEP	OCT	NOV	DEC	YEAR
Elevation 29 m. (95 ft.)					74°30'N—19°17'E								
TEMPERATURE													
Daily Average Min.°C	-9	-10	-10	-8	-3	1	3	3	2	-1	-4	-7	-4
Daily Average Min.°F	17	15	14	18	27	33	37	38	35	30	25	20	25
Daily Average Max.°C	-4	-4	-4	-2	1	4	7	7	5	2	0	-2	1
Daily Average Max.°F	25	26	25	28	34	40	44	45	40	36	32	29	33
Monthly Average °C	-8	-8	-7	-5	-1	2	4	4	3	0	-3	-7	-2
Monthly Average °F	18	18	19	22	30	35	39	40	37	31	26	20	28
RELATIVE HUMIDITY (%)	87	87	88	87	86	90	93	92	91	87	87	88	89
PRECIPITATION													
Monthly Average mm	28	34	26	20	18	25	28	37	44	43	34	28	365.0
Monthly Average Inches	1.1	1.3	1.0	0.7	0.7	0.9	1.1	1.4	1.7	1.6	1.3	1.1	13.9
Days of 1mm or More	8	10	8	6	5	5	7	7	10	10	9	8	93

BODO

Norway

	JAN	FEB	MAR	APR	MAY	JUN	JUL	AUG	SEP	OCT	NOV	DEC	YEAR
Elevation 33 m. (108 ft.)					67°17'N—14°28'E								
TEMPERATURE													
Daily Average Min.°C	-4	-5	-4	0	3	7	11	10	7	3	-1	-2	2
Daily Average Min.°F	24	23	26	31	38	45	51	50	44	37	29	28	36
Daily Average Max.°C	0	0	2	5	9	13	16	16	12	7	4	2	7
Daily Average Max.°F	32	33	36	41	48	55	61	60	54	45	39	35	45
Monthly Average °C	-3	-2	-1	2	7	10	13	12	9	5	1	-1	4
Monthly Average °F	27	28	31	36	45	51	55	54	48	42	34	30	40
RELATIVE HUMIDITY (%)	76	75	73	69	69	74	74	76	75	75	75	75	74
PRECIPITATION													
Monthly Average mm	83	66	67	53	45	57	97	87	119	143	94	96	1007.0
Monthly Average Inches	3.2	2.5	2.6	2.0	1.7	2.2	3.8	3.4	4.6	5.6	3.7	3.7	39.0
Days of 1mm or More	13	12	12	10	8	11	13	12	16	18	14	15	154

JAN MAYEN

Norway

	JAN	FEB	MAR	APR	MAY	JUN	JUL	AUG	SEP	OCT	NOV	DEC	YEAR
Elevation 23 m. (75 ft.)					70°59'N—8°20'W								
TEMPERATURE													
Daily Average Min.°C	-6	-8	-7	-6	-2	1	4	4	2	-1	-4	-5	-3
Daily Average Min.°F	21	18	19	22	28	33	38	39	36	30	26	22	28
Daily Average Max.°C	-1	-2	-2	-1	2	5	7	8	6	4	2	0	2
Daily Average Max.°F	29	28	29	31	35	41	45	46	43	39	35	32	36
Monthly Average °C	-5	-6	-6	-4	-1	2	4	5	3	0	-3	-5	-1
Monthly Average °F	22	21	22	25	31	36	39	41	37	33	27	23	29
RELATIVE HUMIDITY (%)	83	83	83	81	84	87	89	87	85	83	85	84	84
PRECIPITATION													
Monthly Average mm	63	56	58	42	39	33	45	61	81	83	67	62	690.0
Monthly Average Inches	2.4	2.2	2.2	1.6	1.5	1.2	1.7	2.4	3.1	3.2	2.6	2.4	26.5
Days of 1mm or More	13	11	13	9	7	7	9	10	13	14	13	13	132

OSLO

Norway

	JAN	FEB	MAR	APR	MAY	JUN	JUL	AUG	SEP	OCT	NOV	DEC	YEAR
Elevation 96 m. (314 ft.)					59°54'N—10°42'E								
TEMPERATURE													
Daily Average Min.°C	-7	-7	-4	1	6	10	13	12	8	3	-1	-4	2
Daily Average Min.°F	19	19	25	34	43	50	55	53	46	38	31	25	36
Daily Average Max.°C	-2	-1	4	10	16	20	22	21	16	9	3	0	10
Daily Average Max.°F	28	30	39	50	61	68	72	70	60	48	38	32	50
Extreme Monthly Min.°C	-29	-28	-23	-15	-3	1	6	3	-3	-11	-17	-23	-29
Extreme Monthly Min.°F	-21	-18	-10	5	26	33	42	37	26	12	2	-10	-21
Extreme Monthly Max.°C	12	14	17	24	28	34	33	31	25	21	14	12	33
Extreme Monthly Max.°F	53	57	63	75	83	93	91	88	77	70	57	53	93
Monthly Average °C	-5	-5	0	4	11	15	16	15	11	6	1	-3	6
Monthly Average °F	24	24	31	40	51	59	62	60	52	43	34	27	42
RELATIVE HUMIDITY (%)	82	75	65	56	51	54	57	61	65	72	82	85	67
PRECIPITATION													
Monthly Average mm	47	31	41	40	54	64	83	85	84	84	76	58	747.0
Monthly Average Inches	1.8	1.2	1.6	1.5	2.1	2.5	3.2	3.3	3.3	3.3	2.9	2.2	28.9
Days of 1mm or More	9	6	8	7	8	9	10	10	11	10	10	8	106

TROMSO   Norway

	Elevation 102 m. (335 ft.)					69°39'N—18°57'E							
	JAN	FEB	MAR	APR	MAY	JUN	JUL	AUG	SEP	OCT	NOV	DEC	YEAR
TEMPERATURE													
Daily Average Min.°F	22	21	23	28	35	42	48	47	41	34	28	25	33
Daily Average Max.°C	-2	-2	0	3	7	12	16	14	10	5	2	-1	5
Daily Average Max.°F	29	28	31	37	44	54	61	57	50	41	35	31	42
Monthly Average °C	-4	-4	-2	1	5	9	12	10	7	3	0	-3	3
Monthly Average °F	25	25	28	34	41	48	53	51	44	38	31	27	37
RELATIVE HUMIDITY (%)	79	77	73	68	68	69	72	75	75	78	80	79	74
PRECIPITATION													
Monthly Average mm	99	93	79	57	44	58	71	80	103	131	96	98	1009.0
Monthly Average Inches	3.8	3.6	3.1	2.2	1.7	2.2	2.7	3.1	4.0	5.1	3.7	3.8	39.0
Days of 1mm or More	13	12	12	10	8	10	12	12	14	16	14	14	147

SALALAH   Oman

	Elevation 17 m. (55 ft.)					17°3'N—54°6'E							
	JAN	FEB	MAR	APR	MAY	JUN	JUL	AUG	SEP	OCT	NOV	DEC	YEAR
TEMPERATURE													
Daily Average Min.°C	18	19	21	23	25	26	24	23	23	21	20	19	22
Daily Average Min.°F	64	66	69	73	77	79	75	74	74	69	68	67	71
Daily Average Max.°C	27	28	30	31	32	32	28	27	29	31	30	28	29
Daily Average Max.°F	81	82	86	88	90	89	82	81	84	87	86	83	85
Monthly Average °C	23	23	25	27	29	29	26	25	26	26	25	24	26
Monthly Average °F	73	74	77	81	84	84	79	77	79	78	77	75	78
RELATIVE HUMIDITY (%)	51♦	52	56	61	68	74	85	85	72	60	55	50	64
PRECIPITATION													
Monthly Average mm	0	1	5	7	9	12	28	25	4	8	1	4	104.0
Monthly Average Inches	0.0	0.0	0.1	0.2	0.3	0.4	1.1	0.9	0.1	0.3	0.0	0.1	3.5
Days of 1mm or More	0	0	0	0	0	0	0	0	2	0	1	0	3

KARACHI   Pakistan

	Elevation 4 m. (13 ft.)					24°48'N—66°59'E							
	JAN	FEB	MAR	APR	MAY	JUN	JUL	AUG	SEP	OCT	NOV	DEC	YEAR
TEMPERATURE													
Daily Average Min.°C	13	14	19	23	26	28	27	26	25	22	18	14	21
Daily Average Min.°F	55	58	67	73	79	82	81	79	77	72	64	57	70
Daily Average Max.°C	25	26	29	32	34	34	33	31	31	33	31	27	30
Daily Average Max.°F	77	79	85	90	93	93	91	88	88	91	87	80	87
Extreme Monthly Min.°C	4	6	8	14	18	20	23	23	21	14	9	4	3
Extreme Monthly Min.°F	40	43	47	57	65	68	73	73	69	57	48	39	39
Extreme Monthly Max.°C	32	34	41	44	48	46	43	37	41	42	38	33	47
Extreme Monthly Max.°F	89	93	106	111	118	114	110	99	106	108	100	91	118
Monthly Average °C	18	20	24	28	31	31	30	29	29	28	24	19	26
Monthly Average °F	64	68	76	83	87	88	87	84	84	82	75	67	79
RELATIVE HUMIDITY (%)	45	49	57	62	68	69	73	74	71	57	49	45	60
PRECIPITATION													
Monthly Average mm	6	7	13	4	0	6	92	61	20	4	5	7	225.0
Monthly Average Inches	0.2	0.2	0.5	0.1	0.0	0.2	3.6	2.4	0.7	0.1	0.1	0.2	8.3
Days of 1mm or More	0	0	0	0	0	0	3	3	0	0	0	0	6

LAHORE   Pakistan

	JAN	FEB	MAR	APR	MAY	JUN	JUL	AUG	SEP	OCT	NOV	DEC	YEAR
Elevation 214 m. (702 ft.)					31°35'N—74°20'E								

TEMPERATURE

	JAN	FEB	MAR	APR	MAY	JUN	JUL	AUG	SEP	OCT	NOV	DEC	YEAR
Daily Average Min.°C	4	7	12	17	22	26	27	26	23	15	8	4	16
Daily Average Min.°F	40	44	53	63	72	79	80	78	73	59	47	40	61
Daily Average Max.°C	21	22	28	35	40	41	38	36	36	35	28	23	32
Daily Average Max.°F	69	72	83	95	104	106	100	97	97	95	83	73	90
Monthly Average °C	13	15	21	27	31	34	32	31	30	26	19	14	24
Monthly Average °F	55	60	69	80	88	93	89	87	85	78	67	57	76
RELATIVE HUMIDITY (%)	46	41	29	23	20	22	50	58	43	33	41	49	39

PRECIPITATION

	JAN	FEB	MAR	APR	MAY	JUN	JUL	AUG	SEP	OCT	NOV	DEC	YEAR
Monthly Average mm	25	24	37	18	22	35	194	156	69	13	4	16	613.0
Monthly Average Inches	0.9	0.9	1.4	0.7	0.8	1.3	7.6	6.1	2.7	0.5	0.1	0.6	23.6
Days of 1mm or More	2	3	3	2	3	3	8	8	3	1	0	1	37

PANJGUR   Pakistan

	JAN	FEB	MAR	APR	MAY	JUN	JUL	AUG	SEP	OCT	NOV	DEC	YEAR
Elevation 969 m. (3179 ft.)					26°58'N—64°06'E								

TEMPERATURE

	JAN	FEB	MAR	APR	MAY	JUN	JUL	AUG	SEP	OCT	NOV	DEC	YEAR
Monthly Average °C	10	13	18	24	28	32	32	31	27	22	16	12	22
Monthly Average °F	51	56	65	74	83	89	89	87	81	72	62	53	72

PRECIPITATION

	JAN	FEB	MAR	APR	MAY	JUN	JUL	AUG	SEP	OCT	NOV	DEC	YEAR
Monthly Average mm	14	15	16	7	3	3	25	8	2	0	1	10	104.0
Monthly Average Inches	0.5	0.5	0.6	0.2	0.1	0.1	0.9	0.3	0.0	0.0	0.0	0.3	3.5
Days of 1mm or More	1	2	1	1	0	0	1	0	0	0	0	1	7

PESHAWAR   Pakistan

	JAN	FEB	MAR	APR	MAY	JUN	JUL	AUG	SEP	OCT	NOV	DEC	YEAR
Elevation 354 m. (1161 ft.)					34°1'N—71°34'E								

TEMPERATURE

	JAN	FEB	MAR	APR	MAY	JUN	JUL	AUG	SEP	OCT	NOV	DEC	YEAR
Daily Average Min.°C	4	6	11	16	21	25	26	26	22	14	8	4	15
Daily Average Min.°F	40	43	52	60	70	77	79	78	71	58	46	39	59
Daily Average Max.°C	17	19	24	29	37	41	39	37	36	31	25	19	30
Daily Average Max.°F	63	66	75	85	98	106	103	99	96	88	77	67	85
Monthly Average °C	11	13	17	23	28	33	32	31	29	24	17	13	23
Monthly Average °F	52	56	63	73	83	92	90	88	84	75	63	55	73
RELATIVE HUMIDITY (%)	45	43	43	39	8	25	38	45	39	32	40	42	38

PRECIPITATION

	JAN	FEB	MAR	APR	MAY	JUN	JUL	AUG	SEP	OCT	NOV	DEC	YEAR
Monthly Average mm	25	42	75	51	27	7	42	69	18	9	17	25	407.0
Monthly Average Inches	0.9	1.6	2.9	2.0	1.0	0.2	1.6	2.7	0.7	0.3	0.6	0.9	15.4
Days of 1mm or More	2	4	6	5	3	1	3	4	2	1	1	2	34

CRISTOBAL
Panama (Canal Zone)

	Elevation 11 m. (35 ft.)						9°21'N—79°54'W						
	JAN	FEB	MAR	APR	MAY	JUN	JUL	AUG	SEP	OCT	NOV	DEC	YEAR
TEMPERATURE													
Daily Average Min.°C 24	24	25	25	24	24	24	24	24	24	24	24	24
Daily Average Min.°F 76	76	77	77	78	76	76	76	75	75	75	76	76
Daily Average Max.°C 29	29	29	30	30	30	29	29	30	30	29	29	30
Daily Average Max.°F 84	85	85	86	86	86	85	85	86	86	84	85	85
Extreme Monthly Min.°C 21	21	19	22	22	20	21	21	21	21	21	19	18
Extreme Monthly Min.°F 70	69	67	72	71	68	70	70	70	70	69	66	66
Extreme Monthly Max.°C 31	32	33	34	35	34	33	34	34	35	33	32	35
Extreme Monthly Max.°F 88	90	92	94	95	93	91	93	94	95	92	90	95
Monthly Average °C 27	27	27	28	27	27	27	27	27	27	26	27	27
Monthly Average °F 80	80	81	82	81	81	81	81	81	80	80	80	81
RELATIVE HUMIDITY (%)	81	81	80	82	87	88	88	88	88	89	88	85	85
PRECIPITATION													
Monthly Average mm 75	38	39	93	314	308	389	383	320	431	645	380	3415.0
Monthly Average Inches 2.9	1.4	1.5	3.6	12.3	12.1	15.3	15.0	12.6	16.9	25.4	14.9	133.9
Days of 1mm or More 0	0	0	0	0	0	0	0	0	0	0	0	0

MADANG
Papua New Guinea

	Elevation 6 m. (20 ft.)						5°14'S—145°45'E						
	JAN	FEB	MAR	APR	MAY	JUN	JUL	AUG	SEP	OCT	NOV	DEC	YEAR
TEMPERATURE													
Daily Average Min.°C 24	24	23	23	24	23	23	23	23	24	24	24	24
Daily Average Min.°F 75	75	74	74	75	74	74	74	74	75	75	75	75
Daily Average Max.°C 31	30	31	31	31	31	31	31	31	31	31	31	31
Daily Average Max.°F 87	86	87	88	88	88	88	88	88	88	88	88	88
Extreme Monthly Min.°C 21	21	21	21	21	21	17	21	20	20	21	20	16
Extreme Monthly Min.°F 70	70	70	70	70	69	62	70	68	68	70	68	62
Extreme Monthly Max.°C 34	33	34	34	36	36	37	33	34	34	34	34	36
Extreme Monthly Max.°F 94	92	93	93	96	96	98	92	93	93	93	93	98
Monthly Average °C 26	26	27	27	27	27	26	26	27	27	27	27	27
Monthly Average °F 79	80	80	80	80	80	79	80	80	80	80	80	80
RELATIVE HUMIDITY (%)	78	78	77	77	75	75	74	74	75	74	75	77	76
PRECIPITATION													
Monthly Average mm 362	309	359	427	373	193	164	145	135	280	336	412	3495.0
Monthly Average Inches 14.2	12.1	14.1	16.8	14.6	7.6	6.4	5.7	5.3	11.0	13.2	16.2	137.2
Days of 1mm or More 18	17	19	19	19	14	11	10	9	13	17	19	185

PORT MORESBY
Papua New Guinea

	Elevation 38 m. (126 ft.)						9°29'S—147°9'E						
	JAN	FEB	MAR	APR	MAY	JUN	JUL	AUG	SEP	OCT	NOV	DEC	YEAR
TEMPERATURE													
Daily Average Min.°C 24	24	24	24	24	23	23	23	23	24	24	24	24
Daily Average Min.°F 76	76	76	75	74	74	73	73	74	75	76	76	75
Daily Average Max.°C 32	31	31	31	30	29	28	28	29	30	31	32	30
Daily Average Max.°F 89	87	88	87	86	84	83	82	84	86	88	90	86
Extreme Monthly Min.°C 21	-13	21	18	21	18	19	19	19	20	21	21	17
Extreme Monthly Min.°F 69	9	70	65	70	64	66	66	66	68	69	70	64
Extreme Monthly Max.°C 37	36	36	36	34	33	32	32	34	34	34	36	36
Extreme Monthly Max.°F 98	96	96	96	94	91	90	90	94	94	96	97	98
Monthly Average °C 27	27	27	27	27	26	26	26	26	27	28	28	27
Monthly Average °F 81	81	81	81	81	79	78	79	80	81	82	82	80
RELATIVE HUMIDITY (%)	69	72	73	74	77	77	78	77	77	76	73	69	74
PRECIPITATION													
Monthly Average mm 282	189	219	110	63	48	22	24	45	35	48	127	1212.0
Monthly Average Inches 11.1	7.4	8.6	4.3	2.4	1.8	0.8	0.9	1.7	1.3	1.8	5.0	47.1
Days of 1mm or More 15	15	15	8	7	4	3	3	4	4	4	9	91

ASUNCION   Paraguay

	JAN	FEB	MAR	APR	MAY	JUN	JUL	AUG	SEP	OCT	NOV	DEC	YEAR
			Elevation 139 m. (456 ft.)			25°17'S—57°30'W							

TEMPERATURE

	JAN	FEB	MAR	APR	MAY	JUN	JUL	AUG	SEP	OCT	NOV	DEC	YEAR
Daily Average Min.°C	22	22	21	18	14	12	12	14	16	17	18	21	17
Daily Average Min.°F	71	71	69	65	58	53	53	57	60	62	65	70	63
Daily Average Max.°C	35	34	33	29	25	22	23	26	28	30	32	34	29
Daily Average Max.°F	95	94	92	84	77	72	74	78	83	86	90	94	85
Extreme Monthly Min.°C	12	11	9	6	1	-2	-2	-1	3	3	7	8	-1
Extreme Monthly Min.°F	54	52	49	42	34	29	29	30	37	38	45	47	29
Extreme Monthly Max.°C	43	43	41	40	37	37	39	38	41	41	42	43	43
Extreme Monthly Max.°F	109	109	106	104	99	98	103	101	105	106	108	110	110
Monthly Average °C	28	28	26	23	20	18	19	19	21	24	25	27	23
Monthly Average °F	83	82	79	73	69	65	66	66	70	75	78	81	74
RELATIVE HUMIDITY (%)	56	55	55	59	62	61	56	53	48	50	53	50	54

PRECIPITATION

	JAN	FEB	MAR	APR	MAY	JUN	JUL	AUG	SEP	OCT	NOV	DEC	YEAR
Monthly Average mm	142	157	140	162	106	67	46	64	79	112	168	141	1384.0
Monthly Average Inches	5.5	6.1	5.5	6.3	4.1	2.6	1.8	2.5	3.1	4.4	6.6	5.5	54.0
Days of 1mm or More	6	6	6	6	5	4	4	5	5	6	6	7	66

CUZCO   Peru

	JAN	FEB	MAR	APR	MAY	JUN	JUL	AUG	SEP	OCT	NOV	DEC	YEAR
			Elevation 3226 m. (10,581 ft.)			13°33'S—71°55'W							

TEMPERATURE

	JAN	FEB	MAR	APR	MAY	JUN	JUL	AUG	SEP	OCT	NOV	DEC	YEAR
Daily Average Min.°C	7	7	7	4	2	1	-1	1	4	6	6	7	4
Daily Average Min.°F	45	45	44	40	35	33	31	34	40	43	43	44	40
Daily Average Max.°C	20	21	21	22	21	21	21	21	22	22	23	22	21
Daily Average Max.°F	68	69	70	71	70	69	70	70	71	72	73	71	70
Extreme Monthly Min.°C	3	2	2	-4	-4	-5	-9	-5	-1	-1	1	1	-8
Extreme Monthly Min.°F	37	36	35	25	24	23	16	23	30	30	33	34	16
Extreme Monthly Max.°C	28	27	26	26	26	25	25	25	27	29	28	27	28
Extreme Monthly Max.°F	82	81	79	79	78	77	77	77	81	84	82	81	84
Monthly Average °C	13	13	13	12	11	10	10	11	12	13	14	13	12
Monthly Average °F	55	55	55	54	52	49	49	51	54	56	57	56	54
RELATIVE HUMIDITY (%)	40	37	31	33	29	23	23	24	26	27	26	33	29

PRECIPITATION

	JAN	FEB	MAR	APR	MAY	JUN	JUL	AUG	SEP	OCT	NOV	DEC	YEAR
Monthly Average mm	162	120	98	42	7	1	4	8	21	50	76	120	709.0
Monthly Average Inches	6.3	4.7	3.8	1.6	0.2	0.0	0.1	0.3	0.8	1.9	2.9	4.7	27.3
Days of 1mm or More	18	15	13	7	2	0	1	1	4	8	12	15	96

IQUITOS   Peru

	JAN	FEB	MAR	APR	MAY	JUN	JUL	AUG	SEP	OCT	NOV	DEC	YEAR
			Elevation 126 m. (413 ft.)			3°46'S—73°15'W							

TEMPERATURE

	JAN	FEB	MAR	APR	MAY	JUN	JUL	AUG	SEP	OCT	NOV	DEC	YEAR
Monthly Average °C	27	27	26	26	26	26	25	26	26	27	27	27	26
Monthly Average °F	80	80	79	79	79	78	78	79	79	80	80	80	79

PRECIPITATION

	JAN	FEB	MAR	APR	MAY	JUN	JUL	AUG	SEP	OCT	NOV	DEC	YEAR
Monthly Average mm	266	212	298	320	285	192	179	168	209	253	262	292	2936.0
Monthly Average Inches	10.4	8.3	11.7	12.6	11.2	7.5	7.0	6.6	8.2	9.9	10.3	11.5	115.2
Days of 1mm or More	15	12	12	14	13	11	11	10	9	11	11	12	141

LIMA　　　　　　　　　　　　　　　　　　　　　　　　Peru

	Elevation 120 m. (394 ft.)					12°5'S—77°3'W							
	JAN	FEB	MAR	APR	MAY	JUN	JUL	AUG	SEP	OCT	NOV	DEC	YEAR
TEMPERATURE													
Daily Average Min.°C	19	19	19	17	16	14	14	13	14	14	16	17	16
Daily Average Min.°F	66	67	66	63	60	58	57	56	57	58	60	62	61
Daily Average Max.°C	28	28	28	27	23	20	19	19	20	22	23	26	24
Daily Average Max.°F	82	83	83	80	74	68	67	66	68	71	74	78	75
Extreme Monthly Min.°C	15	15	16	13	11	9	9	10	11	12	11	13	9
Extreme Monthly Min.°F	59	59	61	56	52	49	49	50	51	53	51	56	49
Extreme Monthly Max.°C	32	33	33	34	29	27	27	27	26	26	29	31	33
Extreme Monthly Max.°F	89	92	91	93	84	81	81	81	78	79	85	87	93
Monthly Average °C	21	22	22	20	18	16	15	15	15	16	18	19	18
Monthly Average °F	70	72	72	69	64	61	60	59	59	61	64	67	65
RELATIVE HUMIDITY (%)	69	66	64	66	76	80	77	78	76	72	71	70	72
PRECIPITATION													
Monthly Average mm	0	0	0	0	0	1	2	2	2	0	0	0	7.0
Monthly Average Inches	0.0	0.0	0.0	0.0	0.0	0.0	0.0	0.0	0.0	0.0	0.0	0.0	0.0
Days of 1mm or More	0	0	0	0	0	0	0	0	0	0	0	0	0

TRUJILLO　　　　　　　　　　　　　　　　　　　　　Peru

	Elevation 26 m. (85 ft.)					8°7'S—79°2'W							
	JAN	FEB	MAR	APR	MAY	JUN	JUL	AUG	SEP	OCT	NOV	DEC	YEAR
TEMPERATURE													
Monthly Average °C	21	22	22	20	19	18	18	17	17	17	18	20	19
Monthly Average °F	70	72	72	69	66	64	64	62	63	63	65	67	66
PRECIPITATION													
Monthly Average mm	8	1	17	0	0	0	0	0	0	0	0	0	26.0
Monthly Average Inches	0.3	0.0	0.6	0.0	0.0	0.0	0.0	0.0	0.0	0.0	0.0	0.0	0.9
Days of 1mm or More	0	0	1	0	0	0	0	0	0	0	0	0	1

APARRI　　　　　　　　　　　　　　　　　　Philippines

	Elevation 5 m. (17 ft.)					18°22'N—121°38'E							
	JAN	FEB	MAR	APR	MAY	JUN	JUL	AUG	SEP	OCT	NOV	DEC	YEAR
TEMPERATURE													
Daily Average Min.°C	20	21	22	23	24	24	24	24	24	23	23	21	23
Daily Average Min.°F	68	69	71	73	75	76	76	76	75	74	73	70	73
Daily Average Max.°C	27	28	30	32	34	34	33	33	32	30	28	27	31
Daily Average Max.°F	81	83	86	90	93	93	91	91	90	86	83	81	87
Monthly Average °C	23	24	25	28	29	29	29	28	28	27	26	24	27
Monthly Average °F	73	75	78	82	84	85	84	83	82	81	78	76	80
RELATIVE HUMIDITY (%)	74	70	69	66	67	65	69	69	71	75	78	77	71
PRECIPITATION													
Monthly Average mm	139	76	45	36	118	147	183	212	235	334	335	205	2065.0
Monthly Average Inches	5.4	2.9	1.7	1.4	4.6	5.7	7.2	8.3	9.2	13.1	13.1	8.0	80.6
Days of 1mm or More	12	7	4	3	8	11	11	13	11	15	17	17	129

ILOILO

Philippines

	Elevation 14 m. (45 ft.)					10°42'N—122°34'E							
	JAN	FEB	MAR	APR	MAY	JUN	JUL	AUG	SEP	OCT	NOV	DEC	YEAR
TEMPERATURE													
Daily Average Min.°C	23	23	23	24	25	24	24	24	24	24	24	23	24
Daily Average Min.°F	73	74	74	76	77	76	76	76	76	75	75	74	75
Daily Average Max.°C	29	31	31	33	33	32	31	31	31	31	31	30	31
Daily Average Max.°F	85	87	88	92	91	89	87	87	88	88	87	86	88
Monthly Average °C	26	26	27	29	29	28	27	27	27	27	27	27	27
Monthly Average °F	79	79	81	83	84	82	81	81	81	81	81	80	81
RELATIVE HUMIDITY (%)	68	63	59	59	67	71	75	74	75	73	72	70	69
PRECIPITATION													
Monthly Average mm	41	21	36	50	103	289	323	336	267	247	176	79	1968.0
Monthly Average Inches	1.6	0.8	1.4	1.9	4.0	11.3	12.7	13.2	10.5	9.7	6.9	3.1	77.1
Days of 1mm or More	7	4	3	4	7	17	18	18	17	17	12	10	134

MANILA

Philippines

	Elevation 16 m. (52 ft.)					14°35'N—120°59'E							
	JAN	FEB	MAR	APR	MAY	JUN	JUL	AUG	SEP	OCT	NOV	DEC	YEAR
TEMPERATURE													
Daily Average Min.°C	21	21	22	23	24	24	24	24	24	23	22	21	23
Daily Average Min.°F	69	69	71	73	75	75	75	75	75	74	72	70	73
Daily Average Max.°C	30	31	33	34	34	33	31	31	31	31	31	30	32
Daily Average Max.°F	86	88	91	93	93	91	88	87	88	88	87	86	89
Extreme Monthly Min.°C	14	16	16	17	20	22	21	21	21	19	17	16	14
Extreme Monthly Min.°F	58	60	61	63	68	71	69	69	69	67	62	60	58
Extreme Monthly Max.°C	35	36	37	38	38	38	36	35	35	35	34	34	38
Extreme Monthly Max.°F	95	96	98	100	101	100	97	95	95	95	93	94	101
Monthly Average °C	26	26	27	29	29	29	28	27	28	27	27	26	27
Monthly Average °F	78	79	81	84	85	83	82	81	82	81	80	78	81
RELATIVE HUMIDITY (%)	63	59	55	55	61	68	74	73	73	71	69	67	66
PRECIPITATION													
Monthly Average mm	15	3	5	13	110	258	356	389	301	216	97	53	1816.0
Monthly Average Inches	0.5	0.1	0.1	0.5	4.3	10.1	14.0	15.3	11.8	8.5	3.8	2.0	71.0
Days of 1mm or More	2	0	1	1	6	16	19	21	18	14	11	6	115

Pitcairn Island

	Elevation 73 m. (240 ft.)					25°4'S—130°4'W							
	JAN	FEB	MAR	APR	MAY	JUN	JUL	AUG	SEP	OCT	NOV	DEC	YEAR
TEMPERATURE													
Daily Average Min.°C	22	23	22	21	20	24	18	18	18	18	19	21	20
Daily Average Min.°F	71	74	72	69	68	76	64	64	64	65	67	70	68
Daily Average Max.°C	28	28	28	26	25	23	22	22	3	24	26	27	24
Daily Average Max.°F	82	83	83	79	77	74	72	72	73	75	78	80	77
Monthly Average °C	23	24	23	22	21	20	19	18	19	20	21	22	21
Monthly Average °F	74	74	74	72	69	67	66	65	66	67	69	72	70
RELATIVE HUMIDITY (%)	83	82	80	78	84	81	84	82	80	79	84	85	82
PRECIPITATION													
Monthly Average mm	124	149	129	142	132	159	144	124	136	155	130	134	1658.0
Monthly Average Inches	4.8	5.8	5.0	5.5	5.1	6.2	5.6	4.8	5.3	6.1	5.1	5.2	64.5
Days of 1mm or More	0	0	0	0	0	0	0	0	0	0	0	0	0

BRESLAU (WROCLAW)   Poland

Elevation 119 m. (390 ft.)   51°6'N—17°0'E

	JAN	FEB	MAR	APR	MAY	JUN	JUL	AUG	SEP	OCT	NOV	DEC	YEAR
TEMPERATURE													
Monthly Average °C	-4	-2	1	10	12	17	18	17	14	9	5	-3	8
Monthly Average °F	25	29	35	50	54	63	65	63	57	48	41	28	46
PRECIPITATION													
Monthly Average mm	16	32	35	35	80	71	53	82	37	37	47	25	550.0
Monthly Average Inches	0.6	1.2	1.3	1.3	3.1	2.7	2.0	3.2	1.4	1.4	1.8	0.9	20.9
Days of 1mm or More	5	8	7	7	11	8	9	8	7	8	11	6	95

GDANSK   Poland

Elevation 9 m. (29 ft.)   54°23'N—18°40'E

	JAN	FEB	MAR	APR	MAY	JUN	JUL	AUG	SEP	OCT	NOV	DEC	YEAR
TEMPERATURE													
Monthly Average °C	-1	-6	2	6	13	14	17	17	12	10	3	0	7
Monthly Average °F	30	22	35	43	55	58	63	63	54	49	38	32	45
PRECIPITATION													
Monthly Average mm	43	17	31	42	75	71	49	76	75	26	36	39	580.0
Monthly Average Inches	1.6	0.6	1.2	1.6	2.9	2.7	1.9	2.9	2.9	1.0	1.4	1.5	22.2
Days of 1mm or More	12	6	8	8	9	10	7	8	11	6	9	8	102

SZCZECIN   Poland

Elevation 7 m. (22 ft.)   53°24'N—14°36'E

	JAN	FEB	MAR	APR	MAY	JUN	JUL	AUG	SEP	OCT	NOV	DEC	YEAR
TEMPERATURE													
Daily Average Min.°C	-3	-5	-1	2	7	11	13	13	9	6	2	-1	4
Daily Average Min.°F	26	24	30	36	45	51	56	55	49	42	35	29	40
Daily Average Max.°C	2	2	7	12	18	22	23	23	19	13	7	3	13
Daily Average Max.°F	35	36	45	53	65	71	74	73	66	55	44	38	54
Monthly Average °C	-1	-1	3	7	13	16	18	17	14	9	4	1	8
Monthly Average °F	29	31	37	45	55	61	64	63	57	49	40	33	47
RELATIVE HUMIDITY (%)	82	78	66	63	56	59	64	64	65	75	82	85	70
PRECIPITATION													
Monthly Average mm	35	25	29	38	55	54	64	57	43	41	43	42	526.0
Monthly Average Inches	1.3	0.9	1.1	1.4	2.1	2.1	2.5	2.2	1.6	1.6	1.6	1.6	20.0
Days of 1mm or More	9	6	7	8	9	8	9	8	8	7	10	9	98

WARSAW   Poland

	JAN	FEB	MAR	APR	MAY	JUN	JUL	AUG	SEP	OCT	NOV	DEC	YEAR
Elevation 107 m. (351 ft.)					**52°12'N—21°0'E**								
TEMPERATURE													
Daily Average Min.°C	-6	-6	-2	3	9	12	15	14	10	5	1	-3	4
Daily Average Min.°F	22	21	28	37	48	54	58	56	49	41	33	28	40
Daily Average Max.°C	0	0	6	12	20	23	24	23	19	13	6	2	12
Daily Average Max.°F	31	33	42	53	67	73	75	73	66	55	42	35	54
Extreme Monthly Min.°C	-30	-22	-20	-4	-1	3	7	5	0	-8	-17	-21	-30
Extreme Monthly Min.°F	-22	-8	-4	24	30	37	44	41	32	17	1	-5	-22
Extreme Monthly Max.°C	10	12	21	24	34	32	35	37	31	25	16	11	36
Extreme Monthly Max.°F	50	54	69	75	93	90	95	98	88	77	60	51	98
Monthly Average °C	-4	-3	2	8	13	17	18	17	13	8	3	-1	8
Monthly Average °F	25	27	35	46	56	62	64	63	56	47	38	30	46
RELATIVE HUMIDITY (%)	84	80	70	61	56	59	63	63	64	73	83	87	70
PRECIPITATION													
Monthly Average mm	22	21	27	32	59	70	69	58	39	39	38	32	506.0
Monthly Average Inches	0.8	0.8	1.0	1.2	2.3	2.7	2.7	2.2	1.5	1.5	1.4	1.2	19.3
Days of 1mm or More	6	5	6	6	9	9	9	8	7	7	8	8	88

BRAGANCA   Portugal

	JAN	FEB	MAR	APR	MAY	JUN	JUL	AUG	SEP	OCT	NOV	DEC	YEAR
Elevation 720 m. (2362 ft.)					**41°48'N—6°48'W**								
TEMPERATURE													
Daily Average Min.°C	0	1	3	5	7	11	13	13	10	7	3	1	6
Daily Average Min.°F	0	33	38	40	45	51	55	55	50	44	38	33	40
Daily Average Max.°C	8	11	13	16	19	24	28	28	24	18	12	8	17
Daily Average Max.°F	46	51	55	60	65	75	82	83	74	64	53	46	63
Extreme Monthly Min.°C	-12	-9	-4	-2	-2	3	3	1	1	-3	-6	-8	-12
Extreme Monthly Min.°F	10	16	24	29	28	38	37	33	33	26	22	17	10
Extreme Monthly Max.°C	8	18	25	28	31	36	39	37	33	28	22	17	39
Extreme Monthly Max.°F	46	65	77	83	88	96	103	99	92	82	72	62	103
Monthly Average °C	5	6	8	10	14	18	21	20	17	13	8	4	12
Monthly Average °F	40	42	46	50	56	64	70	69	63	56	46	40	53
RELATIVE HUMIDITY (%)	80	73	68	59	59	53	47	47	55	66	74	81	64
PRECIPITATION													
Monthly Average mm	125	102	75	56	55	40	15	10	35	55	88	67	723.0
Monthly Average Inches	4.9	4.0	2.9	2.2	2.1	1.5	0.5	0.3	1.3	2.1	3.4	2.6	27.8
Days of 1mm or More	12	9	8	7	11	5	2	2	5	6	8	5	80

FARO   Portugal

	JAN	FEB	MAR	APR	MAY	JUN	JUL	AUG	SEP	OCT	NOV	DEC	YEAR
Elevation 36 m. (118 ft.)					**37°0'N—8°0'W**								
TEMPERATURE													
Daily Average Min.°C	9	10	11	13	14	18	20	20	19	16	13	10	14
Daily Average Min.°F	48	49	52	55	58	64	67	68	65	60	55	50	58
Daily Average Max.°C	15	16	18	20	22	25	28	28	26	22	19	16	21
Daily Average Max.°F	60	61	64	67	71	77	83	83	78	72	66	61	70
Monthly Average °C	12	12	13	15	18	21	23	24	21	19	15	12	17
Monthly Average °F	54	54	56	59	65	69	74	75	71	66	58	54	63
RELATIVE HUMIDITY (%)	72	70	72	67	67	65	62	63	66	68	70	70	68
PRECIPITATION													
Monthly Average mm	94	69	51	38	23	16	0	1	10	51	70	76	499.0
Monthly Average Inches	3.7	2.7	2.0	1.4	0.9	0.6	0.0	0.0	0.3	2.0	2.7	2.9	19.2
Days of 1mm or More	7	9	7	4	4	1	0	0	1	4	6	4	47

LISBON   Portugal

	Elevation 77 m. (253 ft.)						38°42'N—9°6'W						
	JAN	FEB	MAR	APR	MAY	JUN	JUL	AUG	SEP	OCT	NOV	DEC	YEAR
TEMPERATURE													
Daily Average Min.°C	8	8	10	12	13	15	17	17	17	14	11	9	13
Daily Average Min.°F	46	47	50	53	55	60	63	63	62	58	52	47	55
Daily Average Max.°C	14	15	17	20	21	25	27	28	26	22	17	15	21
Daily Average Max.°F	57	59	63	67	71	77	81	82	79	72	63	58	69
Extreme Monthly Min.°C	-1	-2	1	4	6	9	11	13	11	6	1	-1	-1
Extreme Monthly Min.°F	30	29	34	40	42	49	52	55	51	43	34	31	29
Extreme Monthly Max.°C	19	23	28	31	34	37	39	38	37	32	25	19	39
Extreme Monthly Max.°F	66	73	83	87	94	99	103	100	99	89	77	66	103
Monthly Average °C	11	12	15	15	17	21	22	23	23	18	15	12	17
Monthly Average °F	52	54	58	60	63	69	72	73	73	65	60	54	63
RELATIVE HUMIDITY (%)	72	66	63	58	57	53	48	46	53	59	68	72	60
PRECIPITATION													
Monthly Average mm	94	112	36	73	40	12	3	7	25	51	128	89	670.0
Monthly Average Inches	3.7	4.4	1.4	2.8	1.5	0.4	0.1	0.2	0.9	2.0	5.0	3.5	25.9
Days of 1mm or More	8	10	5	8	5	2	0	1	3	8	9	10	69

PORTO   Portugal

	Elevation 95 m. (312 ft.)						41°8'N—8°36'W						
	JAN	FEB	MAR	APR	MAY	JUN	JUL	AUG	SEP	OCT	NOV	DEC	YEAR
TEMPERATURE													
Daily Average Min.°C	5	5	8	9	11	13	15	15	14	11	8	5	10
Daily Average Min.°F	40	41	46	48	51	56	58	58	56	51	46	42	50
Daily Average Max.°C	13	14	16	18	20	23	25	25	24	21	17	14	19
Daily Average Max.°F	56	58	61	65	67	73	76	77	75	69	62	57	66
Monthly Average °C	9	10	11	13	15	17	19	19	18	16	12	10	14
Monthly Average °F	49	50	52	55	59	63	67	66	64	61	53	49	57
RELATIVE HUMIDITY (%)	69	65	65	61	64	65	60	60	63	64	68	70	64
PRECIPITATION													
Monthly Average mm	180	180	136	97	86	54	13	18	60	122	138	175	1259.0
Monthly Average Inches	7.0	7.0	5.3	3.8	3.3	2.1	0.5	0.7	2.3	4.8	5.4	6.8	49.0
Days of 1mm or More	15	15	13	9	9	6	2	2	6	9	11	12	109

ARECIBO   Puerto Rico

	Elevation 5 m. (16 ft.)						18°28'N—66°43'W						
	JAN	FEB	MAR	APR	MAY	JUN	JUL	AUG	SEP	OCT	NOV	DEC	YEAR
TEMPERATURE													
Monthly Average °C	24	23	24	25	26	27	27	27	27	26	26	24	25
Monthly Average °F	74	74	75	77	79	80	80	81	80	80	78	76	78
PRECIPITATION													
Monthly Average mm	105	52	78	95	144	121	100	86	115	109	232	219	1456.0
Monthly Average Inches	4.1	2.0	3.0	3.7	5.6	4.7	3.9	3.3	4.5	4.2	9.1	8.6	56.7
Days of 1mm or More	0	0	0	0	0	0	0	0	0	0	0	0	0

PONCE   Puerto Rico

	Elevation 9 m. (29 ft.)					18°1'N—66°37'W							
	JAN	FEB	MAR	APR	MAY	JUN	JUL	AUG	SEP	OCT	NOV	DEC	YEAR
TEMPERATURE													
Monthly Average °C	25	25	25	26	27	28	28	28	27	27	26	25	26
Monthly Average °F	76	76	77	78	80	82	82	82	81	81	79	78	79
PRECIPITATION													
Monthly Average mm	22	15	26	23	87	72	70	128	116	153	102	26	840.0
Monthly Average Inches	0.8	0.5	1.0	0.9	3.4	2.8	2.7	5.0	4.5	6.0	4.0	1.0	32.6
Days of 1mm or More	0	0	0	0	0	0	0	0	0	0	0	0	0

SAN JUAN   Puerto Rico

	Elevation 25 m. (82 ft.)					18°29'N—60°7'W							
	JAN	FEB	MAR	APR	MAY	JUN	JUL	AUG	SEP	OCT	NOV	DEC	YEAR
TEMPERATURE													
Daily Average Min.°C	21	21	21	22	23	24	24	24	24	24	23	22	23
Daily Average Min.°F	70	70	70	72	74	75	75	76	75	75	73	72	73
Daily Average Max.°C	27	27	27	28	29	29	29	29	30	29	29	27	28
Daily Average Max.°F	80	80	81	82	84	85	85	85	86	85	84	81	83
Extreme Monthly Min.°C	17	17	17	18	19	19	21	20	21	20	19	17	16
Extreme Monthly Min.°F	63	62	63	65	66	66	70	68	69	68	66	62	62
Extreme Monthly Max.°C	31	33	33	34	34	34	33	34	34	34	34	32	34
Extreme Monthly Max.°F	88	91	91	93	94	93	92	93	94	94	93	90	94
Monthly Average °C	25	25	26	26	27	28	28	28	28	28	27	26	27
Monthly Average °F	77	77	78	79	81	82	82	82	82	82	80	78	80
RELATIVE HUMIDITY (%)	75	74	74	75	75	77	78	77	77	76	76	77	76
PRECIPITATION													
Monthly Average mm	69	50	53	93	152	109	115	137	135	148	150	118	1329.0
Monthly Average Inches	2.7	1.9	2.0	3.6	5.9	4.2	4.5	5.3	5.3	5.8	5.9	4.6	51.7
Days of 1mm or More	12	8	8	8	13	11	14	15	13	13	14	13	142

ST. DENIS   Reunion

	Elevation 10 m. (33 ft.)					20°54'S—55°31'E							
	JAN	FEB	MAR	APR	MAY	JUN	JUL	AUG	SEP	OCT	NOV	DEC	YEAR
TEMPERATURE													
Daily Average Min.°C	23	23	23	21	20	18	17	17	17	19	20	22	20
Daily Average Min.°F	73	73	73	70	67	65	63	63	63	66	68	71	68
Daily Average Max.°C	31	34	34	33	32	31	29	28	30	31	31	30	31
Daily Average Max.°F	88	93	93	91	90	87	84	83	86	88	88	87	88
Monthly Average °C	26	26	26	25	23	22	21	21	21	22	24	25	24
Monthly Average °F	79	79	79	77	74	71	70	70	71	72	75	78	74
RELATIVE HUMIDITY (%)	53	47	52	59	65	71	76	78	74	69	67	62	64
PRECIPITATION													
Monthly Average mm	319	270	249	191	93	78	73	62	43	42	84	164	1668.0
Monthly Average Inches	12.5	10.6	9.8	7.5	3.6	3.0	2.8	2.4	1.6	1.6	3.3	6.4	65.1
Days of 1mm or More	14	14	13	11	8	9	10	9	7	6	7	12	120

BUCHAREST

Romania

Elevation 92 m. (301 ft.)   44°30'N—26°6'E

	JAN	FEB	MAR	APR	MAY	JUN	JUL	AUG	SEP	OCT	NOV	DEC	YEAR
TEMPERATURE													
Daily Average Min.°C	-7	-5	-1	5	10	14	16	15	11	6	2	-3	5
Daily Average Min.°F	19	23	30	41	51	57	60	59	52	43	35	26	41
Daily Average Max.°C	1	4	10	18	23	27	30	30	25	18	10	4	17
Daily Average Max.°F	34	38	50	64	74	81	86	85	78	65	49	39	62
Extreme Monthly Min.°C	-28	-24	-14	-6	0	4	8	7	-2	-11	-18	-27	-27
Extreme Monthly Min.°F	-18	-12	6	22	32	40	46	44	29	13	0	-16	-18
Extreme Monthly Max.°C	16	22	27	33	36	41	41	41	36	31	29	21	40
Extreme Monthly Max.°F	61	72	80	91	96	105	105	105	97	88	85	69	105
Monthly Average °C	-2	0	4	11	17	21	22	22	18	12	6	1	11
Monthly Average °F	28	31	40	52	62	69	72	71	64	53	42	33	51
RELATIVE HUMIDITY (%)	87	84	73	63	63	62	58	59	63	73	85	89	72
PRECIPITATION													
Monthly Average mm	46	38	34	45	69	87	60	61	34	27	45	43	589.0
Monthly Average Inches	1.8	1.4	1.3	1.7	2.7	3.4	2.3	2.4	1.3	1.0	1.7	1.6	22.6
Days of 1mm or More	7	8	7	9	8	10	9	7	4	6	6	9	90

CLUJ

Romania

Elevation 315 m. (1033 ft.)   46°48'N—23°36'E

	JAN	FEB	MAR	APR	MAY	JUN	JUL	AUG	SEP	OCT	NOV	DEC	YEAR
TEMPERATURE													
Daily Average Min.°C	-8	-6	-2	4	9	12	14	13	8	4	0	-4	4
Daily Average Min.°F	18	20	29	38	48	54	56	55	47	39	32	25	38
Daily Average Max.°C	0	2	10	16	21	24	27	26	22	16	8	3	14
Daily Average Max.°F	32	36	49	60	71	75	80	78	71	61	47	37	58
Extreme Monthly Min.°C	-26	-32	-22	-8	-3	2	6	4	-2	-6	-12	-28	-32
Extreme Monthly Min.°F	-15	-26	-8	17	27	35	42	40	29	21	10	-18	-26
Extreme Monthly Max.°C	12	17	24	31	33	34	38	36	34	28	23	13	37
Extreme Monthly Max.°F	54	62	76	88	91	94	100	97	93	83	74	56	100
Monthly Average °C	-4	-2	4	9	14	17	19	18	14	9	4	-1	8
Monthly Average °F	24	29	38	49	58	63	66	64	57	48	38	30	47
RELATIVE HUMIDITY (%)	87	82	70	65	66	68	63	67	69	75	83	87	73
PRECIPITATION													
Monthly Average mm	29	27	24	43	74	79	85	67	30	34	30	32	554.0
Monthly Average Inches	1.1	1.0	0.9	1.6	2.9	3.1	3.3	2.6	1.1	1.3	1.1	1.2	21.2
Days of 1mm or More	6	6	5	9	11	11	10	9	6	6	7	8	94

CONSTANTA

Romania

Elevation 32 m. (104 ft.)   44°12'N—28°42'E

	JAN	FEB	MAR	APR	MAY	JUN	JUL	AUG	SEP	OCT	NOV	DEC	YEAR
TEMPERATURE													
Daily Average Min.°C	-4	-3	1	6	11	16	18	17	14	9	4	-1	7
Daily Average Min.°F	25	28	33	42	52	60	64	63	57	49	40	31	45
Daily Average Max.°C	3	4	8	13	19	24	27	27	23	17	11	6	15
Daily Average Max.°F	37	40	46	56	66	75	81	80	73	63	51	43	59
Extreme Monthly Min.°C	-21	-26	-13	-4	2	7	9	8	1	-12	-12	-17	-26
Extreme Monthly Min.°F	-5	-15	9	24	35	44	49	46	34	10	10	2	-15
Extreme Monthly Max.°C	17	23	24	29	33	34	38	37	34	33	26	21	38
Extreme Monthly Max.°F	62	73	76	84	92	94	101	98	93	91	78	70	101
Monthly Average °C	0	1	4	9	15	20	22	22	18	13	8	3	11
Monthly Average °F	33	34	39	49	59	68	72	72	65	56	47	38	53
RELATIVE HUMIDITY (%)	89	87	83	82	81	78	73	75	79	84	89	90	83
PRECIPITATION													
Monthly Average mm	39	40	22	31	42	40	29	22	25	30	39	44	403.0
Monthly Average Inches	1.5	1.5	0.8	1.2	1.6	1.5	1.1	0.8	0.9	1.1	1.5	1.7	15.2
Days of 1mm or More	0	0	4	0	0	0	0	0	0	0	0	0	4

JASSY   Romania

	JAN	FEB	MAR	APR	MAY	JUN	JUL	AUG	SEP	OCT	NOV	DEC	YEAR
Elevation 103 m. (337 ft.)					47°12'N—27°36'E								
TEMPERATURE													
Daily Average Min.°C	-8	-6	-2	4	10	13	15	15	10	5	1	-4	5
Daily Average Min.°F	18	21	28	40	49	56	60	58	51	41	33	25	40
Daily Average Max.°C	0	2	8	16	23	26	28	28	23	16	8	2	15
Daily Average Max.°F	31	35	46	61	73	78	83	82	73	60	46	36	59
Monthly Average °C	-4	-2	3	10	16	19	21	20	16	10	4	0	9
Monthly Average °F	25	28	37	50	60	66	69	68	60	50	40	31	49
RELATIVE HUMIDITY (%)	83	81	71	62	61	62	60	63	66	73	81	85	71
PRECIPITATION													
Monthly Average mm	33	31	29	47	60	96	79	56	42	25	41	30	569.0
Monthly Average Inches	1.2	1.2	1.1	1.8	2.3	3.7	3.1	2.2	1.6	0.9	1.6	1.1	21.8
Days of 1mm or More	6	6	6	7	8	9	8	6	5	4	5	8	78

SULINA   Romania

	JAN	FEB	MAR	APR	MAY	JUN	JUL	AUG	SEP	OCT	NOV	DEC	YEAR
Elevation 2 m. (7 ft.)					45°12'N—29°42'E								
TEMPERATURE													
Daily Average Min.°C	-4	-3	0	6	12	16	18	18	13	8	4	-1	7
Daily Average Min.°F	25	26	32	44	54	61	65	64	56	47	39	30	45
Daily Average Max.°C	3	4	7	14	20	25	28	27	23	17	11	6	15
Daily Average Max.°F	38	39	45	56	68	76	82	80	73	62	51	42	59
Monthly Average °C	0	1	4	10	16	20	22	22	18	13	8	3	11
Monthly Average °F	33	33	39	49	60	68	72	71	65	56	46	38	52
RELATIVE HUMIDITY (%)	87	85	83	79	78	75	74	77	79	82	86	87	81
PRECIPITATION													
Monthly Average mm	25	21	15	19	27	40	28	30	32	18	24	28	307.0
Monthly Average Inches	0.9	0.8	0.5	0.7	1.0	1.5	1.1	1.1	1.2	0.7	0.9	1.1	11.5
Days of 1mm or More	6	6	4	4	5	6	6	4	3	3	4	6	57

APIA   Samoa

	JAN	FEB	MAR	APR	MAY	JUN	JUL	AUG	SEP	OCT	NOV	DEC	YEAR
Elevation 2 m. (6 ft.)					13°48'S—171°46'W								
TEMPERATURE													
Daily Average Min.°C	24	24	23	24	23	23	23	24	23	24	23	23	24
Daily Average Min.°F	75	76	74	75	74	74	74	75	74	75	74	74	74
Daily Average Max.°C	30	29	30	30	29	29	29	29	29	29	30	29	30
Daily Average Max.°F	86	85	86	86	85	85	85	84	84	85	86	85	85
Monthly Average °C	27	27	27	27	27	26	26	26	26	26	26	27	26
Monthly Average °F	80	80	80	80	80	79	79	78	79	79	80	80	80
RELATIVE HUMIDITY (%)	79	78	78	76	76	73	75	73	75	76	75	77	76
PRECIPITATION													
Monthly Average mm	415	310	355	223	172	146	118	151	160	241	264	383	2938.0
Monthly Average Inches	16.3	12.2	13.9	8.7	6.7	5.7	4.6	5.9	6.3	9.4	10.3	15.0	115.0
Days of 1mm or More	21	19	19	17	14	13	11	11	12	16	15	19	187

SAO TOME
Sao Tome/Principe

		Elevation 8 m. (26 ft.)					0°23'N—6°43'E						
	JAN	FEB	MAR	APR	MAY	JUN	JUL	AUG	SEP	OCT	NOV	DEC	YEAR
TEMPERATURE													
Daily Average Min.°C	22	22	22	22	22	21	20	20	21	22	22	22	22
Daily Average Min.°F	72	72	72	72	72	70	69	69	70	71	71	71	71
Daily Average Max.°C	30	30	30	30	30	28	28	28	29	29	29	29	29
Daily Average Max.°F	85	86	87	87	85	83	82	82	84	84	84	84	84
Monthly Average °C	26	26	26	26	26	25	24	24	25	25	25	25	25
Monthly Average °F	79	79	79	79	79	76	75	76	77	77	78	78	78
RELATIVE HUMIDITY (%)	78	76	74	77	78	74	71	71	74	78	79	79	76
PRECIPITATION													
Monthly Average mm	79	84	134	139	132	18	0	0	22	102	107	99	916.0
Monthly Average Inches	3.1	3.3	5.2	5.4	5.1	0.7	0.0	0.0	0.8	4.0	4.2	3.8	35.6
Days of 1mm or More	6	7	8	10	10	1	0	0	3	7	9	7	68

HAIL
Saudi Arabia

		Elevation 971 m. (3185 ft.)					27°30'N—42°2'E						
	JAN	FEB	MAR	APR	MAY	JUN	JUL	AUG	SEP	OCT	NOV	DEC	YEAR
TEMPERATURE													
Daily Average Min.°C	4	4	8	11	17	21	23	22	19	16	12	6	13
Daily Average Min.°F	39	39	46	52	63	70	73	71	67	61	54	42	56
Daily Average Max.°C	17	19	24	28	33	38	38	39	37	33	24	17	29
Daily Average Max.°F	62	66	75	82	92	101	101	102	98	91	75	63	84
Monthly Average °C	10	12	16	21	26	31	30	31	30	24	17	12	22
Monthly Average °F	50	54	62	70	80	87	86	89	85	75	62	53	71
RELATIVE HUMIDITY (%)	40	32	28	21	26	15	11	13	10	16	36	46	25
PRECIPITATION													
Monthly Average mm	28	13	18	30	19	0	0	0	0	14	70	14	206.0
Monthly Average Inches	1.1	0.5	0.7	1.1	0.7	0.0	0.0	0.0	0.0	0.5	2.7	0.5	7.8
Days of 1mm or More	2	1	2	3	2	0	0	0	0	0	4	1	15

JIDDA
Saudi Arabia

		Elevation 6 m. (20 ft.)					21°28'N—39°10'E						
	JAN	FEB	MAR	APR	MAY	JUN	JUL	AUG	SEP	OCT	NOV	DEC	YEAR
TEMPERATURE													
Monthly Average °C	23	24	26	28	30	31	32	32	31	30	27	25	28
Monthly Average °F	74	75	78	82	86	88	89	89	88	85	81	77	83
PRECIPITATION													
Monthly Average mm	12	6	3	1	1	0	0	0	0	0	19	17	59.0
Monthly Average Inches	0.4	0.2	0.1	0.0	0.0	0.0	0.0	0.0	0.0	0.0	0.7	0.6	2.0
Days of 1mm or More	1	0	0	0	0	0	0	0	0	0	1	1	3

RIYADH   Saudi Arabia

Elevation 609 m. (1998 ft.)					24°39'N—46°42'E								
	JAN	FEB	MAR	APR	MAY	JUN	JUL	AUG	SEP	OCT	NOV	DEC	YEAR
TEMPERATURE													
Daily Average Min.°C	8	9	13	18	22	25	26	24	22	16	13	9	17
Daily Average Min.°F	46	48	56	64	72	77	78	75	72	61	55	49	63
Daily Average Max.°C	21	23	28	32	38	42	42	42	39	34	29	21	32
Daily Average Max.°F	70	73	82	89	100	107	107	107	102	94	84	70	90
Extreme Monthly Min.°C	-7	-2	1	2	15	19	19	17	17	10	2	0	-7
Extreme Monthly Min.°F	19	29	33	36	59	67	67	62	63	50	35	32	19
Extreme Monthly Max.°C	30	33	38	40	43	45	45	44	44	38	34	31	45
Extreme Monthly Max.°F	86	91	101	104	110	113	113	112	111	101	94	87	113
Monthly Average °C	14	16	21	25	31	34	35	35	31	26	20	15	25
Monthly Average °F	58	61	70	77	87	92	95	94	89	79	69	59	77
RELATIVE HUMIDITY (%)	44	37	36	34	31	31	19	19	24	25	33	52	32
PRECIPITATION													
Monthly Average mm	18	9	29	30	11	0	0	0	0	1	6	12	116.0
Monthly Average Inches	0.7	0.3	1.1	1.1	0.4	0.0	0.0	0.0	0.0	0.0	0.2	0.4	4.2
Days of 1mm or More	2	1	4	4	1	0	0	0	0	0	1	1	14

DAKAR   Senegal

Elevation 24 m. (78 ft.)					14°44'N—17°30'W								
	JAN	FEB	MAR	APR	MAY	JUN	JUL	AUG	SEP	OCT	NOV	DEC	YEAR
TEMPERATURE													
Daily Average Min.°C	17	17	17	18	20	23	25	25	24	24	23	20	21
Daily Average Min.°F	63	63	63	65	68	74	76	76	76	76	73	67	70
Daily Average Max.°C	25	25	25	25	26	29	30	30	30	30	29	27	28
Daily Average Max.°F	77	76	77	78	79	84	86	86	87	87	84	80	82
Extreme Monthly Min.°C	13	14	15	16	16	18	21	21	21	21	18	12	11
Extreme Monthly Min.°F	56	58	59	61	61	65	69	69	69	70	64	53	53
Extreme Monthly Max.°C	39	38	43	38	38	38	37	37	38	38	37	35	42
Extreme Monthly Max.°F	102	100	109	101	100	100	99	99	100	101	99	95	109
Monthly Average °C	21	21	21	22	23	26	27	27	27	27	25	22	24
Monthly Average °F	69	69	70	71	73	78	81	81	81	81	78	72	75
RELATIVE HUMIDITY (%)	55	60	63	67	70	69	71	75	75	72	61	52	66
PRECIPITATION													
Monthly Average mm	2	1	0	0	0	11	70	191	139	40	1	0	455.0
Monthly Average Inches	0.0	0.0	0.0	0.0	0.0	0.4	2.7	7.5	5.4	1.5	0.0	0.0	17.5
Days of 1mm or More	0	0	0	0	0	1	4	10	8	2	0	0	25

TAMBACOUNDA   Senegal

Elevation 44 m. (144 ft.)					13°46'N—13°41'W								
	JAN	FEB	MAR	APR	MAY	JUN	JUL	AUG	SEP	OCT	NOV	DEC	YEAR
TEMPERATURE													
Daily Average Min.°C	15	18	21	23	25	24	23	22	22	22	18	15	21
Daily Average Min.°F	59	65	70	74	78	76	73	72	72	71	65	59	69
Daily Average Max.°C	35	37	39	41	40	36	32	31	32	34	36	34	36
Daily Average Max.°F	94	99	103	105	104	97	90	88	89	93	97	93	96
Monthly Average °C	25	28	30	32	33	30	28	27	27	28	27	25	28
Monthly Average °F	78	83	86	90	91	87	82	80	80	82	81	77	83
RELATIVE HUMIDITY (%)	17	17	17	21	33	54	71	76	74	61	36	21	41
PRECIPITATION													
Monthly Average mm	0	1	0	1	18	106	187	233	202	59	2	0	809.0
Monthly Average Inches	0.0	0.0	0.0	0.0	0.7	4.1	7.3	9.1	7.9	2.3	0.0	0.0	31.4
Days of 1mm or More	0	0	0	0	1	8	11	13	12	4	0	0	49

ZIGUINCHOR Senegal

Elevation 10 m. (33 ft.)						12°35'N—16°16'W							
	JAN	FEB	MAR	APR	MAY	JUN	JUL	AUG	SEP	OCT	NOV	DEC	YEAR
TEMPERATURE													
Daily Average Min.°C	16	17	18	19	21	23	23	23	23	23	21	17	20
Daily Average Min.°F	60	62	64	66	70	73	73	73	73	73	70	62	68
Daily Average Max.°C	32	35	37	37	36	33	31	30	31	32	33	32	33
Daily Average Max.°F	90	94	98	98	96	92	88	86	87	90	91	89	92
Monthly Average °C	24	25	26	27	28	28	27	26	26	27	26	24	26
Monthly Average °F	75	78	79	81	82	82	81	79	80	81	79	74	79
RELATIVE HUMIDITY (%)	42	39	39	42	52	64	76	81	77	71	58	45	57
PRECIPITATION													
Monthly Average mm	0	0	0	0	3	112	325	435	314	103	5	0	1297.0
Monthly Average Inches	0.0	0.0	0.0	0.0	0.1	4.4	12.7	17.1	12.3	4.0	0.1	0.0	50.7
Days of 1mm or More	0	0	0	0	0	8	18	21	18	8	0	0	73

MAHE ISLAND Seychelles

Elevation 3 m. (9 ft.)						4°37'S—55°27'E							
	JAN	FEB	MAR	APR	MAY	JUN	JUL	AUG	SEP	OCT	NOV	DEC	YEAR
TEMPERATURE													
Daily Average Min.°C	25	25	25	25	25	25	24	24	24	24	24	24	25
Daily Average Min.°F	76	77	77	78	78	76	75	75	76	75	74	76	76
Daily Average Max.°C	29	29	30	31	30	28	28	28	28	29	29	29	29
Daily Average Max.°F	84	84	86	87	86	83	82	82	82	83	85	85	84
Monthly Average °C	26	27	27	28	27	26	26	26	26	26	26	26	27
Monthly Average °F	80	80	81	82	81	79	78	78	79	79	79	79	80
RELATIVE HUMIDITY (%)	79	77	75	74	74	75	76	77	76	77	75	77	76
PRECIPITATION													
Monthly Average mm	364	248	206	181	160	82	58	79	111	172	208	305	2174.0
Monthly Average Inches	14.3	9.7	8.1	7.1	6.3	3.2	2.2	3.1	4.3	6.7	8.1	12.0	85.1
Days of 1mm or More	18	16	12	15	11	11	10	12	14	15	19	13	166

MESSINA Sicily

Elevation 51 m. (167 ft.)						38°12'N—15°36'E							
	JAN	FEB	MAR	APR	MAY	JUN	JUL	AUG	SEP	OCT	NOV	DEC	YEAR
TEMPERATURE													
Daily Average Min.°C	9	10	11	13	16	20	23	23	21	18	14	11	16
Daily Average Min.°F	49	49	51	55	61	67	73	74	69	64	58	52	60
Daily Average Max.°C	14	14	16	18	22	26	29	30	27	23	19	15	21
Daily Average Max.°F	56	58	60	65	72	79	85	85	80	73	66	60	70
Monthly Average °C	12	12	13	15	19	23	26	26	24	20	16	14	18
Monthly Average °F	53	53	55	59	66	73	78	79	75	67	61	56	65
RELATIVE HUMIDITY (%)	67	68	63	61	60	54	54	56	59	66	66	63	61
PRECIPITATION													
Monthly Average mm	118	100	84	56	34	15	17	28	56	107	102	120	837.0
Monthly Average Inches	4.6	3.9	3.3	2.2	1.3	0.5	0.6	1.1	2.2	4.2	4.0	4.7	32.6
Days of 1mm or More	11	10	9	7	3	2	1	3	5	8	10	12	81

SINGAPORE

Singapore

			Elevation 10 m. (33 ft.)				1°18'N—103°50'E						
	JAN	FEB	MAR	APR	MAY	JUN	JUL	AUG	SEP	OCT	NOV	DEC	YEAR
TEMPERATURE													
Daily Average Min.°C	23	23	24	24	24	24	24	24	24	23	23	23	23
Daily Average Min.°F	73	73	75	75	75	75	75	75	75	74	74	74	74
Daily Average Max.°C	30	31	31	31	32	31	31	31	31	31	31	31	31
Daily Average Max.°F	86	88	88	88	89	88	88	87	87	87	87	87	88
Extreme Monthly Min.°C	20	19	19	21	21	21	24	21	21	21	21	21	18
Extreme Monthly Min.°F	68	66	67	70	70	70	75	69	69	69	69	69	66
Extreme Monthly Max.°C	34	34	34	35	36	35	34	34	34	34	33	34	36
Extreme Monthly Max.°F	93	94	94	95	97	95	93	93	93	93	92	93	97
Monthly Average °C	26	27	27	28	28	28	28	28	27	27	27	26	27
Monthly Average °F	79	80	81	82	82	83	82	82	81	81	80	79	81
RELATIVE HUMIDITY (%)	78	71	70	74	73	73	72	72	72	72	75	78	73
PRECIPITATION													
Monthly Average mm	329	64	191	111	161	95	107	107	206	151	228	264	2014.0
Monthly Average Inches	12.9	2.5	7.5	4.3	6.3	3.7	4.2	4.2	8.1	5.9	8.9	10.3	78.8
Days of 1mm or More	10	5	11	11	11	10	11	10	15	12	15	16	137

HONIARA

Solomon Islands

			Elevation 58 m. (190 ft.)				9°26'S—159°57'E						
	JAN	FEB	MAR	APR	MAY	JUN	JUL	AUG	SEP	OCT	NOV	DEC	YEAR
TEMPERATURE													
Monthly Average °C	27	27	27	27	27	26	26	26	26	27	27	27	27
Monthly Average °F	80	80	80	80	80	79	79	79	79	80	80	80	80
PRECIPITATION													
Monthly Average mm	281	286	358	225	129	95	99	90	94	150	152	217	2176.0
Monthly Average Inches	11.0	11.2	14.0	8.8	5.0	3.7	3.8	3.5	3.7	5.9	5.9	8.5	85.0
Days of 1mm or More	17	16	18	13	9	8	10	10	8	11	11	16	147

MOGADISHU

Somalia

			Elevation 17 m. (56 ft.)				2°2'N—45°21'E						
	JAN	FEB	MAR	APR	MAY	JUN	JUL	AUG	SEP	OCT	NOV	DEC	YEAR
TEMPERATURE													
Daily Average Min.°C	23	23	26	27	26	24	24	23	24	25	25	24	24
Daily Average Min.°F	73	74	78	80	78	76	74	74	75	77	77	75	76
Daily Average Max.°C	29	30	31	32	31	29	28	28	29	30	30	30	30
Daily Average Max.°F	85	85	87	90	89	85	83	83	85	86	86	86	86
Monthly Average °C	27	27	28	28	28	27	26	26	26	27	27	27	27
Monthly Average °F	80	80	82	83	82	80	78	78	79	80	80	80	80
PRECIPITATION													
Monthly Average mm	0	0	3	51	73	81	83	44	18	38	48	10	449.0
Monthly Average Inches	0.0	0.0	0.1	2.0	2.8	3.1	3.2	1.7	0.7	1.4	1.8	0.3	17.1
Days of 1mm or More	0	0	0	2	9	10	9	11	4	8	2	0	55

CAPE TOWN   South Africa

					Elevation 44 m. (145 ft.)		33°58'S—18°36'E						
	JAN	FEB	MAR	APR	MAY	JUN	JUL	AUG	SEP	OCT	NOV	DEC	YEAR
TEMPERATURE													
Daily Average Min.°C	15	15	14	11	9	7	7	7	8	10	13	15	11
Daily Average Min.°F	60	59	57	52	48	45	44	45	47	50	55	58	51
Daily Average Max.°C	26	26	25	23	20	18	17	18	19	21	24	25	22
Daily Average Max.°F	79	79	78	73	67	64	63	64	67	70	74	77	71
Extreme Monthly Min.°C	7	5	6	3	-1	-2	-2	-1	1	1	4	5	-2
Extreme Monthly Min.°F	44	41	42	38	31	29	29	31	33	34	40	41	28
Extreme Monthly Max.°C	37	38	39	39	35	29	29	32	34	32	34	38	39
Extreme Monthly Max.°F	99	100	103	102	95	85	84	89	93	90	93	100	103
Monthly Average °C	20	20	19	17	14	13	12	12	14	16	18	19	16
Monthly Average °F	69	68	66	62	58	55	53	54	57	60	64	67	61
RELATIVE HUMIDITY (%)	52	53	52	55	63	63	63	62	58	55	53	53	57
PRECIPITATION													
Monthly Average mm	14	17	19	37	71	93	73	75	36	33	16	18	502.0
Monthly Average Inches	0.5	0.6	0.7	1.4	2.7	3.6	2.8	2.9	1.4	1.2	0.6	0.7	19.1
Days of 1mm or More	3	2	3	7	8	9	9	9	7	4	3	4	68

JOHANNESBURG   South Africa

					Elevation 1692 m. (5550 ft.)		26°08'S—28°14'E						
	JAN	FEB	MAR	APR	MAY	JUN	JUL	AUG	SEP	OCT	NOV	DEC	YEAR
TEMPERATURE													
Daily Average Min.°C	14	14	13	10	7	4	4	6	9	11	13	14	10
Daily Average Min.°F	58	57	55	50	45	39	40	43	48	52	55	57	50
Daily Average Max.°C	25	25	24	21	19	16	17	19	23	24	24	25	22
Daily Average Max.°F	78	77	75	69	65	60	62	67	73	75	75	76	71
Monthly Average °C	19	19	18	15	13	10	10	12	16	17	18	19	16
Monthly Average °F	67	66	64	60	55	49	50	54	60	63	64	66	60
RELATIVE HUMIDITY (%)	50	52	49	48	39	35	32	28	29	37	47	50	41
PRECIPITATION													
Monthly Average mm	124	91	87	53	13	7	4	6	30	74	121	107	717.0
Monthly Average Inches	4.8	3.5	3.4	2.0	0.5	0.2	0.1	0.2	1.1	2.9	4.7	4.2	27.6
Days of 1mm or More	12	8	8	6	1	1	0	1	2	6	11	11	67

PIETERSBURG   South Africa

					Elevation 1230 m. (4034 ft.)		23°52'S—29°27'E						
	JAN	FEB	MAR	APR	MAY	JUN	JUL	AUG	SEP	OCT	NOV	DEC	YEAR
TEMPERATURE													
Daily Average Min.°C	16	16	15	12	7	4	4	6	10	13	15	16	11
Daily Average Min.°F	62	61	58	53	45	39	39	42	49	56	59	61	52
Daily Average Max.°C	28	27	26	25	22	20	20	22	25	27	27	27	25
Daily Average Max.°F	82	81	79	76	72	67	68	72	77	80	80	81	76
Monthly Average °C	22	21	20	18	15	12	12	14	17	19	20	21	18
Monthly Average °F	71	70	68	64	58	53	53	57	63	67	69	70	64
RELATIVE HUMIDITY (%)	51	51	49	46	40	38	35	34	33	39	46	49	43
PRECIPITATION													
Monthly Average mm	85	60	51	31	12	4	3	5	17	42	86	91	487.0
Monthly Average Inches	3.3	2.3	2.0	1.2	0.4	0.1	0.1	0.1	0.6	1.6	3.3	3.5	18.5
Days of 1mm or More	8	6	6	4	2	0	0	0	1	5	8	8	48

PORT ELIZABETH   South Africa

		Elevation 60 m. (197 ft.)				33°59'S—25°36'E						
	JAN	FEB	MAR	APR	MAY	JUN	JUL	AUG	SEP	OCT	NOV	DEC	YEAR
TEMPERATURE													
Daily Average Min.°C	17	17	16	13	11	8	8	9	11	12	14	16	13
Daily Average Min.°F	62	63	61	56	51	47	46	48	51	54	57	60	55
Daily Average Max.°C	25	25	25	23	21	20	19	20	20	21	22	24	22
Daily Average Max.°F	77	77	76	73	71	68	67	67	68	69	72	75	72
Extreme Monthly Min.°C	7	8	7	6	-1	1	0	0	2	4	6	7	0
Extreme Monthly Min.°F	45	46	45	42	31	33	32	32	35	39	42	44	31
Extreme Monthly Max.°C	34	40	40	38	35	30	32	37	39	36	40	36	40
Extreme Monthly Max.°F	94	104	104	101	95	86	90	98	103	97	104	96	104
Monthly Average °C	21	21	20	18	16	14	14	14	15	17	18	20	17
Monthly Average °F	70	70	68	65	61	58	57	58	60	62	65	68	63
RELATIVE HUMIDITY (%)	65	67	67	65	61	56	57	61	65	68	66	65	64
PRECIPITATION													
Monthly Average mm	39	37	57	56	66	59	50	69	61	57	44	37	632.0
Monthly Average Inches	1.5	1.4	2.2	2.2	2.5	2.3	1.9	2.7	2.4	2.2	1.7	1.4	24.4
Days of 1mm or More	5	5	6	7	5	5	5	7	6	7	7	5	70

PRETORIA   South Africa

		Elevation 1368 m. (4488 ft.)				25°45'S—28°14'E						
	JAN	FEB	MAR	APR	MAY	JUN	JUL	AUG	SEP	OCT	NOV	DEC	YEAR
TEMPERATURE													
Daily Average Min.°C	16	16	14	11	6	3	3	5	9	13	14	15	10
Daily Average Min.°F	60	60	57	51	42	37	37	42	49	55	57	59	50
Daily Average Max.°C	28	28	26	24	21	19	19	22	25	27	27	28	24
Daily Average Max.°F	82	82	79	75	70	66	67	71	77	80	80	82	76
Extreme Monthly Min.°C	9	9	6	1	-3	-4	-4	-2	-1	3	5	6	-4
Extreme Monthly Min.°F	49	49	43	33	26	24	24	28	30	37	41	43	24
Extreme Monthly Max.°C	35	33	33	28	26	25	24	28	32	33	36	35	35
Extreme Monthly Max.°F	95	91	91	83	79	77	75	83	89	92	96	95	96
Monthly Average °C	22	22	21	18	14	11	11	14	18	20	21	22	18
Monthly Average °F	72	71	69	64	58	52	53	58	65	68	69	71	64
RELATIVE HUMIDITY (%)	49	50	49	44	37	34	31	28	29	35	42	46	39
PRECIPITATION													
Monthly Average mm	142	72	77	52	14	5	3	5	22	72	106	111	681.0
Monthly Average Inches	5.5	2.8	3.0	2.0	0.5	0.1	0.1	0.1	0.8	2.8	4.1	4.3	26.1
Days of 1mm or More	11	7	7	5	2	0	0	1	2	6	9	10	60

MOKP'O   South Korea

		Elevation 33 m. (107 ft.)				34°47'N—126°23'E						
	JAN	FEB	MAR	APR	MAY	JUN	JUL	AUG	SEP	OCT	NOV	DEC	YEAR
TEMPERATURE													
Daily Average Min.°C	-2	-2	2	7	13	17	22	23	18	12	6	1	9
Daily Average Min.°F	28	29	35	45	55	63	71	74	65	54	42	33	49
Daily Average Max.°C	5	6	10	17	21	25	28	31	27	21	14	8	18
Daily Average Max.°F	41	43	50	62	70	77	83	87	80	70	58	46	64
Monthly Average °C	1	3	6	12	17	21	25	26	22	16	10	5	14
Monthly Average °F	34	37	43	53	63	70	77	79	72	61	50	40	56
RELATIVE HUMIDITY (%)	71	70	70	75	77	82	86	82	77	73	72	71	75
PRECIPITATION													
Monthly Average mm	34	52	55	104	90	155	198	162	142	51	53	33	1129.0
Monthly Average Inches	1.3	2.0	2.1	4.0	3.5	6.1	7.7	6.3	5.5	2.0	2.0	1.2	43.7
Days of 1mm or More	6	7	6	8	6	8	10	8	7	5	6	7	84

PUSAN

South Korea

	JAN	FEB	MAR	APR	MAY	JUN	JUL	AUG	SEP	OCT	NOV	DEC	YEAR
Elevation 13 m. (41 ft.)					35°6'N—129°1'E								
TEMPERATURE													
Daily Average Min.°C	-2	-1	3	8	13	17	22	23	18	12	6	1	10
Daily Average Min.°F	29	31	37	47	55	62	71	73	65	54	43	33	50
Daily Average Max.°C	6	7	12	17	21	24	27	29	26	21	15	9	18
Daily Average Max.°F	43	45	53	62	69	75	81	85	78	70	59	48	64
Extreme Monthly Min.°C	-14	-12	-7	-2	6	9	14	16	9	2	-3	-12	-13
Extreme Monthly Min.°F	7	11	19	29	42	49	57	60	49	36	26	10	7
Extreme Monthly Max.°C	18	18	21	26	29	33	34	36	32	27	24	19	35
Extreme Monthly Max.°F	65	64	69	78	84	92	94	96	90	80	75	67	96
Monthly Average °C	2	3	8	13	17	20	24	26	22	17	11	5	14
Monthly Average °F	36	38	46	55	63	69	75	78	71	63	51	41	57
RELATIVE HUMIDITY (%)	41	45	50	59	59	71	76	71	64	54	52	49	58
PRECIPITATION													
Monthly Average mm	29	37	76	147	158	215	249	209	190	79	58	24	1471.0
Monthly Average Inches	1.1	1.4	2.9	5.7	6.2	8.4	9.8	8.2	7.4	3.1	2.2	0.9	57.3
Days of 1mm or More	4	5	6	8	7	9	12	9	7	4	5	3	79

SEOUL

South Korea

	JAN	FEB	MAR	APR	MAY	JUN	JUL	AUG	SEP	OCT	NOV	DEC	YEAR
Elevation 87 m. (285 ft.)					37°34'N—126°58'E								
TEMPERATURE													
Daily Average Min.°C	-9	-7	-2	5	11	16	21	22	15	7	0	-7	6
Daily Average Min.°F	15	20	29	41	51	61	70	71	59	45	32	20	43
Daily Average Max.°C	0	3	8	17	22	27	29	31	26	19	11	3	16
Daily Average Max.°F	32	37	47	62	72	80	84	87	78	67	51	37	61
Extreme Monthly Min.°C	-22	-19	-15	-4	2	9	13	14	3	-4	-12	-24	-24
Extreme Monthly Min.°F	-8	-3	5	25	36	49	55	58	38	25	11	-12	-12
Extreme Monthly Max.°C	12	16	22	28	32	37	37	37	33	30	23	14	37
Extreme Monthly Max.°F	54	61	72	83	90	98	98	99	91	86	74	58	99
Monthly Average °C	-4	-1	4	11	17	21	24	25	20	14	7	-1	12
Monthly Average °F	26	30	39	52	63	70	76	77	69	57	44	31	53
RELATIVE HUMIDITY (%)	51	47	46	46	51	54	67	62	55	48	52	52	53
PRECIPITATION													
Monthly Average mm	20	27	48	104	87	150	383	262	160	48	42	23	1354.0
Monthly Average Inches	0.7	1.0	1.8	4.0	3.4	5.9	15.0	10.3	6.3	1.8	1.6	0.9	52.7
Days of 1mm or More	0	0	0	0	0	0	0	0	0	0	0	0	0

ALICANTE

Spain

	JAN	FEB	MAR	APR	MAY	JUN	JUL	AUG	SEP	OCT	NOV	DEC	YEAR
Elevation 82 m. (269 ft.)					38°24'N—0°30'W								
TEMPERATURE													
Daily Average Min.°C	6	6	8	11	13	17	20	20	18	14	10	8	13
Daily Average Min.°F	43	43	47	51	56	63	68	69	65	58	51	46	55
Daily Average Max.°C	16	17	19	21	24	28	31	32	29	25	20	17	23
Daily Average Max.°F	60	63	67	70	76	83	88	89	84	76	69	63	74
Monthly Average °C	12	12	14	16	19	22	25	26	23	19	15	12	18
Monthly Average °F	53	54	57	60	66	72	77	78	74	66	59	54	64
RELATIVE HUMIDITY (%)	57	56	56	57	57	57	57	58	60	58	57	56	57
PRECIPITATION													
Monthly Average mm	17	28	24	32	31	23	5	8	41	73	44	31	357.0
Monthly Average Inches	0.6	1.1	0.9	1.2	1.2	0.9	0.1	0.3	1.6	2.8	1.7	1.2	13.6
Days of 1mm or More	3	3	3	4	4	2	0	1	2	4	4	4	34

ALMERIA   Spain

	JAN	FEB	MAR	APR	MAY	JUN	JUL	AUG	SEP	OCT	NOV	DEC	YEAR
Elevation 7 m. (22 ft.)					36°48'N—2°30'W								
TEMPERATURE													
Daily Average Min.°C	8	9	11	13	15	18	21	22	20	16	12	9	14
Daily Average Min.°F	46	47	51	55	59	65	70	71	68	60	54	49	58
Daily Average Max.°C	16	16	18	20	22	26	29	29	27	23	19	17	22
Daily Average Max.°F	60	61	64	68	72	78	83	84	81	73	67	62	71
Extreme Monthly Min.°C	2	2	3	6	8	12	14	15	10	8	4	3	1
Extreme Monthly Min.°F	35	36	37	43	47	53	58	59	50	46	40	37	34
Extreme Monthly Max.°C	23	24	27	29	34	42	42	40	36	33	26	24	42
Extreme Monthly Max.°F	74	76	80	85	93	107	108	104	96	91	78	76	108
Monthly Average °C	12	13	14	16	19	22	25	26	23	20	16	13	18
Monthly Average °F	54	55	58	61	66	71	77	78	74	67	60	56	65
RELATIVE HUMIDITY (%)	66	65	64	62	63	64	64	65	65	67	68	66	65
PRECIPITATION													
Monthly Average mm	29	19	25	25	18	8	1	3	7	29	22	33	219.0
Monthly Average Inches	1.1	0.7	0.9	0.9	0.7	0.3	0.0	0.1	0.2	1.1	0.8	1.2	8.0
Days of 1mm or More	3	3	3	3	2	1	0	0	1	3	4	4	27

BARCELONA   Spain

	JAN	FEB	MAR	APR	MAY	JUN	JUL	AUG	SEP	OCT	NOV	DEC	YEAR
Elevation 95 m. (311 ft.)					41°24'N—2°12'E								
TEMPERATURE													
Daily Average Min.°C	6	7	9	11	14	18	21	21	19	15	11	8	13
Daily Average Min.°F	43	45	48	52	57	65	69	69	66	58	51	46	56
Daily Average Max.°C	13	14	16	18	21	25	28	28	25	21	16	13	20
Daily Average Max.°F	55	57	60	65	71	78	82	82	77	69	62	56	68
Extreme Monthly Min.°C	-4	-2	0	2	5	9	12	13	9	4	-1	-4	-4
Extreme Monthly Min.°F	24	29	32	35	41	49	54	56	49	39	31	25	24
Extreme Monthly Max.°C	22	25	26	28	32	35	36	37	32	28	27	23	36
Extreme Monthly Max.°F	71	77	79	82	90	95	96	98	89	82	80	73	98
Monthly Average °C	10	11	12	14	17	21	24	24	22	18	13	10	16
Monthly Average °F	50	51	54	57	63	70	75	75	71	64	56	51	61
RELATIVE HUMIDITY (%)	60	59	61	61	61	61	61	63	64	66	63	60	62
PRECIPITATION													
Monthly Average mm	36	40	43	49	53	41	25	52	70	87	67	50	613.0
Monthly Average Inches	1.4	1.5	1.6	1.9	2.0	1.6	0.9	2.0	2.7	3.4	2.6	1.9	23.5
Days of 1mm or More	4	4	5	5	5	5	2	4	5	5	5	5	54

MADRID   Spain

	JAN	FEB	MAR	APR	MAY	JUN	JUL	AUG	SEP	OCT	NOV	DEC	YEAR
Elevation 657 m. (2155 ft.)					40°24'N—3°42'W								
TEMPERATURE													
Daily Average Min.°C	2	2	5	7	10	15	17	17	14	10	5	2	9
Daily Average Min.°F	35	36	41	45	50	58	63	63	57	49	42	36	48
Daily Average Max.°C	9	11	15	18	21	27	31	30	25	19	13	9	19
Daily Average Max.°F	47	52	59	65	70	80	87	85	77	65	55	48	66
Extreme Monthly Min.°C	-10	-7	-4	-2	0	4	8	9	4	-1	-4	-9	-10
Extreme Monthly Min.°F	14	19	25	29	32	40	47	49	39	30	25	16	14
Extreme Monthly Max.°C	18	21	26	29	33	37	38	39	36	30	22	18	38
Extreme Monthly Max.°F	64	70	78	85	91	98	101	102	96	86	72	64	102
Monthly Average °C	6	7	10	12	16	21	24	24	20	14	9	6	14
Monthly Average °F	43	45	50	54	61	69	76	74	68	58	49	43	57
RELATIVE HUMIDITY (%)	71	64	58	52	51	43	37	36	47	57	68	73	55
PRECIPITATION													
Monthly Average mm	47	46	35	48	42	28	14	13	33	50	59	52	467.0
Monthly Average Inches	1.8	1.8	1.3	1.8	1.6	1.1	0.5	0.5	1.2	1.9	2.3	2.0	17.8
Days of 1mm or More	7	8	6	7	6	4	2	1	4	6	7	7	65

PALMA   Spain

		Elevation 10 m. (33 ft.)				39°33'N—2°39'E							
	JAN	FEB	MAR	APR	MAY	JUN	JUL	AUG	SEP	OCT	NOV	DEC	YEAR
TEMPERATURE													
Daily Average Min.°C	6	6	8	10	13	17	20	20	18	14	10	8	13
Daily Average Min.°F	43	44	46	51	55	62	67	68	65	57	50	46	55
Daily Average Max.°C	14	15	17	19	22	26	29	29	27	23	18	15	21
Daily Average Max.°F	57	59	62	66	71	79	84	84	80	73	65	59	70
Monthly Average °C	11	11	13	15	18	22	25	25	23	19	14	12	17
Monthly Average °F	52	52	55	59	64	71	77	77	73	66	58	54	63
RELATIVE HUMIDITY (%)	72	70	69	66	67	65	65	65	69	71	72	72	69
PRECIPITATION													
Monthly Average mm	31	33	28	33	27	16	4	17	50	82	48	48	417.0
Monthly Average Inches	1.2	1.2	1.1	1.2	1.0	0.6	0.1	0.6	1.9	3.2	1.8	1.8	15.7
Days of 1mm or More	4	5	6	8	4	2	1	2	4	7	4	7	54

SEVILLE   Spain

		Elevation 13 m. (42 ft.)				37°24'N—6°0'W							
	JAN	FEB	MAR	APR	MAY	JUN	JUL	AUG	SEP	OCT	NOV	DEC	YEAR
TEMPERATURE													
Daily Average Min.°C	6	7	90	11	13	17	20	20	18	14	10	7	19
Daily Average Min.°F	42	44	194	52	56	63	67	68	64	57	50	44	67
Daily Average Max.°C	15	17	20	24	27	32	36	36	32	26	20	16	25
Daily Average Max.°F	59	63	69	74	80	90	98	97	90	78	68	60	77
Extreme Monthly Min.°C	-3	-2	0	4	3	5	11	12	9	6	0	-3	-2
Extreme Monthly Min.°F	27	29	32	39	37	41	52	54	48	43	32	27	27
Extreme Monthly Max.°C	23	27	30	33	39	45	46	47	43	39	28	22	47
Extreme Monthly Max.°F	73	80	86	91	102	113	114	117	109	102	82	72	117
Monthly Average °C	11	12	14	16	20	23	27	27	24	19	14	11	18
Monthly Average °F	51	54	57	61	67	74	80	80	76	67	58	52	65
RELATIVE HUMIDITY (%)	77	72	75	67	64	50	45	45	55	67	76	79	64
PRECIPITATION													
Monthly Average mm	91	83	61	52	32	16	2	7	18	69	87	85	603.0
Monthly Average Inches	3.5	3.2	2.4	2.0	1.2	0.6	0.0	0.2	0.7	2.7	3.4	3.3	23.2
Days of 1mm or More	7	7	6	6	3	1	0	0	2	5	6	7	50

ZARAGOZA   Spain

		Elevation 258 m. (846 ft.)				41°42'N—0°50'W							
	JAN	FEB	MAR	APR	MAY	JUN	JUL	AUG	SEP	OCT	NOV	DEC	YEAR
TEMPERATURE													
Daily Average Min.°C	2	3	6	8	11	15	18	17	15	11	6	3	10
Daily Average Min.°F	36	38	42	47	53	59	64	63	59	51	43	38	49
Daily Average Max.°C	10	13	17	19	23	27	31	30	27	20	14	10	20
Daily Average Max.°F	50	55	62	67	73	81	87	86	80	69	58	50	68
Monthly Average °C	6	7	10	13	17	21	24	24	21	15	10	7	14
Monthly Average °F	42	45	51	55	63	70	75	74	69	59	49	44	58
PRECIPITATION													
Monthly Average mm	24	19	29	31	33	37	13	15	29	40	35	29	334.0
Monthly Average Inches	0.9	0.7	1.1	1.2	1.2	1.4	0.5	0.5	1.1	1.5	1.3	1.1	12.5
Days of 1mm or More	8	5	2	4	3	2	5	0	3	12	5	8	57

COLOMBO
Sri Lanka

	Elevation 6 m. (19 ft.)					6°54'N—79°52'E							
	JAN	FEB	MAR	APR	MAY	JUN	JUL	AUG	SEP	OCT	NOV	DEC	YEAR
TEMPERATURE													
Daily Average Min.°C	22	22	23	24	26	25	25	25	25	24	23	22	24
Daily Average Min.°F	72	72	74	76	78	77	77	77	77	75	73	72	75
Daily Average Max.°C	30	31	31	31	31	29	29	29	29	29	29	29	30
Daily Average Max.°F	86	87	88	88	87	85	85	85	85	85	85	85	86
Extreme Monthly Min.°C	15	16	18	21	21	22	22	22	22	21	19	17	15
Extreme Monthly Min.°F	59	61	64	70	69	72	71	71	71	69	66	63	59
Extreme Monthly Max.°C	34	36	36	33	33	32	31	31	32	32	32	33	35
Extreme Monthly Max.°F	94	96	96	92	91	89	88	88	89	89	90	91	96
Monthly Average °C	27	27	28	28	28	28	28	28	27	27	27	27	27
Monthly Average °F	80	80	82	83	83	82	82	82	81	80	80	80	81
RELATIVE HUMIDITY (%)	67	66	66	70	76	78	77	76	75	76	75	69	73
PRECIPITATION													
Monthly Average mm	64	85	116	247	413	172	139	111	234	382	308	166	2437.0
Monthly Average Inches	2.5	3.3	4.5	9.7	16.2	6.7	5.4	4.3	9.2	15.0	12.1	6.5	95.4
Days of 1mm or More	5	4	8	13	16	16	11	11	15	18	15	10	142

TRINCOMALEE
Sri Lanka

	Elevation 7 m. (22 ft.)					8°35'N—81°15'E							
	JAN	FEB	MAR	APR	MAY	JUN	JUL	AUG	SEP	OCT	NOV	DEC	YEAR
TEMPERATURE													
Daily Average Min.°C	24	24	24	26	26	26	26	25	25	24	24	24	25
Daily Average Min.°F	75	76	76	78	79	79	78	77	77	76	75	75	77
Daily Average Max.°C	27	28	29	32	33	33	33	33	33	31	29	27	31
Daily Average Max.°F	80	82	85	89	92	92	92	92	92	88	84	81	87
Monthly Average °C	26	27	28	29	30	31	30	30	30	28	27	26	28
Monthly Average °F	79	80	82	85	87	87	86	86	85	83	80	79	83
RELATIVE HUMIDITY (%)	78	70	70	68	61	54	53	56	61	69	78	79	66
PRECIPITATION													
Monthly Average mm	154	106	50	49	48	24	59	86	101	232	357	350	1616.0
Monthly Average Inches	6.0	4.1	1.9	1.9	1.8	0.9	2.3	3.3	3.9	9.1	14.0	13.7	62.9
Days of 1mm or More	8	4	4	5	4	1	4	6	6	12	17	16	87

ASCENSION ISLAND
St. Helena

	Elevation 17 m. (56 ft.)					7°55'S—14°25'W							
	JAN	FEB	MAR	APR	MAY	JUN	JUL	AUG	SEP	OCT	NOV	DEC	YEAR
TEMPERATURE													
Daily Average Min.°C	23	23	24	24	24	23	22	22	21	21	21	22	22
Daily Average Min.°F	73	73	75	75	75	73	72	71	71	70	70	72	73
Daily Average Max.°C	30	30	31	30	30	29	29	28	28	28	27	29	29
Daily Average Max.°F	85	85	88	85	87	85	83	82	82	82	81	84	84
Monthly Average °C	26	27	28	28	27	26	25	25	24	24	25	25	26
Monthly Average °F	79	81	82	82	81	79	78	76	76	76	77	78	79
RELATIVE HUMIDITY (%)	63	62	62	64	62	61	62	62	64	64	63	62	63
PRECIPITATION													
Monthly Average mm	3	5	27	23	11	15	14	11	8	7	4	3	131.0
Monthly Average Inches	0.1	0.1	1.0	0.9	0.4	0.5	0.5	0.4	0.3	0.2	0.1	0.1	4.6
Days of 1mm or More	0	0	0	0	0	0	0	0	0	0	0	0	0

EL FASHER　　　　　　　　　　　　　Sudan

		Elevation 730 m. (2395 ft.)					13°38'N—25°20'E						
	JAN	FEB	MAR	APR	MAY	JUN	JUL	AUG	SEP	OCT	NOV	DEC	YEAR
TEMPERATURE													
Daily Average Min.°C	9	11	15	18	21	23	22	21	20	18	13	10	17
Daily Average Min.°F	49	52	59	64	70	73	72	70	69	65	56	50	62
Daily Average Max.°C	31	32	35	38	39	38	35	32	35	36	33	31	35
Daily Average Max.°F	87	90	96	100	101	101	94	90	95	97	92	87	94
Monthly Average °C	19	21	25	28	30	30	28	27	28	27	23	19	25
Monthly Average °F	66	70	77	83	86	87	82	80	82	81	73	66	78
RELATIVE HUMIDITY (%)	20	15	15	13	15	23	39	51	36	23	20	21	24
PRECIPITATION													
Monthly Average mm	0	0	0	2	6	14	89	93	29	10	0	0	243.0
Monthly Average Inches	0.0	0.0	0.0	0.0	0.2	0.5	3.5	3.6	1.1	0.3	0.0	0.0	9.2
Days of 1mm or More	0	0	0	0	1	2	7	8	3	0	0	0	21

JUBA　　　　　　　　　　　　　　　Sudan

		Elevation 457 m. (1499 ft.)					4°51'N—31°37'E						
	JAN	FEB	MAR	APR	MAY	JUN	JUL	AUG	SEP	OCT	NOV	DEC	YEAR
TEMPERATURE													
Daily Average Min.°C	20	21	23	23	22	22	21	21	21	21	20	20	21
Daily Average Min.°F	68	70	73	73	72	71	69	69	69	69	69	67	70
Daily Average Max.°C	37	37	37	35	33	32	30	30	32	33	35	36	34
Daily Average Max.°F	98	99	98	94	91	89	87	87	90	92	94	96	93
Monthly Average °C	27	28	29	28	27	26	25	25	25	26	26	27	27
Monthly Average °F	81	83	84	82	80	78	76	77	78	79	79	80	80
RELATIVE HUMIDITY (%)	24	24	34	48	56	57	61	63	56	53	43	32	46
PRECIPITATION													
Monthly Average mm	4	11	41	101	145	115	119	146	117	100	46	8	953.0
Monthly Average Inches	0.1	0.4	1.6	3.9	5.7	4.5	4.6	5.7	4.6	3.9	1.8	0.3	37.1
Days of 1mm or More	1	1	5	9	10	9	11	10	8	9	5	1	79

KASSALA　　　　　　　　　　　　　Sudan

		Elevation 500 m. (1640 ft.)					15°28'N—36°24'E						
	JAN	FEB	MAR	APR	MAY	JUN	JUL	AUG	SEP	OCT	NOV	DEC	YEAR
TEMPERATURE													
Daily Average Min.°C	16	16	19	22	25	25	23	23	23	23	20	17	21
Daily Average Min.°F	61	61	66	72	77	77	74	73	73	73	69	63	70
Daily Average Max.°C	34	36	39	41	42	40	35	33	36	39	37	35	37
Daily Average Max.°F	94	96	101	106	107	104	96	92	97	102	99	95	99
Monthly Average °C	24	25	28	31	33	31	29	27	29	30	28	25	28
Monthly Average °F	75	78	83	88	91	88	83	81	84	86	83	77	83
RELATIVE HUMIDITY (%)	25	23	18	16	17	25	42	51	39	25	24	26	28
PRECIPITATION													
Monthly Average mm	0	0	0	4	14	29	96	103	54	8	3	0	311.0
Monthly Average Inches	0.0	0.0	0.0	0.1	0.5	1.1	3.7	4.0	2.1	0.3	0.1	0.0	11.9
Days of 1mm or More	0	0	0	0	2	3	7	8	3	1	0	0	24

KHARTOUM
Sudan

Elevation 380 m. (1246 ft.)					15°36'N—32°33'E								
	JAN	FEB	MAR	APR	MAY	JUN	JUL	AUG	SEP	OCT	NOV	DEC	YEAR
TEMPERATURE													
Daily Average Min.°C	16	17	20	23	26	27	26	25	25	25	21	17	22
Daily Average Min.°F	61	62	68	74	79	81	78	77	78	77	70	62	72
Daily Average Max.°C	32	33	37	40	42	41	38	36	38	39	35	32	37
Daily Average Max.°F	89	91	98	104	107	107	100	96	100	102	96	90	98
Monthly Average °C	22	24	28	32	34	34	32	31	32	32	28	24	29
Monthly Average °F	72	76	82	89	93	93	89	87	89	89	82	75	85
RELATIVE HUMIDITY (%)	21	16	13	13	14	18	31	42	30	20	21	23	22
PRECIPITATION													
Monthly Average mm	0	0	0	0	5	9	51	68	17	7	0	0	157.0
Monthly Average Inches	0.0	0.0	0.0	0.0	0.1	0.3	2.0	2.6	0.6	0.2	0.0	0.0	5.8
Days of 1mm or More	0	0	0	0	3	1	4	4	2	1	0	0	15

PORT SUDAN
Sudan

Elevation 5 m. (16 ft.)					19°31'N—37°13'E								
	JAN	FEB	MAR	APR	MAY	JUN	JUL	AUG	SEP	OCT	NOV	DEC	YEAR
TEMPERATURE													
Daily Average Min.°C	19	19	20	21	23	25	28	29	27	25	24	21	24
Daily Average Min.°F	66	66	67	70	74	77	82	85	80	77	75	71	74
Daily Average Max.°C	27	27	29	31	35	39	41	41	38	34	31	29	34
Daily Average Max.°F	81	81	83	89	95	101	105	106	100	93	88	83	92
Extreme Monthly Min.°C	10	11	12	14	15	20	20	19	14	16	11	12	10
Extreme Monthly Min.°F	50	52	53	58	59	68	68	67	57	61	52	53	50
Extreme Monthly Max.°C	32	32	35	38	44	47	47	47	45	42	36	34	47
Extreme Monthly Max.°F	89	90	95	101	111	117	117	117	113	107	96	93	117
Monthly Average °C	23	23	24	27	29	32	34	34	32	29	27	25	28
Monthly Average °F	73	74	75	80	85	89	93	93	89	85	81	76	83
RELATIVE HUMIDITY (%)	67	68	64	60	54	45	45	45	54	64	68	68	59
PRECIPITATION													
Monthly Average mm	13	1	1	2	2	0	5	2	0	15	41	23	105.0
Monthly Average Inches	0.5	0.0	0.0	0.0	0.0	0.0	0.1	0.0	0.0	0.5	1.6	0.9	3.6
Days of 1mm or More	0	0	0	0	0	0	0	0	0	0	3	1	4

WAU
Sudan

Elevation 438 m. (1437 ft.)					19°36'N—37°12'E								
	JAN	FEB	MAR	APR	MAY	JUN	JUL	AUG	SEP	OCT	NOV	DEC	YEAR
TEMPERATURE													
Daily Average Min.°C	18	19	22	24	23	22	21	21	21	21	20	18	21
Daily Average Min.°F	64	67	72	75	74	72	70	70	70	70	68	64	70
Daily Average Max.°C	36	37	38	37	35	33	31	31	32	34	35	35	34
Daily Average Max.°F	97	98	100	99	94	91	88	87	90	93	95	96	94
Monthly Average °C				30	28	26	25	24	25	25	25	25	19
Monthly Average °F				86	83	79	76	75	76	78	76	77	67
RELATIVE HUMIDITY (%)	17	15	22	34	45	54	60	61	55	48	31	21	39
PRECIPITATION													
Monthly Average mm				64	76	285	87	134	198	170	1		1015.0
Monthly Average Inches	0.0	0.0	0.0	2.5	2.9	11.2	3.4	5.2	7.7	6.6	0.0	0.0	39.5
Days of 1mm or More	0	0	0	1	9	12	10	16	12	9	1	0	70

PARAMARIBO

Suriname

				Elevation 4 m. (12 ft.)			5°49'N—55°9'W						
	JAN	**FEB**	**MAR**	**APR**	**MAY**	**JUN**	**JUL**	**AUG**	**SEP**	**OCT**	**NOV**	**DEC**	**YEAR**
TEMPERATURE													
Daily Average Min.°C	22	22	22	23	23	23	23	23	23	23	23	22	22
Daily Average Min.°F	72	71	72	73	73	73	73	73	73	73	73	72	73
Daily Average Max.°C	29	29	29	30	30	30	31	32	33	33	32	30	31
Daily Average Max.°F	85	85	85	86	86	86	87	89	91	91	89	86	87
Extreme Monthly Min.°C	17	17	17	17	18	19	17	18	18	19	19	17	16
Extreme Monthly Min.°F	62	63	62	62	64	66	62	65	65	67	66	63	62
Extreme Monthly Max.°C	35	33	34	34	34	34	34	34	35	37	37	34	37
Extreme Monthly Max.°F	95	92	94	93	94	94	94	94	95	98	99	94	99
Monthly Average °C	26	26	27	27	27	27	27	27	28	28	28	27	27
Monthly Average °F	79	80	81	81	80	80	81	81	82	82	81	80	81
RELATIVE HUMIDITY (%)	77	74	75	75	79	80	76	70	66	67	71	77	74
PRECIPITATION													
Monthly Average mm	248	132	83	130	278	328	180	171	92	94	101	161	1998.0
Monthly Average Inches	9.7	5.1	3.2	5.1	10.9	12.9	7.0	6.7	3.6	3.7	3.9	6.3	78.1
Days of 1mm or More	0	0	0	0	0	0	0	0	0	0	0	0	0

KARLSTAD

Sweden

				Elevation 47 m. (154 ft.)			59°24'N—13°30'E						
	JAN	**FEB**	**MAR**	**APR**	**MAY**	**JUN**	**JUL**	**AUG**	**SEP**	**OCT**	**NOV**	**DEC**	**YEAR**
TEMPERATURE													
Daily Average Min.°C	-8	-8	-6	0	6	10	13	12	8	3	0	-4	2
Daily Average Min.°F	19	18	22	0	42	50	55	53	46	38	31	26	33
Daily Average Max.°C	-1	-1	3	9	16	20	22	21	16	10	5	2	10
Daily Average Max.°F	30	31	38	49	60	67	72	69	61	50	40	35	50
Extreme Monthly Min.°C	-29	-27	-27	-18	-5	1	6	3	-3	-10	-19	-25	-29
Extreme Monthly Min.°F	-21	-17	-17	-1	23	34	43	37	27	14	-2	-13	-21
Extreme Monthly Max.°C	9	11	17	23	27	32	34	32	24	20	13	9	33
Extreme Monthly Max.°F	48	52	63	73	81	90	93	89	75	68	55	48	93
Monthly Average °C	-5	-5	-1	4	10	15	16	15	11	7	2	-2	6
Monthly Average °F	23	23	30	39	50	59	61	60	52	44	35	28	42
RELATIVE HUMIDITY (%)	83	75	65	56	52	54	58	62	66	71	82	85	67
PRECIPITATION													
Monthly Average mm	43	27	36	36	42	49	60	76	66	67	76	51	629.0
Monthly Average Inches	1.6	1.0	1.4	1.4	1.6	1.9	2.3	2.9	2.5	2.6	2.9	2.0	24.1
Days of 1mm or More	9	5	7	7	7	8	8	9	10	10	11	8	99

OSTERSUND

Sweden

				Elevation 338 m. (1109 ft.)			63°12'N—14°39'E						
	JAN	**FEB**	**MAR**	**APR**	**MAY**	**JUN**	**JUL**	**AUG**	**SEP**	**OCT**	**NOV**	**DEC**	**YEAR**
TEMPERATURE													
Daily Average Min.°C	-12	-11	-8	-3	2	7	10	9	5	1	-4	-8	-1
Daily Average Min.°F	11	12	17	28	36	45	51	48	42	33	26	18	30
Daily Average Max.°C	-5	-4	1	6	13	17	20	18	13	6	1	-2	7
Daily Average Max.°F	23	25	33	43	55	62	68	65	55	43	33	28	44
Monthly Average °C	-9	-8	-4	1	7	12	14	13	8	4	-2	-6	2
Monthly Average °F	15	18	25	34	45	54	56	55	47	39	28	21	36
RELATIVE HUMIDITY (%)	85	81	72	66	55	59	62	64	71	78	87	87	72
PRECIPITATION													
Monthly Average mm	30	23	26	31	37	61	83	61	59	44	40	40	535.0
Monthly Average Inches	1.1	0.9	1.0	1.2	1.4	2.4	3.2	2.4	2.3	1.7	1.5	1.5	20.6
Days of 1mm or More	7	6	7	7	7	9	11	9	10	9	8	9	99

STOCKHOLM   Sweden

	Elevation 44 m. (144 ft.)					59°24'N—18°6'E							
	JAN	FEB	MAR	APR	MAY	JUN	JUL	AUG	SEP	OCT	NOV	DEC	YEAR
TEMPERATURE													
Daily Average Min.°C	-5	-5	-4	1	6	11	14	13	9	5	1	-2	4
Daily Average Min.°F	23	22	26	34	43	51	57	56	49	41	34	29	39
Daily Average Max.°C	-1	-1	3	8	14	19	122	20	15	9	5	2	18
Daily Average Max.°F	30	30	37	47	58	67	251	68	60	49	40	35	64
Extreme Monthly Min.°C	-32	-30	-26	-22	-7	0	4	2	-3	-9	-18	-23	-32
Extreme Monthly Min.°F	-26	-22	-14	-8	20	32	40	36	26	16	0	-9	-26
Extreme Monthly Max.°C	11	12	15	25	29	33	36	33	29	20	14	11	36
Extreme Monthly Max.°F	51	54	59	77	84	91	97	91	84	68	57	52	97
Monthly Average °C	-3	-3	0	4	10	15	17	16	12	7	3	-1	6
Monthly Average °F	27	26	31	40	51	60	63	61	54	45	37	30	44
RELATIVE HUMIDITY (%)	82	75	67	62	54	55	59	64	68	76	84	86	69
PRECIPITATION													
Monthly Average mm	39	26	24	31	29	47	69	73	50	49	52	46	535.0
Monthly Average Inches	1.5	1.0	0.9	1.2	1.1	1.8	2.7	2.8	1.9	1.9	2.0	1.8	20.6
Days of 1mm or More	9	6	6	6	6	7	9	9	9	8	11	10	96

VISBY (GOTLAND)   Sweden

	Elevation 28 m. (91 ft.)					57°42'N—18°18'E							
	JAN	FEB	MAR	APR	MAY	JUN	JUL	AUG	SEP	OCT	NOV	DEC	YEAR
TEMPERATURE													
Daily Average Min.°C	-3	-4	-2	1	3	10	14	13	10	6	3	0	5
Daily Average Min.°F	27	26	28	34	37	50	57	56	51	43	37	32	40
Daily Average Max.°C	1	1	3	8	14	18	21	20	16	11	6	3	10
Daily Average Max.°F	34	33	37	46	56	65	70	68	60	51	43	38	50
Extreme Monthly Min.°C	-17	-17	-16	-15	-3	0	6	5	-1	-7	-12	-13	-17
Extreme Monthly Min.°F	1	1	3	5	27	32	42	41	30	19	10	9	1
Extreme Monthly Max.°C	8	9	16	23	27	31	30	31	25	21	15	11	31
Extreme Monthly Max.°F	47	48	61	73	81	88	86	87	77	70	59	52	88
Monthly Average °C	-1	-2	0	4	9	14	16	16	12	9	4	1	7
Monthly Average °F	30	29	33	39	48	57	61	61	54	47	40	34	45
RELATIVE HUMIDITY (%)	83	79	75	71	65	66	71	71	73	77	81	84	75
PRECIPITATION													
Monthly Average mm	53	30	34	29	31	27	49	49	57	47	54	53	513.0
Monthly Average Inches	2.0	1.1	1.3	1.1	1.2	1.0	1.9	1.9	2.2	1.8	2.1	2.0	19.6
Days of 1mm or More	11	7	8	6	6	5	7	7	9	8	11	11	96

GENEVA   Switzerland

	Elevation 405 m. (1328 ft.)					46°12'N—6°12'E							
	JAN	FEB	MAR	APR	MAY	JUN	JUL	AUG	SEP	OCT	NOV	DEC	YEAR
TEMPERATURE													
Daily Average Min.°C	-2	-1	2	5	9	13	15	14	12	7	3	0	6
Daily Average Min.°F	29	30	36	42	49	55	58	58	53	44	37	31	44
Daily Average Max.°C	4	6	10	15	19	23	25	24	21	14	8	4	16
Daily Average Max.°F	38	42	51	59	66	73	77	76	69	58	47	40	58
Extreme Monthly Min.°C	-16	-18	-12	-5	-2	2	6	5	0	-7	-8	-15	-18
Extreme Monthly Min.°F	3	-1	10	23	29	36	42	41	32	20	17	5	-1
Extreme Monthly Max.°C	17	20	24	27	32	36	38	36	33	26	23	18	38
Extreme Monthly Max.°F	62	68	76	81	89	96	101	97	91	79	74	64	101
Monthly Average °C	1	2	5	9	13	17	19	18	15	10	5	2	10
Monthly Average °F	33	36	41	48	55	62	66	64	59	50	41	35	49
RELATIVE HUMIDITY (%)	78	71	61	55	57	55	55	57	63	69	76	78	65
PRECIPITATION													
Monthly Average mm	83	77	80	62	74	91	69	89	88	73	93	87	966.0
Monthly Average Inches	3.2	3.0	3.1	2.4	2.9	3.5	2.7	3.5	3.4	2.8	3.6	3.4	37.5
Days of 1mm or More	11	8	10	7	12	10	8	9	7	9	9	9	109

ZURICH   Switzerland

		Elevation 493 m. (1617 ft.)				47°24'N—8°36'E							
	JAN	FEB	MAR	APR	MAY	JUN	JUL	AUG	SEP	OCT	NOV	DEC	YEAR
TEMPERATURE													
Daily Average Min.°C	-3	-2	1	4	8	12	14	13	11	6	2	-2	5
Daily Average Min.°F	26	28	34	40	47	53	56	56	51	43	35	29	41
Daily Average Max.°C	2	5	10	15	19	23	25	24	20	14	7	3	14
Daily Average Max.°F	36	41	51	59	67	73	76	75	69	57	45	37	57
Monthly Average °C	-1	1	4	8	12	16	18	17	14	9	4	1	9
Monthly Average °F	31	34	39	46	54	60	64	62	57	49	39	33	47
RELATIVE HUMIDITY (%)	74	65	55	51	52	52	52	53	57	64	73	76	60
PRECIPITATION													
Monthly Average mm	76	73	69	91	105	130	117	139	92	70	83	76	1121.0
Monthly Average Inches	2.9	2.8	2.7	3.5	4.1	5.1	4.6	5.4	3.6	2.7	3.2	2.9	43.5
Days of 1mm or More	11	10	11	12	13	12	11	12	8	8	10	10	128

DAMASCUS   Syria

		Elevation 720 m. (2362 ft.)				33°30'N—36°20'E							
	JAN	FEB	MAR	APR	MAY	JUN	JUL	AUG	SEP	OCT	NOV	DEC	YEAR
TEMPERATURE													
Daily Average Min.°C	2	4	6	9	13	16	18	18	16	12	8	4	11
Daily Average Min.°F	36	39	42	49	55	61	64	64	60	54	47	40	51
Daily Average Max.°C	12	14	18	24	29	33	36	37	33	27	19	13	25
Daily Average Max.°F	53	57	65	75	84	91	96	99	91	81	67	56	76
Extreme Monthly Min.°C	-6	-5	-2	1	7	9	13	13	10	6	-2	-5	-6
Extreme Monthly Min.°F	21	23	28	33	44	48	55	55	50	42	28	23	21
Extreme Monthly Max.°C	21	30	28	35	38	39	42	45	39	34	30	21	42
Extreme Monthly Max.°F	69	86	83	95	101	102	108	113	102	93	86	69	108
Monthly Average °C	8	10	14	19	21	25	26	27	25	19	14	8	18
Monthly Average °F	47	50	56	66	71	77	79	80	77	66	58	47	64
RELATIVE HUMIDITY (%)	57	53	42	32	26	22	19	21	24	31	46	59	36
PRECIPITATION													
Monthly Average mm	42	18	47	4						15	25	26	177.0
Monthly Average Inches	1.6	0.7	1.8	0.1	0.0	0.0	0.0	0.0	0.0	0.5	0.9	1.0	6.6
Days of 1mm or More	0	0	0	0	0	0	0	0	0	0	0	0	0

TAINAN   Taiwan

		Elevation 14 m. (45 ft.)				44°6'N—96°48'E							
	JAN	FEB	MAR	APR	MAY	JUN	JUL	AUG	SEP	OCT	NOV	DEC	YEAR
TEMPERATURE													
Monthly Average °C	17	18	21	24	27	28	28	28	28	25	22	19	24
Monthly Average °F	63	64	70	75	81	82	83	83	82	78	72	66	75
PRECIPITATION													
Monthly Average mm	15	24	38	78	202	442	405	407	207	34	22	22	1896.0
Monthly Average Inches	0.5	0.9	1.4	3.0	7.9	17.4	15.9	16.0	8.1	1.3	0.8	0.8	74.0
Days of 1mm or More	0	0	0	0	0	0	0	0	0	0	0	0	0

TAIPEI Taiwan

		Elevation 9 m. (29 ft.)				25°2'N—121°31'E							
	JAN	FEB	MAR	APR	MAY	JUN	JUL	AUG	SEP	OCT	NOV	DEC	YEAR
TEMPERATURE													
Daily Average Min.°C	12	12	14	17	21	23	24	24	23	19	17	14	18
Daily Average Min.°F	54	53	57	63	69	73	76	75	73	67	62	57	65
Daily Average Max.°C	19	18	21	25	28	32	33	33	31	27	24	21	26
Daily Average Max.°F	66	65	70	77	83	89	92	91	88	81	75	69	79
Extreme Monthly Min.°F	37	32	35	46	50	60	67	66	56	51	34	35	32
Extreme Monthly Max.°C	30	31	33	35	37	37	38	38	36	35	33	31	38
Extreme Monthly Max.°F	86	88	91	95	98	99	101	100	97	95	92	88	101
Monthly Average °C	15	15	18	21	25	27	29	28	27	23	21	17	22
Monthly Average °F	59	60	64	70	77	80	83	83	81	74	69	63	72
RELATIVE HUMIDITY (%)	71	75	69	71	68	68	62	64	66	65	65	69	68
PRECIPITATION													
Monthly Average mm	93	137	135	136	196	291	256	230	264	123	80	75	2016.0
Monthly Average Inches	3.6	5.3	5.3	5.3	7.7	11.4	10.0	9.0	10.3	4.8	3.1	2.9	78.7
Days of 1mm or More	10	10	11	8	11	13	9	8	12	9	8	10	119

DAR ES SALAAM Tanzania

		Elevation 58 m. (190 ft.)				6°53'S—39°12'E							
	JAN	FEB	MAR	APR	MAY	JUN	JUL	AUG	SEP	OCT	NOV	DEC	YEAR
TEMPERATURE													
Daily Average Min.°C	24	24	23	23	21	19	19	18	19	20	22	23	21
Daily Average Min.°F	76	75	74	73	71	67	65	65	66	68	71	74	70
Daily Average Max.°C	31	32	32	31	30	29	29	29	30	30	31	31	30
Daily Average Max.°F	88	89	89	87	86	85	84	85	85	87	87	88	87
Extreme Monthly Min.°C	21	20	21	19	18	16	16	15	16	17	19	21	15
Extreme Monthly Min.°F	69	68	69	66	64	60	60	59	61	62	66	69	59
Extreme Monthly Max.°C	35	35	36	35	33	32	32	32	33	33	34	35	35
Extreme Monthly Max.°F	95	95	96	95	91	90	90	89	91	92	94	95	96
Monthly Average °C	27	28	27	27	25	24	24	24	24	25	26	27	26
Monthly Average °F	81	82	81	80	78	75	74	75	76	77	79	81	78
RELATIVE HUMIDITY (%)	69	68	70	75	68	60	58	57	58	61	66	69	65
PRECIPITATION													
Monthly Average mm	73	62	135	274	157	34	30	26	28	57	127	100	1103.0
Monthly Average Inches	2.8	2.4	5.3	10.7	6.1	1.3	1.1	1.0	1.1	2.2	5.0	3.9	42.9
Days of 1mm or More	6	4	12	18	12	4	4	4	6	6	8	8	92

DODOMA Tanzania

		Elevation 1120 m. (3674 ft.)				6°10'S—35°46'E							
	JAN	FEB	MAR	APR	MAY	JUN	JUL	AUG	SEP	OCT	NOV	DEC	YEAR
TEMPERATURE													
Daily Average Min.°C	18	18	18	18	16	14	13	14	15	16	18	18	16
Daily Average Min.°F	65	64	64	64	61	57	55	57	59	61	64	65	61
Daily Average Max.°C	29	29	29	29	28	27	27	27	29	31	32	30	29
Daily Average Max.°F	84	84	85	84	83	81	80	81	85	87	89	86	84
Monthly Average °C	24	23	24	24	23	21	20	23	22	24	25	24	23
Monthly Average °F	74	74	75	75	73	70	68	73	72	75	76	76	73
RELATIVE HUMIDITY (%)	53	55	54	54	47	41	40	38	35	33	35	45	44
PRECIPITATION													
Monthly Average mm	135	119	99	46	4	0	0	0	0	2	19	122	546.0
Monthly Average Inches	5.3	4.6	3.8	1.8	0.1	0.0	0.0	0.0	0.0	0.0	0.7	4.8	21.1
Days of 1mm or More	10	7	8	2	1	0	0	0	0	0	4	7	39

MWANZA

Tanzania

Elevation 1140 m. (3740 ft.)				2°28'N—32°55'E								
	JAN	FEB	MAR	APR	MAY	JUN	JUL	AUG	SEP	OCT	NOV	DEC	YEAR

TEMPERATURE

	JAN	FEB	MAR	APR	MAY	JUN	JUL	AUG	SEP	OCT	NOV	DEC	YEAR
Daily Average Min.°C	18	18	18	18	18	16	15	16	18	18	19	18	18
Daily Average Min.°F	65	65	65	65	64	61	60	62	64	65	65	65	64
Daily Average Max.°C	27	28	28	28	28	28	28	28	29	29	28	27	28
Daily Average Max.°F	81	82	82	82	82	83	83	83	83	83	82	81	82
Monthly Average °C	23	23	23	23	23	22	22	23	12	24	23	23	22
Monthly Average °F	73	74	74	73	73	72	72	73	53	74	74	74	72
RELATIVE HUMIDITY (%)	64	63	63	67	63	54	49	52	53	55	61	65	59

PRECIPITATION

	JAN	FEB	MAR	APR	MAY	JUN	JUL	AUG	SEP	OCT	NOV	DEC	YEAR
Monthly Average mm	98	115	137	184	91	15	14	20	33	94	142	147	1090.0
Monthly Average Inches	3.8	4.5	5.3	7.2	3.5	0.5	0.5	0.7	1.2	3.7	5.5	5.7	42.1
Days of 1mm or More	10	8	12	17	6	1	3	1	2	8	12	13	93

SONGEA

Tanzania

Elevation 1067 m. (3500 ft.)				10°41'S—35°35'E								
	JAN	FEB	MAR	APR	MAY	JUN	JUL	AUG	SEP	OCT	NOV	DEC	YEAR

TEMPERATURE

	JAN	FEB	MAR	APR	MAY	JUN	JUL	AUG	SEP	OCT	NOV	DEC	YEAR
Daily Average Min.°C	18	18	18	17	15	12	12	13	15	17	18	18	16
Daily Average Min.°F	65	65	64	63	58	54	53	55	59	62	65	65	61
Daily Average Max.°C	27	27	27	26	25	23	23	24	26	29	29	28	26
Daily Average Max.°F	81	81	80	78	76	74	73	75	79	83	84	82	79
Monthly Average °C	23	23	22	22	20	18	17	19	21	23	24	23	21
Monthly Average °F	73	73	72	71	67	64	63	65	69	73	75	74	70
RELATIVE HUMIDITY (%)	64	65	68	65	58	53	50	46	42	39	44	58	54

PRECIPITATION

	JAN	FEB	MAR	APR	MAY	JUN	JUL	AUG	SEP	OCT	NOV	DEC	YEAR
Monthly Average mm	258	230	249	137	11	1	3	0	2	5	51	202	1149.0
Monthly Average Inches	10.1	9.0	9.8	5.3	0.4	0.0	0.1	0.0	0.0	0.1	2.0	7.9	44.7
Days of 1mm or More	18	17	18	12	2	0	1	0	0	1	5	14	88

TABORA

Tanzania

Elevation 1190 m. (3904 ft.)				5°5'N—32°50'E								
	JAN	FEB	MAR	APR	MAY	JUN	JUL	AUG	SEP	OCT	NOV	DEC	YEAR

TEMPERATURE

	JAN	FEB	MAR	APR	MAY	JUN	JUL	AUG	SEP	OCT	NOV	DEC	YEAR
Daily Average Min.°C	17	17	17	17	16	14	14	16	18	19	19	18	17
Daily Average Min.°F	63	63	63	63	61	58	57	60	64	66	66	64	62
Daily Average Max.°C	28	28	28	28	28	29	29	30	31	32	31	28	29
Daily Average Max.°F	82	83	83	83	83	83	83	85	88	90	87	83	84
Monthly Average °C	23	23	23	23	22	22	21	23	24	25	24	23	23
Monthly Average °F	73	73	73	73	72	71	70	73	76	78	76	73	73
RELATIVE HUMIDITY (%)	56	56	57	56	47	38	34	33	31	31	41	55	45

PRECIPITATION

	JAN	FEB	MAR	APR	MAY	JUN	JUL	AUG	SEP	OCT	NOV	DEC	YEAR
Monthly Average mm	149	138	169	150	40	0	1	0	4	26	115	186	978.0
Monthly Average Inches	5.8	5.4	6.6	5.9	1.5	0.0	0.0	0.0	0 1	1.0	4.5	7.3	38.1
Days of 1mm or More	13	12	13	11	3	0	0	0	0	3	11	16	82

BANGKOK Thailand

Elevation 2 m. (7 ft.) 13°45'N—100°28'E

	JAN	FEB	MAR	APR	MAY	JUN	JUL	AUG	SEP	OCT	NOV	DEC	YEAR
TEMPERATURE													
Daily Average Min.°C	20	22	24	25	25	24	24	24	24	24	22	20	23
Daily Average Min.°F	68	72	75	77	77	76	76	76	76	75	72	68	74
Daily Average Max.°C	32	33	34	35	34	33	32	32	32	31	31	31	32
Daily Average Max.°F	89	91	93	95	93	91	90	90	89	88	87	87	90
Extreme Monthly Min.°C	13	13	17	19	22	21	22	22	21	18	13	11	11
Extreme Monthly Min.°F	55	56	62	67	71	70	71	72	69	64	56	52	52
Extreme Monthly Max.°C	38	41	40	41	41	38	38	37	37	38	37	38	41
Extreme Monthly Max.°F	100	106	104	106	106	100	101	99	98	100	99	100	106
Monthly Average °C	26	28	29	30	30	29	29	29	28	28	27	26	28
Monthly Average °F	79	82	85	87	86	85	84	84	83	83	81	79	83
RELATIVE HUMIDITY (%)	53	55	56	58	64	67	66	66	70	70	65	56	62
PRECIPITATION													
Monthly Average mm	9	24	25	62	205	152	156	196	338	234	54	12	1467.0
Monthly Average Inches	0.3	0.9	0.9	2.4	8.0	5.9	6.1	7.7	13.3	9.2	2.1	0.4	57.2
Days of 1mm or More	0	2	1	4	12	12	13	14	17	13	5	1	94

CHIANG MAI Thailand

Elevation 314 m. (1030 ft.) 18°47'N—98°59'E

	JAN	FEB	MAR	APR	MAY	JUN	JUL	AUG	SEP	OCT	NOV	DEC	YEAR
TEMPERATURE													
Daily Average Min.°C	13	14	17	22	23	23	23	23	23	21	19	15	20
Daily Average Min.°F	56	58	63	71	73	74	74	74	73	70	66	59	68
Daily Average Max.°C	29	32	34	36	34	32	31	31	31	30	28	28	32
Daily Average Max.°F	84	89	94	97	94	90	88	88	88	87	86	83	89
Monthly Average °C	21	23	27	28	29	28	28	27	27	26	24	22	26
Monthly Average °F	70	74	80	82	84	83	82	81	81	80	76	71	79
RELATIVE HUMIDITY (%)	52	44	40	49	60	67	69	73	72	69	63	57	60
PRECIPITATION													
Monthly Average mm	12	1	13	46	150	127	165	234	236	115	50	22	1171.0
Monthly Average Inches	0.4	0.0	0.5	1.8	5.9	5.0	6.4	9.2	9.2	4.5	1.9	0.8	45.6
Days of 1mm or More	1	0	1	4	11	12	14	17	14	8	4	2	88

PHITSANULOK Thailand

Elevation 50 m. (164 ft.) 16°50'N—100°15'E

	JAN	FEB	MAR	APR	MAY	JUN	JUL	AUG	SEP	OCT	NOV	DEC	YEAR
TEMPERATURE													
Monthly Average °C	25	27	30	31	30	29	29	28	28	28	27	25	28
Monthly Average °F	76	81	85	89	87	85	84	83	83	83	80	76	83
PRECIPITATION													
Monthly Average mm	7	10	28	51	186	186	197	245	264	141	33	4	1352.0
Monthly Average Inches	0.2	0.3	1.1	2.0	7.3	7.3	7.7	9.6	10.3	5.5	1.2	0.1	52.6
Days of 1mm or More	1	1	2	3	11	13	14	16	15	8	2	1	87

SONGKHLA — Thailand

		JAN	FEB	MAR	APR	MAY	JUN	JUL	AUG	SEP	OCT	NOV	DEC	YEAR
Elevation 10 m. (32 ft.)	7°12'N—100°36'E													
TEMPERATURE														
Monthly Average °C	27	27	28	29	29	28	28	28	28	27	27	27	28
Monthly Average °F	80	81	82	83	84	83	83	83	82	81	80	80	82
RELATIVE HUMIDITY (%)														
PRECIPITATION														
Monthly Average mm	82	31	43	65	114	106	96	99	126	288	569	442	2061.0
Monthly Average Inches	3.2	1.2	1.6	2.5	4.4	4.1	3.7	3.8	4.9	11.3	22.4	17.4	80.5
Days of 1mm or More	6	3	3	5	10	9	8	9	11	17	19	17	117

ATAKPAME — Togo

		JAN	FEB	MAR	APR	MAY	JUN	JUL	AUG	SEP	OCT	NOV	DEC	YEAR
Elevation 400 m. (1312 ft.)	7°35'N—1°7'E													
TEMPERATURE														
Daily Average Min.°C	21	22	21	21	21	20	20	20	20	20	21	21	21
Daily Average Min.°F	69	71	71	70	70	68	68	67	68	68	69	69	69
Daily Average Max.°C	33	34	34	32	31	29	28	28	29	30	32	32	31
Daily Average Max.°F	91	94	92	90	88	85	82	82	84	86	90	90	88
Monthly Average °C	27	28	27	27	26	25	24	24	24	25	26	26	26
Monthly Average °F	80	82	81	80	79	76	75	74	75	77	79	79	78
RELATIVE HUMIDITY (%)	43	45	55	62	66	73	76	77	76	69	57	49	62
PRECIPITATION														
Monthly Average mm	9	39	93	121	136	197	213	180	203	127	35	16	1369.0
Monthly Average Inches	0.3	1.5	3.6	4.7	5.3	7.7	8.3	7.0	7.9	5.0	1.3	0.6	53.2
Days of 1mm or More	0	2	6	7	8	11	14	14	13	8	1	0	84

LOME — Togo

		JAN	FEB	MAR	APR	MAY	JUN	JUL	AUG	SEP	OCT	NOV	DEC	YEAR
Elevation 21 m. (68 ft.)	6°10'N—1°15'E													
TEMPERATURE														
Daily Average Min.°C	22	24	24	24	23	22	22	22	22	23	23	23	23
Daily Average Min.°F	72	74	75	75	74	72	72	71	72	73	74	73	73
Daily Average Max.°C	31	32	32	32	31	30	28	28	29	29	31	31	30
Daily Average Max.°F	88	89	90	89	87	86	82	82	84	85	87	88	86
Monthly Average °C	27	28	28	28	27	26	25	25	25	26	27	27	27
Monthly Average °F	80	82	82	82	81	78	77	77	78	79	81	80	80
RELATIVE HUMIDITY (%)	64	66	67	69	73	78	78	75	74	72	68	63	71
PRECIPITATION														
Monthly Average mm	14	36	69	98	142	262	92	31	60	88	24	9	925.0
Monthly Average Inches	0.5	1.4	2.7	3.8	5.5	10.3	3.6	1.2	2.3	3.4	0.9	0.3	35.9
Days of 1mm or More	0	1	4	5	9	12	7	4	6	5	1	1	55

SOKODE   Togo

	Elevation 403 m. (1322 ft.)					8°58'N—1°8'E						
	JAN	FEB	MAR	APR	MAY	JUN	JUL	AUG	SEP	OCT	NOV	DEC	YEAR
TEMPERATURE													
Daily Average Min.°C	17	19	21	22	21	21	21	21	20	20	18	17	20
Daily Average Min.°F	62	66	70	71	71	69	69	69	68	68	65	62	67
Daily Average Max.°C	34	35	35	33	32	30	28	28	29	31	33	33	32
Daily Average Max.°F	93	95	95	92	89	86	83	82	84	88	92	92	89
Monthly Average °C	26	27	28	28	27	25	24	24	25	25	25	25	26
Monthly Average °F	78	81	83	82	80	78	76	75	76	78	78	77	78
RELATIVE HUMIDITY (%)	32	36	49	57	64	70	74	76	74	62	45	34	56
PRECIPITATION													
Monthly Average mm	6	22	62	103	139	198	235	261	255	108	20	17	1426.0
Monthly Average Inches	0.2	0.8	2.4	4.0	5.4	7.7	9.2	10.2	10.0	4.2	0.7	0.6	55.4
Days of 1mm or More	0	1	4	7	10	12	16	17	15	7	1	0	90

NUKU'ALOFA   Tonga

	Elevation 3 m. (9 ft.)					21°8'S—175°12'W						
	JAN	FEB	MAR	APR	MAY	JUN	JUL	AUG	SEP	OCT	NOV	DEC	YEAR
TEMPERATURE													
Daily Average Min.°C	22	23	23	22	20	18	18	18	18	19	21	21	20
Daily Average Min.°F	72	73	73	71	68	65	64	65	64	67	69	69	68
Daily Average Max.°C	29	29	29	28	26	25	25	24	25	26	27	28	27
Daily Average Max.°F	84	85	84	82	79	77	77	76	77	78	81	82	80
Monthly Average °C	26	26	26	25	23	23	21	21	22	22	24	25	24
Monthly Average °F	78	79	79	77	74	73	70	70	71	72	74	76	74
RELATIVE HUMIDITY (%)	74	75	77	73	74	74	71	72	72	71	70	72	73
PRECIPITATION													
Monthly Average mm	204	235	232	168	94	88	97	107	112	130	101	135	1703.0
Monthly Average Inches	8.0	9.2	9.1	6.6	3.7	3.4	3.8	4.2	4.4	5.1	3.9	5.3	66.7
Days of 1mm or More	0	0	0	0	0	0	0	0	0	0	0	0	0

PIARCO AIRPORT   Trinidad and Tobago

	Elevation 12 m. (39 ft.)					10°37'N—61°21'W						
	JAN	FEB	MAR	APR	MAY	JUN	JUL	AUG	SEP	OCT	NOV	DEC	YEAR
TEMPERATURE													
Daily Average Min.°C	20	21	21	22	23	23	23	22	23	22	22	21	22
Daily Average Min.°F	68	69	69	71	73	73	73	72	73	72	71	70	71
Daily Average Max.°C	30	30	31	32	32	31	31	31	32	32	31	30	31
Daily Average Max.°F	86	86	88	89	89	87	87	88	89	89	88	86	88
Monthly Average °C	25	25	26	26	27	26	26	26	26	26	26	25	26
Monthly Average °F	76	77	78	80	80	79	79	79	79	79	78	77	79
RELATIVE HUMIDITY (%)	65	62	58	57	65	73	73	73	70	71	72	70	67
PRECIPITATION													
Monthly Average mm	71	37	29	43	105	250	262	234	185	177	219	128	1740.0
Monthly Average Inches	2.7	1.4	1.1	1.6	4.1	9.8	10.3	9.2	7.2	6.9	8.6	5.0	67.9
Days of 1mm or More	11	7	5	6	11	19	21	19	16	15	16	15	161

GABES

Tunisia

		Elevation 5 m. (16 ft.)					33°53'N—10°6'E						
	JAN	FEB	MAR	APR	MAY	JUN	JUL	AUG	SEP	OCT	NOV	DEC	YEAR
TEMPERATURE													
Daily Average Min.°C	6	8	10	13	16	21	22	23	21	17	12	8	15
Daily Average Min.°F	44	46	51	56	62	70	72	74	71	62	53	46	59
Daily Average Max.°C	16	18	20	22	24	28	31	31	30	26	22	17	24
Daily Average Max.°F	61	64	67	71	76	82	87	88	85	78	71	63	75
Extreme Monthly Min.°C	-3	-2	2	4	4	6	9	14	12	6	1	0	-2
Extreme Monthly Min.°F	27	28	36	39	39	43	48	57	54	43	34	32	28
Extreme Monthly Max.°C	27	31	37	42	43	46	50	47	49	44	36	27	50
Extreme Monthly Max.°F	81	88	99	108	109	115	122	117	120	111	97	81	122
Monthly Average °C	11	13	15	17	21	24	27	27	26	21	16	12	19
Monthly Average °F	53	55	59	63	69	75	80	81	78	70	61	54	67
RELATIVE HUMIDITY (%)	54	51	53	58	62	63	60	61	61	59	53	54	57
PRECIPITATION													
Monthly Average mm	17	17	18	22	6	1	0	0	28	49	18	26	202.0
Monthly Average Inches	0.6	0.6	0.7	0.8	0.2	0.0	0.0	0.0	1.1	1.9	0.7	1.0	7.6
Days of 1mm or More	2	2	2	3	0	0	0	0	2	4	2	3	20

GAFSA

Tunisia

		Elevation 314 m. (1030 ft.)					34°25'N—8°49'E						
	JAN	FEB	MAR	APR	MAY	JUN	JUL	AUG	SEP	OCT	NOV	DEC	YEAR
TEMPERATURE													
Daily Average Min.°C	4	5	8	11	15	19	21	22	19	14	9	5	13
Daily Average Min.°F	39	41	47	52	58	67	70	71	66	58	48	41	55
Daily Average Max.°C	14	17	20	23	28	33	36	36	32	25	20	15	25
Daily Average Max.°F	57	62	68	74	83	92	97	96	89	78	68	59	77
Monthly Average °C	9	11	13	17	22	26	29	29	25	19	14	9	19
Monthly Average °F	49	52	56	62	71	79	84	84	77	66	57	49	65
RELATIVE HUMIDITY (%)	56	47	43	43	37	33	31	33	41	49	50	57	43
PRECIPITATION													
Monthly Average mm	12	12	21	18	11	8	2	5	19	26	11	27	172.0
Monthly Average Inches	0.4	0.4	0.8	0.7	0.4	0.3	0.0	0.1	0.7	1.0	0.4	1.0	6.2
Days of 1mm or More	2	2	3	2	1	1	0	0	3	2	1	3	20

TUNIS

Tunisia

		Elevation 4 m. (13 ft.)					36°50'N—10°14'E						
	JAN	FEB	MAR	APR	MAY	JUN	JUL	AUG	SEP	OCT	NOV	DEC	YEAR
TEMPERATURE													
Daily Average Min.°C	7	7	9	11	14	18	20	21	20	16	12	9	14
Daily Average Min.°F	44	45	48	51	57	65	69	70	68	60	53	47	57
Daily Average Max.°C	15	16	18	21	25	29	32	32	30	25	21	16	23
Daily Average Max.°F	59	62	65	69	77	84	90	90	85	77	69	62	74
Extreme Monthly Min.°C	-1	0	1	3	6	9	10	11	11	7	1	-1	-1
Extreme Monthly Min.°F	30	32	34	37	43	48	50	52	52	45	34	30	30
Extreme Monthly Max.°C	25	29	33	40	40	43	48	47	44	40	32	27	47
Extreme Monthly Max.°F	77	84	91	104	104	109	118	117	111	104	90	81	118
Monthly Average °C	11	12	13	15	19	23	26	26	24	20	16	12	18
Monthly Average °F	52	53	56	59	66	73	79	80	75	68	60	54	65
RELATIVE HUMIDITY (%)	68	64	61	60	53	50	45	48	54	59	63	67	58
PRECIPITATION													
Monthly Average mm	59	59	51	41	22	12	2	6	36	71	58	58	475.0
Monthly Average Inches	2.3	2.3	2.0	1.6	0.8	0.4	0.0	0.2	1.4	2.7	2.2	2.2	18.1
Days of 1mm or More	8	9	8	5	3	1	0	1	3	6	6	7	57

ANKARA   Turkey

Elevation 861 m. (2825 ft.)   39°57'N—32°54'E

	JAN	FEB	MAR	APR	MAY	JUN	JUL	AUG	SEP	OCT	NOV	DEC	YEAR
TEMPERATURE													
Daily Average Min.°C	-4	-3	-1	4	9	12	15	15	11	7	3	-2	6
Daily Average Min.°F	24	26	31	40	49	53	59	59	52	44	37	29	42
Daily Average Max.°C	4	6	11	17	23	26	30	31	26	21	14	6	18
Daily Average Max.°F	39	42	51	63	73	78	86	87	78	69	57	43	64
Extreme Monthly Min.°C	-25	-24	-16	-7	-1	2	7	4	-2	-3	-18	-25	-25
Extreme Monthly Min.°F	-13	-12	3	20	31	35	44	40	29	27	0	-13	-13
Extreme Monthly Max.°C	15	18	27	32	34	37	38	38	36	32	26	17	37
Extreme Monthly Max.°F	59	64	80	89	94	98	100	100	96	89	78	63	100
Monthly Average °C	0	2	6	11	16	20	23	23	18	13	8	3	12
Monthly Average °F	33	35	42	52	60	67	73	73	65	55	46	37	53
RELATIVE HUMIDITY (%)	70	67	52	40	38	34	28	25	31	37	52	71	45
PRECIPITATION													
Monthly Average mm	51	37	37	44	52	37	14	8	19	25	30	49	403.0
Monthly Average Inches	2.0	1.4	1.4	1.7	2.0	1.4	0.5	0.3	0.7	0.9	1.1	1.9	15.3
Days of 1mm or More	8	7	7	7	9	5	2	1	2	4	5	7	64

ANTALYA   Turkey

Elevation 40 m. (131 ft.)   36°54'N—30°42'E

	JAN	FEB	MAR	APR	MAY	JUN	JUL	AUG	SEP	OCT	NOV	DEC	YEAR
TEMPERATURE													
Daily Average Min.°C	6	7	8	11	16	19	23	22	19	15	11	8	14
Daily Average Min.°F	43	44	46	52	60	67	73	72	67	59	52	46	57
Daily Average Max.°C	15	16	18	21	26	30	34	33	31	27	22	17	24
Daily Average Max.°F	59	60	64	70	78	86	93	92	87	80	71	62	75
Monthly Average °C	10	10	13	16	20	25	28	28	24	20	15	12	18
Monthly Average °F	50	51	55	61	69	77	82	82	76	68	60	53	65
RELATIVE HUMIDITY (%)	70	69	65	67	68	64	60	61	59	64	68	70	65
PRECIPITATION													
Monthly Average mm	269	188	95	48	25	8	3	1	14	83	122	241	1097.0
Monthly Average Inches	10.5	7.4	3.7	1.8	0.9	0.3	0.1	0.0	0.5	3.2	4.8	9.4	42.6
Days of 1mm or More	10	9	7	4	3	1	0	0	1	3	5	9	52

ERZURUM   Turkey

Elevation 1952 m. (6402 ft.)   39°54'N—41°18'E

	JAN	FEB	MAR	APR	MAY	JUN	JUL	AUG	SEP	OCT	NOV	DEC	YEAR
TEMPERATURE													
Daily Average Min.°F	8	12	18	32	41	46	53	53	46	37	29	16	33
Daily Average Max.°C	-4	-2	2	10	17	21	26	27	22	15	7	-1	12
Daily Average Max.°F	24	28	35	50	62	70	78	80	72	59	45	31	53
Extreme Monthly Min.°C	-30	-27	-25	-18	-6	1	3	1	-4	-12	-23	-26	-30
Extreme Monthly Min.°F	-22	-17	-13	-1	22	34	37	34	25	10	-10	-14	-22
Extreme Monthly Max.°C	6	9	18	22	26	30	34	34	32	26	19	12	33
Extreme Monthly Max.°F	42	49	64	71	78	86	93	93	89	79	66	54	93
Monthly Average °C	-8	-7	-2	6	11	15	19	19	15	8	2	-5	6
Monthly Average °F	17	19	29	42	51	59	67	67	59	47	36	23	43
RELATIVE HUMIDITY (%)	74	71	69	51	45	37	29	28	30	39	55	64	49
PRECIPITATION													
Monthly Average mm	23	24	30	50	74	51	25	19	23	43	31	19	412.0
Monthly Average Inches	0.9	0.9	1.1	1.9	2.9	2.0	0.9	0.7	0.9	1.6	1.2	0.7	15.7
Days of 1mm or More	5	5	7	9	12	8	3	2	3	6	5	4	69

ISTANBUL   Turkey

	JAN	FEB	MAR	APR	MAY	JUN	JUL	AUG	SEP	OCT	NOV	DEC	YEAR
Elevation 114 m. (374 ft.)					41°6'N—29°6'E								
TEMPERATURE													
Daily Average Min.°C	3	2	3	7	12	16	18	19	16	13	9	5	10
Daily Average Min.°F	37	36	38	45	53	60	65	66	61	55	48	41	50
Daily Average Max.°C	8	9	11	16	21	25	28	28	24	20	15	11	18
Daily Average Max.°F	46	47	51	60	69	77	82	82	76	68	59	51	64
Extreme Monthly Min.°C	-8	-7	-6	0	3	9	13	12	8	2	-4	-8	-8
Extreme Monthly Min.°F	18	20	21	32	38	48	56	53	47	35	25	17	17
Extreme Monthly Max.°C	19	21	28	35	34	37	38	38	38	29	25	21	37
Extreme Monthly Max.°F	66	69	82	95	94	99	100	100	100	85	77	70	100
Monthly Average °C	6	6	7	12	17	21	23	23	19	15	12	8	14
Monthly Average °F	42	42	45	53	62	70	74	73	67	60	54	47	57
RELATIVE HUMIDITY (%)	75	72	67	62	61	58	56	55	59	64	71	74	64
PRECIPITATION													
Monthly Average mm	108	67	65	48	31	21	23	32	44	69	81	119	708.0
Monthly Average Inches	4.2	2.6	2.5	1.8	1.2	0.8	0.9	1.2	1.7	2.7	3.1	4.6	27.3
Days of 1mm or More	13	10	9	6	5	3	2	3	3	6	8	11	79

VAN   Turkey

	JAN	FEB	MAR	APR	MAY	JUN	JUL	AUG	SEP	OCT	NOV	DEC	YEAR
Elevation 1732 m. (5682 ft.)					38°30'N—43°21'E								
TEMPERATURE													
Daily Average Min.°C	-8	-8	-5	1	6	10	14	14	9	5	1	-6	3
Daily Average Min.°F	18	17	23	34	43	50	57	57	49	41	33	22	37
Daily Average Max.°C	1	2	4	11	18	24	28	28	24	17	11	3	14
Daily Average Max.°F	34	35	40	52	65	75	83	83	76	62	52	38	58
Monthly Average °C	-4	-4	1	7	13	18	22	21	17	10	4	-1	9
Monthly Average °F	25	25	34	45	55	64	71	70	62	50	40	30	48
RELATIVE HUMIDITY (%)	73	73	73	69	60	51	45	41	43	61	69	70	61
PRECIPITATION													
Monthly Average mm	33	32	40	53	53	19	5	3	12	42	46	31	369.0
Monthly Average Inches	1.2	1.2	1.5	2.0	2.0	0.7	0.1	0.1	0.4	1.6	1.8	1.2	13.8
Days of 1mm or More	5	6	8	8	8	3	0	0	1	6	7	5	57

CHARLOTTE AMALIE   U.S. Virgin Islands

	JAN	FEB	MAR	APR	MAY	JUN	JUL	AUG	SEP	OCT	NOV	DEC	YEAR
Elevation 5 m. (16 ft.)					18°21'N—64°56'W								
TEMPERATURE													
Monthly Average °C	25	25	25	26	27	28	28	28	28	28	27	26	27
Monthly Average °F	77	77	78	79	80	82	82	83	82	82	80	78	80
PRECIPITATION													
Monthly Average mm	69	44	44	58	115	76	88	124	145	142	110	80	1095.0
Monthly Average Inches	2.7	1.7	1.7	2.2	4.5	2.9	3.4	4.8	5.7	5.5	4.3	3.1	42.5
Days of 1mm or More	0	0	0	0	0	0	0	0	0	0	0	0	0

ENTEBBE   Uganda

Elevation 1146 m. (3759 ft.)					0°3'N—32°27'E								
	JAN	FEB	MAR	APR	MAY	JUN	JUL	AUG	SEP	OCT	NOV	DEC	YEAR

TEMPERATURE

	JAN	FEB	MAR	APR	MAY	JUN	JUL	AUG	SEP	OCT	NOV	DEC	YEAR
Daily Average Min.°C	17	18	18	18	18	17	16	16	17	17	17	17	17
Daily Average Min.°F	63	63	64	64	64	63	61	61	62	63	63	63	63
Daily Average Max.°C	27	27	27	26	25	25	25	25	26	26	26	26	26
Daily Average Max.°F	80	80	80	78	78	78	77	77	79	79	79	79	79
Monthly Average °C	22	22	22	22	22	21	21	21	21	22	22	22	22
Monthly Average °F	71	72	72	72	71	70	69	69	70	71	71	71	71
RELATIVE HUMIDITY (%)	63	63	65	70	71	68	67	68	66	65	65	65	66

PRECIPITATION

	JAN	FEB	MAR	APR	MAY	JUN	JUL	AUG	SEP	OCT	NOV	DEC	YEAR
Monthly Average mm	83	94	166	263	246	111	74	87	78	114	167	114	1597.0
Monthly Average Inches	3.2	3.7	6.5	10.3	9.6	4.3	2.9	3.4	3.0	4.4	6.5	4.4	62.2
Days of 1mm or More	8	8	14	17	16	10	6	6	7	11	14	10	127

GULU   Uganda

Elevation 1105 m. (3625 ft.)					2°45'N—32°20'E								
	JAN	FEB	MAR	APR	MAY	JUN	JUL	AUG	SEP	OCT	NOV	DEC	YEAR

TEMPERATURE

	JAN	FEB	MAR	APR	MAY	JUN	JUL	AUG	SEP	OCT	NOV	DEC	YEAR
Daily Average Min.°C	16	17	18	18	18	17	17	17	17	17	16	16	17
Daily Average Min.°F	61	63	64	64	64	63	62	62	62	62	62	61	62
Daily Average Max.°C	32	32	31	29	28	28	27	27	28	29	30	30	29
Daily Average Max.°F	89	90	88	85	83	82	80	81	83	84	85	87	85
Monthly Average °C	24	24	24	23	23	22	22	22	22	23	23	23	23
Monthly Average °F	75	76	76	74	73	72	71	71	72	73	73	74	73
RELATIVE HUMIDITY (%)	33	34	42	56	61	61	63	63	58	54	47	41	51

PRECIPITATION

	JAN	FEB	MAR	APR	MAY	JUN	JUL	AUG	SEP	OCT	NOV	DEC	YEAR
Monthly Average mm	16	32	91	173	174	161	175	240	199	197	102	39	1599.0
Monthly Average Inches	0.6	1.2	3.5	6.8	6.8	6.3	6.8	9.4	7.8	7.7	4.0	1.5	62.4
Days of 1mm or More	2	4	8	14	15	12	13	16	16	18	11	4	133

KAMPALA   Uganda

Elevation 1312 m. (4304 ft.)					3°30'N—39°6'E								
	JAN	FEB	MAR	APR	MAY	JUN	JUL	AUG	SEP	OCT	NOV	DEC	YEAR

TEMPERATURE

	JAN	FEB	MAR	APR	MAY	JUN	JUL	AUG	SEP	OCT	NOV	DEC	YEAR
Extreme Monthly Min.°C	12	14	13	14	15	12	12	12	13	13	14	12	11
Extreme Monthly Min.°F	54	57	56	57	59	53	53	53	56	56	58	53	53
Extreme Monthly Max.°C	33	36	33	33	29	29	29	29	31	32	32	32	36
Extreme Monthly Max.°F	92	97	92	91	84	85	85	85	88	90	89	90	97
Monthly Average °C	22	22	22	21	21	21	20	20	21	21	22	22	21
Monthly Average °F	72	72	72	70	70	69	68	68	69	70	71	71	70
RELATIVE HUMIDITY (%)	54	56	62	69	72	69	66	66	65	64	63	62	64

PRECIPITATION

	JAN	FEB	MAR	APR	MAY	JUN	JUL	AUG	SEP	OCT	NOV	DEC	YEAR
Monthly Average mm	50	56	112	181	139	74	49	85	98	108	114	96	1162.0
Monthly Average Inches	1.9	2.2	4.4	7.1	5.4	2.9	1.9	3.3	3.8	4.2	4.4	3.7	45.2
Days of 1mm or More	0	0	0	0	0	0	0	0	0	0	0	0	0

ABERDEEN, SCOTLAND   United Kingdom

			Elevation 59 m. (193 ft.)				57°10'N—2°4'W						
	JAN	**FEB**	**MAR**	**APR**	**MAY**	**JUN**	**JUL**	**AUG**	**SEP**	**OCT**	**NOV**	**DEC**	**YEAR**
TEMPERATURE													
Monthly Average °C	3	3	4	6	9	12	14	14	12	9	5	4	8
Monthly Average °F	37	37	40	44	48	54	57	56	53	48	41	38	46
PRECIPITATION													
Monthly Average mm	83	52	59	53	59	52	66	75	68	77	78	79	801.0
Monthly Average Inches	3.2	2.0	2.3	2.0	2.3	2.0	2.5	2.9	2.6	3.0	3.0	3.1	30.9
Days of 1mm or More	13	9	11	10	10	9	10	10	11	11	13	13	130

BIRMINGHAM, ENGLAND   United Kingdom

			Elevation 163 m. (535 ft.)				52°30'N—1°56'W						
	JAN	**FEB**	**MAR**	**APR**	**MAY**	**JUN**	**JUL**	**AUG**	**SEP**	**OCT**	**NOV**	**DEC**	**YEAR**
TEMPERATURE													
Daily Average Min.°C	2	2	3	5	7	10	12	12	10	7	5	3	7
Daily Average Min.°F	35	35	37	40	45	51	54	54	50	45	40	37	44
Daily Average Max.°C	5	6	9	12	16	19	20	20	17	13	9	6	13
Daily Average Max.°F	42	43	48	54	60	66	68	68	63	55	48	44	55
Extreme Monthly Min.°C	-12	-11	-7	-2	-1	3	7	6	3	-2	-4	-7	-11
Extreme Monthly Min.°F	11	13	19	28	30	37	44	42	37	28	25	20	11
Extreme Monthly Max.°C	15	15	21	24	29	31	33	33	28	26	19	14	33
Extreme Monthly Max.°F	59	59	70	75	85	87	92	91	83	79	67	58	92
Monthly Average °C	3	3	5	8	11	14	16	16	13	10	6	4	9
Monthly Average °F	38	38	42	46	51	57	61	60	56	50	43	40	48
RELATIVE HUMIDITY (%)	82	77	67	66	63	63	65	65	68	73	80	84	71
PRECIPITATION													
Monthly Average mm	60	46	50	47	56	56	48	69	58	54	62	67	673.0
Monthly Average Inches	2.3	1.8	1.9	1.8	2.2	2.2	1.8	2.7	2.2	2.1	2.4	2.6	26.0
Days of 1mm or More	12	9	11	7	10	9	7	9	8	10	10	11	113

EDINBURGH, SCOTLAND   United Kingdom

			Elevation 134 m. (440 ft.)				55°55'N—3°11'W						
	JAN	**FEB**	**MAR**	**APR**	**MAY**	**JUN**	**JUL**	**AUG**	**SEP**	**OCT**	**NOV**	**DEC**	**YEAR**
TEMPERATURE													
Daily Average Min.°C	1	1	2	4	6	9	11	11	9	7	4	2	6
Daily Average Min.°F	34	34	36	39	43	49	52	52	49	44	39	36	42
Daily Average Max.°C	6	6	8	11	14	17	18	18	16	12	9	7	12
Daily Average Max.°F	42	43	46	51	56	62	65	64	60	54	48	44	53
Extreme Monthly Min.°C	-8	-9	-6	-4	-1	3	6	4	1	-2	-4	-7	-9
Extreme Monthly Min.°F	17	15	21	25	30	37	42	40	33	28	24	20	15
Extreme Monthly Max.°C	14	14	20	22	24	28	28	28	26	22	19	14	28
Extreme Monthly Max.°F	57	57	68	72	76	83	83	82	79	71	67	58	83
Monthly Average °C	3	3	5	7	10	13	15	14	12	10	6	4	9
Monthly Average °F	37	38	41	45	50	55	58	58	54	49	42	39	47
RELATIVE HUMIDITY (%)	84	83	81	76	76	73	77	79	80	81	83	84	80
PRECIPITATION													
Monthly Average mm	52	38	49	40	50	50	60	65	67	62	66	59	658.0
Monthly Average Inches	2.0	1.4	1.9	1.5	1.9	1.9	2.3	2.5	2.6	2.4	2.5	2.3	25.2
Days of 1mm or More	12	8	12	7	10	8	8	10	10	11	11	12	119

LONDON, ENGLAND   United Kingdom

	Elevation 59 m. (193 ft.)					51°30'N—0°10'W							
	JAN	FEB	MAR	APR	MAY	JUN	JUL	AUG	SEP	OCT	NOV	DEC	YEAR
TEMPERATURE													
Daily Average Min.°C	2	2	3	4	7	11	13	12	11	5	4	2	6
Daily Average Min.°F	35	35	37	40	45	51	55	54	51	44	39	36	44
Daily Average Max.°C	5	7	11	13	17	21	23	22	19	14	9	7	14
Daily Average Max.°F	44	45	51	56	63	69	73	72	67	58	49	45	58
Extreme Monthly Min.°C	-12	-13	-6	-4	-2	2	7	4	1	-5	-5	-8	-12
Extreme Monthly Min.°F	11	9	21	25	28	35	44	39	34	23	23	18	9
Extreme Monthly Max.°C	15	17	22	29	33	34	35	37	32	29	20	16	37
Extreme Monthly Max.°F	59	62	72	84	91	93	95	99	89	84	68	60	99
Monthly Average °C	4	4	6	8	11	14	16	16	14	11	7	5	10
Monthly Average °F	38	39	42	46	52	58	62	61	57	51	44	40	49
RELATIVE HUMIDITY (%)	80	72	63	58	57	57	55	58	63	70	79	81	66
PRECIPITATION													
Monthly Average mm	73	47	61	53	59	57	45	57	71	73	81	79	756.0
Monthly Average Inches	2.8	1.8	2.4	2.0	2.3	2.2	1.7	2.2	2.7	2.8	3.1	3.1	29.1
Days of 1mm or More	12	8	10	9	10	8	7	8	9	9	11	11	112

MANCHESTER, ENGLAND   United Kingdom

	Elevation 77 m. (252 ft.)					53°30'N—2°15'W							
	JAN	FEB	MAR	APR	MAY	JUN	JUL	AUG	SEP	OCT	NOV	DEC	YEAR
TEMPERATURE													
Monthly Average °C	4	4	6	8	11	14	16	16	14	11	7	5	10
Monthly Average °F	39	39	42	47	52	58	60	60	57	51	44	40	49
PRECIPITATION													
Monthly Average mm	68	49	55	49	61	66	68	82	75	75	79	80	807.0
Monthly Average Inches	2.6	1.9	2.1	1.9	2.4	2.5	2.6	3.2	2.9	2.9	3.1	3.1	31.2
Days of 1mm or More	14	9	11	10	12	11	9	11	11	12	13	12	135

MELO   Uruguay

	Elevation 94 m. (308 ft.)					32°22'S—54°11'W							
	JAN	FEB	MAR	APR	MAY	JUN	JUL	AUG	SEP	OCT	NOV	DEC	YEAR
TEMPERATURE													
Monthly Average °C	24	23	21	17	14	11	12	12	14	17	19	22	17
Monthly Average °F	75	74	70	63	57	52	53	54	58	63	67	71	63
PRECIPITATION													
Monthly Average mm	89	94	108	95	113	116	119	112	131	117	92	79	1265.0
Monthly Average Inches	3.5	3.7	4.2	3.7	4.4	4.5	4.6	4.4	5.1	4.6	3.6	3.1	49.4
Days of 1mm or More	7	8	5	6	6	7	7	6	7	6	7	5	77

MERCEDES   Uruguay

	Elevation 22 m. (72 ft.)					33°40'S—65°28'W							
	JAN	FEB	MAR	APR	MAY	JUN	JUL	AUG	SEP	OCT	NOV	DEC	YEAR
TEMPERATURE													
Monthly Average °C	25	24	22	18	14	11	11	12	14	17	20	23	18
Monthly Average °F	77	75	71	65	58	52	53	54	58	63	69	74	64
PRECIPITATION													
Monthly Average mm	98	138	115	99	92	62	71	73	71	103	87	100	1109.0
Monthly Average Inches	3.8	5.4	4.5	3.8	3.6	2.4	2.7	2.8	2.7	4.0	3.4	3.9	43.0
Days of 1mm or More	6	6	5	7	6	6	6	6	5	8	7	5	73

MONTEVIDEO   Uruguay

Elevation 22 m. (72 ft.)						34°52'S—56°12'W							
	JAN	FEB	MAR	APR	MAY	JUN	JUL	AUG	SEP	OCT	NOV	DEC	YEAR
TEMPERATURE													
Daily Average Min.°C	17	16	15	12	9	6	6	6	8	9	12	15	11
Daily Average Min.°F	62	61	59	53	48	43	43	43	46	49	54	59	52
Daily Average Max.°C	28	28	26	22	18	15	14	15	17	20	23	26	21
Daily Average Max.°F	83	82	78	71	64	59	58	59	63	68	74	79	70
Extreme Monthly Min.°C	8	8	4	2	-2	-4	-3	-4	-2	-2	3	5	-3
Extreme Monthly Min.°F	46	46	40	36	29	25	26	25	29	29	38	41	25
Extreme Monthly Max.°C	43	41	38	37	31	27	28	26	30	34	37	39	42
Extreme Monthly Max.°F	109	105	101	98	87	81	83	79	86	94	98	102	109
Monthly Average °C	23	23	21	17	14	11	11	12	14	16	19	22	17
Monthly Average °F	74	73	70	63	58	52	52	54	57	61	66	71	63
RELATIVE HUMIDITY (%)	53	55	57	61	66	69	69	67	65	62	56	52	61
PRECIPITATION													
Monthly Average mm	96	98	98	91	100	98	82	90	85	113	80	75	1106.0
Monthly Average Inches	3.7	3.8	3.8	3.5	3.9	3.8	3.2	3.5	3.3	4.4	3.1	2.9	42.9
Days of 1mm or More	5	6	6	6	6	7	7	5	6	7	6	6	73

PASO DE LOS TOROS   Uruguay

Elevation 79 m. (259 ft.)						32°49'S—56°31'W							
	JAN	FEB	MAR	APR	MAY	JUN	JUL	AUG	SEP	OCT	NOV	DEC	YEAR
TEMPERATURE													
Monthly Average °C	25	24	22	18	15	12	12	12	14	17	20	23	18
Monthly Average °F	76	75	71	64	58	53	53	54	58	63	67	73	64
PRECIPITATION													
Monthly Average mm	107	129	123	100	108	111	130	104	90	122	111	91	1326.0
Monthly Average Inches	4.2	5.0	4.8	3.9	4.2	4.3	5.1	4.0	3.5	4.8	4.3	3.5	51.6
Days of 1mm or More	6	9	5	5	7	7	8	6	6	8	7	6	80

SALTO   Uruguay

Elevation 46 m. (150 ft.)						31°23'S—57°58'W							
	JAN	FEB	MAR	APR	MAY	JUN	JUL	AUG	SEP	OCT	NOV	DEC	YEAR
TEMPERATURE													
Monthly Average °C	25	24	21	18	15	12	12	13	15	18	20	23	18
Monthly Average °F	77	75	71	64	59	53	54	55	59	64	69	74	64
PRECIPITATION													
Monthly Average mm	112	119	136	140	104	87	82	66	105	123	125	145	1344.0
Monthly Average Inches	4.4	4.6	5.3	5.5	4.0	3.4	3.2	2.5	4.1	4.8	4.9	5.7	52.4
Days of 1mm or More	6	7	6	6	6	6	6	5	6	7	7	7	75

TREINTA Y TRES   Uruguay

Elevation 57 m. (187 ft.)						33°14'S—54°23'W							
	JAN	FEB	MAR	APR	MAY	JUN	JUL	AUG	SEP	OCT	NOV	DEC	YEAR
TEMPERATURE													
Monthly Average °C	23	23	21	17	14	11	11	12	14	16	18	21	17
Monthly Average °F	73	73	69	63	57	52	52	54	57	61	64	70	62
PRECIPITATION													
Monthly Average mm	94	106	96	87	95	128	127	120	121	128	109	98	1309.0
Monthly Average Inches	3.7	4.1	3.7	3.4	3.7	5.0	5.0	4.7	4.7	5.0	4.2	3.8	51.0
Days of 1mm or More	7	8	6	5	7	7	8	8	7	8	7	6	84

ARCHANGEL   USSR

Elevation 13 m. (42 ft.)						64°36'N—40°30'E						
	JAN	FEB	MAR	APR	MAY	JUN	JUL	AUG	SEP	OCT	NOV	DEC	YEAR

TEMPERATURE

	JAN	FEB	MAR	APR	MAY	JUN	JUL	AUG	SEP	OCT	NOV	DEC	YEAR
Daily Average Min.°C	-20	-18	-13	-4	2	6	10	10	5	-1	-7	-15	-4
Daily Average Min.°F	-5	0	8	24	35	44	50	49	41	31	20	6	25
Daily Average Max.°C	-12	-10	-4	5	12	17	20	19	12	4	-2	-8	4
Daily Average Max.°F	10	13	25	41	53	63	68	65	53	40	29	18	40
Monthly Average °C	-15	-13	-7	0	7	12	16	13	8	1	-4	-11	1
Monthly Average °F	6	9	20	32	44	54	60	56	46	34	24	13	33
RELATIVE HUMIDITY (%)	81	75	70	60	55	53	58	65	73	83	88	83	70

PRECIPITATION

	JAN	FEB	MAR	APR	MAY	JUN	JUL	AUG	SEP	OCT	NOV	DEC	YEAR
Monthly Average mm	30	25	23	26	39	56	59	65	61	54	47	37	522.0
Monthly Average Inches	1.1	0.9	0.9	1.0	1.5	2.2	2.3	2.5	2.4	2.1	1.8	1.4	20.1
Days of 1mm or More	8	8	7	7	8	9	8	11	12	13	13	12	116

GORKIJ   USSR

Elevation 82 m. (269 ft.)						56°12'N—43°48'E						
	JAN	FEB	MAR	APR	MAY	JUN	JUL	AUG	SEP	OCT	NOV	DEC	YEAR

TEMPERATURE

	JAN	FEB	MAR	APR	MAY	JUN	JUL	AUG	SEP	OCT	NOV	DEC	YEAR
Daily Average Min.°C	-17	-15	-9	1	8	11	14	13	8	1	-4	-12	0
Daily Average Min.°F	1	5	17	34	47	52	57	55	46	34	24	10	32
Daily Average Max.°C	-11	-8	-2	10	18	21	23	22	16	7	0	-7	8
Daily Average Max.°F	13	18	29	50	65	69	73	71	61	45	0	20	43
Monthly Average °C	-11	-11	-5	5	13	17	19	17	11	4	-3	-8	4
Monthly Average °F	11	12	22	41	55	63	66	63	52	40	26	17	39
RELATIVE HUMIDITY (%)	75	67	67	56	43	49	55	51	61	71	84	82	63

PRECIPITATION

	JAN	FEB	MAR	APR	MAY	JUN	JUL	AUG	SEP	OCT	NOV	DEC	YEAR
Monthly Average mm	27	22	16	18	45	60	66	48	44	42	30	30	448.0
Monthly Average Inches	1.0	0.8	0.6	0.7	1.7	2.3	2.5	1.8	1.7	1.6	1.1	1.1	16.9
Days of 1mm or More	0	0	0	0	0	0	0	0	0	0	0	0	0

KIEV   USSR

Elevation 179 m. (587 ft.)						50°24'N—30°27'E						
	JAN	FEB	MAR	APR	MAY	JUN	JUL	AUG	SEP	OCT	NOV	DEC	YEAR

TEMPERATURE

	JAN	FEB	MAR	APR	MAY	JUN	JUL	AUG	SEP	OCT	NOV	DEC	YEAR
Daily Average Min.°C	-10	-8	-4	5	11	14	15	14	10	6	0	-6	4
Daily Average Min.°F	14	17	25	41	51	56	59	58	50	42	32	22	39
Daily Average Max.°C	-4	-2	3	14	21	24	25	24	20	13	6	-1	12
Daily Average Max.°F	24	28	37	56	69	75	77	76	68	56	42	30	53
Monthly Average °C	-6	-5	0	9	15	18	19	19	14	8	2	-2	8
Monthly Average °F	22	24	32	47	59	65	67	65	56	47	36	28	46
RELATIVE HUMIDITY (%)	81	75	69	56	50	51	53	55	54	65	82	84	65

PRECIPITATION

	JAN	FEB	MAR	APR	MAY	JUN	JUL	AUG	SEP	OCT	NOV	DEC	YEAR
Monthly Average mm	46	44	35	45	52	63	84	69	42	38	52	45	615.0
Monthly Average Inches	1.8	1.7	1.3	1.7	2.0	2.4	3.3	2.7	1.6	1.4	2.0	1.7	23.6
Days of 1mm or More	9	7	7	8	8	9	10	7	8	6	8	8	95

KIROV   USSR

	Elevation 164 m. (538 ft.)					58°39'N—49°36'E						
	JAN	FEB	MAR	APR	MAY	JUN	JUL	AUG	SEP	OCT	NOV	DEC	YEAR
TEMPERATURE													
Daily Average Min.°C	-20	-17	-10	-1	6	10	13	11	6	-1	-6	-15	-2
Daily Average Min.°F	-4	1	14	30	43	50	56	51	43	31	21	5	28
Daily Average Max.°C	-13	-10	-3	8	17	20	23	21	14	5	-2	-9	6
Daily Average Max.°F	9	15	27	46	62	69	73	69	58	40	29	16	43
Monthly Average °C	-14	-12	-6	3	11	16	18	15	9	2	-5	-10	2
Monthly Average °F	7	10	22	38	52	60	64	60	49	35	23	13	36
RELATIVE HUMIDITY (%)	81	75	70	59	47	48	60	55	68	75	85	82	67
PRECIPITATION													
Monthly Average mm	35	26	25	43	45	63	106	60	65	51	46	43	608.0
Monthly Average Inches	1.3	1.0	0.9	1.6	1.7	2.4	4.1	2.3	2.5	2.0	1.8	1.6	23.2
Days of 1mm or More	11	8	7	11	8	10	11	9	11	12	12	11	121

LENINGRAD   USSR

	Elevation 4 m. (13 ft.)					59°58'N—30°18'E						
	JAN	FEB	MAR	APR	MAY	JUN	JUL	AUG	SEP	OCT	NOV	DEC	YEAR
TEMPERATURE													
Daily Average Min.°C	-13	-12	-8	0	6	11	13	13	9	4	-2	-8	1
Daily Average Min.°F	8	11	18	33	42	51	55	55	47	39	28	18	34
Daily Average Max.°C	-7	-5	0	8	15	20	21	20	15	9	2	-3	8
Daily Average Max.°F	19	22	32	46	59	68	70	69	60	48	35	26	46
Extreme Monthly Min.°C	1	-34	-32	-22	-7	0	6	3	-2	-13	-22	-38	-37
Extreme Monthly Min.°F	33	-30	-25	-7	20	32	43	37	29	9	-8	-36	-36
Extreme Monthly Max.°C	6	6	13	23	30	33	32	32	27	21	12	7	32
Extreme Monthly Max.°F	43	42	56	73	86	91	90	90	81	70	54	45	91
Monthly Average °C	-8	-8	-3	4	11	15	18	16	11	5	0	-5	5
Monthly Average °F	17	18	27	39	52	59	64	61	51	42	32	24	41
RELATIVE HUMIDITY (%)	84	73	70	65	57	53	61	61	68	78	85	86	70
PRECIPITATION													
Monthly Average mm	38	28	30	33	37	56	72	79	63	62	50	45	593.0
Monthly Average Inches	1.4	1.1	1.1	1.2	1.4	2.2	2.8	3.1	2.4	2.4	1.9	1.7	22.7
Days of 1mm or More	9	8	8	7	6	8	10	10	12	11	11	12	112

MINSK   USSR

	Elevation 234 m. (767 ft.)					53°54'N—27°30'E						
	JAN	FEB	MAR	APR	MAY	JUN	JUL	AUG	SEP	OCT	NOV	DEC	YEAR
TEMPERATURE													
Daily Average Min.°C	-13	-11	-7	2	8	11	12	12	8	4	-1	-8	1
Daily Average Min.°F	8	12	20	35	46	51	54	53	46	39	30	18	34
Daily Average Max.°C	-7	-4	1	11	18	22	23	22	17	11	3	-3	9
Daily Average Max.°F	19	25	33	51	64	71	73	71	63	51	38	26	49
Extreme Monthly Min.°C	-33	-28	-32	-12	-2	0	6	3	-3	-8	-20	-30	-32
Extreme Monthly Min.°F	-27	-18	-25	11	28	32	43	37	27	18	-4	-22	-27
Extreme Monthly Max.°C	4	6	17	24	31	32	33	33	28	23	12	8	33
Extreme Monthly Max.°F	40	42	63	75	87	89	92	91	83	74	53	46	92
Monthly Average °C	-7	-6	-2	6	13	16	17	17	12	6	1	-4	6
Monthly Average °F	19	21	28	42	55	61	63	62	53	43	33	24	42
RELATIVE HUMIDITY (%)	81	76	71	62	53	50	52	56	55	76	87	87	67
PRECIPITATION													
Monthly Average mm	40	31	39	41	64	72	102	73	49	49	48	48	656.0
Monthly Average Inches	1.5	1.2	1.5	1.6	2.5	2.8	4.0	2.8	1.9	1.9	1.8	1.8	25.3
Days of 1mm or More	10	8	9	10	9	10	10	8	9	10	10	11	114

MOSCOW   USSR

Elevation 156 m. (511 ft.)							55°45'N—37°36'E						
	JAN	FEB	MAR	APR	MAY	JUN	JUL	AUG	SEP	OCT	NOV	DEC	YEAR
TEMPERATURE													
Daily Average Min.°C	-16	-14	-8	1	8	11	13	12	7	3	-3	-10	0
Daily Average Min.°F	3	8	18	34	46	51	55	53	45	37	26	15	32
Daily Average Max.°C	-9	-6	0	10	19	21	23	22	16	9	2	-5	9
Daily Average Max.°F	15	22	32	50	66	70	73	72	61	48	35	24	47
Extreme Monthly Min.°C	-33	-27	-29	-13	-4	-1	6	2	-3	-8	-21	-33	-32
Extreme Monthly Min.°F	-27	-17	-20	8	25	31	43	36	26	17	-5	-27	-27
Extreme Monthly Max.°C	4	4	12	27	30	34	35	36	30	23	8	6	35
Extreme Monthly Max.°F	39	40	53	80	86	94	95	96	86	74	47	42	96
Monthly Average °C	-10	-8	-3	6	13	17	18	16	11	5	-1	-6	5
Monthly Average °F	15	18	26	42	56	62	65	62	51	41	29	21	41
RELATIVE HUMIDITY (%)	77	66	64	54	43	47	54	55	59	67	79	83	62
PRECIPITATION													
Monthly Average mm	43	34	30	38	58	75	86	73	61	56	51	48	653.0
Monthly Average Inches	1.6	1.3	1.1	1.4	2.2	2.9	3.3	2.8	2.4	2.2	2.0	1.8	25.0
Days of 1mm or More	10	7	7	8	9	10	12	9	10	10	11	11	114

ODESSA   USSR

Elevation 64 m. (209 ft.)							46°30'N—30°38'E						
	JAN	FEB	MAR	APR	MAY	JUN	JUL	AUG	SEP	OCT	NOV	DEC	YEAR
TEMPERATURE													
Daily Average Min.°C	-6	-4	-1	6	12	16	18	18	14	9	4	-2	7
Daily Average Min.°F	22	25	31	43	53	60	64	64	56	47	40	29	44
Daily Average Max.°C	0	2	5	12	19	23	26	26	21	16	10	4	14
Daily Average Max.°F	32	35	41	54	66	74	79	78	71	60	50	39	56
Extreme Monthly Min.°C	-24	-25	-15	-4	3	8	10	8	0	-6	-14	-21	-25
Extreme Monthly Min.°F	-11	-13	5	25	38	46	50	47	32	21	6	-5	-13
Extreme Monthly Max.°C	12	15	21	24	33	33	37	36	33	30	21	16	37
Extreme Monthly Max.°F	54	59	70	75	91	92	99	96	91	86	70	60	99
Monthly Average °C	-1	-1	2	9	15	19	22	21	17	11	6	2	10
Monthly Average °F	29	30	36	48	59	67	71	70	62	52	43	35	50
RELATIVE HUMIDITY (%)	80	81	73	67	66	61	55	56	59	66	79	81	69
PRECIPITATION													
Monthly Average mm	45	41	27	33	39	40	47	35	35	23	44	46	455.0
Monthly Average Inches	1.7	1.6	1.0	1.2	1.5	1.5	1.8	1.3	1.3	0.9	1.7	1.8	17.3
Days of 1mm or More	7	6	5	6	6	6	5	4	3	3	5	6	62

OMSK   USSR

Elevation 85 m. (279 ft.)							54°58'N—73°20'E						
	JAN	FEB	MAR	APR	MAY	JUN	JUL	AUG	SEP	OCT	NOV	DEC	YEAR
TEMPERATURE													
Daily Average Min.°C	-26	-23	-18	-6	4	11	13	11	5	-3	-13	-22	-5
Daily Average Min.°F	-14	-9	0	21	40	51	56	52	41	27	8	-7	22
Daily Average Max.°C	-18	-14	-7	4	15	21	23	21	16	4	-8	-15	3
Daily Average Max.°F	-1	6	19	39	59	69	74	70	60	40	18	5	38
Extreme Monthly Min.°C	-49	-43	-39	-25	-13	-1	3	2	-6	-19	-40	-44	-48
Extreme Monthly Min.°F	-56	-45	-39	-13	9	31	38	35	22	-3	-40	-48	-56
Extreme Monthly Max.°C	2	3	13	29	31	36	39	34	29	22	9	2	38
Extreme Monthly Max.°F	35	37	55	84	88	96	102	94	85	72	49	36	102
Monthly Average °C	-18	-17	-9	3	12	18	19	16	10	1	-8	-15	1
Monthly Average °F	0	2	16	37	53	64	67	61	51	34	18	5	34
RELATIVE HUMIDITY (%)	82	80	75	64	49	53	52	54	55	67	79	84	66
PRECIPITATION													
Monthly Average mm	18	14	12	21	27	57	67	53	33	31	26	19	378.0
Monthly Average Inches	0.7	0.5	0.4	0.8	1.0	2.2	2.6	2.0	1.2	1.2	1.0	0.7	14.3
Days of 1mm or More	6	5	4	5	6	8	8	8	7	8	8	6	79

UFA
USSR

			Elevation 197 m. (646 ft.)			54°45'N—56°0'E							
	JAN	FEB	MAR	APR	MAY	JUN	JUL	AUG	SEP	OCT	NOV	DEC	YEAR
TEMPERATURE													
Daily Average Min.°C	-20	-20	-12	-2	7	10	14	10	6	-1	-7	-16	-3
Daily Average Min.°F	-5	-4	11	29	44	51	57	51	42	31	19	3	27
Daily Average Max.°C	-12	-9	-2	10	20	23	25	23	18	7	0	-8	8
Daily Average Max.°F	11	17	29	50	67	73	78	73	64	45	32	18	46
Monthly Average °C										3			0
Monthly Average °F										37			32
RELATIVE HUMIDITY (%)	76	72	72	55	47	49	59	47	49	67	79	79	63
PRECIPITATION													
Monthly Average mm										10			10.0
Monthly Average Inches	0.0	0.0	0.0	0.0	0.0	0.0	0.0	0.0	0.0	0.3	0.0	0.0	0.3
Days of 1mm or More	0	0	0	0	0	0	0	0	0	3	0	0	3

LUGANVILLE
Vanuatu

			Elevation 146 m. (479 ft.)			9°54'S—68°48'W							
	JAN	FEB	MAR	APR	MAY	JUN	JUL	AUG	SEP	OCT	NOV	DEC	YEAR
TEMPERATURE													
Monthly Average °C	26	26	26	25	25	24	23	23	24	25	25	26	25
Monthly Average °F	79	79	79	78	76	75	74	74	75	76	77	78	77
PRECIPITATION													
Monthly Average mm	348	328	343	322	217	205	172	138	160	207	215	234	2889.0
Monthly Average Inches	13.7	12.9	13.5	12.6	8.5	8.0	6.7	5.4	6.3	8.1	8.4	9.2	113.3
Days of 1mm or More	18	15	17	15	14	11	15	8	11	11	12	16	163

CARACAS
Venezuela

			Elevation 1042 m. (3418 ft.)			10°30'N—66°56'W							
	JAN	FEB	MAR	APR	MAY	JUN	JUL	AUG	SEP	OCT	NOV	DEC	YEAR
TEMPERATURE													
Daily Average Min.°C	13	13	14	16	17	17	16	16	16	16	16	14	15
Daily Average Min.°F	56	56	58	60	62	62	61	61	61	61	60	58	60
Daily Average Max.°C	24	25	26	27	27	26	26	26	27	26	25	26	26
Daily Average Max.°F	75	77	79	81	80	78	78	79	80	79	77	78	78
Extreme Monthly Min.°C	8	8	7	11	11	12	11	12	12	12	11	8	7
Extreme Monthly Min.°F	47	46	45	51	52	53	52	53	53	54	51	47	45
Extreme Monthly Max.°C	28	31	33	32	32	30	29	30	29	30	29	28	32
Extreme Monthly Max.°F	83	88	91	89	89	86	84	86	85	86	84	83	91
Monthly Average °C	19	20	20	21	22	21	21	21	22	21	21	20	21
Monthly Average °F	66	67	69	71	71	70	70	70	71	70	69	67	69
PRECIPITATION													
Monthly Average mm	21	14	9	31	94	103	96	111	93	121	85	43	821.0
Monthly Average Inches	0.8	0.5	0.3	1.2	3.7	4.0	3.7	4.3	3.6	4.7	3.3	1.6	31.7
Days of 1mm or More	0	0	0	0	0	0	0	0	0	0	0	0	0

MARACAIBO — Venezuela

	JAN	FEB	MAR	APR	MAY	JUN	JUL	AUG	SEP	OCT	NOV	DEC	YEAR
Elevation 6 m. (20 ft.)						10°39'N—71°36'W							
TEMPERATURE													
Daily Average Min.°C	23	23	23	24	25	25	24	25	25	24	24	24	24
Daily Average Min.°F	73	73	74	76	77	77	76	77	77	76	76	75	76
Daily Average Max.°C	32	32	33	33	33	34	34	34	34	33	33	33	33
Daily Average Max.°F	90	90	91	92	92	93	94	94	94	92	91	91	92
Extreme Monthly Min.°C	19	20	19	20	20	21	21	21	20	20	21	20	18
Extreme Monthly Min.°F	66	68	67	68	68	69	70	69	68	68	70	68	66
Extreme Monthly Max.°C	37	36	37	39	38	38	38	39	39	37	37	36	38
Extreme Monthly Max.°F	98	97	98	102	100	100	101	102	102	99	98	96	102
Monthly Average °C	27	27	27	28	28	28	29	28	28	28	27	27	28
Monthly Average °F	80	80	81	82	83	83	83	83	83	82	81	81	82
RELATIVE HUMIDITY (%)	61	61	61	61	63	60	62	62	62	62	63	62	62
PRECIPITATION													
Monthly Average mm	5	2	7	46	64	63	22	53	86	126	64	27	565.0
Monthly Average Inches	0.1	0.0	0.2	1.8	2.5	2.4	0.8	2.0	3.3	4.9	2.5	1.0	21.5
Days of 1mm or More	1	0	0	4	6	4	3	5	7	9	5	2	46

SANTA ELENA — Venezuela

	JAN	FEB	MAR	APR	MAY	JUN	JUL	AUG	SEP	OCT	NOV	DEC	YEAR
Elevation 859 m. (2816 ft.)						4°36'N—61°7'W							
TEMPERATURE													
Daily Average Min.°C	16	17	18	18	18	18	17	17	17	17	17	17	17
Daily Average Min.°F	61	62	64	64	65	64	62	63	63	63	62	63	63
Daily Average Max.°C	30	31	31	30	29	28	28	28	29	29	30	29	29
Daily Average Max.°F	86	87	88	86	84	82	82	83	84	85	86	84	85
Extreme Monthly Min.°C	13	13	12	14	14	15	14	12	13	13	13	14	8
Extreme Monthly Min.°F	55	55	53	57	57	59	57	54	56	55	55	57	48
Extreme Monthly Max.°C	33	33	35	34	32	31	30	31	33	34	34	32	35
Extreme Monthly Max.°F	91	91	95	93	89	88	86	88	92	93	93	90	95
Monthly Average °C	22	22	22	22	22	21	21	21	21	21	22	21	22
Monthly Average °F	71	71	72	72	71	70	70	70	70	71	71	70	71
RELATIVE HUMIDITY (%)	63	62	57	61	69	73	73	74	59	55	57	61	64
PRECIPITATION													
Monthly Average mm	59	49	73	173	205	242	216	169	98	104	113	76	1577.0
Monthly Average Inches	2.3	1.9	2.8	6.8	8.0	9.5	8.5	6.6	3.8	4.0	4.4	2.9	61.5
Days of 1mm or More	8	6	8	11	17	22	20	18	11	10	10	10	151

DA-NANG — Vietnam

	JAN	FEB	MAR	APR	MAY	JUN	JUL	AUG	SEP	OCT	NOV	DEC	YEAR
Elevation 7 m. (22 ft.)						16°4'N—108°13'E							
TEMPERATURE													
Monthly Average °C	21	22	24	26	28	29	29	29	27	26	24	22	26
Monthly Average °F	70	72	76	79	83	85	85	84	81	78	75	72	78
PRECIPITATION													
Monthly Average mm	103	32	27	32	67	86	91	104	307	591	354	222	2016.0
Monthly Average Inches	4.0	1.2	1.0	1.2	2.6	3.3	3.5	4.0	12.0	23.2	13.9	8.7	78.6
Days of 1mm or More	8	3	2	3	6	6	6	7	11	18	18	15	103

HANOI   Vietnam

		Elevation 16 m. (53 ft.)					21°2'N—105°52'E						
	JAN	FEB	MAR	APR	MAY	JUN	JUL	AUG	SEP	OCT	NOV	DEC	YEAR
TEMPERATURE													
Daily Average Min.°C	13	14	17	21	23	26	26	26	24	22	18	15	21
Daily Average Min.°F	56	58	63	69	74	78	78	78	76	71	64	59	69
Daily Average Max.°C	20	21	23	28	32	33	33	32	31	29	26	22	27
Daily Average Max.°F	68	69	74	82	90	92	91	90	88	84	78	72	82
Extreme Monthly Min.°C	6	6	12	10	16	21	22	21	17	14	7	7	5
Extreme Monthly Min.°F	42	43	53	50	60	69	71	70	63	57	44	44	42
Extreme Monthly Max.°C	33	34	37	39	43	40	40	38	37	36	36	37	42
Extreme Monthly Max.°F	92	94	98	103	109	104	104	101	99	96	97	98	109
Monthly Average °C	16	17	20	24		29	29	29	27	25	23	18	21
Monthly Average °F	61	62	69	75		84	84	84	81	77	73	64	70
RELATIVE HUMIDITY (%)	68	70	76	75	69	71	72	75	73	69	68	67	71
PRECIPITATION													
Monthly Average mm	13	13	21	95		259	163	358	249	75	35	0	1281.0
Monthly Average Inches	0.5	0.5	0.8	3.7	0.0	10.2	6.4	14.0	9.8	2.9	1.3	0.0	50.1
Days of 1mm or More	4	3	7	9	0	13	7	12	11	7	4	0	77

SAIGON   Vietnam

		Elevation 9 m. (30 ft.)					10°47'N—106°42'E						
	JAN	FEB	MAR	APR	MAY	JUN	JUL	AUG	SEP	OCT	NOV	DEC	YEAR
TEMPERATURE													
Daily Average Min.°C	22	22	23	24	24	24	24	24	23	23	23	22	23
Daily Average Min.°F	70	71	74	76	76	75	75	75	74	74	73	71	74
Daily Average Max.°C	32	33	34	35	33	32	31	31	31	31	31	31	32
Daily Average Max.°F	89	91	93	95	92	89	88	88	88	88	87	87	90
Extreme Monthly Min.°C	14	16	18	20	21	21	19	20	21	20	18	14	13
Extreme Monthly Min.°F	57	61	64	68	70	69	67	68	69	68	64	57	57
Extreme Monthly Max.°C	37	39	39	40	39	38	35	35	36	34	35	36	40
Extreme Monthly Max.°F	98	102	103	104	102	100	95	95	96	94	95	97	104
Monthly Average °C	26	27	28	29	28	28	27	27	27	27	26	26	27
Monthly Average °F	78	80	82	84	83	82	81	81	80	80	79	79	81
RELATIVE HUMIDITY (%)	61	56	58	60	71	78	80	78	80	80	75	68	70
PRECIPITATION													
Monthly Average mm	11	7	10	48	213	300	279	269	314	262	111	37	1861.0
Monthly Average Inches	0.4	0.2	0.3	1.8	8.3	11.8	10.9	10.5	12.3	10.3	4.3	1.4	72.5
Days of 1mm or More	1	0	1	3	14	18	19	19	20	18	8	5	126

BERLIN   West Germany

		Elevation 58 m. (190 ft.)					52°27'N—13°18'E						
	JAN	FEB	MAR	APR	MAY	JUN	JUL	AUG	SEP	OCT	NOV	DEC	YEAR
TEMPERATURE													
Daily Average Min.°C	-3	-3	0	4	8	12	14	13	10	6	2	-1	5
Daily Average Min.°F	26	26	31	39	47	53	57	56	50	42	36	29	41
Daily Average Max.°C	2	3	8	13	19	22	24	23	20	13	7	3	13
Daily Average Max.°F	35	37	46	56	66	72	75	74	68	56	45	38	55
Extreme Monthly Min.°C	-17	-26	-14	-7	-2	2	6	6	-1	-9	-13	-19	-26
Extreme Monthly Min.°F	1	-15	7	20	28	35	43	43	31	15	8	-3	-15
Extreme Monthly Max.°C	13	17	23	28	33	34	36	34	34	25	18	14	35
Extreme Monthly Max.°F	55	62	73	83	92	93	96	94	94	77	64	58	96
Monthly Average °C	-1	0	3	9	14	17	18	18	14	9	4	1	9
Monthly Average °F	30	32	38	48	56	63	65	64	58	49	40	34	48
RELATIVE HUMIDITY (%)	82	78	67	60	57	58	61	61	65	73	83	86	69
PRECIPITATION													
Monthly Average mm	43	42	32	43	51	71	67	69	42	40	51	46	597.0
Monthly Average Inches	1.6	1.6	1.2	1.6	2.0	2.7	2.6	2.7	1.6	1.5	2.0	1.8	22.9
Days of 1mm or More	0	0	0	0	0	0	0	0	0	0	0	0	0

FRANKFURT   West Germany

Elevation 110 m. (360 ft.)					50°6'N—8°36'E								
	JAN	FEB	MAR	APR	MAY	JUN	JUL	AUG	SEP	OCT	NOV	DEC	YEAR
TEMPERATURE													
Daily Average Min.°C	-2	-1	2	6	9	13	15	14	11	7	3	0	6
Daily Average Min.°F	29	30	35	42	49	55	58	57	52	44	38	32	43
Daily Average Max.°C	3	5	11	16	20	23	25	24	21	14	8	4	15
Daily Average Max.°F	38	41	51	60	69	74	77	76	69	58	47	39	58
Extreme Monthly Min.°C	-20	-22	-11	-4	-1	4	6	7	2	-6	-13	-18	-21
Extreme Monthly Min.°F	-4	-7	13	24	30	40	43	44	35	21	9	0	-7
Extreme Monthly Max.°C	14	19	24	29	34	34	38	37	35	27	20	17	37
Extreme Monthly Max.°F	57	66	75	84	93	93	100	98	95	80	68	62	100
Monthly Average °C	0	2	4	10	13	17	18	18	15	10	5	0	9
Monthly Average °F	32	35	40	49	56	63	65	64	58	50	40	32	49
RELATIVE HUMIDITY (%)	77	70	57	51	50	52	53	54	60	68	77	81	63
PRECIPITATION													
Monthly Average mm	43	42	48	64	56	77	67	89	52	44	70	51	703.0
Monthly Average Inches	1.6	1.6	1.8	2.5	2.2	3.0	2.6	3.5	2.0	1.7	2.7	2.0	27.2
Days of 1mm or More	0	0	0	0	0	0	0	0	0	0	0	0	0

HAMBURG   West Germany

Elevation 16 m. (52 ft.)					53°36'N—10°0'E								
	JAN	FEB	MAR	APR	MAY	JUN	JUL	AUG	SEP	OCT	NOV	DEC	YEAR
TEMPERATURE													
Daily Average Min.°C	-2	-2	-1	3	7	11	13	12	10	6	3	0	5
Daily Average Min.°F	28	28	31	38	45	51	55	54	49	43	37	31	41
Daily Average Max.°C	2	3	7	13	18	21	22	22	19	13	7	4	13
Daily Average Max.°F	36	37	44	55	64	69	72	72	66	55	45	39	55
Extreme Monthly Min.°C	-18	-17	-12	-6	-1	5	7	6	1	-4	-14	-20	-20
Extreme Monthly Min.°F	-1	2	10	22	30	41	45	42	34	25	7	-4	-4
Extreme Monthly Max.°C	13	15	20	28	32	33	33	32	30	23	17	13	33
Extreme Monthly Max.°F	56	59	68	82	89	92	92	90	86	73	63	55	92
Monthly Average °C	0	1	3	7	12	15	17	17	13	10	5	2	9
Monthly Average °F	32	33	38	45	54	60	62	62	56	49	41	35	47
RELATIVE HUMIDITY (%)	84	80	68	61	57	59	63	63	65	74	83	86	70
PRECIPITATION													
Monthly Average mm	61	38	49	51	58	71	81	74	67	63	69	70	752.0
Monthly Average Inches	2.4	1.4	1.9	2.0	2.2	2.7	3.1	2.9	2.6	2.4	2.7	2.7	29.0
Days of 1mm or More	12	8	10	10	10	10	11	11	10	10	12	12	126

HANNOVER   West Germany

Elevation 55 m. (180 ft.)					52°20'N—9°42'E								
	JAN	FEB	MAR	APR	MAY	JUN	JUL	AUG	SEP	OCT	NOV	DEC	YEAR
TEMPERATURE													
Daily Average Min.°C	-3	-2	0	3	7	10	13	12	9	6	2	-1	5
Daily Average Min.°F	28	28	32	38	45	51	55	54	49	42	36	31	41
Daily Average Max.°C	3	4	8	13	18	21	23	23	19	13	8	4	13
Daily Average Max.°F	37	38	46	56	64	70	73	73	67	56	46	39	55
Monthly Average °C	0	1	4	8	12	16	17	17	14	10	5	2	9
Monthly Average °F	32	33	39	46	54	60	63	62	57	49	41	35	48
RELATIVE HUMIDITY (%)	81	77	67	59	55	57	61	59	64	73	81	84	68
PRECIPITATION													
Monthly Average mm	53	35	43	50	67	70	64	67	48	44	51	58	650.0
Monthly Average Inches	2.0	1.3	1.6	1.9	2.6	2.7	2.5	2.6	1.8	1.7	2.0	2.2	24.9
Days of 1mm or More	11	8	9	10	11	11	10	10	9	8	10	11	118

MUNICH   West Germany

Elevation 529 m. (1735 ft.)					48°6'N—11°42'E								
	JAN	FEB	MAR	APR	MAY	JUN	JUL	AUG	SEP	OCT	NOV	DEC	YEAR
TEMPERATURE													
Daily Average Min.°C	-5	-5	-1	3	7	11	13	12	9	4	0	-4	4
Daily Average Min.°F	23	23	30	38	45	51	55	54	48	40	33	26	39
Daily Average Max.°C	1	3	9	14	18	21	23	23	20	13	7	2	13
Daily Average Max.°F	35	38	48	56	64	70	74	73	67	56	44	36	55
Extreme Monthly Min.°C	-26	-22	-19	-10	-2	2	4	3	-1	-9	-15	-21	-25
Extreme Monthly Min.°F	-14	-7	-2	14	29	35	40	37	30	16	5	-5	-14
Extreme Monthly Max.°C	13	18	21	25	30	31	33	33	28	25	21	14	33
Extreme Monthly Max.°F	55	65	70	77	86	87	91	92	83	77	69	57	92
Monthly Average °C	-2	-1	3	7	12	15	17	17	14	8	3	0	8
Monthly Average °F	29	31	38	45	54	60	63	62	57	47	38	31	46
RELATIVE HUMIDITY (%)	77	71	61	55	57	58	57	58	61	68	78	82	65
PRECIPITATION													
Monthly Average mm	57	51	53	72	106	129	115	115	72	58	59	57	944.0
Monthly Average Inches	2.2	2.0	2.0	2.8	4.1	5.0	4.5	4.5	2.8	2.2	2.3	2.2	36.6
Days of 1mm or More	11	10	10	11	13	13	12	11	8	7	10	10	126

NUREMBERG   West Germany

Elevation 319 m. (1046 ft.)					49°30'N—11°6'E								
	JAN	FEB	MAR	APR	MAY	JUN	JUL	AUG	SEP	OCT	NOV	DEC	YEAR
TEMPERATURE													
Daily Average Min.°C	-4	-4	-1	3	7	11	13	12	9	5	10	-3	5
Daily Average Min.°F	24	25	31	37	44	51	55	53	48	40	50	27	40
Daily Average Max.°C	2	3	9	13	18	22	23	23	20	13	7	3	13
Daily Average Max.°F	35	38	48	56	65	71	74	73	67	56	44	37	55
Extreme Monthly Min.°C	-28	-26	-17	-11	-2	2	4	4	-3	-8	-16	-27	-27
Extreme Monthly Min.°F	-18	-15	2	13	28	36	40	40	27	18	4	-17	-18
Extreme Monthly Max.°C	14	18	23	27	33	33	36	37	34	28	21	18	37
Extreme Monthly Max.°F	58	64	73	81	92	92	97	99	93	82	70	64	99
Monthly Average °C	-1	0	4	8	13	17	18	17	14	9	4	1	9
Monthly Average °F	30	32	39	47	55	62	65	63	57	48	39	33	48
RELATIVE HUMIDITY (%)	77	69	58	55	52	54	56	57	59	68	77	81	64
PRECIPITATION													
Monthly Average mm	47	37	41	45	67	72	69	70	48	47	42	51	636.0
Monthly Average Inches	1.8	1.4	1.6	1.7	2.6	2.8	2.7	2.7	1.8	1.8	1.6	2.0	24.5
Days of 1mm or More	10	8	8	9	10	10	9	9	8	7	9	10	107

STUTTGART   West Germany

Elevation 401 m. (1315 ft.)					48°42'N—9°12'E								
	JAN	FEB	MAR	APR	MAY	JUN	JUL	AUG	SEP	OCT	NOV	DEC	YEAR
TEMPERATURE													
Daily Average Min.°C	-3	-2	1	5	8	12	14	13	10	6	2	-2	5
Daily Average Min.°F	27	28	33	40	47	53	56	56	50	42	36	29	42
Daily Average Max.°C	3	5	10	14	19	22	24	24	20	14	8	4	14
Daily Average Max.°F	38	41	50	58	66	72	75	74	69	58	47	39	57
Monthly Average °C	0	2	5	9	13	16	18	18	15	10	5	1	9
Monthly Average °F	32	35	41	48	55	61	65	64	59	50	41	34	49
RELATIVE HUMIDITY (%)	74	68	57	54	53	56	55	55	59	66	74	78	62
PRECIPITATION													
Monthly Average mm	38	32	37	51	85	93	64	78	51	39	48	37	653.0
Monthly Average Inches	1.4	1.2	1.4	2.0	3.3	3.6	2.5	3.0	2.0	1.5	1.8	1.4	25.1
Days of 1mm or More	9	7	8	9	12	11	10	9	8	7	8	8	106

BELGRADE Yugoslavia

Elevation 139 m. (456 ft.) **44°48'N—20°30'E**

	JAN	FEB	MAR	APR	MAY	JUN	JUL	AUG	SEP	OCT	NOV	DEC	YEAR
TEMPERATURE													
Daily Average Min.°C	-3	-2	2	7	12	15	17	17	13	8	4	0	8
Daily Average Min.°F	26	29	36	45	54	59	62	62	56	47	39	32	46
Daily Average Max.°C	3	5	11	18	23	26	28	28	24	18	11	5	17
Daily Average Max.°F	37	42	52	64	73	79	83	83	76	64	51	42	62
Extreme Monthly Min.°C	-19	-26	-14	-6	-2	5	9	7	2	-13	-11	-19	-25
Extreme Monthly Min.°F	-2	-14	6	21	29	41	49	45	35	9	12	-3	-14
Extreme Monthly Max.°C	17	20	27	31	33	37	39	42	36	34	29	21	41
Extreme Monthly Max.°F	62	68	80	88	92	98	103	107	96	94	85	69	107
Monthly Average °C	0	2	7	12	17	20	22	21	17	12	7	3	12
Monthly Average °F	32	36	44	54	63	68	71	70	63	54	45	37	53
RELATIVE HUMIDITY (%)	75	67	56	49	51	51	47	46	47	58	71	76	58
PRECIPITATION													
Monthly Average mm	52	43	51	57	71	88	68	53	49	41	57	58	688.0
Monthly Average Inches	2.0	1.6	2.0	2.2	2.7	3.4	2.6	2.0	1.9	1.6	2.2	2.2	26.4
Days of 1mm or More	8	7	7	9	10	9	7	6	6	6	8	9	92

SARAJEVO Yugoslavia

Elevation 637 m. (2089 ft.) **43°54'N—18°24'E**

	JAN	FEB	MAR	APR	MAY	JUN	JUL	AUG	SEP	OCT	NOV	DEC	YEAR
TEMPERATURE													
Daily Average Min.°C	-4	-3	0	5	8	12	13	13	10	6	3	-1	5
Daily Average Min.°F	25	26	32	40	47	53	56	56	50	42	37	31	41
Daily Average Max.°C	3	5	10	15	20	24	26	27	23	16	10	6	15
Daily Average Max.°F	37	42	50	59	67	74	79	80	73	61	49	43	59
Monthly Average °C	-1	1	5	9	14	17	19	18	15	10	6	1	10
Monthly Average °F	30	34	41	49	58	63	65	65	59	51	42	34	49
RELATIVE HUMIDITY (%)	75	67	58	54	55	53	49	45	52	62	71	75	60
PRECIPITATION													
Monthly Average mm	77	68	67	74	80	89	85	69	71	77	89	93	939.0
Monthly Average Inches	3.0	2.6	2.6	2.9	3.1	3.5	3.3	2.7	2.7	3.0	3.5	3.6	36.5
Days of 1mm or More	10	10	9	10	10	11	9	8	7	8	10	11	113

SKOPJE Yugoslavia

Elevation 240 m. (787 ft.) **42°0'N—21°30'E**

	JAN	FEB	MAR	APR	MAY	JUN	JUL	AUG	SEP	OCT	NOV	DEC	YEAR
TEMPERATURE													
Daily Average Min.°C	-3	-3	1	5	10	13	15	14	11	6	3	-1	6
Daily Average Min.°F	27	28	33	42	50	56	59	58	52	43	37	30	43
Daily Average Max.°C	5	8	12	19	23	28	31	31	26	19	12	7	18
Daily Average Max.°F	40	47	53	67	74	82	87	88	79	65	53	45	65
Monthly Average °C	0	3	7	12	17	21	23	23	19	13	7	2	12
Monthly Average °F	32	37	45	54	63	70	73	73	65	55	44	35	54
RELATIVE HUMIDITY (%)	76	65	58	48	52	47	42	39	46	59	72	76	57
PRECIPITATION													
Monthly Average mm	39	36	41	39	57	46	35	27	37	43	57	47	504.0
Monthly Average Inches	1.5	1.4	1.6	1.5	2.2	1.8	1.3	1.0	1.4	1.6	2.2	1.8	19.3
Days of 1mm or More	6	6	6	6	8	6	4	4	4	5	6	6	67

SPLIT — Yugoslavia

	JAN	FEB	MAR	APR	MAY	JUN	JUL	AUG	SEP	OCT	NOV	DEC	YEAR
Elevation 129 m. (423 ft.)					43°30'N—16°24'E								
TEMPERATURE													
Daily Average Min.°C	5	5	7	11	16	19	22	22	19	14	10	7	13
Daily Average Min.°F	41	41	45	52	60	66	71	71	66	57	50	45	55
Daily Average Max.°C	10	11	14	18	23	27	30	30	26	20	15	12	20
Daily Average Max.°F	50	51	56	64	73	80	86	86	79	68	59	53	67
Monthly Average °C	7	8	10	14	19	23	25	25	21	17	12	9	16
Monthly Average °F	45	47	51	57	66	73	77	77	70	62	54	48	61
RELATIVE HUMIDITY (%)	60	59	56	55	54	50	45	45	52	60	65	66	56
PRECIPITATION													
Monthly Average mm	86	67	77	71	59	54	31	51	65	80	113	117	871.0
Monthly Average Inches	3.3	2.6	3.0	2.7	2.3	2.1	1.2	2.0	2.5	3.1	4.4	4.6	33.8
Days of 1mm or More	10	9	8	8	7	6	4	5	5	7	9	11	89

TITOGRAD — Yugoslavia

	JAN	FEB	MAR	APR	MAY	JUN	JUL	AUG	SEP	OCT	NOV	DEC	YEAR
Elevation 52 m. (171 ft.)					42°24'N—19°18'E								
TEMPERATURE													
Daily Average Min.°C	2	3	5	9	14	18	21	21	17	12	8	4	11
Daily Average Min.°F	36	37	42	49	56	64	69	69	63	53	46	40	52
Daily Average Max.°C	9	11	14	19	24	29	33	33	28	21	15	12	21
Daily Average Max.°F	48	51	58	67	76	84	91	91	82	70	59	53	69
Monthly Average °C	5	7	10	14	19	23	26	26	21	16	11	7	15
Monthly Average °F	41	44	50	57	66	73	78	78	70	61	51	44	59
RELATIVE HUMIDITY (%)	63	63	54	50	50	43	37	36	45	55	67	67	53
PRECIPITATION													
Monthly Average mm	202	167	164	140	94	66	50	71	116	189	241	233	1733.0
Monthly Average Inches	7.9	6.5	6.4	5.5	3.7	2.5	1.9	2.7	4.5	7.4	9.4	9.1	67.5
Days of 1mm or More	11	10	9	10	7	6	4	5	5	8	11	12	98

KINSHASA — Zaire

	JAN	FEB	MAR	APR	MAY	JUN	JUL	AUG	SEP	OCT	NOV	DEC	YEAR
Elevation 311 m. (1020 ft.)					4°19'S—15°18'E								
TEMPERATURE													
Daily Average Min.°C	22	22	22	22	22	19	17	18	20	21	21	22	21
Daily Average Min.°F	71	71	71	71	71	66	63	65	69	70	71	71	69
Daily Average Max.°C	31	31	32	32	31	28	27	29	30	31	31	30	30
Daily Average Max.°F	87	88	89	89	87	83	81	83	86	87	87	87	86
Extreme Monthly Min.°C	18	18	18	19	18	15	14	14	16	15	17	17	14
Extreme Monthly Min.°F	64	64	64	67	64	59	58	58	61	59	62	63	58
Extreme Monthly Max.°C	36	36	36	36	35	34	32	35	36	36	34	36	20
Extreme Monthly Max.°F	96	97	97	97	95	93	90	95	96	97	94	97	69
Monthly Average °C	25	26	25	25	25	23	22	23	25	25	25	25	24
Monthly Average °F	77	78	77	78	77	73	71	73	76	77	77	77	76
RELATIVE HUMIDITY (%)	71	70	68	68	71	69	66	61	61	65	70	71	68
PRECIPITATION													
Monthly Average mm	142	132	206	226	138	3	2	3	41	127	250	163	1433.0
Monthly Average Inches	5.5	5.1	8.1	8.9	5.4	0.1	0.0	0.1	1.6	5.0	9.8	6.4	56.0
Days of 1mm or More	14	9	14	18	11	0	0	0	6	8	0	13	93

KISANGANI   Zaire

		JAN	FEB	MAR	APR	MAY	JUN	JUL	AUG	SEP	OCT	NOV	DEC	•YEAR
Elevation 396 m. (1299 ft.) 0°31'N—25°11'E														
TEMPERATURE														
Daily Average Min.°C	21	21	21	21	21	22	21	20	20	20	21	21	21	21
Daily Average Min.°F	70	69	70	71	71	69	69	69	69	69	69	69	69
Daily Average Max.°C	31	31	31	31	31	30	29	29	30	30	30	30	30
Daily Average Max.°F	87	88	88	88	87	86	84	84	86	86	86	86	86
Extreme Monthly Min.°C	17	18	17	18	18	18	17	17	17	18	18	16	16
Extreme Monthly Min.°F	63	65	62	64	65	64	63	63	62	64	64	61	61
Extreme Monthly Max.°C	36	36	36	35	34	34	33	33	34	34	35	35	36
Extreme Monthly Max.°F	97	97	96	95	94	93	92	92	93	93	95	95	97
Monthly Average °C	25	25	25	25	25	24	24	24	24	25	24	25	25
Monthly Average °F	77	77	77	77	77	76	75	75	76	76	76	76	76
RELATIVE HUMIDITY (%)	70	67	68	71	71	70	74	73	70	69	70	73	71
PRECIPITATION														
Monthly Average mm	96	107	172	190	161	127	114	178	164	233	206	105	1853.0
Monthly Average Inches	3.7	4.2	6.7	7.4	6.3	5.0	4.4	7.0	6.4	9.1	8.1	4.1	72.4
Days of 1mm or More	9	10	0	22	14	17	14	0	11	16	0	11	124

LUBUMBASHI   Zaire

		JAN	FEB	MAR	APR	MAY	JUN	JUL	AUG	SEP	OCT	NOV	DEC	YEAR
Elevation 1298 m. (4257 ft.) 11°39'S—27°28'E														
TEMPERATURE														
Daily Average Min.°C	17	17	17	15	12	9	9	11	14	16	17	17	14
Daily Average Min.°F	62	62	62	60	53	48	47	51	57	61	62	62	57
Daily Average Max.°C	27	26	27	27	27	25	25	28	31	32	29	27	27
Daily Average Max.°F	80	80	81	81	80	77	78	82	87	89	83	80	81
Monthly Average °C	21	20	21	21	19	17	18	19	22	23	22	20	20
Monthly Average °F	69	69	69	69	66	62	64	66	72	74	71	69	68
RELATIVE HUMIDITY (%)	65	68	64	58	45	41	35	30	28	31	54	64	49
PRECIPITATION														
Monthly Average mm	234	262	204	58	2	1	2	0	2	33	152	251	1201.0
Monthly Average Inches	9.2	10.3	8.0	2.2	0.0	0.0	0.0	0.0	0.0	1.2	5.9	9.8	46.6
Days of 1mm or More	25	19	11	0	0	0	0	0	0	7	0	0	62

LIVINGSTONE   Zambia

		JAN	FEB	MAR	APR	MAY	JUN	JUL	AUG	SEP	OCT	NOV	DEC	YEAR
Elevation 987 m. (3238 ft.) 17°49'S—25°49'E														
TEMPERATURE														
Daily Average Min.°C	19	19	18	15	10	7	7	10	15	19	19	19	15
Daily Average Min.°F	66	66	64	59	51	44	44	49	58	66	67	66	58
Daily Average Max.°C	29	29	30	30	28	25	26	28	32	35	32	30	30
Daily Average Max.°F	85	85	85	86	82	77	78	83	90	94	90	86	85
Monthly Average °C	24	23	23	22	19	16	16	19	24	26	25	24	22
Monthly Average °F	74	73	74	72	66	61	61	66	75	79	77	75	71
RELATIVE HUMIDITY (%)	55	56	44	36	28	28	26	22	18	21	37	52	35
PRECIPITATION														
Monthly Average mm	188	143	81	27	7	0	0	0	2	27	78	176	729.0
Monthly Average Inches	7.4	5.6	3.1	1.0	0.2	0.0	0.0	0.0	0.0	1.0	3.0	6.9	28.2
Days of 1mm or More	14	11	6	2	0	0	0	0	0	3	8	13	57

LUSAKA   Zambia

	JAN	FEB	MAR	APR	MAY	JUN	JUL	AUG	SEP	OCT	NOV	DEC	YEAR
Elevation 1154 m. (3785 ft.) 15°19'S—28°27'E													

Elevation 1154 m. (3785 ft.)   15°19'S—28°27'E

	JAN	FEB	MAR	APR	MAY	JUN	JUL	AUG	SEP	OCT	NOV	DEC	YEAR
TEMPERATURE													
Daily Average Min.°C	17	17	16	15	12	10	9	11	15	18	18	17	15
Daily Average Min.°F	63	63	61	59	54	50	49	53	58	64	64	63	58
Daily Average Max.°C	26	26	26	27	25	23	23	26	29	31	29	27	27
Daily Average Max.°F	79	79	79	80	77	74	74	78	85	89	84	80	80
RELATIVE HUMIDITY (%)	64	65	56	47	38	36	34	29	25	26	44	60	44
PRECIPITATION													
Monthly Average mm	228	169	80	19	5	0	0	0	2	17	81	190	791.0
Monthly Average Inches	8.9	6.6	3.1	0.7	0.1	0.0	0.0	0.0	0.0	0.6	3.1	7.4	30.5
Days of 1mm or More	0	0	0	0	0	0	0	0	0	0	0	0	0

NDOLA   Zambia

Elevation 1270 m. (4166 ft.)   13°0'S—28°39'E

	JAN	FEB	MAR	APR	MAY	JUN	JUL	AUG	SEP	OCT	NOV	DEC	YEAR
TEMPERATURE													
Daily Average Min.°C	17	17	16	14	10	7	7	9	13	15	17	17	13
Daily Average Min.°F	62	62	61	56	49	44	44	48	55	60	62	62	56
Daily Average Max.°C	26	26	27	27	26	24	25	27	30	32	29	27	27
Daily Average Max.°F	79	79	80	81	79	76	76	80	86	89	84	80	81
Monthly Average °C	22	21	21	20	18	15	15	18	21	24	23	22	20
Monthly Average °F	71	71	70	69	64	59	59	64	70	74	74	71	68
RELATIVE HUMIDITY (%)	65	64	57	46	38	36	31	28	24	27	48	63	44
PRECIPITATION													
Monthly Average mm	290	268	168	43	6	0	0	0	2	20	131	273	1201.0
Monthly Average Inches	11.4	10.5	6.6	1.6	0.2	0.0	0.0	0.0	0.0	0.7	5.1	10.7	46.8
Days of 1mm or More	0	0	0	0	0	0	0	0	0	0	0	0	0

SALISBURY   Zimbabwe

Elevation 1479 m. (4851 ft.)   17°56'S—31°5'E

	JAN	FEB	MAR	APR	MAY	JUN	JUL	AUG	SEP	OCT	NOV	DEC	YEAR
TEMPERATURE													
Daily Average Min.°C	16	16	14	13	9	7	6	8	11	15	15	16	12
Daily Average Min.°F	60	60	58	55	48	44	44	47	52	58	60	60	54
Daily Average Max.°C	26	26	26	26	23	21	21	24	27	29	27	26	25
Daily Average Max.°F	79	79	79	78	74	70	71	74	80	84	81	79	77
Extreme Monthly Min.°F	47	49	46	43	36	32	32	34	37	44	46	49	32
Extreme Monthly Max.°C	32	31	30	32	28	26	28	31	33	34	36	33	35
Extreme Monthly Max.°F	90	88	86	89	83	79	82	88	92	93	96	92	95
Monthly Average °C	20	20	20	18	16	13	13	15	19	21	21	20	18
Monthly Average °F	69	68	67	65	60	56	56	60	66	69	69	69	64
RELATIVE HUMIDITY (%)	57	58	49	44	37	37	34	30	26	30	44	56	42
PRECIPITATION													
Monthly Average mm	185	149	91	47	11	2	2	1	9	36	100	180	813.0
Monthly Average Inches	7.2	5.8	3.5	1.8	0.4	0.0	0.0	0.0	0.3	1.4	3.9	7.0	31.3
Days of 1mm or More	14	12	9	5	1	0	0	0	1	4	9	14	69

VII. Major Weather-Related Disasters

The source for the information in this chapter is the Office of Foreign Disaster Assistance, Agency for International Development. The agency used the following criteria to determine inclusion in its report:

- Those events which warranted a U.S. government response;
- Earthquakes and volcanic eruptions which killed at least six people and injured 25 or more, affected at least 1,000 people, or caused damage of $1 million or more;
- Weather disasters except drought in which the number of people killed or injured was at least 50, affected or made homeless was at least 1,000, or damage was $1 million or more; and
- Droughts if the number affected was "substantial."

In the case of small island countries, weather events are listed even if the damage did not measure up to the standards used for larger nations. Weather disasters in small islands can have a significant impact without the numbers required to impact larger countries.

VII. Major Weather-Related Disasters, 1900-1988

AFGHANISTAN

North	Earthquake	1954
Province of Paktia	Drought	1969
Central, Northwest, Northeast	Drought	1969
West	Flood	1972
Khinjan Pass	Landslide	1971
West, Northwest	Drought	1973
Herat, Farah, Kandahar	Flood	1976
Hindu Kush	Earthquake	1976
Central East & Pakistani Border	Flood	1978
3 Southern Provinces	Flood	1980
Hindu Kush	Earthquake	1982
Pakistan/Afghanistan Border	Earthquake	1983
Chitral/Hindu Kush Area	Earthquake	1985

ALBANIA

Albania/Yugoslav Border	Earthquake	1967
Albania	Earthquake	1979

ALGERIA

Constantine	Earthquake	1946
Orleansville	Earthquake	1954
Southern area	Flood	1963
M'sila & environs	Earthquake	1965
West Al-Ashnam	Flood	1966
Aures Samura Constantine	Flood	1967
Algeria	Flood	1969
Northeast Tlemcen	Flood	1973
G. Kabylia & Tlemcen	Flood	1974
Western area	Flood	1979
El Asnam	Earthquake	1980
Northern Algeria	Flood	1982
Western Algeria	Flood	1984
Eastern Algeria	Flood	1985

ANGUILLA

Island-wide	Hurricane	1955
Island-wide	Hurricane	1960

ANTIGUA AND BARBUDA

Island-wide	Hurricane	1950
Island-wide	Hurricane	1960
Island-wide	Hurricane	1966
Island-wide	Drought	1983

ARGENTINA

San Juan	Earthquake	1944
Northwest, Parana & Paraguay Rivers	Flood	1966
Mendoza, Las Cuevas	Landslide	1965
Buenos Aires suburbs	Flood	1967
Mendoza	Flood	1970
Buenos Aires	Heat Wave	1972
Santiago del Estero	Tornado	1973
Santiago del Estero	Storm	1974
Nequen Province	Storm	1975
Parana River; Northeast, Central	Flood	1977
San Juan Province	Earthquake	1977
Central, Northern	Flood	1978
Formosa & Misiones	Flood	1979
Cordoba	Storm	1979
Northwestern	Flood	1980
Buenos Aires Province	Flood	1980
Northeast	Flood	1983
Northeast, Northwest	Flood	1984
Mendoza Province	Earthquake	1985
Buenos Aires	Storm	1985
Buenos Aires Province	Flood	1985
Northern States	Flood	1986
La Rioja Province	Tornadoes	1986
Northwest Buenos Aires Province	Flood	1987
Buenos Aires	Flood	1988

AUSTRALIA

Perth & Meckering	Earthquake	1968
New South Wales,Queensland,Victoria	Flood	1968
New South Wales,Queensland	Flood	1973
Darwin	Cyclone	1974
New South Wales	Flood	1976
Western Australia	Cyclone	1978
3 States	Drought	1982
Sydney	Flood	1984
North Queensland	Cyclone	1986

AUSTRIA

Blons, Langen Valley	Avalanche	1954
Dalaas	Avalanche	1954
Alps	Landslide	1975

BAHAMAS

Nassau	Hurricane	1926
Nassau	Hurricane	1929
Bimini	Hurricane	1935
Bahamas	Hurricane	1945

Bahamas	Hurricane	1963
Eleuthera Abaco Andros	Hurricane	1965
Nassau, Bimini	Hurricane	1967

BANGLADESH

Chittagong & Off-shore Islands	Cyclone	1960
Megna Estuary	Cyclone	1961
Chittagong	Cyclone	1963
Jessore District	Cyclone	1964
Rangpur, Comilla	Flood	1964
Barisal District	Cyclone	1965
Sylhet	Flood	1966
Chittagong, Sandwip	Cyclone	1966
Madaripur, Faridpur	Cyclone	1968
Nationwide	Flood	1968
Nationwide	Flood	1970
Khulna, Chittagong	Cyclone	1970
Mymensingh	Tornado	1972
Faridpur	Storm	1973
South Coast	Cyclone	1973
Nationwide	Flood	1974
East	Floods, Landslides	1976
Brahmputra Valley	Flood	1977
Bay of Bengal	Storm	1977
Ganges River; Western	Flood	1978
South Coast	Flood	1979
Northwestern	Flood	1980
Noakhalis District	Tornado	1981
Rajshahi/Kushita	Flood	1982
Central/Eastern	Flood	1983
Coastal & Off-shore areas	Cyclone	1985
5 Southwestern Districts	Storm	1986
50 of 68 Districts	Flood	1987
Coastal areas	Cyclone	1987
Shylet	Earthquake	1988
Chittagong	Cyclone	1904
Bakerganj	Cyclone	1919
Bhola, E. Meghna Estuary	Storm Surge	1941
Cox's Bazaar/Chittagong	Cyclone	1947
Noakhali & Off-shore Islands	Cyclone	1960

BARBADOS

Island-wide	Hurricane	1955
Island-wide	Flood	1970

BENIN

Atacora Region	Flood	1970
Sahel-Dahomey; Entire Country	Drought	1972
3 Coastal Provinces	Flood	1982

4 Provinces...Flood 1985

BERMUDA
Island-wide ....Hurricane 1948
5 Southeast Parishes.............................Tornadoes.....................................1986
Island-wide ....Hurricane 1987

BELGIUM
Meuse Valley..Storm...1930
Liege...Earthquake..................................1983

BELIZE
Belize City..Hurricane 1931
Corozal Area...Hurricane 1955
Belize, Other Towns.............................Hurricane 1961
Coast Southern Area.............................Hurricane 1974
South & Central Coast...........................Hurricane 1978
Belize Sibun River. ....Flood 1979

BERMUDA
Island-wide ....Hurricane 1948
5 Southeast Parishes.............................Tornadoes.....................................1986
Island-wide ....Hurricane 1987

BOLIVIA
Beni, Mamore & Ibare Rivers ....Floods...1966
Central, Rio Grande Valley ....Flood 1968
Beni, La Paz Oruro ....Flood 1974
Santa Cruz Dept. ....Flood 1977
Countrywide...Flood 1978
Beni/Santa Cruz Depts. ....Flood 1982
Santa Cruz City/Beni Dept....................Flood 1983
Altiplano...Drought..1983
Nation...Drought..1983
3 Provinces...Flood 1986
Cochabamba Dept. Chapare River ....Flood 1987

BOTSWANA
Nationwide ....Drought..1965
Nationwide ....Drought..1968
Nationwide ....Drought..1969
Along Tati & Nise Rivers ....Flood 1972
Nationwide ....Drought..1981
Nationwide ....Drought..1982
Nationwide ....Drought..1983
Nationwide ....Drought..1984
Nationwide ....Drought..1985
Nationwide ....Drought..1986
Nationwide ....Drought..1987

BRAZIL

Northeast Areas...Flood 1975
Recife...Flood 1977
Central & Southern..Drought...............................1978
East-Central, Northeast...................................Flood 1979
Northeastern ....Drought...............................1979
7 North, Central States.....................................Flood 1980
Northeastern ....Flood 1981
Rio de Janeiro State ....Flood 1981
Minas Gerais States...Flood 1983
Southern..Flood 1983
Northeast/Sertao..Drought...............................1979
Santa Catarina..Flood 1984
Northeast Brazil..Flood 1985
Rio Grande do Sul..Drought...............................1985
Petropolis & Rio de Janeiro..............................Flood 1988
10 Northeast States..Drought...............................1988

BULGARIA

Rila Mountains ....Landslide 1965
Svishtov, Ruse ....Earthquake..........................1977
Strazhitsa ....Earthquake..........................1988

BURKINA FASO

Nationwide ....Drought...............................1966
East & North of Ouagadougou.......................Drought...............................1969
Nationwide ....Drought...............................1969
Sahel..Drought...............................1969
Nationwide, except Southwest. ....Drought...............................1977
Northeast Sahel..Drought...............................1983
East, North & NW of Ouagadougou..............Drought...............................1983
Northern area...Flood 1984
Northern regions...Drought...............................1988

BURUNDI

Nationwide ....Drought...............................1943

CANADA

Frank, Alta. ....Landslide 1903
Jean Vianney, Que...Landslide 1971
Ontario..Wind storm..........................1970
Vancouver Island...Storm....................................1975
Edmonton, Alta. ....Tornado 1987

CAMEROON

Nationwide ....Drought................................1971

CAPE VERDE

Nationwide	Drought	1920
South Nicolau, Fogo, Sao Tiago	Drought	1940
Nationwide	Drought	1946
Brava Island	Hurricane	1982
Santo Anteo/Santiago	Tropical Storm	1984

CENTRAL AFRICAN REPUBLIC

Bimbo	Storm	1981

CHAD

Sahel	Drought	1969
Nationwide	Drought	1976
Nationwide	Drought	1980
Nationwide	Drought	1981

CHINA

Yangtze River	Flood	1911
North	Drought	1920
Kansu	Earthquake	1920
Swatow	Storm Surge	1922
Honan, Kansu	Drought	1928
Kansu	Earthquake	1932
Honan Province, Tientsin	Flood	1939
Foochow Coast	Flood	1948
Anhwei Province	Flood	1948
Manchuria	Flood	1951
Nationwide	Flood	1954
Fukien Province	Typhoon	1959
Tientsin	Earthquake	1969
Tangshan, Peking, Tientsin	Earthquake	1976
Anhwei, Kiangsu Province	Drought	1978
Jiangsu Province	Earthquake	1979
Northwest of Shanghai	Earthquake	1979
Minjiang River	Flood	1980
Guandong Province	Typhoon	1980
Central/South China	Flood	1981
Sichuan	Earthquake	1981
Shanzi Province	Flood	1981
Guandong Province	Flood	1982
Yantze River, 7 Provinces	Flood	1982
Heze Area	Earthquake	1983
Yunnan Province	Earthquake	1985
Yunnan Province	Flood	1985
Zhejiang Province	Typhoon	1985
4 Provinces	Flood	1985
USSR/China border	Earthquake	1985
Northwest	Cold wave	1986

Sichuan Province	Storm	1986
2 Provinces	Typhoons	1986
Northeast Province	Flood	1987
Guandong Province	Flood	1987
Ningxia Province	Earthquake	1988

COLOMBIA
Huila Dept.	Earthquake	1967
Magdalena & Cauca Valleys	Flood	1970
Caldas	Flood	1970
Pacific Coast	Earthquake	1979
Northeastern	Flood	1979
West Central	Earthquake	1979
North, East	Floods	1981
Colombia/Venezuela border	Earthqauke	1981
Popayan	Earthquake	1983
Popayan	Earthquake	1984
Volcana Nevada del Ruiz	Volcanic Eruption	1985
4 Eastern Provinces	Storm	1986
All except 2 provinces	Flood	1986
Medellin/Villa Tina Barrio	Landslide	1987
Volcano Nevada del Ruiz	Volcanic Eruption	1988

COMOROS
Islands	Tornado	1951
3 Islands	Cyclone	1983
Anjouan & Grande Comore	Cyclone	1985
Grande Comore, Anjouan, Moheli	Cyclone	1987
Karthala; Grande Comore	Volcanic Eruption	1977

CAYMAN ISLANDS
| Island-wide | Hurricane | 1988 |

COSTA RICA
Meseta Central	Volcanic Eruption	1969
Mt. Areal North	Volcanic Eruption	1968
Pacific Coast	Flood	1969
Central Meseta	Flood	1969
Limon	Flood	1969
Limao Cartago Prov.	Flood	1970
Estrellia Valley	Flood	1970
South of Laguna Arenal	Earthquake	1973
Laguna Arenal	Drought	1973
Mt. Arena	Volcanic Eruption	1976
Mt. Arena	Volcanic Eruption	1975
East Coast	Flood	1980
Southeast of San Jose	Earthquake	1983
San Jose Province	Landslide	1983
Southeast Atlantic Coast	Flood	1988

CUBA

Havana and Suburbs	Hurricane	1926
Santa Cruz del Sur	Hurricane	1932
Isle of Pines	Storm	1944
Isle of Pines	Storm	1948
Entire Island	Hurricane	1963
Southeast, Northeast	Hurricane	1966
Camaron area, Southeast	Earthquake	1976
Eastern Cuba	Flood	1977
Colon	Storm	1978
Alberto, Havana	Hurricane	1982
6 Provinces	Flood	1983
6 Provinces	Hurricane	1985

CYPRUS

Limassol	Windstorm	1969

CZECHOSLOVAKIA

Taira Mountains	Landslide	1974
Topla River	Flood	1987

DENMARK

Elbe Estuary	Storm	1967

DJIBOUTI

Djibouti City	Floods	1977
Djibouti City	Floods	1978
Djibouti City	Floods	1981
Countrywide; esp. Tadjourah	Drought	1980
5 Districts	Drought	1984
5 Districts	Drought	1988

DOMINICA

Entire Island	Hurricane	1963
Entire Island	Hurricane	1979
Entire Island	Hurricane	1980
Entire Island	Hurricane	1984

DOMINICAN REPUBLIC

Santo Domingo	Hurricane	1930
Nationwide	Hurricane	1963
Barahona Neiba Bay	Hurricane	1964
Southeast Coast Barahona	Hurricane	1966
Nationwide	Drought	1968
Nationwide	Hurricane	1979
North Northeast	Flood	1979
Nationwide	Flood	1979

Nationwide ....Hurricane 1987

ECUADOR
Western Ecuador.................................Earthquake............................1942
Peliliep...Earthquake............................1949
Widespread ....Drought................................1964
Milagro...Flood 1967
Guayas, Emeral, Manabi ....Flood 1970
Loja Province ....Earthquake............................1970
Northeast...Flood 1971
Esmeraldas..Earthquake............................1976
South of Quito...................................Earthquake............................1976
5 Provinces, Entire Coast ....Flood 1982
5 Provinces..Earthquake............................1987

EGYPT
Nile River Valley ....Flood 1975
Upper Egypt......................................Flood 1979

EL SALVADOR
Jacuapa...Earthquake............................1951
San Salvador Environs ....Earthquake............................1965
Rio Lempa Southwest Coast.............Hurricane 1969
Sonsonate Ahuachapan ....Flood 1982
San Salvador.....................................Earthquake............................1986

ETHIOPIA
Nationwide ....Drought................................1965
Vicinity of Kelafo.............................Flood 1968
Hamasion Div. ....Drought................................1969
Tigre, Wollo, N. Shoa.......................Drought................................1973
Kangra...Drought................................1975
Gode, Kelafo, Mustahil.....................Flood 1976
Wollo, Tigre Provs............................Drought................................1978
Awash River Valley...........................Floods...................................1977
Wollo, Tigre Provs............................Drought................................1978
Wollo/Gondar ....Drought................................1983
Several Provs. ....Drought................................1983
Ogaden...Drought................................1987
Northeast Sardo.................................Earthquake............................1969

FIJI
Lambasa/Lautoka...............................Cyclone 1931
Viti Levu..Cyclone 1941
Near Suva..Cyclone 1952
Lau Is. ....Cyclone 1958
Viti Levu..Flood 1964
Throughout..Cyclone 1965
Much of nation..................................Cyclone 1972

Savusavu & Bua	Cyclone	1973
Kadavu & South Lau Group	Cyclone	1973
Lau Is.	Cyclone	1975
East, South islands	Cyclone	1979
Vanua Lavu, Viti Levu	Cyclone	1980
Yasawa/Mamanuca	Cyclone	1981
Western & Eastern Divisions	Cyclone	1983
Southern Lau Group	Cyclone	1983
Western Division	Drought	1983
Lautoka Area	Cyclone	1985
Central Division	Flood	1986
North Vaua Levu/Lau Group	Flood	1986

FRANCE

Brittany, Normandy	Windstorm	1969
Val d'Isere	Landslide	1970
Saint-Gervais	Landslide	1970
Southwest	Flood	1977
Marseille	Gales, Flood	1978
Several Districts	Flood	1982
Basque Region	Flood	1983

FEDERAL REPUBLIC OF GERMANY

| South, Rhine River | Flood | 1978 |
| Rhine, Danube | Floods | 1988 |

FRENCH POLYNESIA

Tuamotu/Society Is.	Cyclone	1958
Tuamotu	Cyclone	1983
Moorea/Tetisura	Cyclone	1983

THE GAMBIA

Northwestern region	Drought	1968
Countrywide	Drought	1971
Countrywide	Drought	1980

GHANA

Along coast	Flood	1968
Countrywide	Drought	1971
North & Upper Regions	Drought	1977

GREECE

Greece & Balkan States	Earthquake	1928
Siatista	Hailstorm	1930
Ionian Islands	Earthquake	1953
3 Places	Earthquake	1965
Eurytania Region	Earthquake	1966
Megalopos, Central Greece	Earthquake	1966
Northwest Mountains	Earthquake	1967

Limnos	Earthquake	1968
Salonica	Earthquake	1978
Piraeus	Flood	1977
Southern Greece	Earthquake	1981
Pelopponisis	Earthquake	1986
Greece	Heat wave	1987

GRENADA
Nationwide	Hurricane	1963

GUADELOUPE
Guadeloupe	Hurricane	1928
Guadeloupe	Hurricane	1956
Guadeloupe	Hurricane	1966
Mt. Soufriere	Volcano	1976
St. Martin	Hurricane	1954
St. Martin, Saba	Hurricane	1960

GUAM
	Typhoon	1988

GUATEMALA
Santa Maria	Volcanic Eruption	1902
Pacific Coast	Hurricane	1969
Southwest Coast	Flood	1973
Guatamala City	Earthquake	1976
Southeastern	Earthquake	1979
Western Coast	Flood	1982
Near Quezaltenango	Volcanic Eruption	1983
San Miguel Uspantan	Earthquake	1985
Huehuetenango	Flood	1987
Chuquimula area	Drought	1988

GUINEA-BISSAU
Tombali	Storm	1987

GUINEA
Near Gaoual	Earthquake	1983

GUYANA
East Coast	Flood	1971

HAITI
Cul de Sac Leogane	Hurricane	1909
South Southwest	Hurricane	1915
Jeremie Jacmel	Hurricane	1935
Anse-a-Ceau	Earthquake	1952
Southwest	Hurricane	1954

Southwest	Hurricane	1963
Les Cayes Area	Hurricane	1964
South Hispaniola	Hurricane	1966
Northwest Peninsula	Drought	1968
Les Cayes Region	Flood	1972
Northwest Peninsula	Drought	1974
Countrywide	Drought	1977
North, Northwest, South	Hurricane	1979
Southwest, Port-au-Prince	Hurricane	1980
Southwest	Drought	1980
Les Cayes Area	Flood	1986
Island of La Gonave	Flood	1986
Port-au-Prince	Flood	1987
Southern Haiti	Flood	1987

HONDURAS

South Valle Choluteca	Drought	1965
Central South	Flood	1965
Roatan Utila Guanaja	Hurricane	1969
Widespread	Drought	1972
Widespread	Hurricane	1972
North Coast	Hurricane	1978
North Coast	Flood	1979
Choluteca	Flood	1982
Northeast Honduras Mosquitia	Flood	1986

HONG KONG

	Typhoon	1906
	Typhoon	1961
	Flood	1966
North Point & Tai Po Kan,	Typhoon	1968
Kwungton & Victoria	Landslide	1972
	Typhoon	1971
	Storm	1976
	Storm	1978
	Storm	1978
	Typhoon	1979
	Flood	1982
	Typhoon	1983

ICELAND

Heimaey Is., Helgafell	Volcanic eruption	1973
Neskaupstadhur	Landslide	1974
Kopasker	Earthquake	1976

INDONESIA

Java, Mt. Kelud	Volcanic eruption	1919
Mt. Merapi	Volcanic eruption	1951
Bali, Mt. Agung	Volcanic eruption	1963

Java	Flood	1966
Java, Mt. Kelud	Volcanic eruption	1966
Lombok, South	Drought	1966
Central Java	Flood	1967
East Java	Flood	1968
Donggala	Earthquake	1968
Celebes Is., Madjene	Earthquake	1969
Central Java, Southern Isles	Drought	1972
Irian Jaya	Earthquake	1976
Bali	Earthquake	1976
West Irian	Earthquake	1976
Java, Jakarta	Flood	1977
Nusa Tengarra Is.	Earthquake	1977
Flores, Timor Isl.	Drought	1978
East Java	Flood	1978
Flores Is.	Earthquake	1979
Mt. Sinila, Central Java	Volcanic eruption	1979
Lombok Is.	Earthquake	1979
Irian Jaya	Earthquake	1980
West Java	Earthquake	1980
Central Java	Flood	1980
Irian Jaya	Earthquake	1981
Mt. Semeru	Flood	1981
Mt. Galunggung	Volcanic eruption	1982
Jakarta	Flood	1981
Java	Earthquake	1982
South Sumatra	Flood	1982
Mt. Colo/Una Una	Volcanic eruption	1982
Flores Is.	Earthquake	1982
Mt. Gamalama	Volvanic eruption	1983
Java/Yogyakarta	Flood	1983
West Java	Flood	1984
North Sumatra	Earthquake	1984
Padang Province	Landslides	1987
Eastern Java	Flood	1987
Bengkulu/South Sumatra	Flood	1987
Sulawesi	Floods	1987
Flores Is., Mt. Mandosawu	Volcanic eruption	1987

INDIA

Bengal	Drought	1900
Kangra	Earthquake	1905
Bubonic Plague	Earthquake	1907
Nellore	Cyclone	1927
Baluchistan	Earthquake	1935
Coastal Districts of Madras	Cyclone	1936
Calcutta, Bengal	Drought	1942
West Bengal; Orissa	Cyclone	1942
Rajputana	Cyclone	1943

Assam	Cyclone	1944
Assam, Rima	Earthquake	1950
Tanjore/Tiruchi	Cyclone	1952
Punjab	Cyclone	1955
Tanjore	Cyclone	1955
West Bengal	Cyclone	1956
Maduri/Madras City	Storm	1960
North Kashmir Valley	Earthquake	1963
Orissa/U.P./Punjab	Storm	1963
Rajasthan, 4 central Provs.	Drought	1964
Rameswaram	Cyclone	1964
Nationwide, except South	Drought	1966
Manipur & Assam	Flood	1966
Madras State	Cyclone	1966
Maharashtra, Koynana	Earthquake	1967
North and Central	Flood	1967
Rajasthan, Gujarat North	Flood	1968
Andhra Pradesh/Guntur	Cyclone	1969
8 States	Flood	1970
East Coast, Orrisa State	Cyclone	1971
Central India	Drought	1972
Andhra Pradesh/Orissa	Cyclone	1972
Northwest, Bihar	Flood	1975
Eastern India	Storm	1975
Ganges System	Flood	1977
3 areas	Cyclones	1977
Andhra Pradesh	Cyclone	1979
Northwest, North, Northeast	Flood	1979
Assam	Floods	1979
Northern, Northeast	Flood	1980
Orissa	Flood	1980
10 States	Floods	1981
12 Northeast States	Flood	1982
Orissa State	Storm	1982
9 States	Drought	1982
Gujarat/Maharashtra	Cyclone	1982
Gujarat	Flood	1983
South	Drought	1982
Andhra Pradesh	Cyclone	1983
Northeast States	Flood	1984
Andhra Pradesh	Cyclone	1984
Uttar Pradesh & West Bengal	Flood	1985
Tamil Nadu	Flood	1985
Andhra Pradesh	Flood	1986
West Bengal/Calcutta	Storm	1986
Assam/Bihar/W. Bengal	Flood	1987
15 States	Drought	1987
Andhra Pradesh	Cyclone	1987

IRAN

Khuracan	Earthquake	1947
Meshed	Earthquake	1948
Eastern Iran	Earthquake	1953
Tehran, Kazvin Dist.	Flood	1954
Laristan	Earthquake	1956
Caspian Shores	Earthquake	1957
Western Iran	Earthquake	1957
Lar & Gerash	Earthquake	1960
Northwest, Qazvin	Earthquake	1962
Northeast, Khorassan Prov.	Earthquake	1968
Northeast	Earthquake	1970
Qtr; Southwest Iran	Earthquake	1972
Bandar Abbas	Earthquake	1977
Shahr Kord	Earthquake	1977
Kirman province	Earthquakes	1977
Khorasan Province	Earthquake	1978
Khorasan	Earthquake	1979
Khorasan	Earthquake	1979
Khuzestan	Flood	1980
Kerman Prov.	Earthquake	1981
Kerman Prov.	Earthquake	1981
Fars and Busher Provs.	Floods	1986
Tehran	Flood	1987

IRELAND

East and South Regions	Storm	1986
Northern Ireland	Floods	1987

ISRAEL

Neot Hakikar	Landslide	1970

ITALY

Messina	Earthquake	1908
Avezzano	Earthquake	1915
Naples	Earthquake	1930
Po River Valley	Flood	1951
Vaioni Dam, northern Italy	Landslide	1963
North	Tornado	1965
Rome to Sicily	Flood	1965
Florence, Venice	Flood	1965
Western Sicily	Earthquake	1968
Northeast, Piedmont	Flood	1968
Genoa Provinces	Flood	1970
Toscana	Earthquake	1971
Venice	Cyclone	1970
Sicily, South	Storm	1973
Riviera	Storm	1973

Alps	Landslide	1975
Friuli Region	Earthquakes (2)	1976
Southwest of Turin	Flood	1977
Northern	Flood	1977
Udine	Storm	1978
Mt. Etna	Volcanic eruption	1979
Southern	Earthquake	1980
Avellino/Potenza	Earthquake	1982
Umbria	Earthquake	1982
Ancona	Landslide	1982
Naples	Earthquake	1983
Umbria	Earthquake	1984
South/Central	Earthquake	1984
Venice	Flood	1986

JAMAICA

North Coast	Hurricane	1903
Kingston	Earthquake	1907
West	Hurricane	1912
Northern Areas	Hurricane	1917
Northern	Flood	1987
St. Mary/St. Thomas	Flood	1940
Northern Parishes	Hurricane	1944
South Coast	Hurricane	1951
Entire Island	Hurricane	1963
Nationwide	Drought	1968
Western	Flood	1976
Entire Island	Storm	1973
Western	Flood	1979
Widespread	Flood	1979
North Coast	Hurricane	1980
Entire Island	Flood	1986
Entire Island	Hurricane	1985
Entire Island	Hurricane	1988

JAPAN

Yokohama	Earthquake	1923
Tango, Honshu	Earthquake	1927
Sanriku Coast	Earthquake	1933
Honshu	Typhoon	1934
Honshu	Flood	1947
Honshu	Earthquake	1946
Fukui	Earthquake	1948
Nagoya	Typhoon	1953
Northern	Typhoon	1954
Central Honshu	Typhoon	1958
Central Honshu	Typhoon	1959
Niigata	Earthquake	1964
	Typhoon	1965

South	Flood	1965
Ryukyu Is.	Typhoon	1966
North Aomori Prefecture	Earthquake	1968
Southwest & West	Typhoon	1967
Niigata & Yamagata	Flood	1967
Kyushu	Typhoon	1971
North	Typhoon	1975
South	Typhoon	1976
Ryukyu	Typhoon	1977
Central & Eastern	Flood	1977
Sapporo	Volcanic eruption	1977
Niigata	Flood	1978
Sendai	Earthquake	1978
South	Typhoon	1980
Hokkaido	Typhoon	1981
Central/North	Typhoon	1981
Hokkaido	Earthquake	1982
South/Nagasaki	Flood	1982
Central/Honshu	Typhoon	1982
Kyushu	Typhoon	1982
West	Earthquake	1983
Mt. Oyama	Volcanic eruption	1983
Honshu	Typhoon	1984
Mt. Mihara	Volcanic eruption	1986
Shikoku & Honshu	Typhoon	1987
Near Tokyo	Earthquake	1987

JORDAN

Amman to Ma-an	Flood	1965
Maian	Flood	1966
All Districts	Drought	1969
Zarqa	Flood	1987

KAMPUCHEA

Nationwide	Drought	1987

KENYA

Nyanza & Western Region	Flood	1964
Dry Belt	Drought	1965
Nyanza & Western Provinces	Flood	1968
Countrywide	Drought	1971
Widespread	Flood	1977
Turkana Dist.	Drought	1979
Near Lake Victoria	Flood	1982

LAOS

Mekong River	Flood	1966
South along Mekong River	Flood	1968
Vientiane Plains	Flood	1969

Vientiane and Provs.	Flood	1969
Southern Provinces	Drought	1977
Southern Central	Flood	1978
Southern Central	Flood	1981
Southern Central	Flood	1984
10 Northern Provinces	Drought	1987

LEBANON
| Northern Bekaa Region | Flood | 1987 |

LESOTHO
Throughout	Drought	1968
Mokhotlong District	Flood	1985
Mokhotlong & Other Remote Areas	Flood	1987

LIBERIA
| Talus; near Mano River | Mudslide | 1982 |

LIBYA
| El Marj | Earthquake | 1963 |

MADAGASCAR
Northeast-Andapa, Southwest-Tulear	Cyclone	1968
East to West, Nosy Varika	Cyclone	1968
Central & South Madagascar	Cyclone	1970
Central Region	Cyclone	1972
South Madagascar Tamatave Vicinity	2 Cyclones	1975
North	3 Cyclones	1976
5 Provinces	Cyclone	1977
Tulear Province	Cyclone	1978
Toliary/Tolagnaro	Drought	1981
Countrywide	Cyclone	1981
Countrywide	Cyclone	1983
Northern Madagascar	Cyclone	1984
Toamasina & Coastal Villages	Cyclone	1986
Antananarivo Area	Flood	1986

MALAWI
South along Ruo River	Flood	1967
Shire River Valley	Flood	1969
Lake Malawi Shores	Flood	1979

MALAYSIA
Peninsular East Coast	Flood	1965
Kelantan, Trengganu	Flood	1967
Johore, South Lowlands	Monsoon	1968
West Malaysia, Capital	Flood	1970
Johore Bahru	Flood	1978

East Coast	Monsoon	1983
Trengganu, Kelantan	Flood	1986
East Coast States	Monsoon, Flood	1987

MALDIVES
| Male, 13 other atolls | Flood | 1987 |

MALI
Sahel	Drought	1966
Entire Country	Drought	1969
Niger River Area	Drought	1978
Sahelian/Sudan Zones	Drought	1982
Entire Country	Drought	1982

MARTINIQUE
Entire Island	Hurricane	1960
Entire Island	Hurricane	1963
Entire Island	Hurricane	1967
Entire Island	Hurricane	1970
Entire Island	Hurricane	1979

MAURITANIA
Tichitt & Kandossa	Drought	1965
Countrywide	Drought	1969
Sahel	Drought	1975
Widespread	Drought	1976
Southern	Drought	1978
Nationwide	Drought	1983
Adrar Reg./Atar Village	Flood	1984

MAURITIUS
Rodrigues Island	2 Cyclones	1967
Rodrigues Island	Cyclone	1972
Entire Island	Cyclone	1975
Rodrigues Island	Cyclone	1979
Southwest	Cyclone	1979
Rodrigues Island	Cyclone	1982
Agalega Islands	Cyclone	1982

MEXICO
Colima	Earthquake	1941
Paricutin	Volcanic eruption	1941
East coast	Hurricane	1951
Tampico	Hurricane	1955
Chetumal Area	Hurricane	1955
Jalisco & Colima	Hurricane	1959
Southern Mexico	Hurricane	1961
Guerrero & Michoacan	Earthquake	1964
West & Central	Flood	1965

Yucatan & Tampico	Hurricane	1966
Mexico — U.S. Border	Flood	1967
Chiapas State	Earthquake	1968
South	Storm	1969
Morelia	Landslide	1969
Acapulco	Storm	1971
Mexico City	Flood	1970
Michoacan, Colima	Earthquake	1973
Puebla & Veracruz	Earthquake	1973
Near Acapulco	Storm	1974
Guadalajara	Flood	1973
Irapuato	Flood	1973
Mazatlan	Hurricane	1975
Central & East Region	Storm	1976
La Paz, Baja	Hurricane	1976
3 Northern States	Drought	1978
Mexico City & South	Earthquake	1978
Mexico City & South	Earthquake	1979
Veracruz	Flood	1979
Southeastern	Flood	1980
El Chichon	Volcanic eruption	1982
Sinaloa State	Storm	1981
Central	Earthquake	1981
North Pacific Coast	Hurricane	1982
Manzanillo	Flood	1982
Xicola	Landslide	1983
Mazatlan	Hurricane	1983
11 States	Blizzards	1984
Mexico City & 7 States	Earthquake	1985
Sonora	Flood	1984

MONGOLIA

	Earthquake	1957
Ulan Bator	Flood	1966

MONTSERRAT

Entire Island	Hurricane	1928

MOROCCO

Agadir	Earthquake	1960
Tangier, Gharb Area	Flood	1963
South, along Sous & Ziz River	Flood	1965
Entire Nation	Drought	1966
Coasts, Straits	Earthquake	1969
Northern Regions	Flood	1970
Nationwide	Drought	1971
Western Provinces	Flood	1975
Kenitra, Tetsuan Prov.	Flood	1977

MOZAMBIQUE

Umbeluzi	Flood	1966
Lourenco, Marq. & Gaza	Flood	1967
Zambezia	Flood	1971
Limpopo River	Flood	1977
Zambezi	Flood	1978
Nampula Province	Cyclone	1978
6 Provinces	Drought	1980
Northeast, South, Central Provinces	Drought	1981
South Mozambique	Cyclone	1984
South & Central Mozambique	Flood	1985
Maputo Province	Storm	1985

NEPAL

Mountain Areas	Drought	1964
Nepal-India Border	Earthquake	1966
Western Mountains	Drought	1967
East, Himalayan Watershed	Flood	1968
Southern Nepal	Flood	1970
Lete	Landslide	1970
Hill Area	Drought	1972
Katmandu	Landslide	1975
Pahire Phedi	Landslide	1970
Terao Area	Flood	1978
Countrywide	Drought	1979
Western	Earthquake	1980
Northern Nepal	Flood	1981
Western Districts	Flood	1983
Southern Nepal	Mudslides	1984
Dolakha District	Flood	1985
Nationwide	Flood	1985
Kathmandu Valley	Storm	1988

NETHERLANDS

Zuiderzee Area	Flood	1953

NEW CALEDONIA

Belep/Loyalty Is.	Cyclone	1939
Southern	Cyclone	1948
Central	Cyclone	1951
Southern	Cyclone	1959
Near Ouvea Is.	Cyclone	1969
Ouvea/Grande Terre	Cyclone	1976
Grande Terre	Cyclone	1981
Belep	Cyclone	1981
	Cyclone	1981

NEW ZEALAND
Ruapehu ....Volcanic eruption 1953
Invercargill..Flood 1984
Bay of Plenty ....Earthquake 1987

NICARAGUA
Nation..Earthquake 1931
Managua ....Earthquake 1968
Mistrook, El Salto..Flood 1968
Northwest near Managua ....Volcanic Eruption 1971
Coco R. Valley...Hurricane 1971
Northeast ....Flood 1979
Pacific Coast...Flood 1982

NIGER
Nationwide ....Drought.................................... 1966
North...Drought.................................... 1969
Countrywide ....Drought.................................... 1969
Central Region..Flood 1974
Countrywide ....Drought.................................... 1983
Several Areas ....Drought....................................1988

NIGERIA
Ibadan ....Storm 1978

OMAN
Masirah Is. and South Coast ....Cyclone 1977

PAKISTAN
Karachi..Storm 1926
Quetta, Baluchistan..Earthquake 1935
Hyderabad...Hailstorm 1939
Karachi..Cyclone 1944
Lowarai Pass ....Landslide 1959
Coast, Low Indus. Valley.....................................Cyclone 1964
Lahore District..Flood 1964
Karachi..Cyclone 1965
Karachi Area...Flood 1967
Punjab and Sind..Flood 1976
Widespread ....Flood 1977
Widespread ....Flood 1978
Sind, Punjab ....Heatwave 1975
Northern ....Lightning Strike 1980
Darel/Tangir/Khanbari ....Earthquake 1981
Countrywide ....Flood 1982
Phuban ....Heavy Snowfall.........................1983
Pakistan/Afghan. Border ....Earthquake 1983
Karachi..Flood 1984

Karachi...Dust Storm 1986
Jammu and Kashmir.........................Landslide 1988

PANAMA

Bocas del Toro..................................Tornado 1964
Pacora-Chepo Area ....Flood 1966
Chirqui..Flood 1970
Veraguas Province...........................Flood 1970
Capital, San Miguelit.......................Flood 1972
South Veraguas Province.................Flood 1973
Panama City ....Flood 1978
Panama City ....Flood 1984
Panama City/Los Santos Province....Flood 1986

PARAGUAY

Chaco Region...................................Drought.................................. 1963
Southwest, Parana & Paraguay Rivers.........Flood 1966
Asuncion...Flood 1965
Asuncion & Conception ....Flood 1971
Paraguay River; Northern ....Flood 1979
Paraguay River.................................Flood 1982
Eastern Region ....Flood 1983

PAPUA NEW GUINEA

Ninigo/Awin Is. ....Tsunami 1930
Rabaul...Volcanic eruption 1937
Mt. Lamington ....Volcanic eruption 1951
Manam...Volcanic eruption 1957
Madang..Earthquake............................. 1970
Central Province/Highlands............Drought.................................. 1981
Raboul Volcano................................Volcanic eruption 1983
Northwest ....Earthquake............................. 1983
Bialla Region/New Britain...............Earthquake............................. 1985
East Sepik Province, 8 Villages.......Earthquake............................. 1986
Umboi Is., Huon Peninsula ....Earthquake............................. 1987

PERU

Quiches...Earthquake............................. 1946
Mt. Huascaran ....Landslide 1962
North Coast......................................Earthquake............................. 1966
Widespread ....Flood 1967
Moyobamba.......................................Earthquake............................. 1968
North...Drought.................................. 1969
Huancayo/Pariach ....Earthquake............................. 1969
2 Areas..Flood 1970
Northeastern Peru ....Earthquake............................. 1970
5 Areas..Flood 1971
Piura Tumbes ....Earthquake............................. 1970
Mantaro River..................................Landslide 1974

Cuzco	Flood	1977
San Martin (Northeast)	Flood	1978
North Coast	Flood	1983
Puno Dept.	Drought	1983
Chimbote	Earthquake	1983
Lima	Landslide	1984
Puno & Huanuco/Lake Titcaca	Flood	1986
Cuzco	Earthquake	1986
Lima Area	Flood	1987

PHILIPPINES

Mt. Mayon	Volcanic eruption	1978
Samar/Mindoro/Luzon	Typhoon	1981
Southeast/ North Mindanao	Typhoon	1982
6 Central Provinces	Typhoon	1982
Central/South Luzon	Typhoon	1982
North Luzon	Typhoon	1982
Misamis Oriental	Drought	1983
Ilocos Norte	Earthquake	1983
Southeast Luzon	Typhoon	1983
Northern Luzon & Central Philippines	Typhoon	1984
Undang, Visayas	Typhoon	1984
Luzon	Typhoon	1985
North, Central Luzon, Metro Manila	Typhoon	1986
Luzon, Manila	Typhoon	1986
Nueva Ecija	Typhoon	1986
Central Philippines	Typhoon	1987
Luzon	Typhoon	1986
Bicol Div.	Typhoon	1987
Cagayan & Ilocos Norte	Typhoon	1987

POLAND

Southwest	Flood	1977
Vistula Rver	Flood	1980
Vistula River, Plock	Flood	1982
Baltic Coastline	Storm	1983

PORTUGAL

Lisbon & 3 Other Cities	Flood	1967
Coast Straits	Earthquake	1969
Atlantic Coast	Storm	1973
Madeira Is.	Flood	1979
North Coast & Central	Flood	1979
Lisbon & 3 Cities	Flood	1981
Lisbon Area	Flood	1983

REUNION

| Saint Denis | Cyclone | 1987 |
| La Fournaise; Sainte Rose | Volcanic Eruption | 1977 |

ROMANIA

	Earthquake	1908
	Earthquake	1928
Klausenberg	Storm	1928
	Earthquake	1934
	Earthquake	1940
	Earthquake	1945
30 Counties	Flood	1970
South along Danube	Flood	1975
Bucharest and North	Earthquake	1977

RWANDA

Entire country	Flood	1974
Widespread	Drought	1976

ST. CHRISTOPHER AND NEVIS

Mt. Soufriere, St.Vincent	Volcanic Eruption	1902
Grenadines	Hurricane	1955
St. Vincent	Tropical Storm	1967
Mt. Soufriere, St. Vincent	Volcanic Eruption	1971
Mt. Soufriere, St. Vincent	Volcanic Eruption	1979
St. Vincent	Hurricane	1980
North Leeward District	Floods	1986
St. Vincent	Hurricane	1987

SAO TOME AND PRINCIPE

Countrywide	Drought	1983

SAUDI ARABIA

Nedjaran	Flood	1964

SENEGAL

Saint Louis	Tidal Wave	1966
Northwest	Drought	1966
Nationwide	Drought	1969
Nationwide	Drought	1977
Fleuve/Louga/Senegal Orient	Drought	1979
Matam-Bakel	Flood	1983
4 Depts.	Flood	1983

SIERRA LEONE

Atlantic Coast	Storm	1975

SOMALIA

Nationwide	Drought	1964
East Burao, North Mudugh	Drought	1974
Northwest to Central Areas	Drought	1974

Shabelle, Juba Rivers ....Flood 1977
Hiran/Juba Prov..Flood 1981
12 Central Regions ....Drought................................ 1987

SOUTH AFRICA
Ciskei & Transkei......................................Drought................................ 1964
Umbeluzi River...Flood 1966
Cape Province..Earthquake.......................... 1969
North Natel..Storm 1974
Johannesburg...Flood 1977
Transvaal ....Flood 1978
Cape Province..Flood 1981
Countrywide...Drought................................ 1982
Natal/Kwazulu/Transvaal ....Cyclones.............................. 1984
Natal/Kwazulu..Floods, Landslides................ 1987
Western Deep Leveis Gold Mine..................Earthquake.......................... 1987
Vaal Reefs Gold Mine ....Earthquake.......................... 1988

SOUTH KOREA
Seoul, Kyonggi ....Flood 1966
4 Southern Provinces..................................Drought.................................1967
South ....Drought.................................1968
East and Southeast Coastal Provs. ....Flood 1969
East and Southeast Coast ....Storm 1970
Han River, Seoul..Flood 1972
Pusan..Flood 1972
Seoul Area...Flood 1977
Southern Korea..Typhoon 1979
Central ....Typhoon 1980
North, South Kyonsan Provs. ....Typhoons 1980
South, East, West Coasts/Inland.................Typhoons 1981
Southwest Coast..Typhoons 1982
Nationwide ....Flood 1984
Southern..Flood 1984
Cheju and Coastal Areas ....Typhoons 1985
South Korea...Typhoons 1986
Southeast, Central Seoul............................Typhoons, Floods 1986

SRI LANKA
All Major Rivers in Spate............................Cyclone 1957
Trincomalee and East Coast ....Cyclone 1964
Southwest..Flood 1966
Colombo area; 3 other provs.......................Floods...................................1967
4 Provinces..Flood 1969
Nationwide ....Drought.................................1977
5 Districts..Cyclone 1978
5 Districts..Flood 1982
North Sri Lanka ....Flood 1981
17 Districts..Drought.................................1982

17 Districts	Floods and Landslides	1982
17 Districts	Drought	1983
3 Provinces	Flood	1983
Southwest Districts	Flood	1984
East and Central Regions	Floods	1986
North and Northeast	Drought	1987

SUDAN

Gash River (Central & East)	Flood	1976
West Equatoria Prov.	Flood	1978
Maban	Drought	1983
Kassala	Flood	1983
Northern Regions	Drought	1983
Mundri Dist.	Flood	1983
Kordofan and Darfur	Drought	1987

SURINAME

Suriname	Flood	1969

SWEDEN

Elbe Estuary	Storm	1967
Widespread	Flood	1977
Goteborg	Landslide	1977

SWITZERLAND

Saas-Fee	Landslide	1965
Alps	Landslide	1968
Reckingen	Landslide	1970
Alps	Landslide	1975
Ticino Canton	Hailstorm	1982
4 Cantons	Storm	1984
Fribourg	Storm	1985

TAIWAN

Formosa	Earthquake	1906
	Earthquake	1964
	Typhoon	1965
South Central	Typhoon	1966
	Typhoon	1965
Formosa	Typhoon	1967
	Typhoon	1969
North Taipei	Typhoons	1977
Taipei	Flood	1977
	Typhoon	1983
North	Flood	1984
Near Chusan	Landslide	1986
Central & Southern	Typhoon	1986
Central	Typhoon	1986
Off East Coast	Earthquake	1986

Eastern Turkey	Earthquake	1946
Anatolia	Earthquake	1948
Northwestern turkey	Earthquake	1953
Western Eskuschir	Flood	1964
Southern Turkey	Storm	1964
Western Turkey	Earthquake	1964
Eastern Turkey	Earthquake	1966
Mus Province	Earthquake	1966
3 regions	Earthquake	1967
West Alasehir	Earthquake	1969
West, Central Turkey; Kutahya	Earthquake	1970
Bingol, Erzincan to North	Earthquake	1971
Epicenter-Lice	Earthquake	1975
Northeast Provinces	Earthquake	1976
Central and South Anatolia	Flood	1980
Erzurum/Kars Provs.	Earthquake	1983
Erzurum	Earthquake	1984
Malatya and Adiyaman Provs.	Earthquake	1986

UGANDA

West Bwamba County	Earthquake	1966
Karamoja	Drought	1967
North, Northeast esp. Karamoga	Drought	1967
Karamoja	Drought	1987

USSR

South Ukraine & Volga	Drought	1921
Turkmania/ashkabad	Earthquake	1948
Khait, Tadzhikistan	Landslide	1949
Mt. Bezmianny	Volcanic Eruption	1956
Tashkent	Earthquake	1966
Kum-Dag	Earthquake	1983
Northeast of Moscow	Storm	1983
Widespread	Heavy rains	1985
Tadzhikistan	Earthquake	1985
Moldavia	Earthquake	1986
Soviet Georgia	Flood	1987
Sargazan, Tadzhikistan	Mud avalanche	1987

UNITED KINGDOM

London	Fog	1952
South Wales	Landslide	1966
Scotland	Storm	1968
Southern region	Storm	1987

URUGUAY

| Central and West | Flood | 1967 |
| Eastern & Southern Depts. | Flood | 1986 |

VENEZUELA

Caracas & Macuto................................Earthquake............................... 1967
Llanos Region....................................Flood....................................... 1967
Caracas...Flood....................................... 1981
Caracas & Nearby Coast.....................Flood....................................... 1985
Eastern Venezuela.............................Earthquake............................... 1986
Aragua/Maracay................................Landslide................................. 1987

VIETNAM

Southern Coast..................................Typhoon....................................1953
Central, South China Sea Coast..................Typhoons....................................1964
Near Cambodia Border.......................Flood..1966
5 Northern Provinces.........................Flood..1970
South Vietnam..................................Typhoon....................................1973
Haiphong..Typhoon....................................1977
10 Provinces.....................................Floods.......................................1978
Red River Delta.................................Typhoon....................................1980
Central...Typhoon....................................1980
Central...Torrential Rains........................1980
4 Provinces.......................................Typhoon....................................1982
Central...Whirlwinds................................1984
East of Hanoi....................................Typhoon....................................1984
Central Vietnam................................Flood..1984
Nghia Binh Province..........................Typhoon....................................1984
10 Provinces.....................................Flood..1986
Binh Tria Thien and Nghe Tinh..................Typhoon....................................1985
Binh Tria Thien and Nghe Tinh..................Typhoon....................................1986
Northern Provinces............................Drought, Storms.......................1987
Nghe Binh and Phu Khahu Provs. ....Typhoon....................................1987

WESTERN SAMOA

Windstorm................................. 1964
Cyclone.................................... 1966
Cyclone.................................... 1968

YEMEN ARAB REPUBLIC

South; Taiz-Torba, Tihama.........................Drought.....................................1969
Sana'a Region...................................Flood..1975
Chamar..Earthquake................................1982

YUGOSLAVIA

Skopje..Earthquake............................... 1963
Croatia & Slovenia............................Flood....................................... 1964
Danube system..................................Flood....................................... 1965
Macedonia, Debar..............................Earthquake............................... 1967
Montenegro.......................................Earthquake............................... 1968
Bosnia-Herzegovina...........................Earthquake............................... 1969
Belgrade, Cack..................................Earthquake............................... 1972

VIII. Index